Psychology

FOURTH EDITION

Lester A. Lefton
University of South Carolina

◆

ALLYN AND BACON

Boston   London   Toronto   Sydney   Tokyo   Singapore

Editor Emeritus: Bill Barke
Executive Editor: Susan Badger
Developmental Editor: Elizabeth Brooks
Production Administrator: Susan McIntyre
Cover Administrator: Linda Dickinson
Composition Buyer: Linda Cox
Manufacturing Buyer: Megan Cochran
Illustrators: BostonGraphics, Wayne Clark, William DePippo, Avis Thomas, and Deborah Schneck

Library of Congress Cataloging-in-Publication Data

Lefton, Lester, A.,
    Psychology / Lester A. Lefton. — 4th ed.
      p.   cm.
    Includes bibliographical references and indexes.
    ISBN 0–205–12068–7
    1. Psychology.   I. Title.
BF121.L424   1991
150—dc20   90-44649
                                          CIP

Copyright © 1991, 1985, 1982, 1979 by Allyn and Bacon
A Division of Simon & Schuster
160 Gould Street
Needham Heights, MA 02194

Printed in the United States of America

10 9 8 7 6 5 4 3 2   95 94 93 92 91

CREDITS

2 (p. 34): "Twice Blue" by Obie Simonis, 1989. Photo/Bill Kipp. 3 (p. 70): "Yee" by Tom Holland. Courtesy of Elaine Horwitch Galleries. 4 (p. 118): "Chameleon" by Josette Urso, 1990. Mixed media and canvas. Private Collection. Photo courtesy of Stein Gallery, Tampa, Fla. 5 (p. 152): "Untitled" by Joseph Cornell, 1952. Box construction 19¼ × 12¼ × 4". Photograph courtesy The Pace Gallery. © The Joseph and Robert Memorial Foundation. 6 (p. 198): "Cloister Series—Rush" by Robert Rauschenberg. Photo courtesy of the Lang and O'Hara Gallery, Inc. NYC. 7 (p. 232): "Crown" by John Okulick. Painted wood and metal. 1989. Photograph courtesy of the Nancy Hoffman Gallery, NYC. 8 (p. 266): "Untitled" by Joseph Cornell, mid 1950s. Box construction, 18 × 11½ × 2¾". Photograph courtesy of the Pace Gallery. © The Joseph and Robert Cornell Memorial Foundation. 9 (p. 298): "Questioning Children" by Karel Appel, 1949. The Tate Gallery/Art Resource. 10 (p. 341): "Simple Meaning" by Elizabeth Murray. Collection of Mandy and Cliff Einstein, Los Angeles. Photograph courtesy of Paula Cooper Gallery, NYC. 11 (p. 378): "The House of the Heart" by Miriam Schapiro, 1980. Acrylic and fabric on shaped canvas. Photo courtesy of the Bernice Steinbaum Gallery, NYC. 12 (p. 422): "Persona Box of David" by Maggie Sherman. Private Collection. 13 (p. 464): "Molted Fume" by Charles Arnoldi, 1987–89. Acrylic on plywood. Photo courtesy of Sena Galleries West. 14 (p. 496): "Haute Cinq" by John Chamberlain, 1990. Painted steel. Photo courtesy Pace Gallery. 15 (p. 532): "Shape III" by Yrjo Edelmann. Photo courtesy of the Lillian Heidenberg Gallery. 16 (p. 572): "The Hawthorne Tree #2" by Isaac Witkin, 1990. Bronze. Photo courtesy Patricia Hamilton Gallery, NYC. 17 (p. 610): "Pas Mele," 1990. Welded bronze. Photo courtesy Worth Street Studios.

Please note: In description of his work "Twice Blue", Obie Simonis says that, "The helix or spiral has been a symbol of transcendence and transformation from its appearance as an ancient spiritual image to its present-day use as a model of organic life (DNA). It is as a symbol of change that I use the helix in my compositions." "Twice Blue" is our opening piece for Chapter Two of the text.

PHOTOGRAPHS

ivC: Courtesy of the AT&T Archives; ivR: CNRI-Science Library/Photo-Researchers Inc. v: Sygma. vi: R. Morsch/The Stock Market. vii: J. Parsons/Stock, Boston. viiiL: Psychology Archives; viiiR: J. Caccavo/The Picture Group. ixL: P. Menzel/Stock, Boston; ixC: M. Rogers/TSW-Click, Chicago. xL: Archive/Photo-Researchers; xR: A. Grace/Stock, Boston. xi: D. Dempster/OffShoot Stock. xii: UPI/The Bettmann Archive. xiii: G. Palmer/The Stock Market.
Page 2: T. Van Dyke/Sygma. 5T: The Bettmann Archive; 5B: Psychology Archives. 7L: Library of Congress; 7R: The Bettmann Archive. 8T: The Bettmann Archive; 8B: Historical Picture Service. 12: C. Jones/The Stock Market. 17: A. Reininger/Contact Press-Woodfin Camp & Assoc. 18: Superstock. 25: Courtesy of the AT&T Archives. 37: CNRI-Science Library/Photo-Researchers Inc. 39L: S. Murphy/TSW-Click, Chicago; 39R: L. T. Rhodes/TSW-Click, Chicago. 40L: R. Hutchings/Photo-Researchers Inc., 40R: CNRI-Science Library/Photo-Researchers Inc. 42: Biophoto-Science Library/Photo-Researchers Inc. 50: R. Morsch/The Stock Market. 53L: Superstock; 53R: New York Hospital/Peter Arnold. 54: A. Glauberman/Photo-Researchers Inc. 72: Superstock. 77: J. & L. Weber/Peter Arnold. 89: T. Farmer/TSW-Click, Chicago. 91: Superstock. 92: R. Schwerzel/Stock, Boston. 100: Shostal/Superstock. 102: G. Zimbel/Monkmeyer Press Photo. 112: B. Barnhart/OffShoot Stock. 114: Sygma. 121: D. Woods/The Stock Market. 125: R. Morsch/The Stock Market. 127: G. Hunter/TSW-Click, Chicago. 133: B. Daemmrich/Stock, Boston. 135: A. Reininger/Woodfin Camp & Assoc. 142: A. Glauberman/Photo-Researchers Inc. 145: A. Collins/Monkmeyer Press Photo. 146: R. Morsch/The Stock Market. 147: Tannenbaum/Sygma. 156: Psychology Archives. 163: Courtesy of John Garcia. 167: F. Siteman. 170: Woodfin Camp & Assoc. 171: Stock, Boston. 175: J. Brown/OffShoot Stock. 177: AP/Wide World Photos. 181: M. Winter/Stock, Boston. 182: D. Dempster/OffShoot Stock. 189: D. Kryminec/Photo-Researchers Inc. 193: R. Kopstein/Monkmeyer Press Photo. 201: The Bettmann Archive. 205: D. Parker/Photo-Researchers Inc. 210: D. Schaefer/Monkmeyer Press Photo. 212: C. Morrow/Stock, Boston. 213: Courtesy of NASA. 215: L. Downing/Woodfin Camp & Assoc. 221: DVW/Stock, Boston. 225: D. Dempster/Allyn and Bacon. 227: J. Parsons/Stock, Boston. 234: T. Wurl/Stock, Boston. 235: S. Sutton/Duomo. 237: R. Hutchings/Photo-Researchers Inc. 242: R. Isear/Photo-Researchers Inc. 248: R. Das/Monkmeyer Press Photo. 251: P. Plailly/Photo-Researchers Inc. 256: Corroon/Monkmeyer Press Photo. 258: B. Gallery/Stock, Boston. 262: S. Kuklin/Photo-Researchers Inc. 269: F. Baldwin/Photo-Researchers Inc. 273: Psychology Archives. 279: W. McIntyre/Photo-Researchers Inc. 283: R. Schleipman/OffShoot Stock. 289: R. Pasley/Stock, Boston. 295: J. Coletti/Stock, Boston. 302: Science Library/Photo-Researchers Inc. 303: P. Format-Science Library/Photo-Researchers Inc. 304: J. Stevenson-Science Library/Photo-Researchers Inc. 306: C. Cancellare/The Picture Group. 310: Dr. David Linton. 314: B. Robis/Photo-Researchers Inc. 316: B. Anderson/Monkmeyer Press Photo. 318: D. Goodman/Monkmeyer Press Photo. 330: G. Goodwin/Monkeyer Press Photo. 331: M. Forsyth/Monkmeyer Press Photo. 332: C. Parksa/The Stock Market. 333: J. Caccavo/The Picture Group. 343: H. Rainier/OffShoot Stock. 345: Superstock. 346: El Herwig/Stock, Boston. 349: Courtesy of Harvard University News. 353: T. Friedman/Photo-Researchers Inc. 354: F. Siteman. 356: Allyn and Bacon. 358: F. Siteman. 360: B. Daemmrich/Stock, Boston. 361: Superstock. 363: M. Heron/Woodfin Camp & Assoc. 364: P. Menzel/Stock, Boston. 365: F. Siteman. 368: D. Krakel III/Photo-Researchers Inc. 370: I. Wyman/Sygma. 371: K. Horan/The Picture Group. 372: F. Siteman. 374: P. Damien/TSW-Click, Chicago. 383: Arizona Historical Society Library. 385: Superstock.

(credits continued on last page)

*This book is dedicated
to my wife, Linda Lefton.*

Contents

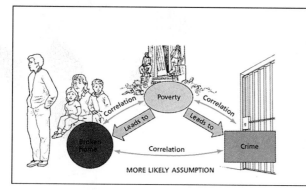  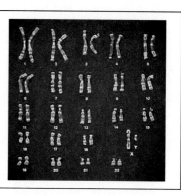

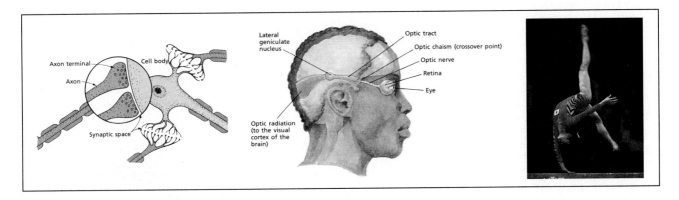

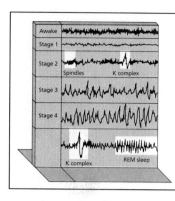

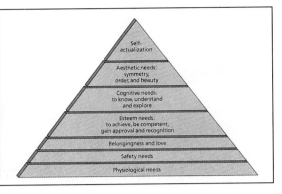

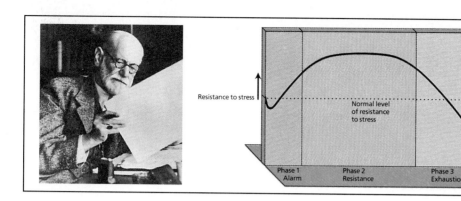

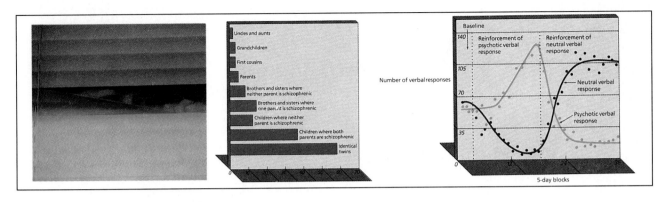

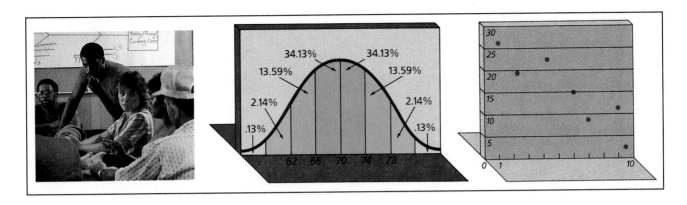

Preface

Writing this text was an exciting, challenging, and fascinating adventure. I had three primary goals for *Psychology*, Fourth Edition. First was to make this complicated science understandable by presenting the nuances of psychology in a straightforward and accessible manner; by explaining principles methodically; and equally important, by systematically going through the facts to teach psychological thinking, the critical process of discovering what is true, and building on current facts and theories. The second was to enrich the student's understanding of the applications of psychology in everyday life and in other fields of study. The third was to show the integration of science and application—that science and application flow from one another, each dependent on the other. To help accomplish these goals, the text is written in a narrative that provides the student with a unitary view, connecting concepts from chapter to chapter.

A New Edition: Writing, Organization, and Content

The fourth edition of *Psychology* has been dramatically revised in form and content. This edition was five years in development, and every word has been considered and reconsidered to make sure that students will find the writing lively and engaging. A lucid, upbeat style is achieved using personal anecdotes, presenting material directly, and always maintaining student interest. In addition, there is a new approach to organizing both the book as a whole and each chapter.

Reorganization The overall table of contents is organized in a new, more logical manner, starting with the basics of psychology (learning, biology, and perception) and moving to the more applied, clinical, and socially relevant chapters. Yet, every chapter is written so that it can stand alone and be read in any order or sequence. Every chapter has been rewritten with the aim of providing a more structured approach, with a smoother, more cohesive flow of information. The internal structure of each chapter attempts to match the way teachers present material; we talked with hundreds of psychology teachers to determine the most logical and sought after structure.

Content This new edition covers the core concepts of psychology in addition to emerging, high-interest topics. The traditional areas of learning, memory, and perception are presented fully and clearly. The applied fields are similarly represented with complete coverage of topics such as child development, gender differences, performance appraisal, and testing issues. New topics such as brief therapy, codependence, and substance abuse are covered, as well as brain plasticity, sexual dysfunctions, and Alzheimer's disease. These high-interest topics are presented in an integrated manner by bringing science and application together and showing how they flow directly from traditional psychology. The content of the text reflects the current status of psychological science without being trendy or neglecting the classics.

Pedagogical Features

A primary aim of *Psychology*, Fourth Edition, is to make psychology both understandable and interesting for students. Nine major pedagogical features have been integrated into *Psychology* to stimulate student involvement and critical thinking about issues, theories, and data.

Critical Thinking Learning about psychology means learning about thinking. Developing critical thinking skills is a major theme in chapter 1 and throughout the book. In addition, each chapter presents material in a special section called "Thinking about Research," which shows students how psychologists use (and sometimes abuse) the scientific method.

Applications Featuring interesting topics such as sleep disorders, managing young children's behavior, or improving memory, special "Applying Psychology" sections focus on how psychology can be applied to everyday life. Applications are a regular theme in the text, and these sections call out and highlight especially interesting examples and place them in context.

Milestones Psychology has had a relatively brief history, yet within its century of life, a number of highly significant people, classic studies, and events have changed its course. The lives of Skinner and Freud, for example, are highlighted in special sections called "Milestones in Psychology." Especially important research such as taste aversion and split-brain research are also featured.

Building Tables Presenting major theories and concepts in a way that shows the development of ideas is a major structural and pedagogical element in this text. Pioneered in previous editions, "Building Tables" have been visually enhanced and expanded. As one set of concepts is mastered, a new set is added on. These tables allow for comparisons and contrasts, while providing a means for integrating concepts. They are also an excellent aid for study and review.

Key Terms in Bold Face Key terms are boldfaced in the text, defined in the margins, and also in the end-of-book glossary. In addition, at the end of each chapter, the key terms are listed with page references to help students review the main concepts.

Focus Questions Throughout the text there are short review sections called "Focus on Learning" which ask the students to pause, review, question, and think about what they have just learned. These sections are nonintrusive and conveniently placed; they provide page references to show where topics are discussed. Answers to these questions are available for teachers in the *Annotated Instructor's Edition*.

Psychology across the Curriculum Psychology has become a diverse discipline that speaks to many issues. Sometimes these issues cross into other disciplines such as education, history, law, medicine, and social work. Special sections in each chapter show the relevancy and connections between psychology and other disciplines.

Chapter Summaries Every chapter has a well-structured chapter summary, organized by section headings with page references to relevant portions of the text.

Connections At the end of each chapter is a connections table that provides cross-references for major, high-interest topics. Students can use connections tables to learn more about various areas of interest and also to see the interrelated nature of psychology.

Supplements for Students

Keeping Pace *Keeping Pace* is an active reading study guide. Now in its fourth edition, this carefully structured study guide helps students participate actively in learning about psychology. It contains book-specific exercises, learning objectives, review sections, and test questions. With page-referenced reviews, *Keeping Pace* guarantees learning for students who use it.

Study Guide for Non-Native Speakers This alternative version of the study guide is an expanded edition of *Keeping Pace* that helps non-native speaking students with North American idioms and phrases linked to the study of psychology and to this textbook.

Studying Psychology A brief how-to manual, provided free to every student, *Studying Psychology: A Manual for Success* is designed to help students develop the skills to master psychology more effectively. With down-to-earth techniques and ideas, this booklet helps students develop effective strategies for studying, listening, dealing with lectures, and preparing for examinations.

Annotated Instructor's Edition and Supplements for Instructors

An Annotated Instructor's Edition is provided to encourage student involvement and understanding. It includes a comprehensive and detailed instructor's section bound into the front of the book and detailed annotations in the margin of each chapter with teaching suggestions, examples, demonstrations, visual aids, and learning objectives. In addition to the *Annotated Instructor's Edition*, a wide array of supplementary materials are available, including a superb set of transparencies; a set of seventy ready-to-duplicate handouts and activities; a lengthy computer-ready test item file; *PsychScience*, an interactive, computer simulation of real-life experiments; and an extensive videotape library. All of these supplements, and more, are keyed to the *Annotated Instructor's Edition*.

Acknowledgments

The cast of characters who helped me prepare this textbook is quite large; some are psychologists, some are students, some are professional textbook developers—including many professionals at Allyn and Bacon. All shaped the direction of this text in important ways.

The psychologists were classroom instructors who used the previous editions of the text, or instructors who read both early and late drafts of chapters. A number of these reviewers were colleagues of mine at the University of South Carolina; I prevailed regularly upon the faculty for guidance—and was given endless help. I especially thank Ernest Furchtgott and Jack Hand, who gave me line-by-line comments on the entire book. I also thank Sandra Kelly, Jay Coleman, Jim Appel, Tom Cafferty, Dave Clement, and Randy Engle, who provided chapter commentary. Most of the reviews that were provided to me came from faculty at other institutions. Some were from research institutions with a focus on graduate study and others were from teaching-oriented community colleges. These psychologists helped me focus my interests, pointed me in new research directions, and queried my logic. They met in focus groups, talked with me individually, and wrote lengthy reviews of each chapter. In immeasurable ways, these reviewers helped make this book better. I thank each of them:

Reviewers of the Fourth Edition

Lewis Aiken
Pepperdine University

Brian Bate
Cuyahoga Community College-
Western Campus

George Bishop
University of Texas-San Antonio

Jay Braun
Arizona State University

John Caruso
Southeastern Massachusetts
University

Winifred Curtis
Community College of Rhode
Island

Donald Devers
Northern Virginia Community
College

Leslie Fisher
Cleveland State University

Linda Flickinger
St. Clair Community College

Mark Garrison
Kentucky State University

Richard Harris
Kansas State University

Morton Hoffman
Metropolitan State College

Kermit Hoyenga
Western Illinois University

William Kalberer
California State University-Chico

Dennis Karpowitz
University of Kansas

Harold Kiess
Framingham State College

Jack Kirshenbaum
Fullerton Community College

James Knight
Humboldt State University

Wayne Lesko
Marymount University

Sheldon Maleve
Westchester Community College

Richard Maslow
Delta College

James Matiya
Moraine Valley Community
College

Robert Meyer
University of Louisville

Jerry Mikosz
Moraine Valley Community
College

Dirk Steiner
Louisiana State University

David Townsend
Montclair State College

Benjamin Wallace
Cleveland State University

William Wallace
Marshall University

John Williams
Westchester Community College

Patrick Williams
Wharton County Junior College

Reviewers of the Previous Edition

Georgia Babladelis
California State University

Lew Barker
Baylor University

William Beatty
North Dakota State University

Richard Bowen
Loyola University

Brian Burnie
George Brown College

Terry Devietti
Central Western University

Thornton Dozier
Michigan State University

Leonard Flynn
Framingham State College

Joy Hammersla
Seattle Pacific University

Charles Hinderliter
University of Pittsburgh

Robert Levy
Indiana State University

Marjorie Lewis
Illinois State University

Cynthia Margolin
San Jose State College

Edward Pollak
West Chester State College

James Roll
William Rainey Harper College

Paul Salmon
University of Louisville

Robert Shaw
Texas Southmost College

Warren Street
Central Western University

David Whitsett
University of Northern Iowa

Joe Rae Zuckerman
Los Angeles Harbor College

With Special Thanks to

Donald Devers
Northern Virginia Community
College

Leslie Fisher
Cleveland State University

Peter Holland
University of Pittsburgh

Ted Lewandoski
Delaware County Community
College

Kevin Williams
Rensselaer Polytechnic Institute

Colleagues Who Participated in Focus Groups

Jean Badry
Indiana University-South Bend

Hal Beck
Appalachian State University

Richard Bowen
Loyola University of Chicago

Lawrence Casler
SUNY-Geneseo

Kathleen Chen
Rochester Institute of Technology

James Corwin
University of New Orleans

Cheryl Dreut
SUNY-Fredonia

James Grosch
SUNY-Geneseo

Ernest Gurman
University of Southern Mississippi

Michael Gurtman
University of Wisconsin-Parkside

Jane Halpert
DePaul University

Kermit Hoyenga
Western Illinois University

Jane Kelly
Hinds Community College

Sal Macias
University of South Carolina-
Sumpter

James Matiya
Moraine Valley Community
College

Harvey Pines
Canisius College

Christopher Rhoades
Hilbert College

Dirk Steiner
Louisiana State University

Michael Stevenson
Ball State University

Andrea Wesley
University of Southern Mississippi

Richard Wesp
Elmira College

The students who read the chapters in this book are my greatest friends and my most important audience. For the past ten years, students in my classroom and in classrooms all over the country have read chapters of this text—both previous editions and drafts of new chapters. They provided criticism and help, and pointed out areas that needed to be strengthened. I am in their debt.

I also thank Marcia Gardner, my administrative assistant; Marcia makes my life easier by attending to details, keeping up my correspondence, and facilitating my work flow. A pillar of strength with an even temper, Marcia keeps me on an even keel and her hard work provides me the time that is needed to write this text. Her editorial suggestions have proved extremely valuable.

My friends at Allyn and Bacon are a team of creative individuals unmatched for their professionalism and commitment to fine book making. Each person with whom I worked was a member of a team that functioned exceptionally well. Many worked behind the scenes and had limited contact with me directly, but I know of their involvement and I am appreciative. I thank the sales force and their experienced managers who gathered information from instructors and students, and Dana Lamothe who coordinated reviews and contacted instructors. The marketing team, especially Diana Murphy, Lou Kennedy, and Sandi Kirshner, has helped immeasurably in gathering information and helping me set the agenda for the text. The design of the text is especially tasteful and pleasing and I thank Catherine Johnson; I also appreciate the superb cover which was designed by Linda Dickinson.

Production is among the most time-consuming and exacting of the processes of putting a textbook together, and every page of the text shows the superb work of Paula Carroll, Judy Fiske, and especially production editor Susan McIntyre. With a fine eye for detail, design, and color, Susan McIntyre managed the myriad of specialized elements in this complicated four-color text. Susan was flexible and responded to dozens of last-minute changes needed to keep the book current and exciting. This was a year-long process and an elaborate book with many innovative elements; Susan far exceeded her challenge—I am most appreciative.

The editorial team at Allyn and Bacon has always been among the best in textbook publishing. I have had the benefit of over ten years of guidance and expertise from top-notch acquisition and developmental editors such as Allen Workman. But this edition of the text was given a special editorial involvement. Every comma, every line, every thought was scrutinized by a number of editors—each took a different role. Sandi Kirshner and Bill Barke launched the revision and set the initial stage for the development of the book; I am thankful for their confidence in the project and in me. But on a day-to-day basis, there were two editors who worked with me to ensure the quality, thematic integrity, and overall direction of the text, Elizabeth Brooks and Susan Badger.

Elizabeth Brooks was my developmental editor and worked with me on a line-by-line basis to make certain that every thought was as precise as could be, that every paragraph was clear, and that every concept was well developed and necessary. Beth regularly made me write and rewrite; she challenged, prodded, and provided advice. Her skill, knowledge, and sound judgment are reflected on every page of text and the book is immeasurably better because of her expertise; I cannot thank her enough.

Every team has to have a leader—someone who will guide, direct, make tough decisions, and challenge its players to new heights. Allyn and Bacon has the best psychology series editor in the business. Executive editor Susan Badger stands without peers. With keen insight into what psychologists want in a text, with understanding of psychological issues and personalities, and with a terrific sense of perspective, Susan Badger led the Allyn and Bacon team. I have never known an editor with Susan's commitment to every detail of the book—manuscript, design, production, and marketing. Her outlook, ideas, and creativity are unmatched. Her imprint is not only stamped on every page of the text, but it has changed the way I think about teaching psychology. She has set a new standard. I thank her.

Last, I dedicate this text to my wife, Linda. A source of sense, sensibility, and strength, Linda helps me keep my focus. My partner, friend, and lover, Linda shares my life in every way and this book would not be the same without her.

1 What Is Psychology?

"Orfeo" by Orlando A. B.

◆

*N*atural disasters cause destruction, untold suffering, and economic hardship, but they can also bring out the best in people. Hurricane Hugo hit the coast of South Carolina in September 1989; less than one month later, an earthquake registering 7.0 on the Richter scale hit the San Francisco area.

In South Carolina, Hurricane Hugo pummeled Charleston and other coastal areas with 135 m.p.h. winds and 17-foot waves. One of the ten worst hurricanes in this century, Hugo demolished beachfront communities, leaving hundreds of people homeless. Electricity and drinking water

Workers dig through the rubble of the collapsed Bay Bridge after the San Francisco earthquake.

were unavailable for days. Food, medical supplies, clothing, and especially money were needed by victims of the hurricane. Damage estimates for the city of Charleston, South Carolina, were over one billion dollars.

In San Francisco, the earthquake destroyed homes and ruptured gas lines, touching off fires throughout the city. A section of the Bay Bridge collapsed, sending cars plunging into the chasm; the upper level of a one-mile stretch of Interstate Highway 880 collapsed onto the lower level, crushing the cars beneath. Amid all this destruction, ordinary people came forward to help: passersby risked their lives to help free survivors trapped beneath the highway; citizens worked alongside fire fighters to put out the raging fires; people with flashlights helped direct traffic at busy intersections; doctors roamed the city looking for those in need of assistance; and hotel managers opened their lobbies to those whose homes were destroyed or inaccessible.

People living hundreds or even thousands of miles away from these two natural disasters responded. Offers of help came from all over the world. Donations came in the form of money, clothing, food, and medical supplies. Architects, builders, medical personnel, and psychologists offered their services as people began the arduous task of rebuilding their lives. The Soviet Union, still recovering from the aftermath of a devastating earthquake in Soviet Armenia, offered to send experts who had gained valuable knowledge in coping with the damage from earthquakes.

What determines when people choose to help or not help? Are people more likely to help in certain situations than in others? Psychologists who study helping behavior say that people's behavior depends on a number of factors, including issues of anonymity, embarrassment, and the number of observers present in a situation. We will examine helping behavior in more detail in chapter 17.

Helping is just one of a multitude of human behaviors that psychologists study. They explore attraction, aggression, and motivation, and study human development from birth to death. They seek answers to questions such as: Why do some siblings turn out so differently from one another? How can we best cope with feelings of depression or anxiety? What is the best way to teach people new behavior? How does memory work? In what ways does the brain affect behavior?

Psychologists try to answer these questions and hundreds more. The focus of psychology is people, their behavior and mental processes. Psychologists try to understand how biology and the physical and social world affect people's day-to-day behavior and interactions. Psychology helps us understand ourselves.

Defining Psychology

Psychology: The science of behavior and mental processes.

What exactly is psychology? The umbrella of psychology is far-reaching, and it is difficult to provide a definition of psychology that includes all its elements. We begin with a simple broad definition: **Psychology** is the science of behavior and mental processes.

Now let's expand on this simple definition. Because psychology is a *science*, psychologists use scientific principles, methods, and procedures. They use precise procedures and carefully defined methods to present an organized body of knowledge and to make inferences (discussed later in the chapter). As a science, psychology is committed to: *objectivity*—evaluating research and theory on their own merits; *accuracy*—gathering data from the laboratory and the real world in precise ways; and *maintaining a healthy skepticism*—cautiously viewing data and theory until results are repeated and verified.

Because psychologists study mental processes and behavior, they observe every aspect of human functioning—overt actions, mental activity, emotional responses, and physiological reactions. *Overt actions* are any directly observable and measurable movements or the products of such movements. Walking, talking, playing, kissing, gestures, and expressions are examples of overt behavior. Products of overt behavior might be term papers that you write, the mess in your bedroom, or your finely tuned body if you exercise regularly. *Mental processes* include your thoughts about being angry or happy or sad; your ideas; or your reasoning processes. *Emotional responses* include anger, regret, lust, happiness, or depression. Psychologists also study *physiological reactions*, which are closely associated with emotional responses and include an increased heart rate when you are excited, biochemical changes when light stimulates your eye, or reactions to stress such as high blood pressure and ulcers.

The first psychologists studied the mind and mental processes. Later psychologists focused only on overt behavior. Today, psychologists study both mental processes and behavior to see how organisms are affected by, and in turn affect, the social, physical, and biological world. Individual behavior affects the social world economically, politically, and educationally. For example, Mother Teresa's acts of self-sacrifice and courage caused great self-examination worldwide. Psychologists also study the effects of the physical environment, such as the effect of temperature and lighting on workers' productivity or the effects of crowding on people's aggressive behavior. Also, drugs, disease, aging, fatigue, diet, and exercise all affect the body—a person's biological world—and have an impact on behavior.

Psychology thus overlaps with other disciplines including biology, medicine, business organization, sociology, and social work. For example, you will see when we examine health psychology that psychologists examine immune system responses to stress in people's lives.

Aims and Scope of Psychology

The goals of psychology are to *describe* the basic components of behavior, to *explain* them, to *predict* them, and, potentially, to *manage* them.

Human behavior is so complex that no single rule, theory, or explanation can account for everything a person feels, thinks, or does. Thoughts and feelings are especially difficult to observe directly. You can describe the steps involved in driving a car, but describing why you chose to attend a particular college or date a certain person is more difficult.

Describing and explaining behavior are prerequisites to predicting behavior and helping people manage it. Therefore, some psychologists do basic research to uncover, explore, and understand the principles of behavior. They measure and describe behavior in a scientific way, using verifiable observations and carefully controlled research methods. Because behavior and mental processes are not always directly observable, psychologists must sometimes infer the thought processes, emotions, and motivations behind the actions they observe in both human and animal subjects (a topic discussed later). From their research, psychologists develop theories to explain, predict, and help manage behavior. A **theory** is a collection of interrelated ideas and facts put forward to explain and predict behavior and mental processes.

Theory: A collection of interrelated ideas and known facts put forward to summarize, explain, and predict behavior and mental processes.

Predicting behavior is important; it enables psychologists to help people anticipate situations and learn how to express their feelings in manageable and reasonable ways. For example, because excessive stress can cause anxiety, depression, and even heart attacks, psychologists use theories about stress to devise specific therapies to help people handle it more effectively.

A general goal of the discipline of psychology is to combine science, the application of science, and professional practice into one organized endeavor (Strickland, 1988). This sometimes means combining divergent interests, values, and approaches to science, for example, taking into consideration issues of public policy, privacy, scientific inquiry, and even religion. This mixture of concerns often is complicated, but it is one of psychology's strengths. Whether psychologists view psychology as a basic research science or an applied science, and whether they work in a laboratory, private practice, university, industry, or mental health facility, all psychologists study behavior and mental processes. They search for information about basic processes that will help practitioners solve day-to-day problems. Examples of how psychology helps people include: the development of management principles that increase worker motivation and productivity (discussed in chapter 17); the formulation of treatment procedures for tension headaches (discussed in chapters 2, 13, and 15); and research showing that the attachments formed between parents and newborns promote healthy emotional growth in children (discussed in chapter 9).

In sum, psychology is a problem-solving science rooted in research and scientific principles. For most psychologists, their work is a search for the causes of behavior. It is an adventure, an exploration into understanding human behavior and mental processes.

Focus on Learning

- ◆ The definition of psychology is extremely broad; give a comprehensive definition. p. 2
- ◆ What are the goals of psychology? p. 3
- ◆ Name a specific research problem that psychology addresses. Identify a specific situation in which psychology may be used to solve a real-life problem. p. 4

A History of Psychology: Schools of Psychological Thought, Past and Present

Psychologists subscribe to many different perspectives in trying to analyze human behavior. These perspectives have been developed over time—across the history of psychology—and serve to orient researchers, providing them with a frame of reference.

A specific approach to the study of behavior is called a *school of psychological thought*. This section discusses the development of schools of psychological thought (summarized in Table 1.1). Table 1.2 presents a time line of important events in the history of psychology. You will see that the study of behavior and mental processes has had a rollercoaster history with emphasis shifting from one topic to another. Initially, psychologists studied only the mind. Later they focused only on overt behavior. Most recently, mental processes are again being carefully considered along with observable behavior.

TABLE 1.1
Summary of Schools of Psychology

School	Focus	Early Leader
Structuralism	Structures of the mind	Wundt
Functionalism	Functions of the mind	James
Gestalt	Properties of the parts of perceptual experience	Wertheimer
Psychoanalysis	Unconscious mental processes	Freud
Cognitive	Thought processes	various
Behaviorism	Overt, observable behavior	Watson
Humanistic	Individual growth, personal responsibility, and free will	Maslow
Biological	Basic biological mechanisms and structures	various

Structuralism: The Contents of Consciousness

The first widely accepted school of thought was developed by Wilhelm Wundt (1832–1920). In 1879, Wundt founded the first psychological laboratory in Leipzig, Germany, and he is considered the founder of the discipline. Before Wundt, the field of psychology did not exist; psychological questions were within the domain of philosophy, medicine, or theology.

Edward B. Titchener (1867–1927) was an Englishman who popularized Wundt's ideas, along with his own, in the United States and the rest of the

Wilhelm Wundt

TABLE 1.2
Important Events in the History of Psychology

Year	Event
1879	Wilhelm Wundt establishes the first psychology laboratory at Leipzig, Germany.
1883	G. Stanley Hall establishes the first American psychology laboratory at Johns Hopkins University.
1887	First professional journal of psychology in the United States is established by G. Stanley Hall (*American Journal of Psychology*).
1890	William James publishes the widely used *Principles of Psychology*.
1892	American Psychological Association is founded by G. Stanley Hall, its first president.
1894	Margaret Floy Washburn is the first woman to receive a Ph.D. in psychology.
1898	Edward L. Thorndike conducts the first experiments on animal learning.
1900	Sigmund Freud introduces his psychoanalytic theory in *The Interpretation of Dreams*.
1905	Alfred Binet and Theodore Simon devise the first intelligence test.
1906	Ivan Pavlov begins to publish his classic studies of animal learning.
1913	John B. Watson champions psychology as the science of behavior.

Edward B. Titchener

English-speaking world. Titchener and other adherents of **structuralism** considered conscious experience the proper subject matter of psychology. Instead of looking at the broad range of behavior and mental processes that psychologists consider today, they tried to "look inside" a person by studying the contents of the mind. They attempted to observe the inner working of the mind to find the elements of conscious experience.

Titchener used a technique called **introspection** or self-examination—the description and analysis by a person of what he or she is thinking and feeling. Wundt and Titchener did some of the first experiments in psychology. They studied the speed of thought by observing reaction times to simple tasks; for example, they changed elements of the environment such as the intensity of a sound to which a person was listening and recorded reaction time.

By today's standards, the structuralists focused too narrowly on conscious experience. They confused many aspects of psychological functioning by changing many things all at once and measuring several things all at once. Further, understanding one person's conscious experiences could tell a psychologist little about another's conscious experiences. Thus, their results allowed for few if any generalizations and they made little progress in describing the nature of the mind.

Functionalism: How Does the Mind Work?

Before long, a new school of thought developed—**functionalism**—bringing with it a new way of thinking about behavior. As an outgrowth of structuralism, functionalism tried to discover how and why the mind functions (hence the name) and its relation to consciousness. Functionalists sought to understand how people adapted to their environment.

With William James (1842–1910) at its head, functionalism was the first truly American psychology. James, a physician and professor of anatomy at Harvard University, argued that knowing the contents of consciousness (structuralism) was too limited; a psychologist had to know how those contents worked together, how they functioned. Through such knowledge, a psychologist could understand how the mind (consciousness) guided behavior.

In 1890, James published *Principles of Psychology* in which he described the mind not as a static group of elements, but as a dynamic set of continuously evolving elements. It was in this work that he coined the phrase *stream of consciousness*, describing the mind as a river, always flowing rather than remaining still.

James broadened the scope of structuralism by attempting to study animals, by applying psychology in practical areas such as education, and by experimenting on overt behavior, not just mental processes. James's ideas influenced the life and writing of another American psychologist, G. Stanley Hall. Hall (1844–1924) was the first to receive a doctorate in psychology and was the founder of the American Psychological Association.

The early schools of psychological thought were soon replaced by different conceptualizations of psychology: gestalt, psychoanalysis, behaviorism, and cognitive and humanistic approaches.

Gestalt Psychology: Examining Wholes

While some psychologists were grappling with structuralism and functionalism, others were developing very different approaches. One such approach was **Gestalt psychology.**

Structuralism: A school of psychology whose ideas were initiated by Wilhelm Wundt (1832–1920) and later put forth by E. B. Titchener; proponents believed that the proper subject matter of psychology was the study of the contents of consciousness.

Introspection: The technique of examining the contents of the mind through self-report and the careful examination of thoughts and feelings.

Functionalism: A school of psychology that grew out of structuralism and was concerned with how and why the conscious mind works; a principal aim was to know how those contents of consciousness worked together.

Gestalt psychology: A school of psychology which argues that behavior cannot be studied in parts, but must be viewed as a whole; Gestalt psychologists focused on the unity of perception and thinking.

William
James

Sigmund
Freud

Like the functionalists, Gestalt psychologists, such as Max Wertheimer and Kurt Koffka, found Wundt's and Titchener's structuralism too limiting. They argued that it is necessary to study a person's total experience—not just parts of the mind or behavior.

Gestalt psychologists suggested that conscious experience is more than simply the sum of its parts. Arguing that the mind takes the elements of experience and organizes them to form something unique, Gestalt psychologists analyzed the world in terms of perceptual frameworks. They proposed that people form simple sensory elements into patterns by which they interpret the world. By analyzing the whole experience (*gestalt* means *whole*), the patterns of a person's perceptions and thoughts, one can understand the mind and its workings.

Eventually Gestalt psychology became a major influence in many areas of psychology, for example, in therapy. A Gestalt-oriented therapist, when dealing with a problem member of a family, might call in an entire family unit to see how the "part" (person with the problem) can be better understood in the context of the "whole" (the entire family). But as broad as its influence would become, Gestalt approaches never achieved as wide a following as psychoanalysis did.

Psychoanalysis: Probing the Unconscious

One of the first researchers to develop a theory about emotional disturbance was Sigmund Freud (1856–1939). Freud was a physician interested in helping people overcome anxiety. He focused on the causes and treatment of emotional disturbances. Freud worked from the premise that unconscious processes direct daily behavior; he ultimately developed techniques such as free association and dream interpretation to explore those unconscious processes. He emphasized the idea that childhood experiences influence future adult behavior and that sexual energy fuels day-to-day behavior.

Freud's approach is called the **psychoanalytic approach,** or psychoanalysis. Psychoanalytic theories assume that maladjustment is a consequence of anxiety resulting from unresolved conflicts and forces of which a person may be unaware. The psychoanalytic perspective has undergone much change since Freud first devised it; at times it seems only loosely

Psychoanalytic approach: The theory developed by Sigmund Freud (1856–1939), who was interested in how personality develops and in the treatment of maladjustment. Freud's approach focused on the unconscious and on how it directs day-to-day behavior.

John B. Watson

B. F. Skinner

connected to Freud's basic ideas. Although contemporary psychoanalysis differs from Freud's original version, its overall focus remains similar. Chapter 12 discusses Freud's theory of personality, and chapter 15 discusses psychoanalysis as the therapeutic technique derived from his theory.

Behaviorism: Observable Behavior

Despite their differences in focus, the structuralists, functionalists, Gestaltists, and psychoanalysts were all concerned with the functioning of the mind. They were all interested in private perception and conscious or unconscious activity. But in the early twentieth century, American psychology moved from studying the contents of the mind to studying overt behavior. At the forefront of that movement was John B. Watson (1878–1958), the founder of **behaviorism.**

Watson was an upstart—clever, brash, and defiant. Trained as a functionalist, he argued that there is no reasonable, objective way to observe the human mind. He contended that observable behavior, not the private contents of the mind, is the proper subject matter of psychology. According to Watson, psychologists should study only activities that can be objectively observed and measured. This was a major break with previous psychologists; it rejected the work of Wundt and most other early psychologists and argued that psychologists should put the study of consciousness behind them.

After Watson, other American researchers extended and developed behaviorism. Behaviorists such as Harvard psychologist B. F. Skinner (1904–1990) attempted to explain the causes of behavior by cataloging and describing the relations among events in the environment (stimuli) and a person's or animal's reactions (responses). Skinner's behaviorism led the way for thousands of research studies on conditioning and human behavior, a special focus on stimuli and responses, and controlling behavior through learning principles.

The behaviorists' perspective focuses on how observable responses are learned, modified, and forgotten. It usually focuses on current behavior and how it is acquired or modified rather than on inherited characteristics or early childhood experiences. A fundamental assumption of behavioral theorists is that disordered behavior can be reshaped and that appropriate, worthwhile behavior can be substituted through the traditional learning techniques described in chapter 5.

Early behaviorists took a stern, unbending view of the scope of psychology by refusing to study mental phenomena (Mahoney, 1989). But other psychologists (non-behaviorists) argued that not all behavior can be explained by stimuli, responses, and their relationship; they focused on such topics as the origins of thought, creativity, and the expression of love. Behaviorists today take a broader view; most behavioral psychologists, including Skinner, are beginning again to study a wider range of human behavior, including mental phenomena and especially thought processes.

Humanistic Psychology: Free Will

Another school of thought that figures into the landscape of modern psychology is **humanistic psychology.** Humanistic psychology arose in response to psychoanalytic and behavioral views. Humanists see people as good and striving to fulfill themselves, whereas psychoanalytically-oriented theorists saw people as fraught with inner conflict, and behaviorists were too stimulus-response bound. Humanistic psychologists see people as having free will, the ability to choose the paths they take in life. In other words, human beings have control of their lives. Humanists focus on individual uniqueness and decision making, and assume that inner psychic forces contribute positively to establishing and maintaining a normal life-style.

Humanistic psychologists assert that human beings are conscious, creative, and born with an innate desire to fulfill themselves. They say that psychologists must examine human behavior individually. Proponents of the humanistic view, such as Abraham Maslow and Carl Rogers (whom we will study in chapter 11), believe that human beings have a desire for **self-actualization,** that is, fulfillment of their human potential, and have the ability to choose their own "reality" (Andrews, 1989).

Cognitive Psychology: Thinking, Again

Many psychologists realized that strict behaviorism had limitations; they especially reacted to its narrow focus on observable behavior. As an outgrowth of behaviorism (and a reaction to it), **cognitive psychology** focuses on thought processes and mental activities involved in perception, memory, learning, and thinking. Cognitive psychology focuses on the mental processes involved in behavior, such as how people solve problems and appraise situations as threatening. Cognitive psychology is sometimes seen as antibehaviorist, but it isn't. Cognitive psychology views the strict behavioral approach as incomplete, missing a key component—mental processes.

Cognitive psychology is not restricted to a single area, but spans many psychological fields. Thus it is hard to identify one person who can be called the leader of the cognitive perspective. However, psychologists such as Albert Bandura, Albert Ellis, Aaron Beck, and Richard Lazarus have taken prominent roles. The cognitive perspective asserts that human beings engage in behavior, both worthwhile and maladjusted, because of ideas and thoughts. Cognitive psychologists may be clinicians working with maladjusted clients to help them achieve more realistic ideas about the world so they might change their behavior. For example, cognitive psychologists may help people with eating disorders realize that they should not measure their successes and failures through weight and food-related activities. Social psychologists with a cognitive emphasis examine how people process, retain, retrieve, and code information about other people (to be discussed in chapter 16).

Biological Perspective: Predispositions

Increasingly, researchers are turning to biology to explain some human behavior. The **biological perspective** (sometimes called a neuroscience perspective) focuses on how physical mechanisms affect emotions, feelings, thoughts, desires, and sensory experiences. Those with a biological perspective tend to examine psychological issues in terms of how inherited and biological structures affect process and behavior. They may focus on genetic abnormalities, central nervous system problems, or hormonal changes. Researchers such as Kety, Gottesman, and Rosenthal (discussed in chapter 15) are often cited as leaders of the biological perspective.

The biological perspective is especially important in studies of sensation and perception, memory, and some types of maladjustment. It is pivotal in examining abnormal behavior such as schizophrenia, which is linked to genetics (at least in part), and alcoholism, which in many cases has biological underpinnings.

Self-actualization: The process proposed by humanistic psychologists by which individuals strive to fulfill themselves.

Cognitive psychology: A school of psychology that focuses on the thought processes and mental activities involved in perception, memory, learning, and thinking.

Biological perspective: Examines psychological issues based on how heredity and biological structures affect behavior; it focuses on how physical mechanisms create emotions, feelings, thoughts, and desires.

Eclecticism: The Best of Everything

Psychologists realize that a complex relationship exists among the factors that affect both overt behavior and mental processes. Therefore, most American psychologists involved in applied psychology, especially clinical psychology, are **eclectic** in their perspective. Instead of studying only one aspect of behavior or taking only one approach to treatment, they use a variety of approaches to evaluate data, theory, and therapy.

An eclectic orientation allows a researcher or practitioner to view a problem from several orientations. Consider depression, the disabling mood disorder in which people become exceedingly sad, which affects ten to twenty percent of men and women in America at some time in their lives (chapter 14 deals at length with depression). From a biological perspective alone, people become depressed because of changes in brain chemistry. From a behavioral point of view alone, people learn to be depressed and sad because of faulty reward systems in their environment. From a psychoanalytic perspective, people become depressed because their early childhood experiences caused them to form a negative outlook on life. Humanists argue that depression is often caused by people choosing inaction because of poor role models. The cognitive perspective suggests that depression is made worse by the interpretations (thoughts) an individual might adopt about a situation. An eclectic position recognizes the complex nature of depression and acknowledges each of the possible contributions; an eclectic practitioner evaluates the person, the depression, and the context in which the person is depressed.

Is Psychology a Unified Science?

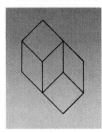

*Y*ou have learned that psychology has a relatively short history (slightly more than 111 years) and that psychologists specialize in different fields, in different settings, with different goals. Some examine fundamental issues in learning, memory, or perception. Others train practitioners to treat learning-disabled children. And there are psychologists who focus solely on the delivery of mental health services.

These divergent interests have caused leading psychologists to speculate whether psychology is a single science or many (Spence, 1987). They ask, "Is there a core of thought to which all psychologists relate?" (Altman, 1987). The sometimes heated debate centers on whether a unified approach to psychology can be maintained. Or is psychology evolving into independent and separate areas? Most psychologists will agree that psychology has many areas of interest and that it is both a basic research science and an applied science. In addition, each area of specialization borrows from others to build the discipline as a whole.

The future of psychology has respected psychologists at odds. I believe that there *is* a core of psychological information and that psychologists use the same techniques and principles regardless of their specialties. Consequently, I view psychology as one science with many applications and many types of psychologists (as does Matarazzo, 1987). In this text, I present the various subdisciplines of psychology in a manner that shows psychology to be a unified discipline with a central core of information.

Eclectic: A combination of theories, facts, or techniques. In clinical psychology, eclecticism usually describes the practice of using whatever therapy techniques are appropriate for an individual client rather than relying exclusively on the techniques of one school of psychology.

You will see that there are central ideas, principles, and procedures that are accepted by all psychologists (Kimble, 1989). After reading this text, you will be familiar with many of these key concepts. Three I mention now. *First*, psychology is the science of behavior and mental processes, and behavior and mental processes can be explained, predicted, and managed, at least to some extent. *Second*, nature puts limits on a person's abilities, but environment influences the extent to which a person's potentials are realized. And *third,* human uniqueness, human values, and the complexity of human behavior require that psychologists rely on scientific methods and procedures in order to understand behavior.

Clearly, researchers have divergent interests. Those who study the effect of television violence on behavior and those who study neurotransmitters and their relation to schizophrenia focus on seemingly unrelated research problems. But both groups use the experimental method, examine effects of these phenomena on behavior, and want to apply these research findings. Both groups call themselves psychologists, and their research findings and ideas are used by practitioners to treat clients with behavior problems. Thus, researchers and practitioners can be said to use the same ideas, principles, and procedures.

Psychology is a science that answers important questions. To do so, it uses a variety of methods, is flexible in explaining behavior; accounts for the complexity of the brain, the environment, and behavior relations; and accommodates competing theories (Kleinginna and Kleinginna, 1988). There are many specialties and interests, but only *one* science of psychology (Fowler, 1990). The diverse range of psychologists' orientations is often reflected in their careers; we shall consider the range of those careers next.   ◆

---

* Identify the assumptions underlying each school of psychological thought. pp. 5–9
* How would the biological, behavioral, and cognitive schools of thought view a specific topic such as depression? pp. 8–9
* In what ways can psychology be viewed as a unified discipline? p. 10

Focus on Learning

Careers in Psychology

Psychologists study nearly every aspect of life, not only to understand how people behave but also to help them lead happier, healthier, more productive lives. Some people mistakenly assume that psychologists primarily assist those suffering from debilitating mental disorders such as schizophrenia or severe depression. Psychologists who help people with severe emotional and behavior problems are called clinical psychologists.

Besides helping people with debilitating disorders, psychologists also help people whose maladaptive habits cause them to suffer from eating disorders, to do poorly in school, or to fail in their relationships. Psychologists also help well-adjusted people lead more exciting, fulfilling lives by providing services such as career counseling and by assisting with community projects such as building shelters for the homeless and aiding schools and communities in coping with natural disasters such as Hurricane Hugo or the San Francisco earthquake. Psychologists seek to provide people with interpersonal skills, knowledge about self-help techniques, and knowledge about how to do and evaluate research. You can see that some psychologists practice psychology, while others teach or do research. Most are involved in a combination of activities, for example, research and teaching.

Psychologists are persons who apply principles of behavior in scientific research or other settings; most have advanced degrees, usually a Ph.D. (Doctor of Philosophy). Many psychologists also train for an additional year or two in a specialized area such as mental health and therapy, perception, physiology, child development, learning, or teaching.

The oldest and largest professional organization for psychologists is the American Psychological Association (APA). Founded in 1892, its purpose is

Psychologist: A person who studies behavior and uses behavioral principles in scientific research or in applied settings for the treatment of emotional problems.

Psychiatrist: A medical doctor who has completed a residency specializing in the study of behavior and the treatment of patients with emotional and physical disorders.

to advance psychology as a science, a profession, and a means of promoting human welfare. Today, the APA has more than 68,000 members, with the majority holding doctoral degrees from accredited universities. In addition, there are more than 25,000 student affiliates.

The APA is not the sole voice of psychology. Many specialty groups have emerged over the years; for example, organizations consisting mainly of developmental, behavioral, cognitive, or neuroscience psychologists have formed. Recently, the American Psychological Society (APS) has formed; it has a large membership of psychologists with academic interests, and focuses on scientific (rather than practice or applied) interests. Among its goals, two that are especially important are to preserve the scientific base of psychology and to promote public understanding of psychology as a science. Some see the formation of this group as a challenge to the APA; others see the APS as an allied organization. The future of the APS is still unclear, but it has great potential for assuming a leadership role as a voice for researchers in psychology.

The Difference between Clinical Psychologists, Psychiatrists, and Psychoanalysts

People often confuse clinical psychologists, psychiatrists, and psychoanalysts. All are mental health practitioners, but each looks at behavior differently. **Psychiatrists** are physicians (medical doctors) who specialize in the treatment of disturbed behavior. Patients who see psychiatrists often have physical and emotional problems. Because of their medical training, psychiatrists can prescribe drugs and can admit patients for hospitalization. Clinical psychologists and psychiatrists often see a similar mix of clients (Knesper, Pagnucco, and Wheeler, 1985) and sometimes work together as part of a mental health team. Most psychologists and psychiatrists support collaborative efforts. However, a friendly rivalry exists between the two disciplines because of their sometimes very different points of view (Berg, 1986).

Clinical psychologists generally have more extensive training in assessment, research, and psychological treatment of emotional problems than

Clinical psychologists generally have extensive training in assessment, research, and psychological treatment of emotional problems.

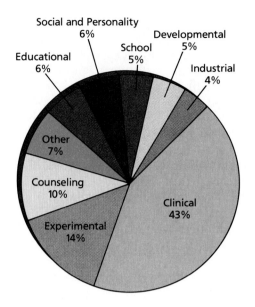

Social and Personality
6%

Developmental
5%

School
5%

Educational
6%

Industrial
4%

Other
7%

Counseling
10%

Clinical
43%

Experimental
14%

FIGURE 1.1
The percentage of psychologists currently working in different branches of psychology is shown here. The human service subfields of clinical, counseling, and school psychology account for more than half of the membership of the APA. (Source: Pion, Bramblett, and Wicherski, 1987)

psychiatrists do. They view their roles in a hospital setting and with patients differently (Kingsbury, 1987). Further, psychiatrists use a medical approach that often involves assumptions about behavior—for example, that abnormal behavior is disease-like in nature—that psychologists do not share.

Psychoanalysts are psychiatrists who have training in a specific method of treating people with emotional problems. Their treatment method, called *psychoanalysis*, was originated by Freud and includes the study of unconscious motivation and dream analysis. Psychoanalysis often requires a course of daily therapy sessions that may last several years. In 1988, psychoanalytic institutes changed their policy and began to accept nonphysicians into their training programs. So while each type of practitioner may treat a similar group of clients, the training and assumptions they bring may vary, and this may be reflected in their choice of treatment.

Psychology as a Career

Psychology is a diverse and exciting field that attracts many college students who like the idea of helping others. Every year almost all the approximately 3,000 new holders of doctorate degrees in psychology accept jobs directly related to their training (Pion, Bramblett, and Wicherski, 1987). There were slightly more than 100,000 psychologists in the United States in 1985 (Stapp, Tucker, and VandenBos, 1985).

If you are considering becoming a psychologist or entering a related field, there is good news: unemployment among psychologists is low and new psychologists continue to find employment in areas related to their graduate training (see Figure 1.1). Most experts agree that employment opportunities will continue to improve in the 1990s (Pion, Bramblett, and Wicherski, 1987).

Training is the key to employment. A psychologist who obtains a Ph.D. from an accredited program in clinical psychology, does an internship in a state hospital, and becomes licensed will have a wide variety of job opportunities available in both the private and the public sectors. Individuals with master's degrees can function in a wide variety of settings, and even those with bachelor's degrees can take an important role in the delivery of psy-

Psychoanalyst: A person (usually a psychiatrist) who has studied the technique of psychoanalysis and uses it in treating people with emotional problems.

chological services. Salary, responsibilities, and working conditions tend to be commensurate with level of training.

Becoming a psychologist is difficult but rewarding. State hospitals employ both bachelor's and master's level psychologists to work with groups of impaired individuals. School systems often hire master's level school psychologists to administer tests and to work with school children. Business and industry employ bachelor's and master's level psychologists in personnel departments and in other positions to evaluate the success of ongoing programs.

Sixty-two percent of the doctoral membership of the APA work in the delivery of human services. Of this number, thirty-nine percent work in clinics, community mental health centers, health maintenance organizations, veterans hospitals, public hospitals, and public and private mental health hospitals. The remainder are private practitioners who maintain offices and work in public and private school settings (Pion, Bramblett, and Wicherski, 1987).

About fourteen percent of psychologists are employed by business, government, and industry. Among those employed by hospitals, most spend their time in the direct delivery of human services, including individual and group therapy. Doctoral-level psychologists provide more than fifty million hours annually for four to ten million people (Howard et al., 1986; Stapp, Tucker, and VandenBos, 1985). Thirty-four percent of the APA are employed by universities in various settings, with nearly half of those in psychology departments. University psychologists spend most of their time researching and teaching.

As a helping profession with strong scientific roots, psychology continues to attract an increasing number of women. The number of women in graduate training programs has doubled in the last twenty years. Data suggest that this trend is likely to continue (Russo and Denmark, 1987). The first women psychologists received training similar to their male colleagues, but were much less likely to achieve a professional status equivalent to that of men (Furumoto and Scarborough, 1986). But today, the research of women such as Mavis Hetherington, Janet Taylor Spence, Elizabeth Loftus, and Sandra Scarr continues to be at the forefront of scientific inquiry.

Today, women are presidents of national, regional, and local organizations, and their thinking and work often dominate the psychological journals (Russo and Denmark, 1987). Although proportionately more women than men are entering psychology, women are also more likely than men to be employed on a part-time basis (Stapp, Fulcher, and Wicherski, 1984).

One Psychologist's Career

My career in psychology began when I was in the tenth grade and conducted a survey of sexual attitudes at my high school. First, I passed out anonymous questionnaires to the juniors and seniors. Then I spent hours collating and summarizing the data. I found the data fascinating (I was about as advanced as my peers) although I did not yet understand how to put them in a framework that would make sense out of them (again, I was only as advanced as my peers).

In college I majored in psychology and was particularly interested in clinical psychology. I took courses in traditional experimental psychology—learning, physiology, perception—but especially enjoyed abnormal psychology, child development, and personality. In addition to classes, I worked in a treatment center for emotionally disturbed children. The work was hard and emotionally demanding, and the pay was not particularly good. Later, as a laboratory assistant, I collected and analyzed data for a psychologist doing research in vision. I loved hunting for answers to scientific questions, speculating about new ideas, designing research questions, and collecting data.

My graduate studies included research in perception, and I studied information processing in vision. In graduate school my intellectual skills were sharpened, my knowledge base expanded, and my interests focused and refined. My teachers were the best in their field and I drew upon their experience and sharp intellects. The fun, challenge, and excitement of graduate school (and the hard work) were an unparalleled experience.

After earning my Ph.D., I became an assistant professor at the University of South Carolina. My research was in cognitive psychology studying perceptual phenomena such as eye movements. At South Carolina I teach, do research in cognitive psychology, and write psychology textbooks. My goal is to share my excitement for psychology in the classroom, in my textbook writing, and in professional journals.

Understanding psychology is one of the main focuses of my life; it enriches me, helps me understand myself and others, and continues to be a fulfilling career. Now, as a professor and chairman of the psychology department, I still find psychology the best of all possible professions. It maintains its challenge; every year it becomes more exciting as new discoveries are made.

Over time my interests changed. At first, I was interested in the delivery of mental health services to children; later I focused on applied research issues, such as eye movements among learning-disabled readers. But my primary focus remains in basic research issues. My change in orientation reflects the three major areas in which psychologists work: the human service fields, the applied fields, and basic experimental research.

What Psychologists Do

The three main fields of psychology—human services, applied research, and experimental psychology—have much in common. All consider research and theory to be the cornerstone of their approach. A human service provider may also do research, and a researcher who works in a university may also provide human services to the university or the community at large. Learning principles discovered in an experimental laboratory may be applied by a human services psychologist to help an alcoholic patient. Similarly, problems discovered by therapists challenge researchers to investigate causes in the laboratory. This cross-fertilization is good. Let's look at each of these areas within psychology.

Human Service Fields

Many psychologists work in settings in which they teach people to cope more effectively by applying behavioral principles. Their aim is to help people solve problems and to promote well-being. Within the human service area are the subfields of clinical, counseling, community, and school psychology.

Clinical Psychology. Clinical psychologists specialize in helping clients with behavior problems such as anger, shyness, depression, or marital discord. Their aim is the promotion of well-being. Clinical psychologists work either in private practice or at a hospital, mental institution, or social service agency. They administer psychological tests, interview potential clients, and use psychological methods to treat emotional problems. Many universities employ psychologists to help students and staff adjust to the pressures of academic life. In universities, clinical psychologists often have laboratories where they research the causes of abnormal behavior.

The subfield of clinical psychology came about as a result of the work of Lightner Witmer (1867–1956), a charter member of the APA, who called for the establishment of a field within psychology that would focus on helping people (McReynolds, 1987). Witmer established the first psychological clinic at the University of Pennsylvania and coined the term *clinical psychologist*. The field of clinical psychology grew in the next eighty years, especially after World War II when training for clinical psychologists began to focus on professional practice and human service needs (Strickland, 1988).

Counseling Psychology. Counseling psychologists, like clinical psychologists, work with people who have emotional problems. Counseling psychologists also help people with career planning, marriage problems, and family planning.

Traditionally, the clients of counseling psychologists have had less serious problems than those of clinical psychologists. However, in the past decade, counseling psychologists have increasingly become engaged in psychotherapy and other activities that were previously performed exclusively by clinical psychologists. According to many practitioners and researchers, counseling and clinical psychology are converging (Fitzgerald and Osipow, 1986). For some psychologists, this is a controversial idea; for others, it is an idea whose time has come (Levy, 1984). Others foresee further mergers with different areas like psychology with its emphasis on interpersonal relations (Leary and Maddux, 1987).

Counseling psychologists may work for public agencies such as mental health centers, hospitals, and universities. Many work in college or university counseling bureaus where they help students adjust to the university atmosphere and provide vocational and educational guidance. Like clinical psychologists, many counseling psychologists continue to explore the causes and treatment of maladjustment through research.

Community Psychology. Community psychologists work for mental health agencies, state governments, and private organizations. They strengthen existing social support networks and stimulate the formation of new networks to meet a variety of challenges (Gonzales et al., 1983). Their goals are to help individuals, and the neighborhoods or communities they live in, to grow, develop, and plan for the future. Community psychology emerged in response to the widespread desire for an action-oriented approach to individual and social adjustment, and one key element of community psychology is community involvement to effect social change. For example, community psychologists have been instrumental in organizing social support groups that help AIDS patients and their families handle the stress and loss of self-esteem produced by this catastrophic illness.

School Psychology. School psychology can be seen as psychology's ambassador to the schools, with the aim of implementing comprehensive services (Fagan, 1986). Many school psychologists see their primary job as helping students, teachers, parents, and others understand each other (Bardon, 1982; Trachtman, 1981). School psychology began in 1896 at the University of Pennsylvania in a clinic founded to study and treat children considered morally or mentally defective (French, 1984). Today there are

Community psychologists help individuals and communities face a variety of challenges, including the formation of support groups.

more than 30,000 school psychologists, most of whom work in educational systems.

School psychologists' jobs vary with their level of training. Those with bachelor's degrees usually only administer tests. Those with master's degrees administer and interpret tests and help teachers with classroom-related problems. Psychologists with Ph.D.s perform all those tasks and also influence school policies and procedures (Bardon, 1983). They establish communication among parents, teachers, administrators, and other psychologists at the school. They also provide information to teachers and parents about students' progress and advise them how to help students achieve more.

Applied Psychology

Applied psychologists do research and use that research to solve everyday practical problems. Psychologists who treat people with emotional problems function as applied psychologists. So do many other psychologists who use psychological principles in business, government, or institutions such as hospitals.

Engineering psychologists (sometimes called human factors psychologists) focus on how to use machines most efficiently (for example, how to design the best automated bank teller or the most pleasing computer screen). *Educational psychologists* focus on how learning proceeds in the classroom, how intelligence affects performance, and the relationship between personality and learning. *Forensic psychologists* focus on legal issues, the court, and correctional systems. They often work with the courts in evaluating whether an inmate is ready for parole, or whether a specific rehabilitation program is achieving its goals. *Health psychologists* focus on the way life-style changes can facilitate health improvement. They devise techniques to help people with medical and psychological problems. *Sports psychology* is an emerging field that focuses on brain behavior interactions, the role of sports in healthful life-styles, and the motivation and preparation of athletes in sports-related activities. *Industrial/organizational* psychologists are concerned with the way

Industrial/organizational psychologists use psychological research to help employers select, evaluate, and motivate workers.

employers evaluate employees; they focus on personnel selection, employee motivation, work behavior, and work appraisals. They apply psychological research and theory to organizational problems (such as productivity, turnover, absenteeism, and management-labor relations) and work in personnel offices, universities, and businesses to help evaluate programs.

Experimental Psychology

Experimental psychology, the other major subfield of psychology, focuses on identifying and understanding the basic processes involved in behavior and thought. Experimental psychology is an approach, not a specific field. When a psychologist says that he or she is an experimental psychologist, it means the researcher uses a set of *techniques*; it does *not* define the *topics* that a psychologist examines. Thus, clinical psychologists are involved in experimental research, as are school psychologists, cognitive psychologists, and physiological psychologists. Many experimental psychologists teach in university settings as well as do research.

Experimental psychology thus covers many areas of interest, some of which overlap with fields outside psychology. An experimental psychologist may be interested in visual perception; in how people learn language or solve problems; in how hormones influence behavior; in the neurochemistry of the brain; in eye movements; or in the components of emotion. Many in the subfields of psychology consider themselves wholly experimentally oriented. These do not, as a general practice, offer help for the emotionally disturbed or offer practical problem-solving applications. Instead, they seek to understand the basic processes of behavior.

The field of *developmental psychology* focuses on the emotional, physical, and intellectual changes that take place over the life span of organisms. Increasingly, psychologists are looking at behavior from a developmental perspective, asking how a particular behavior changes as people mature physically, emotionally, and intellectually. *Social psychology* studies how other people affect individual behavior and thoughts and especially how people interact with one another. Social psychologists examine how the presence of others affects attitude formation, how aggressive behavior emerges, when people are willing to help others, and how and when people form intimate relationships. Social psychology, with its wide scope of interests, has emerged as a dominant field in psychology. *Cognitive psychology* focuses on thought processes, especially the relationship of learning, memory, and perception. Cognitive psychologists often examine how organisms process and interpret information based on some internal representation in memory. *Physiological psychology* (sometimes called neuropsychology) tries to understand the relationship of the brain and its mechanisms to behavior. Drugs, hormones, and even brain transplants are examined. This research often involves specialized techniques for studying behavior, some of which are considered next.

Focus on Learning

- Careers in psychology are diverse and plentiful; identify the major vocational choices available for bachelor's, master's, and Ph.D. level psychologists. p. 13
- Identify the key focus of the human service fields, applied psychology, and experimental psychology. p. 15
- What do psychologists mean when they say that they are experimental psychologists? p. 18

Techniques Used to Study Behavior

If you ever have the opportunity to tour a psychologist's laboratory, take the tour. Even better, if you have an opportunity to assist a psychologist in research, take advantage of it. Although psychologists use some of the same techniques as other scientists, they must refine these techniques to deal with the uncertainties of human behavior. Psychologists have developed an arsenal of techniques and methods for investigating patterns of behavior, some of which are unique to psychology.

Animals and Human Beings

Psychologists study behavior in both animals and human beings. By studying how animals and human beings react under different circumstances, psychologists learn about the basic principles of behavior and the possibilities of their application.

Some experimental psychologists study behavior by observing it first in animals and then generalizing the principles they discover to human behavior. Using animals in research studies allows experimenters to isolate simple aspects of behavior and eliminate the complex distractions and variables that arise in studies involving human beings. It also enables them to control the life history of the organism being studied, to perform autopsies to obtain information, and—since most animals have shorter life spans than human beings—to study several generations in a short time.

Many people object to the use of animals in research, but there are no realistic alternatives (Gallup and Suarez, 1985). For example, experiments on laboratory rats reveal much about the addictive properties of cocaine and its adverse effects on behavior; doing similar experiments on human beings, of course, would be unethical. In addition, many people with incurable diseases and disorders can only hope for a cure through animal research and experimentation (Feeney, 1987). Still, research on animals is only a small part (about seven percent) of the research published in psychological journals (Miller, 1985), and most researchers are sensitive to the needs of animals (Novak and Suomi, 1988). The American Psychological Association has strict ethical guidelines for animal research. There is currently great conflict between researchers who use animal subjects and animal rights activists, but the issue has been around for many years and is likely to be around for many more (Dewsbury, 1990).

Psychologists more often work with human participants, traditionally called **subjects.** In such research, psychologists investigate many of the same processes they do with animals, as well as design experiments specifically for human subjects. Suppose a psychologist decides to test whether an enhanced environment makes organisms smarter—the researcher may use both animals and human subjects. The researcher may first train a rat to run complicated mazes while placing its litter mate in a barren environment. Several months later, the researcher examines the two animals and discovers the maze-running rat's brain cells are larger and have more internal connections. Along the same lines, the psychologist may test whether a decline in IQ scores shown by some nursing home residents can be stopped or reversed by enriching their environment with classes and special activities.

Psychologists do research in both laboratory settings and the real world. They generally try to place their research findings and interpretations in a framework of real-world problems and perspectives. Their ultimate aims are to understand and make reliable predictions about the complexities of human behavior and thus help people manage their lives.

Subject: An individual who participates in an experiment and from whose behavior data are collected; sometimes called a *participant*.

Accidental Discovery

The typical research process is usually systematic and begins with a specific question. But sometimes a researcher searching for the cause of a particular behavior or the answer to a particular question may unexpectedly find an answer to another problem. Such was the case with well-known psychologist Harry Harlow.

Harlow, Terrycloth, and Infant Monkeys. Harry Harlow's (1905–1981) research began in a curious way. He had been breeding a colony of rhesus monkeys which he was going to use for a series of studies on exploration and learning discrimination. To keep the monkeys from transmitting diseases to their offspring, Harlow kept the newborns in "splendidly germ-free isolation from their mothers" (Sears, 1982, p. 1281). The infants thrived but seemed to have "emotional" problems. As adults, for example, they would not mate. Harlow noted that the infant monkeys clung to blankets in their cages and became agitated if the blankets were removed. His intuitive sense told him that their behavior might be important.

Harlow had a new idea—a hypothesis—that the blankets had become surrogate mothers. A **hypothesis** is a tentative idea that expresses a causal relationship between two events or variables. To test his hypothesis, Harlow designed wire mesh "mothers" with nipples that could convey milk; some of the mothers were covered in terrycloth and some were left bare. In a systematic series of experiments he found that infant monkeys became attached to the surrogate mothers and that they became more attached to the cloth-covered ones.

These results stimulated Harlow and others to seek the causes of such behavior, to develop a theory to explain the behavior, and to explore the general nature of early human infant attachment. (Recall that a *theory* is a collection of interrelated ideas and facts put forward to explain and predict behavior and mental processes.) Harlow's early work, his search for causes, led him and other researchers to discover some of the principles of early childhood attachment and to develop a theory about it. (Harlow's research is discussed in more detail in chapter 11.)

Systematic Explorations

Although researchers like Harlow may discover some things accidentally, they always follow up *systematically*; that is, they try to consider all the aspects of a situation that might cause an organism to behave as it does.

Observation may show that two types of behavior often occur together, but this does not necessarily mean that one behavior causes the other. For example, beer consumption increased sharply from 1900 to 1990; at the same time, life expectancy has increased sharply. These two events have paralleled one another, but are unrelated. (Beer consumption was neither the cause of life expectancy increases, nor were life expectancy increases the cause of increased beer consumption.) Only controlled laboratory experiments permit researchers to make *cause-and-effect statements*—to make inferences about the causes of behavior.

Hypothesis: A tentative statement about a causal relationship between two variables or situations to be evaluated in an experiment.

Correlated and Causally Related Events. An important point to remember is that *correlated events are not necessarily causally related.* Two events are *correlated* when the presence of a high value of one variable or situation is regularly associated with a high (or low) value of another. If, for example, a researcher finds that children from broken homes have more emotional

FIGURE 1.2
Correlations do not show causation. When research shows that broken homes and crime are correlated, it does not show causation. Poverty, a third variable, may be the cause of both crime and broken homes.

problems than other children, he or she can state that as a fact; the researcher can say that there is a correlation. But these data do not permit causal statements, that is, we cannot conclude that broken homes cause emotional problems. Even though broken homes provide an atmosphere conducive to emotional stress in children, too many other variables can also contribute to emotional problems, so we cannot state with certainty that broken homes *cause* later emotional disturbances. By contrast, events are causally related when one event makes another event occur—one event or situation is contingent on the other.

Thus, although a correlation shows that a relationship exists between two variables, that relationship may result from a common cause (both variables are affected by a third variable, not by each other) or from the method used to gather the data (see Figure 1.2). Researchers are careful to distinguish between events that are causally related and those that are only correlated. The topic of correlations is discussed further in the Appendix.

Significant Differences. When psychologists suggest that one situation causes another, they have to be sure that certain conditions are met. They pay close attention to how the data are collected and to whether the results of the study are repeatable. Researchers want to be sure that the differences they find are significant. For psychologists, a **significant difference** is the statistically determined likelihood that a behavior has not occurred because of chance alone. For example, when one therapy technique appears to be more effective than another, the researcher wants to be sure that the first technique is significantly different and that the difference is enough to be important. The results are only significantly different if they could not have occurred by chance, by one or two subjects, or by a unique set of subjects. Such conclusions can only come from experiments.

Controlled Experiments

To make meaningful causal inferences, psychologists must create situations in which they can limit the likelihood of obtaining a result that is simply a chance occurrence or due to irrelevant factors. Only by using carefully formulated experiments can psychologists make sound interpretations of their

Significant difference: A statistically determined likelihood that a behavior has not occurred because of chance alone.

results and cautiously extend them to other (sometimes therapeutic) situations. The technique they use more than any other to explore cause-and-effect relationships is the controlled experiment.

An **experiment** is a procedure in which a researcher systematically manipulates elements of a situation in order to discover and describe the relationship between these elements. For example, if a researcher wanted to determine the relationship between a person's eating behavior and his or her weight gains or losses, the researcher could systematically vary how much the person ate and weigh him or her each day. Experiments have specific components and requirements including variables, experimental and control groups, operational definitions, and guidelines for sample sizes.

Variables. Researchers manipulate variables in order to measure how changes in a variable affect behavior. A **variable** is a characteristic of a situation or person that is subject to change. For example, a characteristic of a situation that might change is temperature; temperature is a variable that affects behavior. Another variable is the way people respond to various drug dosages—the dosage level of a drug is a variable. The variable directly and purposely manipulated by the experimenter in a controlled experiment is the **independent variable**—for example, the temperature level, a drug dosage level, or amount of food eaten. It is varied to see what effect it has on behavior—for example, whether the person's activity levels increase or decrease after taking a drug. The behavior (or change) in the organism being measured is the **dependent variable**—the activity level of the person in the above situation.

To see more clearly how variables come into play in an experiment, imagine a simple experiment to determine the effects of sleep loss on behavior. The independent variable (the variable manipulated) might be the number of hours college students were allowed to sleep. The dependent variable could be students' reaction time to a stimulus, such as how quickly they push a button when a light is flashed. The subjects, or participants, in the study might be a large group of college students who normally sleep about seven hours per night.

The tentative idea, or working hypothesis, of the experiment might be that students deprived of sleep will do less well on the reaction time task than those who are allowed to sleep their regular seven hours. Suppose the subjects sleep in the laboratory on four successive nights and are tested each morning in a reaction time task. The subjects sleep seven hours on each of the first three nights, but only four hours on the fourth. If the response times after the first three nights are constant, the researcher can infer that any slowing of reaction time on the fourth test is the result of depriving the subjects of sleep.

If all other factors are held equal, any observed differences in reaction time can be attributed to the independent variable (number of hours of sleep). That is, changes in the independent variable (numbers of hours of sleep) will produce changes in the dependent variable (reaction time). And if the results show that students deprived of sleep respond on the reaction time task one-half second slower than they did after normal sleep, the researcher could feel justified in concluding that sleep deprivation acts to slow down reaction time.

Control and Experimental Groups. Researchers must determine whether it is actually changes in the manipulated variable and not in some unknown extraneous factor that cause a change in the dependent variable. One way

Experiment: A procedure in which a researcher systematically manipulates certain variables to describe objectively the relationship between the variables of concern and the resulting behavior. Well-designed experiments permit inferences about cause and effect and test a hypothesis.

Variables: Conditions or characteristics of a situation (or experiment) that can change.

Independent variable: The variable in an experiment that is directly and purposefully manipulated by the experimenter to see what effect the difference will have on the variables under study.

Dependent variable: The behavior measured by an experimenter to assess whether changes in the independent variable affect the behavior under study.

to do this is to have at least two groups of subjects who are identical in important ways before the experiment begins. The attributes they must have in common depend on what the experimenter is testing. For example, in a sleep experiment, because reflexes slow down as a person grows older, a researcher doing an experiment on reaction times would ensure that the two groups were comprised of subjects who are the same age.

Once the subjects are known to be identical on important attributes that might affect results, they are assigned randomly to either the experimental or the control group. *Random assignment* means that there is no systematic way in which individuals are assigned. Individuals are chosen for groups by chance. An **experimental group** consists of subjects for whom the independent variable is manipulated. A **control group** consists of subjects tested on the dependent variable in the same way as the experimental group but for whom the independent variable is not manipulated; it is a comparison group. In the reaction time experiment, the students who sleep a full seven hours are members of the control group. Those who sleep less are members of the experimental group. By comparing the dependent variable (reaction time) for the experimental and control groups, a researcher can determine whether the independent variable is responsible for any differences in the dependent variable between the groups.

If the researcher is confident that all subjects respond with the same reaction time before the experiment—that is, that the two groups are truly comparable—then the experimenter can conclude that sleep deprivation is the cause of the experimental group's decreased performance. Without comparable groups, the effect of the independent variable is not clear, and few real conclusions can be drawn from data.

Operational Definitions. Another key component of successful scientific research is that all terms used must be given an operational definition. An **operational definition** is the set of methods or procedures used to define a variable. When a researcher manipulates an organism's state of hunger, the concept hunger must be defined in terms of the procedures necessary to produce hunger. For example, a researcher might be interested in the effects of hunger (independent variable) on exploratory behavior in mice (dependent variable). The researcher might deprive mice of food for six, ten, twelve, or twenty-four hours and record the exploratory behavior of the mice under conditions of food deprivation. The researcher would operationally define hunger in terms of number of hours of food deprivation; the dependent variable, exploratory behavior, would be operationally defined in terms of the number of times the mice walked down an alley for more than two feet.

Sample Size. Another important factor in an experiment is the size of the sample. A **sample** refers to the group of subjects who are examined by the researcher, and who are generally representative of the population about which an inference is being made. For example, a researcher studying schizophrenics has to examine a sample of people with that disorder. A psychiatrist who wishes to discover whether murderers have low levels of the neurotransmitter serotonin in their brains would have more luck collecting a relevant sample from a maximum-security penitentiary than from the Ladies' Garden Society.

The number of subjects in a sample is very important. If an effect is obtained consistently with a large enough number of subjects, a researcher can reasonably rule out individual differences and chance as causes. The assumption is that a large sample better represents the population to which

Experimental group: In an experiment, the group of subjects that receives the treatment under investigation and for whom the independent variable has been manipulated.

Control group: In an experiment, the group of subjects that does not receive the treatment under investigation. The control group is used for comparison purposes.

Operational definition: The set of methods or procedures used to define a variable.

Sample: A group of subjects or participants who are generally representative of the population about which an inference is being made.

the researcher wishes to generalize his or her results. (The Appendix found at the end of the book discusses these issues in more detail.)

Designing Successful Experiments: Avoiding Pitfalls. Good experiments often involve several experimental groups, each tested under different conditions, for example, with different dosage levels of a drug such as caffeine or with different treatment procedures applied.

Another study of the effects of sleep deprivation on reaction time, for example, might involve a control group and five experimental groups. The subjects in each one of the experimental groups might be deprived of sleep for a different length of time (sleep deprivation operationally defined in terms of number of hours of sleep lost from the normal number of hours slept). In this way, the researcher can examine the effects of several different periods of sleep deprivation on reaction time.

In a well-designed experiment, the experimenter also looks closely at the nature of the independent variable. Are there actual values of the independent variable above or below which results will differ markedly? For example, in the experiment on sleep deprivation and reaction time, the researcher might find that a one-hour period of sleep deprivation has no effect, two hours of deprivation produce only a modest effect, and thereafter, every additional hour of deprivation markedly slows reaction time. These results would show that reaction time is dependent on the duration of sleep deprivation. Using several groups yields better understanding of how the independent variable (sleep deprivation) affects the dependent variable (reaction time).

Frequently things turn out just the way a researcher expects. Researchers are aware that their expectations about results might influence findings; they fear that they may unwittingly create situations that lead to specific results. They call such an event a **self-fulfilling prophecy.** Teachers, for example, may develop clear expectations for their students' performance early in the year, and students usually confirm those expectations (Jussim, 1989). To avoid self-fulfilling prophecies, researchers often use a **double-blind technique** in which neither the experimenter nor the subjects know who is in the control or experimental group. This is done by having some third individual, for example, another researcher who is not connected with the research project, keep track of which subjects are assigned to which group. This technique minimizes the effect that a researcher's subtle, but nevertheless potent, cues might have on one group of subjects. (In a normal experiment, single-blind, the researcher knows who is in the experimental and who is in the control group but the subjects do not know who is assigned to which group or if they are being presented with a treatment.)

Researchers also try to make sure their studies do not lead to specific results by minimizing the demand characteristics of studies. The **demand characteristics** of a study are the elements of the situation that might clue a subject as to the purpose of the study and elicit specific behavior from the subject. The demand characteristics of a study seem to invite specific behavior. A person who thinks he or she knows the real purpose often tries to behave like a "good" subject, and thus may distort results. The use of computers to minimize interaction with people (subjects are less likely to want to be "good" for a computer), of unobtrusive measures (such as tape recording rather than note taking), and of deception (actually concealing the real purpose of the study) until the end of the research session all minimize the impact of demand characteristics.

Even when demand characteristics are minimized and a double-blind procedure is used, participants behave differently when they are in a research

Self-fulfilling prophecy: The finding that things frequently turn out just the way a person expects they will. Researchers may unwittingly create situations that lead to specific (prophesied) results.

Double-blind technique: A research technique in which neither the experimenter nor the subjects know who is in the control or experimental group, thus minimizing the effects of self-fulfilling prophecies.

Demand characteristics: The elements of the situation that might clue a subject as to the purpose of the study, but especially to behave in specific ways. The elements of the situation that elicit specific behaviors.

study. This finding is called the **Hawthorne Effect,** after some early research studies done at a Hawthorne industrial plant which showed that people behave differently, usually better, when they know they are being observed or are in a new program. Researchers are aware of these effects and attempt to make subjects feel comfortable and natural, and to create experimental situations that minimize the effects of participation. They often do not collect data until after subjects have adapted to the experimental situation and have become less excited about their participation in the research study.

Few people would debate the importance of careful experimentation to scientific research. But experiments affect individuals; just knowing that you are being observed changes behavior (the Hawthorne Effect). Further, some research cannot be conducted on human beings, and arranging conditions to suit an experimenter is not always possible. Experiments are not the only way to collect data about human behavior. Techniques providing information other than cause-and-effect relations also are important. These techniques include questionnaires, interviews, naturalistic observation, and case studies.

The Hawthorne studies alerted researchers to some of the potential problems inherent in the way experiments are designed.

Questionnaires

A **questionnaire,** sometimes called a survey, is used by researchers to gather a large amount of information from many people in a short time. A survey might be used to learn the typical characteristics of psychology students. Such a survey could be sent to students enrolled in an introductory psychology course.

The questionnaire might ask each student to list his or her age, sex, height, weight, previous courses taken, grades in high school, SAT scores, number of brothers and sisters, and parents' financial status. There might also be questions regarding sexual relations, career goals, and personal preferences on topics such as TV shows, clothing styles, and music.

An aim of surveys and questionnaires is to discover relationships among variables. For example, a questionnaire designed to assess aggressiveness may ask respondents to list their gender, the number of fights they might have had in the past, their feelings of anger, and the type of sports they enjoy. When analyzing the questionnaire results, a researcher will check to see if the gender and personality traits of the respondents are related, that is, whether men and women tend to differ in aggressive behaviors.

The strength of a questionnaire is that it gathers a large amount of information in a short time. Its weaknesses are that it's impersonal, it gathers only the information asked by the questions, it limits the subjects' range of responses, it cannot prevent respondents from leaving certain questions unanswered, and it does not provide a structure from which cause-and-effect relationships can be inferred (although correlations may be found).

Interviews

An **interview** is a face-to-face meeting in which an interviewer asks an individual a series of standardized questions. The subject's responses are usually tape recorded or written down. The advantage of an interview over a questionnaire is that it allows the interviewer to ask questions other than the standard ones. If the interviewer notes an exaggerated response, for example, instead of recording a simple answer he or she may decide to ask related questions and thus explore more fully an area that seems important to the subject. However, the interview technique is very time-consuming and, again, no cause-and-effect relationships can be inferred.

Hawthorne Effect: The finding that people behave differently, usually better, when they know they are being observed in an experimental situation.

Questionnaire: A printed form with questions. They are usually given to a large group of people and are a means of gathering a substantial amount of data in a short time.

Interview: A series of open-ended questions used to gather basic detailed information about a person. Though time-consuming, this technique allows the interviewer to probe potentially important issues or problems in depth.

Naturalistic Observation

A seemingly simple way to find out about behavior is to observe it. But people told they are going to be observed tend to become self-conscious and alter their natural behavior. Therefore, psychologists use the technique of **naturalistic observation** by trying to observe from a distance how people or animals behave in their natural settings—the way birdwatchers watch birds—thereby minimizing the effects of their presence on the behavior being observed.

A psychologist conducting research on persuasion may act like a browsing shopper at car lots, furniture stores, and appliance centers to discover how salespeople convince customers to buy expensive products. For example, the researcher may observe that one particularly successful car salesman tends to show budget-minded customers the most expensive automobiles first; mid-priced models then seem more affordable by comparison. A researcher might also simulate naturalistic observation by watching a salesman through a one-way mirror—the kind used to detect thefts in supermarkets.

The strength of naturalistic observation is that the data collected are largely free of contamination. The weakness is that the behavior the psychologist might wish to examine is not always exhibited. Sometimes, for example, animals do not show mating behavior, or groups of people or animals do not migrate, act persuasively, or become aggressive. Naturalistic observation is also very time-consuming.

Naturalistic observers take their data where and how they find them. They cannot manipulate the environment because that might alter the behavior they are observing. Because variables cannot be manipulated, data from naturalistic observation, like those from questionnaires and interviews, do not permit cause-and-effect statements.

Case Studies

The **case study** method involves interviewing subjects to gain information about their background, including data on such things as childhood, family, education, and social and sexual interactions. The information in a case study, or history, describes in detail a specific person's responses to the world and can be used to determine a method of treatment.

The strength of a case history is that the information it provides is complete. A weakness is that the information describes only one individual and his or her unique problem. Since the behavior of one person may be like that of others or may be unique, researchers cannot generalize from one individual to an entire population. Psychologists must be cautious even when generalizing from a large number of case histories.

Combining Techniques

Researchers often use several techniques, either at different times or in combination. When I was an undergraduate in a course on research methods, a group of other students and I tried to examine how hitchhikers' attire affects success at getting rides. We posed as hitchhikers and alternated our clothing from grubby, to moderately pleasant, to dressed up. One of us hid behind a sign and counted the number of cars passing by, the number of cars that stopped to inquire where we were going, and the number of cars that provided a ride (not many).

TABLE 1.3
Five Approaches to Research: Major Strengths and Weaknesses

Approach	Strengths	Weaknesses
Experiment	Manipulation of variables to control extraneous influences; best method for identifying causal relationships	Artificiality of laboratory environment; limited generalizability of findings; manipulation of some variables is unethical or impractical
Correlational Study	Measurement of degree of association among variables; good basis for prediction	Limited opportunity to control third factors; unable to draw conclusions about causal relationships
Questionnaire	Effective means of measuring actions, attitudes, opinions, preferences, and intentions of large number of people	Lack of explanatory power: validity of findings may be limited by sample; reliability difficult to determine; self-report may be inaccurate or biased
Naturalistic Observation	Observation of behavior in its natural context	Little opportunity to control variables; time-consuming
Case Study	Study of rare events; extensive evidence gathered on a single person	Lack of generalizability of findings; time-consuming

Our experiment had many flaws, but it attempted to use the experimental method; that is, it manipulated an independent variable—type of clothes. It also used naturalistic observation, hiding behind the sign and counting. Such mixed use of methods is not only acceptable, it is often desirable and the only way certain types of research can be conducted. See Table 1.3 for a summary of the major approaches to research psychologists use.

Evaluating Psychological Research

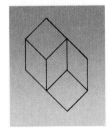

A psychologist, like all scientists, is trained to think and evaluate research critically and put it into a meaningful framework. Whatever the method used to ask questions and to answer research hypotheses, the researcher thinks critically about the question, methods, and results. Psychologists follow a traditional approach to evaluating research; you should use the same critical thinking skills that they do in order to follow their logic, understand their approach, and judge their research using their same mindset.

Critical thinking means evaluating evidence, sifting through choices, assessing outcomes, and deciding if conclusions make sense. When you think critically you are being evaluative, you are not accepting glib generalizations, you are determining the relevancy of facts, and you are looking for biases and imbalances, as well as for objectivity and testable, repeatable results. A critical thinker identifies central issues and is careful not to make cause-and-effect conclusions from correlations.

Whenever you think critically about research, you become a detective sorting through the facts. You look objectively at the facts, question hypotheses and conclusions, avoid oversimplifications, and consider all of the arguments, objections, and counterarguments. You revise opinions when the data and conclusions call for revisions.

As a critical thinker, whenever you have to evaluate a research study in this text, in the popular press, or in a psychological publication, it is helpful to focus on five research criteria: *purpose, methodology, subjects, repeatability,* and *conclusions.*

1. **Purpose.** What is the purpose of this research? What is the researcher trying to test, demonstrate, or prove? Has the problem been clearly defined? Is this researcher qualified to conduct this research?

2. **Methodology.** Is the methodology appropriate and carefully executed? Has the researcher used an appropriate method of investigation? For example, is the method used the most appropriate one for the topic (e.g., case study, survey, experiment)? In addition, has the method been used properly? Is there a control group? Have variables been carefully (operationally) defined? Has the researcher followed ethical guidelines?

3. **Subjects.** Is the sample of subjects properly chosen and carefully described? How is the sample selected? Does the sample accurately reflect the characteristics of the population of individuals about which the researcher would like to make generalizations? Will any generalizations be possible from this study?

4. **Repeatability.** Are the results repeatable? Has the researcher shown the same finding more than once? Have other investigators made similar findings? Are the results clear and unambiguous, that is, not open to criticism based on poor methodology? What additional evidence will be necessary for a psychologist to support the conclusions?

5. **Conclusions.** Are the conclusions, implications, and applications suggested by the study logical? Are they supported by the researcher's data? Has the researcher gone beyond his or her data and drawn conclusions that might fit a predisposed view rather than following logically from the facts of the study? In what ways do the data have implications for psychology as a science, as a profession, and potentially for you as an individual? Has the researcher considered alternative explanations?

Some research is limited in its generalizability because of a small sample size and a biased selection of subjects. Later in this book you will read about autism; you may have seen the movie *Rain Man* in which Dustin Hoffman played an autistic individual. Early studies of autism claimed that autistic children came from homes with cold, unresponsive mothers. But a limited sample of subjects, a lack of control over the home experiences, and a limited opportunity to observe the mothers and the children all led to erroneous conclusions. Recent, more carefully carried out, studies showed the earlier work to be erroneous: parents of autistic children are no more or less responsive than parents of normal children. The findings of earlier studies failed to be replicated.

Think back to the sleep deprivation experiment described earlier. Let's use the five criteria to evaluate this research. The subjects were college students deprived of sleep and tested on an attention, reaction-time task. Think about purpose, methodology, subjects, repeatability, and conclusions. Was the purpose of the study clear? The purpose was to assess the effect of sleep loss on reaction time. Was the methodology appropriate? The method involved depriving subjects of sleep after they had grown used to sleeping in a controlled environment; subjects were tested each morning. The task was carefully operationally defined.

What about the subjects? The subjects were college students who were in good health. Reasonable generalizations might be possible from their reaction times to the reaction times of other similarly aged people. What about repeatability? If the results obtained were found with several groups of subjects, and if the results were consistent within each of those groups, the repeatability of the results seems assured. Last, what about conclusions? Limited conclusions can be drawn from such a research study; there was only one age group, college students; there were no controls on other factors in the students' environment, such as work loads, school pressure, energy expenditures, and history of sleep loss. Simple limited conclusions about sleep deprivation could be drawn such as "Among college students, in controlled research studies, sleep deprivation tends to slow down reaction time." But from the limited study, not much more could be said, and few or no generalizations could be drawn to children, older adults, or populations of the chronically mentally ill. The results of the study do not contradict common sense, but they add little to our overall understanding of attention.

A key to thinking critically about research is to be *evaluative*, to question all aspects of the study. Think about the advantages as well as the limitations of the research method. When a television commercial tells you that nine out of ten doctors recommend brand X, think critically about their claim. What kind of doctors, for what kind of ailment, for what age patients, for what extent of usage?

As you read this text, evaluate research findings. I will present the research in ways that allow you to critically evaluate it and draw your own conclusions. Sometimes I will try to steer you in one direction or another, and you will see my orientation. Knowing that inclinations (mine and yours) exist helps you think about research critically and draw logical conclusions based on facts, not solely on predispositions or prejudices. Remember, thinking critically means evaluating facts and shedding preconceived ideas.

To draw your attention to critical thinking, to remind you to look at all the possibilities, and to stimulate your critical thinking, from time to time in each chapter I will ask you some critical thinking questions. These questions will suggest new ideas and perspectives for you to consider as you evaluate the research studies presented. These are not the only places in the text where you should use your critical thinking skills, but they are good opportunities for you to be especially evaluative. ◆

- ◆ Identify the strengths of five important techniques in doing psychological research. pp. 20–26
- ◆ Name two elements in designing an experiment that are especially important to making generalizations about the results. pp. 22–23
- ◆ Why are psychologists concerned about control groups and sample size? pp. 22–23

Focus on Learning

Applying Research Findings

Psychologists from various fields and perspectives are often both scientists and practitioners. As scientists, they gather basic information about behavior and mental processes; as practitioners, they apply their findings in various disciplines such as law. For example, psychologists influence legal decisions, serve on the faculties of law schools, and are cited in legal case books. Psychologically relevant legal issues include child development, custody, maladjustment, perception of fairness, stereotyping and prejudice, and the accountability of potentially insane criminals (Davis, 1989; Melton, 1987).

Psychology is also applied in public service sectors to help formulate public policy. Psychologists are doing research and serving as consultants on issues that affect the quality of life for people everywhere. They are especially interested in the elderly, health and nursing care, education and learning, and mental health issues (DeLeon, 1988). Psychologists do both laboratory and field-based research to investigate the effects of day care on emotional development, aging on intelligence, preparation courses on intelligence tests and the SAT, drugs such as cocaine on memory, and therapy on mental disorders.

The application of research results requires time and caution. As I have already indicated, psychologists do not have all the answers to questions about human behavior; they have not even defined all the questions that need to be asked. Moreover, before solving actual problems in meaningful ways, researchers must repeat successful experiments to ensure that their findings are reliable. Even after publication and review by professionals, research should be applied cautiously at first. Then, after cautious application, more research is usually conducted.

Researchers in laboratories and health care providers both look at behavior and mental processes with the aim of understanding them and helping people lead more fulfilling, worthwhile, and productive lives. Sometimes this may mean "selling" a position, convincing an agency, a client, or even another group of psychologists. For example, psychologists can help promote safety belt usage by integrating knowledge about safety belts and commitment on the part of the public and by offering useful incentives (Geller et al., 1989). Thus, today, psychologists must do more than just prove a truth, they must deliver the information in a way that will make it accessible to people so that it might be used (Levy-Leboyer, 1988).

Psychology in the Arts and Sciences

Students in colleges and universities are exposed to a broad array of subject matter, regardless of their chosen major. Most students are exposed to English, history, math, science, and social sciences. In each of these disciplines, psychology often plays a prominent role. Understanding psychological concepts helps foster an integration of subject matter across disciplines; thus, in important ways, psychology has become linked to our broad understanding of the liberal arts and sciences. History students try to understand the psychological makeup of dictators and why their populations followed them. In art, students learn the psychology of visual space, in English they study the psychological life of Hemingway, in business they study the psychology of motivation, and in nursing they study the diagnosis and treatment of maladjustment.

Psychology often is interpreted within various fields—math, history, music—by individuals who specialize in both psychology and their own discipline. Academic departments may even offer courses such as Psychology and Art, The Psychology of Business, and Psychology and Women. Psychology helps promote analytical, critical thinking, and it helps students integrate rather than compartmentalize their knowledge. Studying psychology helps students grasp the research process and the processes of inference, and allows students to apply knowledge learned in one discipline to another. Throughout this text I will try to show you these relationships where appropriate.

The Goals of This Book

The primary goal of this book is to introduce you to the basic theories and principles of psychology. Some of what you learn may help you resolve everyday problems. For example, how does your life history affect your future development? How much do your thoughts about yourself and others determine what you will do tomorrow? How can an understanding of personality and motivation help you interact with other people? How can the principles of memory be applied to improving your skills and grades?

An understanding of personality and motivation will help some individuals deal with their underachieving children. Knowledge about depression and its causes will help others cope with rejection in dating. Finally, understanding the origins, symptoms, and treatment of illness will help families deal with feelings about a loved grandmother's Alzheimer's disease.

Psychologists address all of these issues—and many more. In the following chapters, you will explore psychological topics such as the effects of drugs on behavior, the study of mental disorders and therapy, the processes of perception and memory, and the physical, mental, and social development of human beings from birth through death.

What Are Central Issues in Psychology?

It is evident that psychology, with its great diversity and its many subspecialties, is wide-ranging. But with all of its breadth, certain key issues and ideas continue to emerge over and over again in psychology. These ideas, listed below, are presented regularly in this text.

- ◆ The scientific method is a mainstay of psychological research.
- ◆ Psychology is an emerging science based on empirical observation.
- ◆ Psychology theories are diverse, are always expanding, and must be considered in the context of the time at which they are initiated.
- ◆ The relative contribution of the environment versus heredity (nature versus nurture) is frequently questioned by psychologists.
- ◆ People continue to develop through the lifespan, and this is evident in the various subfields of psychology.
- ◆ Aspects of human behavior such as personality and intelligence may be stable and long-lasting, but they are subject to change and must be considered within an environmental context.
- ◆ Thought (cognition) is becoming an increasingly important topic in the study of behavior.
- ◆ Many disorders previously thought to be caused solely by psychological conditions are now known to have a biological component.

Psychology is an exciting, challenging, and diverse discipline. Its terminology may be unfamiliar, and its theories may be new for you. However, you will find that a serious effort to understand psychology will be rewarding and worthwhile. You are faced with a future of challenges. I hope this book will provide you with a fundamental understanding of the principles of human behavior and some effective problem-solving tools you can use for the rest of your life.

Key Terms

Psychology p. 2
Theory p. 3
Structuralism p. 6
Introspection p. 6
Functionalism p. 6
Gestalt psychology p. 6
Psychoanalytic approach p. 7
Behaviorism p. 8
Humanistic psychology p. 8
Self-actualization p. 9
Cognitive psychology p. 9
Biological perspective p. 9

Eclectic p. 10
Psychologist p. 11
Psychiatrist p. 12
Psychoanalyst p. 13
Subject p. 19
Hypothesis p. 20
Significant difference p. 21
Experiment p. 22
Variables p. 22
Independent variable p. 22
Dependent variable p. 22
Experimental group p. 23

Control group p. 23
Operational definition p. 23
Sample p. 23
Self-fulfilling prophecy p. 24
Double-blind technique p. 24
Demand characteristics p. 24
Hawthorne Effect p. 25
Questionnaire p. 25
Interview p. 25
Naturalistic observation p. 26
Case study p. 26

Summary

Defining Psychology

- Psychology is the science of behavior and mental processes, every aspect of an organism's functioning—overt actions, mental activity, emotional and physiological reactions.   p. 2

- *Overt actions* refers to any directly observable and measurable movements in the organism, or the results of such movements. *Mental processes* includes any thoughts about ideas, reasoning processes, and being angry or happy or sad. *Emotional responses* refers to anger, regret, lust, happiness, depression, and so on. Psychologists also study *physiological reactions,* such as an increased heart rate due to excitement or biochemical changes due to light stimulating the eye.   p. 3

- Psychologists attempt to *describe* the basic components of behavior, understand and *explain, predict,* and potentially *manage* them.   p. 3

Schools of Psychological Thought

- Psychology became a field of study in the mid-1800s; since then it has developed into several schools, each with a specific interest or research focus. *Structuralism,* founded by Wundt, focused on the contents of consciousness and was the first true school of psychology. *Functionalism,* with James and others as its spokesmen, stressed *how* and *why* the mind works. *Gestalt psychology* was a reaction to structuralism and functionalism; the early Gestalt psychologists studied perception.   p. 5

- John B. Watson led the revolt in psychology called *behaviorism.* Watson argued that the proper subject of psychology was observable behavior. *Psychoanalysis,* developed by Freud, was both a theory of personality and a treatment procedure.   pp. 7–8

- Psychologists with a biological perspective tend to examine psychological issues based on how heredity and biological structures affect the process under discussion. The *behavioral perspective* concerns how observable responses are learned, modified, and forgotten. The *psychodynamic perspective* assumes that behavior arises because of unconscious conflicts and urges that originated early in life. *Humanistic*

perspectives arose in response to the psychodynamic view and stress the ongoing nature of development. The *cognitive perspective* asserts that human beings engage in both worthwhile and maladjusted behaviors because of ideas and thoughts.   pp. 8–9

Careers in Psychology

- A psychologist has obtained a graduate degree in psychology, typically a Ph.D., and studies behavioral principles; a psychiatrist is a medical doctor who specializes in the treatment of disordered behavior.   p. 11

What Psychologists Do

- The three main fields of psychology—human services, applied research, and experimental psychology—all consider research and theory to be fundamental.   pp. 15–18

- Sixty-two percent of psychologists in the APA are in human service fields such as clinical, counseling, community, and school psychology.   pp. 13–14

Techniques Used to Study Behavior

- Only controlled experiments allow for cause-and-effect conclusions.   p. 20

- An *experiment* is a procedure in which a researcher systematically manipulates variables to discover and describe the relationship between them. A *variable* is a characteristic of a situation or person that is subject to change. An *operational definition* is the set of procedures used to define a variable.   pp. 21–22

- The *independent variable* is directly and purposefully manipulated by the experimenter. The *dependent variable* is observed by the experimenter to determine its response to changes in the independent variable.   p. 22

Applying Research Findings

- Psychologists are both scientists and practitioners. Whether researchers in a laboratory or health care providers, psychologists are doing research and serving as consultants on issues that affect the quality of our lives.   p. 29

Connections

If you are interested in . . .	Turn to . . .	To learn more about . . .
The various schools of psychology and their influence on theory and research	◆ Ch. 3, pp. 96–97 ◆ Ch. 11, pp. 401–405 ◆ Ch. 12, p. 427 ◆ Ch. 15, pp. 543–548	How Gestalt psychology influences the study of perception. Cognitive psychology's explanations of motivation. How Freud's psychoanalytic theory explains personality development. Humanistic theory's influence on therapy techniques.
Careers in the human service subfields of clinical, counseling, community, or school psychology	◆ Ch. 8, p. 273 ◆ Ch. 13, pp. 482–485 ◆ Ch. 15, p. 563	The administration and interpretation of tests. How psychologists help communities meet challenges and prepare for emergencies such as hurricanes. How clinical psychologists help people develop effective coping strategies to deal with stress.
How psychologists use research methods	◆ Ch. 5, p. 162 ◆ Ch. 9, p. 331 ◆ Ch. 11, p. 384	How the experimental method is used to study phenomena such as learning to avoid poisonous foods. How the correlational method is used to study the relationship between fathers and their children. How the experimental method is used to examine the causes of overeating.

2

The Biological Bases
of Behavior

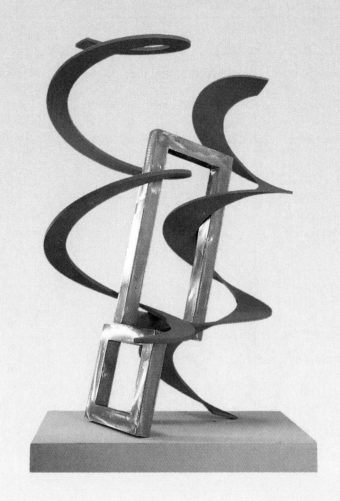

"Twice Blue" by Obie Simonis

---

*I*n 1976, a dangerously violent, mildly retarded mental patient became the first recipient of a brain "pacemaker" when doctors implanted tiny electrodes in the man's brain. The electrodes were wired to a palm-sized battery pack, which stimulated the limbic system (also known as the pleasure center) of his brain every few minutes. After the operation, the patient, who previously had to be tied to his bed because of his violent outbursts, became a calm man. The hospital sent him home, and all went well for several weeks. Then the man went berserk, tried to murder his parents, and seriously wounded his next-door neighbor. Hospital X-rays revealed the problem: the wires between the pacemaker and battery pack had become disconnected. The wires were reattached and the patient's violent attacks ceased.

The impact of biology on behavior is profound. With advances in technology, scientists have the potential to alter a person's biological structures to enhance the quality of life. Biology, particularly genetics, plays a crucial role in shaping our psychological characteristics. In fact, many behavioral, psychological, and physical disorders actually stem from biological factors. A child who acts out in class may have a neurological problem. A person with severe depression may have a chemical imbalance. Recognizing the importance of such factors, psychologists have studied them closely to discover how the biological bases of behavior can be manipulated or controlled. Researchers are working to answer such questions as: Can people intentionally control their own physiological processes? What is the relationship between biological mechanisms and psychological mechanisms? Can diet affect day-to-day behavior?

A complex interplay exists between experience and biology, between conscious voluntary decision making and inherited traits—that is, between nature and nurture. **Nature** refers to a person's inherited characteristics, determined by genetics; **nurture** refers to a person's experiences in the environment. For example, you can lift weights in a gym for years trying to build up physical strength, but your capabilities will always be limited by your inherited body structure. Similarly, people try to maximize their intellectual skills through education, yet not everyone can become a world-renowned brain surgeon. Also, inherited traits may not become evident in behavior unless a person's environment supports and encourages them. Thus, people with special talents must be given opportunities to express and develop them. If Mozart had not had access to musical instruments, his talent might have remained untapped.

In this chapter we will examine the issue of nature versus nurture and then focus on the biological processes that underlie all human behavior and mental processes. Beginning with genetics, then neurons—the building blocks of behavior—we will explore the structure and the functioning of the brain. We will look at how scientists study brain activity, and how various chemical substances affect our behavior.

Nature versus Nurture

Lucy and Max Newman are fraternal twins who attend the same college but have distinctly different talents and interests. Lucy excels at athletics and Max is a gifted scholar. Lucy is leading her team to the state basketball championships, and her admiring coaches claim she is a genius on the court. But Lucy is no genius in the classroom, even though she studies constantly. Max is a straight-A student whose professors predict he will graduate summa cum laude. But Max Newman does not share his twin sister's interest or talent in sports.

Why do the twins differ so much? Their father thinks it's because Lucy has enjoyed sports since she began walking and Max began reading at a very early age. He reasons that Lucy would be just as good a student as Max, and Max just as athletic as Lucy, if their early experiences and interests had been reversed. However, their mother argues that each child was born as either an athlete or scholar, and each is making the most of his or her gifts. The parental debate illustrates a major question in psychology: What is the relationship between biological mechanisms and environmental mechanisms—nature versus nurture?

The debate over what determines our abilities and behavior is actually a debate over the relative contributions of biological and environmental variables. How much of who we are is related to the genes we inherited from our parents? How much is related to the environment in which we were raised? For example, it is clear that biological makeup affects intelligence.

Nature: An individual's genetically inherited characteristics.

Nurture: An individual's experiences in his or her environment.

But can the environment interact with and modify biological makeup? Valid answers to this question must take into account the idea that both nature and nurture affect the expression of traits such as intelligence. Further, the surrounding environment must make it possible for an inherited trait to be expressed in behavior. And last, the complex and constantly changing relationship between biology and environment affects behavior directly. The truth is that genetic traits, inherited abilities, provide the framework for behavior; within that framework, experiences ultimately shape what a person feels, thinks, and does.

Genetics

Genetics is the study of *heredity*, the biological transmission of traits and characteristics. Biologists examine such things as how blue eyes, brown hair, height, and blood pressure problems are transmitted from one generation to the next. Behavioral traits, aspects of personality, and intelligence can also be genetically transmitted, and this is why psychologists are especially interested in heredity. With the exception of identical twins (discussed on p. 38), every human being is genetically unique. Although each of us shares traits with our brothers, sisters, and parents, none of us is identical to them or to anyone else. This occurs because of the large number of genes that determine characteristics.

Chromosomes, which consist of strands of deoxyribonucleic acid (DNA), carry genetic information in their basic functional units—**genes.** Genes are lined up on the chromosomes in the nucleus (or center) of a cell. Each human cell normally contains twenty-three pairs of chromosomes (forty-six total chromosomes), and genes control various aspects of a person's body structure, including eye color, hair color, height, and perhaps basic intellectual abilities.

Traits are determined by pairs of genes. We refer to each member of a pair of genes as an **allele.** Alleles are either *dominant*, that is, expressed in behavior or evident in the person, or *recessive*, that is, not expressed as a trait or in behavior when present singly but transmitted to future generations. When the two alleles of a pair of genes combine, if one member is dominant and the other recessive, the dominant allele will prevail in offspring. Thus, with eye color, brown is a dominant allele and blue a recessive one. If a

Genetics: The study of the potential transmitted from parents to offspring through genes.

Chromosomes: Strands in the nuclei of cells that carry genes. Composed of a DNA core, they are responsible for the hereditary transmission of traits. Found in pairs, they represent the genetic contribution of both parents.

Gene: The unit of heredity transmission carried in chromosomes and consisting of deoxyribonucleic acid (DNA) and protein.

Allele: A single gene and a member of a gene pair that carries a different or alternative genetic code for a particular trait.

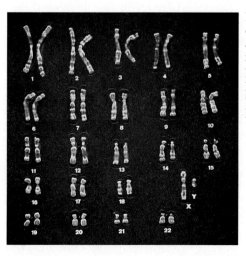

Each human cell contains 23 pairs of chromosomes. The first 22 pairs are alike and transmit similar characteristics in both males and females. The 23rd pair determines sex. In males, the 23rd pair contains one X and Y chromosome (as shown here); in females, the 23rd pair contains two X chromosomes.

brown and a blue allele are paired, the eye color of the offspring will be brown. Only when two recessive alleles are paired will the recessive characteristic be apparent.

Sperm and ova each contain half of the final pairings of genes. The first twenty-two pairs of chromosomes are the same in both males and females. The twenty-third pair, however, differs. This pair of chromosomes determines a person's sex. In females, the twenty-third pair contains two X-type chromosomes; in males, it contains one X- and one Y-type chromosome. In males, when sperm are formed, the pair of chromosomes divides and the twenty-third produces one X-type and one Y-type sperm cell. In females, the twenty-third cell produces an X-type chromosome in each cell. If an X sperm fertilizes an ovum, the result is a female—XX. If a Y sperm fertilizes an ovum, the result is a male—XY.

At the moment of conception, a sperm and an ovum, each containing half of each pair of the parents' chromosomes, combine to form a new organism, and the chromosomes join to form new pairs. There are 8,388,608 possible recombinations of the twenty-three pairs of chromosomes, with a colossal 70,368,744,000,000 possible combinations of genes. You can see that the chances of any two individuals being exactly alike is exceedingly slim.

In an exciting research revolution taking place in the last decade, biological researchers have been trying to map the traits associated with specific chromosomes. They have been trying to map the human *genome*, the DNA blueprint of heritable traits contained in every cell. And they have been modestly successful. More than 400 genetic "markers" or signposts have been discovered on all forty-six chromosomes. Researchers have mapped the exact location of markers for muscular dystrophy, Huntington's disease, some cancers, and some psychological disorders. By understanding the basic biological mechanisms and their relationship to behavior, psychologists can better predict the situations in which maladjustment and some specific behavior disorders might occur.

Twins

Psychologists often rely on studies of twins to assess the contributions of nature and nurture to a person's behavior. Twins make good subjects for these experiments since they begin life in the same uterine environment and share the same nutrition and other prenatal influences. There are two types of twins. **Fraternal twins** occur when two sperm fertilize two ova and the two zygotes (fertilized eggs) implant in the uterus and grow alongside each other. Fraternal twins may be both male, both female, or one male and one female. Their genes are not identical, making them as genetically similar as other brothers and sisters. Only about twelve sets of fraternal twins occur in every 1000 births. **Identical twins** occur when one zygote (fertilized egg) separates into two identical cells. The multiplication of these cells then proceeds normally, and the cells become two genetically identical organisms. If the two cells should also split, the result would be identical quadruplets. Identical twins are rarer than fraternal twins: Only four sets occur in every 1000 births. Of course identical twins can only be both boys or both girls: they share exactly the same genetic heritage.

Researchers at the University of Louisville School of Medicine studied 450 sets of twins—half were identical twins and half were fraternal twins—from infancy through adolescence. The study assessed intelligence as well as home and family variables that might influence intellectual development. By adolescence, identical twins had very similar levels of intellectual achievement. In contrast, fraternal twins' IQs were no more similar than those of

Fraternal twins: Double births resulting from the release of two ova in the female which are then fertilized by two sperm. Fraternal twins are no more or less genetically similar than non-twin siblings.

Identical twins: Double births resulting from the splitting of a zygote into two identical cells that then separate and develop independently. Identical twins have exactly the same genetic makeup.

Fraternal twins (left) occur when two sperm fertilize two ova and both zygotes develop alongside each other in the uterus; they are genetically similar as any two siblings. Identical twins (right) occur when one zygote separates into two identical cells; their genetic make up is the same.

non-twin siblings. The most important conclusion of the Louisville twins study was that although family variables strongly influenced IQ, genetics affected IQ test scores more than environment did (R. S. Wilson, 1983).

Twins' genetic factors (nature) are fixed, but if they are reared apart, their environments (nurture) are different—that is, they will grow up with different families and homes. By comparing psychological characteristics of identical twins who have been reared apart, researchers can assess the extent to which environment affects behavior, perhaps unraveling the nature-nurture puzzle a bit more. Researchers have concluded that significant psychological similarities between identical twins are probably due to biological variables, and significant differences are likely due to environmental variables. For example, the Minnesota adoption studies show that young adopted children are similar intellectually to other children in their adopted family, suggesting that family environment exerts a great influence on young children. By adolescence, however, there is greater variation: Teenagers raised in the same family resemble one another intellectually only if they have common genes (Scarr and Weinberg, 1983). Experts such as Plomin (1989) assert that even though environmental influences on intelligence are strong, heredity exerts a stronger influence.

Our genetic heritage is unaffected by day-to-day experiences. However, over tens of thousands of years humans have evolved a highly organized brain that allows learning to affect their behavior. Our brains act as libraries of information. Each new enriching experience affects our later behavior. Some proponents of the nurture position suggest that people are not limited by their genetic heritage because experience, training, and hard work can stretch their potential to amazing lengths. John B. Watson, a pioneer in the field of behaviorism (which we will examine further in chapter 5), wrote,

> Give me a dozen healthy infants, well-formed, and my own specialized world to bring them up and I'll guarantee to take any one at random and train him to become any type of specialist I might select—doctor, lawyer, artist, merchant-chief and, yes, even beggar man and thief, regardless of his talents, penchants, tendencies, abilities, vocations, and race of his ancestors (1924, p. 104).

Down syndrome: A genetic defect in human beings in which three number twenty-one chromosomes are present. Most individuals with Down syndrome exhibit characteristic physical abnormalities and are mentally retarded.

Phenylketonuria (PKU): A disorder that prevents an individual from metabolizing the amino acid phenylalanine.

Endowed with a fixed genetic heritage, a biology sensitive to change, and a brain sensitive to experience, human beings have the capacity to experience the world in unique ways, to develop new technologies, and, with each new generation, to better the general human condition. Love for other people, desire to do good, and ability to develop high levels of creativity, communication, and technology all reflect human genetic endowment *and* years of learning. Thus, a person's genetic makeup is the foundation on which all his or her behaviors are built.

Genetic Defects

Some scientists are involved in genetic research, attempting to crack the genetic code, manipulate cell structure, and control the transmission of genetic traits. One goal of genetic research is to prevent *genetic defects*—genetically transmitted diseases and behavioral abnormalities. When a person is born with the genetic defect of too few or too many chromosomes, the result is usually dramatic. **Down syndrome** occurs when every cell in the body has an extra copy of chromosome number twenty-one, or when a piece of a twenty-first chromosome breaks off and is joined to another chromosome. This genetic accident occurs in one out of every 660 births. Most people afflicted with Down syndrome have distinct physical features (a short, stocky build, flattened face, and almond-shaped eyes). Many are born with congenital problems, such as heart defects, eye problems, and respiratory disorders. People with Down syndrome also have some degree of mental retardation. Another genetic disorder, **phenylketonuria** (PKU), is caused by the presence of a recessive gene that prevents the individual from processing the amino acid phenylalanine. Unless the disorder is detected soon after birth and the newborn is put on a diet containing low levels of phenylalanine, PKU can cause irreparable mental retardation. Accordingly, in the United States all newborns are given a PKU test. In this case, manipulating the physical environment (through diet) can help control the harmful consequences of a genetic disorder.

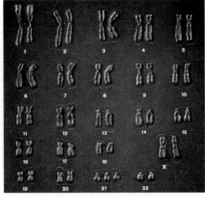

Down syndrome is a genetic defect that most often occurs when every cell in the body has an extra copy of chromosome number 21. Down syndrome causes varying degrees of mental retardation, ranging from mild to severe.

Researchers are also studying a number of other disorders that may have genetic or biological origins. Schizophrenia, for example, has at least a partial genetic basis; some people's genetic inheritance makes them more likely than others to develop schizophrenia. Recent research suggests that a single gene located on chromosome 5 may predispose some individuals to the disorder (Sherrington et al., 1988). Through such genetic research, psychologists may eventually be able to understand and manage severe disorders like schizophrenia.

- ◆ Define the terms *nature* and *nurture* as psychologists use them. p. 36
- ◆ In what way does the twenty-third pair of chromosomes differ from the remaining twenty-two pairs? pp. 37–38
- ◆ Why do twins make good subjects when studying the contributions of nature and nurture to behavior? pp. 38–40

Focus on Learning

Communication in the Nervous System

Before we can fully understand the nature and diversity of human behavior, we must first examine its underlying structure. The nervous system operates behind all of our day-to-day behavior; it allows us to drive a car, pull our hand away from a hot fire, study for a psychology examination, eat when we are hungry, run in a race, and so on. The nervous system acts like a busy air traffic control center, sending, receiving, processing, interpreting, and storing vital information. Many psychologists study how these electrical and chemical signals are used in the brain to represent and process information (Sejnowski, Koch, and Churchland, 1988).

The **nervous system** is composed of structures that act as the communication system for the body and allows for behavior and mental processes. The nervous system enables an organism to coordinate activities, including movement, thought processes, perception of pain, and the consistent beating of the heart. The nervous system is made up of two divisions—the central nervous system (consisting of the brain and spinal cord) and the peripheral nervous system. The peripheral and central nervous systems work in harmony. The central nervous system acts on information provided by the peripheral nervous system and sends out signals that sometimes modify it. The nervous system is composed of billions of cells, each of which receives information from thousands of other cells. The most elementary unit in the nervous system is the neuron, the building block of the entire system.

The Neuron

The basic unit of the nervous system is the nerve cell, or **neuron.** Billions of neurons are found throughout the body, differing in shape, size, and function. There are over 100 billion in the brain alone. Some neurons operate quickly, some relatively slowly; some neurons are large, others are especially small. Neurons are often grouped together in bundles; we call such groups of fibers *nerves.*

Although all of the neurons in your body are alive and active, they are not all activated at once. But they are on alert, ready to convey information and signals to some part of the nervous system. Neuronal firing flows two ways—to the brain from the sense organs and muscles, and from the brain

Nervous system: The structures and organs that act as the communication system for the body, allowing for behavior and mental processes.

Neuron: The basic unit of the nervous system. It is a single cell composed of *dendrites*, which receive neural signals; a *cell body*, which generates electrical signals; and an *axon*, which transmits neural signals.

look this up in other book

diagram backwards

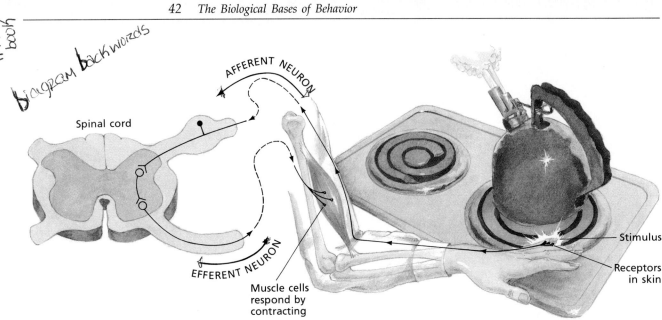

FIGURE 2.1
Afferent neurons carry signals from ~~the muscles and glands to~~ *reseptors to* the spinal cord and brain; *efferent* neurons carry signals from the brain and spinal cord to the muscles and glands.

to the sense organs and muscles with decisions and actions to initiate new behavior. There are three types of neurons: *sensory neurons* convey information inward from the body's outer tissues to the brain and spinal cord; *motor neurons* carry information from the brain and spinal cord to the muscles and glands; and *interneurons* connect neurons together and combine activities of sensory and motor neurons. There are many more interneurons than sensory or motor neurons, and they form the network that allows the neurons to interact with one another. The millions of neurons connected to one another are surrounded by a fourth type of cell called glia. *Glial cells* are small, ten times more numerous than sensory, motor, or interneurons, and act to nourish and help hold the neurons in place. In spite of their important function they appear to play no direct role in behavior. We say that sensory

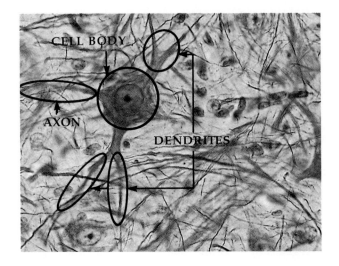

FIGURE 2.2
The basic components of a neuron: dendrites, cell body, and a long, slim axon.

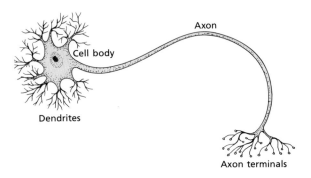

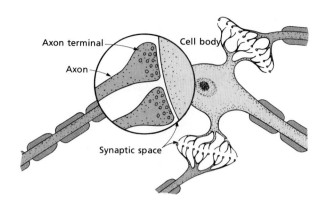

Axon terminal

Axon

Cell body

Synaptic space

FIGURE 2.3
The synapse is very small. Chemicals released by the axon terminal cross the synapse to stimulate the cell body or dendrites of another neuron.

neurons convey **afferent** signals, the messages sent *to* the spinal cord and brain; **efferent** signals are messages sent *from* the brain and spinal cord to other structures in the body (see Figure 2.1). These signals are sent very rapidly and occur at all levels of the nervous system simultaneously.

Typically, a neuron is composed of a cell body (containing a nucleus), dendrites, an axon, and axon terminals. *Dendrites* (from the Greek word tree because of their tree-like appearance) are thin, widely branching fibers that get narrower as they depart from the cell body. They receive information from neighboring neurons and carry it back to the *cell body*. At the cell body the signal is transformed and continues to travel along the long, slim *axon* to the *axon terminals* (Figure 2.2). Many axons, especially the longer ones, are *myelinated;* they are covered with a thin white substance (called a myelin sheath) that allows much faster conduction. The myelin sheath is a form of glial cell and also serves to insulate one neuron from the next.

In almost all neurons, the axon terminals are very close to the receptor site (i.e., dendrites or cell body) of another neuron. The microscopically small space between the axon terminals of one neuron and the receptive site of another is called a **synapse** (Figure 2.3). You can think of many neurons strung together in a long chain as a relay team sending signals, conveying information, or initiating some action in a cell, muscle, or gland. Each neuron receives information from about 1000 neighboring neurons and may synapse on (or transmit information to) as many as 1000 to 10,000 other neurons.

Action Potentials

How do neurons communicate with one another? Each year, scientists learn more about the nature of the neural impulse and how information is transmitted from cell to cell across synapses. The process, which involves both electrical and chemical changes, is sometimes referred to as *electrochemical.* Two types of electrochemical actions take place: the first involves activity within a cell, the second involves transmitter substances (i.e., chemicals) released from the axons of one cell and acting on the cell body or dendrites of another cell.

Understanding electrochemical processes within a cell is essential to explaining the role of the neuron in behavior. The most widely accepted explanation of electrochemical processes is the following: Every cell is surrounded by an extremely thin semipermeable membrane—less than 0.00001 millimeter thick—through which electrically charged ions and small particles in and around the cell pass. Normally the cell is in a resting state, with its

Afferent: Pathways and signals to the central nervous system.

Efferent: Pathways and signals from the central nervous system to other structures in the body.

Synapse: The small space between the axon terminals of one neuron and the receptive site (dendrite, cell body, or axon) of another neuron.

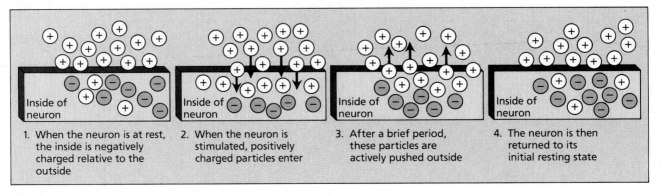

1. When the neuron is at rest, the inside is negatively charged relative to the outside

2. When the neuron is stimulated, positively charged particles enter

3. After a brief period, these particles are actively pushed outside

4. The neuron is then returned to its initial resting state

FIGURE 2.4
(1) When a neuron is at rest, there are more positively charged particles (sodium ions) outside it than inside. Thus, a tiny negative electric charge exists across the cell membrane. (2) When the cell is stimulated, positively charged particles enter. (3) A few milliseconds later, positively charged particles are actively pumped outside. (4) The previous potential is then restored, and the neuron is ready to "fire" once again.

Action potential: An all-or-none electrical current sent down the axon of a neuron, initiated by a rapid reversal of membrane potential. Also called a *spike discharge*.

All-or-none: The principle by which a neuron will fire either at full strength or not at all.

Refractory period: The recovery period of a neuron after it fires, during which time it cannot fire again. It allows the neuron to reestablish electrical balance with its surroundings.

Neurotransmitter: A chemical substance released from the synaptic vesicles that crosses the synaptic space and affects postsynaptic dendrites by binding itself to the postsynaptic dendrite.

inside negatively charged and its outside positively charged, creating a difference in electrical charge across the membrane. We say that the cell is in a state of *polarization*, that is, there exists a difference in the internal state of the cell (negatively charged) compared with the outside. When the cell has been stimulated such that it reaches a threshold, an action potential occurs and travels down the axon. Positively charged sodium ions move through the membrane into the cell, and positively charged potassium ions simultaneously leave the cell, creating a disturbance in the resting level. The rapid reversal of the electrical balance of the cell membrane is the basis of the **action potential,** or *spike discharge*.

A cell does not necessarily fire every time it is stimulated; cells that are stimulated by many other cells are more likely to fire than cells that are less stimulated. If the level of polarization across the cell membrane has not been disturbed enough to generate the action potential, the cell will not fire. When cells do fire, however, they generate action potentials (spikes) in an **all-or-none** fashion—that is, the firing of the cell, like the firing of a gun, occurs at full strength or not at all. Action potentials are completed in two to four milliseconds; generally, neurons cannot fire more than 500 times a second (see Figure 2.4). After each firing the cell goes through a recovery period of a few thousandths of a second, called a **refractory period.** During this period, the chemical balance between the axon and the area around it is reestablished. Action potentials can be blocked by a variety of chemicals at the synapse, an important feature of drugs used to relieve pain and depression.

Neurotransmitters

To transmit information from one cell to the next, neurotransmitters are released. When an action potential moves down the end of an axon, it stimulates chemicals, called **neurotransmitters,** that reside in the axon terminal within *synaptic vesicles,* small storage structures in the axon terminal (Dunant and Israel, 1985). The neurotransmitter is released into the synapse, moves across the synaptic space, and binds to the receptor on the dendrites of the next cell (see Figure 2.5). Dozens of substances, including acetylcholine, norepinephrine, dopamine, and several neuropeptides, are known to

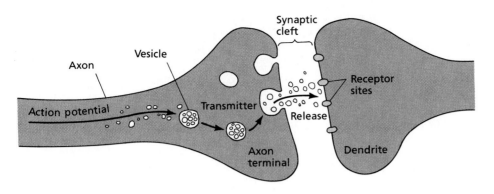

FIGURE 2.5
A typical synapse.

be neurotransmitters. One neurotransmitter, serotonin, has been studied extensively and has been implicated in virtually every class of behavior (McGinty and Szymusiak, 1988). Most well known, however, is acetylcholine which is found in neurons throughout the brain and spinal cord. Acetylcholine is crucial to exciting skeletal muscles, thus allowing us to move. It is also extremely important in day-to-day functions such as memory, learning, and sexual behavior. Its involvement in normal functioning seems crucial, and many memory disorders such as Alzheimer's disease (discussed in chapter 10) are evident when there is a loss of ability to produce it (see Figure 2.6).

The array of neurotransmitters is dazzling; at least fifty have been studied in depth. Serotonin is known to be involved in sleep, norepinephrine influences memory, and GABA is involved in anxiety states. Neuropeptides are chains of amino acids that act as neurotransmitters. Endorphins, one type of neuropeptide, are produced naturally by our bodies and are mimicked by the actions of the narcotic morphine. Endorphins inhibit certain synaptic

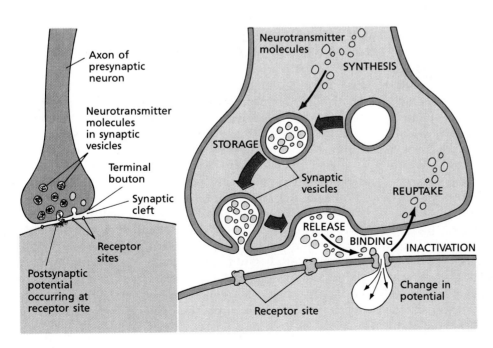

FIGURE 2.6
Synaptic transmission. (a) Neurons transmit information to each other by sending neurotransmitters across a synapse. (b) Following release, a neurotransmitter crosses the synapse, binding with a receptor and altering the electrical potential of the postsynaptic neuron. Most are then reabsorbed by the original neuron.

TABLE 2.1
Five key transmitter substances that play a role in the transmission of information by the nervous system.

Transmitter Substance	Where Found	Effects
Acetylcholine	Brain, spinal cord, autonomic nervous system, target organs of the parasympathetic system	Excitation in brain and autonomic nervous system; excitation or inhibition of target organs
Norepinephrine	Brain, spinal cord, target organs of sympathetic system	Inhibition in brain; excitation or inhibition of target organs
Dopamine	Brain	Inhibition
Serotonin	Brain, spinal cord	Inhibition
GABA	Brain, spinal cord	Inhibition

transmissions, particularly those involving pain. We will discuss pain, endorphins, and pain management in more detail in chapter 3. The study of neurotransmitters may hold the key to our understanding of drug addiction because many drugs such as cocaine affect neurotransmitter actions, which helps explain the addictive nature of the drugs themselves. The study of neurotransmitters may also help us find other drugs that will effectively block powerfully addictive drugs such as cocaine (see Table 2.1).

How do neurotransmitters work? Once released, they move across the synaptic space and attach or bind themselves to receptor sites on the dendrites of the next cell, thereby conveying information to the next neuron. Sometimes the neurotransmitters cause the receptor sites to make the cell more easily penetrable by creating an electrical charge called a *postsynaptic potential (PSP)*.

There are excitatory and inhibitory PSPs. Excitatory PSPs make it easier for the next cell to fire; inhibitory PSPs make it less likely that the next cell will fire. Since thousands of neurons may synapse onto a single cell, a single neuron can receive both excitatory and inhibitory PSPs. If it receives more excitatory ones, another action potential is likely to be generated. If it receives more inhibitory ones, further excitation along the nerve pathway may be ended. Some neurotransmitters appear to be involved in blocking pain; others seem to facilitate sensory experiences. When acetylcholine attaches to muscle cells, for example, it has an excitatory effect. On the other hand, in certain areas of the brain not related to the excitation of muscles, it can have inhibitory effects.

When neurotransmitters were first discovered it was thought that only one type was found in each neuron and acted on one type of receptor. But today we know that a neuron can hold more than one neurotransmitter, which may act on more than one receptor. Some neurotransmitters (especially neuropeptides) are released into the bloodstream, and thus their effects are far-reaching. Researchers are beginning to think of such neurotransmitters as **neuromodulators;** the idea is that a neuropeptide released into the bloodstream affects not only a single cell's immediate ion transfer, but whole classes or groups of cells, and they thus modulate receptor actions to neurotransmitters.

Neuromodulator: A chemical substance whose function is to increase or decrease the sensitivity of widely distributed neurons to the specific effects of neurotransmitters.

Neurotransmitters and Behavior. Although scientists have known about the existence of neurotransmitters for a long time, only recently have they realized their significance in the study of human behavior. For example, researchers have found that serotonin is involved in changes in motivation and mood (e.g., Young et al., 1985) and schizophrenia is thought to be associated with increased levels of neurotransmitter substances. In addition, people with Parkinson's disease, whose symptoms include weakness and uncontrollable shaking, have been found to have low dopamine levels, and treatment with drugs that have the same effects as dopamine (such as L-dopa) alleviates many of their symptoms. Although it is unlikely that one neurotransmitter alone can cause a disorder such as schizophrenia or depression, it may play an important role in the onset or maintenance of such an illness.

Agonist: A chemical that mimics the action of a neurotransmitter, usually by occupying receptor sites.

Antagonist: A chemical that opposes the action of a neurotransmitter, usually by blocking a neurotransmitter from occupying a receptor site.

Psychopharmacology. The study of how drugs affect behavior is called *psychopharmacology.* Many psychoactive (mind-altering) drugs that are abused, cocaine for example, have been studied to learn the physiological mechanisms that cause behavioral reactions. Psychopharmacologists have shown that many common drugs alter the amount of neurotransmitter released at a synapse. Thus a drug changes behavior by changing the way electrical energy is transferred between cells. Drugs can also be used to mimic the role of a neurotransmitter; such drugs are called **agonists.** When an agonist is administered, it is *as if* the neurotransmitter itself has been released. Other drugs, called **antagonists,** act to block or oppose a neurotransmitter from having a specific action. Thus, when an antagonist is administered, a cell's receptor site is blocked and the neurotransmitter cannot have its usual effect. Schizophrenia, a disabling mental disorder, is often treated by the use of antagonists. When exposed to certain drugs that act as antagonists, cells that normally respond to dopamine are blocked from doing so, and symptoms of the disorder are alleviated. This finding led to the *dopamine theory of schizophrenia* (which we will consider in more detail in chapter 14). Last, some drugs block the reabsorption of a neurotransmitter from a receptor site. This action is initiated by some drugs and is useful in the treatment of depression.

The firing of neurons transfers information from the sense organs to the brain and from the brain to the muscular system and the glands. If psychologists knew precisely how this transfer occurred, they could more successfully predict and manage the behavior of people with neurological damage, which in some cases causes learning disabilities (Chalfant, 1989). But the firing of neurons and release of neurotransmitters and neuromodulators do not in themselves explain completely the biological bases of human behavior. The firing of individual neurons is an incomplete picture because it is the brain as a whole that receives, interprets, and makes decisions about those neuronal impulses.

♦ Describe the four basic parts of a neuron. pp. 41–43
♦ Identify the key stages in the generation of an action potential. pp. 43–44
♦ Describe the difference between excitatory and inhibitory postsynaptic potentials. p. 46
♦ Distinguish between a neurotransmitter and a neuromodulator. pp. 44–46

Focus on Learning

Organization of the Nervous System

The nervous system, and especially the brain, controls behavior on a second-by-second basis. Psychologists must therefore understand the organization and functions of the nervous system and its mutually dependent systems and subsystems. Recall that the nervous system is made up of the central nervous system and the peripheral nervous system. The central nervous system is comprised of the brain and spinal cord; the peripheral nervous system connects the central nervous system to the rest of the body. We will examine them both in detail, beginning with the peripheral nervous system.

The Peripheral Nervous System

The **peripheral nervous system** carries information to and from the spinal cord and the brain via spinal nerves attached to the spinal cord and by a system of twelve cranial nerves that carry signals directly to and from the brain (see Figure 2.7). You can think of the peripheral nervous system as containing all nerves that are not in the central nervous system; you should also note that its nerves focus on the periphery or outside parts of the body. The peripheral nervous system actually contains two major systems: the somatic nervous system and the autonomic nervous system.

FIGURE 2.7
Each of the twelve cranial nerves sends information directly to its appropriate location in the brain.

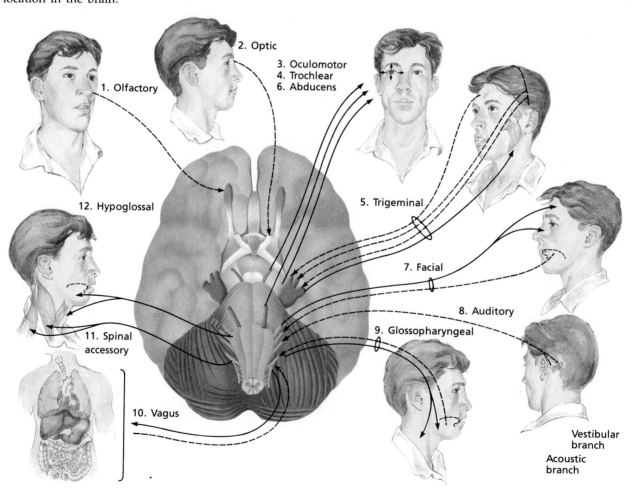

1. Olfactory
2. Optic
3. Oculomotor
4. Trochlear
6. Abducens
5. Trigeminal
7. Facial
8. Auditory
9. Glossopharyngeal
10. Vagus
11. Spinal accessory
12. Hypoglossal

Vestibular branch
Acoustic branch

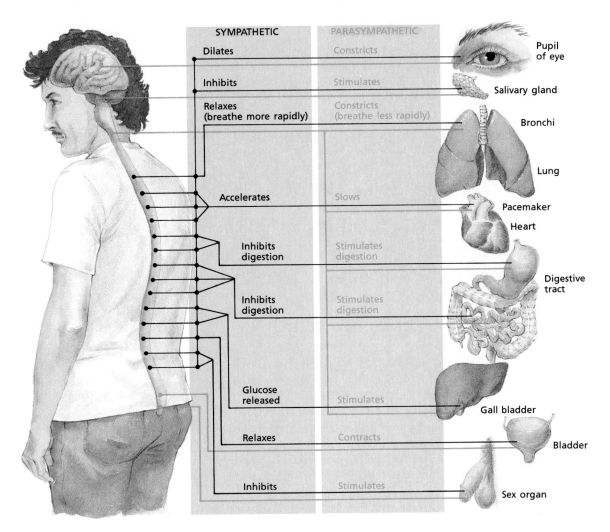

FIGURE 2.8
The activities of the two branches of the autonomic nervous system (ANS).

The Somatic Nervous System. The **somatic nervous system,** which is generally under voluntary control, responds to and acts on the outside world. It is involved in perceptual processing and the control of movement and muscles that are under voluntary control. Consisting of both sensory and motor neurons, it carries information from the sense organs to the brain, and from the brain and spinal cord to the muscles that you control. It is the somatic system that allows you to take off your jacket in the warm afternoon sun and facilitates a quick sprint to class before the instructor starts a lecture.

The Autonomic Nervous System. The **autonomic nervous system,** in contrast to the somatic nervous system, operates involuntarily (although we will see that the technique of biofeedback, discussed in chapter 4, has proven effective in bringing some of these processes under voluntary control). The autonomic nervous system includes internal conditions such as heart rate, blood pressure, and even digestion; the system is called autonomic because many of its systems are self-regulating. It is made up of two divisions: the sympathetic nervous system and the parasympathetic nervous system (see Figure 2.8), which work together in controlling the activities of the muscles and glands.

Somatic nervous system: The part of the peripheral nervous system that carries information to skeletal muscles and thus in turn affects bodily movement.

Autonomic nervous system: The part of the peripheral nervous system that controls the vital processes of the body, such as heart rate, digestive processes, blood pressure, and regulation of internal organs. Its two main subdivisions are the sympathetic and parasympathetic systems.

The sympathetic nervous system is responsible for the body's general preparation for an emergency, known as the fight-or-flight response.

The activities of the **sympathetic nervous system** are easily observed and measured. Activation results in a sharp increase in heart rate and blood pressure, slowing of the digestive processes, dilation of the pupils, and general preparation for emergency—sometimes called the fight-or-flight reflex—usually accompanied by increased flow of adrenaline. The sympathetic nervous system makes your heart pound when you narrowly miss hitting an oncoming car. In contrast, the **parasympathetic nervous system,** which is active most of the time, controls the normal operations of digestion, blood pressure, and heart rate, among other things. The parasympathetic nervous system calms everything down and regulates your heart beat back to normal. In other words, it keeps the body running smoothly. Parasympathetic activity does not show sharp changes on a minute-by-minute basis.

When the sympathetic nervous system is activated and the organism is in a fight-or-flight posture, the somatic nervous system is also activated. For example, when a runner is chased by a large, growling dog and his adrenal glands are stimulated, the burst of energy produced by adrenaline affects the somatic system, making the runner's muscles respond strongly and rapidly. Thus, changes in the autonomic nervous system produce rapid changes in the organism; these changes are usually seen in stress reactions and emotional behavior, which will be discussed more fully in chapters 11 and 13.

The Central Nervous System

The **central nervous system,** consisting of the brain and the spinal cord, serves as the main processing system for most information in the body (see Figure 2.9). Recognizing that the **brain** plays a central role in controlling behavior, psychologists and physiologists are continually trying to understand it better. Some researchers study the brains of people who died of tumors, brain diseases, and trauma (injury) to the brain, hoping to correlate the type of brain damage with the loss of specific abilities such as seeing, reading, or writing. Others observe the behavioral effects of lesions (i.e., damage) to different areas of animals' brains. Still others study the brain-behavior relationships by watching both animals and children interact with their environment and solve problems.

Sympathetic nervous system: The part of the autonomic nervous system that responds to emergency situations. Active only occasionally, sympathetic activity calls up bodily resources as needed.

Parasympathetic nervous system: The part of the peripheral nervous system that controls processes of the body such as heart rate, digestive processes, and blood pressure. Parasympathetic activity usually involves the buildup of energy stores and their maintenance.

Central nervous system (CNS): One of the two major parts of the nervous system, consisting of the brain and spinal cord.

Brain: The part of the central nervous system within the skull.

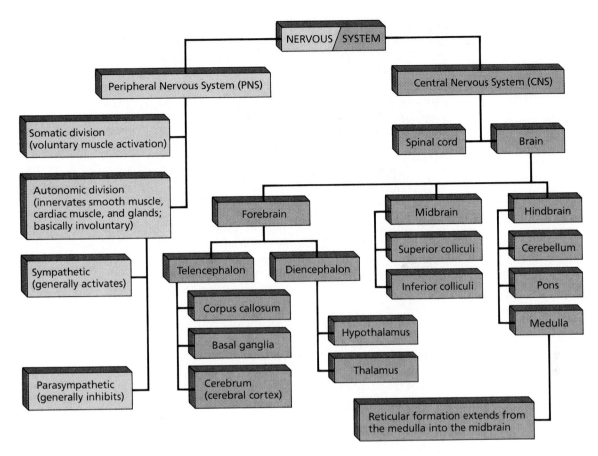

FIGURE 2.9
The basic divisions of the nervous system and their major subdivisions.

Although our understanding of the brain's functions is far from complete, we know that it operates through many mutually dependent systems and subsystems to affect and control behavior. Thousands of brain cells are involved in the performance of even simple activities. When we walk, for example, the visual areas of the brain are activated so that our sight can guide us, motor areas help make our legs move, and the cerebellum helps us keep our balance. It is the central nervous system, communicating with the muscles and glands, that allows all these things to happen. The brain is the control center, but it receives most of its information from the spinal cord, the main communication line to the rest of the body.

The **spinal cord** receives signals from the senses, muscles, and glands and relays the signals to the brain. There are some behaviors which do not involve the brain directly—*spinal reflexes* are actions that are controlled solely by the spinal cord and a system of neurons that create a reflexive response. When you touch a hot stove, a signal goes to the spinal cord and the spinal cord initiates a hand-withdrawing signal to the muscles in the arm and hand. This is a *spinal reflex* linking a sensory input to a motor response. The knee jerk, elicited by a tap on the tendon below the kneecap, is another spinal reflex. Most signals eventually make their way up the spinal cord to the brain for further analysis, but the initial hand withdrawal happens at the level of the spinal cord, before your brain has had time to register and act on pain signals.

Spinal cord: A portion of the central nervous system that is contained within the spinal column. It receives signals from the senses, relays them to the brain, and conveys signals from the brain to the muscles and glands.

Electroencephalogram (EEG): The record of an organism's electrical brain patterns, obtained through electrodes placed on a subject's scalp.

The spinal cord's importance cannot be overstated. When a person's spinal cord is severed, the information exchange between the brain and muscles and glands below the point of damage is halted. Spinal reflexes in such individuals still operate, and knee-jerk responses are evident. But patients who suffer spinal cord damage lose voluntary control over muscles in the lower parts of their bodies. The spinal cord thus serves a key communication function between the brain and the rest of the body; it is the chief trunk line for neuronal activity.

Monitoring Neuronal Activity

While non-living brains can be dissected easily, scientists are more interested in exploring the functions and interconnections of the active central nervous system, a more difficult task. Much of what scientists now know about physiology and behavior, specifically electrical activity in the nervous system, comes from laboratory studies of abnormalities in brain structure and function. In conducting such studies, several basic procedures are used to measure the activity of the nervous system.

One technique for measuring the activity of the nervous system is *single unit recording,* which involves placing a thin wire or needle (a microelectrode) in or next to a single neuron to measure its electrical activity. The data are then recorded on an oscilloscope, which measures changes in electrical voltage. Because neurons fire extremely rapidly, the data are often fed into a computer, which averages the number of times the cell fires in one second or one minute. This technique is usually performed on cats, rats, or monkeys.

Another technique, *electroencephalography,* measures electrical activity in the nervous systems of both human beings and animals. It produces a record of brain-wave activity called an **electroencephalogram,** or **EEG** (*electro* = electrical; *encephalon* = brain; *gram* = record). A small electrode placed on a subject's scalp records the activity of thousands of cells beneath the skull, thus producing an EEG. EEGs, which are generally computer analyzed, are used for a variety of purposes, including the assessment of brain damage, epilepsy, tumors, and other abnormalities (see Figure 2.10).

In normal, healthy human beings, EEGs show a variety of characteristic brain-wave patterns, depending on the subject's level and kind of mental

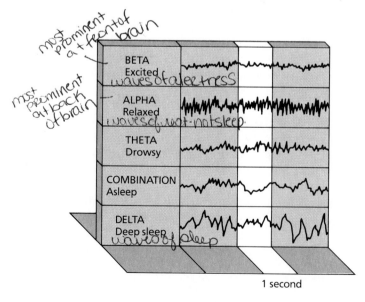

BETA Excited		
ALPHA Relaxed		
THETA Drowsy		
COMBINATION Asleep		
DELTA Deep sleep		

1 second

FIGURE 2.10 Characteristic electrical activity patterns in the EEGs of healthy humans in different states of excitation. High frequency is indicated by the occurrence of a large number of waves within a single unit or period of time.

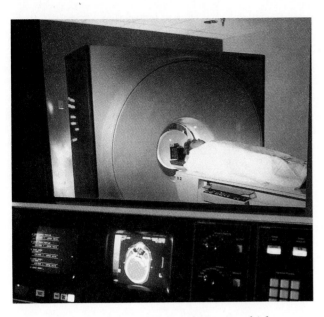

CAT scans are computer-assisted X-rays which allow researchers to view the brain in three dimensions.

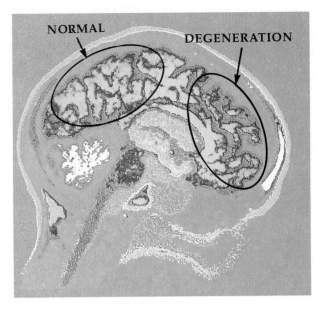

MRI scans are similar to CAT scans, but do not use radiation and produce higher clarity and resolution. This MRI scan reveals degeneration of the frontal lobe, a possible sign of Alzheimer's disease.

activity. Brain waves are usually described in terms of their frequency and amplitude—that is, the number of waves in a unit of time and the height of waves. These brain waves are not yet fully understood, and it must be remembered that they reflect the activity of hundreds of thousands of cells that lie beneath an electrode.

If people are awake, relaxed, and not engaged in active thinking, their EEGs show *alpha waves,* which occur at a rate of eight to twelve cycles per second and are of moderate amplitude. When people are excited, their brain waves change dramatically from alpha waves to high-frequency and low-amplitude waves, called *beta* and *gamma waves.* At different times during sleep, people show patterns of high-frequency and low-frequency waves.

In the last decade, three significant new techniques for measuring the activity of the nervous system have emerged. *CAT scans* (computerized axial tomography) are computer-assisted X-ray procedures used to visualize the brain in three dimensions; they especially help researchers locate specific lesions and tumors in the brain. They are essentially a computerized series of X rays that show slices of the brain photographically. Another technique, *MRI scans* (magnetic resonance imaging), is similar to CAT scans, but does not use radiation and produce higher clarity and resolution. *PET scans* (positron emission tomography), which use radiochemical procedures, enable researchers to watch metabolic changes taking place in an organism as they occur.

These three experimental techniques, CAT, MRI, and PET scans, are making the examination of brain tissue and its processes easier and more precise, thereby providing more information about the brain and its workings. For example, researchers today are showing that small brain lesions are common in elderly people and are a natural part of aging. Further, a tentative link between brain lesions, illness, neurochemistry, and depression is being established (Nemeroff et al., 1988). Today, lawyers are using brain imaging as part of a defense in criminal trials; for example, attorneys now assert that PET scans can show that their client's brain may have damage that traditional neurological tests cannot find. In one California case, a diagnosis of a mental disorder was confirmed through a PET scan and kept a man from going to the gas chamber. The practical applications of such brain imaging techniques are rapidly being put to use by lawers; but in the laboratory, researchers feel that brain scans not only allow better diagnoses of disease and malfunction, but also allow them to continue to examine, map, and study brain structures.

> ◆ Identify the activities of the sympathetic and parasympathetic nervous systems. p. 50
> ◆ Identify the differences between single-unit recording and the EEG. pp. 52–53
> ◆ Describe the difference between CAT, MRI, and PET scans. pp. 53–54

Brain Structures

The structure of the central nervous system and the organization of pathways all seem to point toward the brain. There is no doubt that the brain is the central computing, processing, and storage mechanism that is intimately involved in day-to-day and minute-by-minute behavior. Our understanding of the brain and its relationship to behavior comes about in part through the study of neuroanatomy. *Neuroanatomy* is the study of the structures of the nervous system and uses a wide range of techniques. The principal method of early research was called ablation. In ablation, a portion of an animal's brain is removed and the animal's behavior is studied to determine which behaviors have been disrupted. Today, in addition to ablation we use electrical recording techniques, EEGs, CAT and PET scans, and neurochemical techniques.

We know much about the structure and functions of the brain, and we still have a great deal to learn. On first inspection, it is easy to see that the human brain weighs about three pounds and is relatively fragile. It is composed of two large *cerebral hemispheres,* one on the left side and one on the right side. A large, thick structure called the *corpus callosum* connects the two cerebral hemispheres and permits the transfer of information between them. Besides being divided into right and left halves, the brain can be roughly divided into areas with special functions. Some parts are specialized for visual activities while others are involved in hearing, sleeping, breathing, eating, and a number of other important functions. Some brain activities are localized: speech and language activity, for example, can be pinpointed to a specific area, usually in the left side of the brain. Other activities may occur at several locations: visual activity, for example, occurs in the visual cortex, which occupies both sides of the brain. You will see that psychologists disagree on the extent to which functions are localized within the brain.

We shall examine the brain beginning where the spinal cord and brain meet. You will see that many functions deep within the brain at its core are responsible for basic processes within the body, for example, breathing, sleeping, and eating. As we move higher up through the brain, more complicated structures and functions are found. Organizationally, the brain is traditionally divided into three sections: the hindbrain, the midbrain, and

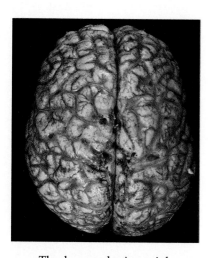

The human brain weighs about three pounds and is composed of two large cerebral hemispheres which are joined by the corpus collosum.

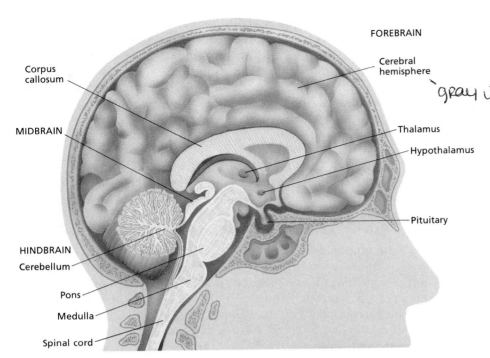

FOREBRAIN

Cerebral
hemisphere

Corpus
callosum

MIDBRAIN

Thalamus

Hypothalamus

Pituitary

HINDBRAIN
Cerebellum

Pons

Medulla

Spinal cord

FIGURE 2.11
The three major sections of
the brain: the hindbrain,
midbrain, and forebrain.

`gray inappearance
& "cover called
cerebral CORTEX
contains all dendrites`

the forebrain, which includes the cortex (see Figure 2.11). Structures found
in the hindbrain and midbrain are often assumed to be organizationally more
primitive and are responsible for more basic, reflexive actions. Structures in
the lower portions of the forebrain are organizationally more complex and
involve higher mental functions. The cortex, which covers the cerebral
hemispheres, serves as the basis for thought processes, a human being's
most advanced abilities.

Hindbrain

The *hindbrain* consists of three main structures: the cerebellum, the medulla,
and the pons. The *cerebellum* is a large structure attached to the back surface
of the brain stem. It influences balance, coordination, and movement, allowing you to do things such as walk in a straight line, type accurately on
a keyboard, and coordinate the many movements involved in dancing. The
cerebellum may also be involved in a number of cognitive or thought operations (Leiner, Leiner, and Dow, 1986).

The *medulla,* through which many afferent and efferent signals pass,
lies just above the spinal cord and controls heartbeat and breathing. Within
the medulla and extending out into the cortex is a lattice-like network of
nerve cells called the *reticular formation,* which directly controls a person's
state of arousal, waking, and sleeping, and bodily functions; damage to it
can result in coma and death. The reticular formation extends into and
through the pons and the midbrain with projections toward the cortex (see
Figure 2.12). Like the medulla, portions of the *pons* are involved in sleep
and dreaming.

Midbrain

The *midbrain* is made up of nuclei (collections of cell bodies) that receive
afferent signals from other parts of the brain and from the spinal cord,

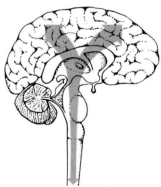

Reticular formation

FIGURE 2.12
Many afferent and efferent
signals pass through the reticular formation.

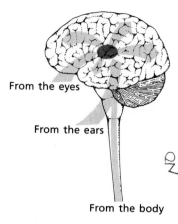

From the eyes

From the ears

From the body

FIGURE 2.13
The thalamus acts as a relay station for sensory information and sends afferent input to the higher centers.

interpret them, and either relay the information to a more complex part of the brain or cause the body to act at once. A portion of the midbrain has been shown to be involved in smooth movement and another in reflexive movements. Movements of the eyeball in its socket, for example, are controlled in part by the superior colliculus, which is a structure in the midbrain. The reticular formation system continues in the midbrain and thus is important in the regulation of attention, sleep, and arousal.

Forebrain

The *forebrain* is the largest and most complicated of the brain structures because of its many related parts: the thalamus and hypothalamus, the limbic system, the basal ganglia and corpus callosum, and the cortex.

Thalamus and Hypothalamus. The *thalamus* acts primarily as a routing station to send information to other parts of the brain, although it probably also performs some interpretive functions (see Figure 2.13). Nearly all sensory information proceeds through the thalamus before going to other areas of the brain. The *hypothalamus* has numerous connections with the rest of the forebrain and midbrain and is involved in many complex behaviors such as motivation, emotion, eating and drinking, and sexual behavior. The hypothalamus has long been known to play a crucial role in the regulation of food intake; disturbances in the hypothalamus often produce sharp eating and drinking behavior changes.

Limbic System. One of the most complex and least understood areas of the brain is the *limbic system.* This system is an interconnected group of structures (including parts of the cortex, thalamus, and hypothalamus) involved in emotional behavior, memory, social behavior, and brain disorders such as epilepsy. Within the limbic system are the hippocampus and the amygdala. In human beings, the *hippocampus* is closely involved in memory functions. The *amygdala* is thought to be involved in the control of emotional behavior. Stimulation of the amygdala in animals produces attack responses, and surgical removal of the amygdala in human beings was once a radical way of treating people who were extremely violent. Stimulation of several areas of the limbic system in rats also produces very pleasurable sensations. Olds and Milner (1954) discovered that rats, when given small doses of electric current in some of the limbic areas as rewards for bar pressing, chose bar pressing over eating, even after having been deprived of food for long periods. They called the areas of the brain being stimulated pleasure centers.

The Basal Ganglia and Corpus Callosum. The *basal ganglia* are a series of nuclei located deep in the brain to the left and right of the thalamus. They control movements and posture and are also associated with Parkinson's disease (see Figure 2.14). Parts of the basal ganglia influence muscle tone and initiate commands to the cerebellum and to higher brain centers. The *corpus callosum* connects and conveys information between the cerebral hemispheres; damage to it results in essentially two separate brains. We will have much more to say about the corpus callosum in a moment.

Cortex. The brain is divided into two major portions, referred to as hemispheres: the left hemisphere and the right hemisphere. The exterior covering

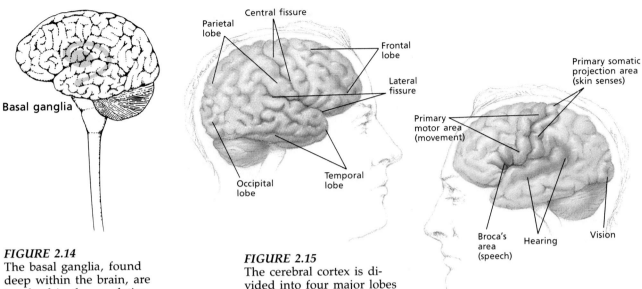

FIGURE 2.14
The basal ganglia, found deep within the brain, are involved in the regulation and control of gross movement. Damage to this important neurological center can have severe behavioral consequences.

FIGURE 2.15
The cerebral cortex is divided into four major lobes (left). Specific areas are concerned with sensory and motor functions (right).

of the cerebral hemispheres, called the *cortex* (or *neocortex*), is about two millimeters thick and consists of six thin layers of cells. A highly developed cortex is evident in human beings, but not all mammals show such specialization. The cortex plays a special role in behavior because it is so intimately involved in thought. The cortex is convoluted or furrowed. These **convolutions** have the effect of creating more surface area in a small space. The overall surface area of the cortex is about 1.5 square feet.

A traditional way to divide the cortex is to consider it as a series of lobes, or areas, each with characteristic structures. The most prominent structures are the two deep fissures—the *lateral fissure* and the *central fissure*— that divide the lobes. These easily recognizable fissures are like deep ravines that run among the convolutions, separating the various lobes. As shown in Figure 2.15, the *frontal lobe* is in front of the central fissure; behind it is the *parietal lobe*. The frontal lobe has some involvement with memory (Lewis, 1989); part of the frontal area is concerned with movement and is sometimes called the *motor cortex*. A lower portion of the left frontal lobe, called *Broca's area*, is involved in speech and language production. The parietal lobe is associated with activities involved in the sense of touch and of body position.

Below the lateral fissure and the parietal lobe is the *temporal lobe*, which is involved in speech, hearing, and the processing of some visual information. At the back of the head, adjacent to the parietal and temporal lobes, is the *occipital lobe*, whose principal responsibility is the visual sense. Other areas of the cortex have less specific functions. For example, the *association cortex* is believed to be involved in complex behaviors that involve thinking *and* sensory processes. These activities may not be strictly visual, auditory, or motor. Instead, they involve the interaction of many different systems or areas.

Convolutions: Characteristic folds in tissues of the cerebral hemispheres and overlying cortex in human beings.

Brain Specialization—The Left and Right of Things

MILESTONES IN PSYCHOLOGY

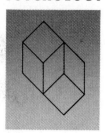

*T*he brain and the body clearly interact with one another on a continuing basis. This two-way street is easily seen when drugs are taken: A person takes a drug which affects brain firing and neurotransmitters; this change makes the person feel different. The person responds to the feeling, and further brain changes take place. A cocaine addict takes the drug, which affects his neurotransmitters, and his brain tells his body to feel a "high" and when it does, he may then behave erratically. The essence is that the brain affects behavior *and* behavior affects the brain. Are there specific places in the brain that control specific behaviors and thoughts? Does one side of the brain have more control than the other?

Early Research on the Cortex. If a cubic centimeter of cortex were removed, how would it affect the ability to think, smell, or see? Although scientists began mapping the brain hundreds of years ago, and we know much about the structure of the brain, research into brain functions did not begin until the 1930s. For example, early researchers asked what happens to visual perception if the cortex of the brain is removed. In 1936 Heinrich Kluver (1897–1979) removed the visual cortex in monkeys and discovered that, although the monkeys lost the ability to discriminate brightness, color, and shape, not all visual functions were impaired. This showed that the cortex is important to vision, but not the only structure involved. Other subcortical structures are important as well.

Kluver was unsure of which brain areas he had destroyed, but today's researchers have sophisticated instruments and techniques that can precisely detail specific brain locations that are destroyed during experimentation. In 1982, Pasik and Pasik extended Kluver's pioneering results. They destroyed monkeys' cortexes and used a series of sophisticated behavioral measures to determine what visual abilities the monkeys lost. They found that monkeys whose visual cortex had been destroyed were still able to discriminate among objects varying in intensity and contrast; respond with eye blinks to increased light intensity; localize an object in space; and discriminate color. They concluded that the cortex in monkeys is crucial for good vision, but that other visual structures can be responsible for certain types of visual discrimination. Most important, they asserted that some sort of reorganization of *other* structures occurs that allows visual functions to take place.

There is no doubt that the cortex is a crucial part of the brain, but only part. By studying victims of accidents, strokes, and brain tumors and then observing their behaviors and mental processes, we have learned a great deal more about the brain. Some of the most exciting work comes from studies that examine differences between the two lobes, the two cerebral hemispheres.

Splitting the Brain. Studies of brain structure show that different areas of the brain are responsible for varying functions. Michael Gazzaniga has been at the forefront of research in brain organization and asserts that the human brain has a modular organization, that it is broken up into discrete units that interact to produce mental activity (Gazzaniga, 1989).

Studies by Sperry (1985) and Gazzaniga (1983) show that in most human beings one cerebral hemisphere—usually the left—is specialized for processing speech and language; the other—usually the right—appears better able to handle spatial tasks and musical and artistic endeavors (see Figure 2.16); (see Hellige, 1990). Some of this evidence comes from studies monitoring brain-wave activity in normal subjects exposed to different kinds of stimuli. When subjects are asked to look at or think about letters or perhaps rehearse a speech, certain characteristic brain-wave activity is produced on the left side of the brain. When they are asked to do creative tasks or are told to reorganize some spatial pattern, brain-wave activity is apparent on the right side of the brain.

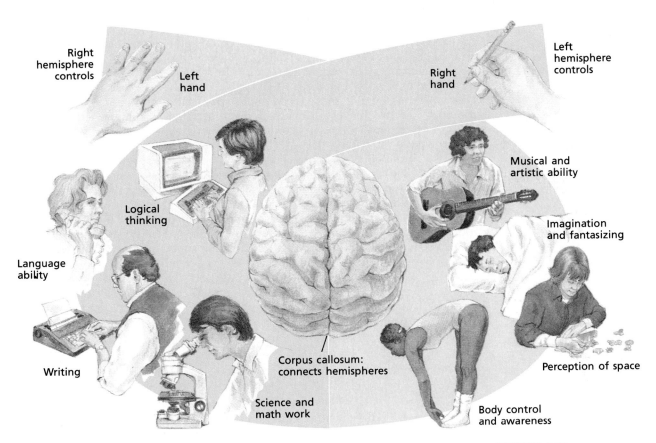

Right hemisphere controls

Left hand

Left hemisphere controls

Right hand

Logical thinking

Musical and artistic ability

Imagination and fantasizing

Language ability

Writing

Corpus callosum: connects hemispheres

Science and math work

Body control and awareness

Perception of space

What happens to behavior and mental processes when connections between the left and right sides are severed and communication between them ceases? A number of important studies have involved **split-brain patients.** In extreme cases, people with uncontrollable, life-threatening epilepsy have undergone an operation to sever the corpus callosum (the band of fibers that connects the left and right hemispheres of the brain) to prevent seizures from spreading across hemispheres. In such cases there was little or no perceptual or cognitive interaction between the hemispheres, and the patients seemed to have two distinct, independent brains, each with its own abilities. Studies of split-brain patients have proven invaluable to scientists who seek to understand how the brain works and how the left and right sides function together. These studies have led to some startling results.

Each cerebral hemisphere is neurologically connected to the opposite side of the body; thus the left hemisphere normally controls the right side of the body. Split-brain patients are unable to use the speech and language capabilities of the left cerebral hemisphere to describe activities carried out by the right one. When stimulus information is presented exclusively to their left hemisphere, they can describe the stimulus, match it, and deal with it in essentially normal ways. However, when the same stimulus is presented to their right cerebral hemisphere, they can perform the matching tasks (saying that two items are identical) but are unable to verbally describe the stimuli (a left-hemisphere task). For example, using simple tests, investigators show that a split-brain subject holding a pencil in the left hand behind a screen cannot describe it. However, the subject can perform a visual matching task easily if the pencil is switched to the right hand. By studying the brain as two separate hemispheres, researchers are discovering the characteristic functions of each.

Studies of split-brain patients show localization of specific functions, but not every behavior can be traced to a single structure in the central nervous

FIGURE 2.16
In most people, lateralization of brain functioning occurs by about age thirteen. The left hemisphere controls language and verbal abilities; the right hemisphere controls spatial, holistic abilities.

Split-brain patients: A term applied to people whose corpus callosum—which normally connects the two cerebral hemispheres—has been surgically severed.

system. Researchers who have studied specific centers in the nervous system, traced pathways, recorded metabolic, electrical, and chemical activity, and examined developmental changes (Clerici and Coleman, 1987) conclude that certain structures (such as the visual cortex and the cerebellum) are strongly involved in specific behaviors, but most behaviors involve the *combined* work of several areas. Although there seem to be some specifically left-brain and right-brain activities, the two halves of our brain work together; although we have localization of functions, we have a unified conscious experience (we will examine consciousness in chapter 4).

There is no doubt that lateralization and specificity of functions exist. There is also no doubt that studying brain functions and the work of Sperry and Gazzaniga have been influential in developing our understanding of brain specificity. Unfortunately, the popular media has simplified, and in some cases trivialized, the specificity of functions to account for school problems, marital problems, artistic abilities, and even baseball batting averages. The extent of hemispheric specialization is yet to be determined, and most scientists and critical thinkers maintain a healthy skepticism about the role of "two minds" in one.   ◆

Plasticity and Change

Do our brains stay the same from birth to death, or can they change, either through experience or simply the passage of time? The basic structure of brain organization is established well before birth and does not change in any substantial ways after birth, but details of its structure and functions, particularly in the cerebral cortex, are subject to change and modification (Kalil, 1989). Psychologists say that the brain is still malleable or teachable during the formative years. Experience with certain stimuli reinforces the development of neural structures. Aoki and Siekevitz (1988) liken the developing brain to a highway system that evolves with use: less traveled roads become abandoned, but popular ones are broadened and new ones added when needed; thus, when neural structures are used, reused, and constantly updated, they become faster and are more easily accessed.

Changes in the brain occur not only in young organisms, but in aging ones as well. As human beings grow older, their central nervous systems function differently, sometimes not as well as before. There are decreases in the number of receptors and cells, for example. Some learning tasks become more difficult for aging animals and human beings. Recent work has identified a drug that facilitates simple learning. When injected into aging rabbits, the drug nimodipine helped them learn simple responses as well as young rabbits do. Nimodipine, used to improve blood flow in human stroke patients, may help learning by blocking calcium transmission to areas of the brain involved in memory. Nimodipine is only one of a large number of drugs that may be used for effective treatment of age-related learning problems (Deyo, Straube, and Disterhoft, 1989) or potential recovery of function after brain damage (LeVere et al., 1989). This work is speculative, new, and exciting; finding specific proteins, specific drugs, and new treatments that alter brain functioning may be a key to our overall understanding of brain development and how that development affects behavior.

Can damage done to the nervous system be repaired? Injury to the brain early in an organism's life is especially detrimental, but recovery depends on the nature of the injury, the age at which the injury takes place, and the presence of certain helping factors, such as the availability of an enriching environment (Kolb, 1989). There is another new line of research that is very exciting, although still somewhat speculative. In a series of studies done mainly with rats, researchers such as Fine (1986) and Bjorkland and his colleagues (1980) have grafted (attached) brain tissue to the central nervous system of rats and other organisms. In some cases the grafts are successful; new tissue grows and repairs old tissue. Someday these methods may be widely used with human beings and offer therapeutic possibilities that exceed organ transplants. Victims of head injuries, brain diseases, and birth defects could all benefit. Research with human beings poses ethical problems, however. There are surgical risks; the techniques are dangerous and as yet unproven, and procedures must be established by physicians and researchers to decide who are the best candidates for such experimentation.

◆ Name the three main structures of the hindbrain. p. 55
◆ What is the role of the corpus callosum and where is it found? p. 56
◆ Describe the overall structure of the cortex, naming two deep fissures. pp. 56–57
◆ What is the potential effect of convolutions of the cortex? p. 57
◆ Name a specific function of the left hemisphere and of the right hemisphere. pp. 58–60

Focus on Learning

Hormones and Glands

In 1978 Dan White fatally shot San Francisco Mayor George Moscone and supervisor/gay activist Harvey Milk. In court, White's attorney successfully argued that a diet of junk food had addled his client's brain and reduced his capacity for moral behavior. White spent only three years in prison for committing a double homicide. Although the "Twinkie defense" is no longer a legal defense in California, White's lawyer capitalized on the fact that a person's body chemistry—even an imbalance in blood-sugar levels—can have a dramatic impact on behavior. In fact, body chemistry, hormones, and learned experiences *can* work together to influence a person, but does this render us unaccountable for our own actions, as Dan White's lawyer claimed?

Combinations of factors are usually the answer to many complex psychological problems, but research shows that some abilities and behaviors have a direct hormonal link. For example, in a paper presented at a scientific meeting in 1988, Kimura reported that when a woman experiences low estrogen levels—during and immediately after menstruation—she excels at spatial tasks but performs less well on motor tasks. The differences are small and do not occur with all women. This work is in its early stages and has yet to be replicated, but it stimulates excitement in the psychological community because of the links shown between hormones and behavior and the differences observed between men and women. These links are mediated by the endocrine glands.

Endocrine Glands

A group of cells that form a bodily structure and secretes a substance is called a *gland*. Substances that communicate information to other glands or organs are part of the endocrine system. There are two types of glands in the human body: those with ducts (such as the tear and sweat glands) and those without ducts, called **endocrine glands**. Psychologists are particularly interested in the endocrine glands, which secrete chemicals called **hormones** directly into the bloodstream and can influence a person's behavior dramatically (see Figure 2.17 on page 62). The hormones travel through the bloodstream to target organs whose cells respond specifically to particular hormones.

Endocrine glands: Ductless glands that secrete hormones directly into the bloodstream.

Hormones: Chemicals that regulate the activities of specific organs or cells. Hormones are produced by the endocrine glands.

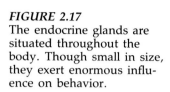

FIGURE 2.17
The endocrine glands are situated throughout the body. Though small in size, they exert enormous influence on behavior.

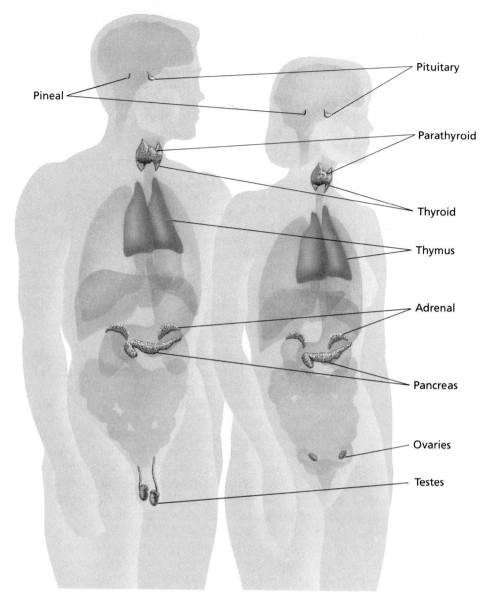

Pituitary Gland. The most important endocrine gland is the *pituitary gland,* sometimes referred to as the body's master gland because it regulates the actions of other endocrine glands. A major function of the pituitary is its control of growth hormones. That's why when teenagers have extreme height or weight problems the pituitary is often suspected (see Figure 2.18).

The pituitary gland is divided into two lobes, the anterior and the posterior. In addition to producing direct changes in bodily functions (e.g., growth), secretions from the lobes of the pituitary affect other glands. The *anterior lobe* produces hormones that stimulate the thyroid and adrenal glands, each of which controls specific behaviors; growth hormones (called somatotrophins) that control the body's development; and sex hormones (called gonadotrophins) that are involved in sexual behavior. A person's psychological state influences the secretions from the anterior pituitary; for example, viewing sexually explicit films can raise subjects' levels of the gonadotrophins (Laferla, Anderson, and Schalch, 1978).

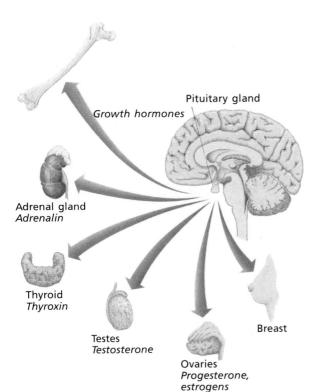

Growth hormones

Pituitary gland

Adrenal gland
Adrenalin

Thyroid
Thyroxin

Testes
Testosterone

Ovaries
*Progesterone,
estrogens*

Breast

FIGURE 2.18
The pituitary is a small gland that directly affects behavior both through the control of other glands and through the release of hormones into the bloodstream.

The *posterior lobe* of the pituitary stores and secretes two major hormones, an antidiuretic hormone (ADH) and oxytocin. ADH acts on the kidneys to increase fluid absorption and decrease the amount of urine produced by the body. Oxytocin stimulates uterine contractions in a pregnant woman and causes labor to begin. Oxytocin also helps nursing mothers release milk.

Pancreas. Another gland, the *pancreas,* is involved in regulating sugar levels. Sugar substances in the blood determine a person's energy level. When blood sugar is high, people are energetic; when it is low, they feel weak and tired. Cells in the pancreas—the islets of Langerhans—control the production of **insulin,** which facilitates the transportation of sugar to the body cells where it is metabolized. When an insufficient amount of insulin is produced, there is too much sugar in the blood, and **diabetes mellitus** occurs. Excess sugar in the blood (or as it is more technically known, **hyperglycemia**) can lead to coma and death if left untreated. Nearly ten million Americans have diabetes and must take daily doses of insulin to ensure that the sugar in their blood can be metabolized properly.

If the pancreas errs in the opposite direction and produces too much insulin, the result is **hypoglycemia,** or very low blood sugar. Hypoglycemic patients have no energy and often feel faint. This condition can usually be controlled through a diet that carefully monitors daily consumption of calories and types of foods.

Adrenal Gland. The *adrenal gland,* located near the kidneys, is also involved with behavior. This gland produces adrenaline (epinephrine), a substance that dramatically alters energy levels and can greatly affect a person's reactions to stress through changes in neuronal firing. Imagine you are being chased through a dark alley. The release of adrenaline causes your heart to pound and gives you a burst of energy to help you outdistance your pursuer.

Insulin: A hormone produced by the pancreas, necessary for the transport of sugar from the blood into body cells so that it can be metabolized.

Diabetes mellitus: A condition in which too little insulin is present in the blood, so that insufficient quantities of sugar are transported into body cells.

Hyperglycemia: A condition in which too much sugar is present in the blood.

Hypoglycemia: A condition usually resulting from the overproduction of insulin, causing very low blood sugar levels.

Hormones Affect Specific Behaviors and One Another. In newborn animals, hormones have an irreversible effect on behavior—they set specific behavior patterns in motion by permanently affecting brain development. In human adults, sexual behavior is to some extent under hormonal control. One study, for example, showed a significant correlation between married couples' hormone levels and frequency of intercourse (Persky, 1978). Although researchers do not know the extent to which hormones control people's behavior, there is no doubt that the glandular system is interconnected. Each hormone affects behavior and eventually other glands. A disorder in the thyroid, for example, affects not only metabolic rate but also the pituitary gland, which in turn affects other behaviors. The glands, the hormones, and target organs are interactive; the brain initiates the release of hormones, which affects the target organs, which affects behavior, which in turn affects the brain, and so on.

Are We What We Eat?

THINKING ABOUT RESEARCH

We all know that food affects us in various ways. A large Thanksgiving meal may make us sleepy. Hungry people feel weak and may cut back on their activities. Parents often say that their children are "off the wall" after consuming candy bars or other high-sugar foods, implying that sugar makes their children hyperactive. Most people agree that food affects behavior. Do some foods affect us more than others? Can some foods be used to help people change their behavior? In the end, are we what we eat?

Early Hypotheses. The possibility of diet as an important variable in shaping children's behavior first emerged in the 1970s, when parents, educators, psychologists, and physicians began seeking new and better ways to treat *attention-deficit hyperactivity disorder,* a disorder estimated to affect from one to fifteen percent of school-age children. Some researchers initially thought hyperactivity was caused by specific food substances (e.g., Feingold, 1976). But studies provided only modest support for dietary modifications. In conducting these studies, researchers learned that there are problems inherent in studies of diet and behavior (e.g., Prinz and Riddle, 1986). For one, it is nearly impossible to have total control over what a child eats and what the food contains. It is also difficult to assess a child's behavior; parents and teachers focus on different behaviors, and children behave differently at home than they do in school. But from this beginning further studies of diet and behavior emerged. Many focused on foods such as breads, starches, and candy—foods made up mostly of carbohydrates.

Hypotheses about Carbohydrates. Many people seem to crave carbohydrates, especially snack foods, to elevate their moods. Foods high in carbohydrates are quick energy sources and provide glucose easily; the brain thrives on and requires glucose (sugar) for neural activity.

People who are obese and those suffering from nicotine withdrawal and postpartum depression all seek out carbohydrates. Carbohydrates are found in table sugar, candy bars, and fruit juices, as well as in potatoes, vegetables, and fruits. Are these people practicing a form of self-medication, providing their bodies with needed foods? First, researchers ruled out the possibility of expectancy and Hawthorne Effects—behavior changes unrelated to the nutrient itself, but due to the expected effect of the carbohydrates. Later, researchers developed the hypothesis that carbohydrates contain substances that alter levels of tryptophan, which ultimately affects behavior. Tryptophan is the amino acid from which serotonin is produced, and when serotonin is released, people often feel calmer and in a better mood. Researchers wished to test the idea that carbohydrate-rich diets alter levels of tryptophan and therefore affect behavior.

Correlational and Experimental Research. Research on the effects of diet has been both correlational and experimental. Tests administered by Prinz and Riddle (1986) showed that children who ate large quantities of sugar demonstrated attention deficits when compared to children consuming low amounts of sugar. This was a correlational study, however, and we cannot draw causal conclusions from it. In an experimental study that attempted to draw causal statements, Ferguson, Stoddart, and Simeon (1986) gave children sugar and compared their behavior to a control group of children, expecting adverse reactions to the sugar. Surprisingly, they found *no differences* between the groups regarding activity levels, behavior ratings made by trained observers, or cognitive activity.

Critical evaluations have led researchers to argue that, in general, carbohydrates appear to have no immediate effect on children's behavior and may even cause a decrease in activity (Behar et al., 1984; Wolraich et al., 1985). So it is generally conceded that carbohydrates are not a cause of hyperactivity. On the physiological side, research shows that people who fast after breakfast and then eat a carbohydrate-rich lunch show marked increases in tryptophan. But for a test meal to reliably elevate tryptophan, it has to be carbohydrate rich *and* protein poor. In adults, experimental studies indicate that consumption of a great deal of carbohydrates induces drowsiness, concentration difficulties, fatigue, and a reduction in pain sensitivity, with maximum effect occurring approximately two hours after intake (Lieberman, Spring, and Garfield, 1986).

Conclusions. The research shows that when people limit their intake of protein (for example, meat) and increase their intake of carbohydrates (for example, pasta), serotonin production increases and mood elevates. After reviewing experimental studies of carbohydrate intake and behavior, Spring, Chiodo, and Bowen (1987) argued that carbohydrates can function like a drug. They can modify brain chemistry and, consequently, mood and behavior. They assert that "as individuals administer drugs, so may they learn to select foods to achieve the same result" (p. 254). An anxious or depressed person may learn that snacking on high-carbohydrate, low-protein foods causes mood enhancement. As little as a piece of toast, a cookie, or a small bowl of pasta provides enough tryptophan for the brain to stimulate production of serotonin. Selective snacking may be used to improve a person's disposition—sometimes for physical reasons and sometimes for psychological ones.

Future Tasks. Researchers continue to ask critical questions about the effects of carbohydrates on behavior: Are there alternative explanations to the current results? Could the effects of carbohydrates and tryptophan be lessened by other foods? Could the behavior being evaluated be the wrong one; that is, would the effects be different if other behaviors were observed? What are the effects of long-term heavy dosages of sugar or carbohydrate consumption? Evaluating the effects of food on behavior is one of the most formidable tasks researchers face because it is difficult to target a specific behavior and draw a causal link to a specific food. Researchers must refine their methods and develop procedures that might remove (or perhaps add) one specific food substance from (or to) a person's diet and then see if behavior changes. The use of the experimental method is essential for psychologists to make causal inferences. Research in this controversial area continues, cutting across the disciplines of nutrition, medicine, nursing, and psychology.   ◆

Psychology in the Biological Sciences

The relationship between psychology and biology has been the focus of this chapter. You can see the interplay of brain-behavior relationships in the regulation of behavior by hormones and drugs. Researchers who study behavior must study biology because the two are so closely connected; for example, the child who is hyperactive may have a glandular disorder; a drug addict is often physiologically as well as psychologically addicted; and a person suffering from migraine headaches can learn to alleviate pain through self-help procedures in addition to drugs.

There has been an especially dynamic melding between psychology and biology. Psychologists work in biology and chemistry departments studying neuroscience. Some brain scientists work in psychology departments focusing on brain anatomy. Whole new departments of neuroscience and brain science are emerging. These researchers are studying how the brain affects behavior and how behavior affects the brain.

The merging of the disciplines is especially apparent in the study of *premenstrual syndrome* (PMS). First described in the medical literature in 1931, PMS is a recurrent, cyclic condition characterized by one or more symptoms that develop during the seven to fourteen days before the onset of menstruation, subside when menstruation occurs, and are then absent for two weeks. The absence of symptoms during the postmenstrual phase is essential to a diagnosis. About one-third of all premenopausal women, primarily those between twenty-five and forty years of age, suffer from symptoms of PMS (Logue and Moos, 1986).

Women who have PMS may experience physical discomfort from water retention, weight gain, breast tenderness, dizziness, headaches, skin disorders, food cravings (including carbohydrates as mood elevators), fatigue, and swollen hands, feet, and ankles. These physical discomforts affect behavior; women suffering from PMS notice depression, irritability, anxiety, tension, mood swings, inability to concentrate, and confusion. As many as 150 different symptoms have been linked to the menstrual cycle (York et al., 1989). The severity of discomfort caused by PMS varies from woman to woman and from month to month.

The relationship of PMS to psychological states and biological mechanisms is striking; researchers in both disciplines are working together more than ever before to better understand the disorder. Researchers are not certain what causes PMS, and considerable controversy exists as to the relationship between symptoms, hormones, and behavior. PMS does not seem to be caused by excesses or deficiencies of a particular hormone, but rather by a change in the way the hormones work. Currently, biological researchers are investigating the possibility that estrogen and progesterone, two hormones produced by the ovaries, may act in combination with neurotransmitters in the brain before menstruation and cause some of the symptoms (Dalton, 1984). Most women who have PMS function effectively despite their discomfort. Understanding the disorder and its symptoms, and being conscious of the physical effects, seem to help (Norris and Sullivan, 1983). Practitioners, researchers, and physicians often report that some women experience physical symptoms without emotional or cognitive symptoms. The physical, emotional, and cognitive changes that take place seem to be somewhat independent—a woman may experience physical maladies without emotional ones, or just the opposite. This is making some researchers begin to consider the possibility of several premenstrual syndromes—not just one.

Psychological issues such as PMS are penetrating through research laboratories, textbooks, and theory. Psychologists are relying on chemists and biologists to develop newer drugs; these scientists are relying on psychologists to evaluate the effectiveness of the drugs on behavior. The cross-fertilization of ideas, theory, and research continues.

- Identify two hormones and describe their effects on behavior. p. 61
- In what ways do food substances such as carbohydrates act like drugs? p. 64
- Describe the physical symptoms that accompany PMS. p. 66

Focus on Learning

Key Terms

Nature p. 36
Nurture p. 36
Genetics p. 37
Chromosomes p. 37
Genes p. 37
Allele p. 37
Fraternal twins p. 38
Identical twins p. 38
Down syndrome p. 40
Phenylketonuria (PKU) p. 40
Nervous system p. 41
Neuron p. 41
Afferent p. 43
Efferent p. 43

Synapse p. 43
Action potential p. 44
All-or-none p. 44
Refractory period p. 44
Neurotransmitter p. 44
Neuromodulators p. 46
Agonist p. 47
Antagonist p. 47
Peripheral nervous system p. 48
Somatic nervous system p. 49
Autonomic nervous system p. 49
Sympathetic nervous system p. 50
Parasympathetic nervous system p. 50

Central nervous system (CNS) p. 50
Brain p. 50
Spinal cord p. 51
Electroencephalogram (EEG) p. 52
Convolutions p. 57
Split-brain patients p. 59
Endocrine glands p. 61
Hormones p. 61
Insulin p. 63
Diabetes mellitus p. 63
Hyperglycemia p. 63
Hypoglycemia p. 63

Summary

Nature versus Nurture

- Psychologists generally assert that human behavior is influenced by both nature (heredity) and nurture (environment). They study the biological bases of behavior to understand how these two variables interact.   p. 36

- Genetics is the study of heredity, the biological transmission of traits. Each person receives traits from his or her parents through the transmission of genes.   p. 37

- The inherited potential of people is carried by chromosomes. Each chromosome contains thousands of genes made up of DNA. The twenty-third pair of chromosomes determines the sex of a fetus.   pp. 37–38

- Identical twins share exactly the same genetic heritage; they come from one ovum and one sperm and are always the same sex. Fraternal twins are produced by two ova and two sperm and can be either both males, both females, or one male and one female.   p. 38

Communication in the Nervous System

- The basic unit of the nervous system is the neuron. The neuron fires in an all-or-none manner and has a refractory period. The space between the axon terminals and the dendrite of another neuron is the synapse.   p. 41

- An action potential stimulates the release of *neurotransmitters* that reside in the axon terminal and synaptic vesicles; neurotransmitters move across the synaptic space and attach, or bind themselves, to receptor sites on the dendrites of the next cell.   p. 44

- Psychopharmacology is the study of how drugs affect behavior. Such research often focuses on agonists and antagonists, how they may be used to learn about drug actions, and how they alleviate symptoms.   p. 47

Organization of the Nervous System

- The nervous system is composed of two subsystems, the central and the peripheral nervous systems. The central nervous system consists of the brain and spinal cord.   p. 48

- The peripheral nervous system carries information to the spinal cord and brain through a series of nerve fibers. The peripheral nervous system is divided into somatic and autonomic nervous systems. The autonomic nervous system is made up of the sympathetic and the parasympathetic nervous systems.   p. 49

Monitoring Neuronal Activity

- One measure of nervous system activity is the electroencephalogram, or EEG. The resulting records of brainwave patterns can be used to assess neurological disorders.   p. 52

- CAT scans (computerized axial tomography) are computer assisted X-ray procedures. MRI scans (magnetic resonance imaging) are similar to CAT scans but do not use radiation. PET scans (positron emission tomography) use radiochemical procedures and allow researchers to watch metabolic changes.   p. 53

Brain Structures

- The brain is usually divided into three sections: hindbrain, midbrain, and the remaining forebrain, including the cortex.   p. 54

- The *hindbrain* consists of the cerebellum, the medulla, and the pons. The *midbrain* is made up of nuclei that receive afferent signals from other parts of the brain and from the spinal cord, interpret them, and either relay the information to other parts of the brain or cause the body to act. The *forebrain* is the largest and most complicated of the brain structures and is comprised of the thalamus and hypothalamus, the limbic system, the basal ganglia and corpus callosum, and the cortex.   p. 55

- The most prominent structures of the cortex are the *lateral fissure* and the *central fissure* that divide the lobes.   pp. 56–57

- Each cerebral hemisphere is neurologically connected to the opposite side of the body.   pp. 58–60

Hormones and Glands

- The endocrine glands affect behavior by secreting hormones. Each controls a different aspect of behavior.   pp. 61–62

- Studies of carbohydrate intake and behavior show that carbohydrates can function like a drug; they can modify brain chemistry and, consequently, mood and behavior.   pp. 64–65

Connections

 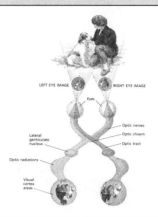 

If you are interested in . . .	*Turn to . . .*	*To learn more about . . .*
The nature versus nurture controversy	◆ Ch. 4, p. 143	The impact of a person's genetic heritage on the likelihood that he or she will become an alcoholic.
	◆ Ch. 7, p. 261	How the study of communication in apes is helping resolve the issue of nature versus nurture.
	◆ Ch. 14, p. 526	The extent to which a person's home environment can increase the likelihood of developing schizophrenia.
Communication between brain structures and the nervous system	◆ Ch. 3, pp. 76–84	How the eyes communicate information to the brain.
	◆ Ch. 11, p. 407	How emotional responses are affected and in turn affect emotion.
	◆ Ch. 13, p. 471	How our bodies' reaction to stressful situations is often arousal, followed by eventual exhaustion.
Brain structures and how they affect behavior	◆ Ch. 4, pp. 139–143	The extent to which alcohol affects higher brain functions.
	◆ Ch. 10, p. 369	The profound effect of Alzheimer's disease on memory.
	◆ Ch. 15, p. 566	The effects of electroconvulsive shock therapy when a person is suffering from depression.

3   *Sensation and Perception*

"Yes" by Tom Holland

◆

*H*ighly trained chemists are cleaning the ceiling of the Sistine Chapel in the Palace of the Vatican in Rome. There are nearly five centuries of grime and dirt on Michelangelo's spectacular frescoes that cover the ceilings and walls. This ambitious art restoration, begun in 1980, is being undertaken inch by inch; the cost of the cleaning will be about three million dollars and will take more than twelve years to complete. As it proceeds, the work is creating a furor in the art world.

Michelangelo's works have been described as dark, deep, and profound. That is, until the restoration began. The removal of soot caused by burning candles and of four hundred years of grime is showing a different Michelangelo. The colors are bright; the contrasts are striking and luminous. The ceiling, which rises sixty-five feet above the floor, is painted in azure, rose, lavender, and pink. The Sistine Chapel is neither dark nor ominous, but glowing with color and excitement. Researchers

Renovation of Michelangelo's paintings in the Sistine Chapel has drastically changed the world's perception of his art.

and art historians now have a new view of Michelangelo, and the restoration is showing his true colors.

As a result of the restoration, Michelangelo's work must now be reinterpreted. Angels once viewed as haunting and austere are now seen as cherubic and lively. Older interpretations of Michelangelo are giving way to newer impressions; Michelangelo is seen with a new clarity. Imagine looking at television through a dirty window or trying to read an illustrated history of North America in a darkened theater. The television picture is visible and the photographs will be seen, but both will be viewed with difficulty and with a loss of detail and visual clarity.

When you walk out of a darkened theater into the daylight you may have trouble seeing until your eyes have adjusted. When you walk into the darkened theater you may also have trouble seeing until your eyes have adjusted. Wearing sunglasses indoors affects your perceptual experience, and your hearing may be impaired for a few hours after a rock concert. Tasting a delicate glass of wine may be nearly impossible after eating Mexican food. Our perception of the visual, auditory, and taste world depends not only on light, sound, and food, but on intervening events (soot and dirt) and continuing events (eating hot tamales).

Whenever you are exposed to a stimulus in the environment, it initiates an electrochemical change in the receptors in your body that, in turn, initiates the processes of sensation and perception. Psychologists study sensation and perception because what people sense and perceive determines how they will understand and interpret the world. This interpretation depends on a combination of stimulation, past experiences, and current interpretations.

Sensation and Perception: A Definition

Traditionally, sensation and perception have been studied together as closely related fields. *Sensation* is the process of stimulation of the sense organ receptor cells and the relaying of initial information to higher centers for further processing; *perception* is the selection and interpretation of sensory input that give it meaning. Thus, sensation provides the stimulus for further perceptual processing. For example, when light strikes the eyeball and initiates electrochemical processes, this is sensation; but our interpretation of that pattern of light and its resulting neural representation as an image (for example, of a barnyard at dusk) is part of perception.

Today, perceptual psychologists generally acknowledge that a strict distinction between sensation and perception is unnecessary. We now think in terms of *perceptual systems*—that is, the sets of structures, functions, and operations by means of which people perceive the world around them. Perception is not merely the firing of one group of neurons but involves sets of neurons and previous experience, as well as stimulation that occurs at our eyes or ears. Psychologists are especially aware that perceptual systems interact. Thus, as researchers gather more sophisticated information about sensation and perception, the boundaries between the two begin to fade.

Sensory and perceptual processes rely so closely on one another that many researchers think about the two processes together as perception. For them, **perception** is the process by which an organism interprets sensory input (which has been converted into electrochemical energy) so that it acquires organization, form, and meaning. It is through perception that people explore the world and discover its rules (Gibson, 1988). This complex process involves the nervous system and one or more of the perceptual or

Perception: The complex process by which an organism interprets sensory input so that it acquires meaning.

sensory systems, that is, vision, hearing, taste, smell, or touch. Although perceptual systems are different, they share common processes. In each case, an environmental stimulus creates an initial stimulation. Receptor cells translate that form of energy into a neuronal impulse, and these impulses are then sent to specific areas of the brain for further processing.

The relationship between the physical stimulus and a person's conscious experience of that stimulus is the focus of **psychophysics.** Psychophysical studies attempt to relate the physical dimension of stimuli to psychological experience. For example, many psychophysical studies attempt to determine the minimum amount of energy necessary to stimulate vision fifty percent of the time, or perhaps eighty percent of the time; in these two cases, the results would be different—it takes more energy to nearly always create a perceptual experience than to create one only half the time. Psychophysical studies show that environmental stimuli are rich with information and cues. These studies also show that human beings (and animals, for that matter) gather information and interpret it in an active, constructive manner. Studies of sensation and perception also show that past experiences affect interpretation and shape our perceptions.

Psychophysics: The study of the relationship between a physical stimulus and a person's conscious experience of the stimulus.

Sensory Experience

Your opponent's serve ricochets off the front wall and whizzes overhead. By the loud smack on the wall behind you, you know instantly that the ball has rebounded too fast to be intercepted at the back of the court. You run to the front of the court, turn, and swat the ball, sending it flying into the left corner. Your opponent raises his racquet in response but is too slow and the ball thumps into his chest. A fast-paced racquetball game provides an exhilarating example of the interaction of perceptual systems. Players must coordinate their hearing, eyesight, motor systems, sense of balance, and posture all at once in order to react effectively to the speeding ball as it bounces off the walls and floor of the court.

Interacting Perceptual Systems

An organism acts on a mixture of perceptual information. Researchers who study the active integration of the perceptual systems find that for the systems to develop fully, they must have varied experiences as well as a way to interact. In a classic study of visual and motor coordination in kittens, Held and Hein (1963) demonstrated the need for the perceptual systems to act together. Pairs of kittens were placed in a circular enclosure, and one of each pair was equipped with a harness and collar that let it move actively as it explored the environment. The other kitten was restrained so that it moved only in response to the movements of the first kitten (see Figure 3.1 on page 74). Active, voluntary movement initiated by the first kitten caused identical, but involuntary, movement by the second kitten. Only the kittens who were allowed to initiate voluntary movements were later able to make good visually-guided motor movements; the others had deficits in their perceptual abilities.

Studies of human beings also show that both varied sensory experiences and interaction among different systems are necessary for perception to develop properly. Von Senden (1932) reported case histories of people who had cataracts (which cloud vision) at birth that were removed in adulthood. These individuals, seeing clearly for the first time as adults, had several

FIGURE 3.1
Held and Hein (1963) raised kittens in a circular enclosure and allowed one kitten active movement, the other only passive movement. Both kittens saw the same view of the world but showed dramatically different types of responses when tested for sensory-motor coordination.

deficiencies. They were unable to recognize simple forms presented in a different color or a different context. These results with human beings parallel those with animals—people need a varied sensory and perceptual experience early in life for normal perceptual experiences to occur in adulthood. The consequences of deprivation and isolation from combined perceptual experiences are debilitating. The effects of limiting stimulation have been followed up with animals and human subjects in studies of restricted environmental stimulation.

Restricted Environmental Stimulation

Throughout the ages, mystics of all kinds have claimed to obtain special trance states by taking vows of silence, adhering to an austere life-style, meditating while sitting stone still for hours, and so on, thereby purposely limiting their sensory experiences. In 1954, neurophysiologist John Lilly enlisted modern technology to find out what would happen if the brain were deprived of all sensory input. He constructed an isolation tank that excluded all light and sound and was filled with heavily salted water which allows for easy floating. In this manmade sea, deprived of all external stimuli, Lilly reported experiencing dreams, reveries, hallucinations, and other altered states. Ten years later, people began enhancing isolation-tank trips by taking drugs such as LSD. During the 1970s, immersion in an isolation tank became a popular means of "expanding" one's consciousness.

The benefits of sensory restriction—isolation from sights, sounds, smells, tastes, and feeling—have been greatly exaggerated, but it can have profound effects on developing animals and humans. Psychologists have used sensory deprivation experiments to test whether certain animal perceptions are innate or learned. For example, animals are deprived of a sensory stimulant, such as light, from birth to six months and then tested on skills that require using the deprived sense, in this case, sight. If the animal performs at the same level as animals that have not been deprived of the stimulus, the experimenters conclude that the perceptual system is inborn. If the animal does not perform well, experimenters conclude that experience is important for the normal development of that perceptual system.

Heron studied the effects of sensory restriction in human beings. College students were confined to a comfortable but dull room. To limit their sensory experiences, they heard only the continuous hum of an air conditioner, they wore translucent plastic visors, and they had tubes lined with cotton placed on their hands and arms. The results were dramatic. Within a few hours the subjects' performance on tests of mental ability was impaired. They became bored and irritable, and many said they saw "images" (Bexton, Heron, and Scott, 1954).

Other studies of sensory restriction placed subjects in identical conditions, *except* that they were told that their deprivation would serve as an aid to meditation. These subjects did not hallucinate or become irritable; in fact, their mental ability improved (Lilly, 1956; Zuckerman, 1969). This study suggests that people do not necessarily become bored because of lack of stimulation. Rather, when people *feel* that their situation is monotonous, they become bored. When given the opportunity to relax in a quiet place for a long time, many people meditate—they find such "deprivation" relaxing. Such findings indicate the need for caution in interpreting data from sensory deprivation studies involving human beings, particularly since subjects approach these situations with strong expectations.

Sensory restriction has proved to have positive effects with some people. Because of the profound relaxation that occurs in an extreme sensory restricted environment, it can be highly effective in helping to modify some habits, including smoking reduction and treating obesity and insomnia (Suedfeld and Coren, 1989). Research shows that sensory restriction does not necessarily produce hallucinations or cognitive impairment, but rather can be facilitative. Research on sensory restriction is exceedingly complicated because so many variables might affect the results. Some subjects may be more likely to benefit than others (men compared with women, older individuals, those with religious backgrounds), and some subjects may be adversely affected. Further, previous experience with sensory restriction may produce a cumulative effect, so that each time a person goes through restriction it has a greater effect.

♦ Explain the traditional view of sensation and perception as separate processes. p. 72
♦ Why have modern researchers viewed perception as a unitary process? pp. 72–73
♦ What are the effects of limiting specific sensory experiences in human beings? pp. 73–75

Focus on Learning

The Visual System

Imagine that you are in a house at night when the power goes out and you are left in total darkness. You hear sounds, but have no idea where they are coming from. You stub your toe on the coffee table, then frantically grope along the walls until you reach the kitchen, where you fumble through the drawers in search of a flashlight.

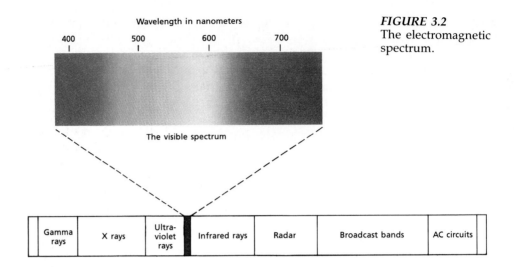

FIGURE 3.2
The electromagnetic
spectrum.

Human beings derive more information through sight than through any other sense. By some estimates, the eyes contain seventy percent of all the body's sense receptors. Although your eyes respond to pressure, the proper or appropriate stimulus for vision is **electromagnetic radiation.** Electromagnetic radiation includes visible light, cosmic rays, X rays, and ultraviolet, infrared, and radar waves. **Light** is the very small portion of those wavelengths that is visible to the eye. It may come directly from a source or be reflected from an object (see Figure 3.2).

The Structure of the Eye

Figure 3.3 shows the major parts of the human eye. Light first passes through the *cornea,* a transparent covering over the pigmented *iris.* The iris constricts or dilates to make the *pupil* smaller or larger as it focuses on objects. Behind the pupil is the *crystalline lens,* which is about four millimeters thick. Together, the cornea and the lens form images in much the same way that a camera lens does. Constriction of the iris makes the pupil smaller, improving the quality of the image on the retina and increasing the depth of focus, that is, the field that is in sharp focus; this action also helps control the amount of light entering the eye.

What happens when people's eyeballs are not perfectly shaped? How does this affect their vision? (See Figure 3.4 on page 78.) Some people are **myopic,** or *nearsighted,* and can see things that are close to them, but have trouble seeing objects at a distance. Others are **hypermetropic,** or *farsighted,* and have trouble seeing things up close, but can see objects that are far away. Near- and farsightedness occur because the image that is cast on the back of the eye is not focused well. In addition, some people have lenses that are irregularly shaped, a condition known as *astigmatism,* which causes distortions in the image. As people grow older, their lenses thicken and become less pliable, causing fuzzy images.

The *retina,* which lines the back of the eye, is like the film in a camera: it captures an image. The retina consists of ten layers of cells; of these, the most important are the photoreceptors, bipolar cells, and ganglion cells. The **photoreceptors** (light receptors) consist of *rods* and *cones.* After light passes

Electromagnetic radiation: The entire spectrum of waves initiated by charged particles, including visible light gamma rays, X-rays, and ultraviolet, infrared, and radar waves.

Light: The portion of the electromagnetic spectrum (ranging from 400 to 750 nanometers) visible to the eye.

Myopic: Unable to see things far away, at a distance; *nearsighted.*

Hypermetropic: Unable to see things that are nearby; *farsighted.*

Photoreceptors: The light-sensitive cells in the retina: rods and cones.

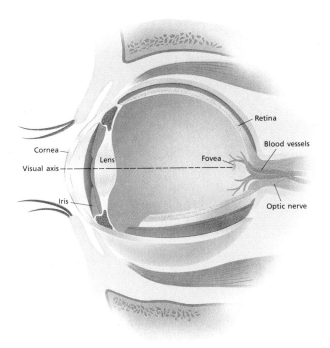

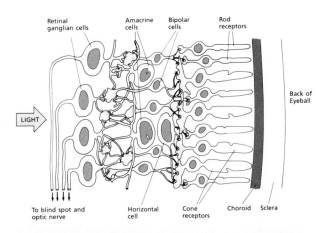

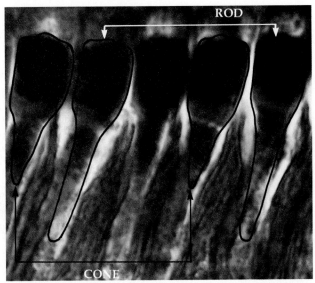

FIGURE 3.3
The main structures of the eye. The fovea is the central portion of the retina. The photoreceptors of the retina connect to higher brain pathways through the optic nerve. Light filters through layers of retinal cells before hitting the receptors (rods and cones), located at the back of the eye and pointed away from the incoming light. The rods and cones pass an electrical impulse to bipolar cells. They relay the impulse to the ganglion cells. The axons of the ganglion cells form the fibers of the optic nerve.

Rods assist in night vision; cones are necessary to day vision, color vision, and fine discrimination.

through several layers of cells it strikes the photoreceptor layer. Here it breaks down photopigments, which cause an electrochemical change in the rods and cones, and the electrical energy is transferred to the next major layer. The process by which the perceptual system analyzes stimuli and converts them into electrical impulses is generally known as *coding*, or more formally, **transduction.**

Each eye contains more than 120 million rods and 6 million cones. These millions of photoreceptors do not have individual pathways to the higher visual centers in the brain. Instead, through the process of convergence, neural energy from rods comes together onto a single *bipolar cell*. At the same time, hundreds of cones synapse and converge onto other bipolar cells.

From the bipolar cells, electrochemical energy is transferred to the *ganglion cell* layer. A number of bipolar cells synapse and converge onto each ganglion cell (there are about one million ganglion cells). The axons of the ganglion cells make up the *optic nerve*, where information that was initially

Transduction: The process by which sensory systems analyze environmental stimuli and convert them into electrical impulses; *coding*.

FIGURE 3.4
The lens focuses light rays directly on the retina in the normal eye. In nearsightedness and farsightedness, the shape of the lens causes the light rays to focus either in front of or behind the retina. Concave or convex lenses correct such visual problems.

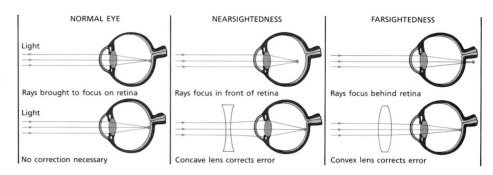

received by the rods and cones is carried via higher pathways in the nervous system, where still further coding takes place, at the **visual cortex** of the brain.

Rods and Cones. The *duplicity theory* of vision states that rods and cones are structurally different and are used to accomplish different tasks. Cones are tightly packed in the center of the retina, or *fovea*, and used for day vision, color vision, and fine discrimination. Rods (and some cones) are found on the rest of the retina, or *periphery*, which is used predominantly for night vision (see Figure 3.5). The fact that cones are especially important

FIGURE 3.5
Top view of the left eye, with the corresponding densities of rods and cones across the retina. (Pirenne, 1967, p. 32)

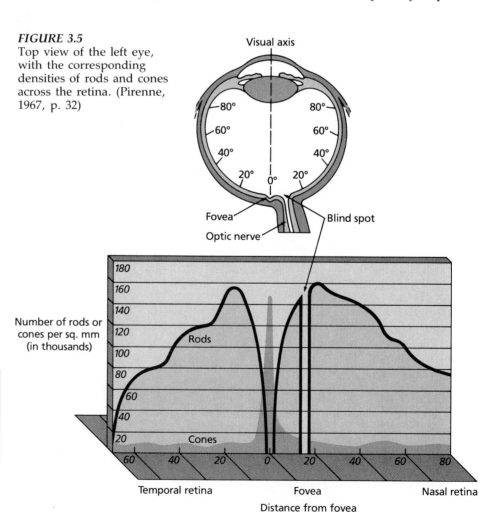

Visual cortex: The first and most important layer of the occipital lobe that receives information from the lateral geniculate nucleus.

in fine visual discrimination is shown in the **visual acuity** tests you take when you apply for a driver's license. A visual acuity test measures the resolution capacity of the visual system, that is, the ability to see fine details. Vision tests may involve reading letters on a Snellen chart or deciding whether a series of closely spaced lines are vertical or horizontal. These abilities are especially mediated by cones. You do best on these tests in a well-lit room (cones operate at high light levels) and when the test is shown in your central (foveal) vision (again, cones occur in the center of your retina more than in any other place).

If you go from a well-lit lobby into a dark theater you will experience a brief period of low light sensitivity and you will be unable to distinguish empty seats. Within thirty minutes you will have fully adapted to the dark and be far more light sensitive. Our eyes are always in some state of light or dark adaptation. Rods and cones are sensitive to light, but in a lighted room they are less sensitive than they are after having been in the dark. **Dark adaptation** is the increase in sensitivity that occurs when the illumination level changes from light to darkness. It is a process by which chemicals in the photoreceptors (rods and cones) regenerate and return to their inactive state and the sensitivity of the visual system increases (see Figure 3.6). Of course, after leaving a dark theater and returning to the afternoon sunlight, you must squint or shade your eyes until they become adapted to the light.

Look at Figure 3.7 on page 80, which shows a dark-adaptation curve. The first part of the curve is determined by cones, the second part by rods. The data for such curves are obtained from experiments with subjects who possess only rods or cones. Typically, a subject is first shown bright light for two minutes. The light is then turned off, and the subject waits in a totally dark room for sixty seconds. Next, a very dim test spot is turned on for half a second and the subject is asked if he or she sees it. Usually, subjects will report seeing the test spot only after several successive presentations, because dark adaptation occurs gradually. Studies in which only cones are stimulated show that the first part of the curve is determined by

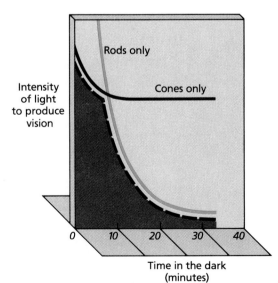

FIGURE 3.6
The dashed line represents a typical overall dark adaptation curve. The two solid lines represent separate dark adaptation for rods and cones. The process of light and dark adaptation occurs continually as people's eyes are exposed to different light intensities. The majority of dark adaptation takes place in the first ten minutes.

Visual acuity: The resolution capability of the visual system in a controlled setting.

Dark adaptation: An increase in sensitivity when a person moves from a light environment to a dark one; chemicals in the photoreceptors regenerate and return to their inactive pre-light adapted state, which results in an increase in sensitivity.

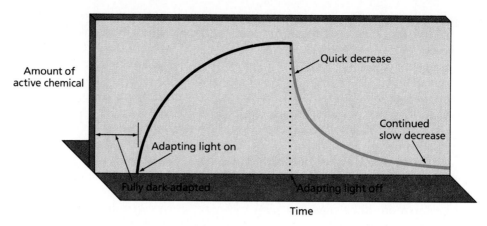

FIGURE 3.7
In the process of dark adaptation, chemicals in the photoreceptors return to a quiet, unactivated state. The fewer the active chemicals, the more sensitive the eye. When a light is turned on, the chemicals become very active; when the light is turned off, there is a quick drop in the amount of active chemical and the eye becomes increasingly more sensitive. (From Cornsweet, 1970, p. 132)

cones and the second part by rods. The speed at which the photochemicals in the rods and cones regenerate determines the shape of the two parts of the curve. This is why when you are driving along a road at night you may have trouble seeing clearly for a few minutes after a car drives toward you with its high beams on; the photochemicals in the rods take some time to regenerate to their dark-adapted state.

Higher Pathways. As electrical impulses leave the retina through the optic nerve, they proceed to higher centers of the brain (see Figure 3.8). Knowledge about the way visual structures are connected to the brain enables physicians to diagnose many conditions, for example, whether a stroke victim with poor vision has a blood clot that is obstructing circulation in the right hemisphere of the brain.

FIGURE 3.8
The major components of the visual system.

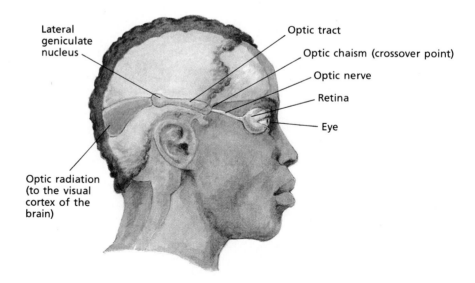

FIGURE 3.9
As this overhead view shows, some information from each eye crosses at the optic chiasm.

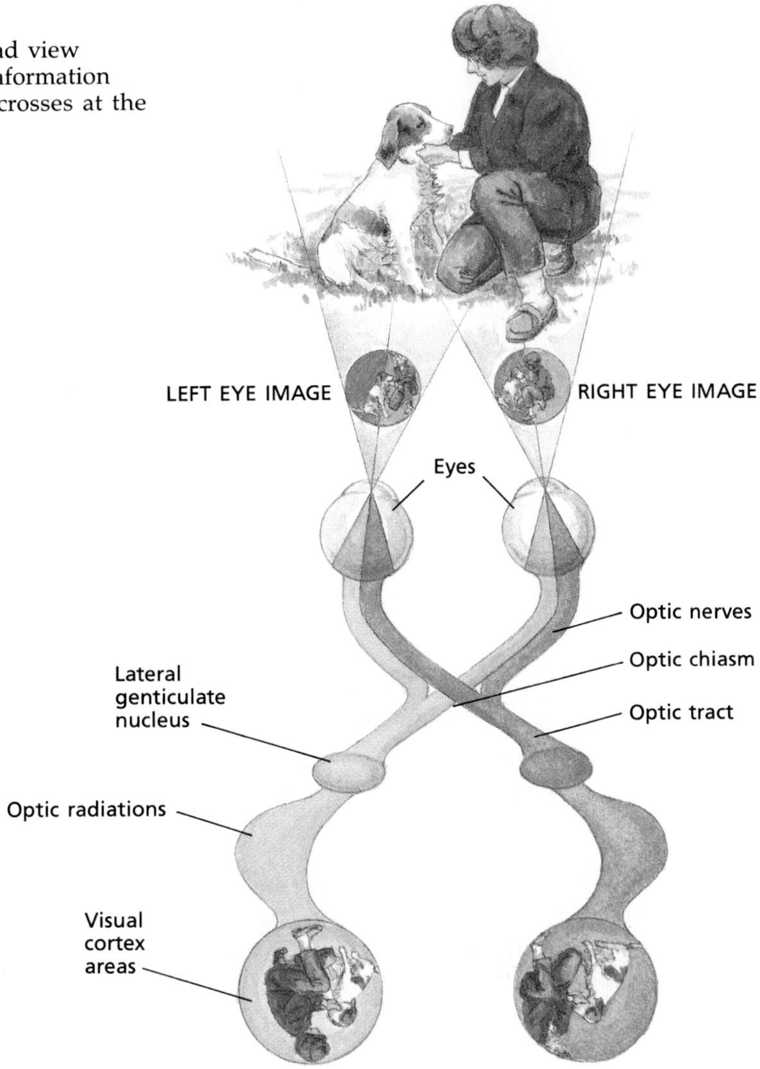

LEFT EYE IMAGE   RIGHT EYE IMAGE

Eyes

Optic nerves

Optic chiasm

Lateral geniculate nucleus

Optic tract

Optic radiations

Visual cortex areas

Each eye is connected to both sides of the brain, with half of its impulses going to the left side of the brain and the other half to the right side. Half of the visual impulses from each eye cross over to the other side of the brain; the point at which the crossover occurs is called the **optic chiasm** (see Figures 3.9, above, and 3.10, on page 82). This crossover of impulses allows the brain to process two sets of signals from an image and helps human beings perceive form in three dimensions. If the optic nerves are severed at the optic chiasm, vision is sharply impaired. Normally, however, impulses proceed to higher brain structures, including the **lateral geniculate nucleus,** the **superior colliculus,** and the **striate cortex.** Of course, people are seldom, if ever, actively aware of the process.

The Electrical Connection

Vision and other perceptual processes are electrochemical in nature. When receptors in the perceptual systems are stimulated, the information is coded and sent to the brain for interpretation and further analysis. Psychologists

Optic chiasm: The point at which the optic nerve fibers from the nasal side of the eye cross over and project to the other side of the brain.

Lateral geniculate nucleus: The first major center at which impulses leaving the eye are processed; sometimes called the *lateral geniculate body.*

Superior colliculus: A secondary part of the visual system that in human beings responds to movement; signals to it are generated from the lateral geniculate nucleus.

Striate cortex: The primary visual cortex to which projections are made in the visual system from the lateral geniculate nucleus.

FIGURE 3.10
As shown in Figure 3.3, the center of the retina (the fovea) contains only cones. At about 18° of visual angle (a measure of the size of images on the retina) there are no receptors at all. This is the place where the optic nerve leaves the eye, called the blind spot. Because the blind spot for each eye is on the nasal side of the eyeball, there is no loss of vision—the two blind spots do not overlap. To demonstrate that you have a blind spot, close one eye and move the page in and out while staring at the point. The black spot will disappear when your eye is about four inches from the page. If you switch eyes, the blind spot for the other eye will be apparent. Once you have located the correct distance, move the tip of a pencil along the page until it reaches the blind spot and watch the tip disappear.

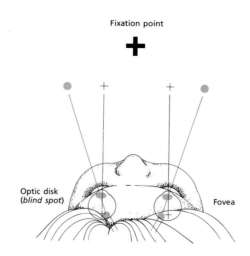

Fixation point

Optic disk
(*blind spot*)   Fovea

are interested in understanding how electrical activity in the nervous system is transmitted and coded because such knowledge helps explain how the perceptual systems operate.

Measuring the electrical activity of the visual system by stimulating it with horizontal, vertical, and slanted lines is, in fact, one way to study how the visual system processes stimuli. Another way is by stimulating the photoreceptors with specific patterns of light, thereby causing a change in electrical activity at all levels of the visual system. Researchers measure this change in activity by means of *single-unit recording*. They place an electrode in or next to a single cell and record its activity in response to stimuli of different sizes and shapes. This process has led to the identification of specific receptive fields involved in the perception of form, shape, and color.

Receptive fields are the areas on the retina that, when stimulated, produce a change in the firing of cells in the visual system (see Figure 3.11 on page 83). For example, certain cells will fire, or become active, if a vertical line is presented at the retina but not if a horizontal line is presented. David Hubel and Torsten Wiesel (1962) found cells in the receptive fields that are sensitive to the position, length, movement, color, or intensity of a line. They characterized the cells as simple, complex, or hypercomplex. *Simple cells* respond to the shape and size of lights that stimulate the receptive field (see Figure 3.12 below). *Complex cells* respond most vigorously to movement of light in one direction. *Hypercomplex cells* are the most specific; they respond

FIGURE 3.12
Receptive fields of "simple" cortical cells: a plus sign means a region in the receptive field that gives an *on* response, and a minus sign indicates an *off* response.

> **Receptive fields:** Areas of the retina that, when stimulated, affect the firing of a single cell in the visual system.

Receptive field shape

Optical stimulus

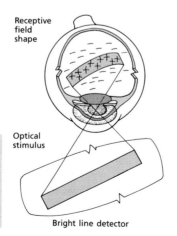

Bright line detector

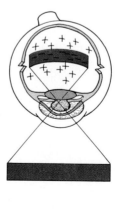

Dark line detector

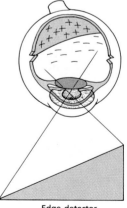

Edge detector

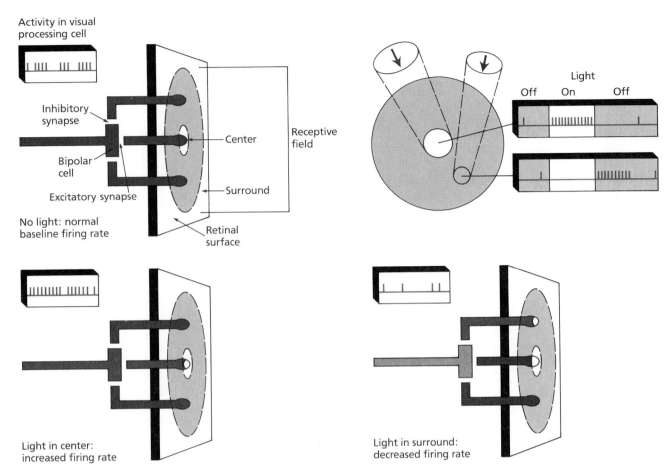

Activity in visual processing cell

Inhibitory synapse

Bipolar cell

Excitatory synapse

No light: normal baseline firing rate

Center

Surround

Receptive field

Retinal surface

Light
Off   On   Off

Light in center: increased firing rate

Light in surround: decreased firing rate

FIGURE 3.11

Hubel and Wiesel (1962) found cells that fire when stimulated in the center of their receptive field but do not fire (and instead produce suppression) when stimulated outside the center area. Receptive fields in the retina are often circular with a center-surround arrangement. Light striking the center of the field produces the opposite result of light striking the surround. Here, light in the center produces increased firing in the visual cell and light in the surround produces decreased firing. The arrangement in other receptive fields may be just the opposite.

only to a line of the correct length and orientation that moves in the proper direction.

Hubel and Wiesel further learned that cells, especially those in the center of the visual cortex, are organized in columns so that lines with a single orientation or width stimulate cells that cut across several, or even all, layers of the visual cortex. Coding becomes more complex as electrical information proceeds through the visual system to higher centers (Burr, Morrone, and Spinelli, 1989). The work of Hubel and Wiesel, which has been supported by other noted researchers (e.g., DeValois, Thorell, and Albrecht, 1985), earned them a Nobel prize in 1981.

Hirsch and Spinelli (1971) conducted a series of experiments in which they controlled the visual experiences of newborn kittens. The kittens wore goggles that let them perceive either vertical lines or horizontal lines. When goggles were later removed, kittens raised with only horizontal experiences bumped into chair legs (vertical) but could leap into a chair seat (horizontal); kittens raised with only vertical experiences had problems with horizontal surfaces (Blakemore and Cooper, 1970). Such studies indicate that although most of the connections in the visual system are present in newborns, the proper functioning of the system is sensitive to and depends on experience.

Eye Movements

Your eyes are constantly in motion. They search for familiar faces in a crowded classroom, scan a page of headlines and articles in a newspaper, and follow a baseball hit high into right field for a home run. Research on eye movements reveals what people are looking at, how long they look at it, and perhaps where they will look next. It also helps psychologists understand certain visual problems, such as dyslexia. Zangwill and Blakemore (1972) studied the eye movements of a man who had difficulty reading. They found that the man was moving his eyes from right to left across a page, rather than in the usual left-to-right direction. Other studies show that poor readers have erratic, even chaotic, eye movements (Lefton, Nagle, Johnson, and Fisher, 1979). We also know that eye movements depend on the context in which they are measured. The eye movements of a reader are different from those of a typist, even when both are reading the same material, because the text viewed by the typist is not processed for meaning the way it is by a reader (Inhoff, Morris, and Calabrese, 1986).

Rapid movements of the eyes from one position to another, called **saccades,** are the most common type of eye movement. These are the voluntary movements people make when reading, driving, or looking for an object. The eye can make only four or five saccades in a second. The movement of the eye takes only about 20–50 milliseconds, but there is a delay of about 200–250 milliseconds before the next movement can be made (Harris et al., 1988).

We use eye fixations to form a stable representation of the visual world by integrating in memory the successive glances (Irwin, Brown, and Sun, 1988). Despite rapid changes in our visual world and the movement of our eyes, head, and body through space, we accumulate the successive glances to form an abstract memory and a stable view of the world.

Perceptual Span. Eye movements have been used to determine the *perceptual span,* that is, the size of the region a person sees when fixating, or staring (for example, the number of letters you see when you fixate at a specific point on this page). Research shows that people use information gathered in both central (foveal) vision and in peripheral vision (noncentral regions of the eye) to determine the location of their next eye movements; this ultimately affects the size of the perceptual span (Pollatsek, Rayner, and Balota, 1986; Rayner and Fisher, 1987). We also know that people tend to direct their gaze to a point just to the left of center of words when they are reading. This site (left of center) may help a reader make inferences about the rest of the word, but the left of center location is probably due to eye movement limitations rather than cognitive decision making on the part of a reader (McConkie, Kerr, Reddix, and Zola, 1988).

In a study of eye movements and perception, Noton and Stark (1971) presented subjects with a series of pictures and told them that they would have to identify the pictures later in different groupings. They recorded the subjects' eye movements during the learning period and in subsequent testing. Each subject fixated on the same area and followed identical scan paths for a specific picture in both phases of the experiment. The researchers suggested that in perceiving and recognizing forms, people use a charac-

Saccades: Rapid movements of the eyes from one point to another. The minimum fixation period between saccades is about one-quarter of a second.

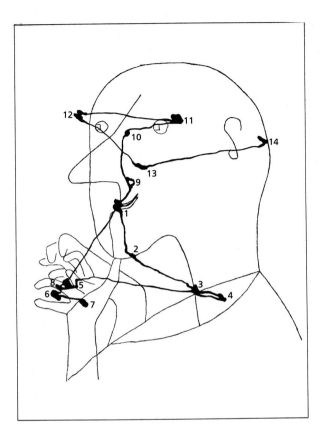

FIGURE 3.13
Eye movements made by a subject viewing a drawing adapted from Paul Klee's *Old Man Figuring*. The numbers show the order of the subject's visual fixations. Lines between the numbers represent saccades, which occupied about 10 percent of the viewing time. The remainder of the time was spent fixating.

teristic pattern of eye movement that follows a fixed path from one feature to the next (see Figure 3.13). Noton and Stark concluded that eye movements are important to the way the brain stores information, and that there are significant individual differences among scan paths. Individual differences are often a key to understanding many perceptual phenomena other than eye movements; this is apparent and prominent when psychologists work with educators to examine perceptual abilities among readers and those who have trouble with reading.

Psychology and Education

A close relationship exists between psychology and education. Many school psychologists have been trained in colleges of education, often in departments devoted exclusively to educational psychology. The cross-fertilization of theories and research becomes especially apparent and important in the study of the perplexing disorder dyslexia, which has often been thought to have a perceptual basis. The term *dyslexia* literally means faulty reading, but the term has taken on a broader meaning. Poor readers, children with emotional problems, and children with learning problems are often diagnosed as dyslexic. Parents are told by educators that the children have perception problems.

The typical child with dyslexia is two years behind in reading ability, has normal intelligence, good health, and no gross neurological problems. Some medical researchers assert that dyslexic children show some central nervous system dysfunctions, evidence of brain damage and asymmetries, and are maturationally slow, although not all agree (Hynd and Semrund-

Clikeman, 1989). Educational researchers focus on different findings: Almost all dyslexic children read slowly, make many pronunciation errors, reverse letters and words, confuse letters of similar shape, and make chaotic eye movements—that is, they make many regressive (backward) fixations and go over and over the same words. Dyslexics obtain less information from the texts they read, obtain faulty information, and fail to master symbol-to-sounds relationships. Dyslexics have trouble naming letters; some studies show that dyslexics have trouble retrieving information about sounds and meanings. They have all these troubles despite a normal vocabulary.

Why are some people dyslexic, and what can be done to assist these individuals? Certain perceptual training helps some dyslexics. For others, drill, repetition and one-on-one supervision are important. Today, researchers in psychology and education are debating the various theories, and they have not yet agreed as to what causes dyslexia or even whether it is a perceptual problem. Psychologists often focus on neurological aspects of dyslexia, such as differences in brain development; others focus on the role of eye movements; still others, on sound-sight language correspondence (e.g., Hynd and Semrund-Clikeman, 1989). Some suggest that dyslexia is more of a subtle language deficiency than a perceptual one (Vellutino, 1987). In education departments the focus is often on training in attention, in comprehension, and in reading. Despite their differences, both psychologists and educators are especially aware of the emotional problems that accompany an inability to read in traditional ways, especially in the classroom, and are using psychological and education theories to solve real problems in education. Thus, psychological ideas are cutting across the curriculum to help dyslexics.

Color Vision

Think of all the different shades of blue—navy blue, sky blue, baby blue, royal blue, turquoise, aqua—that are now apparent in Michelangelo's Sistine Chapel. If you are like most people, you have no trouble discriminating among a wide range of colors. Color depends on the wavelength of light particles that stimulate the photoreceptors. It has three psychological dimensions, *hue, brightness,* and *saturation,* that correspond to three physical properties of light—*wavelength, intensity,* and *purity.* When people speak of the color of an object, they are referring to its **hue**—that is, whether the light reflected from the object looks red, blue, orange, or some other color. Hue is a psychological term, because objects do not themselves possess color. Rather, people's perception of color is determined by how their eyes and brain interpret reflected wavelengths. In the visible spectrum, a different hue is associated with each wavelength. Light with a wavelength of 400 nanometers looks blue; light with a wavelength of 700 nanometers looks red; and so on. (See Figure 3.14.)

The second psychological dimension of color is **brightness.** This refers to how light or dark the hue of an object appears. It is affected by three variables: (1) The greater the intensity of reflected light, the brighter the object. (2) The longer the wavelength of reflected light, the less bright the object. (3) As shown in Figure 3.15, the nearer the wavelengths are to being in the 500–600 nanometer range, the more sensitive the photoreceptors. This is why school buses and fire engines are usually painted yellow—they are more visible to motorists.

The third psychological dimension of color is **saturation,** or purity. Few objects reflect light that is totally pure. Usually they reflect a mixture of

Hue: The psychological property of light referred to as color, determined by the wavelength reflected from an object.

Brightness: The lightness or darkness of reflected light, determined in large part by a light's intensity.

Saturation: The depth of hue of reflected light, as determined by the purity (homogeneity) of the wavelengths contained in the light.

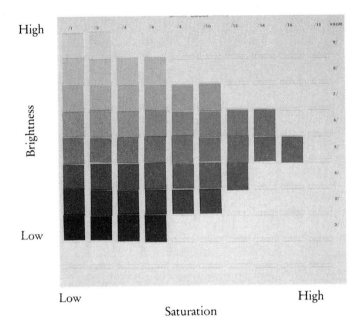

FIGURE 3.14
Hue, brightness, and saturation. These colors have the same dominant wavelength (hue) but different saturation and brightness. (Courtesy of Munsell Color Corporation.)

wavelengths. Pure saturated light has a narrow band of wavelengths and, thus, a narrow range of perceived color. A saturated red light with no blue, yellow, or white in it, for example, appears as a very deep red. Unsaturated colors are produced by a wider band of wavelengths. Unsaturated red light can appear to be light pink or dark red. Or it can look muddy because its wider range of wavelengths makes it less pure.

Color Coding. How does the brain code and process color? Two nineteenth-century scientists, Thomas Young and Hermann Von Helmholtz, working independently, proposed that different types of cones provide the basis for color coding in the visual system. *Color coding* is the ability to discriminate among colors based on differences in wavelength. According to the Young-Helmholtz theory, also called the **trichromatic theory,** all colors can be made by mixing three basic colors: red, green, and blue. (*Trichromatic* means three colors; *tri* means three and *chroma* means color.) All cones are assumed to respond to all wavelengths that stimulate them, but each type of cone—red, blue, or green—responds maximally to the red, blue, or green wave-

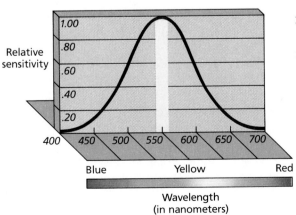

FIGURE 3.15
The average observer's sensitivity to visible light during daylight reaches a peak at 555 nanometers. Thus the normal human eye is more sensitive to yellow wavelengths than to red or blue. Such a curve is called a spectral sensitivity curve.

Trichromatic theory: A theory of color vision developed by Young and Helmholtz which stated that all colors can be made by mixing three basic colors: red, blue, and green.

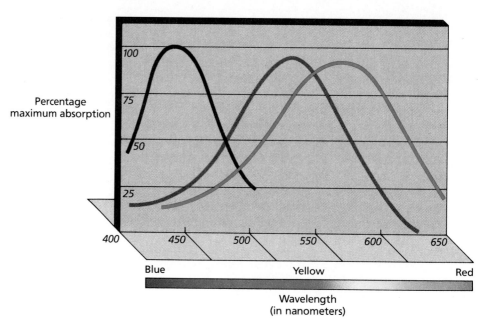

FIGURE 3.16
Each of the three types of cones in the primate eye has peak sensitivity in a different area of the spectrum. Thus certain cells are more responsive to some wavelengths than to others. (MacNichol, 1964)

length (see Figure 3.16). The combined neural output of the three types of cones provides the information that enables a person to distinguish color. If the neural output of one type of cone is sufficiently greater than that of the others, a person's perception of color will be determined mainly by that type of color receptor. Because each person's neurons are unique, it is likely that each of us sees color somewhat differently.

Unfortunately, the trichromatic theory does not explain certain visual phenomena well. For example, it does not explain why some colors look deeper when placed next to other colors (color contrast). It does not explain why people asked to name the basic colors nearly always name more than three. Further, the trichromatic theory does not explain well studies of color blindness (for example, when people have color deficiencies, they often cannot discriminate colors successfully in two areas of the visual spectrum). In response to some of the problems left unresolved, another theory of color vision, the **opponent-process theory,** was proposed by Ewald Herring in 1887. It assumes that there are six primary colors to which people respond, and three types of receptors: red-green, blue-yellow, and black-white. Every receptor fires in response to all wavelengths, but in each pair, one receptor fires maximally to one wavelength. Maximum firing to red, for example, is accompanied by a low rate of firing to green (see Figure 3.17). Opponent-process theory explains color contrast better, and it also helps explain color blindness.

Both the trichromatic theory and the opponent-process theory have received support from research (e.g., Hurvich and Jameson, 1974). Studies of the chemistry and absorptive properties of the retina show three classes of cones. Thus, the trichromatic theory seems to accurately describe coding at the retina (Marks, Dobell, and MacNichol, 1964). Support for the opponent-process theory comes from microelectrode studies of the lateral geniculate nucleus in monkeys. (The lateral geniculate nucleus is one of the major visual projection areas in the visual system of both human beings and monkeys.) Cells in the lateral geniculate nucleus respond differently to various

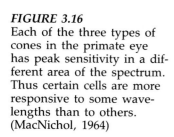

Opponent-process theory: Theory of color stating that color is coded by a series of receptors responding positively or negatively to different wavelengths of light.

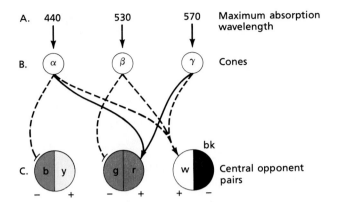

A.   440   530   570   Maximum absorption wavelength

B.   α   β   γ   Cones

C.   b y   g r   w   Central opponent pairs
      –   +   –   +   +   –

FIGURE 3.17
According to an opponent-process model proposed by Hurvich and Jameson (1974), three kinds of cones (alpha, beta, and gamma) respond maximally to light of different wavelengths, indicated at level A. These either stimulate (arrows) or inhibit (dotted lines) three kinds of central opponent pairs—cells that respond to either "blue" or "yellow" (a b/y pair), "green" or "red" (a g/r pair), or "white" or "black" (a w/b pair). This theory is influential because it is compatible with color-blindness data and knowledge of physiology. (After Hochberg, 1978, and Hurvich and Jameson, 1974)

wavelengths. When the eye is stimulated with lights of a wavelength between 400 and 500 nanometers, certain cells in the lateral geniculate nucleus decrease their rate of firing. If stimulated with a longer wavelength, firing rate increases (DeValois and Jacobs, 1968). This change is predicted by the opponent-process theory. Exactly how color information is transferred from the retina to the lateral geniculate nucleus remains to be discovered. Some of the data that helped test the trichromatic and opponent-process theories came from people with abnormal color vision.

Color Blindness. In 1794 John Dalton, founder of the atomic theory of matter, believed he had figured out why he couldn't distinguish his red stockings from his green ones. He reasoned that something blue in his eyeball absorbed red light and prevented him from seeing red. Dalton was not the first person to suffer from red-green color blindness, but he was the first to describe it scientifically.

Most human beings have normal color vision and are called **trichromats.** A very few people (fewer than one percent) do not see any color. These **monochromats** are totally **color blind** and cannot discriminate among wavelengths, often because they lack cone receptors in their retinas (Boynton, 1988). Fortunately, most people with color deficiencies (about eight percent of men and one percent of women) are only partially color deficient (Nathans, 1989). The lack of a specific color-absorbing pigment or chemical in the cones makes accurate color discriminations impossible. **Dichromats** have deficiencies in either the red-green or the blue-yellow area. About two percent of men cannot discriminate between reds and greens (Wyszecki and Stiles, 1967). What does the world look like to a person who is a dichromat? People with color deficiencies see all the colors in a range of the electromagnetic spectrum as the same. For example, to a person with a blue deficiency, all greens, blues, and violets look the same; a person with a red-green deficiency may see red, green, and yellow, as yellow. Many color blind individuals have distorted color responses in several areas of the electromagnetic spectrum, that is, they have trouble with several colors.

The precise role of genetics in color blindness is not clear, but we know that it is transmitted genetically from mothers to their male offspring. The high number of men who are color blind compared to women is due to the way the genetic information is coded and passed on to each generation. The

Trichromats: People who experience color vision the way most other people do, and who require only the three primary colors to see any color.

Monochromats: People whose retinas contain only rods and who therefore cannot perceive hue.

Color blind: Unable to perceive different hues.

Dichromats: People who can distinguish only two of the three basic hues.

Color blindness, the inability to see certain colors, is a hereditary condition in which the proteins of one or more cones either do not function or are inadequate in number. The balloons on the right are shown as they might appear to a dichromat with a red-green deficiency.

genetic transmission occurs on the twenty-third pair of chromosomes and results from inherited alterations in the genes on the X chromosomes that are responsible for cone pigments (Nathans, 1989).

Focus on Learning

- ◆ After electrical impulses are first generated at the retina, they leave the eyeball through what structure, and then proceed to what other brain centers? pp. 78–82
- ◆ What is dyslexia? p. 85
- ◆ Our experience of color is determined by three physical variables; name them and describe their relationship. pp. 86–87
- ◆ Explain the differences between the trichromatic and opponent-process theories of color. pp. 87–89

Visual Perception

The electrochemical processes that stimulate vision and the subsequent changes that take place in the pathways that lead to higher visual centers are all crucial parts of the perceptual process. But many perceptual experiences involve past events in addition to current stimulation. By integrating our previous experiences with new events, perceptual encounters become more meaningful. For example, it is only with experience that people know that an object stays the same size and shape when it is moved away from our immediate vision. We consider next a range of visual perceptual phenomena that are especially dependent on the integration of past experience with current experiences.

Perception of Form: Constancy

Everyday experience shows that people fill in missing information. For example, if your friend is wearing dark sunglasses that conceal most of her face, you will probably still recognize her. Similarly, cartoonists use exaggerated features to portray well-known people, and impressionist artists count on the ability to infer a complete object from dots of paint on canvas. Understanding how human beings perceive form and space helps architects design buildings and designers create furniture and clothes. Perception of form involves the interpretation of stimuli of different sizes, shapes, and depths to create a unit. Two important activities in form perception are recognizing forms at a distance and recognizing forms that appear to have changed size or shape.

People can generally judge the size of an object, even if the size of its image on the retina changes. For example, you can estimate the height of a six-foot-tall man from fifty feet away, with a small image on the retina, as well as from only five feet away, with a much larger image on the retina. **Size constancy** is the ability of the perceptual system to recognize that an object remains constant in size regardless of its distance from the observer or the size of its image on the retina.

Three variables determine a person's ability to maintain size constancy: previous experience with the true size of objects, the distance between the object and the person, and the presence of surrounding objects (Day and McKenzie, 1977). As an object is moved farther away, the size of its image on the retina decreases, while its perceived distance increases. These two processes always work together. Moreover, as an object is moved away, its perceived size does not change in relation to that of other stationary objects. This is why knowing the size of surrounding objects helps people determine their distance from an object as well as the object's actual size.

Researchers have studied how experience helps people establish and maintain size constancy. Bower (1966) trained fifty- to sixty-day-old infants to look toward a specific object by reinforcing their direction of gaze (they were reinforced by an adult saying peek-a-boo). He then placed other objects of different sizes at various distances from the infants so that the sizes of their retinal images varied. Finally, he arranged the objects so that the small ones were close to the infants and the large ones were farther away, causing the sizes of retinal images to be the same. In all these situations the infants showed size constancy. They turned their heads only toward the original reinforced object, not toward the other objects that produced images of the same size on the retina. It is clear that infants have size constancy by the age of six months and probably as early as four months (McKenzie, Tootell, and Day, 1980; Luger, Bower, and Wishart, 1983).

Hollywood special-effects artists use the brain's tendency to judge an object's size by comparing it with surrounding objects to convince moviegoers that a six-inch clay model of an ape is the giant King Kong. However, size constancy can also work to a filmmaker's disadvantage. In the early days of Hollywood, a Western was made that attempted to be humorous by starring a cast of dwarfs. The sheriff, the bad guys, and the heroine were all of diminutive stature. However, because the director also downsized all the props and settings (for example, using Shetland ponies for the horses), the characters appeared normal-sized, and the movie lost its humorous potential.

Another important aspect of form perception is **shape constancy,** which is the ability to recognize a shape despite changes in the angle or position from which it is viewed. For example, even though you usually see trees perpendicular to the ground, you can recognize a tree when it has been chopped down and is lying on the ground. Similarly, a door looks rectangular

Size constancy: The ability of the perceptual system to know that an object remains constant in size regardless of its distance or the size of its image on the retina.

Shape constancy: The ability to recognize a shape despite changes in the orientation or angle from which it is viewed.

At close range Seurat's paintings would appear unintelligible; the forms and objects gain definition when seen as a whole from a distance.

when you view it head-on; nevertheless, you perceive it as a rectangle even when you stand to the side of it.

Depth Perception

For centuries, Zen landscape artists have used the principles of perception to create seemingly expansive, rugged gardens out of tiny plots of land. The gardeners place smaller, less detailed, and darker objects (such as round stones and smooth-barked shrubs) at the rear of the garden and light-colored, well-textured objects (such as craggy rocks and wrinkle-barked trees) near the front to create the illusion of depth. They also make a tapering trail that winds back to the rear of the garden where it disappears behind a rock or tree, leading the viewer to assume it continues for some distance.

Although the Zen landscape artist can fool the eye, you judge the distance of an object every day when you drive a car, catch a ball, or take a picture. You estimate your distance from the object and the distance between that object and another one. Closely associated with these two tasks is the ability to see in three dimensions, that is, in terms of height, width, and depth. Both monocular and binocular cues are used to perceive depth. Binocular cues predominate at close distances and monocular cues are used for distant scenes and two-dimensional fields of view, such as paintings.

Monocular Depth Cues.   Depth cues that do not depend on the use of both eyes are **monocular depth cues** (see Figure 3.18). Two important monocular depth cues deal with motion. The first, *motion parallax,* occurs when a moving observer stares at a fixed point. The objects behind that point appear to move in the same direction as the observer; the objects in front of that point appear to move in the opposite direction. For example, if you stare at a fence while riding in a moving car, the trees behind the fence rails seem to move in the same direction as the car (forward) and the bushes in front of the rails seem to move in the opposite direction (backward). Motion parallax also affects the speed at which objects appear to move. Objects at a greater

The illusion of space is well maintained in a Zen garden. What perceptual cues make this garden seem larger than it actually is?

Monocular depth cues: Depth cues that do not require the use of two eyes.

FIGURE 3.18
Twelve sources of information about an object's distance.

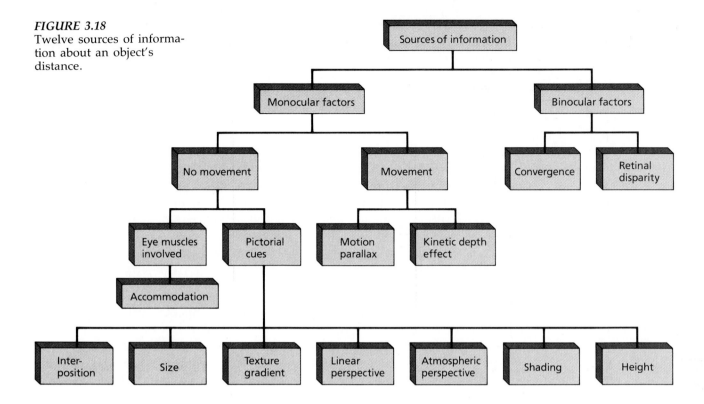

distance from the moving observer appear to move more slowly than objects that are closer.

The second monocular depth cue derived from movement is the *kinetic depth effect.* Objects that look flat when they are stationary appear to be three-dimensional when set in motion. When two-dimensional projects, such as pictures of squares, cubes, or rods shown on a computer screen, are rotated, they appear to have three dimensions.

Other monocular depth cues come from the stimulus itself; they are often seen in photographs and paintings. *Linear perspective* is based on the principle that distant objects appear to be closer together than nearer objects. Two parallel lines in a painting will appear to converge as they recede into the distance (see Figure 3.19).

Another monocular cue for depth is *interposition.* When one object blocks out part of another, the first appears to be closer. A third monocular cue is *texture.* Surfaces that have little texture or detail seem to be in the distance. Artists often use the clues of *clearness* and *shadowing.* Clear objects appear close; objects that are shadowed or dark appear to be farther away. In addition, the perceptual system picks up other information from shadowing, including the curvature of surfaces (Cavanagh and Leclerc, 1989). Still another monocular depth cue is the wavelengths themselves. Distant mountains often look blue, for example, because long (red) wavelengths are more easily scattered as they pass through the air, allowing more short (blue) wavelengths to reach our eyes. Leonardo da Vinci used this phenomenon in his paintings; he even developed an equation for how much blue pigment should be mixed with the normal color of an object so that it would appear as close or far away as he wished. Michelangelo's angels seem to float off the ceiling of the Sistine Chapel because he used color so effectively to portray depth.

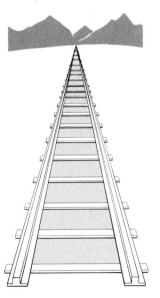

FIGURE 3.19
In a common illusion, parallel railroad tracks appear closer together when they are farther away.

Accommodation: The change in shape of the lens of the eye to keep an object in focus on the retina when the object moves closer to or farther away from the observer.

Retinal disparity: The slight difference in the visual image cast on each eye; a principal binocular cue.

Convergence: The movement of the eyes toward each other to keep corresponding points on the retina as an object moves closer to the observer.

Illusion: A perception of a stimulus that differs from normal expectations about its appearance.

A monocular depth cue not derived from the stimulus is accommodation. If a person looks from one subject to another one at a different distance, the lenses will accommodate, that is, change shape; this cue is available from both of the eyes separately. **Accommodation** is the change in the shape of the lens that enables the observer to keep an object in focus on the retina when the object is moved. It is controlled by muscles attached to the lens, which provide information about the shape of the lens to the higher processing systems in the brain.

Binocular Depth Cues. Most people, even infants, use binocular as well as monocular depth cues. One important binocular depth cue is **retinal disparity,** that is, a slight difference in the image projected on each retina. Retinal disparity occurs because the eyes are separated, causing them to see an object from slightly different angles.

To see how retinal disparity works, hold a finger up in front of some distant object. Examine the object first with one eye and then with the other eye. The finger will appear in different positions relative to the object. The closer objects are to the eyes, the farther apart their images on the retinas will be and the greater the retinal disparity. Objects at a great distance produce little retinal disparity.

Another binocular depth cue is **convergence.** As an object moves closer to a viewer, the viewer's eyes move toward each other, or converge, in order to keep information at corresponding points on the retina. Like accommodation, convergence is controlled by muscles in the eye that convey information to the brain and thus provide a potent physiological depth cue for stimuli close to observers. Beyond twenty or thirty feet, the eyes are aimed pretty much in parallel and the effect of this cue diminishes.

Illusions

When a person's normal visual process and depth cues seem to break down, he or she experiences an optical illusion. An **illusion** is the perception of a physical stimulus that differs from the commonly expected perception; many consider it a misperception of stimulation.

A common illusion is the *Müller-Lyer illusion,* in which two equal-length lines with arrows attached to their ends appear to be of different lengths (see Figure 3.20). A similar illusion is the *Ponzo illusion,* in which two horizontal lines of the same length surrounded by slanted lines appear to be of different lengths (see Figure 3.20). A natural illusion is the *moon illusion.* Although the actual size of the moon and the size of its image on the retina do not change, the moon appears about thirty percent larger when it is over the horizon than when it is overhead. The moon illusion is quite striking. In just a few minutes the size of the moon appears to change from quite large to quite small.

How do visual illusions work? No completely satisfactory explanations have been found. Recent theories account for them in terms of the backgrounds against which the objects are seen. These explanations are based on the observer's previous experiences and well-developed perceptual constancies.

The moon illusion, for example, is explained by the fact that when seen overhead the moon has a featureless background, whereas at the horizon, objects are close to it. Objects in the landscape provide cues about distance that change the observer's perception of the size of the moon (Restle, 1970). To see how the moon illusion depends on landscape cues, try this: When the moon is at the horizon, bend over and look at it from between your

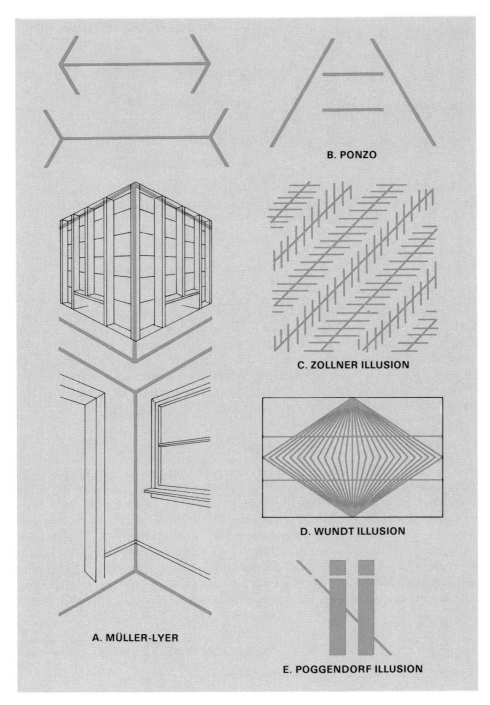

B. PONZO

C. ZOLLNER ILLUSION

D. WUNDT ILLUSION

A. MÜLLER-LYER

E. POGGENDORF ILLUSION

FIGURE 3.20
In the Müller-Lyer and Ponzo illusions at the top, lines of equal length appear different in length. The center and bottom Müller-Lyer illusions show how the arrows usually represent "near corners" and "far corners." In the Zollner illusion, the short lines make the longer ones not seem parallel, even though they are. In the Wundt illusion, the center horizontal lines are parallel, even though they appear bent. In the Poggendorf illusion, the line disappears behind a solid and reappears in a position that seems wrong.

legs. Since that position screens out some of the horizon cues, the magnitude of the illusion will be reduced.

The Ponzo illusion is similarly accounted for by the linear perspective provided by the slanted background lines. The Müller-Lyer illusion occurs because of the angle and shape of the arrows attached to the ends of the lines. Lines angled inward are often interpreted as far corners—those that are distant from the observer. Lines angled outward are commonly interpreted as near corners—those that are close to the observer (see Figure 3.20). Therefore, lines with far-corner angles attached to them appear longer because their length is judged in a context of distance.

FIGURE 3.21
The *Law of Prägnanz:* The
Gestalt principle that items
or stimuli that can be
grouped together as a whole
will be. These sixteen dots are
typically perceived as a square.

FIGURE 3.22
A drawing in which figure
and ground can be re-
versed. You can see either
two faces against a white
background or a goblet
against a dark background.

These are not the only ways of explaining illusions. Some researchers
assert that people see the moon as a different size on the horizon because
they judge it like other moving objects that pass through space. Since the
moon does not get closer to them, they assume that it is moving away.
Objects that move away get smaller, hence the illusion of a change in the
size of the moon (Reed, 1984). This explanation focuses on constancies but
also takes account of movement, space, and the atmosphere.

Gestalt Laws of Organization

Gestalt psychologists (see chapter 1) suggest that conscious experience is
more than the sum of its parts. They argue that the mind takes the elements
of experience and organizes them to form something unique; they thus
analyze the world in terms of perceptual frameworks. Analyzed as a whole
experience, the patterns of a person's perceptions make sense. Gestalt psychologists such as Wertheimer, Koffka, and Kohler greatly influenced early
theories of form perception. These psychologists assumed (wrongly) that
human perceptual processes reflect brain organization and that by studying
perception they could learn about the workings of the brain. They focused

FIGURE 3.23
Two ambiguous figures. (A)
shows a rabbit facing to-
ward the right or a duck
facing toward the left. (B)
shows either an old woman
in profile or a young
woman whose head is
turned slightly away.

A   B

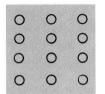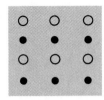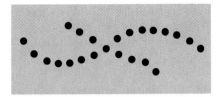

FIGURE 3.24
According to the Gestalt law of proximity, the circles appear to be arranged in vertical columns because items that are close together tend to be perceived as a unit. According to the Gestalt law of similarity, the filled and empty circles appear to be arranged in horizontal rows because similar items tend to be perceived in groups. According to the Gestalt law of continuity, an observer will predict where the next item should occur because the group of items projects into space.

their perceptual studies on the way people experience form and organization. The early Gestaltists believed that people organize a complex visual field into a coherent whole rather than seeing individual, unrelated elements. We see groups of elements, not fragmented parts. According to this idea, called the **Law of Prägnanz,** items or stimuli that can be grouped together and seen as a whole, or a form, will be seen that way. Figure 3.21 shows a series of sixteen dots that people tend to see as a square.

Using the Law of Prägnanz as an organizing idea, Gestalt psychologists developed principles of organization for the perception of figures. They focused on the nature of *figure and ground relationships*, contending that figures are perceived as distinct from the grounds (i.e., backgrounds) on which they are presented (see Figures 3.22 and 3.23). Gestalt psychologists developed the following series of laws for predicting which areas of an ambiguous pattern would be seen as the figure (or foreground) and which as the ground (or background) (Hochberg, 1974, 1979):

- The *law of proximity:* Elements close to one another in space or time will be perceived as groups (see Figure 3.24).
- The *law of similarity:* Similar items will be perceived in groups.
- The *law of continuity:* A string of items will indicate where the next item in the string will be found.
- *Common fate principles:* Items that move or change together will be seen as a whole.
- The *law of closure:* Parts of a figure that are not presented will be filled in by the perceptual system.

A well-known study that examined Gestalt principles was conducted by Beck (1966); you can try it out. Look at Figure 3.25. Divide the patterns into

FIGURE 3.25
In a study asking people to divide these lines into two groups, Beck (1966) found that subjects generally placed the boundary between the upright and tilted T's rather than between the backward L's and upright T's. Beck has argued that this result supports the Prägnanz principle.

Law of Prägnanz: The Gestalt principle that items or stimuli that can be grouped together and seen as a whole, will be.

regions along the most likely boundary. Where do you divide the figure? There are two places in the figure where a boundary might reasonably be placed: between regions that differ in orientation or between regions that differ in shape. The subjects in Beck's study were more likely to place a boundary between the upright T's and the diagonally slanted T's (regions that differ in orientation) than between the backward L's and the upright T's (regions that differ in shape). Beck's work thus verified the Gestalt laws, which predict that people will group together elements they see as being alike.

Beck's work also shows that the Gestalt laws are vague. They apply whether subjects choose orientation or shape to break up the figure, but they do not explain why orientation predominated in Beck's study. Gestalt laws are not always obeyed, nor are they consistent with our current knowledge of brain organization. Nevertheless, these early investigations continue to influence perceptual psychologists. This was the case when psychologists began to study subliminal perception, considered next.

Subliminal Perception

MILESTONES IN PSYCHOLOGY

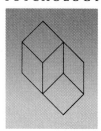

*I*f a visual or auditory stimulus is presented so quickly or at such a low volume that you cannot consciously perceive it, can it affect your behavior? Modern studies of **subliminal perception** (subliminal means below the awareness threshold) began in the 1950s with an innovative advertising ploy. A marketing executive superimposed verbal messages that said things like "buy popcorn" on a regular movie. According to some advertising agents, movie theaters could induce audiences to buy more popcorn by flashing—at speeds too fast to be consciously observed—advertisements on the screen. Although many psychologists dismissed the popcorn marketing campaign as nonsense, it created a sensation and prompted further study.

According to Goleman (1985), subliminal perception is possible, and many cognitive scientists today take unconscious perception for granted. But subliminal perception has had a controversial history.

In the 1950s, when psychologists began to study subliminal perception, they defined it in terms of a threshold below which subjects are unaware of a stimulus fifty percent of the time. Many of the early 1960s studies lacked control groups and did not specify what variables were being manipulated. Some presented stimuli for durations in which several words might easily be seen by one subject and no words by another. Other studies presented "dirty" or taboo words to see if they affected responses more than neutral or emotionally uncharged words did. Portions of results of the taboo word studies could be accounted for by the fact that some subjects were embarrassed to repeat the noxious words to the experimenter (often a person of the opposite sex) and denied having seen them.

To avoid some of these methodological problems, later experiments presented subjects with both threatening and neutral stimuli for very brief durations. The subjects responded by repeating the word or by pressing a button as soon as they saw it. In these experiments, threatening stimuli had to be presented for a longer time or at a greater intensity level than the nonthreatening stimuli to be identified.

If a researcher presents a threatening stimulus, such as a dirty word, it may raise the perceptual threshold above normal levels, making it harder for the subject to perceive subsequent subliminal words. Some researchers suggest that the unconscious or some other personality variable acts as a censor. For example, Silverman (1983) asserts that if an aggressive or sexual message is presented subliminally to subjects, it will affect their subsequent behavior—that unconscious processes are at work. More recently, Balay and Shevrin (1988) suggest that a stage beyond the sensory or perceptual stages affects the perceptual process. They maintain that subliminal perception can be explained in terms of such nonperceptual variables as motivation, previous experience, and unconscious or critical censoring processes that influence perceptual thresholds.

In some controlled situations, subliminal stimuli probably can influence behavior. In the real world, however, we are constantly faced with many competing sensory stimuli, and what grabs our attention depends on many variables, such as importance, prominence, and interest. Should we fear mind control by advertisers or other unsolicited outside stimuli? The answer is probably no. In the end, subliminal perception and any learning that results from it are greatly affected by such nonperceptual variables as motivation, previous experience, personality, and other learned behaviors. However, more research is needed to determine exactly what is taking place when subliminal perception occurs and to what degree subliminal stimuli can influence us, if at all. For example, whether a person is paying attention can have an enormous effect, but what is attention, and how do we know to which stimuli people choose to pay attention? ◆

Attention

People constantly extract signals from the world around them. Although they receive many different messages at once, they can watch, listen, and pay attention only to a selected message. In fact, a person's selective attention is often called the "cocktail party problem." An associated phenomenon inhibits our ability to remember names when being introduced. People often fail to catch the name of someone they are introduced to because they are too preoccupied with thinking of something to say or with appraising the new person.

Perceptual psychologists are concerned with the complex processes involved in extracting information from the environment. They hope to answer the question, "Which stimuli do people choose to listen to?" In selective-listening experiments, subjects wear a pair of headphones and receive different messages simultaneously in each ear. Their task is often to *shadow*, or repeat a message heard in one ear. Typically, they report that they are able to listen to a speaker in either the left or the right ear and can provide information about the content and quality of that speaker's voice. The task of following one message and not the other is easier if the voice in one ear is male and the voice in the other is female, if the pitch of two male voices is different, or if the content of the messages is different. If voice, pitch, intensity, quality, and content are similar in both ears, subjects often shift their attention from one ear to the other. Thus, the more discriminable the two channels, the better the selective attention.

There are several theories about how people are able to attend selectively. The *filter theory* suggests that human beings possess a limited capacity to process information and that perceptual filters must choose between information presented to the left and right ears. The *attenuation theory* states that all the information is analyzed but that only selected information is tuned into and reaches the highest centers of processing.

Hundreds of selective-listening studies have examined the claims of filter versus attenuation theory (e.g., Cherry, 1953; Treisman, 1969). Regardless of whether people filter or attenuate information, selective-attention studies show that human beings must select one of the available stimuli (Duncan, 1980). It is impossible, for example, to pay attention to four lectures at once. A listener can extract information from only one speaker at a time. Admittedly, you can do more than one task at a time, such as drive a car and listen to the radio, but you cannot use the same channel such as vision for several tasks simultaneously (e.g., drive a car, read a book, and inspect photographs).

Attending a three-ring circus is a visual selective attention task. Would you choose one act to concentrate on or be able to pay equal attention to all three acts?

Clearly, both the auditory and visual systems have limited capacities. People have limited ability to divide their attention between tasks and must allocate their perceptual resources for greatest efficiency. How can we do this? How can we structure our world to make the most of our perceptual abilities? These questions are considered by psychologists, who study the relationship of human beings, perception, and machines.

Perception and Machines

APPLYING PSYCHOLOGY

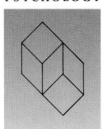

*H*ave you ever stepped into the cockpit of an airplane? To an untrained observer, the visual array is rather bewildering. But if you are a pilot, you know which dials and which levers are most important, and which ones are used for the various functions. This perceptual learning takes place with training and practice. Are there ways to make this training easier? Is the layout of a cockpit the easiest and best suited arrangement for a pilot's perceptual systems? Applied perceptual psychologists speak to this issue directly.

Many psychologists who study perception and attention have focused on an area called ergonomics. *Ergonomics* is the scientific study of work; it is sometimes called engineering psychology, or human factors psychology. The focus of many ergonomic issues is how machines and human beings interact with one another and if there are ways to facilitate that interaction. For example, psychologists have learned that the best way to lay out a typewriter keyboard is not the standard way they are arranged. Research shows that the standard home row of keys—ASDFGHJKL—is inefficient and that far better arrangements are possible and desirable. (Of course, practically speaking, what are we going to do with all those typewriter and computer keyboards all of us have been trained on?) Perceptual psychologists are also examining such issues as the best angle at which to place a computer monitor to avoid eye strain. Like the arrangement of a cockpit, computer keyboards and monitors can be organized to facilitate accurate, efficient use by human beings. Computer keys can be made too big, computer monitors can be placed at poor angles, and cockpit gauges can be dimly illuminated.

An engineering psychologist examines the display considerations (layout, lighting, size), control issues (toggle switches, levers, or push buttons), and limitations of the human beings interacting with it (how tall is an average human being, how far apart can the buttons be, how much weight can a person tolerate). Although perceptual psychologists often focus most of their basic research on how the perceptual system works, they apply that knowledge to machine/human interactions to facilitate work productivity as well as comfort. ◆

◆ What is the difference between a monocular and binocular depth cue? pp. 92–93
◆ Name three monocular depth cues and explain how they aid a person to see depth in a photograph or painting. pp. 92–94
◆ What is the Law of Prägnanz and how does it explain perceptual phenomena? p. 97
◆ What was a major problem with early subliminal perception experiments? pp. 98–99
◆ What happens when a person receives more than one incoming message at the same time? pp. 99–100

Focus on Learning

Hearing

Listening to a Beethoven symphony is delightful and intriguing, but it is difficult because so much is going on at once. With more than twenty instruments playing, the listener must process many sounds, rhythms, and intensities simultaneously. Not all hearing is this difficult, but it is still a complex process. As in seeing, hearing involves converting physical stimuli into a psychological experience.

Suppose a tuning fork is struck or a stereo system booms out a bass note. In both cases, sound waves are being created and air is being moved. The movement of the air and the accompanying changes in air pressure cause the eardrum to move back and forth rapidly. The movement of the eardrum sets in motion a series of electromechanical and electrochemical changes that people experience as sound.

Sound

When any object is set in motion, be it a tuning fork, the reed of a clarinet, or a person's vocal cords, its vibrations cause sound waves. You can place your hand in front of a stereo speaker and feel the displacement of sound waves when the volume is turned up. **Sound** is often thought of in terms of two psychological aspects, pitch and loudness, which correspond to two physical attributes, frequency and amplitude. **Frequency** is the number of times a complete change in air pressure occurs during a given unit of time. Within one second, for example, there may be 50 complete changes (50 cycles per second) or 10,000 complete changes (10,000 cycles per second). Frequency determines the *pitch*, or tone, of a sound; high-pitched tones usually have high frequencies. Frequency is usually measured in hertz (Hz); one Hz equals one cycle per second. Middle C on a piano has a frequency of 262 cycles per second (or 262 Hz). When a short string on a piano is struck, it vibrates at a high frequency and sounds high in pitch; long strings when struck vibrate less frequently and sound low in pitch.

Sound: A psychological term describing changes in pressure through a medium; the medium may be gaseous, liquid, or solid.

Frequency: A measure of the number of complete pressure waves per unit of time, expressed in Hertz (Hz) (pronounced *hurts*), or cycles per second.

High amplitude sound waves, such as those generated by this jazz fusion band, have greater energy and a greater impact on the sensitive structure of our ears.

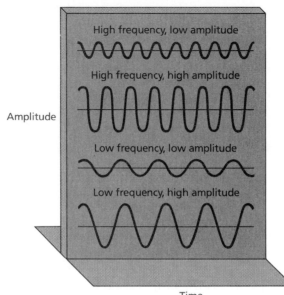

FIGURE 3.26
Frequency and amplitude are independent. High-frequency waves can be of high amplitude (and sound loud) or of low amplitude (and sound quiet).

The **amplitude,** or intensity, of a sound wave determines its loudness. High-amplitude sound waves have more energy; they apply greater force to the ear (see Figure 3.26). Amplitude is measured in decibels. Every increase of twenty decibels corresponds to a tenfold increase in intensity. As shown in Table 3.1, normal speech occurs at about sixty decibels, and painful sounds occur at about 120 decibels.

Amplitude and frequency are related. A low-frequency sound can be very loud or very soft, that is, it can have either high or low amplitude.

TABLE 3.1
Psychological Responses to Various Sound Intensities

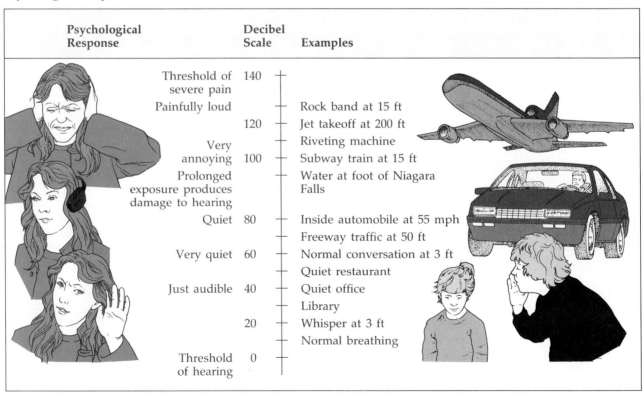

Middle C on a piano, for example, can be loud or soft. The frequency (pitch) of the sound stays the same—it is still middle C; its amplitude (loudness) varies. It is important to note that our psychological experience (i.e., the perception of loudness) depends on other factors, such as background noise and whether we are paying attention. A third psychological dimension, *timbre,* refers to the quality of a sound—the different mixture of amplitudes and frequencies that make up a sound.

> **Amplitude:** The intensity or total energy of a sound wave that determines the loudness of a sound; usually measured in decibels.

Structure of the Ear

The ear is the receptive organ for *audition,* or hearing. It translates physical stimuli (sound waves) into electrical impulses that the brain can interpret. The ear has three major parts: the outer ear, the middle ear, and the inner ear. The tissue on the outside of the head is part of the outer ear. The eardrum (tympanic membrane) is the boundary between the outer and middle ear. When sound waves enter the ear, they produce changes in the pressure of the air on the eardrum. The eardrum responds to these changes by vibrating.

The middle ear is quite small. Within it, tiny bones known as *ossicles* help convert the large forces striking the eardrum into a small force. Two small muscles are attached to the ossicles; these muscles contract involuntarily when a person vocalizes loudly and especially when exposed to an annoying loud noise—they help protect humans from the damaging effects of a loud noise that could overstimulate the delicate mechanisms of the inner ear (Borg and Counter, 1989). Ultimately the ossicles stimulate the *basilar membrane* which runs down the middle of the length of the *cochlea,* a tube in the inner ear. Figure 3.27 shows the major structures of the middle and inner ear.

In the cochlea, which is shaped like a snail's shell and made up of three chambers, sound waves of different frequencies stimulate different areas of the basilar membrane. These areas, in turn, stimulate hair cells that bring

FIGURE 3.27
The major components of the middle and inner ear.

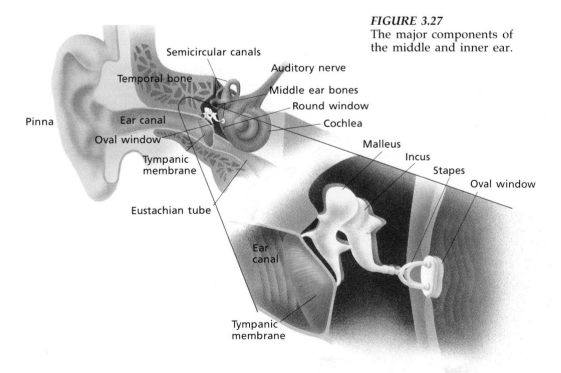

about the initial electrical coding of sound waves. These hair cells are remarkably sensitive. Hudspeth (1983), for example, found that hair cells respond when they are displaced as little as 100 picometers (trillionths of a meter). The hair cells are responsible for the transduction of mechanical energy into electrochemical energy.

Electrical impulses make their way through the brain's auditory nervous system in much the same way that visual information proceeds through the visual nervous system. The neuronal impulses proceed through the auditory nerve to the midbrain and finally to the auditory cortex. Studies of single cells in the auditory areas of the brain show that some cells are more responsive to certain frequencies than to others. Katsuki (1961) found cells that are maximally sensitive to certain narrow frequency ranges; if a sound's frequency is outside that range, the cells might not fire at all. These results are analogous to those reported by Hubel and Wiesel, who found receptive visual fields in which proper stimulation brought about dramatic changes in the firing of a cell.

Theories of Hearing

Most theories of hearing fall into two major classes: place theories and frequency theories. *Place theories* claim that the analysis of sound occurs in the basilar membrane, with different frequencies and intensities affecting different parts of the membrane. They assert that each sound wave causes a traveling wave on the basilar membrane, which in turn causes changes in basilar membrane displacement. The hair cells on the basilar membrane are displaced by the traveling wave, and the displacement of individual hair cells triggers specific information about pitch. By contrast, *frequency theories* maintain that the analysis of pitch and intensity occurs at higher levels of processing (perhaps in the auditory area of the cortex) and that the basilar membrane merely transfers information to those higher centers. Frequency theory suggests that the entire basilar membrane is stimulated and its overall rate of responding is transferred to the auditory nerve and beyond, where analysis takes place (see Figure 3.28).

Both types of theories present theoretical problems and neither explains all the data about pitch and loudness. For example, the hair cells do not act independently (as place theory suggests) but together (as frequency theory suggests). Further, the rate at which hair cells fire is not fast enough to keep up with sound waves (e.g., 1000 cycles per second) as frequency theory

FIGURE 3.28
The basilar membrane. The cochlea unwound and cut open to reveal the basilar membrane, which is covered with thousands of hair cells. Pressure waves in the fluid filling the cochlea cause oscillations to travel in waves down the basilar membrane, stimulating the hair cells.

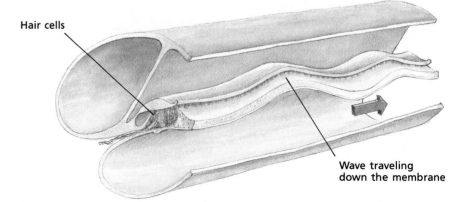

suggests. To get around the difficulties, modern researchers have developed theories of auditory information processing that attempt to explain pitch both in terms of specific action in parts of the basilar membrane *and* in terms of complex frequency analyses at higher levels. Theories that seem at odds with one another can work together to explain pitch and loudness when the best of both theories is combined. (Does this remind you of the debate between the trichromatic theory and the opponent-process theory of color coding?)

Sound Localization

Although not as well tuned as many animals, human beings have amazingly efficient sound localization abilities. How do we know which direction a speaker's voice came from? There are two key facts to remember when considering sound localization: interaural time differences and interaural intensity differences. Because you have two ears, a sound made from the left of your head will arrive at the left ear before the right. Thus you have an *interaural time difference*. In addition, the sound reaches the two ears at different intensities—a sound to the left will be slightly more intense to the left ear than to the right. Thus there is an *interaural intensity difference*. These two pieces of information are analyzed in the brain at nuclei that are especially sensitive to time and intensity differences between the ears.

There are some potential ambiguities. What happens when the sound source is just in front of a person, and thus equidistant from the two ears? It turns out that head and body movements help resolve the source of a sound. People rotate their heads or move their bodies when unsure of the source of a sound. In addition, our external ear has ridges and folds that bounce sounds around just a bit. This creates slight delays that help us localize sounds. Last, sight and past experiences with sounds aid in the task of localizing sounds in space.

Hearing Impairment

Not everyone has perfect hearing. There are about thirteen million hearing impaired people in the United States. The causes of the impairments, which range from minor hearing losses to total deafness, are varied. The two most common causes are conduction deafness and nerve deafness.

Conduction deafness results from interference in the delivery of sound to the neural mechanism of the inner ear. The interference may be caused by something simple, such as a severe head cold or a buildup of wax in the outer ear canal. Or it may be caused by hardening of the tympanic membrane, destruction of the tiny bones within the ear, or diseases that create pressure in the middle ear. **Nerve deafness** results from damage to the cochlea or the auditory nerve. The most common cause is exposure to very high intensity sound, such as a rock band or jet planes. If a loud noise is presented repeatedly for a long time, a person's sound threshold may increase permanently. That is, a higher-amplitude (louder) sound will be required to achieve the same effect as a lower-amplitude (softer) sound in a person with normal hearing. There are about twenty-three million headset radios sold each year in this country and they have the ability to create sound levels so loud that they can bring about hearing loss. The amplitude levels they reach can be as high as 115 decibels. Listening to even moderately loud music for longer than fifteen minutes per day can cause permanent damage.

Conduction deafness: Deafness resulting from interference with the conduction of sound to the neural mechanism of the inner ear.

Nerve deafness: Impairment in hearing as a result of damage to the cochlea of the auditory nerve.

Hearing impairments can create special problems for children and the elderly. Too many schoolchildren have been diagnosed as having low intelligence and labeled as stupid by their classmates when they actually suffer from hearing losses. Sometimes children with partial hearing do not even realize that they are missing much of what is said to them. Older people are more likely to have hearing impairments, particularly for sounds in the high-frequency range. Because normal speech involves primarily the lower frequencies (between 1000 and 5000 Hz), such impairment generally causes few major difficulties.

Hearing is measured by an audiometer, which presents sounds of different frequencies through a headphone, and results are presented as an *audiogram*—a graph showing hearing sensitivity at selected frequencies. The patient's audiogram is compared with that of an adult with no known hearing loss. One simple way to assess and diagnose hearing impairment is to test a person's recognition of spoken words. Typically, a person listens to a tape recording of speech sounds that are standardized in terms of loudness and pitch. Performance is based on the number of words the subject can repeat correctly at various intensity levels. This test can be administered by nonmedical personnel, who then refer individuals who may have hearing problems to a physician.

You can easily see that there are many similarities between the study of hearing and of vision. Physical energy is transduced into electrochemical energy. Coding takes place at several locations in the brain, and people can have impairments in visual or auditory abilities. As we study taste and smell, watch again for similarities among the perceptual systems.

Focus on Learning

- Describe the difference between frequency and amplitude. p. 101
- What is the essential idea of place theory? What is the essential idea of frequency theory? p. 104
- Identify the differences between nerve deafness and conduction deafness. p. 105

Taste and Smell

Try the following experiment. Cut a fresh onion in half and inhale its odor while you have a piece of raw potato in your mouth. Now chew the potato. Does the potato taste like an onion? This experiment demonstrates that taste and smell are closely linked. Food contains substances that act as stimuli for both taste and smell.

Taste

I remember the first time I was in a cheese store. My father was supposed to buy some cheese and crackers because special company was coming for dinner. The store owner allowed me to sample a variety of cheeses: Swiss, blue, cheddar, Gruyere, Gorgonzola, and Brie. The cheddar was too sharp; the blue cheese tasted bitter; and the Swiss was bland in comparison. We finally decided on a large slice of Brie; it was soft and creamy, with a slightly sweet, mild flavor. I was overwhelmed by the quantity of cheeses and their different tastes and smells.

Taste is a chemical sense. Food placed in the mouth is partially dissolved in saliva and stimulates *taste buds*, the primary receptors for taste stimuli. When substances contact taste buds, we experience taste. The taste buds are found on small bumps on the tongue called *papillae*. Each hill-like papilla is separated from the next by a "moat." The taste buds, which can be seen only under a microscope, are located on the walls of these moats. Each taste bud (human beings have about 10,000 of them) consists of several *taste cells*. Taste cells last only about ten days and are constantly being renewed.

Although psychologists still do not know exactly how many tastes there are, most agree that there are four basic ones: sweet, sour, salty, and bitter. Most foods contain more than one primary taste; foods like veal parmigiana, for example, offer a complicated stimulus to the tongue, and as we will see shortly, they also stimulate the sense of smell. All taste cells are sensitive to all taste stimuli, but certain cells are more sensitive to some stimuli than to others. (In this regard they are much like the cones in the retina which are sensitive to all wavelengths, but which are especially sensitive to a specific range of wavelengths.) By isolating stimuli that initiate only one taste sensation, psychologists have found that certain regions of the tongue seem to be more sensitive to particular taste stimuli than others. The tip of the tongue, for example, is more sensitive to sweet tastes than the back of the tongue, and the sides are especially sensitive to sour tastes (see Figure 3.29).

The taste of a particular food or liquid depends on its chemical makeup, but it also depends on our past experiences with this or similar foods, how much saliva is being mixed into the food as we chew, and how long we chew the food. A food that is chewed well tastes stronger than one that is chewed quickly and digested. Food that sits on the tongue for a long time will even lose its flavor—*sensory adaptation* has occurred. Further, a food that loses its texture by being mashed up, blended, or mixed with other foods has less taste and is less appealing to most adults. Thus taste, much like our other perceptual systems, depends not only on a sensory event, but also on past experience and other sensory and perceptual variables.

FIGURE 3.29
The taste buds sensitive to certain basic tastes are distributed unevenly across the tongue. A blowup of a vertical cross-section of one of the tiny bumps (papillae) on the tongue shows that taste buds are found in the little trenches around the papillae.

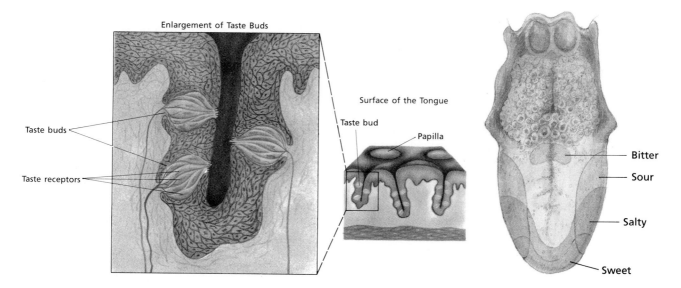

Smell

Like the sense of taste, **olfaction,** or smell, is a chemical sense. That is, the stimulus for smell is a chemical in the air. The olfactory system in human beings is remarkably sensitive and can recognize a smell from as few as forty or fifty molecules of a chemical. For the sensation of smell to occur, chemicals must move toward the receptor cells located on the walls of the nasal passage. This happens when we breathe them in through our nostrils or take them in via the back of our throat when we chew and swallow. When a chemical substance in the air moves past the receptor cells, it is partially absorbed into the mucus that covers the cells, thereby initiating the process of smell.

For human beings to perceive smell, information must be sent to the brain. At the top of the nasal cavity is the *olfactory epithelium*, which contains the olfactory rods, the nerve fibers that transmit information about smell to the brain (see Figure 3.30). There can be as many as thirty million olfactory rods in each nostril, making the olfactory system very sensitive. This fact is dramatically illustrated by perfume manufacturing.

People in the perfume manufacturing business know that making a perfume is complex. They may combine hundreds of scents to make one new perfume; dozens of perfumes have the same basic scent and vary only slightly. The manufacturers' task is to generate a perfume that has a distinctive *top note*, the first impact of a smell. If the substance that creates a smell is not chemically pure, it will be followed by a middle and an end note. The *middle* note follows after the top note fades away, and the *end note* is longlasting, remaining long after the top and middle notes have disappeared.

Theories of smell involve both the stimulus for smell and the structure of the receptor system. Some theories posit a few basic smells; others suggest many, including flowery, foul, fruity, resinous, spicy, and burnt. Psychologists are not unanimous on a single classification system for smells, nor do they completely understand how odors affect the receptor cells. Research into the coding of smell is intense, and physiological psychologists make headway each year. Another area in which important progress has been made is how and if odors affect human behavior. We consider this issue next.

FIGURE 3.30
The olfactory system.

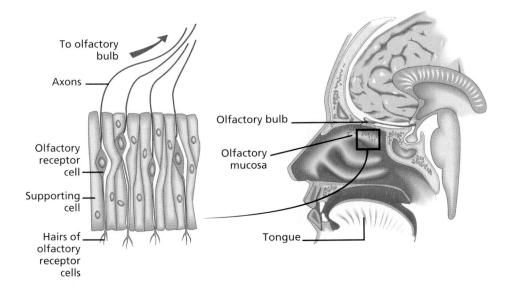

Smell and Communication

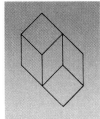

The smells of rotting fish, Limburger cheese, and ammonia probably aren't your favorite fragrances; even the thought of these scents may make you grimace. On the other hand, the smell of a subtle perfume, roasting chicken, or your grandfather's pipe may evoke a pleasant response. Although human beings have a good sense of smell, it pales by comparison to that of some animals. For example, dogs have one hundred times as many olfactory receptors as human beings. Dogs use their sense of smell to recognize objects and other animals. Dogs use their acute smell abilities to sniff out marijuana, cocaine, natural-gas leaks, and bombs (Gibbons, 1986). They can discriminate between dog, cat, and squirrel urine, and through their sense of smell know whether another dog is ready for a sexual encounter.

Pheromones in Animals. Pheromones (pronounced fer-uh-moans) are substances, secreted by animals, that act as communication devices. There are two major kinds of pheromones: primary and releaser. Primary pheromones alter an organism's physiology by releasing hormones that change the way the organism will respond in the future, perhaps in two hours or a day later. Releaser pheromones usually trigger a more or less immediate behavioral response. Pheromones are widely recognized as initiators of sexual activity. For example, female silkworms release a pheromone that can attract a male silkworm from miles away. Similarly, when female hamsters are sexually receptive, they emit a highly odorous substance that attracts males (Montgomery-St. Laurent, Fullenkamp, and Fischer, 1988), and mice are similarly equipped (Coppola and O'Connell, 1988). The impact of the release of a pheromone can be extreme: Early in pregnancy, mice will abort their fetuses rather than let them be attached if they detect the odor of a strange mouse.

Many animals emit pheromones to elicit specific reactions; others, notably dogs, use scents from their feces and urine to maintain territories and identify one another. Beavers attempt to keep strangers out of their territory by depositing foul-smelling substances emitted by sacs near the anus. Reindeer have scent glands between their toes that leave a trail for the rest of the herd. Communication through pheromones is found throughout the animal world, but do human beings share this ability?

Early Ideas. It was generally thought that human beings do not communicate through smell. Researchers have long known that the sexual and aggressive behavior of hamsters is under control of cues from the sense of smell. One study showed that adult male rats who were raised by lemon-scented mothers copulate more effectively with rats that smell of lemons (Fillion and Blass, 1986). People have always said that a kind of "chemistry" exists between close friends, but few really believed that one person's secretions might alter another person's behavior. But groundbreaking research in the 1970s began to change psychologists' thinking about smell and communication. McClintock (1971) found that menstrual periods of women who were either roommates or close friends in a college dormitory become roughly synchronous. That is, after they lived together for several months, their menstrual cycles began and ended at about the same time. McClintock and others began to question whether the synchronization of the menstrual cycles was due to some type of chemical message.

Research Idea. Two studies in the mid-1980s stirred up the pheromone debate. These studies were conducted by two scientists, Cutler and Preti, and focused on a specific issue: Could chemical signals from other people, men and women, alter women's menstrual cycles? They sought to test McClintock's idea that synchronization of the menstrual cycles was caused by some type of chemical message—pheromones. They used a fascinating technique. They swabbed underarm secretions on the lips of women to see if these chemicals affected their menstrual cycles.

In the first study, underarm secretions from men were gathered on swabs that they wore under their armpits (Cutler et al., 1986). This male smell was then swabbed on the upper lips of seven women whose menstrual cycles were either short (under twenty-six days) or long (over 33 days). The female subjects were told that they were receiving a "natural fragrance" that was injected into alcohol. The study was double-blind—neither the subjects nor the experimenter knew which of the subjects were receiving the underarm smell and which were receiving the control smell that had nothing other than alcohol.

Within three months the menstrual cycles of the experimental subjects became similar and approached the norm of 29.5 days. The researchers did a similar study, also double-blind, with secretions from other women (Preti et al., 1986). As in the first study, women were swabbed on their upper lip with underarm secretions or a blank secretion. Results were again similar. The times of menstruation all became similar and approached the norm. Placing the smell affected the women's menstrual cycles; pheromones were causing the change.

One Problem, One Strength. A problem with the Cutler and Preti research is that they used a limited number of subjects; in the first study there were fifteen subjects; in the second, nineteen subjects. Because of this, the researchers were cautious in making generalizations. However, the study was well designed; it had significance because it was double-blind, used an experimental method with control groups, and produced results that could be statistically analyzed.

Implications. These data suggest that the smell of other human beings affects physiological processes in women. The Cutler and Preti studies also suggest that pheromones emitted by a man may also alter a woman's menstrual cycle. The data suggest that women who live with men may have more regular cycles and thus may be more fertile than those who live alone (see Cutler et al., 1986).

Other people's physiological processes may affect us, but the evidence that smell affects human behavior is still suggestive. The effects of pheromones in animals are profound, but the role of pheromones in human beings still remains controversial and is being studied in a wide number of situations (e.g., Makin and Porter, 1989). Nevertheless, perfume makers have been sent into a frenzy of activity trying to make a perfume with pheromone-like abilities. Is it reasonable for them to assert that perfumes, like pheromones, can attract members of the opposite sex? Probably not. Pheromones probably are not as powerful in human beings because so many other environmental stimuli affect human behavior, attitudes, and interpersonal relations.   ◆

The Skin Senses

Our skin contains a wide range of receptors that convey information about touch, pressure, warmth, cold, and pain. In each case, a stimulus is converted into neural energy and then the brain interprets that neural energy into a psychological experience. Skin receptors ultimately send information to the somatosensory cortex of the brain.

Touch

The skin acts as the housing for our *sense of touch,* or *tactile system.* The skin is more than just a binding that holds a person together. Made up of three major layers, the skin of an adult human being measures roughly two square yards and is made up of layers. The top layer, or *epidermis,* consists primarily of dead cells, and varies in thickness. On the face it is thin; on the elbows and heels of the feet it is quite thick. The epidermis is constantly regenerating; in fact, every twenty-eight days or so all of its cells are replaced. The layer underneath the epidermis, called the *dermis,* contains live cells as well as a supply of nerve endings, blood, hair cells, and oil-producing (sebaceous) glands. The dermis and epidermis, which are resilient, flexible, and quite thick, protect the body against quick changes in temperature and pressure. The epidermis in particular guards against pain from small scratches and bumps. The deepest layer, the *hypodermis,* is a thick insulating cushion.

Specialized receptors are responsible for relaying information about the *skin senses*—pain, touch, and temperature (warmth and cold). The receptors for different senses vary in shape, size, number, and distribution. For example, the body has many more cold receptors than heat receptors; it has more pain receptors behind the knee than on top of the nose. In the most sensitive areas of the hand, there are as many as 1300 nerve endings per square inch.

The skin sense receptors appear to interact with one another; sometimes one sensation seems to combine with or change to another. Thus, increasing pressure can become pain. Similarly, an itch seems to result from a low level of irritation of nerve endings in the skin; however, a tickle can be caused by the same stimulus and produce a reflexlike response. Further, we are far more sensitive to pressure in some parts of our bodies than in other parts (compare your fingers to your thigh); the more sensitive areas have more receptors than less sensitive areas do.

Many of our determinations of how something feels are *relative* determinations. When we say that a stimulus is cold, we mean that it is cold compared to normal skin temperature. When we say that an object is warm, it feels warmer than normal skin temperature. When we feel a child's head with the back of our palm and say the child has a fever, we are comparing normal skin temperature to a sick child's elevated skin temperature (and you wouldn't make such a determination right after coming in from twenty degree weather).

Pain

Generally, people look forward to sensory experiences: new smells, sights, tastes, and sounds. One exception is the unpleasant sensation of pain. Pain is the most common symptom in medical settings; nevertheless, pain is adaptive and necessary. In rare cases, people have been born without the ability to feel pain, placing them in constant danger since they do not recognize conditions such as broken bones, serious burns, or the sharp pains that signal appendicitis—pain that would send most of us to the doctor for attention.

Studying pain is difficult because it can be elicited in so many ways. Stomach pains may be caused by hunger or the flu, toothaches by a cavity or abscess, headaches by stress, eye strain, or any number of different causes. Another reason is that myriad kinds of pain exist, including sunburn pain, pain from terminal cancer, labor pains, frostbite, and even pain when a limb is lost as a result of trauma or surgery (Melzack and Loeser, 1978). Psychologists use several kinds of stimuli to study pain. Among them are chemicals, heat and cold, and electrical shock (Flor and Turk, 1989). Most researchers believe that the receptors for pain are the free nerve endings located throughout the body.

Pain is a complex experience both physically and psychologically.

Certain areas of the body are more sensitive to pain than others. For example, the sole of the foot and the ball of the thumb are less sensitive than the back of the knee and the neck. Also, an individual's pain threshold remains fairly constant, but different individuals possess different sensitivities to pain. Some people have a low threshold for pain; they will report a comparatively low-level stimulus as painful. Others have fairly high pain thresholds. But pain is partly psychological, and much depends on a person's experience, attitude, and the situation in which pain occurs. Athletes often report not feeling the pain of an injury until after the competition has ended, for example. What allows pain suppression? How does the body process, interpret, and stop pain? We consider gate control theory as an answer.

Gate Control Theory. A widely accepted explanation of how the body processes pain is the Melzack-Wall gate control theory (Melzack and Wall, 1970). The theory is complex, taking into account the sizes of nerve fibers, their level of development, and the interplay of excitatory and inhibitory cells that can diminish painful sensations. The theory contends that when a signal that might normally indicate a painful stimulus is sent to the brain, it goes through a series of gates. These gates can be opened or closed either fully or partially. How far they open determines how much of the original pain signal gets through. A chemical called substance-P (P stands for pain), which is released by the sensory nerve fibers, transmits pain impulses across the gates. A variety of drugs, electrical stimulation, and acupuncture needles (Omura, 1977) are thought to close the gates partially or fully, making the original painful stimulus less potent.

Many people who suffer chronic, unrelieved pain have sought help from acupuncture. Initially developed in China thousands of years ago, acupuncture is a technique in which long, fine needles are inserted into the body at specific locations in order to relieve pain. Controlled studies of acupuncture have yielded varying results, from the finding of the National Institutes of Health that reported acupuncture no more effective than sugar pills, to a few studies that suggest it helps with mild back pain (Price et al., 1984). Controlled research and results on acupuncture remain inconclusive.

Endorphins. There have been some exciting breakthroughs in research on pain receptors and the nature of pain; consider the study of endorphins. **Endorphins** (from *endogenous*, meaning naturally occurring, and *morphine*, a painkiller) are painkillers naturally produced in the brain and pituitary gland. They help regulate several bodily functions, including the control of blood pressure and body temperature (Bloom, 1981). Endorphins can produce euphoria and a sense of well-being the way morphine does, but to an even greater extent. Stress, anticipated pain, and activities such as running bring about an increased endorphin level. Runners often report feeling "high," a sensation that many believe is directly related to their endorphin level.

Endorphins: Painkillers produced naturally in the brain and pituitary gland.

Endorphins bind themselves to receptor sites in the brain and spinal cord, thereby preventing pain signals from going to higher levels of the nervous system. Naturally produced endorphins include some that increase tolerance to pain and others that actually reduce pain. Enkaphalin, for example, is an innate brain opiate that blocks pain signals (Snyder, 1980). Physicians prescribe synthetic endorphins or endorphin-like substances, such as morphine, to block pain.

Pain Management. Usually the pain resulting from a headache, toothache, or small cut is temporary and can be alleviated with a simple pain medication such as aspirin. For millions of people, however, aspirin is not enough. For those who suffer from constant pain caused by back injury, arthritis, or cancer, drug treatment either is not effective, is dangerous because of the high dosages required, or is not prescribed because of fear of addiction—a fear that is often overstated (Melzack, 1990). Further, each type of pain may require a different treatment (Flor and Turk, 1989).

New technologies are emerging to help people manage pain. Solomon Snyder, a leader in pain research, reasons that something must happen at the site of an injury to trigger endorphin production. What if a drug could stop the whole pain perception process at the actual place where an injury occurs? Solomon, Innis, and Manning are studying the receptor sites in skin tissue and observing how chemicals bind to them (Bishop, 1986). They hope to find compounds that will stop the entire pain perception process, even before endorphin production starts. The compounds they discover may not be total pain relievers, but in combination with other pain medications, such as aspirin, they may be very effective.

Practitioners who deal with pain recognize that it can have both physical and psychological sources. Although pain may initially arise from physical complaints, it can continue because the attention received by the sufferer is reinforcing or because the pain provides a distraction from other problems. Treatment focuses on helping people cope with pain regardless of its origins.

Hypnosis (which will be examined in more detail in chapter 4) has been used to treat patients who suffer pain. They may be instructed to focus on other aspects of their lives and told that after the hypnotic session their pain will be more bearable. Hilgard and Morgan (1975) suggest that two-thirds of patients who are considered highly susceptible to suggestion can experience some relief of pain through hypnosis.

Anxiety and worry can make pain worse. People who suffer from migraine headaches, for example, often make their condition worse by becoming fearful—and therefore tense—when they feel a headache coming on. Researchers find that biofeedback training, which teaches people how to relax and cope more effectively, can help people who suffer from chronic pain and migraine headaches gain some relief (Nuechterlein and Holroyd, 1980) (biofeedback will be discussed further in chapter 4). Other treatments, closely related to biofeedback, are cognitive coping strategies (discussed in chapters 11 and 13). A poor or hopeless attitude can make pain worse. Cognitive coping strategies teach patients to have a better attitude about their pain (Sternbach, 1974). Patients learn to talk to themselves in positive ways, divert their attention to pleasant images, and take an active role in managing their pain and transcending the experience.

Kinesthesis and Vestibular Sensitivity

Kinesthesis refers to awareness aroused by movements of the muscles, tendons, and joints. It is what allows you to touch your finger to your nose with your eyes closed, leap over hurdles during a track and field event, dance without stepping on your partner's feet, and so on. The study of kinesthesis (sometimes called *proprioception*) provides information about bodily movements and internal sensations. The movements of muscles around the eye, for example, help let us know how far away objects are.

Kinesthesis: The awareness aroused by movements of the muscles, tendons, and joints; also called *proprioception*.

Vestibular sense: The sense of bodily orientation and postural adjustment.

Her vestibular sense allows this gymnast to maintain her balance and equilibrium during a difficult routine.

The **vestibular sense** is the sense of bodily orientation and postural adjustment; it helps us keep our balance and sense of equilibrium. The structures essential to these functions are in the ear. Vestibular sacs and semicircular canals, which are associated with the body wall of the cochlea, provide information about the orientations of the head and body relative to the eye-movement and posture systems (Parker, 1980). The vestibular sense allows you to walk the balance beam without falling off, to know which way is up after diving into the water, and to sense that you are over the speed limit when driving on the highway.

Rapid movements of the head bring about changes in the semicircular canals. These changes induce eye movements to help compensate for head changes and changes in body orientation. They may also be accompanied by physical sensations ranging from pleasant dizziness to unbearable motion sickness. Studies of the vestibular sense help scientists understand what happens to people during space travel and under conditions of weightlessness.

Extrasensory Perception

Vision, hearing, taste, smell, touch, and even pain are all part of the normal sensory experience of human beings. But some people claim there are other perceptual experiences that not all normal human beings encounter. People have been fascinated by *extrasensory perception*, or ESP, for hundreds of years.

The British Society for the Study of Psychic Phenomena has investigated reports of ESP since the nineteenth century. Early experimenters tested for extrasensory perception by asking subjects to guess the symbols on what are now called ESP cards, each marked with a star, a cross, a circle, a square, or a set of wavy lines. One of the most consistently successful guessers once guessed twenty-five cards in a row, an event with the odds of nearly 300 quadrillion to one of happening by chance.

ESP includes several different phenomena. *Telepathy* is the transfer of thought from one person to another. *Clairvoyance* is the ability to recognize objects or events, such as the contents of a message in a sealed envelope, that are not present to normal sensory receptors. *Precognition* is unexplained knowledge about future events, such as knowing when the phone is about to ring. *Psychokinesis* refers to the ability to move objects with one's mental powers.

Support for the existence of ESP is generally weak and has not been repeated very often. Moreover, ESP phenomena such as bending a spoon through mental manipulation and "reading people's minds" are not affected by experimental manipulations the way other perceptual events are. In addition, the National Research Council has denounced the scientific merit of most of these experiments. None of these criticisms means that ESP does not exist, and active research using scientific methods continues. But as Child (1985) suggests, psychologists see so much trickery and falsification of data and so many design errors in experiments on this subject that they remain skeptical.

- ◆ Identify behavior in animals that seems to be directly affected by pheromones. p. 109
- ◆ Identify and briefly describe the three major layers of the skin. p. 110
- ◆ Why is pain so difficult to study? p. 111
- ◆ When athletes say they are experiencing a "high," what might be the mechanism that creates it? p. 112
- ◆ If you were an astronaut, would you be more concerned about the activity of the vestibular system or the taste system? p. 113

Focus on Learning

Key Terms

Summary

Sensation and Perception: A Definition
* *Perception* is the process through which people attach meaning to sensory stimuli by use of complex processing mechanisms.   p. 72

Sensory Experience
* Studies of sensory deprivation have shown that an organism's early experience is important in the development and proper functioning of its perceptual systems.   p. 73

The Visual System
* The main structures of the eye are the cornea, iris, pupil, crystalline lens, and retina. The retina is made up of ten layers, of which the most important are the rods and cones, the bipolar layer, and the ganglion cell layer. The ganglion cells make up the nuclei of the long axons that form the optic nerve.   p. 76

* *Receptive fields* are areas on the retina that, when stimulated, produce changes in the firing of cells in the visual system.   p. 82

* The three main psychological characteristics of color—hue, brightness, and saturation—refer to the three physical characteristics: wavelength, intensity, and purity.   p. 86

Visual Perception
* Monocular cues for depth perception include linear perspective, texture, and accommodation. The primary binocular cue is retinal disparity.   p. 92

* Using the Law of Prägnanz as an organizing idea, Gestalt psychologists developed principles of organization for the perception of figures.   p. 97

* If a visual or auditory stimulus is presented so quickly or at such a low volume that you cannot consciously perceive it, we say that it is presented subliminally.   p. 98

Hearing
* *Sound* refers to changes in pressure passing through a gaseous, liquid, or solid medium. The frequency and amplitude of a sound wave principally determine how it will be experienced by a listener.   p. 101

* The ear has three main parts: the outer ear, middle ear, and inner ear. The eardrum or *tympanic membrane* is the boundary between the outer ear and the middle ear. It transmits sound waves to tiny bones in the middle ear, which vibrate and stimulate the *basilar membrane* in the *cochlea*, a tube in the inner ear.   p. 103

* Place theories of hearing claim that the analysis of sound takes place in the inner ear; frequency theories claim that the analysis of pitch and intensity takes place at higher levels of processing.   p. 104

Taste and Smell
* The tongue contains thousands of bumps, or *papillae*, each of which is separated from the next by a "moat." The taste buds are located on the walls of the moats. Each taste bud consists of several *taste cells*.   p. 106

* The *olfactory epithelium* contains the *olfactory rods,* the nerve fibers that process odors.   p. 108

The Skin Senses
* The skin is made up of three major layers; the top layer is called the *epidermis*. The layer underneath the epidermis is called the *dermis*. The deepest layer, called the *hypodermis*, is a thick insulating cushion.   p. 110

* A widely accepted explanation of how the body processes pain is the Melzack-Wall gate control theory.   p. 111

* *Endorphins* are painkillers that are naturally produced in the brain and pituitary gland.   p. 112

* *Kinesthesis* refers to the awareness aroused by movements of the muscles, tendons, and joints. The *vestibular sense* is the sense of bodily orientation and postural adjustment.   p. 112

Extrasensory Perception
* ESP includes several phenomena: telepathy, clairvoyance, precognition, and psychokinesis. Support for the existence of ESP is generally weak.   p. 114

Connections

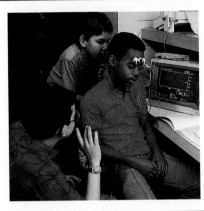
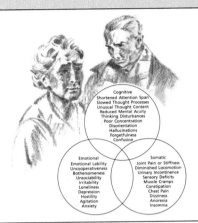

If you are interested in . . .	Turn to . . .	To learn more about . . .
Sensory experiences in human beings	◆ Ch. 4, p. 136	How altered states of consciousness affect perception in both positive and negative ways.
	◆ Ch. 9, p. 308	The effects of early childhood sensory experiences on later perceptual development.
	◆ Ch. 17, p. 632	The impact of too much sensory experience, such as noise.
The operation of our perceptual systems	◆ Ch. 4, p. 132	How feedback from our sensory systems can help manage certain bodily complaints.
	◆ Ch. 6, p. 205	How the initial coding of the visual and auditory world lasts only for a brief time in the sensory register.
	◆ Ch. 17, p. 584	How our perceptions of other people often come from nonverbal visual cues in the environment.
The development of perception	◆ Ch. 7, p. 258	The unfolding of language and thought processes as an individual matures in the environment.
	◆ Ch. 9, p. 308	How the inborn perceptual abilities of children develop over time and through experience.
	◆ Ch. 10, p. 367	How sensory and perceptual abilities decline with advancing age.

4

States of Consciousness

"Chameleon" by Josette Urso

◆

*I*n January 1964, at age seventeen, Randy Gardner hoped to make history, and he did. He decided that he was going to break a world's record by staying awake for more than 260 hours—just short of eleven days. Physically and mentally healthy, Gardner was assured and self-confident. A science fair near his San Diego home was to be the location of his experiment. He enlisted two friends to help keep him awake, and he took no stimulants such as coffee.

After six days, a local physician came to supervise his progress, much to the relief of Gardner's parents. Although he did not suffer any serious physical symptoms, there were marked psychological effects. On day two, he had trouble focusing his eyes; on day three, there were mood changes; on day four, he was irritable and uncooperative. He also began to see images. By day six, Gardner had speech difficulties and memory lapses. By day nine, his thoughts and speech were incoherent. On day ten, blurred vision became more of a problem and he was regularly forgetting things. Mornings were his most difficult time, but at no time did he behave irrationally. Randy Gardner's record is the longest documented account of continuous sleep loss.

One of the most interesting aspects of Randy Gardner's adventure is what happened to his sleep after his deprivation. Sleep researcher William Dement followed Gardner's sleep, mental health, physical recovery, and electroencephalogram for days afterward to see how his subject recovered, what happened to his sleep patterns, and if he made up for lost sleep. Dement found that for the three nights following his deprivation, Gardner slept an extra 6.5 hours, and on the fourth night, an extra 2.5 hours (Gulevich, Dement, and Johnson, 1966; Johnson, Slye, and Dement, 1965).

Following Randy Gardner's sleep loss and his subsequent recovery is part of the history of the study of sleep. Early researchers such as Kleitman and Dement were just beginning to ask interesting questions; they were beginning to realize that sleep and wakefulness follow specific patterns that can be tracked and predicted. They noted that as you move through the day your general awareness—responsiveness, thought processes, and physiological responses—changes. On first waking, you may not be fully aware and responsive. You move sluggishly and are slow to realize that the coffee is perking and your toast is burning. Later, at a job or in class, you are probably alert. But as the day wears on you find your awareness decreasing, and in the evening you may fall asleep in front of the television. Research on sleep is one piece of a larger puzzle of human awareness, human consciousness, and altered states of being. Randy Gardner's goal was to break a world record, which he did, but he also began the modern study of human consciousness.

Consciousness

Human beings are aware (conscious) of the messages that the brain is constantly receiving and sending. The word *conscious* refers to a state of being, and the term has a checkered history in psychology. Early psychologists such as Wilhelm Wundt studied the contents of consciousness, and later psychologists such as William James studied how consciousness operates. However, in the 1920s, behaviorists rejected consciousness as a topic of study. John B. Watson believed that consciousness should be eliminated as a subject of psychological study because it is not a physical structure to be examined, probed, or diagrammed. As the behavioral approach came to dominate American psychology, the study of consciousness and thought was all but forgotten. Only in the 1960s and 1970s was consciousness discussed again as cognitive psychology emerged. The tide has clearly turned; today, consciousness is again a topic of scientific as well as popular interest.

Defining Consciousness

Almost all psychologists agree that a person who is conscious is aware of the environment; for example, we are conscious when we listen to a lecture. But being conscious also refers to inner awareness, that is, knowledge of our own thoughts, feelings, and memories. The word *conscious* is a state of being; we say "I am conscious" or "he was conscious." The word *consciousness* refers to the state of being conscious. So we say that "we are studying consciousness" or "he was in an altered state of consciousness."

When early psychologists studied the mind and its contents, they studied consciousness. Wundt and his students in the late 1880s had subjects report the contents of their consciousness while sitting still, while working, and while falling asleep. At the turn of the century, Sigmund Freud (whom we will study in more depth later) believed that deep within a person's consciousness are needs, wishes, and desires that influence feeling and behavior. According to Freud, people have different levels of consciousness—consciousness they are aware of as well as unconscious thoughts of which they are unaware. Today, cognitive psychologists assert that people are aware of certain mental processes and unaware of others. For example, when you first learn to play tennis, your movements are stilted and often uncoordinated. But with practice you learn to move more automatically. In fact, as a ball approaches, you automatically, unconsciously, approach the ball. Cognitive psychologists generally do not speak about the unconscious but instead refer to (deliberate) controlled versus automatic processes. All these psychologists—the early structuralists, Freud, and even today's cognitive researchers—acknowledge that different levels of consciousness exist.

Each view of conscious behavior depends on a person's orientation to psychology. Rather than taking a specific view, let us take a generally agreed upon view and define **consciousness** as the general state of being aware of and responsive to the environment and our own mental processes. Consciousness can range from alert attention to dreaming, hypnosis, or drug-induced states. We say that a person in a state of consciousness that is different from the usual waking state is in an **altered state of consciousness.** Consciousness and the ongoing biological processes in our bodies are closely linked; our biological processes influence how incoming stimuli affect us and our degree of awareness about the world.

The idea of a continuum guides many researchers who believe that consciousness is made up of several *levels* of awareness, from alertness to total unresponsiveness. Researchers who favor this view suggest, for example, that a person who is drinking heavily enters a lower (or deeper, more profound) *level* of his or her range of conscious levels—that of intoxication. But other researchers believe that distinctly different conscious *states* explain specific behaviors and attention patterns. Researchers who favor this interpretation believe that a heavy drinker has entered a totally different *state* of consciousness. This issue of levels versus states is far from resolved. We will examine the effects of drugs, hypnosis, and meditation on consciousness later in this chapter.

Learning to ride a bike is difficult at first, but eventually the skill becomes automatic.

Theories of Consciousness

As in other areas of psychology, theory guides research in the study of consciousness and its altered states. Several researchers have proposed biologically-based theories of consciousness. Julian Jaynes (1976) suggests that understanding the evolution of the human brain is the key to understanding altered states. He believes that consciousness originates in differences in the function and physiology of the two hemispheres of the brain. Thus, when one structure of the brain is operating, one specific level of consciousness will be revealed; when another structure is operating, other levels will be activated.

Robert Ornstein (1977) suggests that two modes of consciousness exist, each controlled by one side of the brain: the active-verbal-rational mode (called the active mode) and the receptive-spatial-intuitive-holistic mode (called the receptive mode). Ornstein believes that evolution has made the

Consciousness: The general state of being aware of and responsive to events in the environment and one's own mental processes.

Altered state of consciousness: A pattern of functioning that is dramatically different from that of ordinary awareness and responsiveness.

active mode automatic: Human beings limit their awareness automatically in order to shut out experiences, events, and stimuli that do not directly relate to their ability to survive. When people need to gain perspective and judgment about what they are doing, they expand their normal awareness by using the receptive mode. Ornstein believes that techniques such as meditation, biofeedback, hypnosis, and even the use of certain drugs can help people learn to use the receptive mode of their consciousness to balance the more active mode.

Ornstein and his collaborator, David Galin, support many of their ideas with laboratory data showing that the brain is divided and specialized in significant ways; they point out that the left-dominated and right-dominated modes of consciousness operate in a complementary and alternating fashion, one working while the other is inhibited (Galin, 1974; Ornstein, 1976). In Ornstein's model (1977), intellectual activities take place in the active or left-dominated mode, and intuitive activities in the receptive or right-dominated mode; the integration of these two modes underlies the highest human accomplishments. Although the existence of two physiological modes of operation in the brain lends support to Ornstein's ideas, many researchers are skeptical of his theory (Zaidel, 1983). They argue that the structure of the brain does not necessarily explain its function and no data exist to show how the brain actually operates.

Being conscious means being aware, and because human beings are aware they can tell researchers about their experiences. Psychologists can also study a person's consciousness by measuring certain physiological functions. Much of the remainder of this chapter will focus on a wide array of states of consciousness. Some of the research techniques used will be biological, others will be self-report. Some of these conscious states are desirable and normal; others alter human behavior in less positive ways. We begin with an altered state of awareness with which all of us are familiar—sleep.

<table>
<tr><td>

Focus on Learning

</td><td>

◆ How did early psychologists define consciousness? p. 120
◆ What function did Freud believe the unconscious served? p. 121
◆ Robert Ornstein suggests that two modes of consciousness exist, each controlled by one side of the brain. Describe the two modes. pp. 121–122

</td></tr>
</table>

Sleep

In the casinos of Las Vegas it is difficult to tell night from day. There are no windows, activity is at fever pitch twenty-four hours a day, and there are few clocks. People never seem to sleep; it is as if there were no day or night. But people do sleep, and unlike Randy Gardner, people give in to their bodily urges to rejuvenate themselves. Our bodies tell us we are tired without a clock on the wall to remind us.

The Sleep-Wakefulness Cycle: Circadian Rhythms

Human beings are not at the mercy of light and darkness to control activities. There seems to be a biological clock that ticks within us to control the sleep-wakefulness cycle. Some researchers argue that there are two clocks, one controlling a sleep-wakefulness cycle and one controlling various aspects of our physiology. The second clock is supposed to control body temperature, which fluctuates by 1.5 degrees during the day, the lowest temperature occurring while we are sleeping. Whether there exist one or two clocks, neither seems to run on a twenty-four-hour day, and thus the term circadian was born—circadian comes from the Latin *circa diem* (about a day).

Circadian rhythms are internally generated and help control our bodily rhythms, sleep patterns, and body temperature. When time cues are removed from the environment (clocks, windows, temperature changes as the sun goes down) an interesting finding occurs—our circadian rhythm runs a bit slow. When placed in artificial environments and allowed to sleep, eat, and read whenever they want, human beings sleep a constant amount but each "day" they go to sleep a bit later; the full sleep-wakefulness cycle runs at about 24.5 to 25.5 hours. Body temperatures and other bodily functions tend to follow a similar circadian rhythm.

Daylight, clocks, schedules, and erratic work schedules do not allow people's circadian rhythms to control their sleep or wakefulness. But you can see that if this rhythm is thrown off by your having to work through the night, then sleep, then rise, and so forth, your bodily clock may not match your work clock. This becomes especially difficult if you are an airline pilot, a surgeon, or a firefighter.

Consider the air traveler's dilemma: jet lag. If you travel from the East Coast, say New York City, to London, England, the trip will take about six hours. If you leave at 9:00 P.M. you will arrive six hours later, at 3:00 A.M.—at least as far as your body is concerned. You are exhausted. But local time is only 9:00 P.M. People meeting you may want to chat and catch up on friends or business. You stay up till midnight, but as far as your body knows, it is three hours later, 6:00 A.M. You go to bed, sleep seven hours, but your body thinks it is the middle of the day. You experience jet lag as exhaustion and disorientation. You may want to sleep during the day and stay up at night. If you suffer jet lag or if you work long, irregular shifts, your work performance may not be at its peak. We have learned this through studying sleep, the sleep-wakefulness cycle, and sleep deprivation.

Sleep: A Restorative Process

Sleep is a natural state of consciousness experienced by everyone. Some psychologists think that sleep allows the body to recover from the day's expenditure of energy; they see sleep as a restorative process. Others perceive sleep as a holdover from a type of hibernation. They believe an organism conserves energy during sleep, when its expenditure would be inefficient (night is not a good time for animals to catch or produce food). A third view sees sleep as a time when the cortex recovers from exhaustion and overload. They believe that sleep has little effect on basic physiological processes in the rest of the body. These views of physical restoration, hibernation, and cerebral restoration guide researchers' investigations into sleep patterns. But why do some people need more sleep than others?

Everyone needs some sleep. Most of us require about eight hours, but some people can function with only four or five hours and others need as many as nine or ten. Young teenagers tend to sleep longer than college students, and elderly people tend to sleep less than young people. Most young adults (sixty-five percent) sleep between 6.5 and 8.5 hours a night, and about ninety-five percent sleep between 5.5 and 9.5 hours (Horne, 1988).

Although you might think that people who are active and energetic would require more sleep than those who are less active, this is not always

Sleep: A nonwaking state of consciousness characterized by general unresponsiveness to the environment and general physical immobility.

NREM sleep (no rapid eye movements): Four distinct stages of sleep during which no rapid eye movements

REM sleep (rapid eye movements): A stage of sleep characterized by high-frequency, low-voltage brainwave activity, rapid and systematic eye movements, and dreams.

the case. Bedridden hospital patients, for example, sleep about the same amount of time as people who are on their feet all day.

Sleep Cycles and Stages: REM and NREM Sleep

Our sleep-wakefulness cycle is repetitive, determined in part by circadian rhythms, work schedules, and a host of other events. When early sleep researchers such as Nathaniel Kleitman and William Dement studied the sleep-wakefulness cycle, they found stages within sleep that could be characterized through EEGs and by eye movements that occurred during sleep. Researchers working in sleep laboratories study the brain's electrical activity during sleep by attaching electrodes to a subject's scalp and forehead and monitoring his or her brain-wave pattern throughout the night. Experimenters also record eye movements using an electroculogram and muscle tension in the face using an electromyogram (Ogilvie, McDonagh, Stone, and Wilkinson, 1988).

Recordings of sleeping subjects' EEGs (electroencephalograms) have revealed that in an eight-hour period, people typically progress through five full cycles of sleep, with each cycle having four stages (see Figure 4.1) and REM sleep. When people first fall asleep they are in stage 1; their sleep is rather light and they can be wakened easily. Within the next thirty to forty minutes, they pass through stages 2, 3, and 4. Stage 4 is very deep sleep; when subjects leave stage 4 sleep, they pass again through stages 3 and 2. A full sleep cycle lasts approximately ninety minutes. We characterize the first four stages as **no rapid eye movements (NREM) sleep states;** the other pattern is called **rapid eye movement (REM) sleep.** Only during REM sleep do rapid and systematic eye movements occur.

People experience REM sleep for the first time when they leave stage 4 sleep and pass again through stages 3 and 2. Thus, the longer they sleep (and the more sleep cycles they go through), the more REM sleep they experience (Agnew and Webb, 1973). Figure 4.2 shows the distinctive brain-wave patterns of wakefulness, the four stages of NREM sleep, and REM sleep in a normal adult. The waking pattern exhibits a fast, regular rhythm. In stage 1, sleep is light and the brain waves are of low amplitude (height) but relatively fast with mixed frequencies. Sleepers in stage 1 can be wakened easily. Stage 2 sleep shows low-amplitude, nonrhythmic activity combined

FIGURE 4.1
Most people complete about five sleep cycles per night. With each cycle, they spend progressively more time in REM sleep.

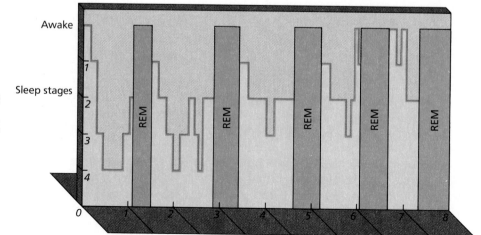

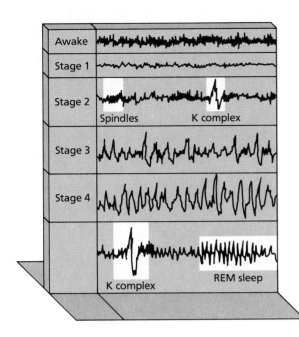

FIGURE 4.2
EEGs show distinctive characteristic patterns for a wakeful state, REM sleep, and each of the four NREM sleep stages. After sleep onset, the EEG changes progressively from a pattern of low voltage and high frequency to one of high voltage and low frequency.

with special patterns called sleep spindles and K complexes. A *sleep spindle* is a rhythmic burst of waves that wax and wane for one or two seconds. A *K complex* is a higher-amplitude burst of activity seen in the last third of stage 2. Sleep spindles and K complexes appear only during NREM sleep. Sleepers in stage 2 are in deeper sleep than in stage 1 but can still be awakened easily.

Stage 3 sleep is a transitional stage between stages 2 and 4, with slower but higher-amplitude activity than at stage 2. Stage 4 sleep, the deepest sleep stage, has even higher-amplitude brain-wave traces, called delta waves. During this stage, people breathe deeply and have slowed heart rate and lowered blood pressure. Stage 4 sleep has two well-documented behavioral characteristics. First, subjects are difficult to awaken. Stage 4 sleep is deep sleep, and wakened subjects often appear confused and disturbed and take several seconds to rouse themselves fully. Second, subjects in stage 4 sleep generally do not dream, although they may report some vague mental activity.

In contrast to stage 4 sleep, subjects who are awakened during REM sleep (after stage 4) can report in great detail the imagery and activity characteristic of a dream state. Because REM sleep is considered necessary to normal physiological functioning and behavior, it might be expected to be a deep sleep; however, it is an active sleep during which the EEG resembles that of an aware person. For this reason, REM sleep is often called *paradoxical sleep*. In REM sleep subjects seem agitated; their eyes move and their heart rate and breathing are variable. Subjects are difficult to awaken during REM sleep.

The bottom pattern in Figure 4.3 shows an EEG transition from NREM stage 2 to REM sleep. The first part of the tracing shows a clear K complex, indicating stage 2 sleep; the last part shows waves characteristic of REM sleep. During periods of sleep in which the high-frequency, low-amplitude waves are apparent, subjects experience rapid eye movements and typically report dreaming. Researchers can identify the stage of sleep an individual is in by watching an EEG recording. If delta waves are present, the subject is in stage 4 sleep. To confirm this, the experimenters may wake the subject and ask if he or she was dreaming.

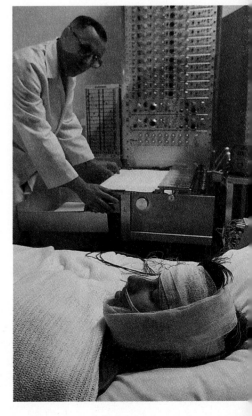

The exact role of sleep in maintaining our physical and mental well-being is still not well understood and scientists continue to study this complex state of consciousness.

Sleep cycles develop from before birth into adulthood. Initially, fetuses show no eye movements. Later they show eye, facial, and body movements. Newborns spend about fifty percent of their sleep time in REM sleep. From age one on, the proportion of REM sleep to stage 4 sleep decreases dramatically (Ellingson, 1975) (see Table 4.1 and Figure 4.3).

One new theory, developed by Horne (1988), asserts that sleep can be divided into two major types, core sleep and optional sleep. *Core sleep* repairs the effects of waking wear and tear on cerebral functions; core sleep is thus restorative. *Optional sleep* fills the time from the end of core sleep till waking. Core sleep has a higher proportion of stage 4 sleep and REM sleep than optional sleep does. This new conceptualization of sleep needs rigorous scientific support, but in the meantime, it has intuitive appeal.

Sleep Deprivation: Doing without REM

The need for sleep is painfully obvious to anyone who has been deprived of it. Just ask Randy Gardner (introduced at the beginning of the chapter) who went without sleep for close to eleven days. When people who normally

FIGURE 4.3
REM sleep (darker areas) occurs cyclically throughout the night at about ninety-minute intervals in all age groups. However, stage 4 sleep decreases with age. In addition, elderly people awaken more often and spend more time awake.

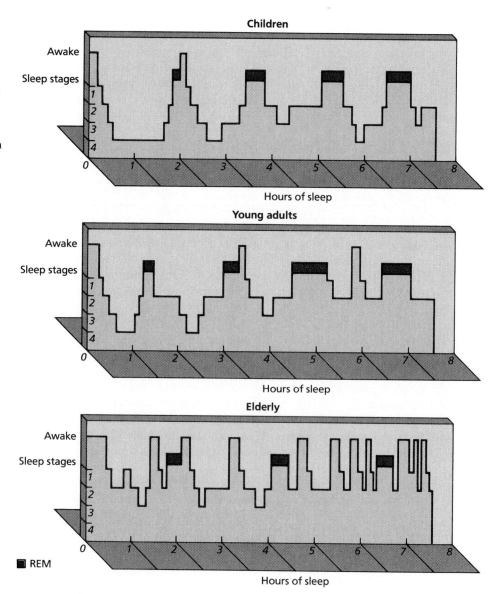

TABLE 4.1
Minutes of REM Sleep, Ages 3 to 15

REM Period	3–5 Yrs.	6–9 Yrs.	10–15 Yrs.	13–15 Yrs.
1	18	18	18	20
2	24	26	29	29
3	27	32	35	30
4	35	35	37	35
5	31	34	32	27
6	29	34	32	27
7	28	58		
8	25			
9	38			

Source: Williams, Karacan, and Hursch, 1974.

sleep eight hours miss a few hours on a particular night, they may be tired the following day but can function quite well. But when people lose a couple of hours of sleep for several nights in a row, they usually look tired, feel lethargic, and are irritable. Remember how you felt the day after pulling an all-nighter to finish a research paper or study for an exam? What effect did sleep deprivation have on your body?

Researchers have investigated what happens to people who are totally or partially deprived of sleep for various amounts of time. The research is generally conducted on laboratory subjects who sleep in a sleep laboratory where their EEGs and eye movements are recorded for several nights. For the first three or four nights, they are allowed to have their normal amount of sleep; the recordings taken during this time provide baseline data. Once sleeping norms are established, the subjects are deprived of sleep (e.g., Webb and Agnew, 1974).

One study deprived subjects of all sleep for 205 hours (8½ days). Researchers found that on the nights immediately after the experiment, subjects spent a greater-than-normal amount of time in REM and stage 4 sleep and the least amount of time in stage 1 and 2 sleep—the lightest stages of sleep (Kales et al., 1970; see also Webb and Agnew, 1975). Similar results were obtained in another study in which subjects were partially deprived of REM sleep. They reported feeling sleepy and spent more time in REM sleep on a subsequent night (Dement, Greenberg, and Klein, 1966); according to Horne (1988), only about thirty percent of lost sleep needs to be recovered, mostly stage 4 sleep and REM sleep.

What happens to subjects who are regularly deprived of core or REM sleep? They become anxious and irritable, report difficulty concentrating, and do worse on tests that involve attention and original responses (May and Kline, 1987). The longer a person is deprived of sleep, the more sleepy, the worse the mood, and the more cognitive difficulties subjects will report (Mikulincer et al., 1989). As soon as they are allowed to have REM sleep again, however, the psychological changes disappear (e.g., Roehrs et al., 1989).

Some researchers suggest that a certain amount of dreaming each night is necessary to psychological well-being. They believe that serious disruptions of personality may occur as a result of prolonged REM sleep deprivation. But other researchers deny that serious psychological changes occur (Bonnet, 1980), and today it is known that serious maladjustments do not occur with

Workers on swing shifts may suffer from decreased attentiveness due to the disruption of their circadian rhythms and sleep patterns.

sleep deprivation. With the exception of brain functions, especially the cortex, sleep deprivation is surprisingly uneventful for the rest of the body. Even more important, whatever changes in cerebral functions do take place with sleep deprivation are reversible after later sleep (Horne, 1988). We saw this in the case of Randy Gardner.

As many as twenty to thirty million American workers have nontraditional work schedules, and they alter their sleep patterns regularly. Studies of circadian rhythms (discussed earlier) generally show that when people put in long hours that stretch through the night into dawn, and when these hours are non-regular, people are less attentive, think less clearly, and may even nod off from time to time. Circadian rhythms and sleep patterns are closely related to and dependent on one another; thus employers, workers, and consumers need to be aware of the potential decreased efficiency of nightworkers, such as airline pilots and medical interns, who often vary their schedules. Decreased efficiency of nightworkers can be accounted for by irregular schedules, but some people exhibit far more serious alterations in their sleep-wakefulness cycle—they exhibit sleep disorders.

Sleep Disorders

APPLYING PSYCHOLOGY

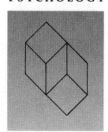

*Y*ou may have a sleep disorder if you snore loudly, sleepwalk, or fall asleep at inappropriate times, such as when driving a car. People who fall asleep suddenly have a disorder known as *narcolepsy*. Narcolepsy is probably a symptom of an autonomic nervous system disturbance and lowered arousal.

Another sleep disorder, *sleep apnea,* causes airflow to stop for at least fifteen seconds so the person ceases breathing. People with this disorder often have as many as 100 apnea episodes in a night; during the day they are exceedingly sleepy and sometimes have memory losses. People with severe apnea may have work-related accidents and severe headaches, and may fall asleep during the day. Drug therapy and some minor surgical techniques for creating better airflow have been used to treat those with sleep apnea. Monitoring equipment for prolonged breathing pauses has also been used to wake the sleeper (Sheridan, 1985). Males are more likely than females to have sleep apnea (Ingbar and Gee, 1985), and sleep apnea is a major hypothesis for explaining SIDS, Sudden Infant Death Syndrome, in which infants die suddenly during sleep for no obvious reason.

Insomnia, a prolonged inability to sleep, is a common sleep disorder often caused by anxiety or depression (Borkovec, 1982). One in ten people report insomnia; they tend to be listless and tired during the day and may use sleeping pills or other drugs to induce sleep (see Coates et al., 1983). Ironically, researchers have found that these drugs do not induce natural sleep: they reduce, instead of increase, the proportion of REM sleep after sleep deprivation (Webb and Agnew, 1975). Because researchers such as Dement found that lack of REM sleep may alter normal behavior, people with chronic insomnia should not use drugs that force sleep. Various researchers have proposed alternative behavioral methods that do not rely on drugs to help insomniacs (e.g., Woolfolk and McNulty, 1983), including relaxation training and self-hypnosis. Other researchers such as Vitiello (1989) assert that diet affects sleep because diet affects sympathetic nervous system activity which may stimulate people in the middle of the night; such research is still in its early stages. However, we saw in chapter 2 (p. 64) that diet (especially carbohydrates) affects mood and sleepiness, so these ideas do have other experimental support.

Night terrors consist of panic attacks that occur within an hour after falling asleep. Sitting up abruptly in a state of sheer panic, a person with a night terror

Insomnia: Prolonged inability to sleep.

may scream, breathe quickly, and be in a total state of fright. Night terrors are especially apparent in young children between ages three and eight. They usually disappear as a child grows older and do not seem to be a symptom of any psychological disorder. The cause of night terrors is not fully established but may be due to electrochemical processes overloading during NREM sleep. ◆

Telling Time and Improving Your Memory While You're Asleep

Since everybody sleeps, it is natural to wonder if we can put this time to good use. Can we program ourselves to wake, to learn, to be more efficient?

Telling Time. Can you awaken every morning at a predetermined time? Can you tell time even in your sleep? Psychologists doubt it, and respond that some *external* cue such as birds chirping or sunlight usually helps people wake up. In a research study to assess if subjects had the ability to wake themselves at a predetermined time, electroencephalographic readings were made of the sleeping subjects (Zepelin, 1986). No subject was consistently able to wake at a predetermined time, although some subjects could wake up at the proper time some of the time. The researchers found that subjects were able to awaken themselves most easily when they were in REM sleep. The cyclical occurrence of REM sleep may be an aid. Being in REM sleep probably facilitated their ability to recall the intention to wake and perhaps the act of waking itself.

Sleep and Memory. Magazines often run ads for "learn while you sleep" programs. Desperate students tape record their class notes and play them the night before an exam while they sleep. But does this technique work? Most research shows that claims for real, long-lasting learning occurring during sleep are false at worst and exaggerated at best (Aarons, 1976; Bierman and Winter, 1989). Research examining subjects who slept and listened to tapes found that learning did not occur. Sleep can, however, aid memory and learning in a different way.

Research in the 1920s showed that sleeping before a test is better than being involved in other kinds of activities. In a now classic study, Jenkins and Dallenbach (1924) had two subjects learn lists of nonsense syllables and recall them either immediately after presentation or up to eight hours later. During the period between learning and recall, the subjects either slept or engaged in normal waking activities. The performance of the subject who slept during the delay period was better than that of the subject who stayed awake; the waking subject's intervening activity affected his memory.

Even more interesting are the results of a study by Benson and Feinberg (1977), who had subjects learn lists of paired associates either in the morning just after sleep or at night just before sleep. Subjects were tested on their recall after eight, sixteen, or twenty-four hours. Those who learned the lists in the morning and were tested at night did worse than those who learned the material at night and were tested in the morning. Moreover, after twenty-four hours, when all subjects had had an equal amount of sleep and waking activity, subjects who learned the paired associates just before sleeping still showed better recall. The researchers concluded that sleep not only insulates subjects from interfering activity but also provides a period during which information can be consolidated. Studies such as this show clearly that sleep is an important aid to memory, although psychologists do not yet know exactly how. A good night's sleep will not guarantee learning or excellent memory, but lack of it surely will impair performance.

Focus on Learning

♦ Describe five distinct patterns of EEG activity that occur during sleep. pp. 124–125
♦ What happens when people are deprived of sleep for one hour a night? p. 126
♦ Name two sleep disorders and describe their symptoms. p. 128

Dreams

Why do some people rarely remember their dreams while other people can recall theirs in vivid detail? Do our dreams have hidden meaning and mysterious symbols to be unraveled? Sometimes life-like, sometimes chaotic, sometimes incoherent, dreams may replay a person's life history or may venture into the unknown. Dreams have long occupied an important place in psychology, but only in the last four decades have they come under close scientific scrutiny.

What Is a Dream?

A **dream** is a state of consciousness that occurs largely during REM sleep and is usually accompanied by vivid visual imagery, although the imagery may be tactile or auditory. During a dream there is an increase in heart rate, the appearance of rapid eye movements, a characteristic brain-wave pattern, and a lack of body movements. Although dreams occur most often in REM sleep, they can also occur in NREM sleep, but they tend to be less visual and more thinking oriented during NREM sleep. REM sleep dreams are intensely visual, may be action-oriented, and are more likely to be emotional than NREM dreams.

Most people dream four or five times a night. Dreams last from a few seconds to several minutes. The first dream of a typical night occurs ninety minutes after you have fallen asleep and lasts for ten minutes. With about four dreams per night and 365 days per year, a person dreams more than 100,000 dreams in a lifetime. But we remember only a few; usually people recall a dream because they woke in the middle of it or because a specific dream had extremely powerful imagery.

Content of Dreams

Sometimes the content of a dream is related to day-to-day events, to a desire that a person wishes would be fulfilled, or to reliving an unpleasant experience. Sometimes a person experiences the same dream over and over again, or a sequence of related dreams. Most dreams are commonplace and focus on people and events with whom we come into contact frequently—family, friends, or co-workers. Common themes include sex, aggressive incidents, and misfortunes. Sounds and other sensations from the environment that do not wake a sleeper are often incorporated into a dream. When a researcher sprayed water on the hands of sleepers, forty-two percent of those who did not wake later reported dreaming about swimming pools, baths, or rain (Dement and Wolpert, 1958).

Dream: A state of consciousness that occurs largely during REM sleep and is usually accompanied by vivid visual, tactile, and auditory experiences.

Dreams are mostly visual and they occur mostly in color. Dement and Kleitman (1957) found that subjects' patterns of rapid eye movements related to the visual imagery of their dreams. When a subject dreamed about climbing a series of ladders, eye movements were vertical; when a subject dreamed about two people throwing tomatoes at each other, eye movements were horizontal. Blind individuals, or those who lost their sight before age five, tend to have dream imagery that is mostly auditory.

Lucid Dreams

Sometimes people report that they are aware of dreaming while it is happening; this is called a **lucid dream.** Most people have had a lucid dream at one time or another. People are often overpowered by the compelling imagery of lucid dreams. Gackenbach and Bosveld (1989) assert that such events are quite spectacular and exciting.

When people experience a lucid dream they often later report that they were inside and outside the dream at the same time. For some people this is upsetting, and they often wake from the dream. Some people attempt to navigate or control their lucid dreams. They tell themselves before going to sleep that they will remember their dreams, they lie quietly after waking up, they let their thoughts wander—this helps them to recall all of their dreaming.

Theories

Some psychologists assume dreams express desires and thoughts that may be unacceptable to the conscious mind. Therapists who interpret and analyze dreams assume that dreams represent some element of a person that is seeking expression. The meaning of a dream will depend on a psychologist's orientation. Some see much symbolism in dreams and assert that the overt content of the dream hides the true meaning. Other psychologists find dreams meaningless.

Freud. Sigmund Freud made his position on dreams very clear: he described dreams as "the royal road to the unconscious." For Freud, a dream expressed desires, wishes, and unfulfilled needs that exist in the unconscious. In his book *The Interpretation of Dreams* (1900), Freud spoke about the manifest and latent content of dreams. The **manifest content** of a dream is its overt storyline, characters, and setting; it is the obvious, clearly discernible events of a dream. The **latent content** of a dream is its deeper meaning, usually involving symbolism, hidden content, and repressed or obscured ideas and wishes—often uncomfortable ones. You will see in chapters 12 and 15 that Freud uses dreams extensively in his theory of personality and in his treatment approach. Freudian psychoanalysts use dream analysis as a therapeutic tool in the treatment of emotional disturbance. Many contemporary therapists use patients' dreams to understand current problems and may see the dream only as a jumping-off point. They see the overt content of a dream, the part easily remembered, as only a topic not fully analyzed in day-to-day experience that needs to be addressed.

Jung. Carl G. Jung (1875–1961) was trained in Freudian approaches to therapy and personality analysis, and he too considered the dream a crucial way to understand human nature. But Jung, more than Freud, focused on the meaning of dreams and took for granted the idea that a dream was nature's

Lucid dream: A dream in which people are aware of their dreaming while it is happening.

Manifest content: Overt storyline, characters, and setting of a dream; the obvious, clearly discernible events of a dream.

Latent content: Deeper meaning, usually involving symbolism, hidden content, and repressed or obscured ideas and wishes of a dream.

way of communicating with the unconscious. Each thing a person dreams has a meaning, so dreams are the language through which an individual expresses his or her deepest feelings in an uncensored form. The dream gives visual expression to a person's instinct. Jungian therapy focuses on dream analysis as an approach to understanding the human condition. We will consider Jung in more detail in chapter 12.

Activation-Synthesis. Two researchers from Harvard Medical School, Allan Hobson and Robert McCarley, believe dreams have a physiological basis (1977). They argue that during periods of REM sleep, the parts of the brain responsible for long term memory, vision, audition, and perhaps even emotion are spontaneously stimulated (activated) from cells in the hindbrain, especially the pons. The cortex tries to make some sense out of the messages (synthesis). Because this activity is not organized by any external stimuli, the resulting dream is often fragmented and incoherent (Hobson, 1989).

The activation-synthesis model necessitates the involvement of the cortex in dreams. The theory is supported by researchers who assert that during sleep the brain (especially the cortex) scans previous memories, refreshes old storage mechanisms, and keeps active memory. But other researchers point out that dreamlike activity occurs even when cells in the pons are not active. This controversial approach is still being actively researched.

Focus on Learning

+ When do dreams occur during the night? p. 130
+ What is a lucid dream? p. 131
+ What did Freud mean when he said that dreams were the "royal road to the unconscious"? p. 131

Controlling Consciousness: Biofeedback, Hypnosis, and Meditation

Can people actually control their consciousness? Can they manipulate their mental states to achieve certain bodily reactions? There are research and anecdotal data to suggest that they can. People have long been taught to relax and breathe deeply when they are in pain. People have long known that races have been won through intense concentration that allowed human beings to endure especially difficult circumstances. Laboratory research also shows that people can bring some bodily states under conscious control through a technique called biofeedback.

Psychology and Medicine: Biofeedback

Imagine a special clinic that teaches people to treat themselves for such ailments as headaches, nearsightedness, high blood pressure, and stress-related illness. By learning to influence consciously what are normally involuntary actions, patients can cure themselves. Such a psychological-medical clinic may exist in the future if biofeedback proves to be the healing tool some researchers predict it will be.

Physicians and psychologists have traditionally assumed that most biological functions, especially those involving the autonomic nervous system, cannot be voluntarily controlled except through drugs or surgery. In the last two decades, however, studies with **biofeedback** have explored the extent to which subjects can learn to control their bodily functions—and thus behavior—by monitoring their neuronal (brain-wave) activity and other physiological responses. A well-known psychologist, Neal Miller, was one of the first researchers to train rats to control certain glandular responses. Miller (1969) suggested that the same techniques could be used to help human beings manage their bodies and behavior. Since then, studies have shown that human beings can manipulate the electrical activity of their bodies by changing their level of excitation.

A relaxed person viewing alpha waves on an oscilloscope, for example, can change those alpha waves to high-frequency waves by becoming more alert and paying attention. Similarly, a subject whose heart rate is displayed on an oscilloscope can watch the rate decrease as he or she relaxes, thereby learning what physiological states allow the body to work easily and efficiently. The person can learn which behaviors relax the heart muscles and lower blood pressure and in time can learn to control them by reproducing behaviors associated with reduced heart rate.

Some researchers (e.g., Drennen and Holden, 1984) contend that biofeedback training is not effective, but others have used it successfully to treat people with stress-related symptoms, hyperactivity, stuttering, depression, nearsightedness, and learning disabilities. For example, Dietvorst (1978) successfully used biofeedback to help recent heart attack victims reduce their anxiety and fear of the future. He trained subjects to decrease their level of arousal, and thus their level of anxiety, by monitoring one measure of their autonomic activity, hand temperature.

Although a number of laboratory studies have demonstrated biofeedback's effectiveness in helping people manage a wide range of problems, only carefully controlled research will ultimately answer persistent questions about its long-term effects. Few physicians use biofeedback in their practices today (Weinman, Mathew, and Claghorn, 1982), but biofeedback may be incorporated into medical and mental health plans in the future. There are still many issues to be resolved in biofeedback. For example, under what conditions, with what types of problems, and with what type of clients is biofeedback effective? Methodological issues, such as those described in chapter 1 (Hawthorne Effects, for example) make this a challenging research area.

Through biofeedback, people attempt to learn how to control what are normally involuntary actions.

Hypnosis

"You are falling asleep. Your eyelids are becoming heavy. The strain on your eyes is becoming greater and greater. Your muscles are relaxing. You are feeling sleepier and sleepier. You are feeling very relaxed."

These instructions are typical of those used in *hypnotic induction*, that is, the process used to hypnotize people. The generally accepted view of **hypnosis** is that individuals are in a semi-mystical or altered state of consciousness and no longer have control over their behavior. They are aware of their surroundings and are conscious, but their level of awareness and willingness to follow instructions are altered. A person's willingness to follow unconventional instructions, such as acting out, making funny noises, and doing what he or she is told by the hypnotist, is called **hypnotic susceptibility** or **suggestibility.** Most people can be hypnotized to some extent (Hilgard, 1965); children between seven and fourteen are the most susceptible; those who daydream for recreation are also especially susceptible (Hoyt et al., 1989).

Biofeedback: The general technique by which individuals can monitor and learn to control the involuntary activity of certain organs and bodily functions.

Hypnosis: An altered state of consciousness brought about by trance-induction procedures. Subjects' responsiveness to a hypnotist's suggestions increases as they become more deeply hypnotized.

Hypnotic susceptibility: The willingness to follow unconventional instructions while under hypnosis.

Age regression: The ability, sometimes induced by hypnosis, to return to an earlier time in one's life and report events that occurred.

Effects of Hypnosis. People who have been hypnotized report that they know they have been hypnotized and are aware of their surroundings. Some report a special, almost mystical state, and most report a sense of time distortion (Bowers, 1979). A time distortion effect of hypnosis is **age regression,** the ability to report details about an experience that took place many years earlier, or to be and feel like a child. Since few studies reporting age regression during hypnosis have been controlled for accuracy of recall, the authenticity of age regression has been questioned (Nash, 1987). *Heightened memory* is another effect of hypnosis. Evidence indicates that hypnosis helps subjects recall information (e.g., McConkey and Kinoshita, 1988). But techniques that do not involve hypnosis may work just as well for this purpose.

In a study by Putnam (1979), hypnotized and nonhypnotized subjects were asked to recall events they had seen earlier on a videotape. Hypnotized subjects made more errors when answering leading questions than nonhypnotized subjects. Putnam suggests that hypnotized subjects not only make more errors (misrecollection), but they mistakenly believe their memories to be accurate (McConkey and Kinoshita, 1988). These results have led researchers to question the use of hypnosis in courtroom settings (Smith, 1983), and many states do not allow the testimony of hypnotized subjects as evidence (Sanders and Simmons, 1983).

A third effect of hypnosis is pain reduction. In a case reported by E. F. Siegel (1979), hypnosis successfully reduced lower-leg pain in a woman who had undergone an above-the-knee amputation. (This phenomenon, called *phantom pain*, is apparent in some amputees.) Hypnosis has also been used to reduce pain from heat, pressure, and childbirth. Few studies of pain management, however, are conducted with adequate experimental rigor. Most patients showed signs of pain even when hypnotized. And in many cases, analgesic drugs (pain relievers) were used along with hypnotism. Some researchers (especially Barber, considered next) challenge the ability of hypnosis to reduce pain and reason that relaxation and a subject's positive attitude and lowered anxiety account for reported reductions in pain.

Cognitive-Behavioral Viewpoint. Theodore Xenophon Barber, one of the major skeptics of traditional theories of hypnotism, contends that the concepts of hypnosis and the hypnotic trance are meaningless and misleading. According to Barber, behaviors of hypnotized subjects are no different from behaviors of subjects willing to think about and imagine themes suggested to them. If subjects' attitudes toward the situation lead them to expect certain effects, those effects will be more likely to occur. Barber's approach is called the *cognitive-behavioral viewpoint* (Barber, Spanos, and Chaves, 1974).

Barber's studies show that subjects given task-motivating instructions perform similarly to subjects undergoing hypnotic induction. More than fifty percent of the subjects in experimental groups showed responsiveness to task suggestions, in contrast to sixteen percent in the control groups who were given no special instructions. From the results, Barber concluded that task-motivation instructions are almost as effective as hypnotic-induction procedures in increasing subjects' responsiveness to task suggestions.

Barber's studies have received support from other research. Salzberg and DePiano (1980), for example, found that hypnosis did not facilitate performance more than task-motivation instructions did. In fact, they argued that for cognitive tasks, task-motivating instruction is more effective than hypnosis. The evidence showing that hypnosis-like effects can be achieved in various ways (e.g., Bryant and McConkey, 1989) does not mean psychologists must discard the concept or use of hypnosis. It means that they should reconsider traditional assumptions.

Hypnosis continues to be widely used as an aid in therapy. Most clients report that it is a pleasant experience; therapists assert that in some cases it can be an important mechanism to help focus clients' energy on a specific topic, it can be an aid in memory, and it can help children cope with the aftereffects of child abuse. Many therapists use hypnosis to change behavior, including helping patients relax, remember, reduce stress and anxiety, lose weight, and stop smoking. Research into the process of hypnosis and its effects continues with an emphasis on defining critical variables in hypnosis and in subjects who are most and least easily hypnotized (e.g., Spanos, Perlini, and Robertson, 1989) as well as potential negative effects (e.g., Owens et al., 1989). Psychologists who are skeptical about hypnosis may have the same attitude toward another closely related practice, meditation.

> **Meditation:** A state of consciousness induced by a variety of techniques and characterized by concentration, restriction of sensory stimuli, and deep relaxation.

Meditation

Despite prescription drugs and frequent doctor visits, Carolyn found little relief from the searing migraines, stomach pains, and high blood pressure that afflicted her during stressful periods. Then, in a stress-management clinic, Carolyn discovered how to ease her tensions through meditation. Now, instead of popping a pill, she meditates at the onset of a headache.

Meditation involves intense concentration, restriction of incoming stimuli, and deep relaxation to produce a sense of detachment. Meditation has been used for centuries to alter consciousness and help relieve health problems. Practitioners report that it can reduce anxiety, tension from headaches, backaches, asthma, and the need for sleep. It can also increase self-awareness and feelings of inner peace (West, 1980, 1982).

There are several forms of meditation, each using different techniques to induce an altered state of awareness (Delmonte, 1983). They all direct the focus of attention away from the outside world by using intense concentration (Schuman, 1980). The forms of meditation now practiced in the Western world derive from the Eastern religions of Buddhism and Hinduism. Zen, yoga, and transcendental meditation are especially popular among people interested in holistic health.

People using Zen Buddhist techniques concentrate on their breathing and count their breaths with the aim of focusing attention very carefully on a specific stimulus. People using yoga focus their attention by gazing at a

Yoga uses physical and mental exercises to alleviate stress.

fixed stimulus. Yoga also involves special physical and breathing exercises with attempts to control autonomic physiological processes such as heart rate and blood pressure; yoga may also require a special seating position. Those using transcendental meditation use techniques similar to those of yoga and may repeat a phrase over and over to themselves, although they do not have to meditate in a specific posture.

Supporters of meditation claim that it is a unique state, capable of causing profound physiological and psychological changes. But a study comparing the physiological responses of meditators with those of hypnotized subjects found them to be nearly identical (Holmes, 1984). Experimental studies also show that individuals trained to simply relax and concentrate have been able to achieve bodily states similar to those of meditators (Fenwick et al., 1977).

Although most theories that explain the nature of meditation and its effects rely on concepts that are not scientifically measurable or observable, some controlled studies have been done. The data from these studies have shown that meditators can alter physiological responses, including oxygen consumption, brain-wave activity, and sleep patterns (Pagano et al., 1976). Follow-up studies of those who use self-hypnosis or meditation to relieve stress found that it continues to exert beneficial effects among those who continue its practice (Soskis, Orne, Orne, and Dinges, 1989). Such evidence encourages some scientists to continue to investigate meditation for relieving tension, anxiety, and arousal.

Focus on Learning

- How is biofeedback used to treat various disorders? p. 132
- Describe three effects of hypnosis. p. 133
- Identify the key point of view in the cognitive-behavioral approach to hypnosis. p. 134
- What are the key effects of meditation? p. 135

Substance Abuse

Each year for the last decade, physicians wrote more than two billion prescriptions for drugs. In the 1980s, almost fifty million prescriptions were written yearly for the tranquilizer diazepam (Valium). At least one-third of all U.S. citizens between the ages of eighteen and seventy-four regularly use some kind of consciousness altering drug that changes both brain activity and daily behavior.

In the United States, people consume caffeine-laden coffee and cola drinks, inhale nicotine, and drink beer, wine, and other alcoholic beverages daily. Although many of these drugs are not considered dangerous, they are far more potent than you may think. A **drug** is any chemical substance that alters normal biological processes. Many widely used drugs are both psychoactive and addictive. A **psychoactive drug** alters behavior, thought, or emotions; such drugs affect behavior by altering biochemical reactions in the nervous system, and this affects consciousness.

Whenever a behavior is a repetitive action or habit that increases the risk of disease or social or personal problems, psychologists consider it an **addictive behavior**. This includes a whole array of behaviors such as gambling, overeating, sexual disorders, and especially substance abuse. Substance abuse usually causes a loss of control, despite a person's attempt to control it. There are often short-term rewards (such as feeling good), followed by long-term deleterious effects (such as memory loss or kidney damage).

Drug: Any chemical substance that alters normal biological processes.

Psychoactive drug: A drug that alters behavior, thought, or emotions; a psychoactive drug affects behavior by altering biochemical reactions.

Addictive behavior: A repetitive action or habit that increases the risk of disease or social or personal problems.

Substance Use and Abuse

There is no doubt that the United States is a drug culture. We use drugs to help us wake up in the morning, to get us through stresses in the day, and to help us sleep. Drugs may be legal or illegal; they may be used responsibly or abused with tragic consequences. In studying substance use, we have to consider the drug itself, its properties, and the context of its use. Not all people respond in the same way to the same drug, and one person may respond differently on different occasions. Does the drug produce dependence? And, finally, are there adverse reactions to the drug for the user, other people, or society (Newcomb and Bentler, 1989)?

There is no single explanation for substance abuse. Societal factors, individual family situations, medical problems, and genetic heritage are all potentially part of a person's reason for abusing drugs. Issues of use and abuse become more sharply delineated when we look at children who have to sort out the conflicting messages our society delivers. Newcomb and Bentler argue:

> Adolescents are quite adept at spotting hypocrisy and may have difficulty understanding a policy of "saying no to drugs" when suggested by a society that clearly says "yes" to the smorgasbord of drugs that are legal as well as the range of illicit drugs that are widely available and used (1989, p. 242).

Who Are the Substance Abusers?

Complex reasons determine why people overuse and rely on drugs; when people do so we call them **substance abusers.** Most of these people turn to alcohol and readily available drugs such as cocaine and marijuana, but substance abuse is not confined to these drugs. Psychologists are seeing a growing number of people abusing legal drugs, such as tranquilizers and diet pills, as well as illegal drugs, such as amphetamines and heroin. A person is a substance abuser if:

1. the substance has been used for at least one month
2. the substance use has caused legal difficulties or social or vocational problems
3. there is recurrent use in hazardous situations such as driving a car.

Substance abuse can lead to psychological dependence, pathological use, or both. **Psychological dependence** is a compelling desire to use the drug, along with an inability to inhibit that desire. **Pathological use** refers to out-of-control episodes, such as an alcohol binge. Most drugs produce a physiological reaction when they are no longer administered; this reaction is generally called **dependence.** Without the drug, a dependent person suffers from **withdrawal symptoms**—physical reactions that may include headaches, nausea, and an intense craving for the withheld drug.

In addition, **addictive** drugs usually produce **tolerance,** a progressive insensitivity to repeated use of the drug in the same dosage. Tolerance forces an addict to use an increasingly greater amount of the drug to achieve the same effect. Alcoholics must consume larger amounts of alcohol to become drunk. Most addictive drugs produce both withdrawal symptoms and tolerance. Whenever a person shows evidence of substance abuse and withdrawal symptoms or tolerance, the person is exhibiting **substance dependence.**

Substance abusers: People who overuse and rely on drugs to deal with their stress and anxiety.

Psychological dependence: A compelling desire to use a drug along with an inability to inhibit that desire.

Pathological use: Out-of-control episodes, such as extensive periods of substance abuse, perhaps for days on end.

Dependence: Reliance on regular use of a drug, without which the individual suffers a psychological or physiological reaction, or both.

Withdrawal symptoms: A variety of physical states that occur when a drug is no longer administered to a person who has developed a physiological dependence on it.

Addictive: Causing a compulsive physiological need. Withholding an addictive drug produces withdrawal symptoms. Addictive drugs usually produce tolerance.

Tolerance: A state of progressive insensitivity to the effects of a specific drug and dosage when that drug is administered repeatedly.

Substance dependence: A state in which there is evidence of substance abuse and withdrawal symptoms or tolerance.

Each time people take a drug, they change their ability to function normally. Specifically, drugs change behavior by altering physiology and the normal state of consciousness. Some drugs increase alertness and performance; others relax people and relieve high levels of arousal and tension. Some produce physical and psychological dependence. But all drugs alter a person's thoughts and mood; they are all considered consciousness altering.

Illicit drug use dropped during the late 1980s for most drugs except cocaine. This is probably in response to national media campaigns, school- and community-based drug programs, and interventions in the workplace. But drug abuse is still a major problem, with millions of people using illicit drugs on a regular basis (U.S. Dept. of Health and Human Services, 1989).

Why Do People Abuse Drugs?

There are physiological and psychological reasons for drug abuse. Some people are considered high-risk—they are more likely to develop a substance abuse problem for physiological and genetic reasons. Others are victims of the numerous emotional problems caused by stress—boredom, loneliness, despair, anxiety. Sadly, many people believe alcohol and drugs provide a quick fix for these problems. People may turn to drugs to relax, be sociable, forget their worries, feel confident, or lose weight. Parental drug use, peer drug use, poor self-esteem, stressful life changes, divorce, poverty, and social isolation have all been implicated. Our society and its materialistic values also contribute to the problem.

Most researchers argue that no single explanation can account for drug use and abuse (Marlatt et al., 1988). Few substance abusers have similar abuse patterns. Some people use alcohol or only one drug. Others are *polydrug* abusers and take several drugs. A polydrug abuser who is a heroin addict, for example, might also take amphetamines. When amphetamines are difficult to obtain, he or she might switch to barbiturates. Kitty Dukakis, wife of 1988 Democratic presidential candidate Michael Dukakis, fought off an amphetamine addiction only to face alcohol addiction. Some researchers assert that many people are addiction prone (Sutker and Allain, 1988); they assert that later addictive behavior can even be predicted from antisocial childhood behavior (Nathan, 1988).

Focus on Learning

◆ What are the properties of a psychoactive drug? p. 136
◆ What defines a person as a substance abuser? p. 137
◆ Describe a polydrug abuser. p. 138

Altered Consciousness with Drugs

Drugs are often categorized by their effects on human behavior and by their chemical makeup. A wide range of substances are abused, and their effects and chemical compositions vary extensively. To understand drug abuse and its relationship to consciousness, researchers must consider the physiological effects of the drug, the social setting in which the drug is used, and the personal factors and physiological makeup of the addict.

All the drugs discussed here are capable of creating a dependence that can alter the course of a person's life and dismantle a normal family structure.

Drug abuse has been under the critical eye of psychologists, physicians, politicians, and law enforcement officials for many years. Education programs for young people, designed to prevent abuse, are generally thought to be the most effective solution, and communication training and family therapy are often important adjuncts.

Alcohol Use and Abuse

Sedatives-hypnotics are drugs that relax and calm people, and in higher doses, induce sleep. The most widely used sedative-hypnotic is alcohol. Even conservative people who do not think of themselves as drug users often turn to alcohol. Alcohol is used by thousands of people to help relieve stress. As a depressant, alcohol helps people rid themselves of tension and anxiety, to move from a state of active consciousness to one in which they do not have tension, but are less aware and alert. After several drinks, they may behave in erratic, irrational ways that are dangerous both for themselves and others around them.

Because alcohol is easily available, relatively inexpensive, and socially accepted, addiction to the drug is easy to establish and maintain. In fact, most U.S. inhabitants consider some alcohol consumption appropriate; they often consume alcoholic beverages before, during, and after dinner, at weddings and funerals, at religious events, and during sports events.

Statistics. Alcohol consumption in the United States has been at an all-time high for more than a decade. According to the Department of Health and Human Services, about 80 percent of urban U.S. adults report having used alcohol at some time. It is estimated that 10 million people in the United States over age eighteen are problem drinkers or alcoholics (Barnes, 1988). Most studies of alcoholics have been with men. Those studies that focus on women show that they are much less likely than men to develop an alcohol addiction, possibly because they drink less frequently and in smaller amounts than men (Wilsnack, Wilsnack, and Klassen, 1986).

Effects. Alcohol is absorbed into the bloodstream from the stomach and small intestines. In general, alcohol, which is a central nervous system depressant, decreases inhibitions and thus increases some behaviors that are normally under tight control. It takes away people's fears. The effects of alcohol vary with the amount of alcohol in the bloodstream and the weight and gender of the user (see Table 4.2 on page 140). After equal amounts of alcohol consumption, women have higher blood alcohol levels than men do, even with allowance for differences in body weight (Frezza et al., 1990). Table 4.3 on page 141 shows various blood alcohol levels and the behavior associated with them.

With increasing amounts of alcohol in the bloodstream, people typically exhibit progressively slowed behavior; often they exhibit severe motor disturbances, such as staggering. Blood alcohol levels greater than .10 percent usually indicate that the person has consumed too much alcohol to function responsibly. In most states, a .10 percent blood alcohol level legally defines intoxication; police officers may arrest drivers who have this level of blood alcohol.

The nervous system becomes less sensitive to, or accommodates, alcohol with increased usage. After months or years of drinking, a person has to consume ever increasing amounts of alcohol to achieve the same effect. Thus

Sedatives-hypnotics: A class of drugs that relax and calm people and in higher doses induce sleep.

TABLE 4.2
Relationships between Alcohol Consumption and Blood Alcohol Level, by Gender and Weight

Absolute Alcohol (oz.)	Beverage Intake in 1 Hour	Blood Alcohol Levels (mg/100 ml)					
		Female (100 lbs.)	Male (100 lbs.)	Female (150 lbs.)	Male (150 lbs.)	Female (200 lbs.)	Male (200 lbs.)
1/2	1 oz. spirits* 1 glass wine 1 can beer	.045	.037	.03	.025	.022	.019
1	2 oz. spirits 2 glasses wine 2 cans beer	.090	.075	.06	.050	.045	.037
2	4 oz. spirits 4 glasses wine 4 cans beer	.180	.150	.12	.100	.090	.070
3	6 oz. spirits 6 glasses wine 6 cans beer	.270	.220	.18	.150	.130	.110
4	8 oz. spirits 8 glasses wine 8 cans beer	.360	.300	.24	.200	.180	.150
5	10 oz. spirits 10 glasses wine 10 cans beer	.450	.370	.30	.250	.220	.180

* All spirits are assumed to be 100 proof.

when not in an alcoholic state, a heavy drinker develops anxiety, cravings, and other withdrawal symptoms (Levin, 1990). When people exhibit such dependency and withdrawal symptoms we say that they are having alcohol-related problems and are probably alcoholics.

Problem Drinkers versus Alcoholics. Alcohol-related problems are medical, social, or psychological problems associated with alcohol use. A person who shows an alcohol-related problem, such as missing work occasionally, spending a paycheck to buy drinks for friends, or losing his or her driver's license because of drunk driving, is said to be involved in *alcohol abuse*. Alcohol-related problems may include a deteriorating liver condition, memory loss, and significant mood swings (Nace, 1987). Thirty-six percent of U.S. inhabitants eighteen and older who drink are potential problem drinkers. The percentage is higher for men (forty-four percent) than for women (twenty-seven percent) and for people eighteen to twenty than for those in any other age group.

A person with alcohol-related problems who also has a physiological and psychological need to consume alcoholic products and experience their effects is an **alcoholic.** All alcoholics are problem drinkers, but not all problem drinkers are alcoholics (Wanberg and Horn, 1983). Without alcohol, alcoholics develop physiological withdrawal symptoms. In addition, they often develop tolerance, whereby a single drink or even a few will not affect them. Alcoholics are often unable to face the world without alcohol.

Social and Medical Problems. From both a medical and psychological standpoint, alcohol abuse is one of the greatest social problems in the United

Alcoholic: A problem drinker who also has a physiological and psychological need to consume alcohol and experience its effects.

TABLE 4.3
Behavioral Effects of Various Blood Alcohol Levels

Percentage of Blood Alcohol	Behavioral Effects
.05	Lowered alertness, impaired judgment, release of inhibitions, good feelings
.10	Slowed reaction times and impaired motor function, less caution
.15	Large, consistent increases in reaction time
.20	Marked depression in sensory and motor capability, decidedly intoxicated behavior
.25	Severe motor disturbance and impairment of sensory perceptions
.30	Stuporous but conscious—no comprehension of events in the environment
.35	Surgical anesthesia; lethal dose for about 1 percent of the population
.40	Lethal dose for about 50 percent of the population

States. Drunkenness is the biggest law enforcement problem today, accounting for millions of arrests each year. The Department of Transportation has estimated that alcohol is involved in more than 28,000 automobile deaths and more than 80,000 automobile accidents each year. In addition, more often than not, people involved in violent crimes and suicide are found to have been drinking.

Although alcoholism is seen as a social disease because of its devastating social consequences, it is also a medical problem. Biomedical researchers look for the effects of alcohol on the brain, as well as anything about the brains of alcoholics that may predispose them to alcoholism. Researchers know that chronic excessive drinking is associated with loss of brain tissue, liver malfunctions, and impaired cognitive and motor abilities (e.g., Ellis and Oscar-Berman, 1989).

Looking at alcoholism as a medical problem shifts the focus toward treatment and away from moral issues. That is, it allows people to view the problem as treatable from both a medical and psychological perspective (Nace, 1987). Consequently, alcoholism is widely recognized as a major health problem, and millions of federal dollars are spent on the treatment of alcoholism. Very little money, however, is spent on prevention.

Teenagers, Drinking, and Driving. Alcohol is the drug of choice among teenagers. In a recent survey, about one-fourth of eighth-grade students and more than one-third of tenth-grade students reported having had five or more drinks on at least one occasion during the past two weeks (Landers, 1988b). A critical problem associated with teenage drinking is driving while intoxicated (DWI). The motor vehicle is the number one killer of Americans aged fifteen to nineteen. And nearly fifty percent of all car deaths in the United States involve drinking. Although teenagers drink and drive less often than older drivers do, their risk of a crash is higher (Williams, 1986); because teenagers are relatively inexperienced both as drivers and as drinkers, they are at higher risk for accidents.

The liver at the top is normal. Excessive alcohol consumption has caused the middle liver to be fatty and unhealthy and the liver at the bottom to be cirrhotic.

Even though drinking and driving is widespread, most teenagers recognize the dangers. One national survey found that forty-four percent of teenagers surveyed would like to see the restrictions for obtaining a driver's license made tighter. Laws are, in fact, being tightened. Most states have raised their drinking age to twenty-one to try to keep alcohol out of the schools, but with limited success. Drunk driving remains a national problem. Socially-oriented political groups like MADD (Mothers Against Drunk Drivers) and SADD (Students Against Drunk Drivers) have begun to exert pressure on both the local and national levels and are effecting changes, but these changes are slow in coming.

Causes. The causes of alcoholism are complex; heredity, parental alcohol abuse, societal pressures, and antisocial behavior are only some. There is no single personality type for all alcoholics, and alcoholism cuts across socioeconomic lines (Graham and Strenger, 1988). Researchers know that alcoholism runs in families. A son of an alcoholic parent is four times more likely to develop alcoholism than a son of a nonalcoholic parent. If that son is involved in criminal behavior as well, he is far more likely to become an alcoholic himself. Nevertheless, about 60 percent of alcohol abusers are from families in which no other member shows signs of abuse (Cadoret, Troughton, and O'Gorman, 1987).

Treatment. For some alcoholics, psychological and medical treatment is successful. The most widely known program is Alcoholics Anonymous, which helps individuals abstain from alcohol by providing a therapeutic and emotionally warm environment. Begun in 1935, Alcoholics Anonymous includes 600,000 members, and its success rate is considerably better than that of many other treatment programs. Programs such as Alcoholics Anonymous make abstinence their goal. The fundamental assumptions, based on the difficulty alcoholics have controlling their drinking, are that an alcoholic is an alcoholic forever and that alcoholism should be considered disease-like in nature and thus incurable (Peele, 1984).

Some practitioners, on the other hand, believe that limited, non-problem drinking should be the goal of treatment programs (Vaillant and Milofsky, 1982). This view assumes that alcohol abuse is a learned behavior and can therefore be unlearned. It also assumes that abstinence is an unattainable goal. Those who prefer controlled use claim that alcohol abuse is merely a symptom of a larger underlying problem such as poor self-esteem and family instability (Sobell and Sobell, 1982). However, most researchers hold that controlled drinking is not a reliable answer for most alcoholics, although it might be a reasonable alternative for young, heavy drinkers who are not yet alcoholics (Nathan and Skinstad, 1987).

Family therapy is generally considered an important part of treatment for alcoholism because one family member's problem with alcohol becomes a problem for the entire family. A multi-modal approach is often the best treatment plan; that is, combining individual or group therapy with Alcoholics Anonymous or some other self-help group (Levin, 1990). Few systematic, carefully controlled studies of alcoholism and procedures for its treatment exist. Some researchers are investigating the use of drugs and behavioral therapies to control alcohol intake (e.g., Weins and Menustik, 1983; Wilson, 1987). Others are studying detoxification centers and halfway houses as treatments for alcoholics. Still others are examining who is at risk—who is likely to become an alcoholic. Table 4.4 lists the warning signs of alcoholism.

TABLE 4.4
Warning Signals of Alcoholism

The following are some of the warning signals that a drinking problem is developing:
You drink more than you used to and tend to gulp your drinks.
You try to have a few extra drinks before or after drinking with others.
You have begun to drink alone.
You are noticeably drunk on important occasions.
You drink the "morning after" to overcome the effects of previous drinking.
You drink to relieve feelings of boredom, depression, anxiety, or inadequacy.
You have begun to drink at certain times, to get through difficult situations, or when you have problems.
You have weekend drinking bouts and Monday hangovers.
You are beginning to lose control of your drinking; you drink more than you planned and get drunk when you did not want to.
You promise to drink less but do not.
You often regret what you have said or done while drinking.
You are beginning to feel guilty about your drinking.
You are sensitive when others mention your drinking.
You have begun to deny your drinking or lie about it.
You have memory blackouts or pass out while drinking.
Your drinking is affecting your relationship with friends or family.
You have lost time at work or school because of drinking.
You begin to stay away from people who do not drink.

Who Is at Risk for Alcoholism?

THINKING ABOUT RESEARCH

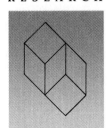

*A*re some people more likely to develop substance abuse problems such as alcoholism than other people? The answer is yes, according to researchers who study the biological side of alcoholism. Researchers have long asserted that genetics, blood and brain chemistry, and certain brain structures predispose certain people to alcoholism.

Correlational Studies. Some of the most interesting research on alcoholism comes from studies that focus on high-risk individuals—people who seem more at risk for a disorder. (For example, the culturally disadvantaged and the economically poor are at high risk for substance abuse because they often live in urban environments that expose them to street-wise drug dealers and crime.) Who is at high risk for alcoholism? Children of alcoholics are more likely to be alcoholics, even if they are raised by nonalcoholic, adoptive parents. The correlations suggest that genetics may be a key factor in the development of alcoholism. Further, psychologists have speculated that there may be something about the physiology of alcoholics and their children that predispose them to alcoholism.

Experimental Research. Studies have shown that alcoholics, more than nonalcoholics, tend to respond with physiological arousal to stress and other aversive stimulation. Finn and Pihl (1987), two McGill University researchers, decided to test the hypothesis that men with extensive family histories of alcoholism were more reactive physiologically to aversive stimulation than control subjects. Further, they attempted to see if alcohol reduces physiological responses more for men with a family history of alcoholism than for control subjects. Their overall aim was to find out if certain people are at high risk for alcoholism.

They divided men up into three groups based on family history: high, moderate, and low risk for alcoholism. The high-risk subjects had alcoholic fathers and grandfathers, and at least one other male alcoholic in the family. The moderate-risk subjects had one alcoholic parent, and no other close alcoholic relative. The low-risk subjects had no identifiable alcoholics in the two previous generations of their family trees.

Finn and Pihl investigated two physiological responses, heart rate and blood volume, of subjects who knew they were going to receive mild electrical shocks. Anticipating a shock induces a physiological response in nearly everybody. But are the responses more pronounced in high-risk subjects? Adding another dimension to the experiment, some subjects were given a moderate level of alcohol (the amount was adjusted for body weight) to bring blood alcohol to a level of 0.07. Would the high-risk subjects show more physiological reaction to the impending shock than the low-risk subjects? Would alcohol consumption affect the responses of the high-risk subjects more than it did those of the low-risk subjects?

Results. The results showed that sober high-risk subjects were more cardiovascularly reactive than sober moderate-risk subjects. In addition, alcohol consumption led to a reduction in physiological response in the high-risk group only. In the moderate- and low-risk groups, alcohol consumption increased physiological responses.

Conclusions and Implications. According to Finn and Pihl, when a strict criterion for selecting high-risk subjects is used, a different pattern of alcohol sensitivity may result than when a one-generation-alcoholic-father criterion is used. Men at high genetic risk for alcoholism in stressful situations show a consistent reduction in physiological responses when they consume alcohol. This finding suggests a genetic predisposition to be calmed by alcohol when faced with stressful or aversive stimulation. The researchers assert that a high-risk label should be assigned to an individual only if two prior generations have been considered. They were able to show a difference between the high-risk (two generations) and the moderate-risk (one generation) subjects when comparing them to control low-risk subjects. They extended their findings in another sample of subjects with a different task, lending support to their earlier findings (Finn, Zeitouni, and Pihl, 1990).

Place a man who is genetically at high risk for alcoholism in a stressful situation, provide that man with alcohol, and the reinforcing effects of stress reduction are likely to make alcohol a highly prized and rewarding substance. Some questions still remain to be answered. For example, are there high-risk, higher-risk, and extremely high-risk individuals? In addition, researchers could use other measures of reactivity that might be more sensitive. The research continues; this study is just one of hundreds that examine risk factors and the genetic side of alcoholism. ◆

Barbiturates and Tranquilizers

Most barbiturates and tranquilizers are considered to be in the class of drugs that relax and calm individuals, and often, when taken in higher doses, induce sleep. Like alcohol, they are in the class of sedative-hypnotics. Barbiturates decrease the excitability of neurons throughout the nervous system. They calm an individual by being a central nervous system depressant. Used as sedatives, drugs such as phenobarbital have largely been replaced by another class of drugs called *tranquilizers*.

Tranquilizers are a chemical class of drugs (technically, benzodiazepines) that sedate, calm, and relax people. With a somewhat lower potential for abuse and for central nervous system depression, they are sometimes called minor tranquilizers. Valium and librium are two of the most widely used tranquilizers prescribed by physicians for relief of mild stress. Such drugs have been widely abused by all segments of society because of their availability.

Narcotic drugs: Drugs with sedative properties that are addictive and produce tolerance.

Opiates: Heroin

Heroin is the most widely known derivative of opium, a drug that dulls the senses, relieves pain, tranquilizes, and induces euphoria. Most opiates are **narcotic drugs;** narcotic drugs generally have sedative properties, are addictive, and produce tolerance. Like many other addictive drugs, heroin is stimulating and considered biologically reinforcing; many researchers feel it is this reinforcing property that keeps people addicted (Wise and Bozarth, 1987).

In the past, opium has been used for everything from relieving children's crying to reducing pain from headaches, surgery, childbirth, and menstruation. Today, opium is illegal, but heroin and other opiates such as morphine (although illegal when not prescribed by a physician) are readily available on the street. The high cost of these drugs has led many addicts to crime to support their habits.

Heroin can be smoked or eaten, but typically it is injected into a vein. Heroin addicts tend to be young, poor, and uneducated. Most become addicts as a result of peer pressure and a desire for upward mobility within their groups. Estimates of the number of heroin addicts vary dramatically from half a million to thirteen million active users. Heroin users often use other drugs, including alcohol, amphetamines, barbiturates, and cocaine, in combination with heroin. *Polydrug* use makes it difficult to classify heroin users as addicts of one drug or another. Moreover, even when classification is possible, treatment is complicated by the medical, psychological, and social problems associated with using many drugs simultaneously.

The major psychological effect of heroin is impaired functioning of the respiratory system. Other effects are some deleterious changes in the heart, arteries, and veins and possible constipation and loss of appetite. Few heroin addicts die of overdoses. A lethal dose of the drug would be much larger than that injected by even heavy users. More often than not, heroin addicts die from taking a mixture of drugs (such as heroin and alcohol) or from disease, especially AIDS, contracted from non-sterile needles and other paraphernalia used in injecting the substance into the bloodstream. Some lawmakers are advocating community programs to distribute sterile needles to drug users to prevent the spread of AIDS but, as you might expect, such programs are controversial.

The only major successful treatment program for heroin addiction is methadone maintenance. Like heroin, methadone is an addicting drug and must be consumed daily or withdrawal symptoms will occur. But unlike heroin, methadone does not produce euphoria or tolerance in the user, and daily dosages do not need to be increased. Because methadone blocks the effect of heroin, a normal injection of heroin has no effect on individuals

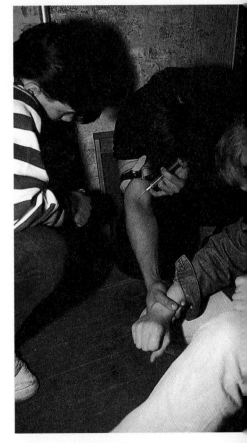

Peer pressure and unsatisfactory social and economic conditions often contribute to people's involvement in heroin use.

on a methadone maintenance program. As a result, methadone-treatment patients (there are about 100,000 such individuals) who might be tempted to use heroin to achieve a high do not do so. Moreover, because methadone is legal, many of the patients are able to hold jobs to support themselves and stay out of jail. Research suggests that methadone treatment combined with psychotherapy and behavior-modification techniques to reduce illicit drug use (Stitzer, 1988) may be far more effective than methadone by itself.

Marijuana

Consciousness-altering drugs that affect moods, thoughts, memory, and perception are called *psychedelics,* or *hallucinogens.* Perhaps the most widely used is marijuana. Because of its widespread use (nearly twenty percent of the population has tried it), we will examine it in more detail.

Marijuana is the dried leaves and flowering tops of the *cannabis sativa* plant whose active ingredient is **THC, tetrahydrocannabinol.** Marijuana can be ingested, but in the United States it is most commonly smoked. It is interesting to note that smoking marijuana is inefficient because twenty to eighty percent of the active ingredient, THC, is lost in the smoke.

In the 1800s, marijuana was used as pain relief for everything from toothaches to childbirth in the United States. Not until the early twentieth century did people begin to fear the potential hazards of its use. The 1930s witnessed the passage of strict laws prohibiting the possession or sale of marijuana. Marijuana was virtually forgotten until it was rediscovered by young people in the 1960s. Since then, it has become one of the most widely used illegal drugs in the United States. More than twenty million adults have used marijuana; nearly ten percent of high school seniors use it daily, and fifty percent have tried it (U.S. Department of Health and Human Services, 1988).

People smoke marijuana to alter their consciousness, alleviate depression, or just as a distraction. Some users report a sense of elation and well-being; others assert that it induces psychoses. And some report adverse reactions such as sleeplessness, bad dreams, and nausea. Marijuana's effects are felt about one minute after smoking, begin to diminish within an hour, and disappear almost completely after three to five hours, although traces of THC can be detected in the body for weeks afterward.

Individuals under the influence of marijuana demonstrate impaired performance on simple intellectual and psychomotor tasks. They become less task oriented and have slower reaction times. Marijuana also interferes with memory. Little is known about how marijuana affects fetal development or its long-term effects on people who use it from early adolescence to middle age. Marijuana has been used extensively only since the late 1960s; it will take a couple of generations before we know all of its long-term effects.

Although researchers agree that marijuana is not physiologically addictive like heroin, many argue that it produces psychological dependence. People become dependent on marijuana for a variety of reasons. One is that it is more easily available than substances such as barbiturates and cocaine. Another is the desired relief of tension that marijuana users experience. Further, most people believe that the drug has few, if any, long-lasting side effects.

Despite considerable social acceptance of marijuana use in the United States, its sale or possession is still against the law in most states. In several

Smoking marijuana interferes with mental processes and the ability to perform simple psychomotor tasks.

THC (tetrahydrocannabinol): The active ingredient in marijuana.

states, **decriminalization** of marijuana has meant that possession is treated as a civil violation instead of a crime. There are no arrests, jail sentences, bail, or trials, but its use is still illegal. For the most part, laws against the sale or possession of marijuana have been ineffective, and the drug is widely available across the United States in both urban and rural areas. Another option, legalization, is even being considered by some experts (Nadleman, 1989), although few legislators take the idea seriously.

Decriminalization: The act of reducing the legal offense of an activity to that of a civil violation (such as a traffic violation).

Psychostimulant: A drug that in low to moderate doses increases alertness, reduces fatigue, and is considered a mood elevator.

Amphetamines and Cocaine

Amphetamines and cocaine are considered psychostimulants and are highly addictive. A **psychostimulant** is a drug that in low to moderate doses increases alertness, reduces fatigue, and is considered a mood elevator. Acting on the central nervous system, *amphetamines* are a chemical grouping of drugs (such as Dexedrine) that increase excitability, depress appetite, and increase alertness and talkativeness. They increase blood pressure and heart rate. After long-term use, individuals have cravings for the drug and experience exhaustion, lethargy, and depression without it.

Cocaine was widely abused in the 1980s. At least fifteen percent of high school seniors have used cocaine at least once. Admissions to cocaine treatment centers have increased sharply, as have deaths associated with cocaine abuse. Crack, the processed and smokable form of cocaine, is also widely used; it is potent, and readily available (especially in the schools).

A central nervous system stimulant and an anesthetic, cocaine increases heartbeat, decreases appetite, and raises blood pressure. It is smoked, sniffed, or injected; when sniffed, it temporarily numbs the user's nasal passage. Sniffing it up the nostrils—snorting—is the most popular method of using cocaine. Once inhaled, it is absorbed into the tiny blood vessels that line the nose. Within five minutes a user starts to feel the effects; the peak effect is in fifteen minutes and may last twenty to thirty minutes. The

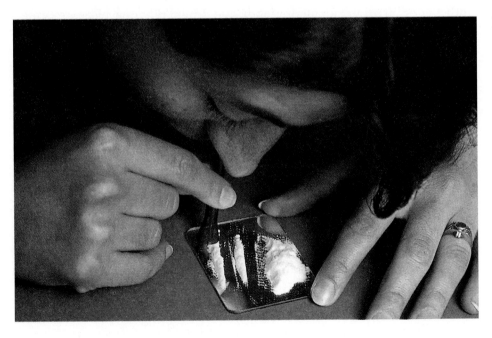

Cocaine and crack are highly addictive, yet became popular in the late 1980s despite the fact that their usage leads to an alarming range of dangerous consequences.

smokable form of cocaine, crack, delivers an unusually large dose and induces euphoria in a matter of seconds. Cocaine produces an exceptional high, but it is short lived and the user's mood drops rapidly. Since cocaine is soluble in water, it can also be injected; however, due to the concern about contracting AIDS through infected needles, such intravenous injections are now less common (Washton, 1989).

Cocaine acts on neurotransmitters in the brain such as norepinephrine and dopamine. It also stimulates sympathetic activity in the peripheral nervous system, causing increased heart rate, blood pressure, blood sugar, and dilation of the pupils. It produces a light-headed feeling, a sense of alertness, increased energy, and sometimes a sense of infallibility. People who use cocaine report feeling a sense of new confidence and self-worth, increased energy, increased awareness, and sexual arousal.

Why is cocaine use so prevalent in our society? First, cocaine acts as a powerful reward. For example, animals will work incessantly, even to the point of exhaustion, to obtain cocaine. A cocaine high is pleasurable, but also brief—users wish to repeat the sensation. When the cocaine wears off, it is replaced by unpleasant feelings (known as crashing). These unpleasant feelings can be alleviated through more cocaine. Second, cocaine produces tolerance and potent urges and cravings. Third, in our pleasure now, pay later society, instant gratification through drug use seems appropriate (Washton, 1989) to some people.

Cocaine is classified as a drug with high abuse potential and little medical value. The drug causes problems due to overdoses (heart attacks, hemorrhage, and heat stroke), due to complications associated with its administration (nose sores, lung damage, infection at injection sites, and AIDS), and due to its use during pregnancy (premature birth, malformations of the fetus, and spontaneous abortions). At a minimum, the drug is addictive, produces irritability, and eating and sleeping disturbances. It also seems to precipitate other disturbances such as panic attacks. Further, cocaine can produce serious mental disorders including paranoia, agitation, and suicidal behavior.

Treatment for cocaine addiction first requires getting the cocaine addict into therapy, providing a structured program, and making sure that the addict goes off all mood-altering addictive drugs. Blocking pleasure centers with a drug such as methadone is not realistic because cocaine works through most of the major neurotransmitter systems. If such a drug could be found, it would probably make the person spiritless. Because a drug treatment for this addiction is so hard to achieve, this places even more of a burden on psychological therapy. Treatment usually means a strong educational involvement, family involvement, group and individual therapy, and long-term follow-up—it is time intensive and expensive.

Nicotine

The most commonly abused substance after alcohol is tobacco. Nicotine, the active ingredient in tobacco, is considered a psychostimulant and is addicting. According to the surgeon general of the United States (1988), more than 300,000 people die prematurely each year because of illnesses such as lung cancer that are related to smoking. One third of thirty-five-year-old heavy smokers will die of diseases caused by their smoking (Mattson, Pollack, and Cullen, 1987).

With dozens of active chemicals in a cigarette, the reinforcing and addictive properties are not fully understood. Human beings respond in different ways to nicotine with both excitatory and inhibitory effects. As a conse-

TABLE 4.5
Commonly Abused Drugs

Type	Drug		Tolerance	Physiological Dependence
Sedatives	Alcohol	Reduces tension	yes	yes
	Barbiturates (e.g., Seconal)	Reduces tension and induces sleep	yes	yes
	Tranquilizers (e.g., Valium)	Alleviates tension and induces relaxation	yes	yes
Psychostimulants	Amphetamines	Increased feelings, feelings of alertness	yes	yes
	Cocaine	Increased alertness, decreased fatigue, stimulates sex drive	yes	yes
Narcotics	Opium Morphine Heroin	Alleviates pain and tension, achieves a high	yes	yes
Psychedelics	Marijuana	Changes in mood and perception	no	no

Note: Even though a drug may not produce physiological dependence, it may produce a psychological need that compels repeated use.

quence, quitting smoking is extremely difficult, and eighty percent of smokers who stop will relapse within one year (Schwartz, 1987); when they do quit, they are likely to gain weight (Klesges et al., 1989).

See Table 4.5 for an overall summary of the effects of commonly abused drugs.

- ◆ What are the effects of sedative-hypnotics on behavior? p. 139
- ◆ As a central nervous system depressant, alcohol has what effect on behavior? pp. 139–140
- ◆ What is *physiological reactivity*? pp. 143–144
- ◆ What are the properties of a narcotic drug? p. 145
- ◆ What are the principal risks of cocaine? p. 147

Focus on Learning

Key Terms

Summary

Consciousness

- Consciousness is a general awareness of and responsiveness to the environment. Consciousness can range from alert attention to altered states like dreaming, hypnosis, or drug-induced conditions.   p. 120

- Normal consciousness and altered states are linked to the ongoing biological processes in our bodies.   p. 121

Sleep

- Circadian rhythms are internally generated and help control our bodily rhythms and sleep patterns.   p. 122

- Recordings of sleeping subjects' EEGs have revealed five distinct patterns of electrical activity. Four are called no rapid eye movements (NREM) sleep states; the other pattern is called rapid eye movement (REM) sleep.   p. 124

- A full sleep cycle takes about ninety minutes, and thus five complete sleep cycles occur in an average night's sleep. Subjects deprived of REM sleep tend to catch up on subsequent nights.   p. 125

- If you snore loudly, sleepwalk, or fall asleep at inappropriate times (e.g., when driving a car) you may have a sleep disorder.   p. 128

Dreams

- A dream is a state of consciousness that occurs largely during REM sleep and is usually accompanied by visual imagery, although imagery may be tactile or auditory.   p. 130

- Most people dream four or five times a night. The first dream of a typical night occurs ninety minutes after you fall asleep and lasts for ten minutes.   pp. 130–131

- The manifest content of a dream is its overt storyline; the latent content of a dream is its deeper meaning.   p. 131

Controlling Consciousness: Biofeedback, Hypnosis, and Meditation

- Biofeedback studies have explored the extent to which subjects can learn to control their bodily functions and behavior by monitoring their neuronal activity.   p. 132

- Hypnosis is traditionally viewed as a special state of consciousness brought about by trance-induction methods. Hypnosis can produce special effects such as age regression.   p. 133

- Meditation has its roots in the Eastern religions of Buddhism and Hinduism. Those who practice it claim that it induces inner peace and tranquility.   p. 135

Substance Abuse

- Whenever a behavior is repetitive and increases the risk of disease or social or personal problems, psychologists consider it addictive.   p. 136

- A person is a *substance abuser* if: the substance has been used for at least one month; the substance use has caused legal difficulties or social or vocational problems; and there is recurrent use in hazardous situations.   p. 137

- Researchers agree that no single explanation can account for drug use and abuse; a multiple explanation approach is necessary.   p. 137

Altered Consciousness with Drugs

- Alcohol affects behavior in proportion to its level in the bloodstream. Alcohol can become physiologically addictive, and many people are psychologically dependent on the drug. pp. 138–139

- Barbiturates and tranquilizers are drugs that relax and calm individuals, and when taken in higher doses often induce sleep.   p. 144

- Although heroin is addictive, its use, in and of itself, is not usually lethal. Heroin addiction has been successfully treated with methadone, which blocks heroin's effects. Although addictive, methadone is legal, medically safe, and does not induce tolerance.   p. 145

- Smoking marijuana produces a high feeling, increased heart rate, and dilation of some small blood vessels. The drug's long-term effects are still unknown.   p. 146

- A psychostimulant is a drug that in low to moderate doses increases alertness, reduces fatigue, and is considered a mood elevator. Cocaine is such a drug, with high abuse potential and little medical value.   p. 147

Connections

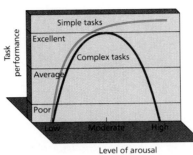

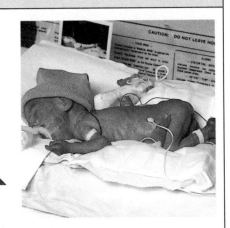

If you are interested in . . .	Turn to . . .	To learn more about . . .
Sleep and dreaming	◆ Ch. 12, pp. 433–434	How personality researchers use dreaming as an important part of their personality theories.
	◆ Ch. 13, p. 469	How stress affects sleep and dreams.
	◆ Ch. 14, p. 518	The impact of depression on sleep.
	◆ Ch. 15, p. 540	Why Freud's interpretation of dreams is used as a therapeutic technique by many therapists.
Consciousness	◆ Ch. 13, p. 74	How biological underpinnings of normal everyday awareness depend on normal consciousness.
	◆ Ch. 13, p. 475	How everyday awareness is affected in adverse ways when people are under stress.
	◆ Ch. 15, p. 538	How treatment procedures for maladjustment sometimes rely on the notion of an *un*conscious to direct day-to-day behavior.
Substance abuse	◆ Ch. 9, p. 304	How drug use by pregnant women affects their unborn children.
	◆ Ch. 13, pp. 469–471	Why people turn to substances such as alcohol to help relieve stress.
	◆ Ch. 17, pp. 575–576	How people's attitudes about lifestyles, including substance use and abuse, are influenced by parents and peers.

5

Learning

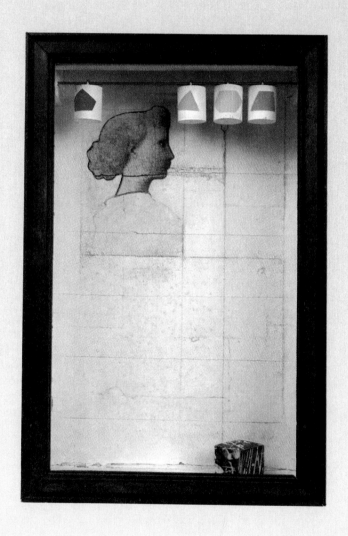

"Untitled" by Joseph Cornell

◆

While walking across campus to his psychology class, Tyson wonders how he can get Cathy to notice him. He has made one strategic move to gain her attention by wearing his blue argyle sweater. The sweater became his favorite after he was complimented on it by several female friends. As he climbs the carpeted stairs to class, he passes Ray, an upperclassman Tyson admires. Noticing that Ray has his jacket collar up, Tyson flips his own collar up as he reaches for the metal knob on the classroom door. He touches the knob and, expecting a shock, instantly jerks back his hand. Tyson had been shocked often as he touched this particular doorknob, but not today. He solves the mystery when he remembers that he is wearing sneakers instead of his leather-soled loafers.

By wearing the blue argyle sweater, adjusting his jacket collar, and jerking his hand back from the doorknob, Tyson has demonstrated three types of learning that involve associations: cognitive learning, operant conditioning, and classical conditioning. By the time we're adults, experience has taught us a large number of simple, predictable associations. We know, for example, that a day at the beach without sunblock will result in a painful sunburn, that staying up late the night before an exam will not help our grades, and that a gas station should be our next stop when the fuel gauge reads empty. We have also learned sophisticated, complicated processes, such as how to drive a car, play baseball, use a computer, and appreciate music from Bach to Springsteen. Some people learn socially nonproductive behaviors such as stealing and drug abuse. We also learn how others view us and how they respond to our actions.

Psychologists define **learning** as a relatively permanent change in the organism that occurs as a result of experience; this change is often seen in overt or observed behavior, but not always. For example, a child may learn good table manners, but only show them on special occasions. The definition of learning has three important parts: experience in the environment, change in the organism, and permanence. First, in order for learning to occur, the organism must experience something in the environment (Tyson observed that Ray was wearing his jacket collar up). Second, to say that learning has occurred, some measurable change in the organism must be evident (Tyson flips his own jacket collar up). The third component is permanence (weeks after seeing Ray, Tyson may still be wearing upturned collars).

Because the internal processes of learning cannot be seen, psychologists study the *results* of learning, including overt behavior such as solving an algebra problem or throwing a ball, and measure physiological changes such as brainwave activity, heartbeat, and temperature. It is important to remember that practice and repeated experiences sharpen our skills and ensure that newly acquired learning, information, and skills are remembered and easily exhibited. Also remember that when learning has occurred, some process within you has changed, and a physiological change has occurred as well.

Behavior is always being modified; new experiences affect learning, and what is learned may be forgotten. Further, an organism's motivation, abilities, and physiological state also influence its ability to learn. For example, if you are tired, learning the material in this chapter will be especially difficult.

The factors that affect learning are often studied in animal behavior because the genetic heritage of animals is easy to control and manipulate, and an animal's history and environmental experiences are known. Although some psychologists claim that different processes underlie animal and human learning, most believe—and experiments show—that those processes are similar. Differences become apparent and especially important when complex behaviors are being evaluated and experiments require the use of language.

As the example of Tyson illustrates, learning results from one of three basic processes: classical conditioning, operant conditioning, and cognitive learning. There are some important similarities among these processes and some sharp differences. These processes are the subject of this chapter. Other topics related to basic learning processes, such as verbal learning, creativity, problem solving, and concept formation, are discussed in chapters 6 and 7. Our emotional responses, which are often conditioned, are discussed in chapter 11.

Learning: A relatively permanent change in an organism that occurs as a result of experiences in the environment; this change is often seen in overt behavior.

Classical Conditioning

In the example at the beginning of this chapter, Tyson jerked his hand back from a doorknob in anticipation of a shock. His reaction was elicited by the presence of the doorknob. In the past, Tyson had been shocked when he touched this particular doorknob. Now he reacts in a reflexive manner when he touches it, whether it shocks him or not. He learned this relationship through a process known as classical conditioning.

People generally experience suspense or fear when they hear sinister music during a horror movie. They may feel envious when seeing a sleek red sports car, and nervous at the thought of taking a final exam. Such responses to music, cars, exams, and other objects and events have been learned. Psychologists say that these types of learned responses have been *conditioned*; they are termed *conditioned responses*.

In a general sense, psychologists use the term conditioning to mean learning. But **conditioning** is a systematic procedure through which associations and responses to specific stimuli are learned. Conditioning is one of the simplest forms of learning. For example, consider what generally happens when a man dressed in black enters a scene on television. We know that something evil will soon happen, and we become alarmed or fearful. We have been conditioned to feel that way toward a villain. In the terminology used by psychologists, the villain is the *stimulus*, and alarm or fear is the *response*.

When psychologists first studied conditioning, they found definite relationships between certain stimuli and certain responses. Each time the stimulus occurs, the same reflexive response, or behavior, follows. For example, the presence of food in the mouth leads to salivation; a tap on the knee leads to a knee jerk; a bright light in the eye leads to contraction of the pupil.

In contrast to **reflexes,** which are not learned, conditioned behaviors *are* learned. Many people, for example, have learned the response of fear to the stimulus of sitting in a dentist's chair; they have learned to associate the chair with drilling and pain. A chair by itself does not elicit fear, but when associated with pain it becomes a stimulus that can elicit fear. This is an example of conditioning—the procedure by which a person learns an association and a response (such as fear) to a neutral stimulus (such as a dentist's chair).

Conditioned behaviors may occur so automatically that they appear to be reflexive, such as Tyson's jerk away from the doorknob. Like reflexes, conditioned responses are involuntary, but unlike reflexes, they are learned. In classical conditioning, previously neutral stimuli like chairs, lights, and buzzers become associated with certain events and lead to responses like fear, eye blinks, and nervousness.

Conditioning: A systematic procedure through which new responses to stimuli are learned.

Reflex: An involuntary, automatic behavior in response to stimuli that occurs without prior learning; such behaviors usually show little variability from instance to instance.

Pavlovian or Classical Conditioning

In 1927 Ivan Pavlov (1849–1936), a Russian physiologist, summarized a now famous series of experiments in which he uncovered a basic principle of learning—conditioning. His research began quite by accident in a series of studies on how saliva and gastric secretions work on the digestive processes of dogs. He knew that it is normal for dogs to salivate when they eat—salivation is a reflexive behavior that aids digestion—but the dogs were salivating *before* they tasted food. Pavlov reasoned that this might be happening because the dogs had learned to associate the trainers, who brought them food, with the food itself. Anxious to know more about the basic form of learning, Pavlov abandoned his medical research and redirected his efforts into conditioning, or teaching, dogs to salivate to a new stimulus, such as a bell.

Ivan Pavlov (center), shown here at the 1932 International Congress of Psychology, reported some of the first systematic studies of classical conditioning.

Classical conditioning: A conditioning process in which an originally neutral stimulus, by repeated pairing with a stimulus that naturally elicits a response, comes to elicit a similar or even identical response; sometimes called *Pavlovian conditioning.*

Unconditioned stimulus: A stimulus that normally produces an involuntary, measurable response.

Unconditioned response: The unlearned or involuntary response to an unconditioned stimulus.

Conditioned stimulus: A neutral stimulus that, through repeated association with an unconditioned stimulus, becomes capable of eliciting a conditioned response.

Conditioned response: The response elicited by a conditioned stimulus.

What Pavlov discovered was **classical conditioning,** also called *Pavlovian conditioning.* In classical conditioning, a stimulus can bring about a response that was initially evoked by another stimulus. The process happens like this: When a neutral stimulus such as a bell, buzzer, or light is associated with a stimulus such as food that naturally brings about a response, the neutral stimulus (the bell) over time will bring about the same response. Pavlov called the natural stimulus (e.g., food) an **unconditioned stimulus** and the natural response (e.g., salivating) an **unconditioned response.** The unconditioned response occurs naturally, without learning, to the unconditioned stimulus.

Pavlov started with a relatively simple experiment to teach dogs to salivate in response to a bell. First he attached tubes inside the dogs' mouths to measure the amount of saliva produced by the unconditioned stimulus, food. He then introduced the new stimulus, a bell (see Figure 5.1). He called this a *neutral stimulus,* since the sound of a bell is not necessarily related to salivation. Pavlov then measured the amount of saliva the dogs produced when a bell was rung by itself; the amount was negligible. He then began the conditioning process by ringing the bell and *immediately* placing food in the dogs' mouths. After this was done several times, the dogs salivated in response to the sound of the bell alone. The dogs had learned that the bell meant that food was coming. Pavlov called the bell, which elicited salivation as a result of learning, a **conditioned stimulus.** He called salivation, the learned response to the sound of the bell, a **conditioned response.** From his experiments, Pavlov discovered that the conditioned stimulus (the bell) brought about a similar but somewhat weaker response than the unconditioned stimulus (the food). The process of Pavlovian conditioning is outlined in Figure 5.2.

The key characteristic of classical, or Pavlovian, conditioning is the use of an originally neutral stimulus (e.g., a bell) to elicit a response (e.g.,

FIGURE 5.1
Pavlov attached a tube to a dog's cheek and measured the number of drops of saliva produced in response to food paired with the sound of a bell and to the sound of the bell alone. The dog learned to associate the ringing of the bell with the presentation of food. This kind of association is a fundamental component of classical conditioning.

salivation) through repeated pairing of the neutral stimulus with an unconditioned stimulus (e.g., food) that elicits the response naturally. On the first few trials of pairings, conditioning is unlikely to occur. With additional trials, there is a greater likelihood that conditioning will occur. After dozens or even hundreds of pairings, the neutral stimulus will yield a conditioned response. We generally refer to this process as the *acquisition process*; we say

FIGURE 5.2
In classical conditioning, there are three basic stages by which a neutral stimulus eventually leads to a conditioned response such as salivating.

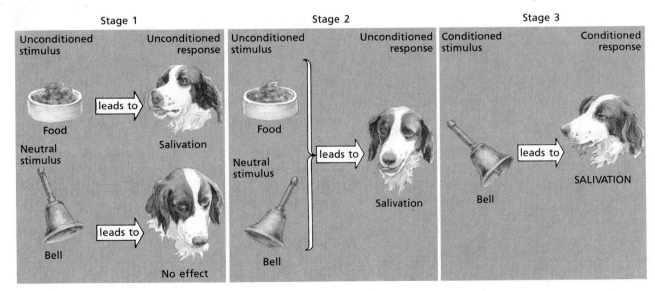

FIGURE 5.3
The graph to the right, sometimes called an *acquisition curve*, shows the course of acquisition of a conditioned response. In classical or Pavlovian conditioning, the first pairings of the conditioned stimulus with the unconditioned stimulus do not bring about a conditioned response. Thus, if presented with the conditioned stimulus alone, an organism in the early days of conditioning might make few if any conditioned responses. However, over many days or trials, the likelihood of a conditioned response increases significantly.

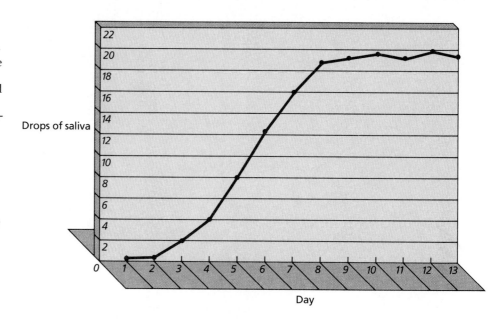

that an organism has acquired a response. Figure 5.3 shows a typical acquisition curve.

Classical conditioning occurs regularly in the everyday world. Your cat or dog may be conditioned to the sound of an electric can opener, which sends it running for food. Similarly, when we hear a siren, we pull over to the side of the road because we expect to see an ambulance, fire truck, or police car behind us. When classical conditioning occurs, behavior changes.

Conditioning in Human Beings

A friend of mine, a former Marine, made a surprising and public demonstration of the power of classical conditioning. This Marine had been a sniper in Vietnam, where he learned to dive for cover at the sound of gunfire. Gunfire was a stimulus followed by death and destruction, and soldiers quickly learned to seek cover on hearing it. While on leave in Houston, this Marine heard a car backfire as he walked down a sidewalk. He instantly dived for cover, right through a storefront window. Fortunately, he wasn't seriously injured, but he certainly startled those around him. Both common sense and laboratory experimentation tell us that my Marine friend was conditioned.

After Pavlov's success with conditioning in dogs, psychologists were able to see that conditioning also occurs in human beings. In 1931, for example, D. P. Marquis showed classical conditioning in infants. Marquis knew that when an object touches an infant's lips, the infant immediately starts sucking because the object is usually the nipple of a breast or bottle from which the infant gets milk. The nipple, an unconditioned stimulus, elicits sucking, an unconditioned response. After repeated pairings of a sound or light with a nipple, infants were conditioned to suck when only the sound or light was presented.

Sucking is only one of many reflexive behaviors in human beings, and hence it is only one of many responses that can be conditioned. Newborns show reflexive responses to loud noises, pain, falling, and even strange people or surroundings (we will examine newborns' reflexes in chapter 9).

For example, a loud noise naturally elicits a startle response—an outstretching of the arms and legs associated with changes in heart rate, blood pressure, and breathing. Have you ever jumped at the sound of a sudden clap of thunder? Any of these responses can be elicited through conditioning procedures.

All kinds of neutral stimuli can become conditioned stimuli that elicit either pleasant or defensive reactions. A puff of air delivered to the eye, for example, produces an unconditioned response: an eye blink. When a light or buzzer is paired with puffs of air to the eye, it will eventually elicit the eye blink by itself. This effect can be produced in many animals (see Figure 5.4), as well as in human adults and infants (Hilgard and Marquis, 1935; Lintz, Fitzgerald, and Brackbill, 1967).

Some psychologists believe that both pleasant and unpleasant emotional responses can be classically conditioned. Consider the following: If a child who is playing with a favorite toy is repeatedly frightened by a sudden loud noise, the child may be conditioned to be afraid each time he or she sees the toy. This type of relationship was explored in 1920 by Watson and Raynor in an experiment with little Albert. Eleven-month-old Albert was given a series of toys to play with, including a live white rat. One day, as Albert reached for the rat, the experimenters made a sudden loud noise that frightened Albert. After repeated pairing of the noise and the rat, Albert learned the relationship. The rat served as a conditioned stimulus, the loud noise as the unconditioned stimulus, and presentation of the rat evoked a response of fear on each subsequent presentation.

Think about the well-known relationship between letter carriers and dogs. Dogs deliver an unconditioned stimulus (a bite) that elicits an unconditioned response (pain). Through repeated *pairings* of stimulus and response, dogs can become conditioned stimuli. At that point, the mere sight of a dog will elicit in the letter carrier a series of defensive reactions associated with fear and pain, including increased heart and respiration rates and sweating.

An example of a pleasant reaction is the beer commercial that applies conditioning principles by featuring beautiful people enjoying their favorite beer while frolicking on a warm, sunny beach or socializing in a cozy ski

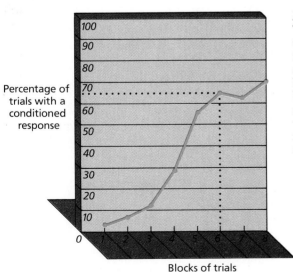

Percentage of
trials with a
conditioned
response

Blocks of trials

FIGURE 5.4
This acquisition curve plots the development of a conditioned eye-blink response in a rabbit in a series of eight blocks of trials. By the sixth block, eye-blinks occur sixty-five percent of the time. (Data from Schneiderman, Fuentes, and Gormezano, 1962.)

Higher-order conditioning:
The process by which a neutral stimulus takes on conditioned properties through pairing with a conditioned stimulus.

chalet. The producers hope that when viewers associate the beer (a neutral stimulus) with an unconditioned stimulus that naturally elicits a positive emotional response (the pleasant scene), it, too, will elicit a positive response. In other words, they hope to condition people to feel good whenever they think about this beer. The powerful role of classical conditioning in advertising has been supported by experimental studies with adults in the laboratory (Stuart, Shimp, and Engle, 1987).

Higher-Order Conditioning

After a neutral stimulus becomes a conditioned stimulus, it is likely to elicit the conditioned response whenever it is presented. Moreover, through a process known as **higher-order conditioning,** when another neutral stimulus is associated with a well-established conditioned stimulus, it can also take on conditioning properties. Thus, higher-order conditioning permits increasingly remote associations, which can result in a complex network of conditioned stimuli and responses. At least two factors determine the extent of higher-order conditioning: (1) the similarity between the higher-order stimulus and the original conditioned stimulus, and (2) the frequency and consistency with which the two conditioned stimuli are paired (Rescorla, 1978).

The following is an example of higher-order conditioning. A light is paired with mild electric shocks so that on seeing the light, a dog exhibits fear; the light has thus become a conditioned stimulus that elicits a set of fear responses. If, after repeated pairings of the light and the shock, a bell is presented with or before the light, the new stimulus (the bell) can also take on properties of the conditioned stimulus (the light). After repeating pairings, the dog will learn to associate the two events, the light and the bell, and either event by itself will elicit a fear response. When a third stimulus—say, an experimenter in a white lab coat—is introduced, the dog may learn to associate the experimenter with the bell or light. After enough trials, the dog may have conditioned fear responses to each of the three stimuli: the light, the bell, and the experimenter (Pavlov, 1927; Rescorla, 1977).

Higher-order classical conditioning is common in our daily lives. For example, a driver who has received several expensive speeding tickets from the Highway Patrol may reflexively slow down whenever he sees a patrol car. If the same driver repeatedly observes a Highway Patrol car parked inconspicuously on a particular stretch of road, he may start slowing down whenever he drives that stretch of road, whether or not he sees a patrol car. The stretch of road becomes another stimulus that induces the driver to ease up on the gas pedal; even the model of the car that the Highway Patrol uses may elicit the response. We will discuss complex conditioning situations further, but you can see that successful pairing of conditioned and unconditioned stimuli—that is, successful classical conditioning—involves many variables.

Focus on Learning

♦ Identify the three important parts of the definition of learning. p. 154
♦ Distinguish between a conditioned and an unconditioned response. p. 156
♦ Provide an example of how higher-order conditioning occurs. p. 160

Variables That Affect Classical Conditioning

Classical conditioning is not a simple process. How loud does the buzzer have to be? How long does the bell have to ring? How sinister must sinister music be? How many times must someone sit in a dentist's chair to become afraid of dentists? How strong does the pain have to be? How would a driver react to the sight of a highway patrolman if her only encounter with one had occurred when her car broke down on a cold, stormy night and she was aided by a patrolman? As with other psychological phenomena, situational variables affect when, if, and under what conditions classical conditioning will occur. Some of the most important variables in classical conditioning are the strength, timing, and frequency of the unconditioned stimulus. When these variables are optimal, conditioning occurs easily.

Strength of the Unconditioned Stimulus. A puff of air delivered to the eye will easily elicit an unconditioned response, but only if the puff of air (i.e., the unconditioned stimulus) is sufficiently strong. Research shows that when the unconditioned stimulus is strong and elicits a quick and regular reflexive (unconditioned) response, conditioning of the neutral stimulus is likely to occur. On the other hand, when the unconditioned stimulus is weak, it is unlikely to elicit an unconditioned response, and conditioning of the neutral stimulus is unlikely to occur. Pairing a neutral stimulus with a weak unconditioned stimulus will not reliably lead to conditioning.

Timing of the Unconditioned Stimulus. For conditioning to occur, an unconditioned stimulus must usually be paired with a conditioned stimulus close enough in time for the two to become associated; we say that they must be temporally contiguous, or close in time. (In Pavlov's experiment, conditioning would not have occurred if the bell and food had been presented an hour apart.) The two stimuli may be presented together or separated by a brief interval. The actual time between the onset of the two stimuli varies from one study to another and depends on many variables, including the type of conditioned response sought. Some types of conditioning can occur with fairly long delays, but a general guideline for achieving a strong conditioned response is that the conditioned stimulus should occur about half a second before the unconditioned stimulus and overlap with it, particularly for reflexes like the eye blink.

Frequency of Pairings. Merely pairing a neutral stimulus with an unconditioned stimulus at close intervals does not result in conditioning; generally speaking, frequent pairings and pairings that establish a relationship between the unconditioned and conditioned stimulus are necessary. If, for example, food and the sound of a bell are paired on every trial, a dog is conditioned more quickly than if the stimuli were paired on every other trial. The frequency of the natural occurrence of the unconditioned stimulus is also important. If the unconditioned stimulus does not occur frequently, but is always associated with the conditioned stimulus, more rapid conditioning is likely because one "predicts" the other (Rescorla, 1988). Once the conditioned response has reached its maximum strength, additional pairings of the stimuli do not increase the likelihood of a conditioned response. There are exceptions to this general rule, and certain one-time pairings can produce learning.

Predictability

A key determining factor in whether conditioning will occur is the predictability of the association of the unconditioned and conditioned stimulus. Closeness in time and a regular frequency of pairings promote conditioning, but these are not enough. Predictability facilitates, and turns out to be a central factor in, conditioning (Rescorla, 1988).

Pavlov thought that classical conditioning was based on timing. But research now shows that if the unconditioned stimulus (such as the food) can be predicted by the conditioned stimulus (such as the bell), then conditioning is rapidly achieved. Conditioning is not achieved because of the number of times the two events have occurred, but rather because of the reliability with which the conditioned stimulus predicts the unconditioned stimulus.

Imagine that walking to class each day you see Carla, and then you see Jose. Carla is always about thirty seconds ahead of Jose. When you walk to class tomorrow and you see Carla, you expect to see Jose. You have learned an association, a predictability of events. Pavlov's dogs learned that bells were good predictors of food; the conditioned stimulus (bells) predicted the unconditioned one (food) well, so conditioning was quickly achieved because the conditioned stimulus reliably predicted the unconditioned stimulus.

From Rescorla's view (1988), what is learned in conditioning is the predictability of events—bells predicting food, light predicting eye blinks, dentist chairs predicting pain, and Carla predicting Jose. The predictability of events becomes especially important in learned behaviors such as food aversions, considered next.

Taste Aversion Challenges the Principles of Learning

MILESTONES IN PSYCHOLOGY

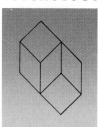

*M*y daughter Sarah has hated mustard ever since her sixth birthday party. After her friends and their mothers left the party, we sat down for a ham sandwich with lettuce and mustard. Two hours later she was ill—fever, vomiting, chills, and swollen glands. It was the flu, but as far as Sarah was concerned it was the mustard that had made her sick. To this day she refuses to eat mustard.

This association of mustard and nausea is an example of conditioned taste aversion. John Garcia's research on conditioned taste aversion helped him win the American Psychological Association's Distinguished Scientific Contribution Award in 1980. Garcia gave animals specific foods or liquids to eat or drink and then induced nausea (usually by injecting a drug or by providing irradiated water to drink). He found that after only one pairing of a food or drink (the conditioned stimulus) and the drug or irradiated water (the unconditioned stimulus), the animals avoided the food or drink that preceded the nausea (see, for example, Linberg, Begg, Chezik, and Ray, 1982; Garcia and Koelling, 1971).

Two aspects of Garcia's work startled the psychological community. First, Garcia showed that conditioned taste aversion could be obtained even if the nausea was induced several hours after the food or drink had been consumed. This contradicted the previously held assumption that the time interval between the unconditioned stimulus and the conditioned stimulus had to be short, especially if conditioning was to occur quickly.

Garcia also proved that not all stimuli can serve as conditioned stimuli, as most learning psychologists believed. He tried to pair bells and lights with nausea to produce an aversion in rats, but he was unable to do so. This led him to conclude, "Strong aversions to the smell or taste of food can develop even when illness is delayed for hours after consumption [but] avoidance reactions do not develop for visual, auditory, or tactile stimuli associated with food" (Garcia and Koelling, 1971, p. 461). Garcia had disproved two accepted principles of learning.

The Garcia Effect. Conditioned taste aversion, sometimes called the *Garcia effect,* has adaptive value. In one trial or instance animals learn to avoid foods that make them sick by associating the smells of poisonous food with the foods themselves. This clearly has inborn survival value. Conditioned taste aversion is unaffected by intervening events during the delay between the taste and the illness (Holder et al., 1989). Human beings quickly learn to associate rancid smells with the illness caused by spoiled food. Anyone who has had food poisoning will attest to the lasting memory of the food or meal that caused it!

Conditioned taste aversion has practical uses. Coyotes and wolves often attack sheep and lambs, destroying entire flocks. Garcia laced lamb meat with a substance that causes a short-term illness and put the food on the outskirts of sheep ranchers' fenced-in areas. Coyotes who ate the lamb became sick and developed a lamb aversion. After this experience, they approached the sheep as if ready to attack, but they nearly always backed off (see, for example, Garcia, Gustavson, Kelly and Sweeney, 1976). By using conditioned taste aversion Garcia deterred coyotes from eating sheep.

John Garcia

Learning, Weight Loss, and Cancer. Patients who have cancer often undergo chemotherapy; an unfortunate side effect of the chemotherapy is vomiting and nausea. They often lose weight and their appetite during their treatment. Is it possible that cancer patients lose so much weight during their treatments because of a conditioned taste aversion? According to researcher Ilene Bernstein (1988), cancer patients become conditioned to avoid food. They often check into a hospital, have a meal, are given chemotherapy, become sick, and then avoid the food that preceded the chemotherapy. Bernstein conducted research with children and adults who were going to receive chemotherapy. Her research showed that patients developed specific aversions to those foods given before their therapy, compared to control groups who were not given those foods but who received chemotherapy.

Patients develop food aversions despite their specific knowledge about the side effects and the fact that it is chemotherapy that induces nausea. Bernstein suggests an intervention based on learning theory: Patients could be given "scapegoat" food just before chemotherapy so that any conditioned taste aversion develops to a low frequency, nutritionally unimportant food, rather than to proteins, carbohydrates, or other nutritious foods. When Bernstein (1988) tried this procedure, results were successful. ◆

Extinction and Spontaneous Recovery

Some conditioned responses last for a long time, while others disappear rather quickly. Much depends on whether a conditioned response can still predict the unconditioned one. Consider the following: What would have happened to Pavlov's dogs if he had rung the bell each day but never followed the bell with food? What would happen if you went to the dentist every day for two months, but the dentist only brushed your teeth with a pleasant tasting toothpaste and never drilled?

If a researcher continues Pavlov's experiment by presenting the conditioned stimulus (bell) but no unconditioned stimulus (food), the likelihood of a conditioned response decreases with every trial. In classical conditioning, the term **extinction** refers to the process through which withholding the unconditioned stimulus gradually reduces the probability (and often the strength) of a conditioned response. Imagine a study in which a puff of air is associated with a buzzer that consistently elicits the conditioned eye-blink response. If the unconditioned stimulus (the puff of air) is no longer deliv-

Extinction: In classical conditioning, the process of reducing the likelihood of a conditioned response to a conditioned stimulus by withholding the unconditioned stimulus.

Spontaneous recovery: The recurrence of a conditioned response following a rest period after extinction.

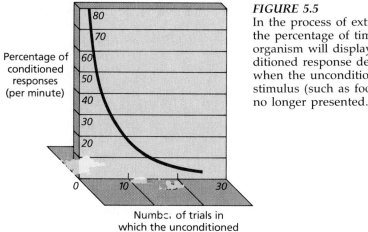

Percentage of conditioned responses (per minute)

Number of trials in which the unconditioned stimulus is not presented

FIGURE 5.5
In the process of extinction, the percentage of times an organism will display a conditioned response decreases when the unconditioned stimulus (such as food) is no longer presented.

ered, the likelihood that the buzzer will continue to elicit the eye-blink response decreases over time (see Figure 5.5). When presentation of the buzzer alone no longer elicits the conditioned response, we say that the conditioned response has been extinguished.

A conditioned response that has undergone extinction can recur, especially after a rest period; in classical conditioning this phenomenon is called **spontaneous recovery.** For example, when a dog has been conditioned to salivate in response to the sound of a bell and then experiences a long series of trials in which food is not paired with the bell, the dog makes few or no responses to the bell: the behavior has been extinguished. If the dog is placed in the experimental situation again after a rest period of twenty minutes, its salivary response to the bell will recur briefly (although less strongly than before). This behavior shows that the effects of extinction are not permanent and that the learned association is not totally forgotten (see Figures 5.6 and 5.7).

FIGURE 5.6
Once a conditioned response extinguishes, an organism will show the response again after a rest interval. This recurrence of a conditioned response is called *spontaneous recovery.* After each successive rest interval, the rate of response decreases and extinction occurs more quickly.

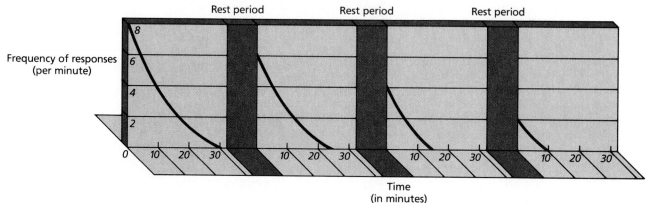

Frequency of responses (per minute)

Time (in minutes)

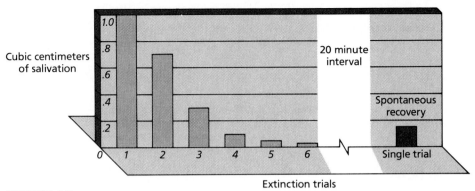

FIGURE 5.7
In a series of trials at three-minute intervals, Pavlov extinguished a conditioned salivary response by omitting presentation of the unconditioned stimulus (food). After a rest interval of twenty minutes, the salivary response recurred, but it was not as strong as in earlier trials. (Data from Pavlov, 1927, p. 58.)

Stimulus Generalization and Stimulus Discrimination

Imagine that a three-year-old child pulls a cat's tail and receives a painful scratch. It would not be surprising if the child developed a fear of that cat, or even of all cats. It is possible that she might even develop a fear of other four-legged animals. People may respond in the same way to similar stimuli, a phenomenon that psychologists call stimulus generalization.

Stimulus generalization occurs when an organism exhibits a conditioned response to a stimulus that is similar, but not identical, to the original conditioned stimulus. The extent to which an organism responds to a stimulus similar to the original one depends on how alike the two stimuli are. If, for example, a loud tone is the conditioned stimulus for an eye-blink response, somewhat lower but similar tones will also produce the eye-blink response. A less frequent and totally dissimilar tone will produce little or no response. (Likewise, the Marine responded to the sound of a car backfiring because it was similar to the sound of gunfire.) See Figure 5.8 for another

FIGURE 5.8
Stimulus generalization occurs when an organism emits a conditioned response to stimuli similar to but not identical to the conditioned stimulus. The bar graph shows the responses of an organism trained with a 1,000-hertz tone. When the organism was later presented with tones of different frequencies, its percentage responses decreased as the tone's frequency became increasingly different. (Data from Jenkins and Harrison, 1960.)

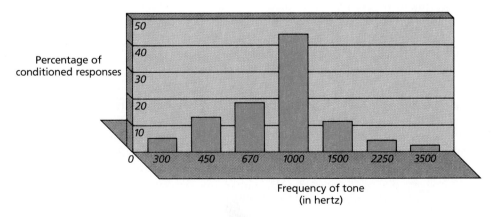

Stimulus generalization: The occurrence of a conditioned response to stimuli similar to, but not the same as, the training stimulus.

TABLE 5.1
Four Important Properties of Classical Conditioning

Property	Definition	Example
Extinction	The process of reducing the probability of a conditioned response by withholding the unconditioned stimulus (the reinforcer)	An infant conditioned to suck in response to a light is no longer given the unconditioned stimulus of stroking the lips; the infant stops sucking in response to the conditioned stimulus.
Spontaneous recovery	The recurrence of a conditioned response following a rest period after extinction	A dog's conditioned salivary response has undergone extinction; after a rest period the dog again salivates in response to the conditioned stimulus, though less than it did before.
Stimulus generalization	The process by which an organism learns to respond to stimuli similar to but not identical to the training stimulus.	A dog conditioned to salivate in response to a high-pitched tone also salivates to a lower-pitched tone.
Stimulus discrimination	The process by which an organism learns to respond to a specific stimulus and then to no other similar stimulus; the complementary process to stimulus generalization	A goat is conditioned to salivate only in response to lights of high intensity and not to lights of low intensity.

example of stimulus generalization and Table 5.1 for a summary of important properties of classical conditioning.

Stimulus discrimination is the process by which an organism responds differently to dissimilar stimuli. Pavlov showed that animals that have learned to differentiate between pairs of stimuli display frustration or even aggression when discrimination is made difficult or impossible. He trained a dog to discriminate between a circle and an ellipse and then changed the shape of the ellipse on successive trials to look more and more like the circle. Eventually, the animal was unable to discriminate between the shapes; it randomly chose one or the other, and also became aggressive.

Human beings exhibit similar disorganization in behavior when placed in situations in which they feel compelled to make a response, but do not know how to respond correctly. In such situations, where discrimination becomes impossible, behavior can become stereotyped and limited in scope; people may choose either not to respond to the stimulus or to respond always in the same way (Lundin, 1961; Maier and Klee, 1941). Often, therapists must teach maladjusted people to learn to be more flexible in their responses to difficult situations. (For a summary of classical conditioning, see Building Table 5.1.)

Conditioning Physical Symptoms

Think of Tyson's hand on the doorknob, the Marine's reaction to a loud noise, and a person's fear of the dentist's chair. You can see that classical conditioning explains a wide range of human behaviors, including some of the physical symptoms people exhibit.

Physical responses to the world, such as heart rate acceleration and changes in blood pressure, can be altered through classical conditioning. Substances such as pollen, dust, cat fur, or mold initiate an allergic reaction in many people. Cat fur naturally elicits an allergic reaction, such as an inability to breathe, in asthmatics. Asthma attacks, like other behaviors, can

Stimulus discrimination: The process by which an organism learns to respond only to a specific reinforced stimulus; the complementary process to stimulus generalization.

be conditioned to occur. If fur is *always* found in Lindsay's house (a regular pairing), classical conditioning theory predicts that an asthmatic individual entering Lindsay's house would have an allergic reaction. (A conditioned stimulus, the house, predicts an unconditioned response, the asthma.) Researchers have shown that people with severe allergies can have an allergic reaction merely from the sight of a cat (or Lindsay's house), regardless of the presence of fur.

Even the body's immune system can be conditioned. Normally our bodies release antibodies to fight disease when toxic substances are found in the blood. This is an involuntary activity independent of the nervous system. In a striking series of studies, animals were classically conditioned in a way that altered their immune responses (Ader, Cohen, and Bovbjerg, 1982). Ader paired a sweet-tasting solution with a drug that produced illness and as a side effect also suppressed the immune response. The animals quickly learned to avoid the sweet-tasting substance that seemed to predict illness. When later presented with the sweet-tasting substance alone, there was a reduction of immune system antibodies. Ader had classically conditioned an immune system response that was previously thought not to be under nervous system control.

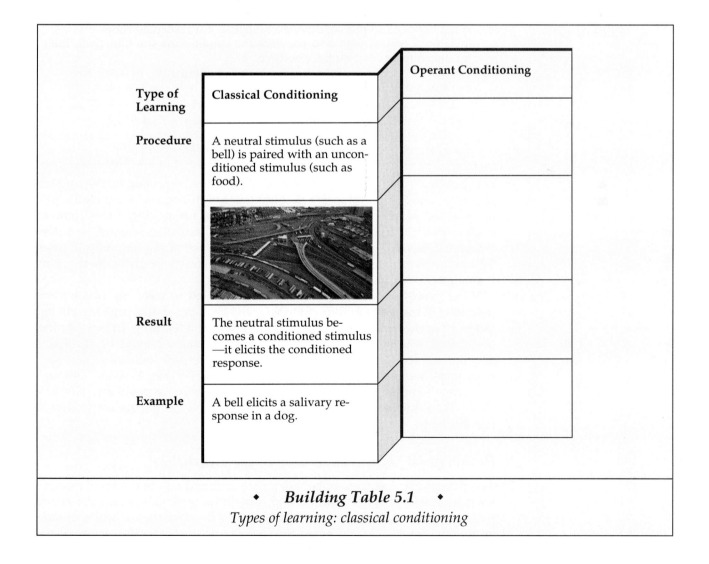

Type of Learning	Classical Conditioning	Operant Conditioning
Procedure	A neutral stimulus (such as a bell) is paired with an unconditioned stimulus (such as food).	
Result	The neutral stimulus becomes a conditioned stimulus—it elicits the conditioned response.	
Example	A bell elicits a salivary response in a dog.	

♦ ***Building Table 5.1*** ♦

Types of learning: classical conditioning

it is unlikely to elicit an unconditioned response & conditioning of the neutral stimulus is unlikely to occur

2. ★ predictability of the association of the unconditioned & conditioned stimulus

New research also shows that drug users condition themselves. When heroin addicts inject heroin, their bodies produce an anti-opiate substance to protect them from overdose; this is a natural response. Siegel (1988) has shown if the addict always injects his drug in the same room, the place itself may serve to initiate an anti-opiate response, without heroin ever actually being administered. Therefore, the location of a user's heroin administration can serve as a conditioned stimulus for the anti-opiate response. When an anti-opiate response occurs, an addict may develop withdrawal symptoms, which in turn may create an even greater "need" for the drug. The stimulus for the increased use may have merely been the location of the drug consumption.

Classical conditioning in its simplest form explains a wide range of phenomena, but not all of our behaviors are the result of such associations. Many complex behaviors result from another form of learning, called *operant conditioning*, which is discussed next.

Focus on Learning

- 1 ◆ What happens when an unconditioned stimulus (e.g., a puff of air) is not sufficiently strong? p. 161
- 2 ◆ Closeness in time and a regular frequency of pairings promote conditioning, but what third variable is especially important in establishing an association of the unconditioned and conditioned stimulus? p. 162
- 3 ◆ What happens to the conditioned response if a researcher does a Pavlovian-type experiment and presents the conditioned stimulus (bell) but no unconditioned stimulus (food)? p. 163
- 4 ◆ Conditioned taste aversion is a powerful phenomenon; describe the process. pp. 162–163

3. Extinction occurs

4.

Operant Conditioning

Let's return to Tyson, the student described at the beginning of the chapter. Tyson was wearing a blue argyle sweater, which became his favorite after he received several compliments on it. Unlike his jerking away from an electric shock, Tyson's decision to wear that particular sweater is a non-reflexive behavior and cannot be attributed to classical conditioning. Rather, Tyson was reinforced in wearing his blue sweater through operant, or instrumental, conditioning.

The process by which Tyson was conditioned to wear his sweater was described in the 1930s by B. F. Skinner, who challenged and began to change the way psychologists think about conditioning and learning. In fact, Skinner questioned whether Pavlovian (classical) conditioning should be studied at all. Skinner focused only on an organism's *observable* behavior. Skinner's early work was in the tradition of strict behaviorists like Watson, although ultimately Skinner modified some of his most extreme positions. His 1938 book, *The Behavior of Organisms*, continues to have an impact on studies of conditioning.

Pioneers: B. F. Skinner and E. L. Thorndike

According to Skinner, many behaviors are acquired and maintained through what he called operant conditioning, not through Pavlov's classical conditioning. He used the term *operant conditioning* because the organism *operates* on the environment, with every action followed by a specific event or consequence. In **operant conditioning,** an increase or decrease in the likelihood that a behavior will recur is affected by the delivery of a rewarding or punishing event as a consequence of the behavior. Moreover, the conditioned behavior is usually voluntary, not reflexlike as in classical conditioning. Consider what happens when a boss rewards and encourages her overworked employees by giving them unexpected cash bonuses. If the bonuses improve the employees' morale and induce them to work harder, then the employer's conditioning efforts are successful. In turn, the employees could condition the boss by rewarding her bonus-paying behavior through increasing their productivity, thereby encouraging her to continue paying bonuses.

In the laboratory, researchers have studied similar sequences of behaviors followed by rewards. One of the most famous experiments was conducted by the American psychologist E. L. Thorndike (1874–1949), who pioneered the study of operant conditioning during the 1890s and first reported his work in 1896. Thorndike placed hungry cats in boxes and put food outside the boxes. The cats could escape from the boxes and get food by hitting a lever that opened a door in the box. The cats quickly performed the behavior Thorndike was trying to condition (hitting the lever), because hitting the lever (at first by accident and then deliberately) gave them access to food. Because the response, hitting the lever, was important (i.e., instrumental) in obtaining the reward, Thorndike used the term *instrumental conditioning* and called the behaviors *instrumental behaviors*.

Although Skinner spoke of operant conditioning and Thorndike of instrumental conditioning, the two terms are often used interchangeably. What is important is that both theorists acknowledged that first the behavior is *emitted* or displayed, and then a consequence (e.g., a reward) follows. This is unlike classical (Pavlovian) conditioning, in which first there is a change in the environment (e.g., bells and food are paired) and then the conditioned behavior (usually a reflexive response) is *elicited* (see Figure 5.9).

In operant conditioning like that in Thorndike's experiment with cats, an organism emits a behavior and a consequence follows. The *type* of consequence that follows the behavior is crucial, since it determines whether the behavior is likely to recur. The consequence can be a *reinforcer* or a *punisher*. As in classical conditioning, a reward acts as a reinforcer, increasing the likelihood that the behavior targeted for conditioning will recur; in Thorndike's experiment, food was the reinforcer for hitting the lever. A punisher, on the other hand, decreases the likelihood that the targeted behavior will recur. If an electric shock is delivered to the feet of a cat each time the cat touches a lever, the cat quickly learns not to touch the lever. Parents use reinforcers and punishers when they link the behavior of their teenaged children to the use of the family car. A teenager on a date is more likely to return home at an appropriate hour if he or she knows doing so will ensure use of the car again. We will discuss punishment and its consequences in more detail later in this chapter.

The Skinner Box and Shaping

Much of the research on operant conditioning has used an apparatus called a **Skinner box.** A Skinner box usually contains a mechanism for delivering a consequence whenever the animal in the box makes a readily identifiable response that the experimenter has decided to reinforce or punish. In studies that involve rewards, the delivery mechanism is often a small lever or bar in the side of the box; whenever the animal presses it, the behavior is

Operant conditioning: A conditioning procedure in which the probability that an organism will emit a response is increased or decreased by the subsequent delivery of a reinforcer or punisher; sometimes called *instrumental conditioning.*

Skinner box: Named for its developer, B. F. Skinner, a box containing a responding mechanism (usually a lever) capable of delivering a reinforcer (often food or water) to an organism.

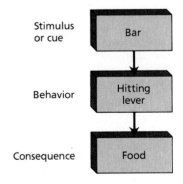

FIGURE 5.9
In instrumental conditioning—unlike classical conditioning—the behavior to be conditioned (such as hitting a lever) is reinforced or punished *after* it occurs.

In the Skinner box, behavior is punished or rewarded after an animal makes a response.

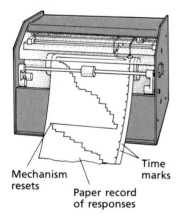

Mechanism resets

Time marks

Paper record of responses

FIGURE 5.10
The cumulative recorder marks each time an organism makes a response. The paper in the device moves constantly; if the organism does not respond, the pen makes a straight line.

Shaping: The gradual training of an organism to give the proper responses by selectively reinforcing behaviors as they approach the desired response.

rewarded. Punishment in a Skinner box often takes the form of electric shocks delivered through a grid on the floor of the box.

In a traditional operant conditioning experiment, a rat that has been deprived of food is placed in a Skinner box. The rat moves around the box, often seeking to escape; eventually it stumbles on the lever and presses it. With that action, the experimenter delivers a pellet of food into a cup. The rat moves about some more and happens to press the lever again; another pellet of food is delivered. After a few trials, the rat learns that pressing the lever brings food. A hungry rat will learn to press the lever many times in rapid succession to obtain food.

Counting lever presses or measuring salivary responses is a tedious but necessary part of studying conditioning. Psychologists have developed a practical and simple device called a *cumulative recorder* to measure animal behavior (see Figure 5.10). These devices were essential for the early progress made in animal learning laboratories. Today, psychologists use computerized devices to quantify behavior like bar pressing and to track the progress that an organism makes in learning a response. Teaching an organism a complex response takes many trials because most organisms need to be taught in small steps through the process of shaping.

Shaping Simple Behaviors. **Shaping** is the process of reinforcing behavior that approximates a desired behavior. To teach a hungry rat to press a bar in a Skinner box, for example, a researcher begins by giving the rat a pellet of food each time it enters the side of the box in which the bar is located. Once this behavior is established, the rat receives food only when it touches the wall where the bar is located. It then receives food only when it approaches the lever, and so on until it receives food only when it actually presses the bar. At each stage, the reinforced behavior (entering the half of the box with food, touching the wall with the food, etc.) more closely approximates the desired behavior (i.e., pressing the lever).

Shaping is effective for teaching animals new behaviors; for example, you use shaping to train a dog to sit on command. This generally is done

His father's attention and praise act as reinforcers to this young boy's involvement in baseball.

by pairing food with a push on the dog's rear while verbally commanding "Sit!" With reinforcement following sitting, the dog begins to sit with less and less pressure applied to its rear, and eventually the dog sits on command. Shaping is also helpful in teaching people new behaviors. Do you remember learning to play baseball? First, you were taught how to hold the bat correctly, then how to swing it, then how to simply make contact with the ball, and finally how to hit the ball for a base hit.

Teaching new behaviors using operant conditioning, especially if they are complex, is time-consuming and often must be done in several stages. For example, a father who wants his son to make his bed neatly will at first reinforce *all* of the child's attempts at bed making, even if the results are sloppy. Over successive weeks, the father will reinforce only the better attempts, until finally he reinforces only neat bed making. Patience is important because it is essential to reinforce all steps toward the desired behavior, no matter how small (Fischer and Gochros, 1975). Shaping embodies a central aspect of behaviorism: reinforced behaviors recur. B. F. Skinner is the individual most responsible for advancing that notion.

B. F. Skinner—The Man and His Ideas

B. F. Skinner awakened at 4:40 every morning so he could work undisturbed before his phone started ringing.

Skinner is arguably the most influential psychologist the United States has ever produced. Although he spent his career studying animals, his writings are all about people. His theories about using principles of operant conditioning to design a utopian society brought him lasting fame.

But Burrhus Frederic Skinner was more an engineer than a theorist. Determining the best time to get up in the morning, inventing a better hearing aid, or designing a comfortable enclosed crib for his daughters were the tasks he found most rewarding. "I don't believe I have a very high IQ," he said.

MILESTONES IN
PSYCHOLOGY

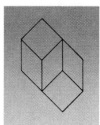

"There are skills I just don't have. Fortunately, I got into a field where I could use the ones I do have—largely practical skills: building apparatuses and so on. I don't think I'm a classical picture of a great thinker or anything of that sort."

Skinner's thinking classified him as a behaviorist. He believed we are what we do and that there is no "self," only a collection of possible behaviors. "People say, 'Do you regard yourself the way you regard your pigeons?' I do! Fortunately, I'm much more complicated than the pigeons."

Skinner was also a determinist. In his view, our actions are more a result of past experiences than genetics. But he took the phrase "a result of" very literally. According to Skinner, our environment completely determines what we do. We control our actions about as much as a rock in an avalanche controls its resting place.

And what about human creativity? Skinner thought we flattered ourselves about freedom and creativity. "If the question is how much the individual contributes," he said, "I think the answer is: nothing." Even Ludwig van Beethoven? "Beethoven was someone who, when he was very young, acquired all the available music at the time, and then, because of things that happened to him personally as accidents and variations, he introduced new things which paid off beautifully. So he went on doing them and he wrote because he was highly reinforced for writing."

Skinner was born March 20, 1904, near Scranton, Pennsylvania. Perhaps the most traumatic period of his life was the year after college, which he called "my Dark Year." While living with his constantly feuding parents, he developed what a nonbehaviorist might call an identity crisis.

"I did not consider actual suicide," he wrote in his autobiography. "Behaviorism offered me another way out: it was not I, but my history that had failed. I learned to accept my mistakes by referring them to a personal history which was not of my making and could not be changed." Skinner found himself abandoning his self.

Skinner had wanted to be a writer but found writing very difficult. After turning toward psychology and getting his Ph.D. from Harvard, Skinner taught at the University of Minnesota and Indiana University before returning to Harvard in 1947. He remained there through the rest of his career.

The personal philosophy that helped Skinner overcome his troubles in early life also made it easier for him to contemplate death. "I'm in good health from the neck down," he would say, half joking. In his later years, he didn't enjoy the theater because his hearing was poor. He didn't dine out because his taste buds had dulled. And he gave up piano because of his failing eyesight. But death didn't scare him, he insisted. "My only fear is that I won't finish the papers I'm writing." Skinner died in August of 1990 at 86 years of age.   ◆

Reinforcement

Operant conditioning depends on the basic principles of reinforcement, that is, rewarding desirable behavior. To psychologists, a **reinforcer** is any event that increases the probability of the recurrence of a response that preceded it. Thus a behavior followed by a desirable event is likely to recur. Examples of reinforcement in our lives abound: A person works hard in a factory and is rewarded with high pay; a student studies long hours for an examination and is rewarded with a top grade; sales agents call on hundreds of clients and sell lots of their product; young children "behave" and their parents reward them with affection and praise. Specific behaviors, like working hard, studying a great deal, calling on clients, or behaving for a parent, are established because of reinforcement. Such behaviors can be taught by using either or both of two kinds of reinforcers: positive and negative.

Reinforcer: Any event that increases the probability of the recurrence of a response that precedes it.

Positive Reinforcement. Most people have used **positive reinforcement** at one time or another. When teaching your dog tricks, you reward it with a biscuit or a pat on the head. When toilet training a two-year-old, a parent often applauds when the child successfully completes a bowel movement; the applause is a reinforcer. Both the dog and the child continue the behaviors because they have been rewarded with something that is important or desired; their behaviors have been positively reinforced.

Some reinforcers are more powerful than others, and a reinforcer for one person may not have reinforcing value for another. Praise from an approving parent may be a powerful reinforcer from a two-year-old; high grades may be the most effective reinforcer for a student; money may be effective for one adult, position or status for another. At many corporations, bonuses for effective performance may include color televisions, cassette tape recorders, or trips to Hawaii.

Negative Reinforcement. Whereas positive reinforcement increases the probability of a response through delivery of a reward, **negative reinforcement** increases the probability of a response through removal of an unpleasant, aversive, or noxious stimulus. Negative reinforcement is reinforcement because it strengthens or increases the likelihood of a response. Suppose a rat is placed in a Skinner box with an electrified grid that delivers a shock every fifty seconds, and the rat can escape the shock by pressing a bar. The behavior to be conditioned is bar pressing; the reinforcement is termination of the painful stimulus. In this case negative reinforcement—termination of the painful stimulus—increases the probability of the response, bar pressing, because that is the way to turn off the unpleasant stimulus.

Noxious or unpleasant stimuli are often used in animal studies of escape and avoidance. In *escape conditioning* the rat in the Skinner box receives a shock just strong enough to cause it to thrash around until it bumps against the bar, thereby stopping the shock. In just a few trials the rat learns to press the bar to *escape* being shocked, to bring an unpleasant situation to an end. In *avoidance conditioning* the same apparatus is used, but a buzzer or some other cue precedes the shock by a few seconds. In this case, the rat learns that when presented with a stimulus or cue such as a buzzer, it should press the bar. Pressing the bar allows it to *avoid* or prevent the shock from occurring.

Avoidance conditioning generally involves escape conditioning: First, the animal learns how to escape the shock by pressing the bar. Then it learns how to avoid the shock by pressing the bar when it hears the buzzer signaling the oncoming shock. In avoidance conditioning the organism learns to respond so that the noxious stimulus is never delivered. For example, to avoid receiving a ticket, a speeding driver may condition herself to slow down whenever her radar detector buzzes. To avoid a bad grade on an English quiz, a student may study before an examination. And when people develop irrational fears, for example, of airplanes or trains, they may avoid those vehicles. However, by getting where they need to go some other way, they may never unlearn their old fears. So avoidance conditioning can explain adaptive behaviors like studying before an exam, and it can also explain why some people maintain irrational fears.

Most children master both escape and avoidance conditioning at an early age. Appropriate signals from a disapproving parent often elicit an avoidance response so that punishment does not follow; for example, a child may decide to take his hand out of the cookie jar when he sees his mother frown.

Positive reinforcement: Presentation of a rewarding or pleasant stimulus to increase the likelihood that a response will occur.

Negative reinforcement: Removal of an aversive stimulus to increase the likelihood that a response will recur.

Similarly, just knowing the possible effects of an automobile accident will make most cautious adults wear seatbelts. Both positive and negative reinforcements *increase* the likelihood that an organism will repeat a behavior. If the reinforcement is strong enough, delivered often enough, and important enough to the organism, it can help maintain behaviors for long periods.

The Nature of Reinforcers. The precise nature of reinforcers is a murky issue. Early researchers recognized events that satisfy biological needs as powerful reinforcers. Later researchers included events that decrease a person's need to meet certain goals, such as conversation that would relieve boredom, sounds that would relieve sensory deprivation, and money that would relieve housing congestion. Then, in the 1960s, researchers acknowledged that many events can be reinforcers. Probable behaviors (that is, behaviors likely to happen, including biological behaviors like eating and social behaviors like reading, knitting, or talking) can reinforce less probable or unlikely behaviors like cleaning closets, studying calculus, or bar pressing (if you are a rodent). Researchers call this idea the *Premack principle*, after David Premack, whose influential writings and research fostered the idea (Premack 1962, 1965). Parents employ the Premack principle when they tell their children they can go outside and play *after* they clean up their rooms.

The Premack principle and its refinements focus on the problem of determining what is a good reinforcer. Therapists and learning theorists know, for example, that something that acts as a reinforcer for one person may not do so for another, and something that acts as a reinforcer on one day may not do so for the same person on the next day. Therefore, they are very careful about determining what events in a client's life—or a rodent's environment—act as reinforcers. If someone were to offer you a reinforcer for some extraordinary activity on your part, what would be the most effective reinforcer? Do reinforcers change because of a person's age and experiences, or do they depend on how often the person has been reinforced?

A reinforcer that is known to be successful may work only in specific situations. The delivery of food pellets to a hungry rat that has just pressed a lever increases the likelihood that the rat will press the lever again. But this reinforcer works only if the rat is hungry; for a rat that has just eaten, food pellets are not reinforcing. Similarly, a salesperson who needs to sell 1000 widgets a month in order to pay his bills and have a predetermined amount of spending money may work overtime to achieve his goal. However, if he sells 1000 widgets in only three weeks, his motivation may decrease and his productivity will likely suffer during the last week of the month. In short, a person or an animal must need or desire a particular consequence if that consequence is to act as a reinforcer.

When studying learning and conditioning, psychologists create the conditions for reinforcement by depriving animals of food or water before an experiment. In doing so, they motivate the animals and allow the delivery of food to take on reinforcing properties. In most experiments the organism is motivated in some way. Chapter 11 discusses the role of an organism's needs, desires, and physiological state in determining what can be used as a reinforcer.

Primary reinforcers are those that have survival value for the organism, such as food, water, or termination of pain; their value does not have to be learned. Food can be a primary reinforcer for a hungry rat, water for a thirsty one. **Secondary reinforcers** are neutral stimuli (such as money or grades) that initially have no intrinsic value for the organism but when paired, coupled, or linked with a primary reinforcer, they too can become a reward.

Primary reinforcer: Any stimulus or event that by its mere delivery or removal acts naturally (without learning) to increase the likelihood that a response will recur.

Secondary reinforcer: A neutral stimulus with no intrinsic value to the organism that acquires reinforcement value through repeated pairing with a reinforcing stimulus.

Many human pleasures are secondary reinforcers that have acquired value, such as leather coats that keep people no warmer than cloth ones and racy sports cars that take people from one place to another no faster than four-door sedans.

Secondary reinforcers are generally used to modify human behavior. An approving nod, unlimited use of the family car, and a promotion are secondary reinforcers that act to establish and maintain a wide spectrum of behavior. People will work long hours when the rewards are significant; successful salespeople may even work seventy-two-hour weeks to reach their sales objectives. This can happen when managers, using basic psychology, offer salespeople a bonus for increasing sales by a certain percentage during a slow month. They reason that by increasing the amount of a reinforcer (money), they may be able to get better performance (higher sales). Research shows that changing the amount of a reinforcer (by increasing it or decreasing it) can significantly alter an organism's behavior.

A chart hanging in the office which acknowledges each department's contribution to sales quotas can act as a reinforcer and motivator.

Superstitious Behaviors. Since reinforcement plays a key role in learning new behaviors, parents and educators try to reinforce children and students on a regular basis. But what happens when a person or animal is unintentionally rewarded for a behavior? What happens when a reward has nothing to do with the behavior that immediately preceded it? Under such conditions people and animals may develop **superstitious behavior.** For example, baseball players try to extend their hitting streak by using the same "lucky" bat. A student may study at the same table in the library because she earned an A after studying there for the last exam. A number of superstitious behaviors—including fear responses to the number 13, black cats, and walking under ladders—are centuries old and have strong cultural associations. These behaviors generally arise from a purely random consequence that occurred immediately after the behavior. Thus, a person who happens to wear the same pair of shoes in two bicycle races and wins both races may come to believe that there is a causal relationship between wearing that pair of shoes and winning a bicycle race.

Animals can learn superstitious behaviors even in a Skinner box. On trials in which a rat was learning the bar-pressing response, it may have

For centuries people have tried to influence the events affecting their lives. The belief that repeating a certain random action such as lighting joss sticks may elicit a positive outcome is known as superstition.

Superstitious behavior: Behavior learned through coincidental association with reinforcement.

Punishment: The process of presenting an undesirable or noxious stimulus, or removal of a positive desirable stimulus, to decrease the probability that a response will recur.

turned its head to the right before pressing the bar and receiving reinforcement. Although the reinforcement actually was contingent only on pressing the bar, to the rat it may have seemed that both the head turning and the bar pressing were necessary (Skinner, 1948). Therefore, the rat will continue to turn its head to the right before pressing the bar.

Punishment

You already know that the consequences of an action, be they rewards or punishment, affect behavior. Clearly rewards can establish new behaviors and maintain them for long periods. How effective is punishment as a way to manipulate behavior? **Punishment,** unlike reinforcement, *decreases* the probability of a particular response. As such, it is one of the most commonly used techniques for teaching children and pets to control their behavior. When a dog growls at visitors, for example, its owner slaps it; when children write on the walls with crayons, their parents may spank them or remove television privileges. In both cases, people indicate displeasure in order to suppress an undesirable behavior.

Researchers use the same technique to decrease the probability that a behavior will recur: They deliver a noxious or unpleasant stimulus, such as a mild electric shock, when an organism displays an undesirable behavior. If an animal is punished for a specific behavior, the probability that it will continue to perform that behavior decreases.

Another form of punishment involves removal of a pleasant stimulus. For example, if a teenager stays out past her curfew, she may be grounded for a week. A child may be forbidden to watch television if he misbehaves. One punishment procedure that has proven effective is *time-out,* in which a person is removed from an environment containing positive events or reinforcers. A child who hits and kicks may be put in a room in which there are no toys, television, or people. Thus, punishment can involve adding a noxious event, such as a slap, or subtracting a positive event, such as television watching. In both cases the aim is to decrease the likelihood of a behavior (see Table 5.2).

TABLE 5.2
Effects of Reinforcement and Punishment

Addition of a Stimulus	Subtraction or Withholding of a Stimulus	Effect
Positive reinforcement Delivery of food, money, or some other reward	*Negative reinforcement* Removal of shock or some other aversive stimulus	Establishes or increases a specific behavior
Punishment Delivery of electric shock, a slap on the hand, or some other aversive stimulus	*Punishment* Removal of automobile, television, or some other pleasant stimulus	Suppresses or decreases a specific behavior

Punishment does not always succeed as a behavior shaping device. Punishment can lead to aggresive behavior such as prison riots.

The Nature of Punishers. Just as reinforcers are used for reinforcement, *punishers* are used for punishment. Punishers can be **primary**—stimuli that are naturally painful to an organism, such as an electric shock to an animal or a spanking to a child—or **secondary**—neutral stimuli that take on punishing qualities, such as a verbal no, a frown, or indifference. Secondary punishers can be effective means of controlling behavior, especially when used in combination with reinforcers for desired behaviors.

Punishment Plus Reinforcement. Some psychologists (e.g., Appel and Peterson, 1965) argue that punishment by itself is not an effective way to control or eliminate behavior. Punishment can suppress simple behavior patterns, but once the punishment ceases, animals often return to their previous behavior. To be effective, punishment must be continuous (Appel and Peterson, 1965). Therefore, those who study children in classrooms urge the combination of punishment for antisocial behavior and reinforcement for prosocial, worthwhile behaviors. A combination of private reprimands for disruptive behaviors and public praise for good behaviors is often the most effective method for controlling classroom behavior.

Limitations of Punishment. A serious limitation of punishment as a behavior-shaping device is that it will only suppress existing behaviors. It cannot be used to establish new, desired behaviors. Punishment also has serious social consequences (Azrin and Holtz, 1966). If parents use excessive punishment to control a child's behavior, for example, the child may try to escape from the home so that punishment cannot be delivered. Punishment may control the child's behavior, but it may also alienate the child from the parents. If ineffectively or inconsistently delivered, it may lead to learned

Primary punisher: Any stimulus or event that by its delivery or removal acts naturally (without learning) to decrease the likelihood that a response will recur.

Secondary punisher: A neutral stimulus with no intrinsic value to the organism that acquires punishment value through repeated pairing with a punishing stimulus.

helplessness, in which a person or animal feels powerless to control the punishment and stops making any response at all. We will discuss learned helplessness in detail in chapter 16.

Punishment can also lead to aggression and other antisocial behaviors. Research shows that children will imitate aggression; thus, parents who punish children physically are more likely to have children who are physically aggressive (Mischel and Grusec, 1966). In addition, a child or institutionalized person may strike out at the person who administers punishment in an attempt to eliminate the source of punishment, sometimes inflicting serious injury.

Punishment can also bring about generalized aggression. For example, if two rats in a Skinner box both receive painful shocks, they will strike out at each other. Similarly, punished individuals are often hostile and aggressive toward other members of their group; this is especially true for prison inmates whose hostility is well recognized and even for class bullies who are often the most strictly disciplined by their parents or teachers.

Skinner (1988) believes that punishment in schools is unnecessary and harmful. He advocates nonpunitive techniques that might involve developing strong bonds between students and teachers and reinforcing school activities at home (Comer, 1988). In general, procedures that lead to a perception of control are much more likely to lead to nonoccurrence of the undesired behavior even when the punishing agent (often Mom or Dad) is not around.

Focus on Learning

1 • In operant conditioning, an organism emits a behavior and it is followed by what event? p. 169 *consequence*
2 • Identify the key processes in shaping. p. 169
3 • Distinguish between primary reinforcers and secondary reinforcers. pp. 172–173 *P.R = survival value to org. (food + water) se = neutral stimuli (money)*
4 • What is the key difference between positive reinforcement and negative reinforcement? p. 173
5 • Identify the key difference between punishment and reinforcement. p. 176

---

*2 * Ex. Give a rat a pellet in the corner of the box where the bar is located.
Give rat pellet when it touches the wall where bar is located.
Give rat pellet when it approaches lever.
Give rat pellet when it touches the lever.
Give rat pellet when it presses lever*

*4 * P.R — rewarding a specific behavior.
N.R — removal of an unpleasant, aversive, or noxious stimuli*

*5 * punishment decreases probability of a particular response*
reinforcement increases prob. of a particular response.

Variables That Affect Operant Conditioning

As with classical conditioning, many variables affect operant conditioning. Most important are the strength, timing, and frequency of consequences (either reinforcement or punishment).

Strength of Consequences. Studies comparing productivity and varying amounts of reinforcement show that the greater the reward, the harder, longer, and faster you will work to complete a task. For example, the more money you receive for mowing lawns, the more lawns you will want to mow. Similarly, the stronger the punishment, the more quickly and longer the behavior can be suppressed (see Figure 5.11). If you receive a heavy fine for speeding, you probably will start to obey the speed limit.

The strength of a consequence can be measured in terms of either time or degree. For example, the length of time a child stays in a time-out room without positive reinforcements affects how soon and for how long an unacceptable behavior will be suppressed. A two-minute stay is not as effective as a ten-minute stay. Likewise, a tentative "Please do not do that" is not as effective as a firm "Don't do that again."

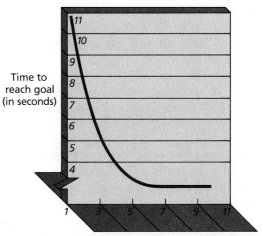

Time to
reach goal
(in seconds)

Magnitude of reinforcement
(number of pellets of food delivered
for each response)

FIGURE 5.11
As the amount of the reinforcer (such as food) in-
creases, an organism's time
to reach a goal usually
decreases.

Punishment, whatever its form, is best delivered in moderation—too
much may be as ineffective as too little. If too much punishment is delivered,
it may cause panic or decrease the likelihood of an appropriate response,
or even elicit behavior that is contrary to the punisher's goals.

Timing of Consequences. Just as the interval between presenting the conditioned stimulus and the unconditioned stimulus is important in classical
conditioning, the interval between a desired behavior and the delivery of
the consequence (reward or punishment) is important in operant conditioning. Generally, the shorter the interval, the greater the likelihood that the
behavior will be learned (see Figure 5.12). If you punish your dog for chewing
up the newspaper several hours after the behavior, it is unlikely that the
punishment will be effective. Similarly, if you reward a child on Wednesday
for eating her green beans the preceding Monday, repeating the good behavior is less likely. (However, an especially large reward or particularly
disagreeable punishment will offset the delay.) (Logan, 1965.)

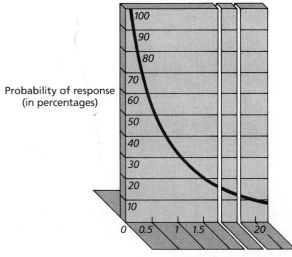

Probability of response
(in percentages)

Delay (in seconds)

FIGURE 5.12
A delay between a response
and reinforcement reduces
the probability that the behavior will recur. Short delays (or no delays) between
a response and reinforce-
ment maximize the chances
that the behavior will recur.

Fixed-interval: A reinforcer is delivered after a specified interval of time, provided that the required response has occurred at least once after the interval has elapsed.

Variable-interval: A reinforcer is delivered after a predetermined but varying interval of time, provided that the required response has occurred at least once after the interval.

Frequency of Consequences. How often do people want to be reinforced? Is a paycheck once a month sufficient? Will people work better if they receive reinforcement regularly or if they receive it at unpredictable times? In the studies discussed so far, we have assumed that a consequence follows each response.

What if people are reinforced some of the time, not continually? When a researcher varies the frequency with which an organism is to be reinforced, the researcher is said to manipulate *schedules of reinforcement* or the pattern of presentation of the reinforcer over time. The simplest and easiest reinforcement pattern is *continuous reinforcement;* this is reinforcement for every occurrence of the targeted behavior. But most researchers, or parents for that matter, do not reinforce a behavior every time it occurs; rather, they reinforce occasionally, or intermittently. What causes the occurrence of reinforcement? Schedules of reinforcement generally are based on either frequency of response or on time. Researchers have devised four basic schedules of reinforcement: two *interval schedules,* which deal with time periods, and two *ratio schedules,* which deal with work output.

The interval schedules can be either fixed or variable. Imagine that a rat in a Skinner box is being trained to press a bar in order to obtain food. If the experiment is on a **fixed-interval** schedule, the reward will follow the first response that occurs after a specified interval of time. That is, regardless of whether the rat works a great deal or just a little, it will be given a reinforcer if it presses the bar at least once after a specified interval. The reinforcement schedule is fixed. As Figure 5.13 shows, output on a fixed-interval schedule follows a scalloping pattern: Just after reinforcement, both animals and human beings typically respond slowly; on the other hand, just before the reinforcer is due, there is an increase in performance.

With a **variable-interval** schedule, a person or an animal is reinforced after varying amounts of time, as long as an appropriate response is made after the variable interval has elapsed. The organism may be reinforced if it makes a response after forty seconds, after sixty seconds, and then after twenty-five seconds. If grades are posted at various unpredictable intervals during a semester, you probably will check the bulletin board at a fairly steady rate.

Rats reinforced on a variable-interval schedule work at a slow, steady rate without showing the scalloping effect of those on a fixed-interval schedule. The delivery of a reinforcer is tied to time intervals rather than work

FIGURE 5.13
The four basic types of reinforcement schedules. The fixed-interval schedule produces a scalloping pattern of responses; the variable-ratio schedule produces high performance rates. Steep slopes represent high work rates. In general, the rate of responding is higher under ratio schedules than under interval schedules. It is also higher under fixed schedules than under variable schedules.

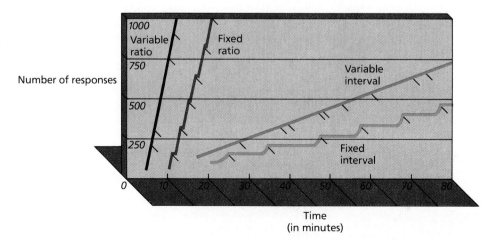

TABLE 5.3
Schedules of Reinforcement

Schedule	Description	Effect
Fixed interval	Reinforcement is given for the first response after a fixed time.	Response rate drops right after reinforcement but increases near the end of the interval.
Variable interval	Reinforcement is given for the first response after a predetermined but variable interval.	Response rate is steady.
Fixed ratio	Reinforcement is given after a fixed number of responses.	Response rate is rapid.
Variable ratio	Reinforcement is given after a predetermined variable number of responses.	Response rate is high and steady.

output, so the work rate is slow. Nevertheless, rats on a variable-interval schedule have a better overall rate of response than those on a fixed-interval schedule.

Ratio schedules, which can also be either fixed or variable, deal with output instead of time. In a **fixed-ratio** schedule, the subject is reinforced for a specific amount of work. For example, a rat in a Skinner box might be reinforced after every tenth bar press. In this case, the rat will work at a fast, steady, regular rate. It has learned that hard work brings the delivery of a reinforcer on a regular basis. Figure 5.13 shows that the work rate of a rat on a fixed-ratio schedule is much higher than that of a rat on an interval schedule. In the same way, a teenager who is paid by the job (i.e., for the amount of work completed) will probably mow more lawns than one who is paid by the hour.

Variable-ratio schedules can achieve very high rates of response. In contrast to a fixed-ratio schedule, a variable-ratio system reinforces the subject after varying amounts of work have been completed. Thus, a rat learns that hard work produces a reinforcer, but it cannot predict when the reinforcer will be delivered. Therefore, the rat's best bet is to work at an even, steady, high rate, thereby generating the highest available rate of response. Sales agents for insurance companies know that the more individuals they approach, the more insurance they will sell. They may not know who will buy, but they do know that a greater number of selling opportunities will result in more sales. Similarly, gamblers pour quarters into slot machines because they never know when they will be reinforced with a jackpot.

An efficient way to teach a response is to have an organism learn the response on a fixed-ratio schedule, and then introduce a variable-ratio schedule. For example, a rat can be reinforced on every trial so that it will learn the proper response quickly. It can then be reinforced after every other trial, then after every fifth trial, and then after a variable number of trials. Once the rat has learned the desired response, very high response rates can be obtained with an infrequent reinforcer. Table 5.3 lists the four basic reinforcement schedules and their effects. These schedules can easily be combined for maximum effect, depending on the targeted behavior.

Lottery participants always hope to be the one lucky person reinforced for having participated.

Fixed-ratio: A reinforcer is delivered after a predetermined number of responses has occurred.

Variable-ratio: A reinforcer is delivered after a predetermined but variable number of responses has occurred.

Anyone working on a commission basis, such as realtors, knows that their earnings don't exist without their own personal effort—the more effort expended, the more likely are higher earnings.

Using Schedules of Consequences. The study of reinforcement has many practical implications. Psychologists use the principles of reinforcement to study frequently-asked questions like "How can I change my little brother's rotten attitude?" "How can I get more work out of my employees?" "How do I learn to say no?" "How do I get my dog to stop biting my ankles?"

To get your brother to shape up, you can shape him. Each time he acts in a way that you like, however slight the action, reward him with praise or affection. When he acts poorly, use an extinction procedure, that is, withhold attention or rewards and ignore him. Continue this pattern for a few weeks, and as he becomes more pleasant, show him more attention. Remember, reinforced behaviors tend to recur.

Most workers get paid a fixed amount each week. They are on a fixed-interval schedule—regardless of their output, they get their paycheck. One way to increase productivity is to place workers on a fixed-ratio schedule. A worker who is paid by the piece, by the report, by the page, or by the widget is going to produce more pieces, reports, pages, or widgets than one who is paid by the hour and whose productivity therefore does not make a difference. Automobile salespeople, who are known for their persistence, work on a commission basis; their pay is linked to their ability to close a sale. Research in both the laboratory and the business world shows that when pay is linked to output, people generally work harder.

Stimulus Generalization and Stimulus Discrimination

Stimulus discrimination:
The process by which an organism learns to respond to a reinforced stimulus and to no other stimulus.

Stimulus generalization:
Responding to stimuli similar to, but not the same as, the training stimulus.

Stimulus generalization and **stimulus discrimination** occur in operant conditioning much as they do in classical conditioning. The difference is that in operant conditioning the reinforcement is delivered only after the animal correctly discriminates between the stimuli. For example, suppose an animal in a laboratory is given either a vertical or a horizontal line and two keys, one to be pressed if the line is vertical, the other, if the line is horizontal. The animal is reinforced for correct responses. The animal will usually make errors at first, but after repeated presentations of the vertical and horizontal lines, with reinforcements given only for correct responses, discrimination will occur. Stimulus discrimination can also be established with colors, tones, and more complex stimuli.

The processes of stimulus discrimination and generalization are evident daily. Children often make mistakes by overgeneralizing. For example, if a baby knows that cats have four legs and a tail, he or she may call all four-legged animals cats. With experience and the help, guidance, and reinforcement of parents, the child will learn to discriminate between dogs and cats, using body size, shape, fur, and sounds. Similarly, you may once have hated all Chinese food, but after several experiences you probably have learned to discriminate among the various dishes. Perhaps you recognize that you like the Hunan dishes and don't like the spicy Szechuan dishes.

Extinction and Spontaneous Recovery

In operant conditioning, if a reinforcer or punisher is no longer delivered—that is, if a consequence does not follow an instrumentally conditioned behavior—the behavior undergoes **extinction** (see Figure 5.14). Suppose, for example, that a pigeon is trained to peck a key whenever it hears a high-pitched tone. Pecking in response to a high-pitched tone brings reinforcement, but pecking in response to a low-pitched tone doesn't. If the reinforcement process ceases entirely, the pigeon will eventually stop working. If the pigeon is on a variable-ratio schedule and thus expects to work for long periods before reinforcement occurs, it will probably work for a very long time before stopping. If it is on a fixed-interval schedule and expects reinforcement within a short time, it will stop pecking after just a few non-reinforced trials.

One way to measure the extent of conditioning is to measure how resistant a response is to extinction; *resistance to extinction* is a measure of how long it takes, or how many trials are necessary, to achieve extinction. Consider a pigeon that is trained to peck when it hears a high-pitched tone and is rewarded each time it pecks correctly. The pigeon is tested for thirty minutes a day for sixty days. On the sixty-first day it is not reinforced for its correct behavior. For the first few minutes the pigeon continues to work normally. But soon its work rate decreases, and by the end of the thirty-minute session it is not pecking at all. When the pigeon is presented with

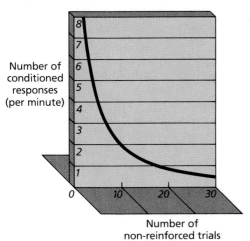

Number of conditioned responses (per minute)

Number of non-reinforced trials

FIGURE 5.14
When an animal's conditioned behavior is not reinforced over several trials, the likelihood of the conditioned response decreases. After many such trials, the behavior undergoes extinction.

Extinction: In operant conditioning, the process in which the probability of an organism emitting a conditioned response is reduced when reinforcement is withheld.

FIGURE 5.15
A child emitted tantrums at bedtime to gain attention. Williams counted the number of minutes the child cried and instructed the parents not to pay attention to the tantrums. After several days the number of minutes the child cried decreased to zero. A week later an aunt put the child to bed; when the child made a fuss (spontaneous recovery), the aunt reinforced the child with attention. The child then had to go through a second series of extinction trials. (Data from C. D. Williams, 1959, p. 269.)

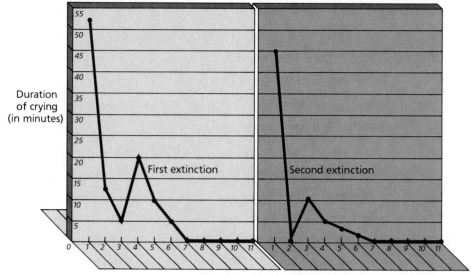

a tone the next day, it again responds with pecking but receives no reinforcer. Within a short time the pecking behavior is extinguished.

Note that the decrease in response is not always immediately apparent. When a reinforcer is withheld, organisms sometimes work harder and show an initial increase in performance. In such cases the curve depicting the extinction process shows a small initial increase in performance, followed by a decrease (Allen, Turner, and Everett, 1970).

As in classical conditioning, **spontaneous recovery** also occurs in operant conditioning. If an organism whose conditioned behavior has undergone extinction is given a rest period and is then retested, it will show spontaneous recovery. If it is put through this sequence several times, its work rate in each spontaneous-recovery session decreases. After one rest period, the organism's work rate almost equals what it was when the conditioned re-

Spontaneous recovery: The recurrence of a conditioned response following a rest period after extinction.

TABLE 5.4
Four Important Properties of Operant Conditioning

Property	Definition	Example
Extinction	The process of reducing the probability of a conditioned response by withholding the reinforcer.	A rat trained to press a bar stops pressing when it is no longer reinforced.
Spontaneous recovery	The recurrence of a conditioned response following a rest period after extinction.	A rat's continued bar-pressing behavior has undergone extinction; after a rest interval, the rat again presses the bar.
Stimulus generalization	The process by which an organism learns to respond to stimuli similar to but not identical to the training stimulus.	A cat presses a bar when presented with either an ellipse or a circle.
Stimulus discrimination	The process by which an organism learns to respond to a specific stimulus and then to no other similar stimulus; the complementary process to stimulus generalization.	A pigeon presses a key only in response to red lights, not to blue or green ones.

sponse was reinforced. But after a dozen or so rest periods (with no rein-forcements) the organism may make only one or two responses; the level of spontaneous recovery will have decreased markedly. Eventually the be-havior will disappear completely (see Figure 5.15).

People also show spontaneous recovery. When you answer a question in class, reinforcement usually follows. The instructor praises you for your extraordinary intelligence. But if the instructor stops reinforcing correct an-swers or does not call on you when you raise your hand, you will probably stop responding (i.e., your behavior will be extinguished). After a vacation, however, you may start raising your hand again (spontaneous recovery), but you will quickly stop if your behavior again is not reinforced (see Table 5.4 for a summary of four important properties of operant conditioning). Instructors learn early in their careers that if they want to have a lively class they need to reinforce not just correct answers, but also attempts at correct answers. In doing so, they help shape or manage their students' behavior.

Managing Children's Behavior

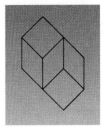

*I*f a child misbehaves constantly, his or her parents may seek the help of a psychologist, read self-help books, or get angry, yell at the child, and hope that the problem goes away. The last approach will not change the way the youngster behaves, but the first two might. Both psychologists and self-help books suggest that misbehavior can be decreased and replaced by more worthwhile behavior by using positive reinforcement to establish and maintain desired behaviors and punishment to suppress or eliminate undesirable ones.

Consider the case of Rochelle. Each morning Rochelle refuses to dress her-self, dawdles over breakfast, and is generally unpleasant and difficult. The entire household's morning routine seems to focus on getting Rochelle out the door and off to school.

Learning theory suggests that Rochelle's behavior could be changed. She could be reinforced for making her bed, dressing herself, and eating breakfast at a reasonable rate. She could also be punished for not making her bed, not getting dressed, and dawdling over breakfast. Therefore, the first thing Rochelle's parents need to do is to decide on a reinforcer. They have several options available: they could allow Rochelle to play outside with friends for a certain amount of extra time, they might read her an extra story at bedtime, they might allow her to choose her clothes for the next day at school, or they might even give her a special food reward like a candy bar. Let us say that they choose the story. Next, they need to decide on an appropriate punisher. Since Rochelle hates being sent to sit in a "thinking chair" in a corner of the family room, her parents will use that as the punisher. They can now begin to implement a serious change in Rochelle's behavior.

Rochelle's parents tell her that if she makes her bed, dresses herself, and eats breakfast quickly she will get to have an extra story read to her at bedtime. They also tell her that if she fails to make her bed, dress herself, and finish breakfast within ten minutes she will be sent to the thinking chair—even if it means being late for school. The procedure is to begin on the following day.

The next morning Rochelle rises quickly, makes her bed, and dresses herself, but breakfast is a half-hour ordeal. Her parents send her to sit in the chair and think about things. Rochelle cries, berates her parents, and laments the misfor-tunes of her life. The next day breakfast is quick, but Rochelle does not make her bed—more time in the thinking chair, no extra stories at bedtime. On the third day Rochelle goes through the morning routine without incident. She is praised and receives hugs from her parents and is read her favorite story that night. After a few weeks of reinforcement and punishment, Rochelle decides that she prefers the extra attention, later bedtime, and an extra story to the think-

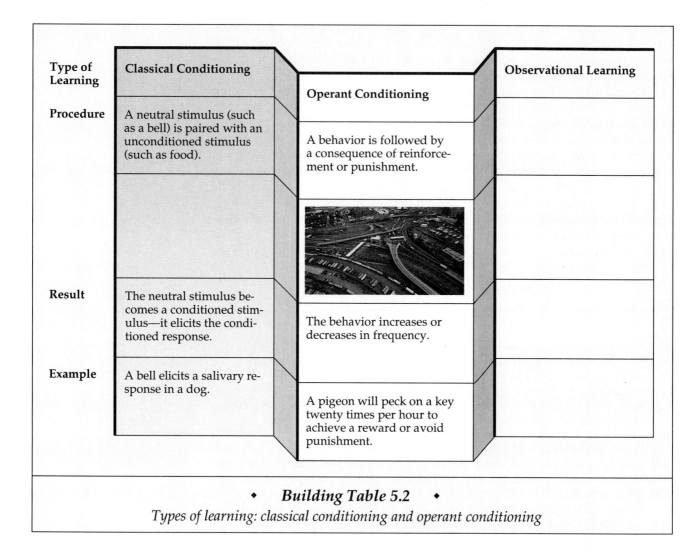

Type of Learning	Classical Conditioning	Operant Conditioning	Observational Learning
Procedure	A neutral stimulus (such as a bell) is paired with an unconditioned stimulus (such as food).	A behavior is followed by a consequence of reinforcement or punishment.	
Result	The neutral stimulus becomes a conditioned stimulus—it elicits the conditioned response.	The behavior increases or decreases in frequency.	
Example	A bell elicits a salivary response in a dog.	A pigeon will peck on a key twenty times per hour to achieve a reward or avoid punishment.	

◆   *Building Table 5.2*   ◆

Types of learning: classical conditioning and operant conditioning

ing chair and that making her bed, after all, takes only 1½ minutes (refer to Building Table 5.2 for a comparison of classical and operant conditioning).   ◆

Intrinsically Motivated Behavior

Psychologists have shown that reinforcement is effective in establishing and maintaining behavior. But some behaviors are intrinsically rewarding; they are performed because they are pleasurable in themselves. People are likely to repeat intrinsically motivated behaviors for their own sake—for example, they work on a project for the feeling of satisfaction it brings. They will perform extrinsically motivated behavior, such as working for a paycheck, only for the sake of the external reinforcement. Interestingly, if reinforcement is offered for intrinsically motivated behavior, performance may actually decrease. Imagine, for example, that a woman performs charity work because it makes her feel good. Paying the woman could cause her to lose interest in the work because it no longer offers the intrinsic reward of selfless behavior. A student pianist may lose his desire to practice when his teacher enters him in a competition; practice sessions become ordeals, and the student may wish to stop playing altogether.

All people are motivated intrinsically. The question is why some are intrinsically motivated to do crossword puzzles and others to climb mountains. One explanation is that as children we are conditioned to feel pleasure, or intrinsic reinforcement, for certain behaviors. Someone who likes crossword puzzles may have been reinforced for accomplishing challenging intellectual tasks; someone who prefers mountaineering may have been reinforced for performing physically demanding feats (in chapter 11 we discuss the conditions under which intrinsically motivated behavior occurs). Next we discuss some of the hidden costs of rewards.

The Hidden Cost of Reward

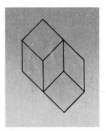

A child may love playing checkers, doing simple crossword puzzles, or coloring in a coloring book. But offer her a dime for doing these things and she may no longer want to play. This effect has been called the hidden cost of offering a reward. Why does this happen? Why do some behaviors seem like fun and others seem like work? Are there things psychologists can do to make events fun? What are the critical variables?

Fundamentals. In general, psychologists find that some behaviors are intrinsically fun—people like to do them for their own reward. Other behaviors, however, are not nearly as much fun and people need to be motivated to perform them, either with reinforcers or with threats of punishment. Psychologists talk about *intrinsic* and *extrinsic* motivation—whether things are done for fun or for rewards. They have found that intrinsically motivated behaviors like doing crossword puzzles are less likely to occur if a reward is offered for doing them.

Hypotheses Are Formed. On the basis of the fundamental findings about intrinsic and extrinsic motivation, some schools have experimented with a grade-free system. But two researchers from Hebrew University of Jerusalem, Butler and Nisan (1986), have found that in some cases rewards encourage learning and performance, although they may decrease creativity. The researchers wanted to know if performance feedback would affect children's willingness to do tasks and how well they did these tasks. They hypothesized that if there is a hidden cost of reward, the feedback should interfere with the students' performance.

Methods. Butler and Nisan asked sixth-grade children to do two word games that involved constructing words from the letters of a longer word. There were two tasks. The first focused on the quantity of words constructed. The second involved more creative thinking; the children were asked to take the first and last letters of the longer word and use those as the first and last letters of still another word. Both of these tasks were repeated each day over a three-day period.

The children were divided into three feedback groups. The first group received *written comments* at the end of a session, such as "The words you wrote were correct, but you did not write many words." The second group of children was given a *numerical grade* on their performance. The third group was given *no feedback* on their performance. Butler and Nisan gave the students an attitude questionnaire at the end of the third session to assess how the students felt about the task. The questions included "How interesting were the tasks?" and "How many more would you like to receive?" The three groups—*comments, numerical grade,* and *no feedback*—were each tested in three sessions. The variables being measured were the total number of words generated and the number of words generated using the first and last letter from a longer word.

Results. The results showed that in the *no feedback* group the number of words for both tasks decreased from the first to the last session; the students became bored with the task. The *comments* students improved their overall performance on both tasks from the first to the last session. Providing *numerical grades* improved performance on the first task (quantity of words), but it decreased performance on the quality task (creative thinking).

Conclusions and Implications. Contrary to the general finding that a reward sometimes decreases performance, results of the Butler-Nisan study show that rewards improve performance on easier tasks. On harder tasks, if feedback is in the form of written comments rather than grades, it also improves performance.

The implications of this experiment are important. School grades may motivate learners, but on tasks that involve creativity they may decrease motivation. The researchers asked students how they felt about both sets of tasks. Generally speaking, students liked getting feedback, and they preferred written comments to grades. However, they would rather get grades than no feedback at all.

Linney and Seidman (1989) assert, "Now more than ever schools need to examine ways to optimize the learning potential of students and facilitate the creation of learning environments that are best matched to their developmental and sociocultural needs" (p. 339). The hidden cost of reward does not have to be evident. School systems that provide interesting tasks are more likely to have motivated students; feedback other than grades can be important in enhancing students' creativity. But most important, learning is facilitated when a task continues to be perceived as challenging and when feedback is given to students who show progress. ◆

Electrical Brain Stimulation

Until the 1950s researchers assumed that reinforcers are effective because they satisfy some need or drive in an organism. Then James Olds (1955, 1969) found an apparent exception to this assumption: He discovered that rats find electrical stimulation of certain areas of the brain rewarding.

Olds implanted an electrode in the hypothalamus of rats and attached the electrodes to a stimulator that provided a small voltage. The stimulator was activated only when the rats pressed a lever in a Skinner box. Olds found that the rats pressed the lever thousands of times in order to continue the self-stimulation. In one study, they pressed it at a rate of 1920 times per hour (Olds and Milner, 1954). Rats will even cross an electrified grid to obtain this reward. Animals who were rewarded with brain stimulation performed better in a maze, running faster with fewer errors. And hungry rats often chose self-stimulation over food.

Stimulation of certain areas of the brain initiates different drives and activities. In some cases, it reinforces behaviors such as bar pressing; in others, it increases eating, drinking, or sexual behavior. Psychologists are still not sure how electrical stimulation reinforces a behavior like lever pressing, but they do know that the area of the brain that is stimulated, the state of the organism, and its particular physiological needs are important. A hungry rat, for example, will self-stimulate faster than a rat that is not hungry. In addition, a hungry rat will generally choose electrical brain stimulation over food but will not starve to death by *always* making this choice (see, for example, Routtenberg and Lindy, 1965).

Psychology in Business and Medicine: Behavioral Regulation

Behavioral regulation theorists assume that people and animals have choices and, if possible, will choose activities that seem optimal to them. Rats, for example, will spend their time eating, drinking, and running on a wheel, activities they find pleasurable. An experiment by Bernstein and Ebbesen

(1978) showed that human beings readjust their activities in a systematic manner. The researchers paid subjects to live in an isolated room twenty-four hours a day, seven days a week, for several weeks. The room had all the usual amenities of a home—bed, tables, shower, books, cooking utensils, and so forth. The experimenters observed the subjects through a one-way mirror and recorded their *base-line activity,* that is, the frequency of certain behaviors when no restrictions are placed on the subjects. They found, for example, that one subject spent nearly twice as much base-line time knitting as studying. The experimenters used the subject's base line to determine the reinforcing event—in this case, knitting.

The experimenters then imposed a contingency. In the case of the subject who liked to knit, they insisted that she study for a certain amount of time before she could knit. If she studied only as much as she did before, she would be able to knit for much less time. As a consequence, the subject altered her behavior so that she could knit more. She began to study for longer periods of time, eventually more than doubling the time she spent studying.

Behavioral regulation has a number of practical applications. For example, if you were a member of Weight Watchers, Alcoholics Anonymous, Gamblers Anonymous, or any other self-help group, you would probably be engaging in some form of self-monitoring or self-regulation. Weight reduction groups often ask people to keep track of when and what they eat, when they have the urge to eat, and what feelings or events precede those urges. The organizers of such groups seek to help people identify the events that lead to eating so they can control it. The aim is to help people regulate themselves and thus manage their lives better.

Medicine. The techniques of self-regulation are based on simple learning principles. You can see how psychologists apply these learning principles when you consider the management of clients with diabetes mellitus. Clients with Type I diabetes require shots of insulin each day. Clients with Type II diabetes account for ninety percent of the diabetic population; these clients are not required to take shots each day but are often obese and must take medication daily and follow a strict diet. In both types, clients' adherence to their self-care regime is poor: eighty percent use unhygienic techniques, fifty-eight percent administer wrong doses of insulin, seventy-five percent do not eat prescribed food, and seventy-seven percent test their urine incorrectly (Wing, Epstein, Norwalk, and Lamparksi, 1986).

Researchers who wish to help diabetics can put some basic psychological principles to work. According to Wing, Epstein, Nowalk, and Lamparksi (1986), if diabetics are to regulate themselves carefully they must self-observe, self-evaluate, and then self-reinforce. The researchers assert that when clients carefully *self-observe* the target behavior, they are better able to *self-evaluate* their progress. After evaluating their progress, it is crucial that they achieve *reinforcement* for adhering to their medical regime. When these procedures are followed, adherence to a medical regime improves.

Business. Economists and business leaders are applying psychological principles to business theory, making predictions about how human beings will distribute their time and effort, money, and work. Schools of business are introducing behavioral regulation theory into their curriculums. Behavioral regulation theory recognizes the interplay of preferences, rewards, schedules of reinforcement, desire for leisure, and motivation.

Can economists explain changes in the stock market through behavioral regulation theory? Hood (1988) asserts that stock prices reflect opinions and

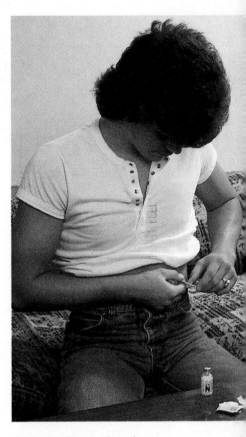

Diabetics know that they must regulate their blood sugar levels by observing a special diet and remembering to take insulin shots.

are subject to the same social pressures as other opinions. According to Hood, the stock market crash of 1987 (when the stock market fell 1000 points in a short period) can be explained by psychological factors rather than economic ones. He asserts that opinions, social pressure, recent history, and emotions drove the stock market down more than fundamental economic reasons, although economic technicalities may have entered into the crash of 1987. Behavioral economists suggest that psychological principles determine how people will spend their effort, distribute their money, and make their stock investments. Investigating these issues in a laboratory has shown that human beings' behavior, and many economic principles, follow from psychological principles. Human beings are decision makers; they can evaluate alternatives and decide how they will distribute effort. This decision process and the focus on thought is clearly seen in studies of cognitive learning, considered next.

Focus on Learning

1. What happens if an organism is reinforced some of the time, not continually? p. 180 ✓ variable-interval
2. When a dog is trained to howl whenever it hears a high-pitched tone and then a low-pitched tone is presented, what will happen? p. 182
3. Distinguish between intrinsically and extrinsically motivated behavior. pp. 186–187
4. In doing human and animal research on learning, researchers often record base-line activity; what is base-line activity? p. 189
   the way you are w/out restrictions

Cognitive Learning

"Enough!" shouted Tyson after four grueling hours of trying to program his personal computer. Errors were rampant in his program and all for the same reason, but he didn't know what. After dozens of trial-and-error manipulations, Tyson turned off the computer and went on to study for his history exam. But then, while staring at a page in the text, he saw the word "while," thought about it, and suddenly realized his programming mistake. His "if-then" statements were missing a necessary comma. After placing the missing comma in all the statements, the program ran flawlessly.

Tyson solved his problem by thinking. His learning was not a matter of simple conditioning of a simple response with a simple reinforcer. Learning researchers have actively focused on learning that involves reinforcement. Conditioning evidenced in studies by Pavlov, Thorndike, and Skinner requires a reinforcer if behavior is to be maintained. Much of the learning literature has focused on stimuli and responses and their relationship, timing, and frequency. But is a reinforcer always necessary for learning? Can a person learn new behaviors just by thinking or using his or her imagination? These questions are problematic for traditional learning researchers, but not for cognitive psychologists or learning researchers who have a cognitive emphasis on learning.

Thinking about a problem allows you to solve the problem and makes other behaviors possible; this thinking becomes crucial to learning and problem solving (Skinner, 1989). The emphasis of cognitive research, evident even in early learning studies, will be shown over and over again as we examine areas of psychology such as motivation, maladjustment, and therapy. Some of the most famous psychologists of the early part of the century examined learning when reinforcement was not evident and behavior was not shown. These early studies focused on *insight* and *latent learning*. Some of these studies gave birth to modern studies of *cognitive mapping.* Other recent research has focused on *observational learning.* Still other cognitive research has focused on problem solving, creativity, and concept formation, which will be covered in chapter 7.

Insight

When you discover a relationship between a series of events, you may say that you had an *insight.* Insights are usually not taught to people, but rather are discovered after a series of events has occurred. Like Tyson discovering his missing comma, many types of learning involve sustained thought and insight.

Discovering the causes of insight was the goal of researchers working with animals in the 1920s. Wolfgang Kohler, a Gestalt researcher, showed that chimps developed insights into methods of retrieving food that was beyond their reach. The chimps discovered that they could pile boxes on top of one another to reach food, or attach poles together, making a long stick to grab bananas. They were never reinforced for the specific behavior, but they learned how to get their food through insight. Once a chimp learns how to pile boxes, or once Tyson realizes his comma error, the insight is not forgotten. The insight occurs through thought, without direct reinforcement. Once the insight occurs, no further instruction, investigation, or training is necessary.

Latent Learning

After a person has an insight, learns a task, or solves a problem (or elements of a problem), that new learning is not necessarily evident. Early researchers were baffled by rats that ran mazes for them and showed the phenomenon of *latent learning.*

Researchers in the 1920s placed hungry rats in mazes and recorded how many trials it took the rats to reach a goal where food was found. It took many days and many trials, but hungry rats learned the mazes well. Other rats were put in the maze, but were not reinforced with food on reaching the goal; they were merely removed from the maze. A third group of rats, like the second group, was not reinforced, but after ten days was given food on reaching the goal. Surprisingly, in one day these rats were reaching the goal with few errors. During the first ten days of maze running they must have been learning something, but not showing it. After being given a reward, they had a reason to reach the goal quickly. Researchers such as E. C. Tolman argued that their learning was latent, that is, it was not demonstrated when it occurred. We call this **latent learning.**

Tolman showed that when a rat is given a reason (such as food) to show learning, the behavior will be evident. In other words, a rat—or a person— without motivation may not show learning, even if it exists. Tolman's work with rats led him to propose the idea that animals and humans develop a type of map of their world, which allows them to navigate a maze, or even a city street. His early work laid the foundation for more modern studies of latent learning (e.g., Chamizo and Mackintosh, 1989) and of cognitive maps that focus on the active decision making of human beings.

Cognitive Maps

Some people are easily disoriented when visiting a new city, while others seem to possess an internal map. These internal maps are sometimes called

Latent learning: Learning that occurs in the absence of any direct reinforcement and that may be demonstrated after the learning occurs, that is, it remains latent.

cognitive maps—cognitive representations that enable some people to navigate from a starting point to an unseen destination. How are these cognitive routes perceived and learned?

Travel routes can be learned through simple associations: this street leads to that street, that street leads to the pizza parlor, and then you go left. But researcher Gary Allen (1987) asserted that learning routes also involves perceptual and cognitive influences, not just rote memorization of turns and signs. He devised a series of studies to demonstrate this.

Slides depicting an actual walk through an urban neighborhood were shown in sequential order to one group of subjects, and then the same slides were shown in random order to a second group. All subjects were then asked to make judgments about the distance from the beginning of the walk to a variety of specific locations. Amazingly, the subjects who viewed the random presentations made judgments that were almost as good as those of subjects who saw the sequential walk. How did they do it?

Allen contends that the subjects form a cognitive map by using visual information from the slides that overlapped with information in other slides. From these they pieced together a map of the neighborhood. (Without the overlap among the scenes, the pictures would have appeared to show a random walk through different neighborhoods.) The random-walk subjects tried to mentally place the slides in order by paying particular attention to parts of the visual world that they had seen in previous slides. In Allen's words, they attempted to impose "order on a collage of perceptual information" (p. 277).

Allen's research on cognitive maps spanned a decade. He showed that human beings pay attention to important landmarks in determining routes and that not all landmarks are equally useful. The value of various types of landmarks is learned during childhood. In one study, Allen and his colleagues discovered that young children do not value landmarks the same way that adults do. As they gain experience, children are more likely to pick landmarks that trigger choices. Human beings also tend to divide portions of a route into segments or chunks, and learn the map of those segments (Allen, 1981). Allen makes a strong case for perceptual and cognitive influences in learning routes. His research suggests that routes are learned by integrating segments of routes and landmarks into cognitive maps. Human beings are active processors of information and that helps them form a cognitive map.

Observational Learning

Let's return to Tyson, whose walk to psychology class was described at the beginning of the chapter. On seeing Ray wearing his jacket collar turned up, Tyson flipped his own collar up to imitate his role model. Tyson learned to change his behavior through observation.

A truly comprehensive learning theory of behavior must be able to explain how people learn behaviors that are not taught. Although Tyson learned to turn his collar up, he was not taught to do so. As another example, everyone knows that smoking cigarettes is unhealthy; smokers regularly try to stop smoking, and for most people the first experience with smoking is unpleasant. But twelve-year-olds light up anyway. They inhale the smoke, cough for several minutes, and feel nauseated. There is no doubt that it is a punishing experience for them. But they try again. Over time they master the technique of inhaling and, in their view, look "cool" with a cigarette. That's the key to the whole situation: The twelve-year-olds observed other people with cigarettes, thought they looked cool, wanted to look cool themselves, and therefore initiated the smoking behavior.

Such situations present a problem for traditional learning theorists. There is little reinforcement to establish smoking behavior; instead, there is punishment (coughing and nausea). But the behavior recurs. To explain this type of learning, Stanford University psychologist Albert Bandura contends that the principles of classical and operant conditioning are just two ways in which people learn. Another way is by observing other people:

> Although it is generally assumed that social behavior is learned and modified through direct reward and punishment of instrumental responses, informal observation and laboratory study of the social learning process reveal that new responses may be rapidly acquired and existing behavior and attitudes exhibited by models. (Bandura, Ross, and Ross, 1963a, p. 527)

During the last twenty-five years, Bandura's ideas, expressed through **observational learning theory** (also called *social learning theory*), have expanded the range of behaviors that can be explained by learning theory (Woodward, 1982). The theory focuses on the role of thought in establishing and maintaining behavior. Bandura and his colleagues conducted important research to confirm their idea that people can learn by observing and then imitating the behavior of others (Bandura 1969, 1977b; Bandura, Ross, and Ross, 1963a). In their early studies they showed one group of children films with aggressive content in which an adult punched an inflated doll, and showed another group films that had neither aggressive nor nonaggressive content. They then compared the play behavior of both groups. The researchers found that the children who had viewed aggressive, violent films tended to be aggressive and violent afterward, whereas the other children showed no change in behavior (Bandura, Ross, and Ross, 1963a; Bandura and Walters, 1963). Bandura's research and many subsequent studies have shown that observing aggression creates aggression in children, but children do not imitate aggressiveness when the person they observe is punished for aggressive behavior.

Everyday experience also shows that people imitate the behavior of others, especially those whom they hold in high esteem. Children emulating Rambo dress in army fatigues and carry toy machine guns. You may buy a particular brand of shampoo because your favorite television star claims to use it. Scores of young girls became interested in gymnastics after watching Olympic star Mary Lou Retton and in track events after watching Florence Griffith Joyner. But unfortunately, not all observational learning is positive: drug and alcohol use often begins when children and teenagers imitate people they admire.

Laboratory studies of observational learning show that people can learn new behaviors by merely observing, without being reinforced. For example, in a study by Bernal and Berger (1976), subjects watched a film of other subjects being conditioned to produce an eye-blink response. The filmed subjects had a puff of air delivered to their eyelids; this stimulus was paired with a tone. After a number of trials, the filmed subjects showed an eye-blink response to the tone alone. The subjects who watched the film also developed an eye blink in response to a tone. Other studies show that cats also learn by observing. John, Chesler, Bartlett, and Victor (1968) found that cats can learn to avoid receiving a shock through a grid floor by watching other cats successfully avoid the shocks by performing some task. People who stutter can decrease their stuttering by watching others do so successfully (Martin and Haroldson, 1977). Even children who fear animals can

Observational learning theory: The process by which organisms learn new responses by observing the behavior of a model and then imitating it; also called *social learning theory.*

These young boys have learned to mimic the traits of the adults around them simply by observing ongoing behavior mannerisms in their community.

learn to be less fearful by watching other children interact with animals (Bandura and Menlove, 1968).

A key point to remember is that if a person observes an action that is not reinforced, but rather punished, it will not be imitated. Children who observe aggression that is punished do not behave aggressively; nevertheless, they may learn aggressive responses that might be evident in the future. Learning may take place through observation, but performance of specific learning may depend on a specific setting and a person's perceived expectations about the effect of exhibiting those behaviors.

Variables That Affect Observational Learning. Observational learning theory has several important elements. One is the type and power of the model employed. Nurturing, warm, and caring models, for example, are more likely to be imitated than nonnurturing, angry ones, and dominant parents are more likely to be imitated than relatively passive ones.

Another element is the learner's personality and degree of independence. Dependent children are more likely to imitate models than are independent children. Generally, the less self-confidence a person has, the more likely he or she is to imitate a model. A third factor is the situation.

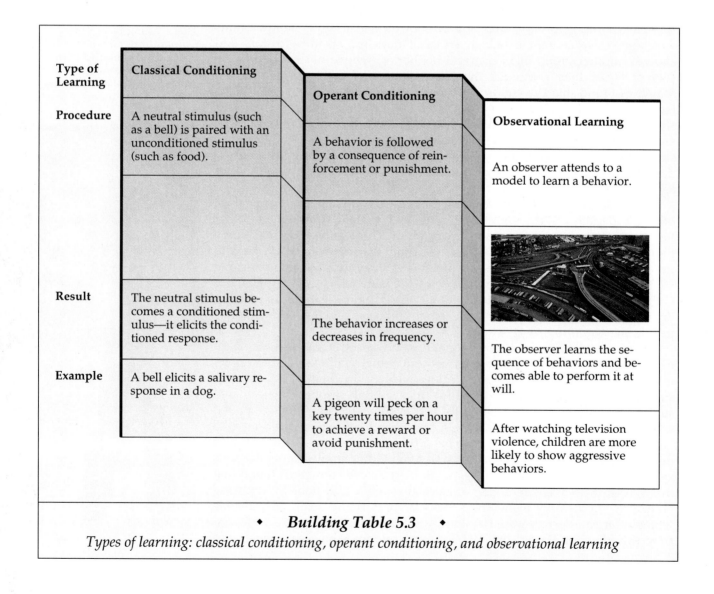

Type of Learning	Classical Conditioning	Operant Conditioning	Observational Learning
Procedure	A neutral stimulus (such as a bell) is paired with an unconditioned stimulus (such as food).	A behavior is followed by a consequence of reinforcement or punishment.	An observer attends to a model to learn a behavior.
Result	The neutral stimulus becomes a conditioned stimulus—it elicits the conditioned response.	The behavior increases or decreases in frequency.	The observer learns the sequence of behaviors and becomes able to perform it at will.
Example	A bell elicits a salivary response in a dog.	A pigeon will peck on a key twenty times per hour to achieve a reward or avoid punishment.	After watching television violence, children are more likely to show aggressive behaviors.

♦   ***Building Table 5.3***   ♦

Types of learning: classical conditioning, operant conditioning, and observational learning

People are more likely to imitate others when there is uncertainty about correct behavior. A teenager going on his or her first date, for example, takes cues from peers about dress and imitates their behavior. And when a person who has never been exposed to death loses someone close, he or she may not know what to say or how to express feelings. Watching other people express their grief provides a model for behavior.

Traditional versus Observational Learning. Psychologists were initially slow to explain behavior patterns in terms of observational learning, possibly because the process of observational learning is more difficult to describe than the process of classical conditioning (Bandura, 1971). Also, early attempts to examine observational learning in the laboratory were not very successful. Perhaps most important, the study of observational learning requires that the psychologist study thinking itself, which is difficult to manipulate, measure, and describe.

1. learning that was not demonstrated when first learned occurred.

2. when punishment is present.

Today, cognitive approaches to understanding learning are gaining an ever more important role in learning theory. Even die-hard learning researchers who have been doing work on operant conditioning for years acknowledge that some learning takes place through thought processes involving observation. Observational learning theorists are not interested in replacing traditional learning theory; rather, they want observational learning to stand alongside classical and operant conditioning as another way of explaining human learning and behavior. Psychologists are concluding that observational learning in combination with classical and operant conditioning can account for nearly all learned behavior (see Building Table 5.3).

Bandura's explanation of learning through observation (1977b) has filled a large gap in psychologists' understanding of the role of thought in how learning occurs. But it has also raised questions. Psychologists need to identify the variables involved in observational learning and understand what people think about the events they observe. In chapters 12 and 15 we will discuss more fully Bandura's research on observational learning and its effects on social behaviors.

> ◆ Identify the key finding in studies of latent learning. p. 191
> ◆ When is reinforcement necessary in observational learning? p. 192
> ◆ For a behavior to be learned through observational learning, who would make the best type of model? pp. 192–194
>   *children + teens*

Focus on Learning

Key Terms

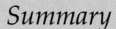

Summary

Classical Conditioning

- Learning is a relatively permanent and stable change in an organism that usually, but not always, can be seen in behavior; it occurs as a result of experience and interaction with the environment.   p. 154

- Reflexes occur involuntarily, quickly, and *without learning* in response to some stimulus.   p. 155

- Classical conditioning involves the pairing of a neutral stimulus (e.g., a bell) with an unconditioned stimulus (e.g., food) so that the unconditioned response (e.g., salivation) becomes a conditioned response. In higher-order conditioning, a second neutral stimulus takes on reinforcing properties by being associated with the conditioned stimulus.   pp. 155–156

- For conditioning to occur, the unconditioned stimulus and the conditioned stimulus must be presented in rapid sequence, and the conditioned stimulus must predict the occurrence of the unconditioned stimulus.   p. 161

- The most important variables in classical conditioning are the strength, timing, and frequency of the unconditioned stimulus. When these variables are optimal, the conditioned stimulus will predict the likelihood of an unconditioned stimulus.   p. 161

- Extinction is the process of reducing the probability that a conditioned response will recur. Spontaneous recovery is the recurrence, after a rest period, of a conditioned response that has undergone extinction.   p. 163

Operant Conditioning

- In operant conditioning, an organism emits or shows a particular behavior which is then followed by a consequence (reward or punishment). The term *reinforcer* refers to any consequence that increases the probability that the response that preceded it will occur. Shaping is the process of reinforcing behavior that approximates a desired behavior.   p. 168

- Positive reinforcement increases the probability that a desired response will occur by introducing a rewarding or pleasant stimulus. Negative reinforcement increases the probability that a desired behavior will occur by removing an aversive stimulus.   pp. 172–173

- Primary reinforcers are those that have survival value for the organism; their value does not have to be learned. Secondary reinforcers are neutral stimuli that initially have no intrinsic value for the organism, but when paired, coupled, or linked with a primary reinforcer, they too become rewards.   pp. 174–175

- The most important variables affecting operant conditioning are the strength, timing, and frequency of consequences. Schedules of reinforcement may be of two types: interval schedules and ratio schedules. Interval schedules provide reinforcement after fixed or variable time periods; ratio schedules provide reinforcement after fixed or variable amounts of work.   pp. 178–182

- Psychologists have shown that reinforcement, or extrinsic motivation, is effective in establishing and maintaining behavior. But some behaviors are intrinsically motivated; they are performed because they are pleasurable in themselves.   pp. 186–187

- Behavioral regulation theorists assume that organisms have choices and, if possible, will engage in the activities that seem optimal to them. If they are prevented from performing a desired activity, they will readjust their activities in a systematic manner.   pp. 188–190

Cognitive Learning

- Cognitive learning psychologists focus on thought processes that help process, establish, and maintain learning. Some of the early studies focused on *insight* and *latent learning* and gave birth to modern studies of *cognitive mapping*.   pp. 190–192

- Observational learning, also called social learning, is the acquisition of new responses by observing and then imitating the behavior of a model.   p. 192

- Some of the key elements of social learning theory are the characteristics and power of the model, the learner's own personality and independence, and the situations in which people find themselves.   pp. 192–195

Connections

If you are interested in . . .	Turn to . . .	To learn more about . . .
Classical conditioning	◆ Ch. 7, p. 256	How theories of language development depend on the idea of higher-order generalization.
	◆ Ch. 12, p. 452	Why behavioral theories of personality depend on the idea that predictability in the environment determines personality.
	◆ Ch. 13, pp. 462, 482–484	How a person's physical responses to the stresses in his or her life can be conditioned, and reversed.
	◆ Ch. 15, pp. 552–553	How treatment for phobias relies on reconditioning individuals.
Operant conditioning	◆ Ch. 7, p. 259	How conditioning has played a crucial role in the development of theories of how people learn language.
	◆ Ch. 11, p. 403	The impact of providing reinforcement to people when they already find a behavior rewarding.
	◆ Ch. 17, pp. 618–621	When, and under what conditions, attitudes such as prejudice are shaped by a parent's use of reinforcement.
Cognitive learning	◆ Ch. 7, p. 240	How people develop reasoning processes and gain insight into problem-solving tasks.
	◆ Ch. 12, p. 447	Why behavior that is observed, imitated and then reinforced becomes part of an individual's personality.
	◆ Ch. 17, p. 627	How aggression researchers have used observational learning theory to show that watching television violence has a deleterious influence on children's behavior.

6 *Memory*

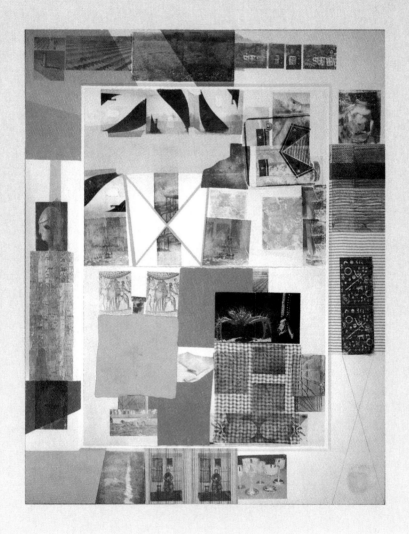

"Cloister Series—Rush 9" by Robert Rauschenberg

◆

*I*t was afternoon and twelve-year-old Martha stood in the kitchen stirring cookie dough while her mother greased a baking sheet. Her father was in the living room, listening to a televised broadcast of a concert. Suddenly, the music stopped and an announcer, his voice charged with excitement, told listeners that Neil Armstrong in Apollo 11 had just landed on the moon. Her mother rushed to her father's side; Martha followed, still holding the bowl of batter as she knelt down by the television to watch the news.

Those childhood images recalled from events that happened more than twenty years before flashed in Martha's mind as she rewrote modern American history class lecture notes. In class, she had been the center of attention because she was the only person, other than the professor, old enough to remember the day United States astronauts landed on the moon. Although Martha could remember an event that occurred two decades earlier, she often had to make a concerted effort to memorize important lecture points heard only hours before.

Psychologists have long recognized that recalling well-learned facts can be easy or difficult. Even though something has been *learned*, it may not always be *remembered*. A person may easily remember the Pledge of Allegiance, but forget the chemical formula for sugar. That's because learning and memory are two separate processes. From chapter 5, recall that *learning* is a relatively permanent change in the organism that occurs as a result of experience; this change is often seen in overt or observed behavior, but not always. And **memory** is the ability to remember past events or previously learned information or skills; memory is also the storage system that allows for retaining and retrieving previously learned information.

As we saw in chapter 5, psychologists studying learning and memory usually use performance (such as the score on an SAT test) to infer that an organism (such as a student) can maintain previously learned information or skills. In animals, physical performance is the only indication of memory, since their communication skills are limited. However, human beings can demonstrate memory in verbal and written performance. This chapter examines the more complex learning found in human beings which leads to memory.

Early memory studies focused on how quickly people learned lists of nonsense words and how long they remembered them or how quickly they forgot them. Later studies focused on variables such as organization of material that affected retention and forgetting. Recent research is focusing on how people code information and use memory aids, imagery, and other learning cues to retrieve information from memory. Researchers are also examining the biological basis of memory. They now use different tasks to examine memory because they know that the various memory tasks require different kinds of knowledge from subjects (Richardson-Klavehn and Bjork, 1988).

Memory: Retaining Information

It would be wonderful to have a perfect memory, right? Not necessarily. Soviet psychologist A. R. Luria studied a man who possessed a memory far surpassing that of normal humans. Shereshevskii, better known as S, could repeat back strings of seventy digits or letters and recite entire conversations verbatim. Even years after hearing a list, S could repeat it, backward or forward! But the remarkable memory also proved an intellectual hindrance. S had to devise ways to forget lists, for example, by writing down the words and then burning the paper. He found it difficult to carry on a simple conversation because a single word triggered a flood of memories, causing him to lose the gist of what was being said.

Few individuals have a memory like S's. Most people learn things through the processes discussed in chapter 5. And, unlike S, just because a person acquires some knowledge does not mean he or she can call it forth at will. Learning can be forgotten or retained. What variables determine what is remembered and what is forgotten? The first research started at the very founding of psychology.

Early Studies: Focus on Forgetting

Some of the first experiments in psychology studied learning, memory, and forgetting. Sometimes these tasks involved paper and pencil, but more often

Memory: The ability to recall or remember past events, images, ideas, or previously learned information or skills; the storage system that allows for retention and retrieval.

they merely involved a subject and an experimenter and some information to be learned. Computers were unheard of, and techniques that psychologists use today, such as the lexical decision task which we will examine later, would not have been understood. Let us follow the development of memory studies through history.

Relearning. Through the technique of *relearning,* Hermann Ebbinghaus (1850–1909) studied how well people learn stored information. Ebbinghaus earnestly believed that the contents of consciousness could be studied by scientific principles. He tried to quantify how quickly subjects could learn, relearn, and forget information. Ebbinghaus was the first person to investigate memory scientifically and systematically, making his technique as important as his findings. Some of his early ideas are still evident in modern conceptions of memory.

In his early studies, in which he was both researcher and subject, Ebbinghaus assigned himself the task of learning lists of letters in order of presentation. First, he strung together groups of three letters to make nonsense syllables such as *nak, dib, mip,* and *daf.* He then recorded how many times he had to present the lists to himself before he could remember them perfectly. Ebbinghaus found that when the lists were short, learning was nearly perfect in one or two trials. When they contained more than seven items, however, he had to present them over and over in order to achieve accurate recall.

Later, Ebbinghaus did learning experiments with other subjects. He had them learn lists of words and then, after varying amounts of time, measured how quickly they relearned the original list. If a subject relearned the list quickly, Ebbinghaus concluded that he or she still had some memory of it. He called this learning technique the *saving method* because what was initially learned was not totally forgotten (see Figure 6.1).

Practice. Following Ebbinghaus's lead, from the 1930s through the 1960s many researchers investigated the best ways for people to learn new material and relearn forgotten skills. In one study in 1966, Baddeley and Longman wanted to learn which resulted in more optimal learning and retention—intensive practice at one time or practice over several intervals—that is,

Hermann Ebbinghaus was the first person to scientifically investigate how people store information.

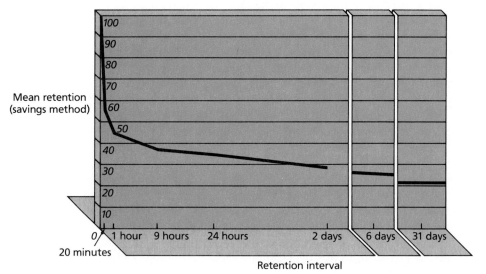

FIGURE 6.1
Ebbinghaus's Forgetting Curve: Ebbinghaus found that most forgetting occurs during the first nine hours after learning.

massed versus distributed practice. To answer this question they taught postal workers to touch-type.

The subjects were divided into four groups: one group practiced typing one hour a day, a second practiced two hours at a time once a day, a third one hour twice a day, and a fourth two hours twice a day. Thus, subjects used either concentrated massed practice or distributed practice over seven days. The dependent variable was how well they typed—that is, the number of accurate keystrokes per minute. A typing test showed that distributed practice was most effective. From the typing experiment and others, researchers have learned that the effectiveness of distributed practice depends on several variables, including the method, order, and speed of presentation. Distributed practice is especially effective in perceptual motor skills where eye-hand coordination is important.

In the 1970s researchers began to study the best way to present information to be learned. (This interest paralleled the innovations being carried out in public schools including open classrooms, new math, and cooperative learning.) For example, researchers found that if one item in a list differs from the others (such as a list of ten animal names and one plant name), the one item that is different is learned more easily. This phenomenon is called the *von Restorff effect.*

Measures of Retention

Psychologists study retention by measuring people's ability to relearn information through several techniques: recall, recognition, reconstruction, and pictorial memory. The most widely investigated techniques have been recall and recognition. *Recall* involves remembering the details of a situation or idea and placing them together in a meaningful framework (usually without any cues or aids). Asking someone to name the craft in which United States astronauts first landed on the moon is a test of recall. *Recognition* involves remembering whether one has seen a stimulus before, that is, whether the stimulus is familiar. Asking someone whether it was Neil Armstrong who landed on the moon in 1969 is a test of recognition.

Recall. In recall tasks, subjects have to remember previously presented information such as strings (i.e., lists) of digits or letters. (Essay exams also require recall.) A typical study might ask subjects to remember ten nonsense syllables, each of which was presented on a screen every ½ second. They would then have to repeat the list at the end of the five seconds.

Three widely used recall tasks are free recall, serial recall, and paired associates. In *free-recall tasks* subjects can recall items in any order, much as you might recall the items on a grocery list. *Serial recall* tasks are more difficult because the items must be recalled in the order in which they were presented, just as you would a telephone number. In *paired-associate tasks,* subjects are given a cue to help them recall the second half of a pair of items. In the learning phase of a study the experimenter would pair the words "tree" and "shoe." In the testing phase, subjects would be presented with the word "tree" and have to respond with the correct answer, "shoe." Table 6.1 lists typical items and requirements used in the three main types of recall tasks.

Recognition. In a multiple choice test you are asked to recognize relevant information. Psychologists have found that recognition tasks can help them measure differences in memory ability better than recall tasks. That's because although a person may recognize a previously studied fact, he or she may

TABLE 6.1
Three Types of Traditional List-Learning Tasks, Materials, and Requirements

Type of Task	Material	Example	Requirement
Serial recall	Nonsense syllables	GIP MAG DEC LIG DEL VEH	Subject learns the items in the order in which they were presented; often items are nonsense syllables, but not always.
Free recall	Words	Ghoul Vanquish Painless Telephone Burp	Subject learns the items in any order.
Paired associate	Nonsense syllables or words	GIP/MAG LIG/ZEP Hall/pencil Coffee/plant	Subject learns to associate the second item of the pair with the first.

Based on Hall, 1982, p. 153.

be unable to recall the associated details contained in the fact. Asked to name the state capital of Maine, you would probably have a better chance of answering correctly if given four items to choose from: Columbus, Annapolis, Helena, or Augusta.

Reconstruction. Here's a test of your memory: What did Neil Armstrong say when he first landed on the moon (his "one small step for a man" speech)? Few of us can recall Armstrong's words exactly, but most can probably recognize them, or reconstruct them approximately. Researchers have shown that people often construct memories of past events that are close approximations but not exact memories. For example, you might construct the gist of the speech by saying that Armstrong said something about man's first steps on the moon being important for all mankind. (Just for the record, his exact words were: That's one small step for a man, one giant leap for mankind.)

In the 1930s, English psychologist Sir Frederick Bartlett (1932) found that when college students tried to recall stories they had just read, they would change them in interesting ways. They shortened and simplified details, a process called *leveling;* they focused on or overemphasized certain details, a process called *sharpening;* and they altered facts to make the stories fit their own views of the world, a process called *assimilation.* In other words, the students constructed memories that distorted the events to some degree.

Contemporary explanations of *reconstructive memory* have focused on the constructive nature of the memory process and how people develop a **schema,** or conceptual framework, that organizes and makes sense of the world. Since we cannot remember *all* the details of an event or situation, we keep key facts and lose minor details. By developing schemas, we group key pieces of information together. In general, we try to fit the entire memory into some schematic that will be available for later recall. For example, Martha's schema for life in the United States during 1969, the year the United States landed on the moon, might include memories of such events as watch-

Schema: Conceptual framework that organizes information and makes sense out of the world by laying out a general framework in which events can be coded.

ing Walter Cronkite's news reports, listening to the Beatles, and reading about urban unrest.

Picture Memory. Related to reconstruction is the study of *picture memory*, whereby researchers see how well people can remember pictures. The results of these studies show that people are amazingly good at recognizing pictures they have previously seen. Ralph Haber found that subjects can recognize hundreds or even thousands of pictures with almost one hundred percent accuracy.

In 1970, Standing, Conezio, and Haber showed subjects thousands of slides, each for a few seconds. They then presented pairs of slides, only one of which the subjects had seen before, and asked the subjects to identify which of the pair they had seen. The subjects recognized the previously seen slides with better than ninety-five percent accuracy. Recent studies repeated Standing's results and developed other approaches (Standing, 1973; Intraub, 1980; Intraub and Nicklos, 1985); they suggest that pictorial information may be coded, stored, and retrieved differently from other information; this is why recognition memory may be so good. The processes of coding, storage of information, and retrieval are important concepts in the information-processing approach examined next.

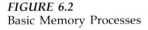

Focus on Learning

> ◆ Distinguish between learning and memory. p. 200
> ◆ Distinguish between massed versus distributed practice. p. 202
> ◆ Identify the key difference between recall and recognition. p. 202
> ◆ What is a schema? p. 203

The Information-Processing Approach to Memory

For many years researchers thought of the brain as a huge map with certain areas that code vision, others that code auditory events, and still others that code, analyze, and store memory. Their research goal was to discover the spatial layout of the brain and how it operates.

But in the 1960s and 1970s, researchers shifted from the map analogy and began to compare the brain to a computer, with complex interconnections and processing abilities. They compared memory in human beings to information processed by computers, with analogies made to computer encoding, storage, and retrieval. Human brains, of course, are not computers, nor do they work exactly the way computers do. They make mistakes and are affected by biological, environmental, and interpersonal events. Never-

FIGURE 6.2
Basic Memory Processes

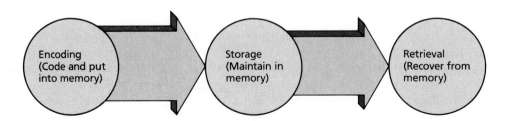

Researchers often compare the human brain to a computer, complete with encoding, storage, and retrieval mechanisms.

theless, enough similarities exist between human brains and computers for psychologists to discuss learning and memory in terms of information processing. The *information-processing approach* typically talks about stages (sensory-register, short-term memory, and long-term memory) in learning and memory and assumes that each stage is separate, although related, and analyzable by scientific methods. Within each stage three processes occur: encoding, storage, and retrieval (see Figure 6.2).

Encoding involves organizing information so that the nervous system can process it. Encoding can be visual or acoustic, or it can include taste, touch, or temperature information; encoding is the first step in establishing memory. **Storage** is the process of maintaining information in memory, for a few seconds or for many years. **Retrieval** is the process by which stored information is recovered from memory. Recalling your Social Security number, the details of a phone call, or the names of the U2 band members are all retrieval tasks. Think of information stored in the brain as books in a library. Books can be checked out and new ones added. Similarly, the books can deteriorate with age, be misplaced, or be difficult to locate. Books used frequently will often be easier to find—you'll know exactly where to look—than those used infrequently. Sometimes you may reorganize the books and store them differently. To better understand how the information-processing approach views encoding storage and retrieval, let us examine the three main stages of memory.

The Sensory Register

There are three stages in memory—the sensory register, short-term memory, and long-term memory—each responsible for different functions. The sensory register provides initial encoding of information and brief, temporary storage. Later, short-term memory provides coding and temporary storage for about thirty seconds. Long-term memory may preserve information for

Encoding: The process by which information is placed into memory; it is the initial transduction of an event into electrochemical energy that allows for mental representations.

Storage: The process of maintaining information in memory for a period of time.

Retrieval: The process by which information is recovered from memory at a time after it is stored.

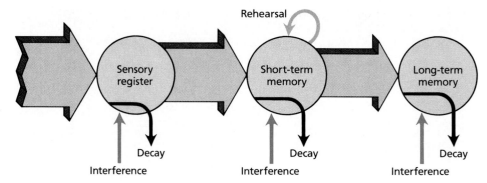

FIGURE 6.3
The information-processing approach stresses analysis by stages in which each level can be examined separately. When information enters the memory-processing system, it proceeds from the sensory register to short-term memory and then to long-term memory. At each stage decay or interference may be operative.

a lifetime (see Figure 6.3). Within each of these three stages, encoding, storage, and retrieval are possible.

As demonstrated by George Sperling in the early 1960s, the purpose of the **sensory register** is to perform initial encoding and brief storage from which human beings can retrieve information. Sperling and other researchers visually presented letters to subjects briefly and found they were able to recall more than three items from just a fifty-millisecond presentation. From his studies and others that followed, researchers claimed the existence of a brief (250 millisecond), rapidly decaying sensory store (see Figure 6.4). This brief image of a stimulus appears the way lightning does on a dark evening; the lightning occurs and you have a brief (250 millisecond) continuing image of it. Although some researchers have challenged the existence of the sensory register and its physiological basis (Sakitt and Long, 1979), most researchers still hold that it is the first stage of encoding.

Encoding and Storage

The sensory register transforms a visual, auditory, or chemical stimulus into a form the brain can interpret. Consider the visual system. The initial coding usually contains information in a picturelike representation. The sensory register establishes the stimulus in an electrical or neural form and stores it for 0.25 second (250 milliseconds) with little interpretation, still in an almost photographic manner. This visual sensory register is sometimes called the *icon*, and the storage mechanism is called *iconic storage*. The storage mech-

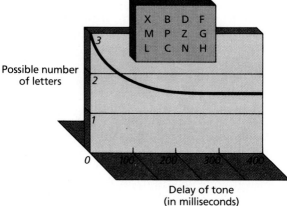

Sensory register: The mechanism that performs initial coding and brief storage of stimuli (for about 0.25 seconds in the visual system).

FIGURE 6.4
This graph plots Sperling's subjects' accuracy in reporting one four-letter row of letters as a function of the delay of the tone telling subjects which row to report. Note that there are no further decreases in accuracy after 250 milliseconds. (Data from Sperling, 1960, p. 11.)

anism for the auditory system is called *echoic storage;* it stores an auditory representation for about three seconds.

The sensory register is temporary and fragile. Once information is established there, it must be transferred elsewhere for additional coding and storage or it will be lost. For example, when you look up an address in a telephone book, it is established in the visual sensory register, but unless you quickly transfer it to short-term memory by repeating it over and over to yourself, you will forget it.

Retrieval

After the stages of encoding and storage, retrieval is possible from the sensory register. How this storage is used remains controversial. One of the first researchers to explore it in depth now suggests that its importance is minimal (Haber, 1983), but this notion is hotly debated (Loftus, 1985). Loftus and her colleagues and Cowan (1988) argue that perhaps the first one hundred milliseconds may be important. This debate is continuing with new theories and interpretations being offered regularly.

<table>
<tr><td>

◆ What are the assumptions of the *information-processing approach*? p. 204
◆ Define encoding, storage, and retrieval. p. 205
◆ What is the purpose of the sensory register? pp. 205–207

</td><td>

Focus on Learning

</td></tr>
</table>

Short-Term Memory

After the sensory register, stimuli either decay and are lost or they are transferred to a second stage called short-term memory. In **short-term memory** information is further encoded, then stored or maintained for about twenty to thirty seconds. In short-term memory, active processing takes place. A person may decide that a specific piece of information is important; if it is complicated or lengthy, it needs to be actively repeated or rehearsed. **Rehearsal** is the process of repeatedly verbalizing or thinking about information. Generally, researchers agree that the more rehearsal, the greater a person's memory for the item to be recalled (Greene, 1987) and that not all items are recalled equally well (Cowan, 1988).

Short-Term Memory Is Discovered

For decades researchers had been studying memory and retrieval, but it was not until 1959 that Margaret and Lloyd Peterson presented evidence for the existence of short-term memory. The Petersons asked subjects to recall a three-consonant sequence, such as *xbd,* after a varying time interval. During a time that ranged from no delay to eighteen seconds, the subjects were required to count backward by threes. The aim of counting backward was to prevent the subjects from repeating or rehearsing the sequence.

The Petersons' aim was to examine recall when rehearsal was not possible. Figure 6.5 on page 208 presents their results. As the interval between presentation and recall increased, accuracy of recall decreased. The Petersons interpreted these results as evidence for the existence of a short-term memory. Using the library analogy, short-term memory could be likened to books

Short-term memory: The memory storage system and process that temporarily holds current or recently attended information for immediate or short-term use. The duration of short-term memory is about thirty seconds; its capacity is limited to from nine to five items.

Rehearsal: Repetitive review through repeated verbalizing or thinking about information or previously learned information; the goal is to keep the information in memory.

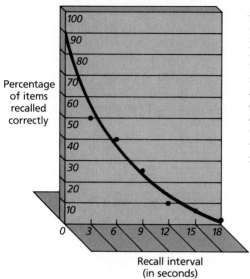

FIGURE 6.5
Peterson and Peterson found that when they delayed the report of three-letter syllables by having subjects count backward, accuracy of recall decreased over the first eighteen seconds. They interpreted these results as evidence for the existence of short-term memory.

that are on loan for a very brief period, then removed unless they are transferred to the library's permanent collection.

Short-term memory as a brief repository, a way-station for memory, has intuitive appeal. But more tasks, more competing events, and much more processing occurs in everyday life than in laboratory studies. If you think this is true, you might find appealing the working memory conception of short-term memory discussed next.

Short-Term Memory as Working Memory

Baddeley and Hitch (1974) think of short-term memory as a **working memory** in which several substructures operate to maintain information while it is being processed. One subsystem may code auditory information; another may be a visual-spatial scratch pad that stores information for a very brief time and is written to, and then rewritten to over and over. Baddeley demonstrated the several components of working memory by having subjects recall digits while doing some other type of reasoning task. He showed that people have limited capacities. If one mental task is demanding, performance on the other will suffer.

Baddeley's introduction of a working memory expanded the concept of short-term memory, focusing on its complexity and how single tasks analyze only single components of a multistage system. Psychologists often focus on those single tasks, trying to understand each of the components in encoding, storage, and retrieval. But Baddeley's conception of working memory goes beyond individual stages and describes the active integration of both conscious processes (such as repetition) and processes that a person is unaware of (such as retrieval of general knowledge about mathematical relationships). Repetition or practice turns out to be an important component of developing some type of working memory (Carlson, Sullivan, and Schneider, 1989).

Baddeley and other researchers argue that within working memory there is a central processing mechanism, like an executive, that controls the work flow, and the distinction between short-term memory and long-term memory is blurred (Cowan, 1988). This notion of an executive suggests that people can control the processing flow of information and adjust it when necessary.

Working memory: A new and broader conception of short-term memory that focuses on the executive processing capacities of memory and uses the idea of memory as a "scratch pad," a holding place for information while other information is being processed and directed for further processing.

Other researchers suggest that the traditional views of short-term memory and even the broader view of working memory is still too limiting. For example, one theory invoking both neurophysiology and attentional mechanisms asserts that localization of function plays an important role (Schneider and Detweiler, 1987); other researchers are examining the possibility that animals have a working memory (Green and Stanton, 1989). These newer theories do not discount sensory, short-term, and long-term memory; rather, they refocus, refine, and elaborate on them.

Encoding and Storage

As we said earlier, storage of information in the sensory register is temporary, and the information is either lost through decay or transferred to the second stage—short-term memory. In short-term memory, semipermanent storage exists in which information is actively processed, that is, further encoded and stored for a bit longer—about twenty to thirty seconds. At this stage people rehearse important information to make sure they remember it because if they do not, it will be lost (Greene, 1987).

To understand the encoding that takes place in short-term memory, imagine a waiter who is given a lengthy and complex order. When the order is in short-term memory, it is unlikely that the waiter will remember it after about two minutes. Thus, he might repeat the order over and over, rehearsing it until he is able to write it down or give it to the chef. Because of the limitations of short-term memory, rehearsal of information is crucial for encoding and keeping the information active. Thousands of research studies have been done on the components and characteristics of storage in short-term memory. They led researchers to conclusions that focus on duration, capacity, and rehearsal in short-term memory.

Duration. The Petersons' experiment showed that information contained in short-term memory is available for no more than thirty seconds. After that, it must either be transferred and stored permanently in long-term memory, or it is lost. (Of course, it could be maintained indefinitely if a person were to rehearse it over and over again until recall was necessary.)

Capacity. In 1956, George Miller argued that human beings can retain about seven (plus or minus two) items in short-term memory. Subsequent research confirmed that claim. The brief and limited number of items that can easily be reproduced after presentation is called the immediate **memory span.** The immediate memory span usually contains a single **chunk,** that is, a manageable and meaningful unit of information. A chunk can be a letter, a group of numbers and words, or even sentences organized in a familiar way for easy coding, storage, and retrieval. Many people remember their Social Security number in three chunks, and their telephone number in two chunks. Chunks can be made up of groupings based on meaning, perception, rhythm, or some arbitrary scheme devised by a learner to help code large amounts of data (Schweickert and Boruff, 1986). Determining what is a chunk is sometimes difficult because what is perceptually or cognitively grouped together for one individual may be different for other individuals.

Rehearsal. *Rehearsal* is the process of actively repeating, reviewing, or thinking about items to be remembered. People will quickly forget a list of meaningless letters and symbols, such as *xbdfmpg,* unless they use rehearsal to maintain the list in short-term memory. Actively rehearsed items can be

Memory span: The brief and limited number of items that can be easily reproduced after presentation in short-term memory, usually confined to a chunk of information.

Chunk: A manageable, familiar, and meaningful unit of information; these units are organized in a way that allows them to be grouped together for easy coding, storage, and retrieval.

maintained in short-term memory almost indefinitely. In general, however, the information entered in short-term memory is either transferred to long-term memory or is lost.

There are two types of rehearsal: maintenance and elaborative. **Maintenance rehearsal** is repetitive review with little or no interpretation; this shallow form of rehearsal involves the physical stimulus, not its underlying meaning. It is the type of rehearsal that goes on principally in short-term memory, for example, when repeating a list of meaningless numbers to be recalled. A more complex **elaborative rehearsal** involves repetition in which the stimulus may be associated with other events and further processed; this type of rehearsal is more typical of long-term memory and the processes of encoding information into long-term memory. Maintenance rehearsal alone is usually not sufficient for items to be transferred into long-term memory and permanently stored.

Retrieval

As in the sensory register, retrieval is the process by which something previously learned is recalled, recognized, or reproduced. When a person has to retrieve a piece of information from memory, there are vast amounts to search through. Using the library analogy, the stacks of books seem endless. One way of retrieving an item in short-term memory is to search through memory *exhaustively*, looking at all the items stored there and then choosing the desired one. Another type of retrieval search is *self-terminating;* that is, searching for something and ending the search as soon as the needed item is found. These two approaches to memory retrieval are being actively examined; understanding the differences between exhaustive and self-terminating searches helps researchers comprehend how retrieving information from memory can be done so rapidly.

We will examine the loss of information from short-term memory in a later section on forgetting. To summarize: four things can happen to information that enters short-term memory. First, it can decay (be lost over time) and be forgotten. Second, it can be confused with other information of a similar nature (interference) and be partially forgotten. Third, it can be rehearsed and used. Or last, as is often the case, it can be rehearsed and transferred to long-term memory (see Figure 6.6). We will have much more to say about these processes when we look at long-term memory, considered next.

Lengthy information, such as a script, must be rehearsed repeatedly in order to pass beyond short-term memory.

Maintenance rehearsal: Repetitive review of information in short-term memory with little or no interpretation.

Elaborative rehearsal: Rehearsal involving repetition in which the stimulus may be associated with other events and further processed; this type of rehearsal is more typical of long-term memory and the processes of encoding information into long-term memory.

FIGURE 6.6
Information maintained in short-term memory can be transferred into more permanent long-term memory. Long-term memory is subject to both decay and interference.

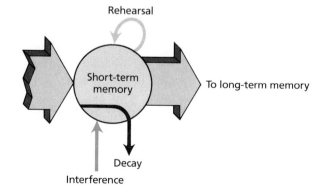

- What is the primary purpose of short-term memory? p. 207
- In the Petersons' experiment, subjects counted backward by threes for what purpose? pp. 207–208
- In what way is working memory a broader conception than short-term memory? p. 208
- Distinguish between maintenance and elaborative rehearsal. p. 210

Focus on Learning

Long-Term Memory

Information stored in **long-term memory,** such as names, faces, dates, places, smells, and both important and trivial events, is encoded in a relatively permanent form. The duration of long-term memory is indefinite—much information in long-term memory lasts for a lifetime. The capacity for long-term memory is seemingly infinite; the more information we acquire, the easier it is to learn. Using the library analogy again, long-term storage includes all the books that are part of the library's permanent collection.

Encoding and Storage

The information typically encoded and stored in long-term memory is either important, such as a friend's birthday, or is used frequently, such as your telephone number. An item such as the price of bananas will probably not be entered in long-term memory. Encoding information into long-term memory often involves rehearsal or repetition, but sometimes a salient or important event is immediately etched into long-term memory.

Several types of information are stored in long-term memory. People remember how to operate a tape deck, sing the words to a Billy Joel song, and define the meaning of the word "sanguine." Each of these types of information seems to be stored and called on in a different way. Psychologists explain the different types of long-term memory by dividing them into procedural and declarative memory.

Procedural memory is storage for the perceptual, motor, and cognitive skills necessary to complete a task (see Figure 6.7). Learning how to drive an automobile, wash the dishes, and swim involves a series of steps that include perceptual, motor, and cognitive skills, and thus procedural memory. Acquiring such skills is usually time consuming and difficult at first, but once the skills are learned they are relatively permanent. Coding of procedural information and its retrieval is indirect; it is not stored all together and must be assembled (Richardson-Klavehn and Bjork, 1988).

FIGURE 6.7
A Tentative Model of Memory: Declarative memory includes what can be declared or brought to mind as a fact. Procedural memory includes motor skills and cognitive skills.

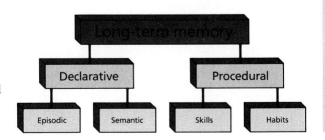

Long-term memory: The memory storage system and process that keeps a relatively permanent record of information.

Procedural memory: Storage for the perceptual, motor, and cognitive skills to complete a task.

Declarative memory, the ability to recall specific facts, allows these players to challenge each other at a game of Trivial Pursuit.

Declarative memory is memory for specific facts, such as "Jimmy Carter was President" or "Neil Armstrong was accompanied to the moon by Edwin Aldrin and Michael Collins." The memory is established quickly and the information is more likely to be forgotten than that in procedural memory. It is easier to examine declarative memory than procedural memory since people can quickly relate a specific fact but have more trouble explaining how to swim, for example. We consider declarative memory in more detail next.

Declarative Memory: Episodic and Semantic Memory

In 1972, Tulving suggested that there are two kinds of declarative long-term memory: episodic and semantic. **Episodic memory** covers specific events, objects, and situations such as what you had for breakfast, the movie you saw last night, or what you did on vacation last summer. Studies of memory for events long past show that people remember them well, especially information about themselves (Barclay and Wellman, 1986). Episodic memory is often specific; a person can say when an event happened, where it happened, and the circumstances surrounding it. It may deal with an individual's personal experiences or his or her memory for experiences of other people.

When researchers have examined people's ability to remember real-world events (rather than artificially created laboratory situations), results show amazingly good recognition memory. These studies often come under the general topic of *autobiographical memory studies* because they have often examined people's memory for their past. People can recognize with good accuracy a person, situation, or event for years after its occurrence. However, recall performance is not as accurate. Studies of autobiographical memory suggest that long-term memory is especially durable and fairly easy to access if a retrieval cue is available (as in a recognition task). The more clearly and sharply defined our memory cues are, the better our recall will be and the less likely retrieval failures will be. We will discuss this issue later in this chapter when we examine forgetting.

Declarative memory: Memory for specific facts; distinct from memory for skills to complete tasks.

Episodic memory: Memory for specific events, objects, and situations; time and place of events is often coded.

Semantic memory covers the memory of ideas, rules, and general concepts about the world. Semantic memory must be based on a set of generalizations relying on previous events, experiences, and learned knowledge. Thus, it develops after episodic memory and is more global. It is not time specific and refers to knowledge that may have been gathered over days, weeks, or even a lifetime.

Semantic memory seems to be stored at different *levels* of memory, like sections or floors of a library, so that a person needing information must go to different levels to access it. For example, is the following sentence true or false? "U.S. astronauts Armstrong, Collins, and Aldrin were the first to land on the moon and did so on July 20, 1969, at 4:18 P.M. eastern standard time." You would need to access classes of information concerning time, dates, people, and historical events which may be complex. Your response time will depend in part on the number of levels that must be examined to verify the accuracy of the sentence (Tilley and Warren, 1983) and the complexity of the information. The idea that there are levels of processing became very popular in the 1970s. In chapter 7 (on p. 236), we examine the *levels-of-processing* idea more fully.

An influential theory of how semantic memory operates comes from the work of Morton (1970), who proposed that memory exists in units called *logogens*. Building on that assumption, other theorists suggested that a *spreading activation*, or excitation, occurs from one unit of memory to another. In other words, when one logogen is activated in memory, related logogens are also activated. When activated, a person's logogen for "Neil Armstrong" may excite related logogens for "Apollo 11" and "moon landing."

An alternative theory, known as *location shifting theory*, maintains that when a person is presented with a word, he or she focuses only on that logogen. Attention must be shifted from one logogen to another before that information can be extracted from memory (Schvaneveldt and Meyer, 1973). Presented with the phrase "Apollo 11," a person would have to shift to other words in his or her memory to construct the events of the famous moon landing.

Psychologists use *lexical decision tasks* to investigate these theories. A typical lexical decision task presents subjects with words in succession. The first is called the *prime;* the second, the *target.* Subjects are asked to decide as quickly as possible if the target is a word or a nonword. Generally, reaction time is the dependent measure. The classical finding in lexical decision tasks is that subjects more quickly identify the target as a word or nonword when the preceding prime is associated with it than when the prime and the target are unassociated. Thus, a subject shown a target such as "doctor" reacts faster to identify it as a word if it is preceded by a prime that is a related word, such as "nurse" (Balota, 1983; Neely, 1976). These findings suggest that spreading activation occurs between closely associated logogens, but that attention shifts take over when unrelated logogens precede a target. Research continues to refine the distinction between semantic and episodic memory and shows that semantic memory can be a powerful memory aid in recalling other material (Groninger and Groninger, 1988).

The semantic-episodic distinction becomes blurred in situations where you expect people to use episodic information, but they use semantic information. For example, ask someone about the last time they saw a doctor and you expect them to tell you about an episode—a specific time. But most people will tell you about what happens in general, for example, by saying things such as "I usually get a cold once or twice a year, and if it's really bad, I take a day off." Such responses suggest that people are drawing on

Is it easier to remember what Neil Armstrong said when he first landed on the moon, or the details of the exact date and time?

Semantic memory: Memory for ideas, rules, and general concepts about the world; this storage mechanism contains the meaning of words and is not time or date specific.

Primacy effect: The more accurate recall of items presented first in a list.

Recency effect: The more accurate recall of items presented at the end of a list.

semantic memory and reconstructing or creating what *might* have happened. They are using schemas, or conceptual frameworks, that organize and make sense of the world (Means et al., 1989).

Retrieval

Encoding and storing information in long-term memory are primary tasks for a person learning a new skill, language, or set of facts. But all the study time and rehearsal is wasted if the information cannot be retrieved. Some interesting findings about retrieval from long-term memory have emerged.

Primacy and Recency Effects. Generally, psychologists researching long-term memory study people of normal intelligence and behavior, such as college students. In a typical experiment a subject may be asked to study a list of thirty or forty words, one presented every two seconds. A few minutes later, the subject is asked to recall the list. Such experiments typically show an overall recall of twenty percent. However, recall is higher for words at the beginning of a list than for those at the middle, a phenomenon called the **primacy effect.** This occurs when no information is stored in short-term memory; at the moment a new task is assigned, the subject's attention to a new stimuli is at its peak. Recall is even higher for words at the end of a list (see Figure 6.8), a tendency called the **recency effect.** This is due to the active rehearsal of the information in short-term memory and its subsequent coding into long-term memory.

Campaign managers attempt to capitalize on the primacy and recency effects in speeches. For example, they urge their candidate to speak both very early in the campaign and late, just before people vote. If several candidates are to speak back-to-back, campaign managers will try to schedule their candidate either first or last; primacy effects suggest that attention is at its peak at the beginning; recency effects suggest that speaking last will be effective because such a speech is more likely to be remembered with no one following the speaker.

Extraordinary Memory. As noted earlier, a nearly perfect recall, like S's, is rare. But is it possible for an average person to develop a remarkable memory? In a famous series of studies, chess players were asked to reproduce the places of pieces on a chess board from a replica of an actual game of chess. The same task was then given to subjects but with randomly placed pieces.

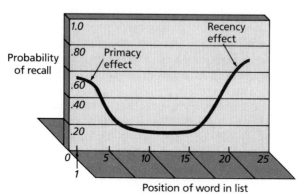

Position of word in list

FIGURE 6.8
A Serial-Position Curve: The probability of recalling an item is plotted as a function of its serial position on a list of items. Generally, the first several items are likely to be recalled (the primacy effect) and the last several are recalled very well (the recency effect).

Candidates speaking first or last will have an advantage due to primacy and recency effects.

In the first case (a real chess game), people with differing chess skills diverged widely in their ability to remember piece positions. Expert players could place four times as many pieces as could novice players. In the random chess board, however, the chess skill levels made no difference. Thus, previous experience with patterns of chess pieces seemed to be crucial; the expert subjects were obviously *chunking* the data in some strategic way. Random placements were equally difficult for all players (Chase and Simon, 1973(a); DeGroot, 1965).

Extraordinary memory and the use of chunking has also been seen with memory span experiments. We saw earlier that memory span for most adults is limited to a chunk containing seven items, plus or minus two. Recent research shows, however, that with practice and special use of chunking strategies, memory span can be increased sharply. One study increased memory span to seventy-nine digits (Ericsson, Chase, and Faloon, 1980), another to as many as 106 digits (Staszewski, 1987). The subjects in these experiments developed strategies for effective, efficient encoding and efficient retrieval of meaningful chunks of information; this entire process was effortful, deliberate, and effective. Subjects in these studies were using exceptionally efficient retrieval structures.

Attempting to increase digit span is a time-consuming process—in the Ericsson study it took twenty months; in the Staszewski study, five years—and the results do not carry over to other materials. But exceptional memory skills can be seen in other research domains. For example, Staszewski (1988) presented research on "lightning mental calculators," individuals who can solve an arithmetic problem such as $54,917 \times 63$ with remarkable speed and accuracy. The key to such achievement is steady practice, efficient use of memory, and extensive knowledge of numerical relationships. A person can't train to be a lightning-fast mental calculator without *extensive* daily and weekly practice. Nor can a person learn to calculate calendar date problems (On what day of the week was July 27, 1946?) without extensive practice and considerable knowledge of day, date, and calendar rules (Howe and Smith, 1988.)

Is There a Special Flashbulb Memory?

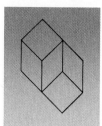

*W*here were you when you learned that President Ronald Reagan had been shot, that the space shuttle *Challenger* had exploded, or that the San Francisco earthquake had occurred? How did you hear about the events? What were you doing? What were your first thoughts?

People vividly remember the circumstances in which they learned of major personal and public events. This phenomenon is often called *flashbulb memory,* and among the first to research it were Brown and Kulik (1977). They argued that there is a special type of memory for events that possess a critical level of surprise and "consequentiality." Most people believe they have flashbulb memories, and the Brown and Kulik work generated an avalanche of debate and research.

Theories. There are two basic theories to explain flashbulb memory. The first focuses on emotion, the second on rehearsal. The emotion approach, sometimes called the Now-Print Theory, suggests that recall is facilitated when extraordinary cognitive information overactivates the limbic system (the brain's emotion center). In addition, information associated with strong emotions may be talked about more; rehearsing information facilitates recall. The second theory focuses on rehearsal and reconstruction. This Reconstructive-Script Theory focuses on people telling and retelling the story, and gradually filling in, or reconstructing, their story to match a standard story format.

Research after the Fact. To determine which of these two approaches is correct, J. N. Bohannon (1988) of the Virginia Polytechnic Institute conducted a study of 279 subjects and their memories of the space shuttle *Challenger* disaster. Subjects were tested at two weeks and then at eight months following the explosion. They were asked to estimate both their emotions on hearing the news (to test the Now-Print Theory) and the number of times they retold the story (to test the Reconstructive-Script Theory). The subject's memory was assessed on three basic tasks: (1) free recall of the story, (2) probed recall of the story (recall when given hints), and (3) probed recall of specific facts about the accident itself.

Results. The results were dramatic. Subjects who rated themselves as more shocked by the shuttle accident remembered more details, were more confident of their answers, and had more complete stories at both testing times than did subjects who rated themselves as less upset. These results, which focus on emotion, support the Now-Print approach. However, the Reconstructive-Script Theory was also supported. This theory suggests that subjects organize their memory and fill in the details. The study's results showed that free recall at eight months was just as good as within two weeks of the explosion, but accurate responses to questions asking for specific details declined over testing times. With short delays, either factor (emotion or rehearsal) is *sufficient* to generate flashbulb memories. But after a delay of eight months, *both are required.*

Conclusions. Simple emotional responses without rehearsal, according to researcher Bohannon, produce good short-term recall only. In the same manner, rehearsed information that does not have a strong emotional component results in superior short-lived memory. Bohannon claims that flashbulb events are only maintained over time "if the flashbulb event was important enough to get the person to repeatedly rehearse the information by telling others" (p. 195). Every person experiences events that are emotional, some of which are rehearsed. When the experience of learning about an event is especially significant, and when it is repeatedly rehearsed, both the circumstances and the event have a high probability of being remembered in detail.

Should flashbulb memory be considered a special kind of memory? Researchers like McCloskey, Wible, and Cohen (1988) argue that "there is no qualitative distinction . . . between memories for learning about shocking, important events, and memories for learning about expected, trivial events" (p. 181). They assert that flashbulb memory is an ordinary memory with no special characteristics. Bohannon's findings on flashbulb memories and the role of emotion and rehearsal in maintaining vivid flashbulb memories are consistent with McCloskey's argument. Flashbulb memories may be vivid, but they must be about emotional events and must be rehearsed. The research suggests that there is no special location or coding mechanism responsible for them. ◆

Imagery: A cognitive process in which a mental picture is created of a sensory event.

◆ What is the difference between procedural and declarative memory? pp. 211–212
◆ How do semantic memories seem to be stored? p. 213
◆ How do primacy and recency effects affect recall? p. 214
◆ What is flashbulb memory? p. 216

Focus on Learning

Imagery

People use perceptual **imagery** every day as a long-term memory aid. In imagery, people create, re-create, or conjure up a mental picture of a sensory or perceptual experience to be remembered. They constantly invoke images to recall things they did, said, read, or saw. People's imagery systems can be activated by visual, auditory, or olfactory stimuli or by other images. Even lack of sensory stimulation can produce vivid imagery. Your imagery helps you answer questions such as: Which is darker, a green pea or a Christmas tree? Which is bigger, a tennis ball or an orange? Imagery is used in memory retrieval when the information sought is a subtle visual property and as an aid in visual perception, for example, to "see" where a ball might hit (Kosslyn, 1987). How can a psychologist measure this mental phenomenon?

Measuring Imagery. More than fifty years ago Gestalt psychologists, with their interest in form perception, recognized the importance of imagery; its importance is being acknowledged once again. The difficulty for psychologists today is to devise techniques and experimental manipulations to measure imagery. One technique, used extensively by Stephen Kosslyn of Harvard University, is to ask subjects to imagine objects of varying size, for example, an animal such as a rabbit next to either an elephant or a fly. In a 1975 study, subjects reported that when they imagined a fly, plenty of room remained in their mental image for a rabbit. But when they imagined an elephant, it took up most of the space. One particularly interesting result was that the subjects required more time and found it harder to "see" the nose of the rabbit when it was next to an elephant than when it was next to a fly because it appeared so small (see Figure 6.9).

In another series of experiments, Kosslyn (1978) asked subjects first to imagine an object at a distance and then to imagine that they were moving toward the object. The subjects were next asked if the object seemed larger to them than before and if it "overflowed" their mental visual field so they could no longer see all of it. The subjects were instructed to stop "mentally walking" at the point at which the object seemed to overflow. By having the subjects estimate the size of the object and the distance at which the images seemed to overflow the mental image frame, Kosslyn was able to estimate the size of a visual image that people can imagine.

FIGURE 6.9
Kosslyn had subjects imagine elephants and flies; a rabbit that was subsequently imagined appeared small in size next to the elephant and large in size in relation to a fly. (Source: Kosslyn, 1975, after Solso, 1979.)

Using this mental walk technique, Kosslyn found a limited image space. Larger objects tended to overflow at greater imagined distances. He also learned that images overflowed in all directions at about the same size. Perhaps the most important finding from Kosslyn's research is that images possess spatial properties. Although they are mental, not physical, phenomena, they have edges—points beyond which visual information ceases to be represented (Kosslyn, 1987). People can construct mental images, transform them, and interpret what they look like (Finke, Pinker, and Farah, 1989). We use our mental imagery ability to decide whether our new station wagon will fit into our single car garage or to count the number of windows in our new apartment, and we do so in three dimensions, regardless of the angle from which we view these objects (Roth and Kosslyn, 1988). The ability to use mental imagery and rotation (see Figure 6.10) helps people recognize misoriented objects (Farah and Hammond, 1988) regardless of their number of dimensions (Shepard and Metzler, 1988), their complexity and familiarity (Bethell-Fox and Shepard, 1988), or their orientation (Takano, 1989; Koriat and Norman, 1989). Mental rotation is a key factor in our ability to perceive the world, understand its transformations, and understand a view of the world that has been transformed from its previously viewed orientation (Tarr and Pinker, 1989).

Imagery as a Memory Aid. Imagery is an important perceptual memory aid. In fact, a growing body of evidence suggests that it is a means of preserving perceptual information that might otherwise decay. According to Paivio (1971), a person told to remember two words may form an image combining those words. If someone is told to remember the words "house" and "hamburger," for example, he or she might form an image of a house made of hamburgers or of a hamburger on top of a house. When later presented with the word "house," the word "hamburger" will come to mind. Paivio suggests that words paired in this way are conceptually linked, with the mediation factor being the image.

How images facilitate recall and recognition is not yet fully understood; an image could add another code to semantic memory. Thus with two codes, semantic and imaginal, a person has two ways to access previously learned information. Some researchers argue that imagery, verbal coding mechanisms, and semantic memory operate together to code and to aid retrieval (Marschark, Yuille, Richman, and Hunt, 1987).

Test for yourself the mnemonic effectiveness of imagery with this example: Suppose you park in section E-17 of an airport parking lot. Now memorize E-17 by visualizing an elephant sitting in your car and reading *Seventeen* magazine. Later in this chapter you'll be asked where you parked.

Eidetic Imagery. In the 1960s, while Paivio was trying to make the study of imagery respectable to behavioral colleagues who preferred to avoid such mentalistic concepts, other researchers were investigating a different kind of imagery: *photograph-like imagery.* If everyone could maintain a photograph-like image of each glimpse of the world, how easy learning and memory would be. Although many people say they have photographic memories, no one reports having an image of everything ever seen. Most reports of photographic memory are normal vivid imagery. But Ralph Haber (1969, 1979) of the University of Illinois showed that some children do have a special kind of imagery called eidetic imagery. *Eidetic imagery,* found in fewer than four percent of schoolage children, is vivid, long-lasting, and complete.

Haber's basic procedure was to place a picture on an easel for about thirty seconds, instruct the children to move their eyes so that they would

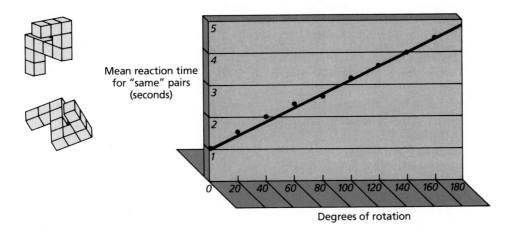

FIGURE 6.10
In exploring the nature of imagery, researchers such as Roger Shepard have drawn pairs of visual stimuli like those shown on the left so that one appears to have been rotated in space. Shepard and Metzler asked subjects to say as quickly as possible whether such stimuli were in fact the same stimuli rotated or different stimuli. Sometimes the stimuli were drawn rotated in space only slightly; at other times the rotations were as much as 180°. Subjects' reaction times to respond correctly varied with the amount of rotation involved. The graph at the right plots the reaction time for "same" pairs as a function of degrees of rotation. This was one of the first of several studies in the 1970s that began to explore visual image ability in a systematic and carefully controlled way.

see all the details in the picture, and then remove the picture. As the subjects continued to look at the blank white easel, they were asked about the nature of their imagery. Children who were eventually termed *eidetic* reported that their images lasted from a half minute to a full minute. Their imagery was so vivid that they could describe even minute details of the pictures. If the picture showed a cat with a striped tail, for example, they could report how many stripes were on the tail. A few eidetic children were even able to develop three-dimensional images. Children who could not remember parts of a picture said they had not looked at those parts long enough. And when they were told to move their image from the easel to another surface, they said that it fell off the edge of the easel. Recently, young adults with eidetic capabilities have been identified by Japanese researchers (Matsuoka, Onizawa, Hatakeyama, and Yamaguchi, 1987).

State-Dependent Learning

Distinguished psychologist Gordon Bower used the following example to describe a phenomenon known as state-dependent learning (Bower, 1981, p. 129):

> When I was a kid I saw the movie *City Lights* in which Charlie Chaplin plays the little tramp. In one very funny sequence, Charlie saves a drunk from leaping to his death. The drunk turns out to be a millionaire who befriends Charlie, and the two spend the evening together drinking and carousing. The next day, when sober, the millionaire does not recognize Charlie and even snubs him. Later the millionaire gets drunk again, and when he spots Charlie treats him as his long-lost companion. So the two of them spend another evening together carousing and drinking and then stagger back to the millionaire's mansion to sleep. In the morning, of course, the sober millionaire

State-dependent learning:
The tendency to recall information learned in a particular physiological state more accurately when one is again in that physiological state.

again does not recognize Charlie, treats him as an intruder, and has the butler kick him out by the seat of his pants.

The millionaire remembers Charlie only when he is intoxicated, the same state in which he originally met him. Psychologists find that information learned while a person is in a particular physiological state is recalled better when the subject is again in that physiological state. This phenomenon, known as **state-dependent learning,** is associated among other states with drugs, time of day (Holloway, 1977), mental illness (Weingartner, 1977), and electroconvulsive shock (Robbins and Meyer, 1970).

In a typical state-dependent learning study, Weingartner, Adefris, Eich, and Murphy (1976) had four groups of subjects learn lists of high- and low-imagery words. To induce intoxication, all subjects except those in the control group drank vodka and fruit juice. The control group learned and recalled while sober; a second group learned and recalled while intoxicated; a third learned while sober and recalled while intoxicated; and a fourth learned while intoxicated and recalled while sober. The results showed that subjects recalled the lists best when they were in the same state in which they had learned the lists.

Several theories attempt to explain state-dependent learning. A widely accepted explanation focuses on how altered or drugged states affect the storage process. According to this view, part of learning involves the coding of stimuli in specific ways at the time of learning; to access the stored information, a person must evoke the same context in which the coding occurred. When you are studying for an examination with music in the background, but are tested in quiet conditions, is your recall not as good? The answer to this question is as yet unresolved, but studies of state-dependent learning may hold the key, and recent studies of mood-dependent memory suggest that the answer may be yes (Eich and Metcalfe, 1989).

Improving Memory

APPLYING
PSYCHOLOGY

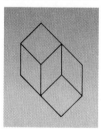

*R*esearchers who study memory often focus on how our brains process and retain information. And their work has direct applications. For example, there are several techniques that can improve memory. We have been examining them throughout this chapter. Here are some of the most powerful ones; they move from simple strategies to more complex overall approaches. Try using them to learn this chapter's concepts.

Rehearse, Rehearse, Rehearse. We defined rehearsal as the repetitive review of previously learned information through repeatedly verbalizing or thinking about the information. There is no substitute for rehearsal, especially for important information. Rehearsing nonsense syllables will facilitate recall, but when you rehearse meaningful and important information, the effect of rehearsal is even greater.

Distribute Practice over Time. You should review newly presented information as soon after it has been presented as possible. After class, review your notes. After reading an article, write a summary of it. Then spread out later repetitions or reviews. Earlier we discussed *massed* versus *distributed* practice and showed that distributed practice is especially effective, but that students and teachers often do not optimize the use of this principle. Don't cram. If you distribute your learning sessions over time, rather than cramming them all into one short spell, you'll do better on most memory and learning tasks.

Focus. Because we have so much to learn when we are in college and we have so little time to learn it, it is not surprising that there is sometimes confusion. We all know that it makes sense not to take Introductory French and Introductory Spanish at the same time. Our limited memory capacity makes us susceptible to interference or confusion with other learned items. Focus on one course or one learning task at a time. When studying for a big Shakespeare test, don't start studying psychology. Organize your studying into coherent chunks; this will allow you to keep structured the information that you are trying to enter into long-term memory.

Use Mnemonics. Make to-be-learned information important and meaningful by using techniques to make difficult or abstract material personally meaningful. *Mnemonics* combines items into an established format, rhyme, or jingle containing the information to be remembered. Most children, for example, learn the notes of the musical scale E G B D F by using a mnemonic jingle such as "Every good boy does fine." Or you may have learned to spell the word *principal* with the ending *pal* because the principal is your pal! Relate the information to be recalled to your personal experiences.

Use Mediation and Imagery. Mediation is a bridging technique; associate two items to be remembered by using a third that ties them together. Cermak (1975) uses the names John and Tillie as an example. John reminds someone of a bathroom, which can be associated with tiles, which sounds and looks like Tillie. Remembering a tiled bathroom helps people remember the two names John and Tillie. Imagery involves making mental pictures of events or things to remember, such as the person standing in a tiled bathroom with John and Tillie.

Review in Different Contexts and Modalities. The place where you learned something can be an important retrieval cue. (When you see your favorite bank teller in a department store you may not be able to remember who he or she is.) Try to review and rehearse in different settings. Study in different modalities. If you heard a lecture, write down the contents. If you have been developing mnemonics on paper, try saying them out loud. If you have been outlining a chapter verbally, try outlining it in writing. As Brown (1989) argues, you should set aside time to reflect on your learning and experiences; hearing yourself retell the information will strengthen the concept regardless of the modality or place in which it was learned.

Prepare the Environment. Because there is so much to learn and remember, you can facilitate the task if you prepare your world (Brown, 1989). Limit the number of opportunities for people to grab your attention. Study in a quiet place where there are few people. Avoid visual clutter in your study area; it is a distraction from the task at hand. Limit the number of tasks you are working on so as to focus your attention and thus stay tuned into one task. Finish those tasks that you start so you bring them to completion and they will not take further attention. Last, keep a notebook handy to jot down ideas, insights, and potential mnemonics.

SQ3R Method. The *SQ3R method*—survey, question, read, recite, and review— is a systematic way to learn and remember new material. To use the SQ3R method, break a task into small units, perhaps one chapter a week.

- Quickly *survey* the material within each unit.
- Ask *questions* about the most important aspects of what was surveyed.
- *Read* the material carefully.
- *Recite* the important points out loud.
- *Review* all material covered.

To improve your memory, prepare your environment. Limit interruptions, study in quiet, create an uncluttered workplace, and focus.

Skinner and Behavioral Memory Management. Recall from chapter 5 that B. F. Skinner (1983) asserts that people need to use a technology of behavior to manage their lives. They need to create an environment with proper rewards and punishers that will help them cope better. Part of his management proposal is managing memory in old age, but his ideas about memory management hold true for people of all ages.

As an example, suppose you had to introduce a friend to a person whose name you forgot. You could manage the situation by flattering the person. You could say that you have noticed that the more important a person is, the easier it is to forget his or her name. Or you could take Skinner's suggestion of recalling a story of how you forgot your own name when asked it by a store clerk. Skinner's idea is to create a situation that doesn't punish you for being forgetful but instead flatters (rewards) the listener.

Skinner also suggests ways to help remember things. For example, if you tend to forget your books in the morning, you should place them near the door. People who often forget what they were going to say in a conversation should practice saying it over to themselves until the other person is finished talking. People who tend to forget what they want to say because they love to tell stories and digress should refrain from digressing. Another way to manage memory is to prepare notes. Students take notes in class; executives make lists of what to do; shoppers make lists of what to buy at the grocery store.   ◆

Focus on Learning

> ◆ How has imagery been measured? p. 217
> ◆ What is state-dependent learning? p. 219
> ◆ Name and describe three techniques that can be used to increase memory. pp. 220–221

Forgetting—The Loss of Memory

Quick! Name your first-grade teacher . . . your Social Security number . . . your telephone number . . . your mother's birthday . . . where you went on your last vacation. In general, our memories serve us amazingly well. Nevertheless, at times you may have trouble recalling the name of someone you know well, where you read an interesting article, or the phone number of a close friend. Have you ever begun an examination only to suddenly "go blank"? In each of these cases, there is a memory failure.

There are many causes of forgetting, such as not rehearsing information well enough, or not using it for a long time. Forgetting also occurs because of interference from newly learned information, or because the information is unpleasant, or because of physiological problems. Moreover, forgetting occurs in both short- and long-term memory.

Reasons for Memory Loss

Researchers recognize that data are lost from both short- and long-term memory, but they want to find out how and why that loss happens. Two concepts, decay and interference, help explain the loss (see Figure 6.11).

Decay: The loss of information from memory as a result of the passage of time and/or disuse.

Decay of Information. According to the **decay** theory, information is lost through *disuse* over time. Unimportant events fade from memory; details become lost, confused, or fuzzy. Another way to look at the decay theory

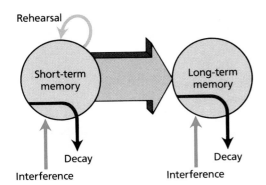

FIGURE 6.11
When information enters short-term memory, it is subject to decay, interference, rehearsal, or transfer into long-term memory.

is that memory exists in the brain in a physiological form known as a memory trace. With the passage of time and a lack of active use, the trace disintegrates, fades, and is lost.

The decay hypothesis was popular for many years but is not widely accepted today. Many early studies did not acknowledge important variables that affect memory processes, such as rate and mode of stimulus presentation. Although decay will form a small part of the final explanation of forgetting, it is probably less important than other factors, such as interference.

Interference in Memory. According to the **interference** explanation, the limited capacity of short-term memory makes it susceptible to interference or confusion between learned items. That is, when competing information is stored in short-term memory, the resulting crowding will affect a person's memory for particular items. For example, if someone looks up a telephone number and is then given another number to remember, the second number will probably interfere with the ability to remember the first one. Moreover, interference in memory is likely to occur when a person is presented with a great deal of new information. (In this text you are being provided with a great deal of new information; organizing your studying into coherent chunks is important so as not to confuse information that you are trying to enter into long-term memory.)

Research on interference theory shows that the extent and nature of a person's experiences both before and after learning are important. For example, a subject given a list of nonsense syllables may recall seventy-five percent of the items correctly. However, if the subject was given twenty similar lists to learn earlier, the number of items correctly recalled will be lower; the previous lists will interfere with recall. If the subject is given additional lists to learn, recall will be even lower. Psychologists call these interference effects proactive and retroactive inhibition. **Proactive inhibition** is the decrease in accurate recall as a result of previous events interfering with a to-be-remembered one. **Retroactive inhibition** is the decrease in accurate recall of an item as a result of later presentation of other items (see Figure 6.12 on page 224).

To understand proactive and retroactive inhibition, suppose someone were to hear a series of lectures, each five minutes long. According to psychological research, the proactive and retroactive inhibition (interference) effects would make a person most likely to remember the first and last speeches. There would be no proactive inhibition on the first speech and no retroactive interference on the last speech. All the middle speeches would

Interference: The suppression or confusion of one bit of information with another received either earlier or later.

Proactive inhibition: The decrease in accurate recall of a target list as a result of previous events that interfere with the recall of target list.

Retroactive inhibition: The decrease in accurate recall of a target list as a result of subsequent presentation of material.

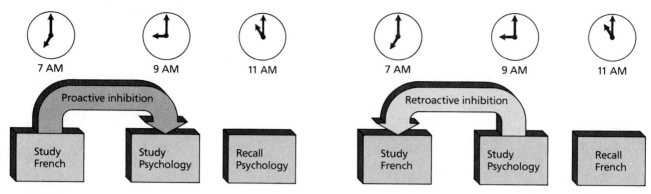

FIGURE 6.12
Proactive and retroactive inhibition or interference occur in memory when old or new information interferes with (or inhibits recall of) to-be-learned material. Proactive inhibition refers to the finding that old information interferes with learning new information. Retroactive inhibition occurs when new information inhibits (interferes with) the recall of previously learned information. Thus, studying French, followed by studying psychology, interferes with your recall of psychology—proactive inhibition. And studying French, followed by studying psychology, interferes with or inhibits your recall of French—retroactive inhibition.

Amnesia: A loss of memory, usually due to traumatic injury.

Retrograde amnesia: Loss of memory for events and experiences preceding the amnesia-causing event.

Anterograde amnesia: Loss of memory for events and experiences following the amnesia-causing event.

have both proactive and retroactive inhibition; thus, the first and last speeches would be remembered best. (Don't forget that there are also primacy and recency effects that will aid in their recall; see page 214.)

Retrieval Failure. Some contemporary researchers assert that every memory is retained and available, but that some information is just less accessible than others. Think of the library analogy: all the books in the library are there, but some cannot be found, or perhaps are misshelved, making retrieval difficult or impossible.

Research on retrieval failures focuses on how people code information, and what cues help in retrieval. If you are given a cue for retrieval and the originally stored information contains that cue, retrieval is easier, faster, and more accurate. The value of a specific retrieval cue depends on how well it compares with the original memory code; this notion is referred to as the *encoding specificity* hypothesis. The more clearly and sharply defined our memory cues are, the better our recall will be and the less likely retrieval failures will be. To increase access to information stored in memory, a person should match the test situation to the original learning situation as much as possible.

Motivated Forgetting and Amnesia. Freud (1933) was the first to formally suggest the idea of *motivated forgetting;* that unwanted or unpleasant events might be lost in memory simply because people wanted to forget them. He stated that such loss occurs through repression, the burying of unpleasant ideas in the unconscious where they remain inaccessible. Although most researchers agree that motivated forgetting probably exists in some form, they have found it hard to measure and are thus far unsuccessful in demonstrating it. Motivated forgetting is hard or impossible to produce in the laboratory, but a related phenomenon, amnesia, can be examined in the laboratory.

Television soap operas frequently portray people with amnesia, but in fact the condition is relatively rare. **Amnesia** is the inability to remember events from the past, usually because of physiological trauma (such as an auto accident, a blow to the head, or a fall from a height). Typically it involves loss of memory for all events within a specific period. There are two kinds of amnesia: retrograde and anterograde.

Retrograde amnesia is the inability to remember events that preceded a traumatizing event (what might be called "soap opera loss"). Loss of memory can cover only the period just before the accident or it can cover several years. Retrograde amnesia can be caused by injuries to the head, carbon monoxide poisoning, or certain kinds of shock therapy in patients with depressive problems. Recovery is generally gradual, with older events remembered first.

Anterograde amnesia is the inability to remember events after an injury or brain damage. People suffering from anterograde amnesia are "stuck" in the life they lived before being injured; new events are often utterly forgotten. For example, if the onset of the amnesia occurred in 1990, the sufferer may be able to remember clearly events in 1989, but have a difficult time recalling what he or she did only half an hour before. The victim may meet someone for the hundredth time, yet think he is being introduced to a perfect stranger.

In studying patients with brain damage or those who have undergone surgery for major epileptic attacks, researchers find that the region of the brain called the *hippocampus* may be responsible for the transfer of new information to permanent memory. Milner (1966) showed that if certain regions of the brain are damaged or removed, people can remember old information but not new information (Milner, Corkin, and Teuber, 1968). The ability to remember remote events seems to depend on brain mechanisms that are separate and distinct from those required for new learning of recent events (Shimamura and Squire, 1986). These data do not conclusively confirm separate places or processes in the brain for different types of amnesia or memory, but they are suggestive. The ability to remember remote events seems particularly important in studies of eyewitness testimony where people try to remember real-life past events.

Both field-based research and laboratory simulations are needed in order to determine the accuracy of eyewitness recollections.

Psychology and Law: Eyewitness Testimony

We saw earlier that in Bartlett's laboratory, subjects sometimes constructed and altered their memories. The constructive nature of memory can have serious consequences for real-life situations, especially eyewitness testimony. If someone sees an accident or crime, for example, can he or she accurately report the facts of the situation to the police or the court? The answer is both yes and no. The police and the court have generally accepted *eyewitness testimony* as some of the best evidence that can be presented. They are hearing from people who saw the crime, have no bias or grudge, and are sworn to tell the truth. But do they?

Some studies of eyewitnesses show that witnesses often recall events incorrectly and identify the wrong people (Bekerian and Bowers, 1983; Loftus, 1979). In fact, eyewitnesses of the same event often report seeing different things. Langman and Cockburn (1975) recorded the eyewitness testimony of people who reported seeing Sirhan Sirhan shoot Senator Robert F. Kennedy in 1968. Even though many of them were standing next to each other, they reported seeing different things.

To complicate the matter, eyewitnesses often enhance their memories over time (recall Bartlett's theory of assimilation). Harvard law professor Alan Dershowitz asserts that the memories of witnesses—particularly those of witnesses with a stake in the eventual outcome—tend to get better with the passage of time. Dershowitz calls this process memory enhancement and states that it occurs when people fit their hazy memories into a coherent theory and pattern of other results. A witness's initial recollections of an event may be vague, for example. But as a trial approaches, he or she is coached and rehearsed and tends to remember "better," with more clarity and less ambiguity. According to Dershowitz, "what began as a hazy recollection becomes frozen into crystalline clarity." The result in the courtroom, however, may be slightly inaccurate, biased, or, at worst, untrue testimony (Dershowitz, 1986); that is, it may be constructed testimony. Ironically, the more detailed a witness is (even about irrelevant details) the more credible that witness is assumed to be, even if the witness recalled things inaccurately (Bell and Loftus, 1989). Complicating the interpretation of results still further is the finding that events (especially wrong information) after an initial episode impair memory for the initial event. Whether the memory is weakened, clouded, or confused, or whether retrieval processes are impaired is still not clear (Belli, 1989; Zaragoza and McCloskey, 1989), but as Loftus and Hoffman (1989) argue: "that people come to accept misinformation and adopt it faithfully as their own is an important phenomenon in its own right."

Despite the strong evidence of errors in eyewitness testimony, two researchers from the University of British Columbia assert that eyewitness testimony can be accurate and that it is the laboratory studies of eyewitness testimony that may be inaccurate. Yuille and Cutshall (1986) argue that laboratory studies generally use simulated events, films of events, television presentations, and slide shows to study eyewitness testimony, which is not the same as actually having seen a crime or accident. They further state that real events are well remembered and that researchers who study eyewitness testimony have to do field work before they make further claims.

Generalizing from field-based situations is difficult because of the number of uncontrolled variables; generalizing from laboratory situations is difficult because of the artificial nature of the situation (Banaji and Crowder, 1989). Today, researchers are insisting on both. Before the issue is resolved, however, more field-based research *and* further laboratory simulation studies are needed.

Focus on Learning

> ◆ Explain the interference theory of memory failure. p. 223
> ◆ Distinguish between proactive and retroactive inhibition. pp. 223–224
> ◆ Distinguish between the two basic kinds of amnesia: retrograde and anterograde. p. 224

The Physiology of Memory

Memories are stored in electrochemical form in the brain. Many psychologists who study the biological bases of behavior now believe that most, if not all, memories are retained at least in some manner. Today, researchers are exploring the neurobiological basis of memory—How does the brain store memories? Where are memories stored?

Consolidation Theory and Coding

Memories are not physical things; rather, most researchers believe memories are made up of unique groupings of neurons in the brain. Based on this fact, in 1949 Canadian psychologist Donald Hebb (1904–1985) presented one of the major psychological and physiological theories of memory. Hebb suggested that when groups of neurons are stimulated, they form patterns of activity. If this pattern of neural activity fires frequently, a reverberating and regular neural circuit is established. This evolution of a temporary neural circuit into a more permanent structure is called **consolidation.**

According to Hebb, consolidation serves as the basis of short-term memory and permits **coding** of information into long-term memory. If Hebb is correct, when people first see or hear a new stimulus, only temporary changes in neurons takes place; with repetition, consolidation occurs and the temporary circuit becomes a permanent structure.

Many psychologists believe that the consolidation process provides the key to understanding learning and memory—that individual differences in ability to learn or remember may be due to differing abilities to consolidate new information properly. Confirmation comes from studies using electro-convulsive shock to disrupt consolidation, which results in impaired memory in both human beings and animals. Further support comes from studies showing that recent memories are more susceptible to amnesic loss than older memories (Milner, 1989).

The consolidation process has been further examined when researchers study the brains of animals raised in enriched environments compared with animals raised in deprived environments. In an enriched environment, toys and objects are available for the animals to play with and learn from. Enriched environments may create more opportunities for brain elaboration. The brains of animals raised in such environments have more dendrites and more synapses with other neurons (Turner and Greenough, 1985). This means that when a neuron is stimulated over and over again, it is enriched and may branch out and become more easily accessible.

If a neuron is stimulated, the biochemical processes that are involved make it more likely to respond later than would nonstimulated neurons; further, the number of dendrites of that cell increases because of previous stimulation (Lynch and Baudry, 1984). This suggests that biochemical actions and repeated use may make learning and memory easier, a conception that fits perfectly with Hebb's suggestions. In addition, clear evidence exists that certain protein synthesis occurs just after learning and that long-term memory depends on this protein synthesis (Matthies, 1989). Psychologists now generally accept the idea that the structure of synapses changes after learning, and especially after repeated learning experiences. As Hebb said in 1949, "some memories are both instantaneously established and permanent. To account for permanence, some structural change seems necessary" (p. 62).

Consolidation theory has been refined, extended, and supported by research. For example, we know that a single neuron has many synaptic sites on its dendrites; Alkon (1989) showed that there is extensive interaction among those sites and with sites of other neurons. He argues that the spread of electrical and chemical activity from one site to another—without activity or firing of the neurons—seems to be critical for initiating memory storage. He asserts that on a given neuron a huge number of different incoming signals can be received and stored. Alkon has been developing mathematical and computer models to simulate neuronal coding for memory and to study animal memory. This exciting work extends Hebb's ideas one step further.

Location of Memory in the Brain

The search for the location of memory—that is, the memory trace—has been longstanding. Early researchers such as Penfield (1958) looked for a single place in the brain; later researchers discovered that memory resides in many areas. Some areas might involve every memory; others are used to remember only one type of memory, for example, visual or auditory memories. In

When an animal is raised in an environment that offers novelty and stimulation, the cortical neurons increase in number.

Consolidation: The evolution of a temporary neural circuit into a more permanent circuit.

Coding: The organization of information and the rules for organization by which the initial stimulus is transformed into some other form.

addition, because of the many steps involved, procedural information is probably stored in many more locations than is declarative information.

Studies focusing on a distinction between short-term and long-term memory provide anatomical evidence about the locations of memory. Baddeley and Warrington (1970), for example, conducted memory experiments comparing normal subjects with amnesiac subjects who had various types of brain damage. Their results showed that amnesiac patients had intact short-term memories but grossly defective long-term memories.

Milner (1966) reported the case of a brain-damaged adult whose short-term memory was intact but who was unable to form new long-term memories. As long as the subject was able to rehearse information and keep it in short-term memory, his recall performance was normal. But as soon as he could no longer rehearse and had to use long-term memory, his recall was very poor. Milner's data provide neurological support for a distinction between short- and long-term memory. They also focus researchers' attention on the action of specific brain centers and cells, and on how cells might change through time and experience.

Until recently, psychologists only asked questions about how cells and synapses changed in response to environmental changes, such as deprivation of sound or light. Now, however, researchers use a variety of techniques to investigate the physiological basis of memory (Zola-Morgan et al., 1982). For example, McGaugh (1983) contends that hormones (chemicals in the bloodstream) may affect the way memories are stored, pointing out that newly established memories are particularly sensitive to chemical and electrical stimulation of the brain. Other researchers are attempting to arrange computer models of the neural networks of the brain; their attempts are fascinating but limited in scope to related groups of brain cells (Sejnowski, Koch, and Churchland, 1988). Also, such work doesn't explain many kinds of learning and memory phenomena, such as state-dependent learning, memory for remote events, or extraordinary memory; the theories that follow from such research help explain a limited range of psychological information about memory (Watkins, 1990).

We will further examine early research on the location of memory. But before we do, a quick test of your memory. Can you recall the letter and number of the airport parking section described earlier?

Where Does Memory Reside? The Penfield Studies

MILESTONES IN PSYCHOLOGY

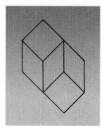

*E*arly researchers tried in vain to determine exactly where memory resides in the brain. They hoped to find the location of the memory trace, or as it was sometimes called, the engram. Although the ultimate goal was not achieved, the research took some important and fascinating turns. Wilder Penfield was one of the principal players in the memory-trace hunt.

During brain surgery on patients suffering from epilepsy, Penfield and his colleagues were able to explore the cortex with electrodes. Electrodes were used to stimulate specific cortical neurons. The patients received only local anesthetic and were conscious during surgery because the brain contains no pain receptors. When Penfield stimulated the temporal lobe cortex (either left or right side), patients reported seeing images, coherent perceptions of experiences. They also reported visual and auditory perceptions that included speech or music. Familiar and unfamiliar experiences were often intermixed with unrealistic and even strange circumstances (Penfield, 1958; Penfield and Jasper, 1954; Penfield and Mathieson, 1954; Penfield and Milner, 1958; Penfield and Perot, 1963).

Penfield interpreted these reports as true perceptions of past events. His patients were reporting memories elicited by the stimulation (Squire, 1987). Penfield concluded that temporal lobe stimulation triggered the memory retrievals. The concept of specific brain locations storing memories that could be accessed by stimulation was revolutionary.

The initial excitement soon dissipated, however. Penfield's patients may not have been retrieving memories at all. Even Penfield acknowledged that the reported memories were dreamlike. Experiences were said to seem familiar, but were not necessarily specific past occurrences. Further, stimulation of different brain sites often brought about the same perception. In addition, removal of specific sites (due to the surgery) failed to destroy the memory for the experience (Squire, 1987).

More recent research using similar techniques has shown that patients report mental images when stimulated with small electrical charges, and they are more likely to report these images with greater stimulation or repeated stimulation. But when the same site is stimulated repeatedly, different mental images are reported! No consistent mental image has been associated with specific anatomical locations (see Halgren, Walter, Cherlow, and Crandall, 1978). One study found that reports of visual effects occurred only when stimulation of the cortex was great enough to spread to visual areas of the brain (Gloor et al., 1982). Experiences seemed to be reported only when structures deep within the brain, in the limbic system, were also stimulated. (Remember that Penfield searched *only* through the temporal cortex.)

Penfield's conclusion that the temporal lobe holds the memory trace has been contested for several reasons. First, destruction of tissue at these locations did not destroy the memory. Second, nearly half the reported visual images occurred when stimulation spread from the cortex to other areas of the brain. Third, structures in other parts of the brain, especially the limbic system, seem to be involved in producing mental images. Penfield's work was a landmark. It gave impetus to additional research, speculation, controversy, and excitement. But subsequent work showed that many brain areas other than the cortex are involved in memory, especially the limbic system. No one area holds the memory trace. Wilder Penfield's conclusions were wrong, but his work was significant and important. ◆

- ◆ What is consolidation? p. 226
- ◆ When organisms are raised in an enriched environment, what happens to their dendrites and synapses? p. 227
- ◆ What was Wilder Penfield's conclusion about the location of memory? Was he correct? pp. 228–229

Focus on Learning

Key Terms

Memory p. 200	Maintenance rehearsal p. 210	State-dependent learning p. 220
Schema p. 203	Elaborative rehearsal p. 210	Decay p. 222
Encoding p. 205	Long-term memory p. 211	Interference p. 223
Storage p. 205	Procedural memory p. 211	Proactive inhibition p. 223
Retrieval p. 205	Declarative memory p. 212	Retroactive inhibition p. 223
Sensory register p. 206	Episodic memory p. 212	Amnesia p. 224
Short-term memory p. 207	Semantic memory p. 213	Retrograde amnesia p. 224
Rehearsal p. 207	Primacy effect p. 214	Anterograde amnesia p. 225
Working memory p. 208	Recency effect p. 214	Consolidation p. 227
Memory span p. 209	Imagery p. 217	Coding p. 227
Chunk p. 209		

Summary

Memory: Retaining Information

- *Memory* is the ability to remember past events or previously learned information or skills; memory is also the storage system that allows retention and retrieval.   p. 200

- *Recall* involves remembering the details of a situation or idea and placing them together in a meaningful framework (usually without any cues or aids). *Recognition* involves remembering whether a stimulus is familiar. *Reconstructive memory* focuses on how people develop a *schema,* or conceptual framework, that organizes the world.   p. 202

The Information-Processing Approach to Memory

- The *information-processing approach* assumes that each stage of learning and memory is separate, although related, and analyzable by scientific methods.   p. 204

- *Encoding* involves organizing information so that the nervous system can process it. *Storage* involves maintaining information in memory. *Retrieval* is the process by which stored information is recovered from memory.   p. 205

The Sensory Register

- The *sensory register* performs initial encoding and brief storage from which human beings can retrieve information.   pp. 205–206

- The visual sensory register may be called the *icon,* and the storage mechanism is called *iconic storage.* The storage mechanism for the auditory system is called *echoic storage.*   p. 206

Short-Term Memory

- In short-term memory, information is further encoded, then stored or maintained for about twenty to thirty seconds; short-term memory is an active processing stage.   p. 207

- Working memory is a broader conception of short-term memory focusing on executive processing capacities of memory and using the idea of memory as a "scratch pad."   p. 208

- The brief and limited number of items that can be reproduced easily after presentation is called the immediate *memory span.* It usually contains a single *chunk,* a manageable and meaningful unit of information.   p. 209

- *Rehearsal* is the process of actively repeating and reviewing items to be remembered. *Maintenance rehearsal* is repetitive review with little or no interpretation. *Elaborative rehearsal* involves repetition in which the stimulus may be associated with other events and further processed.   pp. 209–210

Long-Term Memory

- *Procedural memory* is storage for the perceptual, motor, and cognitive skills necessary to complete a task; *declarative memory* is memory for specific facts.   pp. 211–212

- *Episodic memory* covers specific events, objects, and situations; *semantic memory* covers ideas, rules, and general concepts.   p. 212

- A *primacy effect* is the more accurate recall of items presented first in a list; a *recency effect* is the more accurate recall of items presented at the end of a list.   p. 214

- People's imagery systems can be activated by visual, auditory, or olfactory stimuli.   p. 217

- *State-dependent learning* is the tendency to recall information learned in a particular physiological state more accurately when one is again in that physiological state.   p. 219

Forgetting—The Loss of Memory

- According to the *interference explanation,* the limited capacity of short-term memory makes it susceptible to interference. *Proactive inhibition* is the decrease in accurate recall as a result of previous presentation of material. *Retroactive inhibition* is the decrease in accurate recall as a result of subsequent presentation.   p. 223

- *Retrograde amnesia* is the inability to remember events that preceded a traumatizing event; *anterograde amnesia* is the inability to remember events after an injury or brain damage.   p. 224

The Physiology of Memory

- *Consolidation* is the evolution of a temporary neural circuit into a permanent one.   p. 226

- When Penfield stimulated the temporal lobe cortex, patients reported seeing images. More recent research shows, however, that no consistent mental image was associated with specific anatomical locations.   p. 228

Connections

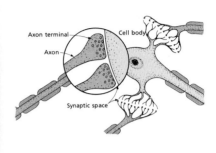

If you are interested in . . .	Turn to . . .	To learn more about . . .
The role of memory in everyday life	◆ Ch. 3, pp. 96–98	How Gestalt psychologists developed theories of perception based on past experiences.
	◆ Ch. 4, p. 146	The effects of drug abuse on long-term memory.
	◆ Ch. 12, pp. 425–433	How personality theorists such as Freud suggested that everyday memories are buried deep within the unconscious.
Forgetting	◆ Ch. 10, p. 369	How Alzheimer's disease has such a profound effect on people's ability to remember past events.
	◆ Ch. 15, pp. 538–543	Why certain personality approaches to treatment rely on the ability to recall events that were forgotten and perhaps dismissed to the unconscious.
The biological basis of memory	◆ Ch. 2, pp. 47, 64–67	How psychobiologists study the biochemical bases of behavior, including memory, to understand the role of biology in memory.
	◆ Ch. 11, p. 411	How theories of emotion depend, in part, on a person's memory for past events and the subsequent interpretation of new events.
	◆ Ch. 15, p. 566	How electroconvulsive shock therapy has been used to treat people who have been seriously depressed and at the same time wipes out many past memories.

7 Cognition and Language

"Crown" by John Okulick

◆

*B*lindfolded, facing twelve to sixteen opponents at one time, Harry Pillsbury played chess. He was able to remember all of his moves and to play skillfully. George Koltanowski played fifty opponents at once while he was blindfolded—in this instance he played with a limit of ten seconds per move—and he won forty-three of the games. Pillsbury was the United States chess champion from 1897 to 1906; Koltanowski in the 1950s was a master chess player himself; both regularly played blindfolded chess and memorized all the moves. In blindfolded chess, a player does not see the board, the pieces, or the opponent, but rather is told his opponent's moves by a third person. This amazing ability is a testament to these players' skill at chess and their extraordinary memory.

    Chess is a game of skill, knowledge, and imagination. It requires a player to think not only of his or her own moves, but of the opponent's

Understanding how the brain comprehends a game of chess gives psychologists one window into its overall workings.

moves and responses. The game is usually divided into three parts, the opening moves, the middle game in which strategies are played out, and the end game when a skillful player can use his or her few remaining pieces to win.

Chess was one of the first games that human beings played against a computer. It was a logical choice: Chess has a finite number of rules; there is a clear playing field (the chessboard); the game is extremely complex (so that the computer doesn't always win); and the rules are rational. Human beings often lose to computers. Whenever I play computer chess, I invariably lose, even on the lowest difficulty level. But through playing computer chess and by studying the computer's responses, I have learned a great deal. One thing I have learned is that I usually have not looked at all the alternatives before making a move. The chess game that I own allows me to "see" the computer's logic by showing me its first, second, and third choice moves. This allows me to trace the logic of the computer program—exactly what psychologists attempt to do when they study thought, reasoning, and language. They try to "see" inside the human brain by devising tasks that will reveal human logic and reasoning. They try to map human strategies and listen to human speech with the aim of getting a glimpse inside the mind.

Thought and language are two separate processes but they are closely related. Thoughts are generally, but not always, expressed in language. Language gives human beings a unique vehicle for planning for the future and analyzing the past. This chapter covers cognition—especially thought related to learning, perceiving, remembering, and using information—and language, the symbolic system people use to communicate their thoughts verbally.

Cognitive Psychology: An Overview

How are a tiger and a domestic cat physically similar? Who is the U.S. Secretary of State? How do you make an omelette?

Answering each of these questions requires a different mental procedure. To answer the first question, you probably drew mental images of both felines and then compared the images. In answering the second question, you may simply have known the right name or called forth a list of cabinet members and chosen from the list. The third question may have required you to mentally walk through the procedure of preparing an omelette and describe each step out loud. The thinking you used to answer these questions required the use of knowledge, language, and images.

Cognitive psychology is the study of the overlapping fields of learning, memory, perception, and thought. Its roller coaster history began in the late 1800s. At the dawn of the study of psychology, the main areas of study were mental processes, thought, and the internal working of the mind. In the 1920s, behaviorism became mainstream psychology and there was little if any reference to cognitive and thought processes. Discussion and research of such "mentalistic" topics were avoided. Then, in the 1960s, with the introduction of modern high-speed computers, analogies related the brain to a computer, and research in thought began again. Researchers now examine questions such as "How do we read?" "How do we know that a robin has wings?" Today, cognitive psychology is a dominant force in psychological study; it affects the way psychologists study language, thought, problem solving, and maladjustment.

Cognitive psychology: The study of encoding, storage, analysis, recall, reconstruction, elaboration, and memory of events. A broad-ranging field, it is involved in theories of personality, social psychology, and maladjustment.

Basic Assumptions of Cognitive Psychologists

Cognitive psychologists study thinking; cognitive researchers assume that mental processes exist, that we are active processors, and that we can study cognitive processes through time and accuracy measures (Ashcraft, 1989). A cognitive psychologist assumes that *mental processes* are systematic, and that they can be studied scientifically. Cognitive psychologists also believe that we are *active participants* in analyzing our world. We do not sit back passively and have the world impose order on us, but rather, we actively construct reality by making associations and generalizations. They also believe that through measures of performance such as *time and accuracy*, a researcher can learn about mental processing. This might mean measuring how long it takes someone to perform a task, how accurately the person does it, and what other factors affect mental activity.

Cognitive Psychology Evolves

Cognitive psychology began with the study of *human information processing*, which focuses on a stage analysis of sensory and perceptual processes. This approach breaks perception into a series of discrete stages that can be examined for time, operating, and methodological characteristics. A stage can be analyzed for its duration, variables that affect its deterioration, or other factors that interfere with it. Chapter 3, Sensation and Perception, examined human information processing stages, and chapter 6, Memory, further analyzed these stages.

Today, psychologists such as Michael Posner do not subscribe to one global theory of cognition; rather they define thought-oriented topics and examine them individually. For example, in the memory area they are interested in how memories are stored. Are they organized in an orderly, systematic fashion, or are they organized simply by the order in which they were entered into memory? Researchers study both declarative and procedural knowledge. Recall from chapter 6 that *declarative knowledge* is factual information that can be coded, recoded, and recalled in various ways like naming the hometown of President Lincoln. *Procedural knowledge* underlies skills like skiing or driving a car.

Cognitive researchers are interested in processes that are automatic compared with those that are controlled. *Controlled processes* require a great deal of effort and attention; *automatic processes* take little effort and happen without conscious awareness—although there are physiological changes that accompany both processes (Strayer and Kramer, 1990). Many difficult tasks were initially controlled processes; after hundreds of repetitions, they became automatic and easy, requiring little or no attention. Contemporary cognitive psychologists want to find out how once-difficult tasks like reading, driving a car, and word processing become automatic.

Closely associated with controlled and automatic processes is the role of *attention*. Limited mental resources must be divided up so that memory can be utilized efficiently. Once something is stored in memory, cognitive researchers want to know how we make inferences from our knowledge and how we *represent knowledge*. Even monitoring one's own awareness, a process called *metacognition*, has become an active focus for cognitive researchers.

Clinical psychologists are using cognitive psychological approaches to treat clients, as you will see in chapter 16. Personality theorists examine cognitive processes, focusing on how personalities are formed by ideas and

For Olympic skater Brian Boitano, performing triple jumps has become nearly automatic, but a quadruple jump still takes great concentration and practice.

perceptions gathered from others (chapter 12) and how self-perceptions are affected by other people (chapters 16 and 17).

It is easy to see that the circle of cognitive psychology is far-reaching. Contemporary cognitive psychologists do research in areas such as memory, maladjustment, computers, and personality, to name just a few. This chapter concentrates on a series of cognitive topics that show the breadth of cognitive psychology—the diversity of thought processes being examined and the topics emerging in the 1990s. Some of today's research questions have their roots in studies of levels of processing; other foci of cognitive psychology examine related areas, concentrating on storage and retrieval of thoughts. Since the levels-of-processing idea has generated so much research and so many new ideas, let's examine it before we go any further.

Levels of Processing

MILESTONES IN PSYCHOLOGY

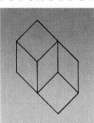

*D*oes the human brain process some information at a deeper, more complex level than other information? Are thinking processes dependent on the depth of storage? For more than five decades, from the 1940s on, researchers have tried to distinguish between short-term memory and long-term memory. But during the 1970s, a new approach to explaining memory coding and retrieval, called *levels of processing*, changed the course of research and thinking.

Researchers Craik and Lockhart (1972) argued that a person can process a stimulus in different ways, to different extents, and at different levels. For example, if presented with a display flashed on a computer screen that says "Cast your vote for Smith, the candidate of distinction," a person will analyze the display on several levels, in several ways. The lines and angles of the display are coded at one level, the words are coded for basic meaning and categorized at another level, and at still another, deeper level, the meaning of the display is analyzed, stored, and coded.

The levels-of-processing approach suggests that distinctions in memory stores may not be as important as the *operations* that are involved in storing thoughts and perceptions. Craik and Lockhart supported their argument with studies of incidental learning. Test subjects are less likely to remember items not processed semantically (for meaning) than items processed for meaning or items that the subjects are told might have to be recalled.

Cognitive psychologists began to equate the depth of processing with the degree of semantic analysis. When the level of processing becomes more complex, the code goes deeper in memory. Thus, the memory for the lines and angles of the computer screen (sensory memory) may be fleeting and short-lived; the memory for the words themselves may be longer (short-term memory); and the memory for the content of the words (semantic components of long-term memory) may be long-lasting. According to Craik and Lockhart, coding in various memory levels involves different operations, and memory features are stored in different ways and for different durations.

The level of processing is dictated by task demands, and each processing level results in a different memory trace with different characteristics. If a person does not care about the meaning of a flashed campaign message, he or she might not code it into long-term memory. But a favorite candidate's message may be analyzed, repeated, and pondered for several seconds, or even minutes.

The levels-of-processing approach was appealing and generated an enormous amount of research. It explained why some information is retained for long periods while other information is quickly forgotten. It was consistent with an information-processing structural analysis and explained the varying decay rates of memory stages. It showed that when people are asked to code information in only one way, they do not code it in other ways (e.g., Kanwisher and

Potter, 1990). Thus, when people are not asked to code words for meaning, they can recall very few of them. This helps explain why some problems tend to be solved only in one way.

However, not every researcher was enamored of the levels-of-processing approach. It was a concept that was impossible to define, and some researchers did not find the same results as Craik and Lockhart. Refinements were suggested focusing on how memory codes are established, how they are elaborated on or made distinctive, and how recall of codes take place. The initial levels-of-processing theory dealt primarily with establishing codes in memory. Later research focused on how those codes were used in recall from memory.

The landmark levels-of-processing research of the early 1970s still shapes the way cognitive researchers think about memory and thought. The traditional short-term and long-term memory distinction suggested a structural difference in memory stores. The levels-of-processing approach, however, states that the way information is coded may determine how it is stored, recalled, and processed. The coding of information becomes crucial when a person has to form a concept to make a decision, the topic we consider next.   ◆

> **Concept:** A classification of objects or ideas that distinguishes them from others on the basis of some common feature.

Concept Formation

Each day, people make hundreds of decisions, solve problems, and behave quite logically; the steps in decision making and problem solving are complicated, but orderly. Before we can better understand these more complex forms of reasoning, we have to realize that every decision involves our ability to form, manipulate, transform, and relate concepts. **Concepts** are the mental categories people use to classify events and objects with respect to common properties. The study of *concept formation* is the examination of the way people organize and classify events and objects, usually in order to solve problems. How do you plan a winning strategy in a game of chess? How do you decide whether you are for or against the death penalty?

Concepts help people organize their thinking and thus make events in the world more meaningful. People develop progressively more complex

On a daily basis, we make many complex decisions almost automatically.

Sample

FIGURE 7.1
In a typical classification task given to first- or second-graders, the task is to circle the picture that is most like the sample.

concepts throughout life. Infants learn the difference between parents and strangers very early. Within a year they can discriminate among objects, colors, and people, and comprehend simple concepts such as animals and flowers. By age two they can verbalize these differences.

Much of what we teach young children involves classification, because this is the key to organizing and understanding our complex world (see Figure 7.1). Think back to your early school years and to current educational television shows such as *Sesame Street*. You were taught to classify the range of colors; different farm animals (and their sounds); shapes such as triangles, circles, and squares; and the letters in the alphabet. You learned to organize the people in your house—mother, father, sister, brother—into a group called a family. You learned that the world is made up of a multitude of countries, states, and towns, and that there are both "bad guys" and "good guys" in the world. The process of concept formation is lifelong and always changing. But what is the best way to study the processes by which children or adults classify and organize information?

Studying Concept Formation

To study concept formation in a carefully controlled environment, psychologists design laboratory studies in which the subject's task is to form a concept using a wide range of tasks. Suppose you are the subject in a laboratory experiment. You might be asked to make judgments of "Who belongs to this category?" or "Is a bicycle a toy or a vehicle?" A concept formation task might ask you to classify colors: "Is aqua more blue or more green?" "Do you place yellow next to blue or next to red?" Here is a common task used in laboratory investigations of concept formation: An experimenter presents you with objects of different shapes, sizes, and colors and says that some characteristics of some of those objects make them similar. You are asked to identify this characteristic.

Each time the researcher presents a stimulus, you ask whether it has the property being targeted and the experimenter answers yes or no. Suppose, for example, the first stimulus is a large red triangle. The experimenter

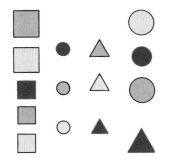

FIGURE 7.2
In a concept-formation task, the subject is asked to classify objects of various shapes, sizes, and colors.

Positive instance: A stimulus that is an example of the concept under study.

Negative instance: A stimulus that is not an example of the concept under study.

Dimension: A conceptual feature that distinguishes an object or phenomenon from others lacking that feature.

tells you that it is a **positive instance** (an example of the concept being sought). You now know that the concept may be largeness, redness, or triangularity. The second stimulus is a small red triangle; the experimenter says that this too is a positive instance. You now know that size is not important. The third stimulus is a large blue triangle; it too is a positive instance. You surmise that the relevant dimension is triangularity. When on the fourth trial the stimulus is a large blue circle and the experimenter responds that it is a **negative instance** (a stimulus that is not an example of the concept), you can say with conviction that triangularity is the concept.

Stimuli vary along dimensions. A **dimension** is some feature that sets an object apart from others. For example, a large red triangle has three dimensions: size, shape, and color (see Figure 7.2). Within each dimension there are different *values* or *attributes*. The color dimension may have red, blue, and green attributes. The size dimension may have large, medium, and small attributes. The shape dimension may have triangular, circular, and square attributes. In the given example, you had to learn that the relevant dimension was shape.

Two variations of the procedure of forming concepts are used in concept formation tasks. The *reception method* presents subjects with a series of instances, the task being to classify each as a positive or negative instance. Subjects are told after each trial whether or not their response was correct. For example, a researcher might show a subject thirty objects, one at a time. After ten or twenty correct responses, the researcher can be certain that the subject has learned the concept.

The *selection method* presents all the possible instances at once (Figure 7.3). Usually the experimenter designates one of the stimuli as a positive instance at the outset. After guessing what the concept is, the subject chooses a second stimulus and asks whether it is a positive instance. After learning whether the second stimulus is positive or negative, the subject picks a third, a fourth, and a fifth instance. This less structured procedure allows an experimenter to examine the hypotheses or strategies that a subject uses in forming a concept.

Concept Formation Theories

As in other areas of psychology, theory has guided research. Over the last fifty years, theory has changed substantially in concept formation from mediation theories to hypothesis-testing theories.

Mediation Theory. Can people form concepts about situations without much effort, simply by absorbing new ideas? If so, then concept formation

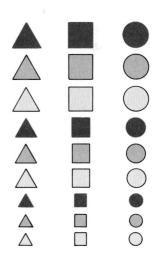

FIGURE 7.3
In a selection task, all the possible combinations of the dimensions are shown at once. The subject chooses which instance to examine next.

Mediation: The process of creating or discovering a connection between previously unconnected things.

Conservative focusing: A strategy for problem solving that involves the elimination of alternative possibilities.

Reasoning: The process by which we generate and evaluate arguments, and reach conclusions.

Logic: The procedure that we use to reach a valid conclusion.

Decision making: The assessment of and choice among alternatives sometimes involves the probability of occurrence of some event and expected value.

is simply the association of certain stimuli and responses. According to **mediation** theory, people use internal bridging thought processes to connect a stimulus (for example, a German shepherd) to a concept response (dog). Mediation theory thus suggests that a link exists between specific instances of a category and the general category. Mediation theory was popular in the 1950s and 1960s, but it has been replaced by the more sophisticated hypothesis-testing theory.

Hypothesis-Testing Theory. The hypothesis-testing theory views concept formation as an active rather than automatic process. It assumes that people acquire new information by generating hypotheses about stimuli, testing those hypotheses, discarding old hypotheses if necessary, and making an inference regarding the stimuli. Levine (1975) identified three hypothesis-testing strategies in adults. In *hypothesis checking,* an unsophisticated strategy that resembles gambling, subjects test one hypothesis at a time. In *dimension checking,* subjects test the hypotheses of a single dimension. In *global focusing,* the most efficient strategy, subjects keep all possible hypotheses in mind but focus on one at a time, ruling out alternatives as they are given feedback. To be an efficient global focuser, a person has to be actively involved in seeking solutions and in forming concepts.

Another type of strategy, **conservative focusing,** is the elimination of possibilities. It is efficient for a limited range of concepts. If you are asked to identify a number from one to ten, for example, the best strategy is first to ask if the number is greater than five. The answer eliminates half the possibilities. If the answer is yes, the next question should be, "Is the number greater than eight?" again eliminating half the possibilities. If the response is yes, only one other question is necessary: "Is the number nine?" By narrowing the choices in this way, the number can be guessed in three tries. A less efficient approach is to guess each number: "Is the number six? Is the number seven? Is the number two?" and so on. Of course, this entire process is part of thinking and decision making, the topic we'll consider next.

<table>
<tr><td>

Focus on Learning

</td><td>

* Name three assumptions that cognitive psychologists make about thought. p. 235
* What is the fundamental idea behind a levels-of-processing approach? p. 236
* Distinguish between a positive and a negative instance of concept formation. p. 239
* In concept formation, what is a dimension? p. 239
* Name the basic, underlying idea of hypothesis-testing theory. p. 240

</td></tr>
</table>

Decision Making

We are generally unaware of our cognitive processes; we don't usually think about thinking. And yet we are thinking all the time, sorting through choices, deciding where to go, what to do, and when to do it. In general, *thinking* refers to reasoning, decision making, and problem solving (Galotti, 1989). **Reasoning** is the process by which we generate and evaluate arguments and reach conclusions; the procedure that we use to reach a valid conclusion is called **logic. Decision making** is the assessment of and choice among alternatives; we make decisions that sometimes involve the probability of occurrence of some event (will my friends want to go on this trip with me) and expected value (how important is this trip, rather than some other one). Our decisions vary from the trivial to complex: what to eat for breakfast, what courses to take in a semester, what career to pursue, what to buy a friend for a birthday present, what jacket to wear, and whether to enter into marriage. The trivial decisions are usually made quickly, without much effort, and unconsciously. The complicated ones require thought and effort. Often our reasoning, thought, and decision making are logical, but at other times our decisions are uncertain; we are not sure how things will work out or whether our reasoning is valid.

Psychologists have devised techniques to look inside the thought processes of individuals, especially reasoning. We will examine two; the first technique involves formal thought, syllogisms, where there is a correct answer. The second technique examines situations where the answer or decision is less certain, estimating possibilities.

Syllogisms: Formal Reasoning

One of the traditional ways to study reasoning, decision making, and thinking processes is to provide subjects with deduction tasks such as syllogisms. *Syllogisms* are a series of statements, or premises, followed by some conclusion; the task is to decide (deduce) if the conclusion is warranted. By asking subjects to describe their thinking and decision-making processes during syllogisms, psychologists can trace people's cognitive processes. They can analyze each decision in the processes and thus "trace" thought. People are not especially good at solving syllogisms, especially those in an abstract form, but when made more concrete, syllogisms are easier to follow. Consider the following:

> Premise 1: All poodles are dogs.
>
> Premise 2: All dogs are animals.
>
> Conclusion: All poodles are animals.

Is the conclusion a logical statement? Does the truth of the two premises (assume that both are true) allow someone to conclude that poodles are animals? When researchers study syllogisms they trace a person's logical steps. In the above example it is easy to see that the conclusion is accurate. You can devise a syllogism where the logic follows—that is, the conclusion follows from the premises—but the conclusion is really false.

People can learn how to use logic and how to be critical thinkers and decision makers. One way is to be skeptical about conclusions and to evaluate premises systematically. Another way is to think the way a detective does, eliminating possibilities one by one, thus using logical decision-making skills.

Logical Decision Making

When making a decision, people are often faced with outcomes that have various attributes, pro and con. On the simplest level, decision making entails adding up the positive attributes of the alternatives and then making a decision. For example, each breakfast meal involves a cereal decision for me, Wheaties versus Fruit Loops. (This is hardly a major life decision, but it shows us the process.) Wheaties have more protein and less sugar than Fruit Loops, but Wheaties do not taste as good. Of course, most decisions involve more complicated variables than the cereal dilemma. For example, when buying a bicycle one has to decide about cost, weight, look, and security, as well as preference for a specific brand. Each of these factors must be considered and weighed for its relative importance.

A decision-making approach in which some variables or characteristics take on more importance than others is called a *compensatory model.* In the bicycle example, it might involve giving importance to each of several factors (weight, cost, looks), evaluating the factors, and then seeing which bicycle has the greatest overall positive score. Another approach to decision making involves ruling out alternatives that do not meet minimum criteria. For example, if you are interested in purchasing a mountain bike, you need not consider a high-performance racing bike. Alternatively, if you cannot spend more than $250 for the bicycle, you can rule out all the higher-priced models. This approach, called *elimination by aspects,* is generally a fast and efficient way to make decisions. It is logical and it helps people reduce any uncertainty they have about a pending decision.

Uncertainty: Estimating Probabilities

How do we decide what to wear, where to go, or how to answer a test item on the SAT? How do we decide when something is bigger, longer, or more difficult? Many decisions are based on formal logic, some on carefully tested hypotheses, and some on educated guesses. Making an educated guess implies knowing something based on past experiences. When someone sees rain clouds, for example, he or she guesses—but cannot be one hundred percent sure—it will rain. The likelihood of rain is expressed as a percentage, that is, as a probability.

Psychological factors, especially previous events, affect how people estimate probabilities. Consider a study by Tversky and Kahneman (1973). Subjects were given names of forty famous people, twenty men and twenty women. In one case, subjects read a list in which the men were more famous than the women; in another, the subjects read a list in which the women were more famous. After reading their respective lists, the subjects were asked if the list contained more names of men or of women.

The subjects who read the list with better-known famous men said there were more men on the list, while those who read the list with better-known famous women said there were more women on the list. The critical variable that affected results was the familiarity of the names of the famous people. In other words, the fact that one gender on the list was more famous affected the subjects' perceptions.

We make probability estimates of all types of behaviors and events. In election years, we make guesses about the likelihood of a Democratic or Republican victory; each spring we place bets on the likelihood that our team will win the World Series; we evaluate the chances of an A on our last exam. From past experience, we estimate the probability of staying on a diet, an exercise regime, or a study schedule. We can judge that the probability of a certain event, given another event, increases or decreases. For example, the probability that there will be rain, given that there are thunder clouds, high winds, and low barometric pressure, is much higher than the probability of rain with just thunder clouds.

When subjects are asked to make probability judgments about the real world, not the laboratory, they sometimes fall down on the task. Human beings make mistakes and errors in judgment, and they may act irrationally.

In order to succeed in the stock market, analysts must learn to estimate probabilities with the least chance of error.

People may ignore key pieces of data and thus make bad (i.e., irrational) decisions not based on the probabilities. For example, when dealing with world affairs, the President may err on the conservative side, not taking chances with important situations (although some presidents have been risk takers). Sometimes people's world views color their probability decision making. If an ethical system, religious belief, or political view is pointed in one direction (e.g., capitalism versus communism or Christianity versus Buddhism), a person's strategies and decision estimates will be affected. Finally, human beings are not machines or computers; their creativity, past experiences, and humanness affect results, sometimes in unpredictable ways. But cognitive psychologists suggest ways for people to become the most efficient learners and thinkers they can be—they are focusing on learning how to learn.

Learning to Learn

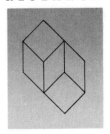

*M*ost college seniors feel they are much better students than they were as freshmen. What makes the difference? How do students learn to learn better? Today, educators and cognitive researchers are focusing on how information is learned as opposed to what is learned. To learn new information, students generate hypotheses, make interpretations, make predictions, and revise earlier ideas. They are active learners (Wittrock, 1987).

Hypotheses Are Formed. Human beings learn how to learn; they learn special strategies for special topics and general rules that depend on their goals (McKeachie, 1988). The techniques for learning foreign languages are different from those needed to learn mathematics. Are there general cognitive techniques that students can use to learn better? McKeachie, Pintrich, and Lin (1985) argued that lack of effective learning strategies is a major cause of low achievement by university students. They conducted a study to see if overall grades improved when rote learning, repetition, and memorization were replaced by more efficient cognitive strategies.

Method. To help students become better learners, McKeachie, Pintrich, and Lin developed a course on learning to learn that provided practical suggestions for studying and a theoretical basis for understanding learning. It made students aware of the processes used in learning and remembering. This awareness is called *metacognition*. Learning-skills practice, development of motivation, and development of a positive attitude were also included. Among specific topics were: learning from lectures, learning from textbooks, test taking, self-monitoring, test anxiety, learning styles, and traditional ideas like SQ3R (survey, question, read, recite, and review). The course focused on learning in general, not on specific courses such as history or chemistry. The goal was to develop generalized strategies or plans to facilitate learning.

One hundred and eighty students enrolled in the learning-to-learn course were tested at the beginning and end of the semester and compared with control groups enrolled in other psychology classes. Varied measures were used to assess whether the course had any impact on SAT scores, reading test scores, anxiety scores from an anxiety test, and especially, grades.

Results and Conclusions. The results showed that learning-to-learn students made gains in a number of areas, including grades and motivation. In later semesters, the students continued to improve. This straightforward study tells an important story about psychology in general, and cognitive psychology in particular. First, it shows that psychologists are engaged in activities that help people, not just esoteric laboratory studies. Second, it evidences a shift in emphasis from studies of learning specific facts, specific stimuli and responses, to studies of learning strategies. Third, it shows that research into thought processes can lead to more effective thought and, subsequently, to high levels of motivation. And last, this simple study shows that people can be taught to be more efficient learners.

McKeachie, Pintrich, and Lin argued that "the cognitive approach has generated a richer, deeper analysis of what goes on in learning and memory, increasing our understanding and improving our ability to facilitate retrieval and use of learning . . . we need to be aware of several kinds of outcomes—not just *how much knowledge* was learned, but *what kinds of learning* took place" (p. 602). Students can better grasp history, chemistry, or economics if they understand *how* to go about studying these topics. Law, psychology, and medicine require different learning strategies. After we learn how to learn, the differences come into sharp focus. Learning how to learn mathematics is one area that students seem to avoid more than any other, and it has unfavorable consequences for individuals and for our society as a whole.   ◆

Psychology and Mathematics

We often make choices and decisions based on numbers and mathematics. When we are told one brand of cereal costs twice as much as another brand, most of us understand the implications. When we are told that the cost of implementing a new program in government costs 3.75 billion dollars, do we understand the size of these numbers? According to John Paulos (1988), we don't. Paulos asserts that people are unable to deal comfortably with the fundamental assumptions about numbers, and especially probability. He calls this inability **innumeracy.**

When confronted with large numbers, and especially probability, our educational system often leaves us lacking. Compare the risk of being killed in a car crash, dying in a bicycle crash, or being killed by a terrorist. The television and print media spend a great deal of time reporting on terrorism, and yet the probability of being killed in a car crash is one in 5,300, dying in a bicycle accident, one in 7,500, and being killed by a terrorist, one in 1.6 million. Because people do not have a good grasp of probability they often have difficulty comparing situations, evaluating risk, and estimating likelihoods.

Why are people innumerate? Why can people not think well about large numbers? According to Paulos, the answer lies in mathematics education. Math teachers rarely go beyond the simple formulas and rarely teach students to think about mathematics. Teachers in elementary school are seldom prepared to ask mathematical questions, in part because they have not had sufficient math background, and in part because they do not realize the importance of mathematics. Paulos argues that students have math anxiety and may have been intimidated by misguided teachers.

He also maintains that people learn to compute and understand mathematics through practice. Thus, when people have learned about probability, they are less likely to attribute causation to events that are only correlated. Psychologists today are working with mathematics educators to develop new materials, to invigorate the mathematics curriculum, and to relate mathematics to real-world problems such as decision making and problem solving.

Innumeracy: The inability to deal comfortably with the fundamental assumptions about numbers and probability.

Focus on Learning

Problem Solving

How do you study for your psychology exam when you have an English paper due tomorrow? How should you handle a friend whose feelings were hurt by something you said? How can you arrange your miniscule closet so that all of your clothes and other belongings will fit? Your car gets a flat tire; what should you do? These are problems to be solved. In important ways, they represent some of the highest levels of cognitive functioning.

Human beings are wonderful at **problem solving;** they excel at confronting a situation that requires an insight to solve it. Because we can form concepts and group things together in logical ways, we are able to organize our thoughts and attack a problem to be solved. Psychologists believe that there are four stages to problem solving. First, you have to realize that a problem exists. Second, you have to assess its complexity. Third, you have to devise ways of solving the problem (which might include a number of strategies leading to insight) and actually implement the problem-solving strategy. And fourth, you have to assess whether your problem-solving approach has been successful.

Huge differences exist in people's problem-solving abilities, but understanding the processes of thought, problem solving, and thinking enables psychologists to help everyone become effective problem solvers. Recall from chapters 1 and 3 that Gestalt psychologists analyzed the world in terms of perceptual frameworks and argued that the mind takes the elements of experience and organizes them to form something unique. Kohler, a Gestalt researcher, showed that chimps could solve problems by developing insights into methods of retrieving food that was beyond their reach. The chimps discovered that they could pile boxes on top of one another to reach food, or attach poles together, making a long stick to grab bananas. Once the insight occurred, no further instruction, investigation, or training was necessary. Kohler's studies focused on insight (see chapter 5) which is essential to problem solving. Although our problem-solving abilities are usually quite good, obstacles such as functional fixedness and psychological set can interfere. Researchers study these obstacles to gain a better understanding of the processes of problem solving.

Functional Fixedness: Cognition with Constraints

When my daughter Sarah was four years old, she observed me taking her raincoat out of the closet before our trip to the zoo. Sarah insisted that it was not raining outside, and that raincoats are for rain. I explained that the coat could also be used as a windbreaker or a light spring jacket. Reluctantly, she put on the coat. In this exchange, Sarah exhibited a basic characteristic of most people: functional fixedness. **Functional fixedness** is the inability to see that an object can have a function other than its stated or usual one.

Problem solving: The behavior of individuals when confronted with a situation or task that requires some insight to solve.

Functional fixedness: The inability to see that an object can have a function other than the one normally associated with it.

When people are functionally fixed, they limit their choices and conceptual framework.

Names and Functions. Studies of functional fixedness show that the name given to a tool often limits its function. A typical study presents a subject with a task and provides tools that can be used in various ways. Duncker (1945), for example, asked two groups of subjects to attach three candles to a door at eye level for an experiment in vision. Each subject was given several objects, including tacks and three small boxes of different shapes and colors. The correct solution was to tack the boxes onto the door (at eye level) and use them as platforms for the candles.

The experimental group received boxes filled with tacks, candles, and matches; the control group received empty boxes accompanied by the other items. Duncker's hypothesis was that the experimental subjects would see the boxes only as containers for the tacks and candles, which would interfere with their ability to think of them as potential tools. His hypothesis was confirmed when all the subjects in the control group solved the problem and only forty-three percent of those in the experimental group solved it. According to Duncker, when an object is used for a specific function, the probability of its being considered for use in another way is decreased.

Two-String Problem. A typical laboratory problem is the two-string problem. In this task, the subject is put in a room in which there are two strings hanging from the ceiling and some objects lying on a table (see Figure 7.4). The task is to tie the two strings together, but it is impossible to reach one string while holding the other. The only solution is to tie a weight, such as a magnet or a pair of pliers, to one string, set it swinging back and forth, take hold of the second string, and wait until the first string swings within reach. This task is difficult because people's previous experience with an object (such as pliers) may prevent them from considering the object as a potential tool in new problem-solving situations.

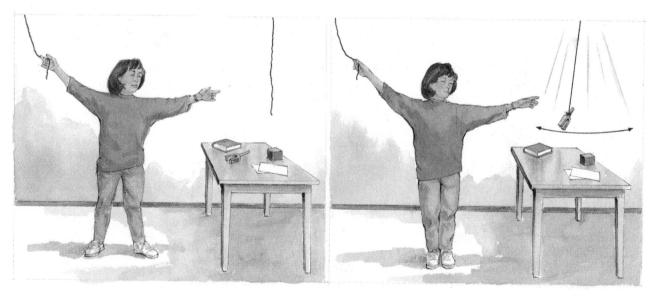

FIGURE 7.4
In the two-string problem the subject must set one string in motion in order to tie both strings together.

Labeling. Functional fixedness can also limit people's flexibility in responding to other people and situations through labeling. Labeling often leads to stereotyped ideas about social conditions. For example, people may see poverty as a human condition that cannot be changed because it has always existed. Or they may think mentally retarded people are beyond help. Avoiding the trap of functional fixedness requires thinking about objects and people in new ways, which can reap surprising benefits. For example, Arm & Hammer dramatically increased sales of its baking soda by showing consumers that the product can be used for more than baking, for instance, to absorb refrigerator odors, brighten teeth, freshen laundry, and improve the smell of cat litter boxes.

Psychological Set

Psychologists have found that most individuals are flexible in their approach to solving a problem. In other words, they do not use preconceived or "set" solutions. However, thinking about objects, people, and situations in new ways becomes especially important when we realize that people sometimes develop a rigid strategy or approach to certain types of problems. Avoiding a rigid, fixed approach allows a painter to work in charcoal, pastels, latex, and oils all at once. A flexible scientist will rely on existing technology, technology that needs to be developed, and even technology beyond the realm of modern science. And politicians such as John F. Kennedy can conceive innovative solutions such as the Peace Corps to complex problems. But all these solutions require limber thought processes.

Creative thinking requires that people break out of their psychological set, that is, their limited ways of thinking about possibilities. Psychological set is the opposite of creativity. According to the principle of *psychological set*, prior experience predisposes a person to make a particular response. Most of the time this predisposition or readiness is useful and adaptive; for the most part, what worked in the past will work in the future. Sometimes, however, the biasing effect of a set is not productive. It limits innovation and prevents a person from solving new and complex problems (M. K. Holland, 1975).

Here's a problem that is difficult because of a psychological set. In Figure 7.5, draw no more than four lines that will run through all nine dots without lifting your pen from the paper. The answer is provided on page 249.

FIGURE 7.5
The Nine-Dot Problem: In this problem, try to connect all nine dots with no more than four lines running through them, and do it without lifting your pen from the paper.

Brainstorming: Thinking without Barriers

Committees formed to evaluate problems and recommend solutions are often composed of people with different viewpoints. After the committee members define the problem, they may write down all possible solutions, rank-order them, and evaluate the possibilities. They have used an effective problem-solving tool called brainstorming. **Brainstorming** is a problem-solving technique whereby people consider all possible solutions without making any initial judgments about the worth of those solutions. As a technique, brainstorming can be used to illuminate alternative solutions to problems as diverse as a city's waste disposal or a topic for a group project. The rationale behind brainstorming is that people will produce more high-quality ideas if they feel unrestrained and do not have to evaluate the suggestions immediately. Brainstorming is a cognitive technique to release the potential of the participant, to free the person from a potential functional fixedness, to increase the diversity of ideas, and to promote creativity.

Brainstorming: A technique for problem solving that involves considering all possible solutions without making prior evaluative judgments.

Brainstorming can be an effective problem solving process for groups in diverse settings.

Creative Problem Solving

The owners of a high-rise professional building were deluged with complaints that the building's elevators were too slow. The owners called in a consultant who researched the problem and discovered that tenants often had to wait several minutes for an elevator. Putting in new, faster elevators would cost tens of thousands of dollars, which exceeded the owner's budget. Eventually, the consultant devised a creative solution that ended the complaints but cost only a few hundred dollars—he installed wall mirrors by each elevator stop so that people could look at themselves while waiting.

Creativity is the process of developing original, novel, and appropriate responses to a problem. An original response is one that is not usually given. A novel response is one that is new or that has no precedent. Unless an original and novel solution is also appropriate, however, it cannot be called creative. An appropriate response is one that is deemed reasonable in terms of the situation. Building a house of toothpicks may be an original and novel idea, but it is clearly not appropriate. A key issue in creativity is how people become more creative in their thinking (Greeno, 1989).

A person doesn't have to be an Einstein or a Picasso to be creative, as the consultant described above demonstrates. Those who are especially careful form a hypothesis and then test it to evaluate potential solutions. For a particularly difficult problem, they may arrive at a creative solution, one that makes others say, "Why didn't I think of that?" Creativity is a different way of thinking. Not all problems demand creative solutions. The question "How much is seventy-five plus twenty-five?" has only one correct answer. But an architect who has to design a new museum for a community can produce a variety of solutions, most of which are creative.

Creativity: A characteristic of thought and problem solving, generally considered to include originality, novelty, and appropriateness.

Creativity as a Three-Stage Process. Morris Stein (1974) defined creativity as a process involving three stages: hypothesis formation, hypothesis testing, and communication of results. In hypothesis formation, a person tries to formulate a new response to a problem, not an easy task. A person must confront a situation and think of it in nonstereotyped ways, explore paths not previously explored.

Next, the hypothesis must be tested against reality. At this stage it is crucial to apply the criterion of appropriateness. If the result is novel, original, and appropriate, the person can move toward the third stage, the communication of results. A creative idea or expression is worthless if it is not shared with other people.

Providing public transportation for people with wheelchairs required creative problem solving skills. The solution—kneeling buses!

Creativity as Divergent Thought. When people sort through alternatives or try to solve a problem, they attempt to focus their thinking. We say that they converge on an answer or that they use convergent thinking skills. *Convergent thinking* involves narrowing down choices and alternatives to arrive at a suitable answer. **Divergent thinking,** in contrast, is the approach in which a person widens the range of possibilities and expands his or her options for solutions. Guilford (1967) defined creative thinking as divergent thinking. According to other psychologists, any solution to a problem that can be worked out only with time and practice is not a creative solution. To foster creativity people need to rethink their whole approach to a task (Greeno, 1989). Successful entrepreneurs know this to be the case (McClelland, 1987), and those who develop new technologies, products, and services are well rewarded for their creativity. Schools of business are paying closer attention to developing creativity in marking courses.

Brain Structure and Creativity. Are some people born creative? It is not clear whether the brain is organized in some special way in highly creative individuals. Researchers have conducted electroencephalographic studies to see if there are any observable differences in the brain waves of gifted and talented people. So far, problems in clearly defining both the subject population (see Young and Ellis, 1981) and appropriate tasks for testing affect the validity of the findings. Moreover, individual differences in brain-wave patterns of normal subjects are sufficiently great that a difference in the brain-wave pattern of an especially creative or talented individual would not necessarily be significant. Also, no firm evidence exists that creative individuals are either more or less intelligent than other people. The data relating to IQ scores and creativity are inconclusive.

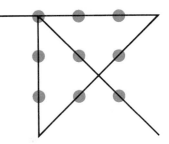

FIGURE 7.6
Here is a creative solution to the nine-dot problem found on p. 247. Notice that you have to think beyond your normal psychological set and not see the nine dots as a square.

Problem Solving and Computers

Given the fact that it is human beings who determine the ways computers accept, store, process, and retrieve data, it is not surprising that computers handle information in much the same manner as the human brain. By simulating specific models of the human brain, computers help psychologists understand human thought processes. Specifically, computers help shape theoretical development (as in the information-processing and stage analysis of perception), assist researchers in investigating how people solve problems, and enable psychologists to test models of aspects of behavior such as memory. Researchers who program computers to work like a human brain are involved in the process of *computer simulations.* Those who program computers to carry out certain types of human activity in optimal ways are involved in *artificial intelligence (AI).* Their task is formidable because, as we saw in chapter 2, the brain is exceedingly complex, with billions of interconnections. We also saw in chapters 3 and 6 that researchers break many perception and memory problems down into small steps using the information-processing approach.

Divergent thinking: According to Guilford, the production of new information from known information, or the generation of logical possibilities, which serves as the basis of creativity.

Information Processing. The information-processing approach to perception, memory, and problem solving is a direct outgrowth of computer simulations. Flowcharts showing how information from the sensory register reaches short- and long-term memory rely implicitly on a computer analogy. Those who study memory extend the computer analogy further by referring to storage areas as buffers, central processors, and memory elements.

In addition, computers have been programmed to understand and produce human language. These programs store information in their memories about the rules for generating English sentences and even speech. For example, programs exist for blind people—information is typed at the keyboard, and the computer vocalizes what has been typed.

Computer Programs. The most widely investigated aspect of computer simulation and artificial intelligence is problem solving. As we saw at the beginning of the chapter, chess was one of the first problems attacked by computers. Computers have been taught to play other games, such as checkers and backgammon, and to solve simple number-completion tasks. They also solve complicated problems involving large chunks of memory. The most sophisticated studies attempt to incorporate aspects of human memory systems into computer programs.

Two basic approaches exist in problem-solving programs: algorithms and heuristics. **Algorithms** are procedures that provide a solution to a problem by examining every possible outcome or way of attacking a problem. Algorithms are precise and exhaustive; in a chess game, for example, an algorithmic approach requires that the computer examine every permutation and combination of possible ways to decide if one move has the highest probability of success. Algorithms are used in a wide variety of real-life problems, from increasing the output of a recipe, to writing a computer program. Because algorithms are a set of rules that *must* be followed, they are often impractical. Human problem solvers, such as chess master Harry Pillsbury, often know things that do not require them to make exhaustive attempts to solve a problem; they have rules-of-thumb that facilitate their work. Thus, they follow heuristics.

Heuristics are sets of strategies that act as guidelines—not strict rules—for problem solving. Heuristic procedures reflect the processes used by the human brain; they are selective and sometimes incorrect. In chess, a heuristic approach suggests that a play has to be considered in terms of the most likely and most successful approaches. Moves are evaluated in terms such as, "Does this move increase my strategic position in the game?" Attacking a queen and castling a king are generally perceived to be important heuristic strategies.

A number of heuristic approaches exist. In **subgoal analysis** a problem is broken down into several smaller steps. In **means-end analysis** a person's (or computer's) current position is compared with the end point of the problem (the goal). The idea is to reduce the number of steps to reach the goal. A **backward-search** involves working backward from the goal or end point to one's current position, both to analyze the problem and to reduce the steps to get from the goal to one's current position. Human beings often use all three of these heuristic approaches, but human beings can become functionally fixed. They may use only one approach or problem-solving set. Human beings are also hampered by their limited attention span and limited ability to work on a number of tasks at one time. Computers, in contrast, can have hundreds or even thousands of processors operating at once. To-

Algorithms: Simple, specific, exhaustive procedures that provide a solution to a problem after a step-by-step analysis.

Heuristics: Sets of selective strategies that act as guidelines for decision making, but are not strict rules.

Subgoal analysis: A heuristic procedure in which a task is broken down into smaller, more manageable parts.

Means-end analysis: A heuristic procedure in which efforts are made to move the problem solver closer to a solution by finding the intervening steps and making changes that will bring about the solution as efficiently as possible.

Backward-search: A heuristic procedure in which a problem solver starts at the end of a problem and systematically works in reverse steps to discover the subparts necessary to achieve a solution.

TABLE 7.1
Algorithms and Heuristics Are Two Different But Equally Viable Approaches to Problem Solving

	Procedure	**Advantages**	**Disadvantages**	**Example**
Algorithms	Exhaustive, systematic consideration of all possible solutions; a set of rules	Solution is guaranteed	Can be very inefficient, effortful, time consuming	Computer chess program is typically based on a set of predefined rules and moves
Heuristics	Strategies; rules of thumb which have worked in the past	Efficient; saves effort and time	Solution not guaranteed	Person who attempts to fix a broken car uses past experience to rule out a whole range of potential problems

day's supercomputers are made up of as many as one thousand powerful computers operating at once, solving problems in parallel.

In computer situations, heuristic approaches are especially effective. In chess and other problem-solving situations they save time and are efficient, and they more accurately reflect the processing approaches of human beings. Although a mindless computer can perform millions of instructions per second, can operate twenty-four hours per day, and can have hundreds of processors operating at the same time, it is still less efficient than a human being. Table 7.1 summarizes the major advantages and disadvantages of algorithms and heuristics.

Although computers can be programmed to process information the way human beings do, they lack human ingenuity and spontaneity. In addition, computers do not have a referential context in which to judge situations. When you say to a grocer, "Halibut?" and the grocer responds, "Wednesday, after four o'clock, downtown only," you understand that halibut will be available on Wednesday, after four o'clock shipment, to the

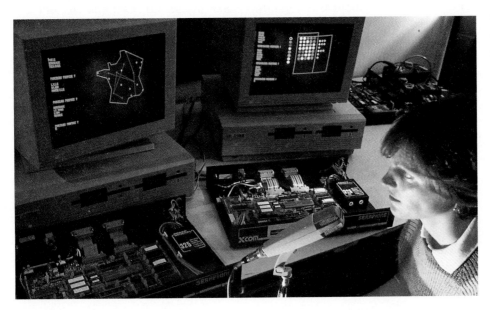

To improve the computer's ability to receive and program information the way humans do, this Seraphine computer is being developed so that it can recognize human voice patterns.

downtown branch of the grocery chain. Human beings understand the context of fresh fish being shipped in only occasionally, to some stores, at certain times during the week. They understand the context of branch stores, shipments, fresh fish, and selective shipments. Computers do not have such contexts. Further, they cannot evaluate their own ideas and improve their own problem-solving abilities by developing heuristics.

Improve Your Problem-Solving Abilities

APPLYING PSYCHOLOGY

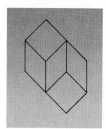

*E*ach of us solves problems on a daily basis; it makes sense to be the best problem solver possible. Problem solving is deliberate and time consuming, and affects day-to-day decisions. Ashcraft (1989) has suggested ways for people to improve their problem-solving abilities.

Increase Your Knowledge. A person with limited knowledge about a topic is far less able to solve problems than a well-informed problem solver. Learn about bicycles if you are going to buy one. Study computer programming if you are going to program a computer.

"Automate" Some Tasks. Become an expert at some simple tasks involved in solving your problem. Because you have limited capacities of attention (chapter 3), you should free mental resources to solve more complex aspects of a problem by automatically solving smaller goals. In chess, have a couple of opening moves prepared; in studying, always make an outline first—these tasks will then be routine and automatic.

Follow a Plan. Have a plan of action. If your problem is remembering material from an exam, use the SQ3R approach (chapter 6, p. 221). Identify the problem, explore alternative approaches, look at the effects, be a critical thinker (see chapter 1, p. 27).

Draw Inferences and Develop Subgoals. Try to draw inferences about the facts that are known and possible ways to solve the problem. Then break large problems down into smaller, more manageable tasks. In planning a Thanksgiving dinner, think first about the appetizers, then about the main course, and last about the desserts.

Work Backward. Trace a solution in reverse order, working backward toward the fact that you know. In writing a computer program, decide what the output should look like first and then decide what steps would get that output.

Search for Contradictions and Relations. Are there possibilities that can be ruled out right away because they violate basic rules, guidelines, or assumptions? Actively consider things you already know to help you rule out inconsistencies. This means using your existing framework of knowledge to help you solve new problems.

Reformulate the Problem and Represent It Physically. Go back to the beginning of the problem and try to restate it, rethink it, in different terms. If you have been thinking in terms of building with wood, think about other materials to achieve a fresh look. Draw, build, or in some way represent the problem physically. Don't use just your brain to solve a problem. Some of the most creative solutions have been sketched out on napkins by problem solvers attempting to represent the problem in some other, new way.

Practice. To be good at problem solving, practice doing it. Practice makes perfect, or at least makes you better at a task. The more often you solve algebra word problems that focus on solving two unknowns, the better you will be at doing the task. (Remember innumeracy discussed above!)   ◆

- ◆ When a person develops a psychological set, what happens to his or her thinking? p. 247
- ◆ What is the rationale behind brainstorming? p. 247
- ◆ What are the traditional criteria for a response to be considered creative? pp. 248–249
- ◆ Distinguish between heuristics and algorithms. pp. 250–251
- ◆ Name five ways to improve your problem-solving abilities. p. 252

Focus on Learning

Language

The doorbell rings. You open the door and see a friend wearing sunglasses, a T-shirt, and pink-and-green neoprene swim trunks. Your friend says, "Get your stick. It's six foot and glassy." Some people might interpret this to mean that they'd better arm themselves with a club because a shiny six-foot monster is running loose. But a surfer would grab his surfboard and head out to the beach, where six-foot-high waves are breaking on a beautiful, windless day. Although the friend's words sound the same to surfer and nonsurfer alike, the interpretation made by each is radically different because surfers use special expressions when talking about their sport. If a surfer and nonsurfer who speak the same language use different expressions to describe surf conditions, does this mean they think about the ocean in different ways? Does language determine thought, or do all people think alike, regardless of their language?

Thought and Language

When researchers discovered that Eskimos had many more words than English-speaking people to describe snow, anthropologist and linguist Benjamin Whorf hypothesized that verbal and language abilities affect thought directly. In Whorf's view, the structure of the language that people speak directly determines their thoughts and perception (Whorf, 1956).

To investigate Whorf's claim, cognitive psychologist Eleanor Heider Rosch studied the language structure and color-naming properties of two cultures with different languages (Heider, 1971, 1972; Heider and Olivier, 1972; Rosch, 1973). Every language has ways of classifying colors, although no language includes more than eleven basic colors (Berlin and Kay, 1969). Rosch's subjects were English-speaking Americans and members of the Dani, a primitive Stone Age tribe in Indonesian New Guinea. In Dani, there are only two basic color names: *mola* for bright colors and *mili* for dark colors. In English, there are many ways of classifying color, such as red, blue, yellow, green, turquoise, pink, and brown. If language determines thought, as Whorf claimed, then the English speakers and the Dani would show two different ways of thinking about color.

Rosch showed both groups of subjects single-color chips for five seconds. After thirty seconds she asked the subjects to pick the same color from a group of forty chips. Whorf's hypothesis predicted that since the Dani have only two basic color-naming words, they would confuse colors within a group. Two different colors from *mola* would be considered the same basic color, *mola*. Neither the Dani nor the English-speaking subjects, however, confused colors within categories. The Dani's two-color language structure did not limit their ability to discriminate, remember, or think about colors.

Rosch's studies showed that language does not determine thought. Although various languages have developed specific grammars and thought processes, they have probably done so in response to specific environments, events, and cultures. It is adaptive for Eskimos to discriminate among many kinds of snow, but their language does not determine their thoughts. Rather, their thoughts about snow help shape their language and the words in it.

In the same manner, even though human beings are sensitive to odors, they have a rather impoverished language structure to describe them. Research shows that although odors are easily detected, descriptions are difficult, often based on personal experiences and sometimes coded in terms of a personal biographical event (for example, grandad's pipe tobacco, mother's perfume, Aunt Bea's upstairs attic) (Richardson and Zucco, 1989). Linguistic processes play a limited role in the processing of smell, and like the description of snow, our language of odors is determined by other factors. But linguistic processes are far from simple and have undergone much careful research and study, as you will see in the following sections.

Linguistics

Tens of thousands of years ago, our cave-dwelling ancestors used to put their thoughts into words to organize hunting parties. Several millennia later, Egyptian scribes used hieroglyphics to represent the spoken word. Still later, Socrates was sentenced to drink hemlock for preaching corrupting ideas to the youth of ancient Greece. Today, world leaders such as Pope John Paul II and Mikhail Gorbachev employ oratory to rouse their constituencies to moral behavior and social progress; professors verbally instruct students in the various fields of human knowledge; and people from all walks of life use language to exchange ideas with others or mentally solve problems. Throughout the ages and in every culture, human beings have rendered their thoughts into language and employed words to order their thoughts. Without this ability, human civilization could never exist. In many ways, language and thinking define humanity.

We learn language as children; children are astonishingly adept at understanding and utilizing the basic rules of language. A three-year-old, noticing that many nouns can be turned into verbs by adding a suffix, may say "It sunned today" to mean it was a sunny day. The miracle of language acquisition in children has long puzzled linguists and psycholinguists.

Linguistics is the study of language, including speech sounds, meaning, and grammar. **Psycholinguistics** is the study of how language is acquired, perceived, understood, and produced; psycholinguists such as Noam Chomsky seek to discover how children learn the complicated rules necessary to speak correctly. Their studies during the past two decades show that children acquire the simple aspects of language first, followed by progressively more complex elements and capabilities.

Studies have also revealed *linguistic structures*, the rules and orderly regularities that exist in, and make it possible to learn, a language. This section examines the study of three major linguistic structures: *phonology*, the study of the sounds of language; *semantics*, the study of the meanings of words and sentences; and *syntax*, the study of the relationships among words and how they combine to form sentences.

Linguistics: The study of language including speech sounds, meaning, and grammar.

Psycholinguistics: The study of how language is acquired, perceived, comprehended, and produced.

Phonology

The gurgling, spitting, and burping noises infants first make are caused by air passing through the vocal apparatus. At about six weeks, infants begin to make speechlike cooing sounds. During their first twelve months, infant vocalizations become more varied and frequent. Eventually, they combine sounds into pronounceable units.

Phonemes: The basic units of sound in a language.

Morphemes: The basic units of meaning in a language.

Phonemes. The basic units of sound that compose the words in a language are called **phonemes**. In English, phonemes are the sounds of single letters, such as *b, p, f,* and *v,* and of combinations of letters, such as *t* and *h* in *th*ese. Forty-five phonemes express all the sounds in the English language; of those, just nine make up nearly half of all words.

Morphemes. At about one year of age, children make the first sounds that psychologists classify as real speech. Initially, they utter only one word. But soon they are saying as many as four or five words. Words consist of **morphemes,** the basic units of meaning in a language. A morpheme consists of one or more phonemes combined into a meaningful unit. The morpheme *do,* for example, consists of two phonemes, the sounds of the letters *d* and *o.* Other words can be formed by adding prefixes and suffixes to morphemes. Adding *ing* or *er* to the morpheme *do,* for example, gives *doing* or *doer.*

It is interesting to note that no matter what language people speak, one of their first meaningful utterances is the morpheme *ma.* It is coincidental that *ma* is a word in English. Other frequently heard words of English-speaking people are *bye-bye, mama,* and *bebe.* In any language, the first words children speak often refer to a specific object or person, especially food, toys, and animals. In the second year, children's vocabulary increases to about fifty words, and in the third year to as many as one thousand words (see Figure 7.7)

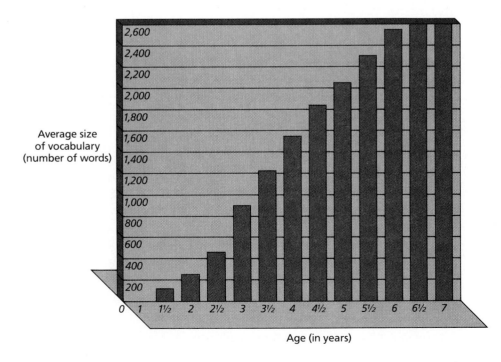

Average size of vocabulary (number of words)

Age (in years)

FIGURE 7.7
Children's average vocabulary increases rapidly from age 1½ to 6½. (Adapted from Moskowitz, 1978, on work by Smith.)

Semantics

At first, infants do not fully understand what their parents' utterances mean. But as more words take on meaning, they develop semantic capability. **Semantics** is the analysis of the meaning of individual words, of the relationship among words, and of the placement of words in a context that generates thought.

Consider how a four-year-old child might misconstrue her father when he says to her mother, "What a terrible day I've had. First, the morning traffic made me a nervous wreck. Then, I got into an argument with my boss, who became so furious he almost fired me." The child might think her dad got into a car accident and was nearly set on fire. In trying to understand the meaning of utterances, a child is faced with understanding not only the meanings of single words, but also their relationship to other words. As everyone who has attempted to learn a new language knows, the meaning of a sentence is not the same as the definitions of the individual words added together. Words mean different things, depending on their sentence context. For example, a Chinese student studying English at a California college needed a light for his cigarette and followed these directions printed on a red box: PULL FOR FIRE. He was astonished to hear a clanging alarm!

Syntax

Once children can use words that have distinct meanings, they begin to combine those words into short sentences such as "Mama look" or "Bye-bye, mama." That is, they develop a syntactic capability. **Syntax** is the study of how words and groups of words combine to form phrases, clauses, and sentences. Syntactic capability enables children to convey more meaning. For example, children acquire a powerful new way of making their demands known when they learn the words "I want" or "give me." Suddenly they can ask for cookies, toys, or mommy, without any of those things being within sight. The rewards that such linguistic behavior brings children are powerful incentives for them to learn more language. Children begin to use

A child's acquisition of language is a marvel to families and scientists alike.

TABLE 7.2
Language Milestones

Age	Language Activity
12 weeks	Smiles when talked to; makes cooing sounds spontaneously
16 weeks	Turns head in response to human voices
20 weeks	Makes vowel and consonant sounds while cooing
6 months	Changes from cooing to babbling
12 months	Imitates sounds; understands some words
18 months	Uses from 3 to 50 words; understands basic speech
24 months	Uses more than 50 words; uses two-word phrases
30 months	Uses new words daily; has very good comprehension of speech
36 months	Has vocabulary of over 1000 words; makes grammatical mistakes, but the number of grammatical mistakes decreases significantly with each passing week

sentences at different ages, but once they begin, they tend to develop at similar rates (R. Brown, 1970). Moreover, the average length of sentences increases at a fairly regular rate as children grow older.

Early studies of children's short sentences suggested that a description of the position of the words and their types could characterize early speech, but later analyses showed these descriptions to be inadequate. Later investigations suggested that young children possess an innate grammar and that they use grammatical relationships in much the same ways that adults do (McNeill, 1970). **Grammar** is the linguistic description of a language; it contains the rules for how a language works. Table 7.2 presents some of the major linguistic milestones in a child's life.

Transformational Grammar

In 1957, linguist Noam Chomsky described a radical approach to grammar that changed many psychologists' view of language development. Chomsky claimed that each person is born with the ability to transform the underlying basis or kernel of meaning into an infinite number of meaningful sentences. In Chomsky's grammar, the message of a sentence is stored differently from the words used to compose it. Psychologists are especially interested in transformational grammar because it helps explain the potential uniqueness of human language.

Surface and Deep Structures. The fundamental idea of Chomsky's **transformational grammar** is that each sentence has both a surface structure and a deep structure. The **surface structure** is the actual sentence: e.g., *Alex gave Mary a dog.* It shows the words and phrases that can be analyzed through the diagramming procedures often learned in junior high school. The **deep structure** is the underlying pattern of the words that helps convey meaning. Thus, the sentences *Alex gave Mary a dog* and *Alex gave a dog to Mary* have different surface structures, but the same deep structure.

To understand transformational grammar more clearly, consider the simple sentence, *Visiting relatives can be a pain.* Although simple, the sentence can have two distinct meanings. It might mean that relatives who visit can be annoying guests or, alternatively, that going to visit relatives is an an-

Grammar: The linguistic description of how a language functions, especially the rules for how all acceptable sentences are generated.

Transformational grammar: Developed by Chomsky, an approach to the study of language that assumes that each surface structure of a sentence has a deep structure associated with it. This grammar includes transformational rules for generating surface structures from deep structures.

Surface Structure: The organization of a sentence that is closest to its written or spoken form.

Deep structure: The organization of a sentence that is closest to its underlying meaning.

Does this sign really mean that the children are slow? Common usage can change the meaning of words and word groupings.

noying chore. Transformational grammar accounts for these two meanings by showing that for the same surface structure there are two possible deep structures. To a great extent, the meaning of a word or a sentence is far more important than its form or structure. There is no doubt that the structure of a sentence conveys meaning, but semantic factors (meaning) help convey the abstract significance of a word or sentence.

Abstraction in Language. Imagine that a friend calls you on the telephone to tell you about a severe storm warning that he just heard over the radio. Most likely your friend won't recite the radio announcement verbatim, but instead will relay in his own words such details as estimates of the storm's arrival, wind velocities, and probable amount of precipitation. That is, your friend will tell you what he remembers best from the announcement, its concepts, not its exact wording. This suggests that our memory of verbal exchanges is not literal minded and passive but, rather, an active compilation of concepts.

Researchers more than fifty years ago made the same argument. In 1932, English psychologist F. C. Bartlett published results from studies that made history and are consistent with recent studies. Bartlett had his subjects read short stories packed with information about a plot. After a few minutes the subjects had to recall the story. They retold the story to another subject, who retold it to another, and so forth. Bartlett examined the retelling of the story from person to person to see what happened to the details as time passed. Bartlett found that the stories grew shorter, less detailed, more informal; some events were altered, and others were made up to fit the altered story line. He argued that his subjects built a *schema*, an organized structure in memory of the events of the story, and the schema was what was remembered. Bartlett thus asserted that his subjects had abstracted the key elements for memory organization and recall.

Focus on Learning

- ◆ What evidence did Whorf use to claim that the structure of the language that people speak directly determines their thoughts and perception? p. 253
- ◆ What are the principal tasks of a psycholinguist? p. 254
  Distinguish among phonology, syntax, and semantics. p. 255
- ◆ Distinguish between surface and deep structure. p. 257

Language Acquisition: Nature versus Nurture

Research shows that language and thought are sensitive to both experience (nurture) and genetic factors (nature.) As in other areas of human behavior, the debate continues about the relative contribution of each factor. If language is based on biology, two things should be true: (1) Many aspects of language ability should be evident early in life. (2) All children, regardless of their culture or language, should develop a grammar in a similar way. On the other hand, if environmental factors account for language acquisition, the role of learning should be preeminent.

Consider what happens when people take their first course in Spanish, French, or Latin. They recognize that there will be a new language in which they will learn to communicate: grammar, reading, pronunciation. Students may buy study aids: books, dictionaries, and tapes. They may read about the country of the new tongue, talk to someone who speaks the language, and rely on foreign language teachers. In general, a student prepares to acquire the new language. But is a newborn already prepared? Researchers who try to resolve this nature/nurture debate over language acquisition study the development of language through observational studies of infants and children, case histories of sensory-deprived infants, studies of reading-disabled or brain-damaged individuals, and experiments with chimpanzees.

Learning Theories

Learning theories stress the role of environmental influences, or nurture, in language acquisition. The basic idea is that language is not a magic process but a natural unfolding of traditional learning.

One learning theory, the *conditioning approach,* stresses the importance of language experiences during the formative years. According to this theory, both other-person reinforcement (in the form of parental approval) and self-reinforcement (in the form of speech) increases the probability that children will emit words and sentences. As the sole explanation of language, the conditioning approach has one serious weakness. Slobin says, "A mother is too engaged in interacting with a child to pay attention to the linguistic form of his utterances" (1975, p. 290). Nevertheless, despite inattention to reinforcing language structure, children eventually learn to form sentences.

Another learning theory claims that children acquire language through *imitation,* that is, by copying adult speech. Through imitation children learn to use the proper forms of language, and although reinforcement occurs, it is not necessary for learning. An example of learning by imitation is picking up regional terminology, such as "Y'all come back, now."

Studies have examined the ability of adults and children to use new words grammatically. Brown and Berko (1960) presented adults and children with a sentence containing real words and nonsense words, such as "Let's wug some fish," then asked them to use the nonsense word correctly in another sentence. Both adults and children responded with sentences such as "The fish were wugged yesterday," using *wug* as a verb, as in the original sentence. Brown and Berko also found that scores on this type of test improved regularly with age. They concluded that formal changes in word associations and skill in placing words in their proper grammatical context are part of a child's developing ability to use English syntax. Children develop the ability to use abstract rules in addition to their growing vocabulary.

Learning approaches have several weaknesses, however. They do not explain how children, who learn grammar in a short period of time using a small sample of sentences, are able to generate an infinite number of new sentences. Additionally, learning approaches do not take into account biological or maturational readiness. If readiness were not to some extent biologically determined, parents could teach their child to speak, read, and write soon after birth.

Biological Theories

Psychologist George Miller (1965) asserts that human beings have an innate, unique capacity to acquire and develop language. Although he does not exclude experience as a factor in shaping children's language, Miller claims that it is human nature itself that allows children to pay attention to language in their environment and ultimately to use it.

Lateralization: The concentration of a particular brain function in one hemisphere.

Even the strongest proponents of the nature (biological) argument do not contend that a specific language is inborn. Rather, they agree that a predisposition toward language exists and that a blueprint for language is preprinted. As a child matures, this blueprint provides the framework through which learning a language and its rules takes place. Three major sources of evidence support the biological side of the nature versus nurture debate:

1. studies of brain structure and lateralization,
2. studies of readiness, and
3. language acquisition in children and chimpanzees.

Brain Structure and Lateralization. As early as the 1800s, researchers knew that the brain of a human being is specialized for different functions. At that time researchers began mapping the brain and discovered that if certain areas were damaged (usually through accidents), the person had severe disorders in language abilities. Later work, for example, that of Norman Geschwind (1972), led to the idea of **lateralization**, the concentration of a particular brain function in one hemisphere.

As we saw in chapter 2, considerable evidence suggests that the left and right sides of the brain (normally connected by the corpus callosum) handle distinctly different functions. The left side appears to be organized for speech and language activities, the right side for processing music and spatial tasks. Geschwind (1970) found that in ninety-seven percent of cases of language impairment resulting from a head injury, the injury involved the left hemisphere. Other studies have shown that when the corpus callosum is surgically severed, information transmitted to only one hemisphere is unavailable to the other. To some extent, the left and right hemispheres function independently.

Some researchers argue that studies of laterality show that the brain has unique processing abilities in each hemisphere. For example, language functions are predominantly, but not exclusively, left-hemisphere functions. But as Goodglass and Butters (1988) argue, the available data do not make an airtight case; each hemisphere seems to play a dominant role in some functions and to interact in others.

Learning Readiness. Researchers such as Erik Lenneberg (1921–1975) claim that human beings are born with a grammatical capacity and a readiness to produce a language (Lenneberg, 1967). They claim that language simply develops as people interact with their environments. One important aspect of this theory is that a child's capacity to learn language depends on maturation of certain neurological capacities. For example, maturation at about eighteen to twenty-four months permits children to acquire grammar so they can interact linguistically with others. On the other hand, lack of maturity in certain structures limits infants' ability to speak in the first months of life. Lenneberg's view derives in part from observations that most children learn the rules of grammar at a very early age.

Lenneberg believes that the brain continues to develop from birth until about age thirteen, with optimal development at age two. During this period children develop grammar and learn the rules for language. After age thirteen, there is little room for improvement or change in their neurological structure. Lenneberg supports his argument with the observation that brain-damaged children can relearn some speech and language, whereas brain-damaged adults or adolescents who lose language and speech are unable to regain the lost ability.

Lenneberg's view is persuasive, but some of his original claims have been seriously criticized, particularly his idea of how a critical readiness period in language development operates (e.g., Kinsbourne, 1975). Some researchers claim that not only human beings but also other organisms are born with a grammatical capacity and a readiness for language, for example, chimpanzees.

Studies with Chimpanzees

Do animals communicate with one another through language? If they do, is that language the same as, similar to, or totally different from the language of human beings? And most important, what can human beings learn from animals about the inborn aspects of language?

The biological approach to language suggests that human beings are prewired, born with a capacity for language. Experience is the key that unlocks this existing capacity and makes it available for expression. The arguments for and against the biological approach to language acquisition use studies showing that chimpanzees naturally develop some language abilities. Researchers can control and shape the environment in which language learning occurs with chimps, something they cannot do in studies involving human subjects.

Chimpanzees are generally considered among the most intelligent animals; in addition, they resemble human beings more closely than any other animal. Playful and curious, chimps share many common physical and mental abilities with human beings. For these reasons, they have been the species of choice when psychologists have studied language in animals.

Until the last two decades, all attempts to teach language to animals have failed, which has led most psycholinguists to conclude that only human beings have the capacity to acquire language. However, some major research projects show that even though chimpanzees lack the necessary vocal apparatus to speak, they can learn to use different methods of communication (Rumbaugh and Savage-Rumbaugh, 1978).

Washoe. From age one, the chimpanzee Washoe was raised like a human child in the home of Allen and Beatrice Gardner (1969). During the day Washoe was in the house or the large fenced yard. At night she slept in a trailer. The Gardners and their research assistants did not speak to Washoe. Instead, they used Ameslan, the American Sign Language. Rather than being taught to speak words, Washoe was taught to make signs that stood for words, simple commands, and concepts such as more, come, give me, flower, tickle, and open.

Within seven months Washoe learned four signs; after twelve months she had learned twelve. At twenty-two months, she had a vocabulary of thirty-four signs; by age four she knew eighty-five signs; and by the end of her fifth year, Washoe had accumulated 160 signs (Fleming, 1974). Washoe learned a large number of signs that refer to specific objects or events. She was able to generalize these signs and combine them in a meaningful order to make sentences. There is no proof, however, that Washoe used a systematic grammar (rules to transform and generate sentences).

Sarah. The chimp Sarah was raised in a cage, with more limited contact with human beings than Washoe had. Psychologist David Premack (1971) used magnetized plastic symbols and instrumental training methods to teach Sarah words and sentences (see Figure 7.8). Initially, Premack placed several

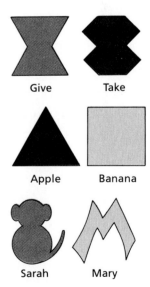

Give   Take

Apple   Banana

Sarah   Mary

FIGURE 7.8
Sarah learned to construct sentences by using pieces of plastic that varied in color, size, and shape.

Studies with chimps such as Nim Chimpsky have raised questions concerning the chimps' ability to truly learn language as opposed to merely mimicking words.

plastic symbols on a board in front of Sarah and placed a banana slightly out of reach. Each time Sarah chose the appropriate symbol, he would give her the banana as a reward. Eventually, Sarah came to associate a specific symbol with a banana, and learned to place the token on the board when she wanted a banana.

Gradually Sarah developed a small but impressive vocabulary. She learned to make compound sentences, to answer simple questions, and to substitute words in a sentence construction, such as, "Place banana dish," "Place apple dish," and "Place orange dish." There is no evidence, however, that she could generate a new sentence, such as, "Is the apple in the dish?" or "Where are the apples?"

Lana. Lana the chimp learned to interact with a computer at the Yerkes Primate Research Center. Researchers Rumbaugh, Gill, and Von Glaserfeld (1973) gave Lana six months of computer-controlled language training. Lana learned to press a series of keys with imprinted geometric symbols. Each symbol represented a word in an artificial language called Yerkish. The computer varied the location of each Yerkish word and the color and brightness of the keys. Through instrumental conditioning, Lana was able to demonstrate some of the rudiments of language acquisition. However, like Washoe and Sarah, Lana did not show that she could manipulate grammatical relations in meaningful and regular ways.

So far most studies of chimps show that their language is similar to that of young children: It is concrete, specific, and limited. Chimps, however, do not show the ability to generate an infinite number of grammatically correct sentences, an ability that human beings acquire with age.

Nim. A Columbia University psychologist, H. S. Terrace (1979, 1980), claims that even the limited results with apes are greatly overvalued. He suggests that apes do not have language abilities and that the data reported so far with chimps show only that they were mimicking their teachers' signs.

Terrace reports significant differences between chimp language and that of young children. In raising his chimp, Nim Chimpsky (named after famous linguist Noam Chomsky), he found that Nim's utterances did not increase in length as young children's do. Nim acquired many words, but she did not use them in longer and longer sentences as time passed. In addition, only twelve percent of Nim's utterances were spontaneous; the remaining eighty-eight percent were responses to her teacher. Terrace points out that a significantly greater percentage of children's utterances are spontaneous. Terrace also found no evidence of grammatical competence either in his own data or in that of other researchers.

Kanzi. Recent work with a little known species of ape, the Pygmy chimpanzee, shows that chimps can acquire symbols without training. According to well-known language researcher Sue Savage-Rumbaugh, these chimps comprehend symbols before they produce them, and they also comprehend human speech. In Savage-Rumbaugh's view (1987), they have the ability to construct a rudimentary grammar.

Kanzi, a pygmy chimp, was provided a keyboard to talk to his human trainers. His keyboard has 256 symbols and he has mastery of more than 150. Recording and interacting with Kanzi has shown that he comprehends both individual words and sentences and responds appropriately. He learned his language by being enmeshed in a language environment, not through training procedures. His unique contribution is that he understands human speech and syntax and has learned to do so without training. He learned his languages steadily and rapidly, and Savage-Rumbaugh feels that this sets him apart from all other apes who have learned language and shown that learning through production of language (e.g., moving symbols).

Chimp Language? Terrace's work challenged the findings of previous investigators and made them think about language in new ways. Others at the Yerkes Regional Primate Center at Emory University have presented additional challenges to primate language acquisition (Savage-Rumbaugh et al., 1983), claiming that not only is chimp language different from that of human beings, but also that the purpose of chimp language is different.

Unlike young children, who spontaneously learn to name and point to objects (often called *referential naming*), chimps do not spontaneously develop such communication skills. For Savage-Rumbaugh and her colleagues, such skills are crucial components of human language. Terrace (1985) agrees that the ability to name is a basic part of human consciousness. He argues that as part of our socialization, we learn to refer to our various inner states: our feelings, thoughts, and emotions.

Chimps can be taught some naming skills, but the procedure is long and tedious. Children, on the other hand, develop this skill easily and spontaneously at a young age. Accordingly, researchers such as Sanders (1985) assert that chimps do not interpret the symbols they use the way children interpret them. These researchers question the comparability of human and chimp language.

Although few psychologists are completely convinced about the role of language in chimps, their criticisms do not diminish the chimps' language abilities or accomplishment in other areas like mathematics (Rumbaugh, Savage-Rumbaugh, and Hegel, 1987; Boysen and Berntson, 1989). They also do not rule out language and speech processing in some chimps (Savage-Rumbaugh, 1987). Chimp language remains an emerging part of psychology where the answers are far from complete, but the quest is exciting.

- ◆ Describe two learning approaches to language acquisition. p. 259
- ◆ What is the crucial assumption of biological approaches to language acquisition? pp. 259–260
- ◆ Terrace claimed an important difference between chimps' language and that of human children. What is that difference? p. 262

Focus on Learning

Key Terms

Cognitive psychology p. 234
Concept p. 237
Positive instance p. 239
Negative instance p. 239
Dimension p. 239
Mediation p. 240
Conservative focusing p. 240
Reasoning p. 240
Logic p. 240
Decision making p. 240
Innumeracy p. 244

Problem solving p. 245
Functional fixedness p. 245
Brainstorming p. 247
Creativity p. 248
Divergent thinking p. 249
Algorithms p. 250
Heuristics p. 250
Subgoal analysis p. 250
Means-end analysis p. 250
Backward-search p. 250
Linguistics p. 254

Psycholinguistics p. 254
Phonemes p. 255
Morphemes p. 255
Semantics p. 256
Syntax p. 256
Grammar p. 257
Transformational grammar
  p. 257
Surface structure p. 257
Deep structure p. 257
Lateralization p. 260

Summary

Cognitive Psychology: An Overview

* Cognitive psychology is the study of the overlapping fields of learning, memory, perception, and thought.   p. 234

* Cognitive psychologists study thinking; they assume that mental processes exist, that they are systematic, and that they can be studied scientifically. They believe that we are active participants in analyzing our world and that through measures of performance a researcher can learn about mental processing.   pp. 234–235

Concept Formation

* In concept formation, people try to classify objects by grouping them with or isolating them from others on the basis of a common feature.   p. 237

* In concept-learning studies, stimuli vary along dimensions; features of an object set it apart from others. Within each dimension are different values or attributes.   pp. 238–239

Decision Making

* *Reasoning* is the process by which we evaluate and generate arguments and reach conclusions; the procedure we use to reach a valid conclusion is called *logic*. *Decision making* is the assessment of and choice among alternatives.   p. 240

* *Syllogisms* are a series of statements followed by a conclusion; the task is to decide if the conclusion is warranted.   p. 241

* A decision-making approach in which some variables or characteristics take on more importance and can make up for others is called a *compensatory model*. In another approach, people rule out alternatives that do not meet minimum criteria; this approach, called *elimination by aspects*, is generally a fast and efficient way to make decisions.   p. 242

* *Innumeracy* is an inability to deal with fundamental assumptions about numbers.   p. 244

Problem Solving

* Problem solving implies confronting a situation that requires insight. Problem solving consists of recognizing that a problem exists, assessing its complexity, devising and implementing solutions, and assessing results.   p. 245

* Functional fixedness is an inability to see that an object can serve more than its stated or usual purpose.   p. 245

* Brainstorming is a problem-solving technique whereby people consider all possible solutions without making initial judgments.   p. 247

* Creative responses are original, novel, and appropriate. According to Guilford, creative thinking is divergent thinking.   p. 248

* *Algorithms* provide a solution to a problem by examining every possible outcome or way of attacking a problem. *Heuristics* are sets of strategies that act as guidelines, not strict rules, for decision making.   p. 250

Language

* *Psycholinguistics* is the study of how people acquire, perceive, comprehend, and produce language. *Grammar* is the linguistic description of a language.   p. 254

* *Phonemes* are the basic units of sounds in a language. *Morphemes* are the basic units of meaning. *Semantics* is the study of the meaning of components of language. *Syntax* is the relationship of groups of words and the way in which words are arranged into phrases and sentences.   p. 255

* *Transformational grammar*, developed by Chomsky, is an approach to studying the structure of a language.   p. 257

Language Acquisition: Nature versus Nurture

* People have the ability to generate an infinite number of correctly formed sentences in their language. Because this ability cannot be acquired through mere imitation or instruction, it suggests the presence of an innate grammar, or language ability.   p. 260

* Few psychologists are completely convinced about the role of language in chimps, but their criticisms do not diminish the chimps' language abilities or accomplishment in other areas like mathematics.   p. 261

Connections

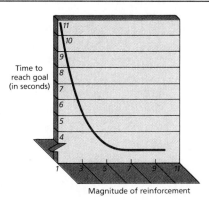

If you are interested in . . .	Turn to . . .	To learn more about . . .
Thought processes	◆ Ch. 5, pp. 190–195	The ways cognitive psychologists approach traditional learning questions.
	◆ Ch. 11, pp. 394–402	How motivational researchers are considering the role of thought in determining a person's day-to-day decision making.
	◆ Ch. 13, p. 466	Why stress is considered an interpreted state.
	◆ Ch. 17, p. 639	How business managers and personnel officers are taking into account the way people remember, code, and interpret information.
Decision making and problem solving	◆ Ch. 5, pp. 187–188	How reinforcement for problem solving can get in the way of a person's intrinsic enjoyment of a task.
	◆ Ch. 8, pp. 278–281	How psychologists use problem solving to help determine intelligence.
	◆ Ch. 15, pp. 549–558	How psychologists consider many maladjustments as a series of problems to be solved.
The role of language in everyday life	◆ Ch. 5, p. 183	How operant learning principles can be used to explain language acquisition.
	◆ Ch. 8, pp. 280, 282	The crucial role of language in determining a person's intelligence.
	◆ Ch. 17, p. 584	The various ways of communicating without overt vocalizations.

8 *Intelligence*

"Untitled" by Joseph Cornell

◆

*M*aria Vega waits anxiously but quietly as her high school adviser examines her school records. Finally, the adviser tells Maria that her intelligence test score is well above average and high enough for the accelerated physics class; students in that class are required to have an IQ test score of 125 or more, a recommendation from the school psychologist, and permission from the instructor. The adviser notes that Maria excels in creative pursuits, and knows that she is keenly interested in science and has always received A's in science. The adviser seeks the approval of the physics teacher and Maria is thrilled when the teacher grants her request.

Through diligent studying, Maria manages to score consistently in the top third of the class on the course exams. But her best talents are revealed when the physics class is divided into groups and assigned projects for the school science fair. Maria is nominated leader of her group, and she thinks of an especially creative experiment that wins first place. Estimating intellectual capabilities is a complex task, but there is more to intelligence than a single test score. Intelligence tests do not measure several mental characteristics that are important to success such as motivation, creativity, and leadership skills.

Intelligence is difficult to measure because it is hard to define. Consider many of the generalized, and often inaccurate, attributes some people use to evaluate intelligence. Sometimes shy, quiet people or especially attractive ones are assumed to be slow-witted, while others, perhaps because they earn a high income, are judged to be bright. Yet looks, income, and talkativeness provide little or no gauge of an individual's intelligence. People demonstrate effective and intelligent behavior in many ways, but not necessarily in all areas. Some people, for example, can write a complicated computer program, but not a short story or an essay. Moreover, intelligence must be defined in terms of the situation in which people find themselves. Intelligent behavior for a dancer is very different from intelligent behavior for a scientist, and both types of behavior are different from intelligent behavior for a child with a learning disability.

What all this means is that no single test—such as a test of verbal ability, English literature, or math—is a clear measure of intelligence. Psychologists therefore use a variety of tests as well as other data such as interviews, teacher evaluations, and writing and drawing samples to evaluate an individual's current standing, to make predictions about future performance or behavior, and to offer suggestions for remedial work or therapy. And in spite of their drawbacks, tests have strong predictive value; for example, intelligence tests can *generally* predict academic achievement, and achievement tests can *generally* predict whether someone will profit from further training in a specific area.

The focus of this chapter is intelligence: theories, tests, and controversies about intelligence. We also examine two special populations with respect to intelligence, the gifted and the mentally retarded. We begin with the question, "What is intelligence?"

What Is Intelligence?

Why do two students who study the same material for the same amount of time get different scores on an examination? Why do some people succeed in medical school and others have difficulty finishing high school? One factor might be that one person is more intelligent than the other, and high intelligence enhances a person's chances to succeed.

Intelligence is one of the most widely used yet highly debated concepts in science and everyday life. In 1921, a group of psychologists attempting to answer the question, "What is intelligence?" could not come to an agreement. Sixty-five years later, Sternberg and Detterman (1986) posed the same question to twenty-five respected researchers, but they still could not reach an agreement.

Defining Intelligence

For some, intelligence refers to all mental abilities; for others, to the basic general factor necessary for all mental activity; for still others, it refers to a group of specific abilities (Jensen, 1987). Quinn McNemar (1964) contended that "All intelligent people know what intelligence is—it is the thing that the other guy lacks!" Varying definitions of intelligence all share certain concepts:

1. Intelligence is defined in terms of observable, objective behavior.
2. Intelligence takes in both an individual's capacity to learn and his or her acquired knowledge.
3. A sign of intelligence is one's ability to adapt to the environment.

Perhaps the most widely accepted definition of **intelligence** is that of the well-known test constructor David Wechsler: *Intelligence is the aggregate or global capacity of the individual to act purposefully, to think rationally, and to deal effectively with the environment* (1958, p. 7). In Wechsler's definition, intelligence is expressed behaviorally—it is the way people act, and their ability to learn new things and to use previously learned knowledge. Most important, intelligence deals with people's ability to adapt to the environment. Wechsler's definition has had far-reaching effects on how test developers devise intelligence tests and investigate the nature of intelligence.

Theories of Intelligence

Human beings show intelligent behavior in a variety of ways, and sometimes they choose not to act intelligently. We cannot say that all people are intelligent all of the time, nor can we specify the exact conditions under which people will exhibit their intelligence. This realization of individual differences in behavior has been a problem for psychology from its beginnings. The early psychologists such as Titchener studied the speed of subjects' mental processes and paid little or no attention to variations (differences) among these subjects. John Watson, known as the father of behaviorism, denied the relevance of individual differences for behaviorism.

But researchers who examine intelligence focus on individual differences. In the early 1900s, a large body of data emerged that described the characteristics thought to be involved in intelligence. The data included information on age, race, sex, socioeconomic status, and environmental factors. From these data, researchers developed theories to describe the nature of intelligence and developed ways in which to test it. Today, the most influential approaches to the study of intelligence are Piaget's and Wechsler's theories, factor theories, Jensen's two-level theory, and the relatively new theory of intelligence proposed by Sternberg.

Piaget. According to Jean Piaget, intelligence is a reflection of a person's adaptation to the environment, with intellectual development consisting of changes in the way the individual accomplishes that adaptation. Every child goes through invariant stages in intellectual development, with different levels of cognitive processes determining the types of intellectual tasks the child can accomplish. (We examine this developmental process in chapter 9). Three-year-olds cannot learn calculus because they are not ready to perform the mental operations needed to grasp the necessary concepts. Piaget's theory of intellectual development focuses on the interaction of biological readiness and learning. In Piaget's view, neither predominates in the development of intelligence; they work together.

Wechsler. David Wechsler viewed intelligence from the perspective of a test examiner. As one of the developers of a widely used and widely re-

Although the Lapp herders of northern Scandinavia take snowmobiles out on herding trips now, they still use traditional tents for shelter and stuff their boots with dried grasses for warmth. Intelligence allows them to cope with the rigors of their environment.

Intelligence: According to Wechsler, "the aggregate or global capacity of the individual to act purposefully, to think rationally, and to deal effectively with the environment."

spected intelligence test, Wechsler knew well that tests were made up of many subparts, each measuring a different aspect of a person's functioning and resourcefulness. He therefore examined closely the components of intelligence and argued that intelligence tests involving spatial relations and verbal comprehension reveal little about someone's *overall* capacity to deal with the world. In Wechsler's view, psychologists need to remember that intelligence is more than simply mathematical or problem-solving ability; it is the broad ability to deal with the world.

Factor Theories. Factor theories of intelligence use a correlation technique known as **factor analysis** to discover what makes up intelligence. Verbal comprehension, spelling, and reading speed, for example, usually correlate highly, suggesting that some underlying attribute of verbal abilities determines a person's score on those three tests.

Early in this century, Charles E. Spearman (1863–1945) used factor analysis to show that intelligence really consisted of two parts: a general factor affecting all tasks and several specific factors necessary to perform specific tasks. According to Spearman, some amounts of both the general and specific factors were necessary for the successful performance of any task. This basic approach to intelligence is called the *two-factor theory of intelligence.*

Louis L. Thurstone (1887–1955) developed Spearman's work further by postulating a general factor analogous to Spearman's, as well as seven other factors, each of which represented a unique mental ability. His theory is known as the **factor-theory approach to intelligence.** In it he developed a computational scheme for sorting out the seven factors that he considered to be the abilities of human beings: verbal comprehension, word fluency, number facility, spatial visualization, associative memory, perceptual speed, and reasoning.

Thurstone's factor-theory approach with its seven abilities led to and culminated in J. P. Guilford's multifactor approach to intelligence testing. Guilford was one of the last students to work with Titchener, and his work focuses on individual mental abilities. He is concerned with developing a testable scheme of intelligence. Guilford gave large numbers of tests to diverse populations and found a whole range of factors that seemed appropriate to describe intelligence. He looked for a structure, a rational scheme of grouping them together; he eventually described a *Structure of Intellect* model. According to Guilford (1967), human intellectual abilities and activities can be described in terms of three major dimensions: the mental operations performed, the content of those operations, and the resulting product of the operations. As Figure 8.1 shows, Guilford's three-dimensional model produces 120 factors, 98 of which have been demonstrated experimentally, according to Guilford. These varieties of intelligence are often, but not always, independent of one another.

Guilford (1985) contends that several scores are necessary for a correct assessment of an individual's intellectual abilities, not one or two, or even four. And so he asserts that intelligence should be defined as "a systematic collection of abilities or functions for processing information of different kinds in different forms" (p. 231). Research supports Guilford's theory and suggests that optimally weighted composite scores may best make predictions about achievement, school learning, and work performance (Guilford, 1980, 1985).

Jensen's Two-Level Theory. Arthur Jensen approaches intelligence testing not from the view of a test constructor, but from the view of a theoretician. Jensen (1969, 1970) suggests that intellectual functioning consists of associ-

Factor analysis: A statistical procedure designed to discover the mutually independent elements (factors) in any set of data.

Factor-theory approach to intelligence: Theories of intelligence based on factor analysis, including those of Spearman and Thurstone.

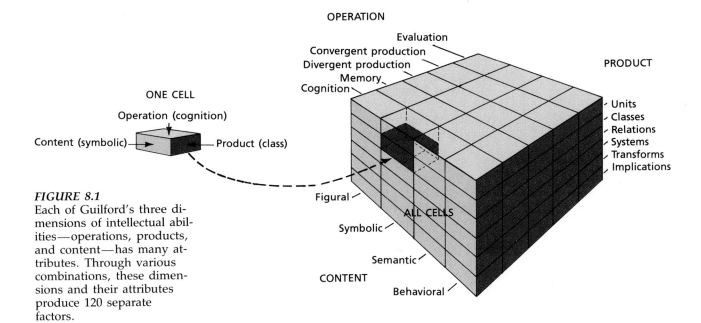

FIGURE 8.1
Each of Guilford's three dimensions of intellectual abilities—operations, products, and content—has many attributes. Through various combinations, these dimensions and their attributes produce 120 separate factors.

ative abilities and cognitive abilities. Associative abilities enable us to connect stimuli and events; they require little reasoning or transformation. Questions testing associative abilities include asking someone to repeat from memory a seven-digit number sequence or to name the first president of the United States. Cognitive abilities, on the other hand, deal with reasoning and problem solving. Solving word problems and defining new words or concepts are examples of cognitive ability tasks.

Jensen's idea is not new; even the founders of the testing movement suggested that different kinds of intellectual functioning are involved in intelligence. What is new is Jensen's claim that associative and cognitive abilities are inherited, adding more information to the nature versus nurture controversy of intelligence (discussed later in this chapter).

Sternberg's View. Robert J. Sternberg takes a new view of intelligence, an information-processing view. He divides intelligence into three dimensions: componential, experiential, and contextual. His aim is to relate a person's intelligence to his or her internal and external world. Sternberg's ideas, which are relatively new in the domain of theories of intelligence, are presented next.

A New Theory of Intelligence

A psychologist in search of a field for important research with far-ranging practical implications could confidently choose intelligence and intelligence testing. Robert J. Sternberg of Yale University did—and his life has never been the same. Fully aware that traditional theories of intelligence are purported to be the building blocks of today's intelligence tests, Sternberg has criticized most widely used tests.

Wrong Focus. Sternberg (1986) finds intelligence tests too narrow and contends they don't adequately account for intelligence in the everyday world. He argues that researchers have focused for too long on *how* to measure intelligence, rather

THINKING ABOUT RESEARCH

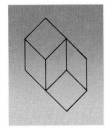

than the more important question of "What is intelligence, how does it change, and what can individuals do to train it?" Sternberg reasons that some tests measure individual mental abilities while other tests measure the way the individual operates in the environment. Sternberg asserts that a solid theory of intelligence must account for both individual mental abilities and the ability of the person to use his or her capabilities in the environment.

New Ideas. Sternberg (1985, 1986) developed a new "triarchic" theory of intelligence, described in his book *Beyond IQ.* Sternberg's theory comprises three subparts, each dealing with a different aspect of intelligence. The three subtheories are contextual, experiential, and componential (see Figure 8.2).

Contextual subtheory deals with an individual's ability to use intelligence to prepare for problem solving in specific situations. This part of the triarchic theory focuses on how people shape their environments so that their competencies can be best utilized. For example, an individual might organize problems in a meaningful way, perhaps by grouping similar items together. This first subtheory, contextual, does not refer to any mental operations that are necessary to carry out problem solving.

The second subtheory, *experiential,* deals with the individual and his or her external world. According to this theory, a test measures intelligence if it assesses a person's ability to deal with novel tasks in an automatic manner. Such a task might involve learning to remember all words containing the letter T in a paragraph. Initially, finding and remembering such words is tedious, but with much practice, the task becomes automatic.

The third subtheory, *componential,* is the glue that holds the other two subtheories together. The componential subtheory describes the mental mechanisms that underlie what are commonly considered intelligent behaviors. A component is a basic method of information processing. It includes a person's ability to

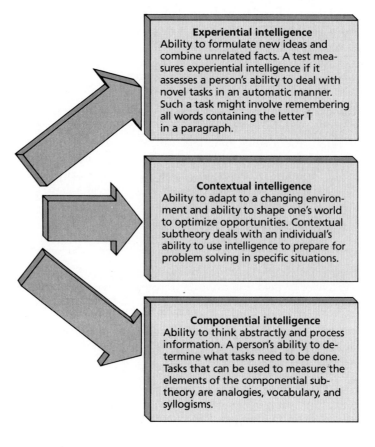

FIGURE 8.2
Sternberg's triarchic theory of intelligence.

Experiential intelligence
Ability to formulate new ideas and combine unrelated facts. A test measures experiential intelligence if it assesses a person's ability to deal with novel tasks in an automatic manner. Such a task might involve remembering all words containing the letter T in a paragraph.

Contextual intelligence
Ability to adapt to a changing environment and ability to shape one's world to optimize opportunities. Contextual subtheory deals with an individual's ability to use intelligence to prepare for problem solving in specific situations.

Componential intelligence
Ability to think abstractly and process information. A person's ability to determine what tasks need to be done. Tasks that can be used to measure the elements of the componential subtheory are analogies, vocabulary, and syllogisms.

determine what tasks need to be done; to determine subtasks that need to be undertaken first; to analyze their subparts; to decide what information should be processed; and to monitor performance. Tasks that can be used to measure the elements of the componential subtheory are analogies, vocabulary, and syllogisms.

To be intelligent, a behavior has to involve all three components—all three subtheories of intelligence. For example, Sternberg suggests that eating is a behavior that is adaptive, but does not show novelty or use of nontrivial abilities. Similarly, turning on a light switch is adaptive, but it is automatic and does not demonstrate the components of intelligence. Few behaviors involve all three components, and so Sternberg asserts that various tasks measure intelligence to a different extent.

Future Tests. Does Sternberg support the continued use of IQ tests? Yes, if the tests are used prudently. Sternberg argues that existing IQ tests do not do justice to the theories from which they evolved and that new tests examining all aspects of intelligent behavior need to be established. Existing IQ tests measure some people's intelligence some of the time, but they are often misleading. From Sternberg's view, new batteries of tests are needed to analyze fully the three basic subcomponents of intelligent behavior. ◆

---

1 ◆ What does Piaget say intelligence reflects? p. 269
2 ◆ What is Wechsler's criticism about the specific parts of intelligence tests? pp. 269–270
3 ◆ In Jensen's view, what is the difference between associative and cognitive abilities? pp. 270–271
4 ◆ Differentiate among the three subtheories of Sternberg's model of intelligence. pp. 271–273

[handwritten margin notes]
1. a person's adaptation to the environment
2. He claims these tests reveal little about someone's overall capacity to deal w/ the world.
3. associative abilities enable us to connect stimuli & events - memory - cognitive abilities deal w/ word problem solving & reasoning

Focus on Learning

Testing   4.

Like Maria Vega, who was profiled at the beginning of this chapter, you probably have taken one or more intelligence tests during your school years. The results of intelligence tests—often rendered in precise numbers—may have determined your educational curriculum from elementary school on. Psychologists are among the first to admit that intelligence tests have shortcomings and researchers continue to revise them to correct inadequacies.

Intelligence tests have had a long and interesting history. In the late nineteenth and early twentieth century, Alfred Binet (1857–1911), a lawyer in France, became interested in psychology and began to study the relationship of physiology and behavior. He later employed Theodore Simon (1873–1961), a physician, and their friendship and collaboration became famous.

Binet and Simon are well known as the founders of the psychological testing movement. Interestingly, the first intelligence tests weren't developed for the general population. In 1904 Binet was commissioned to identify procedures for the education of children with mental retardation in Paris. Binet was chosen for the task because he had been lobbying for action to help the schools; only recently had schools been made public and open to all, and disadvantaged children were doing poorly and dropping out. In 1905 Binet and Simon set a goal to separate normal children from children with mental retardation. As Stagner (1988) suggests, this may have been the first government-sponsored psychological research. Binet and Simon were

Binet worked with Simon and initiated some of the first psychological testing in the 20th century.

concerned only with measuring general intelligence in children, not with why some children were retarded in intellectual development or what their future might be. In 1905, they wrote:

> Our purpose is to be able to measure the intellectual capacity of a child who is brought to us in order to know whether he is normal or retarded. We should, therefore, study his condition at the time and that only. We have nothing to do either with his past history or with his future . . . (p. 194)

Binet coined the phrase "mental age," meaning the age level at which a child is functioning. He and Simon developed everyday tasks, such as counting, naming, and using objects, to determine mental age. The scale they developed can be considered the first useful and practical test of intelligence.

As Binet and Simon's interests broadened and their conception of intelligence matured, their tests became more sophisticated. Eighty years later, psychologists are still following some of their recommendations about how tests should be constructed and administered. In fact, one of the most influential intelligence tests in use today—the Stanford-Binet—is a direct result of Binet and Simon's early tests.

Principles of Test Development

Imagine that you are a seven-year-old child taking an intelligence test and you come to a question that asks, "Which one of the following tells you the temperature?" Below the question are pictures of the sun, a radio, a thermometer, and a pair of mittens. Is the thermometer the only correct answer? Suppose that there are no thermometers in your home, but you often hear the temperature given on radio weather reports. Or imagine instead that you "test" the temperature each morning by standing outside to feel the sun's strength, or that you know it's cold outside when your parents tell you to wear mittens. According to your experiences, any one of the answers to the question might be an appropriately intelligent response.

What Does a Test Measure? The ambiguity and cultural biases of this hypothetical test question illustrate the complexity of intelligence-test development. In general, we say that a *test* is a standardized device for examining a person's responses to specific stimuli, usually questions or problems. Because there are many potential pitfalls in creating a test, psychologists follow an elaborate set of guidelines and procedures to make certain that their questions are properly constructed (see Figure 8.3).

First, a psychologist must decide what the test is to measure. For example, will it measure musical ability, or knowledge of geography, mathematics, or psychology? Second, he or she needs to construct and evaluate items for the test that will give an examiner some reasonable expectation that success on the test means something. Third, standardization must take place.

Standardization. **Standardization** is the process of developing a uniform procedure for administering and scoring a test and for establishing norms. **Norms** are the scores and corresponding percentile ranks of a large and **representative sample** of subjects from the population for whom the test was designed. The people in the sample are matched with regard to variables such as socioeconomic status and age (this idea is also discussed in the appendix). Thus, a test designed for college freshmen might be given to two

Standardization: The process of developing a uniform procedure for the administration and scoring of a test, including the development of norms from a large, representative sample.

Norms: The scores and corresponding percentile ranks or standard scores of the group on whom the test was standardized.

Representative sample: A sample of individuals who match the population with whom they are to be compared with regard to important variables such as socioeconomic status and age.

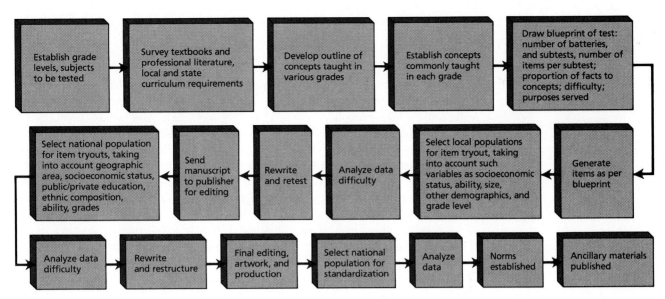

FIGURE 8.3
Procedures for constructing a standardized test. (Source: adapted from Rudman, 1977.)

thousand freshmen, with an equal number of men and women, sixteen- to twenty-year-olds, from large and small high schools, and from different areas of the country. Standardization ensures that there is a basis for comparing future test results with those of a standard reference group.

After a test is designed and administered to a representative sample, the results are examined to establish a norm score for different segments of the test population, for example, for children, adolescents, and adults, or for psychologists, musicians, or geographers. Knowing how people in the representative sample have done allows psychologists and educators to interpret future test results properly. In other words, the scores of those in the sample serve as a reference point for comparing individual scores.

Normal Curve. Test developers generally plot the scores of the representative sample on a graph that shows how frequently each score occurs. On most tests some people do very well, some score very poorly, and most score in the middle. When test scores are distributed that way, psychologists say the data are normally distributed or fall on a normal curve. A **normal curve** is a bell-shaped graphic representation of data arranged so a certain percentage of the population falls under each part of the curve. As Figure 8.4 shows, most people are in the middle range, with a few at each extreme. Tests are often devised so that comparisons can be made of individual scores

Normal curve: A bell-shaped curve arranged so that a certain percentage of the population falls under each part of the curve.

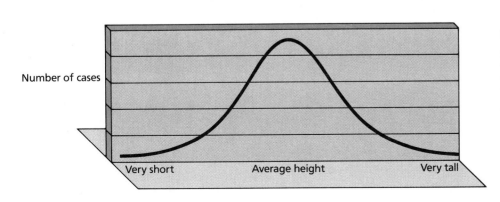

FIGURE 8.4
This bell-shaped curve shows the normal distribution of height in the general population. As with normal distributions of weight or even intelligence, very few people are represented at the extremes.

Raw score: An examinee's unconverted score on a test (such as the number of correct answers).

Standard score: A score that expresses an individual's position relative to the mean based on the standard deviation; it is often derived by converting a raw score to one that can be interpreted on the basis of a population variable (such as age or grade).

Percentile score: A score indicating what percentage of the test population would obtain a lower score.

Deviation IQ: A standard IQ test score that has the same mean and standard deviation at all ages.

against a normal distribution. (The appendix discusses the normal distribution in detail on p. 658.)

Scores. The simplest score on a test is the **raw score**, that is, the number of correct answers. But the raw score is seldom a true indicator of a person's ability. On many tests, particularly intelligence tests, raw scores need to be adjusted to take into account a person's age, sex, and grade level. Such scores are commonly expressed in terms of a **standard score**, indicating an individual's position relative to others. If, for example, a 100-item intelligence test is administered to students in the third and eleventh grades, we would expect those in the eleventh grade to answer more items correctly than those in the third grade. To adjust for the differences, after the test each student's score is compared to the score typically achieved by other students at the same grade level. Thus, if eleventh-graders typically answer seventy questions correctly, an eleventh-grader who answers ninety questions correctly will have done better than most other students at that grade level. Similarly, if third-graders usually answer twenty-five questions correctly, then a third-grader who answers fifteen questions correctly will have performed worse than most other students at that grade level.

A standard score also generally indicates the percentage of other students taking the test who obtain a lower score; this is called a **percentile score**. If, for example, someone's percentile score is eighty-four, then eighty-four percent of people taking the test obtained a lower score.

The Earliest Tests Were Intelligence Tests. Perhaps the oldest and most widely recognized test is the intelligence test. In the early 1900s, intelligence was measured by a simple formula. An intelligence quotient, or IQ, was calculated by dividing a person's mental abilities, or mental age, by his or her chronological age and multiplying the result by one hundred. Mental ages of children were calculated from the number of correct answers on a series of test items; the higher the number answered correctly, the higher the mental age.

A problem with the traditional mental age/chronological age formula is that at each age, the intelligence test shows different variability. Young children are far more variable in their answers than older children or adults are; it is as if their intelligence were less stable, less repeatable, and subject to change. These variations make predictions and comparisons difficult. To simplify measures of IQ, psychologists and testers began using **deviation IQ**, a standard score for which the mean and standard deviation remain constant at all ages. Thus, a child of nine and a child of sixteen, each with an IQ of 115, have the same position relative to others who have taken the same IQ test. Both are in the eighty-fourth percentile; that is, both scored better than eighty-four percent of all others their age who took the same IQ test.

Reliability and Validity

Of all the achievements by psychologists in making tests useful, perhaps the most important is to ensure that tests are both reliable and valid. If a student obtains different scores on two versions (or forms) of the same test, which score is correct? Furthermore, does the test measure what it is supposed to measure and *only* that?

Reliability. **Reliability** refers to the consistency of test scores. In other words, a test is reliable if it yields the same (or very similar) score for the same person in repeated testing, or the same score for the same person using different versions of the test. (Consistency of test scores assumes that the person is in the same emotional and physiological state at each time of administration.) If a test's results are not consistent from one testing session to another, or for two comparable groups of people, meaningful comparisons are impossible.

There are several ways to determine whether a test is reliable. The simplest, called **test-retest,** is to administer the same test to the same person on two or more occasions. If, for example, the person achieves a score of 90 one day and 135 another, the test is probably not reliable. But keep in mind the possibility that the person might have remembered some of the test items from one occasion to the next. To avoid that problem, testers use the **alternative-form** method, which involves giving two different versions of the same test. If the two forms test the same characteristic and differ only in their items, both should yield the same result. Another way to test reliability, the **split-half** method, involves dividing a test into two parts. On a reliable test, the scores from each half yield similar, if not identical, results.

Even the most reliable test will not yield identical results each time it is taken, but a good test will have a relatively small standard error of measurement. The **standard error of measurement** is the number of points a score varies because of imperfect reliability. Consider an intelligence test that has a standard error of measurement of three, for example. If someone scores 115 on that IQ test, a practitioner can state with a high degree of confidence that the individual's real score is between 112 and 118—three points above or below the obtained score.

Validity. If your psychology exam includes questions such as "What is the square root of 647?" and "Who wrote *The Grapes of Wrath?*" it is probably not a valid measure of your knowledge of psychology. That is, it is not measuring what it is supposed to measure.

To be useful, a test must have **validity**—it should measure what it is supposed to measure and predict what it is supposed to predict (see Table 8.1). *Content validity* refers to the test's ability to measure the knowledge or behavior it is intended to measure. A test designed to measure musical aptitude should not include items that assess mechanical aptitude or personality characteristics. Similarly, an intelligence test should measure only

Reliability: The ability of a test to yield the same score for the same individual through repeated testings.

Test-retest: A method of assessing reliability by administering a test to the same group of examinees on two different occasions and computing the similarity between the scores.

Alternative-form: A method of assessing reliability by administering two forms of a test and computing the similarity between the scores.

Split-half: A method of assessing reliability by splitting a test into comparable halves and correlating the scores from each half.

Standard error of measurement: Based on statistical formulas, the number of points that a score may vary because of imperfect reliability.

Validity: The ability of a test to measure only what it is supposed to measure.

TABLE 8.1
Types of Validity Used to Assess Tests

Validity	Aspect Measured
Content validity	The extent to which a test reflects a sample of the actual behavior to be measured
Face validity	The extent to which a test "looks" appropriate just from a reading of the items
Predictive validity	The extent to which a test can predict a person's behavior in some other setting
Construct validity	The extent to which a test actually measures a particular trait (such as intelligence, anxiety, or musical ability)

1. the process of developing a uniform procedure for administering & scoring a test for establishing norms.

2. So that you are matched w/ the correct age, race, + socioeconomic group.

3. Either by raw score, standard score, percentile, or

4. Reliability - consistency of test scores. Validity measure only what is to be measured

intelligence, not musical training, cultural experiences, or socioeconomic status.

In addition to content validity, a test should have *predictive validity*—it should be able to predict a person's future achievements with at least some degree of accuracy. But critics of intelligence tests like to point out that test scores are not always accurate predictors of people's performance. Tests cannot take into account a high level of motivation or creative abilities. Nevertheless, many colleges rely on the SAT scores of high school students to predict their ability to do college-level work, and thus evaluate who should be accepted for admission.

Interpretation

Tests are generally made up of different subtests or subscales, each yielding a score. There may also be one general score for the entire test. All these scores require knowledgeable interpretation; that is, test scores must be placed in a context that is meaningful to the person who receives the information, perhaps a parent or a teacher. Without such a context, the score is little more than a number.

Many intelligence tests provide a single IQ score. These tests, however, contain far more information than that single score. Consider one of the most popular IQ tests for children, the Wechsler Intelligence Scale for Children-Revised, or WISC-R. In addition to an overall IQ score, the WISC-R test yields scores for verbal IQ, performance IQ, and various other subtests.

Although single and multiple scores are useful, researcher Alan Kaufman (1979) suggests that to evaluate an individual accurately, global or overall IQ scores should be de-emphasized and test examiners should look instead at the components of the IQ score. He suggests that the interpretation of test scores is the key to understanding IQs; without such interpretation, a single IQ score can be biased, inaccurate, or misleading.

> ## Focus on Learning
>
> 1 ◆ What is the process of standardization? p. 274
> 2 ◆ Why is a representative sample so important? pp. 274–275
> 3 ◆ How is an intelligence quotient calculated? p. 276
> 4 ◆ Distinguish between reliability and validity. p. 277

Three Important Intelligence Tests

What is the best intelligence test? What does it measure? Can you study for an intelligence test to get a higher score? As in other areas in science, theory leads to application; many intelligence theorists applied their theoretical knowledge to test development. The three tests we shall examine briefly are all based on the theories of their developers.

Stanford-Binet Intelligence Scale

Most people associate the beginning of intelligence testing with Alfred Binet and Theodore Simon. As discussed earlier, in 1905 Binet collaborated with Simon to develop the Binet-Simon Scale. Their original test was actually thirty short tests, arranged in order of difficulty, consisting of tasks such as distinguishing food from nonfood or pointing to objects and naming them.

The Binet-Simon Scale was heavily biased toward verbal questions and was not well standardized. From 1912 to 1916, Lewis M. Terman revised the Binet-Simon Scale and developed an intelligence test now known as the Stanford-Binet. A child's mental age, or intellectual ability, was divided by his or her chronological age and multiplied by 100 to yield an intelligence quotient, or IQ.

For decades psychologists used the original and revised versions of the Stanford-Binet. The Stanford-Binet has traditionally been a good predictor of academic performance, and many of its simplest tests correlate highly with one another. A new version of the Stanford-Binet was published in 1986 with items that minimize gender and racial characteristics. It is comprised of four major subscales and one overall IQ score, and it tests individuals ages two through twenty-three.

Test administration time varies with an examinee's age because the number of subtests given is determined by age. All examinees are first given a vocabulary test, and along with their age, this determines the level at which all other tests begin. There are fifteen possible subtests, which vary greatly in content. Some require verbal reasoning; others, abstract or visual reasoning; and still others, quantitative reasoning. In addition, there are memory tests. Each of the subtests consists of a series of levels with two items at each level. The test begins with test items for each subscale at the entry level and continues until a higher level on each subscale is established (until a prescribed number of items are failed).

Raw scores are determined by the number of items passed and then converted to a standard score for each age group. The new Stanford-Binet is a potent test; one great strength is that it can be used over a wide range of ages and abilities. However, like all tests it has limitations, especially in that not all examinees are given the same battery of tests across age levels. This makes comparing individuals difficult (Sattler, 1988). But the new Stanford-Binet correlates well with the old one, as well as with the WISC-R and the K-ABC, which are discussed next.

Wechsler Scales

David Wechsler (1896–1981), a Rumanian immigrant who earned a Ph.D. in psychology from Columbia University, was influenced by Charles Spearman and Karl Pearson (two English statisticians) with whom he studied. In 1932, Wechsler was appointed chief psychologist at Bellevue Hospital in New York City; there, he began making history. In the 1930s, Wechsler recognized that the Stanford-Binet was inadequate to test the IQ of adults. He also maintained that some of the Stanford-Binet items lacked validity. In 1939, Wechsler developed the Wechsler-Bellevue Intelligence Scale to test the IQ of adults. In 1955, the Wechsler Adult Intelligence Scale (WAIS) was published, which eliminated some technical difficulties of the Wechsler-Bellevue. The 1981 revision of the test is called the WAIS-R.

Wechsler also developed the Wechsler Intelligence Scale for Children. The WISC, which is for children ages six through sixteen, was revised in 1974 as the WISC-R. Table 8.2 on page 280 shows the typical subtests included. In 1967, the Wechsler Preschool and Primary Scale of Intelligence (WPPSI) was developed for children ages four to six-and-a-half and was revised in 1989 as the WPPSI-R.

The Wechsler scales group test items by content: for example, all the information questions are presented together and all the arithmetic problems are presented together. The score on each subtest is calculated and converted

In the 1930s, Wechsler developed a widely used intelligence test for adults. The latest revision of that test is known as the WAIS-R.

TABLE 8.2
Typical Subtest on the WISC-R

Verbal Test		Performance Test	
Subtest	**Type of Task**	**Subtest**	**Type of Task**
Information	Given a question, recall a general fact that has been acquired in both formal and informal school settings.	Picture completion	Given an incomplete picture, point out the part that is missing.
Similarities	Given two ideas, use another concept in describing how both are alike.	Picture arrangement	Given a series of pictures that tell a story, put them in the right sequence.
Arithmetic	Given a word problem, solve it without pencil and paper.	Block design	Given a picture of a block design, use real blocks to reproduce it.
Digit span	Given an orally presented string of digits, recall them.	Object assembly	Given a jigsaw-type puzzle, put the pieces together to form a complete object.
Vocabulary	Given a vocabulary word, define it.	Coding	Given a key that matches numbers to geometric shapes, fill in a blank form with the shapes that go with the numbers.
Comprehension	Given a question requiring practical judgment and common sense, answer it.		

to a standard (or scaled) score, adjusted for the subject's age. These scaled scores allow for comparison of scores across different age levels. Thus an eight-year-old's scaled score of seven is comparable to an eleven-year-old's scaled score of seven.

The Wechsler scales have been well researched; thousands of studies have been conducted to assess their reliability and validity. They are valid cross-culturally (Insua, 1983), for special education students (Covin and Sattler, 1985), learning-disabled students (Clarizio and Veres, 1984), and clinical populations (Eppinger et al., 1987).

The Kaufman Assessment Battery for Children

Many intelligence tests have been criticized for being biased, with some questions geared toward the white middle-class male experience. Psychologists Alan and Nadeen Kaufman contend that their Kaufman Assessment Battery for Children (K-ABC) uses tasks that tap the experience of all people, regardless of their backgrounds. A memory task in the K-ABC, for example, might have a subject look at a picture of a face and a few moments later pick it out from among pictures of other faces.

The K-ABC, which is individually administered, was designed especially for assessment, intervention, and remediation of school problems. School psychologists, who are the primary users of the K-ABC, act as evaluators and consultants to families and schools, helping them to achieve educational goals. The K-ABC consists of four global scales: three measure mental-processing abilities—sequential processing, simultaneous processing, and a composite of the two—and the fourth assesses achievement. The Kaufmans believe that the sequential- and simultaneous-processing scales measure abilities synonymous with intelligence, that is, the ability to process information and solve problems (A. S. Kaufman 1983).

A sequential task requires the manipulation of stimuli in sequential order. For example, a child might be asked to repeat a series of digits in the same order as the examiner presented them. A simultaneous processing task involves organizing and integrating many stimuli at the same time. Here, a child might be asked to recall the placement of objects on a page that was presented only briefly.

The K-ABC assesses how well and in what way an individual solves problems on each task, minimizing the role of language and acquired facts and skills. A separate part of the test, the achievement scale, involves demonstrating skills such as reading comprehension, letter and word identification, and computation. These tasks resemble those typically found on other IQ tests; they are heavily influenced by language experience and verbal ability.

Although early research on the K-ABC shows it to be a promising IQ test (German, 1983; Zins and Barnett, 1983), it is not without its critics. Jensen (1984) and Sternberg (1984) have been especially critical of the assumptions on which the K-ABC is founded, particularly ideas about sequential processing abilities. Kaufman (1984) argues that his test is valid, reliable, and an evolving one that will continue to get better. He wants it to be an alternative to the standard WISC-R and the Stanford-Binet. Many practitioners consider it child-oriented and easy to administer. Final evaluations of the K-ABC are probably still a decade away.

- ◆ In the Stanford-Binet, all examinees begin with what kind of subtest to determine the starting point for all other tests? pp. 278–279
- ◆ How are items grouped in the Wechsler Scales? pp. 279–280
- ◆ What is the chief difference in the Kaufman Assessment Battery for Children (K-ABC), compared to other tests, according to the test developers? pp. 280–281

Focus on Learning

Testing Controversy: Validity and Cultural Biases

In 1986, a federal court in California upheld a 1979 ruling barring administration of IQ tests to black students in the state. According to the judge who made the original ruling, the tests are culturally biased and therefore discriminate against blacks for "special education" purposes, resulting in a disproportionate number of blacks being assigned to classes for the mentally retarded. The California court case illustrates the political, cultural, and scientific issues involved in the debate over what intelligence tests actually measure. The controversy reached a peak in the 1970s. At that time, minority groups joined psychologists and educators in challenging the usefulness of testing in general, and of intelligence testing in particular. The controversy focused on two major issues: the validity of intelligence tests and cultural bias.

Test Validity. There are five basic criticisms of—and defenses for—the validity of tests and testing. The first is that there is no way to measure intelligence because no clear, agreed-upon *definition of intelligence* exists. The defense against this argument, by Mercer (1977) and other researchers, is that although different IQ tests seem to measure different abilities, the major tests have face validity. **Face validity** is the appropriateness of test items "on their face"—that is, do they seem appropriate to experts? Intelligence

Face validity: The appropriateness of test items "on their face"—that is, do they seem appropriate to experts?

Halo effect: The tendency to let one of an individual's characteristics influence the evaluation of other characteristics.

tests have face validity; that is, they generally contain items requiring problem solving and rational thinking, which in Anglo-American society is an appropriate test of intelligence.

The second criticism is that because IQ test items usually consist of *learned information,* they reflect the quality of a child's schooling, rather than actual intelligence. The response to this challenge is that most vocabulary items on IQ tests are learned in the general environment, not in school; moreover, the ability to learn vocabulary and facts seems to depend on the ability to reason verbally.

The third criticism is that *school settings* may adversely affect IQ and other test scores, not only because tests are often administered inexpertly, but also because of halo effects (e.g., Crowl and MacGinitie, 1974). A **halo effect** is the tendency to allow preconceived attitudes about an individual to influence evaluation. A teacher or test administrator can develop a negative (or positive) feeling about a person, a class, or a group of students that might carry over and influence his or her teaching or the administration or interpretation of test scores. People who defend testing against this charge acknowledge that incorrectly administered tests are likely to result in inaccurate IQ test scores, but they claim that these effects are less powerful than opponents claim.

The two other criticisms of testing are less directly related to the issue of validity. One is that some people are *testwise.* They make better use of their time than others do, guess the tester's intentions, and find clues in the test. Practice in taking tests improves these people's performance. The usual responses are that the items on IQ tests are unfamiliar even to experienced test-takers and that the effects of previous practice are seldom or never evident on IQ tests. The final criticism is that individuals' scores often depend on their *motivation to succeed* rather than on actual intelligence. Defenders of IQ tests agree that examinees' attitudes toward a test and their motivation are important, but they deny that the IQ tests themselves influence motivation.

Critics of IQ tests are concerned with the interpretation of scores. They note that test scores without interpretation can foster narrow conceptions regarding students' ability in both students and teachers. One result is the neglect of talents and abilities unmeasured by such tests, perhaps leading to an inappropriate career or wrong placement in school.

Cultural Biases. Another major argument against IQ testing is that tests are culturally biased and thus are used to discriminate against individuals who do not come from certain environments, usually white, middle-class suburban. A test item or subscale is considered culturally biased when, with all other factors held constant, its content is more difficult for members of one group than for another (Kaufman, 1982). To understand how a test can be culturally biased, imagine that an impoverished migrant worker's child is asked the temperature problem posed earlier. If the child is unfamiliar with thermometers and radios, he may choose the sun as the best answer. Based on experiments that have shown some tests to be culturally or racially biased (Shimberg, 1929; Williams, 1970) (see Table 8.3), some educators and parents have urged banning tests in all public schools, especially IQ tests. They argue that certain groups who are not exposed to the same education and experiences as the middle-class group for whom the tests were designed are bound to perform less well.

TABLE 8.3
Myra Shimberg (1929) standardized two tests on urban and rural schoolchildren in New York state. Each test contained twenty-five questions. The examples below show clearly that they test for different kinds of information. Shimberg found that rural children scored significantly lower than urban children on Test A but higher than urban children on Test B. The difference between the scores of the two groups was in part a function of the tests themselves, not of any real difference in the children's intellectual capacities: Test A was biased toward urban children; Test B toward rural children.

Test A	Test B
1. What are the colors in the American flag?	1. Of what is butter made?
2. Who is the president of the United States?	2. Name a vegetable that grows above ground.
3. What is the largest river in the United States?	3. Why does seasoned wood burn more easily than green wood?
4. How can banks afford to pay interest on the money you deposit?	4. About how often do we have a full moon?
5. What is the freezing point of water?	5. Who was president of the U.S. during the World War?
6. What is a referendum in government?	6. How can you locate the pole star?

Clearly, those who interpret IQ tests must be particularly sensitive to any potential biases. But although researchers find differences among the IQ test scores of various racial and cultural groups, they find no conclusive evidence of bias in the tests themselves. Consider one factor thought to be a potential source of test bias, the use of standard English. Research shows that differences in language alone do not account for IQ test score differences (although it could be a contributing factor). Although researchers recognize that the quality of verbal stimulation is probably more important than the quantity, many believe that the language spoken at home, by itself, has little effect on an individual's school performance (F. F. Schachter, 1979).

Also consider that when Jensen (1976) examined the WISC-R scores of a random sample of six hundred white and six hundred black California school children in grades five through twelve, he found that whites scored an average of twelve points higher, but he also found an average twelve-point difference between siblings. The difference between siblings was as great as the difference between racial groups; there is as great variability between individuals as between groups. After examining several other important variables in widely used standardized tests of intelligence, Jensen concluded that "The notion that IQ tests discriminate largely in terms of race or social class is a myth" (p. 340). Jensen does not claim that biases cannot exist—only that they do not exist on tests like the WISC-R. Other well-respected psychologists support his view (Sattler, 1988; Vernon, 1979).

Conclusions. IQ tests cannot predict or explain all types of intellectual behavior. They are derived from a small sample of a restricted range of cognitive activities. As Sattler noted (1988), intelligence can be demonstrated in many ways; an IQ test tells little about someone's ability to be flexible in new situations and to function in mature and responsible ways. Intelligence tests reflect many aspects of a person's environment—how much they are encouraged to express themselves verbally, how much time they spend reading, and the extent to which parents have pressed them to achieve.

In the last two decades, the public, educators, and psychologists have scrutinized the weaknesses of IQ tests and have attempted to eliminate bias

IQ testing has been criticized for not taking cultural differences into account. Faced with the same test questions, two culturally divergent men, such as these British and aboriginal men, are unlikely to perform equally well due to their differing interpretation of the questions posed.

TABLE 8.4
Some Misconceptions about Intelligence Tests and Testing

Misconception	Reality
Intelligence tests measure innate intelligence.	IQ scores measure some of an individual's interactions with the environment; they never solely measure innate intelligence.
IQs are fixed and never change.	People's IQs change throughout life, but especially from birth through age six. Even after this age, significant changes can occur.
Intelligence tests provide perfectly reliable scores.	Test scores are only estimates. Every test score should be reported as a statement of probability, such as: "There is a 90 percent chance that the child's IQ falls between X and Y."
Intelligence tests measure all we need to know about a person's intelligence.	Most intelligence tests do not measure the entire spectrum of abilities related to intellectual behavior. Some stress verbal and nonverbal intelligence but do not adequately measure other areas, such as mechanical skills, creativity, and social intelligence.
A battery of tests can tell us everything we need to know in making judgments about a person's competence.	No battery of tests can give a complete picture of any person. A battery can only illuminate various areas of functioning.

Source: Adapted from Sattler, 1988.

from testing by creating better tests and establishing better norms for comparison. But even the courts acknowledge the complexity of the issues involved in tests and testing (Elliott, 1987). In isolation, IQ scores mean little. Information about an individual's home environment, personality, socioeconomic status, and special abilities is crucial to understanding his or her intellectual functioning. The same argument must be made about the Scholastic Aptitude Test (SAT). The SAT is widely criticized as a predictor of success in college (Nairn, 1980), but other researchers claim that, in combination with high school grades, the SAT is a good predictor of success in college for different ethnic groups and income levels (R. M. Kaplan, 1982).

Critics of standardized testing have been vocal and persuasive, and their arguments cannot be discounted. Research into test construction, test validation, and the causes of differences among individuals' scores continues. Overall, experts see tests as adequately measuring the most important elements of intelligence, despite the flaws of these tests (Snyderman and Rothman, 1987). The components of tests, their subscales, and specific questions not only help researchers evaluate their validity, but also help sort out the components that are most affected by nature from those most affected by nurture. Table 8.4 summarizes some misconceptions about intelligence and testing.

Focus on Learning

1.* Identify three basic criticisms of—and defenses for—the validity of tests and testing. pp. 281–282

2.* When is a test item or subscale considered culturally biased? pp. 282–283

Intelligence: Nature versus Nurture

Scientists now can "see" how hard someone is thinking. In a study conducted at the University of California, Irvine, eight volunteers took a thirty-six-item abstract-reasoning test that required them to complete patterns made by geometric designs. At the start of the test, each volunteer was injected with radioactive glucose, which made the most active parts of the working brains light up on PET scans. Contrary to what you might expect, the brains of those who scored well on the test showed *less* activity overall than those who did poorly. In other words, the high scorers seemed to be more efficient thinkers, while the low scorers seemed to use more brain area to solve the puzzles. Did the high scorers inherit superior mental circuitry or did they learn to use their brains more efficiently, or both?

Some people believe that intelligence cannot be increased with special training, that people are born with all the intelligence they will ever have and that programs such as Head Start, designed to boost scholastic achievement among minorities and the culturally disadvantaged, are a waste of time and money. These people subscribe to the genetic, or *nature*, point of view. Proponents of the genetic view generally assert that intelligence tests portray intelligence accurately. The genetic view seems to offer a simple explanation of why people who receive similar educational opportunities early in life may turn out to have similar IQs as adults.

Other people believe that intelligence is subject to experience and training and is a fluid, changing concept. They believe in the environmental, or *nurture*, point of view. Proponents of this view believe that today's intelligence tests are inadequate—that they do not measure a person's adaptation to a constantly changing environment. That environment is crucial to a person's IQ development seems obvious, because even so basic an intellectual capability as speech must be learned.

Arthur Jensen on the Side of Nature

Psychologists have long recognized that both biological capacities established even before birth (nature) and people's life experiences (nurture) play an important role in intelligence. But as in other areas of psychology, researchers have debated the relative importance of nature and nurture. Arthur Jensen entered the debate in 1969 on the side of nature when he published a controversial article in the *Harvard Educational Review.*

Jensen addressed the issue of the difference in measured IQ scores between blacks and whites. In a study of 1200 California school children, Jensen found that on the average blacks scored sixteen points lower on IQ tests than whites. Jensen concluded that genetic factors are strongly implicated in the difference.

The scientific community's response to Jensen's claim was immediate. Psychologists criticized his logic and challenged the accuracy of the studies he cited and the validity of IQ tests in general. Jensen was called biased. But since 1969 Jensen has continued to maintain that genetic heritage contributes significantly more than environmental factors to the development of intelligence (Jensen, 1976, 1977, 1980). He did a series of research studies which attempted to separate the effects of nature and nurture; each study found evidence in favor of biological contributions. Was Jensen correct? Childrearing studies help answer the question.

Childrearing Environmental Studies

Another way researchers study the relative influence of environment and heredity is by investigating childrearing environments. One type of study compares the intellectual abilities of adopted children with the abilities of their adoptive parents (J. M. Horn, 1983). Many of these studies use identical twins who were separated at birth; because the twins share the same genetic heritage, any differences in IQ test scores must be the result of environmental influences.

One French adoption study showed a fourteen-point increase in IQ test scores in children whose biological parents were unskilled workers but whose adoptive parents were in a higher socioeconomic class (Schiff et al. 1982). This study demonstrated that the effect of the environment is clearly potent. However, other data strongly suggest that home environment has a much *smaller* effect on a child's IQ than the genetic influence of the mother's IQ test score (Longstreath et al., 1981).

Another environmental study administered IQ tests to children reared in different communities in the Blue Ridge Mountains, an isolated area one hundred miles west of Washington, D.C. (Sherman and Key, 1932). Most of the adults in each community were illiterate, and communication with the outside world was limited. The investigators concluded that lack of language training and school experience accounted for the children's poor scores on standardized tests, particularly on tests involving calculation and problem solving. Moreover, because the IQ scores of the children were highest in communities with the best social development and lowest in communities with the least social development, the researchers concluded that the children's IQs developed only as their environment demanded development. Angoff (1988) has similarly asserted that children from impoverished homes can achieve more on IQ tests, the SAT, and other standardized tests if "cognitive training begins early in life and continues for an extended period . . . and is carried out in a continuously supportive and motivating atmosphere"(p. 719).

There is a myth that if a behavior or characteristic is genetic, then it cannot be changed. But as Weinberg (1989) asserts, genes do not fix behavior; they establish a range of possible reactions. Environments determine whether the full range of gene potential is expressed. Table 8.5 summarizes the correlations between IQ scores and childrearing environments for both related and unrelated children in two different studies. If genetics were the sole factor in determining IQ test scores, the correlation for identical twins should be 1.0 whether they were raised together or apart. Also, the correlation should not decrease when any two siblings (twins or not) are brought up apart from one another. But identical twins raised together or apart do not have identical IQ scores. This finding lends strong support to the idea that environment must play an important role in determining IQ scores.

Environment, Family Structure, and Intelligence

Some researchers claim that current theorizing will never resolve the issue of nature's versus nurture's influence on intelligence (Mackenzie, 1984; Vroon, de Leeuw, and Meester, 1986). That's because factors such as family structure, family size, and other environmental variables are also important (Rodgers and Rowe, 1985). For example, an inspiring English teacher, a stimulating television series, or a neighbor with a chemistry set may be

TABLE 8.5
Median Correlations between IQs of Persons of Various Relationships,
Raised Together or Apart

Relationship and Upbringing	Median Correlation	
	Study 1	*Study 2*
Identical twins (monozygotic), reared together	.88	.85
Identical twins (monozygotic), reared apart	.75	.67
Fraternal twins (dizygotic), reared together	.53	.58
Siblings, reared together	.49	.45
Siblings, reared apart	.46	.24
Unrelated children, reared together	.17	.30

Study 1: Loehlin, Lindzey, and Spuhler, 1975. *Study 2:* Bouchard and McGue, 1981.

variables that affect differences between the IQ scores of siblings (McCall, 1983). If such variables affect differences between brothers and sisters, it could be very difficult to estimate how they affect differences between racial or ethnic groups.

Family Size and Structure. Belmont and Marolla (1973) found that children from large families score lower on intelligence tests than those from smaller families and suggest that the third and fourth child have a less optimal intellectual environment than the first or second child. In a later study, Zajonc and Markus (1975) theorized that within a family the intellectual growth of every member depends on the other members. Moreover, they suggested that the overall level of intellectual performance is likely to decrease for each new member of a family.

Consider what happens when two adults have a child. The intellectual climate at home becomes that of two mature adults and a child. Imagine that each adult is assigned thirty units and the child assigned zero units. The average level of intellectual ability in the home drops from thirty to twenty. (See Table 8.6 on page 288.) With a second child, the intellectual average decreases again, and so on.

Because family size has decreased in the past two decades and the spacing between children has increased, Zajonc and Markus predicted that the declining trend in Scholastic Aptitude Test (SAT) scores which began in the late 1960s would be reversed in the late 1980s. In fact, SAT scores did decrease from 1973 to 1979 and then rose from 1980 to 1985. Zajonc (1986) claimed his model predicted the turnaround. But other researchers assert that the model makes wrong predictions, is flawed, and is based on wrong assumptions (Flynn, 1988; Rodgers, 1988).

Keep in mind that the family size model is a statistical one; even Zajonc acknowledges that it will not hold true for all individuals and all families. Even when it does apply, the effects are small, and many researchers discount its importance (e.g., Sattler, 1988). Furthermore, the researchers point out that other important factors, such as increased spacing between the birth of children, can minimize the negative effects. Large families also may con-

TABLE 8.6
The Zajonc-Markus Model of Intellectual Climate in the Home

Year of Birth of Child	Number of Children	Value of intellectual climate	Average No. of Units
		Formula	
1970	1	$\dfrac{\text{Mother (30)} + \text{Father (30)} + \text{Baby (0)}}{\text{Number in family (3)}}$	= 20.0
1972	2	$\dfrac{\text{Mother (30)} + \text{Father (30)} + \text{First child (2)} + \text{Baby (0)}}{\text{Number in family (4)}}$	= 15.5
1974	3	66 ÷ 5	13.2
1976	4	72 ÷ 6	12.0
1978	5	80 ÷ 7	11.4
1980	6	90 ÷ 8	11.3
1982	7	102 ÷ 9	11.3
1984	8	116 ÷ 10	11.6
1986	9	132 ÷ 11	12.0
1988	10	150 ÷ 12	12.5

Note: This example assumes that for each two years of life, a child is credited with two units toward the intellectual climate in the home.

tribute to the growth of individual members in areas other than intelligence by nurturing feelings of social competence, moral responsibility, and ego strength.

Differences Are Small and Narrowing. Black-white differences in IQ scores, SAT scores, and other measures of achievement or ability are narrowing. This may be due to a generation of desegregation, more equal opportunities under the law, federal intervention programs for the culturally disadvantaged, socioeconomic factors that affect home environments, or to other factors (L. V. Jones, 1984). Jones suggests that the more minorities enroll in mathematics courses in high school, the better they will do on achievement tests. Consistent with this reasoning is a cross-cultural study comparing Mexican Americans with Caucasian Americans; it showed that with acculturation to U.S. society, the Mexican-American IQ score differences disappeared (Gonzales and Roll, 1985).

The relative importance of three factors has yet to be established: first, a genetic component may be involved; second, blacks in the United States are disproportionately represented among those who live in culturally impoverished areas; and third, IQ tests may contain a built-in bias against blacks. Perhaps more important than disputing the role of genetics, environment, or test bias is the recognition that within any racial or ethnic group, the differences among individuals are greater than the differences among groups.

Finally, the fact remains that to a great extent, rather than measuring innate intellectual capacity, IQ tests measure the degree to which people adapt to the culture in which they live. All individuals have special capabilities, and how those capabilities are regarded is socially dependent. Being a genius in Africa may mean being a fine hunter or a good storyteller; in the United States, it may mean being an astute and aggressive sales manager.

Too often, the concept of giftedness is attached to high academic achievement alone. This limited conception of intelligence is one reason educators in some settings are placing less emphasis on IQ test scores.

Researchers today assert that typical tests of intelligence are too limited because they do not take into account the many forms of intelligent behavior that occur outside of the testing room (Frederiksen, 1986). Frederiksen suggests that real-life problem situations might be used to supplement the usual psychological tests. This view is consistent with Sternberg's idea (1986) that intelligence must be evaluated on many levels, including the environment in which a person lives and works. This means examining how people solve problems in their world, how they deal with novel situations and everyday problem-solving situations.

Gender Differences

Remember Maria; she excelled at science and her adviser suggested that she take an accelerated physics class. Was Maria's success in science genetically based? As a girl, is she more analytical? Are girls better than boys at some tasks? Are boys better than girls at some tasks? Or are they equal?

The consensus of psychologists has always been that gender differences exist in verbal ability, with girls exceeding boys in most verbal tasks in the early school years. How much of this finding is due to the cultural expectations of parents and teachers? Some of the differences have been due to expectations. For example, parents and teachers alike have encouraged boys more than girls in spatial, mechanical tasks. But two interesting events have occurred in the last two decades. First, parents have been encouraging girls *and* boys in math, verbal, and spatial skills—there has been less gender stereotyping. And second, the observed cognitive differences between boys and girls have been diminishing each year. Referring to girls catching up in mathematical abilities to boys, Rosenthal and Ruben (1982) stated, "We can say that whatever the reason, in these studies females appear to be gaining in cognitive skill relative to males faster than the gene can travel!" (p. 711).

It turns out that the old consensus about gender differences is at a minimum exaggerated, and most likely wrong. Hyde and Linn (1988) ex-

Are women better at analytical tasks, or have gender differences been the result of society's expectations of boys and girls? Recent studies see gender differences as small and disappearing rapidly.

amined 165 research studies on gender differences in verbal ability that tested a total of 1,418,899 subjects. Although they found a gender difference in favor of females, it was so small that they claim it's not worth mentioning. They further argue that more refined tests of intelligence and theories of intelligence are needed to examine any gender differences that might exist. The differences found today exist only in certain special populations, for example, in the very brightest mathematics students where the boys continue to outscore girls (Benbow and Stanley, 1983), or in the grades of juniors and seniors in high school (Kimball, 1989), but these, too, may have a cultural expectation basis (Jacklin, 1989). In general, it is fair to say that differences between the test scores of males and females are disappearing (Feingold, 1988b).

An outcome of Hyde and Linn's findings is the realization that since verbal ability tests provide gender-unbiased measures of cognitive ability, they, rather than mathematical tests (which tend to be gender biased—at least for now), should be used to select students for academic programs. Selection procedures for academic programs become especially important when considering special students, such as the gifted. If you had to design a series of selection procedures for a school, college, or gifted program, what would you use as selection procedures?

The Stability of Intelligence Test Scores

MILESTONES IN PSYCHOLOGY

*N*early every American has taken an intelligence test at some time in his or her academic career. Was the test you took in the second grade still a good predictor of your academic ability when you were a sophomore in high school? Should you have been retested? Does an IQ test score remain stable over a long period of time?

Early examinations of IQ test score stability showed that infant IQ scores did not correlate well with IQ scores of school-age children (Bayley, 1949). Researchers quickly realized that it is not possible to measure the same capabilities in infants that can be measured in older children and adults. Further, correlations of school-age children and adults show that IQ test scores can change, sometimes substantially (Humphreys, 1960). For example, Humphreys (1968) showed that there is a sharp decline in predictive ability of SAT scores from early in college to later in a person's college career. Humphreys and Davey (1988) argue that specialization in college may make senior grades less dependent on general intelligence. In general, psychologists have shown that an individual's intelligence and achievement scores increase with age and then level off in adulthood. Thus, IQ scores stabilize as children mature into adults.

So children's IQ scores may change over time; but what about adults? Do IQ scores remain stable from ages eighteen to age fifty-eight? A forty-year IQ study was conducted by five researchers from Concordia University in Canada (Schwartzman et al., 1987). Two hundred and sixty men who were administered an IQ test when they entered World War II as army recruits were readministered the same test forty years later. The average age of the participants was 64.7 years, and only thirteen percent had received additional formal education after their military service. These same participants had been tested ten and twenty years after military service. Results showed that, in general, intellectual functioning increased a bit around age forty and gradually declined to enlistment age levels when the men were in their fifties. Despite the passage of forty years, cognitive performance remained relatively stable. Regression was evidenced in the performance (nonverbal) sections. Gains came in the vocabulary and mechanical knowledge sections. These results parallel those of earlier studies (Owens, 1966).

Ample evidence now exists to confirm that IQ scores remain stable once test subjects reach adulthood. But the scores of infants and children are so unstable and prone to change that they are not reliable predictors of later IQ scores. Of course, a child who scores high on an IQ test at age nine is likely to do well at age eighteen, and perhaps even better. But the data also show enough fluctuation, especially at younger ages, to make predictions uncertain.   ◆

Focus on Learning

- With respect to intelligence testing, what is the nature versus nurture controversy? p. 285
- What is found when correlations between IQ scores and childrearing environments for both related and unrelated children are examined? pp. 286–287
- Rather than innate ability, intelligence tests measure what? p. 288 *the degree to which people adapt to the culture in which they live*
- What is the current status of gender differences in verbal ability? pp. 289–290 *they are disappearing*

Exceptionality: Giftedness and Mental Retardation

In the movie *Amadeus*, the court composer Salieri is intensely jealous of the musical gifts of his rival Mozart. Salieri is obviously a very intelligent man, an eloquent conversationalist and an accomplished musician. He is cunning in his attempts to ruin Mozart. Conceivably, Salieri would have scored at least as high as Mozart on a traditional IQ test. Yet Mozart's musical talent dwarfed Salieri's. What made Mozart so different?

J. P. Guilford, one of the leading researchers in intelligence testing, whom we discussed earlier, developed a theory about the nature of intellectual functioning. He argued that there is more to intelligence than a high score on a subtest of the WISC-R. He contended that some people are exceptional in traditionally defined ways, such as those measurable by a high IQ score, but that others are exceptional in nontraditional ways, e.g., Mozart who displayed his genius musically and Madame Curie who displayed hers in science.

American society is oriented to education, testing, and looking for the special or exceptional child. As early as the first weeks of the first grade, most students take some kind of reading readiness test; by the end of the fourth grade, they are usually labeled and classified as to their projected future development, again largely on the basis of tests. The term *exceptional* refers to people who are gifted as well as to those who have learning disabilities, physical impairments, and mental retardation.

Children often display their intellectual development in their use of language. For example, a child who learns to read at age three or who can do multiplication at age four is obviously bright, and a child who has not learned to differentiate colors or simple shapes on entering first grade is obviously developing more slowly intellectually than other children.

Defining Giftedness

Gifted individuals represent one end of the continuum of intelligent and talented behavior. But exceptional ability is not limited to cognitive skills. Most six-year-olds enrolled in a ballet class will probably show average ability; dance teachers report that only an occasional child has a natural ability for dance. In the same way, many children and adults learn to play the piano, but few excel. Over a wide range of behaviors, some people excel in a particular area far beyond normal expectations but in other areas are rather average.

The phenomenon of gifted children has been recognized and discussed for centuries. Some, like Mozart, display their genius musically. Others display it in science; many great scientists made their most important theoretical discoveries very early in their careers. Although there is no universally accepted definition of giftedness (just as there is no universally agreed-upon definition of intelligence), one was given in the Gifted and Talented Children's Act of 1978:

> The term "gifted and talented" means children, and whenever applicable, youth, who are identified at the preschool, elementary, or secondary level as possessing demonstrated or potential abilities that give evidence of high performance responsibility in areas such as intellectual, creative, specific academic or leadership ability, or in the performing visual arts and who by reason thereof require services or activities not ordinarily provided by the school. (Section 902)

Thus, gifted children may have superior cognitive, leadership, or performing arts abilities. Moreover, gifted individuals require special education that goes beyond the ordinary classroom. Without special schooling, these children may not realize their potentials.

The United States has a special love-hate relationship with gifted individuals (Gallagher, 1979). Although everyone wants the gifted to succeed and realizes that their successes represent breakthroughs in science and the arts, public schools are designed for the average child and may isolate and even cause ridicule of students who are unique. Moreover, even though the federal government acknowledges the need for special education for gifted individuals, states and communities bear the major financial burden for their education (about ninety-two percent). Some states, including California, Pennsylvania, and Illinois, spend more per year than the federal government on educating gifted and talented students. Nearly every state has a special program for the gifted, but some school systems have none; others allocate special instruction only in brief periods or to small groups. Some systems provide special schools for children with superior cognitive abilities, performing talents, or science aptitude. Most do not offer gifted programs for all grades (Reis, 1989); however, like the needs of students with mental retardation (considered next), the special needs of students who are gifted should not be addressed only on one day a week or only in grades one through six.

Mental Retardation

Mental retardation: Below-average intellectual functioning as measured on an IQ test, accompanied by an impairment in adaptive behavior originating during childhood.

Mental retardation covers a wide range of behaviors, from slow learning to severe mental and physical impairment. Many people with mental retardation are able to cope well with their environments. Most learn to walk and to feed and dress themselves; many learn to read and are able to work. There are a variety of causes for mental retardation, from deprived environments (especially for those with mild retardation) to genetic abnormalities, infectious diseases, and physical trauma (including drugs taken by pregnant women).

A diagnosis of mental retardation involves three criteria: a lower-than-normal (below seventy) IQ test score as measured on a standardized test

TABLE 8.7
Types and Distribution of Mental Retardation as Measured on the Stanford-Binet and Wechsler Tests

Classification	Stanford-Binet IQ	Wechsler IQ	Percentage of the Mentally Retarded	Educational Level Possible
Mild	52–68	55–69	90	Sixth grade
Moderate	36–51	40–54	6	Second to fourth grade
Severe	20–35	25–39	3	Limited speech
Profound	Below 20	Below 25	1	Unresponsive to training

such as the WISC-R or the WAIS-R; difficulty adapting to the environment; and the presence of such problems before age eighteen. There are four basic levels of mental retardation, each corresponding to a different range of scores on a standardized IQ test (see Table 8.7).

Mild Retardation. People with mild mental retardation (Wechsler IQs of fifty-five to sixty-nine) account for approximately ninety percent of people classified as mentally retarded. Through special programs, they are able to acquire academic and occupational skills but generally need some supervision in their work (e.g., Allington, 1981). As adults, people with mild mental retardation function intellectually at the level of a ten-year-old. Thus, with some help from family and friends, most people with mild mental retardation can cope successfully with their environments.

Moderate Retardation. People with moderate mental retardation (Wechsler IQs of forty to fifty-four) account for approximately six percent of those classified as mentally retarded. Most live in institutions or as dependents of their families. Those who are not institutionalized need special classes; some can hold simple jobs, although few are employed. People with moderate mental retardation are able to speak, write, and interact with friends, but their motor coordination, posture, and social skills are clumsy. Their intellectual level is equivalent to that of a five- to six-year-old.

Severe Retardation. Only about three percent of people with mental retardation display severe retardation (Wechsler IQs of twenty-five to thirty-nine). People with severe mental retardation show great motor, speech, and intellectual impairment and are almost totally dependent on others to take care of their basic needs. Severe retardation often results from birth disorders or traumatic injury to the brain.

Profound Retardation. One percent of people with mental retardation are classified as profoundly retarded (IQs below twenty-five). These people are unable to master even simple tasks and require total supervision and constant care. Their motor development and intellectual development are minimal, and many are physically underdeveloped. Physical deformities and other congenital defects (such as deafness, blindness, and seizures) often accompany profound mental retardation.

The Law and Education

Until recently, thousands of children used to be given substandard educations after doing poorly on an intelligence test. Labeled as slow learners or perhaps mentally retarded, these children were given neither special education nor special attention. But in 1975 the federal government passed Public Law 94-142, the Education for All Handicapped Children Act. Originally conceived to improve school programs for physically handicapped children, its passage ensured individualized testing and educationally relevant programs for all children.

The law holds that all school-aged children must be provided an appropriate, free public education. After testing, children with special needs are not to be grouped separately unless they have severe handicaps. Tests for identification and placement must be unbiased. Further, educational programs must be arranged to make them as close to "normal" as possible, with the unique needs of each child considered. An individualized educational program (known as an IEP) must be arranged by the school in consultation with the parents. The law also mandates that schools must follow specific procedures: an explanation of rights, evaluation procedures, regular reevaluation, and reasons for changes in a student's status.

Public Law 94-142 significantly increased the amount of testing in the public school systems, leading to more labeling and classification; many see this as a disadvantage. But the implementation of the law has also guaranteed thousands of children with special needs an appropriate education. This is costly for local school districts, but if a family member needs special education, you can rely on the courts to make sure that the school system provides it.

Since the passage of Public Law 94-142, there has been a shift toward **mainstreaming,** the integration of all children with special needs into regular classroom settings whenever appropriate. Its purpose is to make life as normal as possible for these children by requiring that they and their teachers and classmates cope with their current skill level and expand on it. In mainstreaming, children are assigned to a regular class for at least half of their school day. For the rest of the day, they are often in special education classrooms or in vocational training situations. Although research studies on mainstreaming have produced conflicting data on its effectiveness, psychologists and educators generally support it.

Psychology and Business: Employing Workers with Mental Retardation

Companies are realizing that if people with mental retardation are placed in the right job, properly trained, and effectively motivated, they can be counted on to be good workers. As a result, many companies now hire workers with mental retardation who were once thought unemployable.

Drawbacks do exist in hiring workers with mental retardation. One is that training them often requires extra patience. A more detailed and carefully defined training program is usually necessary; behavioral techniques such as those described in chapter 5 are used extensively. A task may be broken down into thirty or forty individual steps. Workers with mental retardation sometimes need help to keep them focused on their job, such as prompts from supervisors or a checklist. In addition, they may work more slowly than others in the same position and require training in social skills as well,

Mainstreaming: The administrative practice of placing exceptional children in regular classroom settings with the support of special education services.

for example, in being friendly and smiling at coworkers. Also, workers who have lower IQs may be less adept at personal grooming, and may not read, write, tell time, or handle money well.

But there are great successes. Those workers who have been brought through training programs do exceptionally well. Workers with mental retardation are likely to stay with jobs others tire of. They may be more dependable, motivated, and industrious than other workers. After they are trained, they have few problems adjusting to the routine of a nine-to-five job. Owners of fast food restaurants who hire workers with mental retardation, e.g., McDonald's, report that they never come in late and are rarely sick. They consider their new workers reliable and dependable. Marriott Corporation employs more than 1000 workers with mental retardation. In addition, the federal government provides tax benefits to employers of the mentally or physically handicapped. People labelled as mentally retarded and unemployable are working, earning a wage, and handling their lives impressively. They do far better in their lives outside of their jobs than they ever did before—because of the law and mainstreaming.

The federal government has taken an extensive role in the education and support of individuals with mental retardation and provides Supplemental Social Security Income payments to unemployed workers with mental retardation. Advocates of individuals with mental retardation are concerned because the costs of such support programs are rising very quickly. This makes work training programs even more valuable; various states are providing funds heretofore reserved only for institutions to businesses and colleges for the purpose of training workers with mental retardation. Such programs are money-savers for local government; workers who earn money pay taxes and do not require support payments. The task for government is substantial, and the challenge, in terms of numbers and cost, is formidable.

With proper training, many retarded adults are able to successfully get and keep a job.

* What are the superior abilities of gifted children? p. 291
* To whom does the term exceptional apply? pp. 291–292
* Identify the three criteria for making a diagnosis of mental retardation. p. 292
* What does the Education for All Handicapped Children Act mandate? p. 294

Focus on Learning

Key Terms

Intelligence p. 269
Factor analysis p. 270
Factor-theory approach to intelligence p. 270
Standardization p. 274
Norms p. 274
Representative sample p. 274
Normal curve p. 275

Raw score p. 276
Standard score p. 276
Percentile score p. 276
Deviation IQ p. 276
Reliability p. 277
Test-retest p. 277
Alternative-form p. 277
Split-half p. 277

Standard error of measurement p. 277
Validity p. 277
Face validity p. 281
Halo effect p. 282
Mental retardation p. 292
Mainstreaming p. 294

Summary

What Is Intelligence?

- Intelligence is difficult to measure because it is hard to define. Further, no one test is a clear measure of intelligence.   p. 268

- Intelligence must be defined in terms of observable, objective behavior, must take in both an individual's capacity to learn and his or her acquired knowledge, and must indicate ability to adapt to the environment.   p. 269

- Wechsler defined intelligence as the aggregate or global capacity of the individual to act purposefully, to think rationally, and to deal effectively with the environment.   p. 269

- According to Piaget, intelligence is a reflection of a person's adaptation to the environment.   p. 269

- According to Guilford, human intellectual abilities and activities can be described in terms of three major dimensions: the mental operations performed, the content of those operations, and the resulting product.   p. 270

- A factor-analysis approach uses correlational techniques to determine which tasks are involved in intellectual ability.   p. 270

- Sternberg took an information-processing view of intelligence, dividing intelligence into three dimensions: componential, experiential, and contextual.   pp. 271–272

Testing

- Well constructed tests can diagnose specific problems and predict an individual's future performance, perhaps in a job setting. pp. 273–274

- *Standardization* is the process of developing a uniform procedure for the administration and scoring of a test.   p. 274

- A test's validity tells a test developer whether a test measures what it is presumed to measure.   p. 277

- Intelligence tests do not measure the full spectrum of abilities related to intellectual behavior, and do not adequately measure areas such as mechanical skills, creativity, or social intelligence.   pp. 277–278

Three Important Intelligence Tests

- The Stanford-Binet has been a good predictor of academic performance; its newer items minimize gender and racial characteristics. pp. 278–279

- The Wechsler Scales group test items by content. The score on each subtest is calculated and converted to a standard (or scaled) score, adjusted for the subject's age.   pp. 279–280

- The K-ABC consists of four global scales: three measure mental-processing abilities—sequential processing, simultaneous processing, and a composite of the two; the fourth assesses achievement.   pp. 280–281

Intelligence: Nature versus Nurture

- Proponents of the genetic view generally assert that intelligence tests portray intelligence accurately. Proponents of the nurture view believe that today's intelligence tests are inadequate, that they do not measure a person's adaptation to a constantly changing environment.   p. 285

- Many researchers claim that current theorizing will never resolve the issue of nature versus nurture because factors such as family structure, family size, and other environmental variables are important and impossible to measure accurately.   pp. 288–289

- The consensus is that gender differences are at a minimum exaggerated; gender differences in verbal ability are so small that researchers should not say they exist.   pp. 289–290

Exceptionality: Giftedness and Mental Retardation

- Gifted children are those with superior cognitive, leadership, or artistic abilities.   p. 291

- Mental retardation is below-average intellectual functioning together with an impairment in adaptive behavior originating before age eighteen.   p. 292

- Mainstreaming is the integration of exceptional children, especially children with mental retardation, into regular classroom settings. The purpose of mainstreaming is to help normalize the life experiences of such children. p. 294

Connections

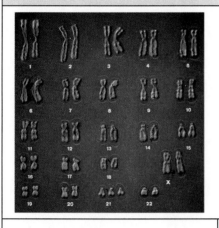

Traditional view

Attitudes → Behavior

Attitudes shape behaviors;
behaviors follow from attitudes

Bem's view

Behavior → Attitudes

Interpretation of situations
happens and then attitudes
are formed

If you are interested in . . .	Turn to . . .	To learn more about . . .
The role intelligence plays in psychological theory	◆ Ch. 2, pp. 36–41	How the study of the biological basis of human behavior focuses on the extent to which inherited structures determine intelligence.
	◆ Ch. 9, p. 316	How theories of child development often focus on intellectual functioning.
	◆ Ch. 10, pp. 367–371	The way developmental psychologists examine growth and maturation by examining issues such as the decline of intellectual functioning that occurs with advanced age or with diseases such as Alzheimer's.
The influence of environment in the development of intelligence	◆ Ch. 9, pp. 322–323	The way early child interactions with parents are important in intellectual functioning.
	◆ Ch. 10, pp. 345–347	How gender differences in social development are often translated into performance differences in intelligence, the workplace, and classroom.
	◆ Ch. 16, pp. 574–583	How many of a person's basic attitudes toward work, school, and intellectual tasks are determined by parents in the early developmental years.
Use of psychological tests	◆ Ch. 12, pp. 458–459	How personality can be examined through projective tests such as the TAT.

9

Child Development

"Questioning Children" by Karel Appel

◆

*D*onna and Peter Bell, and their neighbors BethAnn and Jim Green and Judy and Miguel Guerrera, each have a four-year-old child, but the parents differ radically in their approaches to childhood education. Donna and Peter enrolled their daughter in a preschool that teaches three- to five-year-olds discipline and academic skills, and they expect her to attend a private school for gifted children in two or three years. After her four-hour school day, she attends ballet classes. Donna and Peter argue that an accelerated education will provide their daughter with special advantages and help her become a more successful and capable adult.

In contrast, BethAnn and Jim Green believe that nature has set a timetable for childhood and parents should not try to rush it. Accordingly,

BethAnn and Jim expect the public school system to provide the early education their child needs.

Like the Greens, Judy and Miguel Guerrera believe that childhood development occurs in stages set by nature. But like the Bells, Judy and Miguel also believe that special education and other environmental influences will help their child realize his maximum potential. They enrolled their child in a preschool that stresses playful interaction among the students and is less achievement-oriented than the one the Bells' child attends. Judy and Miguel plan to send their son to a private school when he is six.

Which parents are helping their child the most? Will the Bells' child realize lifelong advantages because of her parents' efforts? Will the Greens' and the Guerreras' children find themselves saddled with disadvantages because their parents weren't "tough" enough on them?

Parents want their children to do well in school and, ultimately, in life. But they often push them too fast and too far. According to David Elkind (1987), a well-known psychologist and professor of child development, pushing children can have adverse consequences. Elkind asserts that parents sometimes take a "superkid" approach to child-rearing. They hurry their children, expecting them to think, feel, and act much older than they are. Elkind's ideas about hurried children are based on the recognition of individual differences among children and their abilities. Some develop slowly; others develop rapidly. Some are cognitively advanced; others are average or slow.

In this chapter and the next we will discuss the processes of human development. This chapter focuses on normal development in children and shows how people's inborn characteristics interact with their environments to produce individuals who are unique in both experience and heredity. The next chapter focuses on adolescence, adulthood, and aging showing that development is a continual process.

Theories of Child Development

Psychologists study development to find out how people change throughout their lives and to learn what causes those changes. They are especially interested in discovering whether the developing infant's abilities, interests, and personality are determined by *nature* (i.e., right from birth) or by *nurture* (i.e., by their experiences after they are born). The nature versus nurture issue has been raised before in chapters 2 and 8. Separating biological from environmental causes of behavior is complicated, and the answer to any specific question about human behavior often involves the interaction of both nature and nurture.

To unravel the causes of behavior, psychologists adopt varying methods and viewpoints in their study of development. Two widely used methods are the cross-sectional method and the longitudinal method. In the *cross-sectional method* subjects of different ages are compared to determine if they differ on some important dimension. In the *longitudinal method* a single group of people is compared at different ages to determine if changes have occurred over time. Each method has advantages and disadvantages. For example, the cross-sectional method suffers from the fact that the subjects' backgrounds (parents, family income, nutrition) differ and they may have learned various things in different ways. Further, the subjects' behavior or performance in a specific task or ability might reflect their predisposition, liking of the task, or some other variable unrelated to changes due to development or aging. Individual differences in this method are impossible to assess. The

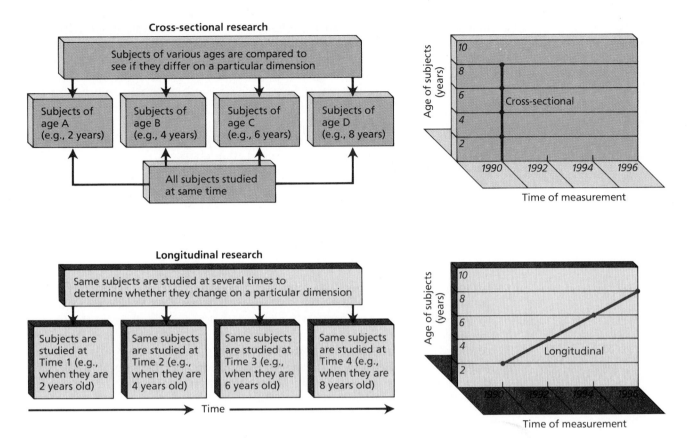

longitudinal method also has problems; it requires repeated access to the same subjects. Some subjects may move, withdraw from the study, even die. After repeated testing on the same task (even though months or years apart), subjects may do better because of practice. Further, longitudinal research sometimes takes years to complete and thus is time-consuming and expensive. See Figure 9.1 for a comparison of cross-sectional and longitudinal approaches.

Regardless of the technique used, most psychologists have a point of view, a theoretical orientation. Some theorists are *reductionistic;* they believe that if we can reduce an organism's behavior to its essential elements, we can explain the behavior. According to the reductionistic (or mechanistic) view, organisms wait for influences in the environment to affect them. All human beings are born alike; differences come about because of different experiences. The mechanistic view of human development tends to support the educational approach taken by Donna and Peter in the example described earlier.

The *organismic view,* in contrast, asserts that people go through development stages that are qualitatively different and cannot be reduced to simple elements. The organism actively affects its world rather than simply waiting for the world to affect it. Development occurs in a series of stages in which key characteristics are likely to emerge. According to the organismic view, BethAnn and Jim are right when they declare that their son's education should be paced with his natural development.

A third way of looking at development is the *contextual view.* Here, all the events in an organism's life are related. The contextualist looks at behavior from the standpoint of the stage of the organism's life and the context

FIGURE 9.1
In *cross-sectional* research, subjects of different ages (for example, ages two, four, six, and eight) are examined to determine if they differ on some specific dimension. In *longitudinal* research, a single group of subjects is examined over time.

Zygote: A fertilized egg.

Embryo: The term used to refer to the human organism from the fifth through the forty-ninth day after conception.

Fetus: The term used to refer to the human organism from the forty-ninth day after conception until birth.

in which the behavior occurs. It blends the reductionistic and organismic view with a third element, social context. In the sample above, Judy and Miguel are taking a contextual view of education. They believe that their son must be mature enough to profit from education and also that the educational environment must be as rich as the boy can handle if he is to achieve his potential.

Each of the families described in our opener, the Bells, Greens, and Guerreras, have a valid point of view, one supported by various psychologists and educators, as you will see in this chapter. We begin looking at events that happened to each of us long before we can remember them. These events are heavily influenced by biology as well as by the environment in which a person lives.

The First Nine Months

Conception occurs when an ovum and a sperm join in the fallopian tube to form a **zygote,** or fertilized egg. During the next five to seven days, the zygote descends through the fallopian tube and implants itself in the bloodlined wall of the uterus. From that time until the forty-ninth day after conception, the organism is an **embryo.** From the eighth week until birth, the organism is a **fetus.** On the average, maturation and development take 266 days; for descriptive purposes these nine months are divided into three trimesters (3-month periods) (see Table 9.1).

The First Trimester

Within minutes after the zygote is formed, basic characteristics—including hair, skin, and eye color; sex; likelihood of being tall or short, fat or lean; and perhaps basic intellectual gifts and personality traits—are established. Within ten hours the zygote divides into four cells. During the first week, about a dozen cells descend from the fallopian tube to the uterus where they begin the process of differentiation in which organs and parts of the

Conception occurs when an ovum and sperm join to form a fertilized egg.

TABLE 9.1
General Stages and Age Spans of Development

Life Stage	Approximate Age
Prenatal period	
Zygote	Conception to day 5 or 6
Embryo	Day 5 to day 49
Fetus	Week 8 to birth
Postnatal period	
Infancy	Birth to age 2
Toddlerhood	Age 2 to 3
Early childhood	Age 3 to 6
Middle childhood	Age 6 to 12
Adolescence	Age 13 to 19
Young adulthood	Age 20 to 40
Middle adulthood	Age 40 to 65
Late adulthood	Age 65 on

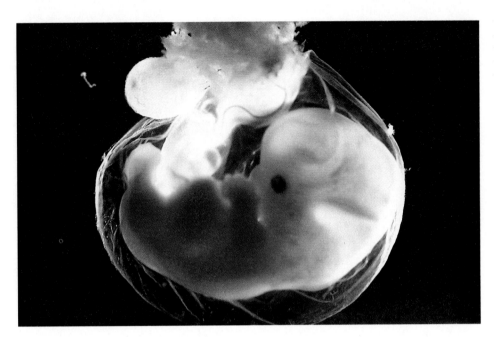

By the time it is five to six weeks old, the embryo has begun to resemble a human being. The heart begins to beat at about four weeks.

body begin to form. Some cells form the *umbilical cord*, a group of blood vessels and tissues that connect the zygote to the placenta. The **placenta** is a mass of tissue in the uterus that acts as the life-support system for the fetus by supplying it with oxygen, food, and antibodies, and eliminating wastes. By the end of the first week, the developing organism is an embryo made up of as many as one hundred cells that are attached to the wall of the uterus.

During the first month, the embryo begins to take shape. Although only a half inch long, it begins to form arms and legs and has the rudiments of eyes, ears, mouth, and brain. By the twenty-fifth day, a primitive version of the heart is beating.

During the second month, the embryo begins to resemble a human being. Each day it grows about a millimeter, and new parts begin to take shape. The nose begins to form about the thirty-third day, and the first true bone cells appear on about the forty-seventh day.

In the third month, growth continues, features become more defined, and sex characteristics begin to appear. The digestive, breathing, and musculature systems become stronger. At the end of the third month, the fetus is about three inches long and weighs one ounce. It can kick its legs, turn its feet, and swallow, although the mother cannot yet feel its movement.

The Second Trimester

During the second three months, the fetus consumes a good deal of food, oxygen, and water through the placenta, increasing in weight and strength. In the fourth month, it can be up to ten inches long, its muscles are significantly stronger, and its heartbeat can be heard with a stethoscope. In the early part of the fourth month, the mother may begin to feel the movement of the fetus.

In the fifth and sixth months, the fetus grows about two inches per month. At the end of the second trimester (about twenty-eight weeks), it is about fourteen inches long and its respiratory system is mature enough to

Placenta: A group of blood vessels and membranes in the uterus connected to a fetus by the umbilical cord and serving as the mechanism for the exchange of nutrients and waste products.

By the fifth month, the fetus has a significant heartbeat and has begun to kick.

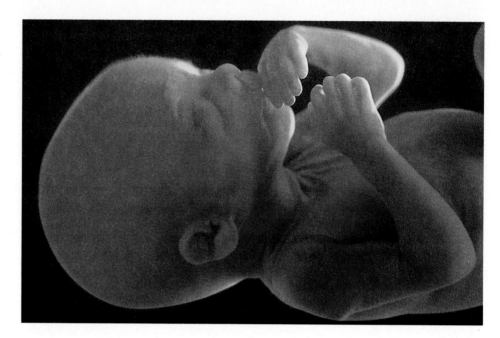

enable it to live outside the uterus, increasing the chances of survival if it is born prematurely.

The Third Trimester

In the last trimester, the fetus gains weight rapidly—usually a pound in the seventh month, two pounds in the eighth, and a pound a week in the ninth. Its respiratory system and internal organs continue to develop, and the muscles mature significantly. The mother can feel strong kicking and movement. Table 9.2 summarizes the major physical developments during the prenatal period.

Pregnancy and Birth: Early Influences

People have long assumed that the behavior of a pregnant woman affected her unborn child's development. Medieval European doctors advised pregnant women that uplifting thoughts would help the baby develop into a good, happy person, while fright, despondency, and negative emotions might disrupt the pregnancy and possibly influence the infant to become sad or mean-spirited. Today, some pregnant women wear audio "fetal belts" so that their unborn children can listen to soothing music and thereby gain a benevolent perspective of the outside world.

While a fetus may not be affected by the mother's condition to the extent suggested by medieval doctors, it is known that from conception until birth, the environment and life-support systems provided by the mother influence the fetus. Environmental factors such as diet, infection, radiation, and drugs affect both the mother and the fetus.

A **teratogen** is a substance, e.g., alcohol, that can produce developmental malformations in a fetus. For example, if the mother drinks alcoholic beverages in early and middle pregnancy, the baby is more likely to be born premature, to have a lower birth weight, and to suffer from mental retardation or hyperactivity (Streissguth, Barr, and Martin, 1983). One study showed that the use of more than 1.5 ounces of alcohol per day during

Teratogen: A substance that can produce developmental malformations in a fetus; such substances are said to be *teratogenic* or to have *teratogenic effects.*

TABLE 9.2
Major Developments during the Prenatal Period

Age	Size	Characteristics
1 week	150 cells	Ovum attaches to uterine lining.
2 weeks	Several thousand cells	Placental circulation established.
3 weeks	1/10 inch	Heart and blood vessels begin to develop. Basics of brain and central nervous system form.
4 weeks	1/4 inch	Kidneys and digestive tract begin to form. Rudiments of ears, nose, eyes are present.
6 weeks	1/2 inch	Arms and legs develop. Jaws form around mouth.
8 weeks	1 inch, 1/30 oz.	Bones begin to develop in limbs. Sex organs begin to form.
12 weeks	3 inches, 1 oz.	Sex distinguished. Kidneys functioning, liver manufacturing red blood cells. Fetal movements.
16 weeks	6½ inches, 4 oz.	Heartbeat may be detected by physician. Bones begin to calcify.
20 weeks	10 inches, 8 oz.	Mother feels movements.
24 weeks	12 inches, 1½ lbs.	Vernix (white waxy substance) protects body. Eyes open, eyebrows and eyelashes form, skin wrinkled and red, respiratory system not mature enough to support life.
28 weeks	15 inches, 2½ lbs.	Fully developed, but needs to gain in size, strength, and maturity of systems.
32 weeks	17 inches, 4 lbs.	Fat layer forms beneath skin to regulate body temperature.
36 weeks	19 inches, 6 lbs.	Settles into position for birth.
38 weeks	21 inches, 8 lbs.	Full term—266 days from conception.

pregnancy was significantly related to a decrease in a four-year-old's intelligence test scores (Streissguth et al., 1989).

Studies show that any drug can affect fetal development; high doses of aspirin, for example, may cause fetal bleeding, although this evidence is controversial (Werler, Mitchell, and Shapiro, 1989). Cigarette smoking constricts the oxygen supply to the fetus. Babies born to mothers who smoke tend to be smaller and may be at increased risk for cleft palate, mental retardation, and hyperactivity (Babson et al., 1980; Hunt, 1983). Cocaine, marijuana, and tranquilizers such as thalidomide can all be teratogenic and produce irreversible major malformations and neurological disorders (Lester and Dreher, 1989; Kopp and Kaler, 1989). The influence of drugs is especially important during the embryonic stage of development when the mother may not realize that she is pregnant.

The Birth Process

Approximately nine months after conception, the mother goes into **labor,** the process in which the uterus contracts to open the cervix and allow the fetus to descend through the birth canal to the outside world. It is divided into three stages: early labor, active labor, and transition. Although each woman's labor is different, all women experience certain characteristic sensations during the three stages.

To allow the fetus to descend through the birth canal, the cervix has to open, or dilate, to about ten centimeters (four inches). In *early labor* the cervix

Labor: The process in which the uterus contracts to open the cervix so that the fetus can descend through the birth canal to the outside world.

Unlike most other infants, "crack babies" are born weak and vulnerable due to the mother's drug use during fetal development.

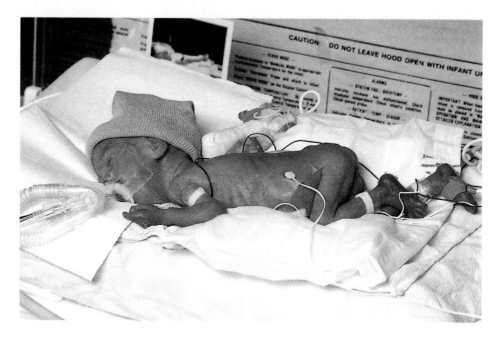

dilates to about three centimeters. Labor pains, or contractions of the uterine muscles, occur at regular intervals, from five to thirty minutes apart, each lasting approximately thirty seconds. In the second stage, *active labor*, the cervix dilates to seven centimeters. Contractions are about three to five minutes apart and more intense. During this stage, the woman usually goes to a hospital or birthing center if she is not giving birth at home. In the third stage, *transition*, the mother is likely to experience major discomfort or pain. During transition the cervix dilates to a full ten centimeters, and contractions are much stronger and last longer.

The baby is now ready to be born. When people speak about the birth of a baby, they are usually referring to the slow descent through the birth canal. For anywhere from five minutes to two hours the mother will bear down with her abdominal muscles, pushing the baby from the uterus through the birth canal. Until delivery, the fetus is attached to its mother by the umbilical cord. Within a few minutes after delivery, the placenta at the other end of the cord detaches from the wall of the uterus and is also delivered.

Natural Childbirth

Throughout most of human history, women delivered babies without the aid of doctors, nurses, or medication. Only during the past seventy years have women in developed countries given birth in hospitals where personnel can respond quickly to complications. In these settings, few babies or mothers die in childbirth.

Since the 1970s a growing movement to keep medical intervention to a minimum during childbirth has developed. A number of techniques help reduce the pain and discomfort of childbirth without using drugs. The best known of these is the *Lamaze method*, which has five basic components: (1) Information about anatomy and physiology to reduce fear of the unknown; (2) Respiratory techniques to maintain a steady oxygen supply during labor; (3) Conditioned relaxation and training to respond to a uterine contraction by relaxing other muscles in the body; (4) A process of cognitive (thought) restructuring, enabling her to distract herself from the activities of the labor room; (5) Social support provided by a labor coach, usually the husband, who attends the Lamaze classes and helps the mother through labor.

The psychological benefits of Lamaze and other natural childbirth methods have not been adequately studied, but most couples who have attended Lamaze classes are thankful for the preparation and feel more confident about the impending birth.

◆ What is a *reductionistic* viewpoint?   p. 301
◆ Compare the *organismic view* and the *contextual view* of development. pp. 300–302
◆ When does a zygote become an embryo, and when does an embryo become a fetus?   p. 302
◆ Describe the three stages of labor.   pp. 305–306
◆ Identify three components of the Lamaze technique.   pp. 306–307

Focus on Learning

Newborns, Infancy, and Early Childhood

Newborns are not nearly as helpless as many people believe. At birth they can hear, see, smell, and respond to the environment in adaptive ways—in other words, they have good sensory systems. But even though their sensory abilities are well developed, they are directly affected by experience. Psychologists are interested in finding out how experience affects the perception of infants and children to help them develop in optimal ways. To do so, they need to know how infants think, what they perceive, and how they react to the world. Psychologists have therefore devised ingenious techniques to "ask" newborns questions about their perceptual world. What are a child's inborn abilities and reflexes? When do inborn abilities become evident? How are inborn abilities affected by the environment?

Newborns' Reflexes

Touch the palm of a newborn baby and chances are you'll find one of your fingers in the surprisingly firm grip of a tiny fist. The baby is exhibiting a reflexive reaction. Babies are born with *primary reflexes,* that is, unlearned responses to stimuli. These reflexes are innate; some help ensure the baby's survival, and most disappear over the course of the first year of life. One primary reflex exhibited by infants is the **Babinski reflex,** a projection of the toes outward and up in response to a touch to the sole of the foot. Another is the **Moro reflex,** an outstretching of the arms and legs and crying in response to a loud noise or change in the environment. Infants also exhibit **rooting,** in which they turn their head toward a stimulus (such as a breast, or hand) that touches their cheek. They show a **sucking** reflex in response to objects that touch their lips and a **grasping** reflex in response to an object touching the palms of their hands. Physicians use the presence or absence of primary reflexes at birth to assess neurological damage and evaluate an infant's rate of development. Table 9.3 on page 308 summarizes the primary reflexes and the ages at which they normally disappear.

Babinski reflex: A reflex in which an infant projects its toes outward and up when the soles of its feet are touched.

Moro reflex: A reflex in which an infant outstretches its arms and legs and cries when there is a loud noise or abrupt change in the environment.

Rooting: A reflex in which an infant turns its head toward a stimulus applied to its lips or cheeks.

Sucking: A reflex in which an infant makes sucking motions when presented with a stimulus to the lips, such as a nipple.

Grasping: A reflex in which an infant grasps vigorously any object touching or placed in its hand.

TABLE 9.3
Newborn Reflexes

Reflex	Initiated by	Response	Duration
Eye blink	Flash a light in infant's eyes	Closes both eyes	Permanent
Babinski	Gently stroke the side of the infant's foot	Flexes the big toe; fans out the other toes	Usually disappears near the end of the first year
Withdrawal reflex	Prick the sole of the infant's foot	Flexes leg	Present during the first 10 days; present but less intense later
Plantar	Press finger against the ball of the infant's foot	Curls all toes under	Disappears between 8 and 12 months
Moro reflex	Make a sudden loud sound	Extends arms and legs and then brings arms toward each other in a convulsive manner	Begins to decline in third month, gone by fifth month
Rooting reflex	Stroke cheek of infant lightly with finger or nipple	Turns head toward finger, opens mouth, and tries to suck	Disappears at approximately 3 to 4 months
Sucking response	Insert finger into the baby's mouth	Sucks rhythmically	Sucking often less intense and less regular during the first 3 to 4 days

Neither a reflex nor a learned behavior, **bonding** is a special process of emotional attachment between parents and babies in the minutes and hours immediately after birth; some psychologists claim that it is inborn. Researchers such as Marshall Klaus and his colleagues (1983) believe that a mother is in a state of heightened sensitivity to her child immediately after delivery, and she begins to form unique, specific attachments to her child. Klaus argues that babies should have as much physical and emotional contact as possible with their mothers and fathers; keeping parents and infant together shortly after birth should be the rule, not the exception (Kennell et al., 1979). Research has not especially supported claims for bonding, but many parents have welcomed the increased contact with their newborns.

At first an infant's abilities and reflexes are biologically determined through genetic transmission. Gradually, learned responses such as reaching for desired objects or grasping a cup replace reflex reactions such as rooting. New experiences in the environment become more important in determining behavior. These complex interactions between nature and nurture follow a developmental time course that continues throughout life (see Table 9.4).

Infants' Perceptual Systems

Bonding: A special process of emotional attachment occurring between parent and child in the minutes and hours immediately after birth.

Long before an infant can explore his surroundings with hands and feet he is busy exploring it with his eyes. What goes on in the infant's mind as he stares, blinks, looks this way and that? Does he sense only a chaotic patchwork of color and brightness or does he perceive and differentiate among distinctive forms? (FANTZ, 1961, p. 66)

Fantz's Viewing Box. Robert Fantz designed a viewing box in which he placed infants and had a hidden observer or camera record their responses

TABLE 9.4

Perceptual-Cognitive Milestones of Infants

First week:

• see patterns, light, dark
• are sensitive to the location of sounds
• can distinguish volume and pitch
• prefer high voices
• will grasp object if they touch it accidentally
• stop sucking to look at a person momentarily

First month:

• become excited at sight of person or toy
• look at objects only if in their line of vision
• prefer patterns to any color, brightness, or size
• coordinate eyes sideways, up and down
• can follow a toy from side to center of body

Second month:

• prefer people to objects
• stare at human face, become quiet to human voice
• startle at sounds and make a facial response
• reach out voluntarily instead of grasping reflexively
• can perceive depth
• can coordinate eye movements
• discriminate voices, people, tastes, and objects

Third month:

• follow moving object
• glance from one object to another
• distinguish near objects from those distant
• search with eyes for sound
• become aware of self through exploration
• show signs of memory

Four to seven months:

• see world in color and with near-adult vision
• can pull dangling objects toward them
• follow dangling or moving objects
• turn to follow sound, vanishing object
• visually search out fast-moving or fallen objects
• begin to anticipate a whole object by seeing only part
• deliberately imitate sounds and movements
• remember a segment representative of an entire situation
• can recall short series of actions
• look briefly for a toy that disappears

Eight to twelve months:

• put small objects into and out of containers
• search behind screen for an object if they see it hidden
• can hold and manipulate one object while looking at a second
• recognize dimensions of objects

One year:

• group objects by shape and color
• have a clear perception of objects as detached and separate
• can relate objects in time and space
• search for object even if they have not seen it hidden
• remember only where object was last seen
• imitate absent models
• solve simple problems

(After Clarke-Stewart, Friedman, and Koch, 1985, p. 191)

to stimuli (see Figure 9.2 on page 310). The exciting part of Fantz's work was not so much that he asked interesting questions but that he was able to get "answers" from the infants. By showing infants various pictures of faces and patterns and recording their eye movements, he discovered the infants' visual preferences. He recorded how long and how often the infants looked at each picture and calculated the total time spent viewing each type of picture. Since they spent more time looking at pictures of faces than at random squiggles, Fantz concluded that they could see different patterns and that they preferred faces.

Ever since Fantz began his work, an avalanche of research on infant perception shows that newborns have surprisingly well-developed perceptual systems. They prefer complex visual fields over simple ones, curved patterns over straight ones, and human faces over random patterns or faces with mixed-up features (Haaf, Smith, and Smitley, 1983). Even in the first few months of life, babies can discriminate among facial features (Nelson,

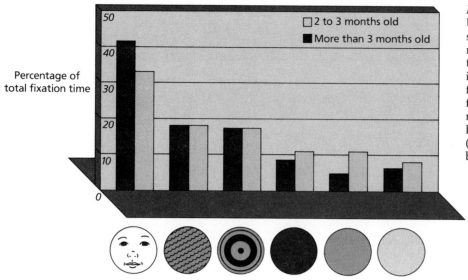

FIGURE 9.2
Using a viewing box to observe newborns' eye movements, Fantz recorded the total time they spent looking at various patterns. He found that they looked at faces or patterned material much more often than at homogeneous fields. (Source: Fantz, 1961; photo by David Linton.)

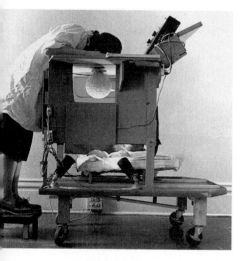

Fantz designed a viewing box which allowed him to record infants' responses to various types of visual stimuli.

1987). Newborns look at pictures of their parents more than at pictures of strangers and at eyes more than at other features (Mauer and Salapatek, 1976). We also know that babies respond to caregivers by imitating their facial gestures some of the time (Kaitz et al., 1988), although research in this area is controversial and the findings are not always consistent (Nelson and Ludemann, 1989).

Using a procedure similar to Fantz's, Walker-Andrews (1986) assessed five- and seven-month-old infants who saw films of people with angry or happy facial expressions making angry or happy sounds. (The lower third of the people's faces was covered so that the infants could not match the sound to the lips.) By observing the infants, the researcher showed that seven-month-old children could tell when the sound and facial expression did not match, but five-month-olds could not. Walker-Andrews' research supports the idea of a timetable by which infants' ability to discriminate among facial expressions develops.

The Visual Cliff. One of the best-known developmental research studies was done by Walk and Gibson in 1961. They devised the *visual-cliff method* to determine the extent of infants' depth perception. The researcher places an infant on a glass surface, half of which is covered with a checkerboard pattern. The same pattern is placed several feet below the transparent half of the glass surface. Infants can crawl easily from the patterned area onto the transparent area. Infants who lack depth perception should be willing to crawl onto the transparent side as often as onto the patterned side. Conversely, infants who have depth perception should refuse to crawl onto the transparent side, even when encouraged to do so by their mothers. Walk and Gibson found that infants who can crawl will show avoidance behavior, thus proving that they have depth perception.

Sorce and his colleagues (1985) used the visual-cliff method to study infants' responses to parents' facial expressions. They placed twelve-month-old babies on the shallow side of the visual cliff and an attractive toy on the deep side, where the mothers were standing. At first, each mother smiled to encourage her baby to crawl toward the toy. When the babies could see the change in depth, some mothers looked fearful or angry while others continued to smile. The researchers found that when the babies were uncertain about what to do at the visual cliff, they used their mother's facial expression to help them decide. If the mother looked fearful or angry, few babies crossed; if the mother smiled, most of the babies crossed. Sorce and his colleagues concluded that the mother's facial expression is a key source of information for infants. Babies are responsive to facial expressions, and even to attractiveness (Longlois, Roggman, and Rieser-Donner, 1990).

Walk and Gibson's visual-cliff method tested whether infants of various ages possessed depth perception.

In sum, newborns enter the world with the ability to experience the environment. They know the difference between warmth and cold, light and dark. Their senses of taste and smell are well developed; they can experience pain; and they can hear. The nervous system, however, will be further developed by experience. After birth, new dendrites proliferate, peripheral nerves mature further, and the capacity of the sensory systems increases. Thus, we can say that the sensory systems of newborns are well formed, but still developing as we will see with the next developmental stages.

Physical and Behavioral Changes: Infancy and Childhood

An infant who weighs seven and a half pounds at birth may weigh as much as twenty or twenty-five pounds by twelve months. At eighteen months the infant is usually walking and beginning to talk. For psychologists, infancy ends when the child begins to represent the world abstractly through language. Thus, *infancy* refers to the period from birth to eighteen months, and *childhood* is the period from eighteen months to about age thirteen, the onset of adolescence.

In the first weeks and months of life, some of the infant's reflexes disappear and new behaviors appear. At about four to eight weeks, infants may sleep for four to six hours during the night, uninterrupted by the need to eat (to the great relief of their weary parents). When awake, they smile at their mothers, stare intently at mobiles and other moving objects, listen attentively to human voices, and reach out to touch objects. At four months they have greater control over head movements and posture, they can sit with support, and they play with toys for longer periods.

At about seven months, infants begin to crawl, giving them more freedom to seek out favorite toys and people and avoid threatening situations The ability to crawl is accompanied by important changes in behavior. Infants now show strong preferences for their mothers or other caretakers. During the period from eight to fifteen months, attachment to the mother may become so strong that her departure from the room causes a fear response known as **separation anxiety.** Some researchers have found that infants who show strong attachment at this age tend to be more curious and self-directed later in life (Ainsworth, 1979). We will discuss attachment processes in more detail in chapter 11.

At the end of the first and beginning of the second year of life, children can walk, climb, and manipulate their environment—skills that often lead to the appearance of safety gates blocking stairways, fasteners closing cabinets, childproof medicine bottles, and a variety of other safety features in the home. There is significant variability in the age at which a child begins to walk or climb; some babies mature early, while others are slow to develop these abilities. The age at which these specific behaviors occur seems un-

Separation anxiety: The fear response in children from eight to fifteen months, displayed when a parent is absent.

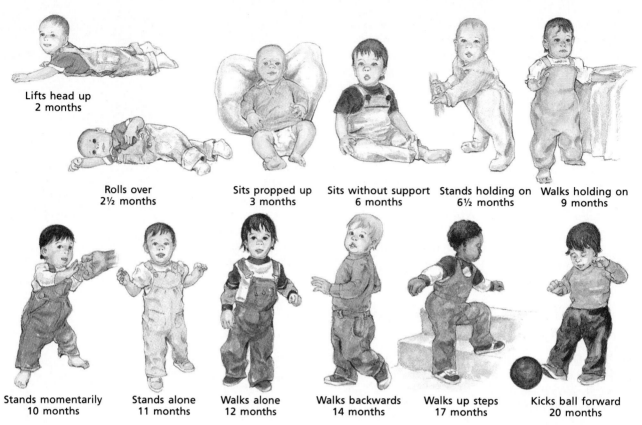

Lifts head up
2 months

Rolls over
2½ months

Sits propped up
3 months

Sits without support
6 months

Stands holding on
6½ months

Walks holding on
9 months

Stands momentarily
10 months

Stands alone
11 months

Walks alone
12 months

Walks backwards
14 months

Walks up steps
17 months

Kicks ball forward
20 months

FIGURE 9.3
Of the 1036 normal Denver babies tested for motor skills in the Denver Development Screening Test, fifty percent had mastered them at the ages indicated. (Source: Frankenberg and Dodds, 1967.)

related to any other major developmental abilities. Figure 9.3 shows the major achievements in motor development for the first fifteen months.

Emotional Changes

The extent to which infants focus on their caretakers increases significantly as they mature. Dialogues in the form of gestures, smiles, and vocalizations become more common. Mothers and fathers initiate these interactions as often as the infants do.

Interactions between parents and babies are important to the child's development. In an experiment in which mothers remained still and expressionless, their infants were sad and turned away from them (Cohen and Tronick, 1983). The implication is that the mere presence of a parent is not enough; the parent must interact both physically and vocally with the infant (Sorce and Emde, 1981) and pay attention (Jones and Raag, 1989). Table 9.5 presents the approximate time at which various emotions emerge in infants.

Several important variables influence the type and amount of interaction between parents and infants. One is the baby's physical attractiveness, or cuteness (Hildebrandt, 1983). People judge especially beautiful babies as more competent, more likeable, and healthier than average or unattractive babies (Stephan and Langlois, 1984). They are more likely to play with, speak to, pinch, jiggle, or smile at attractive children. This is not surprising; psychologists know that people are biased by the attractiveness of others, whether children or adults (Ritter and Langlois, 1988). The baby's own behavior is also important. Clarke-Stewart (1973) found that "the more often

TABLE 9.5
Emergence of Infants' Emotional Expressions

Emotions	Approximate Age of Emergence
Interest	birth
Neonatal smile (a sort of half smile that appears spontaneously)	birth
Distress	birth
Disgust	birth
Social smile	4–6 weeks
Anger	3–4 months
Surprise	3–4 months
Sadness	3–4 months
Fear	5–7 months
Shame	6–8 months
Guilt	Second year

the child looked, smiled, or vocalized to his mother, the more affectionate and attached to the child she became and the more responsive she was to his distress and demands." Tronick and Cohn (1989) concur; they found that infants and mothers both change their behavior in reaction to one another, and argue that neither babies or their mothers are passive recipients of each others's emotions. Both are active participants in forming a relationship, an attachment.

Attachment

A person behaving offensively may be asked, "What's your problem, didn't your mommy and daddly love you enough?" Some psychologists consider the establishment of a close and warm parent-child relationship one of the major accomplishments in the first year of life, and secure babies have mothers who are affectionate and especially responsive (Isabella, Belsky, and von Eye, 1989). This relationship makes later cognitive and emotional development easier (Sroufe and Waters, 1977). Not all researchers agree, but experimental studies show that the quality and nature of the mutual closeness formed between newborns and their mothers can make a big difference in later life (Schwartz, 1983). Children who have not formed warm, close attachments early in life lack a sense of security and become anxious and overly dependent (Bowlby, 1977); as six-year-olds, they are perceived as more aggressive and less competent than their more secure counterparts (Cohn, 1990). Those who have close attachments require less discipline and are less easily distracted (Lewis and Feiring, 1989; Bus and van Ijzendoorn, 1988).

Can adoptive parents form the same type of secure, close attachment to their children as biological parents? Even without the initial postdelivery bonding that Klaus and Kennell describe (p. 308), adoptive parents form supportive, healthy family relationships. A caretaking atmosphere that is warm, consistent, and governed by the infant's needs is the key. Both adoptive and biological parents can provide such an atmosphere, and both adop-

A loving environment that tends to a child's needs can be provided by both biological and adoptive parents.

tive and biological children can form strong attachments to their parents (Singer et al., 1985).

Once established, early attachment is fairly permanent. Brief separations from parents, as in day care centers, do not adversely affect it. Influential psychologists such as Mary Ainsworth (1979) assert that these parental attachments affect the child's later friendships, relations with relatives, and any enduring adult relationship.

Shyness and Temperament

During the earliest months of life, some infants smile or reach out to a new face and readily accept being held or cuddled; others are more inhibited. Still others exhibit extreme reticence, even distress, in the presence of strangers. As adults, the latter infants are likely to be inhibited, meek, and wavering (Caspi, Elder, and Bem, 1988).

Some psychologists believe that each of us is born with a certain temperament: easygoing, willful, outgoing, shy, to mention just a few. Newborns, infants, and children, like the adults they will eventually grow to be, are all different from one another. Generalizations from one child to all children are impossible, and even generalizations from a sample of children must be made with caution. So many variables can affect a child's growth and development that researchers painstakingly try to separate all the important ones. With this caution in mind, let us look at a study of temperament.

To study shyness and temperament in infancy, Daniels and Plomin (1985) conducted a study with adopted infants who were tested for shyness at one and two years of age. They gathered information about both the adoptive and the biological parents of those infants, and also collected data from homes in which children were living with their biological parents. They found that in both biological and adoptive homes, parental ratings of the infant's shyness were associated with the mother's self-reports of *her* shyness.

These findings led them to conclude that the infant's environment plays an important role in the development of shyness.

Many researchers contend that certain personality traits, including shyness, are long-lasting. For example, Jerome Kagan and his colleagues found that two- and three-year-olds who were extremely cautious and shy tended to remain that way for four more years (Kagan, 1989). They also found physiological evidence (increase in autonomic nervous system activity, for example) that these children may be more responsive to change and unfamiliarity (Kagan, Reznick, and Snidman, 1987). Daniels and Plomin (1985) found an important relationship between the biological mothers' shyness and adopted infants' shyness at two years of age. These findings suggest that genetic factors play a role in shyness. But it is important to remember that shyness or any specific temperament can be changed; human behavior is the product of deliberative thought processes as well as biological forces. Parents also recognize that they affect a child's temperament and personality; they assume that their child-rearing practices will have important influences on development.

Child-Rearing Practices

*I*n any bookstore you'll find shelves with how-to books on child rearing. Written by physicians, parents, psychologists, and others, they explain child development and how parents should raise their children. They run the gamut from advocating strong discipline to offering supportive environments where discipline is minimized. Some how-to books stress diet; others emphasize school situations.

The variety of ideas and experts shows that ideas about child rearing are complicated and constantly changing. Today, many researchers and applied psychologists stress that parenting must be considered within the social context of the family. For example, a mother's behavior toward her child is influenced by her own life circumstances, health, education, and ethnicity (Feiring, Fox, Jaskir, and Lewis, 1987) and even the extent to which she thinks she is a controlling parent (Donovan and Leavitt, 1989).

Although hundreds of applied psychology articles have explored issues such as the effects of breast feeding, feeding schedules, and spoiling, the reality is that these topics are less important than the emotional climate in which child rearing takes place. A mother can provide warmth, love, closeness, and nutrients for her infant whether she chooses breast or bottle feeding. The choice to breast or bottle feed is less important than making feeding a pleasurable, relaxed experience for both the parent and the child.

The same rule applies to feeding schedules. Some parents feel that it is important to follow a rigid schedule so that the baby will learn a routine for eating, sleeping, and playing. There is, however, a growing trend toward self-demand schedules, in which the baby is fed whenever he or she is hungry; this is based on research which indicates that parents who are more relaxed and willing to work around the child's own needs produce a warmer, more satisfying emotional climate for their child (Ames, Gillespie, Haines, and Ilg, 1979).

Research into child-rearing practices is difficult because of the wide array of individual variables that affect development. But certain key ideas follow from research: Babies follow a developmental progression; there is much variability among children on developmental issues; and babies are egocentric and unable to delay their gratification. In addition, research shows that a child's home environment, day care situation, and intellectual development all affect how parents interact with their children. ◆

Focus on Learning

- ◆ Identify and describe three primary reflexes.   p. 307
- ◆ Research by Fantz and coworkers shows that infants are born with what perceptual abilities?   pp. 308–310
- ◆ What is attachment and what are its effects?   p. 313
- ◆ Cite evidence to suggest that some traits, such as shyness, are inborn.   p. 314

Intellectual Development

Why do automobiles have childproof locks and windows? Why do parents use gates to guard stairs, and gadgets to keep kitchen cabinets closed? Why are young children's toys made so that small parts cannot come off? The answer: children are curious, inquisitive, and much more intelligent than many people give them credit for being.

The physical and social development of infants is visible and quite dramatic; the parents of infants will tell you that their babies seem to grow and change every day. For this reason, the Bells, Greens, and Guerreras were intent on optimizing chances for their children's development. The changes that occur in young children are less visible, but no less dramatic. Children are continually developing intellectually; the changes they experience center on their ability to cope with an ever-expanding world. Older children can determine the difference between external versus internal causes of behavior more easily than younger children. Much of this difference is intellectually based (Miller and Aloise, 1989).

The noted Swiss psychologist Jean Piaget (1892–1980) believed that the fundamental development of all intellectual abilities takes place during the first two years of life; many psychologists and educators agree. Piaget devised procedures for examining the intellectual development of young children. He described one such procedure as follows:

> Initially we relied exclusively on interviews and asked the children only verbal questions. . . . We now try to start with some action that the child must perform. We introduce him into an experimental setting, presenting him with objects and—after the problem has been stated—the child must do something, he must experiment. Having observed his actions and the manipulation of objects we can then pose the verbal questions that constitute the interview. (PIAGET, 1963, p. 283)

Piaget's theory focuses on *how* people think (thought processes) instead of on *what* they think (content), making it applicable to people in all societies and cultures. But perhaps Piaget's greatest strength is his description of how a person's inherited capacities interact with the environment to produce an intellectually functioning child and adult. Although psychologists were initially skeptical of Piaget's ideas, and some criticisms persist, many researchers show that his assumptions are generally correct and apply cross-culturally. There are dissenters, notably Vygotsky, who stress more of society's role in establishing thought processes (Rogoff and Morelli, 1989).

According to Piaget, both children and adults use two processes to deal with new ideas. One is **assimilation,** in which the person absorbs new ideas and experiences, incorporates them into existing cognitive structures

Piaget studied thought processes in both children and adults, but his focus was on early intellectual development.

Assimilation: According to Jean Piaget, the process by which new concepts and experiences are incorporated into existing ones so as to be used in a meaningful way.

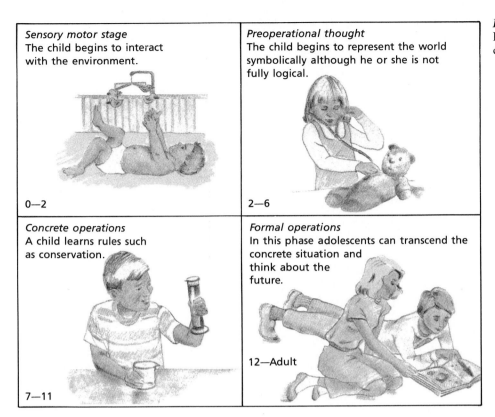

Sensory motor stage
The child begins to interact with the environment.

0—2

Preoperational thought
The child begins to represent the world symbolically although he or she is not fully logical.

2—6

Concrete operations
A child learns rules such as conservation.

7—11

Formal operations
In this phase adolescents can transcend the concrete situation and think about the future.

12—Adult

FIGURE 9.4
Piaget's stages of intellectual development.

(thought processes) and behaviors, and uses them later in similar situations. The second is **accommodation,** the process of modifying previously developed cognitive structures and behaviors so as to adapt them to a new concept. A child who learns to grasp a spoon, for example, demonstrates assimilation by later grasping similar objects such as forks, crayons, and sticks. This assimilated behavior then serves as a foundation for accommodation. The child can learn the new, more complex behavior of grasping a sphere (such as a ball) by modifying her earlier response and widening her grasp. People accommodate new information every day by learning new vocabulary and then assimilating it by using it in their language, only to be confronted with more new information. The two processes alternate in a never-ending cycle of intellectual and behavioral growth. Assimilation and accommodation occur throughout Piaget's four stages of development. Figure 9.4 shows activities typical of each stage.

Piaget's Four Stages

Stages are central to Piaget's theory. Piaget believed that just as standing must precede walking, some stages of intellectual development must precede others. For example, if a parent presents an idea that is too advanced, the child will not understand the new concept and no real learning will take place. A four-year-old who asks how babies are made will probably not understand his mother's biologically accurate explanation and will not learn or remember it. If the same child asks the question a few years later, the

Accommodation: According to Jean Piaget, the process by which new concepts and experiences modify existing cognitive structures and behaviors.

Sensory-motor stage: The first of Piaget's four major stages of intellectual development, covering roughly the first two years of life. During this period the child begins to interact with the environment, and the rudiments of intelligence are established.

explanation will be more meaningful and more likely to be remembered. Piaget's stages are associated with approximate ages and his theory brings the biological component of behavior into sharp focus. Although he acknowledges the role of environmental influences, Piaget clearly has a strong biological bias, especially in referring to stages of development.

The Sensory-Motor Stage. Piaget considered the **sensory-motor stage,** which extends from birth to about age two, to be the most important because the foundation for all intellectual development is established during this period. Consider the enormous changes that take place during the first two years of life. At birth an infant is a totally dependent, reflexlike organism. Within a few weeks infants learn some simple habits. They smile at their mothers or other caretakers; they seek the stimulation offered by a colorful musical mobile hanging overhead; they reach out and anticipate events in the environment, such as their mother's breast or a bottle. At two to three months infants develop rudimentary memory for past events and predict future visual events (Haith and McCarty, 1990). According to Piaget, the acquisition of memory is a crucial foundation for further intellectual development.

By the age of six to eight months, children seek new and more interesting kinds of stimulation. They can sit up and crawl. No longer willing just to watch what goes on around them, they begin to manipulate their environment, attempting what Piaget calls "making interesting sights last." At about eight months, children begin to develop a sense of their own intentions, and they attempt to overcome obstacles to reach goals. They can now crawl to the other side of a room to where the cat is lying or follow their mothers into the next room.

From about nine months on, children develop *object permanence,* the ability to realize that objects continue to exist even when they are out of sight. Prior to object permanence, when a mother leaves the room she has just disappeared. After object permanence develops, the baby realizes that she is just out of view. Although the exact age at which object permanence becomes evident has not yet been established, Baillargeon (1987) showed object permanence for some tasks in four-month-olds—earlier than Piaget believed possible. Various aspects of object permanence evolve gradually throughout the sensory-motor stage (see Figure 9.5).

According to Piaget, children develop object permanence at about nine months of age. At this stage they begin to understand that objects may be out of sight yet still exist.

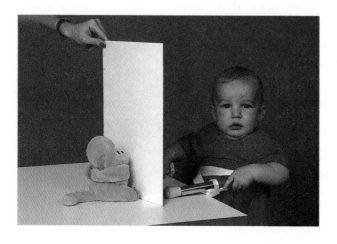
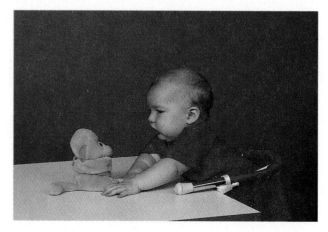

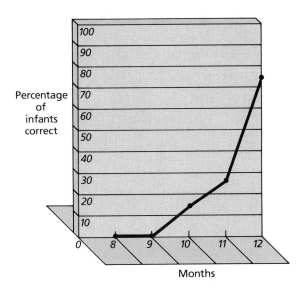

FIGURE 9.5
Object permanence is the ability to know that an object continues to exist even when out of view. Research shows that the ability to remember the location of an object that is subsequently hidden improves over time. Most one-year-olds can remember where an object has been hidden even after a delay of seven seconds. (After Fox, Kagan, and Weiskopf, 1979.)

In the second half of the sensory-motor stage (from about twelve to twenty-four months), children begin to walk, talk, and use simple forms of logic. Object permanence is more fully developed; the child can now follow a ball that rolls away, and search for his mother after she has left the room. Children also begin to use language to represent the world, an ability that takes them beyond the concrete world of visual imagery. By age two, a child can talk about Grandma, Daddy, doggy, cookies, Big Bird, going bye-bye, and other objects and events. No longer an uncoordinated, reflex-oriented organism, the child has become a thinking, walking, talking human being.

Throughout the sensory-motor stage, few demands are made on the child. Self-centeredness, or **egocentrism,** shapes all behavior, and the child is unable to understand that the world does not exist solely to satisfy his or her interests and needs. Children who are egocentric respond to questions such as "Why does it snow?" with answers such as "So I can play in it." For the next few years the child will be unable to see situations from the point of view of another person. Intellectual immaturity makes a young child continue to pester Mom even after she says she has a headache and wants to be left alone (Elkind, 1981a). Children cannot usually put themselves in their mother's (or anyone else's) position.

The Preoperational Stage. At the end of Piaget's sensory-motor stage, children are just beginning to understand the difference between their interests and those of others. This process of **decentration** continues for several years (Ford, 1979). Simultaneously, children may also become manipulative, difficult to deal with, and belligerent. Parents often describe this stage as the terrible twos, characterized by the appearance of the ever-popular word "No!" The child's behavior vacillates between charming and awful. This vacillation and annoying new habits such as being difficult to dress and bathe are signs of normal development and mark the beginning of the stage of preoperational thought.

In the **preoperational stage,** which lasts from about age two to age six or seven, children begin to represent the world symbolically. As preschoolers they play with objects in new ways and try, through let's pretend games, to represent reality. But they remain somewhat egocentric, continue to think

Egocentrism: The inability to perceive a situation or event except in relation to oneself; a characteristic of the sensory motor stage. In infancy, it is the attitude that directs all concerns and behaviors to personal interests and needs.

Decentration: The process, beginning at about age two of changing from a totally self-oriented point of view to one that recognizes other people's feelings, ideas, and viewpoints.

Preoperational stage: Piaget's second major stage of intellectual development, lasting from about age two to age seven, when initial symbolic thought is developed.

FIGURE 9.6
Conservation is the ability to recognize that an object remains the same object regardless of any changes it undergoes, such as a change in shape. When the contents of C are poured into A, young children, who have not yet learned the principle of conservation, will indicate that there is more water in A than in B.

concretely, and cannot deal with abstract thoughts that are not easily represented. They make few attempts to make their speech more intelligible or to justify their reasoning, and they may develop behavior problems such as inattentiveness, belligerence, or temper tantrums. During this stage, adults begin to teach children how to interact with others (Flavell, 1963), but major social and intellectual changes will not become fully apparent until the next stage of development.

The Stage of Concrete Operations. According to Piaget, the preoperational stage is followed by the stage of **concrete operations,** which lasts from about age seven to age eleven. Children in this stage attend school, have friends, can take care of themselves, and may take on many household responsibilities. They can look at a situation from more than one viewpoint and evaluate different aspects of it. This allows more complicated ways of thinking about situations and objects. The child has gained sufficient mental maturity to distinguish between appearances and reality, to think ahead one or two moves in checkers or other games. During this stage children discover constancy in the world; they discover rules and understand the reasons for them. For example, a child learns to wear her raincoat on a cloudy morning, anticipating rain later in the day.

The hallmark of this stage is **conservation,** the ability to recognize that objects may be transformed visually or physically, yet still represent the same amount of weight or volume. This concept has been the subject of considerable research. In a typical conservation task a child is shown two beakers. One beaker is short, squat, and half full of water; the other is tall, thin, and empty (see Figure 9.6). The experimenter pours the water from the short, squat beaker into the tall, narrow one and asks the child, "Which beaker has more water, the first or the second?" A child who does not understand the principles of conservation will claim that the taller beaker contains more water. A child who is able to conserve volume will recognize that the same amount of water was in both beakers and that therefore the amount in both is equal. A child who has mastered one type of conservation (e.g., conservation of volume) often cannot immediately transfer that knowledge to other conservation tasks (e.g., those involving weight.)

When a child masters the concept of conservation, he or she realizes that certain facts are true because they follow logically, not simply because they are observed. Abundant research supports this claim. An example is the work of distinguished psychologist John H. Flavell. Flavell and his col-

Concrete operational stage:
Piaget's third stage of development, lasting from approximately ages seven to eleven. During this stage the child develops the ability to understand constant factors in the environment, rules, and higher-order symbolism (such as arithmetic and geography).

Conservation: The ability to recognize that something changed in some way (such as the "shape" of liquid in a container) is still the same thing with the same weight, substance, or volume.

leagues have been studying a phenomenon closely associated with conservation: the ability of older and younger children to distinguish between appearances and reality. They assert that by the age of six children possess some knowledge about the difference between appearance and reality and can sense what a task is all about. Listen to Flavell (1986):

> Suppose someone shows a three-year-old and a six-year-old a red toy car covered by a green filter that makes the car look black, hands the car to the children to inspect, puts it behind the filter again, and asks, "What color is this car? Is it red or is it black?" The three-year-old is likely to say "black," the six-year-old, "red." (p. 418)

Intellectual abilities continue to develop as a child matures, and slowly in different ways children grasp new and ever more difficult concepts (Flavell, Green, and Flavell, 1989). The development of conservation, in fact, is a necessary prelude to the fourth and final stage of intellectual development, the stage of formal operations.

The Stage of Formal Operations. Piaget's final stage of intellectual development, which starts at about age twelve, is the **formal operational stage.** Unlike concrete operational children, whose thought is still tied to immediate situations, adolescents can engage in abstract thought. They do this by forming hypotheses that allow them to think of different ways to represent situations, organizing them into all possible relationships and outcomes. Adolescents' intellectual worlds are full of informal theories of logic and ideas about themselves and life (Flavell, 1963).

By age twelve the egocentrism of the sensory-motor and preoperational stages has for the most part disappeared, but a new egocentrism develops. According to Piaget, "The adolescent goes through a phase in which he attributes an unlimited power to his own thoughts so that the dream of a glorious future or of transforming the world through ideas (even if this idealism takes a materialistic form) seems to be not only fantasy, but also an effective action which in itself modifies the empirical world" (Inhelder and Piaget, 1958, pp. 345–346). Adolescents' egocentrism and naive hopes eventually decrease as they face and deal with the challenges of life. A summary of some important points about Piaget's theory is presented in Table 9.6.

Formal operational stage: Piaget's fourth and final stage of intellectual development, beginning at about age twelve, when the individual can think hypothetically, can consider all future possibilities, and is capable of deductive logic.

TABLE 9.6

Important Points about Piaget's Theory
1. Cognitive development is a process in which each stage builds on the previous one.
2. The egocentrism of infants is reduced over a period of several years through the process of decentration.
3. The exact age at which each stage of development appears differs from one child to another, but all children in all societies go through the same stages.
4. The actual content of children's thoughts is less important to psychologists than the nature of their thinking. By discovering how children think, psychologists can find ways to facilitate learning

Implications and Criticisms of Piaget's Theory. Parents, educators, and psychologists can enhance children's intellectual development by understanding how cognitive abilities develop. For example, Piaget recognized that parental love and interaction are always important to a child's development, but he asserted that they are *essential* in the first two years of life. He also stressed the importance of providing a great deal of physical and intellectual stimulation, especially stimuli that move and change color, shape, and form. Research confirms that children and animals given sensory stimulation from birth through the early months develop more both intellectually and socially than those who are not given such stimulation. Parents and educators who agree with Piaget have devoted efforts to ensuring that the first years of life for newborns are ones in which stimulation is great, curiosity is encouraged, and opportunities for exploration are maximized. From Piaget's point of view, they are optimizing a child's potential.

While acknowledging that it is possible to accelerate children's development, Piaget stressed that children should not be pushed too fast. Parents serve their children best by providing intellectual stimulation that is appropriate to their current developmental level. Noted psychologist David Elkind (1981b) supports this view in his book *The Hurried Child*, in which he argues that overacceleration ultimately has deleterious effects. Yale psychologist Edward Zigler concurs: "We are driving our children too hard and thereby depriving them of their most precious commodity—their childhood. . . . Children are growing up too fast today, and prematurely placing four-year-olds and five-year-olds into full-day preschool education programs will only compound the problem" (1987, p. 257). In Zigler's view, developmentally appropriate care programs that focus on social interaction and recreation should be the focus for preschoolers. He asserts that the real business of a preschooler is socialization, not education.

Although Piaget's ideas have had an enormous influence on the ways psychologists think about children's development, some researchers have problems with his approach. For example, Fischer and Silvern (1985) remind psychologists that there is enormous variation in maturation and that a strict view of Piaget's stage approach reduces the role of the environment. Other researchers claim that Piaget's specific questions and tasks focus the way people think about children on the wrong abilities and issues. Many studies of young children measure development by giving the same task to children of various ages. Children who cannot do the task are thought to be cognitively deficient. Psychologist Rochel Gelman argues that researchers tend to underestimate younger children's abilities. Studies by Gelman and others show that to understand cognitive development fully, psychologists should ask children of different ages different questions. For example, Shatz and Gelman (1973) found that two-year-olds change the length of their sentences depending on whom they are talking to, using shorter sentences when speaking to younger children; they point to the cognitive maturity of a child who has decentered enough to make such a shift in point of view. Like Gelman, many researchers claim that Piaget may have overestimated the extent of egocentrism in young children. Lempers, Flavell, and Flavell (1977), for example, found that two-year-olds will rotate books they are reading in order to show their mothers the illustrations. Again, such cognitive maturity is impressive in two-year-olds. Can such maturity be enhanced? Can the competency of young children be given a push, a leg up, a head start? The federal government in the 1960s thought it could, and as you will see in the next section, the psychologists who advised the government were correct.

Did Project Head Start Work?

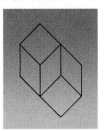

*P*roject Head Start was initiated in the 1960s in an effort to break the poverty cycle by raising the social and educational competency of disadvantaged pre-school children. Head Start has received federal support for more than two decades and is often referred to as a milestone in psychology. The multimillion-dollar project showed what can be done with remedial education, equal educa-tion, and proactive use of child development techniques. But did it really work?

During the past twenty years there have been many reports documenting the success of Head Start. Preschool children score sharply higher at the end of their Head Start year than they did at the beginning (Haskins, 1989). Recently, however, Lee, Schnur, and Brooks-Gunn (1988) questioned whether Head Start actually closed the gap for disadvantaged children. Did it put them on an equal footing with other children?

The investigators reanalyzed the data from Head Start, focusing on intel-lectual differences. They compared gains made by three groups of disadvantaged children: (1) students in Head Start, (2) students who attended no preschool program, and (3) students who attended another preschool program. More than seventy-eight percent of the nine hundred participants were members of minority groups. The aim was to determine whether the Head Start students made gains, and if so, whether those gains were equal to or better than those made by other students from low-income families.

The analysis showed clearly that children enrolled in Head Start programs made important gains and had an advantage over children who did not attend preschool and children who attended another preschool program. However, although they made significant gains in cognitive abilities, Head Start children did not do as well as children from advantaged homes. Head Start did not close the gap. Why? One reason is that Head Start children tended to be especially disadvantaged, even compared with other disadvantaged groups. The research-ers suggest that one year of Head Start may not be enough to close the gap. They argue that their data should be seen "as a mandate for enhancing the program," suggesting that a second year "would be likely to magnify and solidify the Head Start advantage" (Lee et al., 1988, p. 220).

Today, Head Start enrolls about 450,000 children, most of them from the neediest families—mostly black and from the lower classes. As children from other racial minorities and from single-parent homes enter the program, different kinds of gains may be seen. Social class is a critical determinant in school success (Duyme, 1988). Many psychologists consider it imperative that programs such as Head Start and follow-up programs be expanded and funded at higher levels so that they may reach out to a wider community. For example, the school breakfast program that provides nutritious meals for low-income children also produces increases in academic performance (Meyers et al., 1989). As Zigler (1987) has written, "We simply cannot inoculate children in one year against the ravages of a life of deprivation" (p. 258). Clearly, it is essential that economically disadvantaged children be given an equal educational start in life, not only for a year, but also throughout their childhood (Woodhead, 1988).   ◆

Language Development

One of the most important aspects of children's development is the acqui-sition of language, as we discussed in chapter 7. Young children have ways of communicating their desires and needs nonverbally through facial expres-sions, hand motions, and other behaviors, but effective communication be-gins with language acquisition.

In the first few months of life, babies coo and babble. By six months of age, the sounds they make may become differentiated. Very often, six- to eight-month-old babies repeat the same sounds for hours or days at a time. At the end of a year they have learned a few simple words, perhaps including *mama* and *dada*. From this naming stage the child goes on to develop simple two- and three-word sentences that are often characterized as telegraphic because they use few words, as if the child is trying to be economical.

Through their telegraphic two-word sentences, young children can convey an amazingly large number of thoughts. Sentences such as "No peas," "More ice cream," and "Change diaper" are quite explicit and make the child's needs known. But more important than these utterances themselves is the way they evolve into more complex statements as children learn grammar. Children learn grammar, or the rules for generating sentences in a language, at an early age. Although five- and six-year-olds have not yet learned all the grammar of their language, their speech includes nouns, verbs, and adjectives in essentially the correct order. The ability to use language produces dramatic changes in children's lives, allowing them to interact on a more mature level with other people and to represent the world in increasingly complex ways.

Focus on Learning

- Describe the difference between assimilation and accommodation. pp. 316–317
- From Piaget's view, when is the most important time for intellectual development? p. 318
- What is egocentrism and how does it relate to decentration? p. 319
- Identify the characteristics of the *ability to conserve*. pp. 320–321

Moral Reasoning

The physical and intellectual development of childhood is paralleled by growth in the capacity for moral reasoning. From childhood on, people develop **morality,** a set of values that enables them to make decisions about what is right or wrong, good or bad. Morality lets people evaluate situations and behavior and act according to their beliefs.

Attitudes about morals develop and change throughout life. At an early age, children learn from their parents the behaviors, attitudes, and values considered appropriate and correct in their culture. Morality is aided by teachers and bolstered by church and community leaders, as well as by family and friends. As they mature, children acquire new attitudes that accommodate an increasingly complex view of the world and of reality. Your views of morality as a ten-year-old were probably different from your views today. Recognizing the differences in the moral maturity of adolescents and adults, the United States Supreme Court has restricted adolescents' rights to make important life decisions, in part because the court feels that adolescents lack moral maturity (Gardner, Scherer, and Tester, 1989). But do they? Is the reasoning and judgment of a child, a pre-teen, or an adolescent like that of an adult?

Morality: A system of learned attitudes about social practices, institutions, and individual behavior, used to evaluate events as right or wrong.

Piaget and Morality

Piaget examined children's ability to analyze questions of morality and found the results to be consistent with his ideas about intellectual development.

Young children's ideas about morality are rigid and rule-bound. When playing a game, for example, a young child will not allow the rules to be modified. Older children, on the other hand, recognize that rules are established by social convention and may need to be altered, depending on the situation. They have developed a sense of *moral relativity* that allows them to recognize that situational factors affect the way things are perceived (Piaget, 1932).

According to Piaget, as children mature they move from inflexibility toward relativity in their moral judgments; they develop new cognitive structures and assimilate and accommodate new ideas. When young children are questioned about lying, for example, they respond that lying is always and under any circumstances bad—a person should never lie. Sometime between the ages of five and twelve, however, children recognize that lying may be permissible in some special circumstances.

Kohlberg: Heinz's Dilemma

Piaget's theory of moral development was based on descriptions of how children respond to certain kinds of questions and at what age they switch and use other forms of answers. The research of Harvard psychologist Lawrence Kohlberg (1927–1987) grew out of Piaget's work. The central concept in Kohlberg's theory is that of justice. In his studies of moral reasoning Kohlberg presented different types of stories to people of various ages and asked them what the story meant to them and how they felt about it (Kohlberg, 1969). In one story, Heinz, a poor man, stole a drug for his wife who would have died without it:

> In Europe a woman was near death from a special kind of cancer. There was one drug that doctors thought might save her. It was a form of radium that a druggist in the same town recently discovered. The drug was expensive to make, but the druggist was charging ten times what the drug cost him to make. He paid $200 for the radium and charged $2,000 for a small dose of the drug. The sick woman's husband, Heinz, went to everyone he knew to borrow the money, but he could only get together $1,000, which is half of what it cost. He told the druggist that his wife was dying, and asked him to sell it cheaper or let him pay later. But the druggist said. "No, I discovered the drug, and I'm going to make money from it." So Heinz got desperate and broke into the man's store to steal the drug for his wife. (1969, p. 379)

Kohlberg asked his subjects about the morality and justice of Heinz's action: "Would a good husband steal for his wife?" "Was it actually wrong?" "Why?" Adults' interpretations of Heinz's plight differed from those of adolescents and five-year-olds. Children had difficulty seeing that Heinz's circumstances might influence the way his action could be judged (Kohlberg, 1976). Kohlberg found that people's judgments of the behavior of others vary with their level of moral development. Presented with the story of Heinz, children at level one morality either condemn Heinz's behavior, explaining he should be punished because he stole, or justify it, explaining that Heinz was good because he tried to save his wife's life. People at level two morality said that Heinz broke the law by stealing and should go to jail. Only people who have reached level three can see that Heinz was justified in his action (see Figure 9.7 on page 326).

Kohlberg believed that moral development in general proceeds through a series of three levels, each of which is divided into two stages. Young children base their decisions about right or wrong on the likelihood of avoiding punishment and obtaining rewards. This is level one morality, or *pre-*

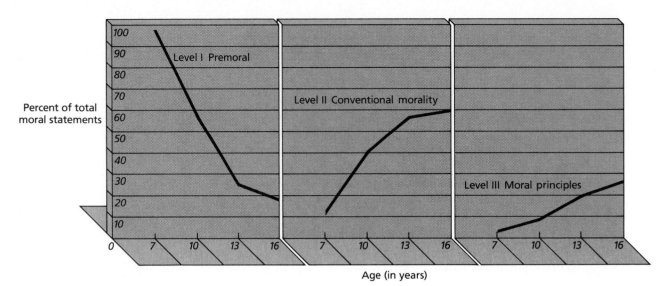

FIGURE 9.7
In Kohlberg's theory of moral development, there is a distinct progression from one stage of morality to another as age increases. Thus, level one morality decreases with age and maturity, and levels two and three continue to increase. (Source: Data from Kohlberg, 1963.)

conventional. A child in this stage would say that it is "bad" to pull the cat's tail, "because mom will spank me." School-age children, who are at level two, adopt *conventional* ideas about morality. They conform to avoid disapproval. At this stage a ten-year-old might choose not to try cigarettes because his parents and friends disapprove of smoking. Level two judgments are governed by a process that considers the implications of a person's behavior. Why did he do it? What will be the consequences for him and for others?

Level three, or *postconventional,* morality is concerned with contracts and laws. In the first stage of level three morality, people make judgments on the basis of their perception of the needs of society, with an end toward maintaining community welfare and order. In the second stage of level three, morality of conscience, people make judgments based on their personal values rather than on those of society. At this stage, a person may be against capital punishment, even though it is legal in some states. Most adults reach at least the first stage of level three. A comparison of Piaget's and Kohlberg's theories on moral development is found in Table 9.7.

TABLE 9.7
A Comparison of Piaget and Kohlberg on Moral Development

Piaget	Kohlberg
Sensory-Motor and Preoperational (birth–7 years)	Level I—Preconventional *Stage 1:* Obedience and punishment orientation *Stage 2:* Naively egoistic orientation
Concrete Operations (8–11 years)	Level II—Conventional *Stage 3:* Good-boy orientation *Stage 4:* Authority-and-social-order-maintaining orientation
Formal Operations (12 years and after)	Level III—Postconventional *Stage 5:* Contractual-legalistic orientation *Stage 6:* Conscience or principle orientation

Research and Challenges

Piaget set the stage for two decades of research by Kohlberg, whose work was monumental in scope. Like other great thinkers, Kohlberg laid down a theory that he knew would be tested, evaluated, and revised, a firm foundation for the next generation of research.

Kohlberg and Piaget. Piaget and Kohlberg studied moral reasoning, not moral behavior. Both theorists focused on how people make decisions, not on the behavior that might result from those decisions. But their theories differ in that Piaget thought of the stages of moral development as discrete, whereas Kohlberg viewed them as overlapping. Kohlberg went further than Piaget in systematizing the development of morality. He elaborated on ideas about how children's interactions with parents and friends may influence their conceptions of morality. For example, when children realize that working within or around the rules affects other family members, their view of the rules changes. Thus, an older girl will spare her mother embarrassment and respond favorably when asked her opinion about her mother's carefully chosen new dress; a younger child will refuse to break the rules about lying and will tell her mother if she thinks the dress looks ugly (Blasi, 1980).

In Kohlberg's view, a child might use earlier levels of moral reasoning from time to time, even though he or she is capable of higher levels, a finding that has been substantiated by the work of De Vries and Walker (1986). They asked university students to fill out an attitude questionnaire and write an essay on capital punishment. The results showed that the subjects had achieved high levels of moral reasoning but often did not reason at those levels in supporting their positions on capital punishment. In fact, twenty-four percent of the subjects used a level of moral reasoning that was a full stage lower than that which they were capable of using. Researchers are expanding on the original Kohlberg research using different contexts such as the classroom, where perceptions of fairness are being evaluated across the age span (Thorkildsen, 1989).

Kohlberg's theory has not gone unchallenged. Some have suggested that his views are culturally bound and that he did not examine issues with which normal adults have to deal. For example, Yussen (1977) has shown that older children and teenagers consider other moral issues in their lives more important than the Heinz dilemma. This criticism does not make Kohlberg's work any less important, but it does raise some important questions.

Lawrence Kohlberg

Gilligan's Work: Gender Differences. A major addition to the study of morality has been the work of Carol Gilligan (1982), who found that people look at more than justice when reasoning moral conflicts. She found that people were also concerned with caring, relationships, and connections with other people. Gilligan focused her research on the differences between girls and boys with respect to their inclinations toward caring and justice.

Although Kohlberg and his colleagues had not reported any gender differences, Gilligan found that girls were more concerned with caring, relationships, and connections with other people. As younger children, girls gravitate toward a morality of caring, while boys gravitate toward a morality of justice. Gilligan asserts that the difference between boys and girls is established by virtue of the child's gender and the child's relationship with the mother. Because of the gender difference, boys see that they are essen-

Carol Gilligan

tially different from other people, whereas girls develop a belief in their similarity or connectedness with others. Gilligan shows that boys respond to the Heinz dilemma by indicating that sometimes people must act on their own to do the right thing. Girls, by contrast, are more likely to look for alternatives, ways to talk out differences, or seek some compromise. Like Kohlberg, Gilligan argues that the development of caring follows a time course with initial caring only toward oneself, later, caring toward others, and ultimately (in some people), a more mature stage of caring for truth. Gilligan's work has been influential in psychologists' evaluations of morality. Some research has been supportive (Ma, 1989), although others find no differences in adult morality of men and women (Boldizar, Wilson, and Deemer, 1989). Some assert that her approach fosters a continuation of sex-role stereotyping—women as caring, men as logical.

Caring and justice are not incompatible values; indeed, they go together. That boys and girls develop them differently need not be seen as negative. Recognizing the differences between boys and girls allows us to expand the horizons of each to the full limits of their human potential (Muuss, 1986; Damon, 1988).

Promoting Morality in Children

Although parents are the main source of children's moral values, Kohlberg suggests that other people can also help promote the development of morality and conscience (Windmiller, 1980). Kohlberg recommends that teachers as well as parents talk to children about moral issues related to situations such as war, death, education, and even cheating on taxes. These discussions are especially worthwhile when adults understand the stages of moral development (Damon, 1980).

Role-taking, the ability to adopt perspectives different from one's own, is another way to foster morality. According to Kohlberg, children who have opportunities in classroom, churches, and at home to consider moral dilemmas from another person's point of view are more likely to develop a mature sense of morality (Kohlberg, 1971). Through such methods people learn not only what society's values are, but also how to think independently. Moreover, they achieve higher levels of moral reasoning, thereby gaining greater flexibility and independence in both judgment and behavior. For example, when older children and teenagers form a self-image and adopt gender-based characteristics, they often rely on the opinions and standards of others. But a study of thirteen-, seventeen-, and twenty-one-year-olds showed that both males and females at higher levels of moral reasoning tended to be less rigid than those at lower levels about incorporating some characteristics associated with the other gender into their self-image (Leahy and Eiter, 1980). They could escape sex-role stereotyping and decide for themselves which characteristics would enhance them as individuals.

*Focus on
Learning*

- ◆ What is morality? p. 324
- ◆ Distinguish among preconventional, conventional, and postconventional morality. pp. 325–327
- ◆ What was Gilligan's criticism of Kohlberg's work? pp. 327–328

Social Development

As society changes, so do ideas and practices related to a child's social development. In a 1959 study of masculinity and father-son relationships, Paul Mussen and Luther Distler concluded that a father's importance and involvement in his son's life are crucial in determining the child's gender-based interests. A generation ago, when Mussen and Distler conducted their research, parents tended to encourage "masculine" traits such as athletic prowess in their sons and "feminine" traits such as shyness in their daughters. They accepted and promoted a gender-based social environment. Today, many parents de-emphasize gender-based interests in their children, seeking to reduce and even eliminate society's tendency to stereotype people, their interests, and their occupations on the basis of sex.

Early Social Development

Social development begins at birth with the development of attachment between parents and their newborn. The nature of a child's beginning and early interactions with parents is a crucial part of personality development. Infants have a great need to be hugged and cuddled, nurtured, and made to feel good, but as psychoanalyst Bruno Bettelheim said, "Love is not enough." Eventually parents must teach their children to interact with others and become independent.

In the first year of life, social interaction is limited because infants are largely egocentric. They seldom distinguish their needs and desires from those of others. About the end of the first year children exhibit strong attachments and fear of strangers. At eighteen to twenty-four months, they have matured sufficiently to have specific desires and needs, but they lack the language skills to make those needs known. A child cannot tell her father, for example, that she wants the green bib, not the blue one, although she can indicate her displeasure, often quite loudly (Ames, Gillespie, Haines, and Ilg, 1979). As early as nine months, infants show that they like to play games by indicating unhappiness when an adult stops playing with them (Ross and Lollis, 1987). They play by themselves, but as they grow older, especially beyond two years of age, they engage in more social play with other children (Howes, Unger, and Seidner, 1989).

By the end of their second year, children have begun to understand that they are separate from their parents. They learn to differentiate themselves from others, to manipulate the world, and to interact with other people. As the child enters the preoperational stage, egocentrism gives way to increased social interaction. Two-year-olds generally play alone or alongside other children, but with little interaction. They prefer to play with an adult rather than with another two-year-old (Jennings, Curry, and Connors, 1986). They are now better at controlling their emotional responses than they were at eighteen months. Gradually they begin to socialize with their peers.

Sharing. Benjamin Spock, noted pediatrician, once said the only two things a child will share willingly are communicable diseases and his mother's age. Actually, from age two until they begin school, children vacillate between quiet conformity and happy sharing, on the one hand, and making stubborn negative demands and exhibiting egocentric behavior on the other (Ames et

Once encouraged to share, children begin to understand that sharing can involve a reciprocal agreement.

al., 1979). Since sharing is a socially desirable behavior, children must learn to share when they enter day care, nursery school, or kindergarten.

Very young children do not understand the concept of sharing, particularly the idea that if you share with another child, he or she is more likely to share with you. In a laboratory study of sharing, researchers observed groups of two children separated by a gate. Initially, one child was given toys and the other wasn't; then the situation was reversed. The researchers found that none of the children shared spontaneously, but sixty-five percent shared a toy when asked to do so by their mothers. Moreover, when deprived of a toy after having shared one, a child often approached another child who had the toy. One child even said, "I gave you a toy, why don't you give me one?" Children do not initiate sharing at a young age, but once they share, they seem to exhibit knowledge about reciprocal arrangements (Levitt, Weber, Clark, and McDonnell, 1985).

Entry into kindergarten helps lead to a breakdown of egocentrism, but many factors can either promote or retard this aspect of development. One variable is the type of toys children play with. Quilitch and Risley (1973) provided young children with two kinds of toys—those that are generally played with by one child at a time (isolate toys) and those that are designed for use by two or more children at the same time (social toys). All the children played with both kinds of toys, but some were first given social toys and others were first given isolate toys. After the initial play period, more of the children who had been given social toys first chose to play with other children. The researchers concluded that the kinds of toys given to children altered the degree of egocentrism exhibited in their play.

Sex Segregation in Play. Children at eighteen months display sex-stereotyped preferences for toys (Caldera, Huston, and O'Brien, 1989); these preferences are also evident in their choice of playmates. Boys and girls don't have much to do with one another during middle childhood. Starting at age three and continuing for several years, they prefer same-sex play partners. According to Eleanor Maccoby and Carol Jacklin (1987), this finding is re-

Young children naturally gravitate toward playmates of the same sex; this natural grouping helps form strong gender-based expectations for behavior.

liable, cuts across a variety of situations, and is difficult to change. Sex segregation does not happen because children have been given "boy" toys or "girl" toys, nor does it result from inborn temperamental differences that lead to rough and tumble play for boys and more sedate play for girls.

The reasons for sex segregation are not fully understood, but Maccoby and Jacklin argue that children know that they are members of one gender or the other. This knowledge binds members of each sex together and differentiates them from members of the other sex. Children with widely different personalities are drawn together solely on the basis of their shared gender. Throughout childhood, temperamental differences interact with social effects, and sex segregation becomes even more pronounced. Sex segregation, gender-based roles, and gender differences are examined in more detail in chapter 10. Although boys and girls don't have much to do with one another during middle childhood, they both share a learning process which helps them become mothers and fathers later in life.

Fathers and Their Children

$\mathcal{T}$he American family is undergoing dramatic changes. During the past two decades, women have entered the workforce in unprecedented numbers and in so doing have changed the shape, structure, and fabric of family life. Women are spending less time with their young children. Are fathers taking up the slack? Do fathers spend enough time with their children? Is it "quality" time?

THINKING ABOUT RESEARCH

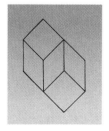

Assertions Lead to Hypotheses. Today's fathers are more interested in their newborns and may be involved in their upbringing from the first moments of the child's life, as evidenced by the fact that many more fathers are now present in the delivery room during their child's birth. They are affectionate and responsive caretakers (Parke and O'Leary, 1976). Two words often used in describing fathers' interactions with children are *quality* and *quantity*. Fathers

As more women enter the workforce, more men are taking the time to develop an intimate relationship with their children.

sometimes assert that they spend limited time with their children, but that this time is quality time. Grossman, Pollack, and Golding (1988) looked at the quality and quantity of interactions between fathers and their firstborn five-year-old children to determine whether this is true.

Methods. The researchers used twenty-three families participating in a Boston University pregnancy and parenthood project. They met with the parents during early pregnancy and within two weeks of the child's fifth birthday. On the first occasion they measured a number of psychological, marital, and sociocultural variables. For example, they examined both the husband's and the wife's adaptation to life as an adult—their levels of anxiety, autonomy, marital adjustment, and age. At the five-year follow-up, they measured both the quantity and the quality of time fathers spent with their children. To measure quantity, the father estimated the average amount of time he spent with his child on weekdays and weekends, with respect to both playtime and caretaking. To measure quality, the researchers had the subjects perform a task that involved both parents and the child in their home. The researchers recorded the quality of the interactions during play in terms of *warmth* (was the parent critical or reinforcing), *attention*, and *responsiveness*.

Results. Quality and quantity of time were not directly related but were affected by numerous variables. Some fathers spent enormous amounts of time with their child, others very little. Some spent quality time; others did not. Men who had been well-adjusted during their wife's pregnancy spent relatively more time with their five-year-olds. Men who enjoyed and were involved in their work spent less time with their children. Interestingly, women played a key role in the amount of time fathers spent with their children. Self-sufficient and autonomous women tended to have husbands who spent less time with their children. These women tended to be very willing and able to "do it all." (Of course, women who "do it all" may create situations that allow husbands to spend less time with their children.) On the quality issue, men who were happy, well-adjusted, and satisfied at work were supportive of their children and spent quality time with them. The same was true of men who valued their own independence.

Conclusions. A striking conclusion of the Grossman, Pollack, and Golding study is that the amount of time men spend with their children is directly affected by their wives. Men married to autonomous, self-sufficient, competent women spent less time with their children. The quality of their time seemed to be affected more by their own feelings of self-worth and adjustment. In sum, the quality and quantity of time men spend with their children cannot be analyzed in simple terms because it is affected by personal psychological variables as well as by marital factors and even the gender of the child (Ross and Taylor, 1989). Parents' interactions with their children must be described in the context of family relationships. There are still unanswered questions: Do some men marry autonomous women because they want little to do with their children? Why does their wives' autonomy keep men from spending time with their children? Do children seek out the more autonomous parent? The research continues.   ◆

Single Parenting

Before this century, fathers were more likely than mothers to head one-parent families. Mothers rarely had the financial means to support children after divorce. High maternal mortality rates at birth also tended to make men the heads of single-parent households.

Today, more children than ever are being raised in single-parent homes. According to the U.S. Department of Commerce, in the decade between 1970 and 1980 the number of single parents raising children increased by at least twenty-eight percent. Only four percent of American households fit the traditional description of a working father, a mother who stays at home, and two or more school-age children; this means that 15 million children in the United States live with one parent. According to the Census Bureau, twenty-four percent of children under the age of six live with just one parent. (U.S. Bureau of the Census, 1989.)

For the millions of divorced, widowed, or never-married parents who are rearing children alone, many of the traditional supports, such as the assistance of grandparents, are unavailable. Single parents tend to work longer hours than married parents (Weinraub and Wolf, 1983), and their own parents and other relatives seldom live in the same community. Still, evidence exists that the effects of single parenthood are indirect and that single parents in some cases can do just as well as, if not better than, they did when they were married (Wilson, 1989). Researchers are just beginning to examine the effects of single parenting; only recently have they realized the extent to which school-age children are being raised by single parents and the extent to which younger children are being cared for in day care centers.

Day Care

According to the Census Bureau (1987), more than 29 million children under age fifteen have a mother who works outside the home. By 1995 it is expected that 34 million children will have working mothers (Hofferth and Phillips, 1987). For families in which both parents work, as well as for single parents, day care can be a necessity; day care centers provide care for about twenty-three percent of preschool children who have working mothers.

Day care situations are becoming increasingly diverse as parents seek alternative arrangements for their children. While their mothers work, most preschool children are cared for in their own or other people's homes, often by baby-sitters, relatives, friends, fathers, ex-spouses, or grandparents (Presser, 1989; U.S. Bureau of the Census, 1987). Many Americans believe that when children are reared by people other than their parents, their development is less than optimal (Kagan, Kearsley, and Zelazo, 1980), but this controversial issue has been the subject of intensive research.

Effects of Day Care. It isn't easy to determine the effects of day care because of a number of variables, including the child's age at entry into a day care program, the child's family background, the security of the child's attachment to parents, and the stability of the child's day care arrangements. All these factors can affect a child's response to the day care experience (Howes and Stewart, 1987; Clarke-Stewart, 1989). Psychologists are especially interested in the relationship of day care and attachment because they believe that a child's emotional security depends on a strong, loving bond with a parent or primary caretaker (Kagan et al., 1980). Contrary to popular belief, studies of attachment behaviors find that nonparental care does not reduce a child's emotional attachment to the mother (Etaugh, 1980). Moreover, there is no firm evidence that temporary separations, such as those caused by day care for preschool children, create later psychological trauma (Lamb et al., 1988).

Considerable evidence suggests that a stimulating, varied environment is necessary for optimal intellectual development and that high-quality day care centers provide a sufficiently stimulating environment. High-quality day

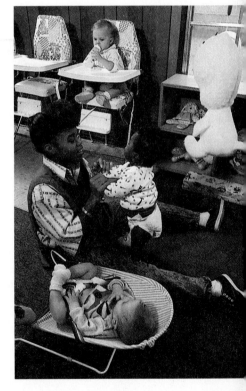

As day care becomes increasingly necessary to the contemporary family, psychologists are studying its effects, both positive and negative.

care means an experienced and highly qualified staff, a low staff-to-child ratio, and low staff turnover (Farber and Egeland, 1982). Belsky and Steinberg (1978) found no differences in intellectual functioning between middle-class children enrolled in quality day care centers and children reared at home. In fact, high-quality day care centers may increase children's positive social interactions with peers (Schindler, Moely, and Frank, 1987), may make them appear happier (Vandell, Henderson, and Wilson, 1988), and may help prevent declines in intellectual functioning that sometimes occur in children from low-income families who are not exposed to varied environments (e.g., Burchinal, Lee and Ramey, 1989).

However, recent research has questioned the conventional wisdom of day care, suggesting that day care centers may have negative effects on social development for children who spend more than twenty hours per week there. Jay Belsky of Pennsylvania State University asserts that extensive nonmaternal care in the first year of life is associated with insecurity in infants. Infants who received more than twenty hours of day care per week displayed more avoidance of their mothers when they were reunited than babies who spent only a couple of hours in day care (Belsky and Rovine, 1988). These results contradict the findings of previous research, and as a result, most psychologists are maintaining an open mind regarding day care and its effects.

Maternal employment is a reality in the 1990s. Thus, the issue for many is not whether infants should be in day care, but rather how to make the best of the day care experience (Clarke-Stewart, 1989). Parents considering day care either as an option or as a necessity should first establish specific care goals both for themselves and for their child. If those goals can be met through day care, they should find the highest-quality day care affordable within a reasonable distance of home and work. Finally, they must also provide a supportive home environment.

Latchkey Children

Millions of children come home from school to empty homes where they take care of themselves until their parents arrive home from work. They are known as self-care, or latchkey, children. Most parents who leave their children in self-care arrangements establish rules for them to follow and maintain telephone contact with them in order to supervise even while they are not present in the home. Do these latchkey arrangements work? Are there behavioral consequences for children left to care for themselves?

Rodman and his colleagues compared self-care children with adult-supervised children. A self-care child is one between the ages of six and thirteen who spends time alone or with a younger sibling on a periodic basis (Rodman, Pratto, and Nelson, 1988). They found children who were alike with respect to age, sex, grade in school, family composition, and mother's and father's occupation and matched them to form comparable groups of self-care and adult-supervised children. When fourth- and seventh-graders in both groups were compared on measures of psychological and social functioning, there were no important differences between the groups. The researchers concluded that "the growing public and professional concern about the negative effects of self-care arrangements is premature and may not be warranted" (Rodman, Pratto, and Nelson, 1985, p. 417; see also Steinberg, 1986). Note that considerable caution must be used in interpreting data on latchkey children because of the immense variability in the situations in which such children are studied. Further, not all researchers find similar results or focus on similar problems; for example, in eighth-grade children, self-care has been implicated in substance abuse (Richardson et al., 1989), but among former latchkey children, college students do not seem to differ on personality or academic variables (Messer, Wuensch, and Diamond, 1989).

The behavioral effects on the child are the true measure of whether day care or self-care makes a difference. Many of these effects will have to be examined a generation from now. For now, the overall developmental effects of self-care for children seem to be minimal or nonexistent (Vandell and Corasaniti, 1988) and those of day care are minimal.

Researchers who study topics such as single parenting, day care, and self-care focus on personality and academic differences between children raised in these environments and children raised in non-day care or non-self-care homes. Their aim is to discern whether differences exist, and if they exist, whether they bring about adverse effects. What are some of the childhood disorders psychologists see? We consider next two of the important disorders of infancy and childhood—hyperactivity and autism.

- ◆ When do children begin to share? p. 329
- ◆ Why does sex segregation occur among boys and girls? pp. 330–331
- ◆ Identify two variables that affect the quality of day care. pp. 333–334
- ◆ Who are latchkey children? pp. 334–335

Focus on Learning

Psychological Disorders of Infancy and Childhood

About 10 million children in the United States suffer from problems that warrant mental health treatment (Tuma, 1989), although fewer than one in five actually receive treatment (Links, Boyle, and Offord, 1989). Researchers are especially interested in disorders occurring during the early years, since environmental experiences are relatively limited and it is easier to isolate the contributions of nature and nurture. Two prominent disorders of infancy and childhood are attention-deficit hyperactivity disorder and autistic disorder, or autism.

Attention-Deficit Hyperactivity Disorder

Although bright, seven-year-old Danny receives poor marks at school and constantly disrupts class by talking, fidgeting, throwing erasers, and picking fights. Danny suffers from **attention-deficit hyperactivity disorder,** also called *hyperkinetic syndrome,* one of the disorders psychologists recognize in infancy and childhood. When a child fails to complete tasks, is easily distracted, needs a lot of supervision, has difficulty sitting still, and generally acts before thinking, he or she may be exhibiting symptoms of attention-deficit hyperactivity disorder (ADHD).

Diagnosis and Symptoms. Attention-deficit hyperactivity disorders appear before age seven and are often evident before age three. They may disappear at puberty or continue into adolescence and adult life. The disorder appears in about three percent of children and is six to nine times more common in boys than in girls.

Attention-deficit hyperactivity disorder: A disorder of infancy, childhood, and adolescence beginning before age seven and characterized by restlessness, inattention, distractibility, and overactivity; also known as *hyperactive syndrome, hyperkinetic syndrome,* or *hyperkineses.*

Teachers are often the first to detect children with ADHD because school settings require attentive, focused behavior. Students with ADHD are unable to remain seated or pay attention, and they make careless, impulsive errors on homework and tests. In addition to having limited attention for schoolwork, they have difficulty in play activities (Lambert, 1988).

Nature or Nurture? Many researchers feel that the influence of biology in ADHD is significant. They support their claims with the following findings:

1. children who exhibit symptoms of ADHD are likely to have another family member with the disorder;
2. symptoms of the disorder are usually evident early in the child's life;
3. parents of these children report that they were unusually active babies;
4. many of these children were born prematurely;
5. many exhibit perceptual and motor deficits;
6. some exhibit abnormalities in their electroencephalograms;
7. these children may poorly tolerate low levels of arousal (Zentall, Faulkenberg, and Smith, 1985); and
8. many have allergy problems (Marshall, 1989).

Treatment. Treatments of ADHD may focus on drugs, diet, or a cognitive (thought) restructuring. The fact that some drugs can relieve symptoms bolsters the hypothesis that the disorder has a biological origin (e.g., Whalen et al., 1989). But the use of drugs often may have the unintentional effect of making youngsters perceive themselves as bad, thus lowering their self-esteem (Jensen, 1989). Currently, the most effective treatment of ADHD is a program of behavior modification at school and home, along with medication.

Autistic Disorder (Autism): A Pervasive Developmental Disorder

Often, children who suffer from problems of maladjustment grow up to be adults who suffer from the same problems. If you saw the 1988 movie *Rain Man* you are probably familiar with some aspects of autistic disorder, which has its origin in childhood. Here is a description of an autistic child; the similarities to the character that Dustin Hoffman played, Raymond Babbit, show the essential accuracy of the film:

> He habitually piled up all furniture and bedding in the center of the room. . . . He played repetitively with the same toys for months, lining things in rows, collected objects such as bottle tops, and insisted on having two of everything, one in each hand. He became extremely upset if interrupted and if the order or arrangement of things were altered. (GAJZAGO AND PRIOR, 1974, p. 264)

An **autistic disorder** (sometimes called *autism, early infantile autism,* or *infantile autism*) is a *pervasive developmental disorder;* that is, psychological development is severely affected in many areas simultaneously. Children with autistic disorder show gross distortions in development, language, communication, perception, motor ability, and reality testing.

Autistic disorder: A disorder of infancy, childhood, and adolescence beginning before age two and a half and characterized by lack of responsiveness to other people, gross impairment in language skills, and bizarre responses to the environment; also known as *early infantile autistic disorder,* or *autism.*

Symptoms. Autistic disorder, which begins before age two and a half, is fairly rare (only four to five cases in ten thousand people). Autistic infants lack the responsiveness of normal babies. They rarely if ever smile, are not cuddly, and seldom vocalize. As these infants mature physically, they communicate little or not at all, make no eye contact, lack play and social skills, and rarely seek comfort when distressed. Autistic children make repetitive motions characterized as bizarre and respond oddly to their environment. They show unusual interest in, and attachment to, various objects.

Nature or Nurture? The causes of autistic disorder are not well understood. Initially, researchers thought that cold, unresponsive parents were the cause (Kanner, 1943), but more recent research shows that parents of autistic children are quite normal (McAdoo and DeMeyer, 1978). Some behavioral researchers suggest that children with autistic disorder are not really withdrawn, but rather choose to manipulate the environment on their own terms—terms that exclude other people.

The causes of autistic disorder are most likely biological. Some assert that it is hard to distinguish autistic disorder from other brain disorders. Although there is probably a biological predisposition to autistic disorder, genetic studies are still inconclusive.

Treatment. Only a few cases of autistic disorder have been treated successfully, and they required an intensive therapeutic environment. Behavioral techniques emphasizing reinforcement of prosocial behaviors are effective in some cases (Schwartz and Johnson, 1985), and long-term follow-up shows that the effects of such behavior modification are long-lasting (Lovaas, 1987). Two-thirds of children with autistic disorder are severely handicapped, unable to lead independent lives. Only seventeen percent (Raymond Babbit would qualify) make adequate social adjustments and can be partially independent as adults.

♦ Identify three symptoms of an attention-deficit hyperactivity disorder (ADHD). p. 335
♦ Identify three symptoms of autistic disorders. p. 336

Focus on Learning

Key Terms

Zygote p. 302
Embryo p. 302
Fetus p. 302
Placenta p. 303
Teratogen p. 304
Labor p. 305
Babinski reflex p. 307
Moro reflex p. 307
Rooting p. 307

Sucking p. 307
Grasping p. 307
Bonding p. 308
Separation anxiety p. 311
Assimilation p. 316
Accommodation p. 317
Sensory-motor stage p. 318
Egocentrism p. 319
Decentration p. 319

Preoperational stage p. 319
Concrete operational stage p. 320
Conservation p. 320
Formal operational stage p. 321
Morality p. 324
Attention-deficit hyperactivity disorder p. 335
Autistic disorder p. 336

Summary

Theories of Child Development

- Psychologists are especially interested in discovering whether a developing infant's abilities, interests, and personality are determined by *nature* or by *nurture.*   p. 300

- *Reductionistic* theorists believe that if we can reduce an organism's behavior to its essential elements, we can explain it. The *organismic view* asserts that people go through qualitatively different developmental stages that cannot be reduced to simple elements. In a *contextual view,* all the events in an organism's life are related.   p. 301

The First Nine Months

- From the fifth through the forty-ninth day after conception, an unborn human being is called an embryo; from then until birth, it is called a fetus.   p. 302

- During the first month, the embryo begins to take shape. During the second month, the embryo begins to resemble a human being. In the third month, growth continues, features become more defined, and sex characteristics begin to appear.   pp. 302–304

Newborns, Infancy, and Early Childhood

- Human infants are born with a set of reflexes that include the rooting, sucking, Babinski, and Moro reflexes.   p. 307

- Newborns have surprisingly well-developed perceptual systems. They prefer complex visual fields, curved patterns, and human faces.   p. 308

- *Infancy* is the period from birth to eighteen months, and *childhood* is the period from eighteen months to about age thirteen.   p. 311

- As infants grow, the extent to which they focus on their caretakers increases significantly, as does their sense of attachment.   p. 313

Intellectual Development

- Piaget identified two processes for gaining new knowledge. Accommodation is modifying existing thought processes and frameworks of knowledge. Assimilation is absorbing, incorporating, and utilizing new information in a meaningful way.   p. 316

- Piaget believed that intellectual development occurs in a series of stages, each of which must be completed before the next stage begins.   p. 317

- At birth, infants are totally egocentric. Toward the end of the sensory-motor period, they begin the process of decentration, gradually moving away from total self-centeredness.   p. 319

Moral Reasoning

- Morality is a system of learned attitudes concerning ideal behavior.   p. 324

- Kohlberg showed that young children base their decisions about right or wrong on the likelihood of avoiding punishment.   pp. 325–326

- Whereas school-age children adopt conventional ideas of morality, adults adopt more mature views.   p. 326

Social Development

- As the child enters the preoperational stage, egocentrism gives way to increased social interaction.   p. 329

- During middle childhood boys and girls prefer same-sex play partners.   p. 330

- As a result of the immense increase in the number of women in the labor force since the 1950s, significant changes have occurred in child care arrangements.   p. 333

Psychological Disorders of Infancy and Childhood

- *Attention-deficit hyperactivity disorder* (ADHD) may be evident when a child fails to complete tasks, is easily distracted, needs a lot of supervision, has difficulty sitting still, and generally acts before thinking.   p. 335

- *Autistic disorder* is a *pervasive developmental disorder* in which development is severely affected in many areas simultaneously. Children with autistic disorders show gross distortions in development, language, perception, motor ability, and reality testing before age two.   p. 336

Connections

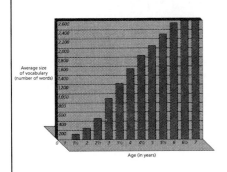

If you are interested in . . .	*Turn to . . .*	*To learn more about . . .*
The role of early childhood experiences in development	◆ Ch. 2, p. 59	The way the brain of a newborn is modifiable and continues to develop until age thirteen.
	◆ Ch. 7, p. 256	How language development proceeds very rapidly once it begins at about eighteen months of age.
	◆ Ch. 17, p. 627	How viewing violence and sexual situations on television proves to have longlasting effects on children.
Social development in childhood	◆ Ch. 11, pp. 394–398	The way children develop specific motives, for example, to achieve, succeed, or be successful.
	◆ Ch. 12, p. 427	Freud's view that the first six years of a child's life is crucial for later personality development.
	◆ Ch. 16, pp. 574–583	How a child's early interactions with parents, peers, church, and school shape his or her attitudes.
Gender differences in development	◆ Ch. 8, p. 289	How psychologists have found that cognitive differences in development are, in most cases, over-exaggerated.
	◆ Ch. 17, p. 628	The aggressive behaviors males and females exhibit and their different modes of expression.

10 Adolescence and Adulthood

"Simple Meaning" by Elizabeth Murray

*I*n the past year Marlene has matured physically into a woman, yet her parents sometimes treat her like a child. She is eager to finish her senior year in high school but worries about leaving friends and family to start college. She constantly asks herself what sort of career she should have. Although she finds her life exciting, Marlene is looking forward to becoming an adult and leaving the uncertainty of adolescence behind.

Like Marlene, Luis is undergoing a transition in his life. Although still physically fit, the thirty-nine-year-old baseball star now needs to wear contact lenses in order to hit a fast pitch, and he finds it increasingly difficult to keep up with the younger players. Luis says he will retire as a baseball player next year and devote more time to coaching and to his family.

At seventy-five, Sierra finds life more rewarding now than ever before. Her youngest child left home to start his own family years ago, and since then Sierra has devoted most of her spare time to painting. She and her husband have opened a gallery in which they sell her artwork. But

Sierra is struggling with the physical challenges of old age, including arthritis, which threatens to end her painting career.

Every age—infancy, childhood, adolescence, early adulthood, and late adulthood—brings its own particular joys and difficulties. Psychologists see aging as a process of continued growth that is influenced by a person's biological inheritance, life experiences, frame of mind, and a certain amount of chance. For example, moving from one state to another changes people's lives; a divorce is unsettling; a death in the family can be devastating; winning the lottery can jolt a person from poverty to luxury and from anonymity to fame. So, in addition to normal predictable maturational and developmental changes, a once-in-a-lifetime happening can permanently alter physical, personality, and social development. In this chapter we will discuss some of the developmental changes that occur during adolescence and adulthood, and trace the psychological processes that underlie these stages of development.

Adolescence

In our culture, the transition from childhood to adulthood brings dramatic intellectual, social, emotional, and physical changes. Generally, this transition occurs between the ages of twelve and twenty, a period known as *adolescence,* when children bridge the gap to adulthood. Although adolescents are in many ways like adults—they are nearly mature physically and mentally, and their moral development is fairly advanced—their emotional development may be far from complete.

Adolescence is often referred to as a time of storm and stress, and for some adolescents this is indeed the case. It is the popular stereotype that adolescents are in a state of conflict resulting in part from the lack of congruity in their physical, intellectual, social, and emotional development. Consider alcohol abuse. Most adolescents know, intellectually, that drinking is illegal, harmful, and potentially deadly when combined with driving. Yet most are not mature enough to stand up to peer pressure by making a conscious decision not to drink.

The idea of storm and stress in adolescence is not the whole picture. Many adolescents go through this period of multiple changes without sig-

FIGURE 10.1
The world of the adolescent has sometimes been characterized as being between childhood and adulthood but belonging to neither.

Children   Adolescents   Adults

nificant psychological difficulty. According to Petersen (1988), adolescence may be a challenging life period, just as adulthood is, but only eleven percent of adolescents have serious difficulties. Thirty-two percent have only sporadic difficulties. And fifty-seven percent of adolescents have basically positive, healthy development during these teenage years. The current consensus among psychologists is that adolescence is not ordinarily a time of great psychological turmoil (Powers, Hauser, and Kilner, 1989).

Adolescence in Cultural Context

Adolescence has not always been seen as a problem period, nor is it considered so in all societies today. Some experts link the "invention" of the adolescent life-stage with social and historical events. In the middle of the nineteenth century, street waifs in large cities roamed the streets as pickpockets, prostitutes, and purse snatchers, and many used drugs, including opium. By 1860, 30,000 young people lived by their wits on the streets of New York City. Their plight led to a reform movement that put many of them in school and helped stretch the age of independence from fourteen to eighteen.

Today, it is common for an American teenager to feel as if "no one understands me," but it's difficult to imagine a teenaged tribeswoman growing up in the jungles of New Guinea expressing the same sentiment. Thus, the problems of adolescence must be considered in a cultural context. Even when they grow up in the same country, adolescents experience life's joys and disappointments in different ways. Some come from disadvantaged cultural or economic groups, perhaps from a Chicago ghetto or an Indian reservation; some grow up in luxury, perhaps in a wealthy suburb of Los Angeles; others are exposed to racial prejudice, drug and alcohol abuse, nonsupportive families, or other stressful situations that lead them to feel powerless in controlling their own lives.

Unfortunately, most of the research on adolescence has been conducted on white, middle-class American teenagers. But researchers now understand that the life experiences of whites, Navajos, Hispanics, African-Americans, Asian-Americans, and other groups are not all alike, and each year more studies compare the experiences of different groups and sensitize both professionals and the public to cultural differences.

Research has concentrated on the life experiences of white, middle-class American teenagers. Recognizing that the lives of adolescents such as this girl growing up on an Indian reservation are different, psychologists are now seeking to expand their understanding of cultural diversity.

Physical Development

The words *adolescence* and *puberty* are often used interchangeably, but in fact they mean different things. **Puberty** is the period during which the reproductive system matures; it occurs at (and signals) the end of childhood. **Adolescence** is the period extending from the onset of puberty to early adulthood. Psychologists observe this distinction when studying adolescence. See Figure 10.1.

The onset of puberty varies widely; some girls begin to mature physically as early as age eight, some boys at nine or ten (Marshall and Tanner, 1969). The average age of puberty is thirteen, plus or minus a year or two. Just before the onset of puberty, boys and girls experience significant growth spurts, gaining as much as five inches in a single year.

By the end of the first or second year of the growth spurt, body proportions, fat distribution, bones and muscles, and physical strength and agility change. In addition, the hormonal system produces secondary sex

Puberty: The period during which the reproductive system matures; it occurs at (and signals) the end of childhood.

Adolescence: The period extending from the onset of puberty to early adulthood.

characteristics. **Secondary sex characteristics** are the physical features of a person's gender identity not directly involved with reproduction. Boys experience an increase in body mass, as well as growth of pubic, underarm, and facial hair. Girls experience an increase in the size of the breasts, widening of the hips, and growth of underarm and pubic hair. Puberty ends with maturation of the reproductive organs, at which time boys produce sperm and girls produce ova and begin to menstruate. These physical changes generally take several years to complete, and the maturing adolescent may find them both exciting and disturbing.

Puberty has received a good deal of research attention. For example, as boys pass through puberty, they feel more positive about their bodies, while girls are more likely to have negative feelings. Researchers assert that puberty itself does not create psychological maladjustment. As Petersen argues (1988), becoming an adolescent means emerging as an adult, socially and sexually; while new forces are coming to bear on the self-images of adolescents, the new status is desirable for most adolescents.

Social Development

In junior high school the most popular boys complete puberty at an early age. Boys who mature early often enjoy several advantages, including increased confidence, superior athletic prowess, greater sexual appeal, and higher expectations from teachers and parents. Early maturing girls, on the other hand, seem to be at a disadvantage because their female peers often treat them as the "odd woman out." Thus, the development of a teenager's personality is affected by both the timing of puberty, a biological factor, and how people react to that timing, an environmental factor. Parents and teachers can help both early- and late-maturing adolescents with feelings about body image. Research shows that involvement with athletics can serve as a buffer against the negative feelings that arise during this period. Increased time spent in sports is associated with increased satisfaction and higher self-ratings of strength and attractiveness. Physical activity is associated with achievement, weight reduction, muscle tone, and stress-reduction, all of which aid a positive self-image (Kirshnit, Richards, and Ham, 1988).

Environmental factors that influence adolescents' social development and self-image affect their later adult behavior. The two most important groups of people who influence the social behavior of adolescents are parents and peers. There is no question that adolescents are responsive to parental influence. If their views are sharply different from their parents' they put up serious resistance only in life-altering decisions (Scherer and Reppucci, 1988). In comparing peer and parental influence, studies disagree, but most indicate that adolescents' attitudes fall somewhere between those of their parents and their peers (e.g., Kelly and Goodwin, 1983).

Peer Groups. The influence of peer groups is formidable; *peer groups* are people who identify with and compare themselves to each other. Peer groups often consist of people of the same age, sex, and race, although adolescents may change their peer group memberships and belong to more than one group. As adolescents spend more time away from parents and home, they experience increasing pressure to conform to the values of their peer group.

Peer groups are a source of information about society, educational aspirations, and group activities. Peers set standards for adolescents; they sometimes praise, sometimes cajole, and constantly pressure one another to

Secondary sex characteristics: The physical features of a person's gender identity that are not directly involved with reproduction, such as pubic hair.

Peer groups exert tremendous influence on adolescents—positive, negative, or even destructive.

conform to behavioral standards, including dress styles, social interaction, and forms of rebellion like drug taking or shoplifting. Most important, they influence the adolescent's developing self-concept. Recognizing the importance of peer pressure among the young, the administrations of Presidents Reagan and Bush attempted to curb drug abuse among teenagers by instituting the "Just Say No" campaign, encouraging teenagers to say no to peers who offered them drugs.

Influence among friends and peers is important, but research (Fisher and Bauman, 1988) indicates that adolescents may align themselves with others who are similar in order to maintain support for their own behavior. Thus, drinkers, marijuana users, or cocaine users might associate with one another, and at the same time, reject others not similarly inclined. This limits the ability of peers to "say no" and influence non-like-minded adolescents.

Gender Differences: Behavior and Mental Processes

Gender differences are differences between males and females in behavior or mental processes. Research on the biological factors that affect gender differences has been extensive, and has shown few if any important differences between the sexes. Learning and experience, the way a person is raised and taught, have a far more profound impact on behaviors in which there seems to be a difference between the genders.

Gender Identity. As noted earlier, a key feature of adolescence is that it is a period of transition and change. Adolescents must develop their own *identities,* a sense of themselves as independent, mature individuals. One important aspect of identity is **gender identity,** a person's sense of being

Gender differences: Differences between males and females in behavior or mental processes.

Gender identity: A person's sense of being male or female.

Gender schema theory: The theory that asserts that children and adolescents use gender as an organizing theme to classify and understand their perceptions about the world.

Sex roles: The full range of behaviors that are generally associated with one's gender; they help people establish who they are; also called *gender roles*.

Sex-role stereotyping: The typical beliefs concerning the patterns of behavior that are expected of persons depending on their gender.

male or female. Children develop a sense of gender identity by age three; by age four or five, children realize that their identity is permanent; and by age eight children know that alteration in their hair, clothes, or behavior does not alter their gender. As we saw in chapter 9, boys and girls separate themselves from one another based on gender—playgrounds of elementary schools are divided on gender lines. In older children and young adolescents, bodies change in appearance rapidly, sometimes in unpredictable ways. During this time, boys and girls often try out various types of behaviors, including those relating to male-female relationships and dating. Some young adolescents become extreme in their orientation toward maleness or femaleness. Boys, especially in groups, may become aggressive and boisterous; girls may act submissive, be overly concerned with their looks, and focus on bonding with other girls. This exaggeration of traditional male or female behaviors is often short-lived.

Many psychologists believe that once gender identity is firmly established, children and then adolescents attempt to bring their behavior and thoughts within generally accepted gender specific roles. **Gender schema theory** asserts that children and adolescents use gender as an organizing theme to classify and understand their perceptions about the world (Bem, 1985; Maccoby, 1988). Young children use gender as a social category. In doing so, appropriate and inappropriate gender behaviors are decided on. In fact, many children's and adolescents' self-esteem and feelings of worth become tied to their gender-based perceptions about themselves, many of which are determined by identification with the same sex parent (Heilbrun, Wydra, and Friedberg, 1989). For example, they may relate their self-worth to how much their behavior matches that of other adult males or females, or how well they fulfill society's view of sex (gender) roles.

Sex Roles. **Sex roles** are the full range of behaviors generally associated with one's gender; they help people establish who they are. But in the course of establishing a sexual identity, people sometimes adopt **sex-role stereotyping.** That is, they learn gender-based behaviors that are strongly expected, regulated, and reinforced by society. Men, for example, may learn to hide their emotions, since society frowns on men who cry in public and reinforces men who appear strong and stoic when faced with sorrow or stress. Gender-based ideas about professions are especially likely to become stereotyped. Even today, how many little girls aspire to be doctors, fire fighters, or president of the United States? Sex-role stereotypes are difficult to change; from the early 1970s to the early 1980s, for example, the percentage of males in nursing, teaching, and social work remained low, even though many people's attitudes became more accepting of men in these professions.

In the workplace, sex-role stereotypes still heavily influence wages and promotions. On average, women earn sixty-six cents for each dollar that a man earns. Although fifty percent of law school classes are women, only about ten percent of partners in large law firms are women (Repa, 1988). Although women are taking positions of higher responsibility in corporate America, still only two percent of senior executives are female.

Parents are the first and most important sources of gender-based stereotyping; they influence a child in the earliest years. Peers and schools are especially important sources of information as well (Maccoby, 1990). In addition, the media, especially television, has a profound impact on people's perceptions. When we view old television shows that portray men and women in strongly sex-stereotyped roles, they sometimes seem ludicrous. Lucy Ricardo always played the scheming, dizzy redhead in *I Love Lucy.*

Sex-role stereotypes are very difficult to change; even today, relatively few women plan to become firefighters and few men intend to teach in day care centers.

June and Ward Cleaver have well-defined, traditional gender roles in *Leave It to Beaver*; you would never find Ward doing the laundry.

Androgynous: The condition in which some typically male and some typically female characteristics are apparent in one individual.

Androgyny. Asserting a gender identity in adolescence has always been part of the transition to adulthood. Today, this task is more complicated, especially for women. In earlier decades women were expected to pursue marriage and homemaking, which were considered full-time careers. Today, women's plans often include a career outside the home, which may be interrupted for childbearing. Since the 1970s, however, many men and women have developed new attitudes about sex roles, encouraging *both* traditionally masculine and traditionally feminine traits. They have deliberately adopted **androgynous** behaviors, those that are shared by both sexes. Thus, both men and women fix cars, have careers, do housework, and help care for children. A number of studies have found that people who rate high in androgynous characteristics tend to feel more fulfilled and more competent when dealing with social and personal issues (Bem, 1975; Worell, 1978).

Differences in Abilities. Often boys and girls align themselves with members of their own gender based on abilities and as a way to compare themselves to each other. But the reality is that cognitive differences between boys and girls, and among male and female adolescents, are minimal, and in most cases nonexistent. As we saw in chapter 8, gender differences in verbal ability are so small that researchers should not say that they exist (Hyde and Linn, 1988) and when they exist in mathematical abilities, differences are very small (Hyde, Fennema, and Lamon, 1990). The differences found today exist only in certain special populations, for example in the very brightest mathematics students where the boys continue to outscore girls (Benbow and Stanley, 1983). In general, whatever cognitive differences may have existed between the sexes are now disappearing (Feingold, 1988b). This does not mean that some differences are not apparent in certain tests (such as the SAT), but that when cultural variables are extracted, the differences are small, unimportant, and refer to overall group differences which obscure individual accomplishments. This means that a specific female may outperform, outanalyze, or outwrite a specific male. Group differences obscure individual accomplishments.

There is no doubt that men and women are different—biological differences certainly exist—but researchers are still trying to sort out basic intellectual differences to determine if they exist and under what conditions. Biologically based mechanisms may account for some gender-based behaviors, but learning is far more potent in establishing and maintaining sex-role stereotypes and gender-specific attitudes (see chapter 5, pp. 192–195). Our society continues to reinforce gender-based activities. This shapes the behavior of children and adolescents into sex roles. But as our society's view changes, so will gender-based activities, including some sexual behaviors, considered next.

Sexual Behavior

In human beings, learned attitudes have a greater influence than biological factors in determining sexual behavior, and people first learn about such relationships at home. Children are affected by their parents' attitudes and behavior—whether, for instance, they hug and kiss openly, seem embarrassed by their bodies, or talk freely about sexual matters. The influence of parents in sexual matters was shown in a study that examined how parents' discipline and control influence teenagers' sexual attitudes and behavior. Miller et al. (1986) surveyed more than two thousand teenagers and their parents about parental discipline and teenage sexual behavior. The results showed that sexual permissiveness and intercourse were more frequent among adolescents who viewed their parents as not having rules or not being strict. Sexual behaviors, especially intercourse, were less frequent among teenagers who reported that their parents were moderately strict. In addition, close relationships with parents and feelings of support have been associated with later ages of first intercourse (Brooks-Gunn and Furstenberg, 1989).

Relaxed Attitudes. American adolescents now view sexual intimacy as an important and normal part of growing up, and premarital heterosexual activity has become increasingly common among adolescents, especially thirteen- to seventeen-year-olds. One study found that sixty percent of white male teenagers had had intercourse by age eighteen, and sixty percent of white girls just a year later, by age nineteen. For blacks, sixty percent of males had had intercourse by age sixteen, and females, sixty percent by age eighteen. There are great individual differences in the age of first intercourse and its subsequent frequency; it is not uncommon for a first intercourse to occur at age fourteen or fifteen, and then for the teenager not to have relations again for a year or two (Furstenberg, Brooks-Gunn, and Chase-Lansdale, 1989). Dreyer (1982) suggests several reasons for early expression of sexual behavior:

1. Adolescents are reaching sexual maturity at younger ages than in previous decades;
2. knowledge and use of contraception are becoming more widespread, thus eliminating fears of pregnancy;
3. adults' sexual attitudes and behavior are changing; and
4. adolescents consider sexual behavior normal in an intimate relationship.

More relaxed attitudes about adolescent sexual behavior have brought about increased awareness of contraception and the problems of teenage pregnancy. Nevertheless, in the late 1980s one in ten teenage girls became pregnant—in fact, by the middle of the decade, nineteen percent of white females and forty-one percent of black females became pregnant by age eighteen (Furstenberg, Brooks-Gunn, and Chase-Lansdale, 1989). More than one million teenage girls become pregnant each year in the United States, and nearly 470,000 give birth. The consequences of childbearing for teen mothers are great; a young woman's chances for future education and employment become more limited, and many young women are forced to rely on public assistance. Most studies indicate that early childbearing women will not achieve economic equality with women who postpone parenthood until they are adults (Furstenberg, Brooks-Gunn, and Chase-Lansdale, 1989).

A variety of trends, including improved transportation and communication, the women's movement, and more equal opportunities in education, are erasing the differences between the sexual behavior of men and women (Sprecher, McKinney, and Orbuch, 1987). Today, almost forty percent of twenty-year-old women have had at least one pregnancy as a teenager—

that is, about one million teenagers—and fifteen percent have had an abortion (Furstenberg, Brooks-Gunn, and Chase-Lansdale, 1989). In fact, current studies show that despite the fear of AIDS, teenagers and college students continue to engage in regular sexual activity.

Contraception. Not using contraception is the principal reason for teenage pregnancy. Morrison (1985) asserts that teenagers are still largely uninformed or ill-informed about reproductive physiology and contraception. Too many underestimate the likelihood of pregnancy and have negative attitudes toward contraception, although they have trouble explaining why. Low levels of self-esteem and feelings of powerlessness and alienation are also associated with the personalities of those who fail to use contraceptives. But as teenagers become older and more sexually active, they tend to use contraception more responsibly (Brooks-Gunn and Furstenberg, 1989). School-based, comprehensive health-care programs that emphasize the complete picture of sexuality (attitudes, contraception, motivation, behavior) reduce the risks of teenage pregnancy (Ford Foundation, 1989). Not surprisingly, younger adolescents in less committed, less stable relationships are less likely to use contraceptives (Milan and Kilmann, 1987), or to make careful decisions about unwanted pregnancies (Gerrard, 1987). The data show that older, more mature men and women are more likely to use contraception (Brooks-Gunn and Furstenberg, 1989), but among college students condom use still does not reach fifty percent (De Buono, et al., 1990).

Erik Erikson and the Search for Identity

Society does not make it easy for adolescents to form an image of who they are and what they want in life. After years of being allowed to behave like children, suddenly they are expected to behave like adults. Trying to achieve the freedom and responsibilities of adulthood, such as taking responsibility for contraception while giving up the security of childhood, can create stress. Marlene, introduced at the beginning of this chapter, is nervous about the enormous decisions she is facing as she prepares to leave high school, friends, and family to attend college and choose a career path.

Erikson's Theory. Perhaps no one is more closely associated with the challenges of adolescence than Erik H. Erikson (1902–), who studied with Freud in Austria. Erikson's theory is noted for its integration of a person's disposition and environment with historical forces in shaping that person's life. With sharp insight, a linguistic flair, and a logical, coherent approach to studying human behavior, Erik Erikson is a key figure in the history of psychology.

Erikson believed in adolescence as a time of identity formation and explained how the "identity crisis" would shape the adult each adolescent would eventually become.

Erikson saw that environment-person relationships were interactive; he asserted that people have to accept responsibility for their lives and their place in history. Nowhere is this idea more evident than in adolescence. According to Erikson, the growth and turmoil of adolescence creates an "identity crisis," and the major task for adolescents is to resolve that crisis successfully by forming an *identity*. Failure to complete the process leaves the adolescent confused about adult roles and unable to cope with the demands of adulthood, including the development of mature relationships with members of the opposite sex (Erikson, 1963, 1968).

Erikson believed that people form self-images from their perceptions of themselves as well as from other people's perceptions of them (expressed through behavior). Membership in political, religious, or ideological groups, for example, helps adolescents discover what they believe in and what satisfies their needs. Erikson maintains that personality development continues throughout life.

Erikson's theory describes a continuum of stages, dilemmas, or crises through which all individuals must pass. Each stage can have either a positive or a negative outcome. New dilemmas emerge as a person grows older and faces new responsibilities, tasks, and social relationships. A person may experience a dilemma as an opportunity and face it positively or view the dilemma as a catastrophe and fail to cope with it effectively. For example, an adolescent may be pressured to engage in drug use or shoplifting; whether the teen succumbs to pressure or emerges as a victor able to withstand peer pressure affects his or her self-image. To emerge as a fully mature, stable adult, a person has to pass through each stage successfully. Table 10.1 lists the stages of Erikson's theory and the important events, crises, dilemmas, and opportunities associated with them. We will take a closer look at each stage.

Erikson's Eight Stages of Development. Stages one through four of Erikson's theory cover birth through age twelve. Stage one involves the development of *basic trust versus basic mistrust.* During their first months,

TABLE 10.1
Erikson's Eight Stages of Psychosocial Development

Stages	Approximate Age	Important Event	Description
1. Basic trust vs. basic mistrust	Birth to 12–18 months	Feeding	The infant must form a first loving, trusting relationship with the caregiver, or develop a sense of mistrust.
2. Autonomy vs. shame/doubt	18 months to 3 years	Toilet training	The child's energies are directed toward the development of physical skills, including walking, grasping, and sphincter control. The child learns control but may develop shame and doubt if not handled well.
3. Initiative vs. guilt	3 to 6 years	Independence	The child continues to become more assertive and to take more initiative, but may be too forceful, leading to guilt feelings.
4. Industry vs. inferiority	6 to 12 years	School	The child must deal with demands to learn new skills or risk a sense of inferiority, failure, and incompetence.
5. Identity vs. role confusion	Adolescence	Peer relationships	The teenager must achieve a sense of identity in occupation, sex roles, politics, and religion.
6. Intimacy vs. isolation	Young adulthood	Love relationships	The young adult must develop intimate relationships or suffer feelings of isolation.
7. Generativity vs. stagnation	Middle adulthood	Parenting	Each adult must find some way to satisfy and support the next generation.
8. Ego integrity vs. despair	Late adulthood	Reflection on and acceptance of one's life	The culmination is a sense of acceptance of oneself as one is and of feeling fulfilled.

infants make distinctions about the world and decide whether it is a comfortable, loving place in which they can feel basic trust. At this stage they develop beliefs about the essential truthfulness of other people. If their needs are adequately met, they learn that the world is a predictable and safe place. Infants whose needs are not met learn to distrust the world. During the second stage, the toddler must resolve the crisis of *autonomy versus shame and doubt*. Success in toilet training and other tasks involving control leads to a sense of autonomy and more mature behavior. Difficulties dealing with autonomy during this stage result in fears and a sense of shame and doubt.

The third stage, which occurs at ages four and five, is that of *initiative versus guilt*, when children develop the ability to use their own initiative. During this stage, they either gain a sense of independence and good feelings about themselves or develop a sense of guilt, lack of acceptance, and negative feelings about their sexuality. If children learn to dress themselves, clean their rooms, and develop friendships with other children, they can feel a sense of mastery; alternatively they can be dependent or regretful. In stage four, *industry versus inferiority*, children either develop feelings of competence and confidence in their abilities or experience failure, inferiority, and feelings of incompetence.

Stage five, *identity versus role confusion*, marks the end of childhood and the beginning of adolescence. At this time adolescents must decide who they are and what they want to do in life. Otherwise, they will become confused and rebellious. The special problems of adolescence—including rebellion, suicide, and drug abuse—must be dealt with. During stage six, *intimacy versus isolation*, young adults begin to select other people with whom they can form intimate relationships. They learn to relate on a warm, social basis with members of the opposite sex. The alternative is to become isolated.

In stage seven, *generativity versus stagnation*, people hope to convey information, love, and warmth to others, particularly their children. As adults they hope to influence their family and the world; otherwise, they will stagnate, feeling that life is unexciting. In Erikson's eighth stage, *ego integrity versus despair*, people decide whether their existence is meaningful, happy, and cohesive or wasteful and unproductive. Many individuals never complete stage eight; those who do feel fulfilled, with a sense that they understand, at least partly, what life is about. Erikson describes this final stage:

> Only he who has somehow taken care of things and people and has adapted himself to the triumphs and disappointments of being, by necessity, the originator of others and generator of things and ideas—only he may gradually grow the fruit of the seven stages. I know no better word for it than integrity . . . It is the acceptance of one's own life cycle and the people who have become significant to it as something that had to be and that, by necessity, permitted no substitutions . . . and an acceptance of the fact that one's life is one's own responsibility. (1959, p. 104)

A key point of Erikson's theory is that people go through each stage, resolving the crises of that stage as best they can. Of course, people grow older whether or not they are ready for the next stage. A person may still have unresolved conflicts, opportunities, and dilemmas from the previous stage. This can cause anxiety and discomfort, and make resolution of advanced stages more difficult. Because adolescence is such a crucial stage for the formation of a firm identity, an adolescent's home environment becomes particularly influential. In the United States today, that experience is often a home with only one parent, or a home with one parent then joined by a step-parent—the topic we consider next.

Life in a One-Parent Family

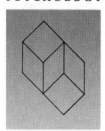

Of the approximately 62 million family households in the United States, about one out of every four is a single-parent household, and most of these parents are women. This family situation can be particularly problematic for some adolescents, although as the number of one-parent families has increased, some of the problems seem to have lessened.

A father's absence may be due to death, desertion, separation, or divorce, among other things. Well-known researcher Mavis Hetherington points out that almost half the children born in the last decade will experience the divorce of their parents (Hetherington, Stanley-Hagan, and Anderson, 1989). Most of these children will also experience the remarriage of their parents. The responses of children to these rapidly changing situations are diverse. Some children of divorced parents seem less able to cope than those who have lost their fathers through death. They often have to deal with parental conflict, the divorce process itself, and continuing disagreements between their parents. They may blame themselves, and as a result, their self-esteem, which is just beginning to strengthen, suffers. Children of divorce often refuse to accept its permanency (Wallerstein and Blakeslee, 1989). This is especially true of emerging adolescents who tend to be affected by a divorce more than very young children or older adolescents.

The negative effects of an absent father are sometimes different for boys than for girls. Boys seem sometimes to have a harder time, perhaps because they do not have as many opportunities to interact with adult men, and they often learn masculine behaviors (sometimes highly stereotyped ones) from peers (Wallerstein and Blakeslee, 1989). Girls can also have a hard time when their father is absent. They see boys as having more freedom and status, while they must struggle for independence. Also, girls from one-parent homes report less positive attitudes toward their fathers, and more sexual experimentation, than girls from two-parent homes. Gender differences do not always appear; sometimes the differences, when apparent, disappear by late adolescence. Wallerstein and Blakeslee argue that girls may not appear to be affected as much as boys, but in later adolescence they show the negative effects. One of the problems in researching children and divorce is that large representative samples are seldom used (Allison and Furstenberg, 1989).

Some children and adolescents exhibit remarkable resiliency. In fact, Hetherington asserts that in the long run, some may actually be strengthened by having to cope with their family transitions (Hetherington, Stanley-Hagan, and Anderson, 1989). The impact of single-parent homes is changing rapidly; whereas two decades ago children of divorce were bound to have a tough time, today many parents and their children are coping well.

In addition, women and their children, who were once at extreme economic disadvantages after a divorce, are faring better due to better education and job opportunities that make them better off financially. Another reason one-parent families are doing better is that parents are increasingly sharing custody and working together toward the best interests of their children. There is a long way to go because many parents still have contentious relationships with spouses, but therapists, the courts, and parents themselves are working in the proper direction. In addition, most people remarry after a divorce; thus, the time a child or an adolescent spends in a single-parent household can be a transitional period between life with a nondivorced, often conflict-ridden parent and life in a step-family. As Hetherington and her colleagues maintain, "Divorce and remarriage can remove children from stressful and acrimonious family relationships and many children eventually emerge as competent or even enhanced individuals" (Hetherington, Stanley-Hagan, and Anderson, 1989, p. 310). ◆

- ◆ Gender-based behaviors are strongly expected, regulated, and reinforced by society. Name three that affect behavior. p. 346
- ◆ What are androgynous behaviors? p. 347
- ◆ In each of Erikson's eight stages, people face dilemmas. What are the overall consequences of a poor outcome at any one stage or dilemma? p. 350

Adulthood

Adults in the 1990s have vastly different life experiences from those of adults of the 1950s whose lives followed predictable and prescribed timetables. People married when they were in their late teens or early twenties and had children soon after. Wives stayed at home to raise the children while their husbands went to work to support the family. Today's adults are marrying later, some not at all, and parenting is being postponed. While some women choose to stay at home to raise the children, many are concentrating on their careers, working side by side with their male coworkers. Many grown children are returning to the nest after college, and divorce has broken up numerous families. The 1950s stereotype of a well-ordered, simple family structure has changed sharply, and in a relatively short period of time.

The American adult life experience of the 1990s is also different from that of other cultures. Americans share some commonalities with people from other Western cultures, but their experience is vastly different from that in third world countries. But these differences have been studied little. Until the 1970s, developmental psychologists focused their work largely on white middle-class children, especially during infancy and early childhood.

Psychologists focus on development throughout the entire life span, recognizing that new challenges are faced in every stage of a person's life. They study adult development by looking at the factors that contribute to

The average American adult leads a vastly different life than that of an adult in any third world country.

	Young Adulthood 18–25	Early Adulthood 25–40	Middle Adulthood 40–65
Physical Change	Peak functioning in most physical skills; optimum time for child-bearing		
Cognitive Change	Cognitive skills high on most measures		
Work Roles	Choose career, which may involve several job changes; low work satisfaction is common		
Personality Development	Conformist; task of intimacy		
Major Tasks	Separate from family; form partnership; begin family; find job; create individual life pattern		

♦   *Building Table 10.1*   ♦

A Summary of Major Changes in Important Domains of Adult Functioning

stability or frustration, to a sense of accomplishment or feelings of despair, and to physical factors that may affect functioning. Researchers today are also examining the differences between men and women, with a special emphasis on the unique experiences of women in U.S. culture. Minorities are being studied and theories now are recognizing and focusing on cultural diversity. Building Table 10.1 summarizes the major changes in adult functioning that occur in young adulthood.

Physical Development

Although physical development in adulthood is slower, less dramatic, and sometimes less visible than in childhood and adolescence, it does occur. Luis, introduced at the beginning of this chapter, is a successful major league baseball player. But at thirty-nine, his batting average is not as impressive as it once was, and he can no longer run as fast as some of his younger teammates. Barbara Newman (1982) traced various types of physical changes that occur in adulthood. Some of her findings are discussed here.

Fitness Changes. Fitness involves both a psychological and a physical sense of well-being. Physically, human beings are at their peak of agility, speed, and strength between ages eighteen and thirty. From thirty to forty there is some loss of agility and speed. And between forty and sixty, much greater losses occur. In general, strength, muscle tone, and overall fitness deteriorate from age thirty on. People become more susceptible to disease; respiratory, circulatory, and blood pressure problems are more apparent; lung capacity and physical strength are significantly reduced.

Sexual Changes. In adulthood, sexual changes occur in adults of both sexes; for example, in women there is often an increase in sexual desire; but in men, erections are less rapidly achieved. In these childbearing years, women and men's sexual desires are sometimes modulated by the stresses of raising a family and juggling a work schedule. For women, mid-life changes in hormones lead to the cessation of ovulation and menstruation at about age fifty, a process known as *menopause*. At about the same age, men's testosterone levels decrease, their ejaculations are weaker and briefer, and their desire for sexual intercourse decreases from adolescent levels.

Sensory Changes. In early adulthood most sensory abilities remain fairly stable, and many women and men increase in fitness and better nutrition. But as the years pass, adults must contend with inevitable sensory losses. Reaction time slows; visual acuity decreases; and the risks of glaucoma and retinal detachment increase. Hearing loss also occurs. By age sixty, most people can no longer hear very high-frequency sounds, and some are unable to hear ordinary speech. During his Presidency, for example, Ronald Reagan suffered from a serious hearing loss despite being in generally good health otherwise.

Social Development: Mid-Life Crises

It is popular to believe that people pass through predictable life crises. In the movies, a mid-life crisis is seen as a time when people reevaluate their choices, change their lives, reorient, become depressed in the process, buy

A mid-life transition, popularly believed to occur around age forty, may or may not be experienced as a crisis.

a fast sports car, and perhaps throw over their spouse for another. The idea that people between thirty-five and forty-five will have a life crisis is widely accepted and considered almost inevitable.

But are crises unavoidable? Does everyone go through a mid-life crisis? We know that people go through transitions. At certain junctures, new decisions must be made and people must reassess who they are, where they are going, and how they want to get there. However, a distinction should be drawn between the idea of a *transition* and a *crisis*. A transition suggests that a person has reached a time in life when old ways of coping no longer work, old tasks have been accomplished, and new methods of living are forthcoming. A person in transition must face new dilemmas, challenges, and responsibilities, which often require reassessment, reappraisal, and development of new skills. A *crisis*, by contrast, occurs when old ways of coping become ineffective and a person is helpless, not knowing what to do, and needing new, radically different coping strategies. Crises are often perceived as painful turning points, catastrophes in a person's life.

Not everyone experiences the infamous mid-life crisis, but most people pass through a mid-life transition, and some pass through two, three, or even more transitions. Often a transition occurs at the beginning of adulthood when people must give up adolescent freedom and accept adult responsibilities. At around age thirty, another transition may occur when career and relationships begun in a person's twenties are reevaluated and sometimes rejected. In the transitions of early and middle adulthood, people reorient their career and family choices—the mid-life "crisis" at about age forty. Sometimes parents experience another transition when their children leave the home—often called the empty nest syndrome. It is less likely to occur in people who are engaged in paid employment outside the home (Adelmann, Antonucci, Crohan, and Coleman, 1989). Transitions also occur at retirement, not only for the retiree, but for his or her spouse.

Consider Sarah. Sarah, a single forty-four-year-old, has operated her own greeting card distributing company for twenty years. Although the company earns her a comfortable living, it has yet to produce enough profits to enable Sarah to establish a retirement fund, and she worries about how she'll make ends meet in another twenty years. Moreover, Sarah would like to try another vocation, perhaps a career in interior decorating. Although she finds the idea of a career change exciting, Sarah questions whether she has the skill and energy to start over. Friends say Sarah is experiencing a mid-life crisis. But Sarah may emerge from her situation a happier, wiser, and more secure adult.

People who experience mid-life transitions normally show no evidence of increased maladjustment, or increased suicides or alcoholism. For some people, however, mid-life changes can be difficult. The mid-life change must be examined for each individual, rather than across all individuals. Like the adolescents in storm and stress, some adults face crises in their lives, while others merely go through transitions that are not perceived as difficult or painful, depending on their unique personalities and ways of coping with the world. The term mid-life crisis may itself be a misnomer; as Levinson (1980) suggests, it should more properly be called a mid-life transition—a transition that may be more difficult for some individuals than others.

Personality Development

A basic tenet of personality theory is that, regardless of day-to-day variations, an individual's personality remains stable over time. That is, despite the frequently observed deviations from "normal" patterns or stages of development, the way people cope with life tends to remain fairly consistent throughout their lifetimes. But research shows that personality may be sensitive to the unique experiences of the individual, especially during the adult years. According to Haan, Millsap, and Hartka (1986), children's and adolescents' personalities tend to remain stable, while those of adults change over time. The researchers collected data from a longitudinal sample of subjects who were asked to describe themselves on variables such as self-confidence, assertiveness, dependability, and warmth. They found important shifts in many variables once the subjects reached adulthood. Adults are likely to be more assertive and self-confident than when they were younger, for example. Further, major life events, such as a child's tragic death, a highly stressful job situation, or a divorce, can alter a person's overall outlook on life. However, the data from this study are not easily generalized because the researchers did not take into account changing societal values and expectations. Nevertheless, the data suggest that the adult years are filled with great personal challenges and opportunities and therefore are the years in which people need to be innovative, flexible, and adaptive.

Positive changes during adulthood—developing a sense of generativity, fulfilling yearnings for love and respect—usually depend on some degree of success at earlier life stages. Adults who continue to operate with youthful ideals and false assumptions are less likely to experience personality growth in later life.

Women have undergone special scrutiny in the last two decades. Researchers now recognize that the male-dominated psychology profession of the 1950s generated a host of personality theories that failed to highlight adequately women's unique personality and development issues. Personality researchers now acknowledge that the life experiences of contemporary women are unique. Women face challenges in the workforce and home that were not conceived of three decades ago. Managing careers, creating homes, and developing a sense of personal satisfaction have given rise to the "supermom" phenomenon, women who are trying to do it all—home, family, career, personal satisfaction. Serious research into supermom and the psychological life of women is just beginning to emerge. Other aspects of

	Young Adulthood 18–25	Early Adulthood 25–40	Middle Adulthood 40–65	Late Adulthood 65–75
Physical Change	Peak functioning in most physical skills; optimum time for childbearing	Still good physical functioning in most areas: health habits during this time establish later risks	Beginning signs of physical decline in some areas—strength, elasticity of tissues, height, cardiovascular function	
Cognitive Change	Cognitive skills high on most measures	Peak period of cognitive skill on most measures	Some signs of loss of cognitive skill on timed, unexercised skills	
Work Roles	Choose career, which may involve several job changes; low work satisfaction is common	Rising work satisfaction; major emphasis on career or work success; most career progress steps made	Plateau on career steps, but higher work satisfaction	
Personality Development	Conformist; task of intimacy	Task of generativity	Increase in self-confidence, openness; lower use of immature defenses	
Major Tasks	Separate from family; form partnership; begin family; find job; create individual life pattern	Rear family; establish personal work pattern and strive for success	Launch family; redefine life goals; redefine self outside of family and work roles; care for aging parents	

♦   ***Building Table 10.2***   ♦

A Summary of Major Changes in Important Domains of Adult Functioning

personality development are discussed in chapter 12. For both men and women, Building Table 10.2 presents a summary of changes in important domains of adult functioning.

Adult Stage Theories

Some people—perhaps the more poetic among us—think of life as a journey that each person takes along a road from birth to death. The concept of a journey through life is similar to Erik Erikson's stage theory, in which people move through a series of stages, resolving a different dilemma in each stage. An important aspect of Erikson's theory is that people progress in a specific direction from the beginning of life to the end.

One noted theorist, Daniel Levinson, has also devised a stage theory of adult development. He agrees that people go through stages and have similar experiences at certain points in their lives. He also agrees that studying those shared experiences allows psychologists to help people manage their lives. But unlike Erikson, Levinson does not see life as a journey toward some specific goal or objective, nor a blueprint that everyone must follow. Rather, a theory of development should lay out the stages, or "eras," during which individuals work out various developmental tasks. In his words:

> We change in different ways, according to different timetables. Yet, I believe that everyone lives through the same developmental periods in adulthood . . . though people go through them in their own ways. . . . (1980, p. 289)

Levinson's Four Eras. Levinson (1978) suggests that as people grow older, they adapt to the demands and tasks of life. He describes four basic eras in the adult life cycle, each with distinctive qualities and different life problems, tasks, and situations; each also brings with it different *life structures,* or unique patterns of behavior and ways of interacting with the world. But since no two people have the same life situation, no two people adapt in exactly the same way. Each person develops a life structure to deal with each era. A young man in his early thirties, for example, may become involved in religious work and learn how groups function to achieve common goals; those skills may be less necessary during his forties, when he concentrates more on his sales career.

In each era, people develop stable life structures that get them through the period successfully. They then enter a new era in which they encounter new life conditions, challenges, and dilemmas. Since the old life structures no longer work, they must go through a period of transition during which they adjust to their new situation. Sometimes the transition is difficult, characterized by anxiety and even depression. Thus, according to this theory, we can think of a person's life as alternating between stable periods and transitional periods. The four eras outlined by Levinson are:

1. ages 11–17   adolescence

2. ages 18–45   early adulthood

3. ages 46–65   middle adulthood

4. ages 65–on   late adulthood

During *adolescence,* young people enter the adult world but are still immature and vulnerable. During *early adulthood* they make their first major life choices regarding family, occupation, and style of living. Throughout this period adults move toward greater independence and senior positions in the community. They raise their children, strive to advance their careers,

During middle adulthood people should be able to see the results of their earlier career decisions. Personal and professional goals often peak in terms of creativity and success during this stage of life.

and launch their offspring into the adult world. Early adulthood is an era of striving, gaining, and accepting responsibility. By the end of this era, at about age forty-five, people may no longer have to care for their children, but instead may assume the responsibility of caring for their parents.

The much-discussed mid-life crisis occurs at the end of early adulthood. During this era people realize that their lives are half over—that if they are to change their lives, they must do so now. Some resign themselves to their original course, while others decide to change, grow, and strive to achieve new goals. (This era is equivalent to Erikson's stage of generativity versus stagnation.)

Middle adulthood spans the years from forty-six to sixty-five. Adults who have gone through a mid-life crisis now live with the decisions they made during early adulthood. Career and family are usually well established. People experience either a sense of satisfaction, self-worth, and accomplishment, or a sense that much of their life has been wasted. It is often during this period that a man or woman reaches his or her peak in creativity and achievement (Simonton, 1988). In the middle of this era, some people go through a crisis similar to that of early adulthood. Sometimes it is a continuation of the earlier crisis; at other times it is a new one.

The years after age fifty are ones of mellowing. People approaching their sixties begin to prepare for late adulthood, making whatever major career and family decisions are necessary before retirement. People in their early sixties generally learn to assess their lives, not in terms of money or day-to-day successes, but according to whether they have been meaningful, happy, and cohesive. At this time, people stop blaming others for their problems. They are less concerned about disputes with other people. They try to optimize their life because they know that at least two-thirds of it has passed, and they wish to make the most of the remaining years. Depending on how well they come to accept themselves, the next decade may be one of great fulfillment or great despair.

Levinson's fourth and final era, *late adulthood*, covers the years from age sixty-five on. During retirement many people relax and enjoy the fruits of their labors. Children, grandchildren, and even great-grandchildren can become the focus of an older person's life.

Gender Differences. Levinson developed his theory by studying forty men in detail over several years. His subjects were interviewed weekly for several months and were then interviewed again after two years. Spouses were interviewed, and extensive biographical data were collected. Levinson's theory has achieved wide acclaim, but it has also been challenged. Psychologists point out that it is based on information gathered from a small sample of middle-class men. It does not consider social class or gender differences.

During late adulthood family relationships again become very important.

Women do not necessarily follow the same life stages or changes as men. As children they are taught different values, goals, and approaches toward life, and these are often reflected later in their choices of vocations, hobbies, and intellectual pursuits (Kalichman, 1989). Women have traditionally sought different career opportunities, although this is changing. In the field of law, for example, women now compose nearly half of all law school students. However, female attorneys often choose careers that do not follow the traditional male associate-partnership ladder.

The developmental course of women, and especially of women's transitions, is similar to that of men, but women tend to experience transitions and life events at later ages and in more irregular sequences than those reported by Levinson. In a major study of women's transitions, Mercer, Nichols, and Doyle (1989) found a developmental progression for women. They especially considered the role of motherhood and how it influences the life courses of women. Mercer, Nichols, and Doyle broke the developmental progression into five eras at which there are important transitions:

1. ages 16–25   launching into adulthood
2. ages 26–30   age 30–leveling
3. ages 36–40   age 40–liberating
4. ages 61–65   regeneration/redirection
5. ages 65–on   age 80–creativity/destructiveness

In *launching into adulthood,* women break away from families to go to school, marry, or work. In *age-30 leveling,* many women readjust their life courses; this is often a time for marriage, separation, or divorce. In *age-40 liberating,* women focus their aspirations and grow personally. In *regeneration/redirection,* women, like men, adjust to their lifetime choices and prepare for retirement and a more leisurely life-style. In *age-80 creativity/destructiveness,* women are challenged to adapt to health changes and loss of spouses and friends, and this time is characterized by a surge of creativity, or sometimes depression. With a five-stage approach, this women's developmental life stage theory is similar to Levinson's, but has its own unique flavor and recognizes differences in the life courses of men and women.

Today, many universities, recognizing that women have special issues that are different from those of men, have departments of women's studies. Women still face discrimination in the workforce, and society continues to vacillate in its expectations for women and childcare. Women still have the burden of family responsibilities, especially childcare; in the aftermath of a divorce, the woman usually gets physical custody of the children. The assumption of childcare after divorce has sharp economic consequences that alter the life-style and course of life stages for women. Clearly there are obvious differences in the life stages of men and women, whether upper-, middle-, or lower-class.

A comprehensive picture of adult development must also include the psychology of minorities and their special life experiences. For example, the life cycle, family responsibilities, and beliefs of a Navajo woman, a recent immigrant from Cuba, or a poor farmer are all different. As they are systematically studied, global theories such as Levinson's will be adjusted to explain adult development more completely.

Divorce

In adult development, no single event has such wrenching effects as divorce. Divorce ends a marriage and begins a new life—offering second chances to the people involved. Divorce affects not only the two individuals divorcing, but also their families, especially the children, as we saw earlier in this chapter.

Divorce begins when a marriage breaks down, often years before the actual legal decree. It also continues to exert influence long afterward. Although the individual who initiated the break-up may initially be relieved, after a year most people who divorce have regrets, feelings of self-recrimination, and sadness over their failed marriage. Economically, men in general see an increase in their living standard, while women see a decrease (Weitzman, 1985).

People first experience either anger or freedom, and conflict between former spouses is common. Sexual and aggressive behaviors are evident that might not have been exhibited before (Wallerstein and Kelly, 1980). Later, adults try to cope with new life-styles and economic situations. This stage is often one of growth, change, and searching—it is a time of transition—and it may last for several years. Eventually, families settle in and find a secure, stable life-style. The two new family units that evolve function adequately, although their functioning is often very different. Single parenthood for those with children (usually the mother) is not easy, but individuals learn to cope with their new situations (Wallerstein and Blakeslee, 1989).

Focus on Learning

- ◆ What happens to an adult's fitness from ages eighteen to sixty? p. 355
- ◆ Distinguish between a transition and a crisis in an adult's life. p. 356
- ◆ Identify Levinson's four eras of adult development and describe an important characteristic of each. p. 359
- ◆ Mercer, Nichols, and Doyle found a developmental progression for women; identify its five stages and describe an important characteristic of each. p. 361
- ◆ When a couple divorces, they go through a three-stage process of adjustment; identify and describe the three stages. p. 362

Aging

As people grow older, they age experientially as well as physically; that is, they gather experiences and expand their worlds (B. F. Skinner, 1983). Nevertheless, in Western society, growing older is not always easy, especially because of the negative stereotypes associated with the aging process.

Although most older adults face aging from a mature and experienced vantage point, are in good health, and look forward to a fruitful retirement, they also face many challenges. Sometimes failing health, their own or a spouse's, complicates life; sometimes society's negative attitudes complicate it. Sierra, introduced at the beginning of this chapter, is happy and well-adjusted. Although her children have left home, she enjoys their visits and keeps busy with her painting. Yet she is faced with nagging health problems, such as arthritis and failing eyesight. In general, being over sixty-five, like being over twenty-one, brings with it new developmental tasks—retirement, health issues, and maintenance of a long-term standard of living.

An Aging Population

How older people view themselves depends, in part, on how society treats them. Many Asian cultures greatly respect the elderly for their wisdom and maturity; in such societies gray hair is a mark of distinction, not embarrassment. In contrast, the United States is a youth-oriented society where people spend a fortune on everything from hair dyes to facelifts to make themselves look younger. However, because the average age of Americans is climbing, how we perceive the elderly and how they perceive themselves may be changing.

In an Asian household, elders are deeply respected.

In the first five years of the 1990s approximately twelve percent of the U.S. population—more than 30 million Americans—will be sixty-five or older. The proportion of elderly people is expected to increase to between twenty and twenty-five percent by 2030, and the number of Americans past sixty-five will exceed 60 million (see Figure 10.2). At present, the average life expectancy at birth in the United States is about 74.7 years. Note that life expectancy is different for men and women—women live about four years longer than men, on the average, and at birth their life expectancy is seven years greater!

For many people the years after age sixty are filled with excitement. Financially, two-thirds of American workers are covered by pension plans provided by their employers. Socially, most maintain close friendships and stay in touch with family members. Some, however, experience financial problems, while others experience loneliness and isolation because many of their friends and relatives have died or they have lost touch with their families. In the United States, there are now as many people over the age of sixty as there are under the age of seven, yet funding for programs involving the health and psychological well-being of older people is relatively limited.

FIGURE 10.2
In the year 2030 the U.S. population will be distributed fairly evenly among ten-year age groups ranging from birth through sixty-nine years old.

A nation growing older
The number of elderly people in the United States will skyrocket in the next century with the aging of the baby boomers.

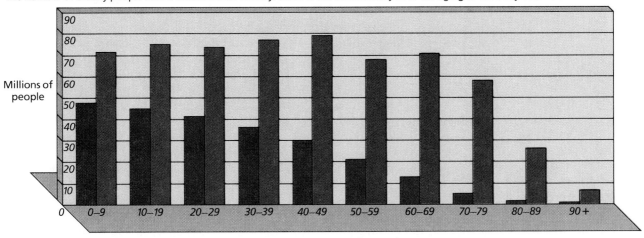

Age (in years)

■ 1930 (Total population 122.8 million)
■ 2030 (Total population 304.8 million)

The growing population of America's elderly have been proving that old age does not automatically relegate older people to their rocking chairs.

Aging: Myths and Realities

In the 1981 movie *On Golden Pond*, Henry Fonda portrayed an eighty-year-old retired university professor named Norman Thayer, Jr. In some ways, Norman is the stereotypical elderly person: he is irascible, dwells on death, has trouble seeing and hearing, and constantly forgets names. Asked how it feels to turn eighty, Norman grumbles, "Twice as bad as it did turning forty." In search of berries for his wife, played by Katharine Hepburn, Norman ventures into the woods he has known for decades but becomes lost, confused, and frightened, all supposed symptoms of old age.

Is Norman typical? When people reach Norman's age do they deteriorate into incompetence? Some do, but consider that Fonda, at age seventy-six, and Hepburn, at age seventy-two, both won Academy Awards for their performances. Shortly after *On Golden Pond* was released, Fonda died. However, his virtuoso acting in the movie shows that, unlike Norman, his mental abilities were sharp even in the last year of his life.

There is a widely held myth that all older people are less intelligent, lacking in common sense, unable to care for themselves, financially insecure, inflexible, and unhealthy. The reality is that many elderly people are as competent and capable as they were in their earlier adulthood. They work, play golf, compete in races, socialize, and stay politically aware and active. Healthy elderly people maintain a good sex life (Bretschneider and McCoy, 1988). As grandparents they may be seen as buffers between children and their parents, as wise advice givers, and as a link to the past. Children, in fact, may have difficulty understanding why older people are viewed so negatively. Building Table 10.3 summarizes important changes in adult functioning from young adulthood to late adulthood.

Perception of Older Adults: Stereotypes

Stereotypes about the elderly have given rise to **ageism,** prejudice against the elderly and the discrimination that follows from it. Ageism is prevalent in the job market, in which older people are not given the same opportunities as their younger coworkers, and in housing and health care. Ageism is exceptionally prevalent in the media—on television and in newspapers, cartoons, and magazines—and in everyday language.

Schmidt and Boland (1986) examined everyday language to learn how people perceive older adults. They found marked inconsistencies. For example, *elder* statesman implies that a person is experienced, intelligent, or perhaps conservative. But *old* statesman might suggest that a person is past his prime, tired, or useless. The term *old people* may allude to positive elements in older adults—for example, the perfect grandparent—or to negative qualities—grouchiness or mental deficiencies. What does *old* mean?

People have a variety of ideas about older adults, and it follows that they may behave differently toward various "types" of older adults. People who are perceived to represent negative stereotypes are more likely to suffer discrimination than those who appear to represent more positive stereotypes. This means that an older person who appears healthy, bright, and alert is more likely to be treated with the same respect shown to younger people. By contrast, an older adult who *appears* less capable may not be given the same respect or treatment. We will see in chapter 16 that first impressions have a potent effect on an individual's behavior. This seems to be particularly true for older people. An older person's physical appearance may invoke ageism and discrimination, whereas a younger person's appearance seems

Ageism: Discrimination on the basis of age, often resulting in the denial of rights and services to the elderly.

	Young Adulthood 18–25	Early Adulthood 25–40	Middle Adulthood 40–65	Late Adulthood 65–75	Late, Late Adulthood 75+
Physical Change	Peak functioning in most physical skills; optimum time for child-bearing	Still good physical functioning in most areas: health habits during this time establish later risks	Beginning signs of physical decline in some areas—strength, elasticity of tissues, height, cardiovascular function	Significant physical decline on most measures	
Cognitive Change	Cognitive skills high on most measures	Peak period of cognitive skill on most measures	Some signs of loss of cognitive skill on timed, unexercised skills	Small declines for virtually all adults on some skills	
Work Roles	Choose career, which may involve several job changes; low work satisfaction is common	Rising work satisfaction; major emphasis on career or work success; most career progress steps made	Plateau on career steps, but higher work satisfaction	Retirement	
Personality Development	Conformist; task of intimacy	Task of generativity	Increase in self-confidence, openness; lower use of immature defenses	Perhaps integrated level; perhaps more inferiority; or perhaps self-actualized; task of ego integrity	
Major Tasks	Separate from family; form partnership; begin family; find job; create individual life pattern	Rear family; establish personal work pattern and strive for success	Launch family; redefine life goals; redefine self outside of family and work roles; care for aging parents	Cope with retirement; cope with declining health; redefine life goals and sense of self	

•   *Building Table 10.3*   •

A Summary of Major Changes in Important Domains of Adult Functioning

less likely to have such an immediate effect. In any case, ageism can be reduced if people recognize the diversity that exists among aging populations (Kimmel, 1988).

Theories of Aging

The quest for eternal youth has inspired extravagant attempts to slow, stop, or reverse the aging process. Ponce de Leon organized an expedition to the New World in 1512 to find the fabled fountain of youth; alchemists in the Middle Ages tried in vain to concoct an elixir of life; and in the past one hundred years, quacks have attempted to reclaim youthful vigor with everything from strong laxative therapy (to clean the colon) to injections of cells from lamb fetuses. In recent years, scientists seem to have increased dramatically the life span of some laboratory animals by feeding them calorie-restricted diets. However, so far the maximum life span attained by human beings is between 100 and 120 years.

Despite the centuries-long search for the secret of eternal youth, psychologists and physicians have been examining the behavioral and physiological changes that accompany aging for only the past two decades. Three basic types of theories have developed to explain why people age. These theories are based on heredity, external factors, and physiology. Although each emphasizes a different cause for aging, it is most likely that aging results from a combination of all three.

Heredity. Genes determine much of a person's physical makeup; thus, it is probable that heredity, to some extent, determines how long a person will live. There exists a strong genetic component to aging and much supporting evidence. For example, we know that long-lived parents tend to have long-lived offspring. But researchers still do not know *how* heredity exerts its influence over the aging process.

External Factors. Kimmel (1980) suggests that external factors affect how long a person will live. For example, people who live on farms live longer than those in cities; normal-weight people live longer than overweight people; and people who do not smoke cigarettes, who are not constantly tense, and who do not expose themselves to disease or radiation live longer than others. Since data on external factors are often obtained from correlational studies, one cannot base cause-and-effect statements on these data, but it is reasonable to assume that external factors such as disease, smoking, and obesity affect a person's life span.

Physiology. Several theories use physiological and genetic explanations to account for aging. Since a person's physiological process depends on both hereditary and environmental factors, these theories rely on both concepts. The *wear-and-tear theory* of aging claims that the human organism simply wears out from overuse, much like the parts of a machine (Rowland, 1977); although a commonsense notion, this view does not have much experimental support. The *homeostatic theory* suggests that the body's ability to adjust to varying situations decreases with age. For example, as the ability to maintain a constant body temperature decreases, cellular and tissue damage occur and aging results. Similarly, when the body can no longer control the use of sugar through the output of insulin, signs of aging appear (Eisdorfer and Wilkie, 1977). On the other hand, aging may be the *cause* of deviations from

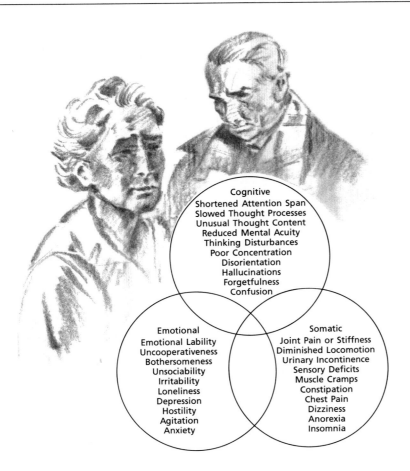

FIGURE 10.3
Symptoms commonly seen in elderly patients. (Source: From Usdin and Hofling, 1978.)

Cognitive
Shortened Attention Span
Slowed Thought Processes
Unusual Thought Content
Reduced Mental Acuity
Thinking Disturbances
Poor Concentration
Disorientation
Hallucinations
Forgetfulness
Confusion

Emotional
Emotional Lability
Uncooperativeness
Bothersomeness
Unsociability
Irritability
Loneliness
Depression
Hostility
Agitation
Anxiety

Somatic
Joint Pain or Stiffness
Diminished Locomotion
Urinary Incontinence
Sensory Deficits
Muscle Cramps
Constipation
Chest Pain
Dizziness
Anorexia
Insomnia

homeostasis, rather than the result. Whatever the causes of aging, people go through a number of predictable changes as they age; these are often called biobehavioral changes, and we consider them next.

Biobehavioral Changes

Elderly people must contend with significant biological changes. These changes include alterations in calcium metabolism, which make the bones more brittle; increased susceptibility to diseases of the joints, such as arthritis and gum disease; decreased elasticity in the skin, creating folds and wrinkles. Some biological changes interact with behavioral ones. For example, people who live alone may not eat properly and may suffer vitamin deficiencies as a result. The changes that come about from the interaction of biology and behavior are called *biobehavioral changes.* Figure 10.3 shows some changes seen in elderly people as a result of aging.

Brain Disorders. Many people wrongly assume that aging is inevitably accompanied by senility, a term once used to describe cognitive changes that occur in older people. Today, these cognitive deficits are known to be caused by brain disorders that occur only in *some* older people. Brain disorders, sometimes called **dementias,** involve losses of cognitive or mental functioning; at a minimum, they are losses of memory. Many people can develop dementias; for example, we know that AIDS patients have a failing immune system that causes brain infections, which in turn lead to dementia. Prac-

Dementias: Impairment in mental functioning and global cognitive (thought) abilities of long-standing duration in an otherwise alert individual. Dementias cause a loss of memory and other related symptoms. The leading cause in the United States is Alzheimer's disease.

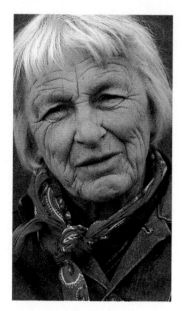

Biobehavioral changes occur as the body ages. Years of hard work in the sun are evident in this elderly rancher's face.

titioners, moreover, realize that some illnesses that cause dementia can be treated and that treatment often halts (but does not reverse) the dementia. Memory loss can occur for recent events (short-term memory) as well as past events. Additional symptoms include loss of language skills, reduced capacity for abstract thinking, personality changes, and loss of a sense of time and place. Severe and disabling dementias affect about 1.5 million Americans; mild or moderate dementias affect an additional 1 to 5 million (U.S. Congress, 1987). With the increasing number of elderly citizens, these statistics are on the rise, and people are recognizing this as a serious national problem.

More than seventy conditions cause dementias. *Reversible dementias,* which are caused by malnutrition, alcoholism, or toxins (poisons), usually affect younger people. *Irreversible dementias* are of two types—multiple infarcts and Alzheimer's disease (to be discussed on p. 369). Multiple infarct dementia is usually caused by small strokes (ruptures of small blood vessels in the brain); it results in a slow degeneration of the brain.

Sensory Abilities. Older people are likely to experience decreased sensory abilities. Their vision, hearing, taste, and smell require a higher level of stimulation to respond the way younger people's senses do. Older people, for example, usually are unable to make fine visual discriminations without the aid of glasses, have limited capacity for dark adaptation, and often have some degree of hearing loss, especially in the high-frequency ranges.

Changes in the Nervous System. One change that can be seen easily in older individuals is a slowing of their reaction time in certain situations. Although the sensory systems themselves may not be impaired, older people respond less quickly to events. In an emergency, for example, an elderly driver may be unable to stop a car as quickly as a younger driver could. Many explanations for this decreased response time have been suggested, but none has been proved conclusively. Other changes include alterations in brain-wave activity, as measured by an EEG, and in autonomic nervous system activity. Some researchers have suggested that older individuals are "under-aroused." However, studies of autonomic nervous system responsiveness in old and young adults show little support for this once popular idea (Powell, Milligan, and Furchtgott, 1980).

Overall Health. People's overall health deteriorates as they age. For men, the probability of dying doubles in each decade after mid-life. Blood pressure rises, cardiac output decreases, and the likelihood of stroke increases. One impact of this deterioration is that cardiovascular disease influences intellectual functioning by decreasing blood flow to the brain (Hertzog, Schaie, and Gribbin, 1978).

Some individuals experience *terminal drop*—a rapid decline in intellectual functioning in the year before death. Some researchers attribute this change to cardiovascular disease, claiming that the decreased blood flow (and resulting decrease in oxygen) to the brain causes declining mental ability and, ultimately, failing health. But although there is evidence for the terminal drop, no satisfactory method exists for predicting death on the basis of poor performance on intelligence or neuropsychological tests (Botwinick, 1984). Next we examine in detail one of the major dementias that affects older people in our society: Alzheimer's disease.

Alzheimer's Disease

THINKING ABOUT
R E S E A R C H

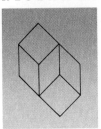

*A*lzheimer's disease is a degenerative disorder of the brain that could well be the most widespread neurological disorder of all time (Bloom, Lazerson, and Hofstadter, 1985). As the population grows older, a result of advanced medical technology, the number of cases of **Alzheimer's disease** increases. Currently, there are about 1.5 to 2 million diagnosed Alzheimer's patients in the United States; in addition, there are a large number of undiagnosed cases. A recent estimate suggested that the numbers may be even greater than once thought: one in ten people over sixty-five may have the disease, and almost one-half of those over age eighty-five may have the disease (Evans et al., 1989). Because it is a degenerative disease, its six- to twenty-year progression cannot be stopped; it is irreversible and ultimately ends in death. To date there is no fully effective method of prevention, treatment, or cure. What causes this disease? What is its impact on our population? How will Alzheimer's disease affect health care delivery in the United States?

What Causes Alzheimer's Disease? A definitive diagnosis of Alzheimer's disease can be made only by examining brain tissue. "Tangled neurons" is the typical explanation, since brain scans usually confirm that the patient's neurons seem to be twisted and gnarled, and cell bodies are loaded with abnormal protein structures called tangles. In addition, the tips of axons that release neurotransmitters are coated with globs of dead and dying nerve terminals called plaque. Levels of neurotransmitter substances are usually lowered.

Correlational research shows that Alzheimer's disease tends to run in families, suggesting a genetic basis or at least a predisposition to the disorder. For example, ten to thirty percent of Alzheimer's patients had parents with the disease. Some researchers posit a depletion of enzymes necessary for the formation of neurotransmitters; others suggest an accumulation of toxins such as aluminum (Neustatler, 1982); and still others have focused on specific neurotransmitters (Gibson, Logue, and Growdon, 1985) and metabolic patterns (Small et al., 1989). Blood supply problems, immune system factors, head injuries, and viruses have also been implicated in the disease. Proteins that accumulate in the brain of Alzheimer's patients are now being found elsewhere in the body, which makes the proteins easier to extract and study. This is a great advantage for Alzheimer's researchers.

Recent *experimental* research shows that certain drugs may halt the progress of Alzheimer's. THA, for example, apparently blocks the action of enzymes that limit the production of acetylcholine, which is thought to be crucial for normal brain functioning. Unfortunately, these and other research efforts remain inconclusive. No one yet knows the causes of Alzheimer's disease or has developed an effective treatment. Researchers are beginning to think that there are many types of Alzheimer's disease, some of which may be hereditary (St. George-Hyslop et al., 1987) and some of which may have been generated by early life events such as a head injury (Roberts, 1988).

Psychological Effects of Alzheimer's Disease. The impact of Alzheimer's disease on the patient is enormous, severely damaging the quality of his or her life. Patients are not necessarily stripped of their vigor or strength, but they slowly become confused and helpless. Initially, they may forget to do things. Later, appointments, anniversaries, and dates for lunch may be forgotten. Such mistakes are often overlooked at first. Jokes cover up memory losses and lapses. The memory losses are not always apparent; some days are better than others. Ultimately the disorder grows worse. Soon Alzheimer's patients have trouble finding their way home and remembering their own names and the names of

Alzheimer's disease: A chronic and progressive disorder that is a major cause of degenerative dementia, currently affecting about two million people in the United States. The disease may be a group of related disorders tied together loosely under one name.

Alzheimer's disease is increasingly prevalent in our society. Alzheimer's victims have difficulty functioning on a daily basis without assistance.

their spouses or children. Patients' personalities also change; they may become abrupt, abusive, and hostile to family members. Within months, or sometimes years, they will lose their speech and language functions. Eventually patients lose all control, especially of memory (e.g., Karlsson et al., 1989) and even of simple bodily functions.

Implications for Families. In addition to studying the effects of Alzheimer's disease on patients, researchers are also studying the impact on the patient's family. Caring for the patient imposes great physical, emotional, and financial hardships on families (Aronson, Levin, and Lipkowitz, 1984). Since families usually cannot care for relatives with Alzheimer's indefinitely, hospitalization or day care is often necessary. The patient's loved ones "walk a tightrope between meeting the patient's needs and preserving their own well-being" (Heckler, 1985, p. 1241). Alzheimer's changes family life and finances in irreversible ways, since most patients are placed in nursing homes after extensive and exhausting care at home. Researchers argue, "In the overwhelming majority of cases, nursing home placement occurs only after responsible family caregivers have endured prolonged, unrelenting caring (often for years) and no longer have the capacity to continue their caregiving efforts" (Brody, Lawton, and Liebowitz, 1984, p. 1331). It is estimated that by 1995 the cost of nursing home care for Alzheimer's patients may be as high as $41 billion per year. America, its aging population, and its health care system are facing a time bomb; although research efforts in Alzheimer's disease are substantial, far more research is needed.   ◆

Intellectual Changes

Perhaps the most distressing change that occurs with aging is a decline in intellectual ability. Many researchers who once believed that general intellectual functioning remains stable throughout life now acknowledge that certain aspects of intelligence deteriorate with age. But it is difficult to know exactly what and how much change occurs.

Many researchers have studied changes in intellectual functioning. A major problem, however, is defining it. Aged people are likely to do poorly on standardized intelligence tests, not because their intelligence is lower, but because the tests require the manipulation of objects during a timed interval, and older people have a slower reaction time or decreased manual dexterity (often because of arthritis). To overcome these disadvantages, researchers have devised different methodologies for studying intelligence in older people.

Although most research indicates that cognitive and intellectual abilities decrease with advancing age, many of the changes are of little importance for day-to-day functioning. For example, overall vocabulary decreases only slightly (Shneidman, 1989). Moreover, some of the changes observed in laboratory tasks (e.g., reaction time tasks) are either small or reversible (Baltes, Reese, and Lipsitt, 1980). Finally, extreme variability in both the types and causes of intellectual deficits suggests that changes in health and family situation may produce the severe biological and psychological consequences that in turn affect intellectual functioning. See Table 10.2 for a summary of age changes in intellectual skills through adulthood.

Whatever the causes, deficits in intellectual functioning that occur with age and influence behavior are seldom devastating. Up to the ages of sixty to sixty-five there is little decline in learning or memory; motivation, interest, and lack of recent educational experience are probably more important in learning complex knowledge than is age.

TABLE 10.2
Summary of Age Changes in Intellectual Skills

Age 20–40	Age 40–65	Age 65 and Older
Peak intellectual ability between about 20 and 35	Maintenance of skill on measures of verbal, unspeeded intelligence; some decline of skill on measures of performance or speeded IQ; decline is usually not functionally significant till age 60 or older	Some loss of verbal IQ; most noticeable in adults with poorer health, lower levels of activity, and less education
Optimal performance on memory tasks	Little change in performance on memory tasks, except perhaps some slowing later in this period	Slowing of retrieval processes and other memory processes; less skillful use of coding strategies for new memories
Peak performance on laboratory tests of problem solving	Peak performance on real-life problem-solving tasks and many verbal abilities	Decline in problem-solving performance on both laboratory and real-life tests

Source: Adapted from Bee (1987).

Despite evidence that old age takes a toll, there exist many remarkable examples of intellectual achievement by people seventy years old or more. Golda Meir, for example, became prime minister of Israel at age seventy; Benjamin Franklin invented bifocal eyeglasses at seventy-four and helped to frame the Constitution of the United States at eighty-one; and Arthur Rubinstein, the Polish-born American concert pianist, gave one of his greatest recitals at New York's Carnegie Hall at age eighty-nine. Elderly people are found in the workplace, in the executive suite, on the road, and in small shops all around the country.

Psychology and Business: Elderly People in the Workplace

Because many employers believe that older adults are less efficient than their younger coworkers, there is widespread discrimination against older workers in industry, according to Ross Stagner (1985), a retired psychology professor at Wayne State University. Much of the following discussion is based on Stagner's analysis of elderly people in the workplace and how businesses treat the elderly.

Job Performance. Some researchers allege that older workers do not perform as well, are less flexible, and are slower to learn new technologies than younger workers. Stagner, however, reports that the work output and quality of older workers is just as good as that of younger workers. He says that the reports are biased because many of the individuals who evaluate the older workers have stereotyped ideas about them: They evaluated them negatively *regardless* of their actual work performance.

Some older workers do show declines in performance. As discussed earlier, older people experience sensory losses that can affect their performance on jobs that require excellent hearing, vision, or motor abilities. Also, in noisy environments in which verbal instructions are given, hearing loss

Elderly workers can perform just as well as their younger counterparts in many jobs. Stability and experience are two important assets of older employees.

	Young Adulthood 18–25	Early Adulthood 25–40	Middle Adulthood 40–65	Late Adulthood 65–75	Late, Late Adulthood 75+
Physical Change	Peak functioning in most physical skills; optimum time for childbearing	Still good physical functioning in most areas: health habits during this time establish later risks	Beginning signs of physical decline in some areas—strength, elasticity of tissues, height, cardiovascular function	Significant physical decline on most measures	Marked physical decline on virtually any measure, including speed, strength, work capacity, elasticity, system functioning
Cognitive Change	Cognitive skills high on most measures	Peak period of cognitive skill on most measures	Some signs of loss of cognitive skill on timed, unexercised skills	Small declines for virtually all adults on some skills	Often significant loss in many areas, including memory
Work Roles	Choose career, which may involve several job changes; low work satisfaction is common	Rising work satisfaction; major emphasis on career or work success; most career progress steps made	Plateau on career steps, but higher work satisfaction	Retirement	Work roles now unimportant
Personality Development	Conformist; task of intimacy	Task of generativity	Increase in self-confidence, openness; lower use of immature defenses	Perhaps integrated level; perhaps more inferiority; or perhaps self-actualized; task of ego integrity	Perhaps integrated or self-actualized, at least for some people
Major Tasks	Separate from family; form partnership; begin family; find job; create individual life pattern	Rear family; establish personal work pattern and strive for success	Launch family; redefine life goals; redefine self outside of family and work roles; care for aging parents	Cope with retirement; cope with declining health; redefine life goals and sense of self	Come to terms with death

◆ *Building Table 10.4* ◆

A Summary of Major Changes in Important Domains of Adult Functioning

Source: Adapted and modified from Korchin, 1975, table 14.2.

can have important implications. On the other hand, even though older adults may experience decreased visual-motor coordination in complex tasks, drill operators over age sixty have been shown to be more accurate than their younger counterparts. Their years of training and perceptual skills make up for lost visual-motor coordination.

Job Satisfaction. Older adults tend to be more satisfied with their jobs than younger workers. They pay more attention to intrinsic characteristics of a job than to extrinsic values such as pay, vacation time, and work environment. Older workers may find more satisfaction in their work because they have had more time to find the "right" job. Moreover, research shows that their mental health tends to be superior to that of younger coworkers.

The motivation, performance, and satisfaction of older workers are much like those of their younger counterparts, and the psychological management principles examined in the laboratory are relevant for older workers as well as for younger ones. Business schools are adjusting their curriculum to reflect this fact; businesses themselves are showing it by hiring older and more experienced workers. Building Table 10.4 summarizes important changes from young adulthood to its final stages.

- Describe ageism. p. 364
- Identify two biobehavioral changes that occur as a result of aging. p. 366
- Describe the key symptoms of Alzheimer's disease, its age of onset, and its prevalence in the population. p. 370
- Sometimes intelligence test scores among aging subjects decrease because of non-intelligence related factors. Identify two. p. 370

Focus on Learning

Dying: The End of the Life Span

Everyone recognizes that death is inevitable, but in the twentieth century few people actually witness death (Aiken, 1985). Before this century, most people died in bed at home, where other people were likely to be with them. Today, nearly eighty percent of people die in hospitals and nursing homes. About eight million Americans experience the death of an immediate family member each year. Every year there are about two million deaths and 800,000 new widows and widowers (Osterweis and Townsend, 1988); we are all affected by death, but most people avoid discussing it.

Thanatology, the study of death and dying, has become an interdisciplinary specialty: Researchers and theorists in several areas—including theology, law, history, psychology, sociology, and medicine—have come together to understand death and dying better. For psychologists, dealing with the process of dying is especially complicated because people do not like to talk or think about death. Nevertheless, considerable progress has been made toward understanding the psychology of dying.

Thanatology: The study of the psychological and medical aspects of death and dying; the study has become increasingly interdisciplinary.

Coping with Death

Elisabeth Kübler-Ross has become famous for her studies of the way people respond psychologically to death and to people who are dying. Kübler-Ross

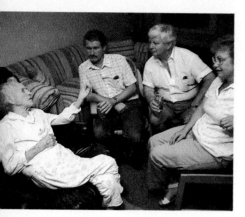

Hospice care provides the dying person with a caring, homelike environment focused on psychological as well as physical needs.

believes that people in Western society fear death because it is unfamiliar, often hidden away in hospitals. She suggests that a way to reduce this fear is to involve members of a dying person's family more closely in what is, in fact, a very natural process. She contends that it is better for people to die at home than in an unfamiliar hospital room.

Kübler-Ross's Stage Theory. Kübler-Ross was one of the first researchers to use a stage theory to discuss people's fear of their own death and that of loved ones. People who learn that they are terminally ill, in Kübler-Ross's view, typically go through five stages: *denial,* which serves as a buffer against the shocking news; *anger* directed against family, friends, or medical staff; *bargaining,* in which a person tries to gain more time by "making a deal" with God, themselves, or their doctors; *depression,* often caused by the pain of their illness and guilt over inconveniencing their family; and finally, *acceptance,* in which the person stops fighting and accepts death.

Criticisms of Kübler-Ross's Theory. Kübler-Ross's theory has been subject to considerable criticism. Not all researchers find the same sequence of events in the dying process (Stephenson, 1985). They argue that the sequence outlined by Kübler-Ross does not work for all people and that the stages are not necessarily experienced in the order she suggested. Others argue that people who are going to die may not experience all of the stages; and even when they do, they do not feel the way Kübler-Ross suggests. But Kübler-Ross contends that her theory was meant to be an overall outline, not a strict set of stages or steps.

Kübler-Ross has also been criticized for her research techniques—her interviews were not very systematic; she offers few statistics; and some of her ideas rely more on intuition than on facts established through scientific methods. Specifically, her data-gathering techniques were highly subjective. Schaie and Willis (1986) have suggested that Kübler-Ross's ideas should not be considered a theory but "an insightful discussion of some of the attitudes that are often displayed by people who are dying" (p. 483). Although Kübler-Ross's ideas about death and dying may not actually be true in every case, many practitioners find them useful in guiding new medical staff through the difficult task of helping the dying, especially those who are facing premature death because of illness such as cancer.

Whether or not one accepts Kübler-Ross's stages as typical, it is clear that, as in all areas of life, people approach death with different attitudes and behaviors. In general, people fear death, although they are more fearful of death in middle age than at any other time in the life cycle. Religious people fear death less than others; older women fear it less than older men; and financially stable people have fewer negative attitudes toward death than poor people. Moreover, most psychologists believe that the ways in which people have dealt with previous stresses in their lives largely predict how they will deal with death.

In addition to imposing emotional stresses on the terminally ill patient, impending death also causes stress for the patient's family. Kübler-Ross has drawn attention to the additional stresses on family members created by interactions with doctors, especially in traditional impersonal hospital settings. Like many other physicians and psychologists, she believes that a more homelike setting can help patients and their families deal better with death. One alternative to the hospital setting is the hospice.

Hospice Care

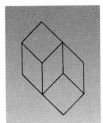

*H*ospices are special facilities established to provide efficient and humane care to terminally ill patients and their families. They address emotional, social, and spiritual needs in addition to physical ones and combine humane treatment with sensitivity to the financial costs of patient care (Butterfield-Picard and Magno, 1982; Smyser, 1982). Hospice care takes psychological principles used in therapy and puts them to work in the day-to-day care of the terminally ill. A hospice often focuses on the psychological needs of the patient, while acknowledging that death is inevitable and imminent.

Hospice care is not appropriate for every dying person. It requires specific kinds of commitment from the patient and family members. Therefore, before admitting a patient, hospices evaluate both the patient and the family. Hospices operate under a different set of guidelines than hospitals and nursing homes that care for the terminally ill (Butterfield-Picard and Magno, 1982):

1. Control of decisions concerning the patient's care rests with the patient and the family.
2. Many aspects of traditional care, such as life-support procedures, are discontinued when the patient no longer desires them.
3. Pain is kept to a minimum so that the patient can experience life as fully as possible until death.
4. A team of professionals provides care around the clock.
5. Surroundings are homelike rather than clinical.
6. When possible, family members and the hospice team are the caregivers.
7. Family members receive counseling before and after the patient dies.

There are more than 440 hospices in the United States today, with at least 360 more under construction, yet relatively few terminally ill patients receive hospice care. For those who do, family members, friends, and practitioners have to answer ethical and practical questions about care and costs, life-support systems, and medications. To help them, researchers and applied psychologists are exploring such issues as exactly when death occurs, how the dying should be treated, and how families can cope better with the dying process. They are examining issues such as how to help the families of the dying patient cope with conflicts about grief over their loss and guilt about their feeling of relief. ◆

- ◆ What is thanatology? p. 373
- ◆ Describe Kübler-Ross's five-stage theory, identifying key behaviors at each stage. pp. 373–374
- ◆ Identify three goals or techniques of hospice care. p. 375

*Focus on
Learning*

Key Terms

Summary

Adolescence

- Changing intellectual abilities, body proportions, and sexual urges (together with parental expectations for more adult behavior) create the classic adolescent identity crisis of Western culture.   pp. 343–344

- Peers and parents are two of the most important influences on adolescent social behavior.   p. 344

- Gender identity is the sense of being male or female; androgyny is the condition in which both typically male and typically female characteristics are apparent in one individual.   p. 345

- Gender schema theory asserts that children and adolescents use gender as an organizing theme to classify and understand their perceptions about the world.   p. 346

- Adolescents view sexual intimacy as a normal part of growing up, and premarital heterosexual activity has become common among adolescents, leading to increased awareness among adolescents about contraception and teenage pregnancy.   pp. 347–348

- Erikson describes psychosocial development throughout life focusing on life's dilemmas. His approach emphasizes the gradual development of complex feelings, beliefs, and experiences, usually through successful completion of one stage at a time.   pp. 349–350

Adulthood

- Development continues throughout adulthood as people learn to maintain their own identity while coping with the demands of jobs, children, other family members, and a constantly changing society.   p. 353

- A distinction should be drawn between the ideas of transition and crisis. A *transition* suggests that a person has reached a time in life when old ways of coping no longer work. A *crisis* occurs when old ways of coping become ineffective and a person is helpless, not knowing what to do.   pp. 355–356

- Daniel Levinson's stage theory of adulthood describes four basic eras: adolescence, early adulthood, middle adulthood, and late adulthood. Women do not necessarily follow the

same life stages as men; consequently, Mercer, Nichols, and Doyle proposed a developmental progression for women broken into five eras: launching into adulthood, age 30–leveling, age 40–liberating, regeneration/redirection, and age 80–creativity/destructiveness.
pp. 359–361

- Divorce begins when a marriage breaks down, often years before the actual legal event. Wallerstein believes that continuing relationships in the post-divorce family are the most likely determiner of whether the children will have problems later in life.   p. 362

Aging

- Changes in overall physical fitness and in sexual and sensory abilities occur in adulthood. Various theories of aging stress the roles of heredity, external factors, and physiology.
pp. 365–367

- Brain disorders, sometimes called *dementias*, involve losses of cognitive or mental functioning. Reversible dementias, caused by malnutrition, alcoholism, or toxins (poisons), usually affect younger people. Irreversible dementias are of two types, multiple infarcts and Alzheimer's disease.   pp. 367–368

- Individuals who suffer from Alzheimer's disease slowly lose their memories. Within months, or sometimes years, they lose their speech and language functions. Eventually they lose all control, especially of memory.
p. 369

Dying: The End of the Life Span

- Elisabeth Kübler-Ross has described dying as a process involving five stages; although controversial, Kübler-Ross's ideas have generated much interest.   p. 373

- A hospice is a special facility established to provide efficient and humane care to terminally ill patients and their families. Hospice care is not appropriate for every dying person. It requires specific kinds of commitment from the patient and family members, including questioning ethical and practical questions about care and costs, life-support systems, and medications.   p. 375

Connections

 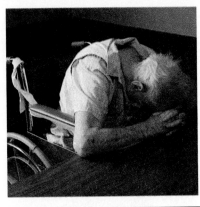 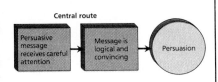

Central route

| Persuasive message receives careful attention | → | Message is logical and convincing | → | Persuasion |

If you are interested in . . .	Turn to . . .	To learn more about . . .
Sexual behavior and the process of development	◆ Ch. 11, pp. 389–390	How many psychological disorders exhibit themselves in the sexual domain of a person's life.
	◆ Ch. 12, pp. 425–427	Freud's argument that a person's life energy is sexual in nature.
	◆ Ch. 17, pp. 613–615	People are attracted to those who share their attitudes and who like them.
Mid-life crises and how people respond to stressful situations	◆ Ch. 11, pp. 411–412	How a person's emotional life is to a great extent determined by how he or she appraises a situation.
	◆ Ch. 13, pp. 471–476	The way people's health can be affected by their reactions to life-cycle events, as well as to stressors in the environment.
	◆ Ch. 14, pp. 516–521	How some people develop symptoms of depression after a major life-cycle crisis.
Stereotypes about certain types of people including adolescents and the elderly	◆ Ch. 5, pp. 172–173	The way operant conditioning, used by parents to reinforce certain ideas in their children, leads to longlasting ideas and evaluations.
	◆ Ch. 16, p. 577	Changing stereotyped ideas, which is possible only when a person views an argument as very powerful and delivered in an expert way by an important communicator.
	◆ Ch. 17, p. 618	How stereotypes, usually based on wrong information from a limited or nonexistent sample of behavior, lead to prejudice.

11 Motivation and Emotion

"The House of the Heart" by Miriam Schapiro

◆

*A*s children most of us have dreams about the future. We think about being athletes, airline pilots, or physicians. We set high goals about which we have little realistic understanding. Jim Abbott had such high goals, and he achieved them. Abbott was the star pitcher on his high school baseball team, he led the U.S. Olympic baseball team to a gold medal, and he has a fastball clocked at ninety-three miles per hour. If these statistics are not enough, the thing that separates Jim Abbott from other athletes is the fact that he has only one hand.

Abbott, whose right arm is ten inches shorter than his left, was never treated as disabled as a youngster; instead, he was encouraged to try harder. He was motivated by his parents and urged to develop a can-do attitude about life. He practiced, practiced, practiced—as all good athletes do. And he is now doing it full time with an incredible degree of success, as a starting pitcher for the California Angels.

Motivation: An internal condition that appears by inference to initiate, activate, or maintain goal-directed behavior.

Why do some people strive to achieve success, while others are content to enjoy life at a more relaxed pace? Why will one person spend a free afternoon watching soap operas and munching potato chips, while another will use the time for a five-mile run and a quick study session before dinner? Why do some people crave the excitement of competition while others seem to shy away from it?

The study of the whys of behavior—that is, motivation—is as old as philosophy. Plato (427–347 B.C.) searched for the location of reason to explain behavior, Descartes (1596–1650) focused on mind-body distinctions, and Wilhelm Wundt (1832–1920), one of the first psychologists, was concerned with the nature of feeling. Many modern theories of motivation have been developed to explain the causes of people's behaviors, but no one theory can explain all behavior. Most psychologists believe it is a combination of inborn motivation and learning that causes people to behave in certain ways. First, let's define motivation.

Motivation: A Definition

Motivation is any condition, internal to an organism, that appears by inference to initiate, activate, or maintain goal-directed behavior. Note that this definition has four basic parts:

1. internal condition,
2. observed by inference,
3. initiation, activation, or maintenance, and
4. goal-directed behavior.

Motivation is usually the result of an *internal condition*. It may develop from physiological needs and drives or from complex desires, such as the desire to help others, obtain approval, or earn a high income. Motivation is an *inferred* concept that links a person's internal conditions to external behavior. Motivation *initiates, activates,* or *maintains* behavior. For example, motivated to become a good ball player, Jim Abbott initiated a regimen of practice, which he maintains throughout the competitive season.

Last, motivation generates *goal-directed* behavior. A goal may be an object such as food, the removal of a painful stimulus, or winning a diving match. The behavior of someone who studies hard, for example, is goal directed: to maximize learning and obtain good grades. The behavior of a person who eats lunch quickly is also goal-directed: to reduce hunger quickly.

Drive reduction theories have focused on an organism's need to act because of a need to establish, balance, or maintain some goal that helps with the survival of the organism or the species. Theories that focus on *learned motives* emphasize choices, especially how an individual's expectation of success or achievement is thought to help determine how he or she will respond. *Cognitive theories* and *humanistic theory* focus on the role of human choice and personal expression. We will examine each of these theories and then look at how a person's motivations affect his or her emotions.

Focus on Learning

- ◆ Define motivation and explain its four basic parts. p. 380
- ◆ What does it mean to say that behavior is goal directed? p. 380
- ◆ Distinguish between drive theories and cognitive theories. p. 380

Hunger, Thirst, and Sexual Motivation

Some of the most influential and best-researched motivation theories are forms of **drive theory.** Drive theories assume that an organism is motivated to act because of a need to attain, reestablish, balance, or maintain some goal that helps with the survival of the organism or the species. Physiological needs are thus said to be *mechanistic* because the organism is pushed, pulled, and energized almost like a machine. Thus, stimuli such as hunger pains create, energize, and initiate behavior. An organism deprived of food for twenty-four hours will spend most of its time looking for food; it is driven to seek food.

A **drive** is an internal condition of arousal that directs an organism to satisfy physiological needs. Drive theories focus on a state of physiological imbalance, a **need,** and they describe an organism motivated by a need as being in a *drive state.* Under conditions of drive, both animals and human beings will show goal-directed behavior. A thirsty animal will seek out water, for example.

In examining the whys of behavior from a drive reduction point of view, psychologists seek to understand simple behaviors such as eating and why people do it when they do. As Maslow suggested (1962, 1969), a person's physiological need for food and water must be satisfied before any others. Let's take a closer look at three important physiological drives—hunger, thirst, and sex—that are motivated by both physiological and psychological factors.

Biological Determinants of Hunger

When you are hungry, you may feel stomach pains or become weak or dizzy—all sensations that cause you to seek food. But what causes the sensations of hunger? Explanations of hunger focus on the glucostatic approach, the role of the brain, and hormones.

Glucostatic Approach. The *glucostatic approach* argues that the principal physiological cause of hunger is the low blood-sugar level that accompanies food deprivation and its creation of a chemical imbalance. Because sugar (later broken down into glucose) is crucial to cellular activity, the body sends signals to the brain warning of a low blood-sugar level, and the brain immediately responds by generating hunger pangs in the stomach. Hunger does not depend directly on the central nervous system but on blood-sugar levels. Experiments with animals whose nerves between the stomach and the brain were severed show that the animals continue to eat at appropriate times—that is, when their blood sugar is low—providing evidence for the glucostatic approach to explaining hunger.

Keep in mind that the amount of food people eat does not determine how hungry they feel. A hungry adult who eats for five minutes may still feel hungry when he or she stops. But thirty minutes later, after the food is converted into sugar, the person may not feel hungry. The type of food eaten determines how soon the feeling of hunger disappears. A candy bar loaded with easily converted sugar will take away hunger faster than foods high in protein, such as meat, cheese, and milk, which take more time to digest and convert into glucose.

The Brain and Hunger. Much of psychologists' understanding of hunger and eating behavior comes from studies of the brain, particularly the region

Drive theory: An explanation of behavior emphasizing internal factors that energize organisms to seek, attain, or maintain some goal. Often the goal is to reestablish a state of physiological balance.

Drive: An internal aroused condition that initiates behavior to satisfy physiological needs. Drives are inferred from behavior.

Need: A physiological condition arising from an imbalance and usually accompanied by arousal.

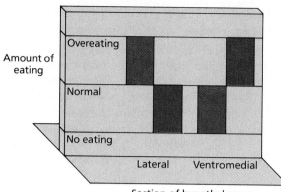

FIGURE 11.1
When the hypothalamus of an animal is either destroyed or activated, an animal's eating behavior is sharply affected.

■ Activation
■ Destruction

of the forebrain called the hypothalamus (see p. 56). Researchers now know that two areas of the hypothalamus are in part responsible for eating behavior. When the stomach becomes full, when the blood-sugar level is high, or when stimulated electrically, the ventromedial hypothalamus, or "stop eating" center, is activated and an organism stops eating. By contrast, when the lateral hypothalamus, the "start eating" center, is activated, the organism starts eating. As Figure 11.1 shows, researchers have also destroyed through lesioning techniques these same areas; destruction caused just the opposite effects of stimulation.

Hormones. Researchers find that the ventromedial hypothalamus may influence eating by stimulating the hormonal and metabolic systems (Powley, 1977). As you recall from chapter 2, insulin is a hormone secreted by the pancreas; it is released into the bloodstream when sugar (glucose) is present to allow blood sugar to be metabolized into the cells. When a person eats food that increases blood-sugar level quickly, this triggers the pancreas to quickly release insulin; a person generally finds that after an initial feeling of relief from hunger, hunger will rapidly recur because blood-sugar level is now low again (often even lower than before eating). The rapid increase in insulin (often too much insulin) allows metabolization of the sugar quickly. Thus eating a sugar-laden candy bar relieves hunger, but may bring a person to an even greater level of hunger within a half hour or so. But what happens when people's motivation for eating, hormonal system, or perhaps genetics lead them to overeating and its resulting condition, obesity?

Obesity

In an address to the American Psychological Association, Yale University psychologist Judith Rodin (1981) summarized the plight of fat people:

> First, heavy people are forced to wear the consequences of their affliction on their body and have probably built up a whole armamentarium of defenses to deal with that circumstance. No other physical characteristic except skin color is so stigmatized in our society. Second is the delightful but problematic fact that food is a positive and reinforcing stimulus for most of us. . . .
> Third, and probably most unfair of all, obesity is unusual because being fat is one of the factors that may keep one fat. . . . the perverse fact is that it often

does take fewer calories to keep people fat than it did to get them fat in the first place. This occurs because obesity itself changes the fat cells and body chemistry and alters level of energy expenditure. (p. 361)

Obesity, whatever its causes, has important psychological and health implications. How do we explain it?

Obesity: Genetic Explanations. Richard Nisbett (1972), a psychologist at the University of Michigan, proposed a *fat cell* explanation, asserting that the number of fat cells people are born with, which differs with each person, determines eating behavior and propensity toward obesity. Body fat is stored in fat cells, so people born with many fat cells are more likely to be obese than are those born with few fat cells. The number of fat cells each person has is genetically determined, but the size of each cell is affected by nutritional experience early in life as well as genetics. Dieting decreases only the *size*, not the *number*, of fat cells. Moreover, the body tends to maintain the size of fat cells at a constant level, so people who have shrunk the normal size of their fat cells by dieting will experience a constant state of food deprivation. Each time there is a significant weight gain, the person may be adding new fat cells. Thus, permanent weight loss becomes extremely difficult. This accounts for the finding that about two-thirds of the people who lose weight will gain it back within one year.

Closely associated with the fat cell explanation of eating and obesity is the view that each person has a *set point*—a level of body weight that is maintained by the body. The set point is determined by many factors, including genetics, early nutrition, current environment, and learned habits. Further, some studies suggest that people can inherit both a tendency to overeat and a slow metabolism. For example, the Pima Indians of Arizona are prone to obesity, with eighty to ninety percent of the tribe's young adults dangerously overweight. According to Ravussin (1988), who spent four years researching their habits, the Indians have unusually low metabolisms. During any twenty-four-hour period, the typical Pima (who is as active as other people) burns about eighty calories less than is considered normal for his or her body size.

People don't have the luxury of choosing their genetic heritage, but that doesn't condemn those who inherit a predisposition toward obesity to becoming fat. Keesey and Powley (1986) agree that the body's natural predisposition is to maintain homeostasis—a steady state or stability—and therefore the individual's attempts to lose weight through intake regulation (such as dieting) are prone to failure. However, Keesey and Powley assert that weight control is achievable by increasing energy expenditure through exercise.

Obesity: Psychological Explanations. Physiological makeup isn't the only important factor in eating behavior; our experiences also "teach" us how to interact with food. The social environment is rampant with food-oriented messages that have little to do with nutritional needs. People use lunch to discuss business and attend dinner parties to celebrate special occasions. Advertisements proclaim that merriment can be found at a restaurant or supermarket. Parents coax good behavior from their children by promising them desserts or fat-laden snacks. Thus, eating acquires a significance that far exceeds its role in satisfying physiological needs; it also serves as a rationale for social interaction, a means to reward good behavior, and a way to fend off unhappy thoughts.

The Pima Indians of Arizona have unusually low metabolisms, resulting in an inherited tendency toward being overweight.

Consider my own attempts to maintain my weight after losing seventy-five pounds through diet and exercise. Suddenly, I noticed food even more than before. Every time I saw food advertised on billboards or television, I wanted to eat. All the social events I attended seemed to feature a delectable spread of appetizers, which I was tempted to sample in order to be "sociable." And whenever I became anxious, my first impulse was to seek the comfort of food. However, by separating eating behaviors linked to hunger from those that were learned responses to emotions, I controlled my eating behavior and avoided gaining weight even two years after my major weight loss. Researchers continue to explore the various causes of overeating, and it has led to some interesting findings, especially when dieters are compared to non-dieters.

What Causes Overeating?

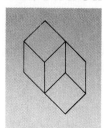

THINKING ABOUT
R E S E A R C H

*T*here are facts of nature that cannot be contradicted. Unfortunately, one fact is that calories not expended will be stored as fat, and a continued imbalance between food intake and calorie expenditure results in obesity. But what causes people to overeat? Through research spanning three decades, answers have slowly evolved.

Initial Studies. Stanley Schachter investigated the eating patterns of obese people. He disguised the true purpose of his experiments because people often alter their behavior when told they are being watched. In one experiment, some subjects were given roast beef sandwiches to eat and others were not. The subjects were then seated in front of bowls of crackers and presented with rating scales. They were told to eat as many of the crackers as necessary to judge whether each bowl contained crackers that were salty, cheesy, or garlicky. The researcher's actual goal was to observe how many crackers the subjects ate in making their judgments.

Initial Results. As Figure 11.2 shows, the normal-weight subjects ate far fewer crackers than they would have if they had not eaten the roast beef sandwiches. In contrast, the obese subjects ate even more than they would have. Schachter concluded that the eating behavior of the obese subjects had little correlation with the actual state of their stomachs, but was determined principally by external factors (Schachter, Goldman, and Gordon, 1968).

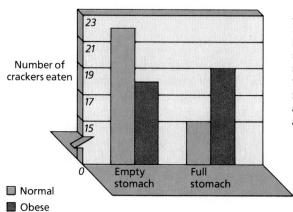

FIGURE 11.2
In an experiment involving normal-weight and obese subjects, normal-weight subjects ate fewer crackers when their stomachs were full, whereas obese subjects ate more when their stomachs were full.

Focus on External Cues. In another study, Schachter asked both obese and normal-weight subjects to sit at a desk and fill out a personality test. The subjects were invited to munch from a bag of almonds while they completed the task. Schachter set up two situations. In one, the almonds were shelled; in the other, they were unshelled. Schachter's question was whether one group would eat more than the other.

About half of the normal-weight subjects ate nuts, whether or not the nuts were shelled. In contrast, nineteen of twenty obese subjects ate the shelled nuts—but only one out of twenty ate the unshelled ones. Schachter concluded that obese people eat more than people of normal weight when food is readily available; less when it is difficult to get. Schachter also showed that obese adults will eat more from a bowl of nuts that is brightly illuminated than from a dimly illuminated bowl. Adults of normal weight are unaffected by the degree of illumination. This evidence led Schachter to infer that the sight of food motivates overweight people to eat; he contended that the availability of food, its prominence, and other *external* cues tell obese subjects when to eat (too much, too fast, and too often). In contrast, normal-weight individuals eat more in response to *internal* physiological mechanisms, such as hunger. This finding suggests that dieters and non-dieters differ in important ways.

Dieters versus Non-dieters. When obese subjects accustomed to constant dieting were told that they had consumed a high-calorie beverage, they were more likely than nonobese people to binge (Spencer and Fremouw, 1979). In contrast, non-dieting obese subjects ate less (rather than more) after receiving such information. Similarly, when a waiter describes a dessert in tempting terms, normal-weight individuals who have just finished a big meal are less likely than obese diners to order the dessert (Herman, Olmsted, and Polivy, 1983). Furthermore, when overweight subjects become upset they are strongly motivated to overeat as a means of coping with their feelings (Grilo, Shiffman, and Wing, 1989). These findings depend on a person's weight, gender, and whether he or she is a regular dieter (Klesges, Klem, and Bene, 1989).

Contradictions. Schachter's work set off wide-ranging research into the psychological variables that cause overeating. It forced psychologists to consider all the factors that motivate people to eat, overeat, and become obese. His work focused on external cues, but other researchers argue that obese people are not necessarily more responsive to external cues than normal-weight people. Stunkard and others suggest that differences between the eating habits of obese and normal-weight individuals are small and inconsistent (Rodin, 1981; Stunkard et al., 1980). They contend instead that the physiological responses of obese individuals may be triggered more quickly than those of normal-weight people. According to physicians Hirsch and Leibel (1988), people who have lost weight often have a lower caloric intake requirement for weight maintenance than those who have never been obese. This means that formerly obese people have a more difficult time keeping their weight down. In addition, Stunkard (Stunkard et al., 1980) argues that genetics may play a stronger role than environmental influences; disorders of the autonomic nervous system may be keeping obese people fat (Peterson, Seligman, and Vaillant, 1988).

The newest research and assertions force a critical evaluation of all previously collected data. They imply that physiological mechanisms may play a much larger role than psychological ones in determining eating behavior. Today, there is no simple answer to the nature versus nurture question of obesity, but the research continues. Some of the latest even suggests a relationship between socioeconomic status and obesity. Sobal and Stunkard (1989) report that in developed societies like the United States, women of lower socioeconomic status are more likely to be obese than women of higher socioeconomic status. Research into the causes for this finding is just beginning. The consequences of eating too much or too little are also being explored in the study of eating disorders, discussed next. ◆

What causes overeating? Some research suggests that overweight people are especially susceptible to external cues that trigger eating.

Eating Disorders

Although she had been fighting the urge all day, Arlene knew she was headed for another eating binge. When her roommates asked her to come with them to a party, Arlene declined, saying she had to study. As soon as her roommates left, Arlene dashed to her car, drove to the corner bakery, and bought a dozen doughnuts. Then she stopped at the grocery store for milk, crackers, ice cream, jam, and half a dozen candy bars. She rushed back home, locked the door, unplugged the phone, and began eating. Within twenty minutes she consumed nearly 7,000 calories. Her stomach painfully swollen, Arlene drank several glasses of water and made herself throw up. Then she swore, for the hundredth time, she would never binge again.

One of the great joys in life, eating, has become the focus of a psychological disorder that is now widely recognized. **Eating disorders** are characterized by gross disturbances in eating behavior and the way in which individuals respond to food. Two such disorders are anorexia nervosa and bulimia nervosa, the disorder that affects Arlene.

Anorexia Nervosa.   **Anorexia nervosa,** or "starvation disease," is an eating disorder characterized by an obstinate and willful refusal to eat. Individuals with the disorder, usually young high school girls from well-educated families, have an intense fear of being fat and relentlessly pursue becoming thinner. As many as forty out of ten thousand young women may develop the disorder. The anorexic's refusal to eat eventually brings about emaciation and malnutrition. Victims can sustain permanent damage to their heart muscle tissue, sometimes dying as a result, as did singer/songwriter Karen Carpenter.

Many therapists believe that anorexia nervosa has strictly psychological origins, citing family interactions and overprotective parents as the main causes (e.g., Brone and Fisher, 1988). Others are exploring both the physiological and psychological origins of the disease, including the many changes taking place at puberty that might influence its emergence (Attie and Brooks-Gunn, 1989), especially the idea that people with eating disorders may lack a hormone thought to induce a feeling of fullness after a meal.

Anorexia nervosa patients need a structured setting and are often hospitalized to help them regain weight. To ensure that the setting is reinforcing, hospital staff members are always present at meals, and individual and family therapy is provided. Clients are encouraged to eat and are rewarded for consuming specified quantities of food. Generally, psychotherapy is also necessary to help these young women maintain a healthy self-image and body weight. Even with treatment, however, as many as fifty percent suffer relapses within a year.

Bulimia Nervosa.   When Arlene made herself vomit, she was showing one of the symptoms of bulimia. **Bulimia nervosa,** another eating disorder, tends to occur in normal-weight women with no history of anorexia nervosa (e.g., Garfinkel, Moldofsy, and Garner, 1980). It involves binge eating (recognized by the person to be abnormal) and a consequent fear of not being able to stop eating. Individuals who engage in binge eating become fearful of gaining weight. Therefore, they often purge themselves of unwanted calories. Methods of purging include vomiting, laxatives, diuretics, compulsive exercising, and weight reduction drugs. Bulimics become depressed (Hinz and Williamson, 1987), and the medical complications are serious, including cardiovascular system changes, gastrointestinal changes, menstrual irregularities,

Eating disorders: A disorder characterized by gross disturbances in eating behavior and the way individuals respond to food.

Anorexia nervosa: An eating disorder characterized by an intense fear of becoming obese, dramatic weight loss, concern about weight, disturbances in body image, and an obstinate and willful refusal to eat.

Bulimia nervosa: An eating disorder characterized by repeated episodes of binge eating and fear of not being able to stop eating, followed by vomiting or use of laxatives, diuretics, compulsive exercising, or weight-reduction drugs.

blood and hormone dysfunctions, muscle and skeletal changes, and sharp swings in mood and personality (Kaplan and Woodside, 1987).

The ratio of female to male bulimics is ten to one (Schlundt and Johnson, 1990). Researchers theorize that women more than men readily believe that fat is bad, and thin is beautiful. Women of higher socioeconomic classes are at greater risk of becoming bulimic, as are professionals whose weight is directly related to achievement, such as dancers, athletes, and models (Striegel-Moore, Silberstein, and Rodin, 1986). Disharmonious family life or having maladjusted parents appears to increase the likelihood of bulimia (Strober and Humphrey, 1987). Bulimics also have lower self-esteem than people who eat normally (Dykens and Gerrard, 1986; Laessle et al., 1989); they come from families they perceive as having poor relationships and a high level of conflict (Johnson and Flach, 1985); and they may have experienced some kind of clinical depression in the past (Walsh et al., 1985). According to Johnson and Larson (1982), some women may eat as a means of lightening their mood swings and regulating tension. After binging, however, they feel guilty. To lessen their guilt and the potential consequence of gaining weight, they "get away with something" by purging themselves. Researchers believe that their purges reduce postbinge anguish. Bulimic women become entirely involved in food-related behaviors to the exclusion of contact with other people.

If an adolescent girl is raised in a family that focuses on dieting, has parents with personality disorders, and is genetically predisposed to weight problems, her likelihood of developing bulimia may be greater than that of the general population (Strober and Humphrey, 1987). Some bulimic women may have disturbed metabolic systems (Devlin et al., 1990) and even disturbances in their perception of taste and feelings of fullness (Rodin, Bartoshuk, Peterson, and Schank, 1990). Efforts to reduce the likelihood that adolescents will develop the disorder continue as does research into its potential biological causes. Researchers (Shissal, Crago, Neal, and Swain, 1987) suggest that prevention programs be established at home, in schools, in colleges, and in the community.

Individuals suffering from anorexia nervosa are unable to see themselves realistically. They compulsively refuse food.

---

1 ◆ What is a mechanistic motivation theory? p. 381
2 ◆ What are the claims of the fat cell theory? p. 383
3 ◆ According to Schachter, what effect do external cues have on the eating behavior of obese subjects? pp. 384–385
4 ◆ Distinguish between anorexia and bulimia. p. 386

Focus on Learning

Thirst

People have many basic needs, among them, the need for water and other fluids. A human embryo is made up of more than eighty percent water; a newborn child, about seventy-five percent water; and a normal adult, about sixty to seventy percent water. Like hunger, thirst serves as a strong drive mechanism in both animals and human beings. Although you can live for weeks without food, you can live only a few days without replenishing your supply of fluid.

A delicate balance of fluid intake is necessary for proper physiological functioning; any imbalance results in a drive to restore the balance. When people experience fluid deprivation and the resulting cellular dehydration, their mouths and throats become dry, cueing them to drink. It is important

1. mechanistic because organism pulled, pushed + energized almost like a machine.
2. # of fat cells person is born with determines eating behavior + propensity towards obesity.
3. sight of food motivates them to eat.
4. anorexia

The human body is extremely sensitive to any loss of water and will always seek to have the balance restored.

to note that thirst is not a *result* of dryness in the throat or mouth, and simply placing water in the mouth will not reduce thirst.

Approximately two-thirds of our body's fluid is contained within the cells, and the remaining one-third is found between the cells. Regulation of fluid within cells is controlled primarily by the hypothalamus (an area of the forebrain, see p. 56); regulation of fluid between cells is controlled primarily by the kidneys and the pituitary. The human body is thus highly sensitive to water losses.

When the body does not have an adequate supply of fluid, cells in the hypothalamus and pituitary respond. Consider fluid loss between cells: Recall from chapter 2 (p. 62) that the pituitary initiates an antidiuretic hormone that acts on the kidneys to increase fluid absorption and decrease the amount of urine produced by the body. Thus, when the pituitary is stimulated in this way, a person urinates less frequently. If a person consumes a great deal of sodium (found in table salt, soy sauce, and many common junk foods), the body responds by needing more fluids—the ratio of the chemical sodium to water content is too great. Again, the body responds by creating a need for fluid and fewer trips to the bathroom.

A key point to remember is that thirst is a response on the part of the body to trigger fluid consumption—it is not the cause or initiator of fluid consumption. Cells in the brain (hypothalamus and pituitary) initiate fluid consumption and respond to cellular changes and ratios of chemicals to fluids in the body. We are motivated to drink because of internal processes. Of course, we can drink too much or too little. We develop many learned preferences, for example, quenching our thirst with Coke versus Pepsi, coffee or tea, or plain unadulterated water. The role of learning and preferences becomes especially important in more complex behaviors, such as sex.

Sexual Motivation and Behavior

The sexual drive in human beings is no longer considered solely or even primarily under physiological control, but is to a great extent under voluntary control. In contrast, the sexual behavior of lower organisms is controlled largely by their physiological and hormonal systems. (See chapter 2 for a review of hormones.)

Sex Hormones. When hormones are released they exert profound effects on behavior. If the hormone-generating testes of male rats are removed, the animals show a marked decrease in sexual activity. In human beings, removal of hormone-generating organs may not affect sexual behavior at all (depending on the person's age at removal). Similarly, most female lower organisms are sexually responsive only when hormones are released into the bloodstream; that is, when they are "in heat." Human beings, on the other hand, can choose whether or not to respond sexually to encounters at any given time.

Generally, the higher the organism on the phylogenetic ladder, the more important sexual experience and learning is to normal sexual behavior later in life. In rats, for example, early experience is not necessary. But if dogs, cats, and monkeys are isolated from sexual experiences early in life, they later show a lack of sexual responsiveness. The human sexual response cycle is far more complex and is made up of a series of stages.

Sexual Response Cycle. When human beings become sexually aroused, they go through a series of four stages known as the sexual response cycle.

In the **excitement phase,** there is increased heart rate, blood pressure, and respiration. A key characteristic of the excitement phase is **vasoconstriction** or engorgement of the blood vessels. In the female, breasts swell and vaginal lubrication increases; in males, there is an erection. The excitement phase is anticipatory and may last from a few minutes to a few hours; it may be initiated by physical contact, fantasy, or any of the senses.

In the **plateau phase,** both men and women are prepared for orgasm. Autonomic nervous system activity increases, for example, with heart rate increasing. In women the vagina becomes engorged and at its full extension; in men, the penis is fully erect and turns a darker color. In the **orgasm phase,** autonomic nervous system activity reaches its peak, and muscle contractions throughout the body occur in spasms. An *orgasm* is the peak of sexual activity in which muscular contractions occur, especially in the genital area. In men, muscles through the reproductive system help expel semen; in women, muscles surrounding the outer vagina contract. Although men experience only one orgasm, women are capable of multiple orgasms. Orgasms are an all-or-none activity lasting only a few seconds; once a threshold for orgasm is reached, it occurs.

After orgasm, a **resolution phase** occurs in which the body naturally returns to its resting or normal state; this takes from one to several minutes and varies considerably from person to person. During the resolution phase, men are usually unable to achieve an erection for a period of time, called a *refractory period.* Like many other physiological responses, the sexual response cycle is subject to considerable variation. Some people have a lengthy plateau phase, while others have a longer resolution phase. People who are unable to normally experience pleasure from sexual activity, and for whom sexual behavior becomes difficult, painful, or aversive, may suffer from a sexual dysfunction.

Sexual Dysfunctions. **Sexual dysfunction** is the inability to obtain satisfaction from sexual behavior, often accompanied by the inability to experience orgasm. Sexual dysfunctions sometimes occur from too much alcohol or drugs; sometimes they occur from fatigue or some other physical ailment. Some sexual dysfunctions are the result of early experience in which faulty sexual behaviors or attitudes are learned. Most people experience some type of sexual problem at one time or another; generally these problems are temporary.

Sexual problems have been carefully researched. Starting with the work of Masters and Johnson (1966, 1970), psychologists and physicians have been attempting to help people with sexual dysfunctions. When a man or a woman comes for treatment, a typical procedure is to treat not only the client but also his or her partner. The Masters and Johnson approach has a strong commitment toward treating pairs of people.

A man is said to suffer from **erectile dysfunction** when he is unable to attain or maintain an erection of sufficient strength to allow him to engage in sexual intercourse. Erectile dysfunction can be caused by anatomical defects, damage to the central nervous system, or the excessive use of alcohol and other drugs. Most often, however, erectile dysfunction is caused by emotional problems.

There are two kinds of erectile dysfunction. A man who suffers from **primary erectile dysfunction** has never had an erection of sufficient strength for sexual intercourse. Masters and Johnson argue that fear and unusual sensitivity or anxiety regarding sexual incidents that may have happened early in a man's life generally contribute to primary erectile dysfunction.

Excitement phase: The stage of the sexual response cycle in which there are initial increases in heart rate, blood pressure, and respiration. *Vasoconstriction* occurs during this stage; erections and vaginal lubrication occur.

Vasoconstriction: In the sexual response cycle, an engorgement of the blood vessels, particularly in the genital area.

Plateau phase: The stage of the sexual response cycle in which both men and women are preparing for orgasm. Autonomic nervous system activity increases and there is further vasoconstriction.

Orgasm phase: The stage of the sexual response cycle in which autonomic nervous system activity reaches its peak, and muscle contractions occur throughout the body in spasms. An *orgasm* is the peak of sexual activity.

Resolution phase: The stage of the sexual response cycle in which the body naturally returns to its resting or normal state.

Sexual dysfunction: The inability to obtain satisfaction from sexual behavior, often accompanied by the inability to experience orgasm.

Erectile dysfunction: In men, the inability to attain or maintain an erection of sufficient strength to allow sexual intercourse.

Primary erectile dysfunction: When a man has never been able to achieve or maintain an erection of sufficient strength for sexual intercourse.

Secondary erectile dysfunction: When a man fails to achieve an erection in twenty-five percent of his sexual attempts, he is said to be suffering from secondary erectile dysfunction.

Premature ejaculation: The condition in which a man cannot delay ejaculation long enough to satisfy his sexual partner in fifty percent of his sexual encounters.

Primary orgasmic dysfunction: The condition in which a woman has never been able to achieve orgasm by any means at any time.

Secondary orgasmic dysfunction: A woman's inability to achieve orgasm, even though she has achieved orgasm in the past by one technique or another; sometimes called *situational orgasmic dysfunction.*

Secondary erectile dysfunction occurs more frequently. Those with **secondary erectile dysfunction** have had successful sexual intercourse in the past but are now incapable of it. When a man fails to achieve penile erection in twenty-five percent of his sexual attempts, he is categorized as having secondary erectile dysfunction. One of the key symptoms and major blocks to curing those with secondary erectile dysfunction is that once a man has had a problem in achieving or maintaining an erection, he becomes overly sensitive and maintains a distinct memory of the incident. The next time he tries to have an erection he fails completely because he fears that he might not be able to maintain it. Thus, a vicious circle is created in which fear produces inability and inability produces fear. Most men, at one time or another, are unable to attain or maintain an erection.

Another common sexual dysfunction is premature ejaculation. **Premature ejaculation** occurs when a man cannot delay ejaculation long enough to satisfy his sexual partner during at least half of his sexual encounters. Many people have assumed that premature ejaculation is caused by either an abnormally sensitive penis or an inability of the man to control himself. However, premature ejaculation is usually caused by emotional and psychological factors; with the cooperation of his partner, a man can learn to withhold orgasm until he wants it to happen. Fear and anxiety caused by previous failures often deprive the man of his "staying power," just as fear can cause secondary erectile dysfunction.

Masters and Johnson's approach to treating erectile dysfunction is to teach men not to fear failure. Both the man and woman are taught the art of giving pleasure in order to receive pleasure. They are taught to relax and to enjoy touching, feeling, and being sexual. In the first stage of treatment they are not encouraged to have intercourse because it may renew past fears. Masters and Johnson argue that once the fear is removed, natural processes will take control and intercourse will follow in due time.

Sexual dysfunctions are not limited to men. When a woman is unable to obtain an orgasm she is said to have orgasmic dysfunction. A woman who has **primary orgasmic dysfunction** never achieves an orgasm through any method of sexual stimulation. Many causes for primary orgasmic dysfunction are physical, but more often, they are psychological and are due to extreme religious orthodoxy, unfavorable communication about sexual activities, or some childhood trauma.

Most orgasmic dysfunctions are categorized as secondary (or situational). **Secondary orgasmic dysfunction** is the inability of a woman who has achieved orgasm by one technique or another in the past to achieve it in a given situation. Thus, a woman who has had an orgasm, even if it is during a homosexual encounter, does not suffer from primary orgasmic dysfunction. Very often the secondary orgasmic dysfunction occurs when a woman is unable to accept her mate because she finds him or her sexually unattractive, undesirable, or in some other way unacceptable. In addition, many women find that orgasm brings about feelings of guilt, shame, and fear. Like her male counterpart, the woman may have experienced traumatic sexually-related events that inhibit her sexual feelings and may bring about fear.

Treatment of female orgasmic dysfunction involves several steps. According to Masters and Johnson, the key is understanding the client's sexual value system and the reasons for her inability and/or unwillingness to achieve orgasm. Masters and Johnson argue that husband, wife, and therapist should take part in a roundtable discussion where the woman discusses her own ideas about sex and what attracts and repels her. Using the woman's own value system, the therapist teaches her to respond to sexual stimulation.

The couple is then directed not to have intercourse; rather, they are told through a series of treatment sessions to seek and sustain pleasure so that in successive days an increasing amount of erotic pleasure is attained. Orgasm is not the focus but ultimately is achieved in an unhurried situation in which pressure to perform is not placed on either partner. Slowly, almost imperceptibly, the partners become more relaxed and willing to experience sexuality. Nearly all sexual behavior focuses on arousal and sensory stimulation, most often creating it; sensory stimulation turns out to be a key component in much of human behavior.

Sensory Stimulation and Arousal Theory

In addition to hunger and thirst, people have complex physiological needs for sensory stimulation. Unlike hunger and thirst, lack of sensory experience does not result in physiological imbalance, yet both human beings and animals seek sensory stimulation. When deprived of a normal amount of visual, auditory, or tactile stimulation, some adults may become irritable and consider their situation or environment intolerable. Kittens like to explore their environment; young monkeys will investigate mechanical devices and play with puzzles; and people seem motivated or impelled toward seeking sensory stimulation. (However, in some situations people seek to avoid stimulation— for example, when they are sick, or need rest.)

Neither a lack of sensory stimulation (previously discussed) nor drive reduction theory explains many basic behaviors. Arousal theory attempts to bridge the gap by explaining the link between our behavior and our state of arousal. Think of some activity that you practice often and occasionally either compete in or perform publicly. For example, you may be a diver, an actor, or a member of a debating team. Chances are, you performed most poorly when you were either not interested in practicing or exceedingly nervous about your performance, such as during competition. Conversely, you probably did your best when you were eager to practice or when you were moderately excited by competition. This explains why some baseball players perform exceptionally well at the beginning of the season, when pressure is only moderately high, and then commit numerous errors when pressure increases, for instance, in the final games of the World Series.

Although it isn't necessary for survival, humans and animals actively seek sensory stimulation.

Arousal is generally thought of in terms of activation of the central nervous system, the autonomic nervous system, and the muscles and glands. The link between performance and arousal was first scientifically explored in 1908 by R. M. Yerkes and J. D. Dodson. They described a relationship, called the Yerkes-Dodson law, between avoidance and learning and task difficulty in mice. Contemporary researchers have extended that relationship (e.g., Brehm and Self, 1989) by suggesting that when a person's level of arousal and anxiety is too high or too low, performance will be poor. Thus, people who do not care about what they are doing have little anxiety, but they also have little arousal and usually perform poorly in both work and play.

Many traditional motivation and learning theorists assume that an increase in drive (and an associated arousal level) will result in increased effectiveness of behavior. Later researchers suggested that drive and ability will predict behavior. According to this simple formulation, as an organism's drive level increases, its performance will improve: The hungrier the rat, the faster it will run down the alley to its food.

Researcher Donald Hebb (1904–1985) suggested that behavior varies from disorganized to effective, depending on a person's level of arousal. He argued that human functioning is most efficient when people are at an optimal level of arousal and, along with other researchers, assumed that people seek, and are most efficient at, specific arousal levels (Anderson, 1990). The inverted U-shaped curve in Figure 11.3 shows the relationship between level of arousal and effectiveness of behavior and is useful in thinking about a broad range of behavioral phenomena.

Fundamental to all arousal theories is the notion that it is not the stimulus but the organism's internal response to the stimulus that determines how the organism behaves. Hebb's idea shifted the focus from stimuli and drives or needs to people's response-determining behavior. For Hebb, arousal energizes behavior, but does not direct it.

The development of optimal arousal theories helped psychologists explain the variation in people's responses to situations in terms of a state of internal arousal rather than solely in terms of the stimuli encountered (see Building Table 11.1). This shift in emphasis marked a subtle but important

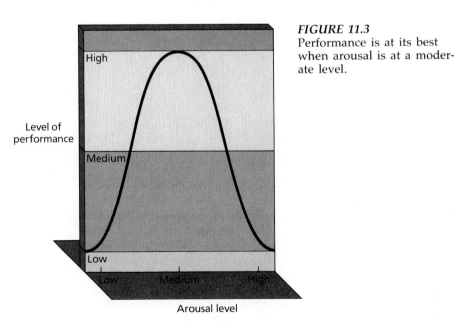

FIGURE 11.3
Performance is at its best when arousal is at a moderate level.

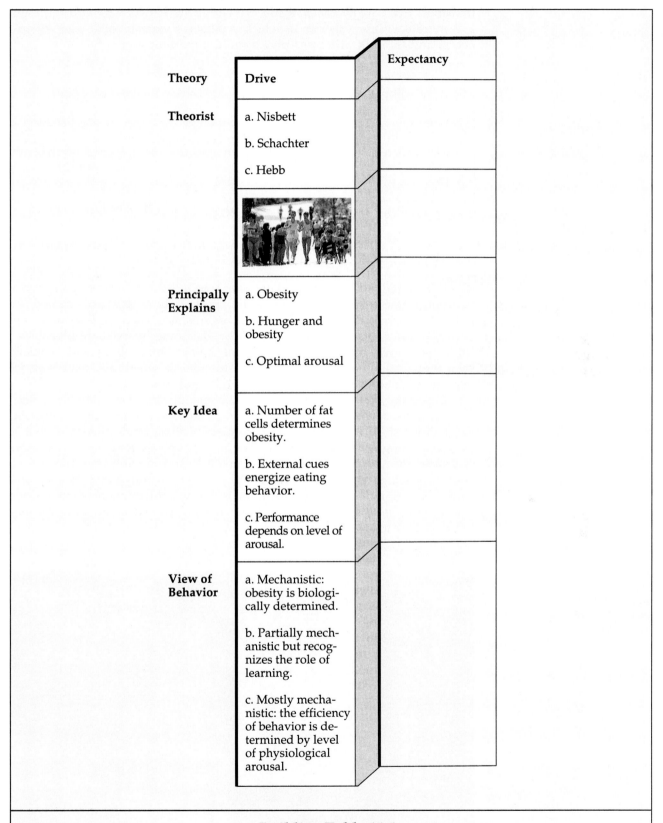

Theory	Drive	Expectancy
Theorist	a. Nisbett b. Schachter c. Hebb	
Principally Explains	a. Obesity b. Hunger and obesity c. Optimal arousal	
Key Idea	a. Number of fat cells determines obesity. b. External cues energize eating behavior. c. Performance depends on level of arousal.	
View of Behavior	a. Mechanistic: obesity is biologically determined. b. Partially mechanistic but recognizes the role of learning. c. Mostly mechanistic: the efficiency of behavior is determined by level of physiological arousal.	

♦   ***Building Table 11.1***   ♦
Drive Theories of Motivation

transition from solely mechanistic drive-reduction theory toward learning and more cognitive theories in which a person's expectations, past experiences, and thought processes play a more important role.

Focus on Learning

- ◆ What will placing water in the mouths of thirsty human beings do? p. 387
- ◆ What two factors play an especially large role in human sexual behavior? p. 388 *physiological & hormonal systems*
- ◆ Distinguish between primary and secondary erectile dysfunction, and between primary and secondary orgasmic dysfunction. pp. 389–390
- ◆ Describe the Yerkes-Dodson law. p. 392

[handwritten notes:]
P.E.D- a guy has never had an erection of sufficient strength for intercourse
S.E.D- have had successful intercourse but are now incaple.
P.O.D- never recieves orgasm through any form of self stimulation
S.O.D- has been able to recieve orgasm by one technique or another but is now unable in certain situations

Learned Motives

If you trace the history of motivation you find a distinct shift back and forth between certain concepts. For example, many early researchers focused on internal conditions, needs, that impel organisms to action. But today researchers recognize and embrace the idea that some motives are physiological, others are learned, and that human beings think about and evaluate their motivations and their behaviors. This idea is most aptly expressed in expectancy theory, which connects thought and motivation.

Expectancy theory focuses on people's need for achievement and success; it suggests that people's expectation of success and the value they place on it direct their behavior. A key element of expectancy theory is that a person's thoughts guide behavior. The social motives and needs a person develops are not physiological in origin; they are not initiated because of some physiological imbalance. Rather, people learn through their interactions in the environment to have needs for mastery, affiliation, or competition. These needs lead to expectations about the future and about how various efforts will lead to various outcomes.

In many cultures, such as the Apache, puberty is celebrated with highly significant rites that help form the young adult's later sexual attitudes.

Expectancy theory: An explanation of behavior that emphasizes a person's expectation of success and need for achievement as energizing factors.

The expression *self-fulfilling prophecy* suggests that those who expect to succeed, will; those who don't, won't. Expectations for success and failure can influence the outcome of an effort if those expectations help shape the person's behavior. Thus, a teacher who expects a student to fail may often treat the student in ways that increase the likelihood of failure; things tend to turn out just the way the teacher expected (or prophesied) they would. Expectancy thus becomes a key component of the whys of behavior.

Motives and Social Needs

To understand some important concepts related to expectancy theories, consider Jim Abbott's desire to be a professional baseball player. The desire, hard work, and long hours of practice meant depriving himself of other pleasures, but winning, being a pro, and being among the best obviously added to Abbott's self-esteem. A **motive** is a specific internal condition that usually involves some form of arousal that directs or impels a person (or animal) toward a goal. Unlike a drive, which has a physiological origin, a **social motive** does not have to have a physiological explanation. Thus, although Abbott was driven to be among the best, there was no urgent physiological need for him to do so.

Jim Abbott was driven by social needs to practice and excel. A **social need** is an aroused condition involving feelings about self, others, and relationships. Abbott's social needs, for example, probably included winning approval from family, friends, and other ball players. These needs for achievement, affiliation, and good feelings about one's self are affected by many factors, including socioeconomic status and race (Littig and Williams, 1978) and experiences from birth onward.

Social Need for Achievement

The most notable expectancy theories focus on the social **need for achievement.** According to achievement theories, people engage in behaviors that satisfy their desires for success, mastery, and fulfillment. Tasks not oriented toward these goals are not motivating and are either not engaged in or are undertaken without energy and commitment.

McClelland. One of the early leaders in studies of achievement motivation was David C. McClelland (1917–   ), whose studies were cited in 1988 by the American Psychological Association for their innovation. McClelland's early research focused on the idea that people have strong social motives for achievement. Ultimately he showed that achievement motivation is learned in a person's home environment during childhood. Adults with high needs for achievement had parents who stressed excellence and provided physical affection and emotional rewards for high achievement. These adults also generally walked early, talked early, and had high needs for achievement even in grammar school (e.g., Teevan and McGhee, 1972). High achievement needs are most pronounced in firstborn children, perhaps because parents typically have more time to give them direction and praise. Achievement motives are often measured through scores derived from coding the thought content of imaginative stories.

TAT. Other early studies of people's need for achievement used the *Thematic Apperception Test,* or TAT. During this test subjects are shown scenes with no captions and vague themes, which are thus open to interpretation. They

Motive: A specific internal condition directing an organism's behavior toward a goal.

Social motive: An internal condition that directs people toward establishing or maintaining relationships with other people and toward establishing feelings about themselves.

Social need: An aroused condition involving feelings about self, others, and relationships.

Need for achievement: A social need that directs a person to strive constantly for excellence and success.

A person's learned need to succeed can be enhanced through competition.

are instructed not to think in terms of right or wrong answers but to answer four basic questions for each picture: What is happening? What has led up to this situation? What is being thought? What will happen? Using a complex scoring system, researchers analyze subjects' descriptions of each scene and find that subjects with high needs for achievement tell stories that stress success, getting ahead, and competition.

High versus Low Need for Achievement. In tests such as the TAT, a researcher can quickly discern high- versus low-need achievement subjects. Lowell (1952), for example, found that when he asked subjects to rearrange scrambled letters (such as *wtse*) to construct a meaningful word (such as *west*), subjects with low needs for achievement did not improve much over successive testing periods. In contrast, subjects who scored high in need for achievement showed regular improvement over several periods of testing (see Figure 11.4). The researchers concluded that when presented with a complex task, subjects with high needs for achievement find new and better ways of performing the task as they practice it, whereas subjects with low needs for achievement try no new methods. High-need achievers constantly strive toward excellence and better performance (McClelland, 1961).

Risk and Achievement. People's need for achievement seems closely related to the amount of risk they are willing to take. Some researchers claim that children exposed to praise are likely to be more achievement oriented and thus willing to take on higher levels of risk. To test this idea, Canavan-Gumpert (1977) presented first- and sixth-grade girls in a New York suburban school with math problems and praised or criticized them for correct or incorrect answers, respectively. After a practice task in which they were praised or criticized, the girls chose problems to do at one of eight difficulty levels.

The praise-success subjects had more optimistic expectations, higher standards, and greater confidence about their future performance. They chose problems at the highest level of difficulty and were willing to take the risk of tough problems and failure. Subjects in the criticism-failure group were dissatisfied with their performance and chose problems at the lowest difficulty level. The most important finding of the Canavan-Gumpert study is that praise and criticism directly affect children's risk-taking behavior and, ultimately, their need for achievement.

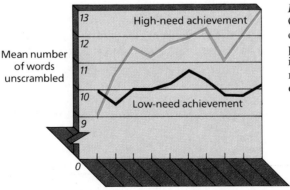

FIGURE 11.4
On scrambled-letter tasks, over successive two-minute periods, low-need achievers improved overall, but high-need achievers improved even more.

The goals people set and the amount of risk they are willing to take are also affected by the kind of needs that motivate them, their past experiences, and even their moods (Hom and Arbuckle, 1988). For example, a person heavily pushed toward success by parents and sports coaches may develop a high need for achievement; after positive experiences in the past, such an individual will typically set challenging, but attainable, goals. Thus, those with high needs for power and public recognition take high risks, and those with high needs for affiliation take low risks.

Importance of Achievement Motivation. For most adults, social motivation, with its emphasis on achievement, focuses on a sense of satisfaction and well-being throughout life. It would thus follow that people whose high needs for achievement are met might be happier. And the data, in fact, show that older individuals with high aspirations are more satisfied with life than are those with low aspirations.

Erikson's theory, studied in chapter 10, postulates middle adulthood as a period of generativity. This can be translated for the motivation researcher as a period of productivity. Late adulthood, from Erikson's view, is a time of integration when achievement is not a focus; however, the data show that achievement motivation does not decrease, or decreases little, with advancing age (Gerrard, Reznikoff, and Riklan, 1982). Life satisfaction is determined by a number of important variables, including income, marital status, and social contacts (Diener, 1983); achievement motivation seems to be highly valued and related to people's sense of well-being. Achievement motivation is affected by many variables such as age, gender, education, and career so that as a concept it still needs much more study. As theories about motivation move away from simple mechanistic explanations, it becomes harder to specify all the potent variables that affect motivation. For example, what happens to people's motivation when they cooperate rather than compete?

Cooperative Learning

*M*ost American classrooms set students against each other by having them compete; when students help each other, it's often called cheating. But research from the University of Minnesota, Johns Hopkins University, and the University of California shows that the interaction between students—not just between student and teacher or student and books—plays a significant role in real learning. Teachers who overlook student-to-student teaching may be failing their own courses (Kohn, 1986).

Studies show that forming teams of students in which no one gets credit until everyone understands the material is far more effective than competitive or individualized learning. Preschoolers or college students, English or physics—students have more fun, enjoy the subject matter more, and learn more when they work together.

What's the secret? Learning stems more from providing explanations than from receiving them. In a cooperative group, everyone has an incentive to help everyone else. The result is that high-, medium-, and low-ability students all benefit from a sharing of skills.

Our society associates excellence with being Number One. But the data show that competition—one student can succeed only if others fail—actually impedes learning. Citing the effectiveness of team learning, David Johnson, a social psychologist and education professor at the University of Minnesota, states,

"There's almost nothing that American education has seen with this level of empirical support. None of us is as smart as all of us" (Kohn, 1986).

Cooperative education isn't simply grouping students around a table and telling them to work together. It means carefully establishing "positive interdependence" that makes each student dependent on and accountable to others in the group. The students start to think of themselves as a team. Knowing they will sink or swim together, they start swimming.

There are several ways to put this theory into practice. One approach, called the jigsaw method, was invented by Elliot Aronson, a social psychologist at the University of California, Santa Cruz. He divided a study project into parts and gave one piece to each student in a group. Then he told them that everyone would be responsible for all the material.

Students had to learn from each other, and they did. But Aronson found other results, too. Self-esteem went up as each student saw that others were depending on him or her. And each one realized that being a good student didn't depend on besting others. Students in the groups also grew to like each other more, including those of different races and ability levels.

When Aronson's experiment was finished, an interesting thing happened. Even though they were free to resume standard teaching methods, some teachers whose classes were used in the study retained cooperative learning. It had worked so well that they decided to keep it.

According to Kohn (1986), competition gets in the way of real learning by making students anxious. It also makes them doubt their own abilities and become nasty toward losers, envious of winners, more prejudiced toward those from other ethnic groups, and suspicious of just about everyone. In a book on competition, Kohn documented the case against competitive learning and asserted that we should move toward cooperative ventures. Cooperation works in a variety of forums; for example, cooperative ventures are better than competitive ones when workers and managers are involved (Tjosvold and Chia, 1989).

Psychologists and educators continue to fine-tune the techniques of cooperative learning. In fact, some of them formed an organization called the International Association for the Study of Cooperation in Education (IASCE). The group conducts research and tries to spread the message that cooperation works better than competition in the classroom.   ◆

| **Focus on Learning** | ◆ What is a self-fulfilling prophecy? p. 395 *those who expect to succeed will*.
 ◆ What does *need for achievement* refer to? pp. 395–396 *people engage in behaviors that satisfy desires*
 ◆ Identify one way cooperative learning can be put to use. p. 397 |

Attributions and Motivation

Expectancy theories show that if people hold beliefs or expectations for success, they will behave, operate, or cooperate in specific ways. But people's beliefs and expectations are in part determined by how they perceive the causes of success or failure. If a person believes that a task is impossible, for example, then the cause of his or her failure has little to do with expectations for success. Similarly, if a person believes that a task is so simple that anyone can do it properly, then success at the task will provide little reward or satisfaction.

Human beings not only have expectancies about their success and failure, but they also hold causal beliefs. They may believe that some tasks are especially easy, that they are especially lucky, or that they are destined for success. Such dispositions to tasks affect behavior directly. We call such general views about the causes of behavior *attributions*. People make attributions, or interpretations, about the causes of behavior. Attribution theory, examined in more detail in chapter 16, can be used here to explain motivation. Consider, for example, a research study by Sandelands, Brockner, and Glynn (1988) in which investigators manipulated participants' perceptions of the likelihood that they would succeed and how persistent they should be in an anagram solution task. The participants were told that some of the trials in the task would be quite difficult. Unknown to the participants, however, all the problems were insoluble.

Half the subjects were told that steady, continuous, and gradual effort would pay off; the other half were told that success would come in an instant as a result of sudden insight. In addition, some subjects were given incentives to perform well and others were not given much incentive. Subjects who were highly involved with the task and told that slow persistence would pay off worked longer on solving anagrams than those who were told that persistence didn't pay off, or who had less incentive. Although persistence is adaptive, when a goal is unattainable, it is perhaps pointless. People often make interpretations (attributions) about the reasons things turn out the way they do, and this affects their day-to-day personality as well as their specific behaviors.

Personality and Motivation

Personality studies (discussed further in chapter 12) provide a wealth of information about what motivates people. Personality, the way people respond to situations most of the time, influences just about everything people do. So although motivated to succeed, a person who has personality characteristics of shyness may be inhibited and reticent about taking a chance. A person who is outgoing, in contrast, may be far more willing to assert herself or himself in a group situation.

Friedman and Rosenman (1974) proposed classifying people according to two distinct personality styles or behavior patterns that can be used to predict the likelihood of suffering a heart attack. They designated people who had a great sense of urgency about all things and were impatient, aggressive, easily aroused to anger, and extremely achievement oriented as Type A, individuals at greater risk for heart attacks. All other people are Type B. Although their primary goal was to help Type A people become Type B people (Kahn et al., 1982), their research also provided information on what motivates people.

Using behavior patterns such as Type A and Type B, psychologists can infer a great deal about individuals' motivations and how they will respond to various situations. Type A people, for example, possess an intense desire to control their environment, and they become irritated and show emotional distress when others slow down their rapid pace (Suls and Wan, 1989; Suarez and Williams, 1989). Furthermore, they find it difficult to develop new motives and new behaviors to help them slow down and relax. Type B people do not seem to be motivated by the same desires for mastery and success. When they desire greatness or achievement, they are willing to pursue these objectives at a far more deliberate pace.

You will see in chapter 13 that the Type A–Type B classification system has become popular, but it lacks rigorous scientific support (e.g., Langeluddecke et al., 1988). It does, however, frame certain key questions for mo-

Theory	Drive	Expectancy	Cognitive
Theorist	a. Nisbett b. Schachter c. Hebb	a. McClelland b. Friedman & Rosenman	
Principally Explains	a. Obesity b. Hunger and obesity c. Optimal arousal	a. Achievment motivation b. The people prone to behavior of Type A coronary heart attack	
Key Idea	a. Number of fat cells determines obesity. b. External cues energize eating behavior. c. Performance depends on level of arousal.	a. Humans learn the need to achieve. b. Time urgency leads to a competitive, unending search for mastery and success, and to heart disease.	
View of Behavior	a. Mechanistic: obesity is biologically determined. b. Partially mechanistic but recognizes the role of learning. c. Mostly mechanistic: the efficiency of behavior is determined by level of physiological arousal.	a. Partly cognitive, partly mechanistic: achievement is a learned behavior b. Partly cognitive, partly mechanistic: Type A behavior is initiated early in life through reinforcement and punishment.	

◆ ***Building Table 11.2*** ◆

Drive and Expectancy Theories of Motivation

tivation researchers. Among those questions are: "Who is likely to be motivated?" "When are people likely to be motivated?" "Can motivation predict behavior?"

Expectancy Theories and Predicting Behavior

One strength of achievement motivation and expectancy theories is their relative precision, which enables psychologists to predict people's behavior. Once they know whether a person's need for achievement is high or low, they can predict the person's behavior in achievement-related activities. For example, once we know that a ball player's need for achievement is very high, we can predict that the athlete will work hard to achieve a goal of winning. Expectancy theories in general achieve precision because they focus on a specific set of behaviors (see Building Table 11.2). An expectancy theory might predict, for example, that Jim Abbott's pitching will be affected by his physiological state, external cues, the occasion, and his desires and expectancies to win.

Expectancy theories are cognitive in the sense that people's expectations of success or failure provide the context in which choices are made. Yet, because they retain certain mechanistic details and descriptions, they do not make the full leap into contemporary cognitive psychology. Cognitive theory places a much greater emphasis on the causal role of thought in behavior.

---

greater risk of heart attack
than all others

- Distinguish between Type A and Type B behavior. p. 399
- How are expectancy theories cognitive? p. 401

Focus on Learning

Cognitive Theory

One of Jim Abbott's goals was to constantly improve his pitching. Pitching well obviously provided him with a sense of accomplishment. The **cognitive theory** of motivation asserts that people are actively and regularly involved in deciding what their goals are and how they will achieve them. Even more than expectancy theory, cognitive theory focuses on thoughts as initiators and determiners of behavior. It emphasizes the role of decision making in all areas of life. For example, you are actively involved in deciding how much time you will spend studying for a psychology exam, how hard you will work to become an accomplished pianist, or how dedicated you will be to a new diet or exercise program.

As early as 1949, Donald Hebb anticipated how cognitive theory would influence psychology to move away from mechanistic views of motivation and behavior:

> As far as one can see at present, it is unsatisfactory to equate motivation with biological need. Theory built on this base has a definiteness that is very attractive; but it may have been obtained at too great a cost. (p. 179)

Hebb recognized that mechanistic drive- or need-reduction theories were incomplete and that other factors, such as arousal and attention, are important determinants of motivation. As a result of Hebb's brilliant theorizing, contemporary researchers emphasize the role of active decision making and

Cognitive theory: An explanation of behavior that emphasizes the role of thoughts and individual choices regarding life goals and the means of achieving them.

the human capacity for abstract thought. These cognitive theorists assume that individuals set their goals and decide how to achieve them.

Cognitive Controls

It may seem like common sense that if you are aware of—and think about— your behavior, motivation, and emotions and attempt to alter your thoughts, you can control your behavior. Cognitive psychologists maintain that if human beings are aware of their thought patterns, they can control their reasoning and ultimately their overt behavior. You will see (in chapter 15) that this idea is used extensively by therapists in helping people with various maladjustments. When explaining motivation, cognitive psychologists show that arousal (which Hebb and other researchers equated with drive) is under voluntary, that is, cognitive, control.

In what is now regarded as a classic study, Lazarus and Alfert (1964) monitored subjects' levels of arousal under conditions capable of inducing great stress. Subjects watched a film showing a primitive ritual called subincision (which involves deeply cutting the penises of adolescents). During the film, which showed five operations, one group of subjects, the *denial commentary* group, heard a commentary during the film that denied that pain and harm were associated with the operation. Another group of subjects, the *denial orientation* group, heard the same commentary before the film. A third group saw the film but did not hear any commentary.

The electrodermal response (EDR) of subjects who saw the film with no commentary increased at once (see Figure 11.5). More important, the increase in EDR for subjects who heard the denial commentary during the film was less than the no-commentary subjects, and the increase was lowest for subjects who heard the denial before the film began (the denial orientation group). Lazarus and Alfert believed that the denial orientation group was able to build up their psychological defenses against the potentially stressful

FIGURE 11.5
Lazarus and Alfert measured the electrodermal response (EDR) of subjects viewing a film of stress-inducing operations. The baseline indicates the level of EDR before the film was shown; with the start of the film, EDR increased in all groups. The increase was greatest in subjects who did not hear a commentary denying the pain. (Lazarus and Alfert, 1964, p. 199.)

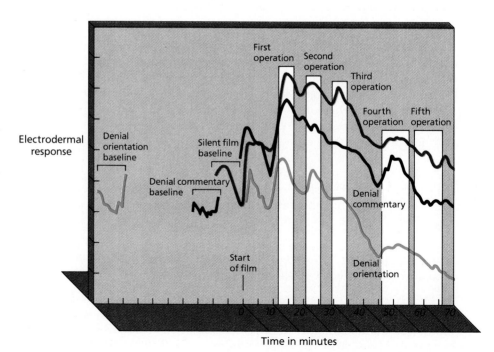

content of the film. In other words, they had some degree of cognitive control over their physiological reactions. Through instruction and self-help techniques, people can alter their behavior by changing their thoughts and thus changing their expectancies (e.g., Norris, 1989). That our thoughts can alter our behavior also becomes evident when people think about reinforcements, their intrinsic and extrinsic motivations.

Intrinsic and Extrinsic Motivation

People engage in a wide variety of behaviors for the fun of it, behaviors that bring no tangible rewards. Infants play with mobiles, children build erector set cities and then take them down, adults do crossword and jigsaw puzzles, and so on. Psychologists call behaviors performed for no apparent reward except the pleasure of the activity itself **intrinsically motivated behaviors.** Edward Deci (1975) suggests that people perform intrinsically motivated behaviors for two reasons: to achieve stimulation and to achieve a sense of accomplishment, competence, and mastery over their environment.

In studies focusing on intrinsic motivation, Deci compared two groups of college-age subjects engaged in puzzle solving. One group received no (external) rewards, and the other group did receive rewards. He found that subjects who were initially given rewards generally spent less time solving puzzles when rewards were no longer given. Those who were never rewarded, on the other hand, spent the same amount of time solving puzzles on all trials (Deci, 1971, 1972). Similar studies of younger children yielded comparable results (Lepper, Greene, and Nisbett, 1973) and also showed that if rewards are expected before the activity is performed, the effect of not giving them is even greater (Ryan, Mims, and Koestner, 1983). Building Table 11.3 on page 404 adds Deci's cognitive theory to the summary of motivation theories.

Other research (e.g., McGraw and Fiala, 1982) shows that offering rewards for engaging in an already attractive task results in a lower level of involvement and often permanent disengagement. Lepper and Greene (1978) refer to this phenomenon as the hidden cost of reward. When people think about the causes of their actions it can alter their behavior. (The hidden cost of reward was examined in more detail in chapter 5, p. 187.)

Extrinsic rewards come from the external environment: praise, a high grade, or money for a particular behavior are extrinsic rewards. Such rewards can strengthen existing behaviors, provide people with information about their performance, and increase feelings of self-worth and competence. On the other hand, when extrinsic rewards are given in a way that will alter a person's motivational orientation, they can decrease intrinsic motivation (Pittman and Heller, 1987). Also, verbal extrinsic rewards (such as praise) are less likely to interfere with intrinsic motivation than are tangible rewards (such as money) (Anderson, Manoogian, and Reznick, 1976).

Psychologists continue to explore the effects of extrinsic rewards for intrinsically motivated behaviors. Baumeister and Tice (1985) showed that people with high self-esteem aspire to excel and seek opportunities to do so when they are rewarded for intrinsically motivated behaviors. But people with low self-esteem aspire to be only adequate or satisfactory when given rewards for intrinsically motivated behavior. It is not surprising, then, that intrinsic motivation is, at least in part, tied up with a person's past experiences and current level of self-esteem. Other variables, such as the type of task a person does and the type of reward a person receives, can influence

Intrinsically motivated behaviors: Behaviors that a person performs in order to feel more competent, satisfied, and self-determined.

Extrinsic reward: A reward that comes from the external environment.

	Drive	Expectancy	Cognitive	Humanistic
Theory				
Theorist	a. Nisbett b. Schachter c. Hebb	a. McClelland b. Friedman & Rosenman	Deci	
Principally Explains	a. Obesity b. Hunger and obesity c. Optimal arousal	a. Achievment motivation b. The people prone to behavior of Type A coronary heart attack	Intrinsic motivation	
Key Idea	a. Number of fat cells determines obesity. b. External cues energize eating behavior. c. Performance depends on level of arousal.	a. Humans learn the need to achieve. b. Time urgency leads to a competitive, unending search for mastery and success, and to heart disease.	Intrinsic motivation is self-rewarding because it makes people feel competent	
View of Behavior	a. Mechanistic: obesity is biologically determined. b. Partially mechanistic but recognizes the role of learning. c. Mostly mechanistic: the efficiency of behavior is determined by level of physiological arousal.	a. Partly cognitive, partly mechanistic: achievement is a learned behavior b. Partly cognitive, partly mechanistic: Type A behavior is initiated early in life through reinforcement and punishment.	Cognitive: motivation is inborn, but extrinsic rewards often decrease it; decision making is crucial.	

◆ **Building Table 11.3** ◆

Drive, Expectancy, and Cognitive Theories of Motivation

the level of intrinsic motivation. A person's intrinsic motivation, external rewards, self-esteem, and perhaps new and competing needs all together affect day-to-day behavior. We consider in chapter 13 (p. 467) what happens if a person's or an animal's goals and needs conflict, and how animals and human beings behave in situations that have both positive and negative aspects. Here we consider the behavior of inaction, of putting off doing something that should be done today.

Procrastination

Jim Abbott is a doer, a person who takes charge of his life, his competitive urges, and his desire to win. But not everybody is so action oriented; people's motivation when they are procrastinating is often to avoid doing something that needs to be done. Motivated behavior is goal directed—people feel impelled or driven to do something. **Procrastination,** on the other hand, is putting off doing something that could and should be done in the present.

Procrastinators tend to rationalize about why something did not get done or did not get done well. Students procrastinate until the night before a term paper is due, then hurriedly write something, receive an average grade, and rationalize by saying, "I could have done better but I didn't have time." Rationalization takes away the student's responsibility for not having achieved full potential and puts it on the clock.

Procrastinators operate under a "magical system," believing that something outside themselves will come through and things will get done, problems will get solved, or the need for something to get done will disappear. Sometimes the magical system works; the problem goes away, the procrastinator is able to sneak through without doing something or without doing it well, or someone does the job for him or her. But successful procrastination sets up a dangerous life-style. Eventually the procrastinating behavior will catch up with the person, and the magical system will no longer work. When that happens, the consequences can be costly. Library books not returned on time bring fines, oil not added to a car destroys the engine, failing to confront the issues in a troubled marriage leads to divorce, and tasks not completed on the job result in being fired.

When negative consequences occur because of procrastination, self-recriminating thoughts may also occur. A cycle begins in which procrastination leads to self-punishment and decreased self-esteem. If the cycle continues, procrastination can become a life-style; the person can be left with a powerful rationalization system, low self-esteem, and an inability to accomplish much. Cognitive theory and humanistic theory are sometimes blended together. For example, humanists emphasize that people try to fulfill themselves and become everything that they might; thus, in breaking away from procrastination people are trying to achieve their potential.

Procrastination: The behavior of putting off until a future time something that could and should be done in the present.

Humanistic theory: An explanation of behavior that emphasizes the role of human qualities such as dignity, individual choice, and self-concept.

Humanistic Theory

Jim Abbott's physiological readiness, his expectations, and his learned behavior all work together to determine his success in baseball. One of the appealing aspects of humanistic theory is that it recognizes the interplay of behavior theories and incorporates some of the best elements of the drive, expectancy, and cognitive approaches to explain behavior.

Humanistic theory emphasizes the entirety of life rather than the components of behavior. Humanistic psychologists insist that individuals' behavior must be viewed within the framework of their environment and values. These psychologists focus both on the dignity of individual choice and freedom and on an individual's feelings of self-worth.

As we saw in chapter 1, one of the leaders and founders of the humanistic approach was Abraham Maslow (1908–1970), who assumed that people are essentially good, that they possess an innate inclination to develop their potential and seek beauty, truth, and goodness. Like other humanistic theorists, Maslow believed that people are innately open and trusting and can experience the world in truly healthy ways. In his words, people are innately motivated toward **self-actualization.** Self-actualized, or self-fulfilled, people are those who achieve their true natures and fulfill their potentials.

Maslow listed the characteristics that he felt distinguished self-actualized people. Although few people have all the following traits, according to Maslow all people strive (and are directed) toward acquiring them. He believed that self-actualized people

Abraham Maslow believed in the humanistic approach, and suggested that people strive for self-actualization.

are realistically oriented	have intimate relationships
accept themselves for what they are	are democratic
are problem centered	do not confuse the means with the end
have a need for privacy	have a good sense of humor
are independent	are creative and nonconformist
have a fresh appreciation of people	appreciate the environment
have spiritual experiences	have thoughts that are unconventional and spontaneous
identify with people	

Maslow's influential theory conceived of people's motives as forming a pyramid-shaped structure, with fundamental physiological needs at the base and needs for love, achievement, and understanding near the top (see Figure 11.6). According to Maslow, as low-level needs are satisfied, people strive

Self-actualization: The process of realizing one's uniquely human potential for good; the process of achieving everything that one is capable of achieving.

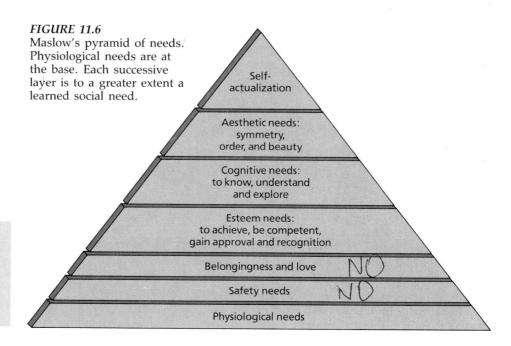

FIGURE 11.6
Maslow's pyramid of needs. Physiological needs are at the base. Each successive layer is to a greater extent a learned social need.

Self-actualization

Aesthetic needs: symmetry, order, and beauty

Cognitive needs: to know, understand and explore

Esteem needs: to achieve, be competent, gain approval and recognition

Belongingness and love

Safety needs

Physiological needs

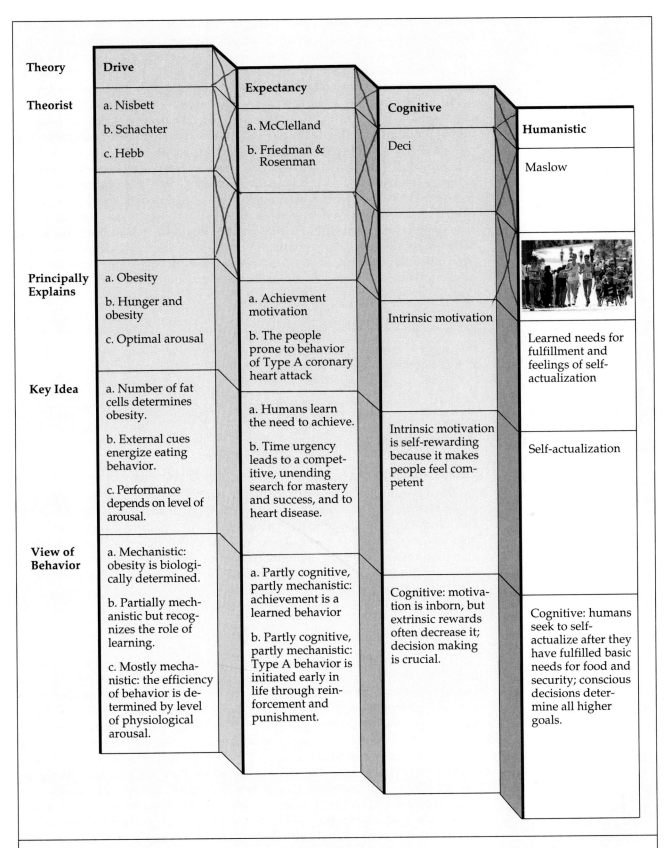

	Drive	Expectancy	Cognitive	Humanistic
Theory				
Theorist	a. Nisbett b. Schachter c. Hebb	a. McClelland b. Friedman & Rosenman	Deci	Maslow
Principally Explains	a. Obesity b. Hunger and obesity c. Optimal arousal	a. Achievment motivation b. The people prone to behavior of Type A coronary heart attack	Intrinsic motivation	Learned needs for fulfillment and feelings of self-actualization
Key Idea	a. Number of fat cells determines obesity. b. External cues energize eating behavior. c. Performance depends on level of arousal.	a. Humans learn the need to achieve. b. Time urgency leads to a competitive, unending search for mastery and success, and to heart disease.	Intrinsic motivation is self-rewarding because it makes people feel competent	Self-actualization
View of Behavior	a. Mechanistic: obesity is biologically determined. b. Partially mechanistic but recognizes the role of learning. c. Mostly mechanistic: the efficiency of behavior is determined by level of physiological arousal.	a. Partly cognitive, partly mechanistic: achievement is a learned behavior b. Partly cognitive, partly mechanistic: Type A behavior is initiated early in life through reinforcement and punishment.	Cognitive: motivation is inborn, but extrinsic rewards often decrease it; decision making is crucial.	Cognitive: humans seek to self-actualize after they have fulfilled basic needs for food and security; conscious decisions determine all higher goals.

◆ ***Building Table 11.4*** ◆

Drive, Expectancy, Cognitive, and Humanistic Theories of Motivation for the next higher level, culminating in self-actualization. He claimed that once someone's basic physiological needs are met, the person is in a better position to satisfy emotional needs. He did not claim that a person's basic physiological needs have to be satisfied completely before he or she can achieve a higher level of fulfillment. But unless their basic physiological needs are met, people are unlikely to grow and develop physically or acquire social and aesthetic motives that might direct behavior. Only if people's needs for food, shelter, and physical safety are met can they attend to developing a sense of self-respect or sense of beauty.

Although Maslow's theory provides an interesting way to organize aspects of motivation and behavior and their relative importance, its global nature makes experimental verification difficult. Moreover, his levels of motivation seem closely tied to middle-class cultural experience, so the theory may not be valid in all cultures. Maslow's theory, like many other motivation theories (see the overview provided in Building Table 11.4), does not explain how other components of our lives interact with behavior; for example, how does motivation to self-actualize affect our emotional experiences? We will discuss emotions next.

Focus on Learning	◆ What is the focus of cognitive theories of motivation? p. 401 ◆ Distinguish between intrinsic and extrinsic motivation. p. 403 ◆ What is self-actualization? p. 406

actively & regularly involved in what their goal are.

pleasure of the activity itself - intrinsic

external environment - external rewards

Emotion

Anger can cause you to hurl an object across the room or lash out at a friend. Happiness can make you smile all day, donate your change to the Salvation Army, and stop to help a motorist with a flat tire. Fear can electrify you, making your legs pump faster as you sprint down a dark, shadowy alley. Although emotions, including love, joy, and fear, can direct people's behavior, these categories remain fuzzy (Rosch, 1978), and even psychologists have difficulty agreeing on definitions.

Elements of Emotion

To some extent the word *emotion* is an umbrella term referring to a wide range of subjective states, such as love, fear, hate, or disgust. We all have emotions, talk about them, and agree on what represents an emotion such as fear, but this is not scientific. The psychological investigation of emotion has led to a more precise definition. An **emotion** is a subjective response, usually accompanied by a physiological change, that is interpreted by the individual, readies the individual toward some action, and has associated with it a change in behavior. People cry when they are sad, find increased energy when they are excited, and breathe faster, sweat, feel nausea, and have decreased salivation (causing a dry mouth) when they are afraid (see Kleinginna and Kleinginna, 1981). Some physiological changes precede an emotional response. Just before a collision in an automobile accident, for example, people show physiological arousal, muscle tension, and avoidance responses—that is, they brace themselves. Other changes are evident only

Emotion: A subjective response, usually accompanied by a physiological change that is interpreted by the individual, readies the individual toward some action, and has associated with it a change in behavior.

TABLE 11.1
The Laws of Emotion

According to Nico Frijda (1988), emotion can be described as a lawful set of behaviors. In Frijda's view, emotion follows a predictable set of courses. This view is yet to be substantiated by research, but provides a comprehensive overview as to how emotion can be examined.

1. Emotions are elicited by specific events.
2. Emotions are specific responses that are subjective in nature.
3. Emotions arise in response to goals or motives important to the individual.
4. Emotions are responses to events appraised as real, and the extent of the emotion is determined by the extent of the realness of the event.
5. Emotions are elicited by people's expectations for change in conditions.
6. Pleasure disappears with continuous satisfaction; pain may persist for longer periods.
7. Emotional events retain their power to evoke emotion indefinitely.
8. One emotion leads to another.
9. When possible, people view a situation in the lightest emotional way.

after an emotion-causing event. It is only after the auto accident that people shake with fear, disbelief, or rage.

People often respond to physiological changes by altering their behavior. When they are afraid, they scream. When they are angry, they seek revenge or retribution. When they are in love, they act tenderly toward others. In some situations, people think about acting out such behaviors but may not express them in directly observable ways. Think about Juliet's claim that "parting is such sweet sorrow"; it appears contradictory. Although emotions may seem written all over people's faces, appearances can be deceiving and difficult to interpret.

Psychologists focus on different aspects of emotional behavior. The earliest researchers cataloged and described basic emotions (Bridges, 1932; Wundt, 1896). Others tried to discover the physiological bases of emotion (Bard, 1934). Still others focused on how people perceive bodily movements (Tagruri, 1968) and on how they convey emotions to others through nonverbal mechanisms such as gestures or eye contact. More recent studies have investigated people's ability to control their emotional responses (Meichenbaum, 1977). Table 11.1 provides a series of laws through which theoreticians have attempted to codify the regularity of emotional behavior (Frijda, 1988).

Many psychologists acknowledge that emotion consists of three elements: feeling, physiological response, and behavior. People experience the same kinds of emotions, but the intensity or quality of those emotions vary. One person's sense of joy is different from another's. Thus, emotions have a private, personal, and unique component. This subjective element is called *feeling*.

Subjective feelings are difficult to measure, so most researchers focus on the other two aspects of emotion—physiological response and behavior. This focus shifts research from the internal process to action or readiness toward action. Physiological responses, such as heart rate and blood pressure, and behavioral responses, such as smiling and crying, are observable and measurable.

Researchers have attempted to quantify the elements of emotion (e.g., Lewis and Michaelson, 1983; Lewis and Saarni, 1985). They suggest that the following five basic elements of emotions must be considered.

1. *Emotional elicitors* are the events that trigger emotions. They include painful as well as pleasant experiences.

2. Brain mechanisms, or *emotional receptors,* are central nervous system mechanisms responsible for processing emotional reactions. (They are discussed later in this chapter.)

3. *Emotional states,* or changes in neural, biochemical, and general physiological activity, occur when the organism is activated emotionally.

4. *Emotional expressions* are observable and measurable changes in the organism that convey information to others about emotional states.

5. *Emotional experience* is a subjective state determined by cognitive and social factors; it is the individual's interpretation and evaluation of an emotional reaction.

Not every researcher considers all elements of a definition of emotion in his or her studies. One may focus on emotional expression; another may focus on emotional experiences. Physiological psychologists sometimes trace pathways and confine their research to brain mechanisms such as the hypothalamus. We consider next those theories that focus on the biological bases of emotion.

Biological Theories of Emotion

The wide range of emotions that human beings express is in large part controlled by a series of neurons located deep within the brain, in an area called the *limbic system.* The limbic system is composed of cells in the hypothalamus, the amygdala, and other cortical and subcortical areas. Studies of these crucial areas began in the 1920s when Bard (1934) found that removal of portions of a cat's cortex produced sharp emotional reactions to simple stimuli such as a touch or a puff of air. The cats would hiss, claw, bite, arch their backs, and growl—and their reaction did not seem directed at any specific person or target. Bard referred to this behavior as sham rage. Later researchers stimulated portions of the brain with electrical current and found that the visual system was also important in emotions. They deduced that the cortex of the brain was integrating visual information and hypothalamic information to produce emotional behavior. In general, two major physiological approaches to the study of emotion developed: the James-Lange theory and the Cannon-Bard theory. Both are concerned with the physiology of emotions and whether physiological change or emotional feelings occur first.

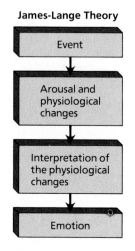

James-Lange Theory

Event

↓

Arousal and physiological changes

↓

Interpretation of the physiological changes

↓

Emotion

FIGURE 11.7
According to the James-Lange theory, arousal precedes interpretation, which precedes emotion.

The James-Lange Theory. According to a theory proposed by William James (1842–1910) and developed with Carl Lange (1834–1900), people experience physiological changes and then interpret them as emotional states (see Figure 11.7). People do not cry because they feel sad; they feel sad because they cry. People do not perspire because they are afraid; they feel afraid after they perspire. In other words, the James-Lange theory says that people do not experience an emotion until after their bodies become aroused and respond with physiological changes. That is, feedback from the body produces feelings or emotions (James, 1884; Lange, 1885/1922). For this approach, *feeling* is the essence of emotion; thus James (1890) wrote: "every one of the bodily changes whatsoever it be is felt, acutely or obscurely, the moment it occurs" (p. 1006).

A modern physiological approach suggests that facial movements by their action create emotions. In some ways this approach is similar to the James-Lange theory. Certain facial movements create a change in blood flow and temperature to the brain; when this occurs, pleasant feelings occur. When a facial movement happens, such as a smile or an eye movement, according to Zajonc, Murphy, and Inglehart (1989), this may release the emotion-linked neurotransmitters. Some neurotransmitters may bring about pleasant, and others unpleasant, emotions. Zajonc and his colleagues argue that facial movements alone are capable of inducing emotions. This theory is still relatively new and has not yet been tested extensively by other researchers.

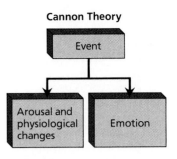

FIGURE 11.8
According to Cannon's theory, arousal and emotion occur simultaneously.

The Cannon-Bard Theory. Physiologists, notably Walter Cannon (1871–1945), were critical of the James-Lange theory. Cannon and P. Bard, a colleague, argued that the physiological changes in many emotional states were identical. They reasoned that if increases in blood pressure and heart rate accompany feelings of both anger and joy, how can people determine their emotional state simply from their physiological state?

Cannon argued that when a person is emotional, two areas of the brain, the thalamus and the cerebral cortex, are stimulated simultaneously (he did not realize the full nature of the limbic system). Stimulation of the cortex produces the emotional component of the experience; stimulation of the thalamus produces physiological changes in the sympathetic nervous system. According to Cannon (1927), emotional feelings *accompany* physiological changes (see Figure 11.8), they do not produce them. A problem with the Cannon-Bard approach is that physiological changes in the brain do not happen exactly simultaneously; further, people report that they often have an experience and then have physiological and emotional reactions to it. Neither the James-Lange nor the Cannon-Bard approach considered the idea that people's interpretation or thoughts about a situation might alter their physiological reactions and emotional responses.

Cognitive Theories of Emotion

Cognitive theories of emotion developed in response to the older biological approaches. They focus on interpretation as well as physiology to explain emotions. They follow logically in the history of psychology because thought processes have become extremely influential in the last three decades.

The Schachter-Singer Approach. The Schachter-Singer view of emotion is a cognitive approach that focuses on emotional activation, incorporating elements of both the James-Lange and Cannon-Bard theories. Stanley Schachter and Jerome Singer observed that people do indeed interpret their emotions but not solely from bodily changes. They argued that people interpret physical sensations within a specific context. Observers cannot interpret what a person's crying means unless they know the situation in which that behavior occurs. If a man cries at a funeral, we suspect he is sad; if he cries at his daughter's wedding, we expect he is joyful.

To prove their contention, Schachter and Singer (1962) injected volunteer subjects with adrenaline, a powerful stimulant that increases signs of arousal such as heart rate, excitement, energy, and even sensations of butterflies in the stomach. The subjects were not aware of the usual results of the injection.

Schachter-Singer Theory

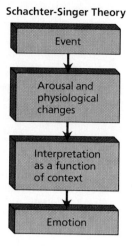

FIGURE 11.9
According to Schachter and Singer, people's interpretations of arousal depend on the context in which they find themselves.

To see if they could affect how subjects interpreted their aroused state, Schachter and Singer manipulated the setting in which the subjects experienced their arousal. They hired undergraduates and paid them to act either happy and relaxed or sad, depressed, and angry. These hired subjects—called stooges—pretended that they, too, were volunteers in the drug study. But they were given injections of saltwater, not adrenaline. Their emotional behavior was strictly an act. The happy stooges shot wads of paper into a wastepaper basket and flew airplanes around the room. The unhappy stooges complained about the questionnaire they had to fill out and voiced their dissatisfaction with the experiment.

All the experimental subjects showed increased physiological arousal. Those with the happy stooges reported that the drug made them feel good; those with the angry stooges reported feeling anger. Schachter and Singer reasoned that when people have no immediate explanation for their physiological arousal, they will label their feelings in terms of the thoughts available to them. The physiological feelings that accompany both joy and anger are the same, but the label attached to the emotion depends on the person's situation. (See Figure 11.9.)

The cognitive view receives support from anecdotal data as well as experiments. When people first smoke marijuana or take other psychoactive drugs, for example, they tend to approach the experience with definite expectations. If told the drug will produce feelings of hunger, new users will report feeling hunger; if told the drug is a downer, users often interpret their bodily sensations as depressive. In Schachter and Singer's view, people thus experience internal arousal, become aware of the arousal, seek an explanation for it, identify an external cue, and then label the arousal. This labeling determines the emotion that is felt.

Other Cognitive Theories of Emotional Behavior. Valins (1966) and Reisenzein (1983) challenged Schachter and Singer's view. Valins showed that thoughts alone are sufficient to produce emotional behavior. He showed male subjects slides of nude women and, at the same time, played a soundtrack of previously recorded heartbeats. The subjects were told that the heartbeats were their own but to ignore them. The heartbeats were speeded up or slowed down as the slides were shown. This meant that the subjects were being cued by the heartbeats as to their supposed arousal level, even though their arousal level may not actually have changed. A control group saw the same slides, heard the same sounds, but was told that the sounds were meaningless and to ignore them.

When the two groups were asked to judge the attractiveness of the nude women, the experimental group rated them more positively than did the control group. Experimental subjects were also more likely than control subjects to want to take copies of the slides home with them. Valins concluded that actual physiological arousal is not a prerequisite for labeling of emotion—cognitive processes alone will suffice (see Harris and Katkin, 1975). Reisenzein (1983) argues that Schachter and Singer's theory overestimates the role of arousal and that arousal at best merely intensifies an emotional experience.

Shaver's Prototypes. Phillip Shaver and his colleagues have sought to identify the basic emotions that all people experience and the ways in which they are experienced. Shaver showed that there are six emotions which almost all people will describe when asked to identify emotions: love, joy,

To understand emotional behavior, Shaver identified six basic emotions that all people recognize and experience: love, joy, anger, fear, sadness, and surprise.

anger, fear, sadness, and surprise (Shaver et al., 1987). Of course, these six categories can overlap, and many other emotional states can be grouped under these six basic categories.

Schwartz and Shaver (1987) contend that people's emotional knowledge is organized around these six emotional categories and that people exhibit characteristic behaviors with each emotion. They also assert that these emotions appear cross-culturally (Shaver and Schwartz, 1988) and that researchers have to understand this overall structure before they can define an overall theory of emotion (Heider, 1990). Every culture may put its own value on an emotion and have traits that trigger that emotion. For example, love is an extremely powerful emotion in the United States, but in Sumatra, one of the chief islands of Indonesia, nostalgia is the most powerful (Heider, 1990).

Shaver asserts that people understand and interpret emotional events by comparing the events to basic emotional concepts. For example, when a mother sees her child fall and start to cry, she rushes toward the child. An observer sees this event and *assumes* that she is frightened and concerned. This inference is based on general knowledge about fear and love. Schwartz and Shaver (1987) claim that people make use of implicit learned knowledge to understand and manage social interactions. Only by understanding this structure of emotion can we begin to place cognitive interpretations within a reasonable framework. Shaver does not deny the role of cognitions; on the contrary, he argues that cognitive interpretations are critical, but before we can understand the cognitions, we have to understand the overall structure and concept of emotion. To some extent, he argues, we have jumped too far into our analysis of emotion, and we need to step back and review the basics.

Frijda: Appraisal and Readiness. Another view of emotion sees appraisal as important, but also takes into consideration the idea that people ready themselves for action. Nico Frijda asserts that every emotional experience is not only a cognitive appraisal of a situation, but also a set of action tendencies or behaviors prepared as the cognitive appraisal takes place.

For Frijda, when a situation is potentially threatening, a person prepares to flee or attack, and autonomic nervous system arousal is invoked (Frijda, Kuipers, and ter Schure, 1989). Frijda supports Shaver's contention that emotions can be arranged into several distinct categories. But he does not suggest that arousal is necessary, nor does he necessarily invoke the limbic system. He supports his ideas by a research study showing that subjects' specific action tendencies are closely associated with specific cognitive appraisals. Thus Frijda has introduced responses along with appraisals. This approach looks again at how emotions develop—an area of research that has often followed different avenues.

Development of Emotional Responses

People's ability to express emotion develops from birth through adulthood. Some aspects seem to be learned, others to be inborn. Naturalistic observations of human infants indicate that they follow a relatively fixed pattern of emotional development. They are born with a startle, or Moro, response; they smile, coo, babble, and gurgle at about six weeks; they develop fear of strangers at six to nine months. Attachment behaviors encouraged in the early weeks and months of life are also nurtured during adolescence and adulthood when people form close loving bonds with others.

Emotional expressions appear in all cultures; fear, joy, surprise, sadness, anger, and disgust are common expressions. These expressions are also found in deaf and blind people, and in people without limbs who therefore have more limited touch experiences (Izard and Saxton, 1988). Because of these findings, most researchers consider those emotional expressions innate even though they unfold slowly over the first year of life and are reinforced by caregivers.

Emotional Development in Rhesus Monkeys. To find out how people develop emotional responses, Harry Harlow (1905–1981), a psychologist at the University of Wisconsin, focused on the development of emotion in rhesus monkeys. (We examined some of Harlow's work in chapter 1.) Harlow's initial studies were on the nature of early interactions among monkeys. He found that monkeys raised from birth in isolated bare wire cages away from their mothers did not survive, even though they were well fed. Other monkeys, raised in the same conditions but with scraps of terry cloth in their cages, survived.

Terry cloth is hardly a critical variable in the growth and development of monkeys, yet its introduction into a wire cage made the difference between life and death for rhesus monkeys. Harlow inferred that the terry cloth provided some measure of security. That conclusion led him to attempt to discover whether infant monkeys had an inborn desire for love or warmth that might be satisfied by soft, warm objects such as terry cloth.

In a classic experiment, Harlow placed infant monkeys in cages along with two wire-covered shapes resembling adult monkeys. One figure was covered with terry cloth; the other was left bare. Both could be fitted with bottles to provide milk. In some cases, the wire mother surrogate had the bottle of milk; in other cases, the terry cloth mother surrogate had the bottle.

Harlow found that the infant monkeys clung to the terry cloth mother surrogates whether or not they provided milk. He concluded that the wire mother surrogate, even with a bottle of milk, could not provide the comfort that a terry cloth–covered mother surrogate could provide (Harlow and Zimmerman, 1958).

Another result of Harlow's experiment was that neither group of monkeys grew up to be totally normal. Harlow's monkeys were more aggressive and fearful than normally raised monkeys. They were also unable to engage in normal sexual relations. And some of the infants raised with wire mother surrogates engaged in self-destructive behaviors (Harlow, 1962).

Harlow next suggested that the emotions of fear, curiosity, and aggression are inborn and that the brain mechanisms underlying them develop over time and in a specific sequence. To test this idea, he isolated monkeys of various ages for different periods of time. As Harlow expected, certain behaviors, such as attachment and nurturing, were more affected by early isolation, and others were more affected by later isolation. When monkeys were deprived of social contacts with other monkeys from ages eighteen to twenty-four months, for example, their later social behaviors relating to mating were essentially normal. Harlow concluded that nature and nurture must interact at specific times (when the relevant brain mechanisms are ready to mature) for normal emotional and social development.

Emotional Development in Human Beings. Although it is a broad leap from Harlow's monkeys to human infants, it is reasonable to assume that infants, like monkeys, have an inborn need for social stimulation. Recall Klaus and Kennell's (1983) theory about attachment and bonding (chapter 9), which suggests that there is a period in which emotional relationships are formed between caregiver and child. They contend that without periods of social stimulation infants will not develop as well emotionally as infants who go through a period of close social attachment. They assert that the first minutes and hours of an infant's life constitute a sensitive period during which close contact allows bonding, that is, attachment between parents and child; their assertion is that the presence or absence of bonding may exert an extraordinary influence later in life (Bornstein, 1989).

Attachment seems to be a reasonable and well-documented process, but because it happens with infants, and cannot be experimented with in the traditional sense, we know less about it than we would, like. It is unclear what physiological mechanisms may influence attachment, but we know that lower animals show regular patterns of behavior in caring for their newborns, such as nesting. Human newborns respond to their mothers through body and eye movements and have a regular communication system (Tronick, 1989). Such responses may strengthen the mother's attachment to her child— a bond already affected by hormonal changes, prevailing cultural biases, and the mother's personal experiences. This early opportunity to form a strong parent-infant attachment may significantly influence both the parent's ability to care effectively for the child and the infant's ability to give and receive affection and love. Parent-infant attachment can be seen on the faces of new parents and on their newborn children.

Harlow studied the emotional development of rhesus monkeys. He discovered that young monkeys raised in sterile environments would not thrive as well as those raised with a terry-cloth-covered wire surrogate mother.

Behavioral Expression of Emotions

Since 1898, psychologists have recognized that facial expressions provide reliable clues to people's feelings. This *behavioral expression* of emotions is easily observed and interpreted by others. Most important, facial expressions are generally an accurate index of a person's emotional state. Recent research suggests that there are asymmetries in facial expressions in infants and adults, and that adults can easily discern those differences. Best and Queen (1989) found that the left side of the face (controlled by the right side of the brain in most people) may be more expressive than the right side of the face, especially in adults (Rothbart, Taylor, and Tucker, 1989). They argue that the right side of the face may be more readily under control by the left side of the brain, and people are able to inhibit right-face expression more easily than left-face expression. But whereas facial expressions (either side) are good indicators of emotion, they are only indicators; real emotions can be masked by a happy face or a turned-down mouth.

People also display emotion through gestures, body language, and voice tone and volume (Izard and Saxton, 1988). Examples include a lowered head, shaking fists, and laughter, as well as clenched teeth, limpness, and loss of energy. Researchers have studied the smiling responses of infants, children, and adults (Carlson, Gantz, and Masters, 1983) by examining when and under what conditions smiling is evoked and then lost. Researchers have studied smiling cross-culturally (Sogon and Masutani, 1989) and have found commonalities in what brings about emotional responses such as smiling. Some researchers have focused on the variables that bring laughter and smiles to people's lives.

Researchers observe animals and human beings in situations that might induce stress and emotional responses. For example, psychologists have studied the emotional expression of store clerks and their responses to customers. In one study (Rafaeli, 1989), a range of variables was considered: clerk gender, wearing a smock with a name tag, presence of other clerks, and customer gender. Although the results were complicated, the emotional expression of the clerks was affected by nearly all the variables. Female clerks displayed positive emotions more often than males; male customers received positive emotional responses more often than female customers; and when especially aware of their role (wearing a smock), clerks were more expressive. The expression of emotion was thus affected by context and subtle variables that are still under scrutiny. Even more measurable than facial expressions and other behavioral responses that can be masked are physiological changes that are hard to mask.

Physiological Expressions of Emotion. Many physiological changes are due to an increase in autonomic nervous system activity. Fear, for example, may slow or halt digestion, increase blood pressure and heart rate, deepen breathing, dilate pupils, decrease salivation (causing a dry mouth), and tense muscles. Researchers recognize that the autonomic nervous system provides direct, observable, measurable responses that can be quantified in a systematic manner. This realization led to the development of the lie detector, for example.

Lie Detectors. A polygraph test, or lie detector, is perhaps the most widely recognized recorder of emotion. This device records changes in the autonomic nervous system activity of subjects. Most autonomic nervous system activity is involuntary, and lying is usually associated with an increase in autonomic activity. A trained polygraph operator compares a person's autonomic responses to a series of relatively neutral questions to his or her responses to questions about the issue being explored. During noncontroversial questions (such as requests for the person's name or address), autonomic activity remains at what is considered baseline level. During critical questions (such as whether the person used a knife as a holdup weapon), however, a person with something to hide usually shows a dramatic increase in autonomic nervous system activity.

A lie detector test can be useful in indicating if a person is lying. Not all people, however, show marked autonomic nervous system changes when emotionally aroused. Habitual liars show little or no change in autonomic activity when they lie; they seem to be able to lie without becoming emotionally aroused. Equally important is the finding that some people who tell the truth may register changes in autonomic nervous system activity because of anxiety. This means that a truthful individual who takes a lie detector test might be called a liar when the individual is in fact telling the truth. The results of a lie detector study (Kleinmuntz and Szucko, 1984) that examined innocent and guilty individuals accused of theft show that although guilty people were often declared guilty by the lie detector, and innocent people often were declared innocent, thirty-seven percent of innocent people were declared guilty! In summary, lie detectors are subject to significant errors in both directions (Szucko and Kleinmuntz, 1981; Kleinmuntz and Szucko, 1984; Patrick and Iacono, 1989).

Today, most states do not accept the lie detector as valid evidence in court, especially in criminal cases. A federal law now restricts businesses from using the polygraph to test prospective employees. The American Psychological Association has also expressed reservations about the use of polygraph tests, asserting that they may cause psychological damage to innocent persons. The association's concerns stem in part from the knowledge that some people can control their emotions and do not respond automatically to external stimuli, and other people are less able to control their emotions and may overreact to external stimuli.

Controlling Emotions

The self-regulation view of emotional expression, another aspect of cognitive theory, stresses that people are not passive, that they do not respond automatically to environmental or internal stimuli. This view asserts that people manage or determine their emotional states in purposeful ways by constantly evaluating their environment and feelings. Through this appraisal of the environment, individuals alter their level of arousal.

Arousal. Arousal is an essential component in emotion, and researchers show that people can use cognitive means to control their arousal level and therefore their emotions. For psychologists studying the behavior of disturbed individuals, the interaction of arousal, emotion, and thought has become increasingly important. Even in normal individuals, too high a level of arousal can produce extreme emotional responses and lead to disorganized behavior (see Figure 11.10 on page 418). Many maladjusted individuals, such as those suffering from the manic stages of a bipolar disorder, have so high a level of arousal that they cannot organize their thinking or behavior (see chapter 14, p. 517). Even young infants show some forms of emotional restraint and control, and an infant's control of emotion continues to develop, especially at the end of the first year (Kopp, 1989).

Some studies show that people can control their body's biochemistry. In the study by Lazarus and Alfert (1964) discussed earlier, for example, subjects were able to manipulate their electrodermal response (EDR) when told in advance about a subincision ritual shown in a film. People also control their emotions because of strong cultural expectations. By using conscious

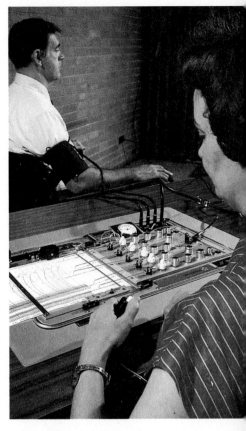

The lie detector test was originally designed to measure physiological responses to emotions, but psychologists today assert that the validity of its findings is highly questionable.

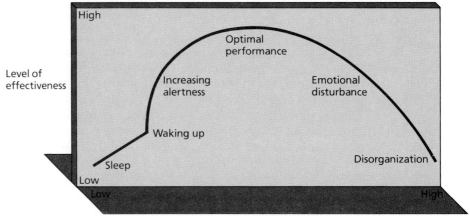

FIGURE 11.10
In accordance with the Yerkes-Dodson law, increases in motivation and arousal often bring increases in emotional feelings. Most important, these increases in arousal change the effectiveness of a person's behavior.

and directed thought, they control their behavior and wait until the proper time and place to express emotions. Thus, emotion and its expression reflect a person's motivations in addition to basic biochemistry (Carver and Scheier, 1990). In the United States, for example, children and women have greater permission to cry and express emotion than men do. But in Latin America, men are expected to be emotional. Expectations and cognitive appraisals of situations seem to be key elements in physiological and subsequent overt behavioral expressions of emotion (Smith, 1989). Expectations that are biased in one direction or another can lead to some unusual consequences; for example, if a person suffers from hypochondriasis (chapter 14, p. 509), any ache, pain, or quickness of breath might lead the person to dire feelings about health.

Facial expressions provide easily recognizable cues to other people's feelings. Posture, tone of voice, and volume can also be used as indicators.

Psychology and the Health Sciences

Applied psychologists, like other health science professionals, are learning that prolonged stress can put people at risk for serious health problems. In chapter 13 we will examine studies that show higher rates of illness among people who have recently lost a spouse or have few close relationships; this implies that both bereavement and social isolation can alter a person's immunity. Some applied psychologists have focused on ways in which simple day-to-day behaviors can facilitate health and improve our emotional lives. For example, noted researcher David McClelland (1989) asserts that a person's motivation, as assessed through his or her thoughts, is associated with health and illness. When diabetic individuals have a relaxed easygoing style, this can lead to proper control of their insulin levels. But when diabetics are strong, willful, and authority seeking, it often leads to sympathetic nervous system activation, a release of stress hormones, depressed immune functions, and greater susceptibility to disease. Thus McClelland argues that our social motives, thoughts, desires, and social needs are implicated in our physiology.

Working together with physicians, social workers, and psychiatrists, psychologists are seeking to improve the health and well-being of people in their daily lives. They are teaching stress management workshops to Type A individuals (to be discussed in chapters 13 and 15), and they are helping people manage their motivations and have realistic ideas about their goals so that they do not develop maladjustment (chapter 14). Health science professionals are focusing on preventive measures to enhance a person's sense of well-being and purpose and to help people manage their motivational and emotional lives in productive, worthwhile ways.

- ◆ Name the five basic elements of emotion. pp. 407–409
- ◆ Compare the key characteristics of the James-Lange, Cannon-Bard, and Schachter-Singer theories of emotion. pp. 410–412
- ◆ Describe the Harlow studies with infant monkeys. pp. 414–415
- ◆ What is the current scientific opinion about lie detectors? p. 416

Focus on Learning

Key Terms

Motivation p. 380	Sexual dysfunction p. 389	Motive p. 394
Drive theory p. 381	Erectile dysfunction p. 389	Social motive p. 394
Drive p. 381	Primary erectile dysfunction p. 389	Social need p. 394
Need p. 381	Secondary erectile dysfunction p. 390	Need for achievement p. 394
Eating disorders p. 386	Premature ejaculation p. 390	Cognitive theory p. 401
Anorexia nervosa p. 386	Primary orgasmic dysfunction p. 390	Intrinsically motivated behaviors p. 403
Bulimia nervosa p. 386	Secondary orgasmic dysfunction p. 390	Extrinsic rewards p. 403
Excitement phase p. 389	Expectancy theory p. 394	Procrastination p. 405
Vasoconstriction p. 389		Humanistic theory p. 405
Plateau phase p. 389		Self-actualization p. 406
Orgasm phase p. 389		Emotion p. 407
Resolution phase p. 389		

Summary

Motivation: A Definition

- Motivation produces goal-directed behavior. It is inferred from behavior and initiated by drives, needs, or desires. A need is an aroused physiological condition involving imbalance.   p. 380

- People's behavior is affected by (1) motivation, (2) emotional state (including arousal), (3) ability, and (4) thought processes. High motivation without ability will not yield high performance, nor will high ability with no motivation.   p. 381

Hunger, Thirst, and Sexual Motivation

- A mechanistic explanation of behavior views the organism as pushed, pulled, and energized almost like a machine.   p. 381

- The glucostatic approach to hunger argues that the principal physiological cause of hunger is the low blood-sugar level that accompanies food deprivation. Researchers know that two areas of the hypothalamus, lateral and ventromedial, arc primarily responsible for the brain's control of eating.   p. 381

- Schachter showed that obese adults tend to eat not only when they are hungry but also whenever food is present. Still, genetics or disorders of the autonomic nervous system may play a strong role.   p. 385

- *Anorexia nervosa*, or "starvation disease," is an eating disorder characterized by obstinate and willful refusal to eat; *bulimia nervosa* involves binge eating (recognized by the person to be abnormal) and a consequent fear of not being able to stop eating. Bulimics often purge themselves of unwanted calories by vomiting and abusing laxatives and diuretics.   p. 386

- Any imbalance in fluid is reflected in a drive to restore the balance, experienced as thirst.   p. 387

- *Sexual dysfunctions* are the inability to obtain satisfaction from sexual behavior. *Erectile dysfunction* is a man's inability to attain or maintain an erection of sufficient strength to perform in sexual intercourse. A woman unable to obtain an orgasm is said to have *orgasmic dysfunction*.   p. 389

- According to optimal arousal theories, individuals seek an optimal level of stimulation. Behavior varies from disorganized to effective to optimal, depending on the person's level of arousal.   pp. 391–392

Learned Motives

- *Expectancy theory* focuses on people's need for achievement and success, suggesting that people's expectations of success and the value they place on it direct their behavior. pp. 394–395

- A social motive is a condition that directs people toward establishing or maintaining relationships with others. A *social need* is an internal aroused condition involving feelings about self, others, and relationships.   p. 395

Cognitive and Humanistic Theories

- Cognitive and humanistic theories move away from mechanistic descriptions of behavior and focus on the role of human choice and expression. Although humanistic theory acknowledges physiological drives, it concerns itself largely with the human qualities of fulfillment and actualization.   pp. 400–405

- Intrinsically motivated behaviors are behaviors that a person performs in order to feel competent and self-determining. Extrinsic rewards decrease the recurrence of intrinsically motivated behavior.   p. 403

- Maslow's humanistic motivation theory assumes that people are basically good and that they strive for self-actualization.   pp. 405–406

Emotion

- Emotions are aroused internal states that may occur in response to either internal or external stimuli, usually accompanied by marked physiological changes.   p. 407

- The James-Lange theory of emotion states that people interpret their emotions in response to physiological changes. The Cannon-Bard theory states that when people experience emotions, two areas of the brain are stimulated simultaneously, one creating an emotional response and the other creating a physiological change.   p. 410

- According to the Schachter-Singer approach, people interpret physiological changes within the context of a situation and infer emotions from these cues.   p. 411

Connections

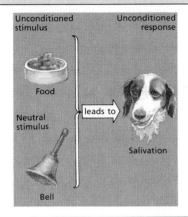  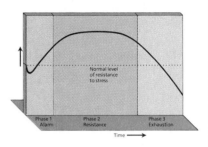

If you are interested in . . .	Turn to . . .	To learn more about . . .
The role of motivation in learning, memory, and intelligence	◆ Ch. 5, pp. 174–175	How an organism in a need state, (for example hungry), learns more, quickly, and better in classical conditioning.
	◆ Ch. 6, p. 220	Ways to improve your memory.
	◆ Ch. 8, p. 285	The relationship between innate intelligence and motivation to succeed on a test.
How thoughts influence motives and behavior	◆ Ch. 5, pp. 190–195	How cognitive learning takes place without specific observable motives or reinforcement.
	◆ Ch. 12, pp. 448–451	How personality theorists are introducing thought into the equation of how a person develops and maintains a personality.
	◆ Ch. 15, pp. 555–558	The way treatment approaches to various disorders consider the role of motivation and a person's appraisal of situations in determining behavior.
The emotional responses people make to various situations	◆ Ch. 4, pp. 132–133	How a person can learn to manipulate his or her body's response and subsequent emotions through techniques such as hypnosis and biofeedback.
	◆ Ch. 13, p. 475	How people's health can be affected by their overall emotional responses when faced with stressful situations.
	◆ Ch. 14, p. 510	The interaction between physiological disorders and emotional responses.

12 Personality and Its Assessment

"Persona Box of David" by Maggie Sherman

◆

Week after week, television evangelist Jim Bakker exhorted his viewers to shun worldly evils, seek peace and pursue it, and then asked for generous donations to help finance his growing ministry. With wife and children at his side, Bakker had a boyish charm and sincerity that many considered infectious and sincere. The downfall of Bakker and his compatriots followed weeks of scandalous headlines on the nightly news. Misuse of funds; overbooking of hotel rooms promised to people who pledged money; then the reports that Bakker had a romantic affair with Jessica Hahn. The nasty details spewed forth: motel rooms, cover-up money, lies, and a wildly extravagant life-style. Before long, boyish Jim Bakker was arrested for misuse of church funds. During his lengthy trial, critics and colleagues proposed a variety of explanations for his behavior. Some said the evangelist was a lecher hiding beneath a pious facade; others proclaimed him a saint who suffered a moral lapse; still others declared the man an egomaniac who believed he could do no wrong. Which of these personality assessments is right? Could each be partly true? Are those who label the evangelist a hypocrite being cynical . . . or just realistic? Did Bakker change or was he always this way?

No other phenomenon is so complex, so resistant to easy definition and assessment, as the human character. Most people describe the way they respond to the world by using catchwords: they say they are shy, or sensitive, or outgoing, or concerned, or aggressive. They also use these words to describe their personalities.

Psychologists describe personality, but they do so in a systematic and scientific way. For psychologists, **personality** is a set of relatively enduring behavioral responses and internal predispositions that characterize how a person reacts to the environment. That is, personality is an individual's behavior in a variety of situations over time. However, psychologists also recognize that an individual's behavior is not consistent all the time or in every situation; a person may "not be herself" on a particular day; a television evangelist may "suffer a moral lapse."

What makes people consistent in their behavior? To answer this question, some personality theorists focus on the day-to-day behaviors that characterize people; others focus on the inner conflicts that shape personality. Some see a human being as an individual who reacts to the environment. Others emphasize the internal, even genetic, influences that impel a person to action. Personality theorists must consider social psychological theories such as attitudes, motivational theories such as expectancy theories, and even biological theories such as those that suggest biological predispositions toward some personality characteristic, e.g., shyness.

The earliest personality theorists (such as Freud) tended to think of personality as something stable within the individual. Later theorists began to recognize that personality depends on a host of environmental situations. Contemporary theorists, especially the behavioral and cognitive ones, often focus more on environmental determinants of personality than on internal dispositions (Kenrick and Funder, 1988).

Personality theories are like all theories; they are a set of interrelated ideas and facts put forward to coherently explain and predict behavior and mental processes. Being able to predict and explain behavior enables psychologists to help people anticipate situations and express their feelings in manageable and reasonable ways. Personality theories focus on a few key questions. Among them are:

Personality: A set of relatively enduring behavioral characteristics and internal predispositions that describe how a person reacts to the environment.

- ◆ Does nature or nurture play a greater role in day-to-day behavior?
- ◆ Do unconscious processes direct behavior?
- ◆ Are human behavior patterns fixed, or are we free to choose our own destinies?
- ◆ Does our behavior depend on our situation?
- ◆ What makes people consistent in their behavior?

No personality theory considers all these issues, nor does every theory explain all of personality. Thus, each theory we consider is incomplete, but each is important because it addresses some key element of our understanding. We begin by examining an approach to personality—psychoanalytic theory—that focuses on the unconscious and how thought and ideas contained in it direct day-to-day behavior. It's the well-known and widely disputed theory of Sigmund Freud.

Psychoanalytic Theory

Freud's influence on psychology is so great that some of his basic ideas and concepts are often taken for granted. Such Freudian terms as *ego, oral fixation, death wish,* and *Freudian slip* and such concepts as *unconscious motivation* and *Oedipus complex* are part of everyday language. But when Freud first introduced his ideas, he was seen as strange, heretical, and simply off base. The psychologists of the time (such as Wundt, Titchener, and Kohler) thought that the proper subject matter of psychology was the study of the mind and ʇʇ it works. Studying the unconscious and suggesting that children have experiences were, to say the least, out of the mainstream.

ʇnd Freud (1856–1939) was an Austrian physician who used hypnosis ᷄   ᵗ people with physical and emotional problems. Most of Freud's patients ᷄   ʿrom the middle and upper classes of Austrian society. Many were socieᵗ᷄ ᵃtrons who, because they lived in a repressive society, had limited opportunities for the release of anxiety and tension. Freud noticed that many of them needed to discuss their problems and often felt better after having done so. From his studies of hypnosis and work with these patients, Freud began to conceptualize a theory of behavior, and many of his early conclusions focused on the role of sexual frustrations in producing physical symptoms. Over time Freud developed an elaborate theory of personality and an accompanying approach to therapy. His approach to personality came to be called *psychoanalytic theory;* his method of therapy, *psychoanalysis.*

Sigmund Freud is best known for his psychoanalytic theory and the therapy method derived from it, psychoanalysis.

Key Concepts

Many psychological theories have a key concept around which the theory grows. Freud's theory had two such key concepts: psychic determinism and unconscious motivation. **Psychic determinism** suggests that all thoughts, feelings, actions, gestures, and speech are determined by some action or event that happened to an individual in the past. Adults, for example, do not have accidental slips of the tongue, nor do they frown or change mood by accident; past events affect all of today's actions. Moreover, most of a person's thoughts and behavior are determined by **unconscious motivation**—thoughts and feelings buried in the mind, or unconscious, the existence of which people are unaware. These two ideas—that behavior is caused by previous events and that people are no longer aware of these events—guided much of Freud's theory.

In addition to his two key concepts, Freud theorized that people are energized and able to act the way they do because of two basic instinctual drives—life and death—with two prominent features, sex and aggression. These instincts are buried deep within the unconscious and are not always socially acceptable. Freud wrote little about aggression until late in his life

Psychic determinism: A psychoanalytic assumption that everything a person feels, thinks, and does has a purpose and that all behaviors are caused by past events.

Unconscious motivation: A psychoanalytic assumption that desires, goals, and internal states of which an individual is unaware determine behavior.

and focused mainly on sexual instincts that he called the **libido** (later in his writings Freud referred to the libido as *life energy*). His critics assert that he was preoccupied with sexual matters.

When people exhibit socially unacceptable behaviors or have feelings that they consider socially unacceptable, especially sexual feelings, they often experience self-punishment, guilt, and anxiety. Freud's theory thus describes conflict between a person's instinctual (often unconscious) needs for gratification and the demands of society for socialization. In other words, it paints a picture of human beings caught in a conflict between basic sexual and aggressive desires and society's demands. A person might wish to strike an offensive drunk, but social rules dictate that he or she should not. For Freud, a person's basic desire is to maximize instinctual gratification while minimizing punishment and guilt.

Structure of Personality

In his theory, Freud considered the sources and consequences of conflict and how people deal with it. For Freud, a person's source of energy to deal with conflict is biologically determined, complex, and lies in the structure of consciousness.

Structure of Consciousness. According to Freud, consciousness consists of three levels. The first level, **conscious** awareness, consists of the thoughts, feelings, and actions of which people are aware. The second level, **preconscious** awareness, is mental activity people can become aware of only if they attend to it closely. The third level, the **unconscious,** is mental activity people are unaware of and can only become aware of through certain techniques such as dream analysis. To illustrate how these behavior levels differ, suppose a woman decides to become a psychotherapist for a *conscious* reason—the reason she gives family and friends: she wants to help people. Later, during an introspective moment, she realizes that her *preconscious* motivation for becoming a psychotherapist stems from a desire to resolve her own unhappiness. Finally, through psychoanalysis, she discovers that she hungers for love and intimacy, which her parents denied her. *Unconsciously,* she hopes her future patients will satisfy that hunger by making her feel needed. Freud's theory focuses on people's unconscious level and how it influences their behavior.

Id, Ego, and Superego. According to Freud's theory, the primary structural elements of personality are three forces that reside, fully or partially, in the unconscious—the id, the ego, and the superego. Each force accounts for a different aspect of functioning. It is important to keep in mind that the id, ego, and superego are concepts, not physical structures.

The **id** is the source of a person's instinctual energy, which, according to Freud, is either sexual or aggressive. The id works on the *pleasure principle,* whereby it tries to maximize immediate gratification through satisfaction of raw impulses. Deep within the unconscious, the demanding, irrational, and selfish id seeks only pleasure. It does not care about morals, society, or other people. Freud might argue that it was Jim Bakker's id that propelled him toward a sexual liaison despite his religious exhortations to others.

While the id seeks to maximize pleasure and obtain immediate gratification, the **ego** (which grows out of the id) works by the *reality principle* and seeks to satisfy the individual's instinctual needs in accordance with reality. The ego acts like a manager, adjusting cognitive and perceptual processes

Libido: In Freud's theory, the instinctual life force that energizes the id. The libido works on the pleasure principle and seeks immediate gratification; the libido is usually sexual in nature.

Conscious: Freud's first level of awareness, which refers to behaviors (feelings and actions) of which a person is aware.

Preconscious: Freud's second level of awareness, which refers to mental activity a person can become aware of by attending to it.

Unconscious: Freud's third level of awareness, which refers to mental activity beyond a person's normal awareness. This material can be made available through psychoanalysis.

Id: In Freud's theory, the source of instinctual energy, which works on the pleasure principle.

Ego: In Freud's theory, the part of personality that seeks to satisfy the id and superego in accordance with reality.

TABLE 12.1
Freud's View of Mental Structures

Structure	Consciousness	Contents and Function
Id	Unconscious	Basic impulses (sex and aggression); seek immediate gratification; immediate, irrational, impulsive
Ego	Mostly conscious	Executive mediating between id impulses and superego inhibitions; tests reality;
		person's conscience

Freud believed that the first stage of development is the *oral stage* during which an infant focuses on oral gratification.

to balance the person's functioning, control the id, and stay in touch with reality. For example, the id of a boy who wakes up shivering may tell him to steal a blanket from his older brother sleeping on the bottom bunk. However, the boy's ego tells him that his older brother might punish him for stealing the blanket. Working on the reality principle, the boy realizes that he can gratify his id most safely by asking his parents for another blanket.

The **superego** is the moral branch of mental functioning taught by parents and society. The superego tells the id and the ego whether gratification in a particular instance is ethical. It attempts to control the id by internalizing parental authority (whether rational or irrational) through the process of socialization and by punishing transgressions with feelings of guilt and anxiety. The superego may tell the boy that stealing a blanket from his brother, who may then become cold, is unethical. By asking his parents for another blanket, the boy can satisfy his id without feeling guilty, fearful, or anxious. The ego and superego attempt to modulate the id and direct it toward more appropriate ways of behaving. (See Table 12.1.)

Development of Personality

Freud strongly believed that if people look at the development of their behavior they can gain insight into their current behavior, and he used this principle with his patients. This belief led him to an elaborate critical stage theory of personality development. Freud believed that the core aspects of personality are established early, remain stable throughout life, and change only with great difficulty. Freud argued that all people pass through five critical stages of personality development: oral, anal, phallic, latency, and genital.

Oral Stage. The first stage is the **oral stage,** based on the fact that newborns' instincts are focused on their mouths—their primary pleasure-seeking center. They receive oral gratification through feeding, thumb sucking, and babbling; during the early months of life, people's basic feelings about the world are established. Freud relied heavily on symbolism, and he contended that an adult who considers the world a bitter place (referring to the mouth and taste senses) probably had difficulty during the oral (location of the taste buds) stage of development. Adults who had difficulty in the oral stage of development would tend to have problems that focus on nurturing and receiving warmth and love.

Superego: In Freud's theory, the moral branch of mental functioning, comprised of the ego ideal and conscience and taught by parents and society.

Oral stage: Freud's first stage of personality development, from birth to about age two, during which infants obtain gratification primarily through the mouth.

Anal Stage. The second major stage of development is the **anal stage.** At about two or three years, children learn to respond to some of society's demands. One parental demand is that children control their bodily functions of urination and defecation.

Most two- and three-year-olds experience pleasure in moving their bowels, with the anal area the focus of pleasurable feelings. This stage therefore establishes the basis for conflict between the id and the ego, between the desire for infantile pleasure and the demand for adult, controlled behavior. Freud claimed that during the anal stage, children develop certain lasting personality characteristics regarding control, such as neatness and an orderliness, that reflect their toilet training. Thus, adults who had difficulty in the anal stage would tend to have problems that focus on orderliness, and might be compulsive in many behaviors.

Phallic Stage. Freud's third stage, the **phallic stage,** centers on the genitals. At about age four or five, children become aware of their sexuality. Freud claimed that during this stage, numerous feelings are repressed so deeply that children, and later adults, are unaware of many of their sexual urges. Nonetheless, sex role development begins during this period.

The **Oedipus complex,** which develops in the phallic stage, is a boy's love for his mother, hostility toward his father, and the consequent fear of castration and punishment by the father. In resolving the Oedipus complex, he eventually accepts his father's close relationship with his mother. Rather than feel excluded by it, he chooses to gratify his need for his mother's attention by identifying with his father. In this way, a young boy begins to identify with and model his behavior after that of his father.

For females, Freud argued that the Oedipus complex, sometimes called the *Electra complex*, follows a slightly different course. When a young girl realizes she has no penis, she develops what Freud called *penis envy*. By attaching her love to her father, she can thereby symbolically acquire a penis. A young girl may ask her father to marry her so they can raise a family together. When she realizes that this is unlikely, she may identify with her mother and copy her mother's behavior as a means of obtaining (or sharing in) her father's affection. Like the young male, the young female identifies with the parent of the same sex in the hope of obtaining affection from the parent of the opposite sex. For both boys and girls, the critical component in resolving the Oedipus complex is the development of identification with the parent of the same sex.

The existence of an Oedipus complex is controversial and widely debated, especially since many people find it sexist and degrading to women. There is no doubt about Freud's views of women; he saw women as weaker and less rational than men and believed that they should be subservient to men. Today, most researchers believe that Freud's notion of penis envy was imaginative, but unconvincing (Stagner, 1988).

Latency Stage. Freud's fourth stage of development, the **latency stage,** lasts from about age seven until puberty. During latency, children develop physically, but sexual urges are inactive. Libidinal urges, sexual fears, and frustrations are repressed, and much of a child's energy is channeled into social or achievement-related activities. Some modern psychoanalysts (considered in the next section) believe that this stage has disappeared from American society because of the fast-paced maturation of children into adolescence. They assert that children move from the phallic stage directly to the genital stage.

Anal stage: Freud's second stage of personality development, from age two to about three, during which children learn to control the immediate gratification obtained through defecation and become responsive to the demands of society.

Phallic stage: Freud's third stage of personality development, from age three to seven, during which children obtain gratification primarily from the genitals. During this stage, children pass through the Oedipus (or Electra) complex.

Oedipus complex: Occurring during the phallic stage, feelings of rivalry with the parent of the same sex and love of the parent of the opposite sex, ultimately resolved through identification with the parent of the same sex; the *Electra complex* is the term used specifically to refer to this process in women.

Latency stage: Freud's fourth stage of personality development, from age seven until puberty, during which sexual urges are inactive.

ORAL 0-2	ANAL 2-3	PHALLIC 3-7		
Infant achieves gratification through oral activities such as feeding, thumb sucking and babling.	The child learns to respond to some of the demands of society (such as bowel and bladder control).	The child learns to realize the differences between males and females and becomes aware of sexuality.	The child continues his or her development but sexual urges are relatively quiet.	The growing adolescent shakes off old dependencies and learns to deal maturely with the opposite sex.

FIGURE 12.1
Freud describes five psychosexual stages of development.

Genital Stage. When people reach the last stage of development, the **genital stage,** the sexuality, fears, and repressed feelings of earlier stages are once again exhibited (see Figure 12.1). Many of an adolescent's repressed feelings of sexuality toward his or her mother and father resurface. During the genital stage, the adolescent shakes off dependence on parents and learns to deal with members of the opposite sex in socially and sexually mature ways. Members of the opposite sex, who may have been ignored during the latency stage, are now seen as attractive and desirable.

During the genital stage, many unresolved conflicts and repressed urges affect behavior. Ideally, if previous stages of development were maneuvered without major incident, people will develop conventional relations with members of the opposite sex. If not, a person may continue to have a series of unresolved conflicts within his or her unconscious.

Unresolved Conflicts

As children proceed from one developmental stage to the next, they adjust their views of the world. But if they do not successfully pass through a stage, a fixation occurs. A **fixation** is an excessive attachment to some person or object that is only appropriate at an earlier level of development. When a person becomes fixated, he or she is said to be arrested at a particular stage of development. Fixation at one developmental stage does not prevent all further development, but unless people master each stage successfully, they cannot fully deal with the later stages. Someone troubled by an unresolved conflict who develops a fixation will find successful completion of later stages more difficult. A child who does not pass successfully through the phallic stage, for example, probably has not resolved the Oedipus complex and may feel hostility toward the parent of the same sex. The child may suffer the consequences of this unresolved conflict throughout life.

According to Freud, good personality adjustment generally involves a balance among competing forces: the child, and later the adult, is neither too self-centered nor too moralistic. Restrictive, punitive, and overbearing

Genital stage: Freud's last stage of personality development, from the onset of puberty through adulthood, during which the sexual conflicts of childhood resurface in adolescents.

Fixation: An excessive attachment to some person or object that is only appropriate to an earlier level of development; a person who becomes fixated is said to be arrested, or halted, at a particular stage of development.

In sublimation, unacceptable desires are rechannelled into proper behaviors. This might explain a prison artist's need to paint rather than expressing himself through violence or theft.

Defense mechanism: A way of reducing anxiety by distorting reality.

Repression: A defense mechanism by which people block anxiety-provoking feelings from conscious awareness and push them into the unconscious.

Projection: A defense mechanism by which people attribute to other people their own undesirable traits.

Denial: A defense mechanism by which people refuse to accept the true source of their anxiety.

Reaction formation: A defense mechanism by which people behave in a manner opposite their true but anxiety-provoking feelings.

Sublimation: A defense mechanism by which people redirect socially unacceptable impulses into acceptable ones.

Rationalization: A defense mechanism by which people reinterpret behavior in terms that render it acceptable.

parents or parents who are indifferent, smothering, or overindulgent produce emotionally disturbed children who have a difficult time coping with life because of fixations. Fixations or partial fixations usually occur because of frustration or overindulgence that hinders the expression of sexual or aggressive energy at a particular psychological stage. What happens when a person becomes fixated? According to Freud, the person develops defense mechanisms and sometimes maladjustment.

Defense Mechanisms   A defense mechanism is a largely unconscious way of reducing anxiety by distorting reality. Everyone defends against anxiety from time to time. Defense mechanisms allow the ego to deal with the uncomfortable feelings anxiety produces. In fact, people are typically unaware that they are using defense mechanisms. But people who use defense mechanisms to such an extent that reality is sharply distorted can become maladjusted.

Freud described many kinds of defense mechanisms, but identified **repression** as most important. In repression, anxiety-provoking behavior or thoughts are totally relegated to the unconscious. When people repress a feeling or desire, they become unaware of it. Thus, a young girl who was taught that assertiveness is inappropriate in women may repress her own assertiveness.

In **projection,** people attribute their own undesirable traits to others. An individual who unconsciously recognizes his or her aggressive tendencies may then see other people acting in an excessively aggressive way. Jim Bakker may have used projection, calling other people sinners against God. In **denial,** a person refuses to accept reality. Someone with strong sexual urges may deny interest in sex rather than deal with those urges. In **reaction formation,** a person defends against anxiety by adopting behaviors opposite to his or her true feelings. A classic example of reaction formation is the behavior of someone with strong sexual urges who becomes extremely chaste, perhaps by becoming a priest. Another example is someone who censures pornographic literature, but has strong desires to read it. In **sublimation,** energy from an impulse that might be considered taboo is channeled or redirected into a socially desirable form; thus, a man who has sexual desires for someone whom he knows may be off limits (perhaps a cousin) channels that sexual energy or drive into painting nudes. In **rationalization,** a person tries to reinterpret undesirable behavior to make it appear acceptable. For example, a thief may rationalize that his victims acquired their wealth through illegal or immoral means or that he needs the money more than they do. Jim Bakker may have rationalized that his followers wanted him to lead a lavish life-style. When people rationalize, they try to make unreasonable feelings or behaviors seem reasonable. When defense mechanisms take over and reality becomes distorted and maladaptive, a person must be concerned about using them.

Freud Today

When it was first published around 1900, Freud's psychosexual theory of development received both favorable and unfavorable attention. It was considered absurd that young children had sexual feelings toward their parents. Freud's theory, however, has to be considered in a cultural context. Austrian society, with its rigid standards of behavior, and Freud's wealthy patients biased him in directions that few theorists would adopt today.

Yet, as we watch young children and the way they identify with their parents, we can see that there are elements of truth to this conception of how personality development proceeds. Little girls do tend to idolize their fathers, and little boys often become strongly attached to their mothers. However, Freud was not nearly as interested in normal development as he was in the pathology, or disorder, that appeared as a result of imperfect development. In many senses, Freud's theory paved the way for other developmental stage theorists, such as Piaget, Levinson, and Erikson, who made more specific predictions about specific behaviors. (See Figure 12.2.)

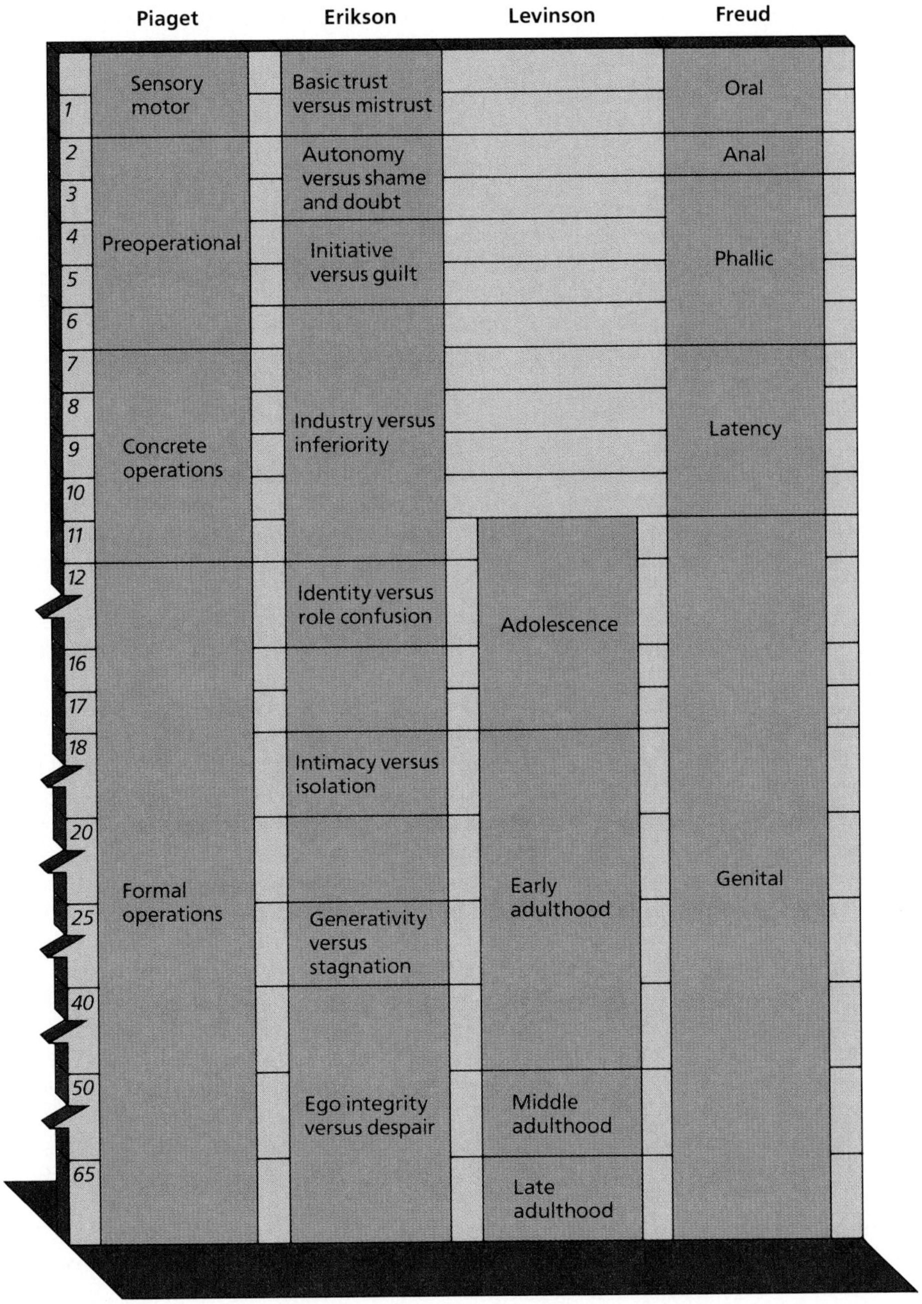

Age	Piaget	Erikson	Levinson	Freud
1	Sensory motor	Basic trust versus mistrust		Oral
2		Autonomy versus shame and doubt		Anal
3	Preoperational			
4		Initiative versus guilt		Phallic
5				
6				
7				
8		Industry versus inferiority		Latency
9	Concrete operations			
10				
11				
12		Identity versus role confusion	Adolescence	
16				
17				
18		Intimacy versus isolation		
20				Genital
25	Formal operations	Generativity versus stagnation	Early adulthood	
40				
50		Ego integrity versus despair	Middle adulthood	
65			Late adulthood	

FIGURE 12.2
The stage theories of Piaget, Erikson, Levinson, and Freud all suggest that individuals must master each stage before they can pass successfully through the next. Notice the similarities among all four theories.

Freud's theories have been sharply criticized for a number of reasons. Some psychologists object to his basic conception of human nature, its emphasis on sexual urges, and his idea that human behavior is biologically determined; others reject his predictions about psychosexual stages and fixations. Psychologists assert that his theory does not account for changing situations and the contexts in which people find themselves. Many people find Freud's ideas about women patently offensive. At a minimum, his ideas are controversial, and many psychologists do not regard them as valid. Almost all agree that his theory makes specific predictions about individual behaviors almost impossible. Regardless of whether Freud's theory is right or wrong, his influence on psychology and on Western culture exceeds that of any other personality theorist, present or past. It weaves together his clinical experiences with patients, his speculations about human nature, and as you will see in the next section, his own extraordinary personality.

The Life of Sigmund Freud

MILESTONES IN PSYCHOLOGY

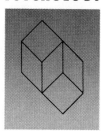

Sigmund Freud is the best-known personality theorist of all time. His mark on psychological thinking was extraordinary, and his insights were unparalleled. The life and personality of Freud were as complex as his theory was profound. He was unhappy, quarrelsome, rebellious, and vindictive. But he was also energetic, loving, thoughtful, and a superb clinician. Many biographers have attempted to portray the complexity of Freud and his theory, but Yale professor Peter Gay has done it best in his 1988 book, *Freud—A Life for Our Time.*

Gay conducted extensive research into Freud's beliefs, life, and papers and letters (many of which were unpublished). He acknowledges *The Interpretation of Dreams*, published in 1899, as "an autobiography at once candid and canny, as tantalizing in what it omits as in what it discloses" (Gay, 1988, p. 104). In it, Freud laid out the keys to psychoanalysis. He made the distinction between the manifest and latent content of dreams. The manifest content is what people remember when they awake; the latent content is the meaning, which requires decoding. From Freud's view, a dream is the disguised fulfillment of a repressed wish. Gay also shows how Freud's extensive reading and study of art, literature, and history affected his theorizing. From 1908 to 1914 Freud worked on papers that dealt with literary characters, including Oedipus, and used the information to build theories on character development, especially ego development.

Gay looks closely at Freud's personal life and recounts Freud's revelation that his father's death was the most significant event, the most decisive loss, of his life. But Freud's failure to deal with the loss of his mother is also important. Gay writes, "Should it really be true that a mother's death is any less poignant? Freud was very much his father's son, dreaming and worrying more about paternal than about maternal relations . . ." (p. 89).

The life of Sigmund Freud must be placed in a historical and cultural context. From his birth in 1856 until his death in 1939, Freud's world underwent vast economic and social changes. He was born into a world of order, but his theorizing took place during a turbulent time—the emergence of World War I. "Freud, a man astonished at very little, was astonished at the hideous spectacle of human nature at war" (p. 355). This experience would later have an impact on his views of preparing for death.

Gay's book allows us to peer into little-known realms of Freud's personal life. Until about 1920, Freud was often seen as radical and extreme—considered an outcast by many. But by the mid-1920s, his celebrity was secure, and Freud acknowledged that he had become a household word. For example, in 1925 Hollywood mogul Samuel Goldwyn asked Freud to write a love story for him, but Goldwyn's extravagant financial offer was refused. The one gratification Freud desired but never achieved was a Nobel prize—a bitter disappointment, according to Gay.

On more than one occasion, Freud destroyed his notes and letters to discourage future biographers. But his expansive correspondence and the volumes he wrote about his theories provided a legacy to document an important chapter of psychology's history. Gay's biography will be a classic because it examines some of the milestone ideas Freud put forth, including fixations, defense mechanisms, and the issue of unresolved conflicts. ◆

---

p. 425
* Identify and describe the primary structural elements of personality from Freud's view. p. 426
* Describe Freud's five-stage theory of personality development. pp. 427–429
* Name and describe three important defense mechanisms. p. 430

Focus on Learning

Psychoanalytic Theory: Dissent and Revision

There is no question that Freud had an enormous impact on psychological thought. But his theory has been attacked by modern theorists, including some of his students who felt that there were serious omissions, errors, and obvious biases in Freudian theory. Many have developed new ideas loosely based on Freud's original conception.

Neo-Freudians

Freud's powerful intellect and key concepts fascinated many psychologists and psychoanalysts. They were not ready to throw good ideas out with bad ones, and where they dissented with Freud, they revised his theories. They became known as **neo-Freudians.**

Some neo-Freudians argued that people are not driven solely by libidinal instincts (Alfred Adler). Others argued that the ego has more of a role than Freud thought in controlling behavior (Erich Fromm). Still others focused on the central role of anxiety in shaping personality and maladjustment (Karen Horney). Many new theories attributed a greater influence to cultural and interpersonal factors (Harry Stack Sullivan). Many of the newer theories were more optimistic and future oriented (Carl Jung). Whereas traditional psychoanalysts begin by focusing on unconscious material in the id and only later try to increase the patient's ego control, many neo-Freudians focus on helping people to develop stronger control of their ego and feel better about their "selves." Carl Jung is one of the best-known theorists who broke with Freud over key issues, and we explore his influential theory next.

Jung's Analytical Psychology

Carl Gustav Jung (1875–1961) was a psychiatrist who became a close friend and follower of Freud. But Jung, a brilliant thinker, ultimately broke with Freud over several key issues. Jung placed relatively little emphasis on sex,

Neo-Freudian: Any person who modified the basic ideas of Freud; the neo-Freudians, sometimes called *neoanalysts,* usually attributed a greater influence to cultural and interpersonal factors.

Carl Gustav Jung deviated from Freud in concentrating on people's attempts to successfully match their basic desires against real-life demands.

at least compared to Freud. He focused on people's desires to blend their basic drives (including sex) with real-world demands; thus Jung saw people's behavior as less rigidly fixed and determined. Jung emphasized the search for meaning in life. When he declared his disagreements with Freud in 1917, he and Freud severed relationships; Freud was intolerant of followers who deviated too much from his position.

Jung chose to differentiate his approach from Freud by calling it an *analytic* approach rather than *psychoanalytic* approach. Like Freud, Jung emphasized unconscious processes as determiners of behavior, and he believed that each person buries past events in the unconscious. Jung's version of the unconscious was slightly different, however; he held that the unconscious anticipates the future and redirects a person when the person is leaning too much in one psychological direction. In addition, Jung developed a new concept central to his ideas, that of the collective unconscious, a layer of unconscious that is even more primitive and deeply hidden from direct examination. The **collective unconscious** is a storehouse, a collection of ideas and images inherited from our ancestors. These inherited ideas and images are called archetypes and are passed from generation to generation. **Archetypes** are emotionally charged ideas and images that have rich meaning and symbolism and are contained within a person's collective unconscious. The archetypes of our collective unconscious emerge in art, religion, and especially in dreams. For example, one especially important archetype is the mandala; the *mandala* is considered a mystical symbol, generally circular in form, and in Jung's view represents the striving for unity within a person's self. Jung pointed out that many religions have mandala-like symbols; indeed, Hinduism and Buddhism use mandala symbols as aids to meditation. Another archetype is the concept of mother; each person is born with a predisposition to react to certain types of people or institutions as mother figures. Mother figures are considered warm and accepting, and nurturing— the Virgin Mary, one's alma mater, or the earth. There are archetypes for wise older men and wizards. Jung found rich symbolism in dreams, and used symbols like the mandala and mothers to help people understand their own mental processes and behavior.

Carl Jung's ideas are widely read, but not widely accepted by mainstream psychologists. Although his impact on psychoanalysis is important, he never achieved prominence in leading psychological thought because his ideas, even more than Freud's, cannot be verified. Some even view them as mere poetic speculation. Another psychologist who broke with Freud but who made a more lasting impact on psychological thought was Alfred Adler, considered next.

Alfred Adler: A Break from Freud

Alfred Adler (1870–1937) was heavily influenced by Freud, and some psychologists consider his theory an extension of Freud's. Adler was a Viennese physician who remembered having an unhappy childhood. He recalled being compared to his older brother, who seemed to be better liked because of his physical prowess and attractiveness. Perhaps his unhappy childhood and feelings of inferiority led Adler to believe that people strive to become the best they can be. When Adler broke with Freudian traditions, he focused much more on human values and social interactions.

Key Concepts. At the turn of the century, physicians believed that diseases attacked weak, or inferior, organs. As a physician, Adler subscribed to this

Collective unconscious: In Jung's theory, a storehouse, a collection of primitive ideas and images in the unconscious that are inherited from our ancestors.

Archetypes: In Jung's theory, emotionally charged ideas and images that have rich meaning and symbolism and are contained within the collective unconscious.

UPWARD STRIVING & Inferiority Complex ASSOCIATED W/ Adler

notion of "organ inferiority" and used it in his personality theory. Adler suggested that people try to strengthen weaknesses both in their organs and in their personality. Thus, a key concept of Adler's theory is that people develop a striving for physical, mental, and psychological superiority; later in his writing he spoke about striving for completion and perfection.

Another key concept of Adler's theory is that people strive to better themselves by focusing not simply on the self (as Freud thought) but on the self *as a member of society*. Adler maintained that people are inherently social beings who seek goals and values that are social in nature. Adler

for perfection.

Adler differed with Freud on two key points. First, Adler viewed human beings as striving to overcome obstacles toward fulfilling themselves, not striving for pleasure. Second, Adler viewed the social nature of human beings as much more important than did Freud. Adler met with Freud on a weekly basis, but in 1911, Freud denounced him because of sharp, irreconcilable differences in their views of personality.

Structure of Personality. According to Adler, people are motivated, or energized, by natural feelings of inferiority, which lead them to strive for completion, superiority, and ultimately perfection. Thus, feelings of inferiority are not always detrimental. A sense of inferiority can compel people to strive for and thereby express their core tendencies, both as individuals and as members of society.

Adler recognized that people seek to express their needs for superiority in different areas of life. Some seek to be superior artists; others seek to be superior social advocates, parents, teachers, or corporate executives. Thus, each person develops a unique life-style in which attitudes and behaviors express a specific life goal or an ideal approach to achieving superiority. Adler eventually sought to develop an "individual" psychology, arguing that people have to be analyzed as unique human beings.

Adler stressed fulfillment through striving toward specific goals. Some life goals, which Adler called *fictional finalism,* are not realistic and are unlikely to be achieved by most, such as winning the Nobel prize for literature, becoming a billionaire, or earning worldwide fame (Adler, 1929/1969). But it is these fictional goals (often unconscious) that motivate people and set up unique patterns of striving.

Development of Personality. Adler felt that children's social interactions are particularly important in determining eventual personality characteristics (later Carl Rogers would come to the same conclusion). Adler and his followers relied heavily on the idea that early relationships with siblings, parents, and other family members determine what life-style an individual eventually chooses. It therefore follows that birth order is important. A firstborn child, for example, is likely to have a different relationship with people, and thus develop a different life-style, from that of a thirdborn child. Firstborns are pushed by parents toward success, leadership, and independence and thus tend to have high needs for achievement. Their early experiences make it likely that they will choose a life-style such as that of a corporate president or U.S. senator, reflecting high needs for achievement. Thirdborn children, on the other hand, are usually more relaxed about achievement. A young child who feels competitive with an older sibling,

Alfred Adler deviated from psychoanalysis moving toward a more humanistic approach to behavior.

however, may develop strong needs for success, mastery, and achievement that drive the child toward success.

Foundations for Other Theories.   To a great extent, psychologists see Adler as stressing an interpersonal route to fulfillment. Adler's ideas of an inferiority complex and of life-style have made their way into other popular theories of psychology. In addition, Adler's key ideas also serve as the foundation of many "Adlerian" childcare development centers. Adler's theory can be thought of as the parent of humanistic theories, such as Carl Rogers's, because it was developed twenty years earlier and laid the foundation for these theories. Adler emphasized an innate social need motivated by feelings of inferiority to strive toward perfection and superiority, but humanistic theories stressed self-actualization.

Humanistic Approaches

Unlike Freudians and neo-Freudians, who wanted to understand relationships between children and parents, theorists such as Abraham Maslow and Carl Rogers were more interested in people's conceptions of themselves and what they would like to become. In general, *humanistic theories* assume that people are motivated by internal forces to achieve personal goals. Humanistic psychology does not focus on disturbed individuals but rather on understanding how healthy people cope with human motives such as self-esteem.

Humanistic theories, which stress fulfillment, developed partly in response to Freud's theory, which stresses the conflict of inner forces. Whereas Freud saw people in conflict warding off evil thoughts and desires with defenses, humanists see people as basically decent and worthwhile (although some of their specific behaviors might not be). Moreover, humanistic fulfillment theories enable theoreticians and practitioners to make predictions about specific behaviors.

Sometimes humanistic theories are also called *phenomenological approaches* because they focus on the individual and his or her unique experiences with and ways of interpreting the world. Humanistic or phenomenological approaches are more likely to examine immediate experiences than past ones, and more likely to deal with an individual's perception of the world than with a therapist's perception of the individual. Finally, they focus on self-determination; people carve their own destinies from their own vantage points and in their own ways. The humanistic approach is represented by two well-known psychologists, Maslow and Rogers, whose theories we examine next.

Abraham Maslow

No single individual is more closely associated with humanistic phenomenological psychology than Abraham Maslow (1908–1970). In chapter 11, we examined Maslow's theory of motivation, which states that human needs are arranged in a pyramidal hierarchy in terms of importance and potency. Lower needs are powerful and drive people toward fulfilling them—food and water, for example. At the middle of the pyramid of needs is safety, then belongingness, and self-esteem. At the top of the pyramid is self-actualization. The higher the need on the hierarchy, the more distinctly human the need.

As a humanist, Maslow felt that human beings were born healthy and undamaged, and he had a strong bias toward studying healthy human beings, rather than those wrapped up in maladjustment. He spoke about personality in terms of human uniqueness and the human need for **self-actualization,** the process of growth, the realization of human potential. He focused not on what was missing from personality or life, but what might be achieved in realizing one's full potential. The process of realizing potential, and of growing, is the process of becoming self-actualized.

Critics of Maslow find his notions too fuzzy and diffuse (as they do Freud's). His approach to psychology is viewed as romantic and never fully developed. A more complete and scientific humanistic approach was presented by Carl Rogers.

Carl Rogers and Self-Theory

Carl Rogers (1902–1987) began to formulate his personality theory during the first years of his practice as a clinician in Rochester, New York. He listened to thousands of patients and was among the first psychologists to record and transcribe interactions with patients. Given the opportunity, Rogers's patients talked about their experiences and thoughts and about themselves. From his experiences with patients, Rogers made three basic assumptions about behavior:

"Self-Theory"= his theory of personality.

- Behavior is goal-directed and worthwhile.
- People are innately good, so they will almost always choose adaptive, enhancing, and self-actualizing behaviors.
- How a person sees his or her world determines how that person will behave.

Key Concepts. Rogers believed that personal experiences provide an individual with a unique, subjective internal frame of reference and world view. He believed that **fulfillment**—an inborn tendency directing people toward actualizing their inherited nature and thus attaining their potential—is the motivating force of personality development. Thus, people strive naturally to express their capabilities, potential, and talents to the fullest extent.

Rogers's personality approach is *unidirectional* because it always moves in the direction of fulfillment. This does not mean that a person's personality undergoes uninterrupted growth. During some periods, no growth is evident. But for Rogers, a person's core tendency is to actualize, maintain, and enhance the experiencing organism. Rogers liked the analogy of a seed, which if watered grows into a plant—a strong, healthy plant, a representative sample of other members of its species.

Structure of Personality. Rogers's theory of personality is structured around the concept of self. What he means by **self** are those perceptions individuals have of themselves and their relationships to people and aspects of life. The self is how people see their own behavior and internal characteristics. As mentioned before, his theory assumes that individuals are constantly engaged in the process of fulfilling their potential, that is, of actualizing their true selves.

Rogers suggested that each person not only has a concept of self, but also of an ideal self. An **ideal self** is the self a person would like to be, such as a competent professional, devoted mate, or loving parent. According to

Self-actualization: The process of becoming everything one might through the realization of innate human potential.

Fulfillment: In Rogers's personality theory, an inborn tendency directing people toward actualizing their inherited natures and thus attaining their potentials.

Self: The main structural component of Rogers's theory of personality. Perceptions that characterize an individual and his or her relationship to other people and to other aspects of his or her life.

Ideal self: The self that a person would ideally like to be.

Carl Rogers developed a personality theory based on his belief in the concept of *self.*

Rogerian theory, each person's happiness lies within his or her conception of self. A person is generally happy when agreement exists between the real (Rogers used the term *phenomenal*) self and the ideal self; great discrepancies between the real and the ideal selves create unhappiness and dissatisfaction, and in extreme cases, major maladjustment.

Rogers's focus on the self led him to his basic principle, which is that people have a tendency to maximize their self-concept through *self-actualization.* In this process, the self grows, expands, and becomes social. People are self-actualized when they have expanded their self-concepts and developed their potentials to approximate their ideal selves. When people's self-concepts are not what they would like them to be, anxiety develops. Like Freud, Rogers saw anxiety as useful because it motivates people to try to actualize their best selves, to become all they are capable of being.

Development of Personality.
Unlike Freud, Rogers suggested that development occurs continuously, not in stages. He contended that personality development involves learning self-assessment techniques to master the process of self-actualization—which takes a lifetime.

Rogers was particularly aware that children develop basic feelings about themselves early in life, which led him to understand the role of social influences in the development of self-concepts. The self-assessments of children who are told that they are beautiful, intelligent, and clever are radically different from those of children who are told that they are bad, dirty, shameful, and a general nuisance. Rogers did not claim that negative feelings toward children's behavior should not be expressed. He suggested that children must grow up in an atmosphere in which they can experience life fully. This involves their recognizing both the good and bad sides of their behavior.

Self-Concepts.
People with rigid self-concepts guard themselves against potentially threatening feelings and experiences. Rogers suggested that these people become unhappy when they are unable to fit new types of behavior into their self-concepts. They then distort their perceptions of their behavior in order to make them compatible with their self-concepts. A person whose self-concept includes high moral principles, rigid religious observances, and strict self-control, for example, probably becomes anxious when he feels envy. Such a feeling is inconsistent with his self-concept. To avoid anxiety he denies or distorts what he is truly experiencing. He may deny that he feels envy, or he may insist that he is entitled to the object he covets.

When a person is faced with a changing world, it may threaten his or her self-concept. The person may then screen out difficult ideas or thoughts, creating a narrow view, a limited conception of the world, and a restriction on personal growth. But individuals can reduce or eliminate their fear by broadening their frame of reference and by considering alternative behaviors. People with healthy self-concepts can allow new experiences in their lives, and can accept or reject them. Such people move in a positive direction. With each new experience, their self-concepts become stronger and more defined, and the goal of self-actualization is brought closer.

Individual Development.
Rogers's concept of personality shows an abiding concern for *individual development.* Rogers stressed that each person must evaluate his or her own situation from a personal (internal) frame of reference, not from the external framework of others.

Approach	Psychoanalytic	Humanistic	Trait
Major Proponent	Sigmund Freud	Carl Rogers	

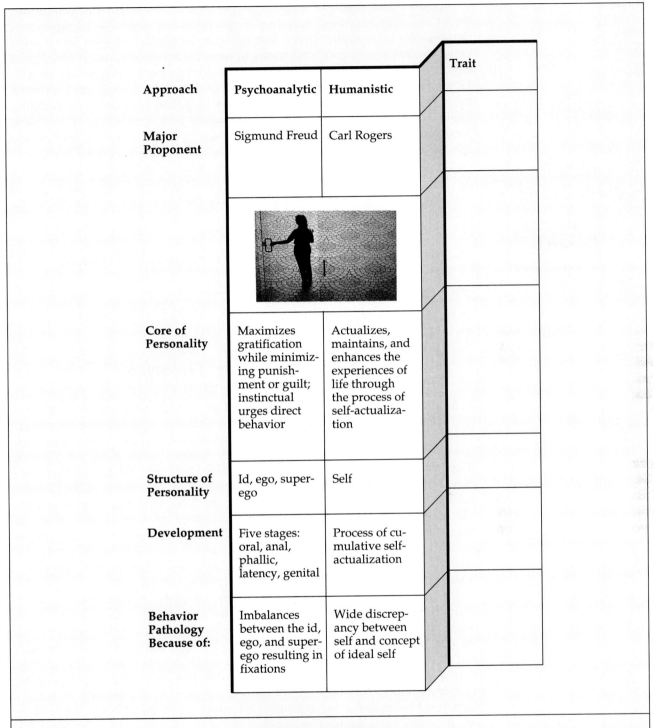

	Psychoanalytic	Humanistic	
Core of Personality	Maximizes gratification while minimizing punishment or guilt; instinctual urges direct behavior	Actualizes, maintains, and enhances the experiences of life through the process of self-actualization	
Structure of Personality	Id, ego, super-ego	Self	
Development	Five stages: oral, anal, phallic, latency, genital	Process of cumulative self-actualization	
Behavior Pathology Because of:	Imbalances between the id, ego, and super-ego resulting in fixations	Wide discrepancy between self and concept of ideal self	

◆ *Building Table 12.1* ◆

Psychoanalytic and Humanistic Theories

Freud's and Rogers's theories of personality make fundamentally different assumptions about human nature and how personality is expressed. Freud saw a biologically driven human being in conflict; Rogers saw human beings as inherently good and trying to be everything they can. Where Freud was strongly deterministic, humanists are strongly oriented toward free will. Humanists believe that people can rise above their biologically inherited traits and use decision-making processes to guide behavior. See Building Table 12.1 for a comparison of psychoanalytic and humanistic approaches. Next, we examine an approach to personality that focuses on traits—the specific behavioral responses individuals make throughout their lives.

Focus on Learning

- ◆ Who were the neo-Freudians, and in reaction to what concepts did their theories develop? p. 433
- ◆ How was Alfred Adler's theory of personality different from Freud's theory? p. 434
- ◆ What is self-actualization according to a therapist such as Rogers? p. 438

Trait and Type Theories

Both ancient philosophers and medieval physicians believed that the proportion of bodily fluids determined a person's temperament and personality. Cheerful, healthy people, for example, were said to have a sanguine personality because blood was their primary humor, while those who had a preponderance of yellow bile were considered hot-tempered. Like their medieval counterparts, some early psychologists based their personality theories on the behaviors people openly exhibit, such as shyness, impulsiveness, and aggressiveness. Research shows that many of these easily observed characteristics predict other behaviors—for example, extremely shy people are more likely to be anxious, lonely, and have low self-esteem (DePaulo, Dull, Greenberg, and Swaim, 1989). Theories based on these observations make intuitive sense and thus have been very popular.

Trait theorists study specific behaviors, or traits. A **trait** is any readily identifiable behavior that characterizes the way an individual differs from other people. Someone might characterize John F. Kennedy as energetic and forward looking, and Margaret Thatcher as tough and practical. Such characterizations present specific ideas about these people's behaviors, that is, their traits. Traits can be evaluated on a continuum, so a person can be extremely shy, very shy, shy, or sometimes shy. Traits become especially important because for some personality theorists, such as Buss (1989), they are the stuff personality is made of.

Type theorists group together traits common to specific personalities. **Types,** therefore, are broad collections of traits loosely tied together and interrelated. Although the distinction between traits and types sometimes blurs, according to Gordon Allport (Allport, 1937), "A man can be said to *have* a trait; but he cannot be said to *have* a type. Rather he *fits* a type" (p. 295). This section examines the theories of two well-known trait psychologists, Gordon Allport and Raymond Cattell, and then examines the broader type theory of Hans Eysenck.

Trait: Any readily identifiable stable behavior that characterizes the way an individual differs from other individuals.

Types: Broad collections of traits tied together loosely and interrelated.

Allport's Trait Theory

The distinguished psychologist Gordon Allport (1897–1967) was a leading trait theorist who suggested that each individual has a unique set of traits. According to Allport (1937), if a person's traits are known, it is possible to predict how he or she will respond to various environmental stimuli. Allport quickly discovered that there are thousands of ways—or traits—to characterize people's behavior, but some seemed more dominant than others.

Allport eventually decided that people's behavior could be categorized into three kinds of traits: *cardinal, central,* or *secondary. Cardinal traits* are ideas and behaviors that determine the direction of a person's life. A clergyman's cardinal trait may be devotion to God; a philosopher's, the need to investigate and explain knowledge; a civil rights leader's, the desire to rectify social and political injustices. Allport noted that many people have no such overall guiding behavior or idea.

The more common *central traits* are reasonably easy to identify behaviors that characterize a person's daily interactions. They are the basic units of personality. Allport believed that central traits, such as controlled, apprehensive, tense, self-assured, forthright, and practical, adequately describe many personalities. For example, boxing legend Muhammad Ali could be characterized as forthright and self-assured; Woody Allen's typical film persona could be described as tense and apprehensive.

Secondary traits are specific behaviors that occur in response to specific situations. For example, a person may have a secondary trait of prejudice toward minorities, a keen interest in psychology lectures, or a love of spectator sports. Being less characteristic of an individual's behavior than central traits, secondary traits are more easily modified and are not necessarily shown on a daily basis.

Everyone has different combinations of traits, which is why Allport claimed that each person is unique. To identify a person's traits, Allport recommended an in-depth study of that individual. If Allport's theory is true, knowing a person's traits would allow a psychologist to predict how that person would respond to the environment, that is, what his or her behavior would be.

Psychologist Gordon Allport was especially well-known as a trait theorist.

Cattell's Factor Theory

Psychologists such as Allport and Raymond B. Cattell (1905–) argue that it is possible to tell a great deal about a person just by knowing a few of his or her traits. Cattell (1965) used the technique of factor analysis, a statistical procedure in which groups of variables, or factors, are analyzed to detect which are related, to show that groups of traits tend to cluster together. Thus, people who describe themselves as warm and accepting also tend to rate themselves as high on nurturance and tenderness but low on aggression, suspiciousness, and apprehensiveness. Researchers also see patterns within professions; for example, artists may see themselves as creative, sensitive, and open, while accountants may describe themselves as careful, serious, conservative, and thorough-minded. Cattell called the obvious, day-to-day cluster of traits *surface traits,* and the higher-order cluster of traits, *source traits.*

Eysenck's Type Theory

Whereas Allport and Cattell focused on the trait level, Hans Eysenck (1916–) focused on higher levels of trait organization, or what he called

Hans Eysenck developed a *type* theory of personality.

types. Eysenck (1970) argued that all personality traits can be reduced to three basic dimensions: emotional stability or emotional instability, introversion or extroversion, and psychoticism.

Emotional stability refers to the extent to which people have control over their feelings. People can be spontaneous, genuine, and warm, or they can be controlled, calm, flat, unresponsive, and stilted. *Introversion* or *extroversion* refers to the extent to which people are withdrawn or open. Introverts are socially withdrawn and shy; extroverts are socially outgoing and open and like to meet new people. Eysenck's third dimension, *psychoticism,* is sometimes called tough- or tender-mindedness. It measures the extent to which people isolate themselves from others. At one extreme, people are troublesome, antiauthority, sensation seeking, insensitive, and risk takers; at the other end, they are warm, gregarious, and tender (see also Howarth, 1986). Each type incorporates elements at a lower level (traits), and each trait incorporates lower order qualities (habits).

Eysenck argues that personality has a biological basis, but emphasizes that learning and experience also shape an individual's behavior. For example, he says that introverts and extroverts possess different levels of arousal in the cortex of the brain. Accordingly, each type seeks the amount of stimulation necessary to achieve their preferred level of arousal. A person with a low level of arousal, where stimulation is less intense, may become a security guard or a librarian; a person with a high level of arousal, which is reflected in his or her outward behavior, may become a race car driver or a politician.

Psychology and History

Famous (and infamous) historical figures are often the focus of in-depth personality studies. Typically the aim is to explain events of history based on specific personality traits involved. When a person's life and history are interpreted in the framework of psychological ideas, we call this a *psychobiography.* The fundamental idea is that some of the underlying psychological conditions within a person shaped the person's life, thinking, and ultimately history. For example, we saw earlier that Peter Gay's account of Freud's life shed light on why Freud developed some of his ideas. A *psychobiography* of Jim Bakker might shed some light on the forces that drove him to extremes and led to the downfall of his ministry.

History is, of course, a set of facts, but not everyone views the facts, let alone their causes, from the same view. Many biographies have been written about Richard Nixon and his presidency; some find his life sympathetic, while others view him with no sympathy. The first step in doing a psychobiography is to determine the true facts of a person's life. But reconstructing the facts is usually only one part; the second step is interpreting those facts and placing them within a context. For example, Adolph Eichmann has been described as a dangerously perverted personality, obsessed with a desire to kill, and as "a cold-blooded scheming plotter, one of the gang of hardened Nazis . . . clamoring . . . to the pinnacle of world conquest" (Hausner, 1966, p. 4).

It is impossible to give a complete description or explanation of a person through a psychobiography—a psychobiographer has to give a selected account, a glimpse, a slice of a person's life. Psychobiographies can help people account for how the subject felt, thought, and acted at a specific point in history—often by using his or her own words as evidence. In doing so, a psychobiographer must account for processes within the individual (as Freud might have), processes within the social environment (as Adler or Mischel might have), and processes of history (as a historian might). Psychobiographers note that Emily Dickinson was extremely shy and notoriously seclusive; she wrote that she used to go to church early to avoid having "to go in after all the people had got there." Still, she was one of the most expressive of all poets.

When evaluating a psychobiography, it is important to recognize the psychobiographer's point of view (Freudian, humanistic, or perhaps behavioral). Thus when Edmund Wilson (1952) wrote that Woodrow Wilson as president of the United States repeated his mistakes as president of Princeton University, he drew allusions to the stability of personality. He also claimed that President Wilson's low self-esteem made him self-defeating and uncompromising (over the League of Nations, for example). President Wilson's psychobiographer ultimately claimed that the former president's maladaptive behavior could be traced to relationships with his father who had been a severe and demanding minister.

Order can be found in the lives of historical figures, even though some argue that the study of individual lives is hopelessly complex (Runyan, 1982). In some ways this is the challenge of a psychobiography—to find order and causation where none seems to exist. Many psychologists find tasks such as evaluating the psychological causes of Hitler's behavior challenging, compelling, and a useful way to view psychology and history. Other psychologists find such analyses far too oriented in one view, too limited in scope, or irresolutely too simple (and thus wrong). Sometimes psychobiographies are written by historians who do not have a full view of psychological theory, or by psychologists who do not have a complete view of history. Although psychobiographies are popular, interesting, and sometimes accurate, most psychologists view them with some degree of skepticism.

Criticisms of Trait and Type Theories

Trait and type theories are appealing because they characterize people in important dimensions and, therefore, provide simple explanations for how individuals behave. However, psychologists have criticized these theories on five basic fronts. First, is trait theory actually a personality theory? Does it make predictions about a behavior and explain why that behavior occurs? Some psychologists claim that trait theory is merely a list of behaviors arranged into a hierarchy. Second, most trait theories do not tell which personality characteristics last a lifetime and which are transient.

Third, if an individual's behavior depends on the situation or context, how can traits predict the individual's acts or behaviors (Epstein and O'Brien, 1985)? Some contend that the failure of trait theory to account for situational differences is a crucial weakness. Fourth, trait theory does not account for changing cultural differences; if you test the same persons ten years apart, their traits are likely to be different, but society is also different, values change, and people adopt new ideas. Trait and type theory do not account for these changing cultural norms. Finally, trait and type theories do not explain why people develop traits or why traits change.

Although trait and type theories continue to evolve, psychologists want a theory that explains the development of personality, how personality theory can predict maladjustment, and especially why a person's behavior can be dramatically different in different situations. Theories that attempt to

Approach	Psychoanalytic	Humanistic	Trait	Behavioral	Cognitive
Major Proponent	Sigmund Freud	Carl Rogers	Gordon Allport		
Core of Personality	Maximizes gratification while minimizing punishment or guilt; instinctual urges direct behavior	Actualizes, maintains, and enhances the experiences of life through the process of self-actualization	A series of interrelated hierarchically arranged traits which characterize the day-to-day behaviors of the individual		
Structure of Personality	Id, ego, super-ego	Self	Traits		
Development	Five stages: oral, anal, phallic, latency, genital	Process of cumulative self-actualization	Process of learning new traits		
Behavior Pathology Because of:	Imbalances between the id, ego, and super-ego resulting in fixations	Wide discrepancy between self and concept of ideal self	Having learned faulty or inappropriate traits		

◆ **Building Table 12.2** ◆

Psychoanalytic, Humanistic, and Trait Theories

describe, explain, and predict behavior with precision tend to be behavioral, the next major group of theories discussed. Building Table 12.2 presents a summary of the theories discussed so far.

+ Distinguish between a *type* and a *trait*. p. 440
+ Identify the central aspect of *cardinal, central,* and *secondary* traits. p. 441
+ Identify and describe the three basic dimensions to which Eysenck argued all personality traits can be reduced. pp. 441–442
+ Identify four criticisms of trait and type theories. p. 443

Behavioral Approaches

The concepts on which some personality theorists focus—inner drives, psychic urges, need for self-actualization—are hard to define, referring to some inner personal characteristic. But another group of personality theorists—the behaviorists—assert that inner forces, hard-to-define constructs, and psychic urges are not the proper subject matter of personality study. Behavioral theorists are practical. They believe that people often need to change aspects of their lives quickly and efficiently, that many do not have the time, money, or energy for a lengthy therapy or personality analysis.

Consider the behavioral self-treatment Redford Williams proposes for people who have Type A personalities—those hard-driving, ambitious, highly competitive people who, according to cardiologists, are at high risk of heart attack (Williams, 1989). Williams says that hostility and cynical mistrust are the lethal elements of Type A personalities, and he outlines steps one can practice to reduce hostility and develop a more trusting attitude and a healthier heart. Among the steps are cynicism monitoring, which entails recording angry feelings in a "hostility" journal, and thought stopping, which involves mentally yelling "Stop!" whenever hostile thoughts start forming. If behaviorists are right in saying that personality is equivalent to habits, then Williams's self-treatment program should help Type A individuals change their health-endangering personalities.

Key Behavioral Concepts

Behavioral personality theorists assert that personality develops as people learn from their environments. The key word is *learn.* According to behaviorists, personality characteristics are not long-lasting or enduring, but are modifiable and subject to change. Personality is the sum of a person's learned tendencies. (Recall from chapter 5 B. F. Skinner's assertion that there is no "self," only a collection of possible behaviors.)

Behaviorists look at personality very differently from any other theorist we have described so far. They generally do not look inward; they look only at overt behavior. Behavioral approaches are often viewed as a reaction to traditional personality theories.

Precisely Defined Elements. Behavioral theories tend to center on precisely defined elements, such as the relationship between stimuli and responses, the strength of stimuli, and strength, duration, and timing of a reinforcer. All these can be tested in a laboratory or clinical setting. By focusing on stimuli and responses, behaviorists avoid conceptualizing human nature and concentrate instead on predicting behavior in specific circumstances. As a result, their assertions are more easily tested. Behaviorists see the development of personality simply as a change in response characteristics—a person learns new behaviors in response to new environments and stimuli.

Responses to Stimuli. For most behaviorists, the structural unit of personality is the response to stimuli. Any behavior, regardless of the situation, is seen as a response to stimuli or a response awaiting reinforcement (or punishment). When an identifiable stimulus leads to an identifiable response, researchers predict that every time that stimulus occurs, so will the response. This stimulus-response relationship helps explain the constancy of personality. If, for example, every time a teenager complains about his financial predicament, his father talks about sports, the teenager may stomp out of the room and slam the bedroom door as he hears his father pronounce, "Teenagers are so moody these days." If this scene is repeated often, it becomes predictable—the stimulus of avoidance (sports talk) leads to the response of withdrawal.

Behavior Patterns. Using a behavioral analysis, psychologists can discover how people develop behavior patterns (such as eating their vegetables or being hostile) and why behavior is in constant flux. The behavioral approach suggests that learning is the process that shapes personality and that learning takes place through experience. Because new experiences happen all the time, a person is constantly learning about the world and changing response patterns accordingly. Just as there are several learning principles involving the use of stimuli, responses, and reinforcement (for a review, see chapter 5), there are several behavioral personality theories based on classical conditioning, operant conditioning, or observational learning.

Classical Conditioning

Most people are fearful or anxious at some time. Some are fearful more often than not. How do people become fearful? What causes constant anxiety and apprehension?

Many behavioral psychologists maintain that people develop anxiety and fear through classical conditioning, in which a neutral stimulus is paired with another stimulus that elicits some response. Eventually, the neutral stimulus can elicit the response on its own. For example, many people fear rats. Because rats are often encountered in dark cellars, people may learn to fear dark cellars—dark cellars become a feared stimulus. Later the person may develop a generalized fear of dark places. If the first time a person sees a train it's in a darkened station that looks like a cellar, the person may learn to fear trains. Classical conditioning thus allows a researcher to explain the predictability of a person's responses when presented with a specific stimulus; it describes the relationship between one stimulus and a human being's expectation of another, and the response that the person makes (Rescorla, 1988).

Operant Conditioning

In operant conditioning, spontaneous behavior is followed with a consequence such as reinforcement or punishment. According to behaviorists, personality can be explained as spontaneous behavior that is reinforced.

When a person is affectionate and that behavior is reinforced, the person is likely to continue to be affectionate.

Time-Out Procedure. Behavioral psychologists often use the operant learning principles of reward and punishment to help children control themselves and shape their personalities. Consider the problem of discipline in school, specifically of a ten-year-old child in the Florida public school system who frequently used obscenities. In an hour's time, the child would utter as many as 150 obscene words and phrases. Each time the child uttered an obscene word, Lahey, McNees, and McNees (1973) took him out of the classroom for a minimum of five minutes and placed him in a well-lit, empty room. The child was told he would be placed in the time-out room every time he made an obscene statement. In a few days, the number of obscenities decreased dramatically, from two a minute to fewer than five an hour. Using a behavioral technique, the researchers modified an element of personality.

The time-out procedure is often used in learning situations in both classrooms and laboratories. As with any reinforcement or punishment procedure, the subject learns that the procedure is contingent on behavior. In the example, time-out was punishing. The child found it rewarding to be in the classroom and punishing to be in the time-out room. To remain in the classroom and avoid being put in the time-out room, he learned not to utter obscenities.

Observational Learning

Observational learning theories assume that people learn new behaviors simply by watching others. The theory contends than an observer will imitate the specific behaviors of a model and thus develop a set of personality characteristics. Personality is thus seen as developing through the process of observation and imitation.

The theory stresses the importance of the relationship between the observer and the model in eliciting imitative behavior. When children view the behavior of a parent or other important figure, their imitative behavior will be significantly more extensive than when they observe the actions of someone less important to them. A son is more likely to adopt his father's hurried behavior than his neighbor's relaxed attitude.

People can learn abnormal, as well as acceptable, behavior and personality characteristics through imitation. In fact, the most notable behavior that people observe and then imitate may be violence on television. As you will see in chapter 17, ample evidence shows that children who observed aggressive violent television programs were more willing to hurt others after watching the program. If children observe people who are reinforced for violent, aggressive behavior, they are likely to imitate that behavior rather than more socially desirable behaviors.

Observational learning theories assume that learning a new response can occur independent of reinforcement. But although personality develops as a function of imitating the behavior of other people, later reinforcement acts to maintain such learned behaviors. Most people, for example, observe aggressive, hostile behavior in others but choose different ways to express emotions. Together, the imitative aspects of observational learning theory and the reinforcement properties of conditioned learning can account for most behaviors. For example, a daughter may become logical and forthright by watching her lawyer mother prepare arguments for a court case, and seeing her win.

Violence on television may actually teach children that violence is acceptable and sometimes even admirable behavior.

Researchers who focus on observational learning recognize that people choose to show some behaviors some of the time and to omit other behaviors. Accordingly, some researchers focus on observational learning with another element—thought. These ideas constitute cognitive theory, a natural reaction to behavioral theory. The cognitive emphasis is on the interaction of a person's thoughts and behavior.

Cognitive Approaches

In some important ways, cognitive approaches to personality appeared as a reaction to strict behavioral models, adding a new dimension. The cognitive emphasis is on the interaction of a person's thoughts and behavior. It considers the uniqueness of human beings, especially their thought processes, and assumes that human beings are decision makers, planners, and evaluators of behavior (strict behavioral approaches did not consider thought processes). Cognitive views have been influenced by the humanist idea that people are essentially good and strive to be better. Many researchers now claim that people can change their behavior, their conceptions of themselves, and their personalities in a short time if they are willing to change their thoughts.

Key Cognitive Concepts

From a cognitive point of view, the mere association of stimuli and responses is not enough for conditioning and learning to occur in human beings—thought processes have to be involved. According to cognitive theory, people exhibit learned behavior based on their situation and personal needs at a particular time. If thought and behavior are closely intertwined, then when something affects a person's thoughts, it should also affect behavior. The man who mentally yells "Stop!" whenever his thoughts become hostile should realize some success in quelling his violent behaviors.

Rotter's Locus of Control

Many classic theories that attempt to explain all aspects of personality and behavior have been criticized because they are difficult to study scientifically. The ego in Freud's theory, for example, is not a physiological object or state that can be manipulated, studied, or examined. Similarly, the concepts of self and maximizing potential in Rogers's theory are difficult to measure and assess. As a reaction to imprecise grand theories, psychologists have developed smaller, well-researched theories. These *microtheories,* some of which follow a cognitive approach, account for specific behaviors in specific situations. Because of their smaller scope, they are easier to test.

One such cognitive-behavioral theory is locus of control, developed by Julian Rotter (1916–). Locus of control involves the extent to which individuals believe that they or that external factors control their lives (Rotter, 1990). Rotter focused on whether people place their locus of control inside themselves (internal) or in their environments (external). Locus of control influences how people view the world and how they identify the causes of success or failure in their lives. In an important way, people's locus of control reflects their personality—their view of, and reactions to, the world. To examine locus of control, Rotter developed a test consisting of a series of statements about oneself and other people. Choosing the statements that best reflect your feelings will help you determine your locus of control:

People's misfortunes result from the mistakes they make.	*versus*	Many of the unhappy things in people's lives are partly due to bad luck.
With enough effort, we can wipe out political corruption.	*versus*	It is difficult to have much control over the things politicians do in office.
There is a direct connection between how hard I study and the grade I get.	*versus*	Sometimes I can't understand how teachers arrive at the grades they give.
What happens to me is my own doing.	*versus*	Sometimes I feel that I don't have enough control over the direction my life is taking.

These statements reflect either an internal (the statements on the left) or an external (the statements on the right) locus of control. People classified as internal (by their choice of statements) feel that they need to control their environment. They are more likely to engage in preventive health measures and dieting than are external people (Balch and Ross, 1975). College students characterized as internal are more likely to profit from psychotherapy (Kilmann, Albert, and Sotile, 1975) and to show high academic achievement (Findley and Cooper, 1983).

People with an external locus of control believe that they have little control over their lives. A college student may attribute his or her poor grade to a lousy teacher, feeling there was nothing he or she could have done to get an A. In contrast, individuals who develop an internal locus of control feel that they can master any course they take because they believe that

Julian Rotter

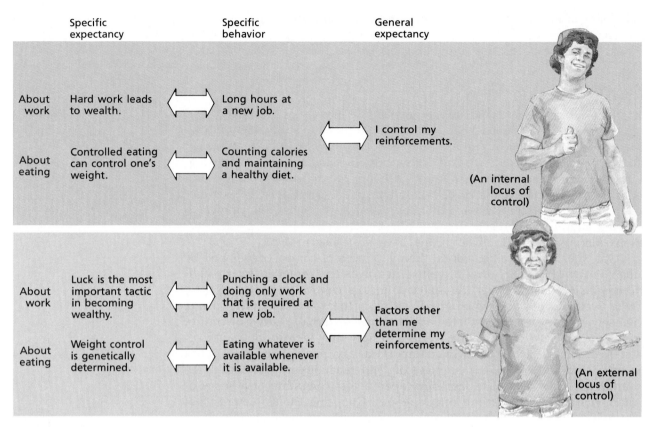

Specific expectancy	Specific behavior	General expectancy

FIGURE 12.3

A person's general expectations about life are determined in a three-stage process: specific expectancies lead to behaviors, which are reinforced. This cycle eventually leads to a general expectancy about life and to an internal or external locus of control.

through hard work they can do well in any subject. People develop expectations based on their beliefs about the sources of reinforcement in their environments. These expectations lead to specific behaviors described as personality. Reinforcement of these behaviors in turn strengthens expectancy and leads to increased belief in internal or external control.

Locus of control elegantly integrates personality theory, expectancy theory, and reinforcement theory (see Figure 12.3). Locus of control describes several specific behaviors, but it is not comprehensive enough to explain all or even most of an individual's behavior. Bandura's theory, discussed next, specifically addresses people's convictions (thoughts) about their own effectiveness.

Bandura's Self-Efficacy

One of the most influential cognitive theories of personality was developed by Albert Bandura (1925–) a former president of the American Psychological Association. His conception of personality began with observational learning theory and the idea that human beings observe, think about, and imitate behavior (Bandura, 1977a). Bandura played a major role in reintroducing thought processes into learning and personality theory.

In 1977, Bandura argued that people's expectations of mastery and achievement and their convictions about their own effectiveness determine the types of behavior they will engage in and the amount of risk they will undertake (Bandura, 1977a, 1977b). He called this self-efficacy. **Self-efficacy** is a person's belief about whether he or she can successfully engage in and execute a specific behavior. Judgments about self-efficacy determine how

Self-efficacy: A person's belief about whether he or she can successfully engage in and execute a specific behavior.

much effort people will expend and how long they will persist in the face of obstacles (Bandura, 1982a, 1982b). A strong sense of self-efficacy allows people to feel free to select, influence, and even construct the circumstances of their own lives. And if a person feels she can control a situation, this increases her perceived self-efficacy to manage it (Bandura and Wood, 1989). Thus, when she has a high level of self-efficacy, she is more likely to attribute success to variables within herself rather than to chance factors and is more likely to pursue a task (Bandura, 1988; McAuley, Duncan, and McElroy, 1989). Because people can think about their motivation, and even their own thoughts, they can effect changes in themselves and persevere in tough times (Bandura, 1989).

Albert Bandura

Bandura's theory is optimistic. It is a long way from Freud's deterministic theory, which argues that biologically based forces locked in conflict determine human behavior. It is also a long way from a strict behavioral theory, which suggests that environmental contingencies shape behavior. Bandura believes that human beings have choices, that they direct the course of their lives. He also believes that society, parents, experiences, and even luck help shape those lives.

Bad luck or nonreinforcing experiences can damage a developing sense of self-efficacy. Observation of positive, prosocial models during the formative years, on the other hand, can help people develop a strong sense of self-efficacy that will encourage and reinforce them to direct their own lives. Bandura's theory allows individual flexibility in behavior. People are not locked into specific responses to specific stimuli as some strict behaviorists might assert. According to Bandura, people choose the behaviors they will imitate, and they are free to adapt their behavior to any situation. Because self-efficacy both determines and flows from feelings of self-worth, a person whom others view as successful may not share that view, and a person who has achieved little of note to society may consider himself a capable and worthy person. Unfortunately, people often develop negative thoughts about themselves and develop a poor sense of self-efficacy, sometimes shown in behaviors that we call shyness.

Overcoming Shyness

APPLYING
PSYCHOLOGY

*A*bout forty percent of adults report being shy, and for at least two million adults, **shyness** is a serious behavior problem that inhibits personal, social, and professional growth. Shy people show extreme anxiety in social situations; they are extremely reticent and often overly concerned with how they look and sound and how others view them. They fear looking, sounding, or acting foolish; as a consequence they may develop clammy hands, dry mouth, excessive perspiration, trembling, nausea, blushing, and a need to go to the bathroom frequently. Shyness keeps people away from social situations and makes them speak softly when they speak at all. Shy people not only hold back from approaching other people, but avoid them (Asendorpf, 1989). Most shy people report that they have always been shy, and half of all shy people feel that they are more shy than other people in similar situations (Carducci and Stein, 1988).

Personality researchers contend that certain personality traits, including shyness, are long-lasting. Jerome Kagan found that two- and three-year-olds who were extremely cautious and shy tended to remain that way for years (Kagan, 1989). Daniels and Plomin (1985) also found an important relationship between biological mothers' shyness and adopted infants' shyness at two years of age. These findings suggest that genetic factors play an important role in shyness.

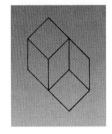

Shyness: Extreme anxiety in individuals who are reticent and often overly concerned with how they look, sound, and appear to others.

The hypersensitivity of shy people can inhibit their personal growth.

Although Kagan suggests that extreme shyness may have a biological basis, we also know that shyness emerges because people develop distorted self-concepts, negative views about their competencies and self-efficacies. Such individuals view themselves in a poor light and see themselves as having few if any social graces. These thoughts combined with actions such as withdrawal and nervousness set a person up for social failure. When such events occur, the person then says "See, I was right." A person's thoughts about his or her shyness, body reactions, and social behaviors thus help maintain the shyness.

People who are shy believe that they can overcome it with some help, and treatment programs exist (Carducci and Stein, 1988). If you are shy, there are some things you can do to help overcome your shyness.

- ◆ Rehearse what you want to say.
- ◆ Build your self-esteem by focusing on your good points.
- ◆ Practice smiling and making eye contact.
- ◆ Use social learning theory concepts—observe the behavior of others whom you admire and copy their behavior.
- ◆ Think about how others feel; remember that about forty percent of all people feel the way you do.
- ◆ Accept who you are and think about your distinctive, positive traits.
- ◆ Engage in relaxation training which might include self-hypnosis, yoga, or even biofeedback.
- ◆ Read self-help books on putting your best foot forward.
- ◆ Think positively; a positive attitude about yourself and other people can go a long way toward helping overcome shyness.   ◆

Mischel's Cognitive Social Learning

Like Bandura, Walter Mischel (1930–) claims that thought is crucial in determining human behavior, but he also believes that both past experiences and current reinforcement are important. What's more, Mischel is an *interactionist*—he focuses on the interaction of people and their environment (Mischel, 1983). Mischel and other cognitive theorists (e.g., Cantor and Kihlstrom, 1982) argue that people respond flexibly to various situations. They change their responses, which are based on their past experiences and their current assessment of the situation, to suit the present situation. This process of adjustment is called *self-regulation*. People make subtle adjustments in their tone of voice and overt behavior (their personality), depending on the context in which they find themselves. Those who tend to be warm, caring, and attentive, for example, can become hostile and aggressive, depending on the situation.

People's personalities and particularly their responses to a stimulus are determined by: *competencies*, what they know and can do; *encoding strategies*, the way they process, attend to, and select information; *expectancies*, their anticipation of outcomes; *personal values*, the importance they attach to various situations; and *self-regulatory systems*, the system of rules they have established for themselves to guide their behavior (Mischel, 1979). Next, we will consider how two researchers studied the constancy of personality by examining the behavioral characteristics of a group of women over twenty years.

Walter Mischel is a cognitive theorist who believes that the interaction of people and their environment shapes day-to-day behavior.

Women's Personality Changes from College to Mid-Life

*D*oes personality change over time or does it stay the same from adolescence through old age? Are personality changes the same for men and women? Trait theorists assume that personality remains much the same over the life span. Shy people stay shy; high school pranksters become retirement home pranksters. A humanist like Erik Erikson and an adult stage theorist Daniel Levinson (chapter 10), on the other hand, contend that people change during the life span. These psychologists believe in an adult life cycle.

THINKING ABOUT RESEARCH

Questions Are Formulated. Unfortunately, most personality and adult life-cycle studies have been conducted with men—who represent less than half the population. Do women's personalities change in a similar way? Do the personalities of career-oriented women change and family-oriented women stay the same? Helson and Moane (1987) from the University of California at Berkeley asked these questions of women from college age to mid-life. Their primary objective was to discover if personality changes are obvious across different life paths and if those changes support theories of adult development and personality. A second goal was to compare the life cycles of men and women because of the failure of previous long-term studies to address the vital issue. They asked if life cycles in adulthood need to be rethought. Do women have mid-life transitions as men do?

Method. Helson and Moane began their work in 1958 at Mills College, a private women's college located in Oakland, California. They gathered information from the same eighty-one women at ages twenty-one, twenty-seven, and forty-three, a longitudinal method where a single group of people is compared at different times to determine if changes have occurred over time. (For a review of this method, see chapter 9, p. 300.) The researchers used several measures of personality, including the California Psychological Inventory, or CPI. The CPI, commonly used to study people from mid-adolescence to old age, is a test of normal personality. Designed to assess effectiveness in interpersonal functioning, it examines confidence, independence, responsibility, socialization, self-control, tolerance, and flexibility, among other dimensions.

Correlational Results. The results, reported as correlations between the different measures of personality, showed interesting stabilities and changes. For example, when the women were between ages twenty-one to twenty-seven they took control of their lives, acknowledged differences in the way the world ought to be and the way it was, and scored higher on tolerance, social maturity, and femininity than they did later in life. At ages twenty-seven to forty-three they scored higher in the areas of dominance, independence, and confidence, but lower on flexibility and femininity. The changes from twenty-seven to forty-three were greater than the changes from twenty-one to twenty-seven. As the women grew older, they became more organized, committed, and work-oriented, but less open to change.

The results of this study are consistent with adult life-cycle theories of development that have focused on men. From ages twenty-one to forty-three there were increases in self-discipline and commitment to duties; this typically occurs with men. The women became more confident, independent, and work-oriented. Until age twenty-seven, changes were small, but after age twenty-seven, the women became less feminine, focusing less on gender-specific tasks, such as childcare, and more on gaining independence and confidence and developing a career.

Conclusions. Helson and Moane (1987) maintain that young to middle-aged women's personalities change in consistent and predictable ways. They feel, for example, that a career requires a women to develop skills, confidence, and insight into others—things that were not necessary at earlier life stages. From Helson and Moane's view, personality is not static but a constantly evolving set of skills and abilities acquired to cope with the demands and dilemmas that face maturing individuals. This is consistent with some stage theorists who have focused on men but presents problems for trait theorists who assert that personality is stable during the life span.

Remaining Issues. Helson and Moane conducted their studies during a time of rapid change in women's roles in society, from 1960 through 1985. Were changes that occurred during this time similar to the changes taking place now or changes that will occur in the next twenty years? Is the United States likely to experience a decade similar to the one that saw the Vietnam war, the Beatles, and Watergate? Today, women ages twenty-one to twenty-seven may not show the same patterns. Research will have to address this possibility.

Helson and Moane used a longitudinal method, a procedure that has problems. There were a limited number of subjects, and those subjects changed as the times did; some dropped out of the research project. Further, after repeated testing on the same task (even though years apart), some of the subjects may have shown spurious results because of practice on the same tests.

There are also variations that this research did not specifically address, e.g., many women opt for careers first and family later. Socioeconomic status and societal changes determine so many life-style, educational, and work issues that this too needs to be examined. Research needs to place results within a historical context, taking into account changing political, social, and moral values. Last, it will take a longitudinal study of college women of the 1980s traced over twenty years to determine if Helson and Moane's findings are still valid for today's generation.   ◆

Cognitive Theories Evolve

From the view of personality theorists such as Rotter, Bandura, and Mischel, human uniqueness can best be explained by the idea that reinforcement, past experience, current feeling, future expectation, and subjective values all influence people's responses to their environments. Human beings have characteristic ways of responding, but those behaviors (their personalities) change, depending on specific circumstances.

Cognitive theories of personality are well researched but not yet complete; they do not, for example, clearly explain the development of personality from childhood to adulthood. They are also not well integrated. Bandura, for example, has shifted his focus from observational learning to self-regulation to self-efficacy without tying together the threads of those research areas. What this incompleteness and lack of coherence signify is that personality research and theory are still in their infancy, with further research and new ideas needed to tie up loose ends and generate more sophisticated, complete theories. See Building Table 12.3 on page 456 for an overall summary of the theories presented in this chapter.

Personality theories are diverse, and their explanations and accounts of specific behaviors vary sharply; each one views the development of personality and maladjustment from a different vantage point. When a practitioner, regardless of his or her orientation, meets a client, there are several ways the client can be evaluated. These techniques are the focus of psychological assessment, the topic considered next.

- For a behaviorist, what explains the constancy of personality? pp. 445–446
- Describe the two kinds of locus of control. p. 449
- What is self-efficacy? p. 450
- Why is Mischel called an interactionist? p. 452

Focus on Learning

Psychological Assessment

Assessment is the process of evaluating individual differences that occur among human beings, using methods such as intelligence tests, interviews, observations, and recording of physiological processes. Psychologists are constantly seeking ways to evaluate personality in order to explain behavior, diagnose and classify maladjusted people, and develop treatment plans when necessary (Haynes, 1984). A number of tests and techniques are used to help assess an individual's personality, and often more than one assessment procedure must be used to provide all the necessary information. Therefore, many psychologists administer a group or *battery of tests.*

A psychologist may assess personality with the Minnesota Multiphasic Personality Inventory-2 (MMPI-2), intelligence with the Wechsler Adult Intelligence Scale-Revised (WAIS-R), and a specific skill, such as coordination, with some other specific test. More confidence can be placed in the data from several tests than in data from a single test; further, with several measures, current levels of functioning are better characterized. It is interesting to note that hundreds of psychological tests exist; according to Barrios (1988), there are more than one hundred tests just for measuring the various elements of anxiety. The purpose of the testing determines the type of tests administered.

Intelligence Tests

Often, the first test given in a psychological assessment is an *intelligence test.* (Chapter 8 is devoted extensively to an examination of intelligence and intelligence tests.) These tests provide specific information about a person's level of intellectual functioning and, therefore, can be good predictors of

Assessment: The process of evaluating individual differences among human beings by using tests and direct observation of behavior. The role of the clinician is central in assessment techniques.

Approach	Psychoanalytic	Humanistic	Trait	Behavioral	Cognitive
Major Proponent	Sigmund Freud	Carl Rogers	Gordon Allport	B.F. Skinnner	Several, including Rotter, Bandura, and Mischel
Core of Personality	Maximizes gratification while minimizing punishment or guilt; instinctual urges direct behavior	Actualizes, maintains, and enhances the experiences of life through the process of self-actualization	A series of interrelated hierarchically arranged traits which characterize the day-to-day behaviors of the individual	Reduction of social and biological needs that energize behavior through the emission of learned responses	Learned responses depend on a changing environment, and person responds after thinking about context of the enviroment
Structure of Personality	Id, ego, super-ego	Self	Traits		
Development	Five stages: oral, anal, phallic, latency, genital	Process of cumulative self-actualization	Process of learning new traits	Responses	Changing responses
				Process of learning new responses	Process of thinking about new responses
Behavior Pathology Because of:	Imbalances between the id, ego, and super-ego resulting in fixations	Wide discrepancy between self and concept of ideal self	Having learned faulty or inappropriate traits	Having learned faulty or inappropriate behaviors	Inappropriate thoughts or faulty reasoning

◆ ***Building Table 12.3*** ◆

Psychoanalytic, Humanistic, Trait, Behavioral, and Cognitive Theories academic achievement—an important part of personality development. They may give an overall IQ score, separate verbal IQ and performance IQ scores (e.g., WISC-R), or all three types of scores. In addition, verbal scores can have subscales that examine specific components of verbal IQ and are thus helpful in assessing the reasons for, say, a student's low grades. But intelligence tests are limited because they provide only a general indication of a person's behavior pattern.

Objective Personality Tests

Next to intelligence tests, the most widely given tests are *objective tests* of personality. These tests, sometimes called *personality inventories,* generally consist of true-false or check-the-best-answer questions. The aim of objective personality tests varies. Cattell developed a test called the 16PF to screen job applicants or to examine individuals who fall within a normal range of functioning. The California Personality Inventory (CPI) is used primarily to identify and assess normal aspects of personality. Using a large sample of normal subjects as a reference group, it examines personality traits such as sociability, self-control, and responsibility.

One of the most widely used and well-researched personality tests is the Minnesota Multiphasic Personality Inventory, or the MMPI. The original MMPI was widely used, and the new MMPI-2 published in 1989 is considered a significant and major revision. The MMPI-2 consists of 567 true-false statements that focus on attitudes, feelings, motor disturbances, and bodily complaints. A series of subscales examine different aspects of functioning and measure the truthfulness of the subject's responses. Typical statements are as follows.

> I tire easily.
>
> I become very anxious before examinations.
>
> I worry about sex matters.
>
> I become bored easily.

The MMPI-2 can be administered individually or to a group. The test takes ninety minutes to complete and can be scored in less than one-half hour. It provides a profile that lets psychologists assess an individual's current level of functioning and characteristic way of dealing with the world, and provides a description of some specific personality characteristics. The MMPI-2 also enables psychologists to make reasonable predictions about a person's ability to function in specific situations, such as working in a mental hospital or as a security guard.

Generally, the MMPI-2 is used as a screening device for maladjustment. The norms for the MMPI-2 are based on the profiles of thousands of "normal" people and a smaller group of psychiatric patients. Each scale tells how most "normal" individuals score; a score far above or below "normal" is an important indicator. In general, a score significantly above "normal" may be considered evidence of maladjustment.

Nearly five thousand published studies have examined the validity and reliability of the original MMPI. The researchers have focused on the predictive value of the MMPI over a wide number of variables, including disorders such as schizophrenia (Walters, 1983); racial differences (Bertelson, Marks, and May, 1982); age, education, and socioeconomic status (Lanyon, 1968); family functioning (Bloomquist and Harris, 1984); and even the likelihood of death from cardiovascular disease (Gillum et al., 1980). For the

FIGURE 12.4
In a Rorschach test, the psychologist asks the subject to describe what he or she sees in an inkblot such as the one above. From these descriptions, the psychologist makes inferences about the subject's drives, motivations, and unconscious conflicts.

most part, these studies have supported the MMPI as a valid and useful predictive tool. The new MMPI now has a better representative sample of minorities that reflects the overall population and a much larger sample (2600 people) of subjects for standardization (the subjects were more representative of the population than were the initial group of subjects used for standardization). The new MMPI adds questions that focus on eating disorders and drug abuse. Older questions that had a gender bias were revised. Newer studies will soon evaluate the MMPI-2; since many of the traditional features of the test remain unchanged, the refinements and modifications should only improve the test's predictive validity (e.g., Butcher et al., 1990).

Projective Tests

The fundamental idea of **projective tests** is that a person's unconscious motives direct daily thoughts and behavior. To uncover those unconscious motives, researchers provide ambiguous stimuli to which examinees can provide responses that might reflect their unconscious. The examinee thus reflects or "projects" unconscious feelings, drives, and motives onto the ambiguous stimulus. Clinicians assess the deeper levels of a person's personality structure and detect motives of which the examinee is not aware. Projective tests are used when it is particularly important to determine whether the examinee is trying to hide something from the psychologist. They tend to be less reliable than objective personality tests, but they help to complete a picture of psychological functioning.

Rorschach Inkblot Test. A widely used projective test is the Rorschach Inkblot Test. Ten inkblots are shown, one at a time, to an examinee. Five are black and white, two have some red ink, and three have various pastel colors. They are symmetrical, with a specific shape or form (see Figure 12.4).

Subjects tell the clinician what they see in the design; a detailed report of the response is made for later interpretation. Aiken (1988) reports a typical response to a Rorschach inkblot:

> My first impression was a big bug, a fly maybe. I see in the background two facelike figures pointing toward each other as if they're talking. It also has a resemblance to a skeleton—the pelvis area. I see a cute little bat right in the middle. The upper half looks like a mouse. (p. 390)

Projective test: A variety of devices or instruments used to assess personality in which an examinee is shown a standard set of ambiguous stimuli and asked to respond in an unrestricted manner.

After the ten inkblots have been shown, the examiner asks specific questions, such as "Describe the facelike figures" or "What were the figures talking about?" Although norms are available for responses, skilled interpretation and good clinical judgment are necessary to place a subject's responses in a meaningful context. Long-term predictions can be formulated only with great caution (Exner, Thomas, and Mason, 1985).

Thematic Apperception Test. The *Thematic Apperception Test,* or TAT (which was discussed in chapter 11 as one way to assess a person's need for achievement), is much more structured than the Rorschach. The TAT consists of black-and-white pictures depicting one or more people in ambiguous situations, and subjects are asked to tell a story describing the situation in each picture. Specifically, they are asked what led up to the situation, what will happen in the future, and what the people are thinking and feeling.

The TAT is particularly useful as part of a battery of tests to examine a person's characteristic way of dealing with others and interacting with the world. To some extent, projective tests have a bad reputation among non-psychologists. Some people feel that interpreting pictures is too subjective and prone to error, and others even suspect a bit of hocus-pocus.

The Thematic Apperception Test (TAT) requires subjects to relate an imagined story to an ambiguous illustration. Responses are interpreted with the intention of gaining a better understanding of the way they deal with people and real-life situations.

Behavioral Assessment

Traditionally, *behavioral assessment* focused on overt behaviors—those that could be examined directly. Today, practitioners and researchers examine cognitive activity as well. Their aim is to gather information both to diagnose maladjustment and to prescribe treatment. Four popular and widely used behavioral assessment techniques are behavioral assessment interviews, naturalistic observation, self-monitoring, and neuropsychological assessment.

Behavioral Assessment Interviews. It is likely that any psychological assessment begins with an interview. Interviews are personal, giving a client (and the client's family) an opportunity to express feelings, facts, and experiences that might not be expressed through other assessment procedures. Interviews yield important information about a client's family situation, occupational stresses, and other events that affect the behavior being examined. They also allow psychologists to evaluate a client's motivations as well as inform the client about the assessment process.

Behavioral assessment interviews tend to be systematic and structured, focusing on overt and current behaviors and paying attention to the situations in which behaviors occur (Haynes, 1984). An interviewer will ask an examinee about the events that led up to a specific response, how the examinee felt as he or she made the response, and whether the same response might occur in other situations. The clinician has the opportunity to select the problems to be faced in therapy and set treatment goals (Morganstern, 1988). Many clinicians consider their first interview with a client a key component in the assessment process.

Interviews reveal only what the interviewee wishes to disclose, however, and are subject to bias on the part of the interviewer. But together with other behavioral measures, interviews are a good starting point.

Naturalistic Observation. In behavioral assessment, *naturalistic observation* involves two or more observers entering a client's natural environment and recording the occurrence of specified behaviors at predetermined intervals. In a personality assessment, for example, psychologists might observe how often a child in a classroom uses obscene words or how often a hospitalized patient refers to his or her depressed state. The purpose of naturalistic observation as a behavioral assessment technique is to observe people without interference by, or the influence of, a psychologist. The strength of the approach is in providing information that might otherwise be unavailable or difficult to piece together. It can help psychologists realize the sequence of actions that may lead up to an outburst of depressed feelings or to antisocial behaviors.

Naturalistic observation is not without its problems, however. How does a researcher record behavior in a home setting without being observed? Do naturalistic samples of behavior represent interactions in other settings? Does the observer have any biases, make inaccurate judgments, or collect enough data? Although naturalistic observation is not perfect, it is a powerful technique of behavioral assessment.

Self-Monitoring. **Self-monitoring** is an assessment procedure in which a person systematically counts and records the frequency and duration of specific behaviors in himself or herself. A person might record the number and duration of specific personality traits or symptoms, such as migraine headaches, backaches, or feelings of panic. Another person might self-monitor eating or sleeping patterns, sexual behavior, or smoking.

Self-monitoring is inexpensive to conduct, easy to do, and applicable for a variety of problems. It reveals information that might otherwise be inaccessible and enables practitioners to probe into the events that preceded the monitored activity to see if some readily identifiable pattern exists. In addition, self-monitoring helps a person become more aware of his or her own behaviors and the situations in which they occur.

Neuropsychological Assessment. The newest branch of assessment is *neuropsychological assessment.* Whereas *neurologists* are physicians who study the brain and its disorders, *neuropsychologists* are psychologists who study the brain and its disorders as they relate to behavior. Neuropsychology is a traditional area in experimental psychology; the difference is that now practitioners routinely watch for signs of neuropsychological disorders.

Often personality changes and some forms of maladjustment result from some type of brain disorder or malfunction in the nervous system (see Table 12.2). The signs may be evident from traditional assessment devices, such as histories (history of headaches), intelligence tests (slow reaction times), or observation of the client during a session (head motions or muscle

TABLE 12.2
Some Brain-Behavior Characteristics for Selected Nervous System Sites

Site	Characteristic
Temporal lobes	These lobes contain auditory reception areas as well as certain areas for the processing of visual information. Damage to the temporal lobe may affect sound discrimination, recognition, and comprehension; music appreciation; voice recognition; and auditory or visual memory storage.
Occipital lobes	These lobes contain visual reception areas. Damage to this area could result in blindness to all or part of the visual field or deficits in object recognition, visual scanning, visual integration of symbols into wholes, and recall of visual imagery.
Parietal lobes	These lobes contain reception areas for the sense of touch and for the sense of bodily position. Damage to this area may result in deficits in the sense of touch, disorganization, and distorted self-perception.
Frontal lobes	These lobes are integrally involved in ordering information and sorting out stimuli. Concentration and attention, abstract-thinking ability, concept-formation ability, foresight, problem-solving ability, speech, as well as gross and fine motor ability may be affected by damage to the frontal lobes.

Source: Adapted from Cohen et al., 1988.

spasms). Thus, when a child is making obscene gestures or remarks frequently and inappropriately and they are accompanied by facial tics, a practitioner may wonder if the neurological disorder Tourette's syndrome, in which such behaviors are often evident, is the cause. When psychologists see evidence of neuropsychological deficit, they will often refer a client to a neuropsychologist or neurologist for further evaluation.

Putting Assessment Techniques to Use

Personality assessment has grown from pencil-and-paper tests, often of intelligence or achievement within a specific discipline, to a wide range of techniques. These techniques are evolving, especially in behavioral assessment. Tests of brain functioning, although not part of a traditional assessment, are also part of the arsenal of psychological instruments. In every area of assessment, new research on new populations is helping personality theorists, applied psychologists, and researchers better understand human behavior and better predict the circumstances under which various behavioral patterns occur.

In the 1990s, a special effort is being made to link assessment to treatment; researchers argue that diagnosis and classification are not enough. A practitioner needs to judge what types of interventions and treatments follow from various diagnostic categories. Both researchers and applied psychologists continue to seek more direct information about behavioral patterns and maladjustment. Applied psychologists are helping school systems, state legislatures, businesses, and universities devise assessment methods to further their goal. This often means using a wide range of techniques including tests, observations, self-monitoring, interviewing, and self-study.

Professionals are often called in to assess the coping mechanisms and the overall effectiveness of office workers.

- ◆ Describe the process of assessment. p. 455
- ◆ Briefly describe the MMPI-2. p. 457
- ◆ What is the aim of a projective test? p. 458
- ◆ Identify and describe two techniques of behavioral assessment. p. 459

Focus on Learning

Key Terms

Personality p. 424
Psychic determinism p. 425
Unconscious motivation p. 425
Libido p. 426
Conscious p. 426
Preconscious p. 426
Unconscious p. 426
Id p. 426
Ego p. 426
Superego p. 427
Oral stage p. 427
Anal stage p. 428
Phallic stage p. 428

Oedipus complex p. 428
Latency stage p. 428
Genital stage p. 429
Fixation p. 429
Defense mechanism p. 430
Repression p. 430
Projection p. 430
Denial p. 430
Reaction formation p. 430
Sublimation p. 430
Rationalization p. 430
Neo-Freudian p. 433
Collective unconscious p. 434

Archetypes p. 434
Self-actualization p. 437
Fulfillment p. 437
Self p. 437
Ideal self p. 437
Trait p. 439
Types p. 439
Self-efficacy p. 450
Shyness p. 451
Assessment p. 455
Projective test p. 458
Self-monitoring p. 460

Summary

Psychoanalytic Theory

* Freud's conflict approach suggests that a person's basic tendency is to maximize instinctual gratification while minimizing punishment and guilt. p. 425

* Freud's structure of personality includes the id, ego, and superego. The id is the source of human instinctual energy. The ego tries to satisfy the id in accordance with reality. The superego acts as the moral branch of mental functioning. p. 426

* According to Freud, the source of life instincts is the libido, which works on the pleasure principle and seeks immediate gratification through the id. p. 426

* Freud described the development of personality in terms of five consecutive stages: oral, anal, phallic, latency, and genital. p. 427

* Defense mechanisms, such as repression, projection, rationalization, denial, and reaction formation, are ways in which people reduce anxiety by distorting reality. p. 430

Psychoanalytic Theory: Dissent and Revision

* According to neo-Freudians, there were serious omissions, errors, and obvious biases in Freudian theory. p. 433

* Jung emphasized unconscious processes as determiners of behavior and believed that each person houses past events in the unconscious. The collective unconscious is a collection of ideas and images inherited from our ancestors, including archetypes, emotionally charged ideas and images that have rich meaning and symbolism. pp. 433–434

* In Adler's theory, people's core tendency is to strive for superiority or perfection. Individuals develop a life-style that allows them to display their life goals. p. 434

Humanistic Approaches

* The humanistic approach of Rogers states that an inborn tendency directs people toward fulfilling their inherited potentials, a process called self-actualization. pp. 436–437

* For Rogers, personality is structured around the idea of self. An ideal self is the individual a person would like to be. p. 438

* According to Rogers, people become unhappy when they are unable to fit new behaviors into their current self-concepts. Persons with rigid self-concepts will evoke defense mechanisms to guard against potentially threatening feelings and experiences. pp. 438–439

Trait and Type Theories

* Personality is a set of relatively enduring behavioral characteristics that describe how a person reacts to the environment. p. 440

* Traits are any readily identifiable behaviors that characterize the way an individual differs from other people; types are broad collections of traits loosely tied together and interrelated. p. 441

Behavioral and Cognitive Approaches

* For behaviorists, the structural unit of personality is the response. All behaviors are seen as responses to stimuli or as responses waiting for reinforcement. p. 445

* Behavioral theories claim that personality development is a gradual process of growth in which certain behaviors are reinforced and others are not. Disturbed behavior is the result of faulty learning patterns. pp. 445–447

* Observational learning theory assumes that people can learn new behaviors by watching others. Unlike classical learning theory, observational learning theory states that (1) learning can occur independent of reinforcement, and (2) thought processes play a significant role in human behavior. p. 448

* The cognitive theories of Bandura, Mischel, and Rotter have reintroduced thought into the equation of personality and situational variables. They especially focus on how people interpret the situations in which they find themselves and then alter their behavior. pp. 450–452

Psychological Assessment

* Assessment is the process of evaluating individual differences among human beings using techniques of intelligence tests, interviews, observations in natural settings, and recording physiological measures. p. 455

* Behavioral assessment may include direct observation, self-evaluation, and interviews. pp. 455–458

Connections

Children   Adolescents   Adults

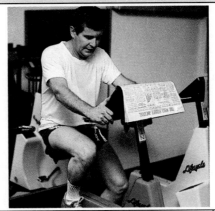

If you are interested in . . .	*Turn to . . .*	*To learn more about . . .*
Freud's psychoanalytic approach and the broad array of theories which developed from it	◆ Ch. 10, p. 350	Erik Erikson's stage theory of adult development.
	◆ Ch. 13, pp. 481–483	How psychologists who teach people to deal with stress realize that many times people use defense-oriented coping skills—some of which are Freudian in nature.
	◆ Ch. 15, pp. 538–543	How Freudian approaches to the treatment of abnormal behavior focus on helping people uncover hidden motivations and biological urges.
The relationship between personality and stress	◆ Ch. 11, pp. 394–398	People who are motivated to compete against others.
	◆ Ch. 13, p. 475	How people with Type A personalities may be at risk for adverse health consequences.
	◆ Ch. 15, p. 557	Stress management, which may involve talking to oneself and trying to maintain composure.
How personality and intelligence are evaluated by psychologists	◆ Ch. 8, p. 278	The way three important tests of intelligence and their various subscales were constructed and how they are administered.
	◆ Ch. 9, p. 316	How Piaget examined intellectual development in children and incorporated these measures into his theory of intellectual development.
	◆ Ch. 15, p. 543	How some therapies require that individuals be motivated and capable of abstract reasoning.

13 *Stress, Coping, and Health*

"Molted Fume" by Charles Arnoldi

———————————————— ◆ ————————————————

*M*ichael Murray is thirty-four years old and has just become a new father. His two-month-old daughter is a source of constant joy; he is amazed by her developing abilities. Yet sometimes he feels as if the walls are closing in. Although his marriage is strong, the strain of balancing two careers and day care, running the household, and coping with the demands of a new baby are beginning to take their toll. Michael is often tired and irritable. Lately, he has begun to depend on several gin and tonics to help him relax at night.

Carolyn Boal is proud of her success. In the five years since she graduated from college, she has worked her way up the corporate ladder to the position of senior marketing analyst, the youngest employee to hold such an important position. But there are never enough hours in the day, and she feels constantly rushed. Because of her demanding schedule, her social life is nonexistent, and she has begun to suffer from migraines during the day and insomnia at night.

Tony Munn returned from Vietnam in 1969 and has worked hard to put the war behind him. He is married, the father of two sons, and holds a good job as a computer programmer. Recently, though, he has begun waking up in the middle of the night drenched in a cold sweat. His dreams are terrifying re-creations of the horrors he witnessed in the war. He has become depressed, unable to concentrate at work, and increasingly withdrawn from his family.

As a student, you may face some special stresses in your life: studying for three final exams in one week, delivering a speech, juggling your studies with a part-time job to help your tight finances, and getting along with your roommate in a small apartment or dorm room. Stress, ranging from the minor hassle of being caught in a traffic jam to the major trauma of war, is a reality for all of us. We can deal with stress in either positive or negative ways. Positive coping can involve exercise, relaxation, and cognitive-coping strategies. Unfortunately, many people (like Michael, Carolyn, and Tony) don't cope effectively with stress. Some suffer from health problems, such as high blood pressure and insomnia. Others try to escape from stress by turning to alcohol and other drugs. This chapter examines the nature of stress, coping with stress, and the relationship of health and stress. It highlights the ways in which motivation, learning, and personality work together to influence people's ability to cope with stress in day-to-day life.

Stress

Eating antacid tablets like candy, launching into tirades at coworkers or friends, fist banging, and nightly cocktails are a way of life for many people who feel that the stress of their jobs, their families, or their financial burdens is too much. Carolyn Boal (introduced earlier) has a high-pressure job that affects her social life and causes daily migraines. A coworker under the same amount of stress may be managing it in more positive ways, without suffering negative health consequences. Herein lies an important difference: Stress can be evaluated and handled in different ways, depending on the person.

What Is Stress?

Stressor: An environmental stimulus that affects an organism in ways that are either physically or psychologically injurious, usually producing anxiety, tension, and physiological arousal.

Stress: A non-specific, often global response by an organism to real or imagined demands made on it; a person has to appraise a situation as stressful for it to be stressful.

Anxiety: A generalized feeling of fear and apprehension that may or may not be related to a particular event or object and is often accompanied by increased physiological arousal.

A **stressor** is an environmental stimulus that acts (or might act) on an organism in physically or psychologically injurious ways. Michael Murray and his wife face several stressors, including the demands of their new baby, day care, careers, and household responsibilities. Stressors *may* induce a response of **stress** in an organism, producing anxiety, tension, and psychological arousal. **Anxiety** is a generalized feeling of fear and apprehension that may or may not be related to a particular event or object and is often accompanied by increased physiological arousal. Whenever something negatively affects someone, physically or psychologically, the person may experience the effect as stress. The key is that not all people view a stimulus or a situation in the same way; *a person has to appraise a situation as stressful for it to be stressful.* This broad definition recognizes that everyone experiences stress at some time, but that stress is an interpreted state, a response on the part of a person.

Appraisal: A Key Component

A key component of stress is that a person has to appraise a situation as stressful for it to be stressful. What is stressful for me—for example, a track meet—may be of little consequence for you. What determines whether a particular event is stressful? When does a person see someone, something, or some time as dangerous or threatening? The answer lies in the extent to which people are familiar with an event, how predictable the event is, and how much they can control the event and themselves.

If you took the SAT or ACT more than once, you probably remember that your apprehension was much greater the first time than the second time—you were less stressed the second time. When people can predict events they feel that they are more in control and can have some impact on the future. This is a two-step process: first you decide if a situation is threatening to your well-being, then you decide if you can cope with it or handle it well.

Types and Sources of Stress

During rehearsal for a choral concert, forty-one grade-schoolers developed nausea, shortness of breath, and abdominal pains. At the choir performance that evening, twenty-nine of the children collapsed on stage. At another school, thirty-four sixth-grade students became dizzy and fainted during their graduation program. Both cases were diagnosed as stress-related disorders. Suffering from stress and trapped in situations that didn't allow them to escape, the children responded with symptoms of physical illness. There are three broad types of stress: *frustrations*, which result when people do not meet their goals; *conflicts*, which result when people must make difficult decisions; and *pressures*, which result from the need to achieve certain goals.

Frustration. When people do not meet a particular goal, they often feel frustrated. **Frustration** is an emotional state that is said to occur when any goal—work, family, or personal—is thwarted or blocked. When people feel that they cannot achieve a goal (often due to situations beyond their control) they may experience frustration and stress. When you are unable to obtain a summer job because of a lack of experience, it can cause feelings of stress; when a grandparent becomes ill, you may feel helpless, and this causes stress. People who seek to get ahead by hard work and education may feel frustrated when opportunities are blocked because of a lack of funds.

Some frustrations are externally caused and there is little a person can do to alleviate them. Your lack of experience for a specific job, your grandparent's illness, or your family's lack of money are external events over which you have little control. Other frustrations are caused by specific people; your boss may be unfair in his appraisal of you, your roommate may be too stingy to chip in for new furniture, or your instructor may be too lenient with people who goof off. You can sometimes alleviate the frustration of dealing with other people by taking some personal action; these actions, however, often place you in conflict and cause stress.

Conflict. When people must make difficult decisions, we say that they are in a state of **conflict** and that this conflict results in feelings of arousal and stress. Consider the difficult decision of those American draftees who did not want to fight in the Vietnam war but did not want to flee to Canada or face imprisonment. What happens if a person's goals and needs conflict— if someone must choose between two equally desirable desserts or two equally difficult academic courses? One of the first psychologists to describe and quantify such conflict situations was Neal Miller (1944, 1959). Miller developed hypotheses about how animals and human beings behave in situations that have both positive and negative aspects. In general, he described three types of situations that involve competing demands.

Frustration: The emotional state or condition resulting from a situation when any goal—work, family, or personal—is thwarted or blocked.

Conflict: The emotional state or condition in which a person has to make difficult decisions about two or more competing motives, behaviors, or impulses.

Neal Miller described conflict by identifying situations which evoke competing demands.

Approach-approach conflicts arise when a person must choose one of two equally pleasant alternatives, such as two wonderful jobs or two good movies. This conflict generates discomfort and a stress response, but people can usually tolerate it because either alternative is pleasant. **Avoidance-avoidance conflicts** occur when a choice involves two equally distasteful alternatives, such as mowing the lawn or painting the garage. **Approach-avoidance conflicts** occur when a particular situation has both appealing and repellant aspects. Studying for an exam, which can lead to good grades but is boring and difficult, is an approach-avoidance situation. All these conflict situations lead to stress.

Miller developed descriptions to predict behavior in conflict situations, particularly in approach-avoidance situations.

1. The closer a subject is to a goal, the stronger the tendency is to approach the goal.

2. When two incompatible responses are available, the stronger one will be expressed.

3. The strength of the tendency to approach or avoid is correlated with the strength of the motivating drive (thus a child who is both hungry and thirsty will seek food if he or she is more hungry than thirsty).

People face such conflict situations regularly. In such situations they may become anxious and upset. Moreover, if their conflicts affect their day-to-day behavior, they may exhibit symptoms of maladjustment.

Pressure: Work, Time, and Life Events. When people feel **pressure** or expectations from others for certain behaviors or results, arousal and stress may occur. Although individual situations differ, certain sources of stress are common to almost everyone; these *sources of stress* are most often associated with work, time, and life events.

Work that is either too burdensome or too light (and therefore understimulating) can cause stress. Work-related stress can also come from fear of retirement, being passed over for promotion, and organizational changes. In addition, the physical work setting may be overstimulating (too noisy or crowded) or understimulating and isolated. As we saw with Carolyn, work-related pressure—deadlines, competition, professional relationships—can cause a variety of physical problems. People suffering from work stress may experience migraines, ulcers, sleeplessness, hunger for sweets, overeating, and intestinal distress. Stress at work often leads to illness, resulting in lost efficiency and absenteeism.

Individuals with high-stress jobs, particularly when stress is constant, show the effects convincingly. Air traffic controllers and surgeons, for example, are responsible for the lives of other people every day and must be alert and organized at all times. If they work too many hours without relief, they may make a fatal mistake. Other high-stress jobs include inner-city high school teachers, customer service agents, waiters and waitresses, and emergency workers, to name just a few.

Lack of time is another common source of stress. Everyone faces deadlines: Students must complete tests before class ends, auto workers must keep pace with the assembly line, and tax returns must by filed by April 15th. A sense of urgency and competitiveness drives some people to speed up their pace continually.

People have only a limited number of hours each day in which to accomplish tasks; therefore, most people carefully allocate their time to re-

Approach-approach conflict: The result of having to choose between two equally attractive alternatives or goals.

Avoidance-avoidance conflict: The result of having to choose between two equally distasteful alternatives or goals.

Approach-avoidance conflict: The result of having to choose a goal that has both attractive and repellent aspects.

Pressure: The emotional state or condition resulting from expectations for success, or specific behaviors or results; the feelings that result from coercion.

Certain jobs, such as this air traffic controller's involve stress levels that not every personality could successfully manage.

duce time pressure. They may establish routines, make lists, set schedules, leave places early, and set aside leisure time in which to rid themselves of stressful feelings. If they do not handle time pressures successfully, they may begin to feel overloaded and stressed.

A third common stress source involves the stages of life, which may be both positive and stressful at the same time. Consider marriage. Marriage gives people a partner, a companion, a lover, a friend, and a person with whom to share future aspirations. But at times one partner may not be fulfilling marital or role obligations or may be causing his or her spouse to feel left out. Both situations bring about stress. We discuss such stressful life events in more detail on page 473.

Responding to Stress

People react to stress in a wide variety of ways. Some experience modest increases in physiological arousal, while others, like Carolyn Boal, may exhibit significant physical symptoms. In extreme cases, people become so aroused, anxious and disorganized that their behavior becomes maladaptive or maladjusted.

Emotion, Physiology, and Behavior. When psychologists study stress, they typically break down a person's reaction to it into emotional, physiological, and behavioral components. *Emotionally,* people's reactions often depend on their frustration, their work-related pressures, and their day-to-day conflicts. When frustrated, people become angry and annoyed; when pressured, they become aroused and anxious; when placed in situations of conflict, they may vacillate or become irritable and sometimes hostile.

Physiologically, the stress response is characterized by arousal. When psychologists refer to arousal, they usually mean changes in the autonomic nervous system, including increased heart rate, breathing, and blood pressure; sweating of the palms; and dilation of the pupils. Arousal is often the first change that occurs when a person feels stressed.

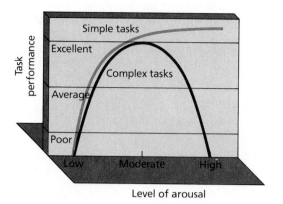

FIGURE 13.1
When arousal is low, task performance is poor or non-existent. Performance is usually best at moderate levels of arousal; at high levels of arousal, on complex tasks, performance usually deteriorates.

Behaviorally, stress and its response of arousal are related. As we saw in chapter 11, psychologist Donald Hebb (1972) argued that effective behavior depends on a person's state of arousal. When people are moderately aroused, they behave with optimal effectiveness; when underaroused, they lack stimulation to behave effectively. Overarousal tends to produce disorganized behavior in which people become ineffective (see Figure 13.1).

A moderate amount of stress is necessary and desirable. Stress and its accompanying arousal is what keeps us active and involved. It impels students to study, drives athletes to excel during competition, and helps business people to strive toward greater heights. In short, stress and arousal can help people achieve their potentials. See Figure 13.2 for an overview of the responses to stressors that occur after an appraisal.

Burnout. A stress reaction especially common to people with high standards is **burnout,** a state of emotional and physical exhaustion, lowered productivity, and feelings of isolation, often due to work-related pressures (Kalimo and Mejman, 1987). People like Carolyn, who daily face high stress levels, often feel enervated, hopeless, emotionally drained, and may eventually stop trying. Although work-related problems and stress are most often the cause of burnout, family, financial, and social pressures can create the same feelings. Burnout victims develop negative self-concepts because they are unable to maintain the high standards they have set for themselves. People with

FIGURE 13.2
After a threat is evaluated, its impact can be seen emotionally, physiologically, and behaviorally.

Burnout: A state of emotional and physical exhaustion, lowered productivity, and feelings of isolation, often due to work-related pressure.

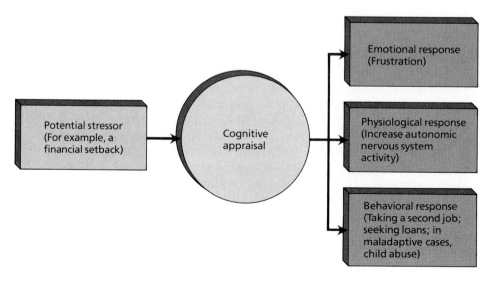

Adults are not the only people subject to stress. Having to perform competitively for his peers and parents may be quite stressful for this young boy.

burnout often cease to be concerned about others and have physical as well as social problems.

Health Consequences. Stress does not cause disease, but it contributes to many diseases, including the six major causes of death in the United States: heart disease, cancer, lung ailments, accidental injuries, cirrhosis of the liver, and suicide. In general, stress affects the immune system, making people more vulnerable to disease (Levy, 1988). It may lead to headaches, backaches, decreased productivity, and family arguments; stress-related illnesses can cause an increase in medical costs for both individuals and employers.

Stress afflicts children as well as adults. Children are usually unable to change or control the circumstances in which they find themselves (Band and Weisz, 1988). A child may experience stress in school, stress owing to abuse by a parent, stress from divorce, or stress from peer pressure. Children, like adults, often show their stress response in physical symptoms.

Studying Stress: Focus on Physiology

Psychologists want to know how today's increasingly harried life-styles affect individual physical and psychological well-being. Does intense competition make business people like Carolyn more susceptible to heart attacks? How can psychologists help people like Michael cope with life stresses, such as having a baby? How can therapists help veterans like Tony who are traumatized by war or other disasters?

Selye's General Adaptation Syndrome. In the 1930s, Hans Selye (1907–1982) began a systematic study of stressors and stress. He investigated the physiological changes in people who were experiencing various amounts of stress. Selye conceptualized people's responses to stress in terms of a *general adaptation syndrome* (1956, 1976). (A *syndrome* is a set of responses. In the case of stress, it is a set of behaviorally defined physical symptoms.) Selye's work initiated thousands of studies on stress and stress reactions, and Selye himself published more than 1600 articles on the topic.

Hans Selye undertook a systematic study of stressors and stress and theorized a *general adaptation syndrome.*

According to Selye, people's response to a stressor can be divided into three stages: an initial short-term stage of alarm, a longer period of resistance, and a final stage of exhaustion. During the initial *alarm stage,* people experience increased physiological arousal. They become excited, anxious, or frightened. Their metabolism speeds up dramatically, and blood is diverted from the skin to the brain, resulting in a pale appearance (the result is much like the fight-or-flight syndrome when the sympathetic nervous system is activated, discussed in detail in chapter 2). People also may experience loss of appetite, sleeplessness, headaches, ulcers, or hormone imbalances; their normal level of resistance to stress decreases. Carolyn's behavior—her headaches and loss of sleep—suggest that she is undergoing the alarm stage of stress.

Since people cannot stay highly aroused for long periods of time, the initial alarm response usually gives way to *resistance.* During this stage, physiological and behavioral responses become more moderate and sustained. People in the resistance stage often are irritable, impatient, and angry, and may experience chronic fatigue. This stage can persist for a few hours, several days, or even years. Couples who suffer traumatic divorces sometimes exhibit anger and emotional fatigue years after the conflict has been resolved in court.

The final stage of Selye's three-part syndrome is *exhaustion.* Stress saps psychological energy; if people don't relieve their stress, they can become too exhausted to adapt. At that point, they again become extremely alarmed, and they finally give up. Maladjustment, withdrawal, or, in extreme cases, death may follow. Tony, the Vietnam veteran, is showing symptoms of exhaustion. Extreme variability exists, however. Not everyone shows the same behaviors in each of Selye's stages. See Figure 13.3 for a graphic view of Selye's three-part syndrome.

Selye inspired others to attempt to identify stressors and refine his theory; one such attempt attributes more specificity to stress than did Selye (Smith, 1989). Another product of continued research is Holmes and Rahe's (1967) Social Readjustment Rating Scale, shown in Table 13.1. This 1960s scale recognized that there are both positive and negative stressful experiences in life. It has been widely used, hotly debated, revised, and has become

FIGURE 13.3
The general adaptation syndrome, according to Selye. During the first phase, the body mobilizes its resources. In the second phase, resistance levels off and eventually begins to decline. In the third phase, resistance is depleted, leading to exhaustion.

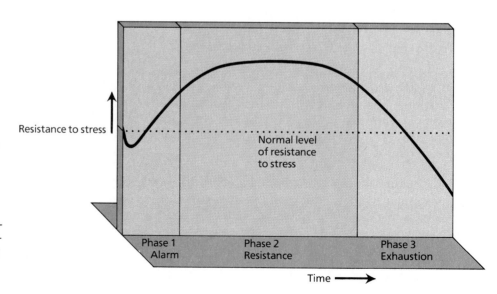

TABLE 13.1
The Social Readjustment Rating Scale

Rank	Life Event	Value	Rank	Life Event	Value
1	Death of spouse	100	23	Son or daughter leaving home	29
2	Divorce	73	24	Trouble with in-laws	29
3	Marital separation	65	25	Outstanding personal achievement	28
4	Jail term	63	26	Wife begins or stops work	26
5	Death of close family member	63	27	Begin or end school	26
6	Personal injury or illness	53	28	Change in living conditions	25
7	Marriage	50	29	Revision of personal habits	24
8	Fired at work	47	30	Trouble with boss	23
9	Marital reconciliation	45	31	Change in work hours or conditions	20
10	Retirement	45	32	Change in residence	20
11	Change in health of family member	44	33	Change in schools	20
12	Pregnancy	40	34	Change in recreation	19
13	Sex difficulties	39	35	Change in church activities	19
14	Gain of new family member	39	36	Change in social activities	18
15	Business readjustment	39	37	Mortgage or loan less than $10,000	17
16	Change in financial state	38	38	Change in sleeping habits	16
17	Death of close friend	37	39	Change in number of family get-togethers	15
18	Change to different line of work	36			
19	Change in number of arguments with spouse	35	40	Change in eating habits	15
			41	Vacation	13
20	Mortgage over $10,000	31	42	Christmas	12
21	Foreclosure of mortgage or loan	30	43	Minor violations of the law	11
22	Change in responsibilities at work	29			

a source of new and important research. Rahe (1989) now uses a list with more than seventy-one life events.

Holmes-Rahe Scale. Holmes and Rahe's basic assumption is that stressful life events to which people must adapt, especially in combination, will damage health. *Stressful life events* are prominent changes in a person's day-to-day circumstances that necessitate change. To test their assumption, the researchers devised a scale on which individuals circle significant life events that they've recently experienced. Each event is rated for its influence on a person. Events such as the death of a spouse, divorce, and illness are rated as high stressors, while events such as changes in eating habits, vacations, and holidays are rated lower. A person's total score is an index of his or her stress level and the likelihood of illness in the next two years. According to Holmes and Rahe, a person who scores above three hundred points will likely suffer stress-induced physical illness.

Although widely used, the Holmes-Rahe scale has been sharply criticized on a number of dimensions. First, for many people who score high on the scale, a direct relationship between health and life events has not been found (Krantz, Grunberg, and Baum, 1985). People have support systems, friends, and activities that influence how, when, and under what conditions stress

Stress is an unavoidable part of our lives. The loss of a home through fire or the assumption of the responsibilities accompanying marriage are both high stress situations.

will affect them. Some psychologists therefore question the validity of the Holmes-Rahe scale in predicting illness (Theorell et al., 1986).

Another criticism stems from the fact that the scale was based on a study of young male navy personnel, whose characteristics do not necessarily match those of the general population, especially older people (Dohrenwend and Shrout, 1985) and young women. In addition, the Holmes-Rahe scale includes only major life events. The stressors faced by most people are seldom crises; they are the day-to-day hassles and irritations that add up over the years (Kanner et al., 1981). Table 13.2 presents the ten most frequent hassles people worry about. The results of a study of the effect of major life events and daily hassles on reported health of elderly subjects showed that hassles are more closely related to psychological and physical health than are major life events (Weinberger, Hiner and Tierney, 1987). In another

TABLE 13.2

Ten Most Frequent Hassles
1. Concerns about weight
2. Health of a family member
3. Rising prices of common goods
4. Home maintenance
5. Too many things to do
6. Misplacing or losing things
7. Yard work or outside home maintenance
8. Property, investment, or taxes
9. Crime
10. Physical appearance

Source: Kanner et al., 1981

study, researchers (DeLongis, Folkman, and Lazarus, 1988) found that flu, headaches, sore throats, and backaches also were significantly related to daily hassles and stress.

Health Psychology, Heart Disease, and Stress

Heart disease and high blood pressure account for more than half the deaths each year in the United States. Among U.S. blacks, high blood pressure is the number one health problem (Anderson, 1989). Physicians and psychologists view this silent killer as a disorder of life-style and quality of life (Kaplan, 1988). Three components of day-to-day life that are particularly important in heart disease are: work-site stress, Type A personality factors, and physiological reactivity.

Work-Site Stress. The likelihood that you will have a heart attack increases significantly if you are an air traffic controller or a surgeon. This occurs because some work is loaded with potential stressors; jobs can demand too little or too much of a worker. Stress is also affected by autonomy, the extent to which a person controls the speed, flow, and level of work. A position with high demands and low controls increases stress. A factory worker, for example, has no control over his work and may experience stress.

Gender differences in heart disease prevalence are apparent, although until the last decade or so, women were more likely to be in jobs (often secretarial) with high demands, low controls, and low pay—key ingredients for stress and stress-related illness (Baruch, Biener, and Barnett, 1987). Placed in similar life situations, however, men and women seem to respond similarly (Hamilton and Fagot, 1988).

Type A Behavior. In the late 1950s, two physicians (Friedman and Rosenman, 1974) identified a pattern of behavior that they believe contributes to heart disease—Type A behavior. **Type A behavior** occurs in individuals who are competitive, impatient, hostile, and always striving to do more in less time. (Alternatively, **Type B behavior** people are calmer, more patient, less hurried.) Do you see yourself as Type A or Type B? Do you know anyone who is Type A?

Early studies of Type A behavior showed a positive association with heart disease; that is, Type A individuals were more likely to have heart attacks. But more recent research suggests that no relationship exists (Matthews, 1988). Some elements of Type A behavior seem related to heart disease or angina (Byrne and Reinhart, 1989), but not the overall Type A behavior pattern. For example, hostility and anger have been related to heart disease (Krantz et al., 1988) as have suspiciousness and mistrust (Weidner et al., 1989).

Has all the Type A research been discredited? No. People who are extremely anxious, depressed, angry, and unhappy have a higher rate of heart disease than normally adjusted people. Type A behavior patterns exist, but a direct relationship to heart disease is minimal or nonexistent. Rather, components of the Type A personality may predict heart disease (Matthews, 1988; Friedman and Booth-Kewley, 1988), and practitioners have been successful at modifying Type A behavior (Friedman et al., 1986).

Physiological Reactions. A possible third factor relating stress to heart disease is how our bodies react to stress. This is called *reactivity*, or physiological reactivity. A situation interpreted as stressful may cause our bodies

Type A behavior: Behavior characterized by competitiveness, impatience, hostility, and striving to do more in less time.

Type B behavior: Behavior that is calmer, more patient, and less hurried than that of Type A individuals.

to react physiologically triggering processes that lead to heart disease. Research shows that Type A behavior patterns are associated with increased physiological reactivity (Contrada, 1989), long-lasting emotional stress (Suls and Wan, 1989), and feelings of anger and hostility (Suarez and Williams, 1989). It is still not clear whether people predisposed to heart disease show reactivity, or whether reactivity predisposes them to heart disease.

Although work-site stress, Type A behavior patterns, and physiological reactivity each may be individually linked to coronary disease, the research suggests that they are interactive (Krantz et al., 1988). From a psychologist's viewpoint, there are important implications. First, much more research is needed to sort out the factors. Second, behavioral factors contribute, although we are not sure how much, to heart disease. Third, and most important, psychologists can suggest interventions that will deter or lessen conditions (typically stress) and significantly alter the likelihood of heart disease. Still another variable, controlling cigarette smoking, is being addressed by psychologists with a number of methods (Burling et al., 1989) but with only moderate success because quitting smoking is so difficult for most people (Epstein and Perkins, 1988). The challenges exist, the research continues, and we all await preventive measures that will help combat heart disease, stress and other disorders, including post-traumatic stress.

Post-Traumatic Stress Disorder

In 1989, a group of army veterans returned with several therapists to Vietnam where they had waged war more than two decades earlier. This time, however, their mission was not to fight an enemy but to heal their own psychological wounds. One veteran reported that he had been haunted for years by nightmares of his combat experiences. This severe stress-related disorder is termed **post-traumatic stress disorder,** a category of mental disorder evident after a person has undergone some type of disaster.

Victims of rape, natural disasters (tornadoes, earthquakes, hurricanes, floods), and disasters caused by human beings (wars, train wrecks, toxic chemical spills) often suffer from this disorder. Many survivors of the 1989 San Francisco earthquake still fear the double-decker freeways of California, which took a heavy toll in the quake; post-traumatic stress disorder is still evident after the 1980 volcanic eruption of Mt. St. Helens (Shore, Vollmer, and Tatum, 1989).

Common symptoms of post-traumatic stress disorder include vivid, intrusive recollections or reexperiences of the traumatic event and occasional lapses of normal consciousness. People may develop anxiety, depression, or exceptionally aggressive behavior; they may avoid situations that resemble the traumatizing event. Such behaviors eventually interfere with daily functioning, family interactions, and health. Research on post-traumatic stress disorder is scanty, with only a few studies focusing on natural disasters such as tornadoes (e.g., Madakasira and O'Brien, 1987) or floods (Solomon et al., 1987); there have been many more studies on Vietnam veterans (e.g., Pitman et al., 1990).

Post-traumatic stress disorder: A category of mental disorders evident after a person has undergone the stress of some type of disaster; common symptoms include vivid, intrusive recollections or reexperiences of the traumatic event and occasional lapses of normal consciousness.

The Vietnam Veteran. Vietnam veterans like Tony (introduced at the beginning of this chapter) are particularly vulnerable to post-traumatic stress disorder. Thousands of the 600,000 Americans who served in that war still suffer feelings of alienation, sleeping problems, reliving of painful experiences, and difficulty concentrating. Most veterans do not suffer from the

Surviving a disastrous experience such as Hurricane Hugo is only the first step in dealing with it. Victims of post-traumatic stress relive the incident countless times, often to their own detriment.

disorder; of those who do, many did not experience symptoms until months or even years after their return home. Those who suffer from the disorder seem more likely to have other stressful events in their lives, which in turn make the disorder worse—a vicious cycle (Solomon et al., 1988).

The Vietnam war created unique psychological problems (Kaylor, King, and King, 1987). Survival—not patriotism—was the primary concern of many military personnel who served. Some servicemen turned to drugs and alcohol to alleviate fear. Moreover, combatants knew that many people in the United States vehemently opposed the conflict. Finally, many veterans were whisked home without ceremony or a chance to reacclimate gradually (Walker and Cavenar, 1982).

For a number of complicated psychological, political, and social reasons, mental health practitioners have tended to be unresponsive to individuals suffering from post-traumatic stress disorder. Too often, clients have been held responsible for how they react to stress. Now that psychologists recognize the disorder, special help in the form of workshops and therapy is becoming available, and drug therapies are being assessed (Lerer et al., 1987). Clients who feel disoriented and disheartened now have options; they need not consider their lives a waste or their situations hopeless.

Psychology and Sociology: Suicide

[handwritten: suicide is most common among elderly]

Fortunately, most people who think about suicide do not actually commit the act; but even the process of contemplating problems can take a heavy toll. When people are depressed during such contemplation, the likelihood that they will actually commit suicide increases. Suicide is traditionally studied in the context of sociology, the study of the structure, function, and organization of society. But suicide is as much a psychological as a sociological phenomenon. Today researchers examine suicide from the point of view of sociology and psychology—in this case the disciplines meld.

Almost everyone who com-
mits suicide shows signs of
depression prior to the
attempt.

According to sociologists, each day about eighty people in the United States commit suicide—that's thirty thousand people each year. These individuals are often lonely, guilty, and depressed. They feel that things cannot and will not get better, and that suicide is their best option. A distinction must be drawn between attempters and completers. *Attempters* try to commit suicide but are unsuccessful; they tend to be young, more often women, impulsive, and more likely to make non-fatal attempts, such as wrist slashing. *Completers* take their lives successfully; they tend to be male and older, and they use lethal techniques of self-destruction, for example, handguns.

Suicide rates in the United States are alarming. More than three times as many men as women actually commit suicide, although four times as many women attempt it (U.S. Department of Health and Human Services, 1986). Among adolescents, suicide is the second leading cause of death (after accidents); one out of every one thousand adolescents attempts suicide each year, and nearly five thousand young people between the ages of fifteen and twenty-four are successful (Stivers, 1988; Allen, 1987). The elderly, divorced, and former patients with psychological disorders have a higher likelihood of attempting and committing suicide. In fact, the elderly make up twenty-three percent of those who commit suicide (U.S. Department of Health and Human Services, 1986). People who have been suffering from major depression are more likely to attempt suicide while they are recovering, when their energy level is higher. At the depths of depression, a person is too weak, divided, and lacking in energy. Although only fifteen percent of depressed people are suicidal, most suicide-prone individuals are depressed.

Are there warning signs of suicide? Psychologists point to several indicators: changes in personal appearance, dramatic drop in schoolwork, changes in drug abuse patterns, decreased appetite, giving away prized possessions, and most important, a depressed attitude. Nearly everyone who is suicidal exhibits depression; such individuals show changes in sleeping patterns, diminished ability to concentrate, fatigue, and feelings of worthlessness. In addition, eighty-six percent of those who are successful have attempted suicide before.

psychological=within
sociological=outside

Causes. The causes of suicide are as complex as the people who commit suicide and may lie both within the individual (psychological) and outside the individual in society (sociological). For some individuals, societal pressures serve as a catalyst, leading them to take their own lives. For others, ill parents, substance abuse which impairs judgment, or traumatic events are the catalysts. For still other people, a long-standing series of psychological disorders may predispose them to suicide. See Table 13.3 for some facts and fables about suicide.

Psychologists cite a broad array of factors that may influence a suicide attempt. *Biological psychologists* assert that certain neurotransmitters have been linked to disorders that predispose an individual to suicide. *Behavioral psychologists* suggest that past experiences with suicide (by observing the effects of suicides on other people) make the behavior reinforcing. Other people who have taken their lives may serve as models for the behavior (Davidson et al., 1989)—this idea is controversial because it is not always the case (Phillips and Paight, 1987; Kessler et al., 1989).

Psychodynamically-oriented psychologists suggest that a person is turning hostility and anger inward. Freud might argue that the act of suicide is the ultimate release of the aggressive instinct. *Cognitive psychologists* assert that suicide is the failure of a person's problem-solving abilities in response to stress, or alternatively, that a person's cognitive assessment is that his or

TABLE 13.3
Facts and Fables about Suicide

Numerous false beliefs persist about suicide. The following list is compiled from numerous sources, but especially from the continuing work of the two most noted names in suicide research, Edwin Shneidman and Norman Farberow.

Fable	Fact
1. Suicide happens without warning.	1. Suicidal individuals give many clues; eighty percent have to some degree discussed with others their intent to commit suicide.
2. Once people become suicidal, they remain so.	2. Suicidal persons remain so for limited periods; thus the value of restraint.
3. Suicide occurs almost exclusively among affluent or very poor individuals.	3. Suicide tends to occur proportionately in all economic levels of society.
4. Virtually all suicidal individuals are mentally ill.	4. As already noted, this is not so.
5. Suicidal tendencies are inherited or run in families.	5. There is no evidence for a direct genetic factor.
6. Suicide does not occur in primitive cultures.	6. Suicide occurs in almost all societies and cultures.
7. Ritual suicide is common in Japan.	7. Ritual suicide is rare in modern Japan; the most common method is barbiturate overdose.
8. Writers and artists have the highest suicide rates because they are "a bit crazy to begin with."	8. Physicians and police officers have the highest suicide rates; they have access to the most lethal means, and their work involves a high level of frustration.
9. Once a person starts to come out of a depression, the risk of suicide dissipates.	9. The risk of suicide is highest in the initial phase of an upswing from the depth of depression.
10. People who attempt suicide fully intend to die.	10. People who attempt suicide have a diversity of motives.

Source: Meyer and Salmon, 1988.

her future is hopeless. *Humanists* see suicide as a waste of a human being's potential, and they attempt to help suicidal and depressed patients focus on the meaning in their lives so that they might fulfill rather than destroy themselves. Many theorists, regardless of orientation, focus on a person's attempt to escape from aversive self-awareness (Baumeister, 1990).

Sociologists tend to focus on society's role in suicide and its prevention. In particular, adolescent suicide has received a great deal of attention. Adolescents who attempt suicide often see a wide discrepancy between their high personal ambitions and meager results. The causes of adolescent suicide are still not fully understood, but the increasing pressures and stress faced by adolescents today certainly contribute to the rising number of suicides. Adolescents face an extremely competitive workforce, a social situation teeming with violence, crime, and drugs, and alternating pressures to conform and to be an individual. Often, angry and frustrated adolescents exhibit other self-destructive behaviors (Stivers, 1988) in addition to feeling hopeless (Kashani, Reid, and Rosenberg, 1989).

Prevention. Most individuals who attempt suicide want to live, but their stress and sense of helplessness about the future tell them that death is the only way out—this is even more true of adults than of adolescents (Cole, 1989). Some are helped by crisis intervention and hot lines (a crisis worker helps a person avoid taking his or her life). Sociologists and psychologists often focus their research efforts on high-risk groups—people suffering from depression or substance abuse. Those who were recently seriously depressed, those who have had a traumatic loss, or those who have been forced into retirement or are suffering ill health are all at greater risk.

When a person makes a suicide threat, take it seriously. Since most people who commit suicide leave clues to their intentions ahead of time, people need to be aware. Statements such as "I don't want to go on" or "I'm a burden to everyone, so maybe I should end it all" should be taken as signs. When people begin to give things away or write letters that have ominous tones to relatives and friends, these too are signs.

If you know someone you think may be contemplating suicide, here are some steps that Curran (1987) suggests you take:

- Talk. Don't be afraid to talk with your friend or relative about suicide; it will not influence him or her to commit suicide.

- Talk with a person who is at risk about stressors; the more an individual talks, the better.

- Help a person who is contemplating suicide seek a psychologist, counselor, or parent. A person thinking of suicide needs counseling.

- Tell your friend's spouse, parent, guardian, or counselor. Unless you are certain that they know, you should tell someone responsible for your friend's welfare.

- Do not keep a contemplated suicide a secret. Resist your friend's attempt to keep you quiet about his or her confidences. Despite a friend's wishes for secrecy, be responsible and tell the friend's relatives or guardian.

Focus on Learning

- Distinguish between *stress* and a *stressor*. p. 466
- Describe Selye's three-part response to stress. p. 471
- Identify the key components of post-traumatic stress disorder. p. 476
- Identify three warning signs for suicide. pp. 477–479

Coping

Most people need a way to cope with anxiety and the physical ailments produced by stress. Some people seek medical and psychological help; others turn to alcohol and drugs. From your own experience, do you know some coping techniques that are more effective than others?

What Is Coping?

In general, coping means dealing with a situation. But for a psychologist, **coping** is the process by which a person takes some action to manage environmental and internal demands that cause, or might cause, stress and will tax the individual's inner resources. This definition of coping involves five important components. First, coping is constantly changing and being evaluated, and is therefore a *process* or *strategy*. Second, coping involves *managing* situations, not necessarily bringing them under complete control. Third, coping is *effortful*; it does not happen automatically. Fourth, coping aims to manage *behavioral as well as cognitive events*. And finally, coping is a *learned* process.

Many types of coping strategies exist; a person may use one, two, or many of them. Coping begins at the biological level. People's bodies respond to stress with specific reactions, including changes in hormone levels, autonomic nervous system activity, and the amount of neurotransmitters in the brain. Effective coping strategies occur at the psychological level when people learn new ways of dealing with their vulnerabilities.

Vulnerability, Coping Skills, and Social Support

A crucial factor that determines how well people cope with their problems is vulnerability. **Vulnerability** is the extent to which people are easily impaired by an event and thus respond maladaptively. Whether or not a person is vulnerable depends on his or her coping skills. **Coping skills** are the techniques people use to deal with stress and changing situations. People with good coping skills to guide them are prepared to deal with stress-related situations and are thus less vulnerable. On the other hand, people with poor coping skills may be extremely vulnerable and not able to deal well with stress at all. In some cases, they even develop a sense of *learned helplessness*, which results from learning that rewards and punishments are not contingent on behavior. Faced with poor coping skills and a loss of control, some people stop responding. (We will discuss learned helplessness further in chapters 14 and 16).

A person's vulnerability is affected by the extent to which he or she has social support. **Social support** is the availability of comfort, recognition, approval, and encouragement. When people feel supported by others with emotional concern, displays of caring, a phone call, or a note, they can cope with extraordinary pressure better—especially when the support is offered by someone who is considered important to the vulnerable person (Dakof and Taylor, 1990). Group therapy (chapter 15) can be especially effective in alleviating anxiety for this reason; in group therapy, other people in similar situations can offer emotional concern and support. According to psychologist Richard Lazarus (1982), people faced with constant stress, whether supported or not, use either defense- or task-oriented coping strategies, considered next.

Coping: The process by which a person manages environmental and internal demands that do, or even might, cause stress.

Vulnerability: The extent to which people are easily impaired by an event, and thus respond maladaptively to external or internal demands placed on them.

Coping skills: The techniques people use to deal with stress and changing situations.

Social support: Providing a person with comfort, recognition, approval, and encouragement.

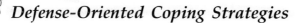

Defense-Oriented Coping Strategies

Defense-oriented coping strategies do not reduce stress, but instead help people protect themselves from its effects. These strategies ease distress, thereby enabling people to tolerate and deal with disturbances. As we saw in chapter 12, Freud and other personality theorists described defense mechanisms by which people distort reality in order to defend themselves against life's pressures. One such mechanism is *rationalization*, whereby people reinterpret reality to make it more palatable. If your boyfriend or girlfriend dumps you, you might cope by telling your friends that you "never really liked him (or her) anyway!" Similarly, a person who is turned down for a job may rationalize that he didn't want to work for the company after all. Another defense mechanism is *reaction formation*. A man who raves about his new job but is feeling stress and fear has developed a reaction formation. He is expressing a feeling that is opposite his true one.

Task-Oriented Coping Strategies

Stress management is becoming increasingly important to highly stressed individuals. Counselors commonly treat stress by identifying the source and then by helping the client modify his or her behavior. Through therapy, a person troubled by stressful situations can learn to cope by untangling personal feelings, understanding the sources of the stress, and then modifying his or her behavior to alleviate it.

Students about to enter college, for example, often show signs of stress. They're worried about academic pressures, social life, and adjustment. At some schools, incoming college students can receive counseling to learn how to deal with their stress. Similarly, stress-management seminars, where psychologists help business executives deal with stress in the corporate world, are becoming increasingly popular. The aim of both programs is the same:

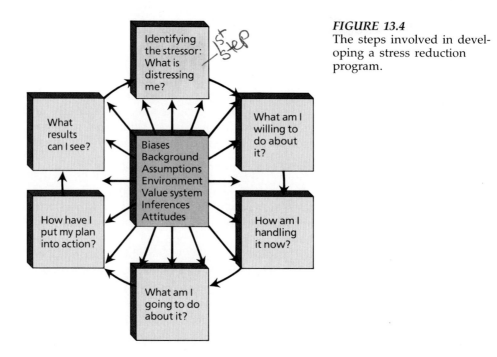

FIGURE 13.4
The steps involved in developing a stress reduction program.

to modify a person's response to stress and replace maladaptive responses with more useful ones.

Most psychologists, especially behavioral psychologists, recommend *task-oriented coping strategies* that often involve stress management. The general strategy usually involves four steps (see Figure 13.4): (1) identifying the source of stress; (2) choosing an appropriate course of action for stress reduction; (3) implementing the plan; and (4) evaluating its success.

Identifying the Source. Since stress-producing situations exist in many areas, identifying the source of stress is often difficult. Someone like Carolyn, for example, may be experiencing problems with her work load, her finances, her social life, and her roommate. She must decide what is causing her the most stress and whether her problems with her social life, for example, are in some way tied to her work situation. It's interesting to note that even with their increased experience, older people seem to have as much difficulty as younger people in identifying and controlling the sources of stress (Lazarus and DeLongis, 1983). *attitude plays role here.*

Adaptive behaviors, such as working out on a regular basis, are preventive measures that protect an individual's overall health. Many companies are recognizing this and provide exercise facilities to their personnel.

Choosing the Action. Once the source of stress is found, people need to choose among several coping strategies. For example, they can withdraw from a competitive, stress-inducing situation by quitting work, leaving a spouse, or declaring bankruptcy. More often, they turn to other people or other methods of coping.

Because stress is usually accompanied by arousal and excitement, people may cope by using *relaxation techniques.* They can learn therapeutic relaxation methods, including biofeedback, hypnosis, or meditation, to refocus their energies (to be discussed shortly). Exercise, such as aerobics, jogging, and racquetball, is another effective way to relax and relieve stress (Dyer and Crouch, 1988).

Many people manage stress and anxiety with *cognitive coping strategies,* whereby they prepare for pressure through gradual exposure to increasingly higher stress levels (Janis, 1982a). Chapter 11 discussed a study in which subjects viewed a film with painful scenes but were able to control their emotional responses (Lazarus and Alfert, 1964). This study suggests that people can learn to manage their stress, to some extent, by using their thought processes. A major goal of current research is to prepare people to react in constructive ways to early warning signs of stress.

Research shows that talking to themselves helps some people cope (Turk, 1978). The self-talk procedure, which is used widely, is effective in helping confront stressors and cope with pain and feelings of being overwhelmed (Turk, Meichenbaum, and Genest, 1983). By talking to themselves, people gain control over their emotions, arousal, and stress reactions; this is especially useful in helping people before noxious or painful medical procedures such as chemotherapy or root canal (Ludwick-Rosenthal and Neufeld, 1988).

Implementing the Plan. Helping people prepare for stressful situations by providing them with new ideas is called stress inoculation. Sometimes **stress inoculation** involves a single technique like breathing deeply and regularly. At other times it is more elaborate, involving graded exposure to various levels of threats or providing detailed information about a forthcoming procedure (Janis, 1985). Janis likens stress inoculation to an antibiotic dose given

Stress inoculation: The procedure of giving people realistic warnings, recommendations, and reassurances to help them prepare for and cope with impending dangers or losses.

to ward off disease. It helps people to defend themselves and to cope with an event when it occurs. Stress inoculation

1. increases the predictability of stressful events,
2. fosters coping skills,
3. generates self-talking,
4. encourages confidence about successful outcomes, and
5. builds a commitment to personal action and responsibility for an adaptive course of action.

It gives people realistic warnings, recommendations, and reassurances to help them prepare and cope with impending dangers or losses.

To cope well both at home and at work, people should be task-oriented, self-monitoring, realistic, open to supportive relationships, and patient (Sarason and Sarason, 1987). They also need to eat sensibly, get enough sleep, stand up to the boss from time to time, find a hobby, take refuge in family, and sometimes, when things get too extreme, quit. Most important, people have to believe in themselves and their ability to cope well with stressors (Bandura et al., 1988).

Evaluating the Success. A well-designed coping plan involves evaluating the plan's success. Have the techniques been effective? Is there still more to do? Are new or further actions needed? All these questions need to be evaluated.

Coping and a Positive Attitude

APPLYING PSYCHOLOGY

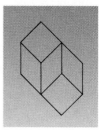

*A*pplied psychologists claim that simply maintaining a positive attitude can have beneficial effects on coping with stress and reducing physical symptoms (Scheier and Carver, 1985). People who feel that they have control over their lives, health, and well-being are more relaxed than those who do not (Rodin, 1986). An upbeat mood, a positive sense of personal control, and even a self-serving bias can facilitate worthwhile behaviors, such as helping others and evaluating people more favorably. Some researchers suggest that people who have positive attitudes may even live longer.

Sometimes reframing or rethinking a situation is a rationalization to make it less anxiety-producing, as shown in chapter 12. One study showed that people engaged in such small self-deceptions, however, may be healthier than people who focus on their anxiety. In a study of people from 1946 through 1988, Peterson, Seligman, and Valliant (1988) reported that those who made excuses for negative events in 1946 had better health in 1988. Such results indicate that people who emphasize the downside of life's events may develop learned helplessness. They may then choose inaction because they believe themselves to be powerless in controlling events. Taking a positive approach and believing in your own abilities helps you to ward off stress and to avoid the fear and arousal that come from feelings of despair and low self-esteem (Bandura et al., 1988). Seligman (1988) argues that optimism helps people achieve goals and cope more effectively—for example, optimistic salespeople substantially outsell their pessimistic colleagues.

Conservation of Resources. People can develop a positive attitude by conserving resources. Hobfoll (1989) suggests that people strive to retain, protect, and build resources; the potential or actual loss of these valued resources is threatening. A person's home, marriage, or status as a community leader are all resources, and from Hobfoll's view, when these resources are under attack, people try to defend themselves. They attempt to ward off the attack or replace the loss of resources by seeking a new marriage or new leadership position, or by gaining some new area of competence or financial strength. Treatment might mean shifting a person's focus of attention and reinterpreting the threat, replacing the lost resources (finding a new job), and reevaluating the threat.

Positive Attitudes and Psychoneuroimmunology. One effect of a positive approach is that it may harness the body's own defense mechanisms. Recent studies of **psychoneuroimmunology** (PNI)—the relationship between the immune system and behavior—have shown that the immune system (which fights disease) responds to a person's moods, stress, and basic attitudes about life. According to PNI researchers, the brain provides information to the immune system about how and when to respond. The two systems seem to be linked together, with each producing substances that alter the other's functions. The brain sends signals to the immune system that trigger its disease-fighting ability. The immune system sends signals to the brain that alter its functioning (Glaser and Kiecolt-Glaser, 1988). Thus, the immune system of a person with a positive, upbeat attitude responds better and faster than that of a person who is depressed and lethargic; a depressed person's immune system slows down. Consider people who have recently lost loved ones to death; they consistently show higher rates of illness. Today, many AIDS patients are provided counseling to bolster their immune systems by improving their attitudes; this may help them live longer.

Positive attitudes and illusions can be beneficial, but they can only go so far (DeAngelis, 1988). Sometimes having a positive attitude and practicing hypnosis, meditation, and the other traditional techniques fail to reduce stress. Sometimes it is because they are tried halfheartedly; at other times they are attempted inexpertly. More often, people just lack coping skills or even knowledge that such skills exist. Wearing rose-colored glasses from time to time can be beneficial, but continuous self-deception can lead to maladjustment, lies, and a truly distorted reality.

Effective Coping Strategies. There are a number of steps you can take to cope, manage stress, and stay healthy.

- **Increase Exercise.** People cope better when they improve physical fitness, usually through exercise. In addition, increased exercise will lower blood pressure and the risk of heart disease.

- **Eat Well.** People feel better and cope better when they eat well and have a balanced diet. This also means not being overweight.

- **Sleep Well.** People react better to life when they have had a good night's sleep—reaction time improves, as does judgment.

- **Learn to Relax.** In our fast-paced society, few people take the time to relax and let uncomfortable ideas and feelings leave them. Learn meditation, yoga, or deep breathing. Schedule some time for yourself each day.

- **Be Flexible.** Our lives are unpredictable; accept that fact, and day-to-day surprises will be easier to handle.

- **Keep Stress at School or the Office.** Work-related pressures should be kept in a work environment. Bringing stress and pressure home will only make the problem worse; people are more likely to be involved in substance abuse and domestic violence when they bring stress home with them.

- **Communicate.** Share your ideas, feelings, and thoughts with the significant people in your life. This will decrease misunderstanding, mistrust, and stress.

Psychoneuroimmunology: The study of how psychological processes and the nervous system affect the body's natural defense system—the immune system—and how, in turn, the immune system influences psychological processes; often referred to as *PNI*.

> ♦ **Seek Support.** Social support from family, friends, and self-help groups helps you to appraise a situation differently. Remember, you have to appraise a situation as stressful for it to be stressful—social support helps you keep stressful situations in perspective. ♦

Focus on Learning

- ♦ Identify the five key components of the definition of coping. p. 481
- ♦ What is vulnerability and how does it affect a person's response to stress? p. 481
- ♦ Distinguish between *defense-oriented coping strategies* and *task-oriented coping strategies*. p. 482
- ♦ What are the effects of stress inoculation? pp. 483–484

Health Psychology

At least half of all deaths in the United States are the result of unhealthy life-styles. In the past, most people died from causes beyond their control—influenza, tuberculosis, and pneumonia, for example. Today, the leading causes of death—heart disease, cancer, stroke, and accidents—can be largely controlled by environmental and behavioral variables. Psychologists believe that there is a direct relationship between people's health and their behavior. **Health psychology** is the study of ideas from many fields that enhance health, prevent illness, diagnose and treat disease, and rehabilitate people.

Traditionally, physicians have looked at health as the absence of disease. If a person was not infected with a virus, bacterial infection, cold, and so on, he or she was considered healthy. Now, however, doctors and psychologists acknowledge that health refers not to the absence of disease, but to the total welfare of a person in terms of social, physical, and mental well-being. Encapsulating social, physical and mental well-being places health and psychology in the same corner (Seeman, 1989). Health is now seen as a condition people can actively pursue by eating right, exercising, and managing stress effectively. Unlike medicine, which focuses on specific diseases, health psychology looks at the broad principles of thought and behavior that cut across specializations of diseases to clarify fundamental psychosocial mechanisms (Taylor, 1990).

Variables That Affect Health and Illness

Health and illness are not single entities affected by single variables. A person's health is affected by complex interrelationships among many events. Accordingly, health researchers have explored four variables that correlate strongly with health and illness: personality, cognitions, social environment, and sociocultural variables (Rodin and Salovey, 1989).

Health psychology: The psychological subfield concerned with the use of psychological principles in health enhancement, illness prevention, diagnosis and treatment of disease, and rehabilitation processes.

Personality. Do certain personality types predispose people to illness? Or does illness predispose people to a specific personality? Some evidence suggests that angry, hostile people are more prone to illness, and optimists are less prone. But which comes first? Perhaps lack of illness causes optimism, or at least positive life-styles. The role of personality variables in illness and health is still unclear, and much more research is needed, as you saw when we examined the role of Type A behavior in heart disease (p. 475). One personality variable that seems important is the extent to which people feel they control their lives, health, and illness. When people have a sense that they can control their health, they are more likely to engage in health-conscious behaviors, such as eating lots of complex carbohydrates, decreasing saturated fat, or exercising more (Taylor, 1990).

Cognitions. People's thoughts and beliefs about themselves, other people, and situations affect health-related behaviors. For example, people with an internal locus of control (discussed in chapter 12) are more likely to take charge of their illnesses and attempt to get better than people with an external locus of control who believe that there is nothing that they can do. People who feel they have control over their health are more likely to lead healthy life-styles.

Social Environment. Family, close friends, and work can be sources of social support, a key element in maintaining health and recovering from illness. Greater self-esteem, positive feelings about the future, and a sense of control are characteristic of people with strong social support. Adults in stable long-term relationships such as marriage are less likely to have illnesses than are people devoid of strong social support networks; in addition, their children are also likely to be healthier (Gottman and Katz, 1989). Support from coworkers and supervisors in the work environment may also facilitate health (Repetti, Matthews, and Waldron, 1989). Individuals with support are more likely to engage in preventive dental health, proper eating habits, and the use of safety practices, such as seat belts.

Sociocultural Variables. Gender, age, ethnic group, and socioeconomic class are also important variables that affect health. Women tend to visit physicians more often than men, although in some non-Western cultures, the quality of their treatment is not equal to that given men. With advancing age, some people are more likely to become ill, but there is great individual variation. Many times, illness among the elderly is affected by other variables, such as loneliness, widowhood, and isolation from family. Ethnicity also seems to be an important sociocultural variable. Ethnic minorities and people from lower socioeconomic groups may lack knowledge, funds, or access to preventive care. In addition, older, less educated, and less affluent individuals are far less likely to engage in exercise, which helps prevent illness. Disease prevention is the focus of many health psychologists. In recent years, preventing the spread of AIDS, considered next, has been of great concern.

AIDS: Acquired Immune Deficiency Syndrome

A recent and major concern of health psychologists is AIDS (*Acquired Immune Deficiency Syndrome*). People who contract this deadly infectious disease generally die within a few years of diagnosis because their immune systems can no longer fight off germs and diseases. Little is known about AIDS, and at present there are no vaccines or cures, and few treatments to slow its destructive course. Moreover, some people, fearing contamination, shun AIDS victims. Because many AIDS victims acquire the disease through homosexual contact or intravenous drug use, some see it as a moral stigma. For all these reasons, AIDS is accompanied by devastating psychological consequences (Schofferman, 1988).

THINKING ABOUT RESEARCH

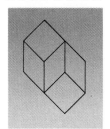

Epidemic. Reports from the Center for Disease Control and the U.S. Department of Health and Human Services (1990) show that more than 81,000 individuals

Health psychologists are attempting to assist individuals and families affected by devastating illnesses and diseases such as AIDS.

have died of AIDS in the United States, and an estimated 1.5 million U.S. inhabitants are infected with the human immunodeficiency virus. Worldwide, five million persons are infected. The Department of Health and Human Services projects that by 1993 at least 450,000 adults in the United States will have been diagnosed with AIDS. Moreover, AIDS-infected mothers will have passed the disease to another 10,000 children by that date (American Psychological Association, 1989). Most AIDS victims are between twenty and forty-nine years of age, and although at present some states such as New York and California have a greater percentage of cases than others, most experts believe that this unevenness will disappear in time.

Psychological Effects. Few other diseases are accompanied by so many losses. AIDS patients face the loss of physical strength, mental acuity, ability to work and care for their families, self-sufficiency, social roles, income and savings, housing, the emotional support of friends and loved ones, and ultimately life itself. Schools have prohibited children with AIDS, or with AIDS in their families, from attending classes. People with AIDS have been fired, coworkers have quit their jobs, and judges have held legal hearings on closed-circuit television to avoid contact with AIDS victims. For many AIDS victims, self-esteem fades rapidly as they blame themselves for having contracted the disease. This self-blame leads to depression, anxiety, self-anger, and a negative outlook on life. Families and friends become similarly affected as they cope with a dying loved one and face their own inability to understand the disease.

Prevention. Psychologists pay particular attention to high-risk behaviors in AIDS prevention. High-risk behaviors directly expose people to the blood or semen of others who are more likely to have been exposed to the virus; in other words, to other people who are likely to have engaged in high-risk behaviors. Often, individuals who have engaged in high-risk behaviors are sexually promiscuous homosexual and bisexual men or present and past intravenous drug abusers. In addition, hemophiliacs are at risk because of the blood transfusions they receive, and so are heterosexuals who have had repeated sexual contact with carriers of AIDS. Ethnic minorities, particularly blacks (twenty-four percent) and Hispanics (fourteen percent), make up a disproportionately large share of AIDS cases in the United States (Peterson and Marin, 1988).

Health professionals agree that the only way to control the spread of AIDS is to decrease the behaviors that put people at risk. People are not likely to get AIDS if they make conscientious decisions about their personal behaviors. Individuals who are not in long-term monogamous relationships must use condoms and avoid oral and anal sex, and intravenous drug users must avoid sharing needles (Fisher, 1988).

Role of the Health Psychologist. Health psychologists can play a major role in setting up AIDS prevention programs, especially for hard-hit groups such as homosexual men and hemophiliacs (Morin, 1988). Adolescents who engage in unprotected sexual activity are especially at risk, and AIDS education aimed at this group is critically important (Flora and Thoresen, 1988). Although AIDS education and prevention campaigns have, in fact, resulted in profound behavior changes among gay men, still not enough is being done (Stall, Coates, and Hoff, 1988). Interestingly, women who have had a previous sexually transmitted disease are more likely than men to alter their high-risk behaviors; men seem more affected by cognitive changes such as fear of the disease (Cochran and Mays, 1989). Thoughts and ideas play an important role in disease prevention and in how people who become sick then respond.   ◆

The Psychology of Being Sick

When a person is sick with an illness that impairs his or her day-to-day functioning, the effects can be devastating. The impact on the individual can be profound both physically and economically. Illness seriously affects both the sick person and his or her family members. Health psychologists are concerned not only with the links between stress and health, but also how people cope with illness when it occurs.

Seeking Health Care. When do people seek health care? What are the variables that prompt a person to become well and healthy? Most people avoid medical care and advice except when absolutely necessary. When a person has a visible symptom (rashes, cuts, swelling, fever) and the symptom appears threatening, painful, and persistent, he or she seeks professional help. People are more likely to seek professional treatment when they are sure that the problem is physical rather than psychological and when medical attention will provide a cure. If they think that medical attention will be a waste of time, or if they dread a diagnosis, they often delay seeking help.

There are gender differences in the willingness to seek medical attention. Women seek medical help more than men do, have more doctor visits, and take more prescription medication (Rosenstock and Kirscht, 1979). Yet men have a shorter lifespan than women do and have higher rates of ulcers, heart disease, and stroke. Men may be less willing to seek medical attention because they perceive it as a weakness in character (it's not strong or macho to admit illness). Because a significant portion of women are not in the workforce, they may have more time to get away for a doctor visit; in addition, women have non-pathological problems throughout their lives (childbirth, menopause) that require medical attention.

The Sick Role. When people do what they feel will help them get well, we say that they are adopting a *sick role*. For most people this means taking specific steps to get well, relieving themselves of normal responsibilities, and realizing that they are not at fault for their illness (Parsons, 1978). (Of course, a person can adopt behaviors associated with illness, when in fact there is no illness or pathology.)

Unfortunately, many people blame the ailing person for being sick, even though the illness may be totally unrelated to any preventive measures a person might have taken. When sick, a person usually is relieved of normal responsibilities such as working or taking care of the family. Although our society fosters an approach that says be cheerful when you are sick, it is normal for people to be slightly depressed or even angry (Lazarus, 1984). Because sickness is generally seen as a temporary state, we expect people to get well and to work toward that end—taking medication, sleeping, and especially, complying with medical advice.

Compliance with Medical Advice. Getting people to adhere to a health regimen has long been a focus of health psychologists. Clients will comply with specific recommendations for a specific disease, such as "Take three tablets a day for ten days." But they are less likely to adhere to general recommendations for diet, exercise, and overall health conditions, such as quitting smoking or relaxing more. The impact of many of the recommendations of physicians is great; for example a ten percent weight reduction in men aged thirty-five to fifty-five through diet and exercise would produce an estimated twenty percent reduction in heart attacks (American Heart Association, 1984). But research shows that clients are more receptive to medical advice and treatment when the treatments are specific, simple, and easy to do and have minimal side effects.

Compliance with medical advice depends on the severity of a problem. When seeking a cure or relief of specific symptoms, people are more likely to be cooperative than when merely seeking wellness or prevention. When exercise is the prescribed treatment, most people drop out of a program within six months. Even when the impact of not taking a medication is serious, people are not especially compliant (Haynes, 1979); this becomes especially true for lengthy or difficult treatments, such as four-times-daily insulin injections (Hanson et al., 1989).

Compliance to a health care regimen is increased when tailored to the life-style and habits of a patient. Even written agreements between practitioners and clients can be helpful. Health psychologists have found clients more likely to adhere to treatments when the doctor's influence and family support systems are substantial. Social support from family and friends turns out to be especially valuable in getting even very sick people to comply with guidelines for treatment (DiMatteo and DiNicola, 1982, 1984). In the next section you will see that health psychologists try to help people be adaptive and cope with their situations.

Health Psychology and Adaptive Behavior

Health psychologists focus on adaptive behaviors that will improve people's day-to-day lives. They encourage preventive programs at work (Antonovsky, 1987) and educate people about ways to manage stress and other positive approaches toward health (Beech, 1987) that will enhance and prolong life. They frequently conduct stress-management workshops to help managers and workers cope with increasing pressures and work loads, and they are involved in helping people quit smoking, control their alcohol intake, follow exercise programs, and practice good nutrition.

Today, health psychologists attempt to change people's behavior *before* it gets out of hand. Health psychology is an action-oriented discipline, and as we enter the 1990s and men and women seek more healthful life-styles, psychologists are playing an instrumental role in that quest. Sometimes they focus on preventive behaviors—using sunscreens when sunbathing, using condoms to prevent the spread of AIDS, exercising regularly. At other times, they help people deal with existing problems such as obesity, diabetes, and high stress levels. Let us examine three of these areas: behavioral interventions, pain management, and stress management.

Behavioral Interventions. To manage existing health disorders and help prevent disease, behavioral interventions are necessary and important. Health psychologists know that many problems are clearly subject to change and modification—these are often considered life-style problems and include obesity, smoking, hypertension, and alcohol and drug abuse.

Consider drug abuse. One sure way to destroy a person's normal health and behavior is through drug use that impairs memory, alertness, and achievement. The principal place where people are introduced to drugs is school, in both city and suburban settings. As a result, in the mid-1980s—under the direction of then Secretary of Education William J. Bennett—a national plan was laid out for achieving drug-free schools. To a great extent, the plan is an effort to help students cope without drugs (see Table 13.4). The plan is action-oriented and incorporates the efforts of education, family, and community in dealing with drug use. The "Just Say No" campaign is only one example of how health psychologists are helping to change people's behavior to improve their health.

TABLE 13.4

A Twelve-Point Plan for Creating Schools without Drugs

Parents

1. Teach standards of right and wrong and demonstrate these standards through personal example.
2. Help children to resist peer pressure to use drugs by supervising their activities.
3. Be knowledgeable about drugs and signs of drug use. When symptoms are observed, respond promptly.

Schools

4. Determine the extent and character of drug use and establish a means of monitoring that use regularly.
5. Establish clear and specific rules regarding drug use that include strong corrective actions.
6. Enforce established policies against drug use fairly and consistently. Implement security measures to eliminate drugs on school premises.
7. Implement a comprehensive drug prevention curriculum from kindergarten through grade twelve.
8. Reach out to the community for support and assistance in making the school's antidrug policy and program work by developing collaborative arrangements.

Students

9. Learn about the effects of drug use, the reasons drugs are harmful, and ways to resist pressures to try drugs.
10. Use an understanding of the danger posed by drugs to help other students avoid them.

Communities

11. Help schools fight drugs by providing them with the expertise and financial resources of community groups and agencies.
12. Involve local law enforcement agencies in all aspects of drug prevention: assessment, enforcement, and education.

Pain Management. Severe and disabling pain is symptomatic of certain illnesses. There is *chronic* pain, which is long-lasting and ever-present. *Periodic* pain comes and goes. And pain may be *progressive*, always present, and increasing in severity as an illness progresses. Pain management is especially important because many people have chronic pain, such as headache pain, lower back pain, and arthritis. Some pain can be treated with drugs, surgery, or other medical interventions. But other types of chronic pain, such as that caused by arthritis and cancer, sometimes call for nontraditional, psychological techniques.

One nontraditional technique is hypnosis, considered in chapter 4. Another approach is biofeedback, also discussed in chapter 4. Other techniques for pain management include behavior modification and cognitive therapy (chapters 5 and 15). Behavior modification uses learning principles to teach people new effective behaviors and to help them unlearn old maladaptive behaviors. People undergoing therapy learn to relax after a twinge of pain rather than focusing on the pain and thus making it worse. Chapter 15 discusses how cognitive therapy uses behavior modification techniques to help people acquire new thoughts, beliefs, and values that can help in pain management.

Stress Management. Because stress exists in all our lives, whether from school exams, parent or peer pressures, natural disasters, illness, death, divorce, inflation, or financial difficulties, many health psychologists focus on stress and its management. With the help of health psychologists, employers are sponsoring programs that focus on managing stress in the workplace (Glasgow and Terborg, 1988). The programs usually involve education, exercise, nutrition classes, and counseling. The results show fewer work days lost to illness and lower health-care costs (Gebhardt and Crump, 1990). Stress management also results in fewer lost lives. When patients who were hospitalized for heart attacks were treated for stress symptoms after their release from the hospital, compared to a control group that did not receive specific stress treatments, they had fewer subsequent heart attacks (Frasure-Smith and Prince, 1989).

The task of managing stress in people's daily lives is becoming greater each day as new and potent forces impinge on people's health (Ilgen, 1990). In the 1990s, people are concerned not only about managing day-to-day illness and stress, but also about potential threats in the food supply and in the environment.

Hazardous Waste, Psychological Distress, and Health

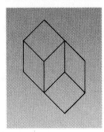

APPLYING PSYCHOLOGY

*H*ow can social scientists help us understand what happened at Love Canal, what happened at Three Mile Island, what is happening in thousands of "Not in My Backyard" incidents? It is hard to be part of a community and not be interested in newspaper stories on global warming, oil spills, or toxic wastes in your own backyard. The general public tends to view these issues as environmental, technological, toxicological, or governmental, but not psychological.

Psychologists know that perceptions of health risks are an important determinant of attitudes and behaviors. Understanding perceptions of health risk has important applied implications for planners, policy makers, and health professionals involved with helping the public cope with emerging technologies. For example, in recent years, toxic hazards and community responses to haz-

ardous waste landfills ha   great deal of attention. Reports on hazardous materials appear   often convey residents' concerns about
health, fear of cancer, un   ing property values, and lack of trust in
the government.

Psychological Studies. Although there have been a few studies of the psychological responses of residents to toxic hazards, most of the information available
comes from media reports or anecdotal evidence. The few psychological studies,
while important, have tended to be descriptive (nonquantitative), based on small
samples, or conducted with activist or litigation groups. Hallman and Wandersman (1989) conducted a psychological study of residents who live near a
hazardous waste landfill in rural South Carolina. Their study provides information about the perception of risk, psychological distress, and level of concern
about possible health effects of the landfill. The results suggest that both distance
from the landfill and perceived exposure are significantly related to perceived
present and future health risks, psychological distress, and fear of cancer. The
results suggest that psychological and health concerns are widespread, rather
than just localized.

People who cope with stress
successfully alleviate their
concern over an issue by
taking positive action and
seeking others' support.

Changing Perceptions. Perceived risks are known to be correlated with active
support of or opposition to technologies; as a result, the ability to predict perceived risks can let policy makers know how receptive a community might be
to proposed or existing technologies and what issues may be critical to residents.
In addition, perceptions of health risks are significantly correlated with higher
levels of psychological distress. Predicting perceived health risks can help identify
people or communities for whom intervention to relieve this distress may be
helpful. Such interventions can take several courses. If people's perceptions of
health risks are based largely on irrational beliefs, then an intervention may be
designed to change these beliefs to better reflect reality. If, on the other hand,
these beliefs appear founded, the logical intervention is to change reality. However, determining whether the beliefs are well-founded is often difficult, given
the uncertainty usually present in hazardous waste disposal situations. This is
particularly true when scientific evidence is equivocal, and the experts themselves
disagree. ◆

- Identify three specific behaviors a person can adopt to enhance health.
  pp. 486–488
- Identify three things that happen when a person adopts a *sick role*.
  p. 489
- Identify two behaviors that can increase compliance with medical advice. p. 490

*Focus on
Learning*

Key Terms

Stressor p. 466
Stress p. 466
Anxiety p. 466
Frustration p. 467
Conflict p. 467
Approach-approach conflict
  p. 468
Avoidance-avoidance conflict
  p. 468

Approach-avoidance conflict
  p. 468
Pressure p. 468
Burnout p. 470
Type A behavior p. 475
Type B behavior p. 475
Post-traumatic stress disorder
  p. 476
Coping p. 481

Vulnerability p. 481
Coping skills p. 481
Social support p. 481
Stress inoculation p. 483
Psychoneuroimmunology
  p. 485
Health psychology p. 486

Summary

Stress

♦ A stressor is a stimulus that acts on an organism in either physically or psychologically injurious ways.   p. 466

♦ Stress is a set of non-specific responses by an organism to environmental demands. Stress is a normal part of living and depends on a person's appraisal of a situation.   p. 466

♦ Approach-approach conflicts arise when a person must choose one of two equally pleasant alternatives. Avoidance-avoidance conflicts occur when a choice involves two equally distasteful alternatives.   p. 468

♦ Physiologically, stress is characterized by arousal. Behaviorally, stress and arousal are related; when moderately aroused, people behave with optimal effectiveness; when underaroused, they lack stimulation to behave effectively. Emotionally, people's reactions often depend on frustration, work-related pressures, and day-to-day conflicts.   p. 469

♦ Selye characterized stress responses as a general adaptation syndrome with three stages: alarm, resistance, and exhaustion.   p. 471

♦ Type A behavior is reflected in people who are competitive, impatient, hostile, and always striving to do more in less time.   p. 475

♦ People exposed to high levels of stress for long periods of time may develop stress-related disorders, including physical illness. Post-traumatic stress disorder may be evident after a person has undergone some type of disaster.   pp. 475–476

♦ A suicide attempter tries to commit suicide but is unsuccessful; completers take their lives successfully. Most suicide completers talk about their death in advance; most want to live, but their sense of helplessness about the future tells them that death is the only way out.   pp. 477–479

Coping

♦ Coping is the process by which a person manages environmental and internal demands that cause, or might cause, stress and will tax his or her inner resources.   p. 481

♦ Defense-oriented coping strategies do not reduce stress, but instead help people protect themselves from its effects. Most psychologists recommend task-oriented coping strategies instead.   p. 482

♦ Stress inoculation increases the predictability of stressful events, fosters coping skills, generates self-talking, encourages confidence about successful outcomes, and builds a commitment to personal action and responsibility to an adaptive course of action.   p. 483

♦ Psychoneuroimmunology is the study of how psychological processes and the nervous system affect the body's immune system, and how, in turn, the immune system influences psychological processes.   p. 485

Health Psychology

♦ Health psychologists employ ideas and principles from many fields to enhance health, prevent illness, diagnose and treat disease, and rehabilitate people.   p. 486

♦ Health psychologists have delineated four variables that seem to correlate strongly with health and illness: personality, cognitive, environmental, and sociocultural variables.
pp. 486–487

♦ Health psychology is an action-oriented discipline that focuses on preventive health measures as well as intervention in existing conditions.   p. 489

♦ When people undertake specific behaviors that they feel will help them get well, we say they are adopting a sick role. Research shows that clients are more receptive to medical treatments when the treatments are specific and simple, with minimal side effects.   p. 489

♦ Perceptions of health risks are an important determinant of attitudes and behaviors toward risky technologies and toward risk behaviors and diseases such as AIDS. If people's perceptions of health risk are based largely on irrational beliefs, then intervention may change these beliefs to better reflect reality.
pp. 490–491

Connections

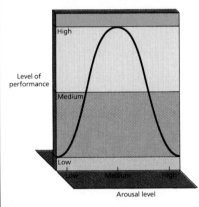

If you are interested in . . .	*Turn to . . .*	*To learn more about . . .*
The role of stress in everyday life	◆ Ch. 11, pp. 390–391, 418	The relationship between arousal and stress.
	◆ Ch. 14, pp. 504–505	How certain psychological disorders have a strong component of anxiety.
	◆ Ch. 17, p. 625	How frustration can lead to stress and ultimately aggression.
How people cope with everyday problems	◆ Ch. 4, pp. 132–135	Various coping techniques (such as biofeedback and self-hypnosis) which can be practiced at home to effectively manage stressors.
	◆ Ch. 8, p. 417	How people can learn to control their emotional responses to situations through self-instruction.
	◆ Ch. 14, pp. 516–521	How seriously depressed people often feel there is no hope and that they cannot cope any longer.
	◆ Ch. 15, pp. 555–559	Cognitive therapy, which focuses on changing people's distorted ideas of reality and helps them to develop positive self-esteem.
Psychology's role in health and well-being	◆ Ch. 5, pp. 166–167	How the immune system can be conditioned to respond to environmental stimulation.
	◆ Ch. 10, pp. 366–368	The inevitable physical deterioration that occurs with aging.
	◆ Ch. 14, p. 509	Various disorders which affect both physical and mental health.

14 *Exploring Psychological Disorders*

"Haute Cinq" by John Chamberlain

U nder a 1987 directive issued by Mayor Edward Koch to help New York City's mentally ill homeless, Joyce Brown was forcibly committed to Bellevue Hospital. The forty-year-old former secretary had lived on a Manhattan sidewalk for a year, feeding herself on seven dollars a day and huddling over a hot-air vent in winter to stay warm. She was dirty and incoherent, cursed at passersby, defecated in her clothes, and tore up and burned dollar bills given to her. But Brown didn't want to be "helped." "Some people are street people," she said. "That's the life they choose to lead."

Brown took her battle to court and the judge found her to be educated, intelligent, and fiercely independent. In explaining her odd behavior, Brown said that after she had eaten enough for the day she tore up any excess money because carrying cash at night was dangerous. She attributed her filthy condition to the inaccessibility of public toilets. Neither suicidal nor malnourished, Brown seemingly posed little threat to herself or others. Three psychiatrists hired by Brown's attorneys testified that the woman was odd but not crazy. Four psychiatrists for the city said she was insane.

The judge ruled in Brown's favor, noting that street life may be aesthetically offensive but that the mentally ill are as entitled as everyone else to freedom.

Brown's case raises an old question about mental illness: how different must a person's behavior be to qualify as abnormal? Is Brown's behavior any stranger than that of an old woman who leaves a multimillion dollar fortune to her cats? Is it any more eccentric than taking a mid-winter bath in an ice-covered lake, as do members of the Polar Bear club, or undergoing extensive cosmetic surgery to obtain a perfect face and body?

What Is Abnormal Behavior?

Is Joyce Brown's behavior merely odd, or is she abnormal? To some extent it depends on where you live, because every society has its own definition of abnormal behavior. In the Soviet Union, for example, people were once regularly placed in mental institutions for political dissent (Farone, 1982). Generally, however, people classified as abnormal have lost touch with reality—their behavior is more than odd. Recent data suggest that in any one month about fifteen percent of the U.S. population eighteen and over meet the criteria for a mental disorder—that is, they exhibit symptoms of abnormality (Reiger et al., 1988). **Abnormal behavior** is behavior characterized as atypical, socially unacceptable, distressing, maladaptive, and the result of distorted cognitions. Let us consider these five distinguishing characteristics of abnormal behavior.

First, abnormal behavior is *atypical*. Many behaviors are unusual, but abnormal behaviors also tend to be statistically uncommon. For example, you would not consider ear piercing among teenage boys to be abnormal; the practice is fairly common in our society today. However, washing one's hands every few minutes during the day until they are raw is abnormal. (Keep in mind that all atypical behavior is not necessarily abnormal. The Olympic feats of runner Florence Griffith-Joyner are statistically uncommon, but not abnormal.)

Second, in addition to being atypical, abnormal behavior is also *socially unacceptable*. Society is fickle. Ideas about what is normal and abnormal vary according to cultural values that are in a constant state of flux. What is normal in one culture may be labelled abnormal in another; consider the Islamic practice of polygamy. Similarly, behavior that was considered abnormal ten years ago, such as male ear piercing, may be considered normal today. For behavior to be judged abnormal, it must be unacceptable to society.

Third, abnormal behavior often causes *distress or discomfort* to the person or to those around him or her. While feelings of anxiety are a normal reaction in many situations, prolonged distress may indicate abnormal behavior. You may feel anxious when preparing to speak in front of a group, but constant, unrelenting anxiety, avoidance of any situations that might require public speaking, and fear of people in general suggests abnormal behavior.

Abnormal behavior: Behavior characterized as atypical, socially unacceptable, distressing, maladaptive, and the result of distorted cognitions.

Is dressing as Spiderman and attempting to climb the sheer walls of city buildings atypical behavior?

Fourth, many psychologists also define abnormal behavior as *maladaptive* or self-defeating to the person exhibiting it. Maladaptive behaviors, such as depression or drug abuse, are harmful and nonproductive. They often lead to more misery and prevent the person from making positive changes in his or her life.

Last, abnormal behavior is often the result of *distorted cognitions.* For example, a young man with distorted cognitions (thoughts) may actually believe that people are out to get him. A woman suffering from major depression may believe that she is worthless, stupid, and unlovable.

In recent years, psychologists have begun to describe behavior in terms of *maladjustment* rather than *abnormality.* The distinction is important because it implies that maladaptive behavior can, with treatment, become adaptive and productive. The term maladjustment also emphasizes specific behaviors rather than labelling the entire person.

To summarize, abnormal behavior is characterized as atypical, socially unacceptable, distressing, maladaptive, and the result of distorted cognitions. There are, of course, exceptions to this definition. For example, we do not hesitate to label drug abuse as abnormal, but unfortunately that behavior is not as atypical as it once was. Nevertheless, this definition provides psychologists with a solid framework from which to explore abnormal behavior and its treatment.

Before prescribing treatment, mental health practitioners want to know why a person is maladjusted because the cause of a disorder can sometimes help define a treatment plan. Therefore, they often turn to theories and models that attempt to explain the causes of abnormality. A **model** is an analogy that helps scientists discover relationships among data; it uses a structure from one field to help describe data in another. Psychologists use models to make predictions about behavior. These models form the basis of **abnormal psychology,** the field of psychology concerned with the assessment, treatment, and prevention of maladaptive behavior. Several models help explain abnormal behavior: medical-biological, psychodynamic, humanistic, behavioral, cognitive, sociocultural, and interactionist.

Model: A perspective or approach derived from data in one field, used to help describe data in another field.

Abnormal psychology: The field of psychology concerned with the assessment, treatment, and prevention of maladaptive behavior.

Medical-biological model:
An approach that considers behavior to be the result of biological and physiological conditions.

Medical-Biological Model

Thousands of years ago, our ancestors believed that abnormal behavior was caused by demons that invaded people's bodies. The "cure" often involved trephination—drilling a hole in the skull to allow the evil force to escape. Even as recently as a few hundred years ago, people with psychological disorders were caged and treated like animals. Early reformists, such as Philippe Pinel advocated the medical model and proposed that abnormal behavior could be treated and cured. When scientists proved that syphilis could cause mental disorders, the medical model gained even greater acceptance and led to more humane treatment and improved conditions for patients.

The **medical-biological model** focuses on the biological and physiological conditions that initiate abnormal behaviors. Over time, mental health professionals have expanded the medical approach to include ideas as initiators of abnormal behavior and maladjustment. This model adequately deals with a range of mental ailments, such as organic psychoses caused by mercury poisoning or viral attacks on brain cells. It focuses on genetic abnormalities, problems in the central nervous system, and hormonal changes. It also helps explain and treat individuals with substance abuse problems and with schizophrenia, two disorders that may have a strong biological component. Proponents of the medical-biological model might explain Joyce Brown's behavior (introduced at the beginning of the chapter) as a result of a chemical or hormonal imbalance that altered her judgment.

Since researchers who subscribe to the biological explanation of maladjustment are interested in how a person's body influences or determines behavior, they suggest treatments using drugs to change biochemical and other bodily functions. This approach serves as the foundation for traditional psychology and psychiatry. Many of the terms and concepts used in psychology and psychiatry are borrowed from medicine, including *treatment, case, symptom, syndrome,* and also the term *mental illness* itself. The medical model assumes that abnormal behavior, like other illnesses, can be diagnosed, treated, and cured.

But the medical approach has not gone unchallenged. Its critics say that the model does not take advantage of modern psychological insights, such as those of learning theory. A major—but not surprising—disadvantage of the medical model is that it emphasizes hospitalization and drug treatment rather than solving psychological problems by psychological means. Use of the medical model also has fostered the notion that abnormal behavior can be infectious, much like a bacterial disease. This contamination analogy portrays the mentally unhealthy person as someone to fear and avoid and hampers treatment programs designed to reintegrate patients back into society.

Psychodynamic Explanation of Abnormality

The *psychodynamic* approach to explaining abnormal behavior is loosely rooted in Freud's theory of personality (discussed in chapter 12). Psychodynamic theories assume that psychological disorders result from anxiety produced by unresolved conflicts and forces a person may not be aware of. They assert that maladjustment occurs when a person relies on too many defense mechanisms or when defense mechanisms fail. Joyce Brown's behavior might be explained as anger turned inward against herself; although she is bright and capable, her behavior might be seen as a reaction to her fears of competing

In the 18th and 19th centuries, Philippe Pinel insisted on treating mental patients as recoverable subjects. His humane treatment of patients fostered a new era of change in the treatment of psychological disorders.

due to low self-esteem that was initiated in childhood. Treatment usually involves helping a patient become aware of motivations, conflict, and desires so that he or she can have a healthier life-style. We will explore psychodynamic approaches in more detail in chapter 15.

Humanistic Explanation of Abnormality

Like psychodynamic theorists, humanists assume that inner psychic forces are important in establishing and maintaining a normal life-style. But unlike psychodynamic theorists, *humanists* believe that people have much more cognitive control over their lives. They focus on individual uniqueness and decision making. Humanists contend that people become maladjusted when their expectations far exceed their achievements; in Joyce Brown's case, a humanist might focus on her dignity, self-respect, and quest for independence. Treatment usually involves helping maladjusted people discover and accept their true selves, formulate more realistic self-concepts and expectations, and become more like their ideal selves.

Behavioral Models

The *behavioral model* states that abnormal behaviors are caused by faulty or ineffective learning and conditioning patterns. Two fundamental assumptions of learning theorists are that disordered behavior can be reshaped and that more appropriate, worthwhile behaviors can be substituted through traditional learning techniques (see chapter 5).

Learning theorists assume that events in a person's environment reinforce or punish various behaviors selectively, and in doing so, they shape personality and may create maladjustment. Behaviorists thus contend that a woman who has learned to avoid people who make her anxious may overgeneralize that behavior and become afraid of all people. Likewise, a boy who receives little reinforcement for his efforts to be good may become pessimistic, introverted, and anxious. An abusive husband may have learned to assert his dominance over women through physical abuse because as a child he was rewarded for typically masculine behaviors (such as fighting) and punished for typically feminine behaviors (such as nurturance). Proponents of the behavioral model might explain Joyce Brown's behavior by noting that she did not find significant or important reinforcers in the work world and she felt she could take care of herself and manage better on a day-to-day basis on the streets.

Cognitive Explanations

The *cognitive* perspective asserts that human beings engage in both prosocial and maladjusted behaviors because of ideas and thoughts. As thinking organisms, individuals decide how to behave, with abnormal behavior based on false assumptions or unrealistic situations.

Practitioners with the cognitive perspective treat people with psychological disorders by helping them develop new thought processes that instill new values. Joyce Brown might be assumed to have developed wrong ideas about the world; these ideas might be irrational and may have led her to what most people consider maladaptive behaviors. A practitioner might assert that a patient (such as Brown) can replace maladjusted behaviors with worthwhile ones. For example, suppose an individual believes that his value as a person hinges totally on his career success. When he falls short of his impossibly high goals, he loses self-esteem, begins drinking, and eventually becomes deeply depressed. Using the cognitive model, a therapist might treat this maladjusted individual by helping him formulate more rational self-concepts and adopt more effective coping strategies.

The Sociocultural Perspective

People develop abnormalities within a context—the context of family, community, and society. Researchers, especially cross-cultural researchers, have shown that people's personality development and their disorders reflect their cultures, the stressors in their societies, and the type of disorders prevalent in their societies.

As researchers examine the frequency and types of disorders that occur in different societies, they note some sharp differences not only between societies, but within societies as a function of the decade being examined, and the age and gender of the clients. For example, in China, depression is relatively uncommon, but stress reactions in the form of physical ailments are common. Understanding cross-cultural perspectives on abnormality helps us better frame our questions and interpretations of data. Thus a sociocultural approach is often illuminating.

The Legal Perspective

Interestingly, the law defines abnormal behavior differently. Think about John W. Hinckley, Jr., the man who attempted to assassinate President Ronald Reagan. A jury declared him "not guilty by reason of insanity" and he was acquitted of murder charges. During the public outcry that followed, states sought to prohibit the insanity plea. At least half the states changed their insanity pleas, and twelve adopted a new plea, "guilty but mentally ill," and three chose to eliminate the insanity plea altogether.

The term *insane* is a legal term, not a psychological one. Insanity refers to a condition that excuses people from responsibility and protects them from punishment. From the legal point of view, a person cannot be held responsible for his or her crime if, at the time of the crime, he or she lacked the capacity to recognize right from wrong or to obey the law.

Think back to the example of Joyce Brown. Do any of the legal criteria describe her? The answer is no. Although useful for judicial purposes, the legal definition of abnormal behavior is too focused to be useful in treating clients.

The Interactionist Perspective

Each of the models we've discussed—medical-biological, psychodynamic, humanistic, behavioral, cognitive, sociocultural, and legal—explains maladjustment from a different perspective. No one model can explain every kind of abnormal behavior, but each has value. For some disorders (such as phobias), learning theory explains the cause and prescribes an effective course of treatment. For other disorders (such as schizophrenia), medical-biological theories explain a significant part of the problem. Consequently, many psychologists take an *eclectic*, or interactionist position, drawing on all these perspectives. For example, a therapist could treat a depressed patient by prescribing antidepressant drugs (medical-biological model); helping the patient develop new, optimistic thought processes (cognitive model); and teaching the patient adaptive behaviors to eliminate depression-inducing stress (behavioral model). As you examine each of the psychological disorders presented in this chapter, think about why you favor one explanation of maladjustment over another. Do you have a cognitive bent, or do you favor a more psychodynamic approach? Perhaps you are more behavioral in your beliefs. Regardless of a practitioner's predispositions, it is important that he or she carefully evaluate symptoms so that proper diagnoses can be made. Considered next is the system developed to aid practitioners in making diagnoses—the DSM-III-R.

◆ Identify and describe the distinguishing characteristics of maladjustment. p. 498
◆ What are the advantages and disadvantages of the medical model of maladjustment? p. 500
◆ Identify the distinguishing characteristics of the psychodynamic, humanistic, and cognitive models of maladjustment. pp. 500–501
◆ What does it mean when a psychologist says that he or she is eclectic? p. 502

Focus on Learning

Diagnosing Abnormal Behavior: DSM-III-R

goal: to improve accuracy of diagnosis

Three psychiatrists hired by Joyce Brown's attorneys testified that she was odd but not crazy. Four other psychiatrists (for the city) said she was insane. This controversy underscores the fact that diagnosing maladjusted behavior is a complicated process. Therefore, the American Psychiatric Association has devised a system for diagnosing maladjusted behavior. The most recent edition of the *Diagnostic and Statistical Manual of Mental Disorders*, published in 1987, is called the DSM-III-R. The goal of DSM-III-R is to improve the reliability of diagnoses by categorizing disorders according to observable behaviors. The system designates nineteen major categories of maladjustment and more than two hundred subcategories. Table 14.1 lists some of the major classifications in the DSM-III-R. DSM-III-R also cites the **prevalence** of a disorder: the percentage of the population displaying a disorder during any specified period. For most psychological disorders, practitioners also know the lifetime prevalence: the statistical likelihood that a person will develop the disorder during his or her lifetime.

TABLE 14.1

Major Classifications in DSM-III-R	
Disorder of Infancy, Childhood, and Adolescence	Anxiety Disorders
Organic Mental Disorders	Somatoform Disorders
Psychoactive Substance Use Disorders	Dissociative Disorders
Schizophrenia	Sexual Disorders
Delusional Disorders	Sleep Disorders
Psychotic Disorders	Factitious Disorders
Mood (Affective) Disorders	Disorders of Impulse Control
Personality Disorders	Adjustment Disorders

Prevalence: The percentage of the population displaying a disorder during any specified period.

Note: Each classification is further broken down into subtypes (with some minor modifications).

You might think that a diagnostic manual is straightforward, like an encyclopedia of mental disorders. But DSM-III-R has met with resistance and controversy (Millon, 1983). Some psychologists applaud its increased recognition of social and environmental influences on behavior (Linn and Spitzer, 1982). Others argue that it is too precise; still others that it is too complicated. Some claim a sexist bias against women (Kaplan, 1983). Others feel that the DSM-III-R should go beyond diagnosis and include problem-oriented and problem-solving information rather than just symptoms (Longabaugh et al., 1986). Many psychologists are unhappy with the continued use of psychiatric terms that perpetuate the use of a medical rather than behavioral model.

Overall, the psychological community would rather have DSM-III-R than not have it (McReynolds, 1989). DSM-III-R is by no means the final word in diagnosing maladjustment and its reliability is not completely known. It is an evolving system and psychologists and psychiatrists are hard at work preparing DSM-IV. The remainder of this chapter explores some of the most important disorders in DSM-III-R and their consequences, beginning with anxiety disorders.

Anxiety Disorders

It had been a stress-filled week for Conrad, and now he was arguing with his wife on the phone. Suddenly, he became short of breath and his heart began to pound vigorously. Certain that he was having a heart attack, Conrad hung up and called an ambulance. At the hospital, the examining doctor informed Conrad that he had suffered nothing more than an anxiety attack.

Psychologists know that almost everyone experiences anxiety. Most people feel anxious in specific situations, such as before taking an examination, competing in a swim meet, or delivering a speech. Although anxiety can be a positive, motivating force, its effects can also be debilitating and, left untreated, may eventually impair a person's health and lead to hospitalization.

Defining Anxiety

Anxiety: A generalized feeling of fear and apprehension that may or may not be related to a particular event or object, often accompanied by increased physiological arousal.

Karen Horney, a neo-Freudian renowned for her work on anxiety, described anxiety as the central factor in both normal and abnormal behavior (Horney, 1937). **Anxiety** is customarily considered a generalized feeling of fear and apprehension, often accompanied by increased physiological arousal, that may or may not be related to a particular event or object. Horney considered it a motivating force, an intrapsychic urge, and a signal of distress. Although DSM-III-R was not written when Horney developed her ideas, Horney would have argued that it is anxiety that underlies many forms of maladjustment. She believed that maladjustment occurs when too many defenses against anxiety pervade an individual's personality.

In contrast, Freud saw anxiety as the result of constant conflict among the id, ego, and superego, and he called nearly all forms of behavior associated with anxiety *neurotic*. Freud's term "neurosis" has made its way into everyday language, and nonpsychologists tend to describe any behavioral quirk as neurotic. Today, psychologists believe that as a catchall, the term neurosis is neither appropriate nor efficient. Precise and consistent diagnosis of maladjustment is essential to appropriate treatment, but anxiety refers to a wide range of symptoms, including fear, apprehension, inattention, palpitation, respiratory distress, dizziness, and fear of death.

Psychologists recognize anxiety as a key symptom of maladjustment—not necessarily the cause of maladjustment. Apprehension, fear, and its accompanying autonomic nervous system arousal are caused by thoughts, environmental stimuli, or perhaps some long-standing and as yet unresolved conflict. This is clearly the case with generalized anxiety disorders, considered next.

Generalized Anxiety Disorder

Every disorder represents a different pattern of behavior and maladjustment, and DSM-III-R classifies them under a variety of diagnostic categories. Those in which anxiety is the prominent feature are designated as **generalized anxiety disorders.** People with a generalized anxiety disorder feel anxious almost constantly. They often report sleep disturbances, excessive sweating, muscle tension, headaches, and insomnia. They are tense and irritable, unable to concentrate, have difficulty making decisions, and may hyperventilate (Rapee, 1986).

For a diagnosis, DSM-III-R states that a person must show persistent anxiety for at least one month. If such chronic anxiety has no obvious source, it is called **free-floating anxiety.** On the other hand, the source of such extreme anxiety may be, and often is, specific stressors in the environment, such as being in a prisoner-of-war camp.

Psychologists describe three areas of functioning in which people with a generalized anxiety disorder show impairment. One is *motor tension,* whereby the person is unable to relax and exhibits jumpiness, restlessness, and tension. The second is *autonomic hyperactivity,* whereby the person sweats, has a dry mouth, has a high resting pulse rate, urinates frequently, and may complain of a lump in the throat. The third is *vigilance,* whereby the person has difficulty concentrating and is irritable and impatient. Unlike people who feel anxious almost constantly, those who suffer from phobic disorders, considered next, have far more focused anxiety and fear.

Karen Horney considered anxiety a central motivating force behind normal and abnormal behavior.

Phobic Disorders

Do you know someone who is petrified at the thought of an airplane ride, who avoids crowds at all cost, or who shudders at the sight of a harmless garden snake? A **phobic disorder** is an anxiety disorder involving the irrational fear of, and consequent attempt to avoid, specific objects or situations. People with phobic disorders exhibit avoidance and escape behaviors, show increased heart rate and breathing patterns, and report thoughts of disaster and severe embarrassment. Many psychologists agree that, once established, phobias are maintained by the relief a person derives from escaping or avoiding the feared situation.

One key to diagnosing a phobic disorder is that the fear must be disproportionate to the situation. Most people who fear heights would not avoid visiting a friend who lived on the top floor of a tall building, but a person with a phobia of heights would. Fear alone does not distinguish a phobia; fear *and* avoidance must be evident.

Mild phobic disorders occur in about 7.5 percent of the population. They are, in fact, relatively common in well-adjusted people. Severe disabling phobias occur in less than 0.05 percent of the population and typically appear in patients with other disorders (Seif and Atkins, 1979). Phobias occur most frequently between the ages of thirty and sixty and about equally in men and women (Marks, 1977). There are an infinite number of objects and

Generalized anxiety disorder: A disorder characterized by persistent anxiety for at least one month, sometimes accompanied by problems in motor tension, autonomic hyperactivity, apprehension, and concentration.

Free-floating anxiety: Persistent anxiety not clearly related to any specific object or situation, accompanied by a sense of impending doom.

Phobic disorder: A disorder characterized by fear and subsequent attempted avoidance of specific objects or situations, acknowledged by the person as unreasonable.

In extreme cases, people suffering from agoraphobia are afraid to leave the safety of their own homes. They are often isolated and depressed.

situations toward which people could become fearful. Because of their diversity and number, DSM-III-R classifies three basic kinds of phobias: agoraphobia, social phobia, and simple phobia; we consider them next.

Agoraphobia. **Agoraphobia** is a marked fear of being in open and public places from which escape might be difficult. It is accompanied by avoidance behaviors that may eventually interfere with normal activities. It can become so debilitating that it prevents the individual from going into any open space, traveling in airplanes, or being in crowds. People with severe cases may decide to never leave their homes. Agoraphobia is often brought on by stress, particularly interpersonal stress. It is far more common in women than in men and is often accompanied by other disorders. A housewife who had agoraphobia for eight years reported the following:

> It causes terrible problems. The children miss out on lots of things, as I can't take them around to parties and so on; and my husband has to take time off to take them to dentists, doctors, and so on. He does all the shopping, and this makes life hard for him. I am in the house all day on my own, with only the dog to talk to, and feel that I am really going mad. The house is like a prison: all I do all day is housework, to keep myself busy. Having agoraphobia makes one very lonely as you can't go out to see anyone. If only I had someone to talk to, it wouldn't be so bad. (MELVILLE, 1977, P. 22)

The disorder brings about hyperventilation, extreme tension, and even cognitive disorganization (Zitrin, 1981). Agoraphobics feel weak and dizzy when they have an attack and often suffer from severe panic attacks (*panic attacks* are characterized as acute anxiety that is not triggered by a specific event). They often are seriously depressed (Breier, Charney, and Heninger, 1984).

Agoraphobia is complicated, incapacitating, and extraordinarily difficult to treat (Mathews, Gelder, and Johnston, 1981). According to Freud and other psychoanalysts, traumatic childhood experiences may cause people to avoid particular objects, events, and situations that produce anxiety. Freudians speculate that agoraphobics may have feared abandonment by a cold or nonnurturing mother and the fear has generalized to a fear of abandonment or helplessness. Most researchers today find Freudian explanations of phobic behavior unconvincing. As an alternative, modern learning theory

Agoraphobia: A disorder characterized by fear of being in public places from which escape might be difficult.

suggests that agoraphobia may develop because people avoid situations they have found painful or embarrassing. Failed coping strategies and low self-esteem have been implicated (Williams, Kinney and Falbo, 1989). Despite much research, no simple cause for the disorder has been found.

evaluated by other

Social Phobia. While a person with agoraphobia may avoid all situations involving other people, a person with a **social phobia** tends to avoid situations in which he or she may be exposed to the scrutiny of other people. A person with a social phobia fears behaving in an embarrassing or humiliating way and avoids eating in public or speaking before other people. The person with a social phobia avoids evaluation by refusing to deal with people or situations in which evaluation might occur.

Simple Phobias. DSM-III-R classifies all specific phobias other than agoraphobia and social phobia as a **simple phobia.** A person with a simple phobia shows an irrational and persistent fear of an object or situation, along with a compelling desire to avoid it. Most people are familiar with simple phobias; they include *claustrophobia*—fear of closed spaces; *hematophobia*—fear of the sight of blood; and *acrophobia*—fear of heights. Table 14.2 lists some common simple phobias. Many develop in childhood, adolescence, or early adulthood. Most people who have fears of heights, small spaces, water, doctors, or flying can calm themselves and deal with their fears; those who cannot (true phobics), often seek the help of a therapist when the phobia interferes with their health or day-to-day functioning. Treatment using behavior therapy is typically effective.

Obsessive-Compulsive Disorders

Being orderly and organized is an asset for most people in today's fast-paced, complex society. But when orderliness becomes the prime concern in a person's life, he or she may be suffering from an obsessive-compulsive disorder. **Obsessive-compulsive disorders** are characterized by the presence of unwanted thoughts, urges, and actions that focus on maintaining order and control.

People with obsessive-compulsive disorders combat anxiety by carrying out ritual behaviors that reduce tension. For example, a man obsessed with

Social phobia: A disorder characterized by fear of, and desire to avoid, situations in which the person might be exposed to scrutiny by others and might behave in an embarrassing or humiliating way.

Simple phobia: A disorder characterized by irrational and persistent fear of an object or situation along with a compelling desire to avoid it.

Obsessive-compulsive disorder: A disorder characterized by persistent and uncontrollable thoughts and irrational beliefs that cause an individual to perform compulsive rituals that interfere with daily life.

TABLE 14.2
Some Common Forms of Object Phobias

Name	Object(s) Feared	Name	Object(s) Feared
Acrophobia	High places	Hematophobia	Blood
Agoraphobia	Open places	Mysophobia	Contamination
Ailurophobia	Cats	Nyctophobia	Darkness
Algophobia	Pain	Pathophobia	Disease
Anthropophobia	Men	Pyrophobia	Fire
Aquaphobia	Water	Thanatophobia	Death
Astraphobia	Storms, thunder, and lightning	Xenophobia	Strangers
Claustrophobia	Closed places	Zoophobia	Animals
Cynophobia	Dogs		

The desk of a person with an obsessive-compulsive disorder will be orderly to an extreme degree. Every apparent element—the scheduling of events, the writing pads and pens ritualistically laid out—is an attempt to alleviate anxiety.

avoiding germs may wash his hands one hundred times a day and wear white gloves to avoid touching contaminated objects. If these compulsive acts are not performed, the person may develop severe anxiety. A woman obsessed with punctuality may become extremely anxious if dinner guests arrive five minutes late. Writing notes is ordinarily helpful in organizing one's life, but one can overdo it as we see from the following account:

> I used to write notes to remind myself to do a particular job, so in my mind there was a real risk that one of these notes might go out of the window or door. . . . My fear was that if one of these papers blew away, this would cause a fatality to the person carrying out my design project. . . . I found it difficult to walk along the street, as every time I saw paper I wondered if it was some of mine. I had to pick it all up, unless it was brown chocolate paper, or lined paper, which I didn't use. And before I got on my bike, I checked that nothing was sticking out of my pocket and got my wife to re-check. . . . I would have to sit in a certain seat on the bus so that, when I walked downstairs, I could look back up and check that no papers were on the seat. I couldn't smoke a cigarette without taking it to bits and checking there was no document between the paper and tobacco. I couldn't even have sex because I thought a piece of paper might get intertwined into the mattress. . . . (MELVILLE, 1977, PP. 66–67)

Freud and other psychodynamic theorists believed that the obsessive-compulsive disorder comes largely from difficulties during the anal stage of development when orderliness and cleanliness are often stressed. Learning theorists argue that bringing order to a person's environment reduces uncertainty and risk and thus is reinforcing. Since reinforced behaviors tend to recur, these behaviors become exaggerated during times of stress. Biologically-oriented theorists believe that factors including chronic elevated levels of arousal are implicated (Turner, Beidel and Nathan, 1985).

Practitioners report that true obsessive-compulsive disorders are relatively rare. Treatment often includes drugs (such as Prosac) in combination with relaxation exercises, as well as helping people change their ideas about stress and the consequences of anxiety (e.g., Christensen, Hadzi-Pavlovic, Andrews, and Mattick, 1987). While obsessive-compulsive disorders are rare, they are relatively easy to understand; today, self-help groups and a greater awareness of the disorder are leading to treatment. Somatoform and dissociative disorders discussed next are also rare, but in some important ways, they are harder to understand and treat.

Focus on Learning

- What are the goals of DSM-III-R and what are its advantages and disadvantages? p. 503
- What are the key characteristics and symptoms of a generalized anxiety disorder? p. 505
- Identify the key characteristics and symptoms of agoraphobia and obsessive-compulsive disorder. p. 506

Somatoform and Dissociative Disorders

If you were a television writer for a soap opera, you might have on your desk a copy of DSM-III-R with the page turned to somatoform and dissociative disorders. These disorders are relatively rare and are studied less than other disorders, but they make for fascinating reading and study. They are naturals for interesting television storylines.

Somatoform Disorders

Somatoform disorders involve real physical symptoms, often pain, that are not under voluntary control and for which no apparent physical cause exists. Evidence suggests that the causes are psychological. Two types of somatoform disorders are somatization disorder and conversion disorder.

Somatization Disorder. **Somatization disorders** involve recurrent and multiple complaints of several years' duration for which medical attention has not been effective. Those with the disorder, however, tend to seek medical attention at least once a year. The disorder typically begins before age thirty, and is diagnosed in only about one percent of females and is even rarer in males. Patients feel sickly for a good part of their lives and may report muscle weakness, double vision, memory loss, and hallucinations. Other commonly reported symptoms include: gastrointestinal problems such as vomiting and diarrhea, painful menstrual periods with excessive bleeding, sexual indifference, and pains in the back, chest, and genitals. Patients are often beset by anxiety and depression. Individuals with somatization disorders often have a host of emotional problems that cause their medical complaints; unfortunately, some of the medical conditions are not psychologically caused, and physicians must be especially careful to treat medically those conditions that need treatment and not dismiss all the patient's problems as psychological.

Conversion Disorder. **Conversion disorders** are the loss or alteration of physical functioning for no apparent physiological reason. People suffering from conversion disorders often lose the use of their arms, hands, or legs, or their vision or another sensory modality. They may develop a combination of ailments. For example, a patient may not only become blind but also deaf, mute, or totally paralyzed.

Although the patient may be unaware of the relationship, conversion disorders are generally considered a way to escape or avoid upsetting situations. Also, the huge amount of attention and support patients sometimes receive because of the symptoms may cause them to maintain the disorder. Conversion disorders are often associated with a history of psychosomatic illness. Men and women are equally likely to develop a conversion disorder, but, like somatization disorder, it is rare.

Hypochondriasis. When a person spends a lot of time going to a physician with all types of bodily complaints for which the physician can find no cause, psychologists suspect hypochondriasis. **Hypochondriasis** is the inordinate preoccupation with health and illness coupled with an excessive concern and anxiety about disease. Such individuals feel that they have grave afflictions. They become preoccupied with minor aches and pains and often miss work and create alarm among family members. Every ache, every minor symptom is examined, interpreted, and feared.

Psychodynamic views of hypochondriasis focus on how the symptoms of the illness keep the person from dealing with some other painful source of stress in his or her life. Behavioral psychologists focus on how the illness can be reinforcing: people are given extra attention and care, and the illness

Somatoform disorder: A disorder characterized by real physical symptoms not under voluntary control and for which no evident physical cause exists.

Somatization disorder: A disorder characterized by recurrent and multiple complaints of several years' duration for which medical attention is ineffective.

Conversion disorder: A disorder characterized by the loss or alteration of physical functioning not due to a physiological disorder, but apparently due to internal psychological conflict.

Hypochondriasis: The inordinate preoccupation with health and illness coupled with excessive anxiety about disease.

diverts attention from other tasks at which the individual may not be succeeding. By focusing on his or her illness, a person may avoid marital problems, financial affairs, and educational goals. Of course, to the hypochondriac the fears and anxiety are real, and only through therapy can the true causes of the overattention to symptoms be dealt with.

Dissociative Disorders

Dissociative disorders involve a sudden but temporary alteration in consciousness, identity, or memory. These disorders are quite noticeable and vivid, although relatively rare.

Psychogenic Amnesia. Psychogenic amnesia, one of several dissociative disorders, used to be grouped with hysterical neuroses. But today psychologists recognize it as a separate disorder. **Psychogenic amnesia** is the sudden inability to recall important personal information. The memory loss is too extensive to be explained by ordinary forgetfulness. Often, the amnesia is brought on by traumatic incidents involving threat of physical injury or death. The condition, relatively rare, is more common during wars or natural disasters and is assumed to be caused by high levels of stress or extreme reactions to a traumatic life event.

Multiple Personality. Another form of dissociative disorder, often associated with psychogenic amnesia but presenting a dramatically different kind of behavior, is multiple personality. A diagnosis of **multiple personality** is made when two or more distinct personalities, each of which is dominant at particular times, exist in a single person. Each personality has a unique style with different memories and behavioral patterns. For example, one personality may be adaptive and efficient at coping with life, while another may exhibit maladaptive behavior. Some people's alternate personalities are of the opposite sex.

Each personality is usually unaware of any other one, although in some cases they eavesdrop on each other (Schacter et al., 1989). The different personalities (when active) acknowledge that time has passed but cannot account for it. The switch from one to the other is usually brought on by stress.

Despite popular movies and books, such as *The Three Faces of Eve* and *Sybil*, multiple personality as a diagnosed disorder is extremely rare, with less than three hundred actual recorded cases in history. The mass media and lay people often confuse multiple personality with schizophrenia, a much more common disorder discussed later in this chapter. Psychologists have little data on the causes of multiple personality and debate how it might best be classified (see Greaves, 1980). There is even controversy as to whether multiple personality actually exists. Some psychologists think that some people invent multiple personalities to avoid taking responsibility for their own behavior, especially in criminal cases; other researchers think that some therapists subtly encourage patients to show symptoms of this disorder so that they (the therapists) might achieve some recognition. Multiple personality is a well-known disorder, vivid and interesting, and much more research is needed before comprehensive theories and effective treatments are available. Multiple personality is sometimes confused with personality disorders that exhibit a different set of symptoms. We consider them next.

Dissociative disorder: A disorder characterized by a sudden temporary alteration in consciousness, identity, or motor behavior.

Psychogenic amnesia: A disorder characterized by the sudden inability, too extensive to be explained by ordinary forgetfulness, to recall important personal information.

Multiple personality: A disorder characterized by the existence within an individual of two or more different personalities, each of which is dominant and directs the individual's behavior at distinct times.

Personality Disorders

People who are inflexible and have long-standing maladaptive ways of relating to the environment may be diagnosed as having a **personality disorder.** Often these disorders begin in childhood or adolescence and persist throughout adulthood. People with personality disorders are easy to spot but difficult to treat because they do not have obvious symptoms or exhibit anxiety or tension—they are just being themselves.

Types of Personality Disorders

People with personality disorders are divided into three broad types: those whose behavior appears odd or eccentric, fearful or anxious, or dramatic, emotional, and erratic. We will consider four specific personality disorders: paranoid, dependent, histrionic, and antisocial.

Paranoid Personality Disorder. People who have unwarranted feelings of persecution and who mistrust almost everyone are said to have paranoid personality disorder. They are hypersensitive to criticism and have a restricted range of emotional responses. They have strong fears of losing control and independence. Sometimes they appear cold, humorless, and even scheming. As you might expect, people with paranoid personality disorder are seldom able to form close, intimate relationships with others.

Dependent Personality Disorder. Fearful or anxious behaviors are characteristic of people with a dependent personality disorder. Such people let others make all important decisions in their lives. They try to appear pleasant and agreeable at all times. They act meek, humble, and affectionate in order to keep their protectors. Battered wives often suffer from the dependent personality disorder.

Histrionic Personality Disorder. The histrionic personality disorder is characterized by dramatic, emotional, and erratic behaviors. These people seek attention by exaggerating situations in their lives. They have stormy personal relationships, are excessively emotional, and demand reassurance and praise.

Closely related to the histrionic personality disorder is the *narcissistic personality disorder.* People with this disorder have an extreme sense of self-importance, an expectation of special favors, a constant need for attention, and a lack of caring for others and react to criticism with rage, shame, or humiliation.

Antisocial Personality Disorder

Perhaps the most widely recognized personality disorder is the **antisocial personality disorder,** whose victims exhibit dramatic, emotional, or erratic behaviors. Although exhibiting destructive and often reckless behavior, such individuals often go unnoticed due to their superficial charm.

A person who frequently changes jobs, does not take proper care of his or her children, is arrested often, fails to pay bills, and lies constantly displays behaviors described in the DSM-III-R as typical of antisocial personality disorder. Such people are relatively unsocialized adults, unwilling to conform

Personality disorder: Inflexible, long-standing, maladaptive behaviors in dealing with the environment that typically cause stress and social or occupational problems.

Antisocial personality disorder: A disorder beginning before age fifteen and characterized by continuous and chronic behavior that violates the rights of other people through lying, theft, delinquency, and other violations of societal rules. The individual lacks feelings of guilt, cannot understand other people, behaves irresponsibly, does not fear punishment, and is often egocentric.

to and live by society's rules, and their behavior often brings them into conflict with society. Antisocial people consistently blame others for their behavior. They seldom feel guilt or learn from experience or punishment. The disorder occurs six times more often in men than in women. Extreme forms are displayed by cold-blooded killers like Charles Manson or Ted Bundy, although most antisocial personalities reveal their sociopathy through less deadly and sensational means.

Nature or Nurture? Adopted children separated at birth from antisocial parents are likely to show antisocial behavior later in life (Cadoret, 1978). This suggests a genetic contribution to the disorder. Another fact that suggests a genetic cause is that the nervous systems of people diagnosed as having antisocial personality disorders may be different from those of normal people. When normal people do something wrong, their autonomic nervous system reacts with symptoms of anxiety, such as fear, heart palpitations, and sweating. Evidence suggests that *decreased* autonomic arousal is characteristic in antisocial personality disorders (Waid, 1976). These people do not function at sufficiently high levels of autonomic nervous system arousal, do not experience the physiological symptoms of anxiety, and thus do not learn to associate those symptoms with antisocial behavior.

On the nurture side, some psychologists believe that child-rearing practices and unstable family situations render individuals with an antisocial personality disorder unable to learn fear, guilt, and punishment avoidance. Such people seem to have learned maladaptive behaviors from their family situations and consequently to have developed inappropriate behaviors. If the environmental viewpoint is correct, then antisocial personality disorder may be a learned behavior. The symptoms of antisocial personality disorder often are seen first in a person's home environment in interactions with family members. Unfortunately, family relationships become strained, and some people suffering with the disorder may become involved in domestic violence and/or child abuse, discussed next.

Psychology and Social Work: Child Abuse

Child abuse is not a DSM-III-R personality disorder, but many child abusers suffer from personality disorders. **Child abuse,** which involves physical, emotional, or sexual mistreatment of children, has been implicated in the development of the antisocial personality disorder. Fifty percent of the families reported for abuse or neglect in New York had at least one child who was later taken to court for conduct disorders or for being ungovernable (Alfaro, 1981). Social workers are on the front lines: They are the practitioners who refer children, their families, and abusers to therapy. Often they are trained in family therapy and provide treatment. Psychiatric social workers are trained in psychological principles to deal with such issues as child, spousal, and sexual abuse.

Child abuse is clearly an important psychological and social problem. Between 350,000 and two million children in the United States are the victims of abuse each year (Helfer, 1987); 1200 children die each year from child abuse and neglect. Research shows that of all the reported cases of child abuse, thirty to forty percent are substantiated by professionals such as social workers (Eckenrode et al., 1988). And not all cases are reported; even some treated cases go unreported by therapists, although they are bound by law to report them (Kalichman, Craig, and Follingstad, 1989).

Child abuse: Physical, emotional, or sexual mistreatment of children.

Prevention of child abuse is more likely when an entire family is willing to consider changing behavior patterns.

The Child Abuser. Who are the child abusers? Only about five percent of child abusers exhibit symptoms of very disturbed behavior. The view of the typical child abuser as a deranged parent is put forth by television shows and the movies (Wolfe, 1985). Most abusive parents seem quite normal by traditional social standards and sometimes have a prominent place in the community.

A distinction must be made between those who physically abuse children and those who sexually abuse them. Physically abusive parents often have unusually high expectations of their children and distorted perceptions of their children's behavior. They are generally less satisfied with their children than nonabusive parents and perceive child-rearing as more difficult than do nonabusive parents (Trickett and Susman, 1988). Abusive parents are not necessarily more discipline-oriented, power-oriented, or authoritarian with their children, but they tend to rely on ineffective child-management techniques, including aversive control, blaming, scapegoating, threats, verbal degradations, and physical punishment (Emery, 1989). Parents who were abused as children are far more likely to be abusers themselves, especially if they do not have a stable, emotionally satisfying, supportive relationship with a mate (Egeland, Jacobvitz, and Sroufe, 1988). Research indicates that thirty to fifty percent of all abusive parents were themselves abused as children (Kaufman and Zigler, 1987).

Prevention. Most psychologists and social workers consider child abuse an interactive process, involving parental incompetence, environmental stress, and poor child-management techniques. Therefore, both psychologists and social workers focus on changing family systems and patterns of interaction (Emery, 1989). Parents can be taught different coping skills, impulse control, effective child-management techniques, and ways to interact with their children constructively. These techniques applied in an early intervention program for parents at risk of child abuse produce encouraging results. Children of potentially abusive parents who have undergone such therapy have fewer and less-intense behavior problems (Wolfe, Edwards, Manion, and Koverola, 1988). School-based prevention programs focus on education and keeping abuse from ever occurring, as well as reporting ongoing or past abuse. Evaluations of such programs are equivocal; Repucci and Haugaard (1989)

Rape: Forcible, sexual assault of an unwilling partner who is usually, but not always, a woman.

conclude, "We cannot be sure whether prevention programs are working, nor can we be sure that they are doing more good than harm" (p. 1274). These researchers argue that extensive investigation of the full range of preventive efforts is urgent. It is impossible not to concur.

Rape

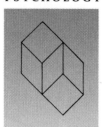

*R*ape is not a DSM-III-R classification. Rape is a crime, often involving an individual with an antisocial personality disorder. **Rape** is forcible sexual assault of an unwilling partner, usually a woman (c.f. Myers, 1989). Most rapes are planned, often in a meticulous manner; they are generally not impulsive acts prompted by a spur-of-the-moment sexual or aggressive feeling. Rape should be considered a violent crime rather than a sexual crime. Labeling rape a sexual assault obscures the violent, brutal nature of the crime and often places the woman on the defensive in the courtroom—*even though she was the victim.*

More than 91,000 cases of rape were reported during 1987, according to the FBI, but many experts assert that this is only one-fourth of the actual number. For example, one research study found that twenty-seven percent of college women had experienced situations in which rape was attempted, and 7.5 percent of college men reported initiating acts that meet the definition of rape (Koss, Gidycz, and Wisniewski, 1987). Although these results are not generalizable to the entire population, rape or attempted rape seems to be far more common than previously believed. Today on college campuses, rape or attempted rape by an acquaintance—sometimes known as date rape—is receiving increased attention; many rape victims know their assailants.

The Rapist. Because rape is such a violent crime, it has come under the critical eye of researchers who have sought to understand the characteristics and motivations of the rapist. Certain facts about rapists are coming into focus. They tend to be young, often between fifteen and twenty-five (Sadock, 1980). Often, rapists are poor, culturally disadvantaged, and uneducated. Many have willing sexual partners and half are married, although their high level of aggressiveness probably precludes a happy and stable marriage or relationship.

Rapists may have some history of sexual dysfunctions, but this finding is not consistent across all studies. Rapists often have committed another sex-related offense, although this finding as well is not consistent across all studies (Furby, Weinrott, and Blackshaw, 1989). They tend to be more responsive to violence than are other men (Quinsey et al., 1984) and less able to understand cues and messages from women who say no. Levels of maladjustment of rapists vary from slight to extreme when measured on psychological tests (Kalichman et al., 1989) and men who assault women and rape them often do not view their attack as rape, but rather as a "mere" assault (Bourque, 1989). Remember, rape is an act of violence; it is not considered a psychosexual disorder like the ones considered in the next section. ◆

Sexual Disorders

Few behaviors arouse more anxiety, fear, and superstition than those involving human sexuality. But many sexual problems, such as orgasmic dysfunction, are often temporary symptoms of some other type of problem that is not sexual in nature, such as anxiety or poor communication between partners. We considered some of the sexual dysfunctions in chapter 11 when we examined sexual motivation (p. 388). We now consider disorders referred to as sexual disorders that focus on sexual behavior.

Sexual deviations (called *paraphilias* in DSM-III-R) are sexual practices directed toward objects rather than people, sexual encounters involving real or simulated suffering or humiliation, or sexual activities with nonconsenting partners. DSM-III-R classifies only a few true sexual deviations; some researchers, however, maintain that there are many more (Money, 1984). A diagnosis of sexual deviation is made when the causes are psychological rather than physical and when these behaviors are the primary source of sexual stimulation or gratification for the individual.

The following are some unconventional sexual activities that characterize sexual disorders. **Fetishism,** which is more common in men, involves sexual arousal and gratification brought about by objects rather than by people. For example, a man may have a fetish about a woman's shoes and receive sexual gratification from them instead of from her.

In **transvestic fetishism,** also known as transvestism or *cross-dressing*, a male receives sexual gratification by dressing in the clothing of a woman. (The number of females so diagnosed is very small.) Interference with this cross-dressing produces frustration. Transvestites consider themselves members of their own sex and most are heterosexual.

A person who achieves sexual satisfaction by watching other people in different states of undress or sexual activity is practicing **voyeurism.** Most voyeurs, or "peeping Toms," are men. Because voyeurs generally do not want to be seen, some researchers suggest that they are excited by the risk of discovery involved in watching other people. Another unconventional sexual activity is **exhibitionism,** in which adult males expose their genitals to unsuspecting observers, who are almost always female. Exhibitionists find the startled reactions of their victims sexually arousing.

Some people derive sexual satisfaction through sexual contact with children, a disorder known as **pedophilia.** Most pedophiles are well-acquainted with the child; sometimes they are even close relatives. Many are married and seemingly well-adjusted, both sexually and socially. Pedophiles may

Sexual deviations: Sexual practices directed toward objects rather than people, sexual encounters involving real or simulated suffering or humiliation, or sexual activity with a nonconsenting partner.

Fetishism: A sexual disorder in which sexual arousal and gratification are brought about by objects.

Transvestic fetishism: A sexual disorder characterized by recurrent and persistent cross-dressing for the purpose of achieving sexual excitement.

Voyeurism: A sexual disorder in which the preferred method of sexual gratification consists of repetitive observations of people in different states of undress or sexual activity.

Exhibitionism: A sexual disorder in which the preferred method of sexual stimulation and gratification consists of repetitive acts of exposing the genitals to strangers.

Pedophilia: A sexual disorder in which the preferred method of sexual gratification consists of repetitive sexual activity with children.

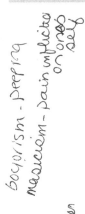

The men in this support group for cross-dressers take pleasure in posing as women even though they do not question their own sexual indentities.

Sexual sadism: A sexual disorder in which an individual inflicts physical or psychological pain on another person in order to achieve sexual excitement.

Sexual masochism: A sexual disorder in which an individual seeks physical or psychological pain, often including humiliation or being bound or beaten, to achieve sexual excitement.

suffer from loneliness or schizophrenia (Regestein and Reich, 1978). Fifty percent were themselves sexually abused as children.

Two other types of paraphilia are **sexual sadism** and **sexual masochism.** A sadist achieves sexual gratification by inflicting pain on a sexual partner. A masochist achieves sexual gratification from experiencing pain inflicted by someone else. Sadists and masochists are often sexual partners; the sadist provides the pain for the masochist and both achieve sexual satisfaction. The pain involved can be physical or emotional.

Nature or Nurture? Most psychologists agree that sexual disorders are learned behaviors. According to Freudians, problems during the Oedipal period create sexual problems later in life. Most behavioral practitioners agree in part with Freud, saying that sexual deviants are people whose normal sex-role stereotyping went haywire early in their lives. They argue that a difficult adolescence and a poor emerging self-concept are learning factors that may predispose an individual to sexual disorders. Individuals who had a difficult time with their parents and peers, for example, may exhibit some of those problems through sexual disorders when they are adults. Often, anger, hostility, shame, and self-doubt are present in people who suffer from sexual disorders.

Unfortunately the causes and treatment of sexual disorders have not been studied much. Thus, psychologists know less than they would like about biological and environmental contributions. Most practitioners focus on behavioral treatments and teaching people new, more adaptive ways of expressing feelings, fears, and sexual urges. These techniques can be effective and do not require hospitalization or drug therapy, unlike treatment for some of the more debilitating disorders considered in the remainder of this chapter.

Focus on Learning

- Distinguish between conversion disorders and somatization disorders. p. 509
- Identify the key characteristics of the antisocial personality disorder. pp. 511–512
- Identify characteristics of child abusers and distinguish them from the characteristics of rapists. p. 512
- Provide a definition of sexual deviations; distinguish between sadism and masochism. pp. 514–516

Mood Disorders

All of us experience depression at one time or another. Ending a long-term intimate relationship, feeling overwhelmed during final exams, mourning the death of a close friend, and experiencing serious financial problems are all sources of depression. When people become so depressed or sad that a change occurs in their outlook and overt behavior, they may be suffering from depression. Depression is considered by DSM-III-R a type of mood disorder (previously known as affective disorders). Depression is often caused or at least initiated by a specific event, although for many individuals the symptoms occur gradually. There are two major types of mood disorders that involve depression: bipolar disorders and depressive disorders.

Bipolar Disorders

Gustav Mahler, the nineteenth-century Austrian composer-conductor, apparently suffered from a bipolar disorder. At age nineteen he wrote to a friend:

> Much has happened within me since my last letter; I cannot describe it. Only this: I have become a different person. I don't know whether this new person is better; he certainly is not happier. The fires of a supreme zest for living and the most gnawing desire for death alternate in my heart, sometimes in the course of a single hour.

Originally bipolar disorders were called manic/depressive disorders, but that term is no longer used. **Bipolar disorder** gets its name from the fact that patients' behavior vacillates between two extremes—mania and depression. The manic phase is characterized by rapid speech, inflated self-esteem, distractibility, impulsiveness, and decreased need for sleep. Patients in a manic phase are easily distracted, get angry when things do not go their way, and seem to have boundless energy. A person in the depressed phase, which often follows the manic phase, is moody and sad, with feelings of hopelessness.

Almost two million Americans suffer from bipolar disorders, which typically begin in late adolescence and continue throughout life. Patients can be relatively normal for a few days, weeks, or months in between episodes of excitement and depression. Or they can rapidly vacillate between excitement and depression. The key component of bipolar disorders is the shift from mania or excited states to depressive states of sadness and hopelessness. Although Mahler's manic depression started much earlier, people who suffer bipolar disorders are often in their late twenties before they begin to manifest symptoms. The disorder seems to have a biological basis (Leber, Beckham, and Danker-Brown, 1985), with patients responding fairly well to drug treatment, especially to Lithium (which will be discussed in the next chapter). Table 14.3 lists the signs and symptoms of mania and depression in bipolar disorders.

Bipolar disorder: A disorder characterized by vacillation between two extremes, mania and depression; originally called manic/depressive disorder.

TABLE 14.3
Bipolar Disorder Involves Cycles of Mania and Depression

	Manic Behavior	Depressive Behavior
Emotional characteristics	Elated, euphoric Very sociable, expansive Impatient	Gloomy, hopeless Socially withdrawn Irritable, indecisive

Cognitive characteristics	Distractible
	Desire for action
	Impulsive
	Talkative
	Grandiose
	Inflated self-esteem
		Slowness of thought
		Obsessive worrying
		  about death
		Negative self-image
		Delusions of guilt
		Difficulty
		  concentrating

Motor characteristics	Hyperactive Decreased need for sleep Sexual indiscretion Fluctuating appetite	Decreased motor activity Fatigue Difficulty in sleeping Decreased sex drive Decreased appetite

Depressive disorders: A general category of disorders in which people show extreme and persistent sadness, despair, and loss of interest in life's usual activities.

Major depression: A disorder characterized by loss of interest in almost all usual activities as evidenced by a sad, hopeless, or discouraged mood. Other symptoms include sleep disturbance, loss of appetite, loss of energy, and feelings of unworthiness and guilt; a subtype of depressive disorders.

Delusion: False beliefs, inconsistent with reality, held in spite of evidence to the contrary.

Depressive Disorder: Major Depression

Bonnie Strickland, former president of the American Psychological Association, said during 1988 APA meetings, "Depression has been called the common cold of psychological disturbances . . . which underscores its prevalence, but trivializes its impact." Strickland noted that at any one time there are about fourteen million people suffering from this disabling disorder. The main difference between **depressive disorders** and bipolar disorders is that people with depressive disorders show no vacillation between excitement and depression; they tend to be depressed constantly. **Major depression,** one of a series of depressive disorders, is eight times more common than bipolar disorders.

The essential characteristics of major depression are a depressed, sad, hopeless mood and a loss of interest in all or almost all usual activities and pastimes. Someone experiencing a major depression is experiencing not merely fleeting anxiety with sadness but displays a relatively extreme reaction to a specific event, such as the loss of a loved one, job, or home, or a failure in life. People experiencing a major depression show at least some impairment of social and occupational functioning, although their behavior is not necessarily bizarre.

Symptoms. Depressed individuals experience symptoms such as poor appetite, insomnia, weight loss, loss of energy, feelings of worthlessness, intense guilt, inability to concentrate, difficulty sleeping, and sometimes thoughts of death and suicide. They have a gloomy outlook on life, especially slow thought processes, an extremely distorted view of current problems, and a tendency to blame themselves (Silberman, Weingartner, and Post, 1983). Depressed people often withdraw from social and physical contact with others. Every task seems to require a great effort.

Depressed people may also have **delusions** or false beliefs that induce feelings of guilt, shame, and persecution. Seriously disturbed patients show even greater disruptions in thought and motor processes (Weingartner et al., 1981) and a total lack of spontaneity and motivation (Cohen et al., 1982). Such patients typically report that they have no hope for themselves or the world; nothing seems to interest them. Some feel responsible for severe world problems, such as economic depression, disease, or hunger. They report strange diseases and may insist that their body is disintegrating or that their brain is being eaten from the inside out. Most people who exhibit symptoms of a major depression can describe their reasons for feeling sad and dejected, but they may be unable to explain why their response is so deep and so prolonged.

Psychologists say that people suffering from major depression are poor at reality testing. *Reality testing* is a person's ability to accurately judge the demands of the environment and his or her ability to deal with those demands. People with poor reality testing are unable to cope with the demands of life in rational ways because their reasoning ability is grossly impaired.

Onset and Duration of Depressive Episodes. A major depressive episode can occur at any age, although major depression usually first occurs before age forty. Symptoms are rapidly apparent and last for a few days, weeks, or months. Because so many circumstances can bring about a depressive reaction, the extent of depression varies dramatically from individual to individual. Episodes may occur once or many times. Sometimes depressive episodes are separated by years of normal functioning followed by two or three brief episodes of depression a few weeks apart. Stressful life events are not good predictions of depression (Swindle, Cronkite, and Moos, 1989). It is important to recognize that depression is not exclusively an adult disorder. Many researchers have found evidence of depression in children.

Children. Research on depression in children is controversial. Lefkowitz and Tessiny (1985) found that five percent of elementary school children were depressed. But although few researchers disagree that children can become sad, some maintain that they do not exhibit true depressive behaviors (Hodges and Siegel, 1985). However, Kovacs (1989) asserts that mood disorders such as depression are persistent and more common than once thought. She asserts that children can exhibit some forms of depression, and generally meet the DSM-III-R criteria for it. When children show depression, they often show other symptoms, especially anxiety and loneliness (Larson et al., 1990). This work remains controversial, and treatment plans must be flexible and account for the wide array of family situations in which children find themselves—divorce or foster homes or an environment of alcoholism or child abuse, for example.

Prevalence. Women, as teenagers and adults, are twice as likely as men to be diagnosed as depressed and are more likely to express feelings of depression openly (Blumenthall, 1975; Allgood-Merten, Lewinsohn, and Hops, 1990). In the United States, about nineteen to twenty-three percent of women and eight to eleven percent of men have experienced a major depressive episode at some time. About six percent of women and three percent of men have experienced episodes sufficiently severe to require hospitalization.

According to a number of studies, Americans born around 1960 suffer up to ten times the incidence of major depression as did their grandparents or great-grandparents. Moreover, people in developing cultures are far less likely to develop the passivity, feelings of hopelessness, diminished self-esteem, and suicidal tendencies that typify Westerners afflicted by major depression. Do you agree or disagree with Seligman (1988), who suggests that the increased incidence of depression in the United States stems from too much emphasis on the individual, coupled with a loss of faith in such supportive institutions as family, country, and religion?

Clinical Evaluation. How does a practitioner know if a person is depressed? A complete clinical evaluation involves three parts: a physical examination, a psychiatric history, and a mental status examination. A *physical examination* is given to rule out thyroid disorders, viral infection, or anemia—all of which cause a slowing down of behavior. A neurological exam checking coordination, reflexes, and balance is part of this exam, to rule out brain disorders. A *psychiatric history* attempts to trace the course of the potential illness, genetic or family factors, and past treatments. Finally, *a mental status examination* examines thought, speaking processes, and memory, and includes interviews, tests for psychiatric symptoms including the MMPI-2, and projective tests such as the TAT.

Theories of Depression

Most psychologists believe that depression is caused by a combination of biological, learning, and cognitive factors. Biological theories suggest that chemical and genetic processes can account for depression. Learning theories suggest that people develop faulty behaviors. Cognitive theories suggest that irrational ideas guide behavior. We will examine each theory in more detail next.

Biological Theories. Are people born with a predisposition to depression? Depression may be biologically or genetically based, according to McNeal and Cimbolic (1986). Weissman et al. (1987) found that children of depressed patients are more likely to be depressed themselves. Other researchers discovered the *norepinephrine hypothesis,* which states that an insufficient amount of norepinephrine (a neurotransmitter in the brain; see chapter 2) may cause depression. Research has shown that if the level of norepinephrine at the receptor site in the brain is increased, depression is alleviated (e.g., Buchsbaum et al., 1978). Since aversive stimuli decrease norepinephrine levels, however, being in a stressful situation could bring about depression. Recent research suggests that although the norepinephrine hypothesis is not false, the biological underpinnings of depression are more complex. That is, depression may be caused by many other substances in the brain, in addition to norepinephrine, that are not functioning properly.

Other evidence for a biological explanation of depression is that antidepressant drugs (tricyclics) seem to help certain types of depressed patients. In one study (DiMascio et al., 1979), severely depressed patients were given one of three treatments: psychotherapy alone, an antidepressant drug alone, or a combination of psychotherapy and drug therapy. The results were dramatic. When compared with a group of control subjects who were not depressed, psychotherapy and drug therapy were equally effective in reducing depressive symptoms. However, a combination of psychotherapy and drug therapy helped most.

Learning and Cognitive Theories. Learning and cognitive theorists argue that people who are depressed learn depressive behaviors and thoughts. People with poor social skills who never learn to express prosocial behaviors and who are punished for the behaviors they do exhibit experience the world as aversive and depressing. For example, Peter Lewinsohn (1974) believes that people who have few positive reinforcements in their lives (often the old, sickly, and poor) become depressed. Other people find them unpleasant and avoid them, thus creating a nonreinforcing environment (Lewinsohn and Talkington, 1979). Lewinsohn stresses that depressed people often lack the social skills needed to obtain reinforcement, such as asking a neighbor or friend for help with a problem. See Figure 14.1 for a summary of this process.

Psychiatrist Aaron Beck has proposed another influential learning theory. Beck suggests that depressed people already have negative views of themselves, the environment, and the future, which cause them to magnify their errors. They compare themselves to other people, usually unfairly, and when they come up short, they see the difference as disastrous. They see the human condition as universally wretched, become angry (Riley, Treiser, and Woods, 1989), and view the world as a place that defeats positive behavior. Their poor self-concept, along with negative expectations about the world, produces negative future expectations that lead to depression.

Beck (1967, 1972, 1976) believes that depression does not cause negative feelings but that negative feelings and expectation *cause* depression. Research supports Beck's theory. Depressed people are harsher on themselves than nondepressed people are, and they have particularly low levels of self-expectation (Space and Cromwell, 1980). They make judgments based on in-

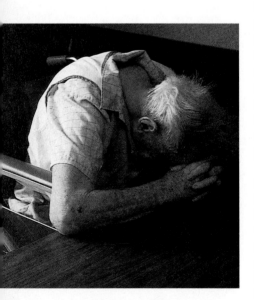

With few positive reinforcements in their lives, the elderly often become depressed and further alienate those people who could be caring for them.

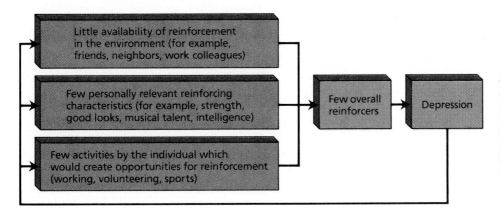

FIGURE 14.1
According to Lewinsohn, few reinforcers in the environment are available for some people and this causes depression, which then leads to even fewer reinforcers.

sufficient data, they overgeneralize, and they exaggerate the negative outcomes in their lives. Being depressed causes poor judgments and thus affects people's cognitions. Beck's theory is influential among psychologists because it is consistent with the notion that depression stems from a lack of appropriate (positive) reinforcements in people's environments and because it acknowledges both cognitive *and* environmental variables.

Learned Helplessness. What happens when a person's hopes and dreams are constantly thwarted, regardless of his or her behavior? What would you do if you failed every exam you took, regardless of your efforts? **Learned helplessness** (discussed in more detail in chapter 16) results when a person learns that rewards and punishments are not contingent on behavior. Faced with a loss of control, some people stop responding.

In one version of learned helplessness, Seligman (1976) suggested that people's beliefs about the causes of their successes or failures determine whether they become depressed. When they attribute their mistakes or failures to conditions within themselves ("my own weakness, which is unlikely to change"), they come to regard themselves with low self-esteem (Raps et al., 1982). That is, when they believe that eventual outcomes are unrelated to anything in their control, people develop learned helplessness. For example, a man who comes to believe that his effort to meet new people by being outgoing and friendly never works, may stop trying. Eventually, he will choose not to respond to the environment because he has learned that his behavior makes no difference (Peterson and Seligman, 1984). Seligman (1988) argues that the environment, rather than genetics, is the cause of depression and helplessness, especially when people believe they are the cause of long-standing failures in many areas of their lives.

The effects of helplessness and depression are poignant and painful. They influence the day-to-day life of the individual, the work environment, and the person's family. These factors and more become especially apparent when studying an even more disabling disorder, schizophrenia.

Learned helplessness: The behavior of giving up or not responding, exhibited by subjects exposed to negative consequences or punishment over which they have no control.

- Identify the key characteristics of a bipolar disorder. p. 517
- What are the essential characteristics of major depression? p. 518
- Describe how the norepinephrine hypothesis accounts for depression. p. 520
- From one learning or cognitive view of depression, explain how depression occurs. pp. 520–521

Focus on Learning

Schizophrenia

Schizophrenia is considered the most devastating, complex, and frustrating mental disorder; people with the disorder lose touch with reality and are often unable to function in a world that makes no sense to them. We often say that such individuals are psychotic; the term **psychotic** refers to the fact that the impairment is gross, and it hinders an individual's ability to meet the ordinary demands of life. Schizophrenia begins slowly, with more symptoms developing as time passes.

Schizophrenia affects one of every one hundred people in the United States. Almost twenty-five percent of patients admitted to mental hospitals each year are diagnosed as schizophrenic (Sartorious, 1982). The diagnosis occurs more frequently among lower socioeconomic groups and nonwhites (Kramer, 1982; Lindsay and Paul, 1989) and more frequently among younger rather than older people.

Essential Characteristics of Schizophrenia

People with a **schizophrenic disorder** display sudden changes in thought, perception, emotion (affect), and overall behavior. Those changes are often accompanied by distortions of reality. Further, there is usually an inability to respond appropriately in thought, perception, or emotion.

Thought Disorders. One of the first signs of schizophrenia is difficulty maintaining logical thought and coherent conversation. People with schizophrenia show disordered thinking and impaired memory (Sengel and Lovallo, 1983). They may have delusions (false beliefs held even in the face of contrary evidence). Many have delusions of persecution and believe that the world is a hostile place.

Delusions of persecution are often accompanied by delusions of grandeur: the patient believes he or she is a particularly important person. This importance becomes the reason for his or her persecution. Sometimes, for example, the patient takes on the role of an important character in history—General Douglas MacArthur, Jesus Christ, or the Queen of England—and deludes him- or herself that people are conspiring to harm him or her.

Perceptual Disorders. Another sign of schizophrenia is the presence of **hallucinations,** which may be visual, tactile, olfactory, or most commonly, auditory. The patient reports hearing voices originating outside his or her head. The voices may comment on the patient's behavior or direct the patient to behave in certain ways (Bentall, 1990). For example, convicted murderer David Berkowitz (known to the media as "Son of Sam") claimed that his neighbor's dog told him to kill. Hallucinations probably have a biological basis and are caused by abnormal brain responses (Assad and Shapiro, 1986).

Emotional Disorders. One of the most striking characteristics of schizophrenia is the display of inappropriate emotional responses, or **affect.** A patient with schizophrenia, for example, may become depressed and cry when her favorite food falls on the floor yet laugh hysterically at the death of a close friend or relative. Some patients show no emotion (either appropriate or inappropriate) and seem incapable of experiencing a normal range of feeling. Their emotional range is constricted, or *flat*. They show blank, expressionless faces, even when presented with a deliberately provocative remark or situation. Other patients show *ambivalent* affect. They have a wide

Psychotic: Behavior and mental processes in which there is a gross impairment of reality testing that interferes with an individual's ability to meet the ordinary demands of life.

Schizophrenic disorders: A group of disorders characterized by lack of reality testing and deterioration of social and intellectual functioning, beginning before age forty-five and lasting at least six months. Schizophrenics often show serious personality disintegration with significant changes in thought, mood, perception, and behavior.

Hallucinations: Compelling perceptual experiences without a real physical stimulus. They may be visual, tactile, olfactory, or most commonly in schizophrenia, auditory.

Affect: A person's emotional response.

range of emotional behaviors in a brief period, seeming happy one moment and sad and dejected the next. An ambivalent affect is usually caused by internal conflicts.

Types of Schizophrenia

The term *schizophrenia* is a catchall for patients displaying many symptoms, but there are actually five types of schizophrenia, each with different symptoms, diagnostic criteria, and causes: disorganized, paranoid, catatonic, residual, and undifferentiated. According to DSM-III-R, a diagnosis of schizophrenia, regardless of the subtype, requires the presence of the following features:

1. lack of reality testing
2. involvement of more than one area of psychological functioning,
3. deterioration in social and intellectual functioning,
4. onset of illness generally before age forty-five, and
5. duration of illness for at least six months.

Disorganized Type. The **disorganized type** of schizophrenia is characterized by severely disturbed thought processes. Patients have hallucinations and delusions and are frequently incoherent. They may exhibit bizarre emotions, with periods of giggling, crying, or irritability for no apparent reason. Their behavior can be silly, inappropriate, or even obscene. Such patients exhibit a severe disintegration of normal personality, a loss of reality testing, and often poor personal hygiene. Their chances for recovery are poor.

Paranoid Type. **Paranoid type** schizophrenics are among the most difficult to identify and study because their outward behavior often seems appropriate to the situation. They may actively seek out other people and not show extreme withdrawal from social interaction. The degree of disturbance of paranoid type patients varies over time. (Note that paranoid type schizophrenia is distinct from another disorder, paranoid delusion disorder, in which there is less likely to be a biological cause for the behavior.)

Paranoid patients may be alert, intelligent, and responsive, but their delusions and hallucinations impair their ability to deal with reality (see Kendler, 1980), and their behavior is often unpredictable and sometimes hostile. Patients diagnosed as paranoid types may see bizarre images and are likely to have auditory hallucinations. They may feel that they are being chased by ghosts or intruders from another planet. Paranoid type patients have extreme delusions of persecution and, occasionally, of grandeur. They may feel that certain events in the world have a particular significance to them. If, for example, the president of the United States makes a speech deploring crime, a paranoid type patient may believe that the president is referring specifically to the patient's crimes. Patients diagnosed as paranoid schizophrenics have a better chance of recovery than do patients with other subtypes of schizophrenia.

Catatonic Type. There are actually two subtypes of **catatonic type** schizophrenia—excited and withdrawn—both of which involve extreme overt behavior. *Excited* catatonic patients show excessive activity. They may talk and shout continuously and engage in seemingly uninhibited, agitated, and aggressive motor activity. These episodes usually appear and disappear sud-

Disorganized type: One of five major subtypes of schizophrenia, characterized by frequent incoherence, absence of systematized delusions, and blunted, inappropriate, or silly affect.

Paranoid type: One of five major subtypes of schizophrenia, characterized by delusions, hallucinations of persecution and/or grandeur, and sometimes irrational jealousy.

Catatonic type: One of five major subtypes of schizophrenia, characterized by stupor, in which the individual is mute, negative, and basically unresponsive, or by displays of excited or violent motor activity.

Residual type: A schizophrenic disorder characterized by inappropriate affect, illogical thinking, or eccentric behavior but with the patient generally in touch with reality.

Undifferentiated type: A schizophrenic disorder characterized by a mixture of symptoms.

denly. *Withdrawn* catatonic patients tend to appear stuporous, mute, and negative. Although they occasionally exhibit signs of the excited phase, they usually show a high degree of muscular rigidity. They are not immobile but have a decreased level of speaking, moving, and responding, although they are usually aware of events around them. Catatonic type patients may use immobility and unresponsiveness to maintain control over their environment since their behavior relieves them of the responsibility of responding to external stimuli.

Residual and Undifferentiated Type.

People who show symptoms attributable to schizophrenia but who remain in touch with reality are characterized as **residual type.** Such patients show inappropriate affect, illogical thinking, or eccentric behavior. They have a history of at least one previous schizophrenic episode.

Sometimes it is difficult to determine which category most appropriately describes a patient (Gift et al., 1980). Some patients exhibit all the essential features of schizophrenia—prominent delusions, hallucinations, incoherence, and grossly disorganized behavior—but do not fall into the categories of disorganized, catatonic, paranoid, or residual type. These individuals are classified as **undifferentiated type** (see Table 14.4).

Causes of Schizophrenia

What causes people to lose their grasp on reality with such devastating results? Are people born with schizophrenia or do they develop it as a result of painful childhood experiences? Theories of schizophrenia take markedly different positions about its origins. Biologically-oriented psychologists focus on chemicals in the brain and a person's genetic heritage—the basic argument is that schizophrenia is a brain disease (Johnson, 1989). Learning theorists argue that a person's environment and early experiences cause

Catatonic patients limit their physical movements until they are actually rigid. This behavior is accompanied by a general decrease in responsiveness even though they retain an awareness of the world around them.

TABLE 14.4
Types and Symptoms of Schizophrenic Disorders as Described in DSM-III-R

Classification	Symptoms
Disorganized	Frequent incoherence, absence of systematized delusions, and blunted, inappropriate, or silly affect
Paranoid	Delusions and hallucinations of persecution or grandeur, and/or unfounded jealousy
Catatonic	Stupor in which there is a marked decrease in reactivity to environment; or an excited phase in which there is excited motor activity, apparently purposeless and not influenced by external stimuli
Residual	History of at least one previous episode of schizophrenia with prominent psychotic symptoms but has at present a clinical picture without any prominent psychotic symptoms, and there is continuing evidence of the illness such as inappropriate affect, illogical thinking, social withdrawal, or eccentric behavior
Undifferentiated	Prominent delusions, hallucinations, incoherence, or grossly disorganized behavior *and* does not meet the criteria for any of the other types, or meets the criteria for more than one type

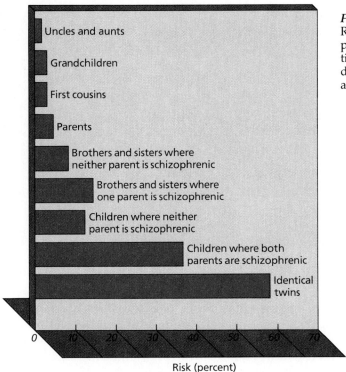

FIGURE 14.2
Risk of developing a schizo-phrenic disorder for rela-tives of a person with the diagnosis. (Source: Tsuang and Vandermey, 1980.)

schizophrenia. The arguments for each approach are compelling, and there are data to support each of the various theories.

Biological Causes. Evidence suggests the presence of some kind of bio-logical determinant or predisposition to schizophrenia (Farone and Tsuang, 1985). People born with that predisposition have a greater probability of developing schizophrenia than do other people; it is now generally accepted that schizophrenia runs in families (Holzman and Bivens, 1988). The children and siblings of schizophrenic patients are more likely to exhibit maladjust-ment and schizophrenic symptoms than are other people (Walker and Emory, 1983). About one percent of the U.S. population are schizophrenic, but when one parent has schizophrenia, the probability that an offspring also will have it increases to between three and fourteen percent. If both parents have schizophrenia, children have about a thirty-five percent probability of de-veloping it (D. Rosenthal, 1970) (see Figure 14.2). (Researchers are aware that the family environments of children of schizophrenics is typically un-usual, and they acknowledge that this evidence is only suggestive.)

However, if schizophrenia were totally genetic, then the likelihood that identical (monozygotic) twins, who have identical genes, would show the disorder would be one hundred percent. (This likelihood is referred to as the **concordance rate**.) Studies of schizophrenia in identical twins show con-cordance rates from zero to eighty-six percent (Dalby, Morgan, and Lee, 1986; Gottesman and Shields, 1982), suggesting that there are other factors involved.

Nevertheless, most researchers agree that genetics is a fundamental cause of the disorder. The concordance rate for schizophrenia in monozygotic (identical) twins is almost five times that in dizygotic (fraternal) twins. More-over, studies of monozygotic twins reared apart from their natural parents and from each other show a higher concordance rate than fraternal twins or control subjects (Kety et al., 1975; Rosenthal et al., 1968; Stone, 1980).

Concordance rate: The per-centage of occasions when two groups or individuals show the same trait.

The Genain quadruplets, all of whom developed some manifestation of schizophrenic disorder, are a classic example of genetic influence.

Other support for a biological basis of schizophrenia comes from researchers who discovered that chemicals in the bloodstream may contribute to the development of schizophrenia. Several studies support the importance of the neurotransmitter *dopamine.* Dopamine pathways are considered one of the main sites of biochemical disturbance in the brain (Bowers, 1982). Drugs called *phenothiazines* appear to block receptor sites in the dopamine pathways. When patients with schizophrenia are given phenothiazines, many of their disturbed thought processes and hallucinations disappear. Conversely, drugs that stimulate the dopamine system (such as amphetamines) aggravate existing schizophrenic disorders. (See Figure 14.3.)

Evidence now shows that certain portions of the brains of schizophrenic patients have abnormalities (although it is not yet clear whether schizophrenia causes the brain changes or the brain changes cause schizophrenia). For example, the brain ventricles, hollow areas normally filled with fluid, are enlarged in some schizophrenic patients. This may limit the amount of brain tissue available for other functions (DeLisi et al., 1986). Another potential cause of schizophrenia, derived from the *viral hypothesis,* states that schizophrenic symptoms may be produced by a virus acting on a genetic predisposition to schizophrenia. According to this theory, people diagnosed as schizophrenic have contracted a virus, either before birth or at some time during their lives (Crow et al., 1979; Kessler, 1980).

Environmental Factors. Some psychologists believe that in addition to genetics, environmental interactions determine the development of schizo-

FIGURE 14.3
In the dopamine hypothesis, schizophrenia is assumed to develop in part from an excess of dopamine in the brain.

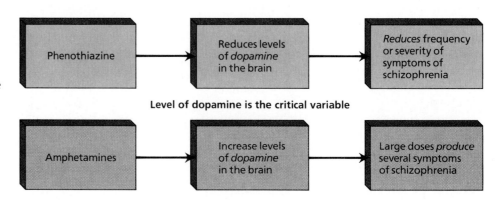

phrenia. Freudian psychologists, for example, suggest that early childhood relationships determine whether a person will become fixated at the oral stage and develop a disorder like schizophrenia. Such a person has not developed an ego and will make judgments based on the id's pleasure principle. Lacking the ego, which uses the reality principle in making judgments, the individual will seek immediate gratification and thus be unable to deal effectively with reality. Freudian psychologists assert that a person who has successfully passed through the oral stage and has developed a strong ego is unlikely to suffer from schizophrenia.

Behavioral explanations of schizophrenia rely on traditional learning principles such as those discussed in chapter 5. This approach argues that faulty reinforcement and extinction procedures, as well as social learning processes, can account for schizophrenia. Imagine a child brought up in a family where the parents constantly argue, where the father is an alcoholic, and neither parent shows much caring or affection for each other or for anyone else. Such a child, receiving no reinforcement for interest in events, people, and objects in the outside world, may become withdrawn and begin to exhibit schizophrenic behavior. Lidz (1973) argues that children who grow up in such homes adopt the family's faulty view of the world and relationships and thus are likely to expect reinforcement for abnormal behaviors. Growing up in such an emotionally fragmented environment may predispose individuals to emotional disorder and eventual schizophrenia (Walker et al., 1983). In addition, if parents themselves are schizophrenic and they mistreat the child, this increases the likelihood of future behavior problems like schizophrenia (Walker, Downey, and Bergman, 1989).

Even in families in which marital conflict is absent, parents sometimes confuse their children. Some parents, for example, place their children in situations that offer two competing messages, called a **double bind.** Initially defined by Bateson, double bind situations usually occur between individuals with a strong emotional attachment, such as child and parents (Mishler and Waxler, 1968). In play, parents may hold up a toy and say, "No, you may not have this," while at the same time smiling and giving other nonverbal assurances that the child may have the toy. Generally, the child understands that the parent is teasing. But not all children understand this and not all situations are so clearly cued. Games like this, if played consistently, may shape an environment of confusion conducive to the development of schizophrenia (Reilly and Muzekari, 1979).

Learning theory suggests that schizophrenics are likely to develop and maintain the disorder because of faulty reinforcement patterns. A person who receives a great deal of attention for behaviors that other people see as bizarre is likely to continue those behaviors. Other reinforcement theories suggest that bizarre behavior and thoughts are themselves reinforcing because they allow the person to escape from acute anxiety and an overactive autonomic nervous system.

Nature or Nurture? Many variables determine whether an individual will develop schizophrenia. Some people, because of either family environment, genetic history, or brain chemistry, are more vulnerable than others (see Figure 14.4 on page 528). The more **vulnerable** the individual, the less necessary are environmental stress or other disorders (such as anxiety) to the initiation of a schizophrenic episode (Zubin and Spring, 1977). When a person develops the disorder, the effect on the individual and his or her family is devastating; the strains on family life are formidable (Lefley, 1989).

Double bind: A situation in which an individual is given two different and inconsistent messages.

Vulnerable: A person's diminished ability to deal with demanding life events.

FIGURE 14.4
According to the biological view of schizophrenia, the environment triggers behaviors in people who are predisposed to schizophrenia. Thus, for people who opt for the combined view of nature and nurture, genetic abnormalities lead to situations in which environmental stressors trigger the behavioral pattern of schizophrenia.

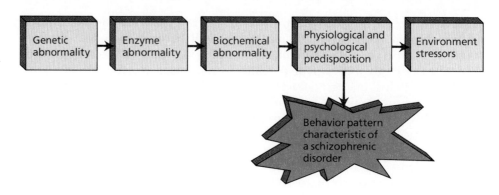

Although the causes of schizophrenia are still undetermined, research suggests the following:

1. A connection exists between genetics and schizophrenia, although genetics alone cannot account for its development.

2. Specific types of chemical substances in the brain are associated with schizophrenia.

3. Environmental factors (such as the presence of marital conflict and double bind) contribute to the development of schizophrenia. Among these factors, early childhood relationships may be especially important.

4. The most likely cause of schizophrenia is a biological predisposition in the individual, aggravated by a climate of emotional immaturity, lack of communication, and emotional instability.

High-Risk Children and Schizophrenia

MILESTONES IN PSYCHOLOGY

*C*an schizophrenia be averted? Do some people have a vulnerability to schizophrenia that is triggered by stressful situations? According to the vulnerability-stress hypothesis, a person's susceptibility to schizophrenia depends on genetic factors, birth factors, and stress during infancy, childhood, and adolescence. This approach assumes that when stressors appear, schizophrenia and its symptoms may appear; the more stressors, the more likely that schizophrenia will surface. Some people can tolerate a great deal of stress, while others can tolerate very little before schizophrenia materializes.

Psychologists have followed children of schizophrenic mothers and fathers from birth to adulthood. These studies, generally called high-risk studies because the subjects are at higher risk than the general population, have produced landmark results. The high-risk approach is effective because:

1. Subjects can be studied before the disorder develops,

2. The data are relatively unbiased because it is not known whether the child will become schizophrenic, and

3. Data can be gathered from the individuals and their families, not from doctors or hospital records.

Many high-risk projects are under way throughout the world, including some started in the 1960s that are now assessing the likelihood of schizophrenia in mature adults. Typical of these studies is the Copenhagen High-Risk Project. Since 1962, Mednick, Parnas, and Schulsinger (1987) have followed a sample of 207 children who were at high risk for schizophrenia, as well as 104 control children. The mothers of the high-risk children were schizophrenic, and the control subjects were matched for age, gender, social class, education, and urban-rural differences. Psychological tests were given at periodic intervals. Results showed that if the child's mother was schizophrenic, the child was at least eight times more likely to develop schizophrenia. If the child's birth experience just preceding, during, or after birth was traumatic, there was increased likelihood of schizophrenia. They also showed that poor parental supervision was related to the development of schizophrenia.

Other high-risk projects show similar results. The University of Rochester Child and Family Study, which began in 1972 (Wynne, Cole, and Perkins, 1987), shows that parental maladjustment predicts children who will need psychological care. The Stony Brook High-Risk Project (Weintraub, 1987) reports that considerable family discord, poor parenting skills, and marital conflict are related to psychological problems in children. The relationship is magnified when there is a schizophrenic parent.

There is no doubt that children of schizophrenic parents are at greater risk for developing schizophrenia. But researchers are most interested in the high-risk children who *never* develop the disorder. What makes them different? Researchers believe that family relationships are an important dimension. If children of schizophrenic parents are in a household filled with discord, fighting, alcoholism, and poor discipline, they are much more likely to develop the disorder. Burman concludes, "Stressful environments will tend to produce schizophrenia in genetically predisposed individuals" (Burman et al., 1987, p. 364). The vulnerability-stress hypothesis might prove to be the most accurate predictor of schizophrenia. It appears that in some people who are more vulnerable than others, stressors may spark the psychiatric disorder (or relapse) as will such events as alcohol abuse (Drake, Osher, and Wallach, 1989). The longitudinal research continues. ◆

- ◆ Identify three symptoms of schizophrenia. pp. 522–523
- ◆ Identify three features that a diagnosis of schizophrenia requires, according to DSM-III-R. p. 523
- ◆ Describe the biological theory of schizophrenia that relies on dopamine as an explanation for the disorder. pp. 525–526
- ◆ Describe the essential results of high-risk studies of schizophrenia. pp. 528–529

Focus on Learning

Key Terms

Abnormal behavior p. 498
Model p. 499
Abnormal psychology p. 499
Medical-biological model
  p. 500
Prevalence p. 503
Anxiety p. 504
Generalized anxiety disorder
  p. 505
Free-floating anxiety p. 505
Phobic disorder p. 505
Agoraphobia p. 506
Social phobia p. 507
Simple phobia p. 507
Obsessive-compulsive disorder
  p. 507
Somatoform disorder p. 509
Somatization disorder p. 509

Conversion disorder p. 509
Hypochondriasis p. 509
Dissociative disorder p. 510
Psychogenic amnesia p. 510
Multiple personality p. 510
Personality disorder p. 511
Antisocial personality disorder
  p. 511
Child abuse p. 512
Rape p. 514
Sexual deviations p. 515
Fetishism p. 515
Transvestic fetishism p. 515
Voyeurism p. 515
Exhibitionism p. 515
Pedophilia p. 515
Sexual sadism p. 516
Sexual masochism p. 516

Bipolar disorder p. 517
Depressive disorders p. 518
Major depression p. 518
Delusion p. 518
Learned helplessness p. 521
Psychotic p. 522
Schizophrenic disorder p. 522
Hallucinations p. 522
Affect p. 522
Disorganized type p. 522
Paranoid type p. 523
Catatonic type p. 523
Residual type p. 524
Undifferentiated type p. 524
Concordance rate p. 525
Double bind p. 527
Vulnerable p. 527

Summary

What Is Abnormal Behavior?

- Abnormal behavior is atypical; it is socially unacceptable and causes distress or discomfort to the person exhibiting the behavior or to those around him or her; it is maladaptive or self-defeating to the person exhibiting it and is often the result of distorted cognitions.   p. 498

Diagnosing Abnormal Behavior: DSM-III-R

- The diagnostic categories of the DSM-III-R are helpful because they describe behavior in terms of its characteristics rather than solely in terms of its frequency.   p. 503

- Abnormal behavior is studied extensively to determine whether its causes are primarily environmental or genetic.   pp. 503–504

Anxiety Disorders

- Anxiety is a generalized feeling of fear and apprehension, often accompanied by increased physiological arousal that may or may not be related to a specific event or object.   p. 504

- A generalized anxiety disorder is characterized by persistent anxiety of at least one month's duration. It can include problems in motor tension, autonomic hyperactivity, apprehension, and concentration.   p. 505

- Phobic disorders are characterized by irrational fear and avoidance of objects or situations. p. 505

- Individuals with an obsessive-compulsive disorder have persistent and uncontrollable thoughts and irrational beliefs, causing them to perform compulsive rituals that interfere with normal daily functioning.   p. 507

Somatoform and Dissociative Disorders

- Somatoform disorders are characterized by real physical symptoms not under voluntary control and for which no evident physical cause exists.   p. 509

- Dissociative disorders are characterized by a sudden temporary alteration in consciousness, identity, or motor behavior.   p. 510

Personality Disorders and Sexual Disorders

- People who have unwarranted feelings of persecution and who mistrust almost everyone are said to have paranoid personality disorder.

Fearful or anxious behaviors are characteristic of dependent personality disorder. Dramatic, emotional, and erratic behaviors are characteristic of histrionic personality disorder.   p. 511

- Antisocial personality disorder is characterized by a history of behavior that violates others' rights. Persons with antisocial personality disorders behave irresponsibly, have no fear of punishment, and are egocentric.   p. 511

- Sexual deviation is a sexual practice directed toward objects rather than people, or involving real or simulated suffering, humiliation, or nonconsenting partners.   p. 514

Mood Disorders

- Bipolar disorder, formerly known as manic/depressive disorder, gets its name from the fact that patients' behavior vacillates between two extremes, mania and depression.   p. 516

- Patients diagnosed as having a major depression disorder have a gloomy outlook on life, especially slow thought processes, an exaggerated view of current problems, and a tendency to blame themselves.   p. 518

- The norepinephrine hypothesis suggests that an insufficient amount of norepinephrine at receptor sites causes depression. Learning theories stress that reinforcement determines the course and nature of depression.   p. 520

Schizophrenia

- Schizophrenia is a group of disorders characterized by lack of reality testing and deterioration of social and intellectual functioning. Such individuals often show serious personality disintegration with significant changes in thought, mood, perception, and behavior. p. 522

- Biological studies suggest that the cause of schizophrenia must be to some extent genetic. This view is supported by higher concordance rates for identical twins than for fraternal twins.   p. 525

- The fact that a drug reduces symptoms of schizophrenic disorder does not conclusively demonstrate that the disorder is biological in origin. Although some genetic contribution to schizophrenia probably exists, environmental factors also seem important.   p. 527

Connections

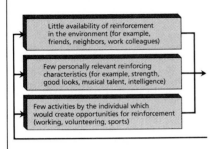

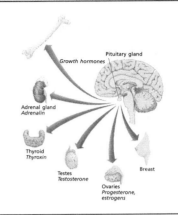

If you are interested in . . .	*Turn to . . .*	*To learn more about . . .*
The role of anxiety in normal behavior and in maladjustment	◆ Ch. 11, pp. 390–391	How behavior is affected when a person is feeling anxious and aroused.
	◆ Ch. 13, pp. 465–471	How a person's health can deteriorate due to continually high levels of anxiety, stress, and autonomic nervous system arousal.
The role of learning in the development of various forms of maladjustment	◆ Ch. 5, p. 185	How children's behavior, both good and bad, is learned through conditioning procedures.
	◆ Ch. 12, pp. 450–451	How self-esteem and self-efficacy—often learned in the formative years of childhood—affect the ability to cope with simple as well as complex demands of life.
	◆ Ch. 16, p. 589	How attitudes and self-perceptions develop through a process of repeated experiences.
The biological bases of psychological disorders	◆ Ch. 2, pp. 60–64	Hormonal and genetic influences on behavior.
	◆ Ch. 11, p. 386	How overeating, or even eating the wrong foods, can affect behavior.
	◆ Ch. 15, p. 567	The use of drugs to treat various forms of maladjustment.

15 *Approaches to Treatment*

"Shape III" by Yojo Edelmann

◆

Ricky Estavez was depressed about his monthly sales totals—at least that's what he told his coworkers. He invited them to join him for a couple of beers after work. Most declined, knowing that Ricky was suffering another bout of depression. Outside the bar, Ricky telephoned his wife to say he was going to be home late. His wife lectured him; this led to harsh words, and Ricky began shouting, then abruptly hung up. Ricky soon began to come in to work late and sometimes skipped out altogether. Angry and anxious about his sales performance, losing sleep, losing weight, and verging on alcoholism, Ricky made an appointment with a counselor at the hospital's Psychological Services Center.

Psychologists recognize that people are vulnerable to numerous coping problems related to stress, maladjustment, peer pressure, and drug and alcohol abuse. Everyone suffers to some degree, but for some people these problems become overwhelming. In such severe cases, the afflicted person may seek professional help.

Therapy Comes in Many Forms

Many types of treatment are available for people like Ricky Estavez who are having difficulty coping with life. When a person seeks help from a physician, mental health counseling center, or drug treatment center, an initial working diagnosis is necessary. Does the person have medical problems? Should the person be hospitalized? Is the person dangerous to himself or others? If talking therapy is in order, what type of practitioner is best suited for the person? There are two broad types of therapy: somatic therapy and psychotherapy.

Somatic Therapy and Psychotherapy

Severely depressed individuals may need tranquilizers; those diagnosed as having a schizophrenic disorder may need antipsychotic drugs; those with less severe disorders may be advised to change their diets and exercise more. These are biologically based therapies, sometimes called *somatic therapies*. We will examine some of these biological therapies later in this chapter; our focus now, however, will be to explore the broad array of psychological therapies that are available for people suffering from maladjustment.

Psychotherapy is the treatment of emotional or behavioral problems through psychological techniques. The goal of psychotherapy is to help people cope better and achieve more emotionally satisfying life-styles, often by helping them relieve stress, improve interpersonal communication, and modify their faulty ideas about the world. Psychotherapy helps people improve their self-images and adapt to new and challenging situations.

Types of Psychotherapy

There are about two hundred different forms of therapy. Some focus on treating individuals, some on groups of individuals, and others on families. Some psychologists even deal with whole communities. A therapist's training will usually determine the type of treatment approach taken. Rather than using just one type of psychotherapy, many therapists take an *eclectic* approach, that is, they combine a number of techniques in their treatment (Norcross, Prochaska, and Gallagher, 1989). Here is an overview of the psychotherapeutic approaches in use today.

Some practitioners use *psychodynamically based approaches* that loosely or closely follow Freud's basic ideas. Their aim is to help patients understand the motivations underlying their behavior. They assume that maladjustment and abnormal behavior occur when people do not understand themselves adequately. *Humanistic* therapists assume that people are essentially good — that they have an innate disposition to develop their potential and seek

Psychotherapy: The treatment of emotional or behavioral problems through psychological techniques.

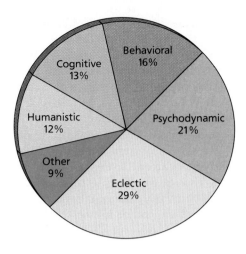

FIGURE 15.1
The primary orientation of 579 clinical psychologists who belong to the American Psychological Association. (Source: Based on data from Norcross, Prochaska, and Gallagher, 1989.)

beauty, truth, and goodness. Humanistic therapy is oriented toward helping people realize their full potential and find meaning in life. In contrast, *behavior therapy* is based on the assumption that most behaviors, whether normal or abnormal, are learned. Behavior therapists encourage their clients to learn new adaptive behaviors. Growing out of behavior therapy and the heavy influence of cognitive psychology is *cognitive therapy*. Cognitive therapy focuses on changing a client's thoughts and perceptions. See Figure 15.1 for a graphic representation of the primary orientations of clinical psychologists.

Some psychologists specialize in *group therapy* and use techniques drawn from psychodynamically-oriented, behavior, and humanistic therapies. Last, *community psychologists* focus on helping individuals, groups, and communities develop a more action-oriented approach to individual and social adjustment.

Which Therapy, Which Therapist?

The appropriate type of therapy and its effectiveness vary with the type of disorder being treated and the goal of the client. Individual psychodynamic therapy has a good success rate for people with anxiety and adjustment disorders; it is less successful for those with schizophrenic disorders. Similarly, long-term group therapy is more effective than short-term individual therapy for people with personality disorders (Piper, Debbane, Bienvenu, and Garant, 1984). Behavior therapy is usually the most effective approach with children (Casey and Berman, 1985). Ricky could receive effective treatment from a variety of therapists. One therapist might focus on discovering the root causes of Ricky's maladjustment, while another therapist might concentrate on eliminating symptoms—depression, drinking, and poor work performance.

Although there are differences among the various psychotherapies, there are also some commonalities. In all the therapies, clients usually expect a positive outcome, which helps them strive for change. In addition, they receive attention, which helps them maintain a positive attitude. Moreover, no matter what type of therapy is involved, certain characteristics must be present in both therapist and client for therapeutic change to occur. Many variables in each therapy can affect the outcome. Among them are the therapist's gender, personality, level of experience, and empathy (e.g., Gurman and Razin, 1977). Good therapists communicate interest, understanding, respect, tact, maturity, and ability to help. They use suggestion, encouragement, interpretation, examples, and perhaps rewards to help clients change or rethink their situations. But clients must be willing to make some changes in their life-styles and ideas. If a therapist is knowledgeable, accepting, and objective, he or she can facilitate behavior change, but the client is the one who makes the changes (Lafferty, Beutler, and Crago, 1989).

Other variables, such as the client's social class, age, education, therapeutic expectations, and level of anxiety, are also important (e.g., Luborsky et al., 1980). Therapists must also be sensitive to current issues and circumstances. For example, they need to be sensitive to the unique life stresses experienced by women (Hare-Mustin, 1983). Similarly, therapists must address the special obstacles facing clients of racial and other minority groups (Sue, 1988). In general, a therapist and client must form an alliance, a joint desire to work purposefully together.

Challenges to Psychotherapy

Is therapy really necessary? Some researchers note that many clients could achieve relief from their symptoms without psychotherapy. Others assert that psychotherapy is more art than science; still others feel that psychotherapy only provides transitory placebo effects.

Placebo Effects. A **placebo effect** is a change in behavior that occurs as a result of a person's *expectations* rather than as a result of a specific treatment. Physicians report that people who are given sugar pills and told that the pills are medicine sometimes experience relief from their symptoms. In much the same way, patients in psychotherapy may show relief from their symptoms simply because they have entered therapy and now expect change. For some people, just the attention of a therapist and the chance to express their feelings can be therapeutic. One research study showed that clients who paid for therapy had a better therapeutic outcome than clients who did not pay (Yoken and Berman, 1984). It is important to note that placebo effects in psychotherapy are likely to be transient. Any long-lasting therapeutic effects will generally come about from the client's and therapist's efforts (Horvath, 1988). Research studies that compare traditional therapies with placebo treatments show that the traditional psychotherapies are more effective (Clum and Bowers, 1990).

Psychotherapy Research. In 1952, an important paper by Eysenck challenged the effectiveness of psychotherapy, claiming that it produces no greater change in maladjusted individuals than naturally occurring life experiences do. Thousands of studies followed that attempted to investigate the effectiveness of therapy.

Research shows what clients and therapists have known for decades. Using sophisticated statistical techniques to analyze large amounts of data, Smith and Glass found psychotherapy effective (Smith, Glass, and Miller, 1980). Although many psychologists challenge the data, techniques, and conclusions of these analyses, most are still convinced that psychotherapy is effective (e.g., Garfield and Bergin, 1986; Matt, 1989; Weisz et al., 1987).

Many researchers contend that most psychotherapies are equally effective; that is, regardless of the approach a therapist uses, the results are often the same. But some researchers disagree; noted psychologist Alan Kazdin

Placebo effect: A nonspecific therapeutic change that occurs as a result of a person's expectations of change rather than as a direct result of any specific treatment.

TABLE 15.1

Signs of Good Progress in Therapy
◆ The client is providing personally revealing and significant material.
◆ The client is exploring the meaning of feelings and occurrences.
◆ The client is exploring material avoided earlier in therapy.
◆ The client is expressing significant insight into personal behavior.
◆ The client's method of communicating is active, alive, and energetic.
◆ There is a valued client-therapist working relationship.
◆ The client feels free to express strong feelings toward the therapist—either positive or negative.
◆ The client is expressing strong feelings outside of therapy.
◆ The client moves toward a different set of personality characteristics.
◆ The client is showing improved functioning outside of therapy.
◆ The client indicates a general state of well-being, good feelings, and positive attitudes.

Source: Mahrer and Nadler, 1986.

(1986) pointed out that research on the effects of psychotherapy is exceedingly difficult to conduct and interpret. Kazdin maintains that such research is often done under less than ideal conditions, or uses highly focused approaches, with clients solicited through newspaper advertisements (Krupnick, Shea, and Elkin, 1986), or under research conditions that do not mimic real-life therapeutic situations. And it is uncertain whether such studies can be generalized to regular client populations (Forsyth and Strong, 1986). Kazdin does not claim that such research should not be done, but rather that it must be carefully evaluated and that new research methodologies are needed that can evaluate small differences (Kazdin and Bass, 1989; Strupp, 1989). But new, more complete psychotherapy research strategies are under development, and as more studies are completed, there will be a clearer picture of how various approaches are best used to treat certain disorders with particular types of clients (Howard, Kopta, Krause, and Orlinsky, 1986). Table 15.1 presents some generally recognized signs of good progress in therapy. Before surveying the therapies, identify things that you think should happen as a result of treatment. What would you expect to gain, lose, or change in therapy?

Outcomes of Therapy

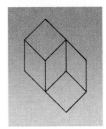

*T*hroughout this text we present research studies that describe experiments in which a treatment is given to one group which is then compared with a control group. The same procedure is used in evaluating therapy outcomes. The general question is, "Is a certain type of therapy effective?" The specific question is usually more precise. For example, the researchers may ask, "Is systematic desensitization more effective than client-centered therapy in treating phobias?" Researchers evaluate the research by asking questions such as: "Are there enough subjects?" "Is there a control group?" "Have the studies been repeated?"

Control Groups. Usually there are at least three groups of subjects. One group is treated with systematic desensitization; another is treated with client-centered

Psychoanalysis: A lengthy insight therapy developed by Freud that aims at uncovering conflicts and unconscious impulses through special techniques including free association, dream analysis, and transference.

Psychodynamically-based therapies: Therapies based loosely on Freud's theory of psychoanalysis; using a part of the approach, some practitioners reject some elements of Freud's theory.

therapy; and the third is placed on a waiting list to receive therapy. The aim is to let time pass and then compare the two experimental groups with the untreated or control group. The control group usually receives treatment after the other two groups have been treated (it would be unethical not to provide treatment for all the participants). Another element of research on the outcomes of therapy is that clients are usually tracked after the termination of therapy. Six-month and one-year follow-ups are common. By these means, a researcher can determine whether or not the effects of therapy are long-lasting.

Difficulties. Outcome studies are difficult. Clients have to be recruited. Therapists have to be trained in specific techniques. Clients have to be evaluated before treatment begins. Clients then must be treated, usually over a ten- to sixteen-week period. Post-treatment evaluations must be conducted, as well as follow-ups six months later. Only then can the results be evaluated. Sometimes a therapy study concerns families, not single individuals. This complicates recruitment, scheduling, retention of subjects, and outcome measures—for example, who has changed, on what dimensions, and to what extent.

Decisions. As you read about a specific therapy, you might ask, "Is it effective?" This is a reasonable question, often asked by professional psychologists. Three researchers at the University of Missouri asked the question about family therapy (Hazelrigg, Cooper, and Borduin, 1987), discussed in greater detail later in this chapter. They searched the psychological literature of the last eighteen years to find every article that dealt with family therapy. In reviewing those articles, they found that family therapy had positive effects as measured by family interactions and behavior ratings. But at the time of post-treatment follow-up, many of the advances exhibited by clients while in therapy had diminished somewhat.

Despite this, family therapy is effective, sometimes more effective than any other treatment procedure, including traditional individual therapy. It took research to show that this is true and to persuade skeptical practitioners to believe it. This is part of the fun of psychology: developing hypotheses about a topic of special interest, testing those hypotheses, publishing the results, reevaluating other psychologists' research, and making meaningful breakthroughs that help improve the human condition. ◆

Focus on Learning

◆ Identify the goals of psychotherapy. p. 534
◆ Identify the fundamental assumption of psychodynamically-based approaches to therapy and behavior therapy. pp. 534–535
◆ What is a placebo effect? p. 536

Psychodynamic Therapy

Classical Freudian **psychoanalysis** focuses on helping the client uncover the unconscious motivations that lead to psychological conflict and maladaptive behavior; it is practiced by therapists who are specifically trained in its theory and practice. There are about three thousand practicing psychoanalysts in the United States, and many other psychologists use a therapy loosely connected to or rooted in Freudian theory. Psychologists refer to these as **psychodynamically-based therapies,** that is, they use theory, approach, or techniques that derive from Freud.

Sigmund Freud believed that the exchange of words in psychoanalysis causes therapeutic change. According to Freud,

The patient talks, tells of his past experiences and present impressions, complains, and expresses his wishes and his emotions. The physician listens, attempts to direct the patient's thought-processes, reminds him, forces his attention in certain directions, gives him explanations and observes the reactions of understanding or denial thus evoked. (FREUD, 1920, P. 21)

Insight therapy: A therapy that attempts to discover relationships between unconscious motivations and current behavior. Insight therapy assumes that abnormal behavior results from individuals' failure to understand their unconscious motivations and needs.

Freud's therapy is an **insight therapy;** insight therapies share two basic assumptions. The first is that becoming aware of one's motivations helps a person change and become more adaptable; the second is that the causes of maladjustment are unresolved conflicts, which the patient was unaware of and therefore was unable to deal with. The goal of insight therapy is to treat the causes of abnormal behavior rather than the behaviors themselves. In general, insight therapists try to help people see life from a different perspective so that they can choose more adaptive life-styles. Because psychoanalysis is based on the development of a unique relationship between the therapist and the patient, compatibility is especially critical; the patient and therapist usually decide within the first few sessions whether they feel comfortable working with each other.

Goals of Psychoanalysis

Many individuals who seek psychotherapy are unhappy with their behavior but are unable to change. As you may recall from our discussion of Freud's theory of personality (chapter 12), Freud believed that conflicts among a person's unconscious thoughts and processes produce maladjusted behavior. The general goal of psychoanalysis, then, is to help patients understand the unconscious motivations that direct their behavior. Only when patients become aware of those motivations can they begin to choose behaviors that will let them lead more fulfilling lives. In psychoanalysis, patients are encouraged to express healthy impulses, strengthen day-to-day functioning based on reality, and perceive the world as a positive rather than a punishing place.

To illustrate the psychoanalytical approach, suppose Ricky seeks the help of a counselor who uses a psychodynamically-based therapy. The psychologist might attempt to discover the source of Ricky's problems by asking him to describe how he relates to his parents. From this description, the psychologist learns that Ricky's father has long expected his son to take over the family business. He also learns that Ricky has sought his father's approval all his life; in fact, that's why he is in the family business. However, Ricky is not sure he wants to be in sales and has always resented his father's insistence that he become a sales manager.

Through therapy, Ricky realizes he is torn between his desire to please his father and his dislike of sales. In fact, Ricky thinks he might prefer being a photographer. Ricky also discovers that he has been incapable of expressing anger toward his father; frustrated, he has lost interest in work and begun using alcohol to numb the pain of his diminishing self-esteem.

Techniques of Psychoanalysis

In general, psychoanalytic techniques are geared toward the exploration of early experiences. In traditional psychoanalysis, the patient lies on a couch and the therapist sits in a chair out of the patient's view. Freud believed

Freud's study in London contained the couch which would later become the symbol of psychoanalysis.

that this arrangement would allow the patient to be more relaxed and less threatened than he or she would be in viewing the therapist. However, many contemporary followers of Freud prefer to face patients rather than use the couch, feeling that this factor was overrated.

Two major techniques used in psychoanalysis are free association and dream analysis. In **free association,** the patient is asked to report whatever comes to mind, regardless of how trivial it might seem or how disagreeable it might feel. A therapist might say, "I can help you best if you say whatever thoughts and feelings come to your mind, even if they seem irrelevant, immaterial, foolish, embarrassing, upsetting, or even if they're about me, even very personally, just as they come, without censoring or editing" (Lewin, 1970, p. 67). The purpose of free association is to help patients learn to recognize connections and patterns among their thoughts and to allow the unconscious to express itself freely.

In **dream analysis,** patients are asked to describe their dreams in detail. Sometimes lifelike, sometimes chaotic, sometimes incoherent, dreams periodically replay a person's life history and at other times venture into a person's current problems. Freud believed that dreams represent some element of the unconscious seeking expression. Psychodynamically-oriented therapists see much symbolism in dreams. They assert that the overt content of the dream hides the true meaning; many therapists use patient's dreams to understand current problems. The goal of dream analysis is to disclose unconscious desires and motivations by discovering the meaning of the patient's dreams.

Both free association and dream analysis involve **interpretation** by therapists. In psychoanalysis, therapists try to make unconscious ideas, feelings, and impulses conscious by providing a context for them; they try to find common threads in a patient's behavior and thoughts. When patients use defense mechanisms (techniques to mask or avoid dealing with anxiety, examined in chapter 12) it often signals an area that may need to be explored. For example, if a patient becomes jittery every time he speaks about women,

Free association: A psychoanalytic technique in which a person reports to the therapist his or her thoughts and feelings as they occur, regardless of how illogical their order or content may seem.

Dream analysis: A psychoanalytic technique in which a patient's dreams are interpreted, used to gain insight into the individual's unconscious motivations.

Interpretation: In Freud's theory, the technique of providing a context, meaning, or cause of a specific idea, feeling, or set of behaviors.

the therapist may speculate that the patient's nervousness results from early difficulties with women, perhaps with his mother. The therapist may then encourage the patient to explore his attitudes and feelings about women in general and about his mother in particular.

Two processes central to psychoanalysis are resistance and transference. **Resistance** is a patient's unwillingness to cooperate with the therapist, sometimes to the point of becoming belligerent. For example, disturbed by his counselor's unsettling interpretations, Ricky might become angry and start resisting treatment by missing appointments.

Analysts usually interpret these behaviors as meaning that the patient wishes to avoid discussing a particular subject, or that an especially difficult stage in therapy has been reached. To minimize resistance, they try to accept the patient's behavior. When the therapist does not judge but merely listens, the patient is more likely to describe feelings thoroughly.

In **transference,** patients transfer feelings from earlier relationships to the therapist. For example, if Ricky's therapist is a man, Ricky may act hostile or competitive toward him, while another client may behave lovingly toward the same therapist. Psychoanalysts would say that in both cases the patients are acting as if the therapist were their father. Because the therapist will respond differently from the way Ricky's father might have, Ricky can experience the conflict differently, leading to a better understanding of the issue. By permitting transference, the therapist gives patients a new opportunity to understand their feelings, and can guide them in the exploration of repressed or difficult material. The examination of thoughts or feelings that were previously considered unacceptable (and therefore were often repressed) helps patients understand and identify the underlying conflicts that direct their behavior.

Therapy, with its slowly gained insights into the unconscious, is gradual and continual. Through their gradual insights, often frequently repeated, patients learn new ways of coping with instinctual urges and develop more mature ways of dealing with anxiety and guilt. The entire process of interpretation, resistance to interpretation, and transference is sometimes referred to as **working through.**

Ego Analysis

Freud's theory has not been universally accepted; even his followers have disagreed with him. One group of psychoanalysts, referred to as **ego-analysts,** or ego-psychologists, have modified some of Freud's basic ideas about psychoanalysis. Like Freud, they assume that psychoanalysis is the appropriate method for treating patients with emotional problems. Unlike Freud, however, they assume that people have voluntary control over when, whether, and in what way their biological urges will be expressed.

A major disagreement has to do with the role of the id and the ego. Whereas traditional psychoanalysts begin by focusing on unconscious material in the id and only later try to increase the patient's ego control, ego-analysis aims at helping patients develop stronger control of their egos. (Recall from chapter 12 that the ego is the part of the personality that operates on the reality principle and tries to control impulsive behavior by responding realistically to the demands of the environment.) From an ego-analyst's point of view, a weak ego is just as likely to cause maladjustment as failure to understand and control the id. Thus, by learning to master and develop their egos—including moral reasoning and judgment—people gain greater control over their lives.

Resistance: In psychoanalysis, an unwillingness to cooperate by which a patient signals his or her reluctance to provide the therapist with information or to help the therapist understand or interpret a situation.

Transference: A psychoanalytic procedure in which a therapist becomes the object of a patient's emotional attitudes about an important person in his or her life.

Working through: The gradual, often repeated, slow process in therapy of interpretation, resistance to interpretation, and transference.

Ego-analysts: Practitioners who use the psychoanalytic approach to therapy that assumes the ego has greater control over behavior than Freud suggested.

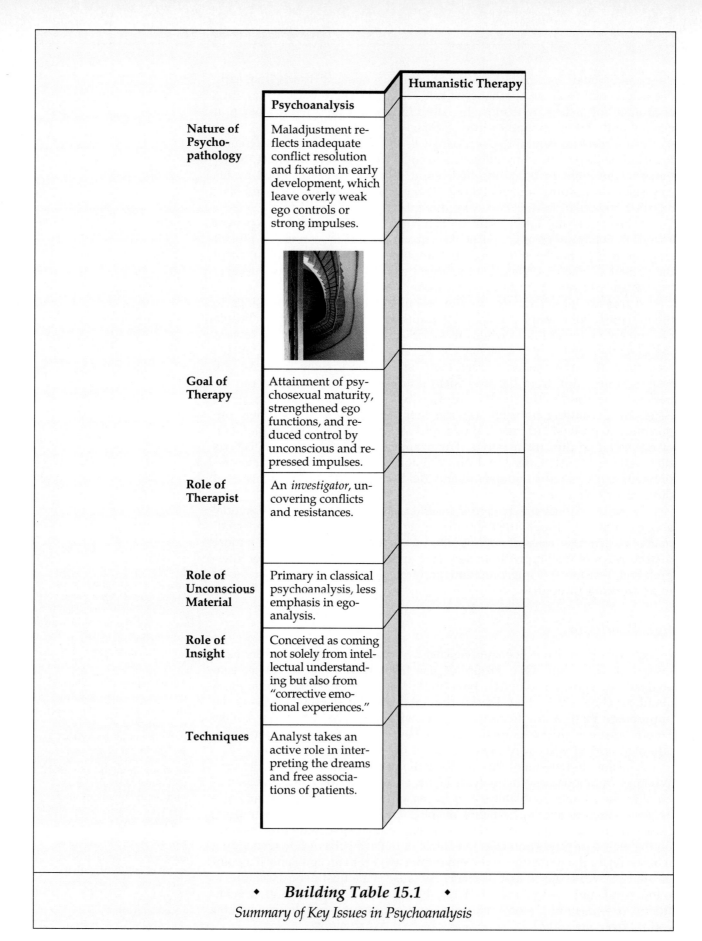

	Psychoanalysis	Humanistic Therapy
Nature of Psycho-pathology	Maladjustment reflects inadequate conflict resolution and fixation in early development, which leave overly weak ego controls or strong impulses.	
Goal of Therapy	Attainment of psychosexual maturity, strengthened ego functions, and reduced control by unconscious and repressed impulses.	
Role of Therapist	An *investigator*, uncovering conflicts and resistances.	
Role of Unconscious Material	Primary in classical psychoanalysis, less emphasis in ego-analysis.	
Role of Insight	Conceived as coming not solely from intellectual understanding but also from "corrective emotional experiences."	
Techniques	Analyst takes an active role in interpreting the dreams and free associations of patients.	

◆ ***Building Table 15.1*** ◆
Summary of Key Issues in Psychoanalysis

Criticisms of Psychoanalysis

Some critics of psychoanalysis contend that the approach is unscientific, lacking in precision, and subjective; they assert that its concepts, such as id, ego, and superego, are not linked to real things or day-to-day behavior. Other critics object to Freud's biologically-oriented approach, which suggests that human beings are bundles of energy caught in conflict and driven toward some hedonistic goal. These critics want to know where the free will in human behavior is. Also, some elements of Freud's theory are sexist and untestable. For example, the Oedipal complex, with its reliance on such concepts as penis envy, is patently sexist and impossible to submit to scientific inquiry. In addition, Freud conceived of men and women in strictly prescribed roles; most practitioners today find such an idea objectionable.

Quite aside from these criticisms, the effectiveness of psychoanalysis is open to question. Research shows that psychoanalysis is selectively effective: It is more effective, for example, for people with anxiety disorders than for those diagnosed as schizophrenic. Also, people who enter analysis with a high level of anxiety show greater overall improvement at the end of therapy than those who enter with a low level of anxiety (Burstein, Coynes, Kernberg, and Voth, 1972). And younger patients improve more than older ones. In general, studies show that psychoanalysis can be as effective as other therapies, but is no more so (Garfield and Bergin, 1986).

One major drawback of psychoanalysis is that it is not suitable for all patients. The problems addressed in psychoanalysis are difficult, and a patient must be highly motivated and articulate to grasp the complicated and subtle relationships explored. Also, since traditional psychoanalysis involves meeting individually with the therapist for one hour, five days a week, for approximately five years, a typical psychoanalysis might cost $100,000. Many people who seek therapy do not want or cannot afford this type of therapy. Building Table 15.1 presents a summary of the key components of the psychoanalytic view of therapy. Humanistic therapies, which we will discuss next, are neither as time consuming nor as comprehensive in their goals.

- What is the goal of psychoanalysis? p. 539
- Identify two major techniques in psychoanalysis. pp. 539–540
- On what issues do ego-analysts disagree with Freud? p. 541
- Identify two major criticisms of Freudian psychoanalysis. p. 543

Focus on Learning

Humanistic Therapy

Humanistic therapies, unlike psychoanalytic therapies, emphasize the uniqueness of the human experience and the idea that human beings have free will to determine their destinies. Humanistic psychologists assert that human beings are conscious, creative, and born with an innate desire to fulfill themselves. To some extent, humanistic approaches are an outgrowth of psychodynamically-based insight therapies: they help people understand the causes of their behavior. But unlike Freud's approach, they assume that people are decision makers, goal setters, and intrinsically good at heart—individuals who can reflect on their problems and make choices about their lives. Client-centered therapy and Gestalt therapy are two types of humanistic therapies.

Client-centered therapy: An insight therapy developed by Carl Rogers that seeks to help people evaluate the world and themselves from their own perspective by providing a nondirective environment and unconditional positive regard for the client; sometimes called *person-centered therapy.*

Nondirective therapy: A form of therapy in which the client determines the direction of therapy while the therapist remains permissive, almost passive, and accepts totally the client's feelings and behavior.

Client-Centered Therapy

Client-centered therapy, also called *person-centered therapy,* was developed by Carl Rogers (1902–1987). Rogers was a quiet, caring man who turned the psychoanalytic world upside down when he introduced his approach. He focused on the person, he listened intently to his clients, and he encouraged them to define their own "cures." Rogers saw people as basically good, competent, social beings who move forward and grow. Throughout life they move toward their ideal selves, maturing into fulfilled individuals through the process of self-actualization.

Rogerian therapists see problem behaviors occurring when the environment prevents a person from developing his or her innate potential. If children are given love and reinforcement only for their achievements, for example, as adults they may see themselves and others only in terms of achievement. Rogerian treatment involves helping people evaluate the world from their own perspective and develop improved self-regard. For example, a Rogerian therapist might treat Ricky by encouraging him to explore his goals, desires, and expectations, and then asking if he can achieve these through sales, photography, or some other option. Ricky may come to realize that he can be a good son even if he doesn't become a sales manager. Table 15.2 presents the basic assumptions underlying Rogers's approach to treatment.

Techniques of Client-Centered Therapy. Because its goal is to help clients discover and actualize their as-yet-undiscovered selves, client-centered therapy is nondirective. In **nondirective therapy** the therapist does not dominate the client, but instead encourages the client's search for growth.

The use of the word *client* rather than *patient* is a key aspect of Rogers's approach to therapy. In psychoanalysis, therapists *direct* the patient's "cure" and help them understand their behavior; in Rogerian therapy, therapists *guide* clients and help them realize what they feel is right for them. The client directs the conversation, and the therapist helps the client organize thoughts and ideas simply by asking the right questions, responding with words such as "Oh," and reflecting back the client's feelings. Even a small movement, such as a nod or gesture, can help the client stay on the right track. The client learns to evaluate the world from his or her own vantage point, with little interpretation by the therapist.

A basic tenet of client-centered therapy is that the therapist must be a warm, accepting person who projects positive feelings toward the client. To

TABLE 15.2

Carl Rogers's Assumptions about Human Beings
1. People are innately good and are effective in dealing with their environments.
2. Behavior is purposeful and goal-directed.
3. Healthy people are aware of all their behavior; they choose their behavior patterns.
4. A client's behavior can be understood only from his or her own point of view. Even if a client has misconstrued events in the world, the therapist must understand how the client sees those events.
5. Effective therapy occurs only when a client modifies his or her behavior, not when the therapist manipulates it.

counteract clients' negative experiences with people who were unaccepting, and thus taught them that they are bad or unlikable, client-centered therapists accept clients as they are, with good and bad points, respect them for their worth as individuals, and show them positive regard and respect. *Empathic understanding*, whereby therapists communicate acceptance and recognition of clients' emotions and encourage them to discuss whatever feelings they have, is an important part of the therapeutic relationship.

Client-centered therapy can be viewed as a consciousness-raising process that helps people expand their awareness. Initially clients tend to express attitudes and ideas they have adopted from other people. Thus, Ricky might say, "I should get top sales figures," implying "because my father counts on my success." As therapy progresses and Ricky experiences the empathic understanding of the therapist, he will begin to use his own ideas when evaluating himself (Rogers, 1951). As a result, he will talk about himself in more positive ways and try to please himself rather than others. He may say, "I should make top sales figures only if they mean something to me," reflecting a more positive, more accepting attitude about himself. As Ricky feels better about himself, he will eventually suggest to the therapist that he knows how to deal with the world and may be ready to leave therapy.

Frederick Perls's Gestalt therapy concentrates on present experiences and feelings.

Criticisms of Client-Centered Therapy. Client-centered therapy is widely acclaimed for its focus on the therapeutic relationship. No other therapy seems to make clients feel so warm, accepted, and safe. These are important characteristics of any therapy, but critics argue that they may not be enough to bring about long-lasting change.

Critics of client-centered therapy assert that lengthy discussions about past problems do not necessarily help people with their present difficulties, and that an environment of unconditional positive regard may not be enough to bring about behavior change. They feel that Rogerian therapy may be making therapeutic promises that cannot be fulfilled and that it focuses on concepts such as self-actualization that are hard to define.

Gestalt Therapy

With the aim of creating an awareness of a person's whole self, **Gestalt therapy** differs significantly from psychoanalysis. It assumes that human beings are responsible for themselves and their lives and that they need to focus not on the past, but on the present. As such, Gestalt therapy is concerned with current feelings and behaviors and their representation in a meaningful coherent whole.

Frederick S. Perls (1893–1970), a physician and psychoanalyst trained in Europe, was the founder and principal proponent of Gestalt therapy. He was a dynamic, charismatic therapist, and many psychologists followed him and his ideas closely. Perls assumed that the best way to help clients come to terms with anxiety and other unpleasant feelings was to focus on their current understanding and awareness of the world, not on past situations and experiences. Building Table 15.2 on page 546 presents a summary of the key components of psychoanalytic and humanistic views of therapy.

Gestalt therapy: An insight therapy founded by Perls that emphasizes the importance of a person's being aware of current feelings and situation.

Goals of Gestalt Therapy. The goals of Gestalt therapy are to help people resolve old conflicts and enable them to resolve future conflicts. It aims at expanding clients' awareness of their current attitudes and feelings so they can respond more fully and appropriately to current situations. Gestalt therapy does not "cure" people; rather, it helps them become complete and

	Psychoanalysis	Humanistic Therapy	Behavior Therapy
Nature of Psychopathology	Maladjustment reflects inadequate conflict resolution and fixation in early development, which leave overly weak ego controls or strong impulses.	Pathology reflects an incongruity between the *real* self and the potential, desired self. The person is overly dependent on others for gratification and self-esteem.	
Goal of Therapy	Attainment of psychosexual maturity, strengthened ego functions, and reduced control by unconscious and repressed impulses.	Fostering self-determination, authenticity, and integration by releasing human potential and expanding awareness.	
Role of Therapist	An *investigator*, uncovering conflicts and resistances.	An *authentic*, empathic person in true encounter with patient, sharing experience.	
Role of Unconscious Material	Primary in classical psychoanalysis, less emphasis in ego-analysis.	Emphasis is primarily on conscious experience.	
Role of Insight	Conceived as coming not solely from intellectual understanding but also from "corrective emotional experiences."	Used by many, but there is more emphasis on *how* and *what* questions rather than *why* questions.	
Techniques	Analyst takes an active role in interpreting the dreams and free associations of patients.	Patient is asked to see the world from a different perspective and is encouraged to focus on current situations rather than past ones.	

♦ *Building Table 15.2* ♦

Summary of Key Issues in Psychoanalysis and Humanistic Therapy enables them to continue to adapt in the future. Gestalt psychologists help people deal with feelings of what Perls called *incomplete Gestalts*, that is, unfinished business or unresolved conflicts, such as previously unrecognized feelings of anger toward a spouse or envy of a brother or sister.

From Perls's point of view, the client needs to expand his or her conscious awareness by reconnecting fragments of past and current experience. He argued that people develop false lives and are not in touch with their real selves. Only when people become aware of the here and now can they become sensitive to the tensions and repressions that made their previous behavior maladaptive. Also, once they become aware of their current feelings and accept themselves, clients can understand earlier behaviors and plan appropriate future behaviors. From a Gestalt viewpoint, healthy people are in touch with their feelings and reality. So a major goal of therapy is to get people in touch with their feelings so that they can construct an accurate picture of their psychological world.

Guided by a Gestalt-oriented therapist, Ricky may explore his relationship with his parents. He may realize that his anger, drinking, and poor sales reflect low self-esteem and hostile feelings toward his father. After constructing an accurate picture of his psychological world, Ricky can adopt new behaviors that will help him explore other careers while continuing his sales work.

Techniques of Gestalt Therapy. Gestalt therapy examines current feelings and behaviors of which a client may be unaware. Usually the therapist asks the client to concentrate on current feelings about a difficult past experience. For example, a Gestalt therapist may ask a client to relive a situation and discuss it as if it were happening in the present. The underlying assumption is that feelings expressed in the present can be understood and dealt with more easily than feelings remembered from the past.

Many Gestalt techniques are designed to help clients become more alert to significant sensations in themselves and to their surroundings. One such technique is to have clients change the way they talk; a client who feels he has trouble expressing aggression might be asked to talk to each member of a group aggressively. Another technique is to ask clients to behave in a manner opposite to the way they feel; a man who feels hostile or aggressive toward his boss, for example, might be asked to behave as if their relationship were warm and affectionate. The man might be asked to talk to an imaginary boss who is sitting in an empty chair across from him. The point is to help clients understand their true feelings and thus enlarge their understanding of the world. By discussing the situation, clients are forced to hear their own feelings out loud. Previously internalized anxiety is experienced in the present and channeled into more prosocial and productive behaviors. For these reasons, Gestalt therapy is considered an experiential therapy.

Hypnosis, while not exactly a psychodynamic or a humanistic technique, is used by many practitioners as adjuncts to their therapies. Gestalt therapists use it from time to time to help bring clients to a more complete awareness of their surroundings. Evidence suggests that a subject's susceptibility to hypnosis can affect the outcome of some therapeutic interventions (although Spanos, Lush, and Gwynn [1989] assert that other techniques work just as well). Therapists may use hypnosis to help clients relax, remember past events, reduce anxiety, quit smoking, raise consciousness, or even lose weight (Cochrane, 1987). We discussed hypnosis in greater detail in chapter 4.

Criticisms of Gestalt Therapy. Gestalt therapy encourages clients to be in touch with their feelings through a number of diverse techniques. This approach is seen as both a strength and a weakness. Some critics feel that Perls was too focused on individuals' happiness and growth, that he encouraged the attainment of these goals at the expense of other goals. Gestalt therapy is also criticized for focusing too much on feelings and not enough on thought and decision making. Some psychologists think that Gestalt therapy might work best for healthy people who want to grow, and that it might not be successful with severely maladjusted people who cannot make it through the day.

Focus on Learning

◆ Why is Rogerian therapy considered client-centered? p. 544
◆ What is the key technique of nondirective therapies? p. 544
◆ What is the aim of Gestalt therapy? p. 545
◆ What is an important criticism of Gestalt therapy? p. 547
◆ Briefly describe the major differences between psychoanalysis, client-centered therapy, and Gestalt therapy. pp. 538–547

Behavior Therapy

Sometimes people have problems, such as fear of heights, anxiety about public speaking, marital conflicts, or sexual dysfunction, that may not warrant an in-depth discussion of early childhood experiences, an exploration of unconscious motivations, a lengthy discussion about current feelings, or a resolution of inner conflicts. In these cases, behavior therapy may be more appropriate than psychodynamically-based or humanistic therapy.

Goals of Behavior Therapy

Behavior therapy, sometimes called *behavior modification*, uses learning principles to help people replace maladaptive behaviors with new ones. Behavior therapists assume that people's behavior is influenced by changes in their environments, in the way they respond to that environment, and in the way they interact with other people (Stolz, Wienckowski, and Brown, 1975). Unlike psychodynamic therapy, behavior therapy aims not to discover the origins of a behavior, only to alter it. For a person with a nervous twitch, for example, the goal would be to eliminate the twitch. Thus, behavior therapists treat people by having them first unlearn old, faulty behaviors and then learn new ones.

Behavior therapy: A therapy based on the application of learning principles to human behavior. Synonymous with behavior modification, it focuses on changing overt behaviors rather than on understanding subjective feelings, unconscious processes, or motivations.

Behavior therapists do not always focus on the problems that caused the client to seek therapy. If they see that the client's problem is caused by some other situation, they may focus on changing that situation. A client may, for example, seek therapy because of a faltering marriage. But the therapist may discover that the marriage is suffering because of the client's excessive arguments with his spouse following heavy drinking, and that the drinking is brought on by a hard day at work, aggravated by the client's excessive expectations for his own performance (Goldfried and Davison, 1976). In this situation, the therapist might focus on helping the client develop standards consistent with his capabilities, past performance, and realistic future performance, which will ease the original cause of the problem—the tension felt at work.

Unlike psychodynamic or humanistic therapy, behavior therapy does not encourage clients to interpret past events to find their meaning. Although a behavior therapist may uncover a chain of events leading to a specific behavior, that discovery will not generally prompt a close examination of the client's early experiences. To illustrate how behavior therapy works, suppose that Ricky Estavez seeks the help of a behavior-oriented counselor. The therapist first might point out that Ricky has adopted self-destructive responses—anger, drinking, lackadaisical work habits—to his father's demands. Then the therapist will help him formulate new, more positive responses. For example, instead of responding angrily when his father inquires about his work, Ricky might learn to answer by thanking his father for showing concern, then switching the conversation to an interest they both share. If they both enjoy golf, for instance, Ricky might relate that he recently reduced his handicap.

When people enter behavior therapy, many aspects of their behavior may change, not just those specifically being treated. Thus, a person who is being treated for extreme shyness might find not only that the shyness decreases, but also that he can engage more easily in discussions about emotional topics and perform better on the job. Behaviorists argue that once a person's behavior has changed, it may be easier to manage attitudes, fears, and intrapsychic conflicts. What are some other aspects of a person's life that might change when they enter behavior therapy?

Behavior Therapy versus Psychodynamic and Humanistic Therapy

Behaviorists are dissatisfied with psychodynamic and humanistic therapies for three basic reasons: (1) psychodynamic and humanistic therapies use concepts that are almost impossible to define and measure (e.g., id, ego, self-actualization); (2) some studies show that patients who do not receive psychodynamic and humanistic therapy improve anyway; and (3) once a person has been labeled as abnormal, the label itself may lead to maladaptive behavior. (Although this is true with any type of therapy, psychodynamic therapy tends to use labels more than behavior therapy does.) Behavior therapists assume that people display maladaptive behavior not because they are abnormal, but because they are having trouble adjusting to their life situations; if they are taught new ways of coping, the maladjustment will disappear.

Most insight therapists, especially those who are psychodynamically based, assume that if only *overt* behavior is treated, as is often done in behavior therapy, symptom substitution may occur. **Symptom substitution** is the appearance of one behavior to replace another that has been eliminated by treatment. Thus, insight therapists argue that if a therapist eliminates a nervous twitch without examining its underlying causes, the client will express the disorder by developing some other symptom, such as a speech impediment. Behavior therapists, on the other hand, contend that symptom substitution does not occur if treatment involves proper use of behavioral principles. Research shows that behavior therapy is at least as effective as insight therapy and in some cases is more effective (e.g., Miller and Berman, 1983; Snyder and Wills, 1989).

Symptom substitution: The appearance of one symptom to replace another that has been eliminated.

Techniques of Behavior Therapy

Behavior therapy uses an array of techniques to help people change their behavior, among them: operant conditioning, counterconditioning, and modeling, often in combination. In addition to using several behavioral techniques, the therapist may use a combination of insight and behavioral techniques. A good psychotherapist will use whatever combination of techniques will help a client most efficiently and effectively. The more complicated the disorder being treated, the more likely it is that a practitioner will use a mix of therapeutic approaches—a *multimodal approach*.

Behavior therapy usually involves three general procedures:

1. identifying the problem behavior and its frequency;
2. treating the client, perhaps by reeducation, communication training, or some type of counterconditioning; and
3. assessing whether there is a lasting behavior change.

If the client exhibits the new behavior for several weeks or months, the therapist concludes that treatment was effective. Let's now discuss the major behavior therapy techniques—operant conditioning, counterconditioning, and modeling—in more detail.

Operant Conditioning

Operant conditioning procedures are used with different people in different settings to achieve a wide range of desirable behaviors, including increased reading speed, improved classroom behaviors, and the maintenance of personal hygiene. As explained in chapter 5, operant conditioning depends on a reinforcer, defined as any event that increases the probability that a particular response will recur. Ricky could employ operant conditioning to help himself adopt more positive responses to his father. For example, he could ask his wife to praise him every time he responds to his father in an appropriate manner.

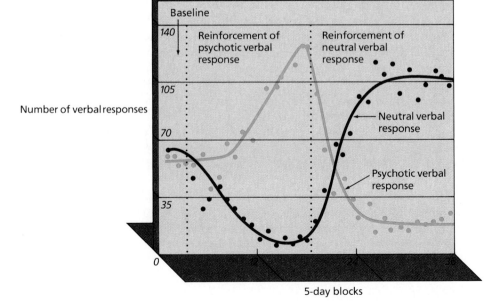

FIGURE 15.2
A study by Ayllon and Haughton found that reinforcement affected the frequency of psychotic and neutral verbal behavior in hospitalized patients.

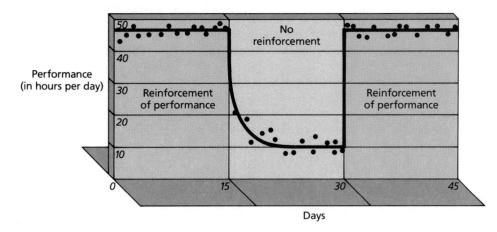

One of the most effective uses of operant conditioning is with children who are antisocial, slow learners, or in some way maladjusted. Operant conditioning is also effective with patients in mental hospitals. Ayllon and Haughton (1964), for example, instructed staff members to reinforce hospitalized patients for psychotic verbalizations during one period and for neutral verbalizations during another. As expected, the frequency of psychotic verbalizations increased when they were reinforced and decreased when they were not reinforced (see Figure 15.2).

Token Economies. Token economies are one way of rewarding adaptive behavior. In a **token economy,** participants receive tokens when they engage in appropriate behavior. Patients can exchange the tokens for desired items or activities, such as candy, new clothes, games, or time with important people in their lives. The more tokens people earn, the more items or privileges they can receive.

Token economies are used to modify behavior in social settings, usually with groups of people. They aim to strengthen behaviors that are compatible with social norms. For example, a patient in a mental hospital might receive tokens for cleaning tables, helping in the hospital laundry, and maintaining certain standards of personal hygiene and appearance. The number of tokens earned is determined by the level of difficulty of the behavior or job and how long the person performs it. Thus, patients might receive three tokens for brushing their teeth but forty tokens for engaging in prosocial helping behaviors. Ayllon and Azrin (1965) monitored the performance of a group of patients for forty-five days. They found that when tokens (reinforcement) were contingent on performance, the patients produced about four times as much work per day as when tokens were not delivered. (See Figure 15.3.)

Extinction and Punishment. As explained in chapter 5, extinction and punishment are operant conditioning techniques that can decrease the frequency of an undesired behavior. If reinforcers are withheld, extinction of a behavior will occur. Suppose a six-year-old refuses to go to bed at the designated time. When she is taken to her bedroom, she cries and screams violently. A therapist might suggest the following approach. If the parents give in and allow her to stay up, they are reinforcing the crying behavior: The child cries, the parents give in. One way to eliminate the crying behavior is to stop reinforcing it by insisting that the child go to bed and stay there. Chances are that the child will cry loudly and violently but the behavior will eventually be extinguished (C. D. Williams, 1959).

Token economy: An operant conditioning procedure in which tokens are given to the patient to reinforce socially acceptable behavior. The tokens are later exchanged for desirable items or privileges.

Time out: A punishment procedure in which a person is removed from a desired or reinforcing situation to decrease the likelihood that an undesired behavior will recur.

Counterconditioning: A process of reconditioning in which a person learns a new response to a familiar stimulus.

Systematic desensitization: A counterconditioning procedure in which a person first learns deep relaxation and then imagines a series of progressively fearful situations. With each successive experience, the person learns relaxation rather than fear as a new response to a formerly fearful stimulus.

Another way to decrease the frequency of undesired behavior is to punish it. Punishment often involves the presentation of an aversive stimulus. In the laboratory, researchers might provide slight electric shocks to get adult subjects to stop performing a specific behavior. Usually, punishment for undesired behaviors is combined with positive reinforcement for prosocial and desired behaviors. A person diagnosed as having a DSM-III-R paraphilia, for example, might receive an electric shock whenever he becomes sexually aroused by an inappropriate object (such as a pair of women's shoes) but be positively reinforced for becoming aroused by a picture of a nude woman.

Time Out. As mentioned in chapter 5, **time out,** the physical removal of a person from sources of reinforcement, is widely used. It decreases the occurrence of undesired behaviors. Suppose a child regularly throws temper tantrums each time she wants a piece of candy, an ice cream cone, or her little brother's toys, and out of frustration and embarrassment her parents often give in. In the time-out procedure, whenever the child misbehaved she would be placed in a room without toys, television, or other people, or in a "thinking chair" away from the rest of her family. She would be kept in the chair or the time-out room for a short period, for example, five or ten minutes; if she left, more time would be added. Not only is the child not getting what she wants, she is also removed from any potential source of reinforcement. Time out is especially effective when combined with positive reinforcers for appropriate behavior and administered by a child care specialist (Crespi, 1988).

Counterconditioning

A second major approach to behavior therapy, **counterconditioning** or reconditioning, teaches people new, more adaptive responses to familiar situations. For example, anxiety is one of the first responses people show when they are maladjusted, fearful, or lacking in self-esteem, so if a therapist can inhibit anxiety by conditioning a person to respond with something other than fear—that is, by *counter*conditioning the person—a real breakthrough in therapy will be achieved.

Joseph Wolpe (1915–) was one of the initial proponents of counterconditioning. His work in classical conditioning, especially situations in which animals show conditioned anxiety responses, led him to attempt to inhibit or decrease anxiety as a response in human beings. His therapeutic goal was to replace anxiety with some other response, such as relaxation, amusement, or pleasure.

Wolpe's work has had a profound impact on behavior therapists. Behavior therapy using counterconditioning begins with a specific stimulus (S_1) that elicits a specific response (R_1). After the person undergoes counterconditioning, the same stimulus (S_1) should elicit a new response (R_2) (Wolpe, 1958). There are two basic approaches to counterconditioning: systematic desensitization and aversive counterconditioning.

Systematic Desensitization. **Systematic desensitization** is a three-stage process in which people are taught to relax when presented with stimuli that formerly elicited anxiety. First the subject learns how to relax; then the subject describes the specific situations that arouse anxiety; and finally the subject, while deeply relaxed, imagines the scenes that elicit anxiety. In this way the subject is gradually, step by step, exposed to the source of anxiety, usually by imagining a series of progressively more fearful or anxiety-provoking situations.

Flying in an airplane, for example, is a stimulus situation (S_1) that can bring about an inappropriate fear response (R_1). With systematic desensitization therapy, the idea of flying (S_1) can eventually elicit a response of curiosity or even relaxation (R_2). The therapist might first ask the client to imagine sitting in an airplane on the ground, then to imagine the airplane taxiing, and eventually to imagine flying though the billowing clouds. As the client realizes that imagining the scene will not result in harm or isolation, he or she becomes able to tolerate more stressful imagery and may eventually perform the imagined behavior, in this case, flying in an airplane.

Systematic desensitization is not effective for all disorders, however. It is most successful for people with problems like anger control or who exhibit forms of anxiety, such as phobias. But it is not especially effective with people who exhibit serious psychotic symptoms, nor is it the best treatment for situations involving interpersonal conflict (Wolpe, 1973). There is much controversy over how systematic desensitization works. Some psychologists suggest that the patient's expectations account for the success of the procedure. Some practitioners think that systematic desensitization is not a form of counterconditioning but an extinction procedure or perhaps a form of cognitive restructuring, discussed later in the chapter.

Using systematic desensitization, a therapist gradually acclimates a client to a previously frightening situation.

Aversive Counterconditioning. The second major type of counterconditioning is **aversive counterconditioning,** in which a stimulus that elicits undesirable behavior is paired with a noxious or aversive stimulus. As with systematic desensitization, the objective is to teach a new response to the original stimulus. A behavior therapist, for example, might use aversive counterconditioning to teach someone like Ricky Estavez a new response to alcohol. The first step might be to teach him to associate alcohol (the original stimulus) with the sensation of nausea (a noxious stimulus). If verbal instruction is not enough, the therapist might administer a drug that causes nausea whenever alcohol is consumed. The goal is to make drinking or the consequences of drinking alcohol (the undesirable behavior) unpleasant. Eventually the treatment will make just the thought of alcohol produce nausea and, thus, avoidance behavior (the new response) (Davidson, 1974).

Modeling

Both children and adults learn behaviors by watching and imitating other people—in other words, by observing models. Children learn table manners, toilet behavior, and appropriate responses to animals by observing and imitating their parents and other models. Similarly, the music you listen to, the clothing styles you wear, and the social or political causes you support are determined, in part, by the people around you.

According to Albert Bandura (1977a), modeling is most effective in three areas: (1) learning new behavior, (2) helping to eliminate fears, especially phobias, and (3) expressing already existing behavior. By watching the behavior of others, people learn to exhibit more adaptive and appropriate behavior. Bandura, Blanchard, and Ritter (1969), for example, asked people with snake phobias to watch other people handling snakes. Afterward, the subjects' fear of snakes was reduced. Jaffe and Carlson (1972) used modeling to treat people with test anxiety; and Wincze and Caird (1976) used it to help people who were experiencing sexual dysfunction.

Aversive counterconditioning: A counterconditioning technique that pairs an aversive or noxious stimulus with a stimulus that elicits undesirable behavior so that the subject will adopt new behaviors in response to the original stimulus.

	Psychoanalysis	Humanistic Therapy	Behavior Therapy	Cognitive Therapy
Nature of Psychopathology	Maladjustment reflects inadequate conflict resolution and fixation in early development, which leave overly weak ego controls or strong impulses.	Pathology reflects an incongruity between the *real* self and the potential, desired self. The person is overly dependent on others for gratification and self-esteem.	Symptomatic behavior stems from faulty learning or learning of maladaptive behaviors. The symptom is the problem; there is no "underlying disease."	
Goal of Therapy	Attainment of psychosexual maturity, strengthened ego functions, and reduced control by unconscious and repressed impulses.	Fostering self-determination, authenticity, and integration by releasing human potential and expanding awareness.	Relieving symptomatic behavior by suppressing or replacing maladaptive behaviors.	
Role of Therapist	An *investigator*, uncovering conflicts and resistances.	An *authentic*, empathic person in true encounter with patient, sharing experience.	A *trainer*, helping subject unlearn old behaviors and learn new ones.	
Role of Unconscious Material	Primary in classical psychoanalysis, less emphasis in ego-analysis.	Emphasis is primarily on conscious experience.	No concern with unconscious processes.	
Role of Insight	Conceived as coming not solely from intellectual understanding but also from "corrective emotional experiences."	Used by many, but there is more emphasis on *how* and *what* questions rather than *why* questions.	Irrelevant and unnecessary.	
Techniques	Analyst takes an active role in interpreting the dreams and free associations of patients.	Patient is asked to see the world from a different perspective and is encouraged to focus on current situations rather than past ones.	Subjects learn new responses; used to establish new behaviors and eliminate "faulty" or undesirable ones.	

❖ *Building Table 15.3* ❖

Summary of Key Issues in Psychoanalysis, Humanistic Therapy, and Behavior Therapy

Behavior is often acquired through modeling, and the choice of model may occur from day-to-day activities such as reading a popular magazine.

One problem with modeling is that people may observe and imitate the behavior of inappropriate models. Many studies show that people imitate violent behaviors that they have observed on television and in movies. Further, many adolescents become involved in alcohol and drug abuse because they imitated their peers. Such imitation often occurs because of faulty thinking about situations, people, or lifelong goals. When people have developed a faulty set of expectations that guide their behavior, cognitive therapy may be in order. Building Table 15.3 presents a summary of the key components of psychoanalytic, humanistic, and behavioral views of therapy.

◆ Identify two reasons why behaviorists are dissatisfied with psychodynamic and humanistic therapies. p. 549
◆ As a behavior therapy technique, operant conditioning is especially effective with what kinds of people or what disorders? p. 550
◆ What takes place in systematic desensitization? p. 552
◆ In what situations is modeling (observational learning) most effective? p. 553

Focus on Learning

Cognitive Therapy

Cognitive psychologists have had a profound impact on many areas of psychology, especially in therapy. In the past, most behavior therapists were concerned only with overt behavior, but many now incorporate thought processes into their treatments. Researchers now suggest that the thought process may hold the key to managing many forms of maladjustment. Therapists who use *cognitive restructuring,* for example, are interested in modifying the faulty thought patterns of disturbed people (Mahoney, 1977). Cognitive restructuring as a therapeutic technique is effective for people who have attached labels to certain situations; for example, they may feel that sex is dirty or that assertiveness is unwomanly. Whenever they are presented with

Albert Ellis developed a cognitive therapy known as rational-emotive therapy. He believed that maladjustment was caused by faulty or irrational assumptions.

a situation that involves sex or assertiveness, they respond in the same way, which is determined by their thoughts about the situation, rather than by facts of the situation.

There are three basic propositions of cognitive therapy (Dobson and Block, 1988). First, cognitive activity affects behavior; second, cognitive activity can be monitored; and third, behavior changes can be effected through cognitive changes. Like other forms of behavior therapy, cognitive restructuring therapy focuses on current behavior and current thoughts. It is not especially concerned with uncovering forgotten childhood experiences, although it can be used to alter thoughts about childhood experiences.

Rational-Emotive Therapy

The best-known cognitive therapy is **rational-emotive therapy,** developed by researcher Albert Ellis (1913–) more than thirty years ago. Most behavior therapists assume that abnormal behavior is caused by faulty and irrational behavior patterns. Ellis and his colleagues, however, assume that it is caused by faulty and irrational thinking patterns (Ellis, 1962, 1970; Ellis and Harper, 1961). They believe that if faulty thought processes can be replaced with rational ideas, maladjustment and abnormal behavior will disappear. Ricky may hold the irrational belief that his father will not love him if he doesn't become a big-time sales manager. This belief could be the source of Ricky's anxiety, hostility, and self-destructive behavior, yet it may be unfounded.

According to Ellis, psychological disturbance is a result of events in a person's life that give rise to irrational beliefs, leading to negative emotions and behaviors. Moreover, they are a breeding ground for further irrational ideas (Dryden and Ellis, 1988). Ellis argues that people invent dogmatic demands on themselves and on other people, and they rigidly hold on to them no matter how unrealistic and illogical they are (Ellis, 1988). So from Ellis's view, if Ricky feels that the only way he can be a success is to please his father and follow in the family business, then he is bound to be unhappy.

Thus, a major goal of rational-emotive therapy is to help a person examine the past events that produced the irrational beliefs. Ellis, for example, tries to zero in on a client's basic philosophy of life and how it is inevitably self-defeating (Ellis, 1990). He thus tries to uncover the client's thought patterns and help the client recognize that his or her underlying beliefs are faulty. In other words, the therapist tries to alter irrational beliefs and thought patterns. When rational-emotive therapy is successful, the client adopts different behaviors based on new, more rational thought processes. Cognitive behavior therapy has been used effectively to treat depression, bulimia, weight loss, anger, and adolescent behavior problems (e.g., Deffenbacher, 1988).

Table 15.3 lists ten irrational assumptions that, according to Ellis, cause emotional problems and maladaptive behaviors. They are based on people's needs to be liked, to be competent, to be loved, and to feel secure. When people place irrational or exaggerated value on these needs, they become maladaptive and lead to emotional disturbance, anxiety, and abnormal behavior. Can you add to Ellis's list of irrational assumptions?

Beck's Approach

Another cognitive restructuring therapy that focuses on irrational ideas is that of Aaron Beck (1963). As described in chapter 14, Beck's theory assumes that depression is caused by people's distorted cognitive views of reality, which lead to negative views about the world, themselves, and the future,

Rational-emotive therapy: A cognitive behavior therapy originated by Albert Ellis that emphasizes the importance of logical, rational thought processes.

TABLE 15.3

Ten Irrational Assumptions Outlined by Albert Ellis
1. It is a necessity for an adult to be loved and approved by almost everyone for virtually everything.
2. A person must be thoroughly competent, adequate, and successful in all respects.
3. Certain people are bad, wicked, or villainous and should be punished for their sins.
4. It is catastrophic when things are not going the way one would like.
5. Human unhappiness is externally caused. People have little or no ability to control their sorrows or to rid themselves of negative feelings.
6. It is right to be terribly preoccupied with and upset about something that may be dangerous or fearsome.
7. It is easier to avoid facing many of life's difficulties and responsibilities than it is to undertake more rewarding forms of self-discipline.
8. The past is all-important. Because something once strongly affected someone's life, it should continue to do so indefinitely.
9. People and things should be different from the way they are. It is catastrophic if perfect solutions to the grim realities of life are not immediately found.
10. Maximal human happiness can be achieved by inertia and inaction or by passively and without commitment "enjoying oneself."

Source: Ellis and Harper, 1961.

and often to gross overgeneralizations. A man who thinks that he has no future, that all of his options are blocked, and who undervalues his intelligence is likely to be depressed. For such individuals, forming appraisals of situations, especially self-appraisals, is distorted and based on insufficient (and sometimes wrong) data. The goal of therapy, therefore, is to help people develop realistic rather than distorted appraisals of the situations they encounter, and to solve problems the way they do in the rest of their lives. The therapist acts as a trainer and co-investigator providing "data" to be examined, a guide to understanding how cognitions influence behavior (Beck and Weishaar, 1989).

According to Beck, successful clients pass through four stages as they correct their faulty views and move toward improved mental health:

> First, he has to become aware of what he is thinking. Second, he needs to recognize what thoughts are awry. Then he has to substitute accurate for inaccurate judgments. Finally, he needs feedback to inform him whether his changes are correct. (BECK, 1976, P. 217)

Meichenbaum's Approach

Some researchers, such as Donald Meichenbaum, believe that what people *say* to themselves determines what they will do. Therefore, a goal of therapy is to change the things people say to themselves. According to Meichenbaum, the therapist has to change the client's self-instructions.

A strength of Meichenbaum's theory is that self-instruction can be used in many settings for many different problems (Dobson and Block, 1988). It can help people who are shy or impulsive, people with speech impediments, and even those who are schizophrenic (Meichenbaum, 1974; Meichenbaum and Cameron, 1973). Rather than attempting to change irrational beliefs,

Aaron Beck based his cognitive restructuring therapy on the theory that individuals may appraise themselves and their life decisions using faulty data.

clients learn a repertoire of activities that they can use to make their behavior more adaptive. For example, they may learn to conduct a private monologue in which they work through adaptive ways of thinking and coping with situations. They can then discuss with a therapist the quality of these self-instructional statements and their usefulness. They may learn to organize their responses to specific situations in an orderly set of steps.

Cognitive therapy in its many forms has been used with adults, children, and specialized groups such as women and the elderly (DiGiuseppe, 1989; Davis and Padesky, 1989; Glantz, 1989). It can be applied to problems such as anxiety disorders, marital relations, chronic pain, and as we saw in Beck's work, depression. Cognitive therapy continues to make enormous strides and influences an increasing number of theorists and practitioners who conduct both long-term and brief therapy, considered next.

Brief Therapy

MILESTONES IN
PSYCHOLOGY

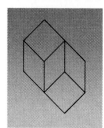

*T*here is a new therapy in town—and it is often a cognitive therapy. Brief therapy rejects many of the traditional ideas of the various therapies we have just discussed. Proponents of brief therapy reject the concept of an ideal therapist who can do all things for all people, the idea that one therapeutic approach can help all people with any behavior or emotional problem, the belief that a person's unconscious or life history must be understood fully before the client can end therapy, and the concept that the therapist and client have only one chance to resolve past or future psychological problems.

In an award-winning address to the American Psychological Association, Nicholas Cummings (1986) described a new model for psychotherapy, **brief intermittent therapy** throughout the life cycle, which is based on a blend of psychotherapeutic orientations and skills. A basic goal of brief therapy is to give clients what they need. The therapy therefore focuses on treating clients' problems efficiently and getting them back on their own as quickly as possible. One of its objectives is to save clients time and money, with the knowledge that they can and will return if they need help in the future. There are, however, no limits on the number of sessions, and the client remains in therapy as long as he or she feels it is necessary. But today more and more therapists think in terms of *planned* short-term treatments (Wells and Phelps, 1990).

In the first session of brief therapy, the therapist makes sure that treatment begins. He or she strives to perform an *operational diagnosis* that answers the question, "Why is the client here today instead of last week or last month, last year, or next year?" The answer indicates to the therapist the specific problem for which the client is seeking help. Also in the first session, "Every client makes a therapeutic contract with every therapist" (Cummings, 1986, p. 430). The goals of therapy are established and agreed on by the client and the therapist.

Because it is relatively new, there is not a great deal of published research on the effectiveness of brief psychotherapy (Koss, Butcher, and Strupp, 1986). Research has been limited to relatively few clients with a narrow range of problems. But researchers have found brief therapy to be effective when treatment goals and procedures are tailored to the client's needs and the time available (Brom, Kleber, and Defares, 1989; Siddall, Haffey, and Feinman, 1988). ◆

Brief intermittent therapy: A therapy approach that focuses on identifying the client's current problem and treating it with the most effective treatment as quickly as possible.

Building Table 15.4 provides an overall summary of the cognitive, humanistic, behavioral, and psychoanalytic approaches to individual therapy. Considered next is group therapy that focuses on treating groups of people rather than individuals.

	Psychoanalysis	Humanistic Therapy	Behavior Therapy	Cognitive Therapy
Nature of Psycho-pathology	Maladjustment reflects inadequate conflict resolution and fixation in early development, which leave overly weak ego controls or strong impulses.	Pathology reflects an incongruity between the *real* self and the potential, desired self. The person is overly dependent on others for gratification and self-esteem.	Symptomatic behavior stems from faulty learning or learning of maladaptive behaviors. The symptom is the problem; there is no "underlying disease."	Maladjustment occurs because of faulty irrational ideas and thinking about the world.
Goal of Therapy	Attainment of psychosexual maturity, strengthened ego functions, and reduced control by unconscious and repressed impulses.	Fostering self-determination, authenticity, and integration by releasing human potential and expanding awareness.	Relieving symptomatic behavior by suppressing or replacing maladaptive behaviors.	To change the way subjects think about themselves and the world.
Role of Therapist	An *investigator*, uncovering conflicts and resistances.	An *authentic*, empathic person in true encounter with patient, sharing experience.	A *trainer*, helping subject unlearn old behaviors and learn new ones.	A *trainer* and coinvestigator helping the client learn new rational ways to think about the world.
Role of Unconscious Material	Primary in classical psychoanalysis, less emphasis in ego-analysis.	Emphasis is primarily on conscious experience.	No concern with unconscious processes.	Little or no concern with unconscious processes.
Role of Insight	Conceived as coming not solely from intellectual understanding but also from "corrective emotional experiences."	Used by many, but there is more emphasis on *how* and *what* questions rather than *why* questions.	Irrelevant and unnecessary.	Irrelevant, but may be used if some insight does occur.
Techniques	Analyst takes an active role in interpreting the dreams and free associations of patients.	Patient is asked to see the world from a different perspective and is encouraged to focus on current situations rather than past ones.	Subjects learn new responses; used to establish new behaviors and eliminate "faulty" or undesirable ones.	Subjects learn to think situations through logically and to reconsider many of their irrational assumptions.

◆ *Building Table 15.4* ◆

Summary of Key Issues in Psychoanalysis, Humanistic Therapy, Behavior Therapy, and Cognitive Therapy

Source: Adapted and modified from Korchin, 1976, table 14-2.

Focus on Learning

- Identify the three basic propositions of cognitive therapy. p. 556
- According to Ellis, what are the consequences of developing irrational beliefs? p. 556
- From the view of a cognitive therapist such as Beck, why do people develop depression? pp. 556–557
- Identify the basic goal and format of brief therapy. p. 558

Group Therapy

When several people meet to receive psychological help, the treatment is referred to as **group therapy.** This technique was introduced around the turn of the century and has become increasingly popular since World War II. One reason for its popularity is that the demand for therapists exceeds the number available. Individually, a therapist can generally see up to forty clients a week for one hour each. But in a group, the same therapist might see eight or ten clients in just one hour. Another reason for the popularity is that the therapist's fee is shared among the members of the group, making it less expensive than individual therapy.

Group therapy is often more effective than individual therapy in the treatment of such problems as interpersonal conflicts (Spiegel and Bloom, 1983). The social pressures that operate in a group can help shape the members' behavior; in addition, group members provide useful models of behavior for each other. Successful helping organizations like Weight Watchers, Gamblers Anonymous, and Alcoholics Anonymous practice a form of group therapy; such self-help groups continue to grow in popularity each year. About six million American adults are currently members of self-help groups, and researchers see the self-help group as an important method for coping with some mental health problems (Jacobs and Goodman, 1989). Ricky might find help for his alcoholism by joining a therapy group that focuses on alcohol and drug abuse problems; with people of similar age and problems, Ricky may find himself not so alone.

Techniques, Goals, and Format of Group Therapy

The techniques used by a therapy group are determined largely by the nature of the group and the orientation of its therapist. The group may follow a psychoanalytic, client-centered, Gestalt, behavior therapy, or other approach. No two groups are alike, and no two groups deal with individual members in the same way.

In traditional group therapy, from six to twelve clients meet on a regular basis (often once a week) with a therapist in a clinic, hospital, or therapist's office. Generally, the therapist selects members on the basis of what they can gain from and offer to the group. The goal is to construct a group whose members are compatible (but not necessarily the same) in terms of age, needs, and problems.

The format of traditional group therapy varies, but generally each member describes his or her problems to the other members, who in turn relate their experiences with similar problems and how they coped with them. This gives individuals a chance to express their fears and anxieties to other people who are warm and accepting; each member eventually realizes that every person has emotional problems. Group members also have opportu-

Group therapy: A method in which several people meet as a group with a therapist for the treatment of emotional and behavioral problems.

nities to role play, or try out, new behaviors in a safe but evaluative environment. In a Vietnam veterans' outreach center, for example, a therapist might help members relive past traumas and cope with their continuing fears. Finally, in group therapy members can exert pressure on an individual to behave in more appropriate ways, or at least more like the group norms. Sometimes the therapist is directive in helping the group cope with a specific problem. At other times he or she allows the group to work through its problems independently.

Nontraditional Group Therapy

Several nontraditional techniques are sometimes used in group therapy. One is **psychodrama,** which stems from the work of J. L. Moreno, a Viennese psychiatrist who used this technique in the 1920s and 1930s. In psychodrama, group members act out situations, feelings, and roles. Those who participate can practice expressing their feelings and responding to the feelings of others. Even those who do not participate can see how others respond to different emotions and situations. Psychodrama can help release the floodgates of emotion and can be used to help refine social skills and define problem areas that need to be worked on further (Naar, 1990).

Another nontraditional approach is **encounter group therapy.** Encounter groups are designed to help people self-actualize and develop better interpersonal relationships. Self-actualization (discussed in chapter 11) is the process by which people move toward fulfilling their potentials. Each encounter group is unique. Some are like regular therapy groups. In others, the leader participates minimally, if at all. Some researchers believe that groups made up of specific types of people, such as female athletes, drug addicts, alcoholics, homosexuals, anorexics, or singles, have an advantage in therapy. It is also important to remember that whatever caused a problem, it may create unhappiness and maladjustment for the individual, and it may affect the person's friends, coworkers, and family (Backer and Richardson, 1989).

Psychology and Social Work: Family Therapy

A special form of group therapy is **family therapy,** in which two or more members of a family are treated at once. A *family* is defined as any group of people who are committed to each other's well-being, preferably for life (Bronfenbrenner, 1989). Widely used by a large number of practitioners, especially social workers, family therapy aims to change the ways family members interact. From a family therapist's point of view, the real patient in family therapy is the family's structure and organization (Jacobson and Bussob, 1983). While parents may identify one member of their family, perhaps a delinquent child, as the problem, family therapists believe that the person, in many cases, may simply be a scapegoat. The "problem" member diverts the family's attention from other problems that are more difficult to confront. Sometimes family therapy is called *relationship therapy* because this is often the focus of the intervention (Becvar and Becvar, 1988).

Social workers and family therapists attempt to change *family systems.* This means that treatment takes place within an ongoing, active "social system" such as a marriage or family. Therapists assume that there are multiple sources of psychological influence—individuals within a family affect family processes and family processes affect individuals. It is an interactive system (Bednar, Burlingame, and Masters, 1988). The family systems approach has become especially popular in universities that have social work

Psychodrama: A group therapy procedure in which members act out their situations, feelings, and roles.

Encounter group: A group of people who meet together to learn more about their feelings, behavior, and interactions.

Family therapy: A special form of group therapy in which two or more people who are committed to each other's well-being are treated at once; family therapy often attempts to change *family systems.*

Family therapy often attempts to deal with the family system as a whole rather than focusing on the needs or problems of any one family member.

colleges, in departments of psychology, and even in colleges of medicine where patients are often seen in a family setting.

Many psychologists, social workers, and psychiatrists use family therapy to help individuals and families change (e.g., Gustafsson, Kjellman, and Cederblad, 1986). However, not all families profit equally from such interventions. Family therapy is difficult, for example, with families that are disorganized or in which not all members participate.

Some researchers feel that the family systems approach is as effective as individual therapy and in some situations more effective (Bednar, Burlingame, and Masters, 1988). A clinician presented with a person with some type of adjustment problem must also consider the impact of this problem on other people, one of the main focuses of the topic we consider next, codependence.

Codependence

APPLYING PSYCHOLOGY

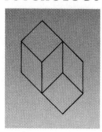

*R*ecently, practitioners have been focusing on families and how they often become wrapped up in a patient's problems—depression, alcoholism, drug abuse, child abuse, or anxiety disorders—that become devastating for them. This is not a DSM-III-R disorder, and the families of people with disorders such as substance abuse have often gone relatively unnoticed. Although practitioners often treat whole families, not just a person suffering from maladjustment, they are facing a new type of adjustment problem, not for the patient, but for his or her family and friends, called *codependence*.

In codependence, families often cling to a person with serious problems in a dependent way. The codependent—the family member or friend—is often plagued by intense feelings of shame, fear, anger, or pain, but cannot express those feelings because of an intense desire to please and care for the person suffering from a disorder or addiction. Codependent persons hope to be perfect in helping the person with the disorder; they feel that if they are perfect, they can help the individual. In some cases, people actually need the patient to stay disordered; for example, families sometimes unwittingly want a patient to maintain dependency on them so that they can stay in a controlling position. A practitioner often has a patient who is facing alcoholism or a cocaine addiction, and a friend or family member who is codependent.

Codependency has long been recognized by psychologists, but Pia Mellody has brought it before practitioners again in a book, *Facing Codependence* (1989). She asserts that families often need therapy and that people who suffer from codependence lack the necessary skills to lead mature, satisfying adult lives. Codependents have difficulty experiencing positive self-esteem; they have difficulty setting psychological boundaries between themselves and others; and they have difficulty defining and meeting day-to-day needs. They become wrapped up in another person and in doing so create suffering for themselves and retard the growth of the original patient. The problem of codependence is just being realized and evaluated; Mellody suggests a therapeutic approach to treat codependency, and future research will evaluate these ideas scientifically. We know that disorders, both mild and severe, affect a person's life, coworkers, family members, and ultimately the community. ◆

- ◆ In what ways can group therapy be more effective than individual therapy? p. 560
- ◆ Describe the makeup of a traditional group meeting for therapy. p. 560
- ◆ What is a family systems approach to family therapy? p. 561

Focus on Learning

Community Psychology

The therapies described in this chapter are based on the assumption that people need help to adapt to society in healthy and productive ways. However, some psychologists try to help people in a broader way. **Community psychology** has emerged in response to a widespread desire for a more action-oriented approach to individual and social adjustment.

In the 1960s many psychologists recognized that individual therapy was at best imprecise and at worst inefficient for treating large numbers of maladjusted people. Researchers and practitioners, as well as politicians, sought a more efficient and effective approach. President John F. Kennedy's 1963 message to Congress called for "a bold new approach" to the treatment of mental illness and was followed by legislation and funding for community mental health centers.

The general aims of community psychology are to strengthen existing social support networks and to stimulate the formation of new networks to meet new challenges (Gonzales et al., 1983). A key element is community involvement to effect social change. A church or synagogue group, for example, could mobilize its senior citizens for a foster grandparent program, and set up support groups of family and friends for patients released from mental hospitals.

Another key element of community psychology is **empowerment,** that is, helping people enhance existing skills and develop new skills, knowledge, and motivation so they can gain control over their own lives (Rappaport, 1987). Community psychology focuses on prevention, early intervention, planning, research, and evaluation. Community psychologists work in schools, churches, planning commissions, and prisons. They plan and set up programs for bringing psychological skills and knowledge into the community.

A special focus of community psychology is *primary prevention*, that is, lowering the rate of new cases of a disorder or counteracting harmful cir-

Community psychology: A branch of psychology that seeks to reach out to society to provide services and especially to effect social change through planning, prevention, intervention, research, and evaluation.

Empowerment: Facilitating the development of skills, knowledge, and motivation in individuals so that they can act for themselves and gain mastery over their own affairs.

cumstances that might lead to maladjustment. Primary prevention usually works on groups rather than on individuals. It may focus on an entire community, on mild-risk groups, such as children from families of low socioeconomic status, or on high-risk groups, such as children of schizophrenic parents.

Community Mental Health Programs

APPLYING
PSYCHOLOGY

*I*n response to growing public awareness of mental health problems, a special kind of service agency—*the neighborhood clinic*—has been developed. Such clinics help communities cope with problems created by mental illness, unemployment, and lack of education. Some clinics provide free, confidential treatment for problems such as drug addiction, alcoholism, and emotional and psychological disorders.

Centers offer various services, including partial hospitalization programs for people who require hospitalization during the day, and outpatient care for people who live at home while receiving therapy. They also offer consultation, education programs, and lectures and literature on topics such as therapy, family planning, and drug rehabilitation.

Crisis intervention centers help people deal with short-term, stressful situations that require immediate therapeutic attention. Often the crisis is a specific event; for example, a man may lose his job, a child may be seriously ill, or a woman may be raped. The focus of crisis intervention is on the immediate circumstances, not on past experiences. Psychologists know that a crisis is a turning point at which things will get better or worse—a point at which change is possible (Pittman et al., 1990). Some studies show that crisis intervention therapy can be especially effective (Sawicki, 1988). One problem in evaluating crisis therapy is that a variety of techniques are used, making controlled comparisons difficult (Slaikeu, 1990).

Applied psychologists often seek to develop human service programs. Although many community psychologists focus on research, many are also involved in intervention, consultation, and developing existing resources. Whether they work in the juvenile justice system, in helping communities deal with the impact of toxic waste, or in the direct delivery of mental health services, community psychologists are generally considered applied psychologists.   ◆

Human Diversity

Community psychologists have been especially sensitive to *human diversity*, that is, the fact that people are not alike and do not have the same needs. A society is made up of individuals from many different cultures, races, religions, and regional heritages. Each subgroup develops its own style of living, which may vary considerably from that of the majority culture (Snowden, 1987) and leads to marked ethnic-related differences in mental health (Snowden and Cheung, 1990).

One special population, the elderly, forms a growing percentage of the general population. In the early 1990s, more than thirty million Americans will be sixty-five or older. The proportion of elderly people is expected to increase by the year 2030, and the number of Americans over sixty-five will exceed sixty million. Community psychologists are developing programs that focus on the special needs of the elderly for social support, physical and psychological therapy, and continuing education.

Another special group, women, accounts for somewhat more than half the general population. However, much more than half of the people seen by mental health practitioners are women. Men are less likely to seek therapy. One reason for this difference may be that changes in sex roles have placed severe stresses on women, many of whom combine the roles of mother, spouse, and wage earner. In addition, as a group, women are paid less than their male counterparts. Single mothers, older women, women members of minority groups, and women homosexuals often have great difficulty getting a job, supporting a family, and finding their own place in a world where societal values and expectations are constantly changing. Of course, making generalizations about special populations such as women, Afro-Americans, or Hispanics is always risky.

Psychology as a Community Activity

One aim of community psychology is to serve all members of the community, including people who might not otherwise be able to afford the services of a psychotherapist or counselor. Community psychologists staff mental health centers, twenty-four-hour hotlines, and suicide prevention centers. They also provide psychological services to groups of alcoholics or drug addicts and establish prevention programs to identify high-risk individuals and provide them with appropriate services before the need for crisis intervention or hospitalization arises.

Community psychologists are change-oriented. Because they believe that some social conditions and organizational procedures result in maladjusted individuals, they often advocate changes in community institutions and organizations. For example, they seek to improve the court system, develop programs to prevent drug use in schools, help energy conservation groups educate the public, consult with industry about reducing stress on the job, help churches develop volunteer programs to aid the homeless, and help hospitals set up preventive medicine programs.

Community psychologists help people deal with crises in their lives that come about because of community situations. Consider Stockton, California. In 1988, a man opened fire on a school playground, killing five children and wounding twenty-nine others. Within hours, community psychologists mobilized to provide support to a city in shock. Hot lines, counseling groups, and discussion forums were set up to help both parents and children cope with their grief and fear. More than a year later, many of the children and their parents were still receiving counseling.

As mentioned earlier, many community psychologists see their task as one of empowerment. That is, they seek to encourage people to develop or improve their skills, knowledge, and motivation so that they can solve their own problems and contribute to the improvement of living conditions for everyone. Community psychologists therefore focus on bringing about change by linking human potential to existing social structures.

Crisis intervention centers such as this battered women's shelter provide immediate assistance to people in need.

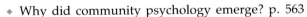

◆ Why did community psychology emerge? p. 563
◆ What is empowerment? p. 563
◆ Identify three settings in which community psychologists might work. pp. 564–565

Focus on Learning

Biologically-Based Therapies

When an individual is referred to a practitioner for help, the usual approach involves some form of psychological treatment. This usually means a talking therapy that may be based on psychodynamic, behavior, cognitive, or humanistic theories. But for some patients, talking therapy is not enough. Some are too depressed; others may be exhibiting symptoms of bipolar disorders; others may need hospitalization because they are suicidal.

Biologically-based therapies may include medication, hospitalization, and the involvement of physicians. Biologically-based approaches are generally not used alone, but in combination with traditional forms of therapy—a multimodal approach. Biological therapies fall into broad classes that vary from those rarely if ever used to those used frequently: psychosurgery, electroconvulsive shock therapy, and drug therapies.

Psychosurgery

Psychosurgery is brain surgery that was once used to alleviate symptoms of mental disorders. In the 1940s and 1950s, *prefrontal lobotomies* were common; this procedure involved removing or surgically severing parts of a patient's frontal lobes from other parts of the brain. Severing the frontal lobes, thought to control emotions, destroyed connections within the brain, making patients docile. Patients lost the symptoms of their mental disorders, but also became calm and wholly unemotional; some became unable to control their impulses, and an estimated one to four percent died from the operation.

Today, despite advances in technology and the precision of the operation, psychosurgery is rarely, if ever, used, for three basic reasons. First, drug therapy has proven more effective than such surgical procedures; second, the long-term effects of psychosurgery are questionable; and most important, the procedure is irreversible and morally objectionable to most practitioners, patients, and their families. Its widespread use earlier in this century is considered by many to have been a serious mistake.

Electroconvulsive Shock Therapy

Shock treatment, or **electroconvulsive shock therapy** (ECT), was once a widely used treatment for depressed individuals. ECT is a treatment for severe mental illness in which a brief application of electricity is used to produce a generalized seizure. The duration of the shock is less than a second; patients are treated in three to twelve sessions over several weeks. In the 1940s and 1950s, ECT was routinely given to severely disturbed patients in mental hospitals. Unfortunately, it was often used with patients who did not need it—far more often with women—and by overzealous physicians to control unruly patients in mental institutions.

Today ECT is not a common treatment. According to the National Institutes of Health, fewer than 2.5 percent of all psychiatric hospital admissions are treated with ECT, about 30,000 patients each year. Is ECT effective at all? Could drug therapy or traditional psychotherapy be used in its place?

ECT is effective in the *short-term* management of severely depressed individuals and is sometimes used when a patient is at risk of suicide. But its effects are transient if it is not followed by drug therapy and psychotherapy. Generally speaking, ECT should be used as a last resort when other

Electroconvulsive shock therapy: A treatment for severe mental illness in which a brief application of electricity is used to produce a generalized seizure. The duration of the shock is less than a second; patients are treated in three to twelve sessions over a period of several weeks.

forms of drug treatment and psychotherapy are ineffective. ECT is not appropriate in the treatment of schizophrenia nor to manage unruly behavior or symptoms of other disorders.

The medical risk of death during the administration of ECT is low. But there is potential for memory loss and a decreased ability to learn and retain new information which may endure for several weeks. In addition, ECT may frighten patients, and can leave feelings of shame and stigma.

Much more research is needed to determine the effects of ECT and the subgroups for whom the treatment is beneficial, if any. If practitioners determine that ECT is warranted, the law requires (and medical ethics demand) that a patient has the right to accept or reject the treatment.

Psychology and Pharmacology: Drug Therapies

Drug therapy attempts to manage psychological problems through the use of drugs. By administering various doses of drugs, therapists can help people who are experiencing symptoms of anxiety, mania, depression, and schizophrenia. Their symptoms are lessened. Drugs for the relief of mental problems are sometimes called *psychotropic drugs* and are usually grouped into four classes: antianxiety, antidepressant, antimania, and antipsychotics. See Table 15.4 for a list of some common drugs used to treat psychological disorders.

Antianxiety Drugs. Calming and anxiety reducing, these tranquilizers are mood-altering substances. Widely used in the United States (and probably over-prescribed by physicians), these drugs (technically anxiolytics) reduce stressful feelings, calm patients, and lower excitability. Tranxene, Librium,

TABLE 15.4
Common Drugs Used to Treat Psychological Disorders

Effect Group	Chemical Group	Generic Name	Trade Name
Antianxiety (*Anxiolytics*)	Propanediols	Meprobamate	Equanil Miltown
	Benzodiazepines	Clorazepate dipotassium Alprazolam Diazepam	Tranxene Xanax Valium
Antidepressants (*Thymoleptics*)	Tricyclics	Amoxapine Nortriptyline Amitriptyline Imipramine Maprotiline	Asendin Aventyl Elavil Tofranil Ludiomil
	Monoamine Oxidase Inhibitors (MAOs)	Phenelzine	Nardil
		Tranylcypromine	Parnate
	Atypicial Antidepressant	Fluoxetine	Prozac
Antimania (*Thymoleptic*)	Lithium Carbonate	Lithium	Eskalith
Antipsychotics (*Neuroleptics*)	Phenothiazines	Chlorpromazine Trifluoperazine Thioridazine	Thorazine Stelazine Mellaril
	Butyrophenones	Haloperidol	Haldol

Valium, and Miltown are some of the most widely used. When taken on occasion to help a person through a stressful situation, such drugs are useful. They also help manage anxiety in a person who is extremely anxious, particularly when the person is also receiving some form of psychotherapy.

To help Ricky deal with his anxiety on a temporary basis, a physician may prescribe an antianxiety drug such as Tranxene. But long-term continued use of antianxiety drugs without some adjunct therapy is usually ill-advised. Today, physicians are increasingly wary of patients who seek antianxiety drugs for management of daily stressors; they worry about substance abuse and an over-reliance on drugs to get through the day.

Antidepressant Drugs. As their name suggests, antidepressants, sometimes considered mood elevators, are used to treat individuals who are extremely depressed. People who take antidepressants (technically thymoleptics) become more optimistic, less sad, and often redevelop a sense of purpose. These medications allow people to function outside of a hospital setting. They can take as long as four weeks to reach their full effectiveness, and a daily dosage is necessary to maintain its benefit.

Antidepressants are from two major categories of drugs, *tricyclics* and *monoamine oxidase (MAO) inhibitors.* Tricyclics are prescribed more often because they pose less danger of medical complications (patients on MAO inhibitors have to adhere to special diets to prevent adverse physical reactions to the drug).

Although they have side effects that include drowsiness, antidepressants lift the spirits of people who are depressed and are an important aid in the recovery of people with mood disorders, such as depression and some anxiety disorders (Swedo et al., 1989). The drugs work by altering levels of neurotransmitters in the brain. To help Ricky with a severe bout of depression, a physician might prescribe a commonly used tricyclic such as imipramine (Tofranil) or amitriptyline (Elavil) or perhaps a new drug Fluoxetine (Prozac) that works with fewer serious side effects and alleviates symptoms in a majority of people with depressive problems.

Antimania Drugs: Lithium. Another drug, lithium carbonate, has come into wide use. Lithium carbonate (technically also a thymoleptic) is widely used with bipolar disorders—it relieves the manic elements. Psychiatrists find that when a daily maintenance dose is taken, lithium is especially helpful in warding off future episodes of mania. The dosage of any drug is important, but in the case of lithium it is especially important. Too much produces side effects, while too little has no effect. No drug, lithium included, will cure depressive individuals of all their symptoms and problems; however, the drug allows patients to cope better, manage symptoms, and seek other therapies that allow them to manage their life-styles in the most productive way possible.

Antipsychotic Drugs. Antipsychotic drugs are used mainly with people who suffer from the disabling disorder of schizophrenia. Such drugs (technically neuroleptics) reduce hostility and aggression in violent patients and make their disorders more manageable. These drugs reduce delusions and in some cases allow a person to manage life outside of a hospital setting.

Antipsychotic drugs are usually *phenothiazines* (the most common is *chlorpromazine*). They seem to work by altering the level of brain neurotransmitter substances and their uptake. As in antidepressants, dosages of antipsychotic drugs are crucial. Further, if patients are maintained on antipsychotic drugs for too long, other problems can emerge, including facial tics and involuntary movements of the mouth and shoulders. This problem is called *tardive dyskinesia.*

Biologically-Based Therapies: A Cure-All?

Drug therapy is the most widely used biologically-based therapy. It is especially effective when used carefully, and as an adjunct to other forms of therapy. But several key issues must be stressed. Dosages are especially important and must be monitored; too much or too little of certain drugs is dangerous. Long-term continued usage of many drugs is ill-advised. Further, no drug will cure, in any lasting way, the maladjustments of a vast majority of people who are not coping well. Last, physicians and psychiatrists must be sensitive to the issues of over-medication and long-term dependency. People usually need to reevaluate their situations, explore the causes of their behavior, and modify existing ideas and behaviors. For disorders such as schizophrenia, antipsychotics are necessary, but for the day-to-day stresses of modern life, drug therapies must be used with caution.

- ◆ What is psychosurgery? p. 566
- ◆ What are the effects of electroconvulsive shock therapy (ECT)? p. 566
- ◆ What are the biological and psychological effects of antidepressants such as *tricyclics* and *monoamine oxidase inhibitors* (MAO inhibitors)? pp. 567–568

Focus on Learning

Key Terms

Psychotherapy   p. 534
Placebo effect   p. 536
Psychoanalysis   p. 538
Psychodynamically-based therapies   p. 538
Insight therapy   p. 539
Free association   p. 540
Dream analysis   p. 540
Interpretation   p. 540
Resistance   p. 541
Transference   p. 541
Working through   p. 541
Ego-analysts   p. 541

Client-centered therapy   p. 544
Nondirective therapy   p. 544
Gestalt therapy   p. 545
Behavior therapy   p. 547
Symptom substitution   p. 549
Token economy   p. 551
Time out   p. 552
Counterconditioning   p. 552
Systematic desensitization   p. 552
Aversive counterconditioning   p. 553

Rational-emotive therapy   p. 556
Brief intermittent therapy   p. 558
Group therapy   p. 560
Psychodrama   p. 561
Encounter group   p. 561
Family therapy   p. 561
Community psychology   p. 563
Empowerment   p. 563
Electroconvulsive shock therapy   p. 566

Summary

Therapy Comes in Many Forms

- Psychotherapy is the treatment of emotional or behavioral problems through psychological techniques.   p. 534

- Insight therapists assume that maladjustment is caused by failure to understand one's own motivations and needs. They believe that once this understanding is achieved, the behavior will change.   p. 534

- Behavior therapists apply learning principles to produce specific changes in behavior. They concentrate on changing people's overt behaviors rather than on understanding their unconscious motivations.   p. 534

Psychodynamic Therapy

- According to Freudian theory, conflicts among a person's unconscious thoughts and processes produce maladjusted behavior.   p. 538

- The process of interpretation, resistance to interpretation, and transference in psychoanalysis is sometimes referred to as *working through.*   p. 538

Humanistic Therapy

- Client-centered therapy, a humanistic approach developed by Carl Rogers, aims at helping clients realize their potential by learning to evaluate the world and themselves from their own point of view.   p. 543

- Gestalt therapy, developed by Frederick S. Perls, encourages individuals to get in touch with their current feelings and become aware of their current situations.   p. 545

Behavior Therapy

- Behavior therapy uses learning principles to help people replace maladaptive behaviors with new ones.   pp. 548–549

- A major technique of behavior therapy is systematic desensitization, in which a person is taught to relax while imagining increasingly fearful situations.   p. 552

- According to social learning theory, modeling is especially effective in three areas: learning new behavior, helping to eliminate fears, especially phobias, and encouraging already existing behavior.   p. 553

Cognitive Therapy

- There are three basic propositions of cognitive therapy: cognitive activity affects behavior; cognitive activity can be monitored; and behavior changes can be brought about through cognitive changes.   p. 555

- Rational-emotive therapy emphasizes the role of rational thought. It assumes that irrational assumptions are the cause of maladjustment.   p. 556

Group Therapy

- Group therapy is used to treat several people simultaneously. Group therapy is often more effective than individual therapy in the treatment of such problems as interpersonal conflicts.   p. 560

- The techniques used by a therapy group are determined by the nature of the group and the orientation of its therapist. The format of traditional group psychotherapy varies widely.   p. 560

- Family therapists attempt to change family systems; treatment takes place within an ongoing, active social system such as a marriage or family because individuals affect family processes and vice versa.   p. 561

Community Psychology

- Community psychology provides mental health services on a continuous basis in an attempt to reach people who might not otherwise seek psychological help.   p. 563

- The general aims of community psychology are to strengthen existing social support networks and to stimulate the formation of new networks to meet new challenges.   p. 564

Biologically-Based Therapies

- Biological therapies include psychosurgery, electroconvulsive shock therapy, and drug therapies.   p. 566

- Drugs for the relief of mental problems are called psychotropic drugs; these include antianxiety, antidepressant, antipsychotic, and antimania drugs.   pp. 567–568

Connections

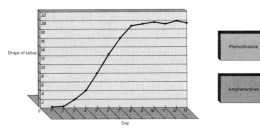

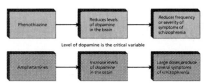

If you are interested in . . .	Turn to . . .	To learn more about . . .
Freud's theory of psychoanalysis as a therapeutic approach	◆ Ch. 12, pp. 426–430	Freud's theory of personality, which later developed into a full-blown treatment approach.
	◆ Ch. 12, p. 430	How defense mechanisms are often overused by individuals in need of therapy.
The behavioral approach to therapy	◆ Ch. 1, p. 8	How early behaviorists focused only on overt, observable behavior.
	◆ Ch. 5, pp. 166–168, 177–178, 193	Classical conditioning, operant conditioning, and modeling which can help explain longstanding behaviors—some of which may become maladaptive.
	◆ Ch. 14, p. 520	How disorders such as depression often have a cognitive basis which requires a change in thought processes and overt behavior.
Biological approaches to therapy	◆ Ch. 2, pp. 45–47	How certain chemicals in the blood and brain which affect behavior can be used as part of a multimodal treatment approach.
	◆ Ch. 13, p. 469	How stress can lead to a number of health-related issues which can be alleviated, in part, through psychotherapy, and in part, through drug treatments.
	◆ Ch. 14, p. 520	Depression's biological basis and how it can sometimes be alleviated through drug therapy.

16

The Social World

"The Hawthorne Tree #2" by Isaac Witkin

*I*n 1978 a team of forty eminent scientists assembled in Turin, Italy, to study a yellowed, fourteen-foot strip of linen bearing the ghostly imprint of a bearded man wearing a crown of thorns. Purported to be Christ's burial cloth, the Shroud of Turin has been worshiped by multitudes since its earliest known exhibit in 1354. After six days of extensive testing—including X-ray fluorescence, surface sampling, photographic computer analysis, and image enhancement—the scientists announced that the cloth's imprint was not paint or pigment and may have resulted from a brief flash of radiation emanating from a body. In a news service interview, the scientific team's leader said, "Every one of the scientists I have talked to believes the cloth is authentic." Convinced that the shroud was genuine, one Jewish member of the scientific team converted to Christianity.

In the fall of 1988, the Vatican permitted small swatches of the shroud to be submitted to a new carbon-14 dating technique (earlier carbon-14 procedures would have destroyed too much of the cloth). All three laboratories that analyzed the linen concluded it was woven between twelve and thirteen centuries after Christ's death. One expert declared the shroud

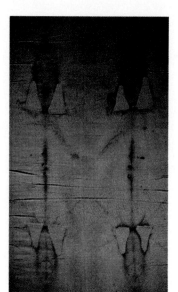

The Shroud of Turin presents a dilemma to believers and unbelievers alike as new evidence corroborates, then denies that this is the shroud of Christ.

to be the work of a brilliant medieval hoaxer. But the new scientific proof didn't shake the faith of those who ardently believed in the shroud legend. Some believers questioned the accuracy of carbon-14 dating; others said that the image—regardless of its age—was created by a miracle.

The Shroud of Turin case exemplifies how humans acquire, maintain, and change their attitudes. On one hand, preliminary "proof" of the shroud's authenticity convinced a well-educated man to change his long-standing religious beliefs. Yet even stronger scientific evidence debunking the shroud proved unpersuasive to others. Why would people hold such strong and different attitudes about a piece of cloth?

Social psychology is the study of how people influence and are influenced by the thoughts, feelings, and behaviors of other people. Your behavior, although it may not always be apparent, is directly affected by the social world you live in. Social psychologists focus on *individual behavior,* on how individuals form attitudes and feelings about themselves and other people, and on individuals' responses to others. Look at what you are wearing right now. Look at what other people are wearing. Are similarities only a matter of chance? On a grander scale, we saw that in the 1988 presidential election Michael Dukakis came to be seen as an ultra-liberal—soft on crime and national defense and strong on wasteful government social programs. How was this image created? How did it come to be adopted by a majority of voters? We also see the power of the social world in the child of an abusive parent who constantly reminds the child that he or she is lazy, stupid, and good for nothing; we know that such children usually come to behave as their parents suggest they do. We also know that thoughts or overt behaviors affect our individual actions. Our social world influences us powerfully, directly, and from the moment we are born.

This chapter provides an overview of some of the traditional topics in social psychology: attitudes, social cognition, social influence, and behavior in groups. These help us form an understanding of behavior when there is more than one person involved—that is, our social world. This chapter focuses on how individual behavior is affected by other people. This is especially evident in the formation of *attitudes* (lasting feelings, beliefs, and behavior tendencies toward other people, ideas, or objects). We will examine *social cognition* (making sense of events and people), *social influence* (efforts to alter the attitudes or behavior of others), and *group behavior* (people working toward a common purpose who are loosely related and have some common goals). We begin with attitudes.

Social psychology: The study of how people influence and are influenced by the thoughts, feelings, and behaviors of other people; social psychologists focus on *individual behavior.*

Attitude: A pattern of relatively enduring feelings, beliefs, and behavior tendencies toward other people, ideas, or objects.

Attitudes

Attitudes determine whether you will respond to a given situation positively or negatively, or with enthusiasm or reluctance. **Attitudes** are lasting patterns of feelings, beliefs, and behavior tendencies toward other people, ideas, or objects. These patterns are shaped by how other people perceive us, and by how we think other people see us. Social psychologists are concerned with how the behavior and attitudes of other people influence individual behavior. The scientist who underwent the religious conversion while studying the Shroud of Turin was undoubtedly influenced by the beliefs of his fellow investigators. Moreover, his attitudes toward the shroud were shaped by professional training that made the existing scientific proofs convincing.

Dimensions of Attitudes

People's attitudes are comprised of different dimensions. Psychologists contend that attitudes are multi-dimensional (Cacioppo, Petty, and Geen, 1989); most believe that there are three basic dimensions: cognitive, emotional, and behavioral.

The *cognitive dimension* of attitudes consists of thoughts and beliefs, such as the belief that science or religious faith can reveal truths. The *emotional dimension* involves feelings of like or dislike. A person may like the idea that the Shroud of Turin is authentic because it makes her or him feel more spiritual. The third dimension, *behavior*, is how people show their beliefs and feelings, such as publicly announcing the shroud's authenticity or undergoing a religious conversion.

When people form attitudes about a group of people, a series of events, or a political philosophy, those attitudes help them categorize, process, and remember the people, events, and ideas (Hymes, 1986). When people have strongly held attitudes and adopt a specific belief, they are said to have a *conviction*. Once people acquire a conviction, they think about it, become involved with it, and may become emotional over it (which makes convictions long-lasting and resistant to change). This is especially true of religious and political convictions (Abelson, 1988). For example, despite strong scientific evidence to the contrary, many people still believe that the Shroud of Turin was Christ's burial cloth.

Individuals do not always publicly display their attitudes, especially when the attitudes are not yet firmly established, or when their attitudes and behaviors are inconsistent. For example, despite widespread support of a nuclear arms freeze, few people give their time, energy, or money to organizations that support this cause (Gilbert, 1988). What variables determine when attitudes are displayed or changed? Why are some attitudes so hard to modify and others relatively easy to change? Most important, how are attitudes formed?

Forming Attitudes

Attitudes are acquired through learning, beginning early in life. Thus, psychologists rely on learning theories to explain how children form attitudes. Three learning theory concepts (discussed in detail in chapter 5) that help explain attitude formation are classical conditioning, operant conditioning, and observational learning.

Classical Conditioning. The pairing of people, events, and ideologies with attitudes often goes unnoticed because it is so effortless. However, such pairings can shape children's views and emotional responses to the world, thereby forming the basis of children's (and later adults') attitudes. See Figure 16.1 on page 576 for an overview of this process. For example, whenever a child overhears a parent make a negative comment about a neighbor, classical conditioning pairs the formerly neutral stimulus (neighbor) with an unconditioned stimulus (negative comment). Because negative comments naturally elicit negative feelings as a response, we may treat the resulting negative feelings as an unconditioned response. If the child overhears such remarks repeatedly, the neighbor eventually evokes a negative response (now a conditioned response) in the child. Likewise, by repeatedly making remarks about specific religious beliefs, parents may condition their children to accept or reject those beliefs.

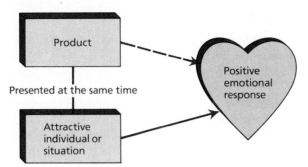

FIGURE 16.1
In attempting to induce positive feelings toward a product or idea, advertisers use classical conditioning techniques—they pair their product or idea with an attractive, desirable state, person, or situation to evoke a pleasant response.

Operant Conditioning. A key principle of operant conditioning states that reinforced behaviors are likely to recur, which helps explain how attitudes are maintained over time. In socializing children, parents express and reinforce ideas and behaviors consistent with their own "correct" view of the world. Such expression and reinforcement helps children adopt those "correct" attitudes. Similarly, therapists reinforce clients' adaptive thoughts, for example, by praising them when they have rid themselves of irrational ideas.

Observational Learning. The social learning point of view asserts that people establish attitudes by watching the behavior of someone they consider significant, and imitating it. The new attitudes people learn eventually become their own. Suppose a young girl sees her father react angrily to a television news story that contradicts the family's religious faith. The next time the child hears a similar argument, she will likely mimic her father's attitude. Children learn about new political ideas and interpersonal relationships through observation, first at home and later at school among friends.

Predicting Behavior from Attitudes

Social psychologists can assess people's attitudes, but whether those attitudes predict behavior depends on a number of variables. For one thing, attitudes are better predictors of behavior when strongly held and there is a minimum of competing outside influence, such as conflicting advertising appeals and advice from friends and relatives. A Catholic who believes strongly in religious miracles will more readily accept the Shroud of Turin's authenticity and revere the shroud if he or she hears only arguments supporting that attitude. Attitudes people consider personally important are more likely to be shown in behavior and stay intact regardless of how situations change over time (Krosnick, 1988).

Also, attitudes are more likely to foretell behavior when the situation requiring a decision closely matches the situation to which the attitude applies. For example, general attitudes about the environment have less impact on an individual's littering behavior than do specific attitudes about littering (Ajzen and Fishbein, 1977). Behavior is also more likely to follow from attitudes if the attitudes are established by personal experience. A person who experiences job discrimination firsthand is more likely to base his or her own hiring practices on an applicant's actual qualifications than is someone who was never unfairly denied employment (Fazio and Zanna, 1981).

Similarly, a person who has been repeatedly misdiagnosed by doctors is more likely to decline a doctor's recommended treatment than someone who has always received effective medical treatment.

Changing Attitudes

It is important to remember that people's attitudes are not always reflected in their behavior, and attitudes can change. Just as people learn attitudes, they can unlearn them and learn new ones. New attitudes may impel a person to try a particular brand of soap, vote Democratic, or undergo a religious conversion. A common avenue by which people's attitudes change is the mass media, particularly television.

The prestige of entertainers and sports figures makes them very effective as communicators—a fact on which advertisers are quick to capitalize.

The goal of television commercials is to change or reinforce people's behavior. Commercials exhort viewers to drink Pepsi, not Coke; to drive a Volvo instead of a SAAB; to say no to drugs; or to vote for Mr. Bush. Their appeal may be cognitive (one product tastes better than the other) or emotional (owning this product will make you feel proud). Whatever their appeal, commercials aim to influence people's convictions and overt behavior. Research shows that television advertising is effective (Barber, Bradshaw, and Walsh, 1989). It is not surprising that television is the most influential medium of attitude change in the Western world, given the fact that in the average American household, the television is on for more than four hours every day and has been shown to affect children profoundly (Huston, Watkins, and Kunkel, 1989).

To change an attitude, a person must be motivated and receptive. Moreover, the person who wishes to effect the change must be persuasive. Social psychologists have often listed the components of attitude change as: the communicator, the communication, the medium, and the audience.

The Communicator. To be persuasive, a communicator—the person trying to influence the attitude change—must project integrity, credibility, and trustworthiness. If people don't trust, respect, or like the communicator, they are unlikely to change their attitudes. An unknown conservationist is less likely to convince an audience of the importance of preserving wildlife than a well-known scientist and environmentalist such as Carl Sagan.

Researchers have found that the perceived power, prestige, celebrity, prominence, and degree of attractiveness of the communicator are extremely important (e.g., Chaiken and Eagly, 1983). Similarly, a speaker regarded as knowledgeable and important, but who speaks inexpertly or uses too technical a vocabulary, is not likely to effect attitude change (Lee and Ofshe, 1981). Ronald Reagan, who often has been called the "Great Communicator," enjoyed effective televised public addresses because viewers perceived him as both powerful and likable and because his speeches were easy to follow.

Well-trained communicators can be especially effective. In a research study promoting energy conservation (Gonzales, Aronson, and Costanzo, 1988), energy auditors were specially trained to change attitudes and help people effectively conserve home energy. The energy auditors learned to communicate vividly, personalize their recommendations, get their clients involved, and induce a sense of economic loss through inaction on the part of the homeowners. The attitude-inducement training had dramatic results. Clients were more likely to become involved in energy conservation measures when their home auditor had the special social psychology training.

The Communication. Presenting a clear, convincing, and logical argument is the most effective tool for changing attitudes. Changing attitudes is more likely when the targeted attitude is not too different from an existing one and when the audience is not highly involved with a particular point of view (Johnson and Eagly, 1989). Thus, political candidates can influence voters to vote for them when their ideas are consistent with those of the voter. Changing the ideas of politically involved citizens (Johnson and Eagly, 1989) is more difficult than altering those of noninvolved citizens, but it is not impossible (Ottati, Fishbein, and Middlestadt, 1988; Zaller, 1987).

Communicating fear is effective in motivating attitude change, especially when health issues are concerned (Robberson and Rogers, 1988) and the communicator does not overdo the fear appeal. For example think of some of the antismoking ads you've seen on television. What techniques do they use to induce fear in the audience? Social psychologist Ronald Rogers (1975) suggests that fear is most effective in changing people's attitudes when (1) the magnitude of the fear-producing event or consequence is sufficiently great, (2) the event or consequence is likely if no adaptive behavior is performed, and (3) the behavior suggested is reasonable and has a good chance of averting the danger (Hass, Bagley, and Rogers, 1975; Rogers and Mewborn, 1976). For example, a dentist may persuade her patients to brush more often by telling them that doing so will prevent cavities, gum disease, and bad breath. Combining fear with the benefits of self-enhancement is an effective way to help modify attitudes. Negative, or fear, approaches work well in changing people's attitudes about their health, but positive approaches stressing enhanced self-esteem also work well (Robberson and Rogers, 1988).

Researchers also find that if people hear an argument, commercial, or political view often enough, they begin to believe it, regardless of its value. Repeated exposure to situations can change attitudes (Bornstein, 1989). For example, after seeing numerous commercials showing one battery brand outperform the competition, a television viewer may change his attitude toward the product from neutral to positive (Petty and Cacioppo, 1981).

The Medium. The way in which communication is presented—its medium—influences people's receptiveness to change. For example, face-to-face communication has more impact than communication through television or in writing. Thus, although candidates for public office rely on TV, radio, and printed ads, meeting people face-to-face is a stronger persuasion tool. And because friends are more trusted than the media, information received from friends is considered more influential. Costanzo et al. (1986) suggest that "Media sources are effective in creating awareness of a new technology, but interpersonal sources exert a far greater influence on the decision to adopt a new technology" (p. 528). Leonard-Barton (1981) showed that the best predictor of whether a customer will purchase solar equipment is the number of acquaintances he or she has who currently own such devices. Are you more likely to buy a particular CD or cassette player if a friend recommends it, rather than listening to a promotional ad?

The Audience. From time to time, people actually *want* to have their attitudes changed; they seek out alternative views. At other times, they fold their arms across their chests and announce, "It's going to take an act of

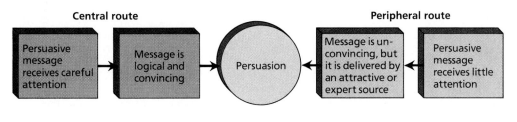

Central route   **Peripheral route**

Persuasive message receives careful attention → Message is logical and convincing → Persuasion ← Message is unconvincing, but it is delivered by an attractive or expert source ← Persuasive message receives little attention

FIGURE 16.2
According to the Petty-Cacioppo model, persuasion can occur through two distinct processes. In the *central* route, it is based on careful attention to logical and convincing messages. In the *peripheral* route, it occurs because individuals are affected by emotional factors such as the appearance or expertise of the source.

Congress to change my mind" (Johnson and Eagly, 1989). This is in part age-related; people are most susceptible to attitude changes in early adult years, and susceptibility to change drops off in later years (Krosnick and Alwin, 1989).

Changing people's attitudes, and ultimately their behavior, can be difficult if they have well-established habits (which often come with advancing age) or are highly motivated in the opposite direction. Consider people's attitudes toward using seat belts. Although the public believes in the effectiveness of seat belts and holds positive attitudes about using them, few people use them all the time. Mittal (1988) showed that getting people to use seat belts takes more than developing positive attitudes, it also takes instilling a use-habit. He argues that the more often people use seat belts, the more likely they will be to use the device in the future. Thus, education and actions to counter forgetting (e.g., warning buzzers) can be helpful (Geller, Patterson, and Talbot, 1982), as can prompting use through signs in an automobile (Rogers et al., 1988) or providing active feedback (Siero et al., 1989).

Petty-Cacioppo Model. Richard Petty and John Cacioppo (1981, 1985) have presented an **elaboration likelihood model** that describes two processes people undergo when changing their attitudes. The first, called *central processes,* emphasizes the conscious and direct information an individual has concerning a given issue. Central processes rely on how effective, authoritative, and logical a communication is. Confronted with scientific evidence that the Shroud of Turin is only six centuries old, many people would conclude through the central process that the relic was not Christ's burial cloth. This is, unless they were highly motivated to believe otherwise, they would conclude that the scientific arguments against the shroud's authenticity are too strong to refute.

Petty and Cacioppo's second route to changing attitudes involves the *peripheral processes* of persuasion and emotion. These processes have an indirect, superficial, but very powerful effect, especially when there are no convincing or powerful arguments that can force the use of central processes, for example, in political messages. (See Figure 16.2.) Whether a person accepts a message depends on how he or she perceives its pleasantness, delivery, the communicator, and similarity to well-established personal attitudes. Peripheral processes also may convince someone that the Shroud of Turin is not genuine, but in this case the disbeliever's attitude stems largely from emotional rather than logical arguments. For example, the person may doubt the shroud's authenticity because a respected religious leader dismisses the relic. Whether a person accepts a message also depends on when the message was delivered. In some cases the passage of time can increase the impact of some messages, a phenomenon we consider next.

Elaboration likelihood model: A theory of attitude change suggesting that there are two routes to persuasion, *central* and *peripheral;* the former focuses on thoughtful, elaborative consideration; the latter, on less careful, more emotional, and even superficial considerations.

The Sleeper Effect

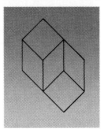

*A*re you influenced to buy shampoo A instead of shampoo B after watching a televised commercial? Do you choose tire X instead of tire Z after reading ads in your daily newspaper? Can you think of one particular ad campaign that has had long-term effects on your attitudes and behavior? Persuasive messages *can* change a person's attitudes, but the effectiveness usually decreases as time passes. However, in the 1940s psychologists discovered that in some cases, the passage of time can *increase* the impact of some messages because of the *sleeper effect*. According to the sleeper effect, the impact of a message delivered by a highly credible source decreases as time passes, but the impact of a low-credibility source message can actually increase. How can this happen?

Consider, for example, a person such as Colonel Oliver North. You may hold the view that Oliver North is a hero having done the correct but controversial thing for his country with respect to the Nicaraguan Contras. During his continuing court battles, you see in the supermarket a tabloid espousing North to be their most admired U.S. citizen. Because you hold the tabloid in such disdain, you discount the message that North was one of the good guys. As time passes, however, you forget who proclaimed North a hero and you are moved to believe that Oliver North was a hero; that is, the source of the message was forgotten, but the message was not. This is the sleeper effect.

For the sleeper effect to occur, the message must have a high impact (North is the greatest U.S. citizen), the low-credibility source (a supermarket tabloid) must be discounted, and the relationship between the message and its deliverer must be disassociated over time (you forget the source of the message) (Gruder et al., 1978). Because of these limiting conditions, the effect is hard to substantiate (Greenwald et al., 1986), but new research does exist.

When the discounting cue, the cue indicating that the message is not credible, such as a counterargument or an undermining of source credibility, is presented *after* the message (instead of before, as is usually the case), reliable sleeper effects can be discerned more easily (Pratkanis et al., 1988). Pratkanis and Ohio State University colleagues showed that sleeper effects are obtainable and more easily explained through what they termed a differential decay interpretation.

The *differential decay interpretation* suggests that sleeper effects are obtained when the message and the discounting cue have opposite, but near equal, immediate impacts that are not well integrated into memory. For the sleeper effect to occur, the discounting cue (a message from a low-class tabloid) must be received after or simultaneously with the message. But the impact of the discounting cue *decays* or lessens faster than the message decays (you continue to remember the idea that North was claimed as the greatest U.S. citizen). With a faster decay rate for the negative influence of the discounting cue, sleeper effects can be obtained. Although another interpretation may emerge that will more powerfully describe and explain the sleeper effect, this interpretation is currently "state of the art" and is based on cognitive research.   ◆

The Search for Cognitive Consistency

Although basic ideas about life and morals are established early, attitudes continually develop and change. Some people seek change, trying to keep pace with friends or relatives; others are resistant. Most people try to maintain consistency between their various attitudes and between their attitudes and behavior. Consistency leads to orderly living and enables people to make decisions about future behavior more easily without having to filter through numerous alternatives (Cialdini, 1988).

Cognitive Dissonance. Imagine the dilemma faced by the scientist who, after discovering preliminary proof of the Shroud of Turin's authenticity in 1978, converted to Christianity. As a scientist, he must have found the physical evidence of the shroud compelling; as a Jew, he must have been bewildered by the "proof" of Christ's divinity. How could he reconcile these two opposite attitudes? Moreover, what further confusion did he suffer when he later learned that the cloth was only six centuries old?

Whenever people realize that their attitudes conflict with each other or with their behavior, they feel uncomfortable. If a student believes he should be saving part of his income toward tuition but spends every dime of it, his attitudes and behavior conflict. He may feel uncomfortable or even upset. Leon Festinger (1919–1989) referred to this feeling as *dissonance*, the discomfort that results when a discrepancy exists between a person's beliefs or between his beliefs and his overt behavior.

Based on the concept that people seek to reduce dissonance, Festinger (1957) proposed a **cognitive dissonance** theory. According to the theory, when people experience conflict between their attitudes and behavior or other attitudes, they are motivated to change either their attitudes or their behavior. Suppose you are a strong proponent of animal rights. You support the ASPCA and Greenpeace, refrain from eating meat, and are repulsed by women in mink coats. Then you win a raffle and are awarded an expensive black leather coat—just like the one worn by your favorite rock star. Wearing the coat goes against all your beliefs, but it feels good, you know it looks great on you, and all your friends admire it. According to cognitive dissonance theory, you are experiencing conflict between your attitudes (animal rights) and your behavior (wearing the coat). To relieve the conflict, you either stop wearing the coat or modify your beliefs. Some psychologists consider cognitive dissonance theory a type of motivation theory because people become energized to do something.

Research supports Festinger's claim that for an attitude or behavior to change, negative consequences (dissonance) have to be associated with maintaining existing attitudes or behaviors. But other studies find that people often engage in activities that help reduce their cognitive discomfort without changing an inconsistent set of beliefs (Steele, 1975). A smoker, for example, might take up jogging to improve his cardiovascular health, but still not change his dissonant smoking habit.

An Alternative to Cognitive Dissonance Theory. Although cognitive dissonance theory has wide popularity, not all psychologists subscribe to it. Social psychologist Daryl Bem (1972) claims that people do not change their attitudes because of internal states such as dissonance. He contends that people often do not understand the causes of their own attitudes and behavior, that they infer their attitudes and emotional states and the causes of their behavior from the situations in which they find themselves. According to Bem, people can perceive their behavior only after the fact and in the context in which it occurred; that is, they can interpret their behavior only in a situational context. His approach is called **self-perception theory.** It suggests that people do not so much change their attitudes after inconsistent behavior but that they simply look at their behavior and say, "If I behaved in this way, I must have had this (consistent) attitude." See Figure

Cognitive dissonance: A state in which individuals feel uncomfortable because they hold two or more thoughts, attitudes, or behaviors that are inconsistent with one another.

Self-perception theory: An approach to attitude formation by which people are assumed to infer their attitudes based on observations of their own behavior.

FIGURE 16.3
In a traditional view of attitudes and dissonance, behavior follows from attitudes. In Bem's approach, attitudes are determined *after* a person appraises his or her situation.

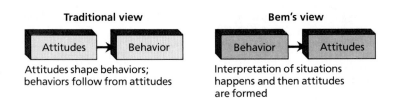

Traditional view

Attitudes → Behavior

Attitudes shape behaviors; behaviors follow from attitudes

Bem's view

Behavior → Attitudes

Interpretation of situations happens and then attitudes are formed

16.3 for an overview of the traditional view of attitude formation compared with Bem's view.

Bem's research is supported to some extent by the work of Stanley Schachter discussed in chapter 11. Schachter showed that subjects infer aspects of their emotional states (at least to some extent) from both their physical states and the situations in which they find themselves. A subject who is physically aroused and surrounded by happy people reports feeling happy. A subject who is physially aroused and in a tense situation reports feeling angry.

Bem's self-perception model is a distinct theoretical alternative to Festinger's cognitive dissonance theory. But research supports both theories. In fact, the results of one study by Tybout and Scott (1983) support both. Tybout and Scott investigated what happened to attitudes when information about the taste of a product was provided or withheld. They discovered that when information was available, internal states such as beliefs and predispositions were the keys to attitude formation and change, much as Festinger suggests. However, when clearly defined information was unavailable, subjects used a process of self-perception such as that described by Bem to determine their attitudes. People may not only infer their own attitudes, but also the thoughts and attitudes of other people, as balance theory suggests.

Balance Theory. **Balance theory** states that we prefer satisfying and harmonious relationships between our beliefs and the beliefs of others whom we like. For instance, if Don likes Paula and Don likes heavy metal music, he will feel a state of cognitive balance if he thinks Paula also likes heavy metal music. However, he will feel a state of imbalance if he thinks Paula does not like heavy metal music (see Figure 16.4). Like cognitive dissonance theory, balance theory can be considered a motivation theory. The unpleasant tension state that results from disagreement motivates people to change. Also, like cognitive dissonance theory, it assumes that people are decision makers whose thoughts ultimately determine their behavior.

According to balance theory, people who wish to maintain stable, balanced relationships must agree in order to avoid unpleasant situations. In fact, research studies on balance theory have shown that friendships are based, in part, on the extent of the perceived agreement between two friends regarding which of their other acquaintances are acceptable. Suppose, for example, Sue likes both Mary and Jeff, but Sue thinks that Mary does not like Jeff. Sue experiences an unpleasant state of tension. Sue can either change her belief about Mary's attitude about Jeff, or she can decide that she herself does not like Jeff. In either case, the imbalance will no longer exist.

Reactance Theory. Have you ever been ordered to do something (perhaps by a parent) that caused you to want to do the exact opposite? According to social psychologist Jack W. Brehm (1966), whenever people feel their freedom of choice is unjustly restricted, they are motivated to reestablish that freedom. Brehm calls this form of negative influence *reactance*. In re-

Balance theory: An attitude theory stating that people prefer to hold consistent beliefs and try to avoid incompatible beliefs.

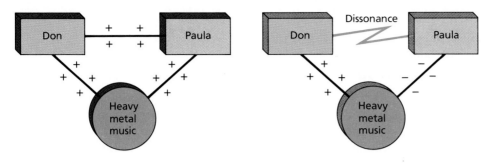

FIGURE 16.4
When Don and Paula both like the same things (heavy metal music, for example), we say their relationship is in balance (plus signs indicate liking; minus signs indicate disliking). But, when Don realizes that Paula doesn't like heavy metal music, he feels some dissonance—an imbalance exists.

actance, what is inconsistent is the image of ourselves as free to choose and the realization that someone is trying to force us to choose an alternative.

Reactance theory is derived from the old notion of forbidden fruit. Whenever people are forbidden to do something, that activity often becomes more attractive. Choosing the forbidden fruit may provide an individual with a sense of autonomy. Thus, if an adolescent is told he cannot be friends with members of a minority group (thereby limiting his freedom of choice), he might seek out members of that group more often; thus, when coercion is used, resistance follows.

According to reactance theory, the extent of reactance is usually directly related to the extent of the restrictions on behavior. If the person does not consider the behavior to be very important and the restriction is slight, little reactance develops. The wording or delivery of the restriction also affects the extent of reactance. A person who is told that she *must* respond in a certain way is more likely to react negatively than if she merely receives a suggestion or is given a free choice in responding.

- ◆ Identify and describe the three dimensions of attitudes. p. 575
- ◆ Describe three of the four factors that affect attitude change. p. 577
- ◆ Distinguish between central and peripheral processes in the elaboration likelihood model. p. 579
- ◆ Identify the key finding in studies of cognitive dissonance. p. 580

Focus on Learning

Social Cognition

After meeting someone for the first time, you might say, "I really like him!" or "I can't explain why, but she rubs me the wrong way." Often first impressions are based on nothing more than the other person's appearance, body language, and speech patterns. Yet these impressions can have lasting effects. How do we form attitudes about others?

Social cognition is the process of making sense of events and people, including ourselves, by analyzing and interpreting those people and events. Social cognition is a thought process that focuses on social information in memory and how it affects judgments, choices, evaluations, and ultimately our behavior (Sherman, Judd, and Park, 1989). The process often begins with our attempts to understand other people's communications, which can be verbal—through words—or nonverbal—through gazes, gestures, body movements, and other means of expression—and form impressions of them. The process by which people use the behavior and appearance of others to

Social cognition: The process of making sense through the interpretation of events, people, ourselves, and the world in general; social cognition is a thought process.

Impression formation: A process by which people use the behavior and appearance of others to infer their internal states and intentions.

Nonverbal communications: Information provided by cues or actions that involve movements of the body, especially the face, and sometimes the vocal cords.

infer their internal states and intentions is known as **impression formation;** usually, but not always, the impressions are accurate.

Nonverbal Communication

Impression formation often begins with **nonverbal communication** or messages. When a person "rubs you the wrong way," it may be due to a gesture, a grimace, or an averting of the eyes that generated your bad feelings. Nonverbal communication comes from many sources: the face, body movements, physical contact, and eye contact.

Facial Expressions. Many of the conclusions we draw from other people's communications are based on their facial expressions. Smiling expresses happiness; furrowed brows and eye twitching suggest anger, disgust, or fear. Recall from chapter 11 that researchers find some people better at interpreting these expressions; similarly, people differ in their ability to convey information through nonverbal mechanisms. But most people can distinguish six basic emotions in the facial expressions of other people—love, joy, anger, sadness, fear, and surprise (Shaver et al., 1987).

A simple gesture such as smiling gives people a powerful cue about a person's truthfulness. Research shows that when people smile, both the smile and muscular activity around the eyes help determine if the truth is being told or if the person is smiling to mask another emotion (Ekman, Friesen, and O'Sullivan, 1988).

Hiding the Truth

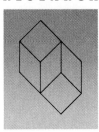

THINKING ABOUT RESEARCH

*C*an you smile while telling a lie? Not very well, according to well-known researchers Ekman, Friesen, and O'Sullivan (1988). More than twenty years ago two of the researchers noted that facial expressions and body movements were important to observers. They contend that facial features and gestures provide complex information to an observer, especially when a person tries to be deceitful. They assert that subtle facial cues accompany various types of smiling and that people cannot mask true emotions with a grin. They tested their idea experimentally by having subjects view people who told about pleasant experiences, and then viewed people who lied about experiences trying to make them seem pleasant; these people were making false smiles.

Method. Ekman and his colleagues distinguish several types of smiles: happy smiles, false smiles, smiles of a listener, and masking smiles. They assert that facial muscles around the eyes and nose signal the real meaning of a smile. The research team videotaped (with a concealed camera) subjects who first truthfully described a film that was mildly enjoyable—they described a nature scene. Then the subjects watched an unpleasant film about skin burns and amputations. They were asked to conceal negative feelings. The researchers were especially concerned with the question: Could the people who were taped convince another person that they were watching a pleasant film?

Procedure. Close-ups of the subjects' faces were scored with respect to which facial muscles moved. The scorer identified the occurrence of particular facial muscle actions, such as pulling brows together, nose wrinkling, and brow raising. The scorer did not know whether the tapes were of truthful or lying subjects. The scorers had no trouble identifying when a muscle had moved and rated the extent to which a muscle had moved.

Results. Muscle movements were categorized into groups, and the results showed that true enjoyment smiles involved eye muscle activity more often than when enjoyment was feigned. When subjects tried to conceal strong emotions with a happy but false smile, there were specific changes in the muscles. The results support the researchers' contention that genuine, happy smiles differ from other smiles in the amount of time it takes for a smile to appear, how long it remains on the face before fading, and the time required for a smile to disappear.

Conclusions. This study shows that smiles are not a unitary phenomenon (a single category of behavior) but are multifaceted. A person can exhibit different social signals through a smile. From a social psychologist's view, this is especially important because it shows that people are tuned in to fine elements of behavior. For example, a person can say that he likes or dislikes your smile. Moreover, another person's smile can affect our own individual behavior. Your boss may be smiling, but a mere lift of an eyebrow or a couple of millimeters of space between the eyebrows can have dramatic impact on your thoughts or overt behavior and research shows that deceptive salespersons can be detected through non-verbal cues (DePaula and DePaula, 1989).   ◆

Of course, not everyone is good at interpreting facial gestures. For example, some children are not good at decoding nonverbal cues, and this leaves their social skills wanting. According to Nowicki and Duke (1989), five- to ten-year-old children sometimes have difficulty interpreting emotional states through facial expressions, posture, and gestures; misjudgments may cause anxiety and confusion that carry over to the classroom and make learning difficult.

Facial expressions are especially potent in televised communication. Mullen et al. (1986) wished to find out if newscasters exhibited biased facial expressions. The researchers asked college students to rate videotaped segments of newscasters while they were referring to candidates; there was no sound from the television monitors. The subjects rated the newscasters' facial expressions on a scale from extremely negative to extremely positive. The results showed that in the 1984 presidential elections, Peter Jennings had a bias in favor of candidate Ronald Reagan. Tom Brokaw and Dan Rather showed no bias; they remained scrupulously neutral.

Although fascinating, the effects of the newscaster experiment were small. Also it is not clear from the study whether viewers' political views influenced their decision to watch Jennings, Brokaw, or Rather in the first place. Moreover, a voter's behavior in the next election is probably going to be based on the candidate, not on the newscaster. But by using a scientific method, the researchers showed a bias and showed that the bias of the newscaster affected the voters' behavior. They suggested that some small portion of voting behavior may be affected by nonverbal gestures, not only of the candidate but also of a television newscaster!

Body Language. Facial expressions are not the only way people communicate nonverbally. They also convey information about their moods and attitudes through body position and gestures—a phenomenon called **body language.** Body movements such as crossing the arms, lowering the head, and standing rigidly can all communicate negative attitudes.

Although small, differences in body language exist based on age and gender. The way younger people walk makes them appear sexier, more carefree, and happier than the way older people walk (Montepare and Zebrowitz-McArthur, 1988). Additionally, research shows that women are

Body language: The communication of information through body positions and gestures.

Facial expressions and eye contact convey as much about our attitudes and intentions as do our spoken words.

often better than men at communicating and interpreting nonverbal messages, especially facial expressions (Hall, 1979). Women are more likely to send nonverbal facial messages but are more cautious in interpreting nonverbal messages sent to them by men (Rosenthal and DePaulo, 1979).

Physical Contact. Argyle (1972) found that individuals convey information nonverbally through physical contact such as touching, hitting, striking, embracing, and kissing and through proximity, that is, the physical distance maintained during interaction with other people. Other ways of giving nonverbal messages include orientation and posture—the angle at which a person sits or stands, such as leaning forward or relaxing backward. The more cues available, the greater the information conveyed (Schwarz, Foa, and Foa, 1983). We will consider some of the cues in more detail in the next chapter. Interestingly, when two people are talking, body movements, hand movements, and other non-verbal gestures decrease when a third person is present, even if that person is passive (Guerin, 1989).

Eye Contact. Researchers are well aware of another form of nonverbal communication—the *eyes* convey a surprising amount of information about feelings. When a person looks at you, he or she may gaze briefly or stare. You might gaze or stare back. Psychologists call this process *making eye contact.* You would probably gaze tenderly at someone you find attractive but avoid eye contact with someone you do not trust or like, or do not know well (Teske, 1988). When people are looked at, they accept it as a sign of being liked. Frequent eye contact between a man and a woman may indicate that they are sexually attracted to each other.

We tend to judge people by the eye contact they make with us. Generally, people prefer modest amounts of eye contact rather than constant or no eye contact. Job applicants, for example, are rated more favorably when they make moderate amounts of eye contact, and speakers who make more rather than less eye contact are preferred. Therapists report that a lack of eye contact in therapy suggests a lack of involvement. Witnesses in a court trial are perceived as more credible when they make eye contact with the attorney. People make inferences from the degree of eye contact about people's internal dispositions—they make attributions.

Attribution

If it's noon and you see someone eating a hamburger and french fries, you can be fairly certain he is eating because he is hungry. Similarly, if you see a student carrying a Koran around campus, you might infer that she is a devout Moslem. In getting to know other people, we often infer the causes of their behavior. When we do, we are making attributions.

Attribution is the process by which someone infers or decides about other people's motives and intentions from observing their behavior, deciding if the causes of behavior are *dispositional* (internal) or *situational* (external). Through attribution, people decide how they will react toward others; they are attempting to evaluate and make sense of their social world.

At first, attribution seems like a fairly straightforward process based on common sense. But keep in mind that it must take into account internal as well as external causes of behavior. If someone makes an *internal attribution,* he or she feels that the behavior comes from within the person, from the individual's personality or abilities. If someone makes an *external attribution,* he or she believes that the person's behavior is caused by outside events

Attribution: The process by which someone infers other people's motives and intentions from observing their behavior. The focus is usually on deciding if the causes of behavior are *dispositional* (internal) or *situational* (external).

such as the weather or luck. In other words, if internal causes seem to predominate, a person's behavior will be attributed to his or her personality or abilities; if external causes predominate, the behavior is attributed to the situation.

People can be mistaken when they infer the causes of another person's behavior. Suppose that the student toting the Koran is actually a Catholic taking a world religion class and uses the Moslem holy book as a text; in that case, our original attribution (that she is a Moslem) could be wrong. To learn about attribution and how it can be more precise, researchers have tried to conceptualize its processes.

Harold Kelley's (1972, 1973) popular theory of attribution contains three criteria to help determine whether the causes of a behavior are internal or external: *consensus, consistency,* and *distinctiveness.* According to Kelley, to infer that someone's behavior is caused by internal characteristics, people must believe that:

- few other people in the same situation would act in the same way (low consensus);
- the person has acted in the same way in similar situations in the past (high consistency);
- the person acts in the same way in different situations (low distinctiveness).

To infer that a person's behavior is caused by external factors, people must believe that:

- most people would act that way in that sort of situation (high consensus);
- the person has acted that way in similar situations in the past (high consistency);
- the person acts differently in other situations (high distinctiveness).

To see how Kelley's theory works, suppose that in a restaurant someone acts rudely to a certain waiter, but other people in the same restaurant are not rude to the waiter (low consensus). Also suppose that the person has acted rudely toward this waiter on other occasions (high consistency). Finally, assume that the person acts rudely to all waiters (low distinctiveness). In such a case, people would no doubt attribute the rudeness to the individual's personality—he or she is simply a rude person.

Now suppose that many other customers act rudely toward the waiter (high consensus) and that our target person has acted rudely toward this waiter in the past (high consistency), but our target person does not act rudely toward any other waiters (high distinctiveness). People would then be more likely to attribute the rudeness to situational factors, such as the waiter's incompetence.

Errors in Attribution. Kelley's theory treats us as if we are scientists who carefully and scientifically go about making attributions. Attribution theory is a rapidly emerging specialty in social psychology and theorists are not all in agreement about the nature of attributions; for example, Hilton (1990) asserts that the traditional view of the individual as a rational scientist trying to sort out relevant facts does not consider factors such as who is doing the explaining, to whom, or why an explanation is needed. He therefore proposes an extension of traditional causal explanation that accounts for the form of attributions, particularly when presented in conversation. His new

Fundamental attribution error: The tendency to attribute behavior to individual dispositional (internal) causes rather than situational (external) causes; this error occurs more often when explaining the behavior of other people.

Actor-observer effect: The tendency for people to attribute the behavior of other people to dispositional causes, while attributing their own behavior to situational causes.

model has an interpersonal focus; it is yet to be fully evaluated by other researchers. Further, social psychologists have found that we are often mistaken or biased in our attributions. Some of the most common types of errors have been identified, including the fundamental attribution error and the actor-observer effect.

When people commit the **fundamental attribution error,** they assume that a person's behavior is caused by internal dispositions—which may or may not be true. They underestimate situational influences and overestimate dispositional influences on other people's behavior. A man may have lost his temper after being overcharged for an item; a woman may have become hostile because the waiter spilled soup on her and did not apologize.

Another kind of error in attribution is the **actor-observer effect,** or the tendency for people to attribute the behavior of others to dispositional causes, but to attribute their own behavior to situational causes. When a young child gets hurt, he or she often says, "You made me hurt myself." But when a friend gets hurt, the same child may say, "You're clumsy." If you fail an exam, you may blame it on your roommate whose radio kept you from concentrating on your studies. But when someone else fails an exam, you may wonder about the person's intelligence. Errors in attribution are often judgments made in a limited context with limited knowledge (Funder, 1987).

Other errors in attribution come from the fact that people generally perceive themselves as having more positive traits and being more flexible in their ability to adapt than other people (Sande, Goethals, and Radloff, 1988); this tendency is seen cross-culturally (Liebrand, Messick, and Wolters, 1986). Can you think of any useful functions that making errors in attribution might serve?

A Just World? According to Melvin Lerner (1970), many people believe that an appropriate relationship exists between what they do and what happens to them. In other words, they believe that the world is just, that people get what they deserve. A negative consequence of the *just-world belief* is that victims of crime, poverty, and other misfortune are often treated as if they brought these things on themselves. People may blame female rape victims for wearing seductive clothing or too much makeup, for acting "too friendly" toward men, or for going out alone after dark. The realization that bad things can happen to good people threatens our belief that the world is just. The ability to see that someone else has been treated unfairly can upset an individual's belief in a just world and perhaps motivate him or her to rectify the situation or compensate someone who was unfairly punished, thus trying to reestablish justice.

Why People Make Attributions. Why do people make attributions? What motivates us to want to know the causes of other people's behavior? A traditional idea is that people engage in the process of attribution to maintain a sense of control over the environment. It helps us feel competent and masterful because we feel that knowledge about the causes of behavior will help us control and predict similar events in the future. Burger and Hemans (1988) showed that subjects who have intense desires to control events around them are more likely to make attributions.

People also make attributions to help maintain a sense of balance, thereby resolving inconsistencies between old and new information about themselves (Snyder and Higgins, 1988). When a person makes an excuse about some personal behavior that has had negative outcomes, he or she has often shifted the cause of the behavior to a less central element of personality or to situational factors. This behavior results in enhanced image building and a sense of control.

Attribution has an important influence on people's judgments about others, especially for juries who must decide the innocence or guilt of defendants. Did John Smith rob the store because he is a violent man? Did he need the money to support his heroin addiction or to pay for his sick child's operation? Did his father beat him as a child? Did his mother abandon him? Is he discouraged over his inability to find a decent job? Is he taking medication that may have altered his behavior? We constantly seek the reasons for people's behavior to help us make judgments about them. You probably reflect on the causes of your own behavior at times; behavior is often shaped by your own self-perceptions.

Self-perception: Attitudes toward and beliefs about oneself, largely formed during childhood and adolescence and often a reflection of other people's perceived attitudes.

Self-Perceptions

How would you describe yourself? **Self-perceptions** are people's attitudes toward and beliefs about themselves, and are greatly affected by how other people perceive them. Thus, when social psychologists study self-perception, they examine how other people and social situations affect how people see themselves, and how that perception influences everyday behavior.

Developing Self-Perceptions. Established early in life and reevaluated frequently, self-perceptions develop over time and from experience. At first, children get answers to questions such as, "Mommy, am I pretty?" or "Mommy, am I smart?" to help form self-perceptions. Adolescents then reassess their early self-perceptions, which enables them to establish a firm identity consistent with both previous attitudes and new values. Successful completion of adolescence (which Erikson calls the identity crisis) results in a person's ability to adapt to new situations while retaining a firm understanding of self and personal values.

A sense of self develops as we become aware of the roles we are often expected to assume.

Role: A set of behaviors expected from a certain category of individuals; a person's roles may change depending on the group within which the person finds himself or herself.

Over the years, people develop a sense of themselves by combining aspects of their family, occupational, recreational, and gender roles. A **role** is a set of behaviors expected from a specific group of individuals. Our culture, for example, has certain expectations for men, women, various ethnic groups, leaders, and those in various social positions. We expect integrity, leadership, and strength from a city mayor; when in 1990 Mayor Marion Barry of Washington, D.C., was arrested for cocaine use, this created a great stir because political leaders are held to high standards, and Mayor Barry disappointed his constituency.

Roles for individuals are sometimes established on the basis of prominent physical cues, such as height, where people expect tall men and women to play basketball and do not expect shorter people to enjoy or play it; in some ways, people are lazy about paying attention to other aspects of a person's behavior (Fiske, 1989). Other roles are defined by the individual; but these, too, often follow from cultural expectations. Research shows these roles to be related to the fact that men often have more status than women and that men are more often engaged in the distinctive behaviors, such as political leadership of national groups (Eagly and Kite, 1987).

People also develop self-perceptions by comparing themselves to others and seeing how they measure up. Thus, athletes compare themselves to better athletes, as well as to less competent ones. And high school juniors compare their academic and social skills both to other juniors and to sophomores and seniors. Individuals also receive feedback from other people that helps them evaluate themselves, but research shows that the extent to which people accept feedback varies with their level of self-esteem—people with higher levels of self-esteem are more willing to accept feedback. Further, when people are in a good mood they are more willing to accept feedback (Esses, 1988).

Perceiving Others. We perceive others in relation to our own value systems and ideas—our self-perceptions. An assertive person, for example, may view other assertive people as expressing normal, appropriate behavior. A quiet, shy, and passive person, on the other hand, may view assertive people as inappropriate, loud, or even aggressive.

A person's frame of reference usually starts with himself or herself, and a comparison is made. Then the person compares an individual to other people or an absolute standard, and makes an overall evaluation. Both children and adults have conceptions of an ideal man or woman; these are determined by one's gender and the culture in which one is nurtured (Gibbons et al., 1988).

Physical Appearance. Many factors determine a person's self-perception, including physical appearance, work habits, athletic abilities, and success as a parent or mate. According to a substantial body of literature, one of these factors—physical appearance—sharply affects people's attitudes toward others. In turn, those attitudes, expressed in behavior, influence how people perceive themselves (Horvath, 1981).

In general, attractive people are judged to have more positive traits and characteristics than are unattractive people, especially when appearance is the first information provided (Benassi, 1982). For example, teachers believe that attractive children get higher marks and misbehave less than unattractive children do. Attractive children are also predicted to have more successful careers (Dion, Berscheid, and Walster, 1972; Lerner and Lerner, 1977). The same process occurs with adults: Attractive people are granted more freedom and liberties and perceived as more fair and competent than unattractive people (Cash and Kehr, 1978).

It is unfortunate that people's self-concepts and their status in other people's eyes may be largely determined by superficial characteristics such as physical attractiveness (Kellerman and Laird, 1982) that can set them up for a lifelong pattern of reinforcement or punishment. Physically unattractive and different people tend to be isolated, to be ignored by members of both sexes, and to have negative traits attributed to them (Krebs and Adinolfi, 1975). In addition, people who perceive themselves as physically unattractive are more likely to have anxiety problems in dealing with members of the opposite sex (Mitchell and Orr, 1976).

How important is attractiveness when it comes to dating? Do people always select the most attractive person for a date? Research shows that people prefer attractive dates, and some studies show that people seek out those of their own level of attractiveness. But other variables seem to play an important role as well; educational level, intelligence, similar socioeconomic status, and commonality of previous experiences all weigh heavily in the choice of whom to date and eventually marry (Feingold, 1988a). Although physical attractiveness is initially important in selecting dates and mates, it is just one variable among many.

Self-Serving Biases. Social psychologists have found that most people are not realistic in evaluating themselves, their capabilities, or their behavior. The **self-serving bias** refers to people's tendency to evaluate their own behavior as worthwhile, regardless of the situation. Most people consider themselves more charitable, more giving, more intelligent, more considerate, more sensitive, more likely to succeed, and more of a leader than they consider most other people.

Psychologists have focused on two possible explanations for the development and role of self-serving biases. First, developing a self-serving bias meets people's *needs for self-esteem* and need to feel good about themselves in comparison to other people. It can be seen as an adaptive response that helps people deal with their limitations and gives them the courage to venture into areas they normally might not explore. The other view—*self-presentation*—is that self-serving biases develop to allow people to present themselves to other people in a positive light (Weary et al., 1982). This allows people to feel that they are presenting themselves well to others in their social world.

Errors in attribution, discussed earlier, contribute to self-serving biases. People tend to take credit for their successes and blame others for their failures, e.g., people assume that good things happen to them because they deserve them and that bad things happen to other people because, in a just world, they deserve them. When something bad happens to you, you may blame it on bad luck or circumstances. When something bad happens to someone else, you may blame it on their careless or reckless behavior. This combination of attribution errors and a self-serving bias helps some people maintain self-esteem and appear competent. Such an attitude, however, may inhibit people from having realistic goals, thus setting them up for disappointment.

Research has shown that although self-serving biases exist, they are not present in all people at all times. People find other ways to cope. Individuals who suffer from depression and loneliness, for example, often have low

Self-serving bias: People's tendency to evaluate their own behavior as worthwhile, regardless of the situation.

levels of self-esteem but do not seem to develop a self-serving bias. Instead, they may develop and exhibit maladjusted or abnormal behavior, as we saw in chapter 14.

Locus of Control. One reason that people may use self-serving attribution biases and errors is to develop a sense of control that enables them to maintain self-esteem and belief in their own ability to succeed and be happy. Therefore, although people misrepresent reality through attribution biases and errors, they feel that they gain control over their lives and their ability to get what they need. Psychologist Julian Rotter (1966) described such misrepresentations in terms of developing an internal locus of control. A person's *locus of control,* which we discussed in chapter 12, influences how he or she views the world and identifies the causes of success or failure in his or her life.

As we discussed, Rotter found that people vary in their sense of being either internal or external in their locus of control, and this affects them in many situations. In therapy, for example, individuals often place the blame for their problems on other people. In daily situations, people with an external locus of control may attribute bad scores on examinations to poor instruction. Those with an internal locus of control, on the other hand, feel that they can master any subject. On the negative side, people with an internal locus of control may also accept blame and intense guilt feelings for various failures in their lives. In general, though, people with an internal locus of control can use that disposition to evaluate situations and be responsive and creative (Strickland, 1989).

Learned Helplessness

Most people feel they can control their environment to a reasonable extent. They develop a successful internal locus of control. But what happens to people in a situation in which they feel they have little control? How do they react when negative things happen to them? Assume that you are a subject in an experiment in which you have to solve puzzles. The puzzles are relatively simple, yet no matter what you do, you cannot find the correct sequence. You probably become frustrated.

Real-life situations in which people have no control over events also create frustration. A university instructor who wants to use audiovisual presentations, for example, may find that the university will not purchase a projector. She will undoubtedly feel some frustration. A student blocked from taking courses she needs to graduate will similarly feel frustrated and helpless.

Research has shown that both people and animals, when put in situations in which they have no control over the negative things happening to them, often stop responding. Martin Seligman (1975) and his colleagues showed, for example, that dogs first exposed to a series of inescapable shocks and then given a chance to escape further punishment fail to learn the escape response. Seligman called this behavior **learned helplessness.** According to Seligman, the major cause of learned helplessness is an organism's belief that its response will not affect what happens to it in the future. In such cases, anxiety, depression, and eventually nonresponsiveness result.

Many researchers believe that Seligman's early views are not comprehensive enough to explain learned helplessness (see Roth, 1980). Thus, other researchers have proposed attribution models of learned helplessness that

Learned helplessness: The behavior of giving up or not responding, exhibited by subjects exposed to negative consequences or punishment over which they have no control.

Feeling overwhelmed and without resources, some people give up on changing the negative aspects of their lives, a behavior known as learned helplessness.

1. the process of making sense of events + people, including ourselves, by analyzing + interpreting those people + events

2.

take into account variables such as the person's locus of control, gender, and previous expectations. For example, people with a strong external locus of control are more likely to develop a sense of learned helplessness than are people with a strong internal locus of control. Further, some researchers argue that repeated failure itself is the critical determinant of helplessness (Kofta and Sedek, 1989). Research on learned helplessness must be expanded to approximate real-life situations more closely than laboratory situations with animals can (Mikulincer and Nizan, 1988).

◆ Define social cognition. p. 583
◆ Describe the difference between *dispositional* and *situational* interpreta-   *internal*   *external*
tions of the causes of behavior. pp. 586–587
◆ Identify the assumptions of the fundamental attribution error. p. 588
◆ What is the principal finding in studies of learned helplessness? p. 592

Focus on Learning

Social Influence

Social influence is the effort on the part of one or more people to alter the attitudes or behavior of others. For example, parents try to instill specific values in their children. Professors attempt to convince students to shed preconceived ideas about subjects. Religious leaders exhort their followers to live in certain ways. Values are long-lasting and for most people are quite stable, changing little over long periods of time (Rokeach and Ball-Rokeach, 1989). People exert a powerful influence on others, and psychologists have attempted to understand how this influence operates. Studies of social influence have focused on three topics: conformity, obedience, and compliance.

Social influence: The effort on the part of one or more people to alter the attitudes or behavior of others.

Conformity

People often conform to the behaviors and attitudes of their peer or family groups. A successful young executive might wear conservative dark suits and drive a BMW in order to fit in with office colleagues. Similarly, the desire to conform can induce people to do things they might not do otherwise. An infamous example is the My Lai massacre, in which American soldiers slaughtered Vietnamese civilians. While several factors account for the soldiers' behavior (including combat stress, hostility toward the Vietnamese, and obedience to authority), the soldiers also yielded to extreme group pressure. The few soldiers who refused to kill the civilians hid that fact from their comrades. One soldier even shot himself in the foot to avoid becoming part of the slaughter.

Conformity occurs when a person changes his or her attitudes or behaviors to be consistent with other people or with social norms. The behaviors they might adopt include positive, prosocial behaviors such as wearing seatbelts, volunteering time and money for a charity, or buying only products that are safe for the environment. Sometimes people conform to counterproductive, antisocial behaviors, such as becoming involved in drugs, hazing in fraternities, or becoming part of an angry mob.

Conformity in Groups. Groups strongly influence conformity. Researcher Solomon Asch found that people in a group adopt its standard, which may be as simple as an individual refraining from speaking during a public address or as pervasive as a whole nation discriminating against a particular ethnic group. Studies also show that individuals conform to group norms even when not pressured to do so. Consider what happens when an instructor asks a class of 250 students to answer a relatively simple question, but no one volunteers. When asked, most students will report that they did not raise their hands because no one else did. Unpressured conformity also is illustrated by the fact that people generally dress appropriately for specific occasions such as weddings, black tie parties, and funerals.

Asch's conformity experiments clearly demonstrated the strength of group influence.

Conforming to Individuals. Asch also found that people imitate the behavior of those whom they respect and value. President Bush's favorite snack, pork rinds, became an instant hit with Americans. When Bush was sworn in as president, makers of pork rinds were deluged with orders from all over the country.

However, in their need to be liked, accepted, and respected, people may allow their behavior to be overly influenced by the irrational ideas of others. Learning to like a new snack food, driving the "in" car, or wearing the latest fashion is relatively harmless. But Asch argued (1955, p. 6) that:

> the tendency to conformity in our society [is] so strong that reasonably intelligent and well-meaning young people willing to call white black is a matter of concern. It raises questions about our ways of education and about the values that guide our conduct.

FIGURE 16.5
Asch's line-drawing task. Subjects were shown these cards and asked to choose the line in the picture on the bottom that was the same length as the line in the picture on the top.

Conformity Experiment. Suppose you have agreed to participate in an experiment of line discriminations. You are seated at the end of a table next to four other students. The experimenter holds up a card and asks each of you to pick which of two lines is longer, A or B. You quickly discover that the task is simple. The experimenter proceeds to hold up successive pairs of lines, with each participant correctly identifying the longest. Suddenly, after several rounds, you notice that the first person has chosen line A instead of line B, which is obviously longer. You are surprised when the second person also chooses line A, then the third, then the fourth. Your turn is next. You are sure that line B is longer. What do you do?

In 1951 Solomon Asch performed a similar experiment to explore conformity. Seven to nine subjects were brought into a room and told that they would be participating in an experiment involving visual judgment, such as that found in Figure 16.5; subjects had to judge which of three lines matched a standard. But only one group member was a naive subject; the others were collaborators of the researcher and they deliberately gave false answers to try to influence the naive subject. Asch found that the naive subject will generally go along with the group, even though the majority answer is obviously wrong and even though the group exerts no explicit or directly observable pressure to do so.

Although only some of the naive subjects conformed in Asch's experiments, enough did so that psychologists have researched the phenomenon further. They have found the number of people in the group to be a critical variable. When one or two individuals collaborate with the researcher, the tendency to conform is considerably less than when ten do. Another important variable is the number of dissenting votes—if even one of fifteen people disagrees with the other collaborating subjects the naive subject is more likely to choose the correct line.

Variables in Conformity. How do groups influence individual behavior? One variable is the amount of information provided when a decision is made. When people are uncertain of how to behave in ambiguous situations, they seek the opinions of others. For example, when they are unsure of how they should vote in an election, people often ask trusted friends for advice.

Another important variable that determines the degree of conformity is the relative competence of the group. People are more likely to conform to the decision of a group if they perceive its members as more competent than themselves. This pressure becomes stronger as group size increases. A student in a large class, for example, may not answer even a simple question if he assumes that his classmates are more competent. Position within a group also affects individual behavior. A person who confidently believes that a group holds her in high esteem will respond independently. If she feels insecure about her status, even though it is high, she may respond as the group does because she fears losing her status.

The extent to which behavior is public also determines people's responses. Individuals are more willing to make decisions that are inconsistent with those of their group when behavior is private. In a democracy, for example, casting a ballot is done privately to minimize group pressure on how individuals vote.

Theories of Conformity. Several theories have attempted to explain why people conform. The *social conformity* approach states that people conform to avoid the stigma of being wrong, deviant, out of line, or different from others. According to this view, people want to do the right thing, and define as right whatever is generally accepted (Festinger, 1954). For example, in high school, a boy might be considered socially correct if he joins the football team, but not if he enrolls in a modern dance class. Neighbors would likely approve if a homeowner built a picket fence that looked like their fences, but would consider the homeowner deviant if he enclosed his property with a ten-foot concrete wall.

Another explanation for the presence or absence of conformity in a group relies on *attribution*. When a person can identify causes for other people's behavior in a group, and he or she strongly disagrees with those causes, conformity disappears (Ross, Bierbrauer, and Hoffman, 1976). Suppose you hear several people argue vehemently for the construction of a toxic-waste incinerator near your town because it will boost the local economy. At first you agree, but you later discover that all the incinerator proponents own land at the proposed building site and stand to make money by selling the land to the incinerator company. After attributing the incinerator proponents' attitude to desire for personal profits, you may no longer agree.

Conformity is the course most people choose to take, but some individuals prefer a greater degree of independence and are willing to risk social disapproval for it.

Mahatma Ghandi is an outstanding example of an individual who changed world history when he presented a dissenting view.

The issue of *independence* also helps explain conformity (or the lack of it). Although people in a group would like to be independent, it is difficult to do so. They would have to face the consequences of their independence, such as serious disapproval, peer pressure to conform, being seen as deviant, and becoming less powerful.

Last, conformity is *expedient* and conserves mental energy. Cialdini (1988) argues that too many events, circumstances, and changing variables exist to analyze all the relevant data. People need shortcuts to help them make decisions. Therefore, it is efficient and easier for people to go along with others whom they trust and respect, especially if key elements of a situation fit in with their views. But not everyone conforms to group pressures all the time—especially when other people disagree with the group.

Dissenting Opinions. Both everyday experience and research show that *dissenting opinions* help counteract group influence and conformity. Even one or two people in a large group can seriously influence decision making. Moreover, when group decision making occurs, a consistent minority can exert substantial influence, even when it is devoid of power, status, or competence (Mungy, 1982). Nelson Mandela provides a clear example of someone who presented a dissenting opinion but was devoid of power for nearly thirty years; he ultimately exerted a profound influence on world politics.

Mahatma Gandhi provides one of the most remarkable examples of a dissenter counteracting group influence. At age twenty-four, after being subjected to humiliating racial discrimination, Gandhi began drafting petitions on behalf of the South African Indian community. A decade later, a South African minister was negotiating with the formerly powerless Gandhi on the issue of Indian rights. Later, Gandhi was instrumental in wresting India's independence from the powerful British. In 1946, Gandhi fasted to stop rioting between Muslims and Hindus during the transfer of British power to India and Pakistan. *The London Times* reported that his lone fast did what several troop divisions could not have done to restore peace. Can you think of any other famous dissenters through history?

Obedience and Milgram's Study

According to psychologists, **obedience** is the process by which a person complies with the orders of another person or group. Stanley Milgram's (1933–1984) studies on obedience are classic. Today, more than twenty-five years later, his results and interpretations still generate debate.

Milgram's work focuses on the extent to which an individual obeys a significant person. His studies, which showed that ordinary people were remarkably willing to comply with the wishes of others, especially if the others were seen as important, reveals a great deal about the social world, social influence in general, and obedience in particular. They also reveal something about an individual's self-perception, values, and early interactions in life.

Milgram (1963) brought two subjects into a laboratory and told them that they were participating in an experiment on paired-associate learning. The subjects drew lots to determine who would be the teacher and who would be the learner. In actuality the drawing was rigged; one subject was collaborating with the experimenter. The naive subject was always the teacher; the collaborator was always the learner.

The learner/collaborator was taken to an adjoining room, where the teacher/naive subject could not see him. The teacher/naive subject was shown a shock generator box containing thirty switches, each labeled with varying shock intensities from low shock to danger—severe shock. The teacher/naive subject was told to shock the learner by hitting one of the switches every time he or she made an error.

A social psychologist and an assistant wearing white lab coats encouraged the naive subject to increase the shock voltage one level each time the learner made a mistake. As the shock level rose, the learner/collaborator screamed *as if* suffering increasing pain. When the shock intensity reached the point of severe shock, the learner stopped responding vocally to the paired-associate stimulus and pounded on the walls of the experimental

Milgram's studies questioned to what degree behavior is sensitive to both authority and peer pressure. Surprisingly, most subjects were willing to deliver extreme levels of shock when told to do so. The man on the right was one of the few subjects who quit the experiment rather than deliver such shocks.

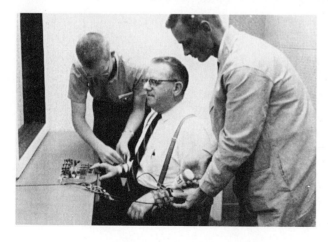

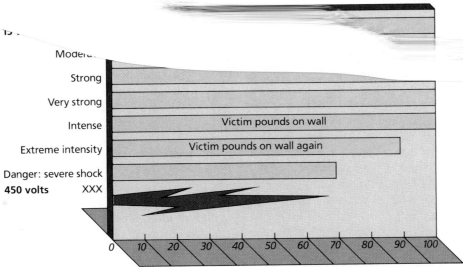

FIGURE 16.6
In a study by Milgram, sixty-five percent of the subjects were willing to use the higher levels of shock
jects were willing to provide shocks they thought to be of moderate or strong intensity. (Source: Data from Milgram, 1963.)

booth. The psychologist directed the teacher to treat the learner's lack of response as an error and to continue to administer increasing levels of shock. As Figure 16.6 shows, sixty-five percent of the subjects continued to shock the learner until all the shock levels were delivered. (You may have guessed by now that the learner/collaborators were not actually receiving shocks; they were only pretending to be in pain.)

Not all Milgram's subjects were obedient. Moreover, the presence of other subjects who refused to participate reduced the probability of obedience to as little as ten percent (Milgram, 1965b; Powers and Geen, 1972). These data suggest that behavior is sensitive to both authority and peer behavior. An individual's ability to resist coercion in the presence of an ally who also refuses to participate indicates the importance of social influences on behavior.

Background Authority. Did conducting the study at prestigious Yale University influence the subjects? Milgram (1965a) suggested that his experiment might have involved a particular type of experimental bias—*background authority.* To investigate the issue, Milgram conducted a second study in an office building in Bridgeport, Connecticut. Subjects were contacted by mail and had no knowledge that Milgram or his associates were from Yale. Forty-eight percent of the office subjects, as compared with sixty-five percent at Yale, delivered the maximum level of shock. Milgram therefore concluded that the perceived function of an institution can induce compliance in subjects. Moreover, an institution's qualitative position within a category (such as a prestigious as opposed to an unknown university) may be less important than the type of institution it is (i.e., a university rather than an office building).

Explaining Milgram's Results. Why did so many subjects in Milgram's experiments obey the wishes of the authority figure? One reason is that the subjects were volunteers, and volunteers often bring undetected biases to an experimental situation, and one such bias is to go along with authority. Another is that the experimental situation can itself bias the outcome. Perhaps the subjects were willing to administer the shocks only because they knew they were participating in an experiment or because they were instructed to do so by the experimenter, and they might not act the same way in real life.

Obedience to authority figures can also be explained by learning theories. Children learn that authority figures, such as teachers and parents, know more than they do and that taking their advice generally proves beneficial. As adults they maintain those beliefs, with the authority figures being employers, judges, government leaders, and so on. Cialdini (1988) also notes that obedience has practical advantages, such as helping people make decisions quickly. "It makes sense to comply with the wishes of properly constituted authorities. It makes so much sense, in fact, that we often do so when it makes no sense at all" (Cialdini, p. 207).

Not only do we obey those in authority, we also take directives from people who merely look authoritative. People who take on the trappings of power (expensive clothes, uniforms, prestigious cars, fancy offices) are often treated as authority figures. We are more likely to heed security guards who dress in uniforms that look like police garb than those who wear clothing of a less official appearance. As we saw in Milgram's conformity studies, people rely on symbols to make quick decisions, although the decisions are sometimes irrational.

Ethical Issues. Milgram's experimental methods raise several ethical questions. The primary issue is deception and potential harm to the subjects who participated. Obtaining unbiased responses in psychological research often requires deceiving naive subjects. After the experiment, subjects are then debriefed. **Debriefing** informs subjects about the true nature of the experiment after its completion. Debriefing preserves both the validity of responses and ethical considerations; of course, debriefing must be done carefully, because if done poorly, it can do more harm than good.

Milgram's subjects were fully debriefed and shown that they had not actually harmed the other person. Nevertheless, critics argue, the subjects realized that they were capable of inflicting severe pain on other people. Milgram therefore had a psychiatrist interview a sample of his obedient subjects a year after the study. No evidence was found of psychological trauma or injury. Moreover, one study reported that subjects viewed participation in the obedience experiment as a positive experience. They did not regret having participated, nor did they report any short-term negative psychological effects (Ring, Wallston, and Corey, 1970).

Implications. Milgram's studies have important implications for social psychologists. They show how people of authority can change the course of events and even influence history; people in positions of power tend to be obeyed.

Moreover, researchers repeated Milgram's methods, and the results of one study suggest that obedience to authority is not specific to Western culture (Shanab and Yahya, 1978). Students at the University of Jordan participated in a similar study, and as in the original Milgram study, about sixty-five percent were willing to give shocks to other students. Milgram's findings are cross-cultural, and apply to men and women, old and young; they show that the social world and our interactions within it are strongly affected by other people. Powerful people in positions of authority can change the course of events and indeed potentially influence history (consider Hitler, Khaddafi, or the pope). Milgram's studies challenge social psychologists to know why people obey and why people in lower positions in

Debriefing: A procedure to inform subjects about the true nature of an experiment after its completion.

authority. They also encourage us to ask how other people influence us to comply with their wishes.

Influence Techniques to Induce Compliance

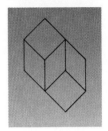

*H*ow can we influence others? How can others influence us? What techniques facilitate compliance or at least attitude change? Managers, salespeople, parents, and politicians all apply the principles of social psychology and influence people daily by using social psychological techniques.

Foot in the Door. To get someone to change an attitude or grant a favor, begin by asking for a small attitude change or a small favor. In other words, get your foot in the door. Ask to borrow a quarter today; a dollar next week; and money for your tuition within a month.

The essence of the *foot-in-the door* effect is that if a person grants a small request, he or she is more likely to comply with a larger request later. It only works, however, if the person first grants the small favor, and it works best if there is some time between the first small request and the later large one. If the person says no to the first favor, it may be even easier to say no to subsequent ones. Although the foot-in-the-door effect is relatively easy to find in American society, cross-cultural studies show that it does not occur as easily in all countries (Kilbourne, 1989).

Door in the Face. To use the *door-in-the-face* technique, first ask for something outrageous; then later ask for something much smaller and more reasonable. That is, use reverse psychology. Ask a friend to lend you $100; after being turned down, ask to borrow $5. Your friend may be relieved to grant the smaller favor.

The principle of the door-in-the-face effect is that a person is more likely to grant a small request if he or she has previously turned down a larger one. It appears to work because people do not want to be seen as turning someone down twice, and it works best if there is little time in between requests. To look good and maintain a positive self-image, they agree to the lesser of two requests.

Ask and You Shall Be Given. When people ask for money for a good cause, whether the request is large or small, they usually will get a response. Ask someone who has given before, and the request is even more likely to be granted (Doob and McLaughlin, 1989). Fund-raisers for universities, churches, and museums know that asking usually will get a positive response.

Low Balling. *Low balling* is a compliance technique by which a person is influenced to make a decision or commitment because of the low stakes associated with it. Once the decision is made, the stakes might increase but the person will likely stick with the original decision. For example, if a man agrees to buy a car for $9000, he may still buy it even if the salesman increases the price to $10,000. Low balling works because people tend to stick to their commitments even if the stakes are raised. Changing one's mind may suggest a lack of good judgment, cause stress, and make the person feel as if he or she were violating an (often imaginary) obligation.

Modeling. Showing someone good behavior, conserving energy, or saying no to drugs increases the likelihood that the person will behave similarly. The person being observed is a model for the desired behavior. *Modeling*, which was discussed in chapter 5, is a powerful technique by which people learn and adopt new behaviors and attitudes by witnessing others engaged in those behaviors and then expressing those attitudes themselves. When well-known athletes publicly declare their attitudes about the scourge of drugs, they act as models for youngsters who aspire to careers such as theirs.

Incentives. Nothing succeeds in eliciting a particular behavior better than a desired incentive. Offering a sixteen-year-old unlimited use of the family car if he or she sets the table every day for dinner usually results in a neatly set dinner table. Offering a large monetary bonus to a sales agent for year-end sales performance usually boosts sales efforts.

We can influence others and induce attitude change by using techniques that researchers have studied in the laboratory. Researchers have shown that the way a request is framed, the approach that a person takes, or the incentives that are offered can be critical in determining if people will comply. Shopkeepers, parents, and politicians all apply these principles to convince and persuade other people. ◆

Social Influence: Implications

Social psychologists know that human behavior is affected by subtle but strong social influences. Consider a worker's mood: Knowing that a person's mood affects absenteeism can alter the way managers deal with employees to improve productivity (George, 1989). The Asch studies showed that people are influenced and conform in their judgments and behavior, even when not directly asked to do so. Milgram's obedience studies showed that people are willing to conform to the desires of a scientific researcher, even though it is psychologically difficult to do so. Social psychologists are not trying to show that humans are callous, irresponsible, or simpleminded. They are trying to uncover and describe the forces at work in social settings that prevent individuals from acting as they might prefer to act if they were alone. Social psychologists acknowledge the importance of the context and the situation in which behavior occurs and try to understand the influence of those variables. You will see in studies of groups, considered next, that many other factors operate to influence individual behavior.

Focus on Learning

- ◆ Identify two variables that affect the extent to which people conform in groups. pp. 593–595 adopting as groups standards, conforming to group norms, even when pressured.
- ◆ Identify the principal finding in studies of obedience. p. 598
- ◆ What is debriefing? p. 600
- ◆ Distinguish between the foot-in-the-door technique and door-in-the-face technique. p. 601

Behavior in Groups

"Membership has its privileges," according to American Express. By appealing to people's desire to be part of a group, the charge-card company is employing psychological principles to sell its product and engender loyalty. To make the American Express group as attractive as possible, the company runs magazine ads featuring famous athletes, actors, politicians, and business people who are card members. Who wouldn't want to identify with such an elite group?

Membership does confer certain advantages, which is why people belong to all kinds of groups. There are formal groups, such as the American

interest. Sports, clubs, business associations, or environmental interests are just a few reasons for people coming together.

Association of University Students, and informal ones, such as peer groups. A **group** can be either a large number of people working toward a common purpose or a small number of people, even two, who are loosely related and have some common goals or interests. Members of groups share characteristics and goals and recognize their relationship with one another and a sense of shared purpose. By joining a group, people indicate that they agree with or have a serious interest in its purpose. If a major function of the American Cancer Society is to raise money for cancer research, a person's membership indicates willingness to raise money for this purpose.

Social Facilitation

Individual behavior is affected not only by joining a group but also by the presence of a group. One effect of the presence of a group is **social facilitation**—a change in performance, either better or worse, because of the presence (or imagined presence) of other people. For example, someone practicing a new sport such as basketball with a degree of success may do even better when other people enter the court. Another person, however, may do worse when other people are around. How the presence of others changes our behavior, and whether it changes for better or worse, is illustrated in Figure 16.7 on page 604, which is based on the generally accepted theory of Robert Zajonc (1965).

According to Zajonc, the presence of others produces heightened arousal, which leads to a greater likelihood of performing a strong or likely response (Jackson and Latane, 1981; Zajonc, 1965). But just what is the nature of the heightened arousal? This is a source of some debate. One theory of social facilitation suggests that fear of evaluation—not the mere presence of people—brings about changes in performance (see Innes and Young, 1975). If an auto mechanic knows that a customer is watching him repair an engine, he will likely increase his work speed to convince the observer of his effi-

Group: A number of individuals, loosely or cohesively related, who share some common characteristics and goals.

Social facilitation: The change in task performance that occurs when people are, or believe they are, in the presence of other people.

According to the *drive theory* of social facilitation, the presence of other people increases our level of motivation or arousal, which, in turn, enhances the performance of our strongest or most likely responses in a given situation. If these responses are correct, performance is enhanced. If they are incorrect, performance is impaired.

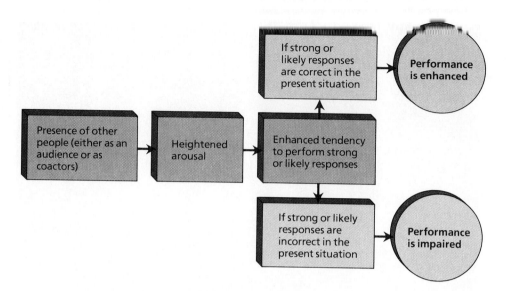

ciency and professionalism. Bond and Titus (1983) suggest that the effects of social facilitation are often overestimated, and the effects of believing oneself to be observed are often underestimated. They caution that a model of social facilitation must take into account the actual and believed presence of observers, as well as the perceived importance of the evaluation being performed.

Social Loafing

A decrease in an individual's effort and productivity as a result of working in a group is called **social loafing.** Social loafing was shown in an early experiment, in which individuals had to pull on a rope either alone or with help. They exerted more effort alone than when other people helped. Similarly, in an experiment in which individuals were instructed to clap their hands and cheer, they clapped and cheered less loudly when they were part of a group (Latane, Williams, and Harkins, 1979).

Most psychologists claim that social loafing occurs when individual performance within a group cannot be evaluated: Poor performance may go undetected, and exceptional performance may go unrecognized. Consequently, people feel less pressure to work hard or efficiently. One study showed that as group size increased, individual members felt their own efforts were more dispensable—the group could function without their help. "Let George do it!" became the prevailing attitude (Kerr and Bruun, 1983).

Social loafing is minimized when the task is attractive and rewarding, and the group is committed to high task performance (Zaccaro, 1984). It is also less apparent when a group is small, when the members know each other well, and when a group leader calls on individuals by name or lets it be known that individual performance may be evaluated (Williams, Harkins, and Latane, 1981). Some researchers have noted decreased social loafing when people have the opportunity to evaluate their own performance relative to other people's, despite the fact that no one else evaluated them (Szymanski and Harkins, 1987), as well as when people evaluated their performance against an objective standard, again when no one else evaluated them (Harkins and Szymanski, 1988).

Social loafing: The decrease in productivity that occurs when an individual works in a group instead of alone.

In groups, people may also be willing to adopt behaviors slightly more extreme than their individual behaviors. They may be willing to make decisions that are risky or even daring. A person who by himself is unwilling to invest money in a venture may change his mind on hearing that other members of the group are investing. Some early research on group decision making focused on the willingness of individuals to accept more risky alternatives when other members of the group did so. Such formulations described individuals as making a *risky shift* in their decisions.

People in a group initially perceive themselves as being more extreme than the other members of the group. They believe they are more fair, more right-minded, more liberal, and so on. When they discover that their positions are not very different from those of others in the group, they shift, or become *polarized*, to show that they are even more right-minded, more fair, or more liberal. They often become more assertive in expressing their views. This phenomenon is known as **group polarization.**

A *persuasive arguments* explanation of group polarization asserts that people tend to become more extreme after hearing views similar to their own. A person who is mildly liberal on an issue becomes even more liberal, more polarized. As more arguments favoring the person's view are presented in the group discussion, the individual is likely to become even more extreme in his or her view. The data, therefore, suggest that instead of becoming more reasonable, people in a group often become more wedded to their initial views. If other people in the group hold similar views, that reinforces the view and may polarize the person even more.

The effects of group polarization are particularly evident in jury rooms. After group discussion, jury members are likely to decide on their initial views and argue for them more strongly. Thus, individual jury members with initially mild views toward a defendant will have an even milder view after group discussions; their initial view becomes a verdict.

Another explanation for group polarization is **diffusion of responsibility,** the feeling individual members have that they cannot be held responsible for the group's actions. If a youth group of a church makes a decision to invest money, for example, no one individual is responsible. Diffusion of responsibility allows the teenagers to make far more extreme decisions as a group than they would individually. *Social comparison* may play a role in group polarization; people compare their view with others whom they respect and who may hold more extreme views than theirs. Feeling as right-minded as their colleagues, they become at least as liberal or fair as their peer group—they polarize their views. After a group becomes polarized, many people in the group may share the same opinion; when such an event occurs (as it often does with government officials), people sometimes fall into a trap called groupthink.

Psychology and Government: The Problem of Groupthink

On the other hand, studies of decision making in government have often focused on the concept of **groupthink,** the tendency of people in a group to seek concurrence with each other when reaching a decision, usually prematurely. Groupthink occurs when group members reinforce commonly held beliefs in the interest of getting along, rather than effectively evaluating

aggeration of individuals' preexisting attitudes as a result of group discussion.

Diffusion of responsibility: The feeling of individuals in a group that they cannot be held individually responsible for the group's actions.

Groupthink: The phenomenon of people in a group reinforcing each other and seeking concurrence and group cohesiveness, rather than effectively evaluating choices and reasoning.

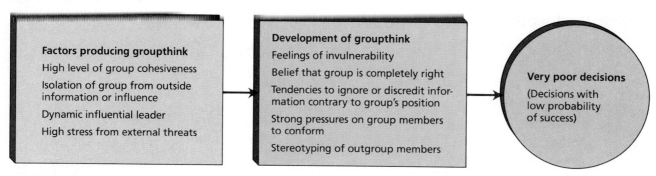

FIGURE 16.8
Factors leading to the development of *groupthink*.

alternative solutions to the problem. The group does not allow its members to disagree or take dissenting opinions and evaluate options realistically (Janis, 1983). It discredits or ignores information not held in common. See Figure 16.8 for a summary of the factors producing groupthink.

Studies of history and government offer several examples of groupthink which led to defective decision making: the Bay of Pigs, North Korea, Pearl Harbor, and Vietnam. In the Bay of Pigs, for example, President Kennedy decided to go ahead with a CIA plan devised by anti-Castro exiles to invade Cuba. When the President asked for counsel from his advisors—an impressive group of wide experience—no one voted against it and the mission was carried out. The Bay of Pigs turned out to be a major political fiasco, which nearly resulted in war between the United States and the Soviet Union. Janis (1982b) and McCauley (1989) cite this as an example of groupthink.

Social psychologist Ivan Steiner (1982) suggests that groupthink occurs when members' overriding concern is to maintain group cohesiveness and harmony. Others maintain that it occurs when individuals in a group feel a sense of cohesiveness and believe that the group cannot make mistakes. Strong leaders often insulate a group from information or other people to keep the group thinking in one direction (McCauley, 1989). Although groupthink is not inevitable, it is common enough that social psychologists consider it an important issue in group influence on decision making. They look at it in terms of group behavior, social influence, and a self-serving and self-reinforcing mechanism. Students of political science, government, and history can use the concept of groupthink to train new leaders and promote more rational decision making.

Deindividuation of members within a group encourages conformity, even at the expense of personal qualms.

Unrestrained Group Behavior

When placed in a group, normally thoughtful people have been known to take part in irrational behaviors. In the early 1970s, for example, streaking became popular on college campuses. A naked person darted out from behind a bush, ran across campus or through a crowded lobby, and disappeared. Soon, streaking groups with hundreds of students began to form. The behavior was not considered a matter of individual responsibility, but a group decision.

A key component of unrestrained behavior such as streaking or mob violence is *anonymity*. Anonymity produces a lack of self-awareness and self-perception that leads to decreased concern with social evaluation. When people have fewer concerns about being evaluated, they are more willing perception, people exhibit behaviors they would normally avoid.

No single individual can be held responsible for the behavior of a group; this view focuses on deindividuation. **Deindividuation** is the process by which individuals lose their distinctive personalities in the context of a group (Diener et al., 1980). Deindividuation (and its accompanying arousal), which can occur in joyous group celebrations, can lead to shifts in people's perceptions of how their behavior will be viewed, and thus to less controlled or less careful decisions about their behavior (see Prentice-Dunn and Rogers, 1984). With deindividuation, people alter their thoughts about decisions.

Groups such as the military and cults use deindividuation to encourage their members to conform. During boot camp, recruits are made to feel that they are there to serve the group, not their individual conscience. In prisons, inmates are made to wear uniforms, cut their hair, and are assigned numbers. With their unique personality stripped away, they are no longer treated as individuals and are made to behave as members of one large prison group. Cults persuade members to go along with group beliefs and a sense of obligation to the group by asking an individual member to perform increasingly more taxing services on the group's behalf.

Deindividuation. The process by which individuals in a group lose their sense of self-awareness and concern with evaluation.

Half the Story

In this chapter we have discussed the components and characteristics that make up the social world of individuals. We have seen that other people affect attitudes, that other people help shape our individual self-perceptions, and that groups of people exert powerful influences on individual behavior. But this is only half the story; in the next chapter we will explore the interactions that occur among individuals and focus on the variables that can influence those interactions.

- ◆ What is the basic finding in studies of social facilitation? p. 603
- ◆ Describe the phenomenon of group polarization and give an example from your own experience. p. 605
- ◆ Describe the phenomenon of groupthink and give an example from your own experience. p. 605
- ◆ Identify two variables that are important in explaining unrestrained group behavior. p. 606

Focus on Learning

Key Terms

Social psychology p. 574
Attitude p. 574
Elaboration likelihood model
   p. 579
Cognitive dissonance p. 581
Self-perception theory p. 581
Balance theory p. 582
Social cognition p. 583
Impression formation p. 584
Nonverbal communications
   p. 584

Body language p. 585
Attribution p. 586
Fundamental attribution error
   p. 588
Actor-observer effect p. 588
Self-perception p. 589
Role p. 590
Self-serving bias p. 591
Learned helplessness p. 592
Social influence p. 593

Obedience p. 598
Debriefing p. 600
Group p. 603
Social facilitation p. 603
Social loafing p. 604
Group polarization p. 605
Diffusion of responsibility
   p. 605
Groupthink p. 605
Deindividuation p. 607

Summary

Attitudes

- Social psychology is the study of how people influence and are influenced by the thoughts, feelings, and behaviors of others. p. 574

- Attitudes are lasting patterns of feelings, beliefs, and behavior tendencies toward people, ideas, or objects. Most psychologists contend that attitudes have three dimensions—cognitive, emotional, and behavioral. p. 574

- Social psychologists categorize the process of attitude change into the factors of the communicator, the communication, the medium, and the audience. pp. 577–578

- The central processes route to attitude change emphasizes rational decision making. The peripheral processes route emphasizes emotional and motivational influences. p. 579

- Cognitive dissonance is a state of discomfort that results when an individual maintains two or more beliefs, attitudes, or behaviors that are inconsistent with each other. p. 580

Social Cognition

- Social cognition is the process of making sense of events and people, including ourselves, through analysis and interpretation. p. 583

- Nonverbal communication is information provided by cues or actions that involve movements of the body, especially the face, and sometimes the vocal cords. Body language is the communication of information through body positions and gestures. p. 584

- Attribution is the process by which someone infers other people's motives and intentions from observing their behavior. p. 586

- The fundamental attribution error is the tendency to attribute behavior to individual dispositional causes rather than situational causes. The actor-observer effect is the tendency for people to attribute the behavior of others to dispositional causes, while attributing their own behavior to situational causes. p. 587

- Early social interactions with parents, peers, and institutions strongly affect self-perception and social behavior later in life. Behavior may be influenced not only by personal beliefs but also by environmental factors such as television, direct reinforcement, or group pressures. p. 588

- Self-perception theory suggests that people observe their own behavior in a situation and then infer their attitudes about the situation from their behavior. Balance theory states that people prefer to hold beliefs that are consistent with those of others. Reactance theory suggests that a person whose freedom of choice is restricted will try to reestablish that freedom. p. 589

- Individuals who place the causes of what happens to them in the outside world are said to have an external locus of control. Those who believe they control what happens to them have an internal locus of control. p. 592

- Learned helplessness is the behavior of giving up or not responding, exhibited by subjects exposed to negative consequences or punishment over which they have no control. p. 592

Social Influence

- Social influence is the effort on the part of one or more people to alter the attitudes or behavior of others. p. 593

- Obedience is the process by which a person complies with the orders of another person or group of people. Conformity occurs when a person changes his or her attitudes or behaviors to be consistent with those of other people or with social norms. pp. 598–602

Behavior in Groups

- Social facilitation is a change in performance, positive or negative, because of the presence of other people. Social loafing is the decrease in individual productivity as a result of working in a group. p. 603

- Group polarization is the exaggeration of preexisting attitudes as a result of group discussion. Groupthink is the tendency of people in a group to seek concurrence when making decisions. p. 605

- Deindividuation is the process by which individuals in a group lose their sense of self-awareness, self-perception, and concern with evaluation. Deindividuation has been used to explain irrational group behavior. p. 607

Connections

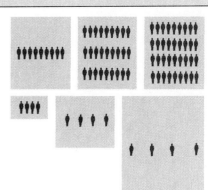

If you are interested in . . .	*Turn to . . .*	*To learn more about . . .*
The formation of attitudes	◆ Ch. 5, pp. 192–193	How social (observational) learning theory claims that people learn attitudes by observing the behavior and attitudes of others.
	◆ Ch. 10, pp. 344–351	The way children's and adolescents' developing attitudes, which are often based on sex role stereotypes, have their roots in childhood learning.
	◆ Ch. 17, p. 618	How prejudices are formed and maintained.
The way people form self-concepts	◆ Ch. 9, pp. 328–332	How early interactions with parents, friends, and relatives help shape a child's developing self-concept.
	◆ Ch. 12, p. 437	How humanists such as Carl Rogers focused their theories around the idea of an emerging and satisfying self-concept.
	◆ Ch. 15, pp. 555–558	How cognitive psychologists claim that a person's self-concept can be bolstered through cognitive (thought) reshaping.
How people behave in groups	◆ Ch. 11, p. 344	Adolescents and peer pressure.
	◆ Ch. 15, pp. 560–563	Why individuals sometimes improve more in group therapy than they do in individual therapy.
	◆ Ch. 17, p. 633	The effects of crowding on individuals.

17 Social Interactions

"Pas Mele" by Bill Barrett

◆

> We killed, killed, killed. The Malays would stop and go through people's
> pockets and take their watches and money. We did not think of watches or
> money. We thought only of killing. . . . we were drunk with blood.

A Semai soldier told that tale to American anthropologist Robert K. Dentan (1968) who lived with the man's tribe for more than a year. What is most remarkable about the story is that the Semais are among the most gentle people on earth. Not a single murder has been recorded among this central Malayan tribe, adults never physically attack one another, children are taught to be nonviolent, and they have no police force. The Semai even regret having to kill their chickens for food.

611

Despite their pacifist heritage, Semai tribesmen were recruited and trained by the British to fight Communist guerrillas in the early 1950s. When their comrades fell in battle, the Semai became "blood drunk" and avenged themselves on the enemy with terrible ferocity. One veteran even reported drinking the blood of a man he killed. Upon their return home, however, the Semai soldiers returned to their pacifist ways.

Like most human beings, the Semai can be either loving or ferocious. Based on social or other environmental influences, an individual can be kind or aggressive, sociable or withdrawn. Social psychologists have shown that human behavior is affected by sometimes subtle, but powerful, social interactions. One aspect of such interaction is relationships and attraction. Another is the way people are hurtful and helpful. One outgrowth of social psychology is environmental psychology. Environmental psychologists study how physical settings like a person's home affect behavior. They are interested in the effects of crowding and how personal space can be changed to meet changing needs. Another outgrowth of social psychology is the more applied field of industrial and organizational psychology. We will take up each of these topics in this chapter.

Relationships and Attraction

What is it about your friends that attracts you and makes you want to maintain a relationship with them? We saw in chapter 11 that people develop relationships to fulfill their needs for warmth, understanding, and emotional security. Social psychologists study **interpersonal attraction**—the tendency of one person to evaluate another person (or symbol or image of a person) in a positive way. Psychologists know that people are attracted to those they consider good looking, who share their attitudes, and with whom they spend time.

Proximity

People are more likely to develop a relationship with a neighbor than with someone who lives several blocks or miles away. Three decades of research show that the closer people are to someone geographically—whether it is where they work or where they live—the more attracted they will be to that person. A simple explanation is that they are likely to see that person often, and repeated exposure leads to familiarity, which leads to attraction. Another reason is that attraction is facilitated by anticipating a relationship with someone one encounters frequently. In addition, if people are members of a group, such as a computer club, a volunteer organization, or an aerobics class, they perceive themselves as sharing the same feelings, attitudes, and values as others in the group. That belief leads to attraction.

Physical Characteristics

Interpersonal attraction: The tendency of one person to evaluate another person (or a symbol of another person) in a positive way.

In addition to liking people who like us, who have views similar to our own, and who live or work close by, we tend to like people we find physically attractive. Numerous experiments have shown that people ascribe more power, status, competence, and personal regard to individuals they find attractive than to those they don't; we saw this in chapter 16 in examining who can best change people's attitudes. Volumes of research show that people are attracted romantically, at least at first, to those whom they find attractive, but research also shows that physical attraction in romantic re-

Physical attraction is defined by the culture in which we live.

lationships is only one important element among many others (Feingold, 1988a).

In a typical physical attractiveness experiment, subjects are given two identical job resumes, each with a different picture attached to it. Results show that people will evaluate the resume of the person they find physically attractive more highly than that of the other person, even though their qualifications are the same. Attractive people are preferred in the work place, as dates, and as friends; they are thought to be less menacing. In one research study (Esses and Webster, 1988), for example, subjects were given information about a hypothetical sex offender, including a facial photograph and a conviction record. The subjects judged physically unattractive sex offenders as less likely to restrain their behavior in the future than better looking but equally dangerous sex offenders. If physical attraction is only one characteristic of attraction, what are others?

Liking Those Who Like Us and Share Our Attitudes

Learning theorists contend that men and women are attracted to and form relationships with those who give them positive reinforcement and dislike those who punish them. The basic idea is simple: People like individuals who like them. Moreover, if someone likes an individual, he or she tends to assume (sometimes incorrectly) that the individual likes him or her in return and that they share similar qualities. This is especially true when a person needs social approval, e.g., when his or her self-esteem is low (Jacobs, Berscheid, and Walster, 1971).

Another attribute that affects the development of relationships is real or perceived similarity in attitudes and opinions. If you perceive someone's attitudes as similar to your own, there is an increased probability that you will like that person. Having similar values, interests, and background is a good predictor of a likely friendship. Similarly, voters who are in agreement with a particular candidate tend to rate him or her as more honest, friendly, and persuasive than politicians with whom they disagree. Researchers have also found that if you already like someone, you will perceive that person's attitudes as similar to your own. Voters who like a particular candidate—perhaps because he or she is warm-hearted or physically attractive—will tend to minimize their attitudinal differences. The slogan "I Like Ike" helped elect Eisenhower, and some political analysts have suggested that George Bush defeated Michael Dukakis in the 1988 presidential election because voters perceived him as being a warmer person.

These phenomena are explained by cognitive consistency theory, which suggests that sharing similar attitudes reduces cognitive dissonance, the phenomenon we discussed in chapter 16. To avoid dissonance, people feel attracted to those they believe share similar attitudes. Shared attitudes in turn lead to attraction and liking. Learning theories also suggest that we like people with similar attitudes because similar attitudes are reinforcing to us. As long as we feel the other person's attitudes are genuine, such liking will continue.

Friendships and the Role of Equity

Friendship is a special two-way relationship between people. A key component of a close relationship or a friendship is the extent to which people are connected with one another's lives. According to one influential group of researchers (Kelley et al., 1983), if two people's behaviors, emotions, and thoughts are related, then the people are dependent on one another, and we can say a relationship exists. Closeness is reported by many researchers as the key variable that defines a relationship, although *close* must be defined operationally so that all researchers mean the same thing when they use the word (Berscheid, Snyder, and Omoto, 1989).

Variables in Friendships. Psychologists Keith Davis and Michael Todd (1984) suggest that, ideally, friends participate as equals, enjoy each other's company, have mutual trust, provide mutual assistance, accept each other as they are, respect each other's judgment, feel free to be themselves spontaneously, understand each other in fundamental ways, and are intimate and share confidences. Reciprocity and commitment between people who

Close friends enjoy each other as equals and are committed to sharing and providing support.

see themselves as equals are essentials of friendship (Hartup, 1989). Compared with casual friends, close friends interact more frequently across a greater range of settings, and are more exclusive and offer each other more benefits (Hays, 1989).

As we saw in chapter 9, friendships among children tend to be of the same sex; cross-sex friendships are rare. With youngsters, friendships lead to cooperation rather than competition, at least more than with non-friends (Hartup, 1989). Among adults, friendships between two women differ from those between two men; both differ from friendships between a man and a woman. Women talk more about family, personal matters, doubts and fears than men do (Aries and Johnson, 1983); men talk more about sports and work. Cultural expectations for specific gender-based behaviors often determine such interactions.

Equity. Equity also plays an important role in relationships. *Equity theory* states that people attempt to maintain stable, consistent, interpersonal relationships in which the ratio of each member's contribution is equal to that of the other members. This ensures that all members are treated fairly. People in close relationships usually have a sense of balance in these relationships and believe they will stay together for a long time (Clark and Reis, 1988).

According to equity theory, one way people maintain a balanced relationship is to make restitution when it is demanded. Apologies help restore a sense of autonomy and fairness to the injured individual. Similarly, people who do favors expect favors in return, often using the principles of equity theory in day-to-day life. When a politician running for reelection responds to her constituents' desires and has a playground built, she expects their votes on election day. Research also shows that when a person feels inequity in a situation, this affects his or her feeling about the other person, especially when the other person is being treated better (Griffeth, Vecchio, and Logan, 1989).

Intimate Relationships and Love

People involved in a close relationship may also be intimate with one another. *Intimacy* generally refers to the willingness of one person to be self-disclosing and to express important feelings and information to another person; in response, the other person usually acknowledges the first person's feelings, making the individual feel valued and cared for (Reis and Shaver, 1988). Self-disclosure and emotional openness are important, key elements in intimate relationships; it comes through direct reports, nonverbal messages, and even touching. Self-disclosure also tends to be reciprocal, so that people who self-disclose to others are usually recipients of intimate information.

Unfortunately, there is little research on intimate relationships outside of marriage. Communication, affection, consideration, and self-disclosure between friends have been studied relatively little. Important individual and gender differences exist in friendships. For example, men are more self-disclosing with a woman than they are with another man (Derlega et al., 1985), and in general men are less likely to be self-disclosing and intimate than women (Aukett, Ritchie, and Mill, 1988). Psychologists know much more about intimate relationships between men and women where sex, marriage, and love become involved.

People in intimate relationships often express feelings in unique ways — they give flowers, take moonlight walks, write lengthy letters, and have

Love may be a state of mind, but it is also a series of behaviors.

romantic dinners. Love, emotional commitment, and sex may be a part of an intimate relationship. According to psychologists, love has psychological, emotional, and social factors.

- Erich Fromm (1956) focused on the idea that mature love is possible only if a person achieves a secure sense of self-identity. He said that when people are in love, they become one and yet remain two individuals.
- Heinlein (1961) wrote that love "is a condition in which the happiness of the other person is essential to your own."
- Branden (1980) suggested that love is "a passionate spiritual, emotional, sexual attachment between a man and a woman that reflects a high regard for the value of each other's person."
- Tennov (1981) believed that the ultimate in romantic love is a state called limerance; this is a head over heels involvement and preoccupation with thoughts of the loved one.
- Davis believed that love is characterized by exclusiveness, fascination, and sexual desire (Davis and Todd, 1982).

Elements in a Love Relationship. Researchers have identified some common elements in love relationships. Love usually involves the idealization of another person; people see their loved ones in a positive light. It also involves caring for another person and being fascinated with that person. And love involves trust, respect, liking, honesty, companionship, and sexual attraction. A central element in love is commitment; however, researchers disagree as to whether love and commitment can be separated, because one usually follows from, or is part of, the other (Fehr, 1988).

Many classifications of love have been suggested and all have some overlapping components. One influential classification is Sternberg's (1986b) view, which sees love as having three components: intimacy, commitment, and passion. Intimacy is a sense of emotional closeness. Commitment refers to the extent to which a relationship is permanent and long-lasting. Passion refers to arousal, some of it sexual, some intellectual, and some motivational.

Love is a state, but is also is an act and a series of behaviors. Thus, although a person may be in love, most psychologists think of love in terms of the behaviors that demonstrate it, including remaining faithful sexually and showing caring behaviors (Buss, 1988). Can you think of other specific behaviors that may demonstrate love?

Process of Love. The process of love begins with infatuation, often based on physical attraction. As people get to know one another, physical attraction may lead into shared interests, liking, companionship, and perhaps sexual intimacy.

Does love have a biological basis? According to David McClelland (1986), two sources exist for understanding love: analytical self-reports governed by the left side of the brain and emotional reports governed by the right side of the brain, a subject we discussed in chapters 2 and 4. From McClelland's view, the right brain can tell us about the emotional experiences that are not consciously processed. He argues that these emotional processes influence physiological processes and behaviors that are not directly under conscious control. In some ways, McClelland argues that there are two psychologies of love, an analytic left-brain understanding and an emotional right-brain understanding. McClelland's view is relatively new, and such a physiologically-based understanding of love has yet to achieve wide acceptance.

Loneliness: An unpleasant experience that occurs when a person's network of social relationships is significantly deficient in either quality or quantity.

Loneliness

People who are not in relationships, as well as some who are, may experience loneliness. Loneliness has no boundaries—it is felt by men and women of all races, socioeconomic levels, and ages. Loneliness has been linked to alcoholism, physical illness, depression, suicide, psychological paralysis, and intensified social isolation.

Perlman and Peplau (1984) define **loneliness** as an unpleasant experience that occurs when a person's network of social relationships is significantly deficient in either quality or quantity, or when there is a discrepancy between a person's needs for social contact and their actual social contact. Loneliness is not synonymous with social isolation. People can be alone and content, or they can be in a crowd and desperately lonely. A person must perceive and interpret his or her situation as lonely for it to be lonely. Thus, cognitive processes play a large role (Marangoni and Ickes, 1989).

Two common types of loneliness are emotional loneliness and social loneliness. *Emotional loneliness* occurs when an individual does not have an intimate relationship with at least one person he or she views as significant. *Social loneliness* occurs when an individual lacks adequate or expected connections with other people, caused by living alone or having no friends or partners.

Brief periods of feeling lonely are normal for everyone. When loneliness persists, however, it becomes a painful and potentially life-threatening problem (Weiss, 1984). Since persistent loneliness is affecting people in epidemic proportions, it cannot be explained only in terms of personality characteristics. It is an inherent problem of modern life and is likely to grow worse in our fast-paced technological society. Major life transitions, as described in chapter 10, and modern life patterns disrupt people's ability to keep consistent intimate relationships. Moreover, earlier retirement, living longer, geographical mobility, and the disintegration of the family can lead to loneliness (Gordon, 1976).

Living alone, working alone, or failing to find friends may create feelings of social loneliness.

Lonely people often perceive themselves as lacking in social skills. A lonely person can find relief by becoming aware of lonely feelings, accepting them, and taking action. One way to overcome loneliness is to reach out and interact with another person by offering a helping hand. When a person reaches out to other people, many old ideas and fears disappear—ideas that may have their roots in prejudice, our next topic.

<table>
</table>

Focus on Learning

◆ Identify two reasons why physical proximity is an aid to developing close relationships. p. 612
◆ Provide one explanation of why, if you perceive someone's attitudes as similar to your own, you will probably like that person. p. 613
◆ Identify three key components of a definition of love. p. 615
◆ Distinguish between emotional loneliness and social loneliness. p. 617

Prejudice

People involved in close relationships know each other well, are attracted to one another, and share ideas, values and activities. But what happens when you do not share ideas, values, or activities with another person or another group of people? What happens when you do not know another group of people well, or at all? Why do some people form negative evaluations of certain groups, such as blacks, Asians, Jews, or homosexuals? What is prejudice and how can it be prevented?

What Is Prejudice?

Prejudice is a negative evaluation of an entire group of people typically based on unfavorable ideas about the group. The negative evaluation is generally based on a small sample of experience, or even no experience, with an individual from the group being evaluated. People sometimes develop prejudices because of stereotypes about others they do not know well. **Stereotypes** are fixed, simple ideas, often about traits, attitudes, and behaviors of groups of people; usually these attributions are oversimplified and wrong. Often such stereotypes are negative. People hold stereotyped ideas about American Indians, Catholics, women, or mountain folk; such stereotypes can lead to prejudice. Stereotypes usually have a historical basis (Helmreich, 1982); for example, the idea that all blacks are natural musicians or athletes probably stems from the fact that historically blacks were barred from avenues of upward mobility except for the entertainment and sports industries.

Prejudice is an attitude; as we saw in chapter 16, an attitude is comprised of a belief (all Xs are stupid—the stereotyped idea), an emotional component (I hate those so-and-so Xs), and often a behavior (I intend to keep those Xs out of my neighborhood). Such prejudice translated into behavior is called discrimination. **Discrimination** is behavior targeted at a person with the aim of holding that person or group apart, treating them differently.

Sometimes people are prejudiced but do not show that attitude in behavior—that is, they do not discriminate. Merton (1949) referred to such individuals as cautious bigots compared to true bigots who are prejudiced and discriminate. And sometimes people show *reverse discrimination*, in which

Prejudice: A negative evaluation of an entire group of people, usually based on a set of negative (and often wrong) ideas about the group.

Stereotypes: Fixed, simple ideas, often about traits, attitudes, and behaviors, that are attributed to groups of people; usually these attributions are oversimplified and are often wrong.

Discrimination: Behavior targeted at a person with the aim of holding that person (or group) apart and treating them differently.

they bend over backward to treat some individual favorably—more positively than they should, based on that person's performance—solely based on preexisting biases or stereotypes (Chidester, 1986). Thus, someone prejudiced toward blacks may treat a black person oversolicitously and evaluate the person with different standards. This, too, is discrimination and has been demonstrated in laboratory studies (Fajardo, 1985). In *tokenism*, prejudiced people engage in positive but trivial actions toward members of a group they dislike. A man may make a token gesture toward the women on his staff, or a manager may hire a token Hispanic. By engaging in tokenism, a person often attempts to put off more important actions, for example, in hiring practices. The trivial behavior justifies, in this person's mind, the idea that he or she has done something for this minority group. Tokenism has negative consequences for the minority person and perpetuates discrimination (Chacko, 1982).

What Causes Prejudice?

The causes of prejudice cannot be tied to a single theory or explanation. Like so many other psychological phenomena, prejudice has multiple causes. We shall consider four theories to explain prejudice: learning theory, motivational theory, cognitive theory, and personality theory.

Learning Theory. According to social learning theory, we learn to be prejudiced; we watch our parents, neighbors, and relatives engaged in acts of discrimination, which often include stereotyped judgments and racial slurs, and we then incorporate those ideas into our own behavioral repertoire. After a child has observed such behaviors, the child is then reinforced (operant conditioning techniques) for exhibiting similar behaviors to classmates or relatives. Thus, through imitation and reinforcement a prejudiced view is transmitted from parents to children, and from one generation to the next.

Motivational Theory. We saw in chapter 11 that people are motivated to succeed, to get ahead, and to provide for basic as well as high-level emotional needs. If people are raised to compete against others for scarce resources, the competition can elicit negative views against competitors. Motivational

We learn attitudes such as racial tolerance. The father shown here has set an example of racial acceptance which his daughter is likely to accept and follow.

theory thus asserts that individuals learn to dislike specific individuals (competitors) and then generalize that dislike to whole classes of similar individuals (races, religions, or colors). This helps make those groups of people (often seen as competitors) into scapegoats—for example, the Jews in Nazi Germany, and blacks in South Africa. Research with children, adolescents, and adults shows that people who are initially seen as friends or neutral are sometimes treated badly when turned into competitors (Sherif et al., 1961; White, 1977). Competition for jobs among immigrants can also create prejudice, particularly in times of economic hardship (Aronson, 1980).

Cognitive Theory. Cognitive theorists assert that people think about individuals and the groups that they come from as a way of organizing the world. Recall from chapter 16 Cialdini's (1988) argument that there are so many events, circumstances, and changing variables in our lives that we cannot easily analyze all the relevant data. People thus devise shortcuts to help them make decisions. One of those shortcuts is to stereotype individuals and the groups they belong to—all Hispanics, all yuppies, all men, all attorneys. By devising such shortcuts in thinking, people develop ideas about who is in an *ingroup,* that is, who is a member of a group to which they belong or want to belong. People tend to see themselves and other members of an ingroup in a favorable light (Wilder and Thompson, 1980). As we saw in chapter 16, when judging other people, individuals make fundamental attribution errors. They assume that other people's behavior is caused by internal dispositions—which may or may not be true—and that other people are all alike (Judd and Park, 1988.) They underestimate situational influences and overestimate dispositional influences on other people's behavior, and then they use those behaviors (Fiske and Taylor, 1984) as evidence for their attitudes (prejudices.) Thus, hostilities between Arabs and Israelis in the Middle East, Catholics and Protestants in Ireland, and blacks and whites in South Africa are perpetuated.

Personality Theory. Some psychologists assert that people develop prejudices because they have a prejudice-prone personality. Some personality tests examine the extent to which people are likely to be prejudiced. For example, one personality trait that appears to be prevalent among prejudiced people is the *authoritarian personality.* People with authoritarian personalities were fearful and anxious as children, and may have been raised by cold, love-withholding parents who regularly used physical punishment. To gain control and mastery as adults, such individuals become aggressive and controlling over others. They see the world in absolutes—good versus bad, black versus white. They also tend to blame others for their problems and become prejudiced toward those people (Adorno et al., 1950). The relationship between personality traits and prejudice has its roots in psychoanalytic theory, but it is not widely accepted by many theorists who study prejudice today. However, the idea that some people have traits that lead them toward prejudice has guided some personality theory research.

Reducing and Eliminating Prejudice

To reduce and eliminate prejudice, we can teach rational thinking, judge people by their behavior, and promote equality. Once people have worked on a community project with an attorney, lived with a person of another race, or prayed with members of a different church, their views of them as individuals change (Wilder and Thompson, 1980).

As students of psychology, we can become especially sensitive to thinking about *individuals* rather than groups. Through examining individuals, we can be sensitive to the wide diversity of human behavior. Although it is tempting to derive broad generalizations about behavior and people when making attributions about the causes of behavior (see chapter 16), we can focus on men and women as individuals, not as members of any particular group. When we focus on individuals, we see that human beings are engaged in a whole array of behaviors—some of them destructive and harmful, and others prosocial, worthwhile, and helpful.

Prosocial Behavior

Are country people more helpful than city people? It turns out that they are (Steblay, 1987), but what factors are at work and under what conditions are people helpful? If a woman is walking down the street with a bag of groceries and drops them, what is the likelihood that someone will stop and pick them up? Will a bystander help if he or she observes an accident or crime? Psychologists who ask these questions want to find out when, and under what conditions, someone will help a stranger. They are examining the likelihood of **prosocial behavior,** an act that benefits someone else or society but generally has no obvious benefit to the person doing it and might even involve some personal risk or sacrifice.

Altruism: Helping without Rewards

Why does Peter Beneson, the founder of Amnesty International, devote so much time and effort to helping "prisoners of conscience" around the world? What compels Mother Teresa to wander Calcutta's streets and attend to the wounds and diseases of people no one else will touch? Who were the people who risked their lives to help the Jews hide from the SS and escape the Nazi death camps during World War II?

Altruistic acts are those behaviors that benefit other people for which there is no discernible reward, recognition, or appreciation. When a person helps someone in need and there is no obvious reward, he or she is generally referred to as being altruistic (Quigley, Gaes, and Tedeschi, 1989). But does an altruistic person truly expect no reward for his or her good acts? Isn't the feeling of well-being after performing an altruistic act a type of reward?

Behavioral Explanations. Behavioral psychologists have a difficult time explaining altruism, since altruistic acts are performed without overt reinforcement or even anticipated reinforcement. Many behaviorists contend that a personality element develops that directs people to seek social approval by helping; for example, self-monitoring individuals tailor their behavior to help other people (White and Gerstein, 1987). People with a high need for achievement are also more likely to be helpful (Puffer, 1987). Some people may develop altruistic behaviors because such actions are self-reinforcing. Research also shows that when we have a relationship with a person, we

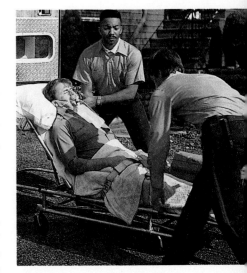

Volunteer emergency medical technicians place the well-being of others before their own.

Prosocial behavior: An act that benefits someone else and often has no obvious benefit to the person doing it; the act might even involve some personal risk or sacrifice.

Altruistic acts: Behaviors that benefit other people for which there is no discernible reward, recognition, or appreciation.

Sociobiology: The theory asserting that even day-to-day behaviors are determined by the process of natural selection; the theory contends that social behaviors that contribute to the survival of our species are passed on through the genes from one generation to the next.

Bystander apathy: The unwillingness of witnesses to an event to help, especially when there are a number of observers (bystanders); the effect increases when there are more observers.

are more likely to be caring and helpful (Batson, 1990). Intrinsically rewarding activities tend to become powerful behavior initiators. Thus, intrinsically rewarding behaviors become established as regular activities, and people are later impelled to help others, such as the homeless, disadvantaged senior citizens, and orphans.

Sociobiology. Consider the following scenario. An infant crawls onto a busy street. A truck is just about to run the infant over when the mother darts in front of the speeding vehicle and carries her child to safety. Most people would say that love impelled the mother to risk her life to save the child. Sociobiologists would argue that the mother committed her heroic deed so that her genes will be passed on to another generation.

Was the mother's brave action altruistic or merely in accordance with her biological drives? The idea that we are genetically predisposed toward certain behaviors was described by Harvard University zoologist Edward Wilson in his 1975 book, *Sociobiology: A New Synthesis.* Wilson argues that biological, genetic factors underlie all behavior, and that human beings are the product of evolution—a tenet of most modern science. But he goes one step further: He asserts that even day-to-day behaviors are determined by the process of natural selection. In other words, social behaviors that contribute to the survival of our species are passed on through the genes from one generation to the next and account for the mechanisms that have evolved to produce behaviors like altruism (Crawford and Anderson, 1989). For the sociobiologist, genetics, not learning, is the key to daily behavior.

At the heart of the **sociobiology** controversy is the issue of altruism. Sociobiologists account for altruism by saying that when a person lays down his or her life for another, that person is passing on the likelihood that the other person's genes will be transmitted to another generation. They point out that people are much more likely to be altruistic toward relatives than strangers; that is, people are instinctively driven to help pass on their family's gene pool to another generation.

Sociobiological theory is hotly debated by psychologists because it places genetics in a position of primary importance and essentially minimizes the role of learning. Psychologists feel strongly that learning plays a key role in the day-to-day activities of human beings. We *learn* to love, to become angry, to help or hurt others, and to develop relationships with those around us. But although sociobiology is too fixed and rigid for most psychologists, it does raise our consciousness about the role of biology and genetics in social behavior. Behavioral theories and sociobiology are two ways of explaining why people help others. Unfortunately, people don't always help. One important area of research is explaining why help is sometimes withheld.

Bystander Apathy: Failing to Help

The study of helping behavior has taken some interesting twists and turns. For example, psychologists have found that in large cities where potentially lethal emergencies, accidents, thefts, or stabbings, occur more frequently, people exhibit bystander apathy—they watch, but seldom help. Bibb Latané and John Darley (1970) investigated **bystander apathy** in a long series of studies. They found that in situations requiring uncomfortable responses, people must choose between helping or standing by apathetically. They must decide whether to introduce themselves into a situation, especially when there are other bystanders.

The Classic Study. Latané and Darley reasoned that when people are aware of other bystanders in an emergency situation, they might be less likely to help because they experience "diffusion of responsibility," a process discussed in the last chapter. To test their hypothesis, they brought college students to a laboratory and told them they were going to be involved in a study of people who were interested in discussing college life. The researchers told the students that in the interest of preserving people's anonymity, a group discussion would be held over an intercom system rather than face to face, and that each person in the group would talk in turn. In fact, there was only one true subject in each experimental session. All the other conversations were prerecorded from assistants who worked for the researchers.

The independent variable in this study was the number of people the naive subject thought were in the discussion group. The dependent variable was whether the subject helped, and the speed with which the naive subject reported the emergency when one of the assistants appeared to have a serious nervous seizure.

The future seizure victim spoke first; he talked about his difficulties getting adjusted to New York City and mentioned that he was prone to seizures, particularly when studying hard. Next, the naive subject spoke, followed by the prerecorded discussions of assistants. Then the seizure victim talked again. After a few relatively calm remarks, his speech became increasingly loud and incoherent; he stuttered and indicated that he needed help because he was having "a-a-a real problem-er-right now and I-er-if somebody could help me out it would-it would-er-er s-sure be good." At this point the experimenter began timing the speed of the naive subject's response.

The naive subjects were led to believe that their discussion group contained two, three, or six people. In the two-person group, they believed they were the only bystander, while in the three-person group, they thought there was one other bystander. When the subjects thought they were the only bystanders, eighty-five percent of the naive subjects responded before the end of the seizure. With one other bystander, sixty-two percent of the naive subjects responded by the end of the seizure. When subjects thought there were four other bystanders, only thirty-one percent responded by the end of the seizure. (Some of the results of this study are presented in Figure 17.1.) Thus, cast in the role of bystanders to an emergency, the naive subjects

Observing someone in need and failing to come to their aid is a common phenomenon. Studies show that the greater the number of observers, the less the chances are that an individual will choose to help.

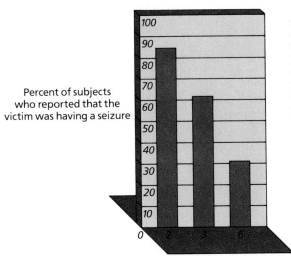

Percent of subjects who reported that the victim was having a seizure

Number of people in group

FIGURE 17.1
In the bystander apathy studies, as the number of people in the group increased, the willingness of naive subjects to inform the experimenter that the victim had suffered a seizure decreased.

were less likely to respond if they thought other people were present who might help. In general, Latané (1981) found that speed of assistance decreases as the number of bystanders believed to be present increases (see Shotland and Heinhold, 1985).

Did these subjects not help because they were cold and callous? Apparently not. They seemed to be very concerned about the seizure victim. Why did they not respond? Latané and Darley suggest that they were worried about the guilt and shame they would feel if they did not help, but also feared making fools of themselves if they did help.

In general, research has shown that bystanders will help under some conditions. For one thing, people's self-concepts and previous experiences affect their willingness to intercede. Bystanders who see themselves as being especially competent in emergencies (such as doctors or nurses) are likely to help a victim regardless of the number of people present (Pantin and Carver, 1982). Also, personality characteristics of the individual involved in a bystander situation are important. Tice and Baumeister (1985) found, for example, that subjects who had a high degree of masculinity were less likely to respond. Researchers contended that highly masculine subjects might be especially fearful of embarrassment. In our society, the personality characteristics of men, in general, stress strength and aggression rather than sensitivity. Last, if the person who needs help has a relationship with the person who can offer help, help is more likely to be given (Batson, 1990).

<table>
<tr><td>

***Focus on
Learning***

</td><td>

♦ Provide a definition of altruism. p. 621
♦ How do sociobiologists account for altruism? p. 622
♦ What is the key explanation for bystander apathy? pp. 622–623

</td></tr>
</table>

Aggression

The Yanomamo Indians of Brazil and Venezuela are among the most violent people on earth; their murder rate is three times that of Detroit's. An estimated forty-four percent of the men aged twenty-five or older have participated in at least one killing. Yet other South American Indian tribes are as peaceful as the Yanomamo are violent. The Semai soldiers discussed at the beginning of the chapter were both brutal killers and compassionate social beings. If people can be either loving or violent, what compels them to act one way or the other?

When people feel unable to control situations that affect their lives, they may become frustrated, angry, and aggressive. Social psychologists define **aggression** as any behavior designed to harm another person or thing. An aggressive person may attempt to harm others physically through force; verbally, through gossip, rumors, or irritating comments; emotionally, by withholding love; or, on a larger scale, by acts of war. Psychologists study aggression to determine what behaviors people are capable of and why those behaviors occur. They have examined three major sources to explain aggressive behavior: instincts, acquired drives, and social learning.

Aggression: Any behavior whose goal is to harm another person or thing.

Instincts

Some psychologists believe that many aspects of behavior, including aggression, are inborn. These *nativists* believe that people are genetically predisposed toward aggression. One nativist, Freud, suggested that people have a destructive release of aggression against themselves, a death instinct he called *thanatos*. However, Freud never fully developed the concept of a death instinct, and today it is not widely accepted.

Another nativist, ethologist and Nobel laureate Konrad Lorenz (1903–1989), investigated aggressive behavior through naturalistic observation. He noted that although animals of the same species fight with each other, they have signals that tell them to stop fighting well before death occurs. In other words, most animals generally do not attempt to kill members of their own species. Human beings are the exception.

According to Lorenz (1964), aggression is instinctive and spontaneous. He contends that the aggressive instinct serves to maximize the use of food, space, and resources. Lorenz stresses the social implications of people's aggressive instincts, focusing on their adaptive rather than maladaptive values.

> **Frustration-aggression hypothesis:** The view that frustration of goal-directed behavior leads to aggression.

Acquired Drives

Another explanation for aggressive behavior is the **frustration-aggression hypothesis,** initially proposed by Dollard et al. (1939). This theory relies on everyday experience demonstrating that people involved in goal-oriented tasks often become aggressive or angry when frustrated. Ordinarily, a driver is unlikely to become upset if another car pulls out into traffic in front of her. However, if the woman is in a hurry to get to work, she might honk angrily at the other driver. On a larger scale, the violence between Catholics and Protestants in Northern Ireland is fueled in part by intense competition for decent jobs in a depressed economy.

Berkowitz (1964) examined the evidence for the frustration-aggression hypothesis and proposed a modified view of it. He suggested that frustration creates a *readiness* for aggressive acts rather than for actual aggression. He showed that even when frustration is present, certain events or situations must be available before aggression occurs, for example, a weapon lying on a table. In a reformulation, Berkowitz (1990) suggests that frustrations generate aggressive inclinations to the extent that they arouse negative feelings. Berkowitz's conception accounts for the reason people don't always become aggressive when frustrated. Many psychologists find the frustration-aggression hypothesis too simple, but it is beneficial, in part, because it has led to other research that helps describe behavior, for example, social learning theory.

Social Learning

Danny is engrossed in watching Andre the Giant in a pro-wrestling match on a Saturday afternoon. Almost without realizing it, Danny lurches over and tackles his sister, Lori. Lori screams, prompting their mother to burst into the room and turn off the TV.

From a psychologist's viewpoint, Danny's mother did the right thing. When children are in situations for which they have not established their own standard responses, they copy behavior. Thus, they imitate characters they see in the movies or on television. According to Bandura, aggressive behavior can be both established and eliminated through *observational learning* as we discussed in chapter 5. Bandura argues that children are not born with aggressive instincts but learn aggression (or nonaggression) by seeing

After watching an adult model take aggressive action against a "Bobo" doll, children became actively aggressive in their own interactions with the doll.

other people, including parents, teachers, and peers, exhibiting such behavior. A child will learn to be aggressive by imitating another child using a toy gun or by watching parents or teachers act aggressively. On the other hand, a child will learn to be nonaggressive if he or she sees parents act nonaggressively or someone being punished for aggressive behavior. Similarly, Semai children learned gentleness from their parents, while Semai soldiers were taught to kill by the British example.

Many researchers point out that conclusions about the effect of social learning and **violence** on children cannot accurately be made from experimental settings. Laboratories are not people's homes, and they have other distracting elements that make them unlike real-life situations. Despite such problems, the results of the studies suggest that children exposed to aggressive situations imitate them in subsequent play. But it is important to note that contrary to widely held beliefs, not all children who grow up in homes in which they are exposed to violence become violent adults (Widom, 1989). It is true that many, if not most, people who are child abusers were abused themselves, but being abused does not make a person an abuser (remember, correlations do not mean causation); a wide array of positive events may mitigate against many early negative experiences.

In a classic study, however, Bandura, Ross, and Ross (1963) found that children who viewed aggression, either live, on films, or in TV cartoons, were nearly twice as aggressive in subsequent play as those who did not view it. Much research supports Bandura's findings. Worchel, Hardy, and Hurley (1976), for example, had adult subjects view films with either violent or nonviolent content and then interact with a series of research assistants. One research assistant was directed to assume a bumbling and inadequate manner by purposely committing mistakes. After the subjects had viewed

Violence: Aggression in which a person seeks to inflict injury through physical force.

and interacted with the assistants, they were asked to rate them to help determine which of the assistants would be rehired. The subjects who had viewed the violent films rated the bumbling assistant lower than those who had viewed the nonviolent films; also, they did not recommend rehiring. Their judgments were more aggressive.

Television and Aggressive Stimuli. Most children spend more hours watching television than they spend in any other activity except sleep (A. C. Nielsen Co., 1988; Liebert, Sprafkin, and Davidson, 1982). Because children watch so much television, it serves as a major source of models for imitative behavior. The fact that television portrays so much aggressive behavior concerns parents and educators, as well as social psychologists. Half of all prime-time television characters are involved in violent activity of some kind; about one-tenth kill or are killed. Moreover, about twenty percent of television males are engaged in law enforcement, whereas fewer than one percent are in law enforcement in the real world (Gerbner and Gross, 1976).

In general, research supports the contention that children who frequently watch violent television programs are more likely to be aggressive than children who see less television violence. One study found that children exposed to large doses of television violence are less likely to help a real-life victim of violence (Drabman and Thomas, 1975), and another found that viewers of violence were less sympathetic to victims than non-viewers (Linz, Donnerstein, and Penrod, 1988). They also are more fearful of becoming victims of violent acts. One study even found that viewing violence at age eight predicted aggressive behavior at age nineteen (Eron and Huesmann, 1980). Children who play violent video games also seem to act more aggressively at later ages (Schutte et al., 1988), and even infants can be affected by watching television (Meltzoff, 1988).

How does watching violence on television affect viewers? How can it increase the likelihood of a person committing violent acts? Baron and Byrne (1987) describe four primary effects of viewing television violence.

- ◆ It weakens the inhibitions of viewers.
- ◆ It may suggest new ideas and techniques to the uninitiated.
- ◆ It may prime or stimulate existing aggressive ideas.
- ◆ It may reduce a person's overall emotional sensitivity to violence.

Television can also have positive effects on children. Children exposed to shows such as *Sesame Street* and *Mister Rogers Neighborhood* that focus on topics like sharing and caring were more likely to engage in prosocial behavior with other children than were children in a control group who did not watch those shows (Coates, Pusser, and Goodman, 1976). Children can also learn vocabulary and language from television (Rice and Woodsmall, 1988).

Research on the effects of television has had important social implications. Children under the age of five believe what they see on television to be "the truth," and thus the content of television shows influences children in profound ways. Further, researchers are concerned about the widespread availability of cable television, which has programs that portray violence more frequently and explicitly than network television does. Such shows can act as a cue for children who might already be aggressive (Josephson, 1987). Social psychologists interested in public policy are suggesting minimum requirements for educational programming on every station, and controls to protect children from advertising that exploits their special vulnerability (Huston, Watkins, and Kunkel, 1989).

Cognitive Psychology and Aggression

Ideas are a highly perishable commodity. They can rapidly become outdated and replaced by newer, more modern ideas. This has been especially true in the study of aggression. Early research was based on learning theory explanations popular in the 1950s and 1960s. Later, with the increasing influence of Skinner's behaviorism, researchers focused on operant interpretations of aggression. They studied the implications of punishing children for aggressive behavior and rewarding them for nonaggressive behavior. A shift toward social learning theory occurred in the 1970s, and the effects of television viewing were a prime focus. In the 1980s, cognitive explanations of aggression became prevalent, and researchers began to speak in terms of cognition, thought, interpretations, and expectations.

Eron's Work on Aggression. Theory generally guides research, and the questions asked in each decade reflect this relationship. Leonard Eron (1987) conducted a longitudinal study of aggression over twenty-two years. He examined and tracked the entire third grade population, 870 students, of Columbia County, a semirural area in New York. Eron's work of the 1960s examined psychological conditions that might cause aggression, especially parental attitudes toward children. He found that children rated as aggressive at age eight were still rated as aggressive at age nineteen, and were three times more likely to have been in trouble with the law as those who were rated as nonaggressive (Lefkowitz et al., 1977).

In the late 1970s, Eron and other aggression researchers looked at the same data in a new light. The full blossoming of the cognitive influence on theory and data collection led them to probe the influences in children's lives that cause them to *interpret* the world in a way that makes them aggressive. They looked at the data with a cognitive frame of reference: An aggressive child responds to the world with combativeness because the child has internalized aggressive ideas. Eron (1987) argued, "It was what the subjects were saying to themselves about what they wanted . . . what might be an effective or appropriate response . . . that helped determine how aggressive they are today" (p. 441).

Eron's work is typical of much social psychological research; he has shifted his explanations from simple drive reduction ideas to social learning ideas, and finally to a cognitive-behavioral analysis of aggression.

Gender Differences in Aggression

Many people believe that men are naturally more aggressive than women. They refer to aggressive contact sports like football and boxing, the aggressive role of men in business, the overwhelming number of violent crimes committed by men, and the traditional view that men are more likely than women to be ruthless and unsympathetic. But are men really more aggressive than women?

To learn more about gender differences in aggression, two psychologists at Purdue University, Alice Eagly and Valerie Steffen (1986), searched the psychological literature over a fifteen-year period for studies of adults exposed to standardized situations designed to induce aggressive behavior. They found sixty-three experiments that compared gender differences in aggressive behavior. Most of the studies were conducted in laboratories, although some were conducted in field settings. The laboratory experiments were often teacher-learner situations, where a teacher had to deliver shocks to a learner (similar to the Milgram studies described in chapter 16). The field experiments typically involved the experimenter cutting in line in front of a naive subject, inciting in him or her mild frustration that could turn into anger and aggression.

Using a painstaking statistical procedure, the researchers discovered what people already expected—men are more physically aggressive than women. But they also found that both men and women use psychological aggression such as verbal abuse and angry gestures. They offer an interesting interpretation of the findings. They suggest that the differences in aggression that appear between men and women are directly related to the perceived consequences of the aggression. Women in our culture have been raised with values that make them feel especially guilty if they induce physical pain; men have not been raised with those values to the same extent. However, gender roles in our society are changing; the number of women in the workforce clearly attests to that fact. Therefore, it is likely that the gender differences in willingness to induce pain—and act aggressively—will diminish in the next decade.

The environment in which people work, study, and live has such a sharp impact that social psychologists have investigated how this affects social behavior. What they have found is that people's environments, including the places where they live and work, alter their aggressiveness and thoughts, and influence their actions. This becomes especially apparent in studying violence and aggression toward women.

The Domestic Assault of Women

MILESTONES IN PSYCHOLOGY

*W*ill today's children create a gentler society? Will they deal with marital conflict through reason and caring? Or will the adults of tomorrow be even more violent than today's adults? Don Dutton, a professor of psychology at the University of British Columbia, is asking these questions to determine the causes of domestic violence, spousal abuse, and the inability of battered women to leave abusive relationships.

Prevalence. Dutton is a social psychologist whose research in aggression and its causes led him to write *The Domestic Assault of Women* (1988) in which he encapsulates current knowledge about why many married women are violently abused. As many as two million women may be beaten by their husbands each year, and nearly thirty percent of all married couples report at least one violent episode (Straus and Gelles, 1986). Sexual abuse and assault have been experienced by thirty-eight to sixty-seven percent of adult women remembering the period before age eighteen, twelve percent of adolescent girls, fifteen percent of college women, and approximately twenty percent of adult women (Koss, 1990). Many women, long before marriage, have thus experienced assault in various forms. High levels of conflict, low socioeconomic status, and exposure to violence as a child are correlated with later domestic violence (Sugarman and Hotaling, 1989). Further, younger adults (under age thirty) are more likely to engage in domestic violence than are older adults (O'Leary et al., 1989) and such behaviors (pushing, shoving, slapping) are fairly stable—a person who is aggressive early in a relationship stays that way.

Causes. Is there some event, action, or predisposition that makes a man abuse his wife? Early explanations of domestic violence focused on *mental disorders,* and many research studies show that men who assault women suffer from personality disorders.

Other explanations of domestic violence focus on *biological predispositions.* The sociobiological theory explains aggressive behaviors as attempts to maximize the likelihood that the aggressors and their offspring will survive. Sociobiologists argue that human beings have a genetic predisposition toward aggression. For example, a man's jealousy about his wife's fidelity, her intention to end a marriage, or the removal of chances for further offspring may create aggression.

Differing from these psychiatric and biological views, many sociologists and psychologists believe that assaults on women by their husbands are generated by the *social rules* supporting male dominance. Although society is changing, a "traditional" wife is submissive and willing to be dominated by her husband. According to this view, aggressive men are merely living up to cultural expectations.

None of these explanations is substantiated by *all* the data, and Dutton proposes a *nested-ecological approach.* This approach views people growing and developing within a social context, and suggests that a valid explanation of domestic violence must examine at least four factors:

1. the cultural values of the individuals (are men and women equal?),
2. their social situation (are they employed?),
3. their family unit (do they communicate as a couple?), and
4. their level of individual development (do they express feelings well, do they excuse violence, have they witnessed family violence?).

In a comprehensive theory of assault, a potentially assaultive male must be evaluated in each of the four areas suggested. Thus, Dutton argues (p. 25):

> Wife assault would be viewed as likely when a male has strong needs to dominate women . . . and exaggerated anxiety about intimate relationships . . . has had violent role models . . . and has poorly developed conflict-resolution skills . . . is currently experiencing job stress . . . is isolated from support systems . . . is experiencing relationship stress . . . and power struggles . . . and exists in a culture where maleness is defined by the ability to respond to conflict aggressively. . . .

Feminists have focused on violence against women as the misuse of power by men (Walker, 1989), but the nested-ecological approach utilizes a complex mix of variables as determinants of assaultive behavior. Unlike most wife-assault models, which focus on one level of analysis (communication, personal values, or perhaps job stress), the nested-ecological approach suggests multiple levels (including feminist views), with the importance of each level differing in each assault case. Although it is tempting to rely on simple models of wife assault, the reality is that human beings are exceedingly complex, and the causes of domestic assault must be understood in a larger context.   ◆

Domestic violence occurs within families, but families live in communities, neighborhoods, cities; each of these units can have an impact on how we live, according to environmental psychologists. We consider their contributions to understanding our social interactions next.

Environmental Psychology

Suppose it is a cool spring day and you are relaxing on a park bench when the baby of the woman seated next to you begins to cry. Now, imagine that it is ninety degrees on a very crowded, stuffy airplane and you have been trying for fifteen minutes to get to your assigned seat when suddenly, the baby of the woman standing next to you starts bawling. The infant in the park was unhappy but cute; the baby on the airplane is a screaming brat. Clearly, environmental conditions can influence reactions. The study of **environmental psychology** is twofold: how physical settings affect human behavior and how people change the environment—often to make it more comfortable and acceptable.

Studying the Environment

Environmental psychologists study the physical and social aspects of the environment, how the individual behaves in it, and how it might be changed. The studies are often conducted in institutional settings, such as schools, hospitals, and churches. For example, consider the design of a nurses' station in hospitals. In traditional hospital floor plans, the nurses' station is the center of activity on each floor and is usually placed between two long corridors. An alternative is to place the nurses' station at the hub of a wheel-like arrangement of rooms. Most of the patient rooms would then be closer to the nursing station, and nurses could service them faster and more efficiently. When Trites and his coworkers (1970) investigated worker satisfaction with different hospital designs, they found a distinct preference for the radial design. Such conclusions led to the redesigning of many hospital wards (Proshansky and O'Hanlon, 1977).

Environmental Variables

The environment represents more than the shape of a building, the layout of a nurses' station or dorm, or the arrangement of buildings in a housing project or shopping mall. It represents variables such as size, shape, furniture and fixtures, climate, noise level, and the number of people per square foot. Environmental psychology is the study of the relationships among such variables. Whether a room is perceived as crowded, for example, is determined not only by the number of people in it but also by the room's size and shape, furniture layout, ceiling height, number of windows, wall colors, lighting, and the time of day. Researchers who look at global environment systems, such as cities, communities, and neighborhoods, must consider all these variables, and more. Two of the easiest environmental variables to control to assure well-being are temperature and noise.

Environmental psychology: The study of how physical settings affect human behavior and how human behavior affects the environment.

Stressor: A stimulus that elicits uncomfortable feelings such as anxiety, tension, and physiological arousal.

Temperature. The consequences of severe physical environments—those with very hot or very cold climates—on behavior can range from annoyance to inability to function. New England industrial workers, for example, would never survive the winter without proper shelter, heating, and clothes, and southern industrial workers would be less productive without air conditioning during the summer.

Environmental variables that impair work performance are called stressors. A **stressor** is a stimulus that elicits uncomfortable feelings such as anxiety, tension, and physiological arousal. Temperature can be a stressor and affect behaviors, including academic performance, driving an automobile, and being attracted toward others. In general, performance is optimal at moderate temperatures and becomes progressively worse at high or low temperatures.

When the temperature rises and people become uncomfortable, they are more likely to make risky decisions, behave erratically, and be less controlled. Research shows that as temperature rises, there are increases in aggression, even rioting (Goranson and King, 1970). Hotter regions of the world show more aggression, and hotter years, months, and days have all been associated with more aggressive behaviors such as murder, riots, and wife beatings (C. A. Anderson, 1989).

Noise. Another environmental variable that can affect performance is *noise*, an unwanted sound, a stressor that can stimulate people to uncommonly high levels of arousal and poor performance. Some noises, such as that of a buzzing fluorescent light, a humming refrigerator, an opening and closing door, a chirping bird, passing cars, or people talking are almost always present in the environment. They are continuous and not too loud, and although they may be unwanted, they are usually not too disruptive, nor are they stressors. Rarely do such noises raise levels of arousal or interfere with daily activities.

Unpredictable and intermittent noise of moderate intensity, however, can impair performance on tasks that involve sustained attention or memory.

Noise, an environmental factor which is sometimes beyond our control, affects us on many levels. It may simply interfere with our concentration, it may arouse us physiologically, and it can cause hearing loss.

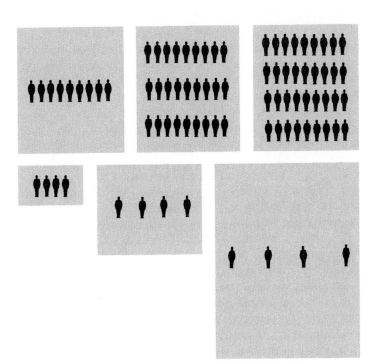

And if noise raises physiological arousal to very high levels, it may impair performance and even cause hearing damage (see chapter 3). Thus, noise acts as a stressor when it interferes with communication, raises physiological arousal, or is so loud it causes pain and headaches. More commonly, noise simply interferes with a person's ability to concentrate.

Crowding

Another environmental variable is the number of people who are around. In some situations in which there are myriads of people, you may feel closed in and crowded. In other situations, the excitement of a crowd may make you feel exhilarated. It is not the size of a space or the number of people that causes you to feel crowded. It is the perception that your space is too limited. Thus, **crowding** is a psychological state. One person might feel crowded and uncomfortable in a mall filled with Christmas shoppers, while someone else may feel that the throngs promote a holiday ambience.

Crowding is affected by both social and spatial density. *Social density* refers to the number of people in a given space; *spatial density* refers to the size of a space with a fixed number of people in it. (See Figure 17.2.) For example, in an empty theater a person may feel lonely, but she may feel crowded when the theater is full, or even half-full. Similarly, the first few people who arrive at a party often feel awkward and ill at ease. Yet within an hour, with perhaps only twenty people there, they may feel closed in. Researchers must be careful to separate the variables of social and spatial density (Baum, 1987).

Crowding in Dorms. An early study on the effects of crowding in dormitories was done in 1973 by Valins and Baum. The dormitories were of two designs: corridors with long hallways, two people per room, thirty-four people per floor, and a shared bathroom and lounge; or suites with four or

Crowding: The perception that one's space is too restricted.

six students sharing a bathroom and lounge, and several suites per floor. Space per student was about the same in both types of dormitories.

The researchers gave freshman students a questionnaire on dorm life. Corridor residents reported too many people on their floor and too many unwanted interactions. Sixty-seven percent of corridor residents found their living space crowded, compared with twenty-five percent of suite residents. Valins and Baum concluded that corridor designs promoted "excessive social interaction and that such interaction is associated with the experience of crowding" (1973, p. 249).

If high-density dormitories produce feelings of crowding, as Valins and Baum suggest, this should be evident in people's behavior. In a now classic study, Bickman et al. (1973) compared the helping behavior shown by students living in high-, medium-, or low-density housing. They used a measure called the *lost-letter technique,* whereby letters were purposely dropped in dormitory corridors. It was reasoned that when someone found the letter, he or she would assume that a person in the dormitory had lost it.

The dependent variable was the number of "lost" letters that were subsequently mailed. The independent variable was the density of housing. The experiment involved high-density (high-rise, twenty-two-story towers, each housing more than 500 students), medium-density (four- to seven-story buildings, each housing about 165 students), and low-density dormitories (two to four stories, with about 58 students each). Letters were dropped unobtrusively in areas near stairwells and elevators, with no more than one letter per corridor. The letters were addressed, sealed, and stamped but had no return address.

The results showed that helping behavior was sixty-three percent in high-density dorms, eighty-seven percent in medium-density dorms, and one-hundred percent in low-density dorms. When questionnaires were distributed to the students in the experiment, answers generally reflected attitudes related to the kind of housing in which students lived; for example, students in high-density dorms reported feeling less trust, cooperativeness, and responsibility. The researchers concluded that students who lived in the higher-density dormitories behaved in a less socially responsible manner toward other dormitory residents.

Controlling the Environment

Although the effects of crowding are not consistent across all situations or populations, certain effects seem to be universal. In high-density situations, people feel stressed, overloaded, and sometimes overaroused. They may feel alone or anonymous and withdraw from the situation. They may become apathetic, exhibit impaired task performance, and sometimes become hostile. Maintaining a sense of control seems to be a crucial variable (Fleming, Baum, and Weiss, 1987).

Personal Space. To help assert individuality and maintain a sense of personal control, human beings generally try to establish appropriate personal spaces. **Personal space** is the area or invisible boundary around an individual that he or she considers private. Encroachment on that space causes displeasure and often withdrawal.

The size of your personal space can change, depending on the situation and the people near you. For example, you may walk arm in arm with a family member but avoid physical contact with a stranger. You may stand

Personal space: The area around an individual that is considered private; the invisible boundary around a person.

close to a friend and whisper in his or her ear, but keep a certain distance from an elevator operator or a store clerk.

Anthropologist Edward Hall (1966) suggested that personal space is a mechanism by which people communicate with others. He proposed that people adhere to established norms of personal space that are learned in childhood. Hall also observed that the use of personal space varies from culture to culture. In the United States, especially in suburban and rural areas, people are used to generous space and large homes. In Japan, on the other hand, where there is little space available per person, people are used to small homes that provide little private space (Aiello and Thompson, 1980). Additionally, Western cultures insist on a fair amount of space for people, reserving proximity for intimacy and close friends, but Arab cultures allow much smaller distances between strangers.

To understand the concept of personal space, Hall classified four *spatial zones*, or distances, used in social interactions with other people: An *intimate distance* (zero to eighteen inches) is reserved for people who have great familiarity with one another. It is acceptable for comforting someone who is hurt, for lovers, for physicians, and for contact sports. The closeness enables a person to hold another person, examine the other's hair and eyes, and hear the other's breath. It also permits opposing team members to tackle each other or a soldier to engage an enemy in hand-to-hand fighting.

An acceptable distance for close friends and everyday interactions is *personal distance* (one and one-half to four feet). It is the distance used for most social interactions. At one and one-half to two feet, someone might tell a spicy story to a close friend. At two feet, people can walk together while conversing. At two to four feet they maintain good contact with a coworker without seeming too personal or impersonal.

Social distance (four to twelve feet) is used for business and interactions with strangers. At four to six feet, people are close enough to communicate their ideas effectively while far enough away to remain separated. Personal space in the social zone may be controlled by physical barriers, such as a desk to separate a clerk, receptionist, or teacher from the people with whom he or she interacts.

Public distance (twelve to twenty-five feet) minimizes personal contact. It is the distance at which politicians speak at lunch clubs, teachers instruct classes of students, and actors and musicians perform. Public distance is sufficiently great to eliminate personal communication between individuals and their audiences. See Figure 17.3 for a presentation of the space that people use when seated or standing.

Acceptable amounts of personal space differs between cultures. Arab cultures typically allow strangers to conduct business in much closer physical proximity than do Western cultures.

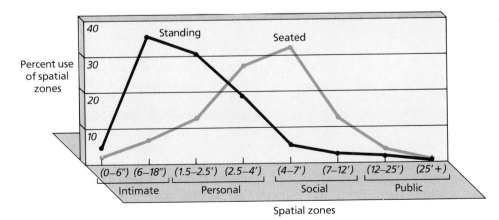

Spatial zones

FIGURE 17.3
While standing, people use primarily the personal and intimate zones. While seated, they use primarily the personal and social zones. (Source: Altman and Vinsel, 1977.)

Privacy: The process of limiting the access of other people by controlling the boundaries between them and oneself.

Territorial behavior: Behavior involved in establishing, maintaining, personalizing, and defending a delineated space.

Privacy. Altman (1975) suggests that the key to understanding why people feel crowded and need personal space is privacy. **Privacy** is the process of controlling boundaries between people so that access is limited. Everyone needs privacy. According to Altman, privacy allows people to develop and nurture a sense of self. Without it, people feel they have no control over who and what can intrude on them. This sense of helplessness can lead to lowered self-esteem and poor social adaptations. Understanding people's need for privacy is central to understanding the behavior of human beings in their environment.

One way people maintain a sense of privacy is to change their immediate environment. When a teenager goes into a room and closes the door, he closes himself off from other people; he limits their access to him. The teenager has set up a boundary—a closed door—behind which he can do what he wants when he wants. Similarly, two people may enter a room and close the door, thereby controlling other people's access to them.

Maintaining a sense of privacy is closely related to territoriality, often an important goal in people's lives. **Territorial behavior** establishes, maintains, personalizes, and defends a definite space. It helps regulate the exclusive use of a specific area by a person or a group of people. Territorial behavior involves marking a space as a private area where intruders are not welcome. Homeowners put up fences and signs that say "No Trespassing"; teenagers lock their bedroom doors; street gangs defend their turfs; and nations wage war in defense of national boundaries. Like personal space behaviors, territorial behaviors are privacy-regulating mechanisms.

Preserving the Environment

An emerging area of environmental research is in controlling people's behavior in the environment; one example is littering. Research studies by Scott Geller at Virginia Polytechnic Institute found that littering can be significantly reduced by providing instructions for proper disposal of objects; the more specific the instructions, the less littering (Geller, 1975; Geller, Witmer, and Tuso, 1977).

Another area of research is finding out what variables make people want to preserve the environment. Consider energy conservation, including driving smaller, fuel-efficient cars and investing in solar panels for the home. Research on these issues has shown that tax laws that reward energy savings, signs, and new equipment such as automatic thermostats help people adopt more energy-saving behaviors. As in the littering issue, when given specific instructions and prompts, people are more likely to comply (Geller, Winett, and Everett, 1982).

Specific behaviors can be targeted for change, and research shows that such a behavioral analysis is effective. But there are tremendous problems that must be solved in our world. Geller (1989) suggests that principles from marketing be added to behavioral analysis to solve these bigger problems. First, promoting socially beneficial ideas and behaviors must be advanced. This means promoting a product or idea by making it affordable, accessible, and desirable. It also means that an analysis must be done of the wants, needs, and perceptions of the people being targeted. After the target population is analyzed and strategies developed, only then should specific interventions be applied. After going through these steps, an evaluation should be done to see if the strategy has been effective. Geller claims that behavioral interventions combined with a social marketing strategy can provide an integrative program for environmental preservation.

- What is the general effect of a stressor such as temperature? pp. 631–632
- Describe the results of the lost-letter experiment. pp. 633–634
- Identify and describe the four spatial zones Hall classified that are used in social interactions with other people. p. 635
- What is the aim of territorial behavior? p. 636

Focus on Learning

Industrial and Organizational Psychology

Many business experts thought that Sharp Corporation of Japan made a big mistake when they built an electronics factory in Memphis. RCA Corporation had built a TV plant in that city, but wildcat strikes, product sabotage, and abysmal quality control forced RCA to shut the factory down. The Japanese plant proved successful, however. What made the difference? One explanation is that Japanese bosses treated their American employees like family, while demanding the highest quality control. In return, the employees were motivated and found their work fulfilling.

Industry, Organizations, and Applications

As productivity becomes increasingly important to American industry, industrial/organizational psychologists are playing more important roles. **Industrial/organizational psychologists** focus on how individual behavior is affected by the work environment, coworkers, and organizations. Industrial/organizational psychology (often called *I/O psychology*) is often thought of as an applied discipline that spans several areas of psychology, including those that deal with work, fatigue, personnel selection, evaluation of programs, consumer surveys, small group processes, and pay and efficiency. I/O psychology has also reached out to government, hospitals, universities, and public service agencies, in addition to traditional business settings. In all these environments, how well individuals perform their duties and relate to one another is a key concern.

Psychology and Business: Selecting Personnel

An important task of industrial/organizational psychologists is to help businesses select well-trained, qualified individuals for specific positions. Today, finding the right people for jobs occurs within the context of an organization's or business's strategic planning. This means forecasting the future needs of an organization, establishing specific objectives, and implementing programs to ensure that appropriate people will be available when the organization needs them (Jackson and Schuler, 1990). Employers want people who will enjoy their work, suit the company's needs, and be productive. To find such employees, I/O psychologists apply learning and motivational theories that deal with reinforcement, for example. Using specific selection procedures, including tests, many develop systems to produce the best match between employers and employees. The selection procedure for a job with a large firm is often complicated and time-consuming. Can even a complex selection process result in serious hiring mistakes?

Selection procedures are aimed at one basic task—predicting the success of a candidate. The key factor is standardization. Employers and researchers

Industrial/organizational psychologists: Applied psychologists who work in industry, government, and public agencies and focus on how individual behavior is affected by the work environment, coworkers, and organizational practices; sometimes called I/O psychologists.

Interviewers are warned not to allow subtle variables such as their own mood to interfere with the interview process.

alike stress that to compare individuals they have to use applications, interviews, work samples, and tests that are alike if reasonable comparisons are to be made. Subtle factors can be at work in selection procedures, and interviewers have to pay particular attention to make sure that factors such as their own moods do not influence their evaluations (Baron, 1987).

Standardized cognitive tests, such as those for general ability and specific knowledge, can be good predictors of academic success. However, the widespread use of tests in industry has raised questions for I/O psychologists concerning whether or not the tests are valid predictors of job performance. This has become especially important given the large number of lawsuits by people who feel that the tests have discriminated against them; these lawsuits challenge the use of tests as selection devices (Guion and Gibson, 1988).

Performance Appraisal

Have you ever been evaluated by an employer? Did your boss appreciate your hard work, dedication to details, and unstinting loyalty? Bosses are sometimes good at making an appraisal of work, but sometimes they forget your good efforts and remember your mistakes, or their poor social skills may not allow them to convey to you accurately how they feel about your performance. What makes a boss good at doing an evaluation? How could a psychologist assess whether a manager is good at his or her assigned task—managing and evaluating?

Performance appraisal: The process by which a supervisor evaluates the performance of a subordinate on a periodic basis.

Performance appraisal is the process by which a supervisor periodically evaluates the performance of a subordinate. Supervisors have been making such appraisals since there have been supervisors, and researchers in the last seventy years have tried to find ways to do it systematically. Performance appraisals are especially important because they are so often used in salary determinations (Cleveland, Murphy, and Williams, 1989). The problem with performance appraisal is that it is generally done inaccurately by people with few skills in evaluation and with few good diagnostic aids. Supervisors generally report that they dislike conducting evaluations. They don't like to review their subordinates; they often acknowledge that they do not have strong evaluative skills; furthermore, some managers have sexist biases (Swim, Borgida, Maruyama, and Myers, 1989). Many companies require periodic evaluations, but reluctant managers do it as infrequently as possible, sometimes in a cursory manner. They often evaluate everybody about the same—average, or perhaps very good. This often leaves employees feeling unappreciated. Ways to improve the process typically involve more active thinking on the part of a supervisor; we see this in the next section.

Performance Appraisal and the Role of Cognition

THINKING ABOUT RESEARCH

I distinctly remember you goofing off last Thursday; on Friday, I saw you behaving rudely to a customer! Don't do it again, do you hear?" exhorted The Boss to an intimidated employee. The frightened clerk shook his head and walked away muttering. He had been out sick on Thursday; further, his boss didn't know the nature of the interaction with the customer who yelled, insulted, and did everything but slap him. He felt that his performance appraisal was inaccurate because of the boss's inaccurate memory and lack of information.

Managers have to observe employees, code in memory their performance, remember it after intervening activities have taken place, and then recall specific behaviors accurately. In general, cognitive processes prove to be crucial in making a performance appraisal (DeNisi and Williams, 1988).

Hypotheses Are Formed. Research shows that when a person makes a performance appraisal of an individual's work, the most recent work has a strong biasing effect. That is, although people's work may be at a distinct level of performance, a good or bad period of performance just before an appraisal can bias an observer toward a good or poor decision. Steiner and Rain (1989) argue that there are recency effects in performance appraisals, just as there are in memory studies. This means that frequent performance appraisals are less likely to be affected by a single episode than a performance appraisal done after a long period of time, when the performance of the last day or two might disproportionately affect results.

Method. Realizing that memory effects are potentially important in performance appraisal, DeNisi, Robbins, and Cafferty (1989) asked subjects to watch videotapes of carpenters who were sawing, sanding, and staining. They were to evaluate the carpenters' performance. The subjects were provided with a guide to "correct" performance and a set of diary cards with tabs on them. The tabbed cards had either the names of the carpenters, task names, or they were blank. There were four groups of subjects, three who used diaries that tracked performance *by task, by person,* and by a *blank* set of cards with no particular orientation, and a *control group* with no diary.

Results and Conclusion. Results showed that the diary conditions produced better recall and improved ratings. Keeping a diary provided a structure for the raters that organized information and made them less dependent on memory. This would obviously help eliminate recency effects found by Steiner and Rain. Performance appraisals are a cognitive task affected by traditional cognitive variables, such as intervening activity, memory loss, and recency effects. Research shows that keeping a diary can minimize the negative effects and may improve performance appraisals.

Implications. Because laws have been passed to protect employees from discrimination according to age, race, gender, and religion, employers have been forced to be more responsive to employees by doing regular performance appraisals. In the process, larger companies with better trained staffs are helping workers by specifying behavioral objectives and tasks to master during the next appraisal period. Industrial/organizational psychologists have also worked to develop better rating forms, to train managers to be better evaluators, and especially to help managers who regularly conduct performance appraisals do so without preconceived biases. They have set up on-the-job training programs for eliminating the biases that might exist. All this can be especially beneficial in motivating workers and helping them find satisfaction in their work, topics we discuss next.   ◆

Motivating Workers

In addition to selecting and appraising personnel, another task of industrial/ organizational psychologists is to motivate workers. One obvious motivator is economics. People need money to live. But a successful employer-employee relationship relies on factors in addition to economic motivation. Performance is also affected by intrinsically motivated behavior, that is, behavior engaged in strictly because it brings pleasure. We examined intrinsic and extrinsic motivation in chapters 5 and 11.

Psychologists know that when intrinsically motivated behaviors are constantly reinforced with direct external rewards (such as money), productivity drops. An extremely well-paid plumber may find her work tedious and unfulfilling and thus be sloppy. In contrast, a lower-paid clerical worker who finds his job important and challenging will perform well and increase his responsibilities.

Employers, often with the help of I/O psychologists, are constantly trying to find ways to motivate employees to be more productive and hence profitable. One theory, initially proposed by Vroom (1964), suggests that job performance is determined by both motivation and ability. Vroom's is an expectancy theory, which we examined in more detail in chapter 11. It states that motivation is determined by what people expect to get from performing a task—a rewarding experience or a frustrating one. According to Vroom, a person must first have the ability to perform the task; without that, the experience will be frustrating and hence nonmotivating.

Lawler and Porter (1967) modified and expanded Vroom's theory. They contend that performance is determined by motivation, ability, and *role perception*—the way people think about themselves and their jobs (see Figure 17.4). Lawler and Porter believe that workers must fully understand the nature of their positions and all that is required of them in performing their jobs. Too often, people fail not because of lack of effort, motivation, or ability, but because they do not know what is expected of them or how to achieve a sense of control or power in an organization (Ragins and Sundstrom, 1989).

Job Satisfaction. Job satisfaction is different from job motivation because performance may or may not be affected by job satisfaction. Motivation, which refers to the internal conditions that direct a person to act, is always shown in behavior. Job satisfaction, which is a person's attitude about his or her work and workplace, may not be shown in behavior. A tired, bored, and overworked electrician may feel discouraged and angry—she may even hate her job—but she can still be motivated to work. Her motivation may stem from the high pay she receives, her obligation to complete a job, or

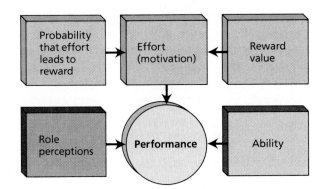

FIGURE 17.4
According to Lawler and Porter's (1967) managerial model, ability, motivation, and role perceptions determine work performance, and the values of a reward and the probability that an effort will be successful affect motivation level. The Lawler and Porter modification of the Vroom expectancy model is widely accepted, but probably not the final word on the variables that affect work performance.

from some other reason. Her motivation and job performance are high—as seen in her work. And although her job satisfaction is low, it does not affect her performance.

Job satisfaction must be viewed within the context of the work setting. Workers' motivation and values have to be consistent with opportunities and resources that are available, thus facilitating potential advancement and satisfaction (Katzell and Thompson,1990). A person's level of satisfaction depends on the extent to which the person sees a discrepancy between his expectations for satisfaction and actual satisfaction. This depends on various facets of a job; people can be pleased or dissatisfied about hours, pay, client contact, promotion opportunities, and other specific facets of a job. People have standards for comparison that determine the extent to which they feel they are doing well or poorly (Rice, McFarlin, and Bennett, 1989). Table 17.1 presents factors that have been shown to be important across a variety of research studies.

Motivation Management. Both employers and psychologists know that people can be motivated by different variables. Monetary rewards are important, for example, but so is the likelihood of success. Psychologists recognize three basic approaches to motivating people, or motivation management: paternalistic, behavioral, and participatory.

TABLE 17.1

Some Key Factors Related to Job Satisfaction Shown to Be Important across a Variety of Research Studies
◆ The work is interesting. ◆ There is adequate recognition. ◆ The work contributes to self-esteem. ◆ There are opportunities for advancement. ◆ The pay is perceived as adequate and equitable. ◆ There is job security. ◆ There are good relationships with supervisory personnel. ◆ There are opportunities for enjoyable social interactions. ◆ There is a positive attitude toward the work environment. ◆ The work is perceived to be challenging. ◆ There are opportunities to apply one's own judgment. ◆ There is some degree of autonomy. ◆ Opportunities exist to influence company policy and procedures. ◆ There is adequate information and equipment. ◆ There is authority to ensure that a job is completed.

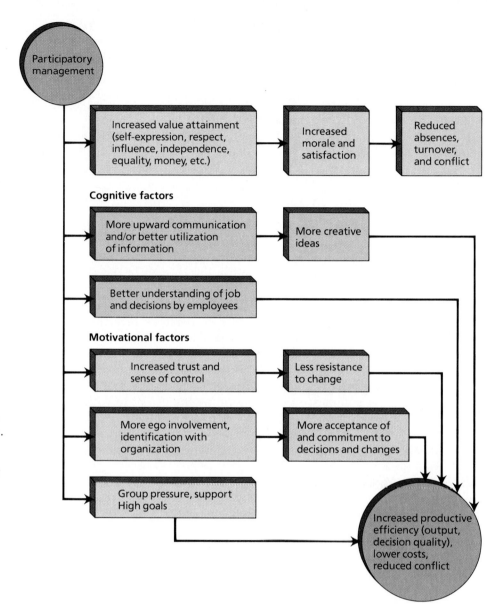

FIGURE 17.5
Participatory management leads to increased work effectiveness and job satisfaction for a variety of reasons. It also leads to many psychological changes; according to Locke and Schweiger (1979), it affects *values, thoughts,* and *motivation.*

The fundamental idea of *paternalistic management* is that a company takes care of its employees' needs and desires in a fatherly manner. This management approach was common in the mining companies of Appalachia, which provided housing, schools, recreation, and churches for employees, not because of individual job performance but simply because they were employees.

The paternalistic management approach is contrary to most psychologists' views on behavior. Instrumental conditioning studies show that for a behavior (such as work) to be established and maintained, reinforcement must be contingent on performance. In a paternalistic system, all employees—productive as well as nonproductive—are given reinforcement. Reinforcement without contingency does not encourage people to work hard.

Behavioral approaches to motivation assume that people will work only if they receive tangible rewards for specific task performance. Examples include paying a factory worker by the piece and a typist by the page. In such a system, hard-working employees obtain more rewards—commissions, salary raises, bonuses, and so on—because they produce more.

Participatory management is based on the belief that individuals who have a say in the decisions that affect their lives are more motivated to work. Participation, it is argued, provides a setting in which managers and employees can exchange information to solve problems (Tjosvold, 1987). Supporters of this approach believe that a sense of competence and self-determination is likely to increase individuals' levels of motivation (Deci, 1975). "Quality circles," whereby workers of all levels assemble to discuss ways to promote excellence, is one technique employers use to involve workers in the management process. Many variables affect the success of participatory management programs: the work setting (e.g., Burgio, Whitman, and Reid, 1983); the individuals involved; the kind of decisions to be made; and the hiring policies (Locke and Schweiger, 1979) (see Figure 17.5). If you were setting up your own company, which type of management style would you use? Would you be The Boss and set objectives to be met, or would you have more participatory management?

In participatory management programs, employees are offered a chance to comment on the business operations that affect them.

◆ What is the basic goal of a selection procedure in industrial/organizational psychology? p. 637

◆ Identify an essential problem with performance appraisal in business and industry. p. 638

◆ Identify the fundamental ideas that underlie paternalistic management, behavioral approaches to management, and participatory management. pp. 641–642

Focus on Learning

Key Terms

Summary

Relationships and Attraction

- Interpersonal attraction refers to the tendency to evaluate another person in a positive way. The process of attraction involves the characteristics of both people involved and the situation.   p. 612

- Research shows that people ascribe more power, status, competence, and personal regard to people they find attractive than to those they don't.   pp. 614–615

- Reciprocity and commitment between people who see themselves as equals are essentials of friendship. Equity theory holds that people attempt to maintain stable, consistent relationships in which the ratio of each member's contribution is equal.   p. 615

- From Sternberg's view, love can be seen as having three components: intimacy (a sense of emotional closeness); commitment (the extent to which a relationship is permanent); and passion (arousal, some of it sexual, some intellectual, and some motivational).   p. 616

- Loneliness is an unpleasant experience that occurs when a person's network of social relationships is deficient in either quality or quantity.   p. 617

Prejudice

- Prejudice is a negative evaluation of an entire group of people that is usually based on a set of negative (and often wrong) ideas about the group. Such ideas are usually based on stereotypes.   p. 618

- Prejudice has multiple causes and can be accounted for, at least to some extent, by learning theory, motivational theory, cognitive theory, and personality theory.   p. 619

Prosocial Behavior

- Prosocial behavior is some act that benefits someone else but generally has no obvious benefit to the person doing it.   p. 621

- Bystander apathy is the unwillingness of witnesses to an event to help, especially when there are a number of observers.   p. 622

Aggression

- Aggression can be viewed as an instinct, an acquired drive, a learned social behavior, or a response to frustration or aggressive stimulation.   p. 624

- Observational learning theory argues that people are not born with aggressive instincts but learn aggression by seeing other people exhibiting such behaviors.   p. 625

- Research shows that children who frequently watch violent television programs are more likely to be aggressive than other children.   p. 627

Environmental Psychology

- Environmental psychologists study how physical settings affect human behavior and how people change their environments to meet their psychological needs.   p. 631

- Crowding is the feeling that one's space is too restricted. Social density refers to the number of people in a given space. Spatial density refers to the variable size of a space that always contains the same number of people.   p. 633

- Personal space refers to the immediate area around an individual at any given time. Hall classified four spatial zones or distances used in social interactions: intimate, personal, social, and public.   p. 634

- Privacy is the process of limiting other people's access by controlling the boundaries between oneself and others.   p. 636

Industrial/Organizational Psychology

- I/O psychology attempts to apply psychological principles in the workplace. I/O psychologists generally use tools like standardized applications, interviews, work samples, and tests.   pp. 637–638

- Performance appraisal is the process by which a supervisor periodically evaluates the performance of a subordinate.   p. 639

- Job satisfaction refers to a person's attitude toward his or her work and workplace. Motivation refers to internal states that direct a person to act.   p. 640

Connections

If you are interested in . . .	Turn to . . .	To learn more about . . .
Gender differences	◆ Ch. 9, p. 330	How sex segregation often begins in childhood years during play.
	◆ Ch. 10, pp. 359–362	Why and when men and women follow different life courses, especially when it comes to midlife transitions.
	◆ Ch. 13, p. 487	The finding that some psychological disorders are more prevalent in women than in men.
The influence of the environment on our perceptions of the world	◆ Ch. 3, pp. 94–96	How our perceptions of the world depend on past experiences in the environment as well as current stimulation.
	◆ Ch. 13, p. 475	The way stressors in the environment such as worksite pressures can eventually lead to health problems.
	◆ Ch. 16, pp. 603–605	How individual behavior changes when a person thinks that he or she is being observed.
Industrial and organizational psychology and the use of tests in the workplace	◆ Ch. 8, pp. 273–291	Using tests to predict specific behaviors; for example, academic achievement or mechanical aptitude.
	◆ Ch. 11, pp. 394–400	How a person's motivation and expectations for success change test results and work performance.
	◆ Ch. 12, p. 457	How personality tests such as the MMPI-2 are used to screen people for maladjustment.

Appendix: Scientific and Statistical Methods

Until recently, Shirley could not hold a job because she suffered from debilitating schizophrenic symptoms, including disordered thinking and bizarre auditory hallucinations. Now, however, Shirley works forty productive hours a week at a floral shop, and she rarely experiences the mental aberrations that once made her life a living hell. Shirley's improvement is due in part to phenothiazine, a drug that helps control the brain's use of the neurotransmitter dopamine, and in part to a caring psychotherapist. But credit must also be given to researchers who discovered that children of schizophrenic parents have a statistically greater risk for developing schizophrenia. By helping uncover the disorder's biological connection, they spurred the search for drugs like phenothiazine.

Scientific progress is in many ways directly linked to our ability to measure and quantify data. In the physical sciences, the need to measure time, weight, and distance precisely has given rise to terms describing mind-boggling minuteness, including femtosecond (one quadrillionth of a second), nanogram (one billionth of a gram), and angstrom (one ten-billionth of a meter.) Examining behavioral phenomena in numerical terms enables scientists to be more exact, consistent, and objective.

Statistics: The branch of mathematics that deals with collecting, classifying, and analyzing data.

Statistics is a branch of mathematics that deals with collecting, classifying, and analyzing data. To rule out coincidence and discover the true causes of behavior, psychologists control the variables in experiments, then use statistics to describe, summarize, and present results.

Conducting Experiments

The following account of a therapy experiment will help illustrate how proper methodology and statistics help scientists interpret results. A psychologist was interested in determining whether a new therapeutic technique he had been using was effective with couples who were experiencing marital conflict. The approach he used focused on relaxation. For three years he had been teaching couples relaxation techniques to help them cope better, and he found it effective—the couples were better able to communicate after they had gone through relaxation exercises. But now he wanted to show it in an experiment; he wanted to show that relaxation training *caused* the marital improvement.

Hypotheses

He hypothesized—that is, developed a tentative idea—that relaxation training can be crucial to communication in marriage. An **hypothesis** is a tentative statement about a causal relationship between two variables or situations which is usually meant to be evaluated in an experiment. Recall that an **experiment** is a procedure in which a researcher systematically manipulates certain variables in order to describe objectively the relation between the variables of concern and the resulting behavior. Well-designed experiments permit inferences about cause and effect.

The psychologist advertised in the newspaper for couples experiencing marital problems. He told the couples who answered the ad that they would be participating in a study of "therapy for marriage difficulties." He informed the potential clients that all the couples would receive effective therapy, although not all at the same time or in the same order, and some would have to be on a waiting list for a few months.

Variables

The psychologist wanted to know if his therapeutic technique (relaxation) would be effective—thus, the independent variable in his study would be the delivery of therapy. Recall from chapter 1 that the **independent variable** is the one directly and purposefully manipulated by the experimenter to see what effect differences in it will have on the variables under study. The **dependent variable** is the behavior measured by an experimenter in order to assess whether changes in the independent variable affect the behavior under study. The dependent variable in this study would be scores in three areas: the couples' level of anxiety, marital satisfaction, and frequency of sexual contact.

To know whether his treatment would be effective, the psychologist asked each of the couples in the study to fill out a battery of questions that measured their anxiety, the level of marital satisfaction, and the frequency of sexual contact. With these he could later assess whether his subjects changed over the course of treatment.

The psychologist divided seventy-five couples into three groups. He put every third couple in a control group and told them that they would have to wait several months for therapy to begin. (The **control group** provides a standard for comparison.) The couples in the other two groups would be compared to those in the control group to see if relaxation produced any measurable effect. These second and third groups were **experimental groups;** they received training in relaxation over a six-month period. One of the experimental groups received relaxation training alone, and the other received relaxation training and also communication exercises.

Hypothesis: A tentative statement about a causal relationship between two variables or situations to be evaluated in an experiment.

Experiment: A procedure in which a researcher systematically manipulates certain variables to describe objectively the relation between the variables of concern and the resulting behavior.

Independent variable: The variable in an experiment that is directly and purposefully manipulated by the experimenter to see what effect the differences in it will have on the variables under study.

Dependent variable: The behavior measured by an experimenter to assess whether changes in the independent variable affect the behavior under study.

Control group: In an experiment, the group of subjects that does not receive the treatment under investigation. The control group is used for comparison purposes.

Experimental group: In an experiment, the group of subjects that receives the treatment under investigation.

Every week for twenty weeks the couples in the two experimental groups were treated. At the end of the study, the researcher again examined the seventy-five couples' level of anxiety, their marital satisfaction, and level of sexual activity. He expected those who received the experimental treatments to do better than the control group. (At the end of twenty weeks, the control group was then given treatment that involved relaxation and communication.)

The researcher found, as expected, that the control group changed very little (or not at all) over the course of the experiment. But the relaxation training groups produced strong effects when compared with the control group. Those who had received relaxation treatment—especially when it was combined with communication training—were less anxious, happier in their marriages, and had more frequent sexual contact. The researcher concluded that the independent variable (the relaxation training) caused a change in the subjects' lives. This experiment is a simple one, and there are other things that the researcher might do to make it better. But it has the elements of a good experiment.

Carefully Conducted Experiments

What makes a good experiment? As mentioned in chapter 1, to be generalizable to a population, a good experiment must have a sufficient number of carefully selected subjects in each group. Experiments have one or more experimental groups and a control group.

Inferences. If researchers are to make valid inferences from the data that are collected, it is important that the subjects come from the same larger population. With human beings, this may mean that the subjects should come from the same socioeconomic status, perhaps the same community, or be nearly the same age; the goal is to provide a balanced group or sample with regard to important characteristics. Thus, a **sample** is a group of subjects or participants who are generally representative of the population about which an inference is being made. Any differences among the groups must be due only to the experimental manipulation. If other variables in the study were properly controlled (i.e., held constant), the researchers could conclude that any difference in the couples' marital relationship at the end of the experiment was a result of therapy. If the sample was not carefully balanced, then it would be difficult or impossible to conclude that therapy alone made the difference.

Subject Selection. Proper selection is a key element of good research. Sometimes subjects are selected randomly; for example, researchers may administer a newly developed achievement test to randomly chosen members of the general population in order to derive an average test score. At other times, subjects are chosen with respect to a specific variable, such as gender or age. In any case, experimental subjects must be representative of the population to which they will be compared, and the researchers must make enough observations to ensure that the behaviors observed are representative and not uncharacteristic.

Carefully Defined Variables. The description of the independent and dependent variables is especially important. The independent variable has to be spelled out accurately, and how it is administered or delivered to subjects has to be equally painstakingly specified. If, for example, the variable is a particular drug dosage, the dosage must be specified carefully. If an experiment states that rats receive 10 milligrams of a drug for each kilogram of body weight, then regardless of its weight, each rat would receive the proper amount of the drug. Similarly, the dependent variable has to be carefully defined; how is it to be

Sample: A group of subjects or participants who are generally representative of the population about which an inference is being made.

measured, with what instruments, how frequently, and by whom? Some dependent variables, such as running speed, are easily specified; others, such as arousal, anxiety, and depression, are more difficult to define precisely. In those cases, researchers offer an **operational definition** of the variable, that is, they provide a concrete description of how the variable being studied will be measured. In the therapy example, marital adjustment could be operationally defined as scores on an adjustment scale or anxiety scale, or self-reports monitored on a weekly basis. If the behavior being measured is anxiety, it can be defined operationally as a change in the electrodermal response (a measure of nervous system arousal).

After researchers have specified the variables and chosen the subjects, they conduct the experiment, hoping it will yield interpretable, meaningful results. But extraneous or irrelevant variables can affect the results, making interpretation difficult. *Extraneous variables* are factors that affect the results of an experiment but are not of interest to the experimenter. A lightning storm that occurs during an experiment in which anxiety is being measured through electrodermal response is an extraneous variable. It would be difficult or impossible for the researchers to ascertain which parts of the increased electrodermal response were due to manipulations of the independent variable and which parts were due to anxiety associated with lightning storms. When extraneous variables occur during an experiment (or just before it), they may *confound* results, making data difficult to interpret.

> **Operational definition:** A definition based on a set of concrete steps used to define a variable.
>
> **Descriptive statistics:** A general set of procedures used to describe and summarize samples of data.

+ Define the terms *hypothesis* and *experiment*. p. 647
+ Distinguish between the independent and the dependent variable. p. 647
+ Why is proper subject selection so important? p. 648
+ How can extraneous variables render an experiment uninterpretable? p. 649

Focus on Learning

Descriptive Statistics

Statistics is a branch of mathematics that researchers use to evaluate and organize experimental data. Specifically, researchers use **descriptive statistics** to summarize, condense, and describe data. Descriptive statistics make it possible for researchers to interpret the results of their experiment. Similarly, your professors use descriptive statistics to interpret exam results. For example, a statistical description of a 100-point midterm exam may show that 10 percent of a class scored more than 60 points, 70 percent scored between 40 and 60 points, and 20 percent scored fewer than 40 points. Based on this statistical description, the professor might conclude that the test was exceptionally difficult and arrange the grades so that anyone who earned 61 points or more receives an A. But before inferences can be drawn or before grades can be arranged, the data from a research study must be organized in a meaningful way.

Organizing Data

When psychologists do research, they often produce large amounts of data that must be assessed. Suppose a social psychologist asks parents to monitor the number of hours their children watch television. The parents might report be-

Frequency distribution: A chart or array, usually arranged from the highest to lowest score, showing the number of instances of each obtained score.

Frequency polygon: A graph of a frequency distribution that shows the number of instances of obtained scores; usually data points are connected by straight lines.

tween 0 and 20 hours of television watching a week. Here is a list of the actual number of hours of television watched by 100 children in a week:

11	18	5	9	6	20	2	5
9	7	15	3	6	11	9	14
6	1	10	3	4	4	10	4
8	8	9	10	13	12	9	8
16	1	15	9	4	3	7	10
10	5	6	12	8	2	13	8
14	12	6	9	8	12	5	17
10	7	3	14	13	7	9	2
10	17	11	13	16	7	5	4
15	11	9	11	16	8	15	17
14	7	10	10	12	8	10	11
11	1	12	7	6	0	5	13
19	18	9	8				

The first step in making these numbers meaningful is to organize them so that we can see the number of times each score occurs. This type of organization is known as a **frequency distribution.** As the frequency distribution in Table A.1 shows, the number 9 occurs more frequently than any other, indicating that more children watched 9 hours of TV a week than any other number of hours.

Researchers often construct graphs from the data in a frequency distribution. Such a graph, called a **frequency polygon,** shows the possible scores (e.g., the

TABLE A.1
A frequency distribution for the number of hours of TV watched by 100 children. (Few individuals score very high or very low; most individuals have scores in the middle range.)

Number of Hours of TV Watching	Number of Individuals Watching	Total Number of Individuals
0	1	1
1	1 1 1	3
2	1 1 1	3
3	1 1 1 1	4
4	1 1 1 1 1	5
5	1 1 1 1 1 1	6
6	1 1 1 1 1 1 1	7
7	1 1 1 1 1 1 1	7
8	1 1 1 1 1 1 1 1 1	9
9	1 1 1 1 1 1 1 1 1 1	10
10	1 1 1 1 1 1 1 1 1	9
11	1 1 1 1 1 1 1	7
12	1 1 1 1 1 1	6
13	1 1 1 1 1	5
14	1 1 1 1	4
15	1 1 1 1	4
16	1 1 1	3
17	1 1 1	3
18	1 1	2
19	1	1
20	1	1

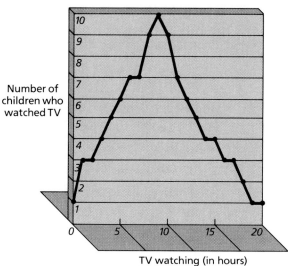

FIGURE A.1
This frequency polygon shows the number of hours of TV watched by 100 children. Frequency is shown on the ordinate or vertical axis; the actual scores occur on the abscissa or horizontal axis.

number of hours children watched TV) on the horizontal axis, or *abscissa*, and the frequency of each score (e.g., the number of children who watched TV for those hours) on the vertical axis, or *ordinate*. Figure A.1 is a frequency polygon of the data from the frequency distribution in Table A.1. Straight lines connect the data points.

Measures of Central Tendency

People use the term "average" to describe a variety of commonalities or tendencies. A wife asks a clerk to help her find a sweater for her average-sized husband. The owner of a new sedan boasts that his car averages 40 miles to a gallon of gasoline. A doctor tells her patient that his serum cholesterol level is average because it falls halfway between low and high measurements. In each of these cases, a person is using "average" to depict a type of norm. A descriptive statistic that tells us which single score best represents an entire set of scores is referred to as a **measure of central tendency.** It is used to summarize and condense data. Also, because almost every group has members who score higher or lower than the group, researchers often use a measure of central tendency to describe the group *as a whole*.

Consider the statement "Men are taller than women." Because we know that some women are taller than some men, we assume that the statement means, *"On the average* men are taller than women." In other words, if we take all the men and all the women in the world and compare their heights, *on the average* men will be taller.

Mean. How would someone investigate the truth of the statement "Men are taller than women"? One way would be to measure the height of thousands of men and women, taking a careful sample from each country, race, and age group. One could then calculate the average heights of the men and women in the sample and plot the results on a graph. Table A.2 has data from a small sample of men and women, and these data are plotted in Figure A.2 (both on page 652). For each group, the heights of the subjects were measured, added together, and divided by the number of subjects in the group. The resulting number, the **mean,** represents the arithmetic average in terms of height for a person in the group. The mean is the most frequently used measure of central tendency.

Measure of central tendency: An index of the average or typical value of a distribution of scores.

Mean: A measure of central tendency calculated by dividing the sum of the scores by the number of scores; the arithmetic average.

Mean height (in inches)

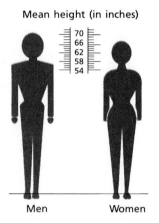

		70	
		66	
		62	
		58	
		54	

Men   Women

FIGURE A.2
These mean heights for men and women reflect an average computed for thousands of people in each group.

TABLE A.2
Calculation of Mean Height for Men and Women, in Inches

Men	Height in Inches	Women	Height in Inches
Davis	62	Hilary	58
Baird	62	Golde	59
Jason	64	Marcy	61
Ross	67	Mickey	64
Paul	68	Sharon	64
Cary	68	Rozzy	66
Mark	69	Bonnie	66
Evan	70	Sue	66
Michael	70	Cheryl	66
Dave	70	Ruth	67
Steven	70	Iris	67
Morry	70	Nancy	67
Alan	70	Theresa	67
Bernie	70	Sylvia	67
Lester	70	Jay	68
Al	70	Linda	68
Arnold	73	Elizabeth	71
Andrew	79	Jesse	75
Corey	79	Gabrielle	76
Stephen	79	Sarah	77
Total height	1400	Total height	1340

$$\text{Mean:} \quad \frac{\Sigma S}{N} = \frac{1400}{20} = 70 \text{ in.} \qquad \text{Mean:} \quad \frac{\Sigma S}{N} = \frac{1340}{20} = 67 \text{ in.}$$

Mode: A measure of central tendency; the most frequent observation.

Median: A measure of central tendency; the point at which 50 percent of all observations occur either above or below.

Mode. Another statistic used to describe the central tendency of a set of data is the mode. The **mode** is the data point most frequently observed. Figure A.3 plots the frequency of different scores for all the data in Table A.2. It shows that only one person is 58 inches tall, three are 79 inches, and more people are 70 inches tall then any other height. The mode of that group therefore is 70 inches.

Median. The **median** is the 50 percent point: Half the observations fall above the median and the other half fall below it. Figure A.4 arranges the data for women in Table A.2 from lowest to highest. It shows that half the data fall above 68 and half fall below 68. The median of the data set, therefore, is 68. You probably have read news reports about median income in the United States being on the rise. For example, a typical news report might be "According to the U.S. Census Bureau, the median income in the United States rose to $30,500 in 1991"; half of the families earn more than this amount, half earn less.

Table A.3 presents a set of data from an experiment on memory. The scores are the number of correctly recalled items. There are three groups of subjects: a control group received no special treatment; the second group received task motivating instructions (such as think hard, focus your attention), and the third group was hypnotized and told under hypnosis that they would recall better. The results of the study show that the task motivating group did slightly worse than the control group (the mean was 10.3 compared with the control group mean of 10.6), but the hypnosis group recalled 15.4 words on average, compared with the control group's recall of 10.6 words, a difference of 4.8 words. Hypnosis seemed to have a positive effect on memory—or did it?

The medians for the control and task motivating group were equal, that is, 10.5 words. If you examine medians, the difference between the control group

TABLE A.3
Calculations of Mean and Median for Three Groups of Subjects

Subject	Control Group	Experimental I (Task motivating)	Experimental II (Hypnosis)
1	10	11	16
2	12	13	14
3	14	14	16
4	10	12	12
5	11	12	10
6	9	8	9
7	5	10	15
8	12	5	12
9	16	10	18
10	7	8	32
Sum	106	103	154
Mean	10.6	10.3	15.4
Median	10.5	10.5	14.5

Control group (scores are re-ordered)

$$\text{Mean} = \frac{5 + 7 + 9 + 10 + 10 + 11 + 12 + 12 + 14 + 16}{10} \quad \frac{106}{10} = 10.6$$

$$\text{Median} = 5 \quad 7 \quad 9 \quad 10 \quad \boxed{10 \quad 11} \quad 12 \quad 12 \quad 14 \quad 16$$
$$\downarrow$$
$$10.5$$

The point at which half the scores fall above and half the scores fall below is 10.5; that is, 10.5 is the median.

Experimental I (scores are re-ordered)

$$\text{Mean} = \frac{5 + 8 + 8 + 10 + 10 + 11 + 12 + 12 + 13 + 14}{10} \quad \frac{103}{10} = 10.3$$

$$\text{Median} = 5 \quad 8 \quad 8 \quad 10 \quad \boxed{10 \quad 11} \quad 12 \quad 12 \quad 13 \quad 14$$
$$\downarrow$$
$$10.5$$

The point at which half the scores fall above and half the scores fall below is 10.5; that is, 10.5 is the median.

Experimental II (scores are re-ordered)

$$\text{Mean} = \frac{9 + 10 + 12 + 12 + 14 + 15 + 16 + 16 + 18 + 32}{10} \quad \frac{154}{10} = 15.4$$

$$\text{Median} = 9 \quad 10 \quad 12 \quad 12 \quad \boxed{14 \quad 15} \quad 16 \quad 16 \quad 18 \quad 32$$
$$\downarrow$$
$$14.5$$

The point at which half the scores fall above and half the scores fall below is 14.5; that is, 14.5 is the median.

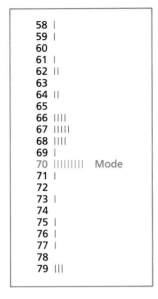

FIGURE A.3
The mode is the data point that occurs with the greatest frequency.

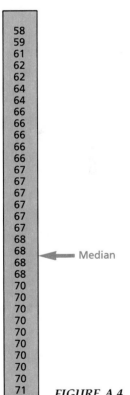

FIGURE A.4
The median is the 50 percent point. It is the point at which half the points fall above and half the points fall below.

and the hypnosis group was 4 words. The median difference (4 words) is smaller than the mean difference (4.8 words.) This occurred because the median discounts very high or very low scores. For example, if you average a zero in with five other test scores (where the average score is about 70), it will drop your *average* substantially; averaging in a 60 would not have as big an impact. But with medians, an extreme score (be it a zero or a 60) would count the same. With a small sample like this one, where a single score can have a big impact, the median is often a better measure of central tendency.

Variability: A measure of the extent to which scores differ from one another and especially the extent to which they differ from the mean.

Range: A measure of variability that describes the spread of scores within a group, calculated by subtracting the lowest score from the highest score.

The mean, mode, and median are descriptive statistics that are measures of central tendency. They each tell researchers something about the average (or typical) subject. Sometimes they are the same number, but more often there exists enough variability (one very tall person, two very short ones) that each central tendency measure yields a slightly different result. If, for example, you had to guess the height of a woman you had never met, a good guess would be the mean, the average height for women. If you were a buyer for a clothing store and had to pick one size dress or one size shoe to order, you might be more likely to pick the modal size, the size that will occur more often than any other.

Measures of Variability

A measure of central tendency is a single number that describes a hypothetical "average" subject. In real life, however, people do not always have scores that reflect the central tendency. Consequently, knowing how an average subject might score is more useful when we know how the scores in the group are distributed relative to one another. If you know that the mean of a group of numbers is 150, you do not know how widely dispersed are the scores that are averaged to calculate that mean.

A statistic that describes the extent to which scores differ from one another in a distribution is called a measure of variability. **Variability** is a measure of the extent to which scores differ from one another and especially the extent to which they differ from the mean. If all the subjects obtain the same score, no variability exists; this, however, is unlikely to occur. It is more usual that in any group of subjects being tested or measured in some way, personal and situational characteristics will cause some to score high and some to score low. If researchers know the extent of that variation, they can estimate the extent to which subjects differ from the mean or "average" subject.

Range. One measure of variability, the **range,** shows the spread of scores in a distribution. The range is calculated by subtracting the lowest score from the highest score. If the lowest score on a test was 20 points, and the highest was 85, the range was 65 points. Whether the mean was 45, 65, or 74 points, the range remained 65. There was always a 65-point spread from the lowest score to the highest.

The range is a relatively crude measure of the extent to which subjects vary within a group. In a group of 100 students, for example, nearly all may have scored within ten points of the mean score of 80. But if the lowest score was 20 and the highest was 85, the range would be 65. More precise measures of the spread of scores within a group are available, however. They indicate how scores are distributed as well as the extent of their spread.

Standard Deviation. Consider a reaction time study that measures how fast subjects press a button when a light is flashed. The following list gives the number of milliseconds it took each of thirty tenth-graders chosen at random to press the button when the light was flashed; clearly, the reaction times vary.

450	490	500
610	520	470
480	492	585
462	600	490
740	700	595
500	493	495
498	455	510
470	480	540
710	722	575
490	495	570

A person who was told only that the mean reaction time is 540 would assume that 540 is the best estimate of how long it takes a tenth-grade student to respond to the light. But these data are variable—not everyone took 540 milliseconds. Some took longer and some took less time. Psychologists say that the data were variable, or that there existed variability.

To find out how much variability exists among data, and to quantify it in a meaningful manner, we need to know the standard deviation. A **standard deviation** is a descriptive statistic that shows the variability of data from the mean of the sample; the standard deviation is calculated by figuring the extent to which each score differs from the mean. The calculations for a standard deviation are shown in Table A.4. The general procedure involves subtracting the mean from each score. You then square that difference. Next, the squared differences are added up and divided by the number of scores minus 1. (In a small sample, to get a better estimate of the population's standard deviation you typically divide by one less than the number of scores.) Last, you take the square root of the answer. You have now calculated a standard deviation.

Table A.5 on page 656 shows the reaction times for two new groups of subjects responding to a light. The mean is the same for both groups, but group 1 shows a large degree of variability while group 2 shows little variability. The standard deviation (i.e., estimate of variability) for group 1 subjects will therefore be substantially higher than that for group 2 subjects because the scores differ from the mean much more in the first group than in the second.

A standard deviation gives information about all the members of a group, not just an average member. Knowing the standard deviation—that is, the variability associated with each mean—enables a researcher to make more accurate predictions. Since the standard deviation for subjects in group 2 is small, a researcher can more confidently predict that a subject will respond to light in

Standard deviation: A descriptive statistic that measures the variability of data from the mean of the sample.

TABLE A.4
The Computation of the Standard Deviation for a Small Distribution of Scores

Score	Score − Mean	(Score − Mean)^2
10	10 − 6 = 4	16
10	10 − 6 = 4	16
10	10 − 6 = 4	16
5	5 − 6 = −1	1
4	4 − 6 = −2	4
4	4 − 6 = −2	4
4	4 − 6 = −2	4
1	1 − 6 = −5	25
48		86

$$\sqrt[2]{\frac{\Sigma(X - \overline{X})^2}{N - 1}}$$

Σ means sum up.
X = score.
Sum of scores = 48.
Mean = sum of scores ÷ 8 = 6.
Sum of squared difference from mean = 86.
Average of squared differences from mean[1] = 86 ÷ 7 = 12.3.
Square root of average squared difference from the mean = 3.5.
Standard deviation = 3.5.

[1] Dividing by the number of scores − 1.

TABLE A.5
Reaction times in milliseconds, mean reaction times, and standard deviations for two groups of subjects. (Group 1 shows a wider range of scores and thus greater variability. Group 2, by contrast, shows a narrow range of scores and little variability.)

Group 1	Group 2
380	530
400	535
410	540
420	545
470	550
480	560
500	565
720	570
840	575
930	580
Mean = 555	Mean = 555
Standard deviation = 197	Standard deviation = 17

about 555 milliseconds (the mean response time.) However, the researcher cannot confidently make the same prediction for subjects in group 1, since that group's standard deviation is high.

Confidence in predictions turns out to be a key issue for statisticians; they want to be as sure as possible that the mean of a group actually represents the mean of the larger population that group (sample) represents. This concern is important because researchers want to make inferences that a difference between a control and experimental group is due to the manipulation of the experimenter, not to chance factors, extraneous variables, or one or two scores that are deviant. It turns out that many of the manipulations and controls that researchers devise are necessary if they wish to make sound inferences, the topic we consider next.

Focus on Learning

- Distinguish between an abscissa and an ordinate. p. 651
- Distinguish between the mean, mode, and median. pp. 651–652
- What is the goal of a measure of variability, such as the standard deviation? p. 654

Inferential Statistics and the Normal Curve

Inferential statistics: Procedures used to reach conclusions (generalizations) about larger populations from a small sample of data with a minimal degree of error.

Researchers use a branch of statistics known as **inferential statistics** in making decisions about data. Inferential statistics are procedures used to reach conclusions (generalizations) about larger populations from a small sample of data, with a minimal degree of error. There are usually two issues to be explored. First, does the mean of a sample, a small group of subjects, actually reflect the mean of a larger population? Second, is a difference found between two means (for example, between a control group and an experimental group) a real and important difference, or is it a result of chance? Psychologists hope to find a

significant difference, which means that a difference in performance between two groups can be repeated experimentally using similar groups of subjects and is not a result of chance variations. Generally, psychologists assume that a difference is statistically significant if the likelihood of its occurring by chance is less than 5 out of 100 times. But many researchers assume a significant difference only if the likelihood of its occurring by chance is fewer than 1 out of 100 times.

It is sometimes difficult to decide whether a difference is significant. Let us refer back to Table A.3 on page 653, in which calculations were performed for a set of data. The data represent scores from a memory study in which the participants had to learn lists of unrelated words. There were three groups of subjects: one was given task motivating instructions to concentrate deeply (experimental group 1), a second group was hypnotized (experimental group 2), and a third group was given no special instructions (the control group). The dependent variable was the average number of words correctly recalled by each subject. The results showed that the task motivated group recalled no more words, on the average, than the control group (in fact, 0.3 words less.) The hypnosis group recalled 4.8 more words, on the average, than the control group.

The hypnosis group did better than the control group. Can we conclude that hypnosis is a beneficial memory aid? Did the hypnosis group do *significantly* better than the control group? Was a 4.8-word difference significant? It is easy to see that *if* the difference between recall was 10 words, and if the variability within the groups was very small, the difference would be considered significant. A one- or two-word difference would not be considered significant if the variability within the groups was large. In the present case, a 4.8-word difference was not significant; the scores were highly variable, and only a small sample of subjects was used. When scores are variable (widely dispersed), both statistical tests and researchers are unlikely to view a small difference between two groups as significant or important (see Figure A.5).

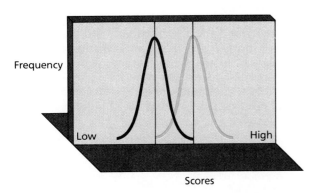

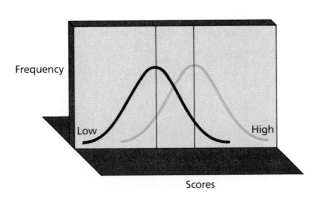

FIGURE A.5
The possible outcomes of two experiments are shown in the two graphs. In both cases, the means are identical. In the first, the scores all cluster around the means—there is little variability. The difference between the means in the first graph is likely to be significant. But the means in the second graph (although identical to the first) are unlikely to be deemed significantly different—the scores are too widely distributed. In the second graph there is too much variability; the means may be affected by an extreme score—thus, a scientist is unlikely to accept them as different from one another.

Normal distribution: A bell-shaped curve drawn as a frequency polygon which depicts the approximated expected distribution of scores when a sample is drawn from a large population; also called *normal curve*.

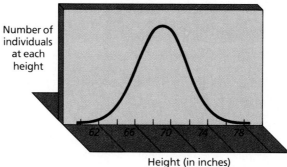

FIGURE A.6
In a normal distribution, or a normal curve, many more people are of average height, weight, or intelligence than are at the extremes.

Height (in inches)

Even if statistically significant differences are obtained, most researchers require that an experiment be repeated with the same results. Repeating an experiment to verify a result is called *replicating* the experiment. If, after replicating an experiment, the same results are obtained, a researcher will generally say that the observed difference between the two groups is important.

The Normal Curve

When a large number of scores are involved, a frequency polygon often takes the form of a bell-shaped curve called a **normal distribution,** or *normal curve*. Normal distributions usually have a few scores at each end and progressively many more scores toward the center. Height, for example, is approximately normally distributed: More people are of average height than are very tall or very short (see Figure A.6.) In addition to height, weight, shoe size, intelligence, and scores on psychology exams tend to be normally distributed.

Characteristics of a Normal Curve

A normal curve has certain characteristics. The mean, mode, and median are assumed to be the same, and the distribution of scores around that central point is symmetrical. Also, most individuals have a score that occurs within six standard deviations—three above the mean and three below it (Figure A.7). To explain, Figure A.8 shows a normal curve for test scores. The mean is 50, and the standard deviation is 10. Note how each increment of 10 points above or

FIGURE A.7
In a normal distribution, or a normal curve, most individuals score within six standard deviations, three on either side of the mean; each standard deviation accounts for a different proportion of the population.

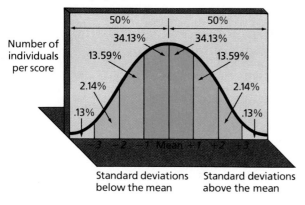

Number of individuals per score

50%   50%
34.13%   34.13%
13.59%   13.59%
2.14%   2.14%
.13%   .13%

Standard deviations below the mean   Standard deviations above the mean

FIGURE A.8
In this normal curve, the standard deviation is 10 points.

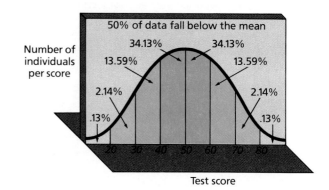

Number of individuals per score

50% of data fall below the mean
34.13%   34.13%
13.59%   13.59%
2.14%   2.14%
.13%   .13%

Test score

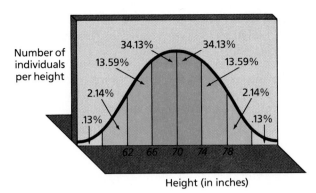

FIGURE A.9
When the mean distribution of height is 70 and the standard deviation is 4, Dennis, who is 74 inches tall, is taller than 84 percent of the sample population (0.13 + 2.14 + 13.59 + 34.13 + 34.13 = 84.12) whereas Rob, who is 66 inches tall, is taller than only 16 percent of the population (0.13 + 2.14 + 13.59 = 15.86).

below the mean accounts for fewer and fewer individuals. Scores between 50 and 60 account for 34.13 percent of those tested; scores of 60 to 70 account for 13.59 percent; and scores above 70 account for only about 3 percent. The sum of these percentages (34.13 + 13.59 + 2.14 + 0.13) represents 50 percent of the scores.

When you know the mean and standard deviation of a set of data, you can estimate where an individual in the sample population stands relative to others. In Figure A.9, Dennis, for example, is 74 inches tall. His height is one standard deviation above the mean, which means that he is taller than 84 percent of the population (0.13 + 2.14 + 13.59 + 34.13 + 34.13 = 84.12 percent.) Rob, who is 66 inches tall, is taller than only 16 percent of the population. His height is one standard deviation below the mean.

Normal Curves: A Practical Example

It is likely that you have dealt with grading on a curve before because your grade on an examination is often determined by how other members of the class do on the same exam. This is what instructors mean when they say that a grade is on a "sliding scale" or "curve." If the average student in a class answers only 50 percent of the questions correctly, a student who answers 70 percent correctly has done a good job. But if the average student scores 85 percent, then someone who scores only 70 percent has not done so well.

When assigning grades on a sliding scale, testing services and instructors generally plot the test results on a graph in order to calculate a mean. They then inspect the scores and "slide the scale" to an appropriate level. Figure A.10

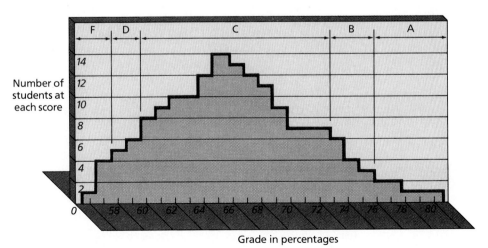

FIGURE A.10
To calculate grades on a sliding scale, instructors often draw a graph showing the number of individuals at each score. They then draw cutoff points for As, Bs, Cs, Ds, and Fs.

Correlation coefficient: A number that expresses the degree and direction of a relationship between two variables; the number ranges from −1.0 (a perfect negative correlation) to +1.0 (a perfect positive correlation); a value of zero indicates no correlation.

shows the scores on a trigonometry test. Since the average score is 65 percent, students who score 65 percent will receive a C, those who do better will receive an A or a B, and those who do worse will receive a D or an F.

For a number of reasons, it is sometimes not practical or possible to collect experimental data that involve control groups or experimental groups, or research that involves manipulations of an experimental variable. In these cases, correlations, considered next, are sometimes calculated, and they can tell a scientist a great deal.

Correlation

Sometimes researchers wish to compare data that were gathered in different surveys and questionnaires. To do so, they perform a *correlation study*. A correlation implies that an increase in the value of one variable will be accompanied by an increase or decrease in the value of a second variable. The degree of relationship between two variables is expressed by a numerical value called the **correlation coefficient.** Correlation coefficients go from −1, through 0, to +1. Any correlation greater or less than 0, regardless of its sign, indicates that the variables are related. When two variables are perfectly correlated, they are said to have a correlation of 1. A perfect correlation occurs when knowing the value of one variable allows one to predict *precisely* the value of the second, but this is a rare occurrence in psychological phenomena.

Most variables are not perfectly correlated; they have a correlation of perhaps .6. Consider height and weight. Although tall people generally weigh more than short people, some tall people weigh less than some short people. Figure A.11 illustrates the fact that knowing a person's height does not enable one to predict his or her weight exactly. The two variables, height and weight, have a correlation of only 0.65.

Another example of imperfectly correlated variables is found in the incidence of children of schizophrenic parents. If a parent is schizophrenic, the likelihood that the child will be schizophrenic increases sharply. Thus, there is a correlation between parents and children with respect to schizophrenia. Because this correlation is not perfect—that is, not every child born to a schizophrenic parent

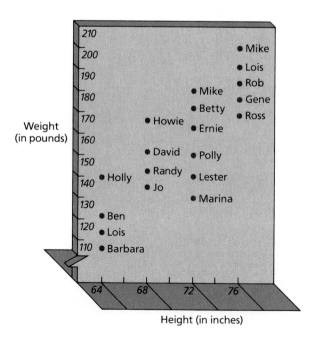

FIGURE A.11
When two variables are related, knowing the value of one helps a person predict the value of the other. A perfect prediction is not available unless the correlation is a correlation of 1.

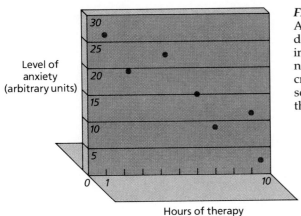

FIGURE A.12
An increase in one variable does not always mean an increase in the other. In a negative correlation, an increase in one variable is associated with a decrease in the other.

will develop the disorder—psychologists believe that genetics is only one of several contributing factors in the development of the disorder.

When one variable shows an increase in value and a second shows an increase, the two variables are positively related, and the relationship is known as a *positive correlation*. Height and weight show a positive correlation: Generally, as height increases, so does weight. On the other hand, if one variable decreases as the other increases, the direction of the correlation is changed: it is a *negative correlation*. The relationship between number of hours of therapy and extent of anxiety shows a negative correlation. As the number of hours of therapy increases, anxiety decreases. These variables have a negative correlation of about -0.6 or -0.7. (See Figure A.12.)

Another example of a negative correlation is that between time and memory. A person might be able to recall an entire list of 10 words immediately after reading it; the next day, he may remember only 5 of the words, and a week later, only one word. As time increases, memory decreases. Similarly, people who live close to an airport report that aircraft noise is painfully loud; those who live farther away report less noise. The loudness of the aircraft noise is negatively correlated to distance from the airport: As distance increases, loudness decreases.

It is important to remember that a correlation of $+0.7$ is no stronger than one of -0.7. The *direction*, not the strength, of the relationship is changed by the plus or minus sign. The strength is determined by the number. The larger the number, the greater the strength of the correlation. A correlation of -0.8 is greater than one of $+0.7$; a correlation of $+0.6$ is greater than one of -0.5.

Some variables show absolutely no correlation; this is expressed by a correlation coefficient of 0. Figure A.13 plots data for height and IQ. The figure

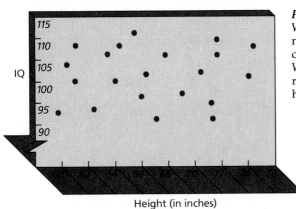

FIGURE A.13
When two variables show no relationship, they have a correlation of 0 (zero). Weight and height are correlated, but IQ and height have a correlation of 0.

FIGURE A.14
The left panel shows a positive correlation: an increase in one variable is associated with an increase in the other. The right panel shows a negative correlation: an increase in one variable is associated with a decrease in the other. The middle panel shows a 0 correlation, with one variable not related to the other.

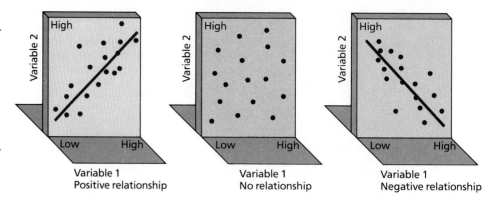

Variable 1
Positive relationship

Variable 1
No relationship

Variable 1
Negative relationship

shows no correlation between IQ and height, so the two variables have a correlation of 0 (see Figure A.14).

As was pointed out in chapter 1, correlation studies make no statements regarding cause and effect. They simply show that if there is an increase in one variable, there will probably be an increase or decrease in another variable. It is only through experimental studies that researchers can make cause-and-effect statements. Many of the studies reported in this text are correlational, but far more are experimental. Whenever possible, researchers wish to draw causal inferences.

Focus on Learning

- Describe the characteristics of a normal curve. p. 658
- Describe positive and negative correlations. p. 661
- In what situation can researchers make cause-and-effect statements? pp. 661–662

Key Terms

Statistics p. 646
Hypothesis p. 647
Experiment p. 647
Independent variable p. 647
Dependent variable p. 647
Control group p. 647
Experimental group p. 647
Sample p. 648

Operational definition p. 649
Descriptive statistics p. 649
Frequency distribution p. 650
Frequency polygon p. 650
Measure of central tendency
  p. 651
Mean p. 651
Mode p. 652

Median p. 652
Variability p. 654
Range p. 654
Standard deviation p. 655
Inferential statistics p. 656
Significant difference p. 657
Normal distribution p. 658
Correlation coefficient p. 660

Summary

Conducting Experiments

♦ An hypothesis is a tentative statement about a causal relationship between two variables or situations to be evaluated in an experiment.   p. 647

♦ A good experiment must have an experimental group, a control group, and a sufficient number of carefully selected subjects in each group. The experiment must include a good sample—a group of subjects or participants who are generally representative of the population about which an inference is to be made.   p. 648

♦ The independent and dependent variables in an experiment must be carefully specified. The independent variable is directly and purposefully manipulated by the experimenter to see what effect differences in it will have on the variables under study. The dependent variable is the behavior measured by an experimenter to assess whether changes in the independent variable affect the behavior under study. If a variable cannot be defined precisely, it must be defined operationally, in the form of a concrete description of how it will be measured.   pp. 647–648

Descriptive Statistics

♦ Researchers use descriptive statistics to summarize, condense, and describe data. A frequency distribution is a way of organizing data to show the number of times each item of data occurs. The graphic version of a frequency distribution is a frequency polygon.   pp. 650–651

♦ A descriptive statistic that indicates which single score best represents an entire set of scores is a measure of central tendency. The most frequently used measure of central tendency is the mean, or arithmetic average. Also used are the mode, or most frequently observed data point, and the median, the 50 percent point.   pp. 652–653

♦ A statistic that describes the extent to which scores differ from one another in a distribution is a measure of variability. One such measure, the range, shows the spread of scores in a distribution. Another, the standard deviation, shows the extent to which all the members of a group will vary from the mean.   p. 654

Inferential Statistics and the Normal Curve

♦ Inferential statistics enable the researcher to determine whether two or more groups differ from one another and whether the difference is a result of chance. When a difference is significant, it can be repeated experimentally using similar groups of subjects. Repeating an experiment to verify a result is called replicating the experiment.   pp. 656–657

♦ On a graph, a normal distribution produces a bell-shaped or normal curve. The mean, mode, and median are generally assumed to be the same, and the distribution of scores around that point is symmetrical.   p. 658

Correlation

♦ Correlation studies compare data that were gathered in different surveys and questionnaires. The correlation coefficient expresses the degree of relationship between two variables. When two variables are perfectly correlated, they are said to have a correlation of 1. p. 660

♦ The direction, not the strength, of a correlation relationship is changed by the plus or minus sign. The strength is determined by the number. The larger the number, the greater the strength of the correlation.   pp. 660–661

♦ Correlation studies make no statements regarding cause and effect. They simply show that if there is an increase in one variable, there will probably be an increase or decrease in another variable. Only through experimental studies can researchers make cause-and-effect statements.   pp. 660–661

Glossary

Abnormal behavior: Behavior characterized as atypical, socially unacceptable, and distressing; the result of distorted cognitions.

Abnormal psychology: The field of psychology concerned with the assessment, treatment, and prevention of maladaptive behavior.

Accommodation: In developmental terms, according to Jean Piaget, the process by which new concepts and experiences modify existing cognitive structures and behaviors; in perception, the change in shape of the lens of the eye to keep an object in focus on the retina when the object moves closer to or farther away from the observer.

Action potential: An all-or-none electrical current sent down the axon of a neuron, initiated by a rapid reversal of membrane potential. Also called a *spike discharge*.

Actor-observer effect: The tendency for people to attribute the behavior of other people to dispositional causes, while attributing their own behavior to situational causes.

Addictive: Causing a compulsive physiological need. Withholding an addictive drug produces withdrawal symptoms. Addictive drugs usually produce tolerance.

Addictive behavior: A repetitive action or habit that increases the risk of disease or social or personal problems.

Adolescence: The period extending from the onset of puberty to early adulthood.

Affect: A person's emotional response.

Afferent: Pathways and signals to the central nervous system.

Age regression: The ability, sometimes induced by hypnosis, to return to an earlier time in one's life and report events that occurred many years earlier.

Ageism: Discrimination on the basis of age. It often results in the denial of rights and services to the elderly.

Aggression: Any behavior whose goal is to harm another person or thing.

Agonist: A chemical that mimics the action of a neurotransmitter, usually by occupying receptor sites.

Agoraphobia (AG-or-uh-FOE-bee-uh): A disorder characterized by fear of being in public places from which escape might be difficult.

Alcohol abuse: Any situation in which a person shows problems related to alcohol.

Alcohol-related problems: Medical, social, or psychological problems associated with alcohol use.

Alcoholic: A problem drinker who also has a physiological and psychological need to consume alcoholic products and experience their effects.

Alcoholism: Physiological addiction to alcohol, usually accompanied by psychological dependence.

Algorithms: Simple, specific, exhaustive procedures that after a step-by-step analysis provide a solution to a problem.

All-or-none: The principle by which a neuron will fire either at full strength or not at all.

Allele: Each member of a pair of genes.

Altered state of consciousness: A pattern of functioning that is dramatically different from that of ordinary awareness and responsiveness.

Alternate-form: A method of assessing reliability by administering two forms of a test and computing the similarity between the scores.

Altruistic acts: Behaviors that benefit other people for which there is no discernible reward, recognition, or appreciation.

Alzheimer's disease: A chronic and progressive disorder that is a major cause of degenerative dementia, currently affecting about two million Americans. The disease may be a group of related disorders tied together loosely under one name.

Amnesia: A loss of memory, usually due to traumatic injury.

Amplitude The intensity or total energy of a sound wave that determines the loudness of a sound; usually measured in decibels.

Anal stage: Freud's second stage of personality development, from ages two to about three, during which children learn to control the immediate gratification obtained through defecation and become responsive to the demands of society.

Antagonist: A chemical that opposes the action of a neurotransmitter, usually by blocking a neurotransmitter from occupying a receptor site.

Androgynous (an-DROJ-ann-us): The condition in which some typically male and some typically female characteristics are apparent in one individual.

Anomalous trichromats: People whose color perception is deficient at various wavelengths and to various extents.

Anorexia nervosa (AN-uh-REX-see-uh-ner-VOH-sah): An eating disorder characterized by an intense fear of becoming obese, dramatic weight loss, concern about weight, disturbances in body image, and an obstinate and willful refusal to eat.

Anterograde amnesia: Loss of memory for events and experiences occurring in a period following the amnesia-causing event.

Antisocial personality disorder: A disorder beginning before age fifteen and characterized by continuous and chronic behavior that violates the rights of other people through lying, theft, delinquency, and other violations of societal rules. The individual lacks feelings of guilt, cannot understand other people, behaves irresponsibly, does not fear punishment, and is often egocentric.

Anxiety: A generalized feeling of fear and apprehension that may or may not be connected to a particular event or object. Often accompanied by increased physiological arousal, these fears and apprehensions are generally attributed to unrealistic sources.

Approach-approach conflict: The result of having to choose between two equally attractive alternatives or goals.

Approach-avoidance conflict: The result of having to choose a goal that has both attractive and repellent aspects.

Archetypes (AR-key-types): In Jung's theory, emotionally charged ideas and images that have rich meaning and symbolism and are contained within a person's collective unconscious.

Assessment: The process of evaluating individual differences among human beings by using tests and direct observation of behavior. The role of the clinician is central in assessment techniques.

Assimilation: According to Jean Piaget, the process by which new concepts and experiences are incorporated into existing ones so as to be used in a meaningful way.

Attention-deficit hyperactivity disorder: A disorder of infancy, childhood, and adolescence beginning before age seven and characterized by restlessness, inattention, distractibility, and overactivity; also known as *hyperactive syndrome* or *hyperkinetic syndrome* or *hyperkinesis.*

Attitude: A pattern of relatively enduring feelings, beliefs, and behavior tendencies toward other people, ideas, or objects.

Attribution: The process by which someone infers other people's motives and intentions from observing their behavior. The focus is usually on deciding if the causes of the behavior are *dispositional* (internal) or *situational* (external).

Autistic disorder (OT-is-tic): A disorder of infancy, childhood, and adolescence beginning before age two and a half and characterized by lack of responsiveness to other people, gross impairment in language skills, and bizarre responses to the environment; also known as *early infantile autistic disorder* or *autism.*

Autonmic nervous system: The part of the peripheral nervous system that controls the vital processes of the body, such as heart rate, digestive processes, blood pressure, and regulation of internal organs. This system is called "autonomic" because many of its systems are self-relating. Its two main subdivisions are the sympathetic and parasympathetic systems.

Aversive counterconditioning: A counterconditioning technique that pairs an aversive or noxious stimulus with a stimulus that elicits undesirable behavior so that the subject will adopt new behaviors in response to the original stimulus.

Avoidance-avoidance conflict: The result of having to choose between two equally distasteful or negative alternatives or goals.

Babinski reflex: A reflex in which an infant projects its toes outward and up when the soles of its feet are touched.

Backward-search: A heuristic procedure in which a problem solver starts at the end of a problem and systematically works in reverse steps to discover the subparts necessary to achieve a solution.

Balance theory: An attitude theory stating that people prefer to hold consistent beliefs and try to avoid incompatible beliefs.

Basal age: The lowest age level on the Stanford-Binet at which all tests are passed.

Behavior: Every aspect of an organism's functioning, including overt behavior, thought, emotion, and physiological activity. These functions may or may not be directly observable.

Behavior therapy: A therapy based on the application of learning principles to human behavior. Synonymous with behavior modification, it focuses on changing overt behaviors rather than on understanding subjective feelings, unconscious processes, or motivations.

Behavioral assessment: Procedures used for diagnosis, evaluation, and intervention in which direct observation, self-evaluation, and interviews are used. The technique avoids interpretation and indirect assessment.

Behaviorism: A school of psychology that rejects the notion that the proper subject of psychology is the contents of consciousness. It maintains instead that psychology can describe and measure only what is observable, either directly or through use of instruments.

Biofeedback: The general technique by which individuals can monitor and learn to control the involuntary activity of certain organs and bodily functions.

Biological perspective: Examines psychological issues from the viewpoint of how heredity and biological structures affect behavior; it focuses on how physical mechanisms create emotions, feelings, thoughts, and desires.

Bipolar disorder: A disorder characterized by vacillation between two extremes, mania and depression; originally called *manic/depressive disorder.*

Body language: The communication of information through body positions and gestures.

Bonding: A special process of emotional attachment occurring between parent and child in the minutes and hours immediately after birth.

Brain: The part of the central nervous system within the skull.

Brainstorming: A technique for problem solving that involves considering all possible solutions without making prior evaluative judgments.

Brief intermittent therapy: A therapy approach that focuses on identifying the client's current problem and treating it with the most effective treatment as quickly as possible.

Brightness: The lightness or darkness of reflected light that is determined in large part by a light's intensity.

Bulimia nervosa (boo-LEE-me-uh ner-VOH-sah): An eating disorder characterized by repeated episodes of binge eating and fear of not being able to stop eating, followed by vomiting or use of laxatives and diuretics, compulsive exercising, and weight reduction drugs.

Burnout: A state of emotional and physical exhaustion, lowered productivity, and feelings of isolation, often due to work-related pressure.

Bystander apathy: The unwillingness of witnesses to an event to help, especially when there are a number of observers (bystanders); the effect increases when there are more observers.

Cardinal traits: In Allport's theory, ideas and behaviors that determine the overall direction of a person's life.

Case study: A method of interviewing a subject to gain information about his or her background, including data on such things as childhood, family, education, and social and sexual interactions.

Catatonic type: One of five major subtypes of schizophrenia, characterized by stupor, in which the individual is mute, negative, and basically unresponsive, or by displays of excited or violent motor activity.

Ceiling age: The age level on the Stanford-Binet above which all tests are failed.

Central nervous system (CNS): One of the two major parts of the nervous system, consisting of the brain and spinal cord.

Central traits: In Allport's theory, behaviors that are reasonably easy to identify that characterize a person's day-to-day interactions.

Child abuse: Physical, emotional, or sexual mistreatment of children.

Chromosomes: Strands in the nuclei of cells that carry genes. Composed of a DNA core, they are responsible for the hereditary transmission of traits. Found in pairs, they represent the genetic contribution of both parents.

Chunk: A manageable, familiar, and meaningful unit

of information; these units are organized in a way that allows them to be grouped together for easy coding, storage, and retrieval.

Classical conditioning: A conditioning process in which an originally neutral stimulus, by repeated pairing with a stimulus that naturally elicits a response, comes to elicit a similar or even identical response; sometimes called *Pavlovian conditioning.*

Client-centered therapy: An insight therapy developed by Carl Rogers that seeks to help people evaluate the world and themselves from their own perspective by providing a nondirective environment and unconditional positive regard for the client; sometimes called *person-centered therapy.*

Coding: The organization of information and the rules for organization by which the initial stimulus is transformed into some other form.

Cognitive dissonance: A state in which individuals feel uncomfortable because they hold two or more thoughts, attitudes, or behaviors that are inconsistent with one another.

Cognitive psychology: The study of the encoding, storage, analysis, recall, reconstruction, elaboration, and memory of events. A broad-ranging field, the study of thought is today involved in personality theory, social psychology, and theories of maladjustment.

Cognitive theory: An explanation of behavior that emphasizes the role of thoughts and individual choice regarding life goals and the means of achieving them.

Collective unconscious: In Jung's theory, a storehouse, a collection of primitive ideas and images that are inherited from our ancestors.

Color blindness: The inability to perceive different hues.

Community psychology: A branch of psychology that seeks to reach out to society to provide service like community mental health centers and especially to effect social change through planning, prevention, intervention, research, evaluation, and empowerment of individuals.

Concept: A classification of objects or ideas that distinguishes them from others on the basis of some common feature.

Concordance rate: The percentage of occasions when two groups or individuals show the same trait.

Concrete operational stage: Piaget's third stage of development, lasting from approximately ages seven to eleven. During this stage the child develops the ability to understand constant factors in the environment, rules, and higher-order symbolism (such as arithmetic and geography).

Conditioned response: The response elicited by a conditioned stimulus.

Conditioned stimulus: A neutral stimulus that, through repeated association with an unconditioned stimulus, becomes capable of eliciting a conditioned response.

Conditioning: A systematic procedure through which new responses to stimuli are learned.

Conduct disorder: A disorder of infancy, childhood, and adolescence usually beginning before age thirteen and characterized by persistent violation of the rights of other people or violation of major age-appropriate norms.

Conduction deafness: Deafness resulting from interference with the conduction of sound to the neural mechanism of the inner ear.

Conflict: The emotional state or condition in which a person has to make difficult decisions about two or more competing motives, behaviors, or impulses.

Conformity: The processes by which a person changes his or her attitudes or behaviors to be consistent with other people or with social norms.

Conscious: Freud's first level of consciousness, which refers to behavior (feelings and actions) of which a person is aware.

Consciousness (CON-shus-ness): The general state of being aware of and responsive to events in the environment; a defining characteristic of being human. Human beings can review the past and their current state of awareness.

Conservation: The ability to recognize that something changed in some way (such as the "shape" of liquid in a container) is still the same thing with the same weight, substance, or volume.

Conservative focusing: A strategy for problem solving that involves the elimination of alternative possibilities.

Consolidation: The evolution of a temporary neural circuit into a more permanent circuit.

Control group: In an experiment, the group of subjects that does not receive the treatment under investigation. The control group is used for comparison purposes so that the observed effects can be traced to the variable under study.

Convergence: The movement of the eyes toward each other to keep information or corresponding points on the retina as an object moves closer to the observer; a binocular depth cue.

Conversion disorder: A disorder characterized by the loss or alteration of physical functioning not due to a physiological disorder, but apparently due to internal psychological conflict.

Convolutions: Characteristic folds in tissues of the cerebral hemispheres and overlying cortex in human beings.

Coping: The process by which a person manages environmental and internal demands that cause stress, or that might cause stress.

Coping skills: The techniques people use to deal with stress and changing situations.

Correlation: A measure of the degree to which two variables are related, expressed in terms of a correlation coefficient that varies from -1 to $+1$. These coefficients express how changes in one variable are associated with changes in another.

Correlation coefficient: A number that expresses the degree and direction of a relationship between two variables; the number ranges from -1.0 (a perfect negative correlation) to $+1.0$ (a perfect positive correlation); a value of zero indicates no correlation. A high number means a change in one variable is associated with a change in the other.

Counterconditioning: A process of reconditioning in which a person learns a new response to a familiar stimulus.

Creativity: A characteristic of thought and of problem solving, generally considered to include originality, novelty, and appropriateness.

Crowding: The perception that one's space is too restricted.

Dark adaptation: An increase in sensitivity when a person moves from a light environment to a dark one; chemicals in the photoreceptors regenerate and return to their inactive pre-light adapted state, which results in an increase in sensitivity.

Debriefing: A procedure to inform subjects about the true nature of the experiment after its completion.

Decay: The loss of information from memory as a result of the passage of time and/or disuse.

Decentration: The process beginning at about age two of changing from a totally self-oriented point of view to one that recognizes other people's feelings, ideas, and viewpoints.

Decision making: The assessment of and choice among alternatives; sometimes involves the probability of occurrence of some event and expected value.

Declarative memory: Memory for specific facts; distinct from memory for skills to complete tasks. See *procedural memory.*

Decriminalization: Reducing the legal offense of an activity to that of a civil violation (such as a traffic violation).

Deep structure: The organization of a sentence that is closest to its underlying meaning.

Defense mechanism: A way of reducing anxiety by distorting reality.

Deindividuation (dee-in-di-vid-you-AY-shun): The process by which individuals in a group lose their sense of self-awareness and concern with evaluation.

Delusion: A false belief, inconsistent with reality, held in spite of evidence to the contrary.

Demand characteristics: The elements of the situation that might clue a subject as to the purpose of the study, but especially to behave in specific ways. The elements of the situation that elicit specific behaviors.

Dementias: Impairment in mental functioning and global cognitive (thought) abilities of longstanding duration in an otherwise alert individual. Dementias cause a loss of memory and other related symptoms. The leading cause in the United States is Alzheimer's disease.

Denial: A defense mechanism by which people refuse to accept the true source of their anxiety.

Dependence: Reliance on regular use of a drug, without which the individual suffers a psychological or physiological reaction, or both.

Dependent variable: The behavior measured by an experimenter to assess whether or not changes in the independent variable affect the behavior under study.

Depressive disorders: A general category of disorders in which people show extreme and persistent sadness, despair, and loss of interest in life's usual activities.

Descriptive statistics: A general set of procedures used to describe and summarize samples of data; generally represented by a single number that represents some aspects of the data.

Deviation IQ: A standard IQ test score that has the same mean and standard deviation at all ages.

Diabetes mellitus: A condition in which too little insulin is present in the blood, so that insufficient quantities of sugar are transported into body cells.

Dichromats: People who can distinguish only two of the three basic hues.

Diffusion of responsibility: The feeling of individuals in a group that they cannot be held individually responsible for the group's actions.

Dimension: A conceptual feature that distinguishes an object or phenomenon from others lacking that feature.

Discrimination: Behavior targeted at a person with the aim of holding that person (or group) apart and treating them differently.

Disorganized type: One of five major subtypes of schizophrenia, characterized by frequent incoherence, absence of systematized delusions, and blunted, inappropriate, or silly affect.

Dissociative disorder: A disorder characterized by a sudden temporary alteration in consciousness, identity, or motor behavior.

Divergent thinking: According to Guilford, the production of new information from known information, or the generation of logical possibilities, which serves as the basis of creativity.

Door-in-the-face effect: The finding that an individual is more likely to grant you a small request if the individual has previously turned you down for a large favor.

Double bind: A situation in which an individual is given two different and inconsistent messages.

Double-blind technique: A research technique in which both the experimenter and the subjects do not know who is in the control or experimental group, thus minimizing the effects of self-fulfilling prophecies.

Down syndrome: A genetic defect in human beings in which three twenty-first chromosomes are present. Most individuals with Down syndrome exhibit characteristic physical abnormalities and are mentally retarded.

Dream: An altered state of consciousness that occurs largely during REM sleep and usually accompanied by vivid visual, tactile, and auditory experiences.

Dream analysis: A psychoanalytic technique in which a patient's dreams are interpreted, used to gain insight into the individual's unconscious motivations.

Drive: An internal aroused condition that initiates behavior to satisfy physiological needs. Drives are inferred from behavior.

Drive theory: An explanation of behavior that emphasizes internal factors that energize organisms to seek, attain, or maintain some goal. Often the goal is to reestablish a state of physiological balance.

Drug: Any chemical substance that alters normal biological processes.

Eating disorder: A disorder characterized by gross disturbances in eating behavior and the way in which individuals respond to food.

Eclectic (ek-LECK-tik): Combination of theories, facts, or techniques. In clinical psychology, this term usually describes the practice of using whatever therapy techniques are appropriate for an individual client rather than relying exclusively on the techniques of one school of psychology.

Efferent: Pathways and signals from the central nervous system to other structures in the body.

Ego (EE-go): In Freud's theory, the part of personality that seeks to satisfy the id and superego in accordance with reality.

Ego-analysis: A psychoanalytic approach to therapy that assumes that the ego has greater control over behavior than Freud suggested and thus is more concerned with reality testing and control over the environment than with unconscious motivations and processes.

Egocentrism: The inability to perceive a situation or event except in relation to oneself; a characteristic of the sensory-motor stage. In infancy, it is the attitude that directs all concerns and behaviors to personal interests and needs.

Elaboration likelihood model: A theory of attitude change which suggests that there exist two routes to persuasions, *central* and *peripheral*; the former focuses on thoughtful, elaborative consideration; the latter, on less careful, more emotional, and even superficial considerations.

Elaborative rehearsal: Rehearsal involving repetition in which the stimulus may be associated with other events and further processed; this type of rehearsal is more typical of long-term memory and the processes of encoding information into long-term memory.

Electroconvulsive shock therapy (eel-EK-tro-cun-VUL-sive): A treatment for severe mental illness in which a brief application of electricity is used to produce a generalized seizure. The duration of the shock is less than a second; patients are treated in three to twelve treatment sessions over a period of several weeks.

Electroencephalogram (EEG) (eel-eck-tro-en-SEFF-uh-low-gram): The record of an organism's electrical brain patterns, obtained through electrodes placed on a subject's scalp.

Electromagnetic radiation: The entire spectrum of waves initiated by charged particles, including visible light gamma rays, X-rays, and ultraviolet, infrared, and radar waves.

Embryo: The term used to refer to the human organism from the fifth through the fortieth day after conception.

Emotion: A subjective response, usually accompanied by a physiological change, that is interpreted by the individual, readies the individual toward some action, and has associated with it a change in behavior.

Empowerment: The process of facilitating the development of skills, knowledge, and motivation in individuals so that they can act for themselves and gain mastery over their own affairs.

Encoding: The process by which information is placed in memory; it is the initial transduction of an event into electrochemical energy that allows for mental representation.

Encounter group: A group of people who meet together to learn more about their feelings, behavior, and interactions.

Endocrine glands: Ductless glands that secrete hormones directly into the bloodstream.

Endocrine system: A system of ductless glands that secrete hormones directly into the blood stream.

Endorphins (en-DOOR-finz): Painkillers produced naturally in the brain and pituitary gland.

Environmental psychology: The study of how physical settings affect human behavior and how human behavior affects the environment.

Episodic memory: Memory for specific events, objects, and situations; time and place of events is often coded.

Erectile dysfunction: In men, the inability to attain or maintain an erection of sufficient strength or quality to allow the act of sexual intercourse.

Excitement phase: The stage of the sexual response cycle in which there are initial increases in heart rate, blood pressure, and respiration. *Vasoconstriction* occurs during this stage, and erections and vaginal lubrication.

Exhibitionism: A psychosexual disorder in which the preferred method of sexual stimulation and gratification consists of repetitive acts of exposing the genitals to strangers.

Expectancy theory: An explanation of behavior that emphasizes a person's expectation of success and need for achievement as the energizing factors.

Experiment: A procedure in which a researcher systematically manipulates certain variables to describe objectively the relation between the variables of concern and the resulting behavior. Well-designed experiments permit inferences about cause and effect.

Experimental group: In an experiment, the group of subjects that receives the treatment under investigation.

Extinction (eggs-STINCK-shun): In classical conditioning, the process of reducing the likelihood of a conditioned response to a conditioned stimulus by withholding the unconditional stimulus.

Extrinsic reward: A reward that comes from the external environment.

Face validity: The appropriateness of test items "on their face"—that is, they seem appropriate to experts.

Factor analysis: A statistical procedure designed to discover the mutually independent elements (factors) in any set of data.

Factor-theory approach to intelligence: Theories of intelligence based on factor analysis, including those of Spearman and Thurstone.

Fetishism: A psychosexual disorder in which sexual arousal and gratification are brought about by objects such as shoes, underwear, or toilet articles.

Fetus: The term used to refer to the human organism from the fortieth day after the conception until birth.

Fixation: An excessive attachment to some person or object that is appropriate at an earlier level of development; when people become fixated, they are said to

be stopped, arrested, or halted at a particular stage of development.

Fixed-interval: A reinforcer is delivered after a specified interval of time, provided that the required response has occurred at least once after the interval has elapsed.

Fixed-ratio: A reinforcer is delivered after a predetermined number of responses has occurred.

Foot in the door effect: The finding that if a person complies with a small request now, the chances increase that the person will later comply with a larger request.

Formal operational stage: Piaget's fourth and final stage of intellectual development, beginning at about age twelve, when the individual can think hypothetically, consider all future possibilities, and is capable of deductive logic.

Fraternal twins: Double births resulting from the release of two ova in the female which are then fertilized by two sperm. Fraternal twins are no more or less genetically similar than nontwin siblings.

Free association: A psychoanalytic technique in which a person reports his or her thoughts and feelings as they occur, regardless of how illogical their order or content may appear.

Free-floating anxiety: Persistent anxiety not clearly related to any specific object or situation, accompanied by a sense of impending doom.

Frequency: A measure of the number of complete pressure waves per unit of time, expressed in Hertz (Hz), or cycles per second.

Frequency distribution: A chart or array, usually arranged from the highest to lowest score, showing the number of instances of each obtained score.

Frequency polygon: A graph of a frequency distribution that shows the number of instances of obtained scores; usually data points are connected by straight lines.

Frustration: The emotional state or condition resulting from a situation when any goal—work, family, or personal—is thwarted or blocked.

Frustration-aggression hypothesis: The view that frustration of goal-directed behavior leads to aggression.

Fulfillment: In Rogers's personality theory, an inborn tendency directing people toward actualizing their inherited nature and thus attaining their potential.

Functional fixedness: The inability to see that an object can have a function other than the one normally associated with it.

Functionalism: A school of psychology that grew out of structuralism and was concerned with how and why the conscious mind works; a principal aim was to know how those contents of consciousness worked together; principal proponents were William James (1842–1910) and G. Stanley Hall (1844–1924).

Fundamental attribution error: The tendency to attribute behavior to dispositions of the individual (internal causes) rather than situational (external) causes; this error occurs more often when explaining the behavior of other people.

Gender differences: Differences between males and females in behavior or mental processes.

Gender identity: A person's sense of being male or female.

Gender schema theory: The theory that asserts that children and adolescents use gender as an organizing theme to classify and understand their perceptions about the world.

Gene: The unit of heredity transmission carried in chromosomes and consisting of deoxyribonucleic acid (DNA) and protein.

Generalized anxiety disorder: A disorder characterized by persistent anxiety for at least one month, sometimes accompanied by problems in motor tension, autonomic hyperactivity, apprehension, and concentration.

Genetics: The study of the potential transmitted from parents to offspring through genes.

Genital stage: Freud's last stage of personality development, from the onset of puberty through adulthood, during which the sexual conflicts of childhood resurface in adolescents.

Gestalt psychology (gesh-TALT): A school of psychology that argues that behavior cannot be studied in parts, but must be viewed as a whole; Gestalt psychologists focus on the unity of perception and thinking.

Gestalt therapy: An insight therapy founded by Perls that emphasizes the importance of a person's being aware of current feelings and situation.

Grammar: The linguistic description of how a language functions; it especially contains rules for how all acceptable sentences are generated.

Grasping: A reflex in which an infant grasps vigorously any object touching or placed in its hand.

Group: A loosely or cohesively related number of individuals who share some common characteristics and goals.

Group polarization: The exaggeration of individuals' preexisting attitudes as a result of group discussion.

Group therapy: A method in which several people meet as a group with a therapist for the treatment of emotional and behavioral problems.

Groupthink: The phenomenon of people in a group reinforcing each other and seeking concurrence and group cohesiveness rather than effectively evaluating choices and reasoning.

Hallucinations: Compelling perceptual experiences without a real physical stimulus. They may be visual, tactile, olfactory, or most commonly in schizophrenia, auditory.

Halo effect: The tendency to let one of an individual's characteristics influence the evaluation of other characteristics.

Hawthorne Effect: The finding that people behave differently, usually better, when they know they are being observed; even if the situation might lead to worse performance, at least initially, being observed in an experimental situation leads to improved performance.

Health psychology: The psychological sub-field concerned with the use of psychological ideas and principles in health enhancement, illness prevention, diagnosis and treatment of disease, and rehabilitation processes.

Heredity: The potential transmitted from parents to offspring through genes.

Heuristics: Sets of selective strategies that act as guidelines for decision making, but are not strict rules.

Higher-order conditioning: The process by which a neutral stimulus takes on conditioned properties through pairing with a conditioned stimulus.

Hormones: Chemicals that regulate the activities of specific organs or cells. Hormones are produced by the endocrine glands and are transported by the bloodstream to their site of action.

Hue: The psychological property of light referred to as color, determined by the wavelength reflected from an object.

Humanistic psychology: The school of psychology that emphasizes the uniqueness of the human experience and the idea that human beings have free will to determine their destiny.

Humanistic theory: An explanation of behavior that emphasizes the role of human qualities, such as dignity, individual choice, self-concept, and self-achievement.

Hyperactivity: An attention deficit disorder whose symptoms include overactivity, distractibility, restlessness, and short attention span.

Hyperglycemia (high-purr-gly-SEEM-me-uh): A condition in which too much sugar is present in the blood.

Hypermetropia: The inability to see things that are nearby; *farsightedness*.

Hypermnesia: Heightened memory, sometimes induced by hypnosis.

Hypnosis: An altered state of consciousness brought about by trance-induction procedures. Subjects' responsiveness to a hypnotist's suggestions increases as they become more deeply hypnotized.

Hypnotic drugs: Drugs such as Miltown and Equanil that induce sleep but reduce or eliminate REM sleep.

Hypnotic susceptibility: The willingness to follow unconventional instructions while under hypnosis.

Hypochondriasis (HI-po-kon-DRY-a-sis): The inordinate preoccupation with health and illness coupled with excessive concern and anxiety about disease.

Hypoglycemia: A condition usually resulting from the overproduction of insulin, causing very low blood sugar levels. It is usually characterized by a lack of energy, and often by faintness and dizziness.

Hypothesis: A tentative statement about a causal relationship between two variables or situations to be evaluated in an experiment.

Id: In Freud's theory, the source of instinctual energy, which works on the pleasure principle.

Ideal self: That self a person would ideally like to be.

Identical twins: Double births resulting from the splitting of a zygote into two identical cells that then separate and develop independently. Identical twins have exactly the same genetic makeup.

Illusion: A perception of a stimulus that differs from normal expectations about its appearance.

Imagery: A cognitive process in which a mental picture is created of a sensory event.

Immune system: The network of organs and specialized glands, white blood cells, and proteins that defend the body against disease.

Implosive therapy: An extinction procedure that aims at reducing (extinguishing) people's fear and avoidance responses by overwhelming them with fearful imagined situations until they learn that they can survive their anxiety and produce other responses.

Impression formation: The process by which people use the behavior and appearance of others to infer their internal states and intentions.

Imprinting: The process by which animals form species-specific behaviors during a critical period early in life. These behaviors are not easily modified.

Independent variable: The variable in an experiment that is directly and purposefully manipulated by the experimenter to see what effect the difference in it will have on the variables under study.

Industrial/organizational psychologists: Applied psychologists who work in industry, government, and public agencies who focus on how individual behavior is affected by the work environment, coworkers, and organizational practices; sometimes called I/O psychologists.

Infantile autism: A disorder of infancy, childhood, and adolescence beginning before age two and a half and characterized by lack of responsiveness to other people, gross impairment in language skills, and bizarre responses to the environment; also known as *early infantial autism or autism*.

Inferential statistics: Procedures used to reach conclusions (generalizations) about larger populations from a smaller set of data with a minimal degree of error.

Innumeracy: The inability to deal comfortably with the

fundamental assumptions about numbers and probability.

Insight therapy: A therapy that attempts to discover relationships between unconscious motivations and current behavior. Insight therapy assumes that abnormal behavior results from individuals' failure to understand their unconscious motivations and needs. Once people understand their motivations, behavior should change.

Insomnia: Prolonged inability to sleep.

Instincts: Inherited, inborn, unlearned, predetermined behavior patterns.

Instrumental conditioning: A conditioning procedure in which the probability that an organism will emit a response is increased or decreased by the subsequent delivery of a reinforcer or punisher; sometimes called *operant conditioning.*

Insulin: A hormone produced by the pancreas, necessary for the transport of sugar from the blood into body cells so that it can be metabolized.

Intelligence: According to Wechsler, "the aggregate or global capacity of the individual to act purposefully, to think rationally, and to deal effectively with the environment."

Interference: The suppression or confusion of one bit of information with another received either earlier or later.

Interpersonal attraction: The tendency of one person to evaluate another person (or a symbol of another person) in a positive way.

Interpretation: In Freud's theory, the technique of providing a context, meaning, or cause of a specific idea, feeling, or set of behaviors; the process of tying a set of behaviors to its unconscious determinant.

Interview: A series of open-ended questions used to gather basic detailed information about a person. Though time-consuming, this technique allows the interviewer to probe potentially important issues or problems in depth.

Intrinsically motivated behaviors: Behaviors that a person performs in order to feel more competent, satisfied, and self-determined.

Introspection: The technique of examining the contents of the mind through self-report and the careful examination of thoughts and feelings.

Kinesthesis (Kin-es-THE-sis): The feelings aroused by movements of the muscles, tendons, and joints; also called *proprioception.*

Labor: The process in which the uterus contracts to open the cervix so that the fetus can descend through the birth canal to the outside world.

Latency stage (LATE-un-see): Freud's fourth stage of personality development, from age seven until puberty, during which sexual urges are inactive.

Latent content: Deeper meaning, usually involving symbolism, hidden content, and repressed or obscured ideas and wishes of a dream.

Latent learning: Learning that occurs in the absence of any direct reinforcement and which may be demonstrated after the learning occurs, that is, it remains latent.

Lateral geniculate nucleus: The first major center at which impulses leaving the eye are processed, sometimes called the *lateral geniculate body.*

Lateralization: The concentration of a particular brain function in one hemisphere.

Law of Pragnanz: The Gestalt principle that items or stimuli that can be grouped together and seen as a whole will be.

Learned helplessness: The behavior of giving up or not responding, exhibited by subjects exposed to negative consequences or punishment over which they have no control.

Learning: A relatively permanent change in an organism that occurs as a result of experiences in the environment; this change is often seen in overt behavior.

Libido: In Freud's theory, the instinctual life force that energizes the id. The libido works on the pleasure principle and seeks immediate gratification.

Light: The portion of the electromagnetic spectrum (ranging from 400 to 750 nanometers) visible to the eye.

Linguistics: The study of language including speech sounds, meaning, and grammar.

Logic: The procedure that we use to reach a valid conclusion.

Loneliness: An unpleasant experience that occurs when a person's network of social relationships is significantly deficient in either quality or quantity.

Long-term memory: The memory storage system and process that keeps a relatively permanent record of information.

Low balling: compliance technique by which a person is influenced to make a decision or commitment because of a low cost associated with it; after the decision is made, the cost is raised and the person is still likely to stick with his or her original decision.

Lucid dream: A dream in which people are aware of their dreaming while it is happening.

Mainstreaming: The administrative practice of placing exceptional children in regular classroom settings with the support of special education services.

Maintenance rehearsal: Repetitive review of information in short-term memory with little or no interpretation; this shallow form of rehearsal typically involves the physical stimulus characteristics, not its underlying meaning.

Major depression: A disorder characterized by loss of interest in almost all usual activities as evidenced by a sad, hopeless, or discouraged mood. Other symptoms include sleep disturbance, loss of appetite, loss of energy, and feelings of unworthiness and guilt.

Manifest content: Overt storyline, characters, and setting of a dream; it is the overt, obvious, clearly discernible events of a dream.

Mean: A measure of central tendency calculated by dividing the sum of the scores by the number of scores; the arithmetic average.

Means-end analysis: A heuristic procedure in which efforts are made toward moving the problem solver closer toward a solution by finding the steps and making changes that will bring about the solution as efficiently as possible.

Measure of central tendency: An index of the average or typical value of a distribution of scores.

Median: A measure of central tendency; the point at which 50 percent of all observations occur either above or below.

Mediation: The process of creating or discovering a connection between previously unconnected things.

Medical-biological model: An approach that considers behavior to be the result of biological or physiological conditions.

Meditation: A state of consciousness induced by a variety of techniques and characterized by concentration, restriction of sensory stimuli, and deep relaxation.

Memory: The ability to recall or remember past events, images, ideas, or previously learned information or skills; the storage system that allows for retention and retrieval.

Memory span: The brief, limited number of items that can be easily reproduced after presentation in short-term memory, usually confined to a chunk of information.

Mental retardation: Below-average intellectual functioning as measured on an IQ test, accompanied by an impairment in adaptive behavior originating during childhood.

Mode: A measure of central tendency; the most frequent observation.

Model: A perspective or approach derived from data in one field, used to help describe data in another field.

Modeling: The social observational learning process by which people behaving can serve as examples (or models) for other people to observe and imitate.

Monochromats: People whose retinas contain only rods and who therefore cannot perceive hue.

Monocular depth cues: Depth cues that do not require the use of two eyes.

Morality: A system of learned attitudes about social practices, institutions, and individual behavior, used to evaluate events as right or wrong.

Moro reflex: A reflex in which an infant outstretches its arms and legs and cries when there is a loud noise or abrupt change in the environment.

Morphemes: The basic units of meaning in a language.

Motivation: An internal condition initiated by drives, needs, or desires and producing goal-directed behavior.

Motive: A specific internal condition directing an organism's behavior toward a goal.

Multiple personality: A disorder characterized by the existence within an individual of two or more different personalities, each of which is dominant and directs the individual's behavior at distinct times.

Myopia: The inability to see things far away, at a distance; *nearsightedness.*

Narcotic drugs: Drugs with sedative properties that are addictive and produce tolerance.

Naturalistic observation: Careful and objective observation of events as they occur in nature, without any intervention by the observer.

Nature: An individual's genetically inherited characteristics.

Need: A physiological condition arising from an imbalance and usually accompanied by arousal.

Need for achievement: A social need that directs a person to strive constantly for excellence and success.

Negative instance: A stimulus that is not an example of the concept under study.

Negative reinforcement: Removal of an aversive stimulus in order to increase the likelihood that a response will recur.

Neoanalyst: Any person who modified the basic ideas of Freud; the neoanalysts, sometimes called *neo-Freudians,* usually attributed a greater influence to cultural and interpersonal factors.

Neo-Freudian: Any person who modified the basic ideas of Freud; the neo-Freudians, sometimes called *neoanalysts,* usually attributed a greater influence to cultural and interpersonal factors.

Nerve deafness: Impairment in hearing as a result of damage to the cochlea of the auditory nerve.

Nervous system: The structures and organs that act as the communication system for the body and allow for behavior and mental processes.

Neuromodulator (NEW-roh-MOD-u-lay-tor): A chemical substance whose function is to increase or decrease the sensitivity of widely distributed neurons to the specific effects of neurotransmitters.

Neuron (NEW-ron): The basic unit of the nervous system. It is a single cell composed of *dendrites,* which receive neural signals; a *cell body,* which generates electrical signals; and an *axon,* which transmits neural signals.

Neuropsychology: The branch of psychology that focuses on the relationship between brain functioning and behavior.

Neurotransmitter (NEW-roh-TRANS-mitt-er): A chemical substance released from the synaptic vesicles that crosses the synaptic space and affects postsynaptic dendrites by binding itself to the postsynaptic dendrite.

Nondirective therapy: A form of therapy in which the client determines the direction of therapy while the therapist remains permissive, almost passive, and accepts totally the client's feelings and behavior.

Nonverbal communications: Information provided by cues or actions that involve movements of the body, especially the face, and sometimes the vocal chords.

Normal curve: A bell-shaped curve drawn as a frequency polygon which depicts the approximated expected distribution of scores when a sample is drawn from a large population. Generally, in a normal distribution the mean, mode, and median are equal and the distribution is symmetrical.

Normal distribution: A bell-shaped distribution of scores, usually obtained only for large sample populations, in which most scores tend to cluster around the mean, with a few scores occurring much higher and a few much lower.

Normal trichromat: An individual who experiences color vision the way most people do, and who requires only the three primary colors to see any color.

Norms: A list of the scores and corresponding percentile ranks or standard scores of the group on whom the test was standardized.

NREM sleep: Four distinct stages of sleep during which no rapid eye movements occur.

Nurture: An individual's experiences in his or her environment.

Obedience: The process by which a person takes orders from another person, or group of people, and complies with the orders; the person or persons influencing the individual usually are perceived to have higher status, and the individual feels obliged to comply.

Observational learning theory: The process by which organisms learn new responses by observing the behavior of a model and then imitating it; also called *social learning theory.*

Obsessive-compulsive disorder: A disorder characterized by persistent and uncontrollable thoughts and irrational beliefs that cause an individual to perform compulsive rituals that interfere with daily life.

Oedipus complex (ED-ih-pus): Occurring during the phallic stage, feelings of rivalry with the parent of the same sex for love of the parent of the opposite sex, ultimately resolved through identification with the parent of the same sex; the *Electra complex* is the term used specifically to refer to this process in women.

Olfaction (ole-FAK-shun): The sense of smell.

Operant conditioning: A conditioning procedure in which the probability that an organism will emit a response is increased or decreased by the subsequent delivery of a reinforcer or punisher; sometimes called *instrumental conditioning.*

Operational definition: A definition based on a set of concrete steps used to define a variable.

Opponent-process theory: The theory of Hering stating that color is coded by a series of receptors responding positively or negatively to different wavelengths of light.

Optic chiasm (k-EYE-asm): The point at which the optic nerve fibers from the nasal side of the eye cross over and project to the other side of the brain

Oral stage: Freud's first stage of personality development, from birth to about age two, during which infants obtain gratification primarily through the mouth.

Orgasm phase: The stage of the sexual response cycle in which autonomic nervous system activity reaches its peak and muscle contractions throughout the body occur in spasms. An *orgasm* is the peak of sexual activity. In men, muscles through the reproductive system help expel semen; in women, muscles surrounding the outer vagina contract.

Paralanguage: Vocal cues that occur along with spoken language that provide information in the processes of impression formation.

Paranoid type: One of five major subtypes of schizophrenia, characterized by delusions, hallucinations of persecution and/or grandeur, and sometimes irrational jealousy.

Paraprofessional: A person who works alongside professional psychologists and aids them in providing psychological services.

Parasympathetic nervous system: The part of the peripheral nervous system that controls processes of the body such as heart rate, digestive processes, and blood pressure; these are the maintenance functions of the body. Parasympathetic activity usually involves the buildup of energy stores and their maintenance.

Pathological use: Out-of-control episodes, such as extensive periods of substance abuse perhaps for days on end.

Pedophilia: A psychosexual disorder in which the preferred method of sexual stimulation and gratification consists of repetitive sexual activity with children.

Percentile score: A score indicating what percentage of the test population would obtain a lower score.

Perception: The complex process by which an organism interprets sensory input so that it acquires meaning.

Performance appraisal: The process by which a supervisor evaluates on a periodic basis the performance of a subordinate.

Peripheral nervous system: One of the two major parts of the nervous system. It carries information to and from the central nervous system through a network of spinal and cranial nerves. It has two functional subdivisions, the somatic and autonomic nervous systems.

Personal space: The area around an individual that is considered private; the invisible boundary around a person.

Personality: A set of relatively enduring behavioral responses and internal predispositions that characterize how a person reacts to the environment.

Personality disorder: Inflexible, long-standing, maladaptive behaviors in dealing with the environment that typically cause stress and social or occupational problems.

Phallic stage (FAL-ik): Freud's third stage of personality development, from ages three to seven, during which children obtain gratification primarily from the genitals. During this stage, children pass through the Oedipus (or Electra) complex.

Phenylketonuria (PKU) (fee-nil-key-tone-NEW-re-uh): A disorder that prevents an individual from metabolizing the amino acid phenylalanine. If not detected and treated shortly after birth, PKU usually results in mental retardation. The condition can be treated successfully by a diet low in phenylalanine (an animo acid present in milk).

Phobic disorder (FOE-bick): A disorder characterized by fear and subsequent attempted avoidance of specific objects or situations, acknowledged by the person as unreasonable.

Phonemes: The basic units of sound in a language.

Photoreceptors: The light-sensitive cells in the retina: rods and cones.

Placebo effect: A nonspecific therapeutic change that occurs as a result of a person's expectations of change rather than as a direct result of any specific treatment.

Placenta: A group of blood vessels and membranes connected to a fetus by the umbilical cord and serving as the mechanism for the exchange of nutrients and waste products.

Plateau phase: The stage of the sexual response cycle in which both men and women are preparing for orgasm; autonomic nervous system activity increases; there is further vasoconstriction; in women the vagina becomes engorged and at its full extension; in men, the penis is fully erect and turns a darker color.

Positive instance: A stimulus that is an example of the concept under study.

Positive reinforcement: Presentation of a rewarding or pleasant stimulus in order to increase the likelihood that a response will occur.

Post-traumatic stress disorder: A category of mental disorders evident after a person has undergone the stress of some type of disaster; common symptoms include vivid, intrusive recollections or reexperiences of the traumatic event and occasional lapses of normal consciousness.

Preconscious: Freud's second level of consciousness, which refers to mental activity of which a person can become aware by attending to it.

Prejudice: A negative evaluation of an entire group of people that is usually based on a set of negative (and often wrong) ideas about the group.

Premature ejaculation: The condition in which a man cannot delay ejaculation long enough to satisfy his sexual partner in one-half of their sexual encounters; ejaculation usually happens at, just before, or just following insertion of the penis.

Preoperational stage: Piaget's second major stage of intellectual development, lasting from about age two to age seven, when initial symbolic thought is developed.

Pressure: The emotional state or condition resulting from feelings or expectations for success, or specific behaviors or results; the feelings that result from coercion from others.

Prevalence: The percentage of the population displaying a disorder during any specified period.

Primary effect: The more accurate recall of items presented first in a list.

Primary erectile dysfunction: When a man has never been able to achieve or maintain an erection of sufficient strength for sexual intercourse.

Primary orgasmic dysfunction: The condition in which a woman has never achieved orgasm by any means at any time.

Primary punisher: Any stimulus or event that by its delivery or removal acts naturally (without learning) to decrease the likelihood that a response will recur.

Primary reinforcer: Any stimulus or event that by its mere delivery or removal acts naturally (without learning) to increase the likelihood that a response will recur.

Privacy: The process of limiting the access of other people by controlling the boundaries between them and oneself.

Proactive inhibition: The decrease in accurate recall of a target list as a result of previous events that interfere with the recall of target list.

Problem drinker: A person who shows alcohol-related problems, which include alcoholism.

Problem solving: The behavior of individuals when confronted with a situation or task that requires some insight to solve.

Procedural memory: Storage for the perceptual, motor, and cognitive skills to complete a task.

Procrastination: The behavior of putting off doing something that could and should be done in the present until a future time.

Projection: A defense mechanism by which people attribute to other people or objects their own undesirable traits.

Projective test: A variety of different devices or instruments used to assess personality in which an examinee is shown a standard set of ambiguous stimuli and asked to respond in an unrestricted manner.

Prosocial behavior: An act that benefits someone else and often has no obvious benefit to the person doing it; the act might even involve some personal risk or sacrifice.

Psychiatrist: A medical doctor who has completed a residency specializing in the study of behavior and the treatment of patients with emotional and physical disorders.

Psychic determinism: A psychoanalytic assumption that everything a person feels, thinks, and does has a purpose, and that all things in behavior are caused by past events.

Psychoactive drug: A drug that alters behavior, thought, or emotions; these drugs affect behavior by altering biochemical reactions in the nervous system.

Psychoanalysis (SIE-co-ah-NAL-ih-sis): A lengthy insight therapy developed by Freud that aims at uncovering conflicts and unconscious impulses through special techniques that include free association, dream analysis, and transference.

Psychoanalyst: A person (usually a psychiatrist) who has studied the technique of psychoanalysis and uses it in treating people with emotional problems.

Psychoanalytic approach (sie-co-an-ah-LIT-ik): The theory developed by Sigmund Freud (1856–1939), who was interested in how personality develops. Freud's approach focused on the unconscious and on how it directs day-to-day behavior.

Psychodrama: A group therapy procedure in which members act out their situations, feelings, and roles.

Psychodynamically based therapies: Therapies based loosely on the theories of Freud and his theory of psychoanalysis; using a part of the approach, some practitioners reject some elements of Freud's theory.

Psychogenic amnesia: A disorder characterized by the sudden inability, too extensive to be explained by ordinary forgetfulness, to recall important personal information.

Psycholinguistics: The study of how language is acquired, perceived, comprehended, and produced.

Psychological dependence: A compelling desire to use a drug along with an inability to inhibit that desire.

Psychologist: One who studies and uses behavioral principles in scientific research or in applied settings for the treatment of emotional problems.

Psychology: The science of behavior and mental processes.

Psychoneuroimmunology: The study of how psychological processes and the nervous system affect the body's natural defense system—the immune system—and how, in turn, the immune system influences psychological processes; often referred to as *PNI*.

Psychophysics: The study of the relationship between a physical stimulus and a person's conscious experience of the stimulus.

Psychostimulant: Drugs which in low to moderate doses increase alertness and reduce fatigue; considered mood elevators.

Psychotherapy: The treatment of emotional or behavioral problems through psychological techniques.

Psychotic (sigh-KOT-ik): Behavior and mental processes in which there is a gross impairment of reality testing that interferes with an individual's ability to meet the ordinary demands of life.

Puberty: The period during which the reproductive system matures; it occurs at (and signals) the end of childhood.

Punishment: The process of presentation of an undesirable or noxious stimulus, or removal of a positive desirable stimulus, in order to decrease the probability that a response will recur.

Questionnaire: A printed form with questions. Usually given to a large group of people, questionnaires are a means of gathering a substantial amount of data in a short time.

Range: A measure of variability that describes the spread of scores within a group, calculated by subtracting the lowest score from the highest score.

Rape: Forcible, sexual assault of an unwilling partner who is usually, but not always, a woman.

Rational-emotive therapy: A cognitive behavior therapy originated by Albert Ellis that emphasizes the importance of logical, rational thought processes.

Rationalization: A defense mechanism by which people reinterpret behavior in terms that render it acceptable.

Raw score: An examinee's unconverted score on a test (such as the number of correct answers).

Reaction formation: A defense mechanism by which people behave in a manner opposite to their true but anxiety-provoking feelings.

Reasoning: The process by which we evaluate and generate arguments and reach conclusions.

Recency effect: The more accurate recall of items presented at the end of a list.

Receptive field: One of many areas of the retina that, when stimulated, affects the firing of a single cell in the visual system.

Reflex: An involuntary, automatic behavior in response to stimuli that occurs without prior learning; such behaviors usually show little variability from instance to instance.

Refractory period: The recovery period of a neuron after it fires, during which time it cannot fire again. This period allows the neuron to reestablish electrical balance with its surroundings.

Rehearsal: Repetitive review through repeatedly verbalizing or thinking about information or previously learned information; the goal is to keep the information in memory.

Reinforcer: Any event that increases the probability of the reoccurrence of a response that precedes it.

Reliability: The ability of a test to yield the same score for the same individual through repeated testings.

REM sleep: A stage of sleep characterized by high-frequency, low-voltage brainwave activity, rapid and systematic eye movement, and dreams.

Representative sample: A sample of individuals who match the population with whom they are to be compared with regard to important variables such as socioeconomic status and age.

Repression: A defense mechanism by which people block anxiety-provoking feelings from conscious awareness and push them into the unconscious.

Residual type: A schizophrenic disorder characterized by inappropriate affect, illogical thinking, or eccentric behavior but with the patient generally in touch with reality.

Resistance: In psychoanalysis, an unwillingness to cooperate by which a patient signals his or her reluctance to provide the therapist with information or to help the therapist understand or interpret a situation.

Resolution phase: The stage of the sexual response cycle in which the body naturally returns to its resting or normal state; this takes one to several minutes and varies considerably from person to person.

Retention: The ability to retrieve learned information.

Retinal disparity: The slight difference in the visual image cast on each eye; a principal binocular cue.

Retrieval: The process of making available previously learned or experienced events.

Retroactive inhibition: The decrease in accurate recall of a target list as a result of subsequent presentation of material.

Retrograde amnesia: Loss of memory for events and experiences preceding the amnesia-causing event.

Role: A set of behaviors that are expected from a certain category of individuals; a person's roles may change depending on the group within which the person finds himself or herself.

Rooting: A reflex in which an infant turns its head toward a stimulus applied to its lips or cheeks.

Saccades: Rapid movements of the eyes from one point to another. The minimum fixation period between saccades is 0.25 second.

Sample: A group of subjects or participants who are generally representative of the population about which an inference is being made.

Saturation: The depth of hue of reflected light, as determined by the purity (homogeneity) of the wavelengths contained in the light.

Schema: A conceptual framework that organizes information and makes sense out of the world by laying out a general framework in which events can be coded.

Schizophrenic disorder: A group of disorders characterized by lack of reality testing and deterioration of social and intellectual functioning, beginning before age forty-five and lasting at least six months. Individuals with this diagnosis often show serious personality disintegration with significant changes in thought, mood, perception, and behavior.

Secondary erectile dysfunction: When a man fails to achieve an erection in 25 percent of his sexual attempts, he is considered to be suffering from secondary erectile dysfunction.

Secondary orgasmic dysfunction: A woman's inability to achieve orgasm, even though she has achieved orgasm in the past by one technique or another; sometimes called *situational orgasmic dysfunction*.

Secondary punisher: A neutral stimulus with no intrinsic value to the organism that acquires punishment value through repeated pairing with a punishing stimulus.

Secondary reinforcer: A neutral stimulus with no intrinsic value to the organism that acquires reinforcement value through repeated pairing with a reinforcing stimulus.

Secondary sex characteristics: The physical features of a person's gender identity that are not directly involved with reproduction, such as pubic hair.

Secondary traits: In Allport's theory, specific behaviors that occur only in response to specific situations.

Sedatives-hypnotics: A class of drugs that relax and calm people and in higher doses induce sleep.

Selective breeding: Controlled breeding to produce the expression of specific genetic traits.

Self: The main structural component of Rogers's theory of personality. A group of perceptions that characterize an individual and his or her relationship to other people and to other aspects of his or her life.

Self-actualization: The process of becoming everything that one might through the realization of human potential; the process of achieving everything that one is capable of achieving.

Self-efficacy (self-EFF-fik-ah-see): The belief that a person has about whether he or she can successfully engage in and execute a specific behavior.

Self-fulfilling prophecy: The finding that frequently things turn out just the way a person expects that they will. Researchers may unwittingly create situations that lead to specific (prophesied) results.

Self-monitoring: An assessment procedure in which a person systematically records the frequency and duration of specific behaviors in himself or herself.

Self-perception: Attitudes toward and beliefs about oneself, largely formed during childhood and adolescence and often a reflection of other people's perceived attitudes.

Self-perception theory: An approach to attitude formation by which people are assumed to infer their attitudes based on observations of their own behavior.

Self-serving bias: People's tendency to evaluate their own behavior as worthwhile, regardless of the situation.

Semantic memory: Memory for ideas, rules, and general concepts about the world; this storage mechanism contains the meaning of words and is not time or date specific.

Semantics: The study of the meaning of components of language.

Sensory-motor stage: The first of Piaget's four major stages of intellectual development, covering roughly the first two years of life. During this period the child begins to interact with the environment, and the rudiments of intelligence are established.

Separation anxiety: The fear response in children from eight to fifteen months, displayed when a parent is absent.

Sex roles: The full range of behaviors that are generally associated with one's gender; they help people establish who they are; also called *gender roles*.

Sex role stereotyping: The typical beliefs concerning the patterns of behavior that are expected of persons depending on their gender.

Sexual deviations: Sexual practices directed toward objects rather than people, sexual encounters involving real or simulated suffering or humiliation, or sexual activity with a nonconsenting partner.

Sexual dysfunction: The inability to obtain satisfaction from sexual behavior, often accompanied by the inability to experience orgasm; sexual inadequacy.

Sexual masochism: A psychosexual disorder in which an individual seeks physical or psychological pain, often including humiliation or being bound or beaten, to achieve sexual excitement.

Sexual sadism: A psychosexual disorder in which an individual inflicts physical or psychological pain on another person in order to achieve sexual excitement.

Shape constancy: The ability to recognize a shape despite changes in the orientation or angle from which it is viewed.

Shaping: The gradual training of an organism to give the proper responses by selectively reinforcing behaviors as they approach the desired response.

Short-term memory: The memory storage system and process that temporarily holds current or recently attended information for immediate or short-term use. The duration of short-term memory is about thirty seconds; its capacity is limited to from five to nine items.

Shyness: Extreme anxiety in individuals who are reticent and often overly concerned with how they look, sound, and appear to others; this anxiety leads to avoidance of social situations.

Significant difference: A statistically determined likelihood that a behavior has not occurred because of a chance alone. A result is said to be significant (trustworthy) if the probability of its occurrence by chance alone is less than 5 times out of 100, or less than 5 percent.

Simple phobia: A disorder characterized by irrational

and persistent fear of an object or situation along with a compelling desire to avoid it.

Situational orgasmic dysfunction: A woman's inability to achieve orgasm even though she has achieved orgasm in the past by one technique or another.

Size constancy: The ability of the perceptual system to know that an object remains constant in size regardless of its distance or the size of its image on the retina.

Skinner box: Named for its developer, B. F. Skinner, a box containing a responding mechanism (usually a lever) capable of delivering a reinforcer (often food or water) to an organism.

Sleep: A nonwaking state of consciousness characterized by general unresponsiveness to the environment and general physical immobility.

Social cognition: The process of making sense through the interpretation of events, people, ourselves, and the world in general: social cognition is a thought process.

Social comparison: The use of other people as a basis for comparing one's own judgments and abilities.

Social facilitation: The change in task performance that occurs when people are, or believe they are, in the presence of other people.

Social influence: The effort on the part of one or more people to alter the attitudes or behavior of others.

Social loafing: The decrease in productivity that occurs when an individual works in a group instead of alone.

Social motive: An internal condition that directs people toward establishing or maintaining relationships with other people and to establish feelings about themselves.

Social need: An aroused condition involving feelings about self, others, and relationships.

Social phobia: A disorder characterized by fear of, and desire to avoid, situations in which the person might be exposed to scrutiny by others and might behave in an embarrassing or humiliating way.

Social psychology: The study of how people influence and are influenced by the thoughts, feelings, and behaviors of other people; social psychologists focus on *individual behavior.*

Social support: The furnishing of a person with comfort, recognition, approval, and encouragement; social support can be provided by friends, family, organizations, and the workplace.

Socialization: The process by which individuals learn the rules of their society and establish and adopt their own values, attitudes, and long-lasting personal characteristics.

Sociobiology: The theory that asserts that even day-to-day behaviors are determined by the process of natural selection; the theory contends that social behaviors that contribute to the survival of our species are passed on through the genes from one generation to the next.

Somatic nervous system: The part of the peripheral nervous system that carries information to skeletal muscles and thus in turn affects bodily movement.

Somatization disorder: A disorder characterized by recurrent and multiple complaints of several years' duration for which medical attention is ineffective.

Somatoform disorder (so-MAT-oh-form): A disorder characterized by real physical symptoms not under voluntary control and for which no evident physical cause exists.

Sound: A psychological term describing changes in pressure through a medium; the medium may be gaseous, liquid, or solid.

Spinal cord: A portion of the central nervous system that is contained within the spinal column. It receives signals from the senses and relays them to the brain, and conveys signals from the brain to the muscles and glands.

Split-brain patients: Term applied to people whose cor-

pus callosum—which normally connects the two cerebral hemispheres—has been surgically severed.

Split-half: A method of assessing reliability by splitting a test into comparable halves and correlating the scores from each half.

Spontaneous recovery: The recurrence of a conditioned response following a rest period after extinction.

Standard deviation: A descriptive statistic that measures the variability of data from the mean of the sample.

Standard error of measurement: Based on statistical formulas, the number of points that a score may vary because of imperfect reliability.

Standard score: A score that expresses an individual's position relative to the mean based on the standard deviation; it is often derived by converting a raw score to one that can be interpreted on the basis of a population variable (such as age or grade).

Standardization: The process of developing a uniform procedure for the administration and scoring of a test, including the development of norms from a large, representative sample.

State-dependent learning: The tendency to recall information learned in a particular physiological state more accurately when one is again in that physiological state.

Statistical model: An approach that specifies behavior deviating from the average as abnormal.

Statistics: The branch of mathematics that deals with collecting, classifying, and analyzing data.

Stereotypes: Fixed, simple ideas, often about traits, attitudes, and behaviors, that are attributed to groups of people; usually these attributions are oversimplified and are often wrong.

Stimulus discrimination: The process by which an organism learns to respond only to a specific reinforced stimulus and to no other stimulus. The complementary process to stimulus generalization.

Stimulus generalization: The occurrence of a conditioned response to stimuli similar to, but not the same as, the training stimulus.

Storage: The process of maintaining information in memory for a period of time.

Stranger anxiety: The fear response in children from age eight to fifteen months, displayed in the presence of strangers.

Stress: A nonspecific, often global response by an organism to real or imagined demands made on it; a person has to appraise a situation as stressful for it to be stressful.

Stress inoculation: The procedure of giving people realistic warnings, recommendations, and reassurances to help them prepare and cope with impending dangers or losses.

Stressor: An environmental stimulus that affects an organism in ways that are either physically or psychologically injurious, usually producing anxiety, tension, and physiological arousal.

Striate cortex: The primary visual cortex to which projections are made in the visual system from the lateral geniculate nucleus.

Structuralism: A school of psychology whose ideas were initiated by Wilhelm Wundt (1832–1920) and put forth by E. B. Titchener; proponents believed that the proper subject matter of psychology was the study of the contents of consciousness. Structuralists developed and used the technique called introspection.

Subgoal analysis: A heuristic procedure in which a task is broken down into smaller, more manageable parts.

Subject: An individual who participates in an experiment and from whose behavior data are collected; sometimes called *participants.*

Sublimation: A defense mechanism by which people redirect socially unacceptable impulses into acceptable ones.

Subliminal perception: Perception of a stimulus that occurs below some level (of duration or luminance) with the result that subjects are unaware of the presentation 50 percent of the time; perception of a stimulus below the awareness threshold.

Substance abusers: People who overuse and rely on drugs to deal with their stress and anxiety.

Substance dependence: Evidence of substance abuse and withdrawal symptoms or tolerance.

Sucking: A reflex in which an infant makes sucking motions when presented with a stimulus to the lips, such as a nipple.

Superego: In Freud's theory, the moral branch of mental functioning.

Superior colliculus: A secondary part of the visual system that in human beings responds to movement; signals to it are generated from the lateral geniculate nucleus.

Superstitious behavior: Behavior learned through coincidental association with reinforcement.

Surface structure: The organization of a sentence that is closest to its written or spoken form.

Sympathetic nervous system: The part of the autonomic nervous system that responds to emergency situations. Active only occasionally, sympathetic activity calls up bodily resources as needed and thus is seen as a process involved only for major energy expenditures.

Symptom substitution: The appearance of one symptom to replace another that has been eliminated.

Synapse (SIN-apps): The small space between the axon terminals of one neuron and the receptive site (dendrite, cell body, or axon) of another neuron.

Syntax: The relation between groups of words, and how those words are arranged in phrases and sentences.

Systematic desensitization: A counterconditioning procedure in which a person first learns deep relaxation and then imagines a series of progressively fearful situations. With each successive experience, the person learns relaxation rather than fear as a new response to a formerly fearful stimulus.

Teratogen: A substance that can produce developmental malformations in a fetus; such substances are said to be *teratogenic* or to have *teratogenic effects.*

Territorial behavior: Behavior involved in establishing, maintaining, personalizing, and defending a delimited space.

Test-retest: A method of assessing reliability by administering a test to the same group of examinees on two different occasions and computing the similarity between the scores.

THC (tetrahydrocannabinol): The active ingredient in marijuana.

Thanatology (THAN-ah-TOL-oh-jee): The study of the psychological and medical aspects of death and dying; the study has become increasingly interdisciplinary.

Theory: A collection of interrelated ideas and known facts put forward to summarize, explain, and predict behavior and mental processes.

Time out: A punishment procedure in which a person is removed from a desired or reinforcing situation to decrease the likelihood that an undesired behavior will recur.

Token economy: An instrumental conditioning procedure in which tokens are given to the patient to reinforce socially acceptable behavior. The tokens are later exchanged for desirable items or privileges.

Tolerance: A progressive insensitivity to the effects of a specific drug and dosage when that drug is administered repeatedly.

Trait: Any readily identifiable stable behavior that characterizes the way that an individual differs from other individuals.

Transduction: The process by which a sensory system analyzes environmental stimuli and converts them into electrical impulses; also known as *coding.*

Transference: A psychoanalytic procedure in which a therapist becomes the object of a patient's emotional attitudes about an important person in his or her life, such as a parent.

Transformational grammar: Developed by Chomsky, an approach to the study of language that assumes that each surface structure of a sentence has associated with it a deep structure. This grammar includes transformational rules for generating surface structures from deep structures.

Transvestic fetishism: A psychosexual disorder characterized by recurrent and persistent cross-dressing to achieve sexual excitement.

Trichromatic theory (try-chrome-MAT-tick): Young and Helmholtz stated that all colors can be made by mixing three basic colors: red, blue, and green.

Type A behavior: Characterized by individuals who are competitive, impatient, hostile, and always striving to do more in less time.

Type B behavior: Characterized by people who are calmer, more patient, less hurried than Type A behavior individuals.

Types: Broad collections of traits that are tied together loosely and interrelated.

Unconditioned response: The unlearned or involuntary response to an unconditioned stimulus.

Unconditioned stimulus: A stimulus that normally produces an involuntary, measurable response.

Unconscious: Freud's third level of consciousness, which refers to mental activity beyond a person's normal awareness. This material can be made available through psychoanalysis.

Unconscious motivation: A psychoanalytic notion that desires, goals, and internal states, of which an individual is not aware, determine behavior.

Undifferentiated type: A schizophrenic disorder characterized by a mixture of symptoms.

Validity: The ability of a test to measure only what it is supposed to measure.

Variability: A measure of the extent to which scores differ from one another and especially the extent to which they differ from the mean.

Variable-interval: A reinforcer is delivered after a predetermined but varying interval of time, provided that the required response has occurred at least once after the interval.

Variable-ratio: A reinforcer is delivered after a predetermined but variable number of responses has occurred.

Variables: Conditions or characteristics of a situation (or experiment) that can change.

Vasoconstriction: In the sexual response cycle, an engorgement of the blood vessels, particularly in the genital area.

Vestibular sense (ves-TIB-you-lar): The sense of bodily orientation and postural adjustment.

Violence: Aggression in which a person seeks to inflict injury through physical force.

Visual acuity: The resolution capability of the visual system in a controlled setting.

Visual cortex: The first and most important layer of the occipital lobe that receives information from the lateral geniculate nucleus; also known as the *striate cortex.*

Voyeurism: A psychosexual disorder in which the preferred method of sexual gratification consists of repetitive observation of people in different states of undress or sexual activity.

Vulnerability: The extent to which people are easily impaired by an event, and thus respond maladaptively.
Vulnerable: Having diminished ability to deal with demanding life events.

Withdrawal symptoms: A variety of physical states that occur when a drug is no longer administered to a person who has developed a physiological dependence on it.
Working memory: A new and broader conception of short-term memory that focuses on the executive processing capacities of memory and uses the idea of memory as a "scratch pad," a holding place for information, while other information is being processed and directed for further processing.
Working through: The gradual, often repeated, slow process in therapy of interpretation, resistance to interpretation, and transference.

Zygote: A fertilized egg.

References

A. C. Nielsen Co. (1988). *1988 Nielsen report on television*. Northbrook, IL: Author.

Aarons, L. (1976). Sleep assisted instruction. *Psychological Bulletin, 83,* 1–40.

Abelson, R. P. (1988). Conviction. *American Psychologist, 43,* 267–276.

Abikoff, H. (1985). Efficacy of cognitive training interventions in hyperactive children: A critical review. *Clinical Psychology Review, 5,* 479–512.

Abramowitz, S. I., & Bell, N. W. (1985). Biofeedback, self-control and tension headache. *Journal of Psychosomatic Research, 29,* 95–99.

Abramson, L. Y., Metalsky, G. I., & Alloy, L. B. (1989). Hopelessness depression: A theory-based subtype of depression. *Psychological Review, 96,* 358–372.

Adelmann, P. K., Antonucci, T. C., Crohan, S. E., & Coleman, L. M. (1989). Empty nest, cohort, and employment in the well-being of mid-life women. *Sex Roles, 20,* 173–180.

Ader, R. (Ed.) (1981). *Psychoneuroimmunology.* New York: Academic Press.

Ader, R., Cohen, N., & Bovbjerg, D. (1982). Conditioned suppression of humoral immunity in the rat. *Journal of Comparative and Physiologial Psychology, 96,* 517–521.

Adler, A. (1969). *The science of living.* Garden City, NY: Anchor Books. (Original work published 1929.)

Adorno, T., Frenkel-Brunswick, E., Levinson, D., & Sanford, R. (1950). *The authoritarian personality.* New York: Harper & Row.

Agnew, H. W., Jr., & Webb, W. B. (1973). The influence of time course variable on REM sleep. *Bulletin of the Psychonomic Society, 2,* 131–133.

Agras, S., Sylvester, D., & Oliveau, D. (1969). The epidemiology of common fears and phobias. Unpublished manuscript, as cited in G. C. Davison & J. M. Neale (1978). *Abnormal psychology: An experimental clinical approach* (2nd ed.). New York: John Wiley & Sons.

Aiello, J. R., & Thompson, D. E. (1980). Personal space, crowding, and spatial behavior in a cultural context. In I. Altman, A. Rapoport, & J. F. Wohlwill (Eds.), *Human behavior and environment: Vol. 2. Advances in theory and research.* New York: Plenum Press.

Aiken, L. R. (1979). *Psychological testing and assessment* (3rd ed.). Boston: Allyn and Bacon.

Aiken, L. R. (1985). *Dying, death, and bereavement.* Boston: Allyn and Bacon.

Aiken, L. R. (1988). *Psychological testing and assessment* (6th ed). Boston: Allyn and Bacon.

Ainsworth, M. D. S. (1979). Infant-mother attachment. *American Psychologist, 34,* 932–937.

Ajzen, I., & Fishbein, M. (1977). Attitude-behavior relations: A theoretical analysis and review of empirical research. *Psychological Bulletin, 84,* 888–918.

Akiskal, H. S. (1979). The biobehavioral approach to depression. In R. A. DePue (Ed.), *Psychobiology of the depressive disorders.* New York: Academic Press.

Albert, I. B. (1975). REM sleep deprivation. *Biological Psychiatry, 19,* 341–351.

Alder, E. M., & Cox, J. L. (1983). Breast feeding and post-natal depression. *Journal of Psychosomatic Research, 27,* 139–144.

Aldwin, C. M., Levenson, M. R., Spiro, A., III, & Bosse, R. (1989). Does emotionality predict stress? Findings from the normative aging study. *Journal of Personality and Social Psychology, 56,* 618–624.

Alfaro, J. D. (1981). Report on the relationship between child abuse and neglect and later socially deviant behavior. In R. J. Hunner & Y. E. Walker (Eds.), *Exploring the relationship between child abuse and delinquency.* Montclair, NJ: Allanheld, Osmun.

Alheid, G. F., McDermott, L. J., Kelly, J., Halaris, A., & Grossman, S. P. (1977). Deficits in food and water intake after knife cuts that deplete striatal DA or hypothalamic NE in rats. *Pharmacological Biochemistry of Behavior, 6,* 273–287.

Alkon, D. L. (1989). Memory storage and neural systems. *Scientific American,* July, 42–50.

Allen, B. P. (1987). Youth suicide, *Adolescence, Vol. XXII,* 271–290.

Allen, G. L. (1981). A developmental perspective on the effects of "subdividing" macrospatial experience. *Journal of Experimental Psychology: Human Learning and Memory, 7,* 120–132.

Allen, G. L. (1987). Cognitive influences on the acquisition of route knowledge in children and adults. In Paul Ellen and Catherine Thinus-Blanc (Eds.), *Cognitive processes and spatial orientation in animal and man, Vol. II, Neurophysiology and developmental aspects.* Boston: Martinus Nijhoff.

Allen, K. E., Turner, K. D., & Everett, P. M. (1970). A behavior modification classroom for Head Start children with problem behaviors. *Exceptional Children, 37,* 119–127.

Allen, M. (1983). Models of hemispheric specialization. *Psychological Bulletin, 93,* 73–104.

Allgood-Merten, B., Lewinsohn, P. M., & Hops, H. (1990). Sex differences and adolescent depression. *Journal of Abnormal Psychology, 99,* 55–63.

Allington, R. L. (1981). Sensitivity to orthographic structure in educable mentally retarded children. *Contemporary Educational Psychology, 6,* 135–139.

Allison, P. D., & Furstenberg, F. F., Jr. (1989). How marital dissolution affects children: Variations by age and sex. *Developmental Psychology, 25,* 540–549.

Allport, G. W. (1937). *Personality: A psychological interpretation.* New York: Holt.

Allport, G. W. (1967). Gordon W. Allport. In E. Boring & G. Lindzey (Eds.), *A history of psychology in autobiography* (Vol. 5). New York: Appleton-Century-Crofts.

Altman, I. (1975). *The environment and social behavior.* Monterey, CA: Brooks/Cole.

Altman, I. (1987). Centripetal and centrifugal trends in psychology. *American Psychologist, 42,* 1058–1069.

Altman, I. & Vinsel, A. M. (1977). Personal space: An analysis of E. T. Hall's proxemics framework. In I. Altman, A. Rapoport, & J. F. Wohlwill (Eds.), *Human behavior and environment: Vol. 2. Advances in theory and research.* New York: Plenum Press.

American Heart Association (1984). *Exercise and your heart.* Dallas, TX: American Heart Association.

American Psychiatric Association (1987). *Diagnostic and statistical manual of mental disorders, revised or DSM-III-R.* Washington, DC.

American Psychological Association (1985). *Violence on TV. A social issue release from the Board of Social and Ethical Responsibility for Psychology.* Washington, DC: Author.

American Psychological Association (1989). Pediatric AIDS and human immunodeficiency virus infection: Psychological issues. *American Psychologist, 44*(2), 258–264.

Ames, L. D., Gillespie, C., Haines, J., & Ilg, F. L. (1979). *The Gesell Institute's child from one to six.* New York: Harper & Row.

Anderson, C. A. (1989). Temperature and aggression: Ubiquitous effects of heat on occurrence of human violence. *Psychological Bulletin, 106,* 74–96.

Anderson, K. J. (1990). Arousal and the Inverted-U hypothesis: A critique of Neiss's "reconceptualizing arousal." *Psychological Bulletin, 107,* 96–100.

Anderson, N. B. (1989). Racial differences in stress-induced cardiovascular reactivity and hypertension: Current status and substantive issues. *Psychological Bulletin, 105,* 89–105.

Anderson, R., Manoogian, S., & Reznick, J. (1976). Undermining and enhancing of intrinsic motivation in pre-school children. *Journal of Personality and Social Psychology, 34,* 915–922.

Andrews, J. D. W. (1989). Integrating visions of reality: Interpersonal diagnosis and the existential vision. *American Psychologist, 44,* 803–817.

Aneshensel, C. S., & Stone, J. D. (1982). Stress and depression: A test of the buffering model of social support. *Archives of General Psychiatry, 39,* 1392–1396.

Angoff, W. H. (1988). The nature-nurture debate, aptitudes, and group differences. *American Psychologist, 43,* 713–720.

Antonovsky, A. (1987). Health promoting factors at work: The sense of coherence. In R. Kalimo, M. A. El-Batawi, & C. L. Cooper (Eds.), *Psychological factors at work and their relation to health.* Geneva: World Health Organization.

Aoki, C., & Siekevitz, P. (1988). Plasticity in brain development. *Scientific American, 12,* 56–64.

Appel, J. B., & Peterson, N. J. (1965). What's wrong with punishment? *Journal of Criminal Law, Criminology, and Police Science, 156,* 450–453.

Arbuthnot, J., & Gordon, D. A. (1986). Behavioral and cognitive effects of a moral reasoning development intervention for high-risk behavior-disordered adolescents. *Journal of Consulting and Clinical Psychology, 54,* 208–216.

Arenberg, D. (1974). A longitudinal study of problem solving in adults. *Journal of Gerontology, 29,* 650–658.

Argyle, M. (1972). Nonverbal communication in human social interaction. In R. Hinte (Ed.), *Nonverbal communication.* New York: Cambridge University Press.

Aries, E. J., & Johnson, F. L. (1983). Close friendship in adulthood conversational content between same-sex friends. *Sex Roles, 9,* 1183–1196.

Arieti, S. (1980). Psychotherapy of schizophrenia: New and revised procedures. *American Journal of Psychotherapy, 34,* 464–476.

Aronson, E. (1980). *The social animal* (3rd ed.). New York: W. H. Freeman.

Aronson, M. K., Levin, G., & Lipkowitz, R. (1984). A community-based family/patient group program for Alzheimer's disease. *The Gerontologist, 24,* 339–342.

Asaad, G., & Shapiro, B. (1986). Hallucinations: Theoretical and clinical overview. *American Journal of Psychiatry, 143,* 1088–1097.

Asch, S. E. (1951). Effects of group pressure upon the modification and distortion of judgments. In J. Guetzkow (Ed.), *Groups, leadership, and men.* Pittsburgh: Carnegie Press.

Asch, S. E. (1955). Opinions and social pressure. *Scientific American, 193*(18), 31–35.

Asendorpf, J. B. (1989). Shyness as a final common pathway for two different kinds of inhibition. *Journal of Personality and Social Psychology, 57,* 481–492.

Ashcraft, M. H. (1989). *Human memory and cognition.* Glenview, IL: Scott, Foresman and Company.

Aslin, R. N., & Jackson, R. W. (1979). Accommodative-convergence in young infants: Development of a synergistic sensory-motor system. *Canadian Journal of Psychology, 33,* 222–231.

Attie, I., & Brooks-Gunn, J. (1989). Development of eating problems in adolescent girls: A longitudinal study. *Developmental Psychology, 25,* 70–79.

Auerbach, S. M., & Kilmann, P. R. (1977). Crisis intervention: A review of outcome research. *Psychological Bulletin, 84,* 1189–1217.

Aukett, R., Ritchie, J., & Mill, K. (1988). Gender differences in friendship patterns. *Sex Roles, 19,* 57–63.

Ayllon, T., & Azrin, N. H. (1965). The measurement and reinforcement behavior of psychotics. *Journal of the Experimental Analysis of Behavior, 8,* 357–383.

Ayllon, T., & Haughton, E. (1964). Modification of symptomatic verbal behavior of mental patients. *Behavior Research and Therapy, 2,* 87–97.

Azrin, N. H., & Holtz, W. C. (1966). Punishment. In Werner K. Honig (Ed.), *Operant behavior: Areas of research and application.* New York: Appleton-Century-Crofts.

Babson, S. G., Pernoll, M. L., Benda, G. I., & Simpson, K. (1980). *Diagnosis and management of the fetus and neonate at risk* (4th ed.). St. Louis: Mosby.

Backer, T. E., & Richardson, D. (1989). Building bridges: Psychologists and families of the mentally ill. *American Psychologist, 44,* 546–550.

Baddeley, A. D. (1976). *The psychology of memory.* New York: Basic Books.

Baddeley, A. D., & Hitch, G. (1974). Working memory. In G. Bower (Ed.), *Recent advances in learning and motivating* (Vol. 8). New York: Academic Press.

Baddeley, A. D., & Longman, D. J. A. (1966). The influence of length and frequency of training session on rate of learning to type. (Unpublished manuscript. Medical Research Council Applied Psychology Unit, Cambridge.) In A. D. Baddeley (Ed.), *The psychology of memory.* New York: Basic Books.

Baddeley, A. D., & Warrington, E. K. (1970). Amnesia and the distinction between long- and short-term memory. *Journal of Verbal Learning and Verbal Behavior, 9,* 176–189.

Baillargeon, R. (1987). Object permanence in 3½- and 4½-month-old infants. *Developmenal Psychology, 5,* 655–664.

Balajthy, E. (1988). Computers and instruction: Implications of the rising tide of criticism for reading education. *Reading Research and Instruction, 28* (1), 49–59.

Balay, J., & Shevrin, H. (1988). The subliminal psychodynamic activation method. *American Psychologist, 3,* 161–174.

Balch, P., & Ross, A. W. (1975). Predicting success in weight reduction

as a function of locus of control: A uni-dimensional and multi-dimensional approach. *Journal of Consulting and Clinical Psychology, 43,* 119.

Balick, L., Elfner, L., May, J. (1982). Biofeedback treatment of dysmenorrhea. *Biofeedback and Self-Regulation, 7,* 499–520.

Balota, D. A. (1983). Automatic semantic activation and episodic memory encoding. *Journal of Verbal Learning and Verbal Behavior, 22,* 88–104.

Balsahm, P. D., & Bondy, A. S. (1983). The negative side effects of reward. *Journal of Applied Behavior Analysis, 16,* 283–296.

Baltes, P. B., Reese, H. W., & Lipsitt, L. P. (1980). Life-span developmental psychology. *Annual Review of Psychology, 31,* 65–110.

Banaji, M. R., & Crowder, R. G. (1989). The bankruptcy of everyday memory. *American Psychologist, 44,* 1185–1193.

Band, E. B., & Weisz, J. R. (1988). How to feel better when it feels bad: Children's perspectives on coping with everyday stress. *Developmental Psychology, 24,* 247–253.

Bandura, A. (1969). *Principles of behavior modification.* New York: Holt, Rinehart & Winston.

Bandura, A. (1971). Analysis of modeling processes. In A. Bandura (Ed.), *Psychological modeling—conflicting theories.* Chicago: Aldine-Atherton.

Bandura, A. (1977a). Self-efficacy: Toward a unifying theory of behavioral change. *Psychological Review, 84,* 191–215.

Bandura, A. (1977b). *Social learning theory.* Englewood Cliffs, NJ: Prentice-Hall.

Bandura, A. (1982a). Self-efficacy: Mechanism in human agency. *American Psychologist, 37,* 122–147.

Bandura, A. (1982b). The psychology of chance encounters and life paths. *American Psychologist, 37,* 747–755.

Bandura, A. (1988). Self-regulation of motivation and action through goal systems. In V. Hamilton, G. H. Bower, & N. H. Frijda (Eds.), *Cognitive perspectives on emotion and motivation* (pp. 37–61). Dordrecht, Netherlands: Kluwer Academic Publishers.

Bandura, A. (1989). Human agency in social cognitive theory. *American Psychologist, 44,* 1175–1184.

Bandura, A., Blanchard, E. B., & Ritter, B. (1969). Relative efficacy of desensitization and modeling approaches for inducing behavioral, affective, and attitudinal changes. *Journal of Personality and Social Psychology, 13,* 173–199.

Bandura, A., Cioffi, D., Taylor, B., & Brouillard, M. E. (1988). Perceived self-efficacy in coping with cognitive stressors and opioid activation. *Journal of Personality and Social Psychology, 55*(3), 479–488.

Bandura, A., & Menlove, F. L. (1968). Factors determining vicarious extinction of avoidance through symbolic modeling. *Journal of Personality and Social Psychology, 8,* 99–108.

Bandura, A., Ross, D., & Ross, S. A. (1963). Imitation of film-mediated aggressive models. *Journal of Abnormal and Social Psychology, 66,* 3–11.

Bandura, A., & Walters, R. (1963). *Social learning and personality development.* New York: Holt, Rinehart & Winston.

Bandura, A., & Wood, R. (1989). Effect of perceived controllability and performance standards on self-regulation of complex decision making. *Journal of Personality and Social Psychology, 56,* 805–814.

Barber, J. G., Bradshaw, R., & Walsh, C. (1989). Reducing alcohol consumption through television advertising. *Journal of Consulting and Clinical Psychology, 57,* 613–618.

Barber, T. X., & Calverley, D. S. (1965). Toward a theory of hypnotic behavior: Effects on suggestibility of defining the situation as hypnosis and defining response in suggestions, it's easy. *Journal of Abnormal and Social Psychology, 29,* 98–107.

Barber, T. X., Spanos, N. P., & Chaves, J. F. (1974). *Hypnosis, imagination, and human potentialities.* New York: Pergamon Press.

Barclay, C. R., & Wellman, H. M. (1986). Accuracies and inaccuracies in autobiographical memories. *Journal of Memory and Language, 25,* 93–103.

Bard, P. (1934). Emotion: 1. The neuro-humoral basis of emotional reactions. In C. Murchison (Ed.), *Handbook of general experimental psychology.* Worcester, MA: Clark University Press.

Bardon, J. I. (1982). The role and function of the school psychologist. In A. Reynolds & T. B. Gutkin (Eds.), *The handbook of school psychology.* New York: John Wiley & Sons.

Bardon, J. I. (1983). Psychology applied to education: A specialty in search of an identity. *American Psychologist, 38,* 185–196.

Barnes, D. M. (1988). Drugs: Running the numbers. *Science, 240,* 1729–1731.

Baron, P., & Joly, E. (1988). Sex differences in the expression of depression in adolescents. *Sex Roles, 18,* 1–7.

Baron, R. A. (1987). Interviewer's moods and reactions to job applicants: The influence of affective states on applied social judgments. *Journal of Applied Social Psychology, 17,* 911–926.

Baron, R. A., & Byrne, D. (1987). *Social psychology: Understanding human interaction* (5th ed.). Boston: Allyn and Bacon.

Barrios, B. A. (1988). On the changing nature of behavioral assessment.

In A. S. Bellack & M. Hersen (Eds.). *Behavioral assessment.* New York: Pergamon Press.

Bartlett, F. (1932). *Remembering: A study in experimental and social psychology.* Cambridge, England: Cambridge University Press.

Baruch, G. K., Biener, L., & Barnett, R. C. (1987). Women and gender in research on work and family stress. *American Psychologist, 42,* 130–136.

Bateson, P. (1990). Obituaries: Konrad Lorenz (1903–1989). *American Psychologist, 45,* 65–66.

Batson, C. D. (1990). How social an animal? *American Psychologist, 45,* 336–346.

Bauer, R. H. (1977). Memory processes in children with learning disabilities: Evidence for deficient rehearsal. *Journal of Experimental Child Psychology, 24,* 415–430.

Bauer, R. H. (1979). Memory, acquisition, and category clustering in learning-disabled children. *Journal of Experimental Child Psychology, 27,* 365–383.

Baum, A. (1987). Crowding. In D. Stokols & I. Altman (Eds.). *Handbook of environmental psychology.* New York: John Wiley & Sons.

Baumeister, R. F. (1990). Suicide as escape from self. *Psychological Review, 97,* 90–113.

Baumeister, R. F., & Tice, D. M. (1985). Self-esteem and responses to success and failure: Subsequent performance and intrinsic motivation. *Journal of Personality, 53,* 450–467.

Bayley, N. (1949). Consistency and variability in the growth of intelligence from birth to eighteen years. *Journal of Genetic Psychology, 25,* 165–196.

Beach, F. A. (1983). Hormones and psychological processes (Daniel Berlyne Memorial Lecture). *Canadian Journal of Psychology, 37,* 193–210.

Beck, A. T. (1963). Thinking and depression: 1. Idiosyncratic content in cognitive distortions. *Archives of General Psychiatry, 9,* 324–333.

Beck, A. T. (1967). *Depression: Clinical, experimental, and the theoretical aspects.* New York: Hober.

Beck, A. T. (1972). *Depression: Causes and treatment.* Philadelphia: University of Pennsylvania Press.

Beck, A. T. (1976). *Cognitive therapy and emotional disorders.* New York: International Universities Press.

Beck, A. T., & Weishaar, M. (1989). Cognitive therapy. In A. Freeman, K. M. Simon, L. E. Beutler, & H. Arkowitz (Eds.), *Comprehensive handbook of cognitive therapy.* New York: Plenum Press.

Beck, J. (1966). Effects of orientation and of shape similarity on perceptual grouping. *Perception and Psychophysics, 1,* 300–302.

Becvar, D. S., & Becvar, R. J. (1988). *Family therapy: A systemic integration.* Boston: Allyn and Bacon.

Bednar, R. L., Burlingame, G. M., & Masters, K. S. (1988). Systems of family treatment: Substance or semantics? *Annual Review of Psychology, 39,* 401–434.

Bee, H. L. (1987). *The journey of adulthood.* New York: Macmillan.

Beeber, A. R., & Pies, R. W. (1983). The nonmelancholic depressive syndromes: An alternative approach to classification. *Journal of Nervous and Mental Disease, 171,* 3–9.

Beech, H. R. (1987). The use of behavioural therapy in somatic stress reactions. In R. Kalimo, M. A. El-Batawi, & C. L. Cooper (Eds.), *Psychological factors at work and their relation to health.* Geneva: World Health Organization.

Beech, H. R., Burns, L. E., & Sheffield, B. F. (1982). *A behavioral approach to the management of stress: A practical guide to techniques.* New York: John Wiley & Sons.

Behar, D., Rapoport, J. L., Adams, A. J., Berg, C. J., & Cornblath, M. (1984). Sugar challenge testing with children considered behaviorally "sugar reactive." *Nutrition and Behavior, 1,* 277–288.

Bekerian, D. A., & Bowers, J. M. (1983). Eyewitness testimony: Were we misled? *Journal of Experimental Psychology: Learning, Memory, and Cognition, 9,* 139–145.

Bell, B. E., & Loftus, E. F. (1989). Trivial persuasion in the courtroom: The power of (a few) minor details. *Journal of Personality and Social Psychology, 56,* 669–679.

Bellak, L. (1983). Psychoanalysis in the 1980s. *American Journal of Psychotherapy, 37,* 476–482.

Belle, D. (1982). The stress of caring: Women as providers of social support. In L. Goldberger & S. Breznitz (Eds.), *Handbook of stress: Theoretical and clinical aspects.* New York: Free Press.

Belli, R. B. (1989). Influences of misleading postevent information: Misinformation interference and acceptance. *Journal of Experimental Psychology: General, 118,* 72–83.

Belmont, L., & Marolla, F. A. (1973). Birth order, family size, and intelligence. *Science, 182,* 1096–1101.

Belsky, J., & Rovine, M. J. (1988). Nonmaternal care in the first year of life and the security of infant-parent attachment. *Child Development, 59,* 157–167.

Belsky, J., & Steinberg, L. D. (1978). The effects of day care: A critical review. *Child Development, 49,* 929–949.

Bem, D. J. (1972). Self-perception theory. In L. Berkowitz (Ed.), *Advances in experimental social psychology.* New York: Academic Press.

Bem, S. L. (1975). Sex-role adaptability: One consequence of psychological androgyny. *Journal of Personality and Social Psychology, 31,* 634–643.

Bem, S. L. (1985). Androgyny and gender schema theory: A conceptual and empirical integration. In T. B. Sonderegger (Ed.), *Nebraska symposium on motivation.* Lincoln, NE: University of Nebraska Press.

Benassi, M. A. (1982). Effects of order of presentation, primacy, and attractiveness on attributions of ability. *Journal of Personality and Social Psychology, 43,* 48–58.

Benawra, R., Mangurten, H. H., & Duffell, D. R. (1980). Cyclopia and other anomalies following maternal ingestion of salicylates. *Journal of Pediatrics, 96,* 1069–1071.

Benbow, C. P., & Stanley, J. C. (1983). Sex differences in mathematical reasoning ability: More facts. *Science, 222,* 1029–1031.

Benjamin, L. T., Jr. (1988). A history of teaching machines. *American Psychologist, 43,* 703–712.

Bennett, W. J. (Secretary). (1986). *What works. Schools without drugs.* Washington, DC: United States Department of Education.

Benson, K., & Feinberg, I. (1977). The beneficial effect of sleep in a Jenkins and Dallenbach paradigm. *Psychophysiology, 14,* 375–384.

Bentall, R. P. (1990). The illusion of reality: A review and integration of psychological research on hallucination. *Psychological Bulletin, 107,* 82–95.

Berbaum, M. L., Moreland, R. L., and Zajonc, R. B. (1986). Contentions over the confluence model: A reply to Price, Walsh, and Vilburg. *Psychological Bulletin, 100,* 270–274.

Berg, M. (1986). Toward a diagnostic alliance between psychiatrist and psychologist. *American Psychologist, 41,* 52–59.

Berkowitz, A., & Perkins, H. W. (1988). Personality characteristics of children of alcoholics. *Journal of Consulting and Clinical Psychology, 56,* 206–209.

Berkowitz, L. (1964). The effects of observing violence. *Scientific American, 2,* 210. San Francisco: W. H. Freeman.

Berkowitz, L. (1989). Frustration-aggression hypothesis: Examination and reformulation. *Psychological Bulletin, 106,* 59–73.

Berkowitz, L. (1990). On the formation and regulation of anger and aggression. *American Psychologist, 45,* 494–503.

Berkowitz, L., & Donnerstein, E. (1982). External validity is more than skin deep: Some answers to criticisms of laboratory experiments. *American Psychologist, 37,* 245–257.

Berlin, B., & Kay, P. (1969). *Basic color terms: Their universality and evolution.* Berkeley: University of California Press.

Berman, J. S., Miller, R. C., & Massman, P. J. (1985). Cognitive therapy versus systematic desensitization: Is one treatment superior? *Psychological Bulletin, 97,* 451–461.

Bernal, G., & Berger, S. M. (1976). Vicarious eyelid conditioning. *Journal of Personality and Social Psychology, 34,* 62–68.

Bernard, M. E., & Joyce, M. R. (1984). *Rational-emotive therapy with children and adolescents: Theory, treatment, strategies, preventative methods.* New York: John Wiley & Sons.

Bernstein, D., & Ebbesen, E. (1978). Reinforcement and substitution in humans: A multiple-response analysis. *Journal of the Experimental Analysis of Behavior, 30,* 243–253.

Bernstein, I. L. (1988). *What does learning have to do with weight loss and cancer?* Paper presented at a Science and Public Policy Seminar sponsored by the Federation of Behavioral, Psychological and Cognitive Sciences, September 9, 1988, Washington, DC.

Berry, D. S., & McArthur, L. Z. (1986). Perceiving character in faces: The impact of age-related craniofacial changes on social perception. *Psychological Bulletin, 100,* 3–18.

Berscheid, E., Snyder, M., & Omoto, A. M. (1989). The relationship closeness inventory: Assessing the closeness of interpersonal relationships. *Journal of Personality and Social Psychology, 57,* 792–807.

Bertelson, A. D., Marks, P. A., & May, G. D. (1982). MMPI and race: A controlled study. *Journal of Consulting and Clinical Psychology, 50,* 316–318.

Best, C. T., & Queen, H. F. (1989). Baby, it's in your smile: Right hemiface bias in infant emotional expressions. *Developmental Psychology, 25,* 264–276.

Bethell-Fox, C. E., & Shepard, R. N. (1988). Mental rotation: Effects of stimulus complexity and familiarity. *Journal of Experimental Psychology: Human Perception and Performance, 14,* 12–23.

Bettelheim, B. (1969). Laurie. *Psychology Today, 2* (12), 24–25, 60.

Bexton, W. H., Heron, W., & Scott, T. H. (1954). Effects of decreased variation in the sensory environment. *Canadian Journal of Psychology, 8,* 70–76.

Bickman, L., Teger, A., Gabriele, T., McLaughlin, C., Berger, M., & Sunaday, E. (1973). Dormitory density and helping behavior. *Environment & Behavior, 5,* 465–466.

Bierman, D., & Winter, O. (1989). Learning during sleep: An indirect test of the erasure-theory of dreaming. *Perceptual and Motor Skills, 69,* 139–144.

Bigham, J. (1894). Memory: Studies from Harvard (II). *Psychological Review, 1,* 453–461.

Binet, A., & Simon, T. (1905). Methodes nouvelles pour le diagnostic de niveau intellectual des anororaux. *L'Annee Psychologique, 11,* 191–244.

Binet, A., & Simon, T. (1905). In E. S. Kite (Trans.), The development of intelligence in children. Baltimore: Williams & Wilkins Co. (Original work published in *L'Annee Psychologique,* 1905, 11, pp. 191–244.)

Birch, H. G., & Rabinowitz, H. S. (1951). The negative effect of previous experience on productive thinking. *Journal of Experimental Psychology, 41,* 121–125.

Birch, J. W. (1974). *Mainstreaming.* Reston, VA: Council for Exceptional Children.

Bishop, J. E. (1986). Technology: Researchers track pain's path, develop new kind of reliever. *The Wall Street Journal,* p. 23.

Bjorklund, A., Dunnett, S. B., Lewis, M. E., & Iversen, S. D. (1980). Reinnervation of the denervated striatum by substantia nigra transplants: Functional consequences as revealed by pharmacological and sensorimotor testing. *Brain Research, 199,* 307–333.

Blakemore, C., & Cooper, G. F. (1970). Development of the brain depends on the visual environment. *Nature, 228,* 477–478.

Blasi, A. (1980). Bridging moral cognition and moral action: A critical review of the literature. *Psychological Bulletin, 88,* 1–45.

Bloom, F. E. (1981). Neuropeptides. *Scientific American, 10,* 148–168.

Bloom, F. E., Lazerson, A., & Hofstadter, L. (1985). *Brain, mind, and behavior.* New York: W. H. Freeman.

Bloomquist, M. L., & Harris, W. G. (1984). Measuring family functioning with the MMPI: A reliability and concurrent validity study of three MMPI family scales. *Journal of Clinical Psychology, 40,* 1209–1214.

Blum, K. (1984). *Handbook of abusable drugs.* New York: Gardner Press.

Blumenthal, M. D. (1975). Measuring depressive symptomatology in a general population. *Archives of General Psychiatry, 32,* 971–978.

Bohannon, J. N., III. (1988). Flashbulb memories for the space shuttle disaster: A tale of two theories. *Cognition, 29,* 179–196.

Boldizar, J. P., Wilson, K. L., & Deemer, D. K. (1989). Gender, life experiences, and moral judgment development: A process-oriented approach. *Journal of Personality and Social Psychology, 57,* 229–238.

Bond, C. F., Jr., & Titus, L. J. (1983). Social facilitation: A meta-analysis of 241 studies. *Psychological Bulletin, 94,* 265–292.

Bonnet, M. H. (1980). Sleep, performance, and mood after the energy-expenditure equivalent of 40 hours of sleep deprivation. *Psychophysiology, 17,* 56–63.

Booth, A., & Edwards, J. N. (1980). Fathers: The invisible parent. *Sex Roles, 6,* 445–456.

Borg, E., & Counter, S. A. (1989). The middle-ear muscles. *Scientific American, 9,* 74–80.

Borkovec, T. D. (1982). Insomnia. *Journal of Consulting and Clinical Psychology, 5,* 880–895.

Borkowski, J. G., & Krause, A. (1983). Racial differences in intelligence: The importance of the executive system. *Intelligence, 7,* 379–395.

Bornstein, M. H. (1989). Sensitive periods in development: Structural characteristics and causal interpretations. *Psychological Bulletin, 105,* 179–197.

Bornstein, R. F. (1989). Exposure and affect: Overview and meta-analysis of research, 1968–1987. *Psychological Bulletin, 106,* 265–289.

Botwinick, J. (1984). *Aging and behavior: A comprehensive integration of research findings* (3rd ed.). New York: Springer.

Bouchard, T. J., Jr., & McGue, M. (1981). Familial studies of intelligence: A review. *Science, 212,* 1055–1058.

Bourque, L. B. (1989). *Defining rape.* Durham, NC: Duke University Press.

Boutin, G. E. (1978). Treatment of test anxiety by rational stage directed hypnotherapy: A case study. *American Journal of Clinical Hypnosis, 21,* 52–57.

Bouton, M. E., & King, D. A. (1983). Contextual control of the extinction of conditioned fear: Tests for the associative value of context. *Journal of Experimental Psychology: Animal Behavior Processes, 9,* 248–265.

Bower, G. H. (1981). Mood and memory. *American Psychologist, 36,* 126–148.

Bower, T. G. R. (1966). The visual world of infants. *Scientific American, 215,* 80–92.

Bowers, K. S. (1979). Time distortion and hypnotic ability: Underestimating the duration of hypnosis. *Journal of Abnormal Psychology, 88,* 435–439.

Bowers, M. B., Jr. (1982). Biochemical processes in schizophrenia: An update. *Schizophrenia Bulletin, 6,* 393–403.

Bowlby, J. (1977). The making and breaking of affectional bonds: Etiology and psychopathology in the light of attachment theory. *British Journal of Psychiatry, 130,* 201–210.

Boynton, R. M. (1988). Color vision. In M. R. Rosenzweig and L. W.

Porter (Eds.), *Annual review of psychology,* Vol. 39. Palo Alto, CA: Annual Reviews, Inc.

Boysen, S. T., & Berntson, G. G. (1989). Numerical competence in a chimpanzee (Pan troglodytes). *Journal of Comparative Psychology, 103,* 23–31.

Brabender, V., & Dickhaus, R. C. (1978). Effect of hypnosis on comprehension of complex verbal material. *Perceptual and Motor Skills, 47,* 1322.

Brackbill, Y. (1979). Obstetrical medication and infant behavior. In J. D. Osofsky (Ed.), *Handbook of infant development.* New York: John Wiley & Sons.

Brackbill, Y., & Nichols, P. L. (1982). A test of the confluence model of intellectual development. *Developmental Psychology, 18,* 192–198.

Branden, N. (1980). *The psychology of romantic love.* Los Angeles: J. P. Tarcher.

Bransford, J. D., & Franks, J. J. (1971). Abstraction of linguistic ideas. *Cognitive Psychology, 2,* 331–350.

Brecher, E. M., & The editors of Consumer Reports. (1975). Marijuana: The legal question. *Consumer Reports, 40,* 265-266.

Brehm, J. W. (1966). *A theory of psychological reactance.* New York: Academic Press.

Brehm, J. W., & Self, E. A. (1989). The intensity of motivation. Annual *Review of Psychology, 40,* 109–131.

Breier, A., Charney, D., & Heninger, G. R. (1984). Major depression in patients with agoraphobia and panic disorder. *Archives of General Psychiatry, 41,* 1129–1135.

Bretl, D. J., & Cantor, J. (1988). The portrayal of men and women in U.S. television commercials: A recent content analysis and trends over 15 years. *Sex Roles, 18,* 595–601.

Bretschneider, J. G., & McCoy, N. L. (1988). Sexual interest and behavior in healthy 80- to 102-year-olds. *Archives of Sexual Behavior, 17,* 109–129.

Bridges, K. M. B. (1932). Emotional development in early infancy. *Child Development, 3,* 324–341.

Brody, E. M., Lawton, M. P., and Liebowitz, B. (1984). Senile dementia: Public policy and adequate institutional care. *American Journal of Public Health, 74,* 1381–1383.

Brody, H. (1978). Cell counts in cerebral cortex and brainstem. In R. Katzman, R. D. Terry, & K. L. Bick (Eds.), *Aging: Vol. 7. Alzheimer's disease: senile dementia and related disorders.* New York: Raven Press.

Brom, D., Kleber, R. J., & Defares, P. B. (1989). Brief psychotherapy for posttraumatic stress disorders. *Journal of Consulting and Clinical Psychology, 57,* 607–612.

Brone, R. J., & Fisher, C. B. (1988). Determinants of adolescent obesity: A comparison with anorexia nervosa. *Adolescence, XXIII,* 155–169.

Bronfenbrenner, U. (1989). *Who cares for children?* Invited address, UNESCO, Paris, September 7, 1989.

Brooks, J. (1985). Polygraph testing. Thoughts of a sceptical legislator. *American Psychologist, 40,* 348–354.

Brooks-Gunn, J., & Furstenberg, F. F., Jr. (1989). Adolescent sexual behavior. *American Psychologist, 44,* 249–257.

Brooks-Gunn, J., & Warren, M. P. (1989). Biological and social contributions to negative affect in young adolescent girls. *Child Development, 60,* 40–55.

Brown, A. S. (1989). *How to increase your memory power.* Glenview, Illinois: Scott, Foresman and Company.

Brown, D. T., & Minke, K. M. (1986). School psychology graduate training. A comprehensive analysis. *American Psychologist, 41,* 1328–1338.

Brown, H. B. (1935). An experience in identification testimony. *Journal of the American Institute of Criminal Law, 25,* 621–622.

Brown, J. (1958). Some tests of the decay theory of immediate memory. *Quarterly Journal of Experimental Psychology, 10,* 12–21.

Brown, R. (1970). The first sentences of child and chimpanzee. In R. Brown (Ed.), *Psycholinguistics: Selected Papers.* New York: Free Press.

Brown, R., & Berko, J. (1960). Word association and the acquisition of grammar. *Child Development, 31,* 1–14.

Brown, R., & Kulik, J. (1977). Flashbulb memories. *Cognition, 5,* 73–99.

Brown, R. W., & Lenneberg, E. H. (1954). A study in language and cognition. *Journal of Abnormal and Social Psychology, 49,* 454–462.

Bryant, R. A., & McConkey, K. M. (1989). Hypnotic blindness: A behavioral and experiential analysis. *Journal of Abnormal Psychology, 98,* 71–77.

Buchsbaum, M. S., Murphy, D. L., Coursey, R. D., Lake, C. R., & Zeigler, M. G. (1978). Platelet monoamine oxidase, plasma dopamine-beta-hydroxylase, and attention in a "biochemical high risk" sample. *Journal of Psychiatric Research, 14,* 214–224.

Buglass, D., Clarke, J., Henderson, A. S., Kreitman, N., & Presley, A. S. (1977). A study of agoraphobic housewives. *Psychological Medicine, 7,* 73–86.

Bulkin, W., & Lukashok, H. (1988). Rx for dying: The case for hospice. *New England Journal of Medicine, 318,* 376–378.

Burchinal, M., Lee, M., & Ramey, C. (1989). Type of day-care and preschool intellectual development in disadvantaged children. *Child Development, 60*, 128–137.

Bureau of the Census (1987). *Statistical Brief*, Survey of Income and Program Participation, SB-2-87, May.

Burger, J. M., & Hemans, L. T. (1988). Desire for control and the use of attribution processes. *Journal of Personality, 56*, 531–546.

Burgio, L. D., Whitman, T. L., & Reid, D. H. (1983). A participative management approach for improving direct-care staff performance in an institutional setting. *Journal of Applied Behavior Analysis, 16*, 37–53.

Burling, T. A., Marotta, J., Gonzalez, R., Moltzen, J. O., Eng, A. M., Schmidt, G. A., Welch, R. L., Ziff, D. C., & Reilly, P. M. (1989). Computerized smoking cessation program for the worksite: Treatment outcome and feasibility. *Journal of Consulting and Clinical Psychology, 57*, 619–622.

Burman, B., Mednick, S. A., Machon, R. A., Parnas, J., & Schulsinger, F. (1987). Children at high risk for schizophrenia: Parent and offspring perceptions of family relationships. *Journal of Abnormal Psychology, 96*, 364–366.

Burns, B. (1987). Is stimulus structure in the mind's eye? An examination of dimensional structure in iconic memory. *Quarterly Journal of Experimental Psychology, 39A*, 385–408.

Burr, D. C., Morrone, M. C., & Spinelli, D. (1989). Evidence for edge and bar detectors in human vision. *Vision Research, 29*, 419–431.

Burstein, E., Coynes, L., Kernberg, O. F., & Voth, H. (1972). The quantitative study of the psychotherapy research project: Psychotherapy outcome. *Bulletin of the Menninger Clinic, 36*, 1–85.

Bus, A. G., & van Ijzendoorn, M. H. (1988). Mother-child interactions, attachment, and emergent literacy: A cross-sectional study. *Child Development, 59*, 1262–1272.

Buss, A. H. (1989). Personality as traits. *American Psychologist, 44*, 1378–1388.

Buss, D. M. (1988). Love acts: The evolutionary biology of love. In R. J. Sternberg & M. L. Barnes (Eds.), *The psychology of love.* New Haven, CT: Yale University Press.

Butcher, J. N., Graham, J. R., Dahlstrom, W. G., & Bowman, E. (1990). Use of the MMPI-2 with college students. *Journal of Personality Assessment.*

Butler, R., & Nisan, M. (1986). Effects of no feedback, task-related comments, and grades on intrinsic motivation and performance. *Journal of Educational Psychology, 78*, 210–216.

Butterfield-Picard, H. & Magno, J. B. (1982). Hospice the adjective, not the noun: The future of a national priority. *American Psychologist, 37*, 1254–1259.

Byrne, D. G., & Reinhart, M. I. (1989). Occupation, Type A behavior and self-reported angina pectoris. *Journal of Psychosomatic Research, 33*, 609–619.

Cabanac, M. (1986). Money versus pain: Experimental study of a conflict in humans. *Journal of the Experimental Analysis of Behavior, 46*, 37–44.

Cacioppo, J. T., Petty, R. E., & Geen, T. R. (1989). *In Attitude Structure and Function:* From the Tripartite to the Homeostasis Model of Attitudes, ed. A. R. Pratkanis, S. J. Breckler, A. G. Greenwald, pp. 275–309. Hillsdale, NJ: Erlbaum.

Cadoret, R. J. (1978). Psychopathology in adopted-away offspring of biologic parents with antisocial behavior. *Archives of General Psychiatry, 35*, 176–184.

Cadoret, R. J., Troughton, E., & O'Gorman, T. W. (1987). Genetic and environmental factors in alcohol abuse and antisocial personality. *Journal of Studies on Alcohol, 48*, 1–8.

Caldera, Y. M., Huston, A. C., & O'Brien, M. (1989). Social interactions and play patterns of parents and toddlers with feminine, masculine, and neutral toys. *Child Development, 60*, 70–76.

Campbell, M., Small, A. M., Green, W. H., Jennings, S. J., Perry, R., Bennett, W. G., & Anderson, L. (1984). Behavioral efficacy of haloperidol and lithium carbonate. A comparison in hospitalized aggressive children with conduct disorder. *Archives of General Psychiatry, 41*, 650–656.

Campbell, S. B. (1985). Hyperactivity in preschoolers: Correlates and prognostic implications. *Clinical Psychology Review, 5*, 405–428.

Canavan-Gumpert, D. (1977). Generating reward and cost orientations through praise and criticism. *Journal of Personality and Social Psychology, 35*, 501–513.

Cannon, W. B. (1927). The James-Lange theory of emotion: A critical examination and an alternative theory. *American Journal of Psychology, 39*, 106–124.

Cantor, N., & Kihlstrom, J. F. (1982). Cognitive and social processes in personality. In G. T. Wilson & C. M. Franks (Eds.), *Contemporary behavior therapy.* New York: Guilford Press.

Cantwell, D. P., Baker, L., & Rutter, M. (1978). Family factors. In M. Rutter & E. Schopler (Eds.), *Autism: A reappraisal of concepts and treatment.* New York: Plenum Press.

Caplan, G. (1976). The family as a support system. In G. Caplan & M.

Killilea (Eds.). *Support systems and mutual help: Multidisciplinary explorations.* New York: Grune & Stratton.

Carducci, B. J., & Stein, N. D. (1988). *The personal and situational pervasiveness of shyness in college students: A nine-year comparison.* Paper presented at the meeting of the Southeastern Psychological Association, New Orleans, April.

Carlson, C. R., Gantz, F. P., & Masters, J. C. (1983). Adults' emotional states and recognition of emotion in young children. *Motivation and Emotion, 7*, 81–102.

Carlson, R. A., Sullivan, M. A., & Schneider, W. (1989). Practice and working memory effects in building procedural skill. *Journal of Experimental Psychology: Learning, Memory, and Cognition, 15*, 517–526.

Carmody, D. P., Nodine, C. F., & Kundel, H. L. (1980). An analysis of perceptual and cognitive factors in radiographic interpretation. *Perception, 9*, 339–344.

Caron, R. F., Caron, A. J., Carlson, V. R., & Cobb, L. S. (1979). Perception of shape-at-a-slant in the young infant. *Bulletin of the Psychonomic Society, 1*, 229–243.

Carver, C. S., & Scheier, M. F. (1990). Origins and functions of positive and negative affect: A control-process view. *Psychological Review, 97*, 19–35.

Casey, R. J., & Berman, J. S. (1985). The outcome of psychotherapy with children. *Psychological Bulletin, 98*, 388–400.

Cash, T. F., & Kehr, J. (1978). Influence of nonprofessional counselors' physical attractiveness and sex on perceptions of counselor behavior. *Journal of Counseling Psychology, 25*, 336–342.

Cashdan, S. (1988). *Object relations therapy.* New York: W. W. Norton.

Caspi, A., Elder, G. H., & Bem, D. J. (1988). Moving away from the world: Life-course patterns of shy children. *Developmental Psychology, 24(6)*, 824–831.

Cattell, R. B. (1965). *The scientific analysis of personality.* Baltimore: Penguin.

Cavanagh, P., & Leclerc, Y. G. (1989). Shape from shadows. *Journal of Experimental Psychology: Human Perception and Performance, 15*, 3–27.

Cermak, L. S. (1975). *Improving your memory.* New York: W. W. Norton.

Chacko, T. I. (1982). Women and equal employment opportunity: Some unintended effects. *Journal of Applied Psychology, 67*, 119–123.

Chaiken, A. L., Sigler, E., & Derlega, V. J. (1974). Nonverbal mediators of teacher expectancy effects. *Journal of Personality and Social Psychology, 30*, 144–149.

Chaiken, S., & Eagly, A. H. (1983). Communication modality as a determinant of persuasion: The role of communicator salience. *Journal of Personality and Social Psychology, 45*, 241–256.

Chaiken, S., & Stangor, C. (1987). Attitudes and attitude change. In M. R. Rosenzweig & L. W. Porter (Eds.), *Annual Review of Psychology.* Palo Alto, CA: Annual Reviews, Inc.

Chalfant, J. C. (1989). Learning disabilities. Policy issues and promising approaches. *American Psychologist, 44(2)*, 392–398.

Chamizo, V. D., & Mackintosh, N. J. (1989). Latent learning and latent inhibition in maze discriminations. *Quarterly Journal of Experimental Psychology, 41B*, 21–31.

Chase, W. G., & Simon, H. A. (1973a). Perception in chess. *Cognitive Psychology, 4*, 55–81.

Chase, W. G., & Simon, H. A. (1973b). The mind's eye in chess. In W. G. Chase (Ed.), *Visual information processing* (pp. 215–281). New York: Academic Press.

Cherry, E. C. (1953). Some experiments on the recognition of speech with one and with two ears. *Journal of the Acoustical Society of America, 25*, 975–979.

Chiam, H. (1987). Change in self-concept during adolescence. *Adolescence, 85*, 69–75.

Chidester, T. R. (1986). Problems in the study of interracial interaction: Pseudo-interracial dyad paradigm. *Journal of Personality and Social Psychology, 50*, 74–79.

Child, I. L. (1985). Psychology and anomalous observations. The question of ESP in dreams. *American Psychologist, 40*, 1219–1230.

Chomsky, N. (1957). *Syntactic structures.* The Hague, Netherlands: Mouton.

Chomsky, N. (1972). *Language and mind* (rev. ed.). New York: Harcourt Brace Jovanovich.

Chomsky, N. (1975). *Reflections on language.* New York: Pantheon Books.

Christensen, H., Hadzi-Pavlovic, D., Andrews, G., & Mattick, R. (1987). Behavior therapy and tricyclic medication in the treatment of obsessive-compulsive disorder: A quantitative review. *Journal of Consulting and Clinical Psychology, 55*, 701–771.

Christiansen, B. A., Smith, G. T., Roehling, P. V., & Goldman, M. S. (1989). Using alcohol expectancies to predict adolescent drinking behavior after one year. *Journal of Consulting and Clinical Psychology, 57*, 93–99.

Cialdini, R. B. (1988). *Influence: Science and practice* (2nd ed.). Glenview, IL: Scott, Foresman, and Company.

Clancy, H., & McBride, G. (1969). The autistic process and its treatment. *Journal of Child Psychology and Psychiatry, 10,* 233–244.

Clarizio, H., & Veres, V. (1984). A short-form version of the WISC-R for the learning disabled. *Psychology in the Schools, 21,* 154–157.

Clark, E. V. (1973). Non-linguistic strategies and the acquisition of word meanings. *Cognition, 2,* 161–182.

Clark, M. S., & Reis, H. T. (1988). Interpersonal processes in close relationships. In M. R. Rosenzweig & L. W. Porter (Eds.), *Annual Review of Psychology, Vol. 39.* Palo Alto, CA: Annual Reviews, Inc.

Clarke-Stewart, A. (1973). Interactions between mothers and their young children: Characteristics and consequences. *Monographs of the Society of Research in Child Development, 38.*

Clarke-Stewart, K. A. (1989). Infant day care: Maligned or malignant? *American Psychologist, 44*(2), 266–273.

Clarke-Stewart, Friedman, & Koch. (1985). *Child development: A topical approach.* New York: John Wiley & Sons.

Clayson, D., & Mensh, I. N. (1987). Psychologists in medical schools. *American Psychologist, 42,* 859–862.

Clerici, W. J., & Coleman, J. R. (1987). Resting and pure tone evoked metabolic responses in the inferior colliculus of young adult and senescent rats. *Neurobiology of Aging, 8,* 171–178.

Cleveland, J. N., Murphy, K. R., & Williams, R. E. (1989). Multiple uses of performance appraisal: Prevalence and correlates. *Journal of Applied Psychology, 74,* 130–135.

Clum, G. A., & Bowers, T. G. (1990). Behavior therapy better than placebo treatments: Fact or artifact? *Psychological Bulletin, 107,* 110–113.

Coates, B., Pusser, H. E., & Goodman, I. (1976). The influence of "Sesame Street" and "Mister Rogers' Neighborhood" on children's social behavior in the preschool. *Child Development, 47,* 138–144.

Coates, T. J., Killen, J. D., Silverman, S., George, J., Marchini, E., Hamilton, S., & Thoresen, C. E. (1983). Cognitive activity, sleep disturbance, and stage-specific differences between recorded and reported sleep. *Psychophysiology, 20,* 243–250.

Cochran, S. D., & Mays, V. M. (1989). Women and AIDS-related concerns. *American Psychologist, 44,* 529–535.

Cochrane, G. J. (1987). Hypnotherapy in weight-loss treatment: Case illustrations. *American Journal of Clinical Hypnosis, 30,* 20–27.

Cohen, J. F., & Tronick, E. Z. (1983). Three-month-old infants' reaction to simulated maternal depression. *Child Development, 54,* 185–193.

Cohen, R. J., Monhague, P., Nathanson, L. S., Swerdik, M. E. (1988). *Psychological testing.* Mountainview, CA: Mayfield Publishing.

Cohen, R. M., Weingartner, H., Smallberg, S., Pickar, D., & Murphy, D. L. (1982). Effort and cognition in depression. *Archives of General Psychiatry, 39,* 593–597.

Cohen, S., & Hoberman, H. M. (1983). Positive events and social supports as buffers of life change stress. *Journal of Applied Social Psychology, 13,* 99–125.

Cohn, D. A. (1990). Child-mother attachment of six-year-olds and social competence at school. *Child Development, 61,* 152–162.

Cole, D. A. (1989). Psychopathology of adolescent suicide: Hopelessness, coping beliefs, and depression. *Journal of Abnormal Psychology, 98,* 248–255.

Cole, R. D. (1979). The use of hypnosis in a course to increase academic and test-taking skills. *International Journal of Clinical and Experimental Hypnosis, 27,* 21–28.

Coleman, J. C., Butcher, J. N., & Carson, R. C. (1980). *Abnormal psychology and modern life* (6th ed.). Glenview, IL: Scott, Foresman.

Comer, J. P. (1988). Educating poor minority children. *Scientific American,* November, 42–51.

Conrad, R., & Hille, B. A. (1958). The decay theory of immediate memory and paced recall. *Canadian Journal of Psychology, 12,* 1–6.

Conrad, R., & Hull, A. J. (1964). Information, acoustic confusion, and memory span. *British Journal of Psychology, 55,* 429–432.

Contrada, R. J. (1989). Type A behavior, personality hardiness, and cardiovascular responses to stress. *Journal of Personality and Social Psychology, 57,* 895–903.

Cook, T. D., Kendziersky, D. A., & Thomas, S. V. (1983). The implicit assumptions of television: An analysis of the 1982 NIMH report on television and behavior. *Public Opinion Quarterly, 47,* 161–201.

Coppola, D. M., & O'Connell, R. J. (1988). Behavioral responses of peripubertal female mice towards puberty-accelerating and puberty-delaying chemical signals. *Chemical Senses, 13*(3), 407–424.

Cornsweet, T. N. (1970). *Visual perception.* New York: Academic Press.

Costanzo, M., Archer, D., Aronson, E., & Pettigrew, T. (1986). Energy conservation behavior. The difficult path from information to action. *American Psychologist, 41,* 521–528.

Covin, T. M., & Sattler, J. M. (1985). A longitudinal study of the Stanford-Binet and WISC-R with special education students. *Psychology in the Schools, 22,* 274–276.

Cowan, N. (1988). Evolving conceptions of memory storage, selective

attention, and their mutual constraints within the human information-processing system. *Psychological Bulletin, 104,* 163–191.

Cowart, V. S. (1982). Stimulant therapy for attention disorders. *Journal of the American Medical Association, 148,* 279–287.

Cowden, R. C., & Ford, L. I. (1962). Systematic desensitization with a phobic schizophrenic. *American Journal of Psychiatry, 119,* 241–245.

Cox, V. C., Paulus, P. B., & McCain, G. (1984). Prison crowding research. The relevance for prison housing standards and a general approach regarding crowding phenomena. *American Psychologist, 39,* 1148–1160.

Craik, F. I. M., & Lockhart, R. S. (1972). Levels of processing: A framework for memory research. *Journal of Verbal Learning and Verbal Behavior, 11,* 671–784.

Crawford, C. B., & Anderson, J. L. (1989). Sociobiology. *American Psychologist, 44,* 1449–1459.

Crespi, T. D. (1988). Effectiveness of time-out: A comparison of psychiatric, correctional and day-treatment programs. *Adolescence, XXIII,* 805–811.

Critchlow, B. (1986). The powers of John Barleycorn. Beliefs about the effects of alcohol on social behavior. *American Psychologist, 41,* 751–764.

Cross, D. G., Sheehan, P. W., & Kahn, J. A. (1980). Alternative advice and counsel in psychotherapy. *Journal of Consulting and Clinical Psychology, 48,* 615–625.

Crow, T. J., Johnstone, E. C., Owens, D. G. C., Ferrier, I. N., MacMillan, J. F., Parry, R. P., & Tyrrell, D. A. J. (1979). Characteristics of patients with schizophrenia or neurological disorder and virus-like agent in cerebro-spinal fluid. *Lancet, 1,* 842–844.

Crowe, L. C., & George, W. H. (1989). Alcohol and human sexuality: Review and integration. *Psychological Bulletin, 105,* 374–386.

Crowl, R. K., & MacGinitie, W. H. (1974). The influence of students' speech characteristics on teachers' evaluations of oral answers. *Journal of Educational Psychology, 66,* 304–308.

Cummings, N. A. (1986). The dismantling of our health system: Strategies for the survival of psychological practice. *American Psychologist, 41,* 426–431.

Cunningham, C. E., Siegel, L. S., & Offord, D. R. (1985). A developmental dose-response analysis of the effects of methylphenidate on the peer interactions of attention deficit disordered boys. *Journal of Child Psychology, 26,* 955–971.

Curran, D. K. (1987). *Adolescent suicidal behavior.* Washington, DC: Hemisphere Publishing.

Curtiss, S. (1977). *Genie: A psycholinguistic study of a modern-day "wild child."* New York: Academic Press.

Cutler, W. B., Preti, G., Krieger, A., Huggins, G. R., Garcia, C. R., & Lawley, H. J. (1986). Human axillary secretions influence women's menstrual cycles: The role of donor extract from men. *Hormones & Behavior, 20,* 463–473.

Cutting, J. E. (1987). Rigidity in cinema seen from the front row, side aisle. *Journal of Experimental Psychology, 13,* 323–334.

Dakof, G. A., & Taylor, S. E. (1990). Victims' perceptions of social support: What is helpful from whom? *Journal of Personality and Social Psychology, 58,* 80–89.

Dalby, J. T., Morgan, D., & Lee, M. L. (1986). Single case study. Schizophrenia and mania in identical twin brothers. *Journal of Nervous and Mental Disease, 174,* 304–308.

Dalton, K. (1984). *The premenstrual syndrome and progesterone therapy.* Chicago: Year Book Medical Publishers.

Dambrot, F. H., Reep, D. C., & Bell, D. (1988). Television sex roles in the 1980s: Do viewers' sex and sex role orientation change the picture? *Sex Roles, 19,* 387–401.

Damon, W. (1980). Structural-development theory and the study of moral development. In M. Windmiller, N. Lambert, & E. Turiel (Eds.), *Moral development and socialization.* Boston: Allyn and Bacon.

Damon, W. (1988). *The moral child.* New York: Free Press.

Daniels, D., & Plomin, R. (1985). Origins of individual differences in infant shyness. *Developmental Psychology, 21,* 118–121.

Darley, J. M., & Berscheid, E. (1967). Increased liking as a result of the anticipation of personal contact. *Human Relations, 20,* 29–40.

Darling, C. A., & Davidson, J. K. (1986). Coitally active university students: Sexual behaviors, concerns, and challenges. *Adolescence, XXI,* 403–419.

Davidson, L. E., Rosenberg, M. L., Mercy, J. A., Franklin, J., & Simmons, J. T. (1989). An epidemiologic study of risk factors in two teenage suicide clusters. *Journal of the American Medical Association, 262,* 2687–2692.

Davidson, W. S. (1974). Studies of aversive conditioning for alcoholics: A critical review of theory and research methodology. *Psychological Bulletin, 81,* 571–581.

Davis, D., & Padesky, C. (1989). Enhancing cognitive therapy with women. In A. Freeman, K. M. Simon, L. E. Beutler, & H. Arkowitz

(Eds.), *Comprehensive handbook of cognitive therapy*. New York: Plenum Press.

Davis, J. H. (1989). Psychology and law: The last 15 years. *Journal of Applied Social Psychology, 19,* 199–230.

Davis, J. M. (1977). Central biogenic amines and theories of depression and mania. In W. E. Fann, I. Karacan, A. D. Pokorny, & R. L. Williams (Eds.), *Phenomenology and treatment of depression*. New York: Spectrum Publications.

Davis, J. R., Wallace, C. J., Lieberman, R. B., & Finch, B. E. (1976). The use of brief isolation to suppress delusional and hallucinatory speech. *Journal of Behavior and Experimental Psychiatry, 7,* 269–275.

Davis, K. (1947). Final note on a case of extreme isolation. *American Journal of Sociology, 52,* 432–437.

Davis, K., & Todd, M. J. (1984). Prototypes, paradigm cases, and relationship assessment: The case of friendship. In S. Duck & D. Perlman (Eds.), *Sage series in personal relationships* (Vol. 1). Beverly Hills, CA: Sage Publications.

Davis, K. E., & Todd, M. J. (1982). Friendship and love relationships. In K. E. Davis & M. J. Todd (Eds.), *Advances in Descriptive Psychology* (Vol. 2). Greenwich, CT: JAI Press.

Davis, S. M., & Drichta, C. E. (1980). Biofeedback theory and application in allied health speech pathology. *Biofeedback and Self-Regulation, 5,* 159–174.

Day, R. H., & McKenzie, B. E. (1977). Constancies in the perceptual world of the infant. In W. Epstein (Ed.), *Stability and constancy in visual perception*. New York: John Wiley & Sons.

Day, R. L., Kitahata, L. M., Kao, F. F., Motoyama, E. K., & Hardy, J. D. (1975). Evaluation of acupuncture anesthesia: A psychophysical study. *Anesthesiology, 43,* 501–517.

de Jong-Gierveld, J. (1987). Developing and testing a model of loneliness. *Journal of Personality and Social Psychology, 53,* 119–128.

de Jong-Gierveld, J., & Van Tilburg, T. (1987). The partner as source of social support in problem and non-problem situations. *Journal of Social Behavior and Personality, 2,* 191–200.

De Vries, B., & Walker, L. J. (1986). Moral reasoning and attitudes toward capital punishment. *Developmental Psychology, 22,* 509–513.

DeAngelis, T. (1988). In praise of rose-colored specs. *APA Monitor*, Vol. 19, 1, 11.

DeBuono, B. A., Zinner, S. H., Daamen, M., & McCormack, W. M. (1990). Sexual behavior of college women in 1975, 1986, and 1989. *New England Journal of Medicine, 322,* 821–825.

Deci, E. L. (1971). Effect of externally mediated rewards on intrinsic motivation. *Journal of Personality and Social Psychology, 18,* 105–115.

Deci, E. L. (1972). Effects of contingent and non-contingent rewards and controls on intrinsic motivation. *Organizational Behavior and Human Performance, 8,* 217–229.

Deci, E. L. (1975). *Intrinsic motivation*. New York: Plenum Press.

Deffenbacher, J. L. (1988). *Cognitive-behavioral approaches to anger reduction: Some treatment considerations*. Paper presented at 96th Annual Convention of the American Psychological Association at Atlanta, GA, August.

deGroot, A. D. (1965). *Thought and choice in chess*. Paris: Mouton & Company.

DeLeon, P. H. (1988). Public policy and public service. *American Psychologist, 43,* 309–315.

DeLisi, L. E., Crow, T. J., & Hirsch, S. R. (1986). The third biannual winter workshop on schizophrenia. *Archives in General Psychology, 43,* 706–711.

DeLisi, L. E., Goldin, L. R., Hamovit, J. R., Maxwell, M. E., Kurtz, D., & Gershon, E. S. (1986). A family study of the association of increased ventribular size with schizophrenia. *Archives in General Psychology, 43,* 148–153.

Delmonte, M. M. (1983). Mantras and meditation: A literature review. *Perceptual and Motor Skills, 57,* 64–66.

DeLongis, A., Folkman, S., & Lazarus, R. S. (1988). The impact of daily stress on health and mood: Psychological and social resources as mediators. *Journal of Personality and Social Psychology, 54,* 486–495.

Dember, W. N. (1974). Motivation and the cognitive revolution. *American Psychologist, 29,* 161–168.

Dement, W., & Wolpert, E. A. (1958). The relation of eye movements, body motility, and external stimuli to dream content. *Journal of Experimental Psychology, 55,* 543–553.

Dement, W. C. (1960). The effect of dream deprivation. *Science, 131,* 1705–1707.

Dement, W. C., Greenberg, S., & Klein, R. (1966). The effect of partial REM sleep deprivation and delayed recovery. *Journal of Psychiatric Research, 4,* 141–152.

Dement, W. C., & Kleitman, N. (1957). The relation of eye movements during sleep to dream activity: An objective method for the study of dreaming. *Journal of Experimental Psychology, 53,* 339–346.

Dempster, F. N. (1988). The spacing effect: A case study in the failure

to apply the results of psychological research. *American Psychologist, 43,* 627–634.

DeNisi, A. S., Robbins, T., & Cafferty, T. P. (1989). Organization of information used for performance appraisals: Role of diary-keeping. *Journal of Applied Psychology, 74,* 124–129.

DeNisi, A. S., & Williams, K. J. (1988). Cognitive approaches to performance appraisal. *Personnel and Human Resources Management, 6,* 109–155.

Denny, N. W., & List, J. A. (1979). Adult age differences in performance on the matching familiar figures test. *Human Development, 22,* 137–144.

Dentan, R. K. (1968). *The Semai: A nonviolent people of Malaya*. New York: Holt, Rinehart & Winston.

DePaulo, B. M., Dull, W. R., Greenberg, J. M., & Swaim, G. W. (1989). Are shy people reluctant to ask for help? *Journal of Personality and Social Psychology, 56,* 834–844.

DePaulo, P. J., & DePaulo, B. M. (1989). Can deception by salespersons and customers be detected through nonverbal behavioral cues? *Journal of Applied Social Psychology, 19,* 1552–1577.

DePietro, J. A., Larson, S. K., & Porges, S. W. (1987). Behavioral and heart rate pattern differences between breast-fed and bottle-fed neonates. *Developmental Psychology, 23,* 467–474.

DePue, R. A., & Monroe, S. M. (1978). The unipolar-bipolar distinction in the depressive disorders. *Psychological Bulletin, 85,* 1001–1029.

Derlega, V. J., Winstead, B. A., Wong, P. T. P., & Hunter, S. (1985). Gender effects in an initial encounter: A case where men exceed women in disclosure. *Journal of Social and Personal Relations, 2,* 25–44.

Derr, A. M. (1986). How learning disabled adolescent boys make moral judgments. *Journal of Learning Disabilities, 19,* 160–163.

Dershowitz, A. M. (1986). *Reversal of fortune inside the Von Bulow case*. New York: Random House.

DeValois, R. L., Thorell, L. G., & Albrecht, D. G. (1985). Periodicity of striate-cortex-cell receptive fields. *Journal of the Optical Society of America (A), 2,* 1115–1123.

DeValois, R. L., & Jacobs, G. H. (1968). Primate color vision. *Science, 162,* 533–540.

Devlin, M. J., Walsh, B. T., Kral, J. G., Heymsfield, S. B., Pi-Sunyer, F. X., & Dantzic, S. (1990). Metabolic abnormalities in bulimia nervosa. *Archives in General Psychiatry, 47,* 144–156.

Dewsbury, D. A. (1989). Comparative psychology, ethology, and animal behavior. In M. R. Rosenzweig & L. W. Porter (Eds.), *Annual review of psychology*, Vol. 40. Palo Alto, CA: Annual Reviews, Inc.

Dewsbury, D. A. (1990). Early interactions between animal psychologists and animal activists and the founding of the APA committee on precautions in animal experimentation. *American Psychologist, 45,* 315–327.

Deyo, R. A., Straube, K. T., & Disterhoft, J. F. (1989). Nimodipine facilitates associative learning in aging rabbits. *Science, 243,* 809–811.

Diener, E. (1983). Subjective well-being. *Psychological Bulletin, 95,* 542–575.

Diener, E., Lusk, R., DeFour, D., & Flax, R. (1980). Deindividuation: Effects of group size, density, number of observers, and group member similarity on self-consciousness and disinhibited behavior. *Journal of Personality and Social Psychology, 39,* 449–459.

Dietvorst, T. F. (1978). Biofeedback assisted relaxation training with patients recovering from myocardial infarction. *Dissertation Abstracts International, 38 (7-B),* 3389.

DiGiuseppe, R. (1989). Cognitive therapy with children. In A. Freeman, K. M. Simon, L. E. Beutler, & H. Arkowitz (Eds.), *Comprehensive handbook of cognitive therapy*. New York: Plenum Press.

DiMascio, A., Weissman, M. M., Prusoff, B. A., Neu, C., Zwilling, M., & Klerman, G. L. (1979). Differential symptom reduction by drugs and psychotherapy in acute depression. *Archives of General Psychiatry, 36,* 1450–1456.

DiMatteo, M. R., & DiNicola, D. D. (1982). *Achieving patient compliance: The psychology of the medical practitioner's role*. New York: Pergamon Press.

DiNicola, D. D., & DiMatteo, M. R. (1984). Practitioners, patients, and compliance with medical regimens: A social psychological perspective. In A. Baum, S. E. Taylor, & J. E. Singer (Eds.), *Handbook of psychology and health: Vol. 4. Social psychological aspects of health*. Hillsdale, NJ: Erlbaum.

Dion, K., Berscheid, E., & Walster, E. (1972). What is beautiful is good. *Journal of Personality and Social Psychology, 24,* 285–290.

Dipietro, J. A. (1981). Rough and tumble play: A function of gender. *Developmental Psychology, 17,* 50–58.

Dise-Lewis, J. E. (1988). The life events and coping inventory: An assessment of stress in children. *Psychosomatic Medicine, 50,* 484–499.

Dobson, K. S., & Block, L. (1988). Historical and philosophical bases of the cognitive-behavioral therapies. In Keith S. Dobson (Ed.), *Handbook of cognitive-behavioral therapies*. New York: Guilford Press.

Doerfler, L. A. (1988). Well-being at work: Profits, programs and prevention. Symposium abstract presented at the Center for Health and

Fitness, Division of Preventative and Behavioral Medicine, University of Massachusetts Medical School, August 14.

Dohrenwend, B. P., & Shrout, P. E. (1985). "Hassles" in the conceptualization and measurement of life stress variables. *American Psychologist, 40*, 780–785.

Dollard, J., Doob, L. W., Miller, N. E., Mowrer, O. H., & Sears, R. R. (1939). *Frustration and aggression.* New Haven, CT: Yale University Press.

Donnerstein, E. (1980). Pornography and violence against women: Experimental studies. *Annals of the New York Academy of Sciences, 347*, 227–288.

Donovan, W. L., & Leavitt, L. A. (1989). Maternal self-efficacy and infant attachment: Integrating physiology, perceptions, and behavior. *Child Development, 60*, 460–472.

Doob, A. N., & McLaughlin, D. S. (1989). Ask and you shall be given: Request size and donations to a good cause. *Journal of Applied Social Psychology, 19*, 1049–1056.

Douce, R. G. (1979). Hypnosis: A scientific aid in crime detection. *Police Chief, 46*, 60–61, 80.

Drabman, R. S., & Thomas, M. H. (1975). The effects of television on children and adolescents: Does TV violence breed indifference? *Journal of Communication, 25*, 86–89.

Drachman, D. A., & Arbit, J. (1966). Memory and the hippocampal complex, 2. *Archives of Neurology, 15*, 52–61.

Drake, R. E., Osher, F. C., & Wallach, M. A. (1989). Alcohol use and abuse in schizophrenia. *Journal of Nervous and Mental Disease, 177*, 408–413.

Dray, S. M., & Taylor, A. N. (1982). ACTH 4-10 enhances retention of conditioned taste aversion learning in infant rats. *Central and Neural Biology, 35*, 147–158.

Drennen, W. T., & Holden, E. W. (1984). Trait/set interactions in EMG biofeedback. *Psychological Reports, 54*, 843–849.

Dreyer, P. H. (1982). Sexuality during adolescence. In B. B. Wolman (Ed.), *Handbook of developmental psychology.* Englewood Cliffs, NJ: Prentice-Hall.

Dryden, W., & Ellis, A. (1988). Rational-emotive therapy. In Keith S. Dobson (Ed.), *Handbook of cognitive-behavioral therapies.* New York: Guilford Press.

Dunant, Y., & Israel, M. (1985). The release of acetylcholine. *Scientific American, 252*, 58–83.

Duncan, J. (1980). The locus of interference in the perception of simultaneous stimuli. *Psychological Review, 87*, 272–300.

Duncker, K. (1945). On problem solving. *Psychological Monographs, 50* (Whole No. 270).

Dush, D. M., Hirt, M. L., & Schroeder, H. (1983). Self-statement modification with adults: A meta-analysis. *Psychological Bulletin, 94*, 3, 408–422.

Dush, D. M., Hirt, M. L., & Schroeder, H. E. (1989). Self-statement modification in the treatment of child behavior disorders: A meta-analysis. *Psychological Bulletin, 106*, 97–106.

Dutton, D. G. (1988). *The domestic assault of women.* Boston: Allyn and Bacon.

Duyme, M. (1988). School success and social class: An adoption study. *Developmental Psychology, 24*, 203–209.

Dyck, P. J., Lambert, E. H., & O'Brien, P. (1976). Pain in peripheral neuropathy related to size and rate of fiber degeneration. In M. Weisenberg & B. Tursky (Eds.), *Pain: Therapeutic approaches and research frontiers.* New York: Plenum Press.

Dyer, J. B., III, & Crouch, J. G. (1988). Effects of running and other activities on moods. *Perceptual and Motor Skills, 67*, 43–50.

Dykens, E. M., & Gerrard, M. (1986). Psychological profiles of purging bulimics, repeat dieters, and controls. *Journal of Consulting and Clinical Psychology, 54*, 283–288.

Eagly, A. H., & Kite, M. E. (1987). Are stereotypes of nationalities applied to both women and men? *Journal of Personality and Social Psychology, 53*, 451–462.

Eagly, A. H., & Steffen, V. J. (1986). Gender and aggressive behavior: A meta-analytic review of the social psychological literature. *Psychological Bulletin, 100*, 309–330.

Easterbrooks, M. A. (1989). Quality of attachment to mother and to father: Effects of perinatal risk status. *Child Development, 60*, 825–830.

Ebbinghaus, H. (1885). *Uberdie gedachtnis.* Leipzig, Germany: Duncker & Humbolt.

Eckenrode, J., Powers, J., Doris, J., Munsch, J., & Bolger, N. (1988). Substantiation of child abuse and neglect reports. *Journal of Consulting and Clinical Psychology, 56*, 9–16.

Edelstein, M. R., & Wandersman, A. (1987). Community dynamics in coping with toxic contaminants. In M. R. Altman and A. Wandersman (Eds.), *Neighborhood and Community Environments.* New York: Plenum Press.

Egeland, B., Jacobvitz, D., & Sroufe, L. A. (1988). Breaking the cycle of abuse. *Child Development, 59*, 1080–1088.

Egger, J., Carter, C. M., Graham, P. J., Gumley, D., & Soothill, J. F. (1985). Controlled trial of oligoantigenic treatment in the hyperkinetic syndrome. *Lancet, 1*, 540–545.

Eich, E., & Metcalfe, J. (1989). Mood dependent memory for internal versus external events. *Journal of Experimental Psychology: Learning, Memory, and Cognition, 15*, 443–455.

Eisdorfer, C. (1983). Conceptual models of aging. *American Psychologist, 2*, 197–202.

Eisdorfer, C., & Wilkie, F. (1977). Stress, disease, aging, and behavior. In J. E. Birren & K. W. Schaie (Eds.), *Handbook of the psychology of aging.* New York: Van Nostrand Reinhold.

Eisenberg, L., & Kanner, L. (1956). Early infantile autism, 1943–1955. *American Journal of Orthopsychiatry, 26*, 556–566.

Ekman, P., Friesen, W. V., & O'Sullivan, M. (1988). Smiles when lying. *Journal of Personality and Social Psychology, 54*, 414–420.

Elkind, D. (1981a). Giant in the nursery—Jean Piaget. In E. M. Hetherington & R. D. Parke (Eds.), *Contemporary readings in child psychology* (2nd ed.). New York: McGraw-Hill.

Elkind, D. (1981b). *The hurried child.* Reading, MA: Addison-Wesley.

Elkind, D. (1987). *Miseducation.* New York: Alfred A. Knopf.

Ellingson, R. J. (1975). Ontogenesis of sleep in the human. In C. G. Lairy & P. Salzarula (Eds.), *The experimental study of human sleep: Methodological problems.* Amsterdam: Elsevier Press.

Elliott, R. (1987). *Litigating intelligence IQ tests, special education, and social science in the courtroom.* Dover, MA: Auburn House Publishing Company.

Ellis, A. (1962). *Reason and emotion in psychotherapy.* New York: Stuart Press.

Ellis, A. (1970). *The essence of rational psychotherapy: A comprehensive approach to treatment.* New York: Institute for Rational Living.

Ellis, A. (1988). *The philosophical basis of rational-emotive therapy (RET).* Paper presented at the 96th Annual Convention of the American Psychological Association in Atlanta, GA, August.

Ellis, A. (1990). *How to stubbornly refuse to make yourself miserable about anything—yes, anything!* New York: Carol Publishing Group.

Ellis, A., & Harper, R. A. (1961). *A guide to rational living.* North Hollywood, CA: Wilshire Book.

Ellis, R. J., & Oscar-Berman, M. (1989). Alcoholism, aging, and functional cerebral asymmetries. *Psychological Bulletin, 106*, 128–147.

Emery, R. E. (1989). Family violence. *American Psychologist, 44*, 321–328.

Emery, R. E. (1989). Family violence: Has science met its match? Edited transcript of a Science and Public Policy Seminar presented by the Federation of Behavioral, Psychological and Cognitive Sciences in the Rayburn House Office Building, Washington, DC, September 15.

Emrick, C. D., & Hansen, J. (1983). Assertions regarding effectiveness of treatment for alcoholism: Fact or fancy? *American Psychologist, 38*, 1078–1088.

Entus, A. K. (1977). Hemispheric asymmetry in processing of dichotically presented speech and nonspeech stimuli by infants. In S. J. Segalowitz & F. A. Gruber (Eds.), *Language development and neurological theory.* New York: Academic Press.

Entwisle, D. R., & Alexander, K. L. (1987). Long-term effects of cesarean delivery on parents' beliefs and children's schooling. *Developmental Psychology, 5*, 676–682.

Eppinger, M. G., Craig, P. L., Adams, R. L., & Parsons, O. A. (1987). The WAIS-R index for estimating premorbid intelligence: Cross-validation and clinical utility. *Journal of Consulting and Clinical Psychology, 55*, 86–90.

Epstein, L. H., & Perkins, K. A. (1988). Smoking, stress, and coronary heart disease. *Journal of Consulting and Clinical Psychology, 56*(3), 342–349.

Epstein, S., & O'Brien, E. J. (1985). The person-situation debate in historical and current perspective. *Psychological Bulletin, 98*, 513–537.

Ericsson, K. A., Chase, W. G., & Faloon, S. (1980). Acquisition of a memory skill. *Science, 208*, 1181–1182.

Erikson, E. H. (1959). Identity and the life cycle: Selected papers. *Psychological Issues, 1*, 1–171.

Erikson, E. H. (1963). *Childhood and society* (2nd ed.). New York: W. W. Norton.

Erikson, E. H. (1968). *Identity: Youth and Crisis.* New York: W. W. Norton.

Erlenmeyer-Kimling, L., & Cornblatt, B. (1987). The New York high-risk project: A followup report. *Schizophrenia Bulletin, 12*, 451–455.

Eron, L. D. (1987). The development of aggressive behavior from the perspective of a developing behaviorism. *American Psychologist, 42*, 435–442.

Eron, L. D., & Huesmann, L. R. (1980). Adolescent aggression and television. *Annals of the New York Academy of Sciences, 347*, 319–331.

Ervin, F. R. (1985). Tryptophan depletion causes a rapid lowering of mood in normal males. *Psychopharmacology, 87*, 173–177.

Esses, V. M. (1988). *Mood moderates the effect of feedback on self-image.* Paper presented at the 96th Annual Convention of the American Psychological Association at Atlanta, GA, August.

Esses, V. M. & Webster, C. D. (1988). Physical attractiveness, dangerousness, and the Canadian criminal code. *Journal of Applied Social Psychology, 18,* 1017–1031.

Etaugh, C. (1980). Effects of nonmaternal care on children. *American Psychologist, 35,* 309–319.

Evans, D. A., Funkenstein, H. H., Albert, M. S., Scherr, P. A., Cook, N. R., Chown, M. J., Hebert, L. E., Hennekens, C. H., & Taylor, J. O. (1989). Prevalence of Alzheimer's disease in a community population of older persons. *Journal of the American Medical Association, 262,* 2551–2556.

Exner, J. E., Jr., Thomas, E. A., & Mason, B. (1985). Children's Rorschachs: Description and prediction. *Journal of Personality Assessment, 49,* 13–14.

Eysenck, H. J. (1952). The effects of psychotherapy: An evaluation. *Journal of Consulting and Clinical Psychology, 16,* 319–324.

Eysenck, H. J. (1970). *The structure of human personality* (3rd ed.). London: Methuen.

Fagan, T. K. (1986). School psychology's dilemma. *American Psychologist, 41,* 851–861.

Fajardo, D. M. (1985). Author race, essay quality, and reverse discrimination. *Journal of Applied Social Psychology, 15,* 255–268.

Fantz, R. L. (1961). The origin of form perception. *Scientific American, 204,* 66–72.

Fantz, R. L., & Miranda, S. B. (1975). Newborn infant attention to form of contour. *Child Development, 46,* 224–228.

Farah, M. J. & Hammond, K. M. (1988). Mental rotation and orientation-invariant object recognition: Dissociable processes. *Cognition, 29,* 29–46.

Farber, B. A. (1983). Introduction: A critical perspective on burnout. In A. P. Goldstein & L. Krasner (Eds.), *Stress and burnout in the human service professions.* New York: Pergamon Press.

Farber, E. A., & Egeland, B. (1982). Developmental consequences of out-of-home care for infants in low-income population. In E. F. Zigler & E. W. Gordon (Eds.), *Day care: Scientific and social policy issues.* Boston: Auburn House.

Farone, S. (1982). Psychiatry and political repression in the Soviet Union. *American Psychologist, 37,* 1105–1112.

Farone, S. V., & Tsuang, M. T. (1985). Quantitative models of the genetic transmission of schizophrenia. *Psychological Bulletin, 98,* 41–66.

Faulkenberry, J. R., Vincent, M., James, A., & Johnson, W. (1987). Coital behaviors, attitudes, and knowledge of students who experience early coitus. *Adolescence, XXIII,* 321–332.

Fazio, R. H., & Zanna, M. P. (1981). Direct experience and attitude-behavior consistency. In L. Berkowitz (Ed.), *Advances in experimental social psychology* (Vol. 14). New York: Academic Press.

Federal Bureau of Investigation (1988). *Uniform crime reports 1987.* Washington, DC: U.S. Department of Justice.

Feeney, D. M. (1987). Human rights and animal welfare. *American Psychologist, 42,* 593–599.

Fehr, B. (1988). Prototype analysis of the concepts of love and commitment. *Journal of Personality and Social Psychology, 55,* 557–579.

Feingold, A. (1988a). Matching for attractiveness in romantic partners and same-sex friends: A meta-analysis and theoretical critique. *Psychological Bulletin, 104,* 226–235.

Feingold, A. (1988b). Cognitive gender differences are disappearing. *American Psychologist, 43,* 95–103.

Feingold, B. F. (1975a). Hyperkinesis and learning disabilities linked to artificial food flavors and colors. *American Journal of Nursing, 75,* 797–803.

Feingold, B. F. (1975b). *Why is your child hyperactive?* New York: Random House.

Feingold, B. F. (1976). Hyperkinesis and learning disabilities linked to the ingestion of artificial food colors and flavors. *Journal of Learning Disabilities, 9*(9), 19–27.

Feiring, C., Fox, N. A., Jaskir, J., & Lewis, M. (1987). The relation between social support, infant risk status and mother-infant interaction. *Developmental Psychology, 3,* 400–405.

Feldman, M. P., & MacCulloch, M. J. (1971). *Homosexual behavior: Therapy and assessment.* Oxford: Pergamon Press.

Fell, J. C. (1985). *Alcohol involvement in fatal accidents 1980–1984.* Washington, DC: National Center for Statistics and Analysis. United States Department of Transportation, National Highway Traffic Safety Administration.

Fenwick, P., Donaldson, S., Gillies, L., Bushman, J., Fenton, G., Perry, I., Tilsley, C., & Serafinowicz, H. (1977). Metabolic and EEG changes during transcendental meditation. *Biological Psychology, 5,* 101–118.

Ferguson, H. B., Stoddart, C., & Simeon, J. G. (1986). Double-bind challenge studies of behavioral and cognitive effects of sucrose-aspartame ingestion in normal children. *Nutrition Reviews, 44* (Suppl.), 144–150.

Festinger, L. (1954). A theory of social comparison processes. *Human Relations, 7,* 117–140.

Festinger, L. (1957). *A theory of cognitive dissonance.* Evanston, IL: Row, Petersen.

Fillion, T. J., & Blass, E. M. (1986). Infantile experience with suckling odors determines adult sexual behavior in male rats. *Science, 231,* 729–731.

Findley, M. J., & Cooper, H. M. (1983). Locus of control and academic achievement: A literature review. *Journal of Personality and Social Psychology, 44,* 419–427.

Fine, A. (1986). Transplantation in the central nervous system. *Scientific American, 255,* 52–67.

Finke, R. A., Pinker, S., & Farah, M. J. (1989). Reinterpreting visual patterns in mental imagery. *Cognitive Science, 13,* 51–78.

Finn, P. R., & Pihl, R. O. (1987). Men at high risk for alcoholism: The effect of alcohol on cardiovascular response to unavoidable shock. *Journal of Abnormal Psychology, 96,* 230–236.

Finn, P. R., Zeitouni, N. C., & Pihl, R. O. (1990). Effects of alcohol on psychophysiological hyperreactivity to nonaversive and aversive stimuli in men at high risk for alcoholism. *Journal of Abnormal Psychology, 99,* 79–85.

Fischer, J., & Gochros, H. L. (1975). *Planned behavior change: Behavior modification in social work.* New York: Free Press.

Fischer, K. W., & Silvern, L. (1985). Stages and individual differences in cognitive development. In M. R. Rosenzweig and L. W. Porter (Eds.), *Annual review of psychology* (Vol. 36). Palo Alto, CA: Annual Reviews, Inc.

Fisher, D. F., Lefton, L. A., & Moss, J. H. (1978). Reading geometrically transformed text: A developmental approach. *Bulletin of Psychonomic Society, 11,* 157–160.

Fisher, D. F., Jarombek, J. J., & Karsh, R. (1974). *Short-term memory (1958–1973); An annotated bibliography.* Aberdeen Proving Ground, MD: U.S. Army Human Engineering Laboratory.

Fisher, E. B., Jr., Delamater, A. M., Bertelson, A. D., & Kirkley, B. G. (1982). Psychological factors in diabetes and its treatment. *Journal of Consulting and Clinical Psychology, 50,* 993–1003.

Fisher, J. F. (1988). Possible effects of reference group-based social influence on AIDS-risk behavior and AIDS prevention. *American Psychologist, 43,* 914–920.

Fisher, L. A., & Bauman, K. E. (1988). Influence and selection in the friend-adolescent relationship: Findings from studies of adolescent smoking and drinking. *Journal of Applied Social Psychology, 18,* 289–314.

Fisher, S., & Greenberg, R. P. (1977). *Scientific credibility of Freud's theory and therapy.* New York: Basic Books.

Fiske, D. W., & Maddi, S. R. (1961). *Functions of varied experience.* Homewood, IL: Dorsey Press.

Fiske, S. T. (1989). Interdependence and stereotyping: From the laboratory to the supreme court (and back). Paper presented at the American Psychological Association Convention, New Orleans, August 13.

Fiske, S. T., & Taylor, S. E. (1984). *Social cognition.* Reading, MA: Addison-Wesley.

Frasure-Smith, N., & Prince, R. (1989). Long-term follow-up of the ischemic heart disease life stress monitoring program. *Psychosomatic Medicine, 51,* 485–513.

Fitzgerald, L. F., & Osipow, S. H. (1986). An occupational analysis of counseling psychology. *American Psychologist, 41,* 535–544.

Flanagan, G. (1962). *The first nine months of life.* New York: Simon & Schuster.

Flannery, R. B., Jr. (1986). Major life events and daily hassles in predicting health status: Methodological inquiry. *Journal of Clinical Psychology, 42,* 485–487.

Flavell, J. H. (1963). *The developmental psychology of Jean Piaget.* New York: Van Nostrand Reinhold.

Flavell, J. H. (1986). The development of children's knowledge about the appearance-reality distinction. *American Psychologist, 41,* 418–425.

Flavell, J. H., Green, F. L., & Flavell, E. R. (1989). Young children's ability to differentiate appearance-reality and level 2 perspectives in the tactile modality. *Child Development, 60,* 201–213.

Fleming, I., Baum, A., & Weiss, L. (1987). Social density and perceived control as mediators of crowding stress in high-density residential neighborhoods. *Journal of Personality and Social Psychology, 52,* 899–906.

Fleming, J. D. (1974). Field report: The state of the apes. *Psychology Today, 7,* 31–46.

Flexser, A. J., & Tulving, E. (1978). Retrieval independence in recognition and recall. *Psychology Review, 85,* 153–157.

Flor, H., & Turk, D. C. (1989). Psychophysiology of chronic pain: Do chronic pain patients exhibit symptom-specific psychophysiological responses? *Psychological Bulletin, 105,* 215–259.

Flora, J. A., & Thoresen, C. E. (1988). Reducing the risk of AIDS in adolescents. *American Psychologist, 43,* 965–970.

Flynn, J. R. (1988). The decline and rise of scholastic aptitude scores. *American Psychologist*, June, 479–480.

Fodor, I. G. (1974). The phobic syndrome in women: Implications for treatment. In V. Franks & V. Burtle (Eds.), *Women in therapy*. New York: Brunner/Mazel.

Ford, D. H., & Urban, H. B. (1963). *Systems of psychotherapy: A comparative study*. New York: John Wiley & Sons.

Ford Foundation. (1989). *The common good social welfare and the American future*. New York: Ford Foundation.

Ford, M. E. (1979). The construct validity of egocentrism. *Psychological Bulletin*, 86, 1169–1188.

Ford, M. R. (1982). Biofeedback treatment for headaches. Raynaud's disease, essential hypertension, and irritable bowel syndrome: A review of the long-term follow-up literature. *Biofeedback and Self-Regulation*, 7, 521–536.

Forgays, D. G. (1983). Primary prevention of psychopathology. In M. Hersen, A. E. Kazdin, & A. S. Bellack (Eds.), *The clinical psychology handbook*. New York: Pergamon Press.

Forsyth, D. R., & Strong, S. R. (1986). The scientific study of counseling and psychotherapy. A unificationist view. *American Psychologist*, 41, 113–119.

Fowler, R. D. (1990). Psychology: The core discipline. *American Psychologist*, 45, 1–6.

Fox, D. K., Hopkins, B. L., & Anger, W. K. (1987). The long-term effects of a token economy of safety performance in open-pit mining. *Journal of Applied Behavior Analysis*, 20, 215–224.

Fox, N. A. (1989). Psychophysiological correlates of emotional reactivity during the first year of life. *Developmental Psychology*, 25, 364–372.

Fox, R., Aslin, R. N., Shea, S. L., & Dumais, S. T. (1980). Stereopsis in human infants. *Science*, 207, 323–324.

Frank, R. A., & Cohen, D. J. (1979). Psychosocial concomitants of biological maturation in preadolescence. *American Journal of Psychiatry*, 136, 1518–1524.

Frankel, F. H., & Misch, R. C. (1973). Hypnosis in a case of long-standing psoriasis in a person with character problems. *American Journal of Clinical and Experimental Hypnosis*, 21, 121–130.

Frankenberg, W. K., & Dodds, J. B. (1967). The Denver Developmental Screening Test. *Journal of Pediatrics*, 71, 181–191.

Frederiksen, N. (1986). Toward a broader conception of human intelligence. *American Psychologist*, 41, 445–452.

Freedman, J. L. (1984). Effect of television violence on aggressiveness. *Psychological Bulletin*, 96, 227–246.

Freedman, J. L. (1986). Television violence and aggression: A rejoinder. *Psychological Bulletin*, 100, 372–378.

French, J. L. (1984). On the conception, birth, and early development of school psychology. With special reference to Pennsylvania. *American Psychologist*, 39, 976–987.

French, S. N. (1980). Electromyographic biofeedback for tension control during fine motor skill acquisition. *Biofeedback and Self-Regulation*, 5, 221–228.

Freud, S. (1900/1953). The interpretation of dreams. In J. Strachey (Ed.), *The standard edition of the complete psychological works of Sigmund Freud* (Vols. 4 and 5). London: Hogarth.

Freud, S. (1920). *A general introduction to psychoanalysis*, authorized English translation of the revised edition by Joan Riviere. New York: Washington Square Press, 1966.

Freud, S. (1933). *New introductory lectures on psycho-analysis*. New York: W. W. Norton.

Frezza, M., di Padova, C., Pozzato, G., Terpin, M., Baraona, E., & Lieber, C. S. (1990). High blood alcohol levels in women. *New England Journal of Medicine*, 322, 95–99.

Friedman, H. S., & Booth-Kewley, S. (1988). Validity of the Type A construct: A reprise. *Psychological Bulletin*, 381–384.

Friedman, M., & Rosenman, R. H. (1974). *Type A behavior and your heart*. Greenwich, CT: Fawcett.

Friedman, M., Thoresen, C. E., Gill, J. J., Ulmer, D., Powell, L. H., Price, V. A., Brown, B., Thompson, L., Rabin, D. D., Breall, W. S., Bourg, E., Levy, R., & Dixon, T. (1986). Alteration of Type A behavior and its effect on cardiac recurrences in post myocardial infarction patients: Summary results of the recurrent coronary prevention project. *American Heart Journal*, 112, 653–665.

Friedrich-Cofer, L., & Huston, A. C. (1986). Television violence and aggression: The debate continues. *Psychological Bulletin*, 100, 364–371.

Frijda, N. H. (1988). The laws of emotion. *American Psychologist*, 43, 349–358.

Frijda, N. H., Kuipers, P., & ter Schure, E. (1989). Relations among emotion, appraisal, and emotional action readiness. *Journal of Personality and Social Psychology*, 57, 212–228.

Fromm, E. (1956). *The art of loving*. New York: Harper & Row.

Funder, D. C. (1987). Errors and mistakes: Evaluating the accuracy of social judgment. *Psychological Bulletin*, 101, 75–90.

Furby, L., Weinrott, M. R., & Blackshaw, L. (1989). Sex offender recidivism: A review. *Psychological Bulletin*, 105, 3–30.

Furchtgott, E., & Busemeyer, J. K. (1979). Heart rate and skin conductants during cognitive processes as a function of age. *Journal of Gerontology*, 34, 182–190.

Furstenberg, F. F., Jr., Brooks-Gunn, J., & Chase-Lansdale, L. (1989). Teenaged pregnancy and childbearing. *American Psychologist*, 44, 313–320.

Furumoto, L., & Scarborough, E. (1986). Placing women in the history of psychology. The first American women psychologists. *American Psychologist*, 41, 35–42.

Gabrenya, W. K., Jr., Latane, B., & Wang, Y. E. (1983). Social loafing in cross-cultural perspective: Chinese on Taiwan. *Journal of Cross-Cultural Psychology*, 14, 368–384.

Gabrielli, W. F., Jr., Mednick, S. A., Volavka, J., Pollock, V. E., Schulsinger, F., & Turan, M. I. (1982). Electroencephalograms in children of alcoholic fathers. *Psychophysiology*, 19, 404–407.

Gackenbach, J., & Bosveld, J. (1989). *Control your dreams*. New York: Harper & Row.

Gajzago, C., & Prior, M. (1974). Two cases of "recovery" in Kanner syndrome. *Archives of General Psychiatry*, 31, 264–268.

Galbraith, R. C. (1982). Sibling spacing and intellectual development: A closer look at the confluence models. *Developmental Psychology*, 18, 181–191.

Galbraith, R. C. (1983). Individual differences in intelligence: A reappraisal of the confluence model. *Intelligence*, 7, 185–194.

Galin, D. (1974). Implications for psychiatry of left and right cerebral specialization: A neurophysiological context for unconscious processes. *Archives of General Psychiatry*, 31, 572–583.

Gallagher, J. J. (1979). Issues and education for the gifted. In A. H. Passow (Ed.), *The gifted and the talented: Their education and development* (78th Yearbook for the National Society for the Study of Education). Chicago: University of Chicago Press.

Gallup, G. G., Jr., & Suarez, S. D. (1985). Alternatives to the use of animals in psychological research. *American Psychologist*, 40, 1104–1111.

Galotti, K. M. (1989). Approaches to studying formal and everyday reasoning. *Psychological Bulletin*, 105, 331–351.

Gamzu, E., Vincent, G., & Boff, E. (1985). A pharmacological perspective of drugs used in establishing conditioned food aversions. In Norman S. Braveman & Paul Bronstein (Eds.), *Experimental assessments and clinical applications of conditioned food aversions*. New York: New York Academy of Sciences.

Garber, J., Miller, W. R., & Seaman, S. F. (1979). Learned helplessness, stress, and the depressive disorders. In R. A. DePue (Ed.), *The psychobiology of the depressive disorders*. New York: Academic Press.

Garcia, J., Gustavson, C. R., Kelly, D. J., & Sweeney, M. (1976). Prey-lithium aversions: I. Coyotes and wolves. *Behavioral Biology*, 16, 61–72.

Garcia, J., & Koelling, R. A. (1971). The use of ionizing rays as a mammalian olfactory stimulus. In H. Autrum, R. Jung, W. R. Loewenstein, D. M. MacKay, H. L. Teuber (Eds.), *Handbook of sensory physiology, Vol. IV*, Chemical Senses, Part 1. New York: Springer-Verlag.

Gardner, R. A., & Gardner, B. T. (1969). Teaching sign language to a chimp. *Science*, 165, 664–672.

Gardner, W., Scherer, D., & Tester, M. (1989). Asserting scientific authority: Cognitive development and adolescent legal rights. *American Psychologist*, 6, 895–902.

Garfield, S. L., & Bergin, A. E. (1986). *Handbook of psychotherapy and behavior change* (3rd ed). New York: John Wiley & Sons.

Garfinkel, P. E., Moldofsy, H., & Garner, D. M. (1980). The heterogeneity of anorexia nervosa. Bulimia as a distinct subgroup. *Archives of General Psychiatry*, 37, 1036–1040.

Gatz, M., & Pearson, C. G. (1988). Ageism revised and the provision of psychological services. *American Psychologist*, 43, 184–188.

Gay, P. (1988). *Freud—a life for our time*. New York: W. W. Norton.

Gazzaniga, M. S. (1983). Right hemisphere language following brain bisection: A 20-year perspective. *American Psychologist*, 38, 525–537.

Gazzaniga, M. S. (1989). Organization of the human brain. *Science*, 245, 947–952.

Gebhardt, D. L., & Crump, C. E. (1990). Employee fitness and wellness programs in the workplace. *American Psychologist*, 45, 262–272.

Geiselman, R. E., MacKinnon, D. P., Fishman, D. L., Jaenicke, C., Larner, B. R., Schoenberg, S., & Swartz, S. (1983). Mechanisms of hypnotic and nonhypnotic forgetting. *Journal of Experimental Psychology: Learning, Memory, and Cognition*, 9, 626–635.

Geller, E. S. (1975). Increasing desired waste disposals with instructions. *Man Environment Systems*, 5, 125–128.

Geller, E. S. (1989). Applied behavior analysis and social marketing: An integration for environmental preservation. *Journal of Social Issues*, 45, 17–36.

Geller, E. S., Kalsher, M. J., Rudd, J. R., & Lehman, G. R. (1989).

Promoting safety belt use on a university campus: An integration of commitment and incentive strategies. *Journal of Applied Social Psychology, 19,* 3–19.

Geller, E. S., Patterson, L., & Talbot. (1982). A behavioral analysis of incentive prompts for motivating safety belt use. *Journal of Applied Behavior Analysis, 15,* 403–415.

Geller, E. S., Winett, R. A., & Everett, P. B. (1982). *Preserving the environment: New strategies for behavior change.* New York: Pergamon Press.

Geller, E. S., Witmer, J. F., & Tuso, M. E. (1977). Environmental intervention for litter control. *Journal of Applied Psychology, 62,* 344–351.

Gendlin, E. T. (1986). What comes after traditional psychotherapy research? *American Psychologist, 41,* 131–136.

George, J. M. (1989). Mood and absence. *Journal of Applied Psychology, 74,* 317–324.

Gerbner, G., & Gross, L. (1976). The scary world of TV's heavy viewer. *Psychology Today,* September, 41–45.

German, D. (1983). Analysis of word-finding disorders on the Kaufman Assessment Battery for Children (K-ABC). *Journal of Psychoeducational Assessment, 1,* 121–134.

Gerrard, C. K., Reznikoff, N., & Riklan, N. (1982). Level of aspiration, life satisfaction, and locus of control in older adults. *Experimental Aging Research, 8,* 119–121.

Gerrard, M. (1987). Sex, sex guilt, and contraceptive use revisited: The 1980s. *Journal of Personality and Social Psychology, 52,* 975–980.

Gershone, J. R., Erickson, E. A., Mitchell, J. E., & Paulson, D. A. (1977). Behavioral comparison of a token economy and a standard psychiatric treatment ward. *Journal of Behavior Therapy and Experimental Psychiatry, 8,* 381–385.

Geschwind, N. (1970). The organization of language in the brain. *Science, 170,* 940–944.

Geschwind, N. (1972). Language and the brain. *Scientific American, 226,* 76–83.

Gherman, E. M. (1981). Stress and the bottom line: A guide to personal well-being and corporate health. New York: AMACOM.

Gibbons, B. (1986). The intimate sense of smell. *National Geographic, 9,* 324–360.

Gibbons, J. L., Stiles, D. A., Schnellmann, J. de la Garza, & Hidalgo, I. M. (1988). *Guatemalan adolescents view the ideal person as hard-working.* Paper presented at the 96th Annual Convention of the American Psychological Association, Atlanta, GA, August.

Gibson, C. J., Logue, M., & Growdon, J. H. (1985). CSF monoamine metabolite levels in Alzheimer's and Parkinson's disease. *Archives of Neurology, 42,* 489–492.

Gibson, E. J. (1988). Exploratory behavior in the development of perceiving, acting, and the acquiring of knowledge. *Annual Review of Psychology, 39,* 1–41.

Gibson, J. J. (1950). *The perception of the visual world.* Boston: Houghton Mifflin.

Gift, T. E., Strauss, J. S., Ritzler, B. A., Kokes, R. F., & Harder, D. W. (1980). How diagnostic concepts of schizophrenia differ. *Journal of Nervous and Mental Disease, 168,* 3–8.

Gilbert, R. K. (1988). The dynamics of inaction. *American Psychologist, 43,* 755–764.

Gilligan, C. (1982). *In a different voice: Psychological theory and women's development.* Cambridge, MA: Harvard University Press.

Gillum, R., Leon, G. R., Kamp, J., & Becerra-Aldama, J. (1980). Prediction of cardiovascular and other disease onset and mortality from 30-year longitudinal MMPI data. *Journal of Consulting and Clinical Psychology, 48,* 405–406.

Glantz, M. D. (1989). Cognitive therapy with the elderly. In A. Freeman, K. M. Simon, L. E. Beutler, & H. Arkowitz (Eds.), *Comprehensive handbook of cognitive therapy.* New York: Plenum Press.

Glaser, R., & Kiecolt-Glaser, J. (1988). Stress-associated immune suppression and acquired immune deficiency syndrome (AIDS). In T. P. Bridge, A. F. Mirsky, & F. K. Goodwin (Eds.), *Psychological, neuropsychiatric, and substance abuse aspects of AIDS.* New York: Raven Press.

Glasgow, R. E., & Terborg, J. R. (1988). Occupational health promotion programs to reduce cardiovascular risk. *Journal of Consulting and Clinical Psychology, 56*(3), 365–373.

Glass, C. R., Gottman, J. M., & Shmurak, S. H. (1976). Response acquisition and cognitive self-statement modification approaches to dating-skills training. *Journal of Counseling Psychology, 23,* 520–526.

Gloor, P., Olivier, A., Quesney, L. F., Andermann, F., & Horowitz, S. (1982). The role of the limbic system in experiential phenomena of temporal lobe epilepsy. *Annals of Neurology, 12,* 129–144.

Goetz, K. L., & van Kammen, D. P. (1986). Computerized axial tomography scans and subtypes of schizophrenia. *Journal of Nervous and Mental Disease, 174,* 31–41.

Golden, M., Rosenbluth, L., Grossi, M., Policare, H., Freeman, H., & Brownlee, E. (1978). *The New York City infant day care study.* New York: Medical and Health Research Association of New York City.

Goldfried, M. R., & Davison, G. C. (1976). *Clinical behavior therapy.* New York: Holt, Rinehart & Winston.

Goldman, M., Cowles, M. D., & Florez, C. A. (1983). The halo effect of an initial impression upon speaker and audience. *Journal of Social Psychology, 120,* 197–201.

Goldstein, A. J., & Chambless, D. L. (1978). A reanalysis of agoraphobia. *Behavior Therapy, 9,* 47–57.

Goldstein, G., & Hersen, M. (1984). Historical perspectives. In G. Goldstein & M. Hersen (Eds.), *Handbook of psychological assessment.* New York: Pergamon Press.

Goleman, D. (1985). *Vital lies, simple truths.* New York: Simon & Schuster.

Gonzales, L. R., Hays, R. B., Bond, M. A., & Kelly, J. G. (1983). Community mental health. In M. Hersen, A. E. Kazdin, & A. S. Bellack (Eds.), *The clinical psychology handbook.* New York: Pergamon Press.

Gonzales, R. R., & Roll, S. (1985). Relationship between acculturation, cognitive style, and intelligence. *Journal of Cross-Cultural Psychology, 16,* 190–205.

Gonzales, M. H., Aronson, E., & Costanzo (1988). Using social cognition and persuasion to promote energy conservation: A quasi-experiment. *Journal of Applied Social Psychology, 18,* 1049–1066.

Goodglass, H., & Butters, N. (1988). Psychobiology of cognitive processes. In R. C. Atkinson, R. J. Herrnstein, G. Lindzey, & R. D. Luce (Eds.), *Stevens' handbook of experimental psychology, 2nd Edition, Volume 2, Learning and Cognition.* New York: John Wiley & Sons.

Goodman, J. (1983). How to get more smileage out of your life: Making sense of humor, then serving it. In P. McGhee & J. Goldstein (Eds.), *Handbook of humor research* (Vol. 2, pp. 1–21). New York: Springer-Verlag.

Goranson, R. E., & King, D. (1970). Rioting and daily temperature: Analysis of the U.S. riots in 1967. Unpublished manuscript, York University, as cited in P. A. Bell, J. D. Fisher, & R. J. Loomis, *Environmental psychology.* Philadelphia: W. B. Saunders, 1978.

Gordon, S. (1976). *Lonely in America.* New York: Simon & Schuster.

Gorney, R., Loye, D., & Steele, G. (1977). Impact of dramatized television entertainment on adult males. *American Journal of Psychiatry, 134,* 170–174.

Gotlib, I. H., Whiffen, V. E., Mount, J. H., Milne, K., & Cordy, N. I. (1989). *Journal of Consulting and Clinical Psychology, 57,* 269–274.

Gottesman, I., & Shields, J. (1982). *Schizophrenia: The epigenetic puzzle.* Cambridge: Cambridge University Press.

Gottheil, E., & Stone, G. C. (1974). Psychosomatic aspects of orality and anality. *Journal of Nervous and Mental Disease, 159,* 182–190.

Gottman, J. M., & Katz, L. F. (1989). Effects of marital discord on young children's peer interaction and health. *Developmental Psychology, 25,* 373–381.

Gottsfeld, M. L. (1978). Treatment of vaginismus by psychotherapy and adjunctive hypnosis. *American Journal of Clinical Hypnosis, 22,* 272–277.

Graham, J. R., & Strenger, V. E. (1988). MMPI characteristics of alcoholics: A review. *Journal of Consulting and Clinical Psychology, 56,* 197–205.

Grant, B. W. (1975). *Schizophrenia: A source of social insight.* Philadelphia: Westminster Press.

Grant, V. W. (1977). *The menacing stranger.* Oceanside, NY: Dabor Science Publications.

Greaves, G. B. (1980). Multiple personality: 165 years after Mary Reynolds. *Journal of Nervous and Mental Disease, 168,* 577–596.

Green, B. L., Lindy, J. D., Grace, M. C., & Gleser, G. C. (1989). Multiple diagnosis in posttraumatic stress disorder: The role of war stressors. *Journal of Nervous and Mental Disease, 177,* 329–386.

Green, R. J., & Stanton, M. E. (1989). Differential ontogeny of working memory and reference memory in the rat. *Behavioral Neuroscience, 103,* 98–105.

Greenberg, M., & Morris, N. (1974). Engrossment: The newborn's impact upon the father. *American Journal of Orthopsychiatry, 44,* 520–531.

Greene, R. L. (1987). Effects of maintenance rehearsal on human memory. *Psychological Bulletin, 102,* 403–413.

Greeno, J. G. (1989). A perspective on thinking. *American Psychologist, 44,* 134–141.

Greenwald, A. G., Pratkanis, A. R., Leippe, M. R., & Baumgardner, M. H. (1986). Under what conditions does theory obstruct research progress? *Psychological Review, 93,* 216–229.

Greif, G. L. (1985). Single fathers rearing children. *Journal of Marriage and the Family,* 185–191.

Griffeth, R. W., Vecchio, R. P., & Logan, J. W., Jr. (1989). Equity theory and interpersonal attraction. *Journal of Applied Psychology, 74,* 394–401.

Griffin, M. L., Weiss, R. D., Mirin, S. M., & Lange, U. (1989). A comparison of male and female cocaine abusers. *Archives of General Psychiatry, 46,* 122–126.

Griffiths, R. R., Bigelow, G., & Liebson, I. (1977). Comparison of social time-out and activity time-out procedures in suppressing ethanol self-administration in alcoholics. *Behavior Research and Therapy, 15,* 329–335.

Grilo, C. M., Shiffman, S., & Wing, R. R. (1989). Relapse crises and coping among dieters. *Journal of Consulting and Clinical Psychology, 57,* 488–495.

Groninger, L. D., & Groninger, L. K. (1988). Autobiographical episodes as mediators in the recall of words. *American Journal of Psychology, 101,* 515–538.

Grossman, F. K., Pollack, W. S., Golding, E. (1988). Fathers and children: Predicting the quality and quantity of fathering. *Developmental Psychology, 1,* 92.

Grossman, F. M. (1983). Percentage of WAIS-R standardization sample obtaining verbal-performance discrepancies. *Journal of Consulting and Clinical Psychology, 51,* 641–642.

Grossman, S. P., & Grossman, L. (1977). Food and water intake in rats after transections of fibers en passage in the tegmentum. *Physiological Behavior, 18,* 647–658.

Gruder, C. L., Cook, T. D., Hennigan, K. M., Flay, B. R., Alessis, C., & Halamaj, J. (1978). Empirical tests of the absolute sleeper effect predicted from the discounting cue hypothesis. *Journal of Personality and Social Psychology, 42,* 412–425.

Guerin, B. (1989). Social inhibition of behavior. *The Journal of Social Psychology, 129,* 225–233.

Guggenheim, F. G., & Babigian, H. M. (1974). Catatonic schizophrenia: Epidemiology and clinical course. *Journal of Nervous and Mental Disease, 158,* 291–305.

Guilford, J. P. (1967). *The nature of human intelligence.* New York: McGraw-Hill.

Guilford, J. P. (1980). Fluid and crystallized intelligences: Two fanciful concepts. *Psychological Bulletin, 88,* 406–412.

Guilford, J. P. (1985). The structure of intellect model. In B. B. Wolman (Ed.), *Handbook of intelligence: Theories, measurements, and applications,* New York: John Wiley & Sons.

Guion, R. M., & Gibson, W. M. (1988). Personnel selection and placement. In M. R. Rosenzweig & L. W. Porter (Eds.), *Annual Review of Psychology.* Palo Alto, CA: Annual Reviews, Inc.

Gulevich, G., Dement, W., & Johnson, L. (1966). Psychiatric and EEG observations on a case of prolonged (264 hours) wakefulness. *Archives of General Psychiatry, 15,* 29–35.

Gunderson, J. G., & Mosher, L. R. (1978). The cost of schizophrenia. In R. Cancro (Ed.), *Annual review of the schizophrenic syndrome (1976-7).* New York: Brunner/Mazel.

Gurman, A. S., & Razin, A. M. (1977). *Effective psychotherapy: A handbook of research.* New York: Pergamon Press.

Gustafsson, P. A., Kjellman, N-I. M., & Cederblad, M. (1986). Family therapy in the treatment of severe childhood asthma. *Journal of Psychosomatic Research, 30,* 369–371.

Haaf, R. A., Smith, P. H., & Smitley, S. (1983). Infant response to facelike patterns under fixed-trial and infant-control procedures. *Child Development, 54,* 172–177.

Haan, N., Millsap, R., & Hartka, E. (1986). As time goes by: Change and stability in personality over fifty years. *Psychology and Aging, 1,* 220–232.

Haber, R. N. (1969). Eidetic images, *Scientific American, 220*(4), 36–44.

Haber, R. N. (1979). Twenty years of haunting eidetic imagery: Where's the ghost? *Behavioral and Brain Sciences, 2,* 583–629.

Haber, R. N. (1983). The impending demise of the icon: A critique of the concept of iconic storage in visual information processing. *Behavioral and Brain Sciences, 6,* 1–54.

Haber, R. N. (1985). An icon can have no worth in the real world: Comments on Loftus, Johnson, and Shimamura's "How much is an icon worth?" *Journal of Experimental Psychology: Human Perception and Performance, 11,* 374–378.

Hahn, W. K. (1987). Cerebral lateralization of function: From infancy through childhood. *Psychological Bulletin, 101,* 376–392.

Haier, R., Siegel, B., Nueckterlein, Haylett, E., Wu, J., Paek, J., Browning, H., & Buchsbaum, M. (1988). Cortical glucose metabolic rate correlates to abstract reasoning and attention studied with positron emission tomography. *Intelligence, 12,* 199–218.

Haith, M. M., & McCarty, M. E. (1990). Stability of visual expectations at 3.0 months of age. *Developmental Psychology, 26,* 68–74.

Halberstadt, A. G., & Saitta, M. B. (1987). Gender, nonverbal behavior, and perceived dominance: A test of the theory. *Journal of Personality and Social Psychology, 53,* 257–272.

Haley, J. (1976). *Problem solving therapy.* New York: W. W. Norton.

Halgren, E., Walter, R. D., Cherlow, A. G., & Crandall, Ph. H. (1978). Mental phenomena evoked by electrical stimulation of the human hippocampal formation and amygdala. *Brain, 101,* 83–117.

Hall, E. T. (1966). *The hidden dimension.* Garden City, NY: Doubleday.

Hall, J. A. (1979). Gender, gender roles, and nonverbal communication skills. In R. Rosenthal (Ed.), *Skill in nonverbal communication.* Cambridge, MA: Oelgeschlager, Gunn & Hain.

Hall, J. F. (1982). *An invitation to learning and memory.* Boston: Allyn and Bacon.

Hall, S. M., Ginsberg, D., & Jones, R. T. (1986). Smoking cessation and weight gain. *Journal of Consulting and Clinical Psychology, 54,* 342–346.

Hall, V. C., & Turner, R. R. (1974). The validity of the "different languages explanation" for poor scholastic performance by black students. *Review of Educational Research, 44,* 69–81.

Hallam, R. S., & Rachman, S. (1976). Current status of aversion therapy. In M. Hersen, R. M. Eisler, & B. M. Miller (Eds.), *Progress in behavior modification* (Vol. 2). New York: Academic Press.

Hallman, W. K., & Wandersman, A. H. (1989). *Hazardous waste: Present risk, future risk, cancer risk or no risk?* Paper presented at the American Psychological Association Conference, New Orleans, August.

Hamburg, D., Bibring, G., Fischer, C., Stanton, A., Wallerstein, R., & Haggart, E. (1967). Report of ad hoc committee on central fact-gathering data of the American Psychoanalytic Association. *Journal of the American Psychoanalytic Association, 15,* 841–861.

Hamilton, S., & Fagot, B. I. (1988). Chronic stress and coping styles: A comparison of male and female undergraduates. *Journal of Personality and Social Psychology, 5,* 819–823.

Hammen, C., & Krantz, S. E. (1985). Measures of psychological processes in depression. In E. E. Beckham & W. R. Leber (Eds.), *Handbook of depression. Treatment, assessment, and research.* Homewood, IL: Dorsey Press.

Hammen, C., & Mayol, A. (1982). Depression and cognitive characteristics of stressful life-events types. *Journal of Abnormal Psychology, 91,* 165–174.

Hanks, R. (1985). Moral reasoning in adolescents: A feature of intelligence or social adjustment? *Journal of Moral Education, 14,* 43–55.

Hanson, C. L., Cigrang, J. A., Harris, M. A., Carle, D. L., Relyea, G., & Burghen, G. A. (1989). Coping styles in youths with insulin-dependent diabetes mellitus. *Journal of Consulting and Clinical Psychology, 57,* 644–651.

Harbin, T. J. (1989). The relationship between the type A behavior pattern and psychological responsivity: A quantitative review. *Psychophysiology, 26,* 110–112.

Hare-Mustin, R. D. (1983). An appraisal of the relationship between women and psychotherapy. *American Psychologist, 38,* 593–601.

Harkins, S. G., & Szymanski, K. (1988). Social loafing and self-evaluation with an objective standard. *Journal of Experimental Social Psychology, 24,* 354–365.

Harlow, H. F. (1962). The heterosexual affectional system in monkeys. *American Psychologist, 17,* 1–9.

Harlow, H. F., & Zimmerman, R. R. (1958). The development of affectional responses in infant monkeys. *Proceedings of the American Philosophic Society, 102,* 501–509.

Harper, R. A. (1975). *The new psychotherapies.* Englewood Cliffs, NJ: Prentice-Hall.

Harris, C. M., Hainline, L., Abramov, I., Lemerise, E., & Camenzuli, C. (1988). The distribution of fixation durations in infants and naive adults. *Vision Research, 28,* 419–432.

Harris, V. A., & Katkin, E. S. (1975). Primary and secondary emotional behaviour: An analysis of the role of autonomic feedback on affect, arousal, and attribution. *Psychological Bulletin, 82,* 904–916.

Hartup, W. W. (1989). Social relationships and their developmental significance. *American Psychologist, 44,* 120–126.

Haskins, R. (1989). Beyond metaphor: The efficacy of early childhood education. *American Psychologist, 44*(2), 274–282.

Hass, J. W., Bagley, G. S., & Rogers, R. W. (1975). Coping with the energy crisis: Effects of fear appeals upon attitudes toward energy consumption. *Journal of Applied Psychology, 60,* 754–756.

Hatch, J. P. (1981). Voluntary control of sexual responding in men and women: Implications for the etiology and treatment of sexual dysfunctions. *Biofeedback and Self-Regulation, 6,* 191–206.

Hatfield, E., Traupmann, J., Sprecher, S., Utne, M., Hay, J. (1985). Equity and intimate relations: Recent research. In W. Ickes (Ed.), *In compatible and incompatible relationships* (pp. 91–117). New York: Springer-Verlag.

Hausner, G., (1966). *Justice in Jerusalem.* New York: Holocaust Library.

Hay, D. A., & O'Brien, P. J. (1983). The La Trobe Twin Study: A genetic approach to the structure and development of cognition in twin children. *Child Development, 54,* 317–330.

Haynes, S. N. (1984). Behavioral assessment of adults. In G. Goldstein & M. Hersen (Eds.), *Handbook of psychological assessment.* New York: Pergamon Press.

Haynes, R. B. (1979). Determinants of compliance: The disease and the mechanics of treatment. In R. B. Haynes, D. W. Taylor, & D. L. Sackett (Eds.), *Compliance in health care.* Baltimore: Johns Hopkins University Press.

Hays, R. B. (1989). The day-to-day functioning of close versus casual friendships. *Journal of Social and Personal Relationships, 6,* 21–37.

Hazan, C., & Shaver, P. (1987). Romantic love conceptualized as an attachment process. *Journal of Personality and Social Psychology, 52,* 511–524.

Hazelrigg, M. D., Cooper, H. M., & Borduin, C. M. (1987). Evaluating the effectiveness of family therapies: An integrative review and analysis. *Psychological Bulletin, 101,* 428–442.

Hebb, D. O. (1949). *Organization of behavior.* New York: John Wiley & Sons.

Hebb, D. O. (1955). Drives and the C.N.S. (conceptual nervous system). *Psychological Review, 62,* 243–254.

Hebb, D. O. (1972). *Textbook of psychology* (3rd ed.). Philadelphia: W. B. Saunders.

Hebb, D. O. (1974). What psychology is about. *American Psychologist, 29,* 71–79.

Heckler, M. M. (1985). Psychology in the public forum. The fight against Alzheimer's disease. *American Psychologist, 40,* 1240–1244.

Heider, E. R. (1971). "Focal" color areas and the development of color names. *Developmental Psychology, 4,* 447–455.

Heider, E. R. (1972). Universals in color naming and memory. *Journal of Experimental Psychology, 93,* 10–21.

Heider, E. R., & Olivier, D. C. (1972). The structure of the color space in naming and memory for two languages. *Cognitive Psychology, 3,* 337–354.

Heider, K. G. (1991). *Landscapes of emotion: Lexical maps and scenarios of emotion terms in Indonesia.* Cambridge, MA: Cambridge University Press.

Heilbrun, A. B., Jr., Wydra, D., & Friedberg, L. (1989). Parent identification and gender schema development. *Journal of Genetic Psychology, 150*(3), 293–299.

Heimberg, R. G., Becker, R. E., Goldfinger, K., & Vermilyea, J. A. (1985). Treatment of social phobia by exposure, cognitive restructuring, and homework assignments. *Journal of Nervous and Mental Disease, 173,* 236–245.

Heinlein, R. (1961). *Stranger in a strange land.* New York: Putnam.

Held, R., & Bauer, J. A. (1967). Visually guided reaching in infant monkeys after restricted rearing. *Science, 155,* 718–720.

Held, R., & Hein, A. (1963). Movement produced stimulation in the development of visually guided behavior. *Journal of Comparative and Physiological Psychology, 56,* 872–876.

Helfer, R. E. (1987). The developmental basis of child abuse and neglect: An epidemiological approach. In R. E. Helfer & R. S. Kempe (Eds.), *The battered child* (4th ed.). Chicago: University of Chicago Press.

Hellige, J. B. (1990). Hemispheric asymmetry. In M. R. Rosenzweig & L. W. Porter (Eds.), *Annual Review of Psychology, 41,* 55–80.

Hellige, J. B., & Wong, T. M. (1983). Hemisphere-specific interference in dichotic listening: Task variables and individual differences. *Journal of Experimental Psychology: General, 112,* 218–239.

Helmreich, W. B. (1982). *The things they say behind your back.* Garden City, NY: Doubleday.

Helson, R., & Moane, G. (1987). Personality change in women from college to midlife. *Journal of Personality and Social Psychology, 53,* 176–186.

Hemshorn, A. (1985). They call it Alzheimer's disease. *Journal of Gerontological Nursing, 11,* 36–38.

Hendler, C. S., & Redd, W. H. (1986). Fear of hypnosis: The role of labeling in patients' acceptance of behavior interventions. *Behavior Therapy, 17,* 2–13.

Hendrick, C., & Hendrick, S. S. (1989). Research on love: Does it measure up? *Journal of Personality and Social Psychology, 56,* 784–794.

Henker, B., & Whalen, C. K. (1989). Hyperactivity and attention deficits. *American Psychologist, 44,* 216–223.

Henry, K. R. (1984). Cochlear damage resulting from exposure to four different octave bands of noise at three ages. *Behavioral Neuroscience, 98,* 107–117.

Herek, G. M., & Glunt, E. K. (1988). An epidemic of stigma. *American Psychologist, 43,* 886–891.

Herman, C. P., Olmsted, M. P., & Polivy, J. (1983). Obesity, externality, and susceptibility to social influence: An integrated analysis. *Journal of Personality and Social Psychology, 45,* 926–934.

Hermann, D. J. (1982). The semantic-episodic distinction and the history of long-term memory typologies. *Bulletin of the Psychonomic Society, 20,* 207–210.

Heron, W. (1957). The pathology of boredom. *Scientific American, 196*(1), 52–56.

Hershman, S. (1955). Hypnosis in the treatment of obesity. *International Journal of Clinical and Experimental Hypnosis, 3,* 136–140.

Hertzog, C., Schaie, K. W., & Gribbin, K. (1978). Cardiovascular disease and changes in intellectual functioning from middle to old age. *Journal of Gerontology, 33,* 872–883.

Heston, L. L. (1966). Psychiatric disorders in foster home reared children of schizophrenic mothers. *British Journal of Psychiatry, 11,* 819–825.

Hetherington, E. M., Stanley-Hagan, M., & Anderson, E. R. (1989). Marital transitions: A child's perspective. *American Psychologist, 44,* 303–312.

Hildebrandt, K. A. (1983). Effect of facial expression variations on ratings of infant's physical attractiveness. *Developmental Psychology, 29,* 414–417.

Hilgard, E. R. (1965). *Hypnotic susceptibility.* New York: Harcourt, Brace & World.

Hilgard, E. R., & Hilgard, J. R. (1975). *Hypnosis in the relief of pain.* Los Altos, CA: William Kaufmann.

Hilgard, E. R., & Marquis, D. G. (1935). Acquisition, extinction, and retention of conditioned lid responses to light in dogs. *Journal of Comparative Psychology, 19,* 29–58.

Hilgard, E. R., & Morgan, A. H. (1975). Heart rate and blood pressure in the study of laboratory pain in man under normal conditions and as influenced by hypnosis. *Acta Neurobiologiae Experimentalis, 35,* 501–513.

Hill, C., & Gormally, J. (1977). Effects of reflection, restatement, probe, and nonverbal behaviors on client affect. *Journal of Counseling Psychology, 24,* 92–97.

Hill, J. H., Liebert, R. M., & Mott, D. E. W. (1968). Vicarious extinction of avoidance behavior through films: An initial test. *Psychological Reports, 22,* 192.

Hill, S. Y., Steinhauer, S. R., & Zubin, J. (1987). Biological markers for alcoholism: A vulnerability model conceptualization. In P. C. Rivers (Ed.), *Alcohol and addictive behavior.* Lincoln, NE: University of Nebraska Press.

Hilton, D. J. (1990). Conversational processes and causal explanation. *Psychological Bulletin, 107,* 65–81.

Hinshaw, S. P. (1987). On the distinction between attentional deficits/hyperactivity and conduct problems/aggression in child psychopathology. *Psychological Bulletin, 101,* 443–463.

Hinz, L. D., & Williamson, D. A. (1987). Bulimia and depression: A review of the affective variant hypothesis. *Psychological Bulletin, 102,* 150–158.

Hirsch, H. V. B., & Spinelli, D. N. (1971). Modification of the distribution of receptive field orientation in cats by selective exposure during development. *Experimental Brain Research, 13,* 509–527.

Hirsch, J., & Leibel, R. L. (1988). New light on obesity. *New England Journal of Medicine, 318,* 509–510.

Hobfoll, S. E. (1989). Conservation of resources: A new attempt at conceptualizing stress. *American Psychologist, 44,* 513–524.

Hobson, J. A. (1989). *Sleep.* New York: W. H. Freeman.

Hobson, J. A., & McCarley, R. W. (1977). The brain as a dream state generator: An activation-synthesis of the dream process. *American Journal of Psychiatry, 134,* 1335–1348.

Hochberg, J. E. (1974). Organization and the Gestalt tradition. In E. C. Carterette & M. P. Friedman (Eds.), *Handbook of perception.* New York: Academic Press.

Hochberg, J. E. (1979). Sensation and perception. In E. Hearst (Ed.), *The first century of experimental psychology.* New York: John Wiley & Sons.

Hodges, K. K., & Siegel, L. J. (1985). Depression in children and adolescents. In E. E. Beckham & W. R. Leber (Eds.), *Handbook of depression. Treatment, assessment, and research.* Homewood, IL: Dorsey Press.

Hofferth, S. L., & Phillips, D. A. (1987). Child care in the United States, 1970 to 1995. *Journal of Marriage and the Family, 49,* 559–571.

Holder, M. D., Yirmiya, R., Garcia, J., & Raizer, J. (1989). Conditioned taste aversions are not readily disrupted by external excitation. *Behavioral Neuroscience, 103,* 605–611.

Holland, M. K. (1975). *Using psychology: Principles of behavior and your life.* Boston: Little, Brown.

Holloway, F. A. (1977). State-dependent retrieval based on time of day. In B. Ho, D. Chute, & D. Richards (Eds.), *Drug discrimination and state-dependent learning.* New York: Academic Press.

Holmes, D. S. (1978). Projection as a defense mechanism. *Psychological Bulletin, 85,* 677–688.

Holmes, D. S. (1984). Meditation and somatic arousal reduction. *American Psychologist, 39,* 1–10.

Holmes, T. H., & Rahe, R. H. (1967). The social readjustment rating scale. *Journal of Psychosomatic Research, 11,* 213–218.

Holyoak, K. J., Koh, K., & Nisbett, R. E. (1989). A theory of conditioning: Inductive learning within rule-based default hierarchies. *Psychological Review, 96,* 315–340.

Holzman, P. S., & Bivens, L. W. (1988). Basic behavioral sciences. *Schizophrenia Bulletin, 14,* 413–426.

Hom, H. L., Jr., & Arbuckle, B. (1988). Mood induction effects upon goal setting and performance in young children. *Motivation and Emotion, 12,* 113–122.

Honig, W. K. (1966). *Operant behavior: Areas of research and application.* New York: Appleton-Century-Crofts.

Hood, D. C. (1988). *Toward understanding stock market movements: A marriage of psychology and economics.* Paper presented at a Science and Public

Policy Seminar sponsored by the Federation of Behavioral, Psychological and Cognitive Sciences, Washington, DC, July 1.

Hoon, E. F. (1980). Biofeedback-assisted arousal in females: A comparison of visual and auditory modalities. *Biofeedback and Self-Regulation, 5,* 175–191.

Horn, J. M. (1983). The Texas adoption project: Adopted children and their intellectual resemblance to biological and adoptive parents. *Child Development, 54,* 268–275.

Horne, J. (1988). *Why we sleep.* New York: Oxford University Press.

Horney, K. (1937). *The neurotic personality of our time.* New York: W. W. Norton.

Horton, D. L., & Mills, C. B. (1984). Human learning and memory. *Annual Review of Psychology, 35,* 361–394.

Horvath, F. S. (1977). The effects of selected variables on the interpretation of polygraph records. *Journal of Applied Psychology, 62,* 127–136.

Horvath, P. (1988). Placebos and common factors in two decades of psychotherapy research. *Psychological Bulletin, 204,* 214–225.

Horvath, T. (1981). Physical attractiveness: The influence of selected torso parameters. *Archives of Sexual Behavior, 10,* 21–24.

Hovland, C. I. (1937). The generalization of conditioned responses: 1. The sensory generalization of conditioned responses with varying frequencies of tone. *Journal of General Psychology, 17,* 125–148.

Howard, K. I., Kopta, S. M., Krause, M. S., & Orlinsky, D. E. (1986). The dose-effect relationships in psychotherapy. *American Psychologist, 41,* 159–164.

Howarth, E. (1986). What does Eysenck's psychoticism scale really measure? *British Journal of Psychology, 77,* 223–227.

Howe, M. J. A., & Smith, J. (1988). Calendar calculating in "idiots savants": How do they do it? *British Journal of Psychology, 79,* 371–386.

Howes, C., & Stewart, P. (1987). Child's play with adults, toys, and peers: An examination of family and child-care influences. *Developmental Psychology, 23,* 423–430.

Howes, C., Unger, O., & Seidner, L. B. (1989). Social pretend play in toddlers: Parallels with social play and with solitary pretend. *Child Development, 60,* 77–84.

Hoyt, I. P., Nadon, R., Register, P. A., Chorny, J., Fleeson, W., Grigorian, E. M., & Otto, L. (1989). Daydreaming, absorption, and hypnotizability. *International Journal of Clinical and Experimental Hypnosis, XXXVII,* 332–342.

Hubel, D. H., & Wiesel, T. N. (1962). Receptive fields, binocular interaction, and functional architecture in the cat's visual cortex. *Journal of Physiology, 160,* 106–164.

Hudspeth, A. J. (1983). The hair cells of the inner ear. *Scientific American, 248,* 54–73.

Huey, E. B. (1972). *The psychology and pedagogy of reading.* Cambridge, MA: MIT Press. (Original work published 1908.)

Humphreys, L. G. (1960). Investigations of the simplex. *Psychometrika, 25,* 475–483.

Humphreys, L. G. (1968). The fleeting nature of the prediction of college academic success. *Journal of Educational Psychology, 59,* 375–380.

Humphreys, L. G., & Davey, T. C. (1988). Continuity in intellectual growth from 12 months to 9 years. *Intelligence, 12,* 183–197.

Humphreys, M. S., Bain, J. D., & Pike, R. (1989). Different ways to cue a coherent memory system: A theory for episodic, semantic, and procedural tasks. *Psychological Review, 96,* 208–233.

Hunt, E. B. (1983). On the nature of intelligence. *Science, 219,* 141–146.

Hurvich, L., & Jameson, D. (1974). Opponent processes as a model of neural organization. *American Psychologist, 30,* 88–102.

Huston, A. C., Watkins, B. A., & Kunkel, D. (1989). Public policy and children's television. *American Psychologist, 44,* 424–433.

Huttunen, M. O., & Niskanen, P. (1978). Prenatal loss of father and psychiatric disorders. *Archives of General Psychiatry, 35,* 429–431.

Hyde, J. S., Fennema, E., & Lamon, S. J. (1990). Gender differences in mathematic performance: A meta-analysis. *Psychological Bulletin, 107,* 139–155.

Hyde, J. S., & Linn, M. C. (1988). Gender differences in verbal ability: A meta-analysis. *Psychological Bulletin, 104,* 53–69.

Hyland, M. E. (1987). Control theory interpretation of psychological mechanisms of depression: Comparison and integration of several theories. *Psychological Bulletin, 102,* 109–121.

Hymes, R. W. (1986). Political attitudes as social categories: A new look at selective memory. *Journal of Personality and Social Psychology, 51,* 233–241.

Hynd, G. W., & Semrud-Clikeman, M. (1989). Dyslexia and brain morphology. *Psychological Bulletin, 106,* 447–482.

Hyona, J., Niemi, P., & Underwood, G. (1989). Reading long words embedded in sentences: Informativeness of word halves affects eye movements. *Journal of Experimental Psychology: Human Perception and Performance, 15,* 142–152.

Ilgen, D. R. (1990). Health issues at work: Opportunities for industrial/organizational psychology. *American Psychologist, 45,* 273–283.

Ingbar, D. H., & Gee, J. B. L. (1985). Pathophysiology and treatment of sleep apnea. *Annual Review of Medicine, 36,* 369–395.

Ingles, T. (1980). St. Christopher's Hospice. In M. Hamilton & H. Reid (Eds.), *A hospice handbook: A new way to care for the dying.* Grand Rapids, MI: Wm. D. Eerdmans.

Ingram, D. (1975). Surface contrasts in children's speech. *Journal of Child Language, 2,* 287–292.

Inhelder, B., & Piaget, J. (1958). *The growth of logical thinking from childhood to adolescence.* New York: Basic Books.

Inhoff, A. W., Morris, R., & Calabrese, J. (1986). Eye movements in skilled transcription typing. *Bulletin of the Psychonomic Society, 2,* 113–114.

Innes, J. M., & Young, R. F. (1975). The effect of presence of an audience, evaluation apprehension, and objective self-awareness on learning. *Journal of Experimental Social Psychology, 11,* 35–42.

Insua, A. M. (1983). WAIS-R factor structures in two cultures. *Journal of Cross-Cultural Psychology, 14,* 427–438.

Intraub, H. (1980). Presentation rate and the representation of briefly glimpsed pictures in memory. *Journal of Experimental Psychology: Human Learning and Memory, 6,* 1–12.

Intraub, H., & Nicklos, S. (1985). Levels of processing and picture memory: The physical superiority effect. *Journal of Experimental Psychology: Learning, Memory, and Cognition, 11,* 284–298.

Irwin, D. E., Brown, J. S., & Sun, J. S. (1988). Visual masking and visual integration across saccadic eye movements. *Journal of Experimental Psychology: General, 117,* 276–287.

Isabella, R. A., Belsky, J., & von Eye, A. (1989). Origins of infant-mother attachment: An examination of interactional synchrony during the infant's first year. *Developmental Psychology, 25,* 12–21.

Israely, Y. (1985). The moral development of mentally retarded children: Review of the literature. *Journal of Moral Education, 14,* 33–42.

Istvan, J. & Matarazzo, J. D. (1984). Tobacco, alcohol, and caffeine use: A review of their interrelationships. *Psychological Bulletin, 95,* 301–326.

Izard, C. E., & Saxton, P. M. (1988). Emotions. In R. C. Atkinson, R. J. Herrnstein, G. Lindzey, & R. D. Luce (Eds.), *Stevens handbook of experimental psychology, 1st Edition, Volume 1, Perception and Motivation.* New York: John Wiley & Sons.

Jacklin, C. N. (1989). Female and male: Issues of gender. *American Psychologist, 44,* 127–133.

Jackson, A. W., & Hornbeck, D. W. (1989). Educating young adolescents. Why we must restructure middle grade schools. *American Psychologist, 44,* 831–836.

Jackson, J. M., & Latane, B. (1981). All alone in front of all those people: Stage fright as a function of number and type of co-performers and audience. *Journal of Personality and Social Psychology, 40,* 73–85.

Jackson, S. E., & Schuler, R. S. (1990). Human resource planning: Challenges for industrial/organizational psychologists. *American Psychologist, 45,* 223–239.

Jacobs, L., Berscheid, E., & Walster, E. (1971). Self-esteem and attraction. *Journal of Personality and Social Psychology, 17,* 84–91.

Jacobs, M. K., & Goodman, G. (1989). Psychology and self-help groups. *American Psychologist, 44,* 536–545.

Jacobson, N. S., & Bussob, N. (1983). Marital and family therapy. In M. Herson, A. E. Kazdin, and A. S. Bellack, *The clinical psychology handbook.* New York: Pergamon Press.

Jaffe, P. G., & Carlson, P. M. (1972). Modeling therapy for test anxiety: The role of model affect and consequences. *Behavior Research and Therapy, 10,* 329–339.

James, J. E. (1981). Behavioral self-control of stuttering using timeout from speaking. *Journal of Applied Behavior Analysis, 14,* 25–37.

James, W. (1884). What is an emotion? *Mind, 9,* 188–205.

James, W. (1890). *Principles of psychology.* New York: Dover Publications.

Janes, C. L., Weeks, D. G., & Worland, J. (1983). School behavior in adolescent children of parents with mental disorder. *Journal of Nervous and Mental Disease, 171,* 234–240.

Janis, I. L. (1982a). *Groupthink* (2nd ed.). Boston: Houghton Mifflin.

Janis, I. L. (1982b). Stress inoculation in health care: Theory and research. In D. Beichenbaum & M. Jaremko (Eds.), *Stress prevention and management. A cognitive behavioral approach.* New York: Plenum Press.

Janis, I. L. (1983). The role of social support in adherence to stressful decisions. *American Psychologist, 38,* 142–160.

Janis, I. L. (1985). Stress inoculation in health care: Theory and research. In A. Monat & Richard S. Lazarus (Eds.), *Stress and coping* (2nd ed.). New York: Columbia University Press.

Jaynes, J. (1976). *The origin of consciousness in the breakdown of the bicameral mind.* Boston: Houghton Mifflin.

Jeffery, R. W. (1988). Dietary risk factors and their modification in cardiovascular disease. *Journal of Consulting and Clinical Psychology, 56(3),* 350–357.

Jenkins, H. M., & Harrison, R. H. (1960). Effect of discrimination training on auditory generalization. *Journal of Experimental Psychology, 59,* 244–253.

Jenkins, J. G., & Dallenbach, K. M. (1924). Oblivescence during sleep and waking. *American Journal of Psychology, 35,* 605–612.

Jennings, K. D., Curry, N. E., & Connors, R. (1986). Toddlers' social behaviors in dyads and groups. *Journal of Genetic Psychology, 147,* 515–528.

Jensen, A. R. (1969). How much can we boost IQ and scholastic achievement? *Harvard Educational Review, 39,* 1–123.

Jensen, A. R. (1970). Can we and should we study race differences? In J. Hellmuth (Ed.), *Disadvantaged child* (Vol. 3). New York: Brunner/Mazel.

Jensen, A. R. (1976). Test bias and construct validity. *Phi Delta Kappan, 58,* 340–346.

Jensen, A. R. (1977). Cumulative deficit in IQ of blacks in the rural South. *Developmental Psychology, 3,* 191–194.

Jensen, A. R. (1980). Can we be neutral about bias? *Contemporary Psychology, 25,* 868–871.

Jensen, A. R. (1984). The black-white difference on the K-ABC: Implications for future tests. *Journal of Special Education, 18,* 377–408.

Jensen, A. R. (1987). Psychometric g as a focus on concerted research effort. *Intelligence, 11,* 193–198.

Jensen, P. S. (1989). Kids talk about the "good pill." Paper presented at the annual meeting of the American Psychiatric Association.

John, E. R., Chesler, P., Bartlett, F., & Victor, I. (1968). Observational learning in cats. *Science, 159,* 1489–1491.

Johnson, B. T., & Eagly, A. H. (1989). Effects of involvement on persuasion: A meta-analysis. *Psychological Bulletin, 106,* 290–314.

Johnson, C., Connoers, M. E., & Tobin, D. L. (1987). Symptom management of bulimia. *Journal of Consulting and Clinical Psychology, 55,* 668–676.

Johnson, C., & Flach, A. (1985). Family characteristics of 105 patients with bulimia. *American Journal of Psychiatry, 142,* 1321–1324.

Johnson, C., & Larson, R. (1982). Bulimia: An analysis of moods and behavior. *Psychosomatic Medicine, 44,* 341–351.

Johnson, D. L. (1989). Schizophrenia as a brain disease. *American Psychologist, 44,* 553–555.

Johnson, J. A., Collins, H. W., Dupuis, V. L., & Johnson, J. H. (1988). *Introduction to the foundation of American education* (7th ed.). Needham Heights, MA: Allyn and Bacon.

Johnson, J. E., Lauver, D. R., & Nail, L. M. (1989). Process of coping with radiation therapy. *Journal of Consulting and Clinical Psychology, 57,* 358–364.

Johnson, L. C., Slye, E. S., & Dement, W. (1965). Electroencephalographic and autonomic activity during and after prolonged sleep deprivation. *Psychosomatic Medicine, 27,* 415–423.

Johnson, M. A. (1989). Variables associated with friendship in an adult population. *Journal of Social Psychology, 129(3),* 379–390.

Johnson, R. F. Q., & Barber, T. X. (1978). Hypnosis, suggestions, and warts: An experimental investigation implicating the importance of "believed in efficacy." *American Journal of Clinical Hypnosis, 20,* 165–174.

Johnston, E., & Donoghue, J. R. (1971). Hypnosis and smoking: A review of the literature. *American Journal of Clinical Hypnosis, 13,* 265–272.

Jones, B. (1983). Measuring degree of cerebral lateralization in children as a function of age. *Developmental Psychology, 19,* 237–242.

Jones, E. E. (1964). *Ingratiation: A social psychological analysis.* New York: Appleton-Century-Crofts.

Jones, L. V. (1984). White-black achievement differences. The narrowing gap. *American Psychologist, 39,* 1207–1213.

Jones, S. S., & Raag, T. (1989). Smile production in older infants: The importance of a social recipient for the facial signal. *Child Development, 60,* 811–818.

Jordan, H. A., Canavan, A. J., & Steer, R. A. (1985). Patterns of weight change: The interval 6 to 10 years after initial weight loss in a cognitive-behavioral treatment program. *Psychological Reports, 57,* 195–203.

Josephson, W. L. (1987). Television violence and children's aggression: Testing the priming, social script, and disinhibition predictions. *Journal of Personality and Social Psychology, 53,* 882–890.

Judd, C. M., & Park, B. (1988). Out-group homogeneity: Judgments of variability at the individual and group levels. *Journal of Personality and Social Psychology, 54,* 778–788.

Jussim, L. (1989). Teacher expectations: Self-fulfilling prophecies, perceptual biases, and accuracy. *Journal of Personality and Social Psychology, 57,* 469–480.

Just, M. A., & Carpenter, P. A. (1980). A theory of reading: From eye fixations to comprehension. *Psychological Review, 87,* 329–354.

Kagan, J. (1988a). Jerome Kagan citation. *American Psychologist, 4,* 223–225.

Kagan, J. (1988b). The meanings of personality predicates. *American Psychologist, 43,* 614–620.

Kagan, J. (1989). Temperamental contributions to social behavior. *American Psychologist, 44,* 668–674.

Kagan, J., Kearsley, R. B., & Zelazo, P. R. (1980). *Infancy: Its place in human development.* Cambridge, MA: Harvard University Press.

Kagan, J., Reznick, J. S., & Snidman, N. (1987). The physiology and psychology of behavioral inhibition in children. *Child Development, 58,* 1459–1473.

Kahn, E. (1985). Heinz Kohut and Carol Rogers: A timely comparison. *American Psychologist, 40,* 893–904.

Kahn, J. P., Kornfield, D. S., Blood, D. K., Lynn, R. B., Heller, S. S., & Frank, K. A. (1982). Type A behavior and the thallium stress test. *Psychosomatic Medicine, 44,* 431–436.

Kahn, S. (1975). Why and how we laugh. New York: Philosophical Library.

Kail, R. (1985). Development of mental rotation: A speed-accuracy study. *Journal of Experimental Child Psychology, 40,* 181–192.

Kaitz, M., Meschulach-Sarfaty, O., & Auerbach, J. (1988). A reexamination of newborns' ability to imitate facial expressions. *Developmental Psychology, 1,* 3–7.

Kales, A., Caldwell, A. B., Preston, A., Healey, S., & Kales, J. D. (1976). Personality patterns and insomnia: Theoretical implications. *Archives of General Psychology, 33,* 1128–1134.

Kales, A., & Kales, J. D. (1974). Sleep disorders: Recent findings in the diagnosis and treatment of disturbed sleep. *New England Journal of Medicine, 290,* 487–499.

Kales, A., Tan, T. L., Kollar, E. J., Naithoh, P., Preson, T. A., & Malmstrom, E. J. (1970). Sleep patterns following 205 hours of sleep deprivation. *Psychosomatic Medicine, 32,* 189–200.

Kalichman, S. C. (1989). Sex roles and sex differences in adult spatial performance. *Journal of Genetic Psychology, 150,* 93–100.

Kalichman, S. C., Craig, M. E., & Follingstad, D. R. (1988). Mental health professionals and suspected cases of child abuse: An investigation of factors influencing reporting. *Community Mental Health Journal, 1,* 43–51.

Kalichman, S. C., Craig, M. E., & Follingstad, D. R. (1989). Factors influencing the reporting of father-child sexual abuse: Study of licensed practicing psychologists. *Professional Psychology: Research and Practice, 20,* 84–89.

Kalichman, S. C., Szymanowski, D., McKee, G., Taylor, J., & Craig, M. E. (1989). Cluster analytically derived MMPI profile subgroups of incarcerated adult rapists. *Journal of Clinical Psychology, 45,* 149–155.

Kalil, R. E. (1989). Synapse formation in the developing brain. *Scientific American,* 76–85.

Kalimo, R., & Mejman, T. (1987). Psychological and behavioural responses to stress at work. In R. Kalimo, M. A. El-Batawi, & C. L. Cooper (Eds.), *Psychosocial factors at work and their relation to health.* Geneva: World Health Organization.

Kalliopuska, M. (1982). Body-image disturbances in patients with anorexia nervosa. *Psychological Reports, 51,* 715–722.

Kamin, L. J. (1974). *The science and politics of IQ.* Hillsdale, NJ: Erlbaum.

Kaminer, Y., Feingold, M., & Lyons, K. (1988). Bulimia in a pair of monozygotic twins. *Journal of Nervous and Mental Disease, 176,* 246–248.

Kandel, D. B., & Raveis, V. H. (1989). Cessation of illicit drug use in young adulthood. *Archives of General Psychiatry, 46,* 109–116.

Kanner, A. D., Coyne, J. C., Schaefer, C., & Lazarus, R. S. (1981). Comparison of two modes of stress measurement: Daily hassles and uplifts versus major life events. *Journal of Behavioral Medicine, 4,* 1–39.

Kanner, L. (1943). Autistic disturbances of affective content. *Nervous Child, 2,* 217–240.

Kanwisher, N. G., & Potter, M. C. (1990). Repetition blindness: Levels of processing. *Journal of Experimental Psychology: Human Perception and Performance, 16,* 30–47.

Kaplan, A. S., & Woodside, D. B. (1987). Biological aspects of anorexia nervosa and bulimia nervosa. *Journal of Consulting and Clinical Psychology, 55,* 645–653.

Kaplan, H. B. (1977). Gender and depression: A sociological analysis of a conditional relationship. In W. E. Fann, I. Karacan, A. D. Pokorny, & R. L. Williams (Eds.), *Phenomenology and Treatment of Depression.* New York: Spectrum Publications.

Kaplan, M. (1983). A woman's view of DSM-III. *American Psychologist, 38,* 786–792.

Kaplan, R. M. (1982). Nader's raid on the testing industry. Is it in the best interest of the consumer? *American Psychologist, 37,* 15–23.

Kaplan, R. M. (1988). Health-related quality of life in cardiovascular disease. *Journal of Consulting and Clinical Psychology, 56(3),* 382–392.

Karabenick, S. A., & Strull, T. K. (1978). Effects of personality and situational variation in locus of control on cheating. Determinants of the "congruence effect." *Journal of Personality, 46,* 72–95.

Karlsson, T., Backman, L., Herlitz, A., Nilsson, L. G., Winblad, B., &

Osterlind, P. O. (1989). Memory improvement at different stages of Alzheimer's disease. *Neuropsychologia, 27,* 737–742.

Kashani, J. H., Reid, J. C., & Rosenberg, T. K. (1989). Levels of hopelessness in children and adolescents: A developmental perspective. *Journal of Consulting and Clinical Psychology, 57,* 496–499.

Katkin, E. S. (1985). Psychology in the public forum. Polygraph testing, psychological research, and public policy. An introductory note. *American Psychologist, 40,* 346–347.

Katsuki, Y. (1961). Neutral mechanisms of auditory sensation in cats. In W. A. Rosenblith (Ed.), *Sensory communication.* Cambridge, MA: MIT Press.

Katzell, R. A., & Thompson, D. E. (1990). Work motivation. *American Psychologist, 45,* 144–153.

Kaufman, A. S. (1979). *Intelligent testing with the WISC-R.* New York: John Wiley & Sons.

Kaufman, A. S. (1982). The impact of WISC-R research for school psychologists. In C. R. Reynolds & T. B. Gutkin (Eds.), *The handbook of school psychology.* New York: John Wiley & Sons.

Kaufman, A. S. (1983). Some questions and answers about the Kaufman Assessment Battery for Children (K-ABC). *Journal of Psychoeducational Assessment, 1,* 205–218.

Kaufman, A. S. (1984). K-ABC and controversy. *Journal of Special Education, 18,* 409–444.

Kaufman, J., & Zigler, E. (1987). Do abused children become abusive parents? *American Journal of Orthopsychiatry, 57*(2), 186–192.

Kaylor, J. A., King, D. W., & King, L. A. (1987). Psychological effects of military service in Vietnam: A meta-analysis. *Psychological Bulletin, 102,* 257–271.

Kazdin, A. E. (1975). Behavior modification in applied settings. Homewood, IL: Dorsey Press.

Kazdin, A. E. (1978a). Behavior therapy: Evolution and expansion. *Counseling Psychologist, 7,* 34–37.

Kazdin, A. E. (1978b). *History of behavior modification. Experimental foundations of contemporary research.* Baltimore: University Park Press.

Kazdin, A. E. (1986). Comparative outcome studies of psychotherapy: Methodological issues and strategies. *Journal of Consulting and Clinical Psychology, 54,* 95–105.

Kazdin, A. E., & Bass, D. (1989). Power to detect differences between alternative treatments in comparative psychotherapy outcome research. *Journal of Consulting and Clinical Psychology, 57,* 138–147.

Kazdin, A. E., Esbeldt-Dawson, K., Sherick, R. B., & Colbus, D. (1985). Assessment of overt behavior and childhood depression among psychiatrically disturbed children. *Journal of Consulting and Clinical Psychology, 53,* 201–210.

Kazdin, A. E., & Wilson, G. T. (1978). *Evaluation of behavior therapy: Issues, evidence, and research strategies.* Cambridge, MA: Ballinger Press.

Kearins, J. M. (1981). Visual spatial memory in Australian aboriginal children of desert regions. *Cognitive Psychology, 12,* 434–460.

Keesey, R. E., & Powley, T. L. (1986). The regulation of body weight. In M. R. Rosenzweig & L. W. Porter (Eds.), *Annual review of psychology.* Palo Alto, CA: Annual Reviews, Inc.

Keith, S. J., Gunderson, J. G., Reifman, A., Bucksbaum, S., & Mosher, L. R. (1976). Special report: Schizophrenia 1976. *Schizophrenia Bulletin, 2,* 509–565.

Kellerman, J. M., & Laird, J. D. (1982). The effect of appearance on self-perceptions. *Journal of Personality, 50,* 296–315.

Kelley, H. H. (1972). Attribution in social interaction. In E. E. Jones et al. (Eds.), *Attribution: Perceiving the causes of behavior.* Morristown, NJ: General Learning Press.

Kelley, H. H. (1973). Process of causal attribution. *American Psychologist, 28,* 107–128.

Kelley, H. H., Berscheid, E., Christensen, A., Harvey, J. H., Huston, T. L., et al. (1983). *Close relationships.* New York: W. H. Freeman.

Kelly, C., & Goodwin, G. C. (1983). Adolescents' perception of three styles of parental control. *Adolescence, 18,* 567–571.

Kelly, J. A., St. Lawrence, J. S., Hood, H. V., & Brasfield, T. L. (1989). Behavioral intervention to reduce AIDS risk activities. *Journal of Consulting and Clinical Psychology, 57,* 60–67.

Kendler, K. S. (1980). The nosologic validity of paranoia (simple delusional disorder): A review. *Archives of General Psychiatry, 37,* 699–706.

Kendler, K. S., Tsuang, M. T., & Hays, P. (1987). Age at onset in schizophrenia. *Archives of General Psychiatry, 44,* 881–882.

Kennell, J. H., Voos, D. K., & Klaus, M. H. (1979). Parent-infant bonding. In J. D. Osofsky (Ed.), *Handbook of infant development.* New York: John Wiley & Sons.

Kenrick, D. T., & Funder, D. C. (1988). Profiting from controversy lessons from the person-situation debate. *American Psychologist, 43,* 23–44.

Kent, M. A., & Peters, M. A. (1973). Effects of ventromedial hypothalamic lesions on hunger-motivated behavior in rats. *Journal of Comparative and Physiological Psychology, 83,* 92–97.

Kerr, N., & Bruun, S. E. (1983). Dispensability of member effort and group motivation losses: Free-rider effects. *Journal of Personality and Social Psychology, 44,* 78–94.

Kessler, R. C., Downey, G., Stipp, H., & Milavsky, J. R. (1989). Network television news stories about suicide and short-term changes in total U.S. suicides. *Journal of Nervous and Mental Disease, 177,* 551–555.

Kessler, S. (1980). The genetics of schizophrenia: A review. *Schizophrenia Bulletin, 6,* 404–416.

Kety, S. S. (1979). The biological substrates of schizophrenia. In T. Fukuda & H. Mitsuda (Eds.), *Schizophrenic psychoses.* New York: Igaku-Shoin.

Kety, S. S., Rosenthal, D., Wender, P. H., Schulsinger, F., & Jacobsen, B. (1975). Mental illness in the biological and adoptive families of adopted individuals who had become schizophrenic: A preliminary report based upon psychiatric interviews. In R. Five, D. Rosenthal, & H. Brill (Eds.), *Genetic research in psychiatry.* Baltimore: Johns Hopkins University Press.

Khachaturian, Z. S. (1985). Progress of research on Alzheimer's disease. Research opportunities for behavioral scientists. *American Psychologist, 40,* 1251–1255.

Kiecolt-Glaser, J., & Glaser, R. (1988). Major life changes, chronic stress, and immunity. In T. P. Bridge, A. F. Mirsky, & F. K. Goodwin (Eds.), *Psychological, neuropsychiatric, and substance abuse aspects of AIDS.* New York: Raven Press.

Kilbourne, B. K. (1989). A cross-cultural investigation of the foot-in-the-door compliance induction procedure. *Journal of Cross-Cultural Psychology, 20,* 3–38.

Kilmann, P. R., Albert, B. M., & Sotile, W. M. (1975). Relationship between locus of control, structure of therapy, and outcome. *Journal of Consulting Psychology, 43,* 588.

Kilmann, P. R., & Sotile, W. M. (1976). The marathon encounter group: A review of the outcome literature. *Psychological Bulletin, 83,* 827–850.

Kimball, M. M. (1989). A new perspective on women's math achievement. *Psychological Bulletin, 105,* 198–214.

Kimble, G. A. (1988). *Psychology from the standpoint of a generalist.* Paper presented at the 96th Annual Convention of the American Psychological Association, Atlanta, GA, August.

Kimble, G. A. (1989). Psychology from the standpoint of a generalist. *American Psychologist, 44,* 491–499.

Kimmel, D. C. (1980). *Adulthood and aging. An interdisciplinary view* (2nd ed.). New York: John Wiley & Sons.

Kimmel, D. C. (1988). Ageism, psychology, and public policy. *American Psychologist, 43,* 175–178.

Kimura, D. (1988). Sex differences and hormonal influences on cognitive brain function. Paper presented at the Society for Neuroscience meeting in Toronto, Canada. *Society for Neuroscience Abstracts, 14,* 239.

Kingsbury, S. J. (1987). Cognitive differences between clinical psychologists and psychiatrists. *American Psychologist, 42,* 152–156.

Kinsbourne, M. (1975). The ontogeny of cerebral dominance. In D. Aaronson & R. W. Rieber (Eds.), *Developmental psycholinguistics and communication disorders. Annals of the New York Academy of Science, 263,* 244–250.

Kinsey, A. C., Pomeroy, W. B., & Martin, C. E. (1948). *Sexual behavior in the human male.* Philadelphia: W. B. Saunders.

Kinston, W., Loader, P., & Miller, L. (1987). Emotional health of families and their members where a child is obese. *Journal of Psychosomatic Research, 31,* 583–599.

Kintsch, W., & van Dijk, T. A. (1978). Toward a model of text comprehension and production. *Psychological Review, 85,* 363–394.

Kirkley, B. G., Schneider, J. A., Agras, W. S., & Bachman, J. A. (1985). Comparison of two group treatments for bulimia. *Journal of Consulting and Clinical Psychology, 53,* 43–48.

Kirshnit, C. E., Richards, M. H., & Ham, M. (1988). *Athletic participation and body-image during early adolescence.* Paper presented at the 96th Annual Convention of the American Psychological Association, Atlanta, GA, August.

Klaus, M. H., & Kennell, J. H. (1983). *Bonding: The beginnings of parent-infant attachment* (rev. ed.), Antonia W. Hamilton (Ed.). New York: New American Library.

Klein, M. (1948). *Contributions to psychoanalysis.* London: Hogarth.

Kleinginna, P. R., Jr., & Kleinginna, A. M. (1981). A categorized list of definitions with suggestions for a consensual definition. *Motivation and Emotion, 5,* 345–380.

Kleinginna, P. R., Jr., & Kleinginna, A. M. (1988). Current trends toward convergence of the behavioristic, functional, and cognitive perspectives in experimental psychology. *Psychological Record, 38,* 369–392.

Kleinke, C. L. (1986). Gaze and eye contact: A research review. *Psychological Bulletin, 100,* 78–100.

Kleinke, C. L., & Staneski, R. A. (1980). First impressions of female bust size. *Journal of Social Psychology, 110,* 123–134.

Kleinmuntz, B., & Szucko, J. J. (1984). Lie detection in ancient and modern times. A call for contemporary scientific study. *American Psychologist, 39,* 766–776.

Klesges, R. C., Klem, M. L., & Bene, C. R. (1989). Effects of dietary restraint, obesity, and gender on holiday eating behavior and weight gain. *Journal of Abnormal Psychology, 98,* 499–503.

Klesges, R. C., Meyers, A. W., Klesges, L. M., & La Vasque, M. E. (1989). Smoking, body weight, and their effects on smoking behavior: A comprehensive review of the literature. *Psychological Bulletin, 106,* 204–230.

Kline, R. B., Canter, W. A., & Robin, A. (1987). Parameters of teenage alcohol use: A path analytic conceptual model. *Journal of Consulting and Clinical Psychology, 55,* 521–528.

Klinnert, M. D., Campos, J., Sorce, J., Emde, R. N., & Svejda, M. (1982). The development of social referencing in infancy. In R. Plutchik & H. Kellerman (Eds.), *Emotion: Theory, research, and experience, Vol. 2. Emotion in early development.* New York: Academic Press.

Kluver, H. (1936). An analysis of the effects of the removal of the occipital lobes in monkeys. *Journal of Psychology, 2,* 49–61.

Knesper, D., Pagnucco, D. J., & Wheeler, J. R. C. (1985). Similarities and differences across mental health service providers and practice settings in the United States. *American Psychologist, 40,* 1352–1369.

Koegel, R. I., & Covert, A. (1972). The relationship of self-stimulation to learning in autistic children. *Journal of Applied Behavior Analysis, 5,* 381–387.

Koenig, K. P., & Masters, J. (1965). Experimental treatment of habitual smoking. *Behavior Research Therapy, 3,* 235–243.

Kofta, M., & Sedek, G. (1989). Repeated failure: A source of helplessness or a factor irrelevant to its emergence? *Journal of Experimental Psychology: General, 118,* 3–12.

Kohlberg, L. (1963). The development of children's orientation toward a moral order: Sequence in the development of moral thought. *Vita Humana, 6,* 11–33.

Kohlberg, L. (1969). The cognitive-developmental approach to socialization. In D. A. Goslin (Ed.), *Handbook of socialization theory and research.* Chicago: Rand McNally.

Kohlberg, L. (1971). From is to ought: How to commit the naturalistic fallacy and get away with it in the study of moral development. In T. Mischel (Ed.), *Cognitive development and epistemology.* New York: Academic Press.

Kohlberg, L. (1976). Moral stages and moralization: The cognitive-developmental approach. In T. Likcona (Ed.), *Moral development and behavior.* New York: Holt, Rinehart & Winston.

Kohn, A. (1986). *No contest: The case against competition.* Boston: Houghton Mifflin.

Kolb, B. (1989). Brain development, plasticity, and behavior. *American Psychologist, 44,* 1203–1212.

Kopp, C. B. (1989). Regulation of distress and negative emotions: A developmental view. *Developmental Psychology, 25,* 343–354.

Kopp, C. B., & Kaler, S. R. (1989). Risk in infancy: Origins and implications. *American Psychologist, 44*(2), 224–230.

Korchin, S. J. (1976). *Modern clinical psychology: Principles in intervention in the clinic and community.* New York: Basic Books.

Koretz, J. F., & Handelman, G. H. (1988). How the human eye focuses. *Scientific American, 7,* 92–99.

Koriat, A., Melkman, R., Averill, J. R., & Lazarus, R. S. (1972). The self-control of emotional reactions to a stressful film. *Journal of Personality, 40,* 601–618.

Koriat, A., & Norman, J. (1989). Establishing global and local correspondence between successive stimuli: The holistic nature of backward alignment. *Journal of Experimental Psychology, Learning, Memory, and Cognition, 15,* 480–494.

Koss, M. P. (1990). The women's mental health research agenda. *American Psychologist, 45,* 374–380.

Koss, M. P., Butcher, J. N., & Strupp, H. H. (1986). Brief psychotherapy methods in clinical research. *Journal of Consulting and Clinical Psychology, 54,* 60–67.

Koss, M. P., Gidycz, C. A., & Wisniewski, N. (1987). The scope of rape: Incidence and prevalence of sexual aggression and victimization in a national sample of higher education students. *Journal of Consulting and Clinical Psychology, 55,* 162–170.

Kosslyn, S. M. (1975). Information representation in visual images. *Cognitive Psychology, 7,* 341–370.

Kosslyn, S. M. (1978). Measuring the visual angle of the mind's eye. *Cognitive Psychology, 7,* 356–389.

Kosslyn, S. M. (1987). Seeing and imagining in the cerebral hemispheres: A computational approach. *Psychological Review, 94,* 148–175.

Kovacs, M. (1989). Affective disorders in children and adolescents. *American Psychologist, 44,* 209–215.

Kramer, J. H., Blusewicz, M. J., & Preston, K. A. (1989). The premature aging hypothesis: Old before its time? *Journal of Consulting and Clinical Psychology, 57,* 257–262.

Kramer, M. (1982). The continuing challenge: The rising prevalence of mental disorders, associated chronic diseases, and disabling conditions. In M. O. Wagenfeld, P. V. Lemkau, & B. Justice (Eds.), *Public mental health: Perspectives and prospects.* Beverly Hills, CA: Sage Publications.

Krantz, D. S., Contrada, R. J., Hill, D. R., & Friedler, E. (1988). Environmental stress and biobehavioral antecedents of coronary heart disease. *Journal of Consulting and Clinical Psychology, 56*(3), 333–341.

Krantz, D. S., Grunberg, N. E., & Baum, A. (1985). Health psychology. *Annual Review of Psychology, 36,* 349–383.

Krebs, D., & Adinolfi, A. A. (1975). Physical attractiveness, social relations, and personality style. *Journal of Personality and Social Psychology, 31,* 245–253.

Kreek, M. J. (1979). Methadone in treatment: Physiological and pharmacological issues. In R. I. Dupont, A. Goldstein, & J. O'Donnell (Eds.), *Handbook on drug abuse.* (NIDA, DHEW, and Office of Drug Abuse Policy, Executive Office of the President.) Washington, DC: U.S. Government Printing Office.

Krosnick, J. A. (1988). Attitude importance and attitude change. *Journal of Experimental Social Psychology, 24,* 240–255.

Krosnick, J. A., & Alwin, D. F. (1989). Aging and susceptibility to attitude change. *Journal of Personality and Social Psychology, 57,* 416–425.

Krueger, L. E., Keen, R. H., & Rublevich, B. (1974). Letter search through words and nonwords by adults and fourth-grade children. *Journal of Experimental Psychology, 102,* 845–849.

Krump, M. A., Chatton, M. J., & Tierney, L. M. (Eds.). (1986). *Current medical diagnosis and treatment.* Los Altos, CA: Lange Medical Publications.

Krupnick, J., Shea, T., & Elkin, I. (1986). Generalizability of treatment studies utilizing solicited patients. *Journal of Consulting and Clinical Psychology, 54,* 68–78.

Kübler-Ross, E. (1969). *On death and dying.* New York: Macmillan.

Kübler-Ross, E. (1975). *Death: The final stage of growth.* Englewood Cliffs, NJ: Prentice-Hall.

Labov, W. (1970). The logic of nonstandard English. In F. Williams (Ed.), *Language and poverty.* Chicago: Rand McNally.

Lachman, S. J. (1983). The concept of learning: Connecting and selectioning. *Academic Psychology Bulletin, 5,* 155–168.

Lader, M. (1975). The nature of clinical anxiety in modern society. In C. D. Spielberger & I. G. Sarason (Eds.), *Stress and anxiety* (Vol. 1). Washington, DC: Hemisphere Publishing.

Laessle, R. G., Tuschl, R. J., Waadt, S., & Pirke, K. M. (1989). The specific psychopathology of bulimia nervosa: A comparison with restrained and unrestrained (normal) eaters. *Journal of Consulting and Clinical Psychology, 57,* 772–775.

Laferla, J. J., Anderson, D. L., & Schalch, D. S. (1978). Psyioendocrine response to sexual arousal in human males. *Psychosomatic Medicine, 40,* 166–172.

Lafferty, P., Beutler, L. E., & Crago, M. (1989). Differences between more and less effective psychotherapists: A study of select therapist variables. *Journal of Consulting and Clinical Psychology, 57,* 76–80.

Lahey, B. B., Green, K. D., & Forehand, R. (1980). On the independence of ratings of hyperactivity, conduct problems, and attention deficits in children: A multiple regression analysis. *Journal of Consulting and Clinical Psychology, 48,* 566–574.

Lahey, B. B., McNees, M. P., & McNees, M. C. (1973). Control of an obscene "verbal tic" through timeout in an elementary school classroom. *Journal of Applied Behavior Analysis, 6,* 101–104.

Lamb, M. E., Hwang, C., Bookstein, F. L., Broberg, A., Hult, G., & Frodi, M. (1988). Determinants of social competence in Swedish preschoolers. *Developmental Psychology, 1,* 58–70.

Lambert, N. M. (1988). Adolescent outcomes of hyperactive children. *American Psychologist, 43,* 786–799.

Landers, S. (1988a). Laboratory animals, NRC report strongly supports use in biomedical, behavioral labs. *American Psychological Association APA Monitor,* November, 11.

Landers, S. (1988b). Survey verifies teen risk-taking. *American Psychological Association APA Monitor,* November, 30.

Landers, S. (1988c). Survey verifies teen risk-taking. *American Psychological Association APA Monitor, 19,* 11, 30.

Lange, C. G. (1922). *The emotion* (English translation). Baltimore: Williams & Wilkins. (Original work published 1885.)

Langeluddecke, P., Fulcher, G., Jones, M., & Tennant, C. (1988). Type A behaviour and coronary atherosclerosis. *Journal of Psychosomatic Research, 32,* 77–84.

Langford, G. W., Meddis, R., & Pearson, A. J. D. (1974). Awakening latency from sleep from meaningful and nonmeaningful stimuli. *Psychophysiology, 11,* 1–5.

Langlois, J. H., Roggman, L. A., & Rieser-Danner, L. A. (1990). Infants' differential social responses to attractive and unattractive faces. *Developmental Psychology, 26,* 153–159.

Langman, B., & Cockburn, A. (1975). Sirhan's gun. *Harper's, 250*(1496). 16–27.

Lanyon, R. I. (1968). *A handbook of MMPI group profiles*. Minneapolis: University of Minnesota Press.

Larson, R. W., Raffaelli, M., Richards, M. H., Ham, M., & Jewell, L. (1990). Ecology of depression in late childhood and early adolescence: A profile of daily states and activities. *Journal of Abnormal Psychology, 99*, 92–102.

Lashley, K. S. (1944). Studies of cerebral function in learning: XIII. Apparent absence of transcortical association in maze learning. *Journal of Comparative Neurology, 80*, 257–281.

Latane, B. (1981). The psychology of social impact. *American Psychologist, 36*, 343–356.

Latane, B., & Darley, J. M. (1970). *The unresponsive bystander: Why doesn't he help?* New York: Meredith.

Latane, B., Williams, K., & Harkins, S. (1979). Many hands make light work: The causes and consequences of social loafing. *Journal of Personality and Social Psychology, 37*, 822–832.

Latimer, C. R. (1988). Methods and designs eye-movement data: Cumulative fixation time and cluster analysis. *Behavior Research Methods, Instruments, & Computers, 20*, 437–470.

Lawler, E. E. (1973). *Motivation in work organizations*. Belmont, CA: Brooks/Cole.

Lawler, E. E., & Porter, L. W. (1967). Antecedent attitudes of effective managerial performance. *Organizational Behavior and Human Performance, 2*, 122–142.

Lazarus, A. A. (1971). *Behavior therapy and beyond*. New York: McGraw-Hill.

Lazarus, R. S. (1974). Cognitive and coping processes in emotion. In B. Weiner (Ed.), *Cognitive views of human motivation*. New York: Academic Press.

Lazarus, R. S. (1982). The psychology of stress and coping, with particular reference to Israel. In C. D. Spielberger, I. G. Sarason, & N. A. Milgram (Eds.), *Stress and anxiety* (Vol. 8). Washington, DC: Hemisphere Publishing.

Lazarus, R. S. (1984). The trivialization of distress. In B. L. Hammonds & C. J. Scheirer (Eds.), *Psychology and health: The master lecture series*. Washington, DC: American Psychological Association.

Lazarus, R. S., & Alfert, E. (1964). Short-circuiting of threat by experimentally altering cognitive appraisal. *Journal of Abnormal and Social Psychology, 69*, 195–205.

Lazarus, R. S., & DeLongis, A. (1983). Psychological stress and coping in aging. *American Psychologist, 38*, 245–254.

Lazarus, R. S., DeLongis, A., Folkman, S., & Gruen, R. (1985). Stress and adaptational outcomes. *American Psychologist, 40*, 770–779.

Leahy, R. L., & Eiter, M. (1980). Moral judgment and the development of real and ideal androgynous self-image during adolescence and young adulthood. *Developmental Psychology, 16*, 362–370.

Leary, M. R., & Kowalski, R. M. (1990). Impression management: A literature review and two-component model. *Psychological Bulletin, 107*, 34–47.

Leary, M. R., & Maddux, J. E. (1987). Progress toward a viable interface between social and clinical-counseling psychology. *American Psychologist, 42*, 904–911.

Leber, W. R., Beckham, E. E., & Danker-Brown, P. (1985). Diagnostic criteria for depression. In E. E. Beckham & W. R. Leber (Eds.), *Handbook of depression. Treatment, assessment, and research*. Homewood, IL: Dorsey Press.

Lee, M. T., & Ofshe, R. (1981). The impact of behavioral style and status characteristics on social influence: A test of two competing theories. *Social Psychology Quarterly, 44*, 73–82.

Lee, P. K., Andersen, T. W., Modell, J. H., & Saga, S. A. (1975). Treatment of chronic pain with acupuncture. *Journal of the American Medical Association, 232*, 1133–1135.

Lee, V. E., Schnur, E., & Brooks-Gunn, J. (1988). Does Head Start work? A 1-year follow-up comparison of disadvantaged children attending Head Start, no preschool, and other preschool programs. *Developmental Psychology, 24*, 210–222.

Leffler, A. S. (1988). *The invisible scars: Verbal abuse and psychological unavailability and relationship to self-esteem*. Paper presented at the 96th Annual Convention of the American Psychological Association in Atlanta, GA, August 15.

Lefkowitz, M. M., Eron, L. D., Walder, L. O., & Huesmann, L. R. (1977). *Growing up to be violent*. New York: Pergamon Press.

Lefkowitz, M. M., & Tesiny, E. P. (1985). Depression in children: Prevalence and correlates. *Journal of Consulting and Clinical Psychology, 53*, 647–656.

Lefley, H. P. (1989). Family burden and family stigma in major mental illness. *American Psychologist, 44*, 556–560.

Lefton, L. A., Nagle, R. J., Johnson, G., & Fisher, D. (1979). Eye movements in good and poor readers: Then and now. *Journal of Reading Behavior, 11*, 319–328.

Lefton, L. A., Spragins, A. B., & Byrnes, J. (1973). English orthography: Relation to reading experience. *Bulletin of the Psychonomic Society, 2*, 281–282.

Leiner, H. C., Leiner, A. L., & Dow, R. S. (1986). Does the cerebellum contribute to mental skills? *Behavioral Neuroscience, 100*, 443–454.

Lemere, F., & Voegtlin, W. (1950). An evaluation of the aversive treatment of alcoholism. *Quarterly Journal of Studies on Alcohol, 11*, 199–204.

Lempers, J. D., Clark-Lempers, D., & Simons, R. L. (1989). Economic hardship, parenting, and distress. *Child Development, 60*, 25–39.

Lempers, J. O., Flavell, E. H., & Flavell, J. H. (1977). The development in very young children of tacit knowledge concerning visual perception. *Genetic Psychology Monographs, 95*, 3–53.

Lenneberg, E. H. (1967). *Biological foundations of language*. New York: John Wiley & Sons.

Lennox, R. (1988). The problem with self-monitoring: A two-sided scale and a one-sided theory. *Journal of Personality Assessment, 52*, 58–73.

Leon, G. R. (1984). *Case histories of deviant behavior* (3rd ed.). Boston: Allyn and Bacon.

Leonard-Barton, D. (1981). The diffusion of active residential solar energy equipment in California. In A. Shama (Ed.), *Marketing solar energy innovations* (pp. 243–257). New York: Praeger.

Lepper, M. R., & Greene, D. (1978). Overjustification research and beyond: Toward a means-end analysis of intrinsic motivation. In M. R. Lepper & D. Greene (Eds.), *The hidden cost of reward*. Hillsdale, NJ: Erlbaum.

Lepper, M. R., Greene, D., & Nisbett, R. E. (1973). Undermining children's intrinsic interest with extrinsic reward: A test of the overjustification hypothesis. *Journal of Personality and Social Psychology, 28*, 129–137.

Lepper, M. R., & Gurtner, J. L. (1989). Children and computers. *American Psychologist, 44*, 170–178.

Lerer, B., Bleich, A., Kotler, M., Garb, R., Hertzberg, M., & Levin, B. (1987). Posttraumatic stress disorder in Israeli combat veterans. *Archives of General Psychiatry, 44*, 976–981.

Lerner, M. J. (1970). The desire for justice and reactions to victims. In J. Macaulay & L. Berkowitz (Eds.), *Altruism and helping behavior: Social psychological studies of some antecedents and consequences*. New York: Academic Press.

Lerner, R. M., & Lerner, J. V. (1977). Effects of age, sex, and physical attractiveness on child-peer relations, academic performance, and elementary school adjustment. *Developmental Psychology, 13*, 585–590.

Lester, B. M., & Dreher, M. (1989). Effects of marijuana use during pregnancy on newborn cry. *Child Development, 60*, 765–771.

Leventhal, E. A., Leventhal, H., Shacham, S., & Easterling, D. V. (1989). Active coping reduces reports of pain from childbirth. *Journal of Consulting and Clinical Psychology, 57*, 365–371.

Levere, T. E., Brugler, T., Sandin, M., & Gray-Silva, S. (1989). Recovery of function after brain damage: Facilitation by the calcium entry blocker nimodipine. *Behavioral Neuroscience, 103*, 561–565.

Levere, T. E., Morlock, G. W., Thomas, L. P., & Hart, F. D. (1974). Arousal from sleep: The differential effect of frequencies equated from loudness. *Physiology and Behavior, 12*, 573–582.

Levin, D. J. (1990). *Alcoholism*. New York: Hemisphere Publishing.

Levine, M. (1975). *Hypothesis testing: A cognitive theory of learning*. Hillsdale, NJ: Erlbaum.

Levinson, D. J. (1978). *The seasons of a man's life*. New York: Alfred A. Knopf.

Levinson, D. J. (1980). Toward a conception of the adult life course. In N. J. Smelser & E. H. Erikson (Eds.), *Themes of work and love in adulthood*. Cambridge, MA: Harvard University Press.

Levitt, M. J., Weber, R. A., Clark, M. C., & McDonnell, P. (1985). Reciprocity of exchange in toddler sharing behavior. *Developmental Psychology, 21*, 122–123.

Levy, L. H. (1984). The metamorphosis of clinical psychology. Toward a new charter as human services psychology. *American Psychologist, 39*, 486–494.

Levy, S. M. (1988). Behavioral risk factors and host vulnerability. In T. P. Bridge, A. F. Mirsky, & F. K. Goodwin (Eds.), *Psychological, neuropsychiatric, and substance abuse aspects of AIDS*. New York: Raven Press.

Levy-Leboyer, C. (1988). Success and failure in applying psychology. *American Psychologist, 43*, 779–785.

Lewin, K. K. (1970). *Brief psychotherapy*. St. Louis: Warren H. Green.

Lewinsohn, P. M. (1974). Classical and theoretical aspects of depression. In I. S. Calhoun, H. E. Adams, & K. M. Mitchell (Eds), *Innovative treatment methods in psychopathology*. New York: Wiley Interscience.

Lewinsohn, P. M., & Talkington, J. (1979). Studies on the measurement of unpleasant events and relations with depression. *Applied Psychological Measurement, 3*, 83–101.

Lewinsohn, P. M., Youngren, M. A., & Grosscup, J. (1979). Reinforcement and depression. In R. A. DePue (Ed.), *The psychobiology of the depressive disorders*. New York: Academic Press.

Lewis, H. (1981). *Freud and modern psychology*. New York: Plenum Press.

Lewis, J. L. (1970). Semantic processing of unattended messages using dichotic listening. *Journal of Experimental Psychology, 85,* 225–282.

Lewis, M., & Feiring, C. (1989). Infant, mother, and mother-infant interaction behavior and subsequent attachment. *Child Development, 60,* 831–837.

Lewis, M., & Michalson, L. (1983). *Children's emotions and moods: Developmental theory and measurement.* New York: Plenum Press.

Lewis, M., & Saarni, C. (1985). Culture and emotions. In M. Lewis and C. Saarni (Eds.), *The socialization of emotions.* New York: Plenum Press.

Lewis, R. S. (1989). Remembering and the prefrontal cortex. *Psychonomic Society, 17*(1), 102–107.

Libert, R. M., Sprafkin, J. N., & Davidson, E. S. (1982). *The early window: Effects of television on children and youth* (2nd ed.). New York: Pergamon Press.

Lidz, T. (1973). *The origin and treatment of schizophrenic disorders.* New York: Basic Books.

Lieberman, H. R., Spring, B. J., & Garfield, G. S. (1986). The behavioral effects of food constituents: Strategies used in studies of amino acids, protein, carbohydrate and caffeine. *Nutrition Reviews, 44* (Suppl.), 61–69.

Liebert, R. M., Sprafkin, J. M., & Davidson, E. S. (1982). *The early window: Effects of television on children and youth* (2nd ed.). New York: Pergamon Press.

Liebrand, W. B. G., Messick, D. M., & Wolters, F. J. M. (1986). Why we are fairer than others: A cross-cultural replication and extension. *Journal of Experimental Social Psychology, 22,* 590–604.

Lilly, J. C. (1956). Mental effects of reduction of ordinary levels of physical stimuli in intact, healthy persons. *Psychiatric Research Reports, 5,* 1–28.

Lindberg, M. A., Beggs, A. L., Chezik, D. D., & Ray, D. (1982). Flavor-toxicosis associations: Tests of three hypotheses of long delay learning. *Physiology and Behavior, 29,* 439–442.

Lindsey, K. P., & Paul, G. L. (1989). Involuntary commitments to public mental institutions: Issues involving the overrepresentation of blacks and assessment of relevant functioning. *Psychological Bulletin, 106,* 171–183.

Links, P. S., Boyle, M. H., & Offord, D. R. (1989). The prevalence of emotional disorder in children. *Journal of Nervous and Mental Disease, 177,* 85–91.

Linn, L., & Spitzer, R. L. (1982). DSM-III: Implications for liaison psychiatry and psychosomatic medicine. *Journal of the American Medical Association, 247,* 3207–3209.

Linn, S., Reznick, J. S., Kagan, J., & Hans, S. (1982). Salience of visual patterns in the human infant. *Developmental Psychology, 5,* 651–657.

Linney, J. A., & Seidman, E. (1989). The future of schooling. *American Psychologist, 44*(2), 336–340.

Linnoila, M., Karoum, F., Rosenthal, N., & Potter, W. Z. (1983). Electroconvulsive treatment and lithium carbonate: Their effects on norepinephrine metabolism in patients with primary, major depressions. *Archives of General Psychiatry, 40,* 677–680.

Lintz, L. M., Fitzgerald, H. E., & Brackbill, Y. (1967). Conditioning the eyeblink response to sound in infants. *Psychonomic Science, 7,* 405–406.

Linz, D. G., Donnerstein, E. D., & Penrod, S. (1988). Effects of long-term exposure to violent and sexually degrading depictions of women. *Journal of Personality and Social Psychology, 55,* 758–768.

Littig, L. W., & Williams, C. E. (1978). Need for affiliation, self-esteem, and social distance of black Americans. *Motivation and Emotion, 2,* 369–374.

Locke, E. A., & Schweiger, D. M. (1979). Participation in decision-making: One more look. In B. M. Staw (Ed.), *Research in organizational behavior* (Vol. 1). Greenwich, CT: JAI Press.

Loehlin, J. C., Lindzey, G., & Spuhler, J. N. (1975). *Race differences in intelligence.* San Francisco: W. H. Freeman.

Loehlin, J. C., Willerman, L., & Horn, J. M. (1988). Human behavior genetics. *Annual Review of Psychology, 39,* 101–133.

Loftus, E. F. (1979). The malleability of human memory. *American Scientist, 67,* 310–320.

Loftus, E. F., & Hoffman, H. G. (1989). Misinformation and memory: The creation of new memories. *Journal of Experimental Psychology: General, 118,* 100–104.

Loftus, G. R. (1985). On worthwhile icons: Reply to Di Lollo and Haber. *Journal of Experimental Psychology: Human Perception and Performance, 11,* 384–388.

Loftus, G. R., Shimamura, A. P., & Johnson, C. (1985). How much is an icon worth? *Journal of Experimental Psychology: Human Perception and Performance, 11,* 1–13.

Logan, F. A. (1965). Decision making by rats: Delay versus amount of reward. *Journal of Comparative and Physiological Psychology, 59,* 1–12.

Logothetis, N. K., & Schall, J. D. (1989). Neuronal correlates of subjective visual perception. *Science, 245,* 761–763.

Logue, C. M., & Moos, R. H. (1986). Perimenstrual symptoms: Prevalence and risk factors. *Psychosomatic Medicine, 48,* 388–414.

Loh, H. H., et al. (1976). Beta-endorphin is a potent analgesic agent. *Proceedings of the National Academy of Science, 73,* 2895–2898.

Longabaugh, R., Stout, R., Kriebel, G. W., Jr., McCullough, L., & Bishop, D. (1986). DSM-III and clinically identified problems as a guide to treatment. *Archives of General Psychiatry, 43,* 1097–1103.

Longstreath, L. E., Davis, B., Carter, L., Flint, D., Owen, J., Rickert, M., & Taylor, L. (1981). Separation of home intellectual environment and maternal IQ as determinants of child IQ. *Developmental Psychology, 17,* 532–541.

Loo, C. (1988). *Socio-cultural barriers to the achievement of Asian-American women.* Paper presented at the 96th Annual Convention of the American Psychological Association in Atlanta, GA August.

Lorenz, K. (1964). Ritualized fighting. In J. D. Carthy & F. J. Ebling (Eds.), *The natural history of aggression.* New York: Academic Press.

Lovaas, O. I. (1987). Behavioral treatment and normal educational and intellectual functioning in young autistic children. *Journal of Consulting and Clinical Psychology, 55,* 3–9.

Lovatt, F. J., & Warr, P. B. (1968). Recall after sleep. *American Journal of Psychology, 81,* 523–527.

Lowell, E. L. (1952). The effect of need for achievement on learning and speed of performance. *Journal of Psychology, 33,* 31–40.

Lowell, S. H., & Paparella, M. M. (1977). Presbycusis: What is it? *Annals of Otology, Rhinology, and Laryngology, 85,* 1710–1717.

Luborsky, L., Mintz, J., Auerbach, A., Christoph, P., Bachrach, H., Todd, T., Johnson, M., Cohen, M., & O'Brien, C. P. (1980). Predicting the outcome of psychotherapy. *Archives of General Psychiatry, 37,* 471–481.

Luborsky, L., & Spence, D. P. (1978). Quantitative research on psychoanalytic therapy. In S. L. Garfield & A. E. Bergin (Eds.), *Handbook of psychotherapy and behavior change: An empirical analysis* (2nd ed.). New York: John Wiley & Sons.

Ludwick-Rosenthal, R., & Neufeld, W. J. (1988). Stress management during noxious medical procedures: An evaluative review of outcome studies. *Psychological Bulletin, 3,* 326–342.

Luger, G. F., Bower, T. G. R., & Wishart, J. G. (1983). A model of the development of the early infant object concept. *Perception, 12,* 21–34.

Lundin, R. W. (1961). *Personality: An experimental approach.* New York: Macmillan.

Lutkenhaus, P., Grossman, K. E., & Grossman, K. (1985). Infant-mother attachment at twelve months and style of interaction with a stranger at the age of three years. *Child Development, 56,* 1538–1542.

Lykken, D. T. (1957). A study of anxiety in the sociopathic personality. *Journal of Abnormal and Social Psychology, 55,* 6–10.

Lynch, G., & Baudry, M. (1984) The biochemistry of memory: A new and specific hypothesis. *Science, 224,* 1057–1063.

Lynch, J. J. (1977). *The broken heart: The medical consequences of loneliness.* New York: Basic Books.

Ma, H. K. (1989). Moral orientation and moral judgment in adolescents in Hong Kong, Mainland China, and England. *Journal of Cross-Cultural Psychology, 20,* 152–177.

Maccoby, E. E. (1988). Gender as a social category. *Developmental Psychology, 24,* 755–765.

Maccoby, E. E. (1990). Gender and relationships. *American Psychologist, 45,* 513–520.

Maccoby, E. E., & Jacklin, C. N. (1987). Gender segregation in childhood. *Advances in Child Development and Behavior, 20,* 239–287.

MacHovec, F. J., & Man, S. C. (1978). Acupuncture and hypnosis compared: Fifty-eight cases. *American Journal of Clinical Hypnosis, 21,* 45–47.

Mackenzie, B. (1984). Explaining race differences in IQ. The logic, the methodology, and the evidence. *American Psychologist, 39,* 1214–1233.

MacKinnon, D. W. (1962). The nature and nurture of creative talent. *American Psychologist, 17,* 484–495.

Mackintosh, N. J. (1986). The biology of intelligence? *British Journal of Psychology, 77,* 1–18.

MacNichol, E. F. (1964). Three-pigment color vision. *Scientific American, 211,* 48–56.

Madakasira, S., & O'Brien, K. F. (1987). Acute posttraumatic stress disorder in victims of a natural disaster. *Journal of Nervous and Mental Disease, 175,* 286–290.

Mahoney, M. J. (1977). Reflections on the cognitive-learning trend in psychotherapy. *American Psychologist, 32,* 5–13.

Mahoney, M. J. (1989). Scientific psychology and radical behaviorism. *American Psychologist, 44,* 1372–1377.

Mahrer, A. R., & Nadler, W. P. (1986). Good moments in psychotherapy: A preliminary review, a list, and some promising research avenues. *Journal of Consulting and Clinical Psychology, 54,* 10–15.

Maier, N. R. F., & Klee, J. B. (1941). Studies of abnormal behavior in the rat: 17. Guidance versus trial and error and their relation to convulsive tendencies. *Journal of Experimental Psychology, 29,* 380–389.

Makin, J. W., & Porter, R. H. (1989). Attractiveness of lactating females breast odors to neonates. *Child Development, 60,* 803–810.

Malamuth, N. M., Check, J. V. P., & Briere, J. (1986). Sexual arousal in response to aggression: Ideological, aggressive, and sexual correlates. *Journal of Personality and Social Psychology, 50,* 330–340.

Mann, H. (1959). Group hypnosis in the treatment of obesity. *American Journal of Clinical Hypnosis, 1,* 114–116.

Marangoni, C., & Ickes, W. (1989). Loneliness: A theoretical review with implications for measurement. *Journal of Social and Personal Relationships, 6,* 93–128.

Marcus, M. D., Wing, R. R., & Hopkins, J. (1988). Obese binge eaters: Affect, cognitions, and response to behavioral weight control. *Journal of Consulting and Clinical Psychology, 56,* 433–439.

Marks, I. M. (1969). *Fears and phobias.* New York: Academic Press.

Marks, I. M. (1977). Clinical phenomena in search of laboratory models. In J. D. Maser & M. E. P. Seligman (Eds.), *Psychopathology experimental models.* San Francisco: W. H. Freeman.

Marks, I. M., Gelder, M. G., & Bancroft, J. (1970). Sexual deviance two years after electrical aversion. *British Journal of Psychiatry, 117,* 73–85.

Marks, W. B., Dobell, W. H., & MacNichol, J. R. (1964). The visual pigments of single primate cones. *Science, 142,* 1181–1183.

Marland, S. P., Jr. (1972). *Education of the gifted and talented* (Vol. 1). Washington, DC: U.S. Government Printing Office.

Marlatt, G. A. (1983). The controlled-drinking controversy: A commentary. *American Psychologist, 39,* 1097–1110.

Marlatt, G. A., Baer, J. S., Donovan, D. M., & Kivlahan, D. R. (1988). Addictive behaviors: Etiology and treatment. *Annual Review of Psychology, 39,* 223–252.

Marquis, D. P. (1931). Can conditioned responses be established in the newborn infant? *Journal of Genetic Psychology, 39,* 479–492.

Marschark, M., Yuille, J. C., Richman, C. L., & Hunt, R. R. (1987). The role of imagery in memory: On shared and distinctive information. *Psychological Bulletin, 102,* 28–41.

Marshall, Paul (1989). Attention deficit disorder and allergy: A neurochemical model of the relation between the illnesses. *Psychological Bulletin, 106,* 434–446.

Marshall, W. A., & Tanner, J. M. (1969). Variations in the pattern of pubertal changes in girls. *Archives of Disease in Childhood, 44,* 291–303.

Martin, R., & Haroldson, S. (1977). Effect of vicarious punishment on stuttering frequency. *Journal of Speech and Hearing Research, 20,* 21–26.

Maslow, A. H. (1962). *Toward a psychology of being.* New York: Van Nostrand.

Maslow, A. H. (1969). Toward a humanistic biology. *American Psychologist, 24,* 734–735.

Massaro, D. W., & Warner, D. S. (1977). Dividing attention between auditory and visual perception. *Perception and Psychophysics, 21,* 569–574.

Masters, W. H., & Johnson, V. E. (1966). *Human sexual response.* Boston: Little, Brown.

Masters, W. H., & Johnson, V. E. (1970). *Human sexual inadequacies.* Boston: Little, Brown.

Matarazzo, J. D. (1987). There is only one psychology, no specialties, but many applications. *American Psychologist, 42,* 893–903.

Mathews, A. M., Gelder, M. G., & Johnston, D. W. (1981). *Agoraphobia: Nature and treatment.* London: Guilford Press.

Matin, E. (1974). Saccadic suppression: A review and an analysis. *Psychological Bulletin, 81,* 899–917.

Matin, E. (1976). Saccadic suppression and the stable world. In R. A. Monty & J. W. Senders (Eds.), *Eye movement and psychological processes.* Hillsdale, NJ: Erlbaum.

Matsuoka, K., Onizawa, T., Hatakeyama, T., & Yamaguchi, H. (1987). Incidence of young adult eidetikers, and two kinds of eidetic imagery. *Tohoku Psychologica Folia, 46,* 62–74.

Matt, G. E. (1989). Decision rules for selecting effect sizes in meta-analysis: A review and reanalysis of psychotherapy outcome studies. *Psychological Bulletin, 105,* 106–115.

Matthews, K. A. (1988). Coronary heart disease and Type A behaviors: Update on and alternative to the Booth-Kewley and Friedman (1987) quantitative review. *Psychological Bulletin, 104,* 373–380.

Matthies, H. (1989). Neurobiological aspects of learning and memory. *Annual Review of Psychology, 40,* 381–404.

Matteson, M. E., Pollack, E. S., & Cullen, J. W. (1987). What are the odds that smoking will kill you? *American Journal of Public Health, 77,* 425–431.

Mauer, D., & Salapatek, P. (1976). Development changes in the scanning of faces by young infants. *Child Development, 47,* 523–527.

May, J., & Kline, P. (1987). Measuring the effects upon cognitive abilities of sleep loss during continuous operations. *British Psychological Society, 78,* 443–455.

May, R. (1982). Anxiety and values. In C. D. Spielberger & I. G. Sarason (Eds.), *Stress and anxiety* (Vol. 8). Washington, DC: Hemisphere Publishing.

McAdams, D. P. (1980). A thematic coding system for the intimacy motive. *Journal of Research in Personality, 14,* 413–432.

McAdoo, W. G., & Demeyer, M. K. (1978). Personality characteristics of parents. In M. Rutter & E. Schopler (Eds.), *Autism: A reappraisal of concepts and treatment.* New York: Plenum Press.

McAuley, E., Duncan, T. E., & McElroy, M. (1989). Self-efficacy cognitions and causal attributions for children's motor performance: An exploratory investigation. *Journal of Genetic Psychology, 150*(1), 65–73.

McCall, R. B. (1983). Environmental effects on intelligence: The forgotten realm of discontinuous nonshared within-family factors. *Child Development, 54,* 408–415.

McCauley, C. (1989). The nature of social influence in groupthink: Compliance and internalization. *Journal of Personality and Social Psychology, 57,* 250–260.

McClelland, D. C. (1961). *The achieving society.* Princeton, NJ: Van Nostrand.

McClelland, D. C. (1986). Some reflections on the two psychologies of love. *Journal of Personality, 54,* 334–353.

McClelland, D. C. (1987). Characteristics of successful entrepreneurs. *Journal of Creative Behavior, 21,* 219–233.

McClelland, D. C. (1989). Motivational factors in health and disease. *American Psychologist, 44,* 675–683.

McClintock, M. K. (1971). Menstrual synchrony and suppression. *Nature, 229,* 244–245.

McCloskey, M., Wible, C. G., & Cohen, N. J. (1988). Is there a special flashbulb-memory mechanism? *Journal of Experimental Psychology: General, 117,* 171–181.

McConkey, K. M., & Kinoshita, S. (1988). The influence of hypnosis on memory after one day and one week. *Journal of Abnormal Psychology, 97,* 48–53.

McConkie, G. W., Kerr, P. W., Reddix, M. D., & Zola, D. (1988). Eye movement control during reading: I. The location of initial eye fixations on words. *Vision Research, 28,* 1107–1118.

McGaugh, J. L. (1983). Preserving the presence of the past. Hormonal influences on memory storage. *American Psychologist, 38,* 161–174.

McGaugh, J. L., & Herz, M. J. (Eds.). (1970). *Controversial issues in consolidation of the memory trace.* New York: Atherton Press.

McGhie, A., & Chapman, J. (1961). Disorders of attention and perception in early schizophrenia. *British Journal of Medical Psychology, 34,* 103–116.

McGinty, D., & Szymusiak, R. (1988). Neuronal unit activity patterns in behaving animals: Brainstem and limbic system. *Annual Review of Psychology, 39,* 135–168.

McGlashan, T. H., & Miller, G. H. (1982). The goals of psychoanalysis and psychoanalytic psychotherapy. *Archives of General Psychiatry, 39,* 377–388.

McGrath, M. J., & Cohen, D. B. (1978). REM sleep facilitation of adaptive waking behavior: A review of the literature. *Psychological Bulletin, 85,* 24–57.

McGraw, K. O., & Fiala, J. (1982). Undermining the Zeigarnik effect: Another hidden cost of reward. *Journal of Personality, 50,* 58–66.

McKeachie, W. J. (1988). Teaching thinking. *Update: National Center for Research to Improve Postsecondary Teaching and Learning, 2,* 1.

McKeachie, W. J., Pintrich, P. R., & Lin, Y. (1985). Learning to learn. In G. d'Ydewalle (Ed.), *Cognition, information processing, and motivation.* North, Holland: Elsevier Science Publishers B.V.

McKenzie, B. E., Tootell, H. E., & Day, R. H. (1980). Development of visual size constancy during the 1st year of human infancy. *Developmental Psychology, 16,* 163–174.

McNeal, E. T., & Cimbolic, P. (1986). Antidepressants and biochemical theories of depression. *Psychological Bulletin, 99,* 361–374.

McNeill, D. (1970). Explaining linguistic universals. In J. Morton (Ed.), *Biological and social factors in psycholinguistics.* London: Logos Press.

McNemar, Q. (1964). Lost: Our intelligence. Why? *American Psychologist, 19,* 871–882.

McReynolds, P. (1987). Lightner Witmer: Little-known founder of clinical psychology. *American Psychologist, 42,* 849–858.

McReynolds, P. (1989). Diagnosis and clinical assessment: Current status and major issues. *Annual Review of Psychology, 40,* 83–108.

Meadow, A., Parnes, S. J., & Reese, H. (1959). Influence of brainstorming instructions and problem sequence on a creative problem solving test. *Journal of Applied Psychology, 43,* 413–416.

Means, B., Nigam, A., Zarrow, M., Loftus, E. B., Donaldson, M. S., & Washington, G. (1989). *Vital and health statistics autobiographical memory for health-related events, Series 6: Cognition and survey measurement No. 2.* Hyattsville, MD: U.S. Department of Health and Human Services.

Meddis, R., Pearson, A. J. D., & Langford, G. N. (1973). An extreme case of healthy insomnia. *EEG in Clinical Neurophysiology, 35,* 213–224.

Mednick, S. A., Parnas, J., & Schulsinger, F. (1987). The Copenhagen high-risk project, 1962–86. *Schizophrenia Bulletin, 13,* 485–495.

Mehrabian, A. (1980). The effects of emotional state on approach-avoidance behaviors. In A. Mehrabian (Ed.), *Basic dimensions for general psychological theory.* Cambridge, MA: Oelgeschlager, Gunn & Hain.

Meichenbaum, D. (1974). *Cognitive behavior modification.* Morristown, NJ: General Learning Press.

Meichenbaum, D. (1975). Self-instructional methods. In F. H. Kanfer & A. P. Goldstein (Eds.), *Helping people change.* New York: Pergamon Press.

Meichenbaum, D. (1977). *Cognitive behavior modification.* New York: Plenum Press.

Meichenbaum, D., & Cameron, R. (1973). Training schizophrenics to talk to themselves: A means of developing attentional controls. *Behavior Therapy, 4,* 515–534.

Melamed, L. E., Haley, M., & Gildrow, W. (1973). An examination of the role of task-oriented attention in the use of active and passive movement in visual adaptation. *Journal of Experimental Psychology, 98,* 125–201.

Mellody, P., Miller, A. W., & Miller, J. K. (1989). *Facing codependence.* New York: Harper & Row.

Melton, G. B. (1987). Bringing psychology to the legal system. *American Psychologist, 42,* 488–495.

Meltzer, H. Y., & Stahl, S. M. (1976). The dopamine hypothesis of schizophrenia: A review. *Schizophrenia Bulletin, 2,* 19–76.

Meltzoff, A. N. (1988). Imitation of televised models by infants. *Child Development, 59,* 1221–1229.

Meltzoff, A. N., & Moore, K. (1983). Newborn infants imitate adult facial gestures. *Child Development, 54,* 702–709.

Melville, J. (1977). *Phobias and compulsions.* New York: Penguin Books.

Melzack, R. (1990). The tragedy of needless pain. *Scientific American, 262,* 27–33.

Melzack, R., & Loeser, J. D. (1978). Phantom body pain in paraplegics: Evidence for a central "pattern generating mechanism" for pain. *Pain, 4,* 195–210.

Melzack, R., & Wall, P. D. (1965). Pain mechanisms: A new theory. *Science, 150,* 971–979.

Melzack, R., & Wall, P. D. (1970). Psychophysiology of pain. *International Anesthesiology Clinics, 8,* 3–34.

Menaghan, E. G., & Lieberman, M. A. (1986). Changes in depression following divorce: A panel study. *Journal of Marriage and the Family, 48,* 319–328.

Mercer, J. R. (1977). The struggle for children's rights: Critical juncture for school psychology. *School Psychology Digest, 6,* 4–19.

Mercer, R. T., Nichols, E. G., & Doyle, G. C. (1989). *Transitions in a woman's life,* Springer Series: Focus on Women, Volume 12. New York: Spring Publishing Company.

Merton, R. K. (1949). Merton's typology of prejudice and discrimination. In R. M. MacIver (Ed.), *Discrimination and national welfare.* New York: Harper & Row.

Messer, S. C., Wuensch, K. L., & Diamond, J. M. (1989). Former latch-key children: Personality and academic correlates. *Journal of Genetic Psychology, 150*(3). 301–309.

Meyer, D. R., & Meyer, P. M. (1984). Bases of recoveries from perinatal injuries to the cerebral cortex. In S. Finger & C. R. Almli (Eds.), *The behavioral biology of early brain damage.* New York: Academic Press.

Meyer, R. (1980). The antisocial personality. In R. Woody (Ed.), *The encyclopedia of mental assessment.* San Francisco: Jossey-Bass.

Meyer, R. G., & Salmon, P. (1988). *Abnormal psychology* (2nd ed.). Boston: Allyn and Bacon.

Meyers, A. F., Sampson, A. E., Wetzman, M., Rogers, B. L., & Kayne, H. (1989). School breakfast program and school performance. *American Journal of Diseases of Children, 143,* 1234–1239.

Miele, F. (1979). Cultural bias in the WISC. *Intelligence, 3,* 149–164.

Mikulincer, M., Babkoff, H., Caspy, T., & Sing, H. (1989). The effects of 72 hours of sleep loss on psychological variables. *British Journal of Psychology, 80,* 145–162.

Mikulincer, M., & Nizan, B. (1988). Causal attribution, cognitive interference, and the generalization of learned helplessness. *Journal of Personality and Social Psychology, 55,* 470–478.

Milan, R. J., & Kilmann, P. R. (1987). Interpersonal factors in premarital contraception. *Journal of Sex Research, 23,* 289–321.

Milgram, S. (1963). Behavioral study of obedience. *Journal of Abnormal and Social Psychology, 67,* 371–378.

Milgram, S. (1965a) Some conditions of obedience and disobedience to authority. *Human Relations, 18,* 57–75.

Milgram, S. (1965b). Liberating effects of group pressure. *Journal of Personality and Social Psychology, 1,* 127–134.

Miller, B. C., McCoy, J. K., Olson, T. D., & Wallace, C. M. (1986). Parental discipline and control attempts in relation to adolescent sexual attitudes and behavior. *Journal of Marriage and the Family, 48,* 503–512.

Miller, G. A. (1965). Some preliminaries to psycholinguistics. *American Psychologist, 20,* 15–20.

Miller, G. A., & Gildea, P. M. (1987). How children learn words. *Scientific American, 9,* 94–99.

Miller, N. E. (1944). Experimental studies of conflict. In J. McV. Hunt (Ed.), *Personality and behavioral disorders* (Vol. 1). New York: Ronald Press.

Miller, N. E. (1959). Liberalization of basic S-R concepts: Extensions to conflict behavior, motivation, and social learning. In S. Koch (Ed.), *Psychology: A study of a science* (Vol. 2). New York: McGraw-Hill.

Miller, N. E. (1969). Learning of visceral and glandular responses. *Science, 163,* 434–445.

Miller, N. E. (1985). The value of behavioral research on animals. *American Psychologist, 40,* 423–440.

Miller, P. H., & Aloise, P. A. (1989). Young children's understanding of the psychological causes of behavior: A review. *Child Development, 60,* 257–285.

Miller, R. C., & Berman, J. S. (1983). The efficacy of cognitive behavior therapies: A quantitative review of the research evidence. *Psychological Bulletin, 94,* 39–53.

Miller, T. W. (1989). Life-event scaling: Clinical methodological issues. In T. W. Miller (Ed.), *Stressful life events.* Madison, WI: International Universities Press.

Miller, W. R. (1985). Motivation for treatment: A review with special emphasis on alcoholism. *Psychological Bulletin, 98,* 84–107.

Millon, T. (1983). The DSM-III: An insider's perspective. *American Psychologist, 38,* 804–814.

Milner, B. (1966). Amnesia following operation on the temporal lobes. In C. W. M. Whitty & O. L. Zangwill (Eds.), *Amnesia.* London: Butterworth.

Milner, B. (1968). Preface material specific and generalized memory loss. *Neuropsychologia, 6,* 175–179.

Milner, B., Corkin, S., & Teuber, H. L. (1968). Further analysis of hippocampal amnesic syndrome: 14-year follow-up study of H.M. *Neuropsychologia, 6,* 215–234.

Milner, P. M. (1989). A cell assembly theory of hippocampal amnesia. *Neuropsychologia, 27,* 23–30.

Mischel, W. (1973). Toward a cognitive social learning reconceptualization of personality. *Psychology Review, 80,* 252–283.

Mischel, W. (1979). On the interface of cognition and personality: Beyond the person-situation debate. *American Psychologist, 34,* 740–754.

Mischel, W. (1983). Alternatives in the pursuit of the predictability and consistency of persons: Stable data that yield unstable interpretations. *Journal of Personality, 51,* 578–604.

Mischel, W., & Grusec, J. E. (1966). Determinants of the rehearsal and transmission of neutral and aversive behaviors. *Journal of Personality and Social Psychology, 3,* 197–205.

Mishler, E. G., & Waxler, N. E. (1968). Family interaction processes and schizophrenia: A review of current theories. In E. G. Mishler & N. E. Waxler (Eds.), *Family processes and schizophrenia.* New York: Science House.

Mitchell, J. E., & Eckert, E. D. (1987). Scope and significance of eating disorders. *Journal of Consulting and Clinical Psychology, 55,* 628–634.

Mitchell, K. R., & Orr, F. E. (1976). Heterosexual social competence, anxiety, avoidance, and self-judged physical attractiveness. *Perceptual and Motor Skills, 43,* 553–554.

Mittal, B. (1988). Achieving higher seat belt usage: The role of habit in bridging the attitude-behavior gap. *Journal of Applied Social Pychology, 18,* 993–1016.

Money, J. (1984). Paraphilias: Phenomenology and classification. *American Journal of Psychotherapy, 38,* 164–168.

Monroe, S. M., & Steiner, S. C. (1986). Social support and psychopathology: Interrelations with preexisting disorder, stress, and personality. *Journal of Abnormal Psychology, 95,* 29–39.

Montepare, J. M., & Zebrowitz-McArthur, L. (1988). Impressions of people created by age-related qualities of their gaits. *Journal of Personality and Social Psychology, 55,* 547–556.

Montgomery-St. Laurent, T., Fullenkamp, A. M., & Fischer, R. B. (1988). A role for the hamster's flank gland in heterosexual communication. *Physiology & Behavior, 44*(6), 759–762.

Mook, D. G. (1983). In defense of external invalidity. *American Psychologist, 38,* 379–388.

Moore, E. G. J. (1986). Family socialization and the IQ test performance of traditionally and transracially adopted black children. *Developmental Psychology, 22,* 317–326.

Moos, R. H., & Finney, J. W. (1983). The expanding scope of alcoholism: Treatment evaluation. *American Psychologist, 10,* 1036–1044.

Morey, L. C., Skinner, H. A., & Blashfield, R. K. (1984). A typology of alcohol abusers: Correlates and implications. *Journal of Abnormal Psychology, 93,* 408–417.

Morganstern, K. P. (1973). Implosive therapy and flooding procedures: A critical review. *Psychological Bulletin, 79,* 318–334.

Morganstern, K. P. (1974). Cigarette smoke as a noxious stimulus in self-managed aversion therapy for compulsive eaters: Technique and case illustration. *Behavior Therapy, 5,* 255–260.

Morganstern, K. P. (1988). Behavioral interviewing. In A. S. Bellack & M. Hersen (Eds.), *Behavioral assessment*. New York: Pergamon Press.

Morin, S. F. (1988). AIDS: The challenge to psychology. *American Psychologist, 43,* 838–842.

Morrison, D. M. (1985). Adolescent contraceptive behavior: A review. *Psychological Bulletin, 98,* 538–568.

Morrison, J. R. (1974). Changes in subtype diagnosis of schizophrenia: 1920–1966. *American Journal of Psychiatry, 131,* 674–677.

Morton, J. A. (1970). A functional model for memory. In D. A. Norman (Ed.), *Models of human memory*. New York: Academic Press.

Moskowitz, B. A. (1978). The acquisition of language. *Scientific American, 239*(5), 92–108.

Mott, T., Jr. (1979). The clinical importance of hypnotizability. *American Journal of Clinical Hypnosis, 21,* 263–269.

Mowrer, O. H., & Mowrer, W. A. (1938). Enuresis: A method for its study and treatment. *American Journal of Orthopsychiatry, 8,* 436–459.

Moyer, W. W. (1978). Effects of loss of freedom on subjects with internal or external locus of control. *Journal of Research and Personality, 12,* 253–261.

Mullen, B., & Suls, J. (1982). The effectiveness of attention and rejection as coping styles: A meta-analysis of temporal differences. *Journal of Psychosomatic Research, 26,* 43–49.

Mullen, B., Tice, D. M., Baumeister, R. F., Dawson, K. E., Riordan, C. A., Radloff, C. E., Goethals, G. R., Kennedy, J. G., & Rosenfeld, P. (1986). Newscasters' facial expressions and voting behavior of viewers: Can a smile elect a president? *Journal of Personality and Social Psychology, 51,* 291–295.

Mungy, G. (1982). The power of minorities. In H. Tajfel (Ed.), *European monographs in social psychology* (Vol. 31). London: Academic Press.

Munroe, R. L., & Munroe, R. H. (1983). Birth order and intellectual performance in East Africa. *Journal of Cross-Cultural Psychology, 14,* 3–16.

Murdock, B. B., Jr. (1974). *Human memory: Theory and data*. Potomac, MD: Erlbaum.

Murphy, E. H. (1985). Effects of pattern deprivation on visual cortical cells in the rabbit: A reevaluation. *Journal of Neurophysiology, 53,* 1535–1550.

Murphy, G. E., Simons, A. D., Wetzel, R. D., & Lustman, P. J. (1984). Cognitive therapy and pharmacotherapy. *Archives of General Psychiatry, 41,* 33–36.

Murray, A. W., & Szostak, J. W. (1987). Artificial chromosomes. *Scientific American, 11,* 62–68.

Murray, E. J., & Berkun, M. M. (1955). Displacement as a function of conflict. *Journal of Abnormal and Social Psychology, 51,* 47–56.

Mussen, P. H., & Distler, L. (1959). Masculinity, identification, and father-son relationships. *Journal of Abnormal and Social Psychology, 59,* 350–356.

Muuss, R. E. (1986). Adolescent eating disorder: Bulimia. *Adolescence, 21,* 257–267.

Muuss, R. E. (1989). Carol Gilligan's theory of sex differences in the development of moral reasoning during adolescence. *Adolescence, 23,* 229–243.

Myer, R. G., & Salmon, P. (1988). *Abnormal psychology* (2nd ed.). Boston: Allyn and Bacon.

Myers, M. F. (1989). Men sexually assaulted as adults and sexually abused as boys. *Archives of Sexual Behavior, 18,* 203–215.

Naar, R. (1990). Psychodrama in short-term psychotherapy. In R. A. Wells & V. J. Giannetti (Eds.), *Handbook of the brief psychotherapies*. New York: Plenum Press.

Nace, E. P. (1987). *The treatment of alcoholism*. New York: Brunner/Mazel.

Nadelmann, E. A. (1989). Drug prohibition in the United States: Costs, consequences, and alternatives. *Science, 245,* 939.

Nairn, A., et al. (1980). *The reign of ETS: The corporation that makes up minds*. Washington, DC: Nader.

Nash, M. (1987). What, if anything, is regressed about hypnotic age regression? A review of the empirical literature. *Psychological Bulletin, 102,* 42–52.

Nathan, P. E. (1983). Failures in prevention: Why we can't prevent the devastating effect of alcoholism and drug abuse. *American Psychologist, 38,* 459–467.

Nathan, P. E. (1988). The addictive personality is the behavior of the addict. *Journal of Consulting and Clinical Psychology, 56*(2) 183–188.

Nathan, P. E., & Skinstad, A. H. (1987). Outcomes of treatment for alcohol problems: Current methods, problems, and results. *Journal of Consulting and Clinical Psychology, 55,* 332–340.

Nathan, P. E., Zare, N., Simpson, H. F., & Andbert, M. M. (1969). A systems analytic model of diagnosis: I. The diagnostic validity of abnormal psychomotor behavior. *Journal of Clinical Psychology, 25,* 3–9.

Nathans, J. (1989). The genes for color vision. *Scientific American, 260,* 42–49.

National Center on Child Abuse and Neglect. (1981). *Executive summary:*

National study of the incidence and severity of child abuse and neglect (DHHS Publication No. OHDS 81-30329). Washington, DC: U.S. Government Printing Office.

Nebes, R. D. (1989). Semantic memory in Alzheimer's disease. *Psychological Bulletin, 106,* 377–394.

Neely, J. H. (1976). Semantic priming and retrieval from lexical memory: Evidence for facilitatory and inhibitory processes. *Memory and Cognition, 4,* 648–654.

Nelson, C., & Horowitz, F. D. (1983). The perception of facial expressions and stimulus motion by two- and five-month-old infants using holographic stimuli. *Child Development, 54,* 868–877.

Nelson, C. A. (1987). The recognition of facial expressions in the first two years of life: Mechanisms of development. *Child Development, 58,* 889–909.

Nelson, C. A., & Ludemann, P. M. (1989). Past, current, and future trends in infant face perception research. *Canadian Journal of Psychology, 43,* 183–198.

Nemeroff, C. B., Knight, D. L., Kirshnan, R. R., Slotkin, T. A., Bissette, G., Melville, M. L., & Blazer, D. G. (1988). Marked reduction in the number of platelet-tritiated imipramine binding sites in geriatric depression. *Archives of General Psychiatry, 45,* 919–923.

Nemeth, C., & Endicott, J. (1976). The midpoint as an anchor: Another look at discrepancy of position and attitude change. *Sociometry, 39,* 11–18.

Neustatler, P. (1982). Aluminum tie to Alzheimer's? Intake of metal now an issue. *Medical Tribune, 23,* 1.

Newcomb, M. D., & Bentler, P. M. (1988). Impact of adolescent drug use and social support on problems of young adults: A longitudinal study. *Journal of Abnormal Psychology, 97,* 64–75.

Newcomb, M. D., & Bentler, P. M. (1989). Substance use and abuse among children and teenagers. *American Psychologist, 44*(2), 242–248.

Newman, B. M. (1982). Mid-life development. In B. B. Wolman (Ed.), *Handbook of developmental psychology*. Englewood Cliffs, NJ: Prentice-Hall.

Nicholson, R. S., & Berman, J. S. (1983). Is followup necessary in evaluating psychotherapy? *Psychological Bulletin, 93,* 261–278.

Nisbett, R. E. (1972). Hunger, obesity, and the ventromedial hypothalamus. *Psychological Review, 79,* 433–453.

Noble, E. P. (Ed.). (1978). *Alcohol and health* (Third Special Report to the U.S. Congress from the Secretary of DHEW). Washington, DC: U.S. Government Printing Office.

Nodine, C. F., Carmody, D. P., & Herman, E. (1979). Eye movements during visual search for artistically embedded targets. *Bulletin of the Psychonomic Society, 13,* 371–374.

Nodine, C. F., Carmody, D. P., & Kundel, H. L. (1978). Searching for NINA. In J. W. Senders, D. F. Fisher, & R. A. Mondy (Eds.), *Eye movements and the higher psychological processes*. Hillsdale, NJ: Erlbaum.

Nolen-Hoeksema, S. (1987). Sex differences in unipolar depression: Evidence and theory. *Psychological Bulletin, 101,* 259–282.

Norcross, J. C., Prochaska, J. O., & Gallagher, K. M. (1989). Clinical psychologists in the 1980s: II. Theory, research, and practice. *Clinical Psychologist, 42,* 45–52.

Norris, J. (1989). Normative influence effects on sexual arousal to nonviolent sexually explicit material. *Journal of Applied Social Psychology, 19,* 341–352.

Norris, R. V., & Sullivan, C. (1983). *PMS/Premenstrual syndrome*. New York: Rawson Associates.

Noton, D., & Stark, L. (1971). Eye movements and visual perception. *Scientific American, 224*(6), 35–44.

Novak, M. A., & Suomi, S. J. (1988). Psychological well-being of primates in captivity. *American Psychologist, 43,* 765–773.

Nowicki, S., Jr., & Duke, M. P. (1989). *A measure of nonverbal social processing ability in children between the ages of 6 and 10*. Paper presented at the American Psychological Society Meeting, Alexandria, VA, June.

Nuechterlein, K. H. (1977). Reaction time and attention in schizophrenia: A critical evaluation of the data theories. *Schizophrenia Bulletin, 3,* 373–428.

Nuechterlein, K. H., & Holroyd, J. C. (1980). Biofeedback in the treatment of tension headache: Current status. *Archives of General Psychiatry, 37,* 866–873.

Nunner-Winkler, G., & Sodian, B. (1988). Children's understanding of moral emotions. *Child Development, 59,* 1323–1338.

O'Brien, F., & Azrin, N. H. (1972). Symptom reduction by functional displacement in a token economy: A case study. *Journal of Behavior Therapy and Experimental Psychiatry, 3,* 205–207.

O'Donohue, W. (1989). The (even) bolder model. *American Psychologist, 44,* 1460–1468.

O'Leary, K. D., Barling, J., Arias, I., Rosenbaum, A., Malone, J., & Tyree, A. (1989). Prevalence and stability of physical aggression between spouses: A longitudinal analysis. *Journal of Consulting and Clinical Psychology, 57,* 263–268.

O'Leary, K. D., & Carr, E. G. (1982). Childhood disorders. In G. T. Wilson & C. M. Franks (Eds.), *Contemporary behavior therapy*. New York: Guilford Press.

Ogilvie, R. D., McDonagh, D. M., Stone, S. N., & Wilkinson, R. I. (1988). Eye movements and the detection of sleep onset. *Psychophysiology, 25,* 81–91.

Olds, J. (1955). Physiological mechanisms of reward. *Nebraska Symposium on Motivation, 3,* 73–139.

Olds, J. (1969). The central nervous system and the reinforcement of behavior. *American Psychologist, 24,* 114–132.

Olds, J., & Milner, P. (1954). Positive reinforcement produced by electrical stimulation of septal area and other regions of rat brain. *Journal of Comparative and Physiological Psychology, 47,* 419–427.

Omura, Y. (1977). Critical evaluation of the methods of measurement of "tingling threshold," "pain threshold," and "pain tolerance" by electrical stimulation. *Acupuncture & Electro-Therapeutic Research International Journal, 2,* 161–236.

Orenstein, H., & Carr, J. (1975). Implosion therapy by tape recording. *Behavior Research and Therapy, 13,* 177–182.

Ornitz, E. M., & Ritvo, E. R. (1976). The syndrome of autism: A critical review. *American Journal of Psychiatry, 133,* 609–621.

Ornstein, R. E. (1976). A science of consciousness. In P. R. Lee, R. E. Ornstein, D. Galin, A. Deikman, & C. T. Tart (Eds.), *Symposium of consciousness*. San Francisco, 1974. New York: Viking Press.

Ornstein, R. E. (1977). *The psychology of consciousness* (2nd ed.). New York: Harcourt Brace Jovanovich.

Ossip-Klein, D. J., Doyne, E. J., Bowman, E. D., Osborn, K. M., McDougall-Wilson, I. B., & Neimeyer, R. A. (1989). Effects of running or weight lifting on self-concept in clinically depressed women. *Journal of Consulting and Clinical Psychology, 57,* 158–161.

Osterberg, O. (1973). Circadian rhythms of food intake in oral temperature in "morning" and "evening" groups of individuals. *Ergonomics, 16,* 203–209.

Osterweis, M., & Townsend, J. (1988). *Health professionals and the bereaved*. Rockville, MD: National Institute of Mental Health.

Ottati, V., Fishbein, M., & Middlestadt, S. E. (1988). Determinants of voters' beliefs about the candidates' stands on the issues: The role of evaluative bias heuristics and the candidates, expressed message. *Journal of Personality and Social Psychology, 55,* 517–529.

Owens, M. E., Bliss, E. L., Koester, P., & Jeppsen, E. A. (1989). Phobias and hypnotizability: A reexamination. *International Journal of Clinical and Experimental Hypnosis, Vol. XXXVII,* 207–216.

Owens, W. A., Jr. (1966). Age and mental abilities: A second adult follow-up. *Journal of Educational Psychology, 51,* 311–325.

Pagano, R. W., Rose, R. M., Stivers, R. M., & Warrenburg, S. (1976). Sleep during transcendental meditation. *Science, 191,* 308–310.

Paivio, A. (1963). Learning of adjective-noun paired-associates as a function of adjective-noun word order and noun abstractness. *Canadian Journal of Psychology, 17,* 370–379.

Paivio, A. (1969). Mental imagery in associative learning and memory. *Psychological Review, 76,* 241–263.

Paivio, A. (1971). *Imagery and verbal processes*. New York: Holt, Rinehart & Winston.

Paivio, A., & Yarmey, A. D. (1966). Pictures versus words as stimuli and responses in paired-associate learning. *Psychonomic Science, 5,* 235–236.

Paivio, A., & Yuille, J. C. (1966). Word abstractness and meaningfulness, and paired-associate learning in children. *Journal of Experimental Child Psychology, 4,* 81–89.

Palermo, D. S. (1978). *Psychology of language*. Glenview, IL: Scott, Foresman.

Palkovitz, R. (1985). Fathers' birth attendance, early contact, and extended contact with their newborns: A critical review. *Child Development, 56,* 392–406.

Pantin, H. M., & Carver, C. S. (1982). Induced competence and the bystander effect. *Journal of Applied Social Psychology, 12,* 100–111.

Papcun, G., Krashen, S., & Terbeck, D. (1971). Is the left hemisphere specialized for speech, language, or something else? UCLA Working Papers in Phonetics, 19 (as cited in D. S. Palmermo. *Psychology of language*. Glenview, IL: Scott, Foresman, 1978).

Pardine, P., Dytell, R., & Napoli, A. (1981). Transfer benefits of biofeedback: A research note. *Perceptual and Motor Skills, 52,* 373–374.

Parke, R. D. (1979). Perspectives on father-infant interaction. In J. D. Osofsky (Ed.), *Handbook of infant development*. New York: John Wiley & Sons.

Parke, R. D., & O'Leary, S. E. (1976). Father-mother-infant interaction in the newborn period: Some findings, some observations, and some unresolved issues. In K. Riegel & J. Meacham (Eds.), *The developing individual in a changing world: Vol. 2. Social and environmental issues*. The Hague, Netherlands: Mouton.

Parker, D. E. (1980). The vestibular apparatus. *Scientific American, 243,*(5), 118–135.

Parkes, K. R. (1982). Occupational stress among student nurses: A natural experiment. *Journal of Applied Psychology, 67,* 784–796.

Parmelee, A. H., & Stern, E. (1972). Development of states in infants. In C. D. Clemente, T. P. Purpara, & F. E. Meyer (Eds.), *Sleep and the maturing nervous system*. New York: Academic Press.

Parson, T. (1978). *Action theory and the human condition*. New York: Free Press.

Pasik, P., & Pasik, T. (1982). Visual functions in monkeys after total removal of visual cerebral cortex. In W. D. Neff (Ed.), *Contributions to sensory physiology*. New York: Academic Press.

Patrick, C. J., & Iacono, W. G. (1989). Psychopathy, threat, and polygraph test accuracy. *Journal of Applied Psychology, 74,* 347–355.

Patterson, G. R., DeBaryshe, B. D., & Ramsey, E. (1989). A developmental perspective on antisocial behavior. *American Psychologist, 44,* 329–335.

Patton, B. L. (1984). *Semantic memory: Neutral primes?* Unpublished master's thesis. University of South Carolina, Columbia.

Paulos, J. A. (1988). *Innumeracy: Mathematical illiteracy and its consequences*. New York: Hill and Wang.

Pavlov, I. P. (1927). *Conditioned reflexes*. London: Oxford University Press.

Peele, S. (1984). The cultural context of psychological approaches to alcoholism. Can we control the effects of alcohol? *American Psychologist, 39,* 1337–1351.

Pelham, B. W., & Swann, W. B., Jr. (1989). From self-conception to self-worth: On the sources and structure of global self-esteem. *Journal of Personality and Social Psychology, 57,* 672–680.

Pelham, W. E., Schendler, R. W., Bologna, N. C., & Contreras, J. A. (1980). Behavioral and stimulant treatment of hyperactive children: A therapy study with methylphenidate probes in a within-subject design. *Journal of Applied Behavior Analysis, 13,* 221–236.

Pendergrass, V. E. (1972). Time out from positive reinforcement following persistent high rate behavior in retardates. *Journal of Applied Behavior Analysis, 5,* 85–91.

Penfield, W. (1958). *The excitable cortex in conscious man*. Illinois: Charles C. Thomas.

Penfield, W., Mathieson, G. (1954). Memory: Autopsy findings and comments on the role of hippocampus in experiential recall. *Archives of Neurology, 31,* 145–154.

Penfield, W., & Milner, B. (1958). Memory deficit produced by bilateral lesions in the hippocampal zone. *Archives of Neurological Psychiatry, 79,* 475–497.

Penfield, W., & Perot, P. (1963). The brain's record of auditory and visual experience. *Brain, 86,* 595–596.

Penfield, W. W., & Jasper, H. (1954). *Epilepsy and the functional anatomy of the human brain*. Massachusetts: Little, Brown.

Perkins, R. E., & Hill, A. B. (1985). Cognitive and affective aspects of boredom. *British Journal of Psychology, 76,* 221–234.

Perlman, D., & Peplau, L. A. (1984). Loneliness research: A survey of empirical findings (pp. 13–46). In L. A. Peplau & S. E. Goldston (Eds.), *Preventing the harmful consequences of severe and persistent loneliness* (DHHS Publication No. ADM 84-1312). Washington, DC: U.S. Government Printing Office.

Persky, H. (1978). Plasma testosterone level and sexual behavior of couples. *Archives of Sexual Behavior, 7,* 157–173.

Petersen, A. C. (1988). Adolescent development. In M. R. Rosenzweig and L. W. Porter (Eds.), *Annual review of psychology* (Vol. 39). Palo Alto, CA: Annual Reviews, Inc.

Petersen, R. C. (1980). *Marijuana and health* (Eighth Annual Review to the U.S. Congress from the Secretary of DHEW, DHEW Publication No. ADM 80–945). Washington, DC: U.S. Government Printing Office.

Peterson, C., & Seligman, M. E. P. (1984). Causal explanations as a risk factor for depression: Theory and evidence. *Psychological Review, 91,* 347–374.

Peterson, C., Seligman, M., & Vaillant, G. E. Unpublished research cited by T. DeAngelis, In praise of rose-colored specs. *Monitor,* 1988, vol. 19, 22.

Peterson, J. L., & Marin, G. (1988). Issues in the prevention of AIDS among black and Hispanic men. *American Psychologist, 43,* 871–877.

Peterson, L. R., & Peterson, M. J. (1959). Short-term retention of individual verbal items. *Journal of Experimental Psychology, 58,* 193–198.

Petty, L. K., Ornitz, E. M., Michaelman, J. D., & Zimmerman, E. G. (1984). Autistic children who become schizophrenic. *Archives of General Psychiatry, 41,* 129–131.

Petty, R. E., & Cacioppo, J. T. (1981). *Attitudes and persuasion: Classic and contemporary approaches*. Dubuque, IA: William C. Brown.

Petty, R. E., and Cacioppo, J. T. (1985). The elaboration likelihood model of persuasion. In L. Berkowitz (Ed.), *Advances in experimental social psychology* (Vol. 19). New York: Academic Press.

Phillips, D. A., & Zigler, E. (1980). Children's self-image disparity:

Effects of age, socioeconomic status, ethnicity, and gender. *Journal of Personality and Social Psychology, 39*, 689–700.

Phillips, D. P., & Paight, D. J. (1987). The impact of televised movies about suicide. *New England Journal of Medicine, 317*, 809–811.

Phillips, E. L. (1988). Length of psychotherapy and outcome: Observations stimulated by Howard, Kopta, Krause, and Orlinsky. *American Psychologist*, August, 669–670.

Piaget, J. (1932). *The moral judgment of the child*. London: Routledge & Kegan Paul.

Piaget, J. (1963). The attainment of invariants and reversible operations in the development of thinking. *Social Research, 30*, 283–299.

Pion, G. M., Bramblett, J. P., Jr., & Wicherski, M. (1987). *Preliminary report: 1985 doctorate employment survey*. Washington, DC: American Psychological Association.

Piper, W. E., Debbane, E. G., Bienvenu, J. P., & Garant, J. (1984). A comparative study of four forms of psychotherapy. *Journal of Consulting and Clinical Psychology, 52*, 268–279.

Pirenne, M. H. (1967). *Vision and the eye*. London: Science Paperbacks.

Pitman, R. K., Orr, S. P., Forgue, D. F., Altman, B., de Jong, J. B., & Herz, L. R. (1990). Psychophysiologic responses to combat imagery of Vietnam veterans with posttraumatic stress disorder versus other anxiety disorders. *Journal of Abnormal Psychology, 99*, 49–54.

Pittman, F. S., III, Flomenhaft, K., & DeYoung, C. D. (1990). Family crisis therapy. In R. A. Wells & V. J. Giannetti (Eds.), *Handbook of the brief psychotherapies*. New York: Plenum Press.

Pittman, T. S., & Heller, J. F. (1987). Social motivation. In M. R. Rosenzweig & L. W. Porter (Eds.), *Annual review of psychology*. Palo Alto, CA: Annual Review, Inc.

Plomin, R. (1989). Environment and genes: Determinants of behavior. *American Psychologist, 44*(2), 105–111.

Pokorny, A. D. (1977). Suicide in depression. In W. E. Fann, I. Karacan, A. D. Pokorny, & R. L. Williams (Eds.), *Phenomenology and treatment of depression*. New York: Spectrum Publications.

Polivy, J., Heatherton, T. F., & Herman, C. P. (1988). Self-esteem, restraint, and eating behavior. *Journal of Abnormal Psychology, 97*, 354–356.

Pollak, J. M. (1979). Obsessive-compulsive personality: A review. *Psychological Bulletin, 36*, 225–241.

Pollatsek, A., & Rayner, K., & Balota (1986). Inferences about eye movement control from the perceptual span in reading. *Perception & Psychophysics, 2*, 123–130.

Pollock, V. E., Schneider, L. S., Gabrielli, W. F., Jr., & Goodwin, D. W. (1987). Sex of parent and offspring in the transmission of alcoholism. *Journal of Nervous and Mental Disease, 175*, 668–673.

Powell, D. A., Milligan, W. L., & Furchtgott, E. (1980). Peripheral autonomic changes accompanying learning and reaction time performance in older people. *Journal of Gerontology, 35*, 57–65.

Power, T. G., & Chapieski, M. L. (1986). Childrearing and impulse control in toddlers: A naturalistic investigation. *Developmental Psychology, 22*, 271–275.

Powers, P. C., & Geen, R. G. (1972). Effects of the behavior and the perceived arousal of a model on instrumental aggression. *Journal of Personality and Social Psychology, 23*, 175–184.

Powers, S. I., Hauser, S. T., Kilner, L. A. (1989). Adolescent mental health. *American Psychologist, 44*, 200–208.

Powley, T. L. (1977). The ventromedial hypothalamic syndrome, satiety, and a cephalic phase hypothesis. *Psychological Review, 84*, 89–126.

Pratkanis, A. R., Greenwald, A. G., Leippe, M. R., & Baumgardner, M. H. (1988). In search of reliable persuasion effects: III. The sleeper effect is dead. Long live the sleep effect. *Journal of Personality and Social Psychology, 54*, 203–218.

Premack, D. (1962). Reversibility of the reinforcement relation. *Science, 136*, 255–257.

Premack, D. (1965). Reinforcement theory. In D. Levine (Ed.), *Nebraska symposium on motivation* (Vol. 13) pp. 123–180). Lincoln: University of Nebraska Press.

Premack, D. (1971). Language in chimpanzees? *Science, 172*, 808–822.

Prentice-Dunn, S., & Rogers, R. W. (1984). Effects of deindividuating situational cues and aggressive models on subjective deindividuation and aggression. *Journal of Personality and Social Psychology, 39*, 104–113.

Presser, H. B. (1989). Some economic complexities of child care provided by grandmothers. *Journal of Marriage and the Family, 51*, 581–591.

Preti, G., Cutler, W. B., Garcia, C. R., Huggins, G. R., & Lawley, H. J. (1986). Human axillary secretions influence women's menstrual cycles: The role of donor extract of females. *Hormones and Behavior, 20*, 474–482.

Price, D. D., et al. (1984). A psychophysical analysis of acupuncture analgesia. *Pain, 19*, 27–42.

Price, R. (1985). *People of the mirror: An intimate look at loneliness*. Far Hills, NJ: New Horizon Press.

Prinz, R. J., & Riddle, D. B. (1986). Associations between nutrition and

behavior in five-year-old children. *Nutrition Reviews, 44* (Suppl.), 151–157.

Prinz, R. J., Roberts, W. A., & Hantman, E. (1980). Dietary correlates of hyperactive behavior in children. *Journal of Consulting and Clinical Psychology, 48*, 760–769.

Proshansky, H. M., & O'Hanlon, T. (1977). Environmental psychology: Origins and development. In D. Stokols (Ed.), *Perspectives on environment and behavior: Theory, research, and application*. New York: Plenum Press.

Puffer, S. M. (1987). Prosocial behavior, noncompliant behavior, and work performance among commission salespeople. *Journal of Applied Psychology, 72*, 615–621.

Putnam, W. H. (1979). Hypnosis and distortions in eyewitness memory. *International Journal of Clinical and Experimental Hypnosis, 27*, 437–448.

Quigley, B., Gaes, G. G., & Tedeschi, J. T. (1989). Does asking make a difference? Effects of initiator, possible gain, and risk on attributed altruism. *Journal of Social Psychology, 129*, 259–267.

Quilitch, H. R., & Risley, T. R. (1973). The effects of play materials on social play. *Journal of Applied Behavior Analysis, 6*, 573–578.

Quinsey, V. L., Chaplin, T. C., & Upfold, D. (1984). Sexual arousal to nonsexual violence and sadomasochism themes among rapists and non-sex-offenders. *Journal of Consulting and Clinical Psychology, 52*, 651.

Rabinowitz, J. C., Mandler, G., & Patterson, K. E. (1977). Determinants of recognition and recall: Accessibility and generations. *Journal of Experimental Psychology: General, 106*, 302–329.

Rachlin, H., Logue, A. W., Gibbon, J., & Frankel, M. (1986). Cognition and behavior in studies of choice. *Psychological Review, 93*, 35–45.

Rachman, S., & DeSilva, P. (1978). Abnormal and normal obsessions. *Behavior Research and Therapy, 16*, 223–248.

Rada, R. T. (1983). Rape. In W. E. Fann, I. Karacan, A. D. Pokorny, & R. L. Williams (Eds.), *Phenomenology and treatment of psychosexual disorders*. New York: SP Medical & Scientific Books.

Rafaeli, A. (1989). When clerks meet customers: A test of variables related to emotional expressions on the job. *Journal of Applied Psychology, 74*, 385–393.

Ragins, B. R., & Sundstrom, E. (1989). Gender and power in organizations: A longitudinal perspective. *Psychological Bulletin, 105*, 51–88.

Rahe, R. H. (1989). Recent life change stress and psychological depression. In T. W. Miller (Ed.), *Stressful life events*. Madison, WI: International Universities Press.

Rapee, R. (1986). Differential response to hyperventilation in panic disorder and generalized anxiety disorder. *Journal of Abnormal Psychology, 95*, 24–28.

Rappaport, J. (1987). Terms of empowerment/exemplars of prevention: Toward a theory for community psychology. *American Journal of Community Psychology, 2*, 121–148.

Rapport, M. D., DuPaul, G. J., Stoner, G., & Jones, J. T. (1986). Comparing classroom and clinic measures of attention deficit disorder: Differential, idiosyncratic, and dose-response effects of methylphenidate. *Journal of Consulting and Clinical Psychology, 54*, 334–341.

Raps, C. S., Reinhard, K. E., Peterson, C., Abramson, L. Y., & Seligman, M. E. P. (1982). Attributional style among depressed patients. *Journal of Abnormal Psychology, 91*, 102–108.

Raskin, M., Bali, L. R., & Peeke, H. V. (1980). Muscle biofeedback and transcendental meditation. *Archives of General Psychiatry, 37*, 93–97.

Ravussin, E., Lillioja, S., Knowler, W. C., Christin, L., Freymond, D., Abbott, W. G. H., Boyce, V., Howard, B. V., & Bogardus, C. (1988). Reduced rate of energy expenditure as a risk factor for body-weight gain. *New England Journal of Medicine, 318*, 467–472.

Rayner, K., & Fisher, D. L. (1987). Letter processing during eye fixations in visual search. *Perception & Psychophysics, 1*, 87–100.

Reed, C. F. (1984). Terrestrial passage theory of the moon illusion. *Journal of Experimental Psychology: General, 113*, 489–516.

Regestein, Q. R., & Reich, P. (1978). Pedophilia occurring after onset of cognitive impairment. *Journal of Nervous and Mental Disease, 166*, 794–798.

Reid, J. B., & Hendriks, A. F. C. J. (1973). Preliminary analysis of the effectiveness of direct home intervention for the treatment of predelinquent boys who steal. In L. Hamerlynck, L. Handy, & E. Mash (Eds.), *Behavioral change: Methodology, concepts, and practice*. Champaign, IL: Research Press.

Reifman, A. S., Larrick, R., & Fein, S. (1988). *The heat-aggression relationship in major-league baseball*. Paper presented at the 96th Annual Convention of the American Psychological Association, Atlanta, GA, August.

Reigier, D. A., Boyd, J. H., Burke, J. D., Rae, D. S., Myers, J. K., Kramer, M., Robins, L. N., George, L. K., Karno, M., & Locke, B. Z. (1988). One-month prevalence of mental disorders in the United States. *Archives of General Psychiatry, 45*, 977–986.

Reilly, S., & Muzekari, L. (1979). Responses of normal and disturbed adults and children to mixed messages. *Journal of Abnormal Psychology, 88*, 203–208.

Reis, H. T., & Shaver, P. (1988). Intimacy as an interpersonal process. In S. Duck (Ed.), *Handbook of personal relationships: Theory, relationships and interventions*. Chichester, NY: Wiley.

Reis, S. M. (1989). Reflections on policy affecting the education of gifted and talented students. *American Psychologist, 44*, 399–408.

Reisenzein, R. (1983). The Schachter theory of emotion: Two decades later. *Psychological Bulletin, 94*, 239–264.

Repa, B. K. (1988). Is there life after partnership? *ABA Journal, 74*, 70–75.

Repetti, R. L., Matthews, K. A., & Waldron, I. (1989). Employment and women's health. *American Psychologist, 44*, 1394–1401.

Reppucci, N. D., & Haugaard, J. J. (1989). Prevention of child sexual abuse. *American Psychologist, 44*, 1266–1275.

Rescorla, R. A. (1977). Pavlovian 2nd-order conditioning: Some implications for instrumental behavior. In H. Davis & H. Herwit (Eds.), *Pavlovian-operant interactions*. Hillsdale, NJ: Erlbaum.

Rescorla, R. A. (1978). Some implications of a cognitive perspective on Pavlovian conditioning. In S. H. Hulse, H. Fowler, & W. Honig (Eds.), *Cognitive process in animal behavior*. Hillsdale, NJ: Erlbaum.

Rescorla, R. A. (1988). Pavlovian conditioning: It's not what you think it is. *American Psychologist, 43*, 151–160.

Restle, F. (1970). Moon illusion explained on the basis of relative size. *Science, 167*, 1092–1096.

Revenson, T. A., & Felton, B. J. (1989). Disability and coping as predictors of psychological adjustment to rheumatoid arthritis. *Journal of Consulting and Clinical Psychology, 57*, 344–348.

Rheingold, H. L., Gewirtz, J. L., & Ross, H. W. (1959). Social conditioning of vocalizations in the infant. *Journal of Comparative and Physiological Psychology, 52*, 68–73.

Rice, M. L. (1989). Children's language acquisition. *American Psychologist, 44*, 149–156.

Rice, M. L., & Woodsmall, L. (1988). Lessons from television: Children's word learning when viewing. *Child Development, 59*, 420–429.

Rice, R. W., McFarlin, D. B., & Bennett, D. E. (1989). Standards of comparison and job satisfaction. *Journal of Applied Psychology, 74*, 591–598.

Richardson, J. L., Dwyer, K., McGuigan, K., Hansen, W. B., Dent, C., Johnson, C. A., Sussman, S. Y., Brannon, B., & Flay, B. (1989). Substance use among eighth-grade students who take care of themselves after school. *Pediatrics, 84*, 556–566.

Richardson, J. T. E., & Zucco, G. M. (1989). Cognition and olfaction: A review. *Psychological Bulletin, 105*, 352–360.

Richardson-Klavehn, A., & Bjork, R. A. (1988). Measures of memory. In M. R. Rosenzweig & L. W. Porter (Eds.), *Annual review of psychology* (Vol. 39). Palo Alto, CA: Annual Reviews, Inc.

Riley, W. T., Treiber, F. A., & Woods, M. G. (1989). Anger and hostility in depression. *Journal of Nervous and Mental Disease, 177*, 668–674.

Ring, K., Wallston, K., & Corey, M. (1970). Mode of debriefing as a factor affecting subjective reaction to a Milgram-type obedience experiment: An ethical inquiry. *Representative Research in Social Psychology, 1*, 67–88.

Ritter, J. M., & Langlois, J. H. (1988). The role of physical attractiveness in the observation of adult-child interactions: Eye of the beholder or behavioral reality? *Developmental Psychology, 24*, 254–263.

Robberson, M. R., & Rogers, R. W. (1988). Beyond fear appeals: Negative and positive persuasive appeals to health and self-esteem. *Journal of Applied Social Psychology, 18*, 277–287.

Robbins, M., & Meyer, D. (1970). Motivational control of retrograde amnesia. *Journal of Experimental Psychology, 84*, 220–225.

Roberts, G. W. (1988). Immunocytochemistry of neurofibrillary tangles in dementia pugilistica and Alzheimer's disease: Evidence for common genesis. *The Lancet*, December 24/31, 1456–1457.

Robins, L. N. (1966). *Deviant children grown up*. Baltimore: Williams & Wilkins.

Robins, L. N. (1970). The adult development of the antisocial child. *Seminars in Psychiatry, 2*, 420–434.

Robins, L. N., Helzer, J. E., Weissman, M. M., Orvaschel, H., Gruenberg, E., Burke, J. D., & Regier, D. (1984). Lifetime prevalence of specific psychiatric disorders in three sites. *Archives of General Psychiatry, 41*, 949–958.

Robinson, N. M., & Robinson, H. B. (1976). *The mentally retarded child* (2nd ed.). New York: McGraw-Hill.

Robinson, R. G., Tortosa, M., Sullivan, J., Buchanan, E., Andersen, A. E., & Folstein, M. F. (1983). Qualitative assessment of psychologic state of patients with anorexia nervosa or bulimia: Response to caloric stimulus. *Psychosomatic Medicine, 45*, 283–292.

Roche, J. P. (1986). Premarital sex: Attitudes and behavior by dating stage. *Adolescence, 21*, 107–121.

Rockstein, M., & Sussman, M. (1979). *Biology of aging*. Belmont, CA: Wadsworth.

Rodgers, J. L. (1988). Birth order, SAT, and confluence: Spurious correlations and no causality. *American Psychologist, 43*, 476–477.

Rodgers, J. L., & Rowe, D. C. (1985). Does contiguity breed similarity? A within-family analysis of nonshared sources of IQ differences between siblings. *Developmental Psychology, 21*, 743–746.

Rodin, J. (1979). *Obesity theory and treatment: An uneasy couple?* Paper presented at the meeting of the Association for the Advancement of Behavior Therapy, San Francisco.

Rodin, J. (1981). Current status of the internal-external hypothesis for obesity: What went wrong? *American Psychologist, 36*, 361–372.

Rodin, J. (1986). Aging and health: Effects of the sense of control. *Science, 233*, 1271–1276.

Rodin, J., Bartoshuk, L., Peterson, C., & Schank, D. (1990). Bulimia and taste: Possible interactions. *Journal of Abnormal Psychology, 99*, 32–39.

Rodin, J., & Salovey, P. (1989). Health psychology. In M. R. Rosenzweig & L. W. Porter (Eds.), *Annual review of psychology*, (Vol. 40). Palo Alto, CA: Annual Reviews, Inc.

Rodman, H., Pratto, D. J., & Nelson, R. S. (1985). Child care arrangements and children's functioning: A comparison of self-care and adult-care children. *Developmental Psychology, 21*, 413–418.

Rodman, H., Pratto, D. J., & Nelson, R. S. (1988). Toward a definition of self-care children: A commentary on Steinberg (1986). *Developmental Psychology, 24*, 292–294.

Roehrs, T., Timms, V., Zwyghuizen-Doorenbos, A., & Roth, T. (1989). Sleep extension in sleepy and alert normals. *Sleep, 12*, 449–457.

Rogers, C. R. (1951). *Client-centered therapy*. Boston: Houghton Mifflin.

Rogers, C. R. (1959). A theory of therapy, personality, and interpersonal relationships, as developed in the clientcentered framework. In S. Koch (Ed.), *Psychology: A study of a science* (Vol. 3). New York: McGraw-Hill.

Rogers, C. R. (1961). *On becoming a person: A therapist's view of psychotherapy*. Boston: Houghton Mifflin.

Rogers, C. R. (1970). The process of the basic encounter group. In J. T. Hart & T. M. Tomlinson (Eds.), *New directions in client-centered therapy*. Boston: Houghton Mifflin.

Rogers, R. W. (1975). Protection motivation theory of fear appeals and attitude change. *Journal of Psychology, 91*, 93–114.

Rogers, R. W., & Mewborn, C. R. (1976). Fear appeals on attitude change: Effects of a threat's noxiousness, probability of occurrence, and efficacy of coping responses. *Journal of Personality and Social Psychology, 34*, 54–61.

Rogers, R. W., Rogers, J. S., Bailey, J. S., Runkle, W., & Moore, B. (1988). Promoting safety belt use among state employees: The effects of prompting and a stimulus-control intervention. *Journal of Applied Behavior Analysis, 21*, 263–269.

Rogoff, B., & Morelli, G. (1989). Perspectives on children's development from cultural psychology. *American Psychologist, 44*(2), 343–348.

Rokeach, M., & Ball-Rokeach, S. J. (1989). Stability and change in American value priorities. *American Psychologist, 44*, 775–784.

Romano, S. T., & Bordieri, J. E. (1989). Physical attractiveness stereotypes and students' perceptions of college professors. *Psychological Reports, 64*, 1099–1102.

Rosch, E. (1973). Natural categories. *Cognitive Psychology, 4*, 328–350.

Rosch, E. (1978). Principles of categorization. In E. Rosch & B. B. Lloyd (Eds.), *Cognition and categorization* (pp. 27–48). Hillsdale, NJ: Erlbaum.

Rosenberg, M. S. (1987). New directions for research on the psychological maltreatment of children. *American Psychologist, 42*, 166–171.

Rosenhan, D. L. (1973). On being sane in insane places. *Science, 179*, 250–258.

Rosenstock, I. M., & Kirscht, J. P. (1979). Why people seek health care. In G. C. Stone, F. Cohen, & N. E. Adler (Eds.), *Health psychology—A handbook*. San Francisco: Jossey-Bass.

Rosenthal, D. (1970). *Genetic theory in abnormal behavior*. New York: McGraw-Hill.

Rosenthal, D., Wender, P. H., Kety, S. S., Schulsinger, F., Welner, J., & Ostergaard, L. (1968). Schizophrenic's offspring reared in adoptive homes. In D. Rosenthal and S. S. Key (Eds.), *The transmission of schizophrenia*. Oxford: Pergamon Press.

Rosenthal, R., & DePaulo, B. M. (1979). Sex differences in accommodation in nonverbal communication. In R. Rosenthal (Ed.), *Skill in nonverbal communication*. Cambridge, MA: Oelgeschlager, Gunn & Hain.

Rosenthal, R., & Rubin, D. (1982). Further meta-analytic procedures for assessing cognitive gender differences. *Journal of Educational Psychology, 74*, 708–712.

Rosenzweig, S. (1986). Idiodynamics vis-à-vis psychology. *American Psychologist, 41*, 241–245.

Rosenzweig, S. (1988). The identity and idiodynamics of the multiple personality "Sally Beauchampt." *American Psychologist, 43*, 45–48.

Rosett, H. L., Weiner, L., Lee, A., Zuckerman, B., Dooling, E., and Oppenheimer, E. (1983). Patterns of alcohol consumption and fetal development. *Obstetrics and Gynecology, 61*, 538–546.

Ross, H., & Taylor, H. (1989). Do boys prefer daddy or his physical style of play? *Sex Roles, 20,* 23–26.

Ross, H. S., & Lollis, S. P. (1987). Communication within infant social games. *Developmental Psychology, 2,* 241–248.

Ross, L., Bierbrauer, G., & Hoffman, S. (1976). The role of attribution processes in conformity and dissent. *American Psychologist, 31,* 148–157.

Roth, J. D., & Kosslyn, S. M. (1988). Construction of the third dimension in mental imagery. *Cognitive Psychology, 20,* 344–361.

Roth, S. (1980). A revised model of learned helplessness in humans. *Journal of Personality, 48,* 103–118.

Rothbart, M. K., Taylor, S. B., & Tucker, D. M. (1989). Right-sided facial asymmetry in infant emotional expression. *Neuropsychologia, 27,* 675–687.

Rotter, J. B. (1964). *Clinical psychology* (2nd ed.). Englewood Cliffs, NJ: Prentice-Hall.

Rotter, J. B. (1966). Generalized expectancies for internal versus external control of reinforcement. *Psychological Monographs, 80* (1, Whole No. 609).

Rotter, J. B. (1990). Internal versus external control of reinforcement. *American Psychologist, 45,* 489–493.

Rounsaville, B. J., Glazer, W., Wilber, C. H., Weissman, M. M., & Kleber, H. D. (1983). Short-term interpersonal psychotherapy in methadone-maintained opiate addicts. *Archives of General Psychiatry, 40,* 629–636.

Routtenberg, A., & Lindy, J. (1965). Effects of the availability of rewarding septal and hypothalamic stimulation on bar pressing for food under conditions of deprivation. *Journal of Comparative and Physiological Psychology, 60,* 158–161.

Rowland, K. F. (1977). Environmental events predicting death for the elderly. *Psychological Bulletin, 84,* 349–372.

Ruback, R. B., & Innes, C. A. (1988). The relevance and irrelevance of psychological research: The example of prison crowding. *American Psychologist, 43,* 683–693.

Ruderman, A. J. (1986). Dietary restraint: A theoretical and empirical review. *Psychological Bulletin, 99,* 247–262.

Rudman, H. C. (1977). The standardized test flap. *Phi Delta Kappan, 59,* 179–185.

Rumbaugh, D. M., Gill, T. V., & Von Glaserfeld, E. D. (1973). Reading and sentence completion by a chimpanzee (PAN). *Science, 182,* 731–733.

Rumbaugh, D. M., & Savage-Rumbaugh, S. (1978). Chimpanzee language research: Status and potential. *Behavior Research Methods and Instrumentation, 10,* 119–131.

Rumbaugh, D. M., Savage-Rumbaugh, S., & Hegel, M. T. (1987). Summation in the chimpanzee (Pan troglodytes). *Journal of Experimental Psychology: Animal Behavior Processes, 13,* 107–115.

Runyan, W. M. (1982). *Life histories and psychobiography.* New York: Oxford University Press.

Russell, G., & Russell, A. (1987). Mother-child and father-child relationships in middle childhood. *Child Development, 58,* 1573–1585.

Russell, G. F. M., Szmukler, G. I., Dare, C., & Eisler, I. (1987). An evaluation of family therapy in anorexia nervosa and bulimia nervosa. *Archives of General Psychiatry, 44,* 1047–1051.

Russo, N. F., & Denmark, F. L. (1987). Contributions of women to psychology. In M. R. Rosenzweig & L. W. Porter (Eds.), *Annual review of psychology* (Vol. 38). Palo Alto, CA: Annual Reviews, Inc.

Russo, N. P., & Sobel, S. D. (1981). Sex preferences in the utilization of mental health facilities. *Professional Psychology, 12,* 7–19.

Ryan, R. M., Mims, V., & Koestner, R. (1983). Relation of reward contingency and interpersonal context to intrinsic motivation: A review and test using cognitive evaluation theory. *Journal of Personality and Social Psychology, 45,* 736–750.

Sadock, V. (1980). Special areas of interest. In H. Kaplan, A. Freeman, & B. Sadock (Eds.), *Comprehensive textbook of psychiatry, III.* Baltimore: Williams & Wilkins.

Sakitt, B., & Long, G. M. (1979). Cones determine subjective offset of a stimulus but rods determine total persistence. *Vision Research, 19,* 1439–1443.

Salter Ainsworth, M. D. (1989). Attachments beyond infancy. *American Psychologist, 44,* 709–716.

Salzberg, H. C., & DePiano, F. A. (1980). Hypnotizability and task motivating suggestions: A further look at how they affect performance. *International Journal of Clinical and Experimental Hypnosis, 28,* 261–271.

Samuels, S. J. (1970). Interaction of list length and low stimulus similarity on the Von Restorff effect. *Journal of Educational Psychology, 61,* 57–58.

Sande, G. N., Goethals, G. R., & Radloff, C. E. (1988). Perceiving one's own traits and others': The multifaceted self. *Journal of Personality and Social Psychology, 54,* 13–20.

Sandelands, L. E., Brockner, J., & Glynn, M. A. (1988). If at first you don't succeed, try, try again: Effects of persistence-performance contingencies, ego involvement, and self-esteem on task persistence. *Journal of Applied Psychology, 73,* 208–216.

Sanders, G. S., & Simmons, W. L. (1983). Use of hypnosis to enhance eyewitness accuracy: Does it work? *Journal of Applied Psychology, 68,* 70–77.

Sanders, R. J. (1985). Teaching apes to ape language: Explaining the imitative and nonimitative signing of a chimpanzee (Pan troglodytes). *Journal of Comparative Psychology, 99,* 197–210.

Sanders, R. W. (1978). Systematic desensitization in the treatment of child abuse. *American Journal of Psychiatry, 135,* 483–484.

Sarason, I. G., & Sarason, B. R. (1987). *Abnormal psychology: The problem of maladaptive behavior* (5th ed.). Englewood Cliffs, NJ: Prentice-Hall.

Sarason, I. G., Sarason, B. R., Potter, E. H., III, & Antoni, M. H. (1985). Life events, social support, and illness. *Psychosomatic Medicine, 47,* 156–163.

Sartorious, N. (1982). Epidemiology and mental health policy. In M. O. Wagenfeld, P. V. Lemkau, & B. Justice (Eds.), *Public mental health: Perspectives and prospects.* Beverly Hills, CA: Sage Publications.

Sartorious, N., Shapiro, R., & Jablewsky, N. (1974). The international pilot study of schizophrenia. *Schizophrenia Bulletin, 1,* 24–34. (Experimental Issue No. 11.)

Satterfield, J. H., Cantwell, D. P., Saul, R. E., & Yusin, A. (1974). Intelligence, academic achievement, and EEG abnormalities in hyperactive children. *American Journal of Psychiatry, 131,* 391–395.

Sattler, J. M. (1982). *Assessment of children's intelligence and special abilities* (2nd ed.). Boston: Allyn and Bacon.

Sattler, J. M. (1988). *Assessment of children* (3rd ed.). San Diego: Jerome M. Sattler.

Savage-Rumbaugh, E. S., Pate, J. L., Lawson, J., Smith, S. T., & Rosenbaum, S. (1983). Can a chimpanzee make a statement? *Journal of Experimental Psychology: General, 112,* 457–492.

Savage-Rumbaugh, S. (1987). A new look at ape language: Comprehension of vocal speech and syntax. In R. A. Dienstbier & D. W. Leger, *Comparative perspectives in modern psychology.* Lincoln, NE: University of Nebraska Press.

Sawicki, S. (1988). Effective crisis intervention. *Adolescence, XXIII,* 83–88.

Saxe, L., Doughtery, D., & Cross, T. (1985). The validity of polygraph testing. *American Psychologist, 40,* 355–366.

Scarr, S., & Weinberg, R. A. (1983). The Minnesota adoption studies: Genetic differences and malleability. *Child Development, 54,* 260–267.

Schacht, T. E. (1985). DSM-III and the politics of truth. *American Psychologist, 40,* 513–521.

Schachter, F. F. (1979). *Everyday mother talk to toddlers.* New York: Academic Press.

Schachter, S. (1971). Some extraordinary facts about obese humans and rats. *American Psychologist, 26,* 129–144.

Schachter, S., Goldman, R., & Gordon, A. (1968). Effects of fear, food deprivation, and obesity on eating. *Journal of Personality and Social Psychology, 10,* 91–97.

Schachter, S., & Singer, J. E. (1962). Cognitive, social, and physiological determinants of emotional state. *Psychological Review, 69,* 379–399.

Schacter, D. L., Kihlstrom, J. F., Kihlstrom, L. C., & Berren, M. B. (1989). Autobiographical memory in a case of multiple personality disorder. *Journal of Abnormal Psychology, 98,* 508–514.

Schaie, K. W., & Willis, S. L. (1986). *Adult development and aging* (2nd ed.). Boston: Little, Brown.

Schalling, D. (1978). Psychopathy-related personality variables and the psychophysiology of socialization. In R. D. Hare & D. Shalling (Eds.), *Psychopathic behavior: Approaches to research.* Chichester, England: John Wiley & Sons.

Scheier, M. F., & Carver, C. S. (1985). Optimism, coping, and health: Assessment and implications of generalized outcome expectancies. *Health Psychology, 4,* 219–247.

Scherer, D. G., & Reppucci, N. D. (1988). Adolescents' capacities to provide voluntary informed consent. *Law and Human Behavior, 12,* 123–141.

Schiff, M., Duyme, M., Dumaret, A., & Tomkiewicz, S. (1982). How much could we boost scholastic achievement and IQ scores? A direct answer from a French adoption study. *Cognition, 12,* 165–196.

Schindler, P. J., Moely, B. E., & Frank, A. L. (1987). Time in day care and social participation of young children. *Development Psychology, 2,* 255–261.

Schlesier-Stroop, B. (1984). Bulimia: A review of the literature. *Psychological Bulletin, 95,* 247–257.

Schlundt, D. G., & Johnson, W. G. (1990). *Eating disorders.* Boston: Allyn and Bacon.

Schmauk, F. J. (1970). Punishment, arousal, and avoidance learning in sociopaths. *Journal of Abnormal Psychology, 76,* 443–453.

Schmidt, D. F., & Boland, S. M. (1986). Structure of perceptions of older adults: Evidence for multiple stereotypes. *Psychology and Aging, 1,* 255–260.

Schneider, W., & Detweiler, M. (1987). A connectionist/ control, architecture and working memory. In G. H. Bower (Ed.), *The psychology of learning and motivation.* San Diego: Academic Press.

Schneiderman, N., Fuentes, I., & Gormenzano, I. (1962). Acquisition and extinction of the classically conditioned eyelid response in the albino rabbit. *Science, 136,* 650–652.

Schofferman, J. (1988). Care of the AIDS patient. *Death Studies, 12,* 433–449.

Schroeder, D. H., & Costa, P. T. (1984). Influence of life event stress on physical illness: Substantive effects or methodological flaws. *Journal of Personality and Social Psychology, 46,* 853–863.

Schuckit, M. A. (1987). Biological vulnerability to alcoholism. *Journal of Consulting and Clinical Psychology, 55,* 301–309.

Schulz, S. C., Van Kammen, D. P., Balow, J. E., Flye, M. W., & Bunney, W. E., Jr. (1981). Dialysis in schizophrenia: A double-blind evaluation. *Science, 211,* 1066–1068.

Schuman, M. (1980). The psychophysiological model of meditation and altered states of consciousness: A critical review. In J. M. Davidson & R. J. Davidson (Eds.), *The psychobiology of consciousness.* New York: Plenum Press.

Schutte, N. S., Malouff, J. M., Post-Gorden, J. C., & Rodasta, A. L. (1988). Effects of playing videogames on children's aggressive and other behaviors. *Journal of Applied Social Psychology, 18,* 454–460.

Schvaneveldt, R. W., & Meyer, D. E. (1973). Retrieval and comparison processes in semantic memory. In S. Kornblum (Ed.), *Attention and performance IV.* New York: Academic Press.

Schwartz, J. C., & Shaver, P. (1987). Emotions and emotion knowledge in interpersonal relations. *Advances in Personal Relationship, 1,* 197–241.

Schwartz, J. L. (1987). *Review and evaluation of smoking cessation methods: The United States and Canada, 1978–1985* (NIH Publication No. 87-2940). Bethesda, MD: Division of Cancer Prevention, National Cancer Institute, U.S. Department of Health and Human Services.

Schwartz, P. (1983). Length of day-care attendance and attachment behavior in eighteen-month-old infants. *Child Development, 54,* 1073–1078.

Schwartz, S., & Johnson, J. H. (1985). *Psychopathology of childhood: A clinical-experimental approach.* New York: Pergamon Press.

Schwartzman, A. E., Gold, D., Andres, D., Arbuckle, T. Y., & Chaikelson, J. (1987). Stability of intelligence: A 40-year follow-up. *Canadian Journal of Psychology, 41,* 244–256.

Schwarz, L. M., Foa, U. G., & Foa, E. B. (1983). Multichannel nonverbal communication: Evidence for combinatory rules. *Journal of Personality and Social Psychology, 45,* 274–281.

Schweickert, R., & Boruff, B. (1986). Short-term memory capacity: Magic number or magic spell? *Journal of Experimental Psychology: Learning, Memory, and Cognition, 12,* 419–425.

Sears, R. R. (1982). Obituary: Harry Fredrick Harlow (1905–1981). *American Psychologist, 37,* 1280–1281.

Seeman, J. (1989). Toward a model of positive health. *American Psychologist, 44,* 1099–1109.

Segal, Z. V. (1988). Appraisal of the self-schema construct in cognitive models of depression. *Psychological Bulletin, 103,* 147–162.

Seidman, L. J. (1983). Schizophrenia and brain dysfunction: An integration of recent neurodiagnostic findings. *Psychological Bulletin, 94,* 195–238.

Seif, M. N., & Atkins, A. L. (1979). Some defensive and cognitive aspects of phobias. *Journal of Abnormal Psychology, 88,* 42–51.

Sejnowski, T. J., Koch, C., & Churchland, P. S. (1988). Computational neuroscience. *Science, 9(9),* 1299–1306.

Seligman, M. (1988). G. Stanley Hall lecture presented at the American Psychological Association Convention, Atlanta, GA, August.

Seligman, M. E. P. (1975). *Helplessness.* San Francisco: W. H. Freeman.

Seligman, M. E. P. (1976). *Learned helplessness and depression in animals and humans.* Morristown, NJ: General Learning Press.

Seligmann, J., Hager, M., & Springen, K. (1986). The fear of forgetting. *Newsweek,* September 29, 51.

Selye, H. (1956). *The stress of life.* New York: McGraw-Hill.

Selye, H. (1976). *Stress in health and disease.* London: Butterworth.

Sengel, R. A., & Lovallo, W. R. (1983). Effects of cueing on immediate and recent memory in schizophrenics. *Journal of Nervous and Mental Disease, 171,* 426–430.

Shakow, D. (1977). Segmental set: The adaptive process in schizophrenia. *American Psychologist, 32,* 129–139.

Shanab, M. E., & Yahya, K. A. (1978). A cross-cultural study of obedience. *Bulletin of the Psychonomic Society, 11,* 267–269.

Shapiro, D. A., & Shapiro, D. (1982). Meta-analysis of comparative therapy outcome studies: A replication and refinement. *Psychological Bulletin, 92,* 581–604.

Shatz, M., & Gelman, R. (1973). The development of communication skills: Modifications in the speech of young children as a function of

listener. *Monographs of the Society for Research in Child Development, 38*(2, Serial No. 152).

Shaver, P., & Schwartz, J. C. (1988). Cross-cultural similarities and differences in emotion and its representation: A prototype approach. To appear in a book edited by R. B. Zajonc and S. Moscovici, based on the Symposium on Social Psychology and Emotions, Paris, January 1987.

Shaver, P., Schwartz, J., Kirson, D., & O'Connor, C. (1987). Emotion knowledge: Further exploration of a prototype approach. *Journal of Personality and Social Psychology, 52,* 1061–1086.

Shaver, P. R., & Hazan, C. (1988). A biased overview of the study of love. *Journal of Social and Personal Relationships, 5,* 473–501.

Shaywitz, S. E., Cohen, D. J., & Shaywitz, B. A. (1980). Behavior and learning difficulties in children of normal intelligence born to alcoholic mothers. *Journal of Pediatrics, 96,* 978–982.

Shebilske, W. L., & Rotondo, J. A. (1981). Typographical and spatial cues that facilitate learning from textbooks. *Visible Language, 15,* 41–54.

Shepard, S., & Metzler, D. (1988). Mental rotation: Effects of dimensionality of objects and type of task. *Journal of Experimental Psychology: Human Perception and Performance, 14,* 3–11.

Sheridan, M. S. (1985). Things that go beep in the night: Home monitoring for apnea. *Health and Social Work,* 63–70.

Sherif, M., Harvey, O. J., White, B. J., Hood, W. E., and Sherif, C. W. (1961). *Intergroup conflict and cooperation: The Robbers Cave experiment.* Norman, OK: Institute of Group Relations.

Sherman, M., & Key, C. B. (1932). The intelligence of isolated mountain children. *Child Development, 3,* 279–290.

Sherman, S. J., Judd, C. M., & Park, B. (1989). Social cognition. *Annual Review of Psychology, 40,* 281–326.

Sherrington, R., Brynjolfsson, J., Petursson, H., Potter, M., Dudleston, K., Barraclough, B., Wasmuth, J., Dobbs, M., & Gurling, H. (1988). Localization of a susceptibility locus for schizophrenia on chromosome 5. *Nature, 336,* 164–167.

Shimamura, A. P., & Squire, L. R. (1986). Memory and metamemory: A study of the feeling-of-knowing phenomenon in amnesic patients. *Journal of Experimental Psychology: Learning, Memory, and Cognition, 12,* 452–460.

Shimberg, M. E. (1929). An investigation into the validity of norms with special reference to urban and rural groups. *Archives of Psychology, 104,* 1–62.

Shissal, C. M., Crago, M., Neal, M. E., & Swain, B. (1987). Primary prevention of eating disorders. *Journal of Consulting and Clinical Psychology, 55,* 660–667.

Shneidman, E. (1989). The Indian summer of life. A preliminary study of septuagenerians. *American Psychologist, 44,* 684–694.

Shock, N. W. (1977). Biological theories of aging. In J. E. Birren & K. W. Schaie (Eds.), *Handbook of the psychology of aging.* New York: Van Nostrand Reinhold.

Shore, J. H., Vollmer, W. M., & Tatum, E. L. (1989). Community patterns of posttraumatic stress disorders. *Journal of Nervous and Mental Disease, 177,* 681–685.

Shotland, R. L., & Heinold, W. D. (1985). Interpersonal relations and group processes. Bystander response to arterial bleeding: Helping skills, the decision-making process, and differentiating the helping response. *Journal of Personality and Social Psychology, 49,* 347–456.

Siddall, L. B., Haffey, N. A., & Feinman, J. A. (1988). Intermittent brief psychotherapy in a HMO setting. *American Journal of Psychotherapy, XLII,* 96–101.

Siegel, E. F. (1979). Control of phantom limb pain by hypnosis. *American Journal of Clinical Hypnosis, 21,* 285–286.

Siegel, O. (1982). Personality development in adolescence. In B. B. Wolman & G. Stricker (Eds.), *Handbook of developmental psychology.* Englewood Cliffs, NJ: Prentice-Hall.

Siegel, S. (1988). State dependent learning and morphine tolerance. *Behavioral Neuroscience, 102,* 228–232.

Siero, S., Boon, M., Kok, G., & Siero, F. (1989). Modification of driving behavior in a large transport organization: A field experiment. *Journal of Applied Psychology, 74,* 417–423.

Silberman, E. K., Weingartner, H., & Post, R. M. (1983). Thinking disorder in depression. Logic and strategy in an abstract reasoning task. *Archives of General Psychiatry, 40,* 775–780.

Silverman, L. H. (1976). Psychoanalytic theory: "The reports of my death are greatly exaggerated." *American Psychologist, 31,* 621–637.

Silverman, L. H. (1983). The subliminal psychodynamic activation method: Overview and comprehensive listing of studies. In J. Masling (Ed.), *Empirical studies of psychoanalytic theories* (Vol. 1, 69–100). Hillsboro, NJ: Erlbaum.

Silverstein, B. (1989). The psychology of U.S. attitudes and cognitions regarding the Soviet Union. *American Psychologist, 44,* 903–913.

Simmons, C. H., & Zumpf, C. (1983). The lost letter technique. *Journal of Applied Social Psychology, 13,* 6, 510–514.

Simonton, D. K. (1988). Age and outstanding achievement: What do we know after a century of research? *Psychological Bulletin, 104,* 251–267.

Singer, L. M., Brodzinsky, D. M., Ramsay, D., Steir, M., & Waters, E. (1985). Mother-infant attachment in adoptive families. *Child Development, 56,* 1543–1551.

Skinner, B. F. (1938). *The behavior of organisms.* New York: Appleton-Century-Crofts.

Skinner, B. F. (1948). Superstition in the pigeon. *Journal of Experimental Psychology, 38,* 168–172.

Skinner, B. F. (1983). Intellectual self-management in old age. *American Psychologist, 38,* 239–244.

Skinner, B. F. (1986). What is wrong with daily life in the Western world? *American Psychologist, 41,* 568–574.

Skinner, B. F. (1988). Skinner joins aversives debate. *American Psychological Association APA Monitor,* June, 22.

Skinner, B. F. (1989). The origins of cognitive thought. *American Psychologist, 44,* 13–18.

Slaikeu, K. A. (1979). Temporal variables in telephone crisis intervention: Their relationship to selected process and outcome variables. *Journal of Consulting and Clinical Psychology, 47,* 193–195.

Slaikeu, K. A. (1990). *Crisis intervention.* 2nd Edition. Boston: Allyn and Bacon.

Slobin, D. I. (1975). On the nature of talk to children. In E. H. Lenneberg & E. Lenneberg (Eds.), *Foundations of language development: A multidisciplinary approach* (Vol. 1). New York: Academic Press.

Slovic, P., Lichtenstein, S., & Fischhoff, B. (1988). Decision making. In R. C. Atkinson, R. J. Herrnstein, G. Lindzey, & R. D. Luce (Eds.), *Stevens' handbook of experimental psychology,* 2nd ed., Vol. 2, *Learning and Cognition.* New York: John Wiley & Sons.

Small, G. W., Kuhl, D. E., Riege, W. H., Fujikawa, D. G., Ashford, J. W., Metter, E. J., & Mazziotta, J. C. (1989). Cerebral glucose metabolic patterns in Alzheimer's disease. *Archives in General Psychiatry, 46,* 527–528.

Smith, C. A. (1989). Dimensions of appraisal and physiological response in emotion. *Journal of Personality and Social Psychology, 56,* 339–353.

Smith, D., & Kraft, W. A. (1983). DSM-III: Do psychologists really want an alternative? *American Psychologist, 38,* 777–785.

Smith, M. C. (1983). Hypnotic memory enhancement of witnesses: Does it work? *Psychological Bulletin, 94,* 387–407.

Smith, M. L., & Glass, G. V. (1977). Meta-analysis of psychotherapy outcome studies. *American Psychologist, 32,* 752–760.

Smith, M. L., Glass, G. V., & Miller, T. I. (1980). *The benefits of psychotherapy.* Baltimore: Johns Hopkins University Press.

Smyser, A. A. (1982). Hospices: Their humanistic and economic value. *American Psychologist, 37,* 1260–1262.

Snowden, L. R. (1987). The peculiar successes of community psychology: Service delivery to ethnic minorities and the poor. *American Journal of Community Psychology, 5,* 575–586.

Snowden, L. R., & Cheung, F. K. (1990). Use of inpatient mental health services by members of ethnic minority groups. *American Psychologist, 45,* 347–355.

Snyder, C. R., & Higgins, R. L. (1988). Excuses: Their effective role in the negotiation of reality. *Psychological Bulletin, 104,* 23–35.

Snyder, D. K., & Wills, R. M. (1989). Behavioral versus insight-oriented marital therapy: Effects on individual and interspousal functioning. *Journal of Consulting and Clinical Psychology, 57,* 39–46.

Snyder, S. H. (1974). *Madness and the brain.* New York: McGraw-Hill.

Snyder, S. H. (1980). Brain peptides as neurotransmitters. *Science, 209,* 976–983.

Snyderman, M., & Rothman, S. (1987). Survey of expert opinion on intelligence and aptitude testing. *American Psychologist, 42,* 137–144.

Sobal, J., & Stunkard, A. J. (1989). Socioeconomic status and obesity: A review of the literature. *Psychological Bulletin, 105,* 260–275.

Sobell, M. B., & Sobell, L. C. (1982). Controlled drinking: A concept coming of age. In K. R. Blanstein & J. Polivy (Eds.), *Self-control and self-modification of emotional behavior.* New York: Plenum Press.

Sogon, S., & Masutani, M. (1989). Identification of emotion from body movements: A cross-cultural study of Americans and Japanese. *Psychological Reports, 65,* 35–46.

Solomon, S. D., Smith, E. M., Robins, L. N., & Fischbach, R. L. (1987). Social involvement as a mediator of disaster-induced stress. *Journal of Applied Social Psychology, 17,* 1092–1112.

Solomon, Z., Mikulincer, M., & Flum, Hanoch, F. (1988). Negative life events, coping responses, and combat-related psychopathology: A prospective study. *Journal of Abnormal Psychology, 97*(3), 302–307.

Solso, R. L. (1979). *Cognitive psychology.* New York: Harcourt Brace Jovanovich.

Sorce, J. F., Emde, R. N., Campos, J., & Klinnert, M. D. (1985). Maternal emotional signaling: Its effect on the visual cliff behavior of 1-year-olds. *Developmental Psychology, 21,* 195–200.

Sosa, R., Kennell, J., Klaus, M., Robertson, S., & Urrutia, J. (1980). The effect of a supportive companion on perinatal problems, length of labor, and mother-infant interaction. *New England Journal of Medicine, 303,* 597–600.

Soskis, D. A., Orne, E. C., Orne, M. T., & Dinges, D. F. (1989). Self-hypnosis and meditation for stress management: A brief communication. *International Journal of Clinical and Experimental Hypnosis, XXXVII,* 285–289.

Source, J. F., & Emde, R. N. (1981). Mother's presence is not enough: Effect of emotional availability on infant exploration. *Development Psychology, 17,* 737–745.

Space, L. G., & Cromwell, R. L. (1980). Personal constructs among depressed patients. *Journal of Nervous and Mental Disease, 168,* 150–158.

Spanos, N. P., DeBeuil, D. L., Saad, C. L., & Gorassini, D. (1983). Hypnotic elimination of prism-induced aftereffects: Perceptual effect or responses to experimental demands? *Journal of Abnormal Psychology, 92,* 216–222.

Spanos, N. P., Lush, N. I., & Gwynn, M. I. (1989). Cognitive skill-training enhancement of hypnotizability: Generalization effects and trance logic responding. *Journal of Personality and Social Psychology, 56,* 795–804.

Spanos, N. P., Perlini, A. H., & Robertson, L. A. (1989). Hypnosis, suggestion, and placebo in the reduction of experimental pain. *Journal of Abnormal Psychology, 98,* 285–293.

Spanos, N. P., Radtke-Bodorik, H. L., Ferguson, J. D., & Jones, B. (1979). The effects of hypnotic susceptibility, suggestions for analgesia, and the utilization of cognitive strategies on the reduction of pain. *Journal of Abnormal Psychology, 88,* 282–292.

Spence, J. T. (1987). Centrifugal versus centripetal tendencies in psychology. *American Psychologist, 42,* 1052–1054.

Spencer, J. A., & Fremouw, W. J. (1979). Binge eating as a function of restraint and weight classification. *Journal of Abnormal Psychology, 88,* 262–267.

Sperling, G. (1960). The information available in brief visual presentations. *Psychological Monographs, 15,* 201–293.

Sperry, R. W. (1985). Consciousness, personal identity, and the divided brain. In D. F. Benson & E. Zaidel (Eds.), *The dual brain: Hemispheric specialization in humans* (pp. 11–26). New York: Guilford Press.

Spiegel, D., & Bloom, J. R. (1983). Group therapy and hypnosis reduce metastatic breast carcinoma pain. *Psychosomatic Medicine, 45,* 333–340.

Spitzer, R. (1981 October). Nonmedical myths and the DMS-III. *APA Monitor, 12,* 3, 33.

Spragins, A. B., Lefton, L. A., & Fisher, D. F. (1976). Eye movements while reading and searching spatially transformed text: A developmental examination. *Memory and Cognition, 4,* 36–42.

Sprecher, S., McKinney, K., & Orbuch, T. L. (1987). Has the double standard disappeared? An experimental test. *Social Psychology Quarterly, 50,* 24–31.

Spring, B., Chiodo, J., & Bowen, D. J. (1987). Carbohydrates, tryptophan, and behavior: A methodological review. *Psychological Bulletin, 102,* 234–256.

Spring, B., Chiodo, J., Harden, M., Bourgeois, M., Lutherer, L., Harner, D., Crowell, S., & Swope, G. (1986). Effects of noon meals varying in nutrient composition on plasma amino acids, glucose, insulin, and behavior. *Psychopharmacology Bulletin, 22,* 1026–1029.

Sprinthall, N. A., & Collins, W. A. (1984). *Adolescent psychology.* Reading, MA: Addison-Wesley.

Squire, L. R. (1987). *Memory and brain.* New York: Oxford.

Sroufe, L. A., & Waters, E. (1977). Attachment as an organizational construct. *Child Development, 48,* 1184–1199.

St. Claire-Smith, R., & MacLaren, D. (1983). Response preconditioning effects. *Journal of Experimental Psychology: Animal Behavior Processes, 9,* 41–48.

St. George-Hyslop, P. H., Tanzi, R. E., Polinsky, R. J., et al. (1987). The genetic defect causing familial Alzheimer's disease maps on chromosome 21. *Science, 235,* 821–944.

Stagner, R. (1985). Aging in industry. In J. E. Birren & K. W. Schaie (Eds.), *Handbook of the psychology of aging* (2nd ed.). New York: Van Nostrand Reinhold.

Stagner, R. (1988). *A history of psychological theories.* New York: Macmillan.

Stall, R. D., Coates, T. J., & Hoff, C. (1988). Behavioral risk reduction for HIV infection among gay and bisexual men. *American Psychologist, 43,* 878–885.

Stampfl, T. G., & Levis, D. J. (1968). Implosive therapy—a behavioral therapy? *Behavior Research and Therapy, 6,* 31–36.

Standing, L. (1973). Learning 10,000 pictures. *Quarterly Journal of Experimental Psychology, 25,* 207–222.

Standing, L., Conezio, J., & Haber, R. N. (1970). Perception and memory for pictures: Single trial learning of 2500 visual stimuli. *Psychonomic Science, 19,* 73–74.

Stanton, H. E. (1978). A one-session hypnotic approach to modifying smoking behavior. *International Journal of Clinical and Experimental Hypnosis, 26,* 22–29.

Stapp, J., Fulcher, R., & Wicherski, M. (1984). Human resources in psychology. The employment of 1981 and 1982 doctorate recipients in psychology. *American Psychologist, 39,* 1408–1423.

Stapp, J., Tucker, A. M., & VandenBos, G. R. (1985). Human resources in psychology. Census of psychological personnel: 1983. *American Psychologist, 40,* 1317–1351.

Staszewski, J. (1987). The psychological reality of retrieval structures: An investigation of expert knowledge (Doctoral dissertation, Cornell University, 1987). *Dissertation Abstracts International, 48,* 2168B.

Staszewski, J. J. (1988). Skilled memory and expert mental calculation. In M. T. H. Chi, R. Glaser, & M. J. Farr, *The nature of expertise.* Hillsdale, NJ: Erlbaum.

Stebbins, W. C. (1970). *Animal psychophysics. The design and conduct of sensory experiments.* New York: Appleton-Century-Crofts.

Steblay, N. M. (1987). Helping behavior in rural and urban environments: A meta-analysis. *Psychological Bulletin, 102,* 346–356.

Steele, C. M. (1975). Name-calling and compliance. *Journal of Personality and Social Psychology, 31,* 261–369.

Stein, M. I. (1974). *Stimulating creativity.* New York: Academic Press.

Steinberg, L. (1986). Latchkey children and susceptibility to peer pressure: An ecological analysis. *Developmental Psychology, 22,* 433–439.

Steinberg, L. (1987). Impact of puberty on family relations: Effects of pubertal status and pubertal timing. *Developmental Psychology, 3,* 451–460.

Steiner, D. D., & Rain, J. S. (1989). Immediate and delayed primacy and recency effects in performance evaluation. *Journal of Applied Psychology, 74,* 136–142.

Steiner, I. D. (1982). Heuristic models of groupthink. In M. Brandstatter, J. H. Davis, & G. Stocker-Kreichgauer (Eds.), *Group decision making.* New York: Academic Press.

Stellar, J. R., & Stellar, E. (1985). *The neurobiology of motivation and reward.* New York: Springer-Verlag.

Stephan, C. W., & Langlois, J. H. (1984). Baby beautiful: Adult attributions of infant competence as a function of infant attractiveness. *Child Development, 55,* 576–585.

Stephenson, J. S. (1985). *Death, grief, and mourning (individual and social realities).* New York: Macmillan.

Stern, M., & Hildebrandt, K. (1984). Prematurity stereotype: Effects of labeling on adults' perceptions of infants. *Developmental Psychology, 20,* 360–362.

Sternbach, R. A. (1974). *Pain patients: Traits and treatment.* New York: Academic Press.

Sternberg, R. J. (1984). The Kaufman Assessment Battery for Children: An information-processing analysis and critique. *Journal of Special Education, 18,* 269–279.

Sternberg, R. J. (1985). *Beyond IQ.* Cambridge, MA: Cambridge University Press.

Sternberg, R. J. (1986a). A triangular theory of love. *Psychological Review, 93,* 119–135.

Sternberg, R. J. (1986b). *Intelligence applied: Understanding and increasing your intellectual skills.* New York: Harcourt Brace Jovanovich.

Sternberg, R. J., & Detterman, D. L. (Eds.). (1986). *What is intelligence? Contemporary viewpoints on its nature and definition.* Norword, NJ: Ablex Publishing Corporation.

Steward, A. L., Greenfield, S., Hays, R. D., Wells, K., Rogers, W. H., Berry, S. D., McGlynn, E. A., & Ware, J. E. (1989). Functional status and well-being of patients with chronic conditions. *Journal of the American Medical Association, 262,* 907–913.

Stewart, M. A., DeBlois, C. S., Meardon, J., & Cummings, C. (1980). Aggressive conduct disorder in children. *Journal of Nervous and Mental Disease, 168,* 604–610.

Stiles, W. B., Shapiro, D. A., & Elliott, R. (1986). Are all psychotherapies equivalent? *American Psychologist, 41,* 165–180.

Stipek, D., & McCroskey, J. (1989). Investing in children: Government and workplace policies for parents. *American Psychologist, 44*(2), 416–423.

Stitzer, M. L. (1988). Drug abuse in methadone patients reduced when rewards/punishments clear. *Alcohol, Drug Abuse, and Mental Health, XIV,* 1.

Stivers, C. (1988). Adolescent suicide: An overview. *Marriage and Family Review, 12,* 135–142.

Stolz, S. B., Wienckowski, L. A., & Brown, B. S. (1975). Behavior modification: A perspective on critical issues. *American Psychologist, 30,* 1027–1048.

Stone, M. H. (1980). *The borderline syndromes.* New York: McGraw-Hill.

Storms, L. H. (1976). Implosive therapy: An alternative to systematic desensitization. In V. Binder, A. Binder, & B. Rimland (Eds.), *Modern therapies.* Englewood Cliffs, NJ: Prentice-Hall.

Stott, D. H., & Latchford, S. A. (1976). Prenatal antecedents of child health, development, and behavior: An epidemiological report of incidence and association. *Journal of the American Academy of Child Psychiatry, 15,* 161–191.

Stott, D. H., & Wilson, D. M. (1977). The adult criminal as a juvenile. *British Journal of Criminology, 17,* 47–57.

Straus, M. A., & Gelles, R. J. (1986). Societal change in family violence from 1975 to 1985 as revealed by two national surveys. *Journal of Marriage and the Family, 48,* 465–479.

Strayer, D. L., & Kramer, A. R. (1990). Attentional requirements of automatic and controlled processing. *Journal of Experimental Psychology: Learning, Memory, and Cognition, 16,* 67–82.

Streissguth, A. P., Barr, H. M., & Martin, D. C. (1983). Maternal alcohol use and neonatal habituation assessed with the Brazelton Scale. *Child Development, 54,* 1109–1118.

Streissguth, A. P., Barr, H. M., Sampson, P. D., Darby, B. L., & Martin, D. C. (1989). IQ at age 4 in relation to maternal alcohol use and smoking during pregnancy. *Developmental Psychology, 25*(1), 3–11.

Strickland, B. R. (1988). Clinical psychology comes of age. *American Psychologist, 43,* 104–107.

Strickland, B. R. (1989). Internal-external control expectancies: From contingency to creativity. *American Psychologist, 44,* 1–12.

Striegel-Moore, R. H., Silberstein, L. R., & Rodin, J. (1986). Toward an understanding of risk factors for bulimia. *American Psychologist, 41,* 246–263.

Strober, M., & Humphrey, L. L. (1987). Familial contributions to the etiology and course of anorexia nervosa and bulimia. *Journal of Consulting and Clinical Psychology, 55,* 654–659.

Strupp, H. H. (1989). Psychotherapy. *American Psychologist, 44,* 717–724.

Stuart, E. W., Shimp, T. A., & Engle, R. W. (1987). Classical conditioning of consumer attitudes: Four experiments in an advertising context. *Journal of Consumer Research, 14,* 334–349.

Stunkard, A., Coll, M., Lundquist, S., & Meyers, A. (1980). Obesity and eating style. *Archives of General Psychiatry, 37,* 1127–1129.

Suarez, E. C., & Williams, R. B. (1989). Situational determinants of cardiovascular and emotional reactivity in high and low hostile men. *Psychosomatic Medicine, 51,* 404–418.

Sue, S. (1988). Psychotherapeutic services for ethnic minorities. *American Psychologist, 43,* 301–308.

Suedfeld, P., & Coren, S. (1989). Perceptual isolation, sensory deprivation, and rest: Moving introductory psychology texts out of the 1950s. *Canadian Psychology, 30,* 17–29.

Sugarman, D. B., & Hotaling, G. T. (1989). Violent men in intimate relationships: An analysis of risk markers. *Journal of Applied Social Psychology, 19,* 1034–1048.

Suls, J., & Wan, C. K. (1989a). Effects of sensory and procedural information on coping with stressful medical procedures and pain: A meta-analysis. *Journal of Consulting and Clinical Psychology, 57,* 372–379.

Suls, J., & Wan, C. K. (1989b). The relation between Type A behavior and chronic emotional distress: A meta-analysis. *Journal of Personality and Social Psychology, 57,* 503–512.

Surgeon General. (1988). The health consequences of smoking: Nicotine addiction. *A Report of the Surgeon General,* Rockville, MD: U.S. Department of Health & Human Services.

Surwit, R. S., Feinglos, M. N., & Scovern, A. W. (1983). Diabetes and behavior: A paradigm for health psychology. *American Psychologist, 38,* 255–262.

Sutker, P. B., & Allain, A. N. (1988). Issues in personality conceptualizations of addictive behaviors. *Journal of Consulting and Clinical Psychology, 56*(2), 172–182.

Swedo, S. E., Leonard, H. L., Rapoport, J. L., Lenane, M. C., Goldberger, E. L., & Cheslow, D. L. (1989). A double-blind comparison of clomipramine and desipramine in the treatment of trichotillomania (hair pulling). *New England Journal of Medicine, 321,* 497–501.

Swim, J., Borgida, E., Maruyama, G., & Myers, D. G. (1989). Joan McKay versus John McKay: Do gender stereotypes bias evaluations? *Psychological Bulletin, 105,* 409–429.

Swindle, R. W., Jr., Cronkite, R. C., & Moos, R. H. (1989). Life stressors, social resources, coping, and the 4-year course of unipolar depression. *Journal of Abnormal Psychology, 98,* 468–477.

Szapocznik, J., Perez-Vidal, A., Hervis, O., Brickman, A. L., & Kurtines, W. M. (1990). Innovations in family therapy: Strategies for overcoming resistance to treatment. In R. A. Wells & V. J. Giannetti (Eds.), *Handbook of the brief psychotherapies.* New York: Plenum Press.

Szucko, J. J., & Kleinmuntz, B. (1981). Statistical versus clinical lie detection. *American Psychologist, 36,* 488–496.

Szymanski, K., & Harkins, S. G. (1987). Social loafing and self-evaluation with a social standard. *Journal of Personality and Social Psychology, 53,* 891–897.

Tagruri, R. (1968). Person perception. In G. Lindzey & E. Aronson (Eds.), *The handbook of social psychology.* Reading, MA: Addison-Wesley.

Tait, M., Padgett, M. Y., & Baldwin, T. T. (1989). Job and life satisfaction: A reevaluation of the strength of the relationship and gender effects as a function of the date of the study. *Journal of Applied Psychology, 74,* 502–507.

Takano, Y. (1989). Perception of rotated forms: A theory of information types. *Cognitive Psychology, 21,* 1–59.

Tanner, J. M. (1962). *Growth at adolescence* (2nd ed.). Oxford: Blackwell.

Tanner, J. M. (1978). *Education and physical growth* (2nd ed.). New York: International Universities Press.

Tarpy, R. M., & Sawbini, F. L. (1974). Reinforcement delay: A selective review of the last decade. *Psychological Bulletin, 81,* 984–997.

Tarr, M. J., & Pinker, S. (1989). Mental rotation and orientation-dependence in shape recognition. *Cognitive Psychology, 21,* 233–282.

Tart, C. T. (1972). States of consciousness and state-specific sciences. *Science, 176,* 1203–1210.

Tart, C. T. (1977). Putting the pieces together: A conceptual framework for understanding discrete states of consciousness. In N. E. Zinberg (Ed.), *Alternate states of consciousness.* New York: Macmillan.

Tarter, R. E. (1988). Are there inherited behavioral traits that predispose to substance abuse? *Journal of Consulting and Clinical Psychology, 56*(2), 189–196.

Taylor, S. H. (1990). Health psychology. *American Psychologist, 45,* 40–50.

Teevan, R. C., & McGhee, P. E. (1972). Childhood development of fear of failure motivation. *Journal of Personality and Social Psychology, 21,* 345–348.

Tennov, D. (1981). *Love and limerance.* Briarcliff Manor, NY: Stein and Day.

Terrace, H. S. (1979). How Nim Chimpski changed my mind. *Psychology Today, 13,* 65–76.

Terrace, H. S. (1980). *Nim.* New York: Alfred A. Knopf.

Terrace, H. S. (1985). In the beginning was the "name." *American Psychologist, 40,* 1011–1028.

Teske, J. A. (1988). Seeing her looking at you: Acquaintance and variation in the judgment of gaze depth. *American Journal of Psychology, 101,* 239–257.

Theorell, T., Svensson, J., Knox, S., Waller, D., & Alvarez, M. (1986). Young men with high blood pressure report few recent life events. *Journal of Psychosomatic Research, 30,* 243–249.

Tholey, P. (1983a). Cognitive abilities of dream figures in lucid dreams. *Lucidity Letter, 2*(4), 71.

Tholey, P. (1983b). Techniques for inducing and manipulating lucid dreams. *Perceptual and Motor Skills, 57,* 79–90.

Tholey, P. (1988). Psychotherapeutic application of lucid dreaming. In J. I. Gackenbach & S. LaBerge (Eds.), *Conscious mind, sleeping brain: Perspectives on lucid dreaming.* New York: Plenum Press.

Thompson, R. F., Donegan, N. H., & Lavond, D. G. (1988). The psychobiology of learning and memory. In R. C. Atkinson, R. J. Herrnstein, G. Lindzey, & R. D. Luce (Eds.), *Stevens' handbook of experimental psychology,* Vol. 2. *Learning and Cognition.* New York: John Wiley & Sons.

Thompson, W. R. (1954). The inheritance and development of intelligence. *Research Publication Association of Nervous and Mental Diseases, 33,* 209–331.

Thorkildsen, T. A. (1989). Justice in the classroom: The student's view. *Child Development, 60,* 323–334.

Thorndyke, P. W. (1977). Cognitive structures in comprehension and memory of narrative discourse. *Cognitive Psychology, 9,* 77–110.

Thyer, B. A., & Geller, E. S. (1987). The "buckle-up" dashboard sticker: An effective environmental intervention for safety belt promotion. *Environment and Behavior, 19,* 484–494.

Tice, D. M., & Baumeister, R. F. (1985). Masculinity inhibits helping in emergencies: Personality does predict the bystander effect. *Journal of Personality and Social Psychology, 49,* 420–428.

Tietze, C. (1978). Teenage pregnancies: Looking ahead to 1984. *Family Planning Perspectives, 10,* 205.

Tilley, A., & Warren, P. (1983). Retrieval from semantic memory at different times of day. *Journal of Experimental Psychology: Learning, Memory, and Cognition, 9,* 718–724.

Tinbergen, N. (1974). Etiology and stress disease. *Science, 185,* 20–27.

Titchener, E. B. (1898). *A primer of psychology.* New York: Macmillan.

Tjosvold, D. (1987). Participation: A close look at its dynamics. *Journal of Management, 13,* 739–750.

Tjosvold, D., & Chia, L. C. (1989). Conflict between managers and workers: The role of cooperation and competition. *The Journal of Social Psychology, 129,* 235–247.

Tomarken, A. J., & Kirschenbaum, D. S. (1984). Effects of plans for future meals on counterregulatory eating by restrained and unrestrained eaters. *Journal of Abnormal Psychology, 93,* 458–472.

Torrey, E. (1983). *Surviving schizophrenia: A family manual.* New York: Harper & Row.

Trachtman, G. M. (1981). On such a full sea. *School Psychology Review, 10,* 138–181.

Treisman, A., & Gormican, S. (1988). Feature analysis in early vision: Evidence from search asymmetries. *Psychological Review, 95,* 15–48.

Treisman, A. M. (1969). Strategies and models of selective attention. *Psychological Review, 76,* 282–295.

Trickett, P. K., & Susman, E. J. (1988). Parental perceptions of child-rearing practices in physically abusive and nonabusive families. *Developmental Psychology, 24,* 270–276.

Trites, D., Galbraith, F. D., Sturdavent, M., & Leckwart, J. F. (1970). Influence of nursing-unit design on the activities and subjective feelings of nursing personnel. *Environment and Behavior, 2,* 203–234.

Tronick, E. Z. (1989). Emotions and emotional communication in infants. *American Psychologist, 44,* 112–119.

Tronick, E. Z., & Cohn, J. F. (1989). Infant-mother face-to-face interaction: Age and gender differences in coordination and the occurrence of miscoordination. *Child Development, 60,* 85–92.

Tulving, E. (1972). Episodic and semantic memory. In E. Tulving & W. Donaldson (Eds.), *Organization and memory.* New York: Academic Press.

Tuma, J. M. (1989). Mental health services for children. *American Psychologist, 44,* 188–199.

Tune, G. S. (1969). Sleep and wakefulness in 509 normal human adults. *British Journal of Medical Psychology, 42,* 75–79.

Tune, L. F. (1989). *Driven off the road by brain disease.* Paper presented at the annual meeting of the American Psychiatric Association.

Turk, D. C. (1978). Cognitive behavioral techniques on the management of pain. In J. P. Foreyt & D. J. Rathgen (Eds.), *Cognitive behavior therapy: Research and application.* New York: Plenum Press.

Turk, D. C., Meichenbaum, D., & Genest, M. (1983). *Pain and behavioral medicine. A cognitive-behavioral perspective.* New York: Guilford Press.

Turnbull, C. M. (1961). Notes and discussions: Some observations regarding the experiences and behavior of the Bambute Pygmies. *American Journal of Psychology, 7,* 304–308.

Turner, A. M., & Greenough, W. T. (1985). Differential rearing effects on rat visual cortex synapses. I. Synaptic and neuronal density and synapses per neuron. *Brain Research, 329,* 195–203.

Turner, S. M., Beidel, D. C., & Nathan, R. S. (1985). Biological factors in obsessive-compulsive disorders. *Psychological Bulletin, 97,* 430–450.

Tversky, A., & Kahneman, D. (1973). Availability: A heuristic for judging frequency and probability. *Cognitive Psychology, 4,* 207–232.

Tybout, A. M., & Scott, C. A. (1983). Availability of well-defined internal knowledge and the attitude formation process: Information aggregation versus self-perception. *Journal of Personality and Social Psychology, 44,* 474–491.

Usdin, G., & Hofling, C. K. (1978). *Aging: The process and the people.* New York: Brunner/Mazel.

U.S. Congress, Office of Technology Assessment. (1987). *Losing a million minds: Confronting the tragedy of Alzheimer's disease and other dementias,* OTA-BA-323. Washington, DC: U.S. Government Printing Office, April).

U.S. Department of Health and Human Services. (1986). *Suicide.* Rockville, MD: National Institute of Mental Health.

U.S. Department of Health and Human Services. (1988). *Facts from the 1987 national high school senior survey.* Rockville, MD: Alcohol, Drug Abuse, and Mental Health Administration.

U.S. Department of Health and Human Services. (1989). Drug use by high school seniors lowest since 1975. *ADAMHA News,* May 1989, XV, #3, p. 10.

U.S. Department of Health and Human Services. (1989). *Illicit drug use in U.S. shows steep drop—except cocaine addiction.* Rockville, MD: Public Health Service Alcohol, Drug Abuse, and Mental Health Administration.

U.S. Department of Health and Human Services. (1989). *Latest ADAMHA research on AIDS reported at Montreal conference.* Rockville, MD: Public Health Service Alcohol, Drug Abuse, and Mental Health Administration.

U.S. Department of Health and Human Services. (1989). *Reducing the health consequences of smoking: 25 years of progress. A report of the surgeon general.* U.S. Department of Health and Human Services, Public Health Service, Centers for Disease Control, Center for Chronic Disease Prevention and Health Promotion, Office on Smoking and Health. DHHS Publication No. (CDC) 89-8411.

U.S. Bureau of the Census. (1989). *Single parents and their children.* Statistical Brief, SB-3-89. Washington, DC: U.S. Government Printing Office.

Vaillant, G. E., & Milofsky, E. S. (1982). The etiology of alcoholism: A prospective view. *American Psychologist, 37,* 494–503.

Valins, S. (1966). Cognitive effects of false heart-rate feedback. *Journal of Personality and Social Psychology, 4,* 400–408.

Valins, S., & Baum, A. (1973). Residential group size, social interaction, and crowding. *Environment and Behavior, 5,* 421–435.

van Doornen, L. J. P., & De Geus, E. J. C. (1989). Aerobic fitness and the cardiovascular response to stress. *Psychophysiology, 26,* 17–28.

Van Praag, H. M. (1978). Neuralendocrine disorders in depression and their significance for the monoamine hypothesis of depression. *Acta Psychiatrica Scandinavica, 57,* 389–404.

Vandell, D. L., & Corasaniti, M. A. (1988). The relation between third graders' after-school care and social, academic, and emotional function. *Child Development, 59,* 868–875.

Vandell, D. L., Henderson, V. K., & Wilson, K. S. (1988). A longitudinal study of children with day-care experiences of varying quality. *Child Development, 59,* 1286–1292.

Varma, V. K., Bouri, M., & Wig, N. N. (1981). Multiple personality in India: Comparison with hysterical possession state. *American Journal of Psychotherapy, 35,* 113–120.

Vellutino, F. R. (1987). Dyslexia. *Scientific American, 256,* 34–41.

Vernon, P. E. (1979). *Intelligence: Heredity and environment.* San Francisco: W. H. Freeman.

Vitiello, M. V. (1989). *Unraveling sleep disorders of the aged.* Paper presented at the annual meeting of the Association of Professional Sleep Societies, Washington, DC.

Von Senden, M. (1932). *Raum-und Gaestaltauffassung bei operierten. Blindgeborenin vor und nach der Operation.* Leipzig, Germany: Barth.

Vroom, V. H. (1964). *Work and motivation.* New York: John Wiley & Sons.

Vroon, P. A., de Leeuw, J., & Meester, A. C. (1986). Distribution of intelligence and educational level in fathers and sons. *British Journal of Psychology, 77,* 137–142.

Wagemaker, H., & Cade, R. (1977). The use of hemodialysis in chronic schizophrenia. *American Journal of Psychiatry, 134,* 684–685.

Wagstaff, G. F. (1983). Suggested improvement of visual acuity: A statistical reevaluation. *International Journal of Clinical and Experimental Hypnosis, 36,* 239–240.

Waid, W. M. (1976). Skin conductance response to both signaled and unsignaled noxious stimulation predicts level of socialization. *Journal of Personality and Social Psychology, 34,* 923–929.

Walk, R. D., & Gibson, E. J. (1961). A comparative and analytical study of visual depth perception. *Psychological Monographs, 75*(15).

Walker, E., Downey, G., & Bergman, A. (1989). The effects of parental psychopathology and maltreatment of child behavior: A test of the diathesis-stress model. *Child Development, 60,* 15–24.

Walker, E., & Emory, E. (1983). Infants at risk for psychopathology: Offspring of schizophrenic parents. *Child Development, 54,* 1269–1285.

Walker, E., Hoppes, E., Mednick, S., Emory, E., Schulsinger, F. (1983). Environmental factors related to schizophrenia in psychophysiologically labile high-risk males. *Journal of Abnormal Psychology, 90,* 313–320.

Walker, J. I., & Cavenar, J. O. (1982). Vietnam veterans: Their problems continue. *Journal of Nervous and Mental Disease, 170,* 174–180.

Walker, L. E. A. (1989). Psychology and violence against women. *American Psychologist, 44,* 695–702.

Walker-Andrews, A. S. (1986). Intermodal perception of expressive behaviors: Relation of eye and voice? *Developmental Psychology, 22,* 373–377.

Wallace, R. K., & Benson, H. (1972). The physiology of meditation. In *Altered states of awareness: Readings from Scientific American.* San Francisco: W. H. Freeman.

Wallerstein, J. S., & Blakeslee, J. (1989). *Second chances.* New York: Ticknor & Fields.

Wallerstein, J. S., & Kelly, J. B. (1980). *Surviving the breakup.* New York: Basic Books.

Walsh, B. T., Roose, S. P., Glassman, A. H., Gladis, M., & Sadik, C. (1985). Bulimia and depression. *Psychosomatic Medicine, 47,* 123–131.

Walters, G. D. (1983). The MMPI and schizophrenia: A review. *Schizophrenia Bulletin, 9,* 226–246.

Wanberg, K. W., & Horn, J. L. (1983). Assessment of alcohol use with multidimensional concepts and measures. *American Psychologist, 38,* 1055–1069.

Wardle, J., & Beales, S. (1988). Control and loss of control over eating: An experimental investigation. *Journal of Abnormal Psychology, 97,* 35–40.

Washton, A. M. (1989). *Cocaine addiction.* New York: W. W. Norton.

Watkins, M. J. (1990). Mediationism and the obfuscation of memory. *American Psychologist, 45,* 328–335.

Watson, D., & Pennebaker, J. W. (1989). Health complaints, stress, and distress: Exploring the central role of negative affectivity. *Psychological Review, 96,* 234–254.

Watson, J. B. (1924). *Behaviorism.* Chicago: University of Chicago Press.

Watson, J. B. (1930). *Behaviorism* (2nd ed.). New York: W. W. Norton.

Watson, J. B., & Rayner, R. (1920). Conditioned emotional reaction. *Journal of Experimental Psychology, 3,* 1–14.

Watson, O. M., & Graves, T. D. (1966). Quantitative research in proxemic behavior. *American Anthropologist, 68,* 971–985.

Weary, G., Harvey, J. H., Schwieger, P., Olson, C. T., Perloff, E., & Pritchard, S. (1982). Self-presentation and the moderation of self-serving biases. *Social Cognition, 1,* 140–159.

Webb, W. B. (1975). *Sleep: The gentle tyrant.* Englewood Cliffs, NJ: Prentice-Hall.

Webb, W. B., & Agnew, H. W., Jr. (1974). Sleep and waking in a time-free environment. *Aerospace Medicine, 45,* 617–622.

Webb, W. B., & Agnew, H. W., Jr. (1975). The effects on subsequent sleep of an acute restriction of sleep length. *Psychophysiology, 12,* 367–370.

Webb, W. B., & Agnew, H. W., Jr. (1977). Analysis of the sleep stages in sleep-wakefulness regiments of varied length. *Psychophysiology, 14,* 445–450.

Webb, W. B., & Kersey, J. (1967). Recall of dreams and the probability of stage 1-REM sleep. *Perceptual and Motor Skills, 24,* 627–630.

Wechsler, D. (1958). *The measurement and appraisal of adult intelligence* (4th ed.). Baltimore: Williams & Wilkins.

Weidner, G., Friend, R., Ficarrotto, T. J., & Mendell, N. R. (1989). Hostility and cardiovascular reactivity to stress in women and men. *Psychosomatic Medicine, 51,* 36–45.

Weil, A. T. (1972). *The natural mind: A new way of looking at drugs and the higher consciousness.* Boston: Houghton Mifflin.

Weil, A. T. (1977). The marriage of the sun and the moon. In N. E. Zinberg (Ed.), *Alternate states of consciousness.* New York: Macmillan.

Weinberg, R. A. (1989). Intelligence and IQ. *American Psychologist, 44,* 98–104.

Weinberger, M., Hiner, S. L., & Tierney, W. M. (1987). In support of hassles as a measure of stress in predicting health outcomes. *Journal of Behavioral Medicine, 10,* 19–31.

Weingartner, H. (1977). Human state-dependent learning. In B. T. Ho, D. Richards, & D. L. Chute (Eds.), *Drug discrimination and state-dependent learning.* New York: Academic Press.

Weingartner, H., Adefris, W., Eich, J. E., & Murphy, D. L. (1976). Encoding-imagery specificity in alcohol state-dependent learning. *Journal of Experimental Psychology, 2,* 83–87.

Weingartner, H., Cohen, R. M., Murphy, D. L., Martello, J., & Gerdt, C. (1981). Cognitive processes in depression. *Archives of General Psychiatry, 38,* 42–47.

Weingartner, H., Rapaport, J. L., Buchsbaum, M. S., Bunney, W. E., Jr., Ebert, M. H., Mikkelsen, E. J., & Caine, E. D. (1980). Cognitive processes in normal and hyperactive children and their response to amphetamine treatment. *Journal of Abnormal Psychology, 89,* 25–37.

Weinman, M. L., Matthew, R. J., & Claghorn, J. L. (1982). A study of physician attitude on biofeedback. *Biofeedback and Self-Regulation, 7,* 89–98.

Weinraub, M., & Wolf, B. (1983). Effects of stress and social supports on mother-child interactions in single- and twoparent families. *Child Development, 54,* 1297–1311.

Weins, A. N., & Menustik, C. E. (1983). Treatment outcome and patient characteristics in an aversion therapy program for alcoholism. *American Psychologist, 38,* 1089–1096.

Weintraub, S. (1987). Risk factors in schizophrenia: The Stony Brook high-risk project. *Schizophrenia Bulletin, 13,* 439–443.

Weiss, A. A. (1978). *Mental retardation.* Paper presented at the meeting of the Implementation of Protection and Advocacy Systems, Columbia, SC, April, 26.

Weiss, B., Williams, J. H., Margen, S., Abrams, B., Caan, B., Citroe, L. J., Cox, C., McKibben, J., Ogar, D., & Schultz, S. (1980). Behavioral response to artificial food colors. *Science, 207,* 1487–1489.

Weiss, R. S. (1984). Loneliness: What we know about it and what we might do about it. In L. A. Peplau and S. E. Goldston (Eds.), *Preventing the harmful consequences of severe and persistent loneliness* (DHHS Publication No. ADM No. 84-1312) (pp. 3–12). Washington, DC: U.S. Government Printing Office.

Weiss, S. R., & Ebert, M. H. (1983). Psychological and behavioral characteristics of normal-weight bulimics and normal-weight controls. *Psychosomatic Medicine, 45,* 293–304.

Weissman, M. M., Gammon, G. D., John, K., Merikangas, K. R., Warner, V., Prusoff, B. A., & Sholomskas, D. (1987). Children of depressed parents. *Archives of General Psychiatry, 44,* 847–849.

Weisz, J. R., & Weiss, B. (1989). Assessing the effects of clinic-based psychotherapy with children and adolescents. *Journal of Consulting and Clinical Psychology, 57,* 741–746.

Weisz, J. R., Weiss, B., Alicke, M. D., Klotz, M. L. (1987). Effectiveness of psychotherapy with children and adolescents: A meta-analysis for clinicians. *Journal of Consulting and Clinical Psychology, 55,* 542–549.

Weitzman, L. J. (1985). *The divorce revolution: The unexpected social and economic consequences for women and children in America.* New York: Free Press.

Wells, K. B., Hays, R. D., Burnam, A., Rogers, W., Greenfield, S., & Ware, J. E., Jr. (1989). Detection of depressive disorder for patients receiving prepaid or fee-for-service care. *Journal of the American Medical Association, 262,* 3298–3302.

Wells, R. A., & Phelps, P. A. (1990). The brief psychotherapies: A selective overview. In R. A. Wells & V. J. Giannetti (Eds.), *Handbook of the brief psychotherapies.* New York: Plenum Press.

Werler, M. M., Mitchell, A. A., & Shapiro, M. B. (1989). The relation of aspirin use during the first trimester of pregnancy to congenital cardiac defects. *New England Journal of Medicine, 321,* 1639–1642.

West, M. (1982). Meditation and self-awareness: Physiological and phenomenological approaches. In G. Underwood (Ed.), *Aspects of consciousness: Vol. 3. Awareness and self-awareness.* London: Academic Press.

West, M. A. (1980). Meditation and the EEG. *Psychological Medicine, 10,* 369–375.

Whalen, C. K., Henker, B., Buhrmester, D., Hinshaw, S. P., Huber, A., & Laski, K. (1989). Does stimulant medication improve the peer status of hyperactive children? *Journal of Consulting and Clinical Psychology, 57,* 545–549.

White, M. J., & Gerstein, L. H. (1987). Helping: The influence of anticipated social sanctions and self-monitoring. *Journal of Personality, 55,* 41–45.

White, R. K. (1977). Misperception in the Arab-Israeli conflict. *Journal of Social Issues, 33,* 190–221.

Whorf, B. L. (1956). *Language, thought, and reality: Selected writings of Benjamin Lee Whorf* (J. B. Carroll, Ed.). New York: John Wiley & Sons.

Wideman, M. V., & Singer, J. E. (1984). The role of psychological mechanisms in preparation for childbirth. *American Psychologist, 39,* 1357–1371.

Widom, C. S. (1989). Does violence beget violence? A critical examination of the literature. *Psychological Bulletin, 106,* 3–28.

Wilcox, C. (1989). Risk taking and presidential voting: Gambling on McGovern and Carter. *Journal of Social Psychology, 129,* 161–168.

Wilder, D. A., & Thompson, J. E. (1980). Intergroup contact with independent manipulations of in-group and out-group interaction. *Journal of Personality and Social Psychology, 38,* 589–603.

Williams, A. F. (1986). Raising the legal purchase age in the United States: Its effects on fatal motor vehicle crashes. *Alcohol, Drugs, and Driving, 2,* 1–12.

Williams, C. D. (1959). Case report: The elimination of tantrum behavior by extinction procedures. *Journal of Abnormal and Social Psychology, 59,* 269.

Williams, K., Harkins, S., & Latane, B. (1981). Identifiability as a deterrent to social loafing: Two cheering experiments. *Journal of Personality and Social Psychology, 40,* 303–311.

Williams, R. (1989). *The trusting heart: Great news about Type A behavior.* New York: Random House.

Williams, R. L. (1970). Black pride, academic relevance, and individual achievement. *Counseling Psychologist, 2,* 18–22.

Williams, S. L., Kinney, P. J., & Falbo, J. (1989). Generalization of therapeutic changes in agoraphobia: The role of perceived self-efficacy. *Journal of Consulting and Clinical Psychology, 57,* 436–442.

Williamson, D. A., Kelley, M. L., Davis, C. J., Ruggiero, L., & Blouin, D. C. (1985). Psychopathology of eating disorders: A controlled comparison of bulimic, obese, and normal subjects. *Journal of Consulting and Clinical Psychology, 53,* 161–166.

Wilsnack, R. W., Wilsnack, S. C., & Klassen, A. D. (1986). Antecedents and consequences of drinking and drinking problems in women: Patterns from a U.S. national survey. In P. C. Rivers (Ed.). *Alcohol and addictive behavior.* Lincoln, NE: University of Nebraska Press.

Wilson, E. (1952). Woodrow Wilson at Princeton. *In shores of light.* New York: Farrar, Straus and Young.

Wilson, E. O. (1975). *Sociobiology: A new synthesis.* Cambridge, MA: Harvard University Press.

Wilson, G. T. (1987). Cognitive studies in alcoholism. *Journal of Consulting and Clinical Psychology, 55,* 325–331.

Wilson, G. T., & Davison, C. G. (1971). Processes of fear reduction in systematic desensitization: Animal studies. *Psychological Bulletin, 76,* 1–14.

Wilson, M. N. (1989). Child development in the context of the black extended family. *American Psychologist, 44*(2), 380–385.

Wilson, R. S. (1983). The Louisville twin study: Developmental synchronies in behavior. *Child Development, 54,* 298–315.

Wincze, J. P., & Caird, W. K. (1976). The effects of systematic desensitization and video desensitization in the treatment of essential sexual dysfunction in women. *Behavior Therapy, 7,* 335–342.

Windmiller, M. (1980). Introduction. In M. Windmiller, N. Lambert, & E. Turiel (Eds.), *Moral development and socialization.* Boston: Allyn and Bacon.

Wing, J. K. (1978). *Reasoning about madness.* Oxford: Oxford University Press.

Wing, L. (Ed.). (1976). *Early childhood autism* (2nd ed.). New York: Pergamon Press.

Wing, R. R., Epstein, L. H., Nowalk, M. P., & Lamparski, D. M. (1986).

Behavioral self-regulation in the treatment of patients with diabetes mellitus. *Psychological Bulletin, 99,* 78–89.

Wise, R. A., & Bozarth, M. A. (1987). A psychomotor stimulant theory of addiction. *Psychological Review, 94,* 469–492.

Wittrock, M. C. (1987). *The teaching of comprehension.* Thorndike Award Address, 1987 American Psychological Association Annual Meeting, New York, August 29.

Woititz, J. G. (1983). *Adult children of alcoholics.* New York: Health Communications.

Wolfe, D. A. (1985). Child-abusive parents: An empirical review and analysis. *Psychological Review, 97,* 462–482.

Wolfe, D. A., Edwards, B., Manion, I., & Koverola, C. (1988). Early intervention for parents at risk of child abuse and neglect: A preliminary investigation. *Journal of Consulting and Clinical Psychology, 56,* 40–47.

Wolfe, J. M. (1983). Hidden visual processes. *Scientific American, 248*(2), 94–103.

Wolkind, S. N. (1974). The components of "affectionless psychopathy" in institutionalized children. *Journal of Child Psychology and Psychiatry, 15,* 215–220.

Wolpe, J. (1958). *Psychotherapy by reciprocal inhibition.* Stanford, CA: Stanford University Press.

Wolpe, J. (1973). *The practice of behavior therapy* (2nd ed.). New York: Pergamon Press.

Wolraich, M. L., Milich, R., Stumbo, P., & Schultz, F. (1985). The effects of sucrose ingestion on the behavior of hyperactive boys. *Journal of Pediatrics, 106,* 862–867.

Woodhead, M. (1988). When psychology informs public policy: The case of early childhood intervention. *American Psychologist, 6,* 443–454.

Woodward, W. R. (1982). The "discovery" of social behaviorism and social learning theory, 1870–1980. *American Psychologist, 37,* 396–410.

Woolfolk, R. L., & McNulty, T. F. (1983). Relaxation treatment for insomnia: A component analysis. *Journal of Consulting and Clinical Psychology, 51,* 495–503.

Worchel, S., Hardy, T. W., & Hurley, R. (1976). The effects of commercial interruption of violent and nonviolent films on viewers' subsequent aggression. *Journal of Experimental Social Psychology, 12,* 220–232.

Worell, J. (1978). Sex roles and psychological well-being: Perspectives on methodology. *Journal of Consulting and Clinical Psychology, 46,* 777–791.

Wozniak, P. R. (1984). Making sociobiological sense out of sociology. *The Sociological Quarterly, 25,* 191–204.

Wundt, W. (1896). *Grundress er psychologie.* Leipzig, Germany: Engleman.

Wyatt, G. E., Peters, S. D., & Guthrie, D. (1988). Kinsey revisited, Part I: Comparisons of the sexual socialization and sexual behavior of white women over 33 years. *Archives of Sexual Behavior, 17,* 201–239.

Wynne, L. C., Cole, R. E., & Perkins, P. (1987). University of Rochester child and family study: Risk research in progress. *Schizophrenia Bulletin, 13,* 463–467.

Wyszecki, G., & Stiles, W. S. (1967). *Color science: Concepts and methods, quantitative data and formulas.* New York: John Wiley & Sons.

Yates, A. J. (1975). *Practice in behavior therapy.* New York: John Wiley & Sons.

Yerkes, R. M., & Dodson, J. D. (1908). The relation of strength of stimulus to rapidity of habit formation. *Journal of Comparative Neurology and Psychology, 18,* 459–482.

Yogman, M., Dixon, S., Tronick, E., Als, H., & Brazelton, T. B. (1977). *The goals and structure of face-to-face interaction between infants and fathers.* Paper presented at the biennial meeting of SRCD, New Orleans.

Yoken, C., & Berman, J. S. (1984). Does paying a fee for psychotherapy alter the effectiveness of treatment? *Journal of Consulting and Clinical Psychology, 52,* 254–260.

Yonas, A., Granrud, C. E., & Petersen, L. (1985). Infants' sensitivity to relative size information for distance. *Developmental Psychology, 21,* 161–167.

York, R., Freeman, E., Lowery, B., & Strauss, J. F. (1989). Characteristics of premenstrual syndrome. *Obstetrics and Gynecology, 73,* 601–605.

Young, A. W., & Ellis, A. W. (1981). Asymmetry of cerebral hemispheric function in normal and poor readers. *Psychological Bulletin, 89,* 183–190.

Young, S. N., Smith, S., Pihl, R. O., & Ervin, F. R. (1985). Tryptophan depletion causes a rapid lowering of mood in normal males. *Psychopharmacology, 87,* 173–177.

Young-Loveridge, J. M. (1985). Use of orthographic structure and reading ability: What relationship? *Journal of Experimental Child Psychology, 40,* 439–449.

Yuille, J. C., & Cutshall, J. L. (1986). A case study of eyewitness memory of a crime. *Journal of Applied Psychology, 71,* 291–301.

Yussen, S. R. (1977). Characteristics of moral dilemmas written by adolescents. *Developmental Psychology, 13,* 162–163.

Zaccaro, S. J. (1984). Social loafing: The role of task attractiveness. *Personality and Social Psychology Bulletin, 10,* 99–106.

Zaidel, E. (1983). A response to Gazzaniga: Language in the right hemisphere, convergent perspectives. *American Psychologist, 38,* 542–546.

Zaidel, S., & Mehrabian, A. (1969). The ability to communicate and to infer positive and negative attitudes facially and vocally. *Journal of Experimental Research and Personality, 3,* 233–241.

Zajonc, R. B. (1965). Social facilitation. *Science, 149,* 269–274.

Zajonc, R. B. (1983). Validating the confluence model. *Psychological Bulletin, 93,* 457–480.

Zajonc, R. B. (1986). The decline and rise of scholastic aptitude scores: A prediction derived from the confluence model. *American Psychologist, 41,* 862–867.

Zajonc, R. B., & Markus, G. B. (1975). Birth order and intellectual development. *Psychological Review, 82,* 74–88.

Zajonc, R. B., Murphy, S. T., & Inglehart, M. (1989). Feeling and facial efference: Implications of the vascular theory of emotion. *Psychological Review, 96,* 395–416.

Zaleska, M. (1978). Some experimental results: Majority influence on group decisions. In H. Brandstatter, J. H. Davis, & H. Schuler (Eds.), *Dynamics of group decisions.* Beverly Hills, CA: Sage.

Zaller, J. R. (1987). Attitudes and social cognition. *Journal of Personality and Social Psychology, 53,* 821–833.

Zangwill, O. L., & Blakemore, C. (1972). Dyslexia: Reversal of eye movements during reading. *Neuropsychologia, 10,* 371–373.

Zaragoza, M. S., & McCloskey, M. (1989). Misleading postevent information and the memory impairment hypothesis: Comment on Belli and reply to Tversky and Tuchin. *Journal of Experimental Psychology: General, 118,* 92–99.

Zental, S. S. (1980). Behavioral comparisons of hyperactive and normally active children in natural settings. *Journal of Abnormal Child Psychology, 8,* 93–109.

Zental, S. S., Falkenberg, S. D., & Smith, L. B. (1985). Effects of color stimulation and information on the copying performance of attention-problem adolescents. *Journal of Abnormal Child Psychology, 13,* 501–511.

Zental, S. S., & Zental, T. R. (1983). Optimal stimulation: A model of disordered activity and performance in normal and deviant children. *Psychological Bulletin, 94,* 446–471.

Zepelin, H. (1986). REM sleep and the timing of selfawakenings. *Bulletin of the Psychonomic Society, 24,* 254–256.

Zigler, E., & Levine, J. (1983). Hallucinations vs. delusions. A developmental approach. *Journal of Nervous and Mental Disease, 171,* 141–146.

Zigler, E., & Muenchow, S. (1983). Infant day care and infant-care leaves: A policy vacuum. *American Psychologist, 38,* 91–94.

Zigler, E. F. (1987). Formal schooling for four-year-olds? No. *American Psychologist, 42,* 254–260.

Zins, J. E., & Barnett, D. W. (1983). The Kaufman Assessment Battery for Children and school achievement: A validity study. *Journal of Psychoeducational Assessment, 1,* 235–241.

Zitrin, C. M. (1981). Combined pharmacological and psychological treatment of phobias. In M. Navissakalian & D. H. Barlow (Eds.). *Phobias: Psychological and pharmacological treatments.* New York: Guilford Press.

Zola-Morgan, S., Squire, L. R., & Mishkin, M. (1982). The neuroanatomy of amnesia: Amygdala-hippocampus versus temporal stem. *Science, 218,* 1337–1339.

Zubin, J., & Spring, B. (1977). Vulnerability—a new view of schizophrenia. *Journal of Abnormal Psychology, 86,* 103–126.

Zucker, R. A., Gomberg, E. S. (1986). Etiology of alcoholism reconsidered. *American Psychologist, 41,* 786–793.

Zuckerman, M. (1969). Variables affecting deprivation results and hallucinations, reported sensations, and images. In J. P. Zubek (Ed.), *Sensory deprivation.* New York: Appleton-Century-Crofts.

Name Index

Subject Index

(credits continued from copyright page)

387: G. Zimbel/Monkmeyer Press Photo. 388: R. Morsch/The Stock Market. 391: M. Rogers/TSW-Click, Chicago. 393: F. Siteman. 394: B. Gillette/Stock, Boston. 396: C. Gupton/Stock, Boston. 400: F. Siteman. 404: F. Siteman. 406: Historical Picture Service. 408: F. Siteman. 413TL: G. Palmer/The Stock Market; TC: K. Harrison/The Image Works; TR: R. Hutchings/Photo-Researchers Inc.; BL: Sygma; BC: R. Morsch/The Stock Market; BR: B. Alper/Stock, Boston. 415: M. Rogers/TSW-Click, Chicago. 417: TSW-Click, Chicago. 418: B. Daemmrich/Stock, Boston. 425: Archive/Photo-Researchers. 427: A. Canavesio/Photo-Researchers Inc. 430: U. Welsch. 434: Archive/Photo-Researchers Inc. 435: UPI/Bettmann Archive. 438: Research Library. 440: F. Siteman. 441: UPI/Bettmann Archive. 442: Historical Picture Service. 444: F. Siteman. 448: D. Dempster/Allyn and Bacon. 449: Historical Picture Service. 451: Historical Picture Service. 452: B. Daemmrich/Stock, Boston. 455: F. Siteman. 459: D. Dempster/Allyn and Bacon. 461: D. Dempster/Allyn and Bacon. 469: J. Brown/OffShoot Stock. 471: L. Kolvoord/The Image Works. 472: UPI/Bettmann Archives. 474L: G. Smith/Stock, Boston; 474R: C. Fishman/Woodfin Camp & Assoc. 478: P. Chauvel/Sygma. 483: A. Grace/Stock, Boston. 488: D. Hudson/Sygma. 490: J. Caccavo/The Picture Group. 493: Sudhir/The Picture Group. 499: C. Ursillo/Photo-Researchers Inc. 500: Mary Evans Picture Library/Photo-Researchers Inc. 505: The Bettmann Archive. 506: D. Dempster/OffShoot Stock. 513: B. Daemmrich/Stock, Boston. 515: P. Yates/The Picture Group. 520: B. Daemmrich. 524: Grunnitus/Monkmeyer Press Photo. 526: The Genain Estate. 540: Mary Evans Picture Library. 542: F. Siteman. 545: Research Library. 548: F. Siteman. 553: R. Howard/OffShoot Stock. 554: F. Siteman. 555: J. Parsons/Stock, Boston. 556: The Bettmann Archive. 557: Research Library. 559: F. Siteman. 562: B. Daemmrich. 565: B. Daemmrich. 574: Tortoni/Photo-Researchers Inc. 577: D. Lyn/Shooting Star. 586 R: Sydney/Stock, Boston. 589: B. Barnhart/OffShoot Stock. 593: D. Grossman/Photo-Researchers Inc. 596: B. Daemmrich. 597: UPI/The Bettmann Archive. 598: The Milgrim Estate. 603: R. Schelipman/OffShoot Stock. 606: P. Conklin/Monkmeyer Press Photo. 613L: J. Curtis/OffShoot Stock; 613R: D. Dempster/OffShoot Stock. 614: B. Daemmrich, Boston. 616: Superstock. 617: B. Stanton/Rainbow. 619: J. Curtis/OffShoot Stock. 621: G. Palmer/The Stock Market. 626: C. Wolinsky/Stock, Boston. 632: G. Greig/Monkmeyer Press Photo. 635: D. Gardner/OffShoot Stock. 638: D. Dempster/OffShoot Stock. 643: G. Palmer/The Stock Market.

Figures, Tables, and Quotations: Chapter 2: FIG. 2.15, P. 57–From Carlson, N. R. *Physiology of behavior,* Second Edition, Boston: Allyn and Bacon, Inc., 1981. QUOTE p. 39–From Watson, J. B. *Behaviorism,* Second Edition, New York: W. W. Norton & Company, Inc., 1930. FIG. 2.18, p. 63–From Lefton, L. and Valvatne, L. *Mastering Psychology,* Third Edition, Boston: Allyn and Bacon, 1988.
Chapter 3: FIG. 3.1, p. 74–From Held, R., and Hein, A. Movement produced stimulation in the development of visually guided behavior, *Journal of Comparative and Physiological Psychology,* 1963, 56, pp. 872–876. Copyright © 1963 by the American Psychological Association. Reprinted by permission. FIG. 3.3B, p. 77–From Pinel, John P. J. *Biopsychology,* Boston: Allyn and Bacon, 1990. FIG. 3.5, p. 78–From Pirenne, M. H. *Vision and the eye,* London: Chapman & Hall, 1967, p. 32. FIG. 3.7, p. 80–From *Visual perception* by Tom N. Cornsweet, copyright © 1970 by Harcourt Brace Jovanovich, Inc., reproduced by permission of the publisher. FIG. 3.10, p. 82–From Carlson, N. R. *Physiology of behavior,* Second Edition, Boston: Allyn and Bacon, Inc., 1981. FIG. 3.11, p. 83–From "The visual cortex of the brain," by David Hubel. Copyright © November 1963 by *Scientific American,* Inc. All rights reserved. FIG. 3.12, p. 82–From *Sensation & Perception,* Second Edition by Stanley Coren, Clare Porac, and Laurence M. Ward, copyright © 1984 by Harcourt Brace Jovanovich, Inc., reproduced by permission of the publisher. FIG. 3.13, p. 83–From "Eye movements and visual perception," by David Noton and Lawrence Stark. Copyright © June 1971 by *Scientific American,* Inc. All rights reserved. FIG. 3.16, p. 88–Reprinted with permission from *Vision Research,* 4, E. F. MacNichol, Jr., Retinal mechanisms of color vision, Copyright 1964, Pergamon Press plc. FIG. 3.17, p. 89–From Hurvich, L., & Jameson, D. Opponent processes as a model of neural organization. *American Psychologist,* 1974, 30, 88–102. Copyright 1974 by the American Psychological Association. Reprinted by permission of the author. FIG. 3.25, p. 97–From Beck, J. Effects of orientation and of shape similarity on perceptual grouping. *Perception and Psychophysics,* 1966, 1, pp. 300–302. Reprinted with permission from the American Psychological Association. FIG. 3.29 (left), p. 107–From Pinel, John P. J. *Biopsychology,* Boston: Allyn and Bacon, 1990. FIG. 3.30, p. 108–From Carlson, N. R. *Psychology: The science of behavior,* Third Edition, Boston: Allyn and Bacon, 1990.
Chapter 4: FIG. 4.1, p. 124–From *Some must watch while some must sleep,* by William C. Dement. Copyright © 1972 by William C. Dement. Used by permission of the Stanford Alumni Association and William C. Dement. FIG. 4.2, p. 125–From *Some must watch while some must sleep,* by William C. Dement. Copyright © 1972 by William C. Dement. Used by permission of the Stanford Alumni Association and William C. Dement. FIG. 4.3, p. 126–From Kales, A., & Kales, J. D. Sleep disorders. Recent findings in the diagnosis and treatment of disturbed sleep. Reprinted by permission of *The New England Journal of Medicine,* 290, 487–499, (1974). TABLE 4.1, p. 127–From *EEG of human sleep,* by R. Williams, I. Karacan, & C. Hursch. New York: John Wiley & Sons, copyright © 1974. TABLE 4.2, p. 140 and Table 4.3, p. 141–From Ray, Oakley: *Drugs, society, & human behavior,* ed. 3, St. Louis, 1983, The C. V. Mosby Co. TABLE 4.4, p. 143–From Rice, F. P. *The adolescent: Development, relationships and culture,* Boston: Allyn and Bacon, 1987, p. 332. QUOTE p. 137–From Newcomb, M. D., & Bentler, P. M. Substance use and abuse among children and teenagers, *American Psychologist,* 1989, 44(2), 242. Copyright 1989 by the American Psychological Association. Reprinted by permission.
Chapter 5: FIG. 5.4, p. 159–From Schneiderman, N., Fuentes, I., & Gormezano, I. Acquisition and extinction of the classically conditioned eyelid response in the albino rabbit, *Science,* 136, 18 May 1962, 650–652. Copyright 1962 by the AAAS. FIG. 5.13, p. 180–From "Teaching machines," by B. F. Skinner. Copyright © November 1961 by *Scientific American,* Inc. All rights reserved.
Chapter 6: FIG. 6.10, p. 219–From Shepard, R. N. & Metzler, J., Mental rotation of three-dimensional objects, *Science,* 171, 19 February 1971, 701–703. Copyright 1971 by the AAAS. QUOTE pp. 219–220–From Bower, G. H. Mood and memory, *American Psychologist,* 1981, 36, 129. Copyright 1981 by the American Psychological Association. Reprinted by permission.
Chapter 7: FIG. 7.7, p. 255–From "The acquisition of language," by Breyne A. Moskowitz. Copyright © November 1978 by *Scientific American,* Inc. All rights reserved. FIG. 7.8, p. 261–From Premack, D., Language in chimpanzees? *Science,* 172, 21 May 1971, 808–822. Copyright by the AAAS.
Chapter 8: FIG. 8.3, p. 275–Adapted from Rudman, H. C. The standardized test flap, *Phi Delta Kappan,* 1977, 59, 179–185. FIG. 8.4, p. 284–Adapted from Sattler, J. M. *Assessment of children's intelligence and special abilities,* Third Edition, San Diego: Sattler, 1988. TABLE 8.5, p. 287–From Loehlin, J. C., Lindzey, G., & Spuhler, J. N. *Race differences in intelligence,* San Francisco: W. H. Freeman, 1975.
Chapter 9: FIG. 9.2, p. 310–From "The origin of form perception," by R. L. Fantz. Copyright © 1961 by *Scientific American,* Inc. Photo by David Linton. All rights reserved. TABLE 9.4, p. 309–From "Child development: A topical approach, by A. Clarke-Stewart, S. Friedman, & J. Koch. New York: John Wiley & Sons, copyright © 1974. QUOTE p. 308–From "The origin of form perception," by Robert L. Fantz. Copyright © 1961 by *Scientific American,* Inc. All rights reserved. QUOTE p. 316–From Piaget, J. The attainment of invariants and reversible operations in the development of thinking, *Social Research,* 30(3) (Autumn 1963), 282–299. QUOTE p. 321–From Flavell, J. H. *American Psychologist,* 1986, 41, 418–425. Copyright 1986 by the American Psychological Association. Reprinted by permission. QUOTE p. 325–From Kohlberg, L. The cognitive-developmental approach to socialization. In D. A. Goslin (Ed.), *Handbook of socialization theory and research.* Chicago: Rand McNally, 1969, p. 379.
Chapter 10: FIG. 10.2, p. 363–From *The 1988 World Book Year Book.* © 1988 World Book, Inc. Reproduced with permission. FIG. 10.3, p. 367–From Usdin & Hofling. *Aging: The process and the people,* Bruner/Mazel, 1978. TABLE 10.2, p. 371–Adapted from Bee, H. L. *The Journey of adulthood,* New York: Macmillan, 1987. QUOTE p. 351–From Erikson, E. H. Identity and the life cycle: Selected Papers, *Psychological Issues,* 1959, 1, 1–171, quote p. 104. Reprinted with permission of International University Press. QUOTE p. 359–From Levinson, D. J. Toward a conception of the adult life course. In N. J. Smelser & E. H. Erikson (Eds.), *Themes of work and love in adulthood.* Cambridge: Harvard University Press, p. 289. QUOTE p. 375–From Butterfield-Picard, H., & Magno, J. B. Hospice the adjective, not the noun: The future of a national priority. *American Psychologist,* 1982, 37, 1254–1259. Copyright 1982 by the American Psychological Association. Reprinted by permission.
Chapter 11: QUOTE p. 382–From Rodin, J. (1981). Current status of the internal-external hypothesis for obesity. *American Psychologist,* 36, (2), 129–148, quote p. 6. Copyright 1981 by the American Psychological Association. Reprinted with permission. FIG. 11.2, p. 384–From Schachter, S. Some extraordinary facts about obese humans and rats. *American Psychologist,* 1971, 26, 129–144. Copyright 1971 by the American Psychological Association. Reprinted by permission. FIG. 11.4, p. 396–From Lowell, E. L. The effect of need for achievement on learning and speed of performance, *Journal of Psychology,* 33, 31–40, 1952. Reprinted with permission of the Helen Dwight Reid Educational Foundation. Published by Heldref Publications, 4000 Albemarle St., N.W., Washington, D.C. 20016. Copyright © 1952. FIG. 11.5, p. 402–From Lazarus, R. S., & Alfert, E. Short-circuiting of threat by experimentally altering cognitive appraisal. *Journal of Abnormal and Social Psychology,* 1964, 69, 195–205. Copyright 1964 by the American Psychological Association. Reprinted by permission. FIG. 11.10, p. 418–Figure 9.11 from *Textbook of Psychology,* Third Edition, by Donald O. Hebb, copyright © 1972 by Saunders College Publishing, a division of Holt, Rinehart and Winston, Inc., reprinted by permission of the publisher. TABLE 11.1, p. 409–From Frijda, N., *American Psychologist.* 1988. Copyright 1988 by the American Psychological Association. Reprinted by permission. QUOTE p. 401–From *Organization of behavior* by D. O. Hebb, New York: John Wiley & Sons, copyright © 1949.
Chapter 12: TABLE 12.2, p. 460–From Cohen, R. J., Montague, P., Nathanson, L. S., Swerdik, M. E. *Psychological Testing,* Mountainview, CA: Mayfield Publishing, 1988. QUOTE p. 458–From Aiken, L. R. *Psychological testing and assessment,* Sixth Edition, Boston: Allyn and Bacon, p. 390.
Chapter 13: TABLE 13.1, p. 473–From Holmes & Rahe. *Journal of Psychosomatic Research.* Pergamon Press, Ltd. TABLE 13.3, p. 479–From Meyer, R. G., & Salmon, P. *Abnormal Psychology,* Second Edition, Boston, Allyn and Bacon, 1988, p. 333. TABLE 13.4, p. 491–From *What works: Schools without drugs.* Washington, D.C.: United States Department of Education, 1986.
Chapter 14: FIG. 14.2, p. 525–From Tsaung & Vandermey. *Genes and the Mind.* 1980. Oxford University Press, Inc. TABLE 14.1, p. 503–From American Psychiatric Association: *Diagnostic and Statistical Manual of Mental Disorders,* Third Edition. Washington, D.C.: American Psychiatric Association, 1988. QUOTE p. 506–From Melville, J. *Phobias and Compulsions,* London: Penguin Books, 1977, p. 22. Reprinted by permission of the Peters, Fraser & Dunlop Group Ltd. QUOTE p. 508–From Melville, J. *Phobias and Compulsions,* London: Penguin Books, 1977, p. 66–67. Reprinted by permission of the Peters, Fraser & Dunlop Group Ltd.
Chapter 15: FIG. 15.2, p. 550–Reprinted with permission from *Behavior Research and Therapy,* 2, Ayllon, T., & Haughton, E., Modification of symptomatic verbal behavior of mental patients, Copyright 1964, Pergamon Press plc. FIG. 15.3, p. 551–From Ayllon, T., & Azrin, N.H. The measurement and reinforcement behavior of psychotics, *Journal of the Experimental Analysis of Behavior,* 1965, 8, 357–383. Reprinted by permission of the Society for the Experimental Analysis of Behavior, Inc. TABLE 15.1, p. 537–Adapted from Mahrer, A. R., & Nadler, W. P. Good moments in psychotherapy: A preliminary review, a list, and some promising research avenues, *Journal of Consulting and Clinical Psychology,* 1986, 54, 10–15. Reprinted by permission of the American Psychological Association. TABLE 15.2, p. 544–From Rogers, Carl R. *On becoming a person: A therapist's view of psychotherapy.* Copyright © 1961 by Houghton Mifflin Company. Used with permission. TABLE 15.3, p. 557–From the book, *A new guide to rational living* by Albert Ellis, Ph.D. & Robert A. Harper, Ph.D. © 1975, 1961. Used by permission of the publisher, Prentice-Hall, Inc., Englewood Cliffs, NJ. BUILDING TABLE 15.3, p. 555–Adapted from *Modern clinical psychology: Principles of intervention in the clinic and community,* by Sheldon J. Korchin. Copyright © 1976 by Sheldon J. Korchin. Reprinted by permission of Basic Books, Inc., Publishers. QUOTE p. 538–539–From Freud, S. *An introduction to psychoanalysis.* In J. Riviere (Ed.), *A general introduction to psychoanalysis.* New York: Liveright Publishers, 1963. (Original work published 1920.)
Chapter 16: Fig. 16.6, p. 599–From Milgram, S. Behavioral study of obedience, *Journal of Abnormal and Social Psychology,* 1963, 67, 371–378. Copyright 1963 by the American Psychological Association. Adapted by permission.
Chapter 17: Fig. 17.3, p. 635–From Altman, I., & Vinsel, A. M. Personal space: An analysis of E. T. Hall's proxemics framework. In I. Altman, A. Rapoport, & J. F. Wohlwill (Eds.), *Human behavior and environment: Vol. 2. Advances in theory and research,* New York: Plenum Press, 1977. FIG. 17.5, p. 642–From Locke, E. A., & Schweiger, D. M. Participation in decision-making. One more look. In B. M. Staw (Ed.), *Research in organizational behavior,* Vol. 1, Greenwich, CT: JAI Press, 1979. QUOTE p. 630–From Donald G. Dutton, *The domestic assault of women: Psychological and criminal justice perspectives.* Copyright © 1988 by Allyn and Bacon. Reprinted with permission.